The Annals of Jan Długosz

The Annals of Jan Długosz

Annales seu cronicae incliti regni Poloniae

An English abridgement
by
MAURICE MICHAEL

With a commentary
by
Paul Smith

IMPublications

6 Charlton Mill, Charlton, Chichester, West Sussex PO18 0HY, UK.

Published by IM Publications
6 Charlton Mill, Charlton, Chichester, West Sussex PO18 0HY, United Kingdom.

First published in MS in Latin in the 15th century as *Annales seu cronicae incliti regni Poloniae*. This edition translated and abridged by Maurice Michael from *Roczniki Czyli Kroniki Sławnego Królestwa Polskiego*, the Polish translation of the Latin by Julia Mrukówna.

Books 1–11 of *Roczniki czyli Kroniki sławnego Królestwa Polskiego* © Polish Scientific Publishers PWN Ltd, Warsaw. Book 12 © Julia Mrukówna.

Edited by Jane Allan

Maurice Michael asserts his moral right to be identified as the author of this work.

ISBN 1 901019 00 4.

British Library Cataloguing in Publication Data.
A catalogue record for this book is available from the British Library.

Printed in the UK by Redwood Books, Trowbridge.

Contents

Preface

I discovered Julia Mrukówna's Polish translation of Jan Długosz's famous medieval chronicle when leafing through its Polish publisher's catalogue. I was fascinated, for I had spent most of the war working with or for the Poles, many of whom were my friends, and sent for a reading copy. The more I read, the more convinced I became that the *Roczniki*, which, I learned, was not only one of the gems of Polish literature, but now placed on a par with the chronicles of Froissart and de Commynes, should be available in English and I conceived a vague plan that one day I should try my hand at translating it. That day came years later, when I accepted partial retirement and, moving house, came across the copy of Volume 3/4 that I had laid aside all those years before. The rest of the text assembled, it was obvious that the enormous length of the whole made a straightforward translation of the *Roczniki* out of the question. However, could I not produce an English version that would act as an introduction to the *Annales*, a guide to the treasures to be found in those thousands of pages? After all, the Latin was always there for those who wished to delve deeper. The Latin text! I realized that, ideally, this was what I should work from, but it was a good fifty years since I had used my Latin and I was reluctant to spend the necessary two years or more in brushing it up and familiarizing myself with medieval Polish Latin, when Julia Mrukówna's excellent Polish translation was there for me to use and I had the necessary Polish. Whatever I attempted, I was going to have to reduce the three million words of the original and its footnotes to a half or three-quarters of a million words so as to allow the book to be published at a price that a private person could afford. Obviously, this was going to necessitate ruthless abridgement, so ruthless that I felt it could best be done by someone like myself who was academically uncommitted and who regarded the *Annales* more as a work of literature, than as an historical source book. To skip what the author himself called "myth" and start with the year A.D. 965 seemed obvious, as it did to remove Długosz' many repetitions and his sometimes lengthy panegyrics of his heroes. I felt, too, that I need include only sufficient accounts of the royal progresses and hunts to indicate their importance, extent and duration. Again, what happened west of the Oder and east of the Dniepr would, surely, be adequately documented elsewhere and need not be included in detail. On the other hand, I felt that all details of morals, customs, ritual, habits, details of climate, husbandry, war, prejudices and superstitions should be given in full, as well as the little insights, like the fact that Prince Andrew of Hungary brought a quantity of "curios" back from the Holy Land, which I found fascinating.

I realized that I was a relative ignoramus, the fool who has felt that he must step in where no academic angel has yet dared to tread. To those who feel outraged by my omissions I can only plead ignorance of the importance of the events in question and crave their indulgence, while hoping that the man with the man with the scythe will allow me to produce a supplementary volume that will make amends for the most grievous of my omissions.

Once I started work, I soon realized that there was much in the medieval terminology that I could not be sure of translating correctly and that my text was going to need careful editing. The Polish Cultural Institute in London put me in touch with Paul Smith, graduate of Oxford and London, who had done original research in Lublin, Prague and Marburg, and he agreed to give advice. The task of editing was undertaken by my daughter, Jane Allan, a medieval history graduate of St. Andrews, who has neglected her domestic duties in order to help. I am deeply indebted to them both, for together they have made this a much better book.

M.M.

Acknowledgements

I gratefully acknowledge the generosity of the private individuals listed below, friends of Poland and the Poles, some themselves Poles, who have sent me contributions towards the cost of producing this book:

The national organization of the Anglo–Polish Society and the members of the branches of that Society in Chester, Dunstable, London, Luton, Raunds, Scunthorpe and Wellinborough, Arthur Andersen & Co., SC, Christopher Beazley, Mrs. K. Downia-Berger, Mrs. Bridget Fiolkowska, Mrs. Anna Frackiewicz, Martin Gilbert C.B.E., Mrs. Nora Grajnert, Professor Dame Elizabeth Hill, Miss Peggy Jacobson, Chris Jurczynski, Legion of Young Polish Women, Chicago, Mrs. Christine Kolczyńska, The Lord Listowel, Mrs. Kazimierz Lubecki, C. Maryszczak, Charles Pick, Jan Pieńkowski, Polish Combatants Association 340, Professor Dr. O. Szemerérenyi, FBA, Mrs. I.H.C. Thornton, M. Wartalski, Adam Watson, C.M. Woods, and Count T. Zamoyski.

Further I must thank the British Academy, which, having taken thought, decided that this was a venture worth supporting, and whose generous grant together with that, equally generous, from the M.B. Grabowski Fund have made publication possible.

For their advice and help over the illustrations I am most grateful to the staffs of the Archiwum Główne Akt Dawnych, Warsaw, Archiwum Państwowe, Olsztyn, Bibliothèque Nationale, Paris, British Library and its Map Room, the Bodleian Library, Oxford, Geheimes Staatsarchiv Preussischer Kulturbesitz, Berlin, The Israel Museum, Jerusalem, the Library and Map Room of the Jagiellonian University, Cracow, the London Library, London, Town Museum, Cracow, Národní Muzeum, Prague, Niedersächsische Staats- und Universitätsbibliothek, Göttingen, Országs Széchényi Kőnyvtár, Budapest, The Board of the Trustees of the Royal Armouries, London, Staats- und Universitätsbibliothek, Carl von Ossietzky, Hamburg, Státní Knihovna Československe, Prague, VDI Verlag, Düsseldorf, and the Základní Knihovna of the Československá Akademie Věd, Prague.

I have, too, to thank Dr. Karol Drozd, Dr. Ryszard Herczyński and Dr. Hanna Mausch of the Polish Cultural Institute, Mrs. Halina Malinowska, Mrs. Ursula Phillips of the School of Slavonic and East European Studies, whose patience I have tested to the limit, and Dr. Edward Schnaydr.

As to the text itself, I am more than grateful to the Editors and to Paul Smith in particular for his help and many suggestions and, especially, for the Commentary he has provided and his detailed work on the index.

M.M.

Calendar of Feasts and Saint's Days

AGNES . . . . January 21
ALEXIS . . . . July 17
ANDREW . . . . November 30
ANNUNCIATION . . . . March 25
ASSUMPTION . . . . August 15
AUGUSTINE . . . . August 28
BARBARA . . . . December 4
BARTHOLOMEW . . . . August 24
DOMINIC . . . . August 7
DRY SUNDAY . . . . 2nd Sunday in Lent
ELIZABETH OF HUNGARY . . . . November 19
EPIPHANY . . . . January 6
FABIAN . . . . January 20
FLORIAN . . . . May 4
FRANCIS . . . . October 4
GALL . . . . October 16
GEORGE . . . . April 23
GERVASE & PROTASE . . . . June 19
GILES . . . . September 1
GOTHARD . . . . May 4
HIPPOLYTUS . . . . August 13
IMMACULATE CONCEPTION . . . . December 8
JACOB . . . . June 23
JADWIGA . . . . October 17
JAMES the GREATER . . . . July 25
JOHN . . . . December 27
JOHN THE BAPTIST . . . . June 24
JOHN & PAUL . . . . June 26
LAURENCE . . . . August 10
LEONARD . . . . November 6
LUCY . . . . December 13
LUKE . . . . October 18
MARGARET . . . . July 20
MARK . . . . April 25
MARTIN OF TOURS . . . . November 11
MATTHEW, the APOSTLE . . . . September 21
MICHAEL . . . . September 29
MARY MAGDALEN . . . . July 22
NATIVITY OF THE VIRGIN . . . . September 8
NICHOLAS . . . . December 6
PETER & PAUL . . . . June 29
PHILIP . . . . May 1
PROCOPIUS . . . . July 8
PURIFICATION OF THE VIRGIN . . . . February 2
REMINISCERE SUNDAY . . . . February 18

Illustrations and Maps

B. Wapowski's redrawing of Ptolemy's map Tabula moderna Polonie, Ungarie, Bohemie, Germanie, Russie, Lit
pages show the northern part and the southern part is reproduced on pages xx–xxi.

07.—Jagiellonian University Library. The map covers the area from the River Oder to the Black Sea; these

B. Wapowski's redrawing of Ptolemy's map Tabula moderna Polonie, Ungarie, Bohemie, Germanie, Russie, Lit
pages show the southern part and the northern part is reproduced on pages xviii–xix.

Quad picta est parva Germania tota tabulla—British Library. This northern portion covers the area from the R

to the west of Russia; the southern portion is on pages xxiv–xxv.

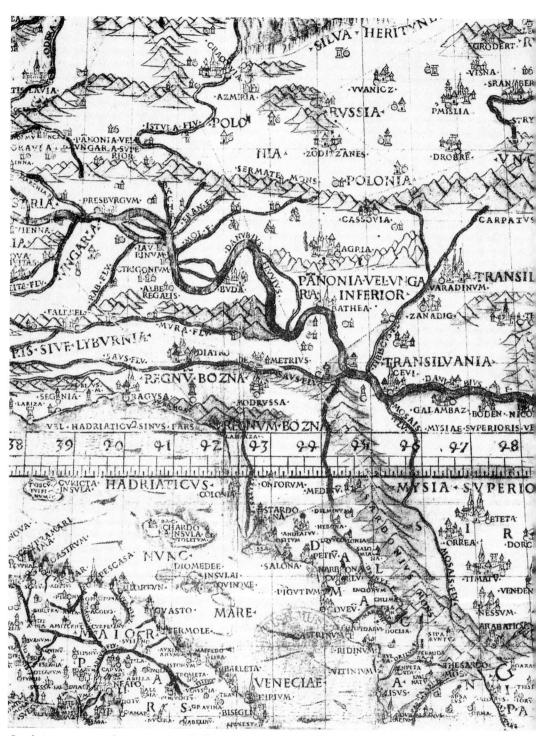

Quad picta est parva Germania tota tabulla—British Library. This southern portion covers the area from the Ri

the Black Sea; the northern portion is on pages xxii–xxiii.

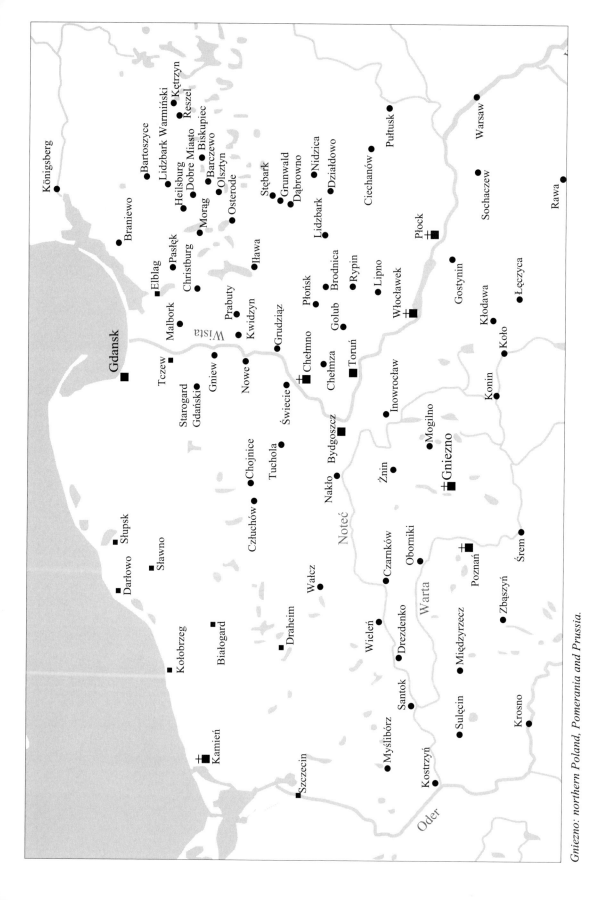

Gniezno: northern Poland, Pomerania and Prussia.

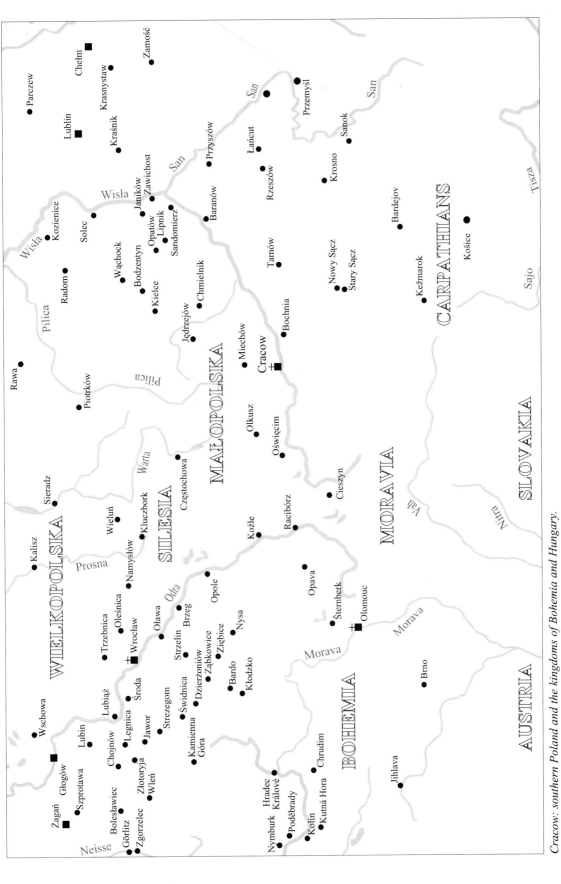

Cracow: southern Poland and the kingdoms of Bohemia and Hungary.

The only surviving contemporary likeness of Jan Długosz is this carving of 1480, the year of his death, on the foundation stone of the Dom Psalterzystów in Cracow. —Muzeum Historyczne m. Krakowa, Cracow.

Jan Długosz' Annales covers more than 500 years of East European history and consists of some three million words. The need for drastic abridgement to enable this English version to be published at a price the individual reader can afford, made it seem appropriate to omit the first of the twelve Books, which is concerned with what the author admits to being myth, thus the English text begins with Book 2 and the year A.D. 965. In Books 2 and 3, where some years record only events outside the immediate scope of this account, these, too, have been omitted.

A.D. 965

The Christian lobby in Poland is now strong enough to enable his councillors to persuade Prince Mieszko to dismiss the seven concubines with whom he currently enjoys carnal love, so that continued association with them should not make him persist in the old pagan ways many wish to see changed. Then envoys are sent to Boleslav of Bohemia, he who murdered his own brother, Václav (the martyr), to ask for his daughter, Dubravka, as Mieszko's sole and lawful wife. These are told that Boleslav will not refuse so eminent a son-in-law provided Mieszko gives up his pagan ways and embraces the Holy Catholic Faith. They receive a similar reply from Dubravka, when they put the proposal to her. She tells them that it does not befit her, a Christian girl, to marry an idolator; but, if Mieszko will let himself be baptized, she will not refuse him.

Mieszko summons his councillors to consider these replies. Several are against accepting the new faith, which to them is suspect; some others consider it too rigorous a regimen for them to live by; while others deplore the discarding of ancestral traditions and the loss of freedom submission to this untried religion would entail. There is such lack of agreement that a decision is postponed until the following day, time enough for Divine Providence, which bestows salvation on kings and princes, to take pity on the Poles, so long in error, and inspire them to accept the Christian faith and thus prevent them becoming an object of contempt for the Bohemians and others, as would have happened had they refused.

An even more numerous embassy is now sent to Prague. The financial arrangements are settled and binding assurances given that not only Prince Mieszko, but the entire Polish nation, will be baptized. Boleslav then hands his daughter over to the Poles, together with her dowry and a trousseau consistent with her position. These then set off on their return journey escorted with extravagant pomp by a number of Bohemian nobles and knights. Mieszko, with many of his barons and nobles, and eminent persons of all estates, rides out from Gniezno to conduct them into the city, where the country's most eminent matrons and maidens, in all their finery, wearing their gold, silver and other ornaments in the bride's honour, as Mieszko has ordered, await the bride.

A few days later, Mieszko, sufficiently instructed in the articles and rites of the true faith by pious men and anchorites already living in the country, who have been summoned to Gniezno for that purpose, together with the greater barons and nobles and the leading citizens of Poland's towns, have their conversion from the darkness of superstition to the light of faith sanctified in the water of baptism. Mieszko, discarding his old name, which is considered too barbaric, re-names himself Mieczysław. His sister adopts both the new faith and a new name, Adelaide. On this same day, Mieczysław takes part in another sacrament, that of matrimony, marrying Dubravka according to the Catholic rite. The celebrations, to which Mieczysław has invited all the neighbouring princes, continue for several days. Each guest is received with rich presents and lavishly entertained. When they finally depart all are loud in their praise of the graciousness and wealth of Prince Mieczysław.

Rigorous measures are now agreed to ensure that all idols and images of the old gods are destroyed. Any who continue to worship them are condemned to lose their estates and heads. All rites, ceremonies and occasions when honour used to be paid to the idols are forbidden, as are divination, enchantments and soothsaying. All games, public or private, that used to be celebrated in honour of the old gods, are similarly prohibited, since our God is not to be mollified by applause, indecent gestures and all the other impieties, as pagan deities are. Nonetheless, almost every town and village still has idols of the old gods and goddesses hidden away in sacred groves, so Mieczysław fixes a day, March 7, on which day in every town and village, before a throng of both sexes, the images of the old gods are to be hacked to pieces and these cast into a lake, bog or marsh, and heaped over with stones. Those who used to make money out of the old idols are sorely aggrieved and weep, but none dares do anything, for fear of the Prince's officials. This destruction of the idols has since been celebrated every Laetare Sunday, when, in many villages, effigies of Dziewanna and Marzanna, are paraded on poles and then cast into a bog and drowned, a custom that persists to this day.

A.D. 966

Mieczysław, encouraged by his faithful wife Dubravka, considers the endowment of the country's sacred sites and the appointment of its holy men. First he founds two metropolitan sees: Gniezno, dedicated to the Blessed Virgin and Cracow to the newly-martyred St. Václav, since he was Dubravka's uncle. He decides that Gniezno is to have the first place and the primatial dignity and Cracow the second, so that through the existence of Cracow Gniezno would not stand alone, while through the existence of Gniezno Cracow would not stand supreme. He establishes seven other sees: Poznań, Smogorzow, which we now call Wrocław, Cruszwic, now Włocawek, Płock, Chełm, Lubusz and Kamień, which are to be subject to the jurisdiction of the metropolitans of Gniezno and Cracow. In addition, he founds collegiate churches, several parishes and churches and monasteries and religious houses.

A.D. 967

Princess Dubravka gives birth to a son, who is christened Bolesław after his grandfather, the Prince of Bohemia, who dies shortly after this and is succeeded by his son, Boleslav, a modest, quiet and pious man, whose younger brother Christinus takes his vows and enters the monastery of St. Emmeramus in Ratisbon, while their sister, Mládá, who is well versed in the holy scriptures, builds a nunnery in Prague and herself enters it. Many Bohemian girls follow her example and devote themselves to virginity and the monastic life.

A.D. 968

Géza, Prince of Pannonia, land of the Huns, who has lost his first wife, having heard reports of the virtue and beauty of Adelaide, sister of Mieczysław of Poland, now sends a formal embassy to the latter asking for her hand in marriage. Having listened to the request, Mieczysław summons his council of nobles and prelates to consider what answer to give. Adelaide herself firmly rejects the idea of marriage to a pagan, and some of Mieczysław's councillors are also against such a union because of the difference in their faiths, but Providence, which can produce good out of evil, induces Mieczysław to agree to the proposal, encouraging his sister with the hope that in the future she will be able to convert Géza and the Huns to the Catholic faith.

The council approves Mieczysław's proposal for such a bond between the two countries, and so Adelaide is sent to Hungary and there marries Géza. She and her entourage are persistent in their attempts to convert the Prince and his people to their faith and in the end they succeed. Géza and many of his nobles allow themselves to be baptized.

A.D. 969

Géza, Prince of Hungary, and his wife Adelaide have a son, Stephen.

A.D. 970

Sviatoslav, the Ruthenian prince, apparently dissatisfied with the lands he has inherited from his father, starts a war against his neighbours, the Bulgarians. He captures eighty of their fortified towns along the Danube and forces these to pay tribute. While he is thus engaged, the Petchenegs attack and besiege Kiev, where the Prince's mother Olga, formerly Helena, is living with her three grandsons, Iaropolk, Oleg and Vladimir. The city is on the point of being starved into surrender, when some Ruthenians serving with the Petchenegs cause panic by spreading a rumour that Sviatoslav and his victorious army have returned from Bulgaria and are in the offing. This sends the Petchenegs fleeing in disarray and the siege is raised; at which point Princess Olga dies.

A.D. 971

Sviatoslav, fearing that on his death his sons will quarrel among themselves, divides his lands between them: Iaropolk, as the eldest, he makes prince in Kiev, his second son, Oleg, he appoints duke of the Drevlianian lands, and the third, Vladimir, duke of the people of Novgorod. Each binds himself by mighty oaths to be satisfied with his share and to refrain from any attempt to take another's.

A.D. 972

Sviatoslav finally returns from his incursion into Bulgaria in possession of considerable booty. However, his homeward progress is barred by a large force of Petchenegs, which easily defeats him, either because his army is overburdened with booty or because the site in which he chooses to do battle is unfavourable. He, himself, in trying to make his men stand firm and so prevent a shameful rout, falls into the hands of his enemies, whose leader, Kura, has Sviatoslav's head severed and made into a goblet, ornamented with gold, from which he, Kura, drinks a daily toast to his triumph.

A.D. 973

Otto I, King of the Romans and Duke of Saxony, suppressed many of the Saxon's sites that were dedicated to idolatry and made them subject to the Christian faith; he founded a metropolitan see in Magdeburg where he is buried in the church of St. Maurice. In this year he is succeeded by his son, the second Otto, a man of probity like his father.

A.D. 974

Moved by the prayers and entreaties of his sister Dubravka, Boleslav endows an epispocal see for Prague in the church of St. Vitus built by St. Václav and endows it generously. Its first bishop is a Saxon monk, Diethmar, who knows something of the Slav tongue.

A.D. 976

The division of lands between the sons of Sviatoslav and their love for each other do not long survive their father's death. Even the broad lands of Ruthenia are too narrow for them and they cannot agree about supremacy. The eldest, Iaropolk, seizes the castle of Warasz, the seat of his brother, Oleg, whom he kills. Then, stained with his brother's blood, he annexes the whole of Drevlianian territory. The youngest, Vladimir, fearing lest Iaropolk sooner or later turn on him, lays siege to Kiev with his brother inside, and, when Iaropolk comes out to him in peace, prompted by Iaropolk's criminal councillor and voivode, Blud, Vladimir kills his brother and so has possession of all three dukedoms. Not content with this, he also takes Iaropolk's pregnant widow and makes her his titular wife, though she could not be more than his concubine, since his real wife, Rogneda, was still alive. Nonetheless, she has her child, a son, whom they christen Sviatopolk.

A.D. 977

Princess Dubravka dies and is buried in the church at Gniezno.

A.D. 978

Vladimir now being a bigamist in Christian eyes, it is logical that he should revert to his old pagan ways and his people with him. Statues and idols are again set up near the castle in Kiev and shrines built in the nearby hills. The chief of the old gods is Piorun, the god of lightning, and his statues are the largest and finest. The entire Ruthenian people honour him and make him burnt offerings and other sacrifices. Vladimir commissions an especially fine statue of him; it is to have a wooden trunk and a silver head with golden ears; other gods have sacred groves allotted to them. Vladimir worships them all, as do his sons and daughters, of whom there are many, for he has taken several wives, one of whom alone gives him four sons and two daughters, while by another he has six sons, besides all the offspring of his numerous concubines. It is said, too, that he is intemperate and unrestrained in his raping of maidens and other people's wives.

A.D. 979

Mieczysław proves a far more scrupulous guide for his people for he is reported to have travelled the country promoting baptism and Christianity and encouraging those already baptised with extra gifts of cloth and money, thereby adding to his own popularity. He introduces or, perhaps, revives what may well have been a pagan custom, according to which, halfway through the service, as the priest chants the Holy Gospel, the knights and barons, still girded with their swords, half draw these from their scabbards, as do men going into battle, and then, as the choir make the response: "Glory unto Thee, O Lord", sheath them again. This practice, the purpose of which is to demonstrate the determination of the nobility to be steadfast in their defence of the Gospel, if necessary giving their lives for it, is to continue almost up to the present day. It is a great shame that it has been abandoned.

A.D. 980

Mieczysław realizes that many of his people, nobles as well as peasants, still cling to the old false gods and make them offerings of incense, drink and perfumes according to the ancient rites, neglecting the boon of baptism, and he now sends officials and heralds to every part of the country with orders that everyone is to assemble at the nearest cathedral church, there to receive a Christian name as a token of Christian faith. Everyone is to be baptised anew, no excuses being allowed, failure to comply with the order is to be punished with confiscation of goods. As a result, many images of the old gods are destroyed, either by fire or by being flung into a bog and so into oblivion.

A.D. 981

Diethmar, first Bishop of Prague, dies and is succeeded by Adalbert, a Bohemian by birth and tongue, who is elected by the clergy and people. He had been baptised Wojciech, but Bishop Albert of Magdeburg, to whom he went as a youth, could not pronounce his name and called him Adalbert instead.

A.D. 984

Bolesław, Mieczysław's son, having observed the six years' mourning ordered for his mother, is told by his father to find himself a wife and if, in doing so, he can revive Poland's ancient friendship with Pannonia, so much the better. Obediently he marries Judith, daughter of Géza of Hungary by his first marriage, a girl of outstanding presence and beauty, who has a rich dowry of gold and silver. The marriage is celebrated in Gniezno with all the requisite pomp in the presence of numerous prelates and barons from Poland and Hungary.

A.D. 985

Vladimir, Prince of Ruthenia, now turns his thoughts to war. He mounts an expedition against Mieczysław, captures the Polish towns of Przemyśl and Cherven and installs strong garrisons in them. He then attacks the Radimichians, who are of Polish extraction, defeats them and exacts tribute.

A.D. 986

Prohorius, the first archbishop of Cracow, dies and is buried in the cathedral. His successor is Prokulf.

A.D. 987

A year of great famine due to man's evil-doing. The harvest fails almost throughout the world, and in certain countries numbers of people die. Poland is one of the countries affected and many villages, even towns, are depopulated. Now, Vladimir of Ruthenia receives envoys representing different religions: the first to arrive are the Mohammedans recommending the false faith of Mahomet; next come the Latins; thirdly the Jews promoting the Hebraic faith and law; and lastly the Greeks who urge the prince to adopt the Christian faith. He treats the delegations graciously and sends them away loaded with gifts. He and his people then deliberate as to which religion to choose, but they cannot make up their minds, so they agree to send emissaries to the various countries to see how they practice their religions. These visit the Bulgars, who are Mohammedans, then the Latins and then the Greeks. The Mohammedan faith they find has much that is reprehensible; the Roman ceremonial is too crude for their liking; but, when they reach Byzantium, the two emperors, Basil and Constantine, guessing their purpose, summon up a throng of priests and monks, arrange great ceremonies and have the Patriarch celebrate Mass in his most splendid vestments. The Ruthenians are invited to witness the ceremony, after which they are sent away loaded with presents and full of the miraculous sweetness of which they were so aware while attending the Greek mass. The conclusion in their report to Vladimir is that the faith of the Mohammedans is not worth considering; while the Greek ceremonial is so much more ostentatious than the Roman, its churches so much better, even lavishly decorated, that the princes recommend the Greek rite and remind the Prince that his grandmother, Olga, was of that persuasion and she was one of the wisest of women. Vladimir recognises the force of the argument and agrees to accept Christianity according to the Greek rite.

A.D. 988

Persistent flooding in many parts of Poland in the previous year caused harvests to be poor or a complete failure. Now comes a spring so unusually dry that the spring sowing is prevented. This is followed by a hot and, for many people, fatal summer, for the result has been famine.

A.D. 989

Wojciech, Bishop of Prague, decides to resign his bishopric and become a monk. He does this, he says, because the Bohemians are such gross, heinous sinners: they take several wives, practice pagan rites, sell Christian boys and girls to the Jews, trade on holy days, choose for themselves graves in ground that has not been consecrated, and pay no attention to the admonitions of their bishop. Wojciech tries to persuade Prince Boleslav's brother, Christinus, to take charge of the see, pointing out it will be easier for him, with his brother's help, to clean up the abuses. Christinus has no wish to concern himself with worldly affairs and refuses, saying he is unequal to such a burden. Wojciech prophesies that since so good a man will not take on the see of Prague, worse will surely follow. So, Wojciech goes to Rome, intending to travel on to Jerusalem, but in Rome he changes his mind and enters the monastery of SS Alexius and Boniface.

A.D. 990

Judith, wife of Bolesław of Poland, having remained childless for five years, gives birth to a son, who is baptised in the font of Gniezno cathedral and christened Mieczysław.

Vladimir, Prince of Ruthenia, who has been assembling a considerable army, now makes a second attack on the Greeks and captures one of their finer cities, Korsun, forcing it and the surrounding country to pay him tribute. He then sends emissaries to Basil and Constantine, the Byzantine emperors, asking for the hand of their sister, Anna, who, he thinks, would make him a suitable third wife. Were this marriage to take place, the emissaries explain, Vladimir would immediately relinquish Korsun and the territories round it that he has conquered. Basil and Constantine reply to the effect that it does not befit them to enter into such a relationship with a pagan and one guilty of idolatry, nor is it fitting for their sister to be wedded to such a person; however, were Vladimir to abandon his pagan errors and adopt Christianity, they would not refuse the request. Vladimir agrees, but wants the two Emperors to come and baptize him themselves. Anna is against the idea altogether and seeks to refuse, but her two brothers prevail on her to accept, pointing out how much good will result from Vladimir's conversion and that of the entire Ruthenian people. So, Basil, Constantine and their sister, Anna, go to Korsun, where they find Vladimir stricken with blindness and beginning to regret his acceptance of the proposal, for is not his blindness a punishment for having abandoned his pagan beliefs? Anna, however, persuades him that his sight will return as soon as he has been baptized. And baptized he is, by the Bishop of Korsun, and immediately he is able to see, and marries Anna. He also builds a church in memory of his conversion, then returns to his own country with his new wife.

A.D. 992

Returned home, Vladimir sets about eradicating the old pagan rites and destroying altars and shrines of the traditional gods. He orders the public destruction of the wonderful statue of Piorun which he had commissioned earlier. This is to be overthrown, tied to the tail of a horse, dragged to the bank of the Dniepr and thrown into its waters. The destruction of the old gods and their idols is not accomplished without tears and lamentations from worshippers of both sexes. Vladimir then issues orders that all members of the tribes subject to him should be marked with the symbol of their new faith and baptism, and that any who disobey are to be regarded as his enemies and have their goods confiscated. This order sends throngs of people pouring into Kiev, where they are all baptized in the Dniepr by the Bishop of Korsun and a team of clergy, trained in the rite, who have been specially sent there from Greece. The heavens resound with the lamentations of the dragon, bewailing the loss of its former power over the Ruthenians, a loss occasioned not by the machinations of apostles or martyrs, but by a mere woman. Vladimir erects the first church to be built there and orders its dedication to St. Basil. Chapels and shrines spring up all over the country. A second church is built in Kiev and suitably endowed, boyars and peasants being ordered to pay their first fruits as tithes. Next, he has twelve of his sons christened. Ruthenian children are now taught to write, and artists are imported from Greece and duly rewarded. Churches are built in brick and stone.

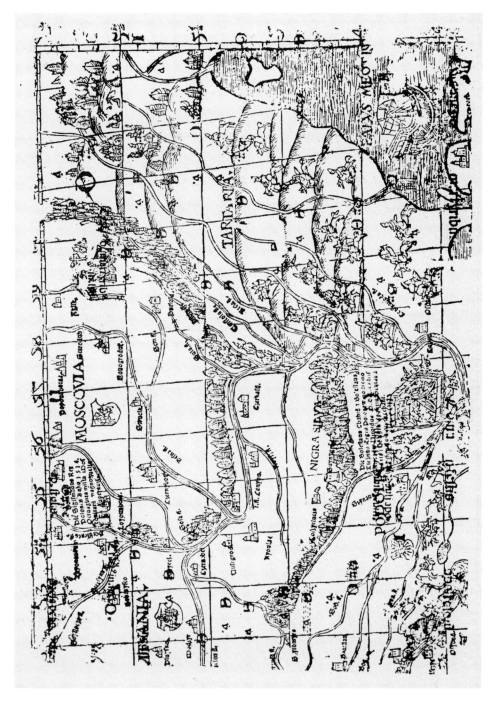

From B. Wapolski's early 16th century map of Eastern Europe.

A.D. 993

It is now five years since Wojciech abandoned the see of Prague and still he has not been replaced. The Bohemians are indignant and lay the blame for a number of misfortunes on this lack of a bishop. Unable to punish a bishop who is not there, they turn on his relatives who are and their possessions. One holy day, a considerable armed throng makes a forcible entry into the town of Libice, where they murder five of the holy Wojciech's brothers. They then go on the rampage, slaughtering 7000 of the inhabitants, regardless of sex or status; and finally set fire to the entire town. This evil deed the Bohemian prince neither condemns nor punishes; however, the Archbishop of Mainz hears of it and officially asks the Pope to send Wojciech back to his flock. The Pope summons Wojciech to him and orders him to return to Prague. Wojciech, however, has other ideas; he explains the nature of the Bohemians to the Pope, telling him how obstinate and savage they are, and how his return would do no good whatever. Instead, he prays that he be allowed to take the word of God to the peoples on the shores of the Northern Seas. The Pope grants his request, provided he first sees what he can do in Prague, so the holy Wojciech leaves his monastery and reluctantly travels to Prague. There, he achieves nothing, except that he is able to buy some Jews who are being sold into slavery and to give them their freedom.

A.D. 994

Wojciech leaves Prague for the second time, having been finally relieved of his see and given permission to preach the word of God to the peoples beyond the boundaries of Poland. With this permit in his wallet, he goes first to Hungary, taking with him a number of monks, the idea being to confirm Géza and his wife Adelaide in their new faith. Géza and Adelaide are delighted. Wojciech confirms their son, Stephen, and then spends the next twelve months preaching to the Slavs and Huns, converting many of them from their idolatry. Wojciech's detractors catch up with him, however, and he leaves Hungary. A few days after his departure, Géza dies of natural causes and is succeeded by his son, Stephen.

A.D. 995

Prokulf, the second archbishop of Cracow, dies and is buried in the cathedral. With the Prince's consent, he is succeeded by Lambert. Robert, the first archbishop of Gniezno, also dies. He, too, is buried in his cathedral.

A.D. 996

Reaching Poland, Wojciech spends some time in Cracow, where he preaches in Czech, which the Poles understand. Eventually, he moves on to Gniezno, the country's other metropolitan seat, where he is rapturously received, and, at Prince Mieczysław's request takes over the vacant see.

A.D. 997

Desiring a martyr's crown, as he himself has said, or, perhaps just remembering the Pope's commission which is still in his wallet, Wojciech leaves Gniezno, and, with an escort of thirty knights and courtiers provided by Mieczysław, heads for the territory of the Prussians beyond Poland's frontiers, across the River Ossa, a tributary of the Vistula. The Prussians are reputed to be a fierce, cruel people, immersed in idolatry and the worship of demons, so blind in their errors that they worship as gods the sun, moon and stars, as well as animals, birds and fire. They hold certain woods, lakes and streams sacred, and in these no man may hunt, fish or cut timber. They have their own language, which is partly derived from Latin and somewhat like the language of the Lithuanians, with whom they have various gods, ceremonies and festivals in common. They have a high priest whose orders must be scrupulously obeyed under penalty of death; he lives in the capital which is called Romowe, after Rome. The word for high priest in their language is Criwe.

The Prussians, Lithuanians and Samogitians have largely the same customs, language and origin. It is said that at the time of the civil war between Caesar and Pompey they left their homes, wherever these were, and came to settle in these lands by the sea, where they now live. They built their settlements deep in the forest, protected by rivers, lakes and swamps. Their pronunciation of words may differ, as it does in Polish, Czech and Ruthenian today, but otherwise their languages are similar in many respects. They do not consider that they have a common stem or language; indeed, the Prussians claim a quite different ancestry, for they will tell you that after the Carthaginian leader, Hannibal, was defeated by the Romans, he fled to Bithynia and found refuge there. He persuaded Prussias, king of the Bithynians, to take up arms against the Romans on his behalf. There was a pitched battle in which the Bithynians were soundly defeated, after which Prussias and most of his people fled to these northern shores where they now live, Prussias, giving his own name to their new country. Traces of these Bithynians are still to be found: indeed some Prussians are still able to speak their old language, to the extent that they can perfectly understand Aeolian, Dorian and Ionian Greek.

The Prussians buy their wives and make them work like slaves. They burn the bodies of the dead together with their horses, arms, clothing and other things dear to their hearts. Otherwise, they are by nature hospitable and friendly. They indulge in bouts of drunkenness, achieved, for wine is not known to them, by drinking fermented mare's milk, which is inebriating. They do not consider that they have been sufficiently hospitable to friend or guest until they see him well and truly intoxicated. Their womenfolk are as ardent topers as the men. Prussians can have an unlimited number of wives, just as many as each can afford to buy; consequently they do not respect them, but force them to perform the servile duties of slaves. Both men and women have a bath every day in order to counter the effects of their drunkenness and so prolong their lives. Begging is prohibited and, indeed, unnecessary, since anyone, however hungry, can be sure of being well entertained in whatever house he cares to enter.

To these people the holy Wojciech now begins to preach through an interpreter provided by Mieczysław, telling them that the sun, moon, animals and fire, which they and their ancestors had worshipped, were in fact creations of his God, who might allow certain demons to inhabit the lakes and forests they considered sacred. It is scarcely to be wondered at that these proud people with their old traditions and ancestry take objection to his preaching and persistent denigration of the gods of their ancestors. Their objection sometimes takes physical form, with the preacher being driven out of the house in which he has been staying and forced to sleep in the open, without a roof over his head, perhaps drenched with rain and shivering with cold. In the end, their high priest, the Criwe, incites the other priests to conspire together to get rid of Wojciech. They achieve this, one day when Wojciech, who by then has traversed more or less the length and breadth of the country proclaiming his objectionable message, comes to a settlement by the sea. There, on April 23, on a cliff by the shore he prepares to say a solemn mass for the conversion of Prussia. The Prussians interpret the ceremonial as a casting of spells and charms intended to destroy them and their gods, and so they fall upon Wojciech and kill him. They sever his head and hang it up in a tree for three days. Then, apprehensive lest they should have to suffer for what they have done, they secretly bury the body in a neighbouring village. Wojciech's six companions and fellow missionaries are expelled from the country under pain of death should they ever dare to return.

Poland under Mieczysław has become so powerful, populous and rich that those who run it, prelates and barons, consider that the time has come for their country to be made one of the Christian Kingdoms and be granted a crown by the Pope. They begin petitioning Mieczysław to send to Rome to ask for such a crown, and this he agrees to do, sending an embassy under Bishop Lambert of Cracow. As the Poles arrive in Rome, an embassy from Prince Stephen of Hungary reaches the Holy City bent on the very same errand. The Pope, Benedict VII, is said to have been inclined at first to grant both petitions: indeed, he seems even to have promised a crown to Poland; but then, reputedly, he has a vision which causes him to change his mind, so that only Hungary receives the coveted crown. In justifying his decision the Pope points out that the Poles are more fond of blood-thirsty hunts than of acts of piety and charity, are more inclined to oppress their subject peoples, more concerned with booty than peace, more prone to mendacity than to telling the truth, have more regard for their cattle and their dogs than for people, and are not averse to shedding blood, and thus not yet worthy of a royal crown.

Fearing that his award of a crown to Prince Stephen and his denial of one to Prince Mieczysław may cause conflict, even warfare between the two, Pope Benedict summons the envoys of both parties and commands them to preserve good relations; whichever party does not will be anathematized. There are those who maintain that the Pope was not persuaded by an angelic vision, but rather heard for a fact that Mieczysław of Poland was dead, and so did not give him a crown, and certainly I have read this account in some of the Polish annals; by the same token the angelic apparition, which adds a certain lustre to the sending of a crown to the Hungarians, may well be something they themselves have dreamed up: for they continue to this day to call their crown "holy", with little justice, for there can be no holiness in a metal object and still less in one gained through usurpation and trickery.

This same year the Ruthenians ravage the lands of the Croats; whereupon the Polovtsy declare war on the Ruthenians. The two armies make contact on the River Trubezh, but with one army on each bank and the river in between there can be no pitched battle; but then, out from the camp of the Polovtsy steps a man of unusual stature, who challenges the Ruthenians to choose a champion from their own ranks to fight a duel with him. Whoever is defeated, his country shall be an object of plunder for three years. A Ruthenian is produced, not from the army there, but sent for from home, and he takes up the challenge. This Ruthenian is of such small stature that the Polovtsian champion treats him with disdain. The duel starts and the little Ruthenian proves the victor, whereupon the Polovtsy take to their heels. The Ruthenians pursue them, killing many and capturing others. Duke Vladimir erects the castle of Pereiaslavl on the site to commemorate the duel.

A.D. 998

On February 7 of this year Boleslav the Pious, brother of Princess Dubravka of Poland, dies in Prague, leaving a son, another Boleslav, to succeed him. According to his uncle, Mieczysław of Poland, the new king of Bohemia is a weakling and allows the country to be exploited by the greedy, rich and powerful. Mieczysław's disapproval of the situation takes practical expression, for he assembles a powerful army and, accompanied by his son, invades Bohemia. Most Bohemian cities welcome the Poles with open arms, but Prague refuses to accept the king's authority and shuts its gates against him. Mieczysław attacks and gains control of the city and its castle. After putting the country's affairs to rights, Mieczysław returns to Poland. No blood has been shed and Mieczysław is greeted like a conquering hero.

The Pechenegs are planning to invade Ruthenia and put it to fire and the sword. Vladimir learning of their intentions, assembles an army and bars the invader's path. There is a bloody battle in which Vladimir flees and has to hide under a bridge to avoid capture. The victorious Pechenegs capture the Ruthenians' train and return home with considerable booty, many captives and a quantity of cattle.

A.D. 999

Mieczysław of Poland dies and is buried in the cathedral in Poznań. After the funeral, his twenty-eight year-old son, Bolesław, is chosen to succeed him. The new king is a paragon of all the virtues: modest, gifted, handsome, pious, generous to the clergy, gracious to knights and open-handed to those of other ranks. He has at his court not only his own knights, but also men to whom he or his father had granted their freedom and these are so numerous as almost to constitute a separate army.

A.D. 1000

The Prussians, learning that Bolesław sets great store on obtaining possession of the body of Bishop Wojciech, whom they murdered three years previously, send ambassadors to Poland to tell the King that it would be pointless to invade Prussia, since the bishop's body is buried in a secret place, but that, to please him, they are prepared to sell the body for its weight in silver. Bolesław agrees and sends priests and knights to Prussia with what is considered a large enough quantity of silver provided by the treasury. When they reach Romowe, the Prussians duly produce the body from its secret burial place, and the Poles have then to identify it, which they do from the wounds known to have been inflicted upon it and by other marks. While this is being done, it is remarked how miraculously sweetly the body smells. The corpse is then placed on the scales, which reveal that it has lost so much weight that only a handful of silver is required to level the balance. Both the Prussians and the Poles are amazed. The Poles proclaim it a miracle. The body is removed from the scales and placed in a coffin of exquisite workmanship specially brought from Poland. The rest of the silver is gathered up and the exultant Poles depart with it, leaving the Prussians feeling cheated, but not daring to restrain them or seize more of the silver.

The bishop's body is first taken to the monastery of the Austin canons in Trzemeszno, and then to Gniezno, where it rapidly becomes an object of pilgrimage from as far away as Hungary and Germany.

A.D 1001

Hearing of the miracles wrought by the body of the martyred Wojciech, the Roman Emperor, Otto III, vows that if he is relieved of the ailment from which he is suffering, he will make a personal pilgrimage to Wojciech's shrine. He does recover and sets off for Poland with a multitude of princes and knights and suitable gifts for the saint, eager to fulfill his vow and to see in person Prince Bolesław of whom he has heard so much. Bolesław prepares a suitably lavish reception for his eminent guest: coming to meet the Emperor with a large detachment of his household knights; providing him with all he needs and conducting him to Poznań. He also covers the seven miles between Poznań and Gniezno with cloth for it was part of the Emperor's vow to walk the whole distance. In Gniezno they are met by Archbishop Gaudentius and the other bishops, prelates and barons and a festive crowd which Bolesław has ordered to gather to greet the Emperor.

When he reaches the cathedral Otto prostrates himself before the body of St. Wojciech and gives thanks for his recovery: each day piling gifts of gold and silver, worthy of an Emperor, before the shrine. Each day, Bolesław gives the Emperor and his retinue gifts of fitting magnificence: gold, silver and gems, horses, falcons and furs. The Emperor is so impressed by Bolesław's munificence, his prudence and fine judgment and the disciplined performance of his knights and servants that he tells his councillors he believes Bolesław is worthy of the dignity of a king. All acclaim his decision.

In Gniezno cathedral, accompanied by a throng of knights and the populace, the Emperor orders Archbishop Gaudentius and the Polish bishops to anoint Bolesław as King of the Poles with sacral chrism and to perform the special prayers reserved for the anointment of kings. Then he seats him on a throne especially elevated so that the throng may see him and, removing a diadem from his own head, places it upon Bolesław's brow, appointing him and his successors kings of Poland, allies and friends of the Roman Empire and subjecting to their rule all the Polish regions and peoples and whatever lands and districts God might allow them in future to acquire among the barbarians, infidels and schismatics. Further he gives him and the whole Polish kingdom the white eagle on a red field which is to be theirs, as the Roman empire has a black eagle which holds all the Teutonic peoples as its subjects. He must spread the Catholic faith among the Slav and barbarian peoples, rule his subjects justly, observe church law and God, if He sees fit, shall reward him by allowing his heirs and descendants to inherit his authority. The special privileges of the Kings and the Kingdom of Poland are recorded in a golden bull which also absolves them from all obedience and subjection to the Roman Emperor and his successors. Thus is the Polish republic fashioned under the laws of kings, and Bolesław set above all other dukes of the Slav race and tongue.

Feeling he would be ashamed if he did not further reciprocate King Bolesław's generosity, Otto formally bethrothes Bolesław's son Mieczysław to his own niece Ryksa, eldest daughter of Herenfried, Count Palatine of the Rhine. Finally he presents King Bolesław with a nail from the True Cross, which pierced the body of Christ, a noble thing the Emperor holds dearer than anything in the world, and the lance of St. Maurice, also precious, to serve him in his wars with the barbarians. In return Bolesław gives the Emperor one of the blessed Wojciech's arms. After this exchange of courtesies, the Emperor sets out for home, accompanied on the journey by a number of Polish knights and dignitaries, who are to escort Ryksa back to Poland. They duly reach Magdeburg, the Emperor's favoured seat, and there Ryksa and her dowry are formally handed over to the escort.

A.D. 1002

Back in Rome after his pilgrimage to Wojciech's shrine, the Emperor finds he has to deal with a certain Crescencius, a Roman, who has suffocated the Pope, John XVI, and seized power in Rome; his ambition is growing and he is aiming to gain control of all Italy, and thus of the Empire. Otto takes counter-measures and succeeds in shutting Crescencius up in Hadrian's old fortress. He then entices him out onto the bridge and kills him. All this would have redounded to his credit, only he spoils it all by yielding to the physical attractions of Crescencius' wife and raping her; after which she avenges herself by giving Otto poison, of which he dies on January 28.

The moment the Emperor is found to be dead, the Archbishop of Cologne, Herbert, takes command. He has the Emperor's body dressed in his purple robes and set on his horse, as if still alive, and so he "rides" out from Rome. Thus is the news of his death kept from the people, who, it is said, would otherwise have been up in arms. The Emperor is conveyed across the Alps to Swabia, where his intestines are interred in Augsburg, while the rest of the body continues on to Aachen and is there buried. Henry II of Bavaria becomes the new Emperor, the eighty-fourth.

The Bohemians are profoundly jealous of Poland and its new dignity, and the councillors of King Boleslav, particularly the barons of the Vršovci and Rawita clans, are keen to sow discord for their own profit: so they advocate war against Poland to increase Bohemia's prestige and perhaps force Bolesław to pay tribute. So, without sufficient, indeed without any, justification, Boleslav assembles an army, invades at Kłodzko and proceeds to lay the country waste. Bolesław of Poland, amazed at such behaviour on the part of someone he has always considered to be a friend and brother, sends ambassadors to require that, in view of past ties and years of peace, the Bohemians abandon their action, return all the booty they have taken, pay compensation for all the damage they have inflicted, and restore peace. The Bohemians reply that they only undertook the war reluctantly and solely in order to right past wrongs and put an end to continual violations by the Poles. Boleslav has no wish to continue hostilities, they say, and is prepared to negotiate a truce, provided he can be suitably compensated. The Poles take this to mean that hostilities are suspended, if not ended; but Boleslav, listening, as before, to his councillors who advise him that the Poles will never dare to defend themselves, assembles an even larger force, breaks the truce and again moves into Poland, laying it waste as he goes. Bolesław, learning of this reverse, furiously calls upon all able-bodied men in the kingdom to rally to the standard and moves in forced marches against the Bohemians. Boleslav, learning from his scouts that the Polish forces are stronger than his, withdraws into his own country, so the Poles, to their chagrin, find him and his army gone. Bolesław vows to treat the other Boleslav not only as an enemy but also a poisonous spy.

A.D. 1003

Prince Bolesław now decides on war against the Bohemians in order to punish them for their treachery and to repay them in kind for the damage they have done to his country. He invades with a huge force and is helped by the Vřsovci whose lands he spares. Many of the towns surrender; those that resist he destroys and burns, hoping thus to make Boleslav come and fight. He, however, shuts himself and his son up in the castle of Vyšehrad, the fortress of Prague. The Poles then invest both the castle and the city, which, after a siege of two years are both starved into submission. Boleslav and his son, Jaromír, are taken prisoner. The Poles occupy the royal residence and take control of the whole country. Many of the Bohemian nobles and barons swear allegiance to the Polish king.

As things settle down, Prince Bolesław appoints Poles and trustworthy Bohemians as his lieutenants and starostas in the principal towns and cities and prepares to return to Poland, taking his army with him. His advisers, particularly the Vřsovci, ask that before he goes, as an insurance against future revolt, he put both Boleslav and his son, Jaromír, to death; but he cannot bring himself to do this, and, instead, has the Bohemian king's eyes put out and hands Jaromír to the Vřsovci to imprison.

A.D. 1004

Considering it inadvisable to leave Moravia independent, Bolesław prepares a considerable force and sets about besieging the few towns that do not voluntarily surrender. Now the revenues of all Bohemia and Moravia are sent to Poland.

Bolesław of Poland is afraid lest the Bohemian king's second son, Oldřich, who has long been in the service of the Emperor and so living outside Bohemia, should become a rallying-point for those Czechs who object to the Polish rule of their country, so he sends emissaries to Henry requesting that Oldřich be handed over to him. The Emperor, who has been showered with gifts, agrees, and poor Oldřich is surrendered and taken to Poland, where he is to live for a number of years in not too rigorous captivity.

A.D. 1005

Poland has six men famed for their piety and holy lives: Benedict, Matthew, John, Isaac, Christian and Barnabas.

Bolesław, hearing reports of the virtues of St. Romuald, sends to ask him for a few of his brethren, who, by their example, may help to strengthen the Polish people, so recently converted, in their faith. The Emperor Henry, who is at this time in Pereum, a waste in the marshes near Ravenna, supports the request with a personal visit to St. Romuald. The saint is unwilling to order any of the brethren to go, but leaves it to them to decide. Though urged by the Emperor, only two volunteer, Brother John and Brother Benedict. These two Bolesław welcomes as if they were angels from Heaven. They are joined by four of the pious Poles already mentioned who teach them their language. The King gives them a site in Wielkopolska, an area surrounded by woods and forests, where the town of Kazimierz now stands, and here they build little huts, one for each, and live the abstemious lives of hermits, maintained by the generosity of the King, teaching the people with such great success that their fame spreads throughout Poland.

They have no possessions of their own, nor any livelihood but alms. Their garments are coarse and rough; their food scant and of the simplest, and they spend their days in prayer and fasting, making the flesh submit to the spirit by flogging their own bodies.

Everyone comes to them: clerics, nobles, peasants, even the King himself. On one occasion, Bolesław spends some days at the hermitage. On leaving, he presents the hermits with an ingot of gold to relieve their poverty. They protest that they have no need of gold and ask the King to take it back and put it to some other purpose. The King replies that it would be unseemly to take what has been offered to God and put it to some secular use, so the gold is left with the hermits. They are appalled at having it, and determine to send it back to the King. Barnabas, the youngest and the one accustomed to dealing with the outside world, is chosen to return the gold and he sets out with it. That night, some men, who know of the King's gift to the hermits and want it for themselves, come like thieves in the night to the hermitage and demand the gold, threatening the hermits with an ugly death, if they do not hand it over. When the hermits tell them that it has already been returned to the King, they do not believe them, but ransack the huts, looking for the gold. Failing to find it, they assume that the hermits have hidden it; so, taking each aside separately, they torture them to make them reveal where the ingot is hidden. The hermits have the courage and endurance to stick to their story; so the angry thieves continue to torture them, beating them and burning them, and eventually kill them. Then, in order to cover up their crime, they set fire to the hermitage, intending to burn the bodies. However, the fire does not consume the bodies, nor will it even burn the wood of the huts. It is as if the walls were made of dressed stone, not wood. The thieves, terrified by the miracle, run away.

Vladimir the Great, of Ruthenia, has twelve sons: four (Izjaslav, Iaroslav, Mstislav and Vsevolod) by his first wife and eight (Vysheslav, Sviatopolk, Sviatoslav, Boris, Gleb, Stanislav, Pozvizd and Sudislav) by his second wife, Anna, sister of Basil and Constantine.

He has governed successfully and made his country happy for a number of years, in the process considerably enlarging its boundaries. Now, fearing lest on his death his children should quarrel among themselves, he distributes his possessions between them, retaining for himself Kiev and Berestovo, which, on his death, are to go to his three youngest sons. Iaroslav, fourth of his sons by his first wife, is disappointed by the arrangement, considering that his share does not correspond to his abilities, and he assembles his men near Kiev and attacks it. He captures the castle and removes all his father's treasure from it. Incensed by this behaviour, Vladimir assembles contingents from all the domains he has just distributed among his children, in order to teach Iaroslav a lesson. But Iaroslav, learning what is afoot, seeks armed assistance from the Pechenegs and Varangians. Learning of this, the wretched Vladimir suffers a stroke, or, at least falls seriously ill, and hands over command of this punitive force to his son, Boris, with orders that he is to attack and deal with Iaroslav. Shortly after this, Vladimir dies in the castle at Berestovo. His body is taken to Kiev and there buried in the church of the Holy Virgin Mary, which he himself had built. Meanwhile, his two sons, Boris and Sviatopolk, still ignorant of their father's death, engage Iaroslav and his allies and rout them. Iaroslav escapes. Sviatopolk goes to Kiev and assumes control there, leaving Boris to see to their father's funeral. While he is busied with this, Sviatopolk treacherously has him assassinated. He then sends for his other brother, Gleb. Gleb, warned by Boris's fate, halts when half way; but Sviatopolk sends some of his henchmen to deal with him and they kill him and cut off his head. Both bodies, those of Boris and Gleb, are taken to Kiev and there buried in one grave in the church of St. Basil, where they are revered as martyrs.

A.D. 1006

King Stephen of Hungary, nephew of Mieczysław of Poland, and brother-in-law of King Boleslav, has a son by his wife, Gisela, sister of the late Emperor, Henry I, named Emeric. This Emeric has now reached man's estate and his father desires that he take a wife and perpetuate the line. Emeric, who ardently desires a life of celibacy, but does not dare go against his father's wishes, marries the girl of his father's choice, but continues his life of celibacy and abstinence, preserving his, and her, body pure and free of sensual corruption. He treats his wife as his sister, and lives with her, as if he were not yet married; thus the two remain pure and virtuous until they die. One must admire them, both eminent personages with the wealth to buy whatever pleasures they might desire and to have all the things that ordinary mortals consider important; yet they preferred to attain eternal bliss through love of the most difficult virtues, amounting to little less than martyrdom.

A.D. 1007

Bolesław of Poland finally takes pity on Oldřich, son of Boleslav of Bohemia, whom he has kept captive all these years, and sets him free against his promise to remain loyal to his erstwhile captor. So Oldřich is sent back to Bohemia suitably equipped with horses, servants, clothes and jewellery befitting his status. No sooner is he out of Poland, however, than he forgets his promise, dismisses all his Polish servants and those knights of his household who are not prepared to break their word, and hounds them from the country. Poland never had a more bitter enemy than Oldřich, who proceeds to imprison his own brother Jaromír, and have both his eyes put out.

A.D. 1008

Iaroslav of Ruthenia gathers together a powerful force and attacks his brother Sviatopolk in an attempt to avenge the murder of his two other brothers, Gleb and Boris. Sviatopolk bars the way to Iaroslav and his allies near the fortress of Liubech on the River Dniepr, which separates the two armies. Neither army dares to attempt a crossing, and there they are encamped with the river between them, and so they remain for three months. Suddenly, Iaroslav manages to move his entire army across the river and mounts a sudden attack on Sviatopolk's forces in their camp, which is sited between two lakes. Sviatopolk's men are surprised and quite unprepared. Many just rush from their tents and dash out onto the ice, for the lakes are now frozen. However, the ice is too thin to bear their weight and most of them drown. Those who do survive, or who do not venture onto the ice, are put to the sword or taken into captivity.

Sviatopolk himself manages to escape and makes his way to Poland, where he seeks the help of King Bolesław, to whom he promises all sorts of inducements. Iaroslav, having defeated Sviatopolk, invests the castle in Kiev, forces it to surrender and himself assumes control.

Meanwhile, Bolesław is gathering together an army of his bravest knights and best infantry from all his domains, and when he has a force he considers strong enough, he invades Ruthenia in order to restore the banished Sviatopolk to his throne and to avenge the conspiracies, attacks, looting and other crimes which Poland has suffered at the hands of the Ruthenians. The units of this great army are so well trained by their officers that they will stand firm, pursue or attack, just as the situation requires. Once inside Ruthenia, Bolesław systematically takes and occupies all the towns, big or small, mostly without resistance. In those days there were no fortified towns in Ruthenia, indeed, scarcely any towns with walls round them, and, although some of the bigger towns were densely populated and contained many buildings, they were defended only by their geographical position, or, at best a wooden palisade doing duty for walls and ramparts. Those towns that Bolesław captures easily he gives to his knights to plunder; others which show signs of serious resistance he leaves alone, for he knows that to invest and storm them will take time, and time is precious to him. Having traversed Ruthenia from end to end in a series of forced marches, despoiling and burning as he goes, Bolesław reaches Volhynia without opposition.

The Prince of the Ruthenians, Iaroslav, is an ardent sportsman, and he is fishing in the Dniepr when the news of Bolesław's invasion reaches him. Appalled, he discards his rod, remarking that this is not the time to be thinking of rods and fish, but rather of how best to deal with one's enemies and prevent them from hooking you! Hastily assembling a considerable force of Ruthenians, Varangians and Pechenegs, he bars Bolesław's advance at the River Bug, hoping to prevent him crossing it, if nothing more. If he should be unable to achieve this, he is prepared to do battle. The two armies are thus halted one on either side of the river, skirmishing, but otherwise doing little more than hurling verbal abuse and the occasional clod or stone at each other.

Iaroslav has with him a foster-child and favourite, a man called Budy. He delights in taking a position on the river's bank and from there scoffing and jeering at Bolesław and his knights, calling them cowards and pampered creatures and adding that if any dare to come and fight, he will slit his fat belly open. No one expects this verbal defiance to have any effect, but Bolesław does let himself be provoked. He summons his knights and harangues them: will they, he asks, allow their King to be insulted like this? They all work themselves into a fury, and, finally, with Bolesław at their head, they plunge into the river and swim across, taking the Ruthenians completely by surprise. A fierce and bitter contest ensues, with fortune favouring now one side, now the other, until, after several hours, the Poles prove victorious. Their justified anger leads them to inflict dreadful slaughter on their enemy, but, even so, many Ruthenians, Pechenegs and Varangians are taken prisoner, while the enemy's camp provides the Poles with rich booty, which they jubilantly carry off.

Iaroslav escapes, but he does not dare remain anywhere in the area; not only because he is afraid lest his own people betray him, but also because he knows that Bolesław will hound him down and lay siege to any town in which he might take refuge; so he goes into hiding in the marshes.

Bolesław, learning from deserters and his own spies that Iaroslav has abandoned his capital, advances swiftly on Kiev and invests it with a ring of camps. At this time, Kiev is large and prosperous and, indeed, developing rapidly, as can be seen by the ruins and walls of some thirty-eight churches that still survive, though now half-dilapidated. The city is now under siege, shut off even from the river, for Bolesław takes particular care that nothing reaches it by water. Its large population, swollen by refugees from outside, will soon eat up what provisions there are and the city be forced to capitulate. Occasional small feint attacks are, indeed, launched, but more for the purpose of frightening the besieged than as genuine attempts to storm the city. The final assault Bolesław postpones till a later date, hoping that hunger will do his work for him. And he is proved right, for large numbers do die of hunger or are overcome by their distress, and the city capitulates. Bolesław in splendid armour and with drawn sword, rides in at the head of various units of his army in full battle array; as he passes through the main gate, which the citizens call "the Golden", he deals it such a hefty blow with his sword that it is scored and splintered, leaving a memorial to his triumphant conquest of the city. He rides on up to the Prince's castle, which he occupies and then empties of its equipment and valuables, which he distributes among his knights to encourage them. Thus is Sviatopolk restored to the throne from which he had been driven.

Winter is now at hand, so, retaining the best of his knights, Bolesław sends the bulk of the army into winter quarters, providing them all with ample provisions and clothing. Iaroslav, learning that the Polish army is going into winter quarters, thus leaving Bolesław with only a small, though picked force in the city itself, scents an opportunity and assembles a small force and brings it secretly to within reach of the city, though still on the far side of the river, hoping to be able to overcome Bolesław one way or another. The latter discovers what is afoot, assembles a picked force, mounts his charger and together they cross the river and fall upon Iaroslav and his men camped on the opposite side. After a fierce struggle, Iaroslav is defeated and his whole force either killed or taken prisoner. By repeatedly changing horses Iaroslav himself manages to escape back to Novgorod. He seems to have completely lost his nerve, for he is afraid to remain even there, lest Bolesław's long arm reach as far, and plans to continue his escape by sea. The people of Novgorod try to restrain him and hold out hope of being able to provide him with a new army, to achieve which they issue an edict requiring every villager to contribute four kunas, every esquire five marks and every starosta ten marks to finance the operation. Having thus collected a considerable sum fairly quickly, they recruit Varangians and others and prepare for war. Iaroslav, however, still under the influence of his recent disasters, fails to cooperate and nothing comes of their endeavours.

Meanwhile, Bolesław is in Kiev busy marking the boundaries of his kingdom by erecting iron pillars, three at the place where the River Sula mouths into the Dniepr and three others to the west of the Solawa, or Saale, a tributary of the Elbe in Saxon territory.

Sviatopolk, frustrated by Bolesław's long sojourn in "his" city, stupidly starts systematically murdering individual knights in their winter quarters, either doing the deed with his own hand or inciting others to do it for him. Disgusted by such behaviour, Bolesław withdraws the cavalry from their winter quarters in preparation for active reprisals, and, when Sviatopolk flees, hands the city of Kiev over to his men to loot. He goes still further, captures other Ruthenian fortresses and allows looting to continue until the entire wealth of the Ruthenians and citizens of Kiev, which has been collected during their many years of prosperity, are in Polish hands. Since this time, Kiev, although restored by various rulers and once more having the appearance of a city worthy of a prince, still bears evidence of the damage done to it by Bolesław.

Bolesław also captures Sviatopolk and Iaroslav's two sisters, Pretslava and Mstislava, and makes them and a number of the more eminent of the boyars and Ruthenians hostages. Enriched by what he has looted, he sets off back to Poland, taking his hostages and numerous prisoners with him, but also leaving strong Polish garrisons in the main fortresses.

A.D. 1009

Iaroslav, seeing Bolesław and his men marching back to Poland with all their booty, hopes by cunning and subterfuge to achieve what he has been unable to accomplish by bravery and force of arms; so, assembling a not inconsiderable mixed force of Ruthenians, Połovtsy, Pechenegs, Varangians and other nations, he keeps careful watch on the Poles and surreptitiously follows them at a distance, hoping to be able to launch a successful attack once they reach the frontier, where, being laden with booty and anxious to get to their homes which they have not seen for so long, he assumes they will disperse. As it happens, his assumption is more or less correct, for Bolesław does give his men permission to disperse when they reach the River Bug, but, knowing that Iaroslav and a largish force are behind him and preparing to attack, he collects a force sufficient for a preemptive blow, attacks and again defeats the Ruthenians, inflicting considerable casualties and taking still more prisoners. Iaroslav again manages to escape.

Back in Poland, Bolesław makes lavish gifts to the churches and publicly rewards those of his knights who have particularly distinguished themselves.

A.D. 1010

The Polish king is known as Bolesław Chrobry, Bolesław the Brave.

Wishing to render thanks to God for all the favours He has showered on his country, Bolesław founds a second Benedictine monastery. The first, which was founded by Sieciech, he moves, with the latter's permission, to a pleasant wooded area on the banks of the Vistula and endows it with the income from several royal villages.

Iaroslav, despite having suffered disastrous defeats in the last few years, assembles yet another army and prepares to attack Sviatopolk and Kiev. Sviatopolk bars his way at the very place where, earlier, he had Boris murdered; there is a pitched battle in which Sviatopolk is defeated and forced to retreat. Not having the audacity to approach Bolesław and the Poles for help, he turns to the Pechenegs and, having hurriedly assembled another army, returns to Ruthenia. Iaroslav and his army advance against him and pitch camp on the banks of the Olsha, intending to do battle on the following day. At sunrise Iaroslav mounts his attack and again defeats Sviatopolk, who escapes to Brześć, where Bolesław maintains a garrison, and from there heads for Poland in the hope of obtaining comfort and help from Bolesław, but on the way there he falls ill and dies. His companions bury him in a deserted, unrecorded place. With Sviatopolk dead and out of the way, Iaroslav ascends the throne in Kiev and thereafter is accepted as the leader of the Ruthenian dukes. He is, however, afraid of Bolesław and never dares take action against him or try to recover any of the Ruthenian castles the Poles have occupied, so these Bolesław and his successors keep, governing them with Polish starostas and Polish military commanders. The occupied territory extends almost as far as Kiev and all this the Poles keep.

A.D. 1011

Iaroslav may have disposed of his main opponent, but he still has another with whom to contend, his nephew, Briacheslav, son of Izjaslav, Duke of Polotsk, who now assembles an army of his own people augmented by contingents of Polovtsy and Varangians, and with it attacks and captures Novgorod. He imposes tribute on the whole duchy and lays most of it waste. He dismisses all its starostas before returning to Polotsk, his father's capital. Iaroslav, very hurt by the loss of the duchy of Novgorod, his inheritance, bars Briacheslav's way at the River Sudomir and after a fierce battle emerges victorious. The defeated Briacheslav escapes to Polotsk, leaving many dead on the field of battle. Iaroslav recovers Novgorod and much of the booty.

Iaroslav now turns his attention on Rededa, a Circassian prince, whom he hopes to make his vassal. The two and their armies agree to their two leaders fighting a duel, each army pledging to accept defeat, if its champion is the one to lose. Iaroslav wins the contest and so all the Circassians pay him tribute.

A.D. 1012

Bolesław, his action against Ruthenia so successfully completed, is afraid lest his army, having nothing to do, should grow soft and lazy, so he decides on yet another war, this time against the as yet untamed Saxons. Having assembled a general levy from all his territories and possessions, he marches into Saxony. Assuming that the Saxons will attack him, he orders his troops to close their ranks and not stray from the standard. His spies then tell him that the Saxons have no intention of offering resistance, but have gone into hiding in the forests and trackless wastes, taking their cattle and possessions with them, and that, before they went, they burned down every town with any pretensions to being a strong-point or fortress, so as to deny it to Bolesław. In this situation Bolesław orders his knights to disperse and wreak havoc everywhere, sparing neither towns, villages nor crops; and this they do from one end of the country to the other without encountering resistance, and finally reach the River Elbe, otherwise known as the Łaba. Having thus humbled the enemy, they return to their own country, pausing on the River Saale, or Soława, which flows down the middle of Saxon territory, to erect iron pillars on the bank both to mark the boundary between Polish and German territory and to serve as a memorial to the feats of the Polish army.

A.D. 1013

Having thus humiliated and subjugated the Saxons, Bolesław remembers that there are other territories which once were in the possession of the Poles and inhabited by them, and he feels it a disgrace to him and his name that these should continue to be ruled by others. He is reminded that long before, just because of the shameful murder of their princes by Popiel, various lands on the Northern Sea, Lower Pomerania and Cassubia, all Slav maritime lands, detached themselves from the kingdom of Poland and its authority; surely these, too, should now be brought back into the fold? So, his armies now head in that direction and he makes one and all submit to him, some by force of arms, others by lavish generosity and kindness, others by fear or by example. The rulers of these territories are all descendants of the twenty princes poisoned by Popiel and so Bolesław treats them with the greatest magnanimity, remembering that they are his relations. From them he demands nothing but their submission and feudal obedience, considering it sufficient if Poland recovers her former possessions.

Bolesław's son, Mieczysław, has long been betrothed to Emperor Otto's niece, Ryksa, who, indeed, has been living at the Polish court. The two have now reached maturity and Bolesław arranges a great wedding to be celebrated in Gniezno, to which all neighbouring rulers and princes are invited.

A.D. 1014

Mstislav, ninth son of Vladimir of Ruthenia and Duke of Tmutarakan, usurps the throne in Kiev, assembles a considerable army of Khazars and Circassians and attacks his brother Iaroslav, Duke of Kiev. Iaroslav seeks assistance in an alliance with Iakun, Prince of the Varangians and ventures a couple of engagements, in both of which he is defeated, so the people of Kiev submit to the rule of the victor, Mstislav. Mstislav, more modest and benevolent after his victory, takes a sudden dislike to the city, which so recently he was bent on possessing, and sends messengers to Iaroslav offering him a safe-conduct to come and meet him. Iaroslav accepts and is received most graciously by Mstislav, who tells him to go back to the capital which, he says, is his by right of seniority and for other reasons, and to enjoy it in peace and as he wishes. He, Mstislav is happy to hand it back. The two brothers are in agreement and Mstislav returns to Chernigov and Iaroslav to Kiev. This same year Iaroslav has a son, whom he names Izjaslav.

A.D. 1015

Bolesław has now united into one country Poland and those neighbouring territories that originally were inhabited by Poles or Slavs. His knights and squires consider that they are due a respite from warring and military service, but Bolesław is still eager for fame and glory, and, being himself no lover of rest, he begins planning further action, this time a war against the Prussians, whom he has not yet fought. Once again, then, his veteran knights are equipped for active service and reinforced with a considerable number of fresh heavy cavalry units from throughout the kingdom. Once these have been properly incorporated into the army, he moves against the Prussians, crossing the frontier at Chełmno. The territory of the Prussians lies to the north of Poland, from which it is separated by the rivers Vistula and Ossa, and in many places reaches the sea. Bounded by the Vistula, which flows down from Poland, and by the Niemen which comes from Ruthenia, Prussia is divided into eight provinces, the southernmost of which was still an uninhabited waste in historical times. At the time with which we are dealing, there are few towns in Prussia and these have been built on naturally defensive sites, surrounded by water or marsh. Such forts as there are, are merely timber-made and Bolesław has no difficulty in capturing them, after which he has them demolished or burned to the ground. Seeing that they do not have the strength to stand up to the

Poles, the Prussians send emissaries beseeching Bolesław to spare their country which is in flames. In return they will accept his supremacy and pay him tribute. Bolesław, who tends to take pity on the unfortunate, receives the Prussian emissaries graciously, fixes the tribute they will have to pay each year and forbids all further destruction of Prussian territory and property. Thus defeated by Polish arms, Prussia is reorganized as a province under the King of Poland with boundaries fixed for all eternity on the River Ossa, in the middle of which Bolesław erects another iron column at a spot a quarter of a mile from the town of Rogoźno.

A.D. 1017

King Bolesław prides himself on tempering justice with mercy, and his queen Judith is equally renowned for this very virtue. Some younger sons of the barons, having run through their own money and exhausted the patience and generosity of their families, take to highway robbery in the hope of thus retrieving their fortunes. Inevitably, they are caught, brought to justice and condemned to death. The Queen, moved by their youth and parentage, has them secretly removed to a place of safety and there hidden. Some time later, the King, who assumes that the sentences of death have been carried out, expresses regrets that these young men, who might have turned into doughty knights, should be thus lost to their country. The Queen then drops to her knees beside him and confesses what she has done and beseeches pardon for herself and the young men. The King consents, the young men are summoned to the presence, thoroughly cleansed in a sauna, provided with new clothes and sent to their homes.

A.D. 1018

Iaroslav of Ruthenia, who has never been able to forgive the Poles for the damage they inflicted on his country in previous years, and is still smarting under the humiliating defeat suffered by his army on the River Bug, is again secretly preparing for war. He arms his own people and arranges for them to be reinforced with contingents from neighbouring states, so that all will be in readiness when the time comes to attack Bolesław and expunge the shame of their defeat. Bolesław's intelligence, however, has long since informed him of what the Ruthenians are planning, but he has refrained from overt action in the hope that Iaroslav might change his mind. However, once convinced that the Ruthenian duke really intends to attack him, since Ruthenian troops are moving up to the Polish frontier, Bolesław sends some crack units that he keeps on permanent alert in readiness for just such an eventuality, to deliver a swift pre-emptive blow and so deprive the Ruthenians of the initiative. As it happens, both sides go on the offensive at more or less the same time, though in ignorance of what the others are doing, until, reaching the banks of the River Bug, they pitch camp and discover that their enemy is there too, though on the opposite bank. It is a Saturday when this happens and as Bolesław does not wish to do battle on a Sunday, he keeps his men in camp with orders not to undertake any offensive action. However, at midday on the Sunday, when the sun is at its height and most of the knights are resting, the camp servants, grooms and cooks crowd down to the river either to quench their own thirst, water their horses or just to clean the carcasses of what game they have killed, and there they begin hurling insults and finally mud and stones at the enemy on the far bank. Gradually tension increases and people begin surreptitiously arming themselves. In the end Bolesław's entire force is under arms; they mount their horses and prepare to do battle. To reach the enemy, however, they have first to cross the river, which involves fording it or swimming. Ignoring the danger, the Poles, in full armour, plunge in. Somehow they get across and fall upon the enemy, who are still unarmed and in no way alive to the situation. There is a panic and the Poles achieve an initial success, seeing which Iaroslav's only thought is of avoiding capture. He decides on flight, and when they see him leaving the battle-field his men take fright, and as a result there is more flight than fight. Bolesław orders a pursuit of several miles. Those they catch, the Poles either put to the sword or take prisoner; but Iaroslav himself and a good proportion of his army manage to escape. The Poles, however, are left with the Ruthenian camp, which provides an enormous booty; this the knights are allowed to keep for themselves. Bolesław then marches deep into Ruthenian territory, capturing fortresses or persuading them to surrender. He so humiliates and threatens the Ruthenians that, doubting their own strength, they are forced to plead for peace and the right to remain within their own boundaries.

Bolesław removes great quantities of cattle and other loot to Poland, where he is again greeted as a conquering hero.

Queen Judith dies, and Bolesław, the widower, sends to Iaroslav of Ruthenia asking for the hand of his sister, a request that Iaroslav declines, ostensibly because of religious differences. Bolesław feels offended by the refusal and resumes hostilities, in which he captures several forts and also Iaroslav's sister, whom he treats as booty, making her his concubine.

A.D. 1019

Bolesław does not let victory go to his head, but behaves to the Ruthenians more as a father than as a conqueror. He imposes very minor tribute on them and releases many of their prisoners-of-war.

Ryksa, Bolesław's daughter-in-law, becomes pregnant a second time and gives birth to a child which dies soon afterwards.

Wishing to put a stop to a series of raids into his country from neighbouring states, Bolesław builds a string of forts along Poland's frontiers and puts strong garrisons in them. He fixes amounts of provisions that have to be supplied for their maintenance each year by the surrounding villages, according to the size and ability of each. This impost is called stroza, guard tax. Many of the villagers and peasants have a further duty imposed on them, namely that of keeping guard at night, which

King Stephen recommending the three young princes, Andrew, Béla and Levente, to leave the country.
—Chronika de Gestis Hungarorum. —*Országos Széchényi Könyvtár.*

they do in turn, calling out or singing at specified times to show that all is well, a most effective arrangement.

A.D. 1020

Bolesław, seeing how the Almighty has so undeservedly showered gifts on him and his country, turns his attention to religion and the affairs of God. Seeing how none of his predecessors, the other kings of Poland, had enjoyed such prosperity or acquired such wealth and success, so many valuables and jewels, thus enabling him to surpass in splendour all other kings and peoples, he decides to render thanks to God for His goodness: he makes additional endowments to the churches and cathedrals founded by himself or his father, giving them towns, villages and farms. He builds and endows numbers of country churches and provides them with the golden and silver vessels needed for the service of God. He will not allow payment of the sheaf tithe to be either diminished through a change in the method of collection or called into doubt in any way in his lands and territories, threatening his sons, grandsons and successors with punishment from God and divine vengeance, should any of them dare to seize or appropriate any of that revenue.

A.D. 1021

Having thus dealt with matters ecclesiastical Bolesław now turns his attention to domestic affairs, in particular that of the castles and forts built on the frontiers to protect the country against hostile raids, issuing further orders for their supply and maintenance, as well as building new ones and giving them strong garrisons. He himself pays frequent visits to these forts and, on occasion, stays in one for a short time, hoping thereby to set a good example. General instructions are now issued whereby every peasant or farmer possessing a whole mansus of land shall at once deliver for each mansus a bushel of clean wheat or oats to the nearest royal warehouse for the use of the army.

A.D. 1022

Many of the Polish nobles, prompted, of course, by the Devil, have come to the conclusion that the sheaf tithe is too onerous a burden, while those of the older generation, especially those brought up in pagan ways, feel that they can no longer stomach the new faith that has been imposed upon them, so together they begin plotting to revert to the old pagan rites. They refuse both to pay sheaf tithe at the appointed time, in the field, or even to go to church. They even evict the priests and their servants from their holy places. When news of all this reaches Bolesław, he decides that such a revolt must be stamped out at once, so he uses the army to hunt down and capture the authors of the conspiracy, who, when caught, are either beheaded or flogged. The less guilty, those who have just followed another's example, he pardons.

Stephen, King of Hungary, has been considering abdicating and transferring all temporal duties to his only surviving son, Emeric, so he himself may devote the rest of his life to prayer and contemplation. In this, however, he is frustrated by the death of Emeric, who, after his marriage has lived in chastity with his wife, treating her as a sister, and thus has no heir.

Emeric is buried in the church at Székesfehérvár, which is famous for the miracles it performs.

A.D. 1024

Bolesław is near to completing sixty years of toil and trouble and his friends have begun telling him that he should allow his tired body some respite and transfer the burden of public affairs to the shoulders of his son, Mieczysław. Nothing they can say will convince Bolesław that they are right. He insists that his mind is still healthy and resolute and capable of overcoming age and any weaknesses of the flesh. When he does feel any loss of physical ability, he will transfer the government to his son and get him to deal with the flood of complaints and quarrels that reach him from all quarters. However, as a first step, at the general assembly in Gniezno, at the request and with the agreement of the prelates and barons, he appoints Mieczysław his successor.

A.D. 1025

King Bolesław is ageing and failing. Now, some grievous ailment attacks him and he spends the next few months in constant pain, which the medicines given him cannot alleviate. Common sense tells the King that his illness is gaining the upper hand, so he makes confession several times and takes communion. He then summons his prelates and barons to him in Poznań, where the illness struck him. They then deliberate how to preserve the kingdom. The King beseeches them, on his death, to transfer their favour and allegiance to his son, Mieczysław, whom he has encouraged to believe that he will inherit the entire kingdom, and also to his little grandson, Casimir, the infant son of Mieczysław and Ryksa. Mieczysław, his wife and infant son are there at the King's deathbed; and Bolesław enjoins them to respect their councillors and to maintain peace and justice. He warns them, however, that unless by force of arms they keep in subjection those adjoining lands that he, Bolesław, has conquered, these will deny the new king's authority and secede. Mieczysław solemnly promises to copy his father's acts and virtues and to see that the Kingdom of Poland comes to no harm. The prelates and barons then swear that they will remain in agreement with one another and honour Mieczysław and his successors as their king. The King makes arrangements for suitable rewards for his domestic and personal servants, but refuses to discuss his own funeral. And so he dies.

The funeral over, a general assembly is called to elect a new king. The consensus is that, because Bolesław had named Mieczysław as his successor and there is a wish to repay the services of the father, Mieczysław should succeed and be proclaimed king and that his wife, Ryksa, should be proclaimed queen since she had influence with the German princes. It is also agreed that they are to be crowned on Palm Sunday. Their coronation is followed by days of lavish feasting of the barons, prelates, knights, squires, indeed of all who have come to Poznań to witness the spectacle. Nor are the poor forgotten, for generous alms are distributed to all in need.

The city of Cracow suffers enormous damage by fire.

A.D. 1026

The new king, Mieczysław, and the whole court go into mourning for one year, at the end of which the King and Queen Ryksa leave the castle in Gniezno, their permanent seat, and go to Cracow, where they spend several months, before moving with a considerable army towards the Ruthenian frontier, where the situation requires their attention, in that as soon as they learned of Bolesław's death, the two Ruthenian dukes, Iaroslav and Mstislav, crossed into Poland with a mixed throng of soldiers and peasantry and captured the Cherven forts and other castles. Having laid the countryside waste, they removed most of the peasants to the far side of the River Ros (Rosia), and put them to till the ground there. The fact is that now that Bolesław is dead, the Ruthenians are trying to cast off the Polish yoke; so, there are numerous secret conspiracies and even open revolt, to put down which Mieczysław now crosses the frontier. He captures several eminent Ruthenians and sends them first to Cracow, and thence to various castles where they are kept prisoner for several years, thus ensuring the obedience of the Ruthenians and that there will be no further revolt. Then, leaving garrisons, well stocked with supplies, in the principal forts and cities, Mieczysław returns to Poland. First, he visits Płock and listens to, and decides, the suits and pleas of his subjects; he then moves through Łęczyca and Kujawy and does the same there, before returning to Gniezno. His son, Casimir, is now seven, so the King sends him to school, appointing serious men as his tutors, so that he should be properly enlightened and thus suitably prepared to rule. He is the first Polish prince known to have been "schooled", so that learning could aid his natural gifts.

From the start of his reign Mieczysław has shown himself to be idle, dull-witted, awkward, lacking in common sense and little concerned with serious matters. Having dismissed his father's old experienced councillors, he now pays more attention to the young and frivolous. This is the main reason why Poland suffers such harm and damage during his time. Not only does he refuse to grow wiser, but he will not respect those who are intelligent.

A.D. 1027

While King Mieczysław is busy dealing with the Ruthenians, the Czechs, ashamed to be paying tribute to the Poles, openly revolt. They throw into prison, or deport, all the Poles living in the country and turn to the two Czech princes, Oldřich and Jaromír, both sons of the Boleslav whom the Polish king of that name had blinded. Oldřich assumes the reins of government, but still he is afraid lest his brother wish to share in ruling the country and thus limit his, Oldřich's, scope so he imprisons his brother, Jaromír, and has his eyes put out, after which the poor wretch leads a solitary and unhappy life. Oldřich already has a grown-up son by a village girl, called Božena. The boy's name is Břetislav, an arrogant, but manly youth, and he now puts himself at the head of the action against the Poles, whom he hates and now persecutes, as he does the Vřsovci and those other Bohemian nobility who had collaborated with them. Břetislav's father, Oldřich, dares not so lightly break the oath he made to Bolesław before his release, for he still fears the latter's power, as he does the punishment for breaking such an oath, which is to have his eyes put out, as was done to his father. Thus, when the Polish king dies, remembering his oath, he still refrains from revolt, but actively supports it and encourages it through his son, Břetislav, inflaming the latter's hatred of the Poles and reminding him of their treatment of his grandfather and father.

Against the advice of his relations, Oldřich marries the village girl, Božena.

A.D. 1028

The Polish king's lackadaisical attitude to what is happening in Bohemia, allows Duke Břetislav to cast off the Polish yoke and stop paying tribute. That he does this with impunity encourages him to be more adventurous. He assembles an army and moves into Moravia, which hitherto has been in the hands of the Poles. He invests the Moravian forts with Polish garrisons, knowing that their civilian inhabitants hate their Polish masters and are longing for a change, so that they will quickly surrender unless the Poles repulse the Czechs. The Polish garrison commanders send messengers to Mieczysław to inform him of the situation and to ask for help, but Mieczysław has other things on his mind and no stomach for waging war in order to retain Moravia. When the people of Moravia realize this, as they quickly do, because they have sent their own people to Poland, they are more and more inclined to favour the Czechs. They enter into secret talks with Břetislav and so, one by one, the towns open their gates to him at night and let his men in. Břetislav is a cruel victor: he murders several of the Polish knights, imprisons and tortures others. Those of lesser importance, those who, so to speak, have acquired Moravian citizenship, he expels and confiscates their property. Others he sells into slavery.

A.D. 1029

Urged on by the barons, Mieczysław finally decides to suppress the revolt. Having collected a considerable force, he invades Moravia, but makes no attempt to capture the towns, knowing that, being guilty of treason, their garrisons will hold out just as long as possible and in this will have the help of Břetislav's men. Instead, he has recourse to fire and the sword. First, he burns the suburbs of the rebel towns, then all the villages and settlements round about them; so, having to a certain degree avenged himself, he and the army return unscathed to Poland, taking considerable booty with them.

A.D. 1030

It is now the turn of the Polabian towns and fortresses to follow the example of the Czechs and Moravians. They are encouraged in this and in their plans for secession by the remissness of Mieczysław and the fact that many of them have been inter-marrying with the Germans. So, when some of their head men are summoned to the King, these refuse to go; they refuse, too, to pay the usual tribute, excusing themselves by pretending that they have had to repel hostile raids across the border at their own expense and with their own men. They make all sorts of ingenious excuses for acting on their own, and even the Polish governors are more or less on their side, seeing their role as that of lords and rulers, rather than representatives of the Polish King, and they now claim independent status and sole authority over the territories on this side of the Elbe for themselves, their children and successors. All this because of the Polish king's slackness. Chief among these new states is the Mark of Brandenburg, in Polish called Zgorzelec.

A.D. 1031

First it was the Moravians, the Czechs and the Polabians; now it is the Cassubians and Sorbs who wish for independence from Poland, as do the peoples inhabiting the islands and coastal areas that have been subject to King Bolesław. Human nature likes change and here are peoples who feel themselves abused by having to be constantly at war with their neighbours, the Germans, and their lands being half destroyed by continual hostile raids from across the border: all because King Mieczysław gives them no protection. Now they wish to withdraw from Polish supremacy. They are at first split up into small units, but then some are forcibly taken under the aegis of the Emperor, or are swallowed up by a neighbouring prince; while others have to submit to their former governors and accept their authority. One by one almost all these lands, torn from the kingdom of Poland, come under the sway of various lords and dukes, and there is no question of them again becoming a whole. The city of Bukowiec, in German called Lübeck, has gained enormously in maritime and terrestrial wealth thanks to its position; it has grown to become a German power, removing itself from the authority of princes and governing itself by its own laws. Likewise the county of Magnopole whose name, part Latin part Polish, comes from its broad extensive lands. When the Roman Emperor Henry was campaigning against the Slav prince of the coast, Nicholas or Mikel who gave his name to Mikkelberg, he annexed some territories to his Empire and gave some to his knights, among which was Magnopole which has kept his name.

A.D. 1032

Prompted by the example of these countries, the people of Pomerania decide that they too will cast off the Polish yoke and free themselves from the authority of King Mieczysław. They select the most excellent of their knights, a man of outstanding wealth, common sense and achievements, and invest him with the symbols of authority and the title of king. This defection grieves the King, when he learns of it, more than that of any of the others, and he finds it more than he can tolerate. In this he is encouraged by his barons and councillors, who keep telling him that he must not let Pomerania go and so lose yet another part of his father's kingdom. So, Mieczysław orders general mobilization throughout his territories, collects a large army which, with the idea of impressing the Pomeranians with his strength, includes three exiled Hungarian princes: Andrew, Béla and Levente, grandchildren of King Stephen, all eager to join the expedition. The "king" of the Pomeranians also gathers a considerable army from his own and neighbouring peoples and decides to measure his strength against that of the Polish king. The two armies engage without delay and the

Pomeranians are soundly beaten. Having achieved such a decisive victory, Mieczysław condemns the ringleaders to death and pardons the others. One of the Hungarian princes, Béla, acquits himself outstandingly in the fighting and for this Mieczysław rewards him by choosing him as his son-in-law and giving him the hand of his daughter, together with the revenues from Pomerania to maintain the couple in fitting, princely style. Other chroniclers relate that Béla and the Pomeranian leader fought a duel, Béla being the champion of the Poles. He won and so earned the gratitude of the Polish king.

A.D. 1033

An uneventful year for the Poles, who have no occasion to wage war, either defensive or offensive, though the defection of subject peoples continues. Mieczysław lacks his father's spirit and accepts these losses with equanimity, preferring not to have recourse to arms or involve himself in derring-do. He is too addicted to revelry and licence, and, some say, abuses the marriage laws and the dignity of the Queen by keeping concubines. This earns him the disrespect of his own people, and causes his country's enemies to fear him less than they had his father. His rule is neglectful and some of his people hate him for that. In this year Queen Ryksa bears him a son, who dies a few months later.

Mstislav, the Ruthenian Prince of Chernigov, is killed while out hunting and buried in the Church of St. Salvator. He leaves no heir, so his inheritance passes to the Prince of Kiev, Iaroslav, who now begins to act as the lord of all Ruthenia. Then, while Iaroslav is in Novgorod a horde of Pechenegs attacks Kiev. An express messenger takes the news to Iaroslav, who assembles an army and marches on Kiev. The Pechenegs come out to confront him and are defeated, many of them being drowned in the river as they seek to escape.

A.D. 1034

King Mieczysław is still anything but an old man. He has no ailment that afflicts him, no particular worries, so there is no reason to expect his early death; indeed, he is full of vigour, yet he dies in his fiftieth year. Whether this is due to some innate propensity, or is a divine visitation; or it could be the result of his profligacy and licentious way of life; whatever the cause he now falls prey to mental aberration. At times his state improves and he appears to have recovered his senses; thus people expect him to be restored to health and this keeps down disloyal thoughts of defection. Meanwhile, the affairs of the kingdom are in the hands of Queen Ryksa; whatever is done, is done with her approval or by her order. Nevertheless, despite what the doctors do and the strength of the herbs that they administer, the King's state deteriorates and on March 15 he dies in the castle of Poznań. The Queen and the nobles grieve over his death, but knowledge of his madness alleviates much of the pain.

The Ruthenian Prince, Iaroslav, having finished warring, turns his attention to domestic affairs. He builds numbers of churches and endows numerous monasteries and nunneries. He also builds a costly brick church, St. Sophia, whose tower has a gilt roof and an interior adorned with golden and silver vessels, books and precious vestments. In order to demonstrate his own wealth and Kiev's importance, he builds on the Polish side an enormously costly gate enriched with gold plate and a gilt roof. This he orders to be called the "Golden Gate".

A.D. 1035

The great and powerful lords of the kingdom of Poland hold meetings in Gniezno and Poznań, to choose a new king to replace Mieczysław. Despite numerous councils and much argument over how to restore order to the kingdom, they are unable to agree among themselves; some are in favour of crowning Mieczysław's son Casimir, now almost twenty years of age; others consider him still too young; others again are afraid lest he should have inherited his father's propensity to madness: opinions being thus divided, Casimir's coronation is postponed, despite people's memories of how a similar postponement so endangered and damaged the kingdom in Bolesław's time as almost to bring about its collapse. It is decided that the highest authority be entrusted to Queen Ryksa and a few councillors chosen from among the barons. Some say that the coronation was not so much postponed, as not allowed to take place, because Queen Ryksa had been instrumental in making her husband impose various levies, dues and taxes on the peasants in the royal villages and those of certain knights. These levies had been imposed to meet the needs of the royal kitchen and table at a time of much ceremonial entertainment, and now, though the King is dead, the Queen wishes these taxes to continue, despite the opposition of the barons and knights; while Casimir, whom she hopes, as he does, will inherit his father's kingdom, does nothing to reduce the expenditure of the royal households, thereby earning himself the hatred of many taxpayers, though they dislike the Queen even more. Feelings are soon running so high that there is talk of expelling the Queen and her under-age son, without paying due attention to the fact that this would only lead to the downfall of those who advocate it and of the state created by Bolesław.

A.D. 1036

The tensions occasioned by the death of Mieczysław increase. Whatever is wrong or goes wrong, is blamed on Queen Ryksa. In the end the knights and barons refuse Casimir the crown and the succession. Though their chief complaint is that they are overburdened with taxes and dues which Ryksa has thought up and introduced, what irks them most is the growing realization that Queen Ryksa has all along, even during her husband's life-time, hated the Poles, despised them and their customs and language, often speaking scornfully and disparagingly of them. Not only that, but she maintains Germans in her Court and employ, often in preference to Poles of the most esteemed and noble families. Every chance newcomer from Germany, they complain, stands a better chance of getting whatever position or largesse is available, than does a Pole, however good his family. This propensity of the Queen had occasioned outrage during the old King's lifetime, but the people accepted it for the King's sake; now tempers begin to boil and hatred of the Queen increases. Finally, the people refuse her obedience and she is divested of authority, deprived of her castles, towns and other possessions and expelled from the Court. Finally, she and her young son are ordered to remove themselves from Polish territory and to go and live with her beloved Germans.

The Queen they are expelling has a very masculine mentality. She is ardent in her Christian faith, devout and virtuous; yet the Poles consider her rule insufficiently prudent and moderate. She rules not as a woman, but as a man; never listening to the wise council of others, but all the time interfering in everything and imposing her own will. The only people in whom she will confide her plans are her Germans. So, in the end, the people have recourse to illegal force and turn her out.

The exiled Queen goes to Saxony. Though she may have been divested of her towns and villages she is still able to take with her a considerable fortune raided from the royal treasury: gold, silver, jewelry and precious stones accumulated by Bolesław and Mieczysław and even by herself. She takes as well all sorts of valuables; vessels, necklaces, ornaments of royalty studded with precious stones, pearls etc. She also takes a considerable quantity of coin.

Arriving in Saxony, she goes to Magdeburg then to Brunswick, where she obtains an audience with the Emperor, who receives her graciously. She presents him with two crowns taken from the Polish treasury and begs his protection for herself and her son. The wealth she has removed from Poland allows her to buy various properties for herself and her son. In order that the latter shall have the best education available, she sends him to study in Paris, where he changes his

Polish-sounding name, which people find barbarous and difficult to pronounce, and calls himself Carol.

Bohemia loses its king, Boleslav, he who had been blinded by order of the Polish king, Bolesław. Another death is that of the King's son, Oldřich, to whom Polish Bolesław had restored his freedom. This leaves Jaromír, who has also been blinded on the orders of his own brother, Oldřich, and is thus unable to rule. Instead, he places on the throne his own nephew, Břetislav, Oldřich's son by Božena, whom he strictly enjoins to make sure that he exterminates the treacherous family of Vršovci, at whose suggestion both he and his father have been blinded. One member of this family, Kochan, incensed by the implied insult and finding himself in a strategic position behind Jaromír as the latter is attending to a call from Nature, runs him through with a sharp spear. Thus, in this one year, Boleslav, King of Bohemia, and his two sons are killed; while the Queen of Poland and her young son are sent into exile. It is not a happy year for the ruling houses of these two countries.

A.D. 1037

Poland, without a king, succumbs to the civil war that has long been smouldering, and the result is anarchy. Class prepares to fight class, if they are not already under arms. At first it is the powerful who fight each other, often in quite bloody affrays; but as the best kill each other off in this way, their place is taken by those who once were slaves or prisoners and have now taken over the estates and possessions of the knights and esquires who have killed each other, murdering their children, if any have survived, and taking their wives and daughters for their own pleasure. When others see that they have been able to commit such crimes with impunity, throngs of peasants desert their fields and ploughs and arm themselves. Under leaders of their own choosing they attack such of the nobles as may have survived, murdering them and robbing them of their possessions and destroying whatever they do not want. They burn down the villages and houses of those out of their reach. They spare neither holy places nor things devoted to God or his servants; they loot the richer churches and murder their priests in all sorts of horrible ways, even stoning some to death. Worse still, some of these who are lacking in faith and religion, now decide to revert to the old pagan rites. Many shrines and churches become the dens and lairs of wild animals. The tumult and clash of civil war takes possession of people's minds, like an epidemic; certain parts of the kingdom fight and destroy each other in bloody clashes of arms and blazing fires. Many parts are no longer safe or accessible to any but the birds. Many of the country people, tormented by these continuous disasters, abandon the land they have so long cultivated by the sweat of their brow and turn themselves into murdering brigands. The countryside becomes depopulated. Families quarrel and brother lifts up hand against brother and his possessions. The turmoil is not confined to the frontier areas, but spreads into the centre. Domestic quarrels, killings and treachery multiply and lead to the ruin of the state that Bolesław had established. To add to these disasters comes war with the Czechs, itself as destructive and disastrous as the civil anarchy.

A.D. 1038

Břetislav, King of Bohemia, seeing that the Kingdom of Poland is being torn asunder by civil conflict and, what is worse, strife between the nobility and the commoners, and so will be an easy prey offering no resistance should he invade it, prompted by memories of the hurt the Polish King Bolesław inflicted on the Czech Boleslav, as well as by greed and ambition, invades with a force of nobles and peasants and burns and devastates Wrocław and Poznań and such towns and villages as had not yet been destroyed by the civil fighting. Finally, he reaches the outskirts of Gniezno, the capital of Poland, and captures it with ease, since it has no proper fortifications and few to defend it, while its situation aids an invader. To his great disappointment in this glorious city he finds none of the treasure and booty he expected, nothing, indeed, but miserable slaves; so, his greed inflamed, he decides to loot the churches. Here the Almighty takes a hand, for, when Břetislav and his knights enter the cathedral church of the Blessed Virgin Mary intending to loot it, one and all are stricken with blindness and numbness, which last for a good three days. During these three days some priests of the cathedral who have not run away, remove the body of St. Wojciech to some inconspicuous place and cover it with earth, fearing that the Bohemians may wish to take possession of it. However, the Bohemians are scared by the blindness that has overcome them and Břetislav gives orders for the surrounding country to be put to fire and the sword and the peasants taken into slavery.

The bishop of Prague, Severus, who is in Gniezno with the King, now intervenes, proclaiming that the three-day blindness was not a divine warning against looting the Gniezno churches, but a punishment for sins previously committed: adultery, murder, marrying those it is not permitted to marry, and being buried in unconsecrated ground hence it is quite all right for the King and his men to go ahead and loot the churches, while a three-day fast will absolve them from all their previous sins. So, they all fast for three days, at the end of which the looting begins. Among the things the Bohemians want is the body of St. Wojciech; but, when they demand it the cathedral officials hand over that of Archbishop Gaudentius, the holy Wojciech's brother, who is also buried in the cathedral in a splendid tomb, so splendid that the Bohemians have no difficulty in accepting his body as that of Wojciech. Among the rest of the loot recorded are the bodies of the Five Martyrs; an effigy of Christ Crucified made of pure gold and weighing 300 pounds, originally commissioned by Bolesław I, three plates of pure gold from the great altar, all sorts of vessels and the cathedral's peal of bells famed for their size and sweet tone. All this is carried off to Prague and deposited in the cathedral there. The Polish peasants who have been taken as slaves are distributed throughout the country. At the urgent request of the Moravians, the body of one of the Five Martyrs, namely that of St. Christian is presented to the church in Ołomouc, which was then not a cathedral, and there it is to this day.

Stephen, King of Hungary, or, rather, of Pannonia, feeling that death is near, decides to make such arrangements as will prevent the country being divided up on his death. With this in view he sends to Nitra, one of the strongest fortresses in Slovakia and seat of an archbishopric, for his nephew, Vazul, whom he had imprisoned there because of his bad behaviour; despite which Stephen considers him a suitable successor. Queen Gisela, however, daughter of William, Duke of Burgundy, wants to thwart her husband's intentions and, instead, place on the throne Peter, her own brother, though by a different mother, Stephen's own sister. So, the Queen has Vazul blinded and his ears cut off, thus leaving him a useless, despised cripple. When King Stephen learns of this, he is filled with grief, contracts a fever and dies in Buda on August 15, having reigned forty-six years. His body is taken to Székesfehérvár) and there buried, while the entire nation mourns. At the end of the period of mourning, there being no direct heir, the three sons of László the Bald being in exile in Poland, and Michael's sons crippled, the Queen's brother, Peter, is with the consent of the Hungarian nobles, elected king and crowned in Székesfehérvár by the archbishop of Esztergom and other Hungarian bishops. He is the first foreigner to become king of Hungary. The Hungarian Chronicles relate that his was not the Burgundian side of the family, but the German, and so he was the nephew of the Burgundian King, Sigismund.

Mieczysław's son Casimir, who now calls himself Carol, has spent two years studying in Paris, where he is generously supplied with money by his mother and is indisputably foremost among his peers both in physique and in attainments; tall and graceful, strongly built, of rude health, and considerable vitality, he cultivates good manners and virtues and learning. Now, fearing lest his rank and origins, which he sensibly has kept secret, should become known, he finds himself on the horns of a dilemma: should he return to his fatherland, go to Germany or stay in

France? Should he opt for the knightly estate or for the clergy? Finally, he decides on the church and leaving France goes to St. Romuald, who is regarded as a person of great saintliness, as, indeed, he is, presents him with a very handsome horse, which he has had sent from Poland, and reveals to him who he is and what he is thinking of doing. Romuald approves of his intentions and gives him his support, with which, and a monk's habit, Carol returns to France, and there, with the permission of his mother, he is admitted into the Benedictine monastery at Cluny, famed for the number of its monks.

The Ruthenian Prince, Iaroslav, seeing that Poland is pre-occupied with war, civil and external, assembles an army and invades Mazovia and puts it to fire and the sword. He collects an enormous booty and numerous slaves of both sexes, and returns to Ruthenia.

A.D. 1039

Appalled by the plundering of his cathedral's treasures by the King of Bohemia and his soldiery, the Archbishop of Gniezno sends emissaries to Rome to lodge a complaint with the Pope and his cardinals and to seek retribution. Reaching Rome, the emissaries obtain an audience with Benedict IX and give him details of the disgraceful behaviour of King Břetislav and his Czechs: theft of the church's treasures, enslavement of orthodox members, general pillage and plunder. They insist that the Bishop of Prague, Severus, is equally guilty in that he was privy to the thefts, some of which he even instigated. As was to be expected, the Pope is deeply moved and takes council with his cardinals and the other prelates who chance to be in Rome. Various forms of retribution are suggested, but the one finally adopted is that both the Bishop and the King are to be excommunicated until such time as all the sacred vessels and the rest of the plunder has been returned. However, since the practice of the Holy See is not to publish its judgments before hearing the other side, the King and Bishop are summoned to Rome to explain themselves. Instead of coming in person, they send representatives, who, though not denying any of the crimes of which the King and Bishop are accused, seek to justify them on the ground that since the King had declared war on Poland, the laws of war permit the removal of such treasures and relics. The Pope pronounces them to be in error and their arguments void of sense or foundation. No war, he tells them, however justified, entitles anyone to rob God's churches of their treasures or to remove the bones of those whom the people revere without the prior permission and approval of the Holy See. War, he says, can be declared on people, but not on objects. They must therefore return all that they have stolen from Gniezno cathedral and other Polish churches, or the Holy See must pronounce excommunication in all its severity on both King and Bishop. The Czech emissaries give verbal promises on behalf of the King and Bishop that all objects removed from Polish churches will be returned, and undertake to see that the promise is kept. No sooner is the audience over than the Czechs start lobbying the cardinals, plying them with gifts and promising them this, that and the other, in the hope that they will vote for abrogation of the papal verdict. The bribed cardinals condemn the severity of the punishment and advise the Pope to mitigate it, saying that it will damage the authority of the Holy See should the Czech King and Bishop feel that they have been unfairly treated, or to have been made ridiculous in the eyes of the rest of the world, and so rebel. It must be remembered that at this time there was more than one claimant to the papal crown: as well as Benedict IX there was the Bishop of Sabina, who had assumed the name of Sylvester, and the archpriest of St. John at the Latin Gate, who styled himself Gregory VI. In these circumstances the bribed cardinals find ready ears for their suggestion that excommunication should not be pronounced, and, indeed, nothing comes of it, largely because the Polish archbishop of Gniezno does not pursue the matter energetically.

A.D. 1040

The Kingdom of Poland, once glorious and admired, is now poor and unhappy, rent by civil strife and devastated by foreign enemies, its more eminent citizens either murdered or taken into captivity. Most of its villages have been destroyed by the peasants themselves. Towns have been reduced to ashes or stand half-burned. Fields are no longer tilled. Its merchants have left the country, and no one now attends the fairs and markets. All is ruin and devastation. No part of the country has been spared. Its neighbours have occupied and annexed whole districts. Many people have had recourse to flight, taking refuge in the marshes and forests, in places difficult of access even for wild animals, where they hope that they and their belongings will be safe. Others have gone even further, taking their children and their possessions across the Vistula to lands adjacent to the Ruthenians and Lithuanians, in the belief that there they will no longer be threatened.

People in Poland feel so helpless and hopeless that no one any longer bothers about law and order, nor seeks to promote the common good. Such dignitaries and people of wealth as remain have shut themselves up in their manor houses or gone into hiding in the marshes and other inaccessible places; but now, as if in answer to a voice from Heaven, the bishops and barons take council together and reach the conclusion that without a king and overlord it will not be possible to end Poland's misfortunes, nor to restore law and order. There are various opinions as to whom to choose or even how to appoint a ruler: some think they ought to choose someone from among their own number; others that they should choose a prince from one of their neighbouring states. This, however, is considered tantamount to laying up trouble for the future. It is felt that any outsider of princely blood would be likely to despise the offer and, probably, would not consider it without proof that the rightful heir is either dead or has renounced any claim to the country's throne; whereas to choose one of themselves would mean that he would be despised and rejected as a commoner. This really leaves no course open to them but to search for Mieczysław's son, Casimir, and, if he is still alive, persuade him to return and assume responsibility for law and order in the country. In the meantime the bishops and voivodes assemble yet again in Gniezno together with the clergy and laity comprising the Polish council. Stephen, the Archbishop of Gniezno urges the assembly to save their fatherland from destruction and spare no effort to find Casimir since he cannot be held responsible for the sins of his mother. Many of the lords concur but a large group says there is not sufficient agreement between the bishops and nobles. However, one and all are convinced that Casimir will forgive them for exiling him along with his mother, which they had done, when they could no longer tolerate her rule, because of the damage it was doing to the country.

First, the emissaries go to Germany to see the Queen, who is living in Brunswick, and acquaint her with all the disasters and misfortunes that have befallen the country, with all of which she must already be acquainted. They then ask her where they can find her son. The Queen is delighted to see them there humbling themselves before her. She tells them that her son is, indeed, alive, but that he has taken his vows and entered a Benedictine monastery in Cluny in France. She doubts whether the offer of any temporal throne will tempt her son to return to secular life and recommends that the emissaries abandon the project. They, however, are undeterred and set out for France. Eventually they reach Cluny and the abbot gives them permission to speak to Casimir, whom they recognize, despite his monk's habit. Having described the situation in Poland and admitted that they and those who sent them had acted unjustly in exiling him along with his mother, they beg him to be magnanimous and more generous than they have been, and to return to his country and take up the reins of government. Casimir points out that it required the abbot's permission for them even to speak to him and that much more will be needed if he is to be allowed to return to secular life. The emissaries then again attend upon the abbot and, after presenting him with suitable offerings, explain why they have come. The abbot tells them that he is willing to help them, but that he does not have the authority to relieve a monk and deacon, for Casimir has already advanced to that degree, of his vows; for this they must apply to the Church's highest authority and tribunal, the Holy See, in Rome. He is confident that the Holy Father will be moved by their predicament, and he himself will advise the Holy Father to relieve Casimir of his vows and to allow him to return to secular life.

Somewhat disappointed, the Polish emissaries set out again, this time for Rome. There, having obtained an audience with Pope Benedict IX, they paint the gloomiest picture of the situation in Poland, stressing how God's holy places are deserted, towns plundered and churches destroyed. To avoid the country coming under the rule of barbarians and schismatics, they beseech His Holiness to restore Prince Casimir to his country.

The Pope, the College of Cardinals and their legal experts give lengthy consideration to the request, which is something of a conundrum. In the end Casimir is pronounced relieved of his vows and free to return to secular life, to marry and have children should he so desire. He may return to the kingdom of his father in order to restore it. In return, in acknowledgment of the graciousness of the Holy See, various individual parts of the country and the kingdom as a whole, must pay annual tribute to St. Peter and his successors—the bishops of Rome—a poll tax from which only the nobility are exempt. Polish men must undertake for the rest of time not to allow their hair to grow long, as barbarians do, but to cut it so that their ears are exposed, following the example of Catholics and the Latin nations; also, on days declared sacred to Christ and his Virgin Mother, they are to cover the nape of their neck with a white linen cloth that hangs down like a stole, acknowledging by these three visible signs that it was with the permission of the Holy See and thanks to its benevolence that a monk and deacon has become their king. The imposition of such a tax in perpetuity is proof that wherever it applies is part of the Kingdom of Poland and thus warns invaders that their invasion amounts to a breach of faith and is an act of impiety.

The Ruthenian Prince, Iaroslav, dissatisfied with his duchy and desirous of fame abroad, although himself unfit to endure the fatigues of campaigning, declares war on his neighbours, the Greeks, and sends his eldest son, Vladimir, with a considerable army embarked in ships, to attack Constantinople. However, a violent storm scatters the fleet and the army has the greatest difficulty in getting itself ashore. Once there, it makes its way home on foot, harassed by detachments of Greek soldiers sent out by the Emperor, which, in a final battle turn and run, leaving the Ruthenians victorious.

A.D. 1041

The jubilant Polish emissaries leave Rome in all haste, in their satchels a number of papal documents: instructions to the abbot at Cluny to release Casimir; directions to the primate, the archbishop of Gniezno, and to all the Polish bishops to crown Casimir king of Poland. Reaching France, they go straight to Cluny and present the abbot with the papal bull, which he hastens to implement. Casimir doffs his monk's habit and dons secular royal clothes; thus is a monk turned into a king, or as good as, a member of a religious order become a layman, one who has promised lifelong chastity become a potential husband, a poor man become a rich one, and one who has embraced a life of contemplation been turned into a man of action.

The Poles and their new king go first to Germany to see Queen Ryksa, Casimir's mother, who lives in Thuringia. The former Queen of Poland does her best to persuade her son not to return to Poland, which is in a hopeless state, but to stay in Germany, where he will have sufficient means to maintain a princely household. However, Casimir will not entertain the idea. Queen Ryksa gives him a considerable quantity of gold, silver and jewellery from her treasury and sends with him a detachment of mounted German knights to provide him with an escort worthy of a king returning to his country.

The next, and essential step is to obtain an audience with the new Roman Emperor, Henry III, in order to ask for the return of the two Polish crowns which Queen Ryksa gave his predecessor at the start of her exile. As it happens, the Emperor is staying on St. Swithbert's Isle and is thus not far away. He receives the Poles, most graciously and makes no difficulty about returning the crowns. Casimir takes the opportunity to lay a complaint against the King of Bohemia for having illegally devastated and plundered Poland during the absence of its rightful king. The Emperor agrees to send an envoy to Břetislav to condemn his devastation of Poland and require that everything he has plundered or removed from there be returned forthwith. He also promises Casimir and future kings of Poland help against the Czechs should that be needed. Feeling that Casimir needs a little splendour to enhance his return, the Emperor sends him on his way with a number of courtiers to wait on him and a considerable number of soldiers to help him deal with rebels and defeat his enemies.

The Emperor's envoy finds Břetislav in Prague, informs him of the Emperor's condemnation of the devastation he has caused in Poland and his requirement that all the treasures taken from Gniezno cathedral and elsewhere be returned. Břetislav, like all Czechs, haughty and stupid, falls into a rage, and the emissary has to point out that the Emperor will have to declare war on him unless everything he has removed from Poland is given back. Břetislav's reply is that his declaration of war on Poland was justified by the damage the Poles had previously inflicted on him and the Czechs, and also because of their having blinded his grandfather. The Emperor, he maintains, has no right to force him to return booty. Also, since Břetislav has duly paid the annual tribute of fifty marks of pure gold and 120 choice oxen imposed on all Czechs, he is not bound to obey the Emperor in other respects. Anyway, he intends to do as he pleases and is prepared to go to extremes to avoid returning the booty.

Having arranged everything to his satisfaction and obtained both the Emperor's permission and that of his mother, Casimir sets out for Poland, where his arrival is awaited eagerly by some and with trepidation by others. Those who have been living by robbery and crime, or have stolen parts of the King's property and other people's goods, are apprehensive.

Casimir is greeted at the Polish frontier by the bishops and barons supported by what troops they have been able to assemble. There are many eloquent pleas to Casimir to forget the wrong done him and his mother. In reply, Casimir points out that he has returned to Poland not solely in response to the pleadings of her emissaries, but on the orders of the Pope, and he assures them that he will not seek to avenge himself or his mother, but forget all the wrongs done them.

Now, with considerable energy Casimir gathers the reins of government into his own hands. His first act in the process of rebuilding the country is to tackle the problem of the fortresses and castles along its frontiers that have been occupied by its enemies or else by brigands and bandits. He uses the German knights who came with him to help him recapture these. Some felons that he captures in them he condemns to the shame of the gallows, others he puts to the sword or mutilates by having their hands and feet cut off to be a dire warning to others. He is so eager and thorough that those with bad consciences take fright: the foreigners withdraw from the lands they have occupied, whilst guilty Poles ask their families to plead with the King and persuade him to pardon them.

When order has thus been restored, Casimir attends upon the Metropolitan and Archbishop of Gniezno, Stephen who, in the presence of the other metropolitan and the remaining bishops acclaims him and pronounces him King of Poland, the first of that name; he is then presented with the royal insignia, anointed and crowned with one of the crowns he brought back.

After the coronation, the bishops and barons urge the King to marry someone of princely rank, in the expectation that the marriage will be fruitful and the succession assured. The Prince of Ruthenia at this time is Iaroslav, the son of Vladimir. He has a pretty and virtuous sister called Maria, whose mother was Anna, sister of the Greek Emperors, Basil and Constantine, and she is suggested as a suitable bride, despite the differences in their faiths, and Casimir marries her. The wedding is held in Cracow with tremendous pomp and at great expense, but here Iaroslav helps by sending Casimir a considerable sum of money, vessels and ornaments of gold and silver, as well as a wardrobe and a stable of horses worthy of his rank. This marriage not only brings wealth to Poland, but strength as well, for Iaroslav sends Casimir troops to help him deal with his neighbours and restore his kingdom to its former state. Maria, now Queen of Poland, renounces her Greek Orthodox beliefs and becomes a Roman Catholic, being christened afresh in Cracow cathedral and taking the name of Dobronega. Casimir has her anointed and crowned Queen, in Gniezno cathedral.

Henry III, enraged by the reply given to his emissary by Břetislav of Bohemia and still wishing to keep his promise that he will assist Casimir, as well as wanting to teach the recalcitrant Czech a lesson, announces a military expedition against the Czechs. He divides his considerable army into two forces and himself assumes command of one. The other is commanded by Othard, Duke of Saxony and a man well-versed in the arts of war. Henry invades Bohemia from Ratisbon, while Othard takes another route. Reaching the River Regen, Henry crosses it and advances into the forest that separates Germany from Bohemia, believing it to present no real obstacle. Not only does he fail to send scouts to reconnoitre ahead of the army, but he even omits to send an advance party to select a camping site. They find every path blocked by trees that have been felled, not just fallen, and the labour of removing these is considerable. Finally, they reach a ridge half-way into the forest from which they can see the Bohemian plain in the distance, and there they pitch camp. The plan is for the Emperor to remain there with the non-combatants, the train and the horses, while the knights don light armour and negotiate the rest of the forest on foot. Ahead of them lies a succession of steep, all but inaccessible ridges or cliffs, so that, what with the effort of climbing these and the heat of the sun, they are all exhausted by the time a halt is called. Unsuspecting, or never thinking that the enemy might be anywhere near, they mount no sentries and everyone is allowed to go to sleep. Břetislav's scouts quickly become aware of the situation and the invaders are attacked. Those who are not killed are taken prisoner or put to flight. When Henry learns of this disaster he withdraws to Germany with the residue of his army. Duke Othard has been more successful and is busy putting Bohemia to fire and the sword. Unopposed, he reaches the River Bělina, but there learns of the disaster that has befallen Henry and withdraws by the way he came, taking considerable booty with him. Břetislav, considering that the local commander has not made any serious attempt to defend this part of the country and thus must have been bribed, orders his eyes to be put out and both hands and feet lopped off. After this he is drowned in the river.

A.D. 1042

The one exception to the general rejoicing at once more having a king are the lands of Płock whose name changed to Mazovia, after Masław a Polish dignitary obsessed with a desire for fame and authority who took advantage of the lawlessness of the years when there was no king and assumed the title of "prince". He now refuses to acknowledge the new king and is prepared to resist should he be attacked. Having some Prussian reinforcements, he is more confident than the circumstances justify; also he is afraid lest Casimir should be unable to forgive the damage he did to the country under Queen Ryksa, and so he decides on a pre-emptive strike and for it recruits not only knights but peasants as well. Casimir, appalled at the thought of having to deal with Masław, also decides on a pre-emptive strike, for which he uses his Germans, his own Poles and some Ruthenian units sent him by his brother-in-law Iaroslav. The two sides engage in a fierce battle, but in the end Casimir gains the upper hand and finally routs the enemy. Masław leaves the field of battle and takes refuge with the Prussians, while the whole province submits to its rightful lord, Casimir.

Henry III, angered rather than dispirited by the disastrous defeat inflicted on him in the Bohemian forest, summons all the princes and subjects of the Roman Empire and Germany to take up arms against the Czechs. Having assembled a considerable force, he divides it into three armies, each of which invades on a different front. Břetislav does not have the courage to fight a pitched battle, but takes refuge in his fortresses, forests and inaccessible places, leaving the country as a whole at the mercy of the invaders, who systematically put it to fire and the sword. Eventually as the invaders are advancing on Prague itself, Bishop Severus slips out of the city, like a deserter, and goes to Henry to whom he promises total obedience. Břetislav, fearing the Bishop's desertion should mean that he has to give up Prague, sends emissaries to Henry to acknowlege his guilt and perform an act of complete submission. The emissaries beseech the Emperor not to drive Břetislav out or destroy him completely, promising that in return Břetislav will do whatever the Emperor commands. Henry, feeling that he has already done enough to avenge Břetislav's earlier crimes and misdeeds, accepts the act of submission. Břetislav is made to provide hostages and has to withdraw from all fortresses or strongholds he has occupied or built on Polish territory and, thirdly, has to pay a fine of 2000 marks of pure silver and 500 marks of pure gold. Once Břetislav has complied with all these conditions, Henry will withdraw his army back to Germany, though Břetislav will have to accompany him as far as Ratisbon, where he must repeat his act of submission and take vows of fealty.

Hungary is now on the brink of civil war. Its king, Peter, ascended the throne thanks to the machinations of Queen Gisela, widow of the previous king St. Stephen, which involved blinding and exiling the more immediate heirs. Since becoming king, he has led a licentious life and shown an unwelcome preference for Germans and Italians, to whom he grants castles and high office over the heads of his own people. Naturally, the Hungarians are deeply resentful. All their protests and requests for justice are contemptuously dismissed and, in the end, the spiritual and lay dignitaries of the country decide to elect their own king, and choose Aba, or Owona, a relative of St. Stephen's sister, there being no closer relation. They take him to Székesfehérvár and there crown him. When he hears of this, Peter flees the country with a considerable retinue and makes for Germany and the Emperor. The new King, Aba, removes the Germans and Italians from their high offices and gives these to Hungarians. He also repeals many of King Peter's edicts.

Queen Dobronega gives birth to her first son, who is named Bolesław after the King's grandfather. The delighted King orders several days of jollification.

A.D. 1043

Masław, self-styled Prince of the lands of Płock, or Mazovia, though defeated in his first encounter with Casimir, is enabled to continue his resistance by the support given him by the Prussians, who are afraid that Casimir may extend his influence and end by making them pay him tribute. Anyway, they dislike the Poles. Masław and his Prussian allies assemble a huge army and invade Mazovia hoping to recover it. Casimir is gravely worried by the news, which makes him fear that, maybe, God has not forgiven him for breaking his monastic vows. However, he assembles as large an army as he can muster and marches against Masław and his barbarian allies. Being considerably outnumbered, he avoids skirmishes, let alone a pitched battle and this makes the enemy believe that he is never going to fight; but one night God speaks to Casimir in a dream, or so he thinks, ordering him to attack. This he does and takes the enemy completely by surprise. The Poles are further encouraged by a vision they see in the sky, a figure in a white cloak astride a white horse and bearing a white standard. Casimir distinguishes himself not only as a commander, but as a warrior, and is so covered with the blood of his enemies that his own people scarcely recognize him. At the end of the day, he is so exhausted that he has to be carried back to his tent on a litter. The battle over, the white figure disappears from the sky.

Masław manages to escape and reaches Prussia, where he hopes to be able to persuade its King to provide him with another army, so that he can make a further attempt to defeat Casimir. In

King Peter of Hungary pursued by Aba Samuel and his troops.
—Chronika de Gestis Hungarorum. —*Országos Széchényi Könyvtár.*

this, however, he is disappointed. The Prussians have had enough of him. He is seized and subjected to all sorts of indignities and torture and finally strung up on a gallows in a public place. After this, Poland has no trouble with its neighbours. Even the Prussians submit and pay it tribute.

Queen Dobronega has a second son, who is christened Władysław.

There is famine in Bohemia. Many people flee the country and go to Poland, Hungary and other neighbouring states. Of those who remain, many starve to death. Altogether Bohemia loses three-quarters of its population.

A.D. 1044

King Casimir decides to found and endow a Benedictine monastery in Poland, as a thanks offering for having been released from his vows and allowed to return to secular life and become king of his country. He sends envoys to Cluny to ask the abbot of his former monastery to send him a number of the brethren, who are to bring with them books of the rules and ritual of the Order, and he will build them a monastery at his own expense and endow it handsomely. The abbot, delighted that his former monk has made such a successful return to secular life, gratefully accepts the offer; so that, when the Polish envoys return home, they have with them twelve of the brethren. Casimir builds them a monastery at Tyniec Hill, overlooking the Vistula, two miles from the royal city of Cracow, and provides it with villages and so many privileges that it is better endowed than any in the country. Its first abbot is Aaron, one of the brethren from Cluny. Casimir then builds a second monastery on the bank of the Oder, which he also endows with a number of villages as well as with the rights to fish in the river and run a ferry across it, to hunt and gather honey in the forest.

Pope Benedict is also delighted that the monk he released from his vows has made such a successful king, and he sends to remind Casimir that one of the conditions for his release was that the Church in Poland should pay a poll-tax for everyone living in its conquered provinces, or in those it should conquer in the future. Casimir summons an assembly of the representatives of all his provinces, who unanimously agree to renew the promise made to the Pope and pay one penny a head for those living in the towns and villages in the provinces of Gniezno and Cracow and their dependencies. Thus does Poland become a vassal paying tribute to the Roman Catholic Church or, rather, to the successor of Jesus Christ, the Supreme Pontiff. The assembly also agrees that on no account is payment of the tribute to be delayed, interrupted or withheld. At first this new tax is thought to be rather onerous, but gradually people come to see that it brings them considerable benefit and they end by regarding it as a blessing from God. This is because in the years following its imposition, the kingdom of Poland is again broken up into a number of principalities and provinces, various parts of it being occupied by its neighbours, particularly the Czechs and the brethren of the Teutonic Order who wear a black cross on a white habit; yet, because the Church there still pays its tax to the Pope, this proves that these lands are rightly part of Poland, whoever is occupying them.

Aba, the German king the Hungarians chose for themselves after driving out Peter, has become so unpopular, even hated, after only four years on the throne, that many of the barons and nobles start conspiring to kill him. The Hungarians are also afraid of the penalties the Holy See is expected to impose on them for exiling Peter, and also of what the Emperor may do, for he is seriously angered by what they have done and may, they fear, declare war on them in support of Peter, who has sought refuge with him, especially as Aba has recently made raids into Austria and Bavaria, which are the Emperor's, and devastated them. That is not all, for since then Aba has sent the Emperor rich gifts and promised to free all the captives he took, yet has failed to keep his promise. The Emperor, however, is preoccupied with his own difficulties, chief of which is the war declared on him by Godfrey of Lorraine, because of which he has had to switch the forces intended for use against Hungary and send them against Godfrey.

Aba, told of the conspiracy against him while spending Lent in Csanad, summons the conspirators to a council in the royal apartments there and has fifty of them seized and bound, after which they are either killed or deprived of limbs, without being given the opportunity to confess or receive communion. Many more Hungarians now go into voluntary exile at the Emperor's court, and there seek help for their fellow countrymen. The Emperor announces a punitive expedition, assembles a huge army and marches on Hungary. Aba bars his advance near Jaurinium and on July 5 engages him in battle. The fight is equal for most of the day; but then a violent wind gets up and blows the dust into the Hungarians' faces and this enables the Emperor to get the upper hand, though at considerable cost. Aba escapes and heads for the Tisa, a tributary of the Danube, but in a cottage there he is strangled by his own men. The Emperor is lenient with the Hungarians and reconciles them with Peter. He even goes to Székesfehérvár and there presents Peter with the royal insignia and with his own hands places the crown on his head. That done, he returns to Ratisbon.

A.D. 1046

Queen Dobronega gives birth to a third son, who is named Mieszko or Mieczysław, after his grandfather.

A.D. 1047

The Hungarians cannot endure being ruled by King Peter, and it is not long before they are discussing whether to expel him or kill him and recall the princes Andrew, Béla and Levente, sons of Lászlo the Bald, who are in exile, living at the court of King Casimir of Poland. Inevitably, the King learns of this and orders the ringleaders to be arrested and hanged, the other plotters he has tortured and blinded. This, however, does not quell the revolt. A large number of the nobility assembles in Csanad and sends envoys to Andrew, Béla and Levente in Poland, informing them of the state of affairs in their country and begging them to return home. Andrew and Levente decide to go back, but Béla elects to remain with his brother-in-law, Casimir. Andrew and Levente are greeted rapturously by crowds demanding the right to abandon Christianity and go on a spree killing bishops and priests and tearing down churches, and so revert to the old pagan rites and honour the old gods because, they say, in the old days, under the old gods, they lived happily and at peace and had plenty of everything. Andrew and Levente consider the proposal disgraceful, but they make no attempt to dissuade the people from going ahead with it; indeed, they even tacitly agree to it. One baron in particular, Wacha of Belus and his son, Janus, indulge in demon-worship and all sorts of sacrilegious acts. All Italian and German officials in the King's employ are sought out and killed. The Bishop of Csanad, Gerard, is placed in a waggon, taken to the top of the Kerendfelud and flung down; after that his chest is pierced. Two other bishops and numerous clergy and lay men are stoned to death or wounded. The King, seeing his life in danger, takes to flight and heads for Austria, but is halted by messengers sent after him by Andrew and Levente, ostensibly to persuade him to return; these come up with him when he is sheltering in a manor house, which they then attack. For three days the King and his retinue beat off their attackers, but are themselves killed one by one and, in the end, King Peter falls alive into the hands of his enemies and has his eyes put out. Thus blinded, he is taken to Székesfehérvár, where he dies of the pain and exhaustion and is buried in the basilica of Five Churches, his own foundation. The widowed queen is turned out of her home and those on duty at the Court either killed or exiled. The Emperor has been too occupied with his own affairs and with preparations for a journey into Italy, to be able to intervene in Hungary.

A.D. 1048

After the disgraceful murder of King Peter, Andrew has himself crowned king in Székesfehérvár, the ceremony being performed by three bishops, all of whom owe him their lives. Once king,

The Scene of Varkony in which King Andrew tests his brother, Béla: will he choose the crown or the sword? —Chronika de Gestis Hungarorum.—*Országos Széchényi Könyvtár.*

however, he sets about restoring the Catholic faith and persecuting those who have been worshipping demons and idols, one of whom is his own brother, Levente, who is killed and buried in unconsecrated ground.

Now do peace and quiet reign in the kingdom of Poland. Queen Dobronega gives birth to a fourth son, Otto, but he dies after only a few months.

A.D. 1049

Having restored order in Hungary, King Andrew sends to his brother, Béla, in Poland, to acquaint him with what he has done and to beg him to come back home. He reminds his brother that Béla has equal rights of inheritance, which rights he will respect. He will, too, accept him as his successor (Andrew at this time is childless) and treat him as a son, rather than as a brother. Béla consults King Casimir and the Queen, who both favour the idea, so he goes back home with his wife and their two sons, Géza and László, both of whom were born in Poland, together with his servants and all his possessions. Andrew receives him rapturously and assigns to him one-third of the revenues of the kingdom. Then Andrew marries Anastasia, daughter of the Prince of Ruthenia, and she bears him two sons, Coloman and David. Béla's wife presents her husband with yet another son, who is named Lambert. Relations between the two brothers remain excellent.

Meanwhile, Emperor Henry, feeling that he must avenge the unworthy murder of King Peter, announces an expedition against Hungary and collects a considerable army. He invades and lays siege to Bratislava and for several months bombards it with crossbows and catapults, while his troops lay the surrounding country waste. However, unable to capture the fortress, he returns to Germany, where he has to start hostilities against Godfrey and Baldwin.

A.D. 1050

The Emperor is persistent if nothing else, for he again proclaims a general expedition against Hungary and King Andrew in order to punish them for reverting to paganism and for the murder of his nephew. When the time comes for the invasion, the Emperor is unable to take part, being preoccupied with various squabbles among the princes and other troubles connected with the Empire, so the invading army is placed under the command of Gebhard, Bishop of Ratisbon, who is the Emperor's cousin. The invasion takes place and the troops start looting, burning and thieving. The Hungarians avoid a pitched battle and shut themselves up in their fortresses and various hideouts, sallying out when occasion offers, both by day and by night, either attacking whole units or capturing and killing small groups, or individuals out foraging. In the end, seeing that he is not getting anywhere, Gebhard marches his men back into Germany.

A.D. 1051

The Emperor makes a further attempt to punish Hungary. Having assembled an even larger army than before, he places himself at its head and invades Hungary. At the same time he has Bishop Gebhard sail a flotilla of river boats with supplies down the Danube, so as to be sure that his army is not going to starve. King Andrew and his brother, Béla, realizing that they cannot meet the Emperor head on, deliberately burn down all the places through which the invading army will have to pass, and encourage the peasants to hide all their cattle and possessions in remote or inaccessible places. All fruits of the soil are similarly destroyed. Meanwhile, Gebhard with his flotilla of supply ships reaches Jaurinium. Not knowing where the Emperor is, he sends a messenger to him with a letter asking for instructions. The messenger is captured and taken to King Andrew, who substitutes another German for the messenger and sends him back to Gebhard with instructions as from the Emperor, to the effect that as war has broken out in Germany, Henry has had to return suddenly and so has abandoned the war against Hungary. The Bishop is instructed to return home as quickly as he can. The result of this subterfuge is that the Emperor's army soon runs out of provisions and then disease begins to take its toll. The Hungarians now go on the offensive, especially at night. They use poisoned arrows, which they shoot from ambushes at those out searching for provisions. No one struck by such an arrow will live. The Emperor, knowing that the bulk of his army has no stomach for a fight and that he lacks the opportunity as well as the provisions to give them the strength, accepts the advice of his officers and withdraws to Germany, intending to return when another opportunity offers.

Iaroslav, Prince of Ruthenia, is seriously ill. Feeling that he may die any day, he sends for his five remaining sons and reminds them that, if they do not agree among themselves once he has gone, their enemies will attack and deprive them of what they have. He dies on November 7 in his seventy-sixth year and is buried in the church of St. Sophia, which he built.

A.D. 1052–1053

The Emperor makes yet another attempt to punish Hungary. He assembles a huge force, which includes units sent by Casimir of Poland and Břetislav of Bohemia, marches into the country and proceeds to lay its towns and villages waste. The Hungarians adopt the same tactics as before: no pitched battle, just ambushes and night attacks, picking off isolated units and small groups; but this time they achieve little, so King Andrew sends emissaries to ask for peace on reasonable terms. The Emperor is a reasonable man and accepts Andrew's submission, calls off the plundering and proclaims an armistice. In order to cement relations between them, he suggests that his daughter, Sophia, would make a good wife for Andrew's son, who is still a minor. After this, the Emperor wages no more war against Hungary.

A.D. 1054

Mstislav, Prince of Smolensk and son of Iaroslav, dies without issue. He is succeeded by his brother, Gregory, who dies shortly afterwards.

A.D. 1055

Queen Dobronega gives birth to a daughter, who is christened Świętochna.

Břetislav, Prince of Bohemia, intending to wage war on the Hungarians, brings a huge army up to Chrudim, on the river Chudimka, but there falls seriously ill and has to abandon the invasion. He dies on January 10 leaving five sons, one of whom, Spytihněv, assumes the throne. Almost his first act is to publish an edict that all persons of German extraction must, on pain of death, leave Bohemia within three days. The Germans at once set about saving their lives, for they know full well that after three days the Czechs will be at their throats. They flee in hordes, abandoning their possessions, houses, lands, whatever they have. To show how impartial he is, Spytihněv has his mother, Judith, daughter of Emperor Otto the Red, whom his father Břetislav once abducted from a convent in Ratisbon, placed in a two-wheeled cart, together with the Abbess of St. George's, daughter of a German, Count Brunin, and drove across the frontier and there abandoned. To avenge this insult, Judith, although well on in years, marries a German. Spytihněv's brother, Vratislav, fearing what Spytihněv will do when he finds him in Moravia, flees to Hungary and King Andrew. Unable to vent his cruelty on his absent brother, Spytihněv takes it out on Vratislav's wife, who has remained in the country. He imprisons her and orders her to be kept in a fortress in the custody of its holder. When she has been there a month, hearing that she is in a decline, Spytihněv orders her release, but, exhausted by the rigours of her treatment, she dies on the journey into freedom. King Andrew, who is fond of Vratislav, tries to comfort him and repair his loss by giving him his own daughter, Adelaide, now aged fifteen, as his bride. Learning of this and fearing Vratislav's growing power and influence, Spytihněv sends emissaries to his brother and effects a reconciliation and returns to him everything in Moravia that rightly belongs to him.

A.D. 1056

In most Christian countries famine is causing people to revolt and invade their neighbours. The Liuticians, a people of Slavic and Polish descent who live along the estuary of the River Elbe declare war on the Saxons and other neighbouring peoples. They win a famous victory and indulge in a massacre. Those who escape their swords drown in the river. Among them is William, Margrave of the Saxons, and many other Saxon dignitaries.

Having settled matters in Italy, the Emperor returns to Germany accompanied, at his request, by Pope Victor. He summons an assembly in Utrecht and there, feeling that his end is near, with the Pope's permission he has his seven year-old son, Henry, son of Agnes, the Emperor's second wife, proclaimed king. Henry dies on October 7 and his body is taken to Speyer and there given a splendid funeral which is attended by the Pope, who then returns to Rome.

A.D. 1057

Henry IV, being so young, is given to his mother to be brought up, and, while he remains a minor, she manages the affairs of state both wisely and energetically.

Henry's sister, Matilda, marries the German prince, Rudolf.

A.D. 1058

King Casimir of Poland has lived and ruled only half his life-span when he falls gravely ill in Poznań. Sensing that he has not long to live, he summons the country's prelates and elder statesmen and beseeches them to maintain justice and unity on his death and to accept his first-born son, Bolesław, as their king. Then, having taken communion and the other sacraments as befits a king, he dies in the royal palace on November 28. The nobility and people in general approve of

Bolesław as king, and the seventeen-year old is crowned and anointed before the high altar in Gniezno cathedral by the two metropolitans and six bishops.

A.D. 1059

The barbarian Polovtsy invade Ruthenia, whose three dukes: Izjaslav of Kiev, Sviatoslav of Smolensk and Vsevolod of Periaslavl, try to bar their advance. There is a fierce battle beside the River Olcha in which the Ruthenians are routed, leaving the victorious barbarians free to pillage and devastate the country. Izjaslav and Vsevolod escape the slaughter and make their way to Kiev, while Sviatoslav returns to Smolensk. Many of the noble and knights assemble in Kiev and ask the two princes to give them arms and horses, so that they can try to eject the barbarians who are roaming the countryside pillaging. The two princes are afraid of suffering a second defeat and refuse. The knights then demand the release of Vseslav, Prince of Polotsk, and his two sons, who were treacherously seized two years before and have been kept imprisoned ever since. When this request is refused, the nobility revolt and the two princes flee the country. Soldiers storm the prison and free Vseslav and his sons, and then loot the castle of all that is in it. Izjaslav takes refuge in Poland with his aunt's brother, Bolesław, who receives him sympathetically. The Polovtsy now attack Smolensk. Sviatoslav, undeterred by his previous defeat and with only 3000 men and knights at his disposal, on November 1 engages battle with 12,000 of the enemy near Snovsko on the river Snov. The Polovtsy are defeated, their king and many of their nobles falling into Sviatoslav's hands, together with all the booty they have collected. Since Izjaslav of Kiev has fled the country with his two sons, his wife and a company of knights and gone to Poland, Vseslav the Prince of Polotsk, now freed from captivity, takes possession of the lands and castles of Kiev and makes this his seat.

On May 15 Aaron, Archbishop of Cracow dies. The electors cannot agree on a successor and the see is left vacant.

A.D. 1060

Andrew, King of Hungary, plans to have his seven-year old son, Coloman, marry the Emperor's daughter, Judith Maria and also to have him crowned king, so as to forestall any attempt by Béla, the king's brother, to get the crown for himself, for the King has long suspected his brother of harbouring such a plan, because he works so hard for the common weal and is loved by the people. He invites Béla, as well as the prelates and barons to attend the coronation. During the ceremony, Béla can scarcely disguise his chagrin and, as soon as the ceremony is over, he leaves and, gathering up his wife and three sons, and all his goods and chattels, departs for Poland, since its king, Bolesław, is a relation of his. There he tells Bolesław and the assembled barons and prelates of the wrongs done him and begs them not to let these go unpunished. Bolesław receives the Hungarians in the kindest possible way and generously provides them with all they need and promises to help them as far as he can.

The electors of Cracow finally agree on Lambert Suła as the next archbishop. However, whether on purpose or out of carelessness, the new appointee fails to claim the archiepiscopal insignia and thus deprives the cathedral of the right to be called metropolitan and of the glory of that title, so that, henceforth, it is merely the seat of a suffragan bishop.

A.D. 1061

After six years of cruel rule, to the delight of his people, Spytihněv dies. His brother Vratislav, in exile in Hungary is summoned home and made prince. He behaves with the greatest moderation to his brothers, giving two of them, Otto and Conrad, Moravia in perpetuity, while the third, Jaromír, who feels that he ought to be treated as generously as the other two, abandons his studies for the church and returns to Bohemia. Vratislav disapproves of this and advises him not to give up a career in the Church for the profession of arms, which for him will now be fraught with difficulties, promising that on the present incumbent's death, which because of his age cannot be long delayed, he shall have the bishopric of Prague. Rather reluctantly, Jaromír lets himself be persuaded and resumes his studies for the Church. However, he soon has second thoughts and, on the advice of certain Czech "friends", decides on apostasy. So, discarding cowl and tonsure, he dons secular dress; but, fearing the wrath of Vratislav, he flees to Poland with a considerable number of Czech friends. Bolesław gives them a friendly reception and generously supplies Jaromír with all that he needs to live according to his status. Poland is now harbouring and maintaining three eminent exiles: one from Hungary, one from Bohemia and one from Ruthenia.

A.D. 1062

Vratislav is incensed by his brother's flight to Poland and by his reception there, which makes him wonder whether he is now going to have the Poles invading his country in support of Jaromír. Being unable to punish Jaromír, he vents his anger on Bolesław by invading Poland with all the forces he can muster. Traversing the Forest of Herczyń, which separates Bohemia and Poland, he lays the entire frontier area waste and all that we now call Silesia. When Bolesław hears of this, he hurriedly gets a scratch force together and tries to bar Vratislav's further advance. Contact is made in a wood, in which the Czechs have camped to allow the troops to rest. Bolesław orders his infantry, of which he has a large number, to fell trees all round the perimeter of the wood so as to shut the enemy in. Seeing what is happening, and realizing that they dare not delay, the Czechs have recourse to subterfuge. At sunset they send heralds to the Poles asking for a meeting on the following day in order to negotiate peace, protesting that they will behave as friends, not enemies. Bolesław refuses to negotiate, but promises to meet them the following day to fight it out. Vratislav then has fires lit over the whole extent of his encampment in order to disguise his true intention, and, in the second half of the night, marches out so quietly as not to alert the enemy, leaving his entire train and all heavy things of lesser value behind. When the Poles discover this at dawn, they set out in pursuit of the enemy and, indeed, capture many of them, especially those who have had to break rank either from exhaustion or to attend to calls of Nature. The pursuit takes them into Moravia, which is enemy territory and the Czechs, who accompany Jaromír, grant Bolesław princely authority. Bolesław burns most of the country and returns to Poland with a huge number of captives and considerable booty.

A.D. 1063

Bolesław, exasperated and rightly indignant at Vratislav's behaviour, begins assembling a great army and informs his knights that he is planning a punitive expedition against Bohemia. Vratislav, a man above all circumspect and sober, learning of the war being prepared against him, uses various common friends to try to negotiate a reconciliation and peace. Despite Jaromír's opposition, peace is concluded on equitable terms, which allow for compensation to be paid for injuries sustained and for the freeing of all prisoners.

In the previous year Vratislav's second wife, Adelaide, daughter of King Andrew of Hungary, died leaving her husband two sons, Břetislav and Vratislav, and the same number of daughters: Ludmila and Judith. Vratislav now marries Casimir's daughter and Bolesław's sister, Świętochna, the marriage being celebrated in Cracow with great pomp and at immense expense. Bolesław generously gives his sister a larger dowry than contracted for. The occasion enables the two kings to get to know each other and they become friends. In her new country the bride is called Svátavá. In the course of time she gives her husband four sons: Břetislav, Bořivoj, Vratislav and Soběslav.

The three brother dukes of Ruthenia: Izjaslav of Kiev, Sviatoslav of Smolensk and Vsevolod, filled with envy of the Prince of Polotsk, assemble an army and march against him, hoping to establish their authority over him and his principality. Their armies assemble in Minsk and together they advance on Polotsk. Vsevolod marches out against them and the two armies make contact near the River Nemija. Battle is engaged and both sides suffer heavy casualties. Vsevolod, defeated, flees. The three dukes send after him ostensibly to request a meeting, deceitfully promising not to harm him. Though uneasy about the promise, Vsevolod crosses the Dniepr to meet them. Breaking their word, the three seize him and imprison him and his two sons in Kiev.

A.D. 1064

The peace concluded with the Czechs is interrupted by war with the Prussians. These barbarians, not content with instigating rebellion and refusing to pay tribute as hitherto, have been making frequent raids into Polish territory to plunder and loot. They have even built a fort at a place called Grodek and installed a strong garrison in it, and from this are inflicting considerable damage. Justifiably incensed by this, Bolesław besieges Grodek, but it is well defended both by its position and by a rampart that has been thrown up, and, when after a considerable time he has still been unable to capture it, he abandons the siege. This makes the barbarians more confident than ever, and, as soon as the Poles have withdrawn, they impose their authority on a considerable part of Pomerania and exact tribute from it. After this, whenever they learn that Bolesław has gone to one of the more distant parts of his kingdom, they extend their grip, until they have subjected almost the whole of Pomerania. The King, hurt by their occupation of his territory and ashamed of his failure at Grodek, tries to devise a way of bringing the Prussians to fight a pitched battle, for, so far, they have confined their activities to cunning sorties and ambushes. His scouts tell him that the barbarians have assembled a large force which is encamped beside the River Ossa, which is in spate, and intend to cross it the next day. Bolesław at once marches into enemy territory and, afraid of the enemy escaping him into the marshes and forests as so often before, orders an immediate onslaught. This involves crossing the river, and, seeing that the depth of the water dampens his troops' ardour, he orders the first rank to swim across in full armour, telling the others to forget their fears. However, most of the first rank drown because of the weight of their armour, so the others, wishing to avoid death, leave their heavy armour on the bank and cross the river in silence. Urged on by the King, they attack the enemy and without much effort inflict such damage on the sleeping, unarmed Prussians that only a handful escape. After this, the barbarians withdraw from Pomerania and pay the King the tribute imposed on them.

A.D. 1065

Prince Béla, his wife and children, have been in Poland for six years now. More and more important Hungarians keep coming to Béla to urge him to return to Hungary. He is well aware that such a return would be fraught with difficulties and even dangers, for he knows that he cannot put much faith in the Hungarians, who are more than fickle. He is frightened, too, by the fact that Andrew is related to both the Emperor and to Vratislav of Bohemia, which means that either, or both, might well lend him their support. Nonetheless, he goes to King Bolesław and begs him as a friend and relative to give him armed assistance in regaining his inheritance, the Kingdom of Hungary, so that old age should not find him and his children in exile. The King realizes that what Béla is asking is far from easy, yet promises him his entire army, especially now that, with the Czechs pacified and the Prussians routed, he and his army will otherwise have time on their hands. A levy is organized throughout the kingdom and then, with three contingents commanded by Wszebór, as voivode and leader of the army, he and Béla invade Hungary. Andrew, learning partly from rumour and partly from Hungarians, that Poland is going to war with him, sends his son, Coloman, with a considerable retinue to the Emperor with the request that in the event of his father being defeated, the Emperor, should look after the boy. At the same time, he asks for help for himself. The Emperor sends him two considerable contingents of Germans and Czechs; while Andrew assembles a third and larger force composed entirely of Hungarians. The Germans are commanded by two princes: Wilhelm and Ponth. The Czechs are led by Conrad, Duke of Moravia, brother of the King. Having such an army, Andrew thinks more of what he will do with his victory, than of how to achieve it. The invading army is smaller and comprises only Poles, who use their three-rank formation, but they are all well-trained and disciplined. With them is a not inconsiderable number of Hungarians who side with Béla, and these Bolesław organizes into a fourth force. These four contingents and their individual commanders are all under the supreme command of Bolesław, now a soldier of considerable talent. The two enemies meet beside the River Tisa and, though Andrew's force considerably outnumbers theirs, Bolesław and Béla decide to attack. For a couple of hours there is no telling where the advantage lies. Losses among the Germans and Czechs are considerable, and they are gradually becoming dispersed. Then the Hungarians, recognizing compatriots among the Poles and fearing that, should Bolesław be victorious, these will take it out on them, cross over to the other side. This gives Béla an easy victory. King Andrew tries to escape to Germany in order not to fall alive into his brother's hands, but is caught and, more cruelly treated than his age justifies, dies after ruling his country for fifteen years. Bolesław behaves with great moderation to the German and Czech prisoners and knights, for all are granted their freedom; but Andrew he cruelly orders to be blinded. Béla is taken from the battlefield straight to Székesfehérvár, where Bolesław has him crowned. Having restored order in the country, Bolesław returns to Poland, laden with gifts from King Béla.

A.D. 1066

The people of Hungary make a second attempt to secede from the Christian faith. When King Béla organizes an early congress in Székesfehérvár, so large a number of disgruntled peasants and others of the lower orders assemble, that the King, his bishops and barons fear for their lives and shut themselves in. The ringleaders of the peasants go to the King demanding permission to kill bishops and priests, destroy churches and bells, and to live according to the old pagan rites without paying tithes, which they consider too onerous. Béla promises them an answer within three days, though it would seem that the rebels' condemnation of the Christian faith and desire to revert to the old pagan cult have the support of the entire people, who are promising themselves that in future they will stick to the old ways. The king, seeing that the orthodox faith and his own position are endangered, decides not to delay in preventing the revolt gaining ground; so, on the day on which he promised to give his reply, he has soldiers arrest all the leaders of the revolt and then has them executed before their followers' eyes. The latter then take to their heels and that is the end of the rebellion.

A comet is seen crossing the sky westwards, thus foretelling disaster in Germany and England. In Britain, which is now called England, King Erald is murdered, and, in Germany the princes are at each others' throats.

A.D. 1067

King Bolesław's lay and spiritual advisers have been urging him to marry and so ensure that his royal line does not die out, for, his second brother, Mieczysław being dead, there are only two surviving members: himself and Prince Władysław, who is still unmarried. The King replies that he is still not of an age when marriage is essential, and that there is yet time before he must assume that burden. Also, he is afraid that, should he be really fond of his future wife, it may make him remiss and negligent in waging such wars as may be necessary. In the end, however, he agrees to marry, but rejects all the suggested brides, until they propose Viszeslawa, only daughter of the Prince of Ruthenia, who will inherit a large part of her father's country, and who, where looks are concerned, is far superior to any of the others they have suggested. The marriage is duly arranged and the wedding celebrated in Cracow, the occasion for several days of junketing and tourneys.

The Emperor, Henry IV, marries Berta daughter of Otto, a man of low degree. The wedding is held in Trier with imperial splendour.

The bishop of Prague, Severus, dies, so the Czech princes who, with Vratislav's agreement have been ruling Moravia, send to their brother Jaromír in Poland, where he has been living more as a layman than as a monk, asking him to return, so that they can help him occupy his promised see. All these years the King of Poland has been providing Jaromír lavishly with whatever he needs and Jaromír has been anticipating spending the rest of his life in Poland; however, he is tempted by the offer of this prestigious post and asks Bolesław's permission to accept it. This Bolesław gives and generously provides Jaromír with money, clothes, horses and other necessities, so that he should not return as an impecunious exile. When Jaromír reaches Moravia, his brothers tell him that in the meantime Prince Vratislav has appointed his personal chaplain, Luczko, a Saxon, to the see. Jaromír, bitterly disappointed, is only prevented from returning to Poland by the princes' promise that they will get the appointment annulled. This they do, Vratislav yielding to their arguments and those of the barons, and so Jaromír does become Bishop of Prague. He is invested in his high office by the Emperor, and is consecrated in Mainz by its bishop, Gebhard, who wishes him to change his name and assume that of the bishop, Gebhard.

A.D. 1068

The Emperor Henry IV, being young, accepts no restrictions on what he does and spends almost almost all his time in hunting, sports and other pleasures. This earns him a host of enemies.

A.D. 1069

The young queen, Viszeslawa, gives birth in Cracow to a son, amid general rejoicing. The infant is christened Mieczysław.

While Béla, King of Hungary, is staying at one of the royal residences a whirlwind demolishes the house and the King is crushed beneath the ruins and seriously injured. Feeling that death is near, he has himself carried on a litter to the River Kymsna to attend to various matters of state, but when he gets there he complains of a stabbing pain, which the doctors cannot alleviate. Indeed, the pain grows worse and he dies.

A.D. 1070

King Bolesław decides to go to war with the Ruthenians so as to recover the whole of the territory which the first Polish king, Bolesław, once conquered. As summer comes, he orders all his knights to assemble under arms for an expedition into Ruthenia. The pretext for the war is that he wishes to return Kiev to Izjaslav. Bolesław meticulously attends to every detail, either personally or through Voivode Wszebór. He lavishes money on his troops so as to make them eager for the enterprise, which, he hopes will make him more renowned than his ancestor of the same name. He announces that all the territory which his ancestor acquired by way of conquest or inheritance and which is now in the possession of the Ruthenian dukes, is occupied by them illegally, even if it was with the knowledge or tacit permission of his father, Casimir. Having himself repeatedly requested its return and been told that the dukes will never agree, he has now assembled an army to recover what is his. After delivering a rousing speech to his troops, the King with Prince Izjaslav and his sons by his side, sets off at the head of his army, under command of Voivode Wszebór, a man well versed in the arts of war and one in whom the King confides his inmost thoughts. For several days they advance into Ruthenia unchecked. Looting is forbidden.

Duke Vseslav of Polotsk, the one who drove Izjaslav out of Kiev, also collects an army, a large one consisting of Ruthenians, Pechenegs and Varangians, and with this moves up to stop the Polish advance. The two armies make contact near Belgorod. When Vseslav sees the mighty Polish host, he loses heart and has no stomach for a fight. Unbeknown to his knights, apart from a few who go with him, he leaves the army and withdraws to Polotsk. His army, disheartened by his absence, scatters in all directions. When Bolesław learns of this from his scouts, he occupies yet more territory. The elders in Kiev now send messengers to Dukes Sviatoslav and Vsevolod, telling them that they will need reinforcements if they are to defend the city; and that, if they do not get them, they will burn the castle and take their families and possessions to Greece by sea. They receive an encouraging reply in that they are told that the two dukes are sending envoys to Izjaslav asking him to halt the Poles' advance and stop his military action, then he may peacefully take over his former possessions. Should he refuse, the two dukes promise to bar his advance by force of arms. The people of Kiev, encouraged by this, decide to stay. When the envoys reach Izjaslav and King Bolesław, the two agree to leave the train and part of the army behind, while the rest advances swiftly on Kiev. Fearing treachery, Izjaslav's son, Mstislav is sent on ahead with a number of Polish and Ruthenian knights to find out whether all is quiet in Kiev and to counter any subterfuge or treachery. Whether there is any or not, when he reaches Kiev, Mstislav wreaks vengeance on seventy of Vsevolod's adherents, many apparently innocent, some of whom he executes, others he blinds. He then reports that all is quiet in Kiev, and Bolesław and Izjaslav come to take possession of the city, the more eminent of the citizens going out seven miles to meet them and present them with valuable gifts. So, on May 2, Bolesław enters the city. There he spends the whole of the summer, autumn and winter, with his army going into winter quarters in the surrounding towns and villages, all being provided with suitable clothing and provisions by the Prince. Izjaslav assists Bolesław in taking action against Vsevolod of Polotsk, who, then, frightened of the power of the Poles, flees the country. Izjaslav captures Polotsk castle and the surrounding country and establishes his second son, Mstislav, there. However, Mstislav dies a few days later and Izjaslav's second son, Sviatopolk is sent to replace him.

When the King of Hungary, Coloman, learns of the death of his uncle, Béla, he beseeches his other uncle, the Emperor Henry, to restore him to the now vacant throne of Hungary. Though prepared in principle to help his nephew, the Emperor delays doing so, because winter is at hand. He promises, however, that he will put him back on the throne in the summer. Indeed, he issues orders that all knights under him should see to their arms and be ready to move with him against Hungary in the early spring.

A.D. 1071

Bolesław moves out of winter quarters in Kiev as soon as conditions allow military action, both he and his men being laden with gifts from Izjaslav. First, Bolesław moves towards Przemyśl, on the way capturing various fortresses along the River San, some of which surrender voluntarily, while others he has to storm. Learning that Przemyśl is harbouring a large number of Ruthenians, who consider its large garrison a guarantee of safety for themselves and their possessions, Bolesław decides to employ his whole force to storm it. At this time, Przemyśl is a large town with a considerable population, well provisioned against a siege and ringed by tall ramparts as well as by the River San. When Bolesław tries to move his army below the town he is prevented by the river being in spate and has to wait until the waters subside. When they do, he gets his army across despite the efforts of the Ruthenians to prevent him, and pitches camp no more than a thousand paces from the town. His policy now is to send out patrols to one side or the other of the town and make surprise attacks at various points. This frightens those living round about and makes them seek refuge in the forest and marshes; while those in the town itself do not dare leave the shelter of its defences. For several days these sorties and skirmishes have no real effect; then, one day, the Ruthenians sally out and hurl themselves at the Polish camp. A regular battle ensues in which the Ruthenians are defeated and, with the Poles at their heels, flee in panic back into the town. Some throw their arms away; others are captured. After this, the King moves his camp closer to the town, which he now surrounds on three sides, the fourth being protected by its fortress. For the next three days he bombards the fortress with missiles, meanwhile razing part of the town to the ground. On the fourth day, the townspeople having withdrawn into the fortress, he occupies the rest of the town, which the soldiers are allowed to loot.

After this, his troops are allowed a rest, while the wounded are attended to and the town walls fortified. The siege, of course, continues, difficult as it is, for the fortress is well defended by its garrison, its position and its many towers. Bolesław maintains the siege all summer, convinced that eventually he will starve them out and that is what happens. Many of the civilians who took refuge in the fortress with their wives and children are now weakened by hunger, while, since the fortress is on a hill and thus has no proper water supply, numbers of people are dying of thirst and disease every day. The commander of the fortress, fearing the spread of disease, begins to despair and sends envoys to Bolesław to arrange for surrender, the condition being that he and his men are allowed to march out with their horses and belongings. The King accepts this condition and, once he has taken possession of the fortress, orders its defences to be repaired and improved, and those parts of the town that have been destroyed or damaged, to be rebuilt. The Polish troops then go into winter quarters in the town, while Bolesław and the barons occupy the fortress.

The Emperor, Henry, wishing to keep his promise to his nephew, assembles a large army of Italians, Germans and troops of other nationalities with which he invades Hungary from Austria, taking Coloman with him. The Hungarians, a fickle people not given to loyalty, desert Prince Géza and his brothers, Lászlo and Lambert, Béla's sons, and give their support to Coloman. Géza, seeing that he has been deserted and how big is the army facing him, after consulting his brothers, decides not to resist; so the three, with a few loyal Hungarians, make their way to Poland, never doubting that they will find shelter and protection there; and, indeed, they are welcomed by Władysław and his mother, Queen Dobronega, in the absence of Bolesław, who is busy fighting the Ruthenians, and generously supplied with everything they need. When the Emperor learns that the Hungarian princes have fled, he takes Coloman to Székesfehérvár and, having summoned the bishops, barons and the more eminent citizens, berates their fickleness and makes them swear allegiance to Coloman. To ensure that there can be no doubt about his previous coronation, he has Coloman crowned a second time in his presence and then returns to Germany, laden with gifts. Géza, after spending some time in Cracow and realizing that Bolesław is not going to return for some time, decides to go to him. He finds him in winter quarters in Przemyśl and begs his help in regaining the throne of Hungary. Bolesław, however, is undecided whether to continue the war against the Ruthenians or to interrupt it in order to help the Hungarian princes.

A.D. 1072

Although he is advised not to abandon the war against the Ruthenians, Bolesław feels that he would be ashamed of himself were he not to honour his obligation to the brothers, who depend on him to restore them to power in Hungary; so, he declares war on King Coloman and sends to Poland for men to replace those he is leaving behind to garrison Przemyśl. The three brothers then set out for Hungary. Many of the rich Hungarians are already disenchanted with Coloman and more than ready to forsake him and go over to the three princes. Coloman has no reinforcements, and, knowing how unreliable is the loyalty of the Hungarians, and also being afraid of his three brothers murdering him if they capture him, he flees from Buda and takes refuge in the fort at Musum. Bolesław has to decide whether or not to try to storm the fort, a difficult undertaking; but, while he is deliberating, the Hungarian bishops, fearing the devastation of civil war, come to him at his camp to try to find a compromise that will allow peace to prevail. Neither side really wishes war, so in the end it is agreed that Coloman, though the youngest, is to retain the crown and title of king and as such rule two-thirds of the kingdom, while Géza, Lászlo and Lambert are each to have the title of prince and together rule one-third of the country. That arranged, Bolesław and his army depart laden with gifts from both parties and return to Przemyśl, where they again go into winter quarters. Coloman is once again crowned king of Hungary.

The quarrel between Sviatoslav and Vsevolod of Chernigov and Izjaslav over their boundary leads to renewed armed skirmishes. Sviatoslav and Vsevolod now assemble an army and move against Izjaslav. He, well aware of the changed situation and of the lack of loyalty of his troops, and also afraid of falling into the hands of his enemies, flees from Kiev, which Sviatoslav and Vsevolod then enter and occupy along with the rest of the principality, thus disregarding the wishes of their father, who had made them all swear not to take each other's territory. Meanwhile, Izjaslav and his wife, children and a considerable number of knights, have gone to Poland, taking with them enough gold, silver and other precious objects to arouse people's envy. All this Izjaslav gives to Bolesław (other accounts have it that the Poles appropriated it!) for distribution among his knights, in the hope that this might induce them to restore him to Kiev.

At the end of this year, Sviatoslav dies in Kiev and is buried in the church of St. Salvator in Chernigov. He is succeeded by his brother, Vsevolod. He has one surviving son, Gleb, who takes over the duchy of Nowogrodek.

A.D. 1073

King Bolesław moves out of Przemyśl, leaving a strong garrison in it, and, leaving Kiev to look after itself, heads for what we now know as Łuck, a rich and substantial region with many villages and towns, most of them unfortified and thus easy to capture. Many, indeed, surrender voluntarily, while those which have Ruthenian garrisons are taken without difficulty. The chief fortresses of the area: Wołyń, Vladimir and Chełm, are all built of baulks of timber and sited on natural eminences, and have strong garrisons. First, the Poles start looting villages and, when they have accumulated a considerable booty in cattle, the King orders it to be driven back to Poland. He then advances on Wołyń and attacks the fort there day and night without intermission. The defenders repel all his attacks and his knights advise the King to give up the siege. This, however, he refuses to do and, after six months, the garrison reckoning on the well-known generosity of the Polish king, propose terms for a surrender, namely that all who wish to go may do so with all their belongings, while those who stay will do military service in the fort on the same terms as Polish serving men, except that the King will pay them an extra two thousand marks. So peace is arranged and the fort at Wołyń surrendered. Vsevolod is eager to fight and moves an army up into the vicinity, but, when he sees how strong the Poles are, he withdraws.

Gebhard, formerly Jaromír, Bishop of Prague, mortified by the separation of the sees of Olomouc and Prague which Vladislav has engineered, accosts the Bishop of Olomouc, berates him and, with the help of his servants, trounces him with his own hands. Vladislav is greatly disturbed by the news and sends people to lodge a complaint with the papal tribunal; however, on Jaromír's orders, his envoys are captured and killed. The Pope, Alexander II, is horrified by this crime and sends Cardinal Rudolf to put matters right. Jaromír refuses to appear before him, when summoned, so the Cardinal deprives him of his rank as bishop and places an interdict on the see of Prague. Later, he relents, lifts the interdict and restores Jaromír to his high office, but only on condition that he appears before the Pope. When he eventually does so, the Pope confirms the sentence depriving him of his rank of bishop; but is then moved to relent by Countess Matilda of Tuscany, who offers the whole of the fortune she inherited from her father to St. Peter, if he will reverse his decision, and thus Jaromír recovers his see, but on condition that the see of Olomouc remains separate and independent.

A.D. 1074

At the onset of summer Bolesław prepares to march out of Wołyń in order to capture the remaining two forts of Vladimir and Chełm. However, envoys from Duke Gregory, to whom these castles belong, arrive to propose that, if Bolesław will remove his troops from the latter's territory and permit no destruction of the country, the Duke will accept Bolesław's authority over his castles and lands and do what Bolesław orders. Bolesław accepts the proposal, as this will hasten his conquest of the other parts of Ruthenia, but with the proviso that he is given hostages.

This last condition causes difficulties; indeed, at first it is considered unacceptable, and the armistice is abrogated. Bolesław then resumes burning towns and villages, at which Gregory goes to him in person, makes an act of submission and provides the necessary hostages. Bolesław is not only gracious to him, but sends him back with handsome presents, while he himself marches swiftly on Kiev, convinced that he will never end the war with the Ruthenians until he has captured their capital.

In these days, because of his extensive lands and large army, Vsevolod is considered the most powerful of the Ruthenian princes. When his intelligence tells him that Bolesław is about to attack him, he orders all under his authority to arm themselves and sends to neighbouring principalities for reinforcements. Apart from these, he has a considerable force of Ruthenian knights who have escaped from Przemyśl and the other areas Bolesław has already captured. Encouraged by the strength of his forces, Vsevolod brings his army close to Bolesław's new camp and prepares for battle. The two armies are more or less equally matched, but in the end Bolesław gains the advantage and breaks through the enemy's ranks. They are routed and many are killed, though there are about a thousand Polish casualties as well. Vsevolod escapes. So, after burying his dead and loading his wounded onto waggons, Bolesław returns to Poland with his victorious army and a huge amount of loot.

Stanisław, Bishop of Cracow, indignant at the king's adulteries and a disgraceful rape, that of Christina, wife of the knight Mścisław of Bużenin, goes to the King and rebukes him like a father; but then, when the King pays no attention to him, threatens him with excommunication. Infuriated, the King vituperates the Bishop and seeks ways of harming him; but the Bishop has led an exemplary life and it is not easy to find anything of which to accuse him. In the end, however, the King does find an excuse: three years previously, the Bishop had bought a village in his diocese from a noble knight called Peter, the sale being concluded in front of a number of witnesses. Shortly afterwards the Knight died. Now, at the instigation of the King, the Knight's heirs are claiming that the sale of the village was illegal. The Bishop is denying this before a tribunal set up by the King, but the witnesses whom he calls are too afraid to give evidence. The Bishop then announces that as his witnesses are too afraid to support his case, he will call upon the person most closely involved, the Knight himself, but for this he will need four days. The members of the tribunal think the Bishop crazed, but they agree to a postponement. The tribunal is to re-convene on the level, marshy ground between what is now Solec in Sandomierz and the disputed village of Piotrawin, in accord with a centuries-old tradition, which allows those who attend such tribunals to have grazing for their horses. Meanwhile, the Bishop goes to the village of Piotrawin, orders a three-day fast for all present and masses to be said. He himself spends the next three days and nights in the chapel weeping and praying. At dawn on the fourth day, he orders the Knight's grave to be opened and the sand removed from the body, which has lain there rotting for three years. This is done in the presence of the clergy and many others. The Bishop falls to his knees and offers a prayer to God that the Knight Peter should rise from the dead and give evidence before the tribunal. Then the Bishop descends

The knight who sold one of his villages to the Bishop of Cracow rising from the grave to give evidence on behalf of the purchaser, when the knight's heirs later contested the legality of the sale.
—*Baptiste Matuani:* Contra poetus impudica scribentes carmen—*Jagiellonian University Library.*

into the grave, touches the knight's corpse with his crozier and says: "In the name of the Father, the Son and the Holy Ghost, rise Knight Peter from your dust." At the sound of the Bishop's voice, the Knight stands up. The Bishop takes his hand and leads him from the grave straight to King Bolesław, and says: "Here, as I promised, is Knight Peter, the most important witness in the case of the sale of the village of Piotrawin, for which I am arraigned, to give evidence of the sale. He is known to many of you, though he has been absent for three years. If anyone doubt, let him touch him and be convinced."

The King and the barons are dumbfounded, almost out of their wits at the miracle, and dare not say or ask anything. Then the Knight breaks the silence: "I", he says, "resurrected from the dead by God's power at the request of this holy man, give witness before you all that I sold the village of Piotrawin, which I inherited from my father, legally and irrevocably, to the Bishop and his see of Cracow, and that I received for it a just sum agreed between him and me, and that my heirs and relations have absolutely no right to it." Then, turning to his descendants who are accusing the Bishop, he says: "How shameless you are! Have you lost your reason to accuse the Bishop of this crime, suppressing the truth! Have no doubt but that if you do not do penance, you shall be suitably punished."

Some, in silence, nod admission of their error: others agree that the Bishop has won his case. The tribunal's judgment is that the village of Piotrawin belongs and shall belong to the Bishop and his church, and to this day it is the property of Cracow cathedral.

Having given his evidence, the Knight is conducted back to the church of St. Thomas in Piotrawin. Before returning him to the grave, the Bishop says: "If you would like, Peter, I can ask my Lord, Jesus Christ, to prolong your life for a couple of years, or to grant you something else that you might like?" The Knight replies: "It would not be right for me to live any more of this life, which is more like death than life compared to the state in which the saints in eternal bliss delight in regarding the Trinity and which I am confident of achieving ere long. I beg you to see that my resurrection is ended at once." He then steps into his grave, lies down and gives up the ghost. The Bishop and the local clergy then sing the psalms of the Catholic rite, cover the corpse with sand and close the grave.

A.D. 1075

Having spent the whole winter and part of the spring at home, King Bolesław sets out with a force of cavalry and infantry greater than before and heads for Ruthenia, which he reaches quickly and at once advances on its capital, Kiev, which he invests. The city's defenders make repeated sorties against the king's camp and some of these skirmishes almost become little battles. In the end hunger begins to make itself felt in the city. The sorties become less frequent and so Bolesław moves his camp closer. Deserters tell of hunger growing more severe, so the King intensifies the siege, closing all ways of getting supplies into the city. He himself is ever on the go, seeing that the soldiers, whose duty it is to make the siege effective, are alert, with the result that the guards and sentries are so afraid of the King appearing unexpectedly, that they are always vigilant. The fields in the plain round the city being empty, it is easy to detect any attempt to bring in provisions by day. At this time the city has many suburbs and no proper walls and so is easy to capture, especially as the troops guarding it are exhausted by the enemy's continual bombardment. Now civilians are dying of starvation and disease, yet they hold out, afraid of falling into the hands of Bolesław and his Poles. In the end, however, they have to send heralds to the King begging for generous treatment if the city surrenders. The King agrees and the city capitulates. Bolesław's formal entry into the city is made at the head of a huge retinue of armed men. Wishing to imitate his great-grandfather, Bolesław I, the King pauses at the iron gate and twice strikes it with his sword, cutting a notch to mark his victory and the submission of the city. The Polish soldiers are forbidden on pain of death to rob or loot: everyone's house and belongings are sacrosanct. This so impresses the people of Kiev that they heap gifts on the King, most of which he hands over to his officers and their men. The whole of Ruthenia is now in Polish hands. A considerable tribute is imposed on it, and the reins of authority are handed over to Prince Izjaslav. The rest of the winter is employed in collecting the huge amount of the tribute from all over the country.

Gleb, son of Prince Sviatoslav, having been horribly murdered by his own men, the throne of Novgorod is given to Izjaslav's son, Sviatopolk, while his second son, Vladimir is installed in Smolensk, and the third, Iaropolk, in Wyszegrod.

A.D. 1076

Bolesław and his army winter in Kiev, where meat, milk, fish, grain and provisions of all kinds are to be had in such profusion as to have sufficed, even if all had been gluttons. Discipline becomes slack and all, from the King down, indulge in riotous living: banquets, drunkenness and fornication. The women of Kiev are tall, dark-haired, pretty and flirtatious. The Poles, entranced by their beauty, give themselves up to a life of licentiousness. The King becomes so self-important that those who apply to him receive their answers through a third person. He even indulges in the disgraceful sin of sodomy, imitating the shameful habits of the Ruthenians among whom the practice is common. His behaviour puts him in danger of losing the respect and affection of his men. Meanwhile, the wives, sisters and daughters of his knights, harrowed by the long absence of their husbands and the fact that for almost seven years they have been denied the comfort of a husband and the possibility of bearing children, knowing of the culpable behaviour of their menfolk, find that their own youthful longings are making rational behaviour more and more difficult. As news comes of this knight dying, that one being killed, of others taking mistresses, some of the wives, tired of waiting for their husbands, give themselves to their servants or retainers. When, eventually, news of this reaches the King's camp in Kiev and is confirmed by messengers from home, there is great indignation and anger. People run frenziedly from tent to tent complaining and telling of their unhappiness and wrongs. A few are so incensed that they leave the army without permission and make their way back to Poland to deal with their wives. Many then follow the example of the first few. Nothing can stop them. When they reach home, many find that they have to wage war against their own servants, which some say is God's punishment for their philandering in Kiev. Those servants and retainers who have been fornicating with the knights' wives are well aware of the severity of the punishment to which they have made themselves liable, so, on the advice and sometimes with the active assistance of the adulterous wives, they arm themselves, shut the gate and refuse the knight entry. The knights, of course, win in the end, but it costs the lives of many of their own retinue, as well as of the servants and retainers they kill and torture, and of their adulterous wives.

A notable exception to the adulterous wives is a certain lady called Margaret, wife of Nicholas of Żębocin, who, to preserve her chastity, while other wives, as she can see, are whoring, shut herself up with two of her sisters in the local stone-built church. Through all the years of her husband's absence with the King, she provisioned herself and her sisters by means of a basket let down from the tower on a rope.

King Bolesław is furious both with the wives and the knights, who in such numbers have abandoned him in enemy country, so, when he gets back to Poland with his depleted army, he accuses these knights, to whom he has given so much loot and so many presents, of exposing him to danger and the possibility of being shamefully captured. He arrests and executes the knights who started the general exodus; others he imprisons or deprives of their estates. Wives with babies fathered by their servants have these taken from them and are made to suckle puppies instead.

Bolesław II, the Bold. A.D. 1058–1079.
—B. Paprochi: Ogród Królewski*—Jagellionian*
University Library.

Poland is now a shameful and sorrowful place. Many of the returning knights decide to spare their wives, but the King orders all of them to be punished. This causes him to be disliked, even hated, all the more so because of the shameful fact that the King himself has not given up the swinish, unnatural vice to which he abandoned himself in Kiev, but indulges in it more and more. There is no eminent churchman or layman who dare reproach the King for his immoral behaviour and cruelty.

The jealousy between Coloman, King of Hungary, and his brothers, Géza and Laszló, caused initially by trifling suspicions, gradually grows until it has become so grave that they are actually at war. In the first encounter, Coloman is the victor; but when Vladislav and the Moravian Prince Otto go to Géza's assistance and Coloman is defeated, the latter seeks refuge in Pozonia. To celebrate his victory, Géza founds and endows a cathedral church in Vác, where the battle was fought. He then has himself crowned king of Hungary. Despite this, the Emperor Henry goes to the help of his son-in-law, but nothing comes of it, since his advisers, bribed by Géza, persuade him to withdraw; thus he goes back to Germany with nothing achieved.

The jealousy and hatred of each other of the Ruthenian princes, Boris and Oleg, provide an opportunity for the barbarian Polovtsy to invade the country and set about destroying it. Vsevolod, Duke of Chernigov, intercepts them on August 25 at a place called Sozica. Battle is engaged and Vsevolod is shamefully routed. Boris and Oleg then go on to capture Smolensk fort. Vsevolod, disheartened, escapes to his brother, Izjaslav of Kiev, who reminds him that he himself once suffered the same fate, but has recovered his possessions with the help of the Poles. He promises to help his brother and collects an army, with which he, his son Iaropolk and Vsevolod with his son, march on Smolensk. Oleg does not want to fight and his advice is that they should parley, but Boris is too proud to hear of any such thing and marches out to do battle. In the fighting, Boris is killed, as well as many knights on either side. Izjaslav has taken his place safely among his infantry, but one of Oleg's men, pretending to be one of Izjaslav's, makes his way among the infantry and runs Izjaslav through between the shoulder blades. This makes Oleg and his troops take to their heels, and so Vsevolod recovers his castle at Chernigov. Izjaslav's body is taken to Kiev and buried in the church of the Holy Virgin. He is succeeded by his brother, Vsevolod, one of whose sons, Vladimir, is installed in Chernigov and the other, Iaropolk, in Turov.

A.D. 1077

The Bishop of Cracow finds himself unable to endure his King's harsh rule and his filthy, immoral way of life, so, though rebuking the King is really the duty of the Metropolitan in Gniezno, who so far has failed to fulfill it, feeling that God expects him to do this instead and disregarding the dangers involved, he goes to the King, and, in private, rebukes him in a gentle, fatherly way and begs him to give up this unnatural vice. If the King needs to satisfy the desires of the flesh, he tells him, let him rather do this in living with his wife and having children. The Bishop also begs the King to stop being so bestially cruel to knights and women. Of course, if the King discovers wrong-doing, it must be punished, but let him not act in such a way that his actions appear to be dictated more by malice than by justice. When he finds that the King is turning a deaf ear to his entreaties, the Bishop repeats his strictures in the presence of witnesses, again exhorting the King to change his habits and abandon the shameful vice of sodomy, as well as to stop oppressing and killing his subjects. This so incenses the King that he attacks the Bishop with the most scurrilous accusations and threatens to do all in his power to get even with him. The gentlemen in the Bishop's retinue do not dare come to his defence.

Sviatoslav's son, Roman, a duke of Ruthenia, having persuaded the Polovtsy to help him, declares war on Vsevolod of Kiev. The latter intercepts the Polovtsy near Pereiaslavl; but here the barons of both sides take a hand in the proceedings and come to an amicable agreement. However, the Polovtsy do not like this and revolt against its implementation, killing Roman for having made peace without their consent.

A.D. 1078

The King's behaviour is becoming worse and worse. He treats his knights and common people with increasing cruelty. His treatment of widows and orphans is equally harsh; but, worst of all, is that he is more and more addicted to sodomy. Bishop Stanisław now comes to the conclusion that he must hesitate no longer, but excommunicate the King; so putting on his full vestments, he goes to the King and again rebukes him and demands that he give up the filthy sin of sodomy, and also that he cease to inflict various dues and taxes on the people, and that he return the estates he has unjustly confiscated from some of his knights. The King cannot contain his anger; indeed, he flies into a rage, almost has a brainstorm: he curses the Bishop and calls him all manner of names; indeed, he all but attacks him physically. When the Bishop sees that he is achieving nothing, he goes to the cathedral and from the pulpit there publicly announces that the King has been expelled from the congregation of the faithful. He orders all the churches throughout all Poland publicly to announce that the King has been excommunicated, and enjoins the faithful of whatever estate to avoid the King's company. The King rages and threatens the Bishop, vowing that if he ever encounters him, he will kill him, wherever it may be. The King then with gifts and promises encourages his myrmidons to kill the Bishop and, in order not to expose the cathedral to an attack, the Bishop goes into hiding, and there he stays for more than a year, all the while praying and saying mass for the repentance of the King.

On April 25, Géza, King of Hungary, dies. Although Géza had children of his own and one of them, Saloman, is still alive, Géza is succeeded by his brother, László; this is because the latter's unusual nobility and integrity have so endeared him to the Hungarians that they will consider no other candidate for the throne. So, Laszló is anointed and crowned in Székesfehérvár. He behaves with great moderation towards his nephew, making sure that he lacks nothing but the title of king.

The Emperor is engaged in a bitter struggle with the Saxon Prince, Rudolf, who has invaded his territory. Rudolf is defeated with the loss of many men, though he himself escapes and is determined to assemble a fresh army.

The body of Bishop Stanisław being hacked into pieces by the King's knights.
From Chronika Polonorum—*Jagiellonian University Library.*

Iaropolk, son of Izjaslav, the former prince of Kiev, has persuaded himself that a great wrong has been done him in that on his father's death the throne went not to him, but to his uncle, so he now assembles an army to try and get the throne for himself. When Vsevolod learns of this, he consults his advisers, one of whom suggests that he go to Iaropolk, pretend to be deserting to his side, and then give him a false account of Vsevolod's strength and suggest that he escape to Poland and ask Bolesław's help in regaining his throne. This plan is adopted and, first placing his wife, children and their household in the castle at Łuck, telling them to resist the enemy as far as they can until he returns with Polish reinforcements, Iaropolk heads for Poland. Vsevolod's son, Vladimir, advances on Łuck with a considerable force and the castle surrenders as soon as he appears. Iaropolk's wife and children and their household are removed to Kiev, where the servants are sold into slavery.

King Bolesław is unable to help Iaropolk personally, being involved in the dispute with his knights, but he provides him with a mixed force with which Iaropolk advances on Łuck. Vladimir does not dare give battle, but sends envoys to make peace. It is agreed that he will hand back Łuck and other fortresses he has taken, and he promises to return whatever else he has belonging to Iaropolk. Peace thus restored, Vladimir returns to Chernigov, while Iaropolk rewards the Poles who have helped him and sends them back to Poland.

In November, Iaropolk and Vladimir set out by carriage for Zvenigorod. While asleep in his carriage, Iaropolk is murdered by his body servant, who then flees to Duke Ruryk. Iaropolk was a gentle man. He loved his brothers and throughout his life paid tithes on all his corn, cattle, herds and all his property.

*Eagles guard the pieces of Bishop Stanisław's body
from dogs and other predators, thus allowing them to
be gathered up and pieced together again.
From Michael Vratislaviensis:* Introductorium dia-
lecticae sive congestum logicum, *1504.* —*Jagiellonian University Library.*

A.D. 1079

One day, King Bolesław, steeped in iniquity and crime, scorning his excommunication, enters the cathedral. This is itself an affront to the authority of the Church and the Bishop hurls an
anathema at the King and orders him out, telling him that if he does not go, he will interrupt the
service. The King and his companions remain where they are, so, on the Bishop's orders, the clergy
fall silent and the Mass is interrupted. The Bishop again harangues the King, who rushes out of the
cathedral quivering with rage, shouting and gesticulating, and dashes into the royal castle, which is
close to the cathedral. He now devotes all his thoughts and energies to finding ways of killing the
Bishop. Despite his reputation, no one really believes that the King will be crazy enough to do what
he threatens. At dawn on May 13, the Bishop and his clergy set out for the church at Skałk, where
they intend to say a solemn mass and pray for the King and his people, rather than do this in the cathedral, where the King might try to prevent them. The church at Skałk stands on an eminence and
is surrounded by fields and level pasture. Bolesław, however, has spies everywhere and is soon
told where the Bishop is. He seizes up his sword and with a larger retinue than usual hurries off, intending to kill the Bishop. When he reaches the church, the Bishop is still saying mass, so the King
and his knights stay outside. Soon, however, the King becomes irritated by the delay, which to him
seems unnecessarily long, and he tells some of the knights to go inside and kill the Bishop, even at
the altar. Inside, they draw their swords and make to strike the Bishop, but their arms seem paralysed; they fall to the floor and crawl out on all fours. Impelled by the King's threats, they pick up
their swords and go back into the church. Again they are forced to the floor and crawl out. The King
curses them, and a third time they go in, and the same thing happens. They tell the King that their
arms are not strong enough to do the deed required of them. The King curses them as weak old
women, and, taking his sword he rushes, raging, into the church which, at his coronation, he had

solemly sworn to protect, and cuts the Bishop's head from its body. The knights who have failed so crassly, feel that they should be accessories to the murder and plunge their swords into the Bishop's body. The other knights then join in and the Bishop's body is hacked into a myriad pieces, which the King orders to be thrown here and there about the city for the dogs, vultures, crows and other predators to eat. This done, the King and his knights return to the royal castle.

On the night of the Bishop's murder, the people of the city see strange lights flickering round each piece of the dismembered body, keeping the dogs, pigs and other scavengers away. In the morning, numbers of huge eagles come circling lower and lower above the place of the Bishop's martyrdom and the pieces of his body wherever they lie, driving away all the vultures, crows and other predators. The people, realizing that a miracle is being performed, despite their fear of the King who wishes to deny the Bishop's body burial, carefully gather up all the red and white pieces, which the eagles are guarding, and putting piece to piece re-construct the whole body. That done, they suddenly see that the pieces have become a whole without trace of scar or wound. Delighted by this fresh miracle, but afraid lest the King forbid them to move the body, they carry it to the church of St. Michael at Skałk in which the Bishop was martyred and bury it in a coffin filled with fragrant essences in the porch outside the door, so that the King cannot order it to be thrown out of the church.

When the Pope, Gregory VII, learns of the Bishop's murder, he and all the cardinals are loud in their grief. After consulting how to punish the King, it is decided that the Pope shall issue a special bull imposing an interdict on the whole province of Gniezno. In addition, the King is deprived of his title of king and all his dukes, barons, vassals and subjects are ordered to refuse him obedience. The sons and descendants unto the fourth generation of the knights who took part in the murder, are denied access to offices or positions in the church, and any who already have benefices are deprived of them. The archbishop of Gniezno and all bishops under him are ordered not to crown or anoint anyone as king of Poland without permission of the Holy See. The archbishop and bishops do not dare disobey the papal interdict and close their churches, suspending all worship, though not without popular complaint.

A.D. 1080

Bolesław, although by papal decree no longer king or to be obeyed by his subjects, remains in effect king and everyone obeys him. Indeed, he complains that the Pope has been unjust and that to kill one crazy, impertinent prelate who deserved to die, does not merit such punishment either of himself or of the knights who helped him. However, he is disquieted by reports of lights continually being seen over the bishop's grave. One night he climbs the watch-tower of Cracow castle and sees them for himself. Then, for the first time, he begins to realise the enormity of the crime he has committed.

A.D. 1081

Now he can see his knights' growing contempt for him and how ordinary people condemn him. Now, too, many of the Ruthenian territories that he himself has conquered, throw off the yoke of subjection and refuse to pay the normal tribute and taxes, while his own barons hate and despise him. The powerful men in his kingdom now conspire together to kill or at least imprison him and his accessories, considering this the only way of regaining the royal crown for the country and saving it from divine punishment. Learning of this conspiracy, Bolesław flees the country with a considerable retinue, mostly of those implicated with him in the murder of the bishop, but also with his only son, Mieczysław, who has just had his eleventh birthday and on whom, he fears, the barons might avenge themselves if he remained behind, and goes to Hungary, where his relation, Laszló has just been made king. Here he is fittingly received, for Laszló readily admits that it was

Bolesław who put him on the throne. More and more things detrimental to Bolesław come to light and people's opinion of him further deteriorates. Finally, leaving his son Mieczysław and the knights who have accompanied him into exile, he dons a shabby old cloak as a disguise and, taking only one servant, goes to Carinthia where he does a round of the monasteries built and endowed by his ancestors, in particular that at Wilten, near Innsbruck, where as his penance, for he is really repentant, he does humble kitchen duties, hoping thus to expiate his crimes. Other writers have it, though, that he goes mad while in Hungary and suffers the torment of craziness until on March 21, while hunting in the forest, he is eaten by his own hounds.

Salomon, the king of Hungary, wishing to regain the ancient power and glory of Hungary, starts plotting the removal of Laszló. When this comes out, he is put in prison; but the gentle Laszló soon sets him free and he takes refuge with the Huns, who are Hungary's enemies. He manages to make a treaty with their leader, Kustek, whereby Saloman gives the latter his daughter for his wife, plus all of Transylvania in return for Kustek's help in regaining his throne. Suborned by such promises, the Huns invade Hungary, but Laszló engages them in battle and Saloman and Kustek are routed. Saloman now takes refuge in Bulgaria, where he and those with him have to make a livelihood by highway robbery. The inhabitants soon become disgusted with them and they are forced to move on. Coming to a certain part of the forest, Saloman orders his few remaining companions to wait for him while he goes on ahead. They never see him again. Indeed, he spends the rest of his life wandering and engaging in pious acts. He reaches the town of Pula on the Adriatic coast and there ends his life and is buried. Neither he nor his brother David had an heir.

The Ruthenian duke, Vasilko, son of Rostislav, learning that Bolesław has left Poland and that the country is rent by disturbances, decides to attack it. Assembling an army of mercenaries of many nationalities, including Polovtsy, he makes a swift and violent incursion, takes and burns several forts, then retires with his booty to Ruthenia.

This was a year of great heat, which set fire to woods and forests and dried out many marshes.

A.D. 1082

Poland has lost her right to be called a kingdom and has disintegrated into several principalities. It is no longer a unit or strong, so the barons set about organizing a new order. All agree on the choice of a prince. The man they choose is Casimir's remaining son and Bolesław's brother, Władysław, who has as his second name, Herman. The barons title him "king", but though he agrees to act as king he will not accept the title because he cannot be crowned and anointed according to custom and because Bolesław may return, so he calls himself not just Prince of Poland but heir to the Kingdom of Poland because the royal authority and honour of kings should pertain to the man and not to the land. He is an unusually pious and religious person and his main concern is to get the interdict lifted from Poland and another bishop appointed to Cracow cathedral, for no one has dared take over as Stanisław's successor. Władysław now sends a formal delegation of clergy and laity to Pope Gregory VII, who is moved by their unusual humility and, getting confirmation that Bolesław has gone into exile and been succeeded by his brother, Władysław, a man of exceptional piety, he lifts the interdict and officially appoints as bishop of Cracow the man elected by a secret vote of the chapter, a Pole called Lambert, a noble. Prince Władysław restores safety to the public highways and protects the weak from the strong. He changes or mitigates many of his brother, Bolesław's edicts.

In this year, the Czech prince Vratislav and his brothers, Conrad and Otto, are engaged in war with Leopold, Margrave of Austria, who has attacked them to avenge injuries done to the Austrian inhabitants of Moravia, who are subjects of Conrad and Otto. In the fighting many fall on either side. The Czechs are victorious and Margrave Leopold seeks safety in flight. Vratislav returns home laden with booty.

A.D. 1083

Władysław, now the only Polish prince, yields to the urgent persuasions of the prelates and barons and agrees to marry, so as to prevent his ancient line from dying out. He chooses Judith, a very pretty girl, daughter of the Czech prince Vratislav by his first wife, Adelaide, whose father was King Andrew of Hungary.

A dreadful epidemic breaks out in Ruthenia and neighbouring countries, and many people of both sexes die. Among its victims is Vsevolod, Prince of Kiev, whose elder son, Vladimir, realizing that, if he succeeds his father, he will probably have to fight Sviatopolk, Izjaslav's son who used to have Kiev, sends for Sviatopolk and hands Kiev back to him, while he himself goes to Smolensk. When Sviatopolk reaches Kiev, its people come out to meet him and present him with gifts.

A.D. 1084

Władysław considers it a shame on him and his family that his nephew, Mieczysław, should be exiled in a foreign country, so he sends to King Laszló of Hungary asking him to send the boy back to Poland together with the Polish knights who are there in exile with him. Mieczysław and these knights have been in exile for two years now, and the King and his two brothers have grown so fond of the boy that they treat him as a son. His physical strength and dexterity are so superior to those of his peers, Polish or Hungarian, and even of those older than he, that he is admired and liked wherever he goes. Everyone loves him and sincerely respects him; but he has a natural desire to return to his fatherland, so, when Laszló is asked to send him back, many people think that he should do so, however much he hates the idea. So, seeing how keen his young relative is to return home, Laszló fits him out with horses, clothes and jewels and sends him to his uncle. Many of the Polish knights go with him and those who do, have their properties, which had been sequestrated by the royal treasury for their implication in the murder of St. Stanisław, restored to them.

A.D. 1085

Once Prince Władysław has more or less restored order to his country, he begins to worry about his unfortunate lack of an heir. He realizes that, as his wife, Judith, has not had any offspring, it is unlikely that she will ever be a mother and so his line will end with him. The Princess, eager to avoid the shame of barrenness, takes to pious deeds, making rich gifts to the church, the poor, orphans, widows, wanderers and all unfortunates. She prays every day, beseeching God to grant her a healthy male child. One day the Bishop of Cracow, Lambert, who has been in France, tells her that near Marseilles, where the Rhône falls into the sea, is a Benedictine monastery which possesses the body of St. Giles. This has such power with the Almighty, that never yet has anyone making a just and reasonable request been refused. The Bishop advises the Princess to prepare gifts for the monastery: a huge goblet of pure gold with the likeness of a child, golden and silver vessels and vestments embroidered with gold and scarlet thread, and to send these by a delegation of both clergy and laymen to the monastery at Saint Gilles. This she does. The delegation reaches Marseilles safely and goes to the monastery. The gifts are handed over to the abbot, who then imposes a three-day fast on the monks, during which time they have to beseech God to grant the request of the Polish delegates, who have come so far. Before the three days are out, one of the monks receives a revelation that St. Giles has removed Princess Judith's sterility and that she and Prince Władysław are to have a child. The abbot assures the delegates that God has granted them what they requested. They then return to Poland as fast as they can and give the glad news. Shortly afterwards, the Princess becomes pregnant.

The barbarian Polovtsy, arch-enemies of the Ruthenians, hearing that on Vsevolod's death the throne has passed to Izjaslav's son, Sviatopolk, assemble a huge army and prepare to devastate

Ruthenia. First, however, they send envoys to Sviatopolk reminding him that it was his father's practice to make peace with them and requesting a reply to an earlier query about unpaid tribute. This infuriates Sviatopolk, who throws the Polovtsian envoys into prison. When news of this reaches their country, there is considerable anger and the Polovtsy start devastating the Ruthenian countryside. Realizing that he has blundered, Sviatopolk releases the envoys and sends them back with a request for the peace he previously refused. When this is refused in its turn, he calls his people to arms, intending to engage the enemy. His more realistic advisers tell him that he cannot defeat the Polovtsy and should send for assistance from the other two dukes, Vladimir and Rostislav. These two combine their forces and bring them to Kiev. They rebuke Sviatopolk for having breached international etiquette by imprisoning the envoys, but agree to let that matter rest, so that they can turn their attention to the defence of their country. The combined Ruthenian army then marches out and makes its first halt at Kolropol on the River Stuca. Here they take the feeling of the troops: are they prepared to fight? Opinions are divided and Vladimir advises that they cross the river and make a treaty with the Polovtsy. The army is then moved across the river, which is in spate, and advances in battle array. Rostislav is in command of the left wing, Sviatopolk of the right wing, and Vladimir of the centre. Battle is finally joined on May 20. The Polovtsy start by sending archers to harry the Ruthenian right wing, which is drawn up between two mounds that they have thrown up. These are Sviatopolk's troops and they cannot face the arrows, but run, Sviatopolk with them. The Polovtsy then attack the left wing and the centre and rout both, Vladimir and Rostislav fleeing with the remaining men. Rostislav takes to the river and gets into trouble in an eddy and his brother is almost drowned in a vain attempt to rescue him; Rostislav drowns as do many of his men. In the meantime Sviatopolk has got to Kolropol and stays there until evening. Then, under cover of night, he manages to reach Kiev. Rostislav's body is recovered from the river, taken to Kiev and buried there in his father's tomb in the Church of St. Sophia.

The victorious Polovtsy continue their destruction and pillaging. They invest the castle of Torchesk, whose garrison soon begins to suffer the pangs of hunger and sends to Sviatopolk for help without which, he is told, they will be unable to hold out. Sviatopolk does send them provisions, but these do not get through the blockade, the roads being too well guarded by the Polovtsy. These then divide their forces. One force continues the siege, while the other marches on Kiev. Sviatopolk sallies out to engage them and is again defeated. However, he manages to get back inside the castle, but with only two of his men, for all his knights have either been killed or taken prisoner. The Polovtsy then go back to Torchesk with their booty and prisoners. When the garrison there sees these and realizes that Sviatopolk has been defeated and that they have no hope of receiving food or help, they surrender the castle. The Polovtsy then burn it and carry many of the Ruthenians back to slavery in their own country, where, the winter being severe, many of them die, those who survive are left filthy and half-naked.

A.D. 1086

Princess Judith, having spent her entire pregnancy in prayer, fasting and vigil, gives birth to a boy on August 12. On Christmas Eve the princess dies. Władysław is distraught and wonders whether he would not have preferred to have remained childless and still have his beloved wife. He orders the infant, Bolesław, to be tended with the greatest care.

Oleg of Kiev, wishing in some way to compensate for his defeats, makes peace with the Polovtsy and to ensure that this will endure, takes the daughter of the Polovtsian prince as his wife. Now, with the help of his wife's people, Oleg attacks the fortress at Smolensk. This Prince Vladimir successfully defends, but Oleg burns all its monasteries and churches and devastates the surrounding fields and villages. Then, realising that his losses are too great, Vladimir sends heralds to

Oleg and makes peace. Oleg then withdraws to Pereiaslavl, though his troops continue devastating the countryside as they go and keep taking captives, who are subsequently sold into slavery.

A further disaster strikes the country, when swarms of locusts arrive and eat up all the produce left in the fields.

A.D. 1087

The Dowager Queen Dobronega, widow of Casimir I, dies and is buried in Cracow cathedral. The Roman Emperor, Henry IV, calls a formal assembly of princes in Mainz. One of those attending is the Czech prince, Vratislav, and he plies the Emperor with gifts of gold, silver, jewels and chased vessels, and asks that he be crowned king. The Emperor agrees and orders the Archbishop of Trier to go to Prague and there anoint and formally crown Vratislav as the first king of Bohemia and his wife, Svatava, as the first queen, the actual crowns being provided by the Emperor. Thus the kingdom of Bohemia comes into being at the same time as the kingdom of Poland ceases to exist, as though Destiny would not tolerate the existence of two separate kingdoms speaking the same tongue.

A.D. 1088

Prince Władysław of Poland, still grieving over the loss of his wife, is persuaded to marry again. His bride is the Hungarian Queen Sophia, who remained in Hungary when Saloman went to Bulgaria and on to Istria. Władysław assures her that she shall be given all the respect due to her family and status, and pays the whole of her dowry out of his own pocket. They marry and go back to Poland. Although she never had any children by Saloman, she eventually gives Władysław three daughters. At this time, too, Prince Mieczysław, son of the late King Bolesław and still scarcely more than a youth, marries Eudoxia, Sviatopolk's sister, in order that the Ruthenian lands conquered by his father should remain part of Poland. The two weddings are the occasion for a huge celebration.

A.D. 1089

Prince Mieczysław dies without progeny and so the line of King Bolesław dies out. At the funeral, as the tomb is being closed on her son, Viszeslawa, the Queen Dowager, is carried out of the church in a dead faint. The bishop conducting the service splashes water on her face, which revives her, but she continues to mourn until her death, which occurs shortly afterwards.

The Polovtsy have now devastated or defeated almost all the dukedoms of Ruthenia, only that belonging to Vladimir remaining unconquered, and on him the two leaders of the Polovtsy, Kytan and Itlar, now declare war. Rather than have the enemy devastate his lands yet again, Vladimir sends envoys to conclude peace on terms that are rather unfair, in that Vladimir has to pay the Polovtsy an annual tribute and provide his son, Sviatoslav, as a hostage. After this, a knight called Slaveta, who has arrived on a mission from Sviatopolk, tells Vladimir's knights that they should kill all the Polovtsy who, feeling secure, are now living scattered about the territory. Vladimir hesitates a long time, but finally gives his assent. First, Slaveta rescues Vladimir's son, the hostage, who is slackly guarded, and then kills Kytan and all with him. Another force kills Itlar, who is then being entertained by one of the Russian boyars, and all his men with him.

Vladimir then asks Oleg to come and help him get rid of the Polovtsy and this Oleg promises to do, but cunningly goes elsewhere. Nonetheless, Sviatopolk and Vladimir together attack the unsuspecting Polovtsian outposts. Having killed most of those who have the courage to resist, they round up the non-combatants, women, youths and children, as well as their cattle, camels and horses, and drive them all back into Ruthenia. Angry with Oleg for having broken his promise, his two brothers send to remind him that he has not been as good as his word and demand that he either hand over or kill the son of Itlar, the Polovtsian prince, whom he is harbouring. Oleg refuses to do either, which makes his brother dukes and all the Ruthenian knights hate him. Meanwhile, the stubborn Polovtsy have assembled another army with which they besiege Sviatopolk's fortress at Yuriev. This would have surrendered had Sviatopolk not sent gifts to placate the Polovtsy and induce them to withdraw. Whilst they are doing this, they are pursued by Prussians, who have invaded Ruthenia with a big army and are proceeding to devastate it. David, Prince of Novgorod, withdraws to Smolensk and, at the request of the inhabitants of Novgorod, Mstislav, Vladimir's son, comes from Rostov and takes over the principality.

A.D. 1090

After King Bolesław fled to Hungary, the loyalty of the Ruthenian territories that had come under the Polish crown by right of inheritance or conquest began to waver and their people started to talk of rebellion. So, when news comes of the death of Prince Mieczysław, to whom both territories belonged by virtue of his recent marriage as well as by inheritance from his father and mother, the Ruthenians openly revolt and publicly proclaim that they are now free of the Polish yoke and no longer owe allegiance to King Bolesław or his son. Not only that, they also take up arms and expel or scare away most of the Polish garrisons with their Polish starostas and captains in their territory; others that they cannot overcome by bribery or trickery they starve into surrender, when their Prince never comes to their help, either because he does not care about them or is too involved in other wars and affairs of state to be able to do so. Thus, in the course of one year, Poland loses all the Ruthenian territories it has possessed for such a long time. The Ruthenians, you must know, loathed Polish rule not only because of its injustices, but also because of the differences in the religions of the two peoples.

The quarrel between the Czech king, Vratislav, and his brother, the Bishop of Prague, Jaromír/Gebhard, breaks out again. Vratislav considers that the Bishop opposes his wishes unnecessarily, is unfriendly, impertinent and arrogant. In order to diminish the latter's standing, Vratislav places his new foundation at Vyshegrod directly under the authority of the Holy See and appoints his royal chaplain to be Bishop of Olomouc, which, at his wish, has been made an independent see. Bishop Jaromír takes umbrage at this and sets out intending to go to the Pope to complain. He turns aside on his journey to seek the assistance of the King of Hungary. The two meet in Esztergom, where the Bishop suddenly falls ill and dies. This resolves the quarrel and the sees of Prague and Olomouc remain separate, each with its own bishop.

A.D. 1091

The success of the revolt in Ruthenia encourages Pomerania and Prussia to attempt the same. They renounce obedience and refuse to pay the usual tribute to the Polish treasury, and then set about killing or shamefully expelling all starostas and captains who will not side with them. Rightly indignant, Władysław declares war on Pomerania and the Prussians. He orders armed units from all his territories to assemble on June 24. With this force he invades Pomerania. Although he takes several forts, devastates fields and burns villages, the Pomeranians and their barbarian allies, the Prussians, decide not to beg for peace, but to fight. They assemble a considerable army and, on August 5, seek to bar the Poles' further advance near Rzeczen. They array their ranks and advance. This being a holy day, Władysław is reluctant to fight, but seeing that his men are endangered, he draws his own sword and a fierce battle begins. This lasts most of the day. Gradually, however, the ranks of the Pomeranians begin to thin; then they break, retreat and finally run. The Poles pursue them for a considerable distance, slaughtering many of them in their rage. Their resources now exhausted, the Pomeranians and Prussians submit once again and beg for forgiveness. This the Prince gladly grants, being convinced that in future they will remain loyal. However, he removes all the main fortresses and castles from their jurisdiction and entrusts these to his tried knights, but burns or demolishes all the forts on the actual frontier. Then, having arranged everything to his satisfaction, he returns home with his victorious army.

Vratislav, King of Bohemia, exasperated by the hostility of his two brothers, Conrad and Otto, and more than disquieted by the suspicion that they are planning to prevent his son ascending the throne on his death, marches into Moravia with a heavily armed force, occupies Olomouc and other towns which belong to Otto, and gives them to his son, Břetislav. Otto is killed in the fighting, leaving two sons; Sviatopolk and Otto the Black. Conrad, Vratislav's surviving brother, is treated with abominable cruelty. During the fighting, Břetislav kills a baron who had rendered his father great service and the King is naturally angry, so angry that his son thinks it politic to move his tents and the greater part of his army to the other bank of the river. He then marches off in the direction of the fortress at Hradec. Vratislav is deeply hurt by his son's behaviour and only lets himself be reconciled with him when his brother, Conrad, takes his nephew's side. However, Břetislav now feels that he can no longer trust his father, so he leaves the country and goes to the King of Hungary, with whom he is to remain until his father dies. As punishment, Vratislav nominates his own younger brother, Conrad, as his successor.

In order to avoid further devastation of their lands by the Polovtsy, two of the Ruthenian dukes, Sviatopolk of Kiev and Vladimir of Smolensk, summon the barons, bishops, clergy and boyars to assemble and confer on ways and means of defending their territories. Oleg does not bother to attend, which so incenses the other two that they go for him instead of the Polovtsy. Oleg takes refuge in Staroduba, where he is besieged for thirty-two days. When, finally, hunger constrains him, he begs for peace and submits to his brothers, who order him to come with his brother David to Kiev. When the latter arrives, he promises them obedience and kisses the cross in token of his sincerity. Meanwhile the Polovtsy under Prince Maniak are attacking Kievan territory and doing considerable damage. They burn down the royal palace at Berestovo and collect huge amounts of booty. At the same time, a second Polovtsian force under their second prince, Tuhortkan, attacks Pereiaslavl. Sviatopolk and Vladimir rush to its defence and, on July 19, battle is joined. This proves disastrous for the Polovtsy, and Tuhortkan and his sons are killed. Undeterred, the Polovtsy assemble yet another army and march on Kiev. They approach in close formation and so quietly that they very nearly surprise and capture the castle. In their disappointment, they burn all the churches, monasteries and villages round about. Oleg, who, having broken his promises, is reluctant to meet his brothers, assembles his own army and attacks Murom, which is held by Vladimir's son, Izjaslav, asserting that it is an inheritance from his father and so belongs to him. Izjaslav bars his advance and there is a battle in which Izjaslav is killed and so it ends in victory for Oleg. The people of Murom open the city's gates to Oleg, who then proceeds to capture Rostov castle. Here again the people of Rostov submit without a fight and promise to pay Oleg tribute. Vladimir's second son, Mstislav, who holds Novgorod, fearing the power and tyrany of Oleg, sends envoys to him promising submission and to reconcile him with his father, apparently seeing no obstacle in the fact that Oleg has killed his own brother; but then murders and killings are frequent not only among princes, but kings and emperors as well. Oleg, however, intending to get Novgorod for himself and hoping that he will find it easy to turn Mstislav out, dismisses the envoys without giving them an answer and then invades Novgorod. He halts at Susdal and sends his brother, Iaroslav, ahead to reconnoitre. Iaroslav goes too far ahead and is captured by Mstislav's knights. This gives Oleg a fright and he withdraws to Rostov, while Mstislav captures Susdal and burns it. To be on the safe side, Oleg now retreats to Murom.

Mstislav again sends envoys to Oleg and this time they make peace and so Mstislav disbands his army. When he learns of this, Oleg breaks their agreement and attacks again. Mstislav recalls his troops and marches against Oleg, but for four days avoids doing battle, as he is hoping for the arrival of reinforcements from Kiev and from the Polovtsy. When these fail to arrive, Mstislav sends in his infantry, which defeats Oleg, who again withdraws to Murom. In the end, the two dukes make it up, but Oleg feels that after all his treachery, he is unlikely to be safe anywhere in Ruthenia and withdraws with some of his knights to Ryazan; but Mstislav sends after him promising that he can live safely in Ruthenia and that he will be forgiven for all that he has done. Oleg lets himself be persuaded and returns together with his knights and establishes himself in the fortress of Novgorod.

A.D. 1092

Having suppressed the revolt of the Prussians and Pomeranians, Prince Władysław is hoping for a period of peace and rest, but, suddenly, he is told that these two are once more talking belligerently and he fears for his starostas and captains. His fears are justified, for all of these are killed, except for the few whose judgments have been impeccable. This incenses Władysław and, having prepared a small force of picked men, he advances into Pomerania despite its being February. There, dividing his force into two and entrusting one half to Sieciech the Voivode of Cracow, they drive in two prongs through the whole of Pomerania and Prussia, the troops being encouraged to loot and burn as they go. This continues throughout Lent, the troops paying no attention to the regulation fast. A great number of captives are taken, and much loot and cattle collected, for the Pomeranians and Prussians have gone into hiding and there is little or no resistance. Władysław then starts on the way back to Poland with his loot; but when he reaches a place called Drzeń near the River Nakło, his rear-guard reports that a considerable enemy force is approaching, indeed is scarcely more than five miles away. Władysław is in two minds, should he fight the enemy which considerably outnumbers his force, or await a better opportunity? The final decision is that it is better to fight nobly and die, than to return home without glory. A long battle ensues, towards the end of which the Pomeranians bring up reinforcements to replace their dead and wounded, and renew their attack. The Poles prepare to sell their lives dearly, and the battle, which began at three in the afternoon, continues until darkness has fallen. In the end the Pomeranians are forced to withdraw, but the Poles, most of whom are wounded, are too exhausted to pursue them. This is a battle in which, unusually, more are killed than are taken prisoner. The Poles consider it a triumph that they have not retreated and have retained their loot.

Władysław now has to decide whether to continue the withdrawal to Poland or to march back into Pomerania, and so give the Pomeranians no time to recover their breath or think what to do. His commanders all favour the second plan; yet the quantity of cattle and the amount of other booty they have taken, the numbers of those wounded and the few serviceable troops left him, as well as the approach of Ascension Day and some bad weather, incline the King to return to Poland, and this he does. After spending several days in Gniezno getting reinforcements, he marches back into Pomerania. The Pomeranians, however, have again gone into hiding and there is no one to fight. More or less all Pomerania has already been ravaged and there is nothing more to destroy, so he lays siege to the fort at Nakło, in which, he is told, is a considerable number of Pomeranians, whose task is to guard the fort and prepare incursions into Poland. Almost every night during the siege, the Poles have to stand to arms because of shadowy figures that appear to be armed men, advancing towards them. Woken thus from their sleep night after night, the men become nervous and are convinced that there are enemies everywhere. This continues until one night some of the braver men pursue the shadows away from the camp and discover that it is their own shadows, cast by the moon which is almost at the full, of which they have been so afraid. While they are out chasing their shadows, the real enemy comes and sets fire to several outposts and soldiers' huts, which are mostly roofed with straw or dried grass, causing a big fire in which a number of people and many things perish. The fire also puts many of the siege engines out of action; so, when winter comes, as it does earlier here than in Poland and is more severe, and the troops begin to feel the effect of a shortage of provisions, and suffer from the cold, Władysław abandons the siege and returns to Gniezno. In a strange way this encourages the Pomeranians and they continue their revolt. Religious people would have it that the Poles' failure was due to their having broken the Lenten fast by excessive eating of meat and milk, which is not allowed.

Vratislav, King of Bohemia, contracts a high fever and dies in Prague on January 14. Some chroniclers have it that his death was not due to a fever, but to a fall from his horse while hunting which broke his neck. The bishops and barons approve his brother, Conrad, as his successor, a thing Vratislav arranged in order to spite his son, Břetislav, now in exile in Hungary. However, Conrad reigns for only seven months and eighteen days, before he, too, dies. Learning of these two deaths, Břetislav leaves Hungary and comes to Prague, where he is recognised as heir to the throne, but not crowned king. He proves a zealous protagonist of the Catholic faith and tries to stamp out all the old pagan customs and superstitions, the sooth-saying and fortune-telling and prophesying, that were so rife in his father's day.

A.D. 1093

In the summer of this year, Prince Władysław invades Pomerania yet again. Having captured all the forts and strong-points that remain, he ravages the fields and burns all isolated and abandoned houses. Having dealt thus with all Pomerania, he turns on the Prussians and devastates the whole of their country, plundering and burning in the same way and carrying off huge numbers of captives and cattle. The Pomeranians and Prussians, who now have lost practically everything they possess, send envoys to Władysław offering complete submission and obedience, if only he will relent. Władysław agrees, but he will not spare the leaders of the rebellion. Everyone else has to come to him and confirm their submission and allegiance, but the leaders of the rebels are either executed or sent into exile.

Břetislav, seeing that Władysław is busy warring deep in Prussia, collects as large a force as he can muster and invades the Polish patrimonial lands on the River Elbe and puts them to fire and the sword, which he does without opposition, since all those able to bear arms are with the king in Prussia. His excuse for the invasion is that these lands have not paid the tribute once imposed on them, but all he really wants is plunder and booty from a land rich in cattle.

A.D. 1094

Prince Władysław is furious at the Czechs' invasion of his territories and assembles every soldier he has and even sends for mercenaries from Hungary and Bohemia, the latter mostly Czechs who dislike Břetislav. While making these preparations for a punitive strike, as well as for another war against Moravia that he is planning for the summer, he suddenly falls ill. However, he does not let this spoil his plans. He puts Sieciech the Voivode of Cracow and commander of the army in charge of a force adequate to invade Moravia. He gives the Voivode his orders for this in the presence of his young son, Bolesław, who listens attentively to all that is said, and, eager to go to war, asks his father to let him accompany the Voivode. At first, Władysław refuses, since Bolesław is his only son and war is a dangerous occupation; but the ten-year old protests that he has the strength and only needs his father's permission, which he finally gets. Throughout the campaign his eagerness to learn the disciplines and arts of war greatly impresses the Voivode. Often Bolesław stays with the men on guard duty at night, going without sleep and suffering the cold with them. If sleep overcomes him, he lies down on the bare earth with only a soldier's coat over him. He badgers the Voivode to be allowed to take part in the fighting, although of an age when he should not have been thinking of such things. The Voivode completes his task of burning and plundering and returns to Poland with many captives and much booty.

It is soon obvious that Bolesław is every inch a prince and has all a prince's qualities of integrity, courage and daring. The moment he ceases to be a child, he takes up arms and enters military service.

The six Ruthenian dukes, Sviatopolk of Kiev, Vladimir, David son of Gregory, Vasilko son of Rostislav and David and Oleg sons of Sviatoslav, meet in Liubech to consider ways of improving the defences of Ruthenia, which has been so gravely ravaged by the barbarian Polovtsy. Having criticized their jealousy of each other, the ambition of some, and the way in which by fighting each other they have allowed the barbarians to be victorious, they agree that each shall be content with what he has inherited from his father and not attempt to get what belongs to one of the others. They make a pact on these terms and swear to abide by it, saying that whoever breaks the pact shall be the enemy of all the others. They then disband their armies. Satan, however, soon sows the seed of fresh disagreement. Sviatopolk, Prince of Kiev, conspires with David to get rid of Vasilko, whose loyalty he suspects; so, when Vasilko comes to Kiev on a peaceful errand, he is arrested and hired assassins are sent to kill him, but Vasilko gets the better of them, only to be taken to Zvenigorod where both his eyes are put out, for they believe that if he is allowed to remain alive, Sviatopolk and his sons will never be safe in Kiev; however, Vasilko does not die but remains a captive. Vladimir protests that Ruthenians have never yet perpetrated so cruel and disgraceful a crime; and he, David and Oleg agree to send envoys to reprimand Sviatopolk, who tells them that he has definite proof that Vasilko was plotting against his life in order to take over his duchy. More disturbed than mollified by this reply, the three dukes assemble their armies and march on Kiev. Sviatopolk prepares to take refuge with the Polovtsy, but the Patriarch and the barons dissuade him, and he goes out to meet the others and begs them to put down their arms and forgive each other and so avoid bloodshed. They then make another pact and withdraw their armies. David, however, cannot forgive the blinding of Vasilko and prepares to invade Kiev on his own, but learning that Vasilko's brother, Volodar, is preparing to ambush him, he halts at Busk, which is at once invested by Volodar, who demands the release of his blinded brother. David acquiesces and the two make it up. Nonetheless, in the early spring, Volodar and his blind brother invade Volhynia which belongs to David. Having captured the fort of Vladimir in Volhynia, they burn it and cruelly murder most of those found in it. They then advance on Vladimir's castle and invest it, telling those inside that they will raise the siege and grant everyone their lives, if they will hand over Vasil and Lazarus, the two responsible for blinding Vasilko. This they do and the siege is raised, while Vasil and Lazarus are strung up and killed with a hail of arrows. Sviatopolk, wishing to avenge himself on David, goes to Brześć, where there is a Polish garrison, and asks for help. He is told to stay where he is, while they send to Prince Władysław for instructions. David, however, has got in ahead of Sviatopolk, by himself going to Władysław and offering him a considerable sum of money for help against Sviatopolk. Władysław does not know what to do, but finally assembles an army and, taking David with him, sets out in the hope of reconciling the two brothers. This he attempts to do while in camp beside the River Bug, but he fails and, deciding not to help either of them, goes back to Poland. David then lays siege to castle at Vladimir and captures it after seven weeks. Next, he attacks Volodar and Vasilko, neither of whom is reluctant to fight. Their armies arrayed, battle is engaged. Vasilko and Volodar are victorious and Sviatopolk retreats with his two sons, the two sons of Iaropolk, David's son and the rest of his knights. They are not pursued because the others are afraid of an ambush, and thus reach Vladimir, in which Sviatopolk installs Mstislav, son of one of his concubines. His second son, Iaroslav, he sends to Hungary to ask for help, while he himself returns to Kiev to assemble a fresh army.

Prince Coloman of Hungary now arrives with an army of 8000 men and two bishops, sets up camp beside the River Wiar and proceeds to lay siege to Przemyśl, in which Volodar has sought safety and where, too, are David's wife and family. David himself has gone to the Polovtsy to ask for their help. Chancing to encounter a Polovtsian force under Prince Boniak, he persuades them to help Volodar. They pitch camp not far from Przemyśl. That night, Boniak goes out into the nearby forest and begins to howl like a wolf. When this brings wolves running in answer to his howls, this is taken as an assurance of victory, and, on his return to the camp, David orders the troops to prepare for battle. He divides the whole force into three units, one of which he sends against the Hungarians, while the other two are to remain in reserve, hidden. The first unit has orders to attack and then retreat, pretending to be defeated. This it does, and the Hungarians take the manoeuvre at its face value and pursue so far that Boniak, his Polovtsians and the Ruthenians are able to get in between the Hungarians and their camp, cutting them off. In the ensuing slaughter many of the Hungarians fall or are drowned in the river. Others flee into the woods and hills. Among the casualties is one of the bishops, Kupan, and many knights of renown. Prince Coloman survives. The Ruthenians and Polovtsy capture the enemy's camp. Sviatopolk's son, Iaroslav, and some of his companions escape to the Poles in Brześć, thinking that Hungary will not be safe enough for them. Encouraged by this victory, David besieges the castle at Vladimir. There are frequent skirmishes between the besiegers and the besieged. One day, Mstislav to whom his father entrusted the castle, while shooting at the enemy from the castle walls, is himself hit by an arrow and killed. His death is concealed for four days, and when, finally, it is known, the hungry besieged decide to surrender. However, afraid of what Sviatopolk may do to them, they first send to him telling him of his son's death and of the garrison's situation, which is such that, unless he can quickly come to their assistance, they will have to surrender. Sviatopolk sends his voivode, Putiata, with reinforcements for the garrison. With them is David's second son, Sviatoslav. Putiata halts before he reaches Vladimir; then on the following day, makes a stealthy advance and a sudden fierce attack, which surprises and routs David's men, and so the siege is raised. Putiata appoints Basil as the new captain for the castle at Vladimir and returns to Kiev, while Sviatoslav returns to Łuck. David takes refuge with the Polovtsy, who are prepared to give him further assistance. He and Boniak then lay siege to Łuck, where is his second son, Sviatoslav, the one responsible for his defeat at Vladimir. Sviatoslav, however, slips out of the castle and goes to Smolensk. David and Boniak then advance on Vladimir, whose starosta Basil flees, leaving the castle to its fate, and it is easily captured.

A.D. 1095

The fort at Międzyrzecz on the Oder, near Saxony, has been taken over by a group of deserters from Pomerania, who have begun pillaging the surrounding country. When told of this, young Prince Bolesław demands that his father give him a force sufficient to recapture the fort. He rejects all his father's objections and finally gets his way, but on condition that he will obey Voivode Sieciech, who is to accompany him and see that the rashness of youth does not spoil the enterprise. The fort is duly invested. Its natural position is a good defence, but those inside build additional ramparts. On Sieciech's advice, Bolesław deploys his force so that it completely surrounds the fort and proceeds to throw up his own ramparts of timber and turf. He then brings up siege machines which keep up a continuous bombardment that finally breaches the fort's defences in several places and kills or wounds most of its defenders. The besiegers grow daily more confident and the besieged daily less so. The surviving Pomeranians then send to Bolesław offering to surrender. Terms are agreed, which allow the garrison to march out with its horses, train and all its equipment. Then, having reoccupied the fort and restored order in the surrounding country, Bolesław returns home. His father is delighted with his achievement and the talent for war and leadership he has shown.

Laszló, King of Hungary, dies after eighteen years of just rule, during which time he has added two kingdoms to his own: Dalmatia and Croatia, the last ruler of which, Zvonimir, having no heir, left them both to his widow, who was Laszló's sister, and she ruled them until her death,

Břetislav II, Duke of Bohemia.
Treacherously murdered in A.D. 1100.
From Alexander Guagninus: Sarmatiae Europeae
descriptio.—*Jagiellonian University Library.*

Sobieslaus, Duke of Bohemia.
A.D. 1125–1140.
From Alexander Guagninus: Sarmatiae Europeae
descriptio.—*Jagiellonian University Library.*

when she left them to her brother. Laszló, having no heir, is succeeded by Coloman's son, Géza, who, having received the necessary dispensation from the Pope, gives up his post as bishop of Waradyn.

A.D. 1096

Fate now turns against Prince Władysław, who has been so successful hitherto in all that he has undertaken. He had a natural son by a concubine before Princess Judith gave him a legitimate heir. Judith hated the concubine and her child, so it was sent to a place of which its mother was kept ignorant. When she dies, the child, Zbigniew, is sent to Cracow to be educated. Then, in order to hide the fact of his being a bastard and to prevent him claiming equal rights with his father's heir, he is sent to Saxony, tonsured and put in a monastery.

At this time there is in Bohemia a considerable number of Polish deserters and exiles, either knights sentenced because of debt or crime, or expelled by the powerful Voivode of Cracow, Sieciech, who has more influence with the King than anyone and is horribly arrogant. Those who he thinks may stand in his way he persecutes with trumped up charges or unjustly deprives of their possessions. Prince Břetislav, considering that his best way of avenging himself on the Poles is to stir up domestic strife among them, suborns these discontents with presents and promises and gets them to try to persuade Władysław's illegitimate son, Zbigniew, to leave his monastery and join them. Some of the discontents now go to the monastery where Zbigniew is and manage to extract him, despite the protests of his fellow monks, and take him to Wrocław, the castle and territories of which are held by a baron called Magnus, who is a bitter enemy of the Voivode of Cracow. Explaining that on his father's death Zbigniew will inherit Magnus' fief and other Polish principalities, they ask Magnus to admit them to the castle and help them put an end to their shameful exile. Magnus hesitates for a long time. He knows that among the exiles are many with whom he is connected and is thus urged in one direction by hope and hatred but on the other hand is restrained by loyalty and honesty. Undecided, he consults the chief citizens of Wrocław. They, too, hate Sieciech and are eager to be rid of him, yet afraid lest Zbigniew and the Polish exiles harm them. However, they unanimously decide to admit Zbigniew and the others, provided that they swear not to do anything prejudicial to Władysław and their fatherland. Magnus agrees and so Zbigniew is installed in Wrocław castle, addressed as Prince and given the means to maintain himself and his companions.

Władysław is furious when he learns of this; but even more angry is Sieciech who knows that the reason for the exiles' action is their hatred of him; but what he fears most is losing his position. Władysław now sends envoys to Wrocław, who accuse Magnus, the nobles, and citizens of Wrocław, of recklessness in admitting Zbigniew and the other exiles and try to persuade them of Sieciech's innocence. They ask whether the King is to regard them as rebels, who wish to give their fatherland to the Czechs, or as his loyal subjects. Magnus replies that, far from acting recklessly, they did what they have done only after lengthy consultation and have no intention of handing Wrocław over to the Czechs, who are their enemies and whose hatred and perversity they know all too well. They have admitted Zbigniew and the others, he says, not as enemies of the Prince and their fatherland, but as survivors of the storm whipped up by Sieciech, so that they might save the fatherland from the shame of having exiles begging for alms abroad. Never, in any circumstances, will they refuse obedience and loyalty to Władysław and his son, Bolesław, but they can no longer stomach the arrogance and wickedness of Sieciech. When the envoys, as ordered by Władysław, try to justify Sieciech's actions, the people of Wrocław become so angry that they begin to pick up stones, and Magnus and his barons have to protect the envoys.

When the envoys return home and report all that has happened, Władysław decides on immediate action. He assembles a force and, leaving his son in Cracow, advances on Wrocław, intending to stifle what he regards as a rebellion. All those living in the outskirts of the city compete to proclaim their loyalty, and, when he reaches the city itself, he is met by a procession of clergy, monks and citizens, headed by the Bishop of Wrocław and is conducted into the city with all due respect. The castle gates stand open and Magnus and his knights receive the Prince humbly and with due deference.

The next morning, Zbigniew and the Polish exiles, realizing that they have lost the support of Magnus and the people of Wrocław, and afraid of what Władysław may do to them, slip away and go to Kruszwica, a populous town with a fort. Władysław relieves Magnus of his post of castellan and replaces him jointly with Bolesław and his tutor, Wojslaw. Zbigniew now invokes the help of the Pomeranians, numbers of whom gather at Kruszwica, bringing some Prussians and other barbarians with them. The Pomeranians are hoping thus to promote civil war, which will make it easier for them to gain their objectives. Encouraged by this extra strength, which means that he now has seven regiments of deserters and exiles, Pomeranians and Prussians, Zbigniew can feel confident of defeating his father and advances against him. Battle is joined by Lake Gopło, not far from Kruszwica. The resulting casualties are so heavy that the lake becomes polluted with blood and corpses and for a long time people cannot drink its water, nor eat its fish. Zbigniew's forces are seriously depleted and in the end he and a few companions withdraw into Kruszwica fortress, in which his father finally captures him alive. The troops are not allowed to loot the town. Zbigniew is sent to Cracow and imprisoned there in the custody of Sieciech.

While father and son have been fighting it out at Kruszwica, Břetislav of Bohemia, fulfilling his promise to his Polish exiles, moves his army into that part of Poland that lies along the River Nysa, looting and pillaging as he goes, aiming at Wrocław. He captures and burns the fort at Bardo on the Nysa, which he finds undefended. A little downstream from Bardo he discovers a cliff as high as a tower, broad at the base and tapering towards the top, then falling steeply into the river below, a natural fortress, to which he adds a stout timber superstructure, and this he calls Kamieniec, a name it has to this day.

Leaving a garrison there, he returns to Bohemia, from which he expels two members of the Vršovci clan, whom he accuses of being pro-Polish and betraying his secrets to the Poles. He also confiscates all their property for the benefit of his treasury. The two exiles eventually reach Poland penniless and in rags. Władysław receives them graciously and provides generously for them and their families.

A.D. 1097

Archbishop Martin announces that the long delayed reconsecration of Gniezno cathedral is to take place on May 1, and invites the Prince, his wife and sons, all the other bishops, the powerful barons and important people of Poland to attend the ceremony. The Pomeranians see this as a splendid opportunity and, on the eve of the ceremony, under cover of darkness they mount a surprise attack on the fortress of Santok, having previously bribed many of those inside: who, at an agreed signal, let down ropes up which the Pomeranians climb into the fortress. Already rejoicing at its capture, they are suddenly overcome with fear by the sight of a huge man in armour, astride a white horse, who brandishes a sword at them. Terrified, they run, and their fleeing footsteps are so loud that the noise rouses the garrison, which pursues them and captures or kills them all. The Poles conclude that their saviour, the knight astride a white horse, must have been St. Wojciech.

After the reconsecration of the cathedral the bishops and other eminent personages of the country all urge the Prince to release Zbigniew, who, indeed, promises that in future he will be a loyal subject of his father. Bolesław agrees and then sends his two sons into Pomerania with an army, but when they return without anything achieved, because they have been continually bickering about seniority, fearing that on his death they will continue to bicker and quarrel, he divides Poland between them. Bolesław is to have Cracow, Wrocław, Sandomierz and Sieradz, that is the greater part of the country, while Zbigniew is to have Pomerania, Wielkopolska, Łęczca, Kujawy and Mazovia. Władysław is to retain control of the whole and continue to receive the revenues of all these territories during his lifetime, the young princes taking over their shares only on his death.

A.D. 1098

Władysław goes to Mazovia, his favourite part of the country. While there, he is told that Břetislav is assembling an army with the intention of invading the country around Wrocław. Władysław alerts his son, Bolesław, who is responsible for that area and tells him to take the necessary action. Bolesław immediately assembles a force and with it marches to the frontier. On this occasion, his tutor, Wojsław, is not with him and the latter's absence starts a rumour that he has defected and gone over to Sieciech, the two princes' arch-enemy. Bolesław's intelligence tells him that all is quiet in Bohemia and no invasion planned. He and Zbigniew make a pact to oppose Sieciech whom they suspect of having planned the whole affair so as to discredit them and let him gain control of Wrocław, as he already has of so many of the country's frontier fortresses and castles, in which he has installed his brothers and relations. By this time the troops have worked themselves into a state of near mutiny and Bolesław has his work cut out to calm them, especially when

Wojsław suddenly arrives and is denied entry into the city. Eventually the misunderstandings are cleared up and Bolesław and his brother, who has now joined him, move their camp to a small village called Żarnowiec, where Władysław and his court happen to be. Władysław refuses to believe his sons' assertions about the evil intentions of Sieciech the Voivode of Cracow; indeed, they almost come to blows over this. In the end, the two princes persuade their father to believe them, who are to succeed him, rather than the Voivode, and there is a great reconciliation. Sieciech then takes refuge in the castle that bears his name, Sieciechów, which is heavily fortified with several moats and ramparts. Bolesław and Zbigniew go after him, but Władysław cannot countenance this and, one night when everyone believes him to be asleep in his tent, he slips out in disguise and has himself and a few trusted servants rowed across the Vistula and so makes his way to Sieciech's castle to give him the moral support of his presence. Bolesław, nonplussed, does not know what to do and finally decides not to attack the castle with his father in it, but instead, to start occupying the castles and frontier fortresses in the territories that are going to be his. Accordingly, he occupies the forts in Cracow, Sandomierz, Sieradz and other parts of his share, while Zbigniew tries to take Płock, to which his father has just gone, but is repulsed.

He and Bolesław then join forces and lay siege to Płock, at which juncture Archbishop Martin, fearing lest the situation deteriorate and harm the country, intervenes and succeeds in reconciling father and sons and persuading the former to honour the agreement he made with his sons concerning Sieciech, who is then sent into exile and finds refuge with the Ruthenians. In early spring, Sviatopolk of Kiev, makes an attempt to recover Vladimir castle and those parts of Volhynia which David had conquered. Unable to rely on his own troops, David goes to Władysław in Poland, leaving his wife and all his possessions in Vladimir castle, which Sviatopolk is thus free to occupy.

A.D. 1099

Everything being quiet, the Pomeranians, who are always ready to raid Poland, though so far without enjoying much success, make an attempt on the fortress at Santok, employing first deception and bribery, and then force. When both fail, for the fortress, being the gateway to Poland, is well garrisoned and fortified, as well as being well sited, the Pomeranians build their own fort despite the efforts of the garrison to stop them, using baulks of oak and other materials of which there is ample to hand. The two forts are so close together that those in them can hear each other talking. The Pomeranians provide their fort with ramparts and a moat, so that when they have captured the Polish fort, the two will make a really strong base for raiding into Poland. When Władysław hears of this new threat, he orders Zbigniew to put an end to the Pomeranians' activities. Zbigniew's force is adequate for the task, but he is too hasty in all that he does and accomplishes nothing. When young Bolesław hears of his brother's lack of success, he hurries there with a small force of picked men and storms the Pomeranians' fort without much effort, for the Pomeranians, seeing how small his force is, sally out and attack him. They are routed and pursued to the very gates of the fort; indeed, Bolesław's men almost get inside with them. Bolesław then tears down part of the bridge the Pomeranians have been building and burns the rest, and then lays siege to the fort. The Pomeranians are so impressed by the courage and skill of the young Polish commander that, feeling that the game is up, they set fire to their own fort and escape under cover of darkness. Břetislav, who is Bolesław's uncle, is delighted when he hears of his nephew's military success and invites him for a visit. When he arrives, Břetislav makes him a present of the fort at Kamieniec on the Nysa and, taking a great liking to him, loads him with gifts, which Bolesław turns over to his troops, when he returns home.

On August 10, four of the Ruthenian dukes meet with their advisers and, after much discussion, settle their differences. Then they send for Duke David, who is in Poland, and when he arrives

Prince Béla of Hungary defeating a Pomeranian knight in single combat.
—Chronika de Gestis Hungaro-
rum. —*Országos Széchényi Könyvtár.*

and asks why he has been summoned, he is told that he has been asked to come so that he may make formal complaint of any wrongs the four may have done him. He has a major complaint; that he has been deprived of his inheritance, the duchy of Vladimir. The four then withdraw to consult. Having done so, they tell David that they have no intention of returning Vladimir to him, since he has been making continual raids into their territories, a thing no one else has done in living memory; on the other hand, they have no wish to harm him, and, although forgiveness is all that the situation calls for, they are prepared to grant him a sufficiency, so that he need no longer roam foreign lands as an exile, a thing that shames them all. So, Sviatopolk grants him four estates, and the others a hundred marks a year each, to which Sviatopolk adds an additional estate, that of Dorogobuzh, where David ends his days.

A.D. 1100

Prince Bolesław is now fifteen years old and renowned far and wide for his military achievements. His father decides to reward him by dubbing him knight. The ceremony is planned for the Feast of the Assumption and is to be held in the cathedral in Płock. The whole court is to be there, as well as all the bishops and persons of eminence, and there are to be splendid tourneys. Suddenly, news comes that the Pomeranians, cunning as ever, are taking advantage of the occasion to attack the fort at Santok, thinking that for several days the Poles will be too busy with the festivities to do anything about this, thus giving them time to capture the fort. Here, Bolesław proves them wrong. He postpones his dubbing, orders all present who are bearing arms to follow him, mounts his horse and sets off to relieve Santok. Reaching it, he attacks at dawn, while the Pomeranians are still asleep in their tents. They are completely routed. Bolesław swiftly rounds them up, capturing indeed almost the entire Pomeranian army, and returns to Płock with his prisoners. The ceremonies and celebrations are resumed. Bolesław presents all the booty to his father, who dubs him knight along with a number of noble youths of Bolesław's age, who had been fighting with him.

King Břetislav of Bohemia dies in this year, unrenowned and an object of pity. He had been on a hunting trip and, on the way back, stopped at the village of Stebna. There, one of his huntsmen, a man named Lorek, bribed by members of the clan, the Vršovci, whom Břetislav had banished to Poland and whose possessions he had confiscated, took a hunting spear and treacherously thrust it into the King's belly, from which wound he died three days later. He is succeeded by his brother, Bořivoj, Vratislav's second son.

Iaroslav declares war on Sviatopolk of Kiev, is defeated and captured, taken to Kiev, put in chains and thrown into prison. Later, at the urgent request of the Patriarch of Kiev he is released against his promise never again to engage in hostilities against Sviatopolk. On September 15 Sviatopolk, Vladimir, David, Oleg and Iaroslav, five of the Ruthenian dukes, meet their Polish counterparts and conclude peace. In order to ensure that each side sticks to the agreement, they exchange hostages.

Vseslav, Prince of Polotsk, dies on April 14.

A.D. 1101

Bolesław has a new enemy to fight, the Polovtsy. They have an army, so large that it cannot be drawn up in one line but has to be divided into four, and these are busy pillaging a large area of Bolesław's territory. By the time the Polovtsy reach the Vistula, they have collected a huge number of captives and an enormous amount of booty. Having thus achieved their objective, they start a slow withdrawal back to their own country, slow because of the vast numbers of cattle and captives they are taking with them. Bolesław has been assembling a force of knights, with which he now sets off in pursuit of the Polovtsy, following them well beyond the Polish frontier. The Polovtsy are especially proud of their enormous booty and Bolesław realizes that he will have to act quickly to prevent it all being dispersed into their many forts and hiding-places. Although his men are wearied by a long forced march, he orders an attack the moment he catches up with them. This is made at dead of night, when the enemy are asleep, and meets with very little resistance. First the princes, then their knights take to flight, leaving the others to be made prisoners. Bolesław then frees the Polish captives, some of whom are women, and returns home. Those he has rescued and the knights he has enriched with booty all agree that Poland will be a happy country, when Bolesław rules it: times will be better and the country will enjoy its old renown, be regenerated and once again play a leading role in affairs. Happy and blessed, they say, is the mother who gave to the world such a brave and successsful warrior.

A.D. 1102

Prince Władyslaw of Poland, also known as Herman, falls gravely ill as his fifty-ninth birthday approaches, and, after a long illness, during which time his son, Bolesław, scarcely leaves his side, he dies on June 4. Some chroniclers assert that he did not die a natural death but was treacherously killed by his bastard son, Zbigniew, whom the Poles nicknamed "the deserter". However that may be, at the funeral Zbigniew's only concern appears to be his inheritance. He quarrels shamefully with his brother, Bolesław, maintaining that since the castle at Płock is part of his inheritance, he should have the whole of the treasure deposited there. The quarrel is resolved thanks to the intervention of Archbishop Martin and the other bishops, who decide that Zbigniew should have half the treasure, though neither town law, nor imperial law nor the common law of nations allow illegitimate sons to inherit. After the funeral, Zbigniew withdraws to Płock and Bolesław to the lands allotted to him by his father, whose death he genuinely mourns, wearing round his neck a chain on which is a golden plaque engraved with his father's likeness, and this he wears day and night.

With his increased duties, Bolesław quickly grows up. He proves to be a skilful and far-sighted politician. Expert in the use of arms, a splendid horseman, incredibly enduring of hardship, he is also a splendid speaker, a persistent seeker after the truth, unusually pious and a skilful ruler.

A.D. 1103

Of all the kings and princes of Poland, none has been a better person, a more experienced general, a more daring soldier, a more ardent patriot or a juster judge, than Bolesław. One corner of his mouth was twisted in a rather attractive way and this earned him the soubriquet of Wry-mouth. His only fault was his credulity, which was sometimes so great that he appeared either thoughtless or lacking in discernment.

A year after his father's death, the prelates and barons begin putting pressure on Bolesław to marry. At first reluctant, because of his age, he agrees to marry Zbyslava, daughter of Sviatopolk, Prince of Ruthenia, a girl famed for her beauty and goodness of heart. He and she are in the fourth degree of consanguinity, which worries the Prince's advisers, but they fear that his noble line may die out. This is an impediment that only a papal dispensation can remove and this the Bishop of Cracow obtains. The wedding is fixed for November 16 in Cracow. Zbigniew is invited and, indeed, arrives, but he just takes some money off his brother and heads for Bohemia, where he uses the money and promises of further payments in the future to bribe the Czech prince, Bořivoj and his nephew, Sviatopolk, to take up arms and invade Bolesław's territory; for, as he sees it, there could never be a better opportunity than now, when Bolesław is occupied with his wedding arrangements. This the two agree to do, but when the Czech army reaches the frontier, the troops begin to complain that they are being used to fight an unjust war, which may well enrich their leaders, but which can do them no good whatever. Fearing that their discontent may end in a mutiny, Bořivoj and Sviatopolk disgracefully abandon Zbigniew to his barren hopes. Telling him that they will try to oblige him another time, they return to Bohemia. Bolesław is thus able to celebrate his marriage with jollifications lasting sixteen days.

The Czechs having failed him, Zbigniew goes to the Pomeranians, Prussians and others, trying to persuade them to take up arms against Bolesław, whose defeat and death would enable him to take over the whole of the country.

In April, the Ruthenian dukes meet in Kiev and decide on a punitive campaign against the Polovtsy, who have been breaking the treaty they made by constantly raiding and plundering Ruthenian territory. Although their commanders tell them that winter is not the right season for waging war, they refuse to wait for the summer. They summon David and Oleg, who did not attend the earlier meeting, and ask them to join them. Each duke now brings his army to Kiev, either overland or in ships. Having disembarked those who have come by water, the combined force advances as far as Suten. There they make contact with the Polovtsian army, which is advancing against them; however, God fills the hearts of the Polovtsy and their horses with fear, so that they have lost heart even before battle is engaged. The result is more a slaughter than a battle. Twenty Polovtsian princes are killed, and the Ruthenians find a large quantity of gold, silver, cattle and camels in their camp, which they carry off home together with a large number of captives.

A.D. 1104

Infuriated by the behaviour of Zbigniew, Bolesław assembles a large army of his best troops, which he sends, under command of Voivode Zelislav, into Moravia, part of Sviatopolk's territory. He is so eager for revenge, that he fails to wait for a suitable season for campaigning, but orders hostilities to start in Lent. The army, in Bolesław's usual formation of three ranks, marches into Moravia, devastating, plundering and looting, throughout Lent and Easter. Having ravaged almost the whole of the country without meeting any resistance, the Poles start withdrawing with a huge amount of booty and a horde of captives. When they are not far from the frontier, their scouts tell them that Sviatopolk is pursuing them with an army composed largely of infantry and that this is now encamped only a few miles away. The Voivode orders an immediate halt. Then, sending the sick and the wounded on ahead with the booty and the captives, he draws up his troops in line of battle and awaits Sviatopolk's onslaught. Battle is engaged at ten o'clock the following morning and continues all day until darkness falls. Many are killed and wounded on either side. The result is a stalemate and each side withdraws: the Bohemians to Bohemia and the Poles to Poland. The grief of the Moravians over the people they have lost is enhanced by their failure to recover the loot taken by the Poles. During the fighting, the Voivode has his right hand cut off, but, using his left arm, he kills the man who severed it. In recognition of his services and to compensate for the loss of his hand, Bolesław gives him not only rich gifts, but a hand of cast gold. So many Poles were killed in the fighting, that their loss is attributed to their having violated Lent by eating dishes made with milk and to further wickednesses they permitted themselves during Easter. Indeed, the Poles add more to their reputation than they gain from the whole enterprise.

Bolesław spends the bulk of his princely revenues not on pleasure and personal satisfaction, but on armour and equipment needed by his knights and commanders. He spares no effort to ensure that he has an efficient army; and to achieve this no difficulty is too great, no danger off-putting. Under no other commander have the Poles shown such courage and enterprise. Not satisfied with the damage his Voivode inflicted on Moravia, Bolesław assembles an even larger force and again invades that country, this time through the mountains of the frontier. So difficult is the terrain that he is the first ever to have made the crossing. Inhabitants of the frontier regions are convinced that Sviatopolk is so weakened by the previous fighting that he will be unable to stand up to the Poles, so they put up no resistance. Bolesław is thus able to burn and loot as he wishes and, having devastated the country without loss, he returns home, enriched by yet more booty.

Back at home, Bolesław finds a papal legate, Guido, Bishop of Beauvais, who has been instructed by Pope Paschal II to carry out a visitation of the Church in Poland. Bolesław receives him graciously and encourages him in punishing any of his bishops whom the legate finds guilty. Two, indeed, are deprived of their sees.

Late in the year Princess Zbyslava gives birth to a fine boy, who is christened in Cracow cathedral by the Papal legate, assisted by several Polish bishops, and given his grandfather's name, Władysław.

A.D. 1105

The Pomeranians, encouraged by Zbigniew and his promises, have for some time been violating the frontier between Pomerania and Poland, so Bolesław now decides on reprisals, but informs only a few of his commanders of his intention. He decides to employ only cavalry as he did against the Czechs, and assembles his force in Głogów, so as to mislead Zbigniew and the Pomeranians as to his objective. When all has been prepared to his satisfaction, he sets out and for the next five days, without a halt, leads his force along shady mountain tracks, across all but inaccessible country, making for the town of Kołobrzeg, famous in those days for its wealth. On the sixth day, they are very close to their objective, but the exhausted men and their horses have to have a rest. He orders them to fortify their souls with Holy Communion and their bodies with food and rest; and then, at dawn the following day, having said the office in honour of the Blessed Virgin, they advance on Kołobrzeg. They have to cross a swollen river, which they do, avoiding the bridge so as not to alert the enemy. The force is then divided into three, two of which are held in reserve and as a rear-guard, while he attacks with the third. He succeeds in breaking down one of the gates, thus opening the way for the rest of his men; but most of those who follow him into the town are more intent on looting than on capturing the town, so that, when the townspeople see how few the enemy are, they are encouraged to resist and, indeed, force the Poles to withdraw; and the Pomeranian duke escapes in the confusion. Bolesław punishes the soldiers whose greed made him loose an excellent opportunity, and renews his efforts to capture the town, using his reserves to replace those who have been wounded or are too exhausted to fight. When evening comes, he has achieved nothing, so, seeing that his efforts have been in vain, he calls off the siege and withdraws, allowing his troops to loot and burn the suburbs as they go. Thus, they return home with only a small number of captives and the conviction that Fate has not wished them to capture Kołobrzeg.

Bolesław now allows his troops a short rest, so that they can recover their strength and repair their weapons. They are then called up again for a further attack on the Pomeranians, who, Bolesław hopes, will consider him incapable of further action for the time being. The excuse for the attack is that, some time before, Sviatobor, prince of the coastal area, a vassal and relation of Bolesław's, had been imprisoned by the Pomeranians because his knights and subjects detested his unjust rule.

From his prison, he has sent letters and messengers to his relative Bolesław, beseeching him to take pity on him. Although Bolesław is well aware that Sviatobor and his whole family have never liked him, indeed have been fickle in their loyalty and inclined to treachery, he uses Sviatobor's appeal for help as an excuse for avenging himself on the Pomeranians. So, he crosses into Pomerania, sending envoys ahead to say that he will declare war on them, unless they hand Sviatobor over to him. The Pomeranians are frightened, not so much by this threat of war, as by the unexpected appearance of Bolesław and his army, so, in order to avoid the threatened destruction of their country, they release Sviatobor and conduct him to Bolesław's camp.

The Roman Emperor, Henry V, elevated to the throne by Pope Paschal II after Henry IV was deposed, now invades and conquers Saxony. He persuades many of the German princes, bishops and barons to switch allegiance from his father and is then able to assert his own authority. Those who oppose him are deprived of their offices and exiled. When the deposed emperor prepares a second army to fight his son and restore the others to their former ranks and stations, the two pitch camp on the bank of the Rhine and prepare to fight it out. The young Emperor, realizing that his father's main strength lies in the troops of the Czech prince, Bořivoj, and those of Margrave Leopold, bribes them both with huge gifts and great promises and so gets them to desert his father and come over to him. Their desertion deprives the old emperor of all further desire to fight and he now disperses his army and withdraws to his castles. From then on, his son enjoys success, while his father gradually declines.

The Moravian prince, Svatopluk, has an ambition to conquer the principality of Bohemia and in this he is encouraged by some of the Czech barons, who wish to see a change of ruler in their country. To achieve this, Svatopluk has to remove his uncle, Bořivoj, who obtained the principality by peaceful means; so he assembles an army and marches into Bohemia, at which many Czechs desert Bořivoj and join his nephew. Proud of his initial success, Svatopluk attempts to capture Prague, and, indeed, he might have succeeded had not Bořivoj got there first, installed a strong garrison and made Bishop Herman of Prague governor of the castle. Svatopluk thus finds the gates shut in his face and withdraws to Moravia. Bořivoj could have chased him back, but, uncertain of the loyalty of his troops, decides not to do so.

A.D. 1106

Bolesław is persuaded not to engage in any more military enterprises for the time being; but takes this to apply to himself personally, so, while he busies himself with Church affairs, he sends a mixed force under Skarbimir, whom he appoints voivode, into Pomerania. This captures various small forts and strong-points and minor fortified towns, which together yield a substantial number of captives and plenty of booty, which Skarbimir removes to Poland. He then marches back into

Pomerania and captures the fort at Bytom, goes on to plunder and burn a number of villages without encountering any resistance and again returns to Poland with the plunder. He seeks out Bolesław to report the success of the expedition and finds him at a banquet, to celebrate a wedding and the dedication of a church, given by one of Bolesław's own knights. Bolesław is delighted with the news, and, the next morning, takes Skarbimir and a hundred young knights hunting in the forest, which abounds in game. There is little danger from the wild animals, but plenty from the Pomeranians, who, after Skarbimir's withdrawal, have stealthily penetrated deep into Polish territory and taken a considerable number of captives. Bolesław all but runs into them, but recognizes their badges and horses in time; yet still has to choose whether to withdraw or fight against their superior numbers. He decides that he prefers death to retreat, and is himself the first to strike a blow; indeed, he fights his way right through the enemy's ranks, an irresponsible thing to attempt, but Fortune is with him. Again and again he attacks, but the ranks of his knights begin to thin and then to give way, and, finally, he finds himself with only five others, one of whom, seeing that Bolesław's horse has been disembowelled, beseeches his Prince for the sake of his country to take his horse and save his own life. At this moment, Bolesław's horse collapses, throwing its rider. Bolesław gets up and mounts the other's horse. Looking round he can see scarcely thirty of his own men and Skarbimir who is weakened by wounds and the loss of his right eye, so together they turn and fight their way out. Meanwhile, the banqueteers, hearing the sounds of battle, have armed themselves and come out to help. They meet Bolesław and the others half way and escort them back to safety. After this near-fatal encounter, many reproach the Prince for his foolhardiness. His only reply is that they will soon have another opportunity to accuse him of foolhardiness. He tells everyone to repair their weapons as quickly as they can and be ready to march with him against the Pomeranians, so as to deprive them of the satisfaction of having defeated the Poles.

News comes that Svatopluk and the Czechs have rid themselves of Prince Bořivoj and are now preparing to invade and ravage Poland with an army encamped near Kłodzko. Meanwhile, Bořivoj, exiled by his nephew, is convinced that he will be able to spend his exile in Poland, at Bolesław's court, where, indeed, he is graciously received. He tells Bolesław of Svatopluk's plans. Now, Bolesław has to decide which enemy to attack first. On the one hand, he does not wish to delay avenging himself on the Pomeranians; yet he does not wish to allow Svatopluk time to mount his invasion; so, in the end, he decides to attack both. He divides his army into two: one he sends against Pomerania under command of Skarbimir, while he assumes command of the other and moves it into Herczyń forest, which separates Poland from Bohemia, at which the Czechs call off the invasion and disband their army. Meanwhile, Skarbimir is harassing and plundering Pomerania, and so that country finally receives its due punishment.

A.D. 1107

Almost every town, castle and fort in Pomerania is ready to surrender to the Polish prince, except for Alba, also called Białogród, whose people stubbornly resist and this encourages others to do the same, so Bolesław invades again. As usual he orders his troops to burn houses and devastate fields; that done, he gathers his forces and lays siege to Białogród, a very rich city. Hoping that those inside are secretly inclined to surrender, Bolesław sends in agents who suggest that it would be better for the besieged not to expose themselves to mortal danger by forcing him to capture the city, spilling the blood of his soldiers as well as theirs, but to surrender instead. His agents are to display a white shield if the people of Białogród choose peace and surrender, or a red one if they choose what he calls their downfall and that of their city. The inhabitants of Białogród are unmoved and tell Bolesław's agents that they will not choose either shield, but now that they know what these signify, they will get a white one by driving Bolesław away, and a red one by slaughtering his men should they persist in besieging their city.

Incensed by this arrogant reply, Bolesław orders mantlets and siege towers to be constructed, which are then pushed up to the town's defences and the moat filled with brushwood. Before the assault begins, Bolesław orders his bowmen to provide cover for those scaling the towers and walls damaged by his siege weapons. He himself, with only a shield to protect him, is first in negotiating the moat and ramparts. Reaching the main gate, he starts hacking at it with his sword. His example encourages others, who assault the gate undeterred by the rain of stones, the hail of arrows or the hot tar and boiling water that the defenders pour on their heads, or by the convulsions of the dying. When the gate finally yields, Bolesław is the first to enter the city, opening the way for the rest of his army. A massacre would have followed, had not the men of Białogród, seeing their city's walls breached and its towers destroyed by the enemy's siege-weapons, thrown down their arms and begged for mercy, not for themselves, but for their wives and children and the non-combatants. The Polish knights want to avenge those of their number the enemy has already killed and urge Bolesław to raze the city and kill everyone in it. He, however, decides to be merciful and grants the citizens their lives and their possessions. He sees that no one suffers at the hands of his men. His kindness and mercy conquer him more towns and forts during the rest of the campaign than does his army.

Koźle, a fort on the frontier with Moravia, is accidentally burned to the ground. Its main defence is its site on the river Oder; so, when Bolesław hears of the fire, he at once suspects that Czech saboteurs have been at work, and with a small force, hurries there and starts rebuilding the fort. To prevent the Czechs attacking him while he is thus engaged, he asks Zbigniew to bring him a small force of knights as his own troops are exhausted after the fighting in Pomerania. Zbigniew, who hates his brother more than ever because of his continuing success and growing fame, sends an insolent reply and no help. Nonetheless, Bolesław quickly rebuilds the fort.

Bolesław now has to decide what to do about Zbigniew. It is common knowledge that he is trying to bribe and persuade the Czechs, Pomeranians and Prussians to help him destroy his brother. It is also clear that he has been advising the Pomeranians when to raid Polish territory, as they have repeatedly done. Again, any prisoners the Pomeranians take are immediately sold by Zbigniew, while those Bolesław happens to take on Zbigniew's territory are returned the moment Zbigniew asks for them. Messages and letters constantly pass between Zbigniew and the Pomeranians with intelligence of what Bolesław is doing; in return for which the Pomeranians give Zbigniew a share of the loot taken from Bolesław.

Most of Zbigniew's plans and intrigues are reported to Bolesław, who is inclined to leave retribution to God, but in the end the situation becomes so serious that he feels threatened and sends to Ruthenia and Pannonia for assistance, either from volunteers or mercenaries. He also tells Svatopluk that he is threatened on three sides and asks him to come to his assistance with the largest army he can muster. He then marches into Pomerania, only to find that the Pomeranians, forewarned, have dispersed; while Zbigniew, assuming that Bolesław cannot possibly forgive him for all that he has done, has fled from Wielkopolska, where he was trying to assemble an army, and gone to Mazovia, where he expects to find refuge. Within a few days Bolesław has captured Gniezno, the capital of Zbigniew's duchies, and its castle, and also another of Zbigniew's castles, and in them installed his own commanders and starostas. While Bolesław is busied with all this, his reinforcements from Ruthenia and Hungary arrive, and with them he crosses the Vistula near Mazovia, intending to expel Zbigniew. By this time Zbigniew has lost all hope and concentrates on trying to save his life. Fortunately for him, the bishops now intercede and bring the two brothers face to face. Bolesław details all Zbigniew's plots and intrigues against himself. Zbigniew then begs for mercy and asks for his life and part of the kingdom, binding himself by the most solemn vows never again to conspire against him. Bolesław is moved by his protestations and agrees to let him have Mazo-

Konrad Keyser's Bellefortis *advocates the use of a deep trench protected by mantlets as the best way of attacking the walls of a fort, a method much used by the Poles.* —VDI Verlag, Düsseldorf.

via, provided that he has nothing more to do with the Czechs and Pomeranians. The brothers thus reconciled, the Hungarian and Ruthenian troops return home.

While on a diocesan tour with his Archdeacon, Martin the Archbishop of Gniezno stops at the parish church of Spycimierz to hear Mass. During the service, the village is raided by Pomeranians, who have learned of the Archbishop's presence and have come to capture him in revenge for his having forced them to renounce paganism and to pay tithes and other ecclesiastical dues. The Archbishop does not know what to do, for his servants have run off and the Archdeacon has rushed outside in all his finery hoping to escape, leaving the Archbishop in the church. The Pomeranians, mistaking the Archdeacon for the Archbishop, stop him and respectfully place him in a waggon to cart him away. They then enter the church in search of others, but find nobody there, for fear has lent the Archbishop's aged muscles strength enough to take refuge under the roof of the chapel, between the timbers of the ceiling, while the chaplain, who was to have said Mass, has hidden between the altar and presbytery; so they snatch up the communion vessels and hurry out and back to Pomerania. Many writers have it that all the Pomeranians, who touched the sacred vessels, had epileptic fits and rolled on the ground, bereft of their wits, while their wives, relatives and children, were similarly affected and attacked each other, driving friends and relatives from their homes or, if unable, to reach them, bit and scratched themselves. Many do die and, realizing that the cause of this is their sacrilegious theft of the sacred vessels, the Pomeranians return them all and, renouncing paganism, accept the true faith, send the archdeacon home and promise to pay tithes and church dues in the future.

Prince Bořivoj, unjustly expelled from Bohemia, goes to Poland with his brother, Soběslav, and a number of Czech barons and gentry who hate the tyrannical Svatopluk. Bolesław receives them readily and provides them with everything they need. He also gives Bořivoj a considerable sum of money. Bořivoj then goes to the Emperor who is in Saxony and informs him of his predicament and seeks his help. The Emperor summons Svatopluk to him, but Svatopluk, suspecting that the reason for the summons is his illegal seizure of power in Bohemia, assembles an army which he places under his brother, Otto, and then presents himself before the Emperor, who promptly puts him prison. The Emperor then sends Bořivoj back to Bohemia with instructions that the Czechs are to acknowledge Bořivoj and none other as their legitimate prince. When Bořivoj and his force of Germans reach the fort at Donin, which is under imperial authority, and advance on Prague, Otto, already informed of his brother's predicament, advances against them. Bořivoj avoids a fight and withdraws to Poland. Meanwhile, Svatopluk has made a deal with the Emperor: he is to pay a fine of 10,000 marks in silver and to assist the Emperor with all his armed forces when the latter eventually attacks Hungary to force Coloman to accept his suzerainty. Svatopluk is then released from prison, but he has to give his brother, Otto, as a hostage. However, Otto is guarded so negligently that he escapes back to Bohemia. Even so, Svatopluk has to empty his treasury and strip the churches of their vessels and treasures, as well as levy a tax on the clergy and the people, just in order to pay the fine.

In the autumn of this year, Bolesław, who already has several Pomeranian towns in his possession, lays siege to Czarnków which, too, belongs to Pomerania. He erects four siege towers, each higher than the fort and the town, which he then bombards day and night until the besieged beg for talks. The fort and town surrender and Bolesław makes Gniewomir and all the people who have not accepted the true faith, receive baptism. He then hands both town and fort back to Gniewomir, who promises him loyalty.

Boniak and other Polovtsian chiefs, wishing to avenge the defeat inflicted on them by the Ruthenians, invade the latter's country and make camp near Labien. The Ruthenian dukes combine their armies and advance as far as the River Sula; then, on August 12, they mount a surprise attack on the Polovtsian camp. Taken unawares, the Polovtsy are unable to form a line of battle or even to fight. Some fling themselves on their horses and ride away; others run off into the nearby woods. The Ruthenians indulge in a grand slaughter of the Polovtsy and pursue the fugitives as far as the River Chorol. They find considerable booty in the Polovtsian camp and carry it back home with them.

A.D. 1108

Coloman, King of Hungary, who is well aware of the enmity of the Emperor, learns that the latter is assembling a huge army of Germans with which to fight him, and that the Emperor is to have the help of Svatopluk of Bohemia and other neighbouring princes.

The cause of the Emperor's justified hostility is the fact that on many occasions German crusaders travelling through Hungary on their way to the Holy Land have been killed, wounded, robbed and in various ways insulted and abused by Hungarians. Also, Coloman has banished his brother, Almus, who has gone to the Emperor and got him to agree to restore him to the throne, and this is another reason for the Emperor's preparing the expedition. Coloman considers it necessary to ask for outside help. All his immediate neighbours are either hostile or suspect, as well as afraid to take up arms against the Emperor; so the Hungarian prelates and barons agree that in this dangerous situation they should ask the Poles for help. Coloman decides to do this in person, but first he sends an envoy to arrange a meeting with Bolesław. The two meet in Spisz and there, after much discussion, they form an alliance promising to help each other against all enemies. The alliance is reinforced by Coloman's eldest son, Stephen, marrying Bolesław's daughter, Judith, whose dowry consists of the town of Spisz and all its lands in Poland which are mostly in the diocese of Cracow, and ever since these have belonged to Hungary.

On his return from Spisz, Bolesław again sends for his brother, Zbigniew, and, in the presence of his advisers and the prelates, reminds him of all the harm his treachery has done him.When Zbigniew tries to justify himself or declare his innocence, he gets in a muddle and makes it look as if he were guilty of even more treachery than that of which he is being accused. The result is that Bolesław banishes him from Mazovia and, indeed, all Poland. With Zbigniew out of the way and therefore having greater security at home, he is able to give Coloman more effective aid. The Emperor now invades Hungary with a huge army, to which Svatopluk contributes the promised Czech contingent. Coloman avoids giving battle, but inflicts considerable losses on the imperial troops by sudden attacks in places of his own choosing. The Emperor wastes a lot of time investing Bratislava, which is well defended. Then he divides his forces and attacks several places simultaneously, burning and spreading destruction mainly in the area between the Danube and the Wag; yet all in all he achieves little and finally returns to Germany. Meanwhile, Bolesław, who has sent a force of picked men to reinforce Coloman, thus fulfilling their agreement, marches into Bohemia with a larger, experienced force, which includes a number of Czech nobles who have sought refuge with him from Svatopluk's tyranny. Svatopluk's two captains, Vaček and Matina, try to bar their advance in the forest between the two countries, but Bolesław has no difficulty in routing them and they seek refuge in Prague; Bolesław is free to continue through the country and all flee at his approach. After laying much of the country waste, he returns to Poland with rich booty. He has with him, two Czech princes, Bořivoj and Soběslav, and various members of the Czech nobility. Svatopluk, scared by the news from home and afraid of losing all Bohemia, deserts the Emperor and returns to Bohemia. The Emperor swears to be avenged on Bolesław and the Poles as soon as he can. Svatopluk is furious not only with the Poles, but also with his two captains, one of whom, Vaček, lays all the blame for the harm the country has suffered, on the other, Matina, and even suggests that Matina helped in the destruction. Matina is imprisoned and condemned to death, as are his two sons and those members of his clan, the Vršovci, whom Svatopluk can capture; the others have a price put on their heads and swiftly depart for Poland, where they change the clan name to Rawita.

Once the Emperor has withdrawn his army, Coloman, eager to be avenged on Svatopluk, invades Moravia and burns or destroys everything there. Svatopluk brings up an army to stop the destruction and while riding through the forest receives a heavy blow in one eye from a branch and this blinds him, so that he has to withdraw his army, leaving the country to the mercy of the Hungarians.

On his return from Bohemia, Bolesław is met with two items of bad news: his wife, Zbyslawa, has died, and the Pomeranians have captured the fortress at Ujście. Apparently, many of those Bolesław left to guard the fortress had gone away to attend to their private affairs, learning this the Pomeranians came and laid siege to it. The besieged are doubtful of the outcome, especially when the commander, who has been bribed by a secret envoy from the Pomeranians, tells the others that the Czechs have defeated Bolesław's army and advises them not to risk their own destruction by continuing the fort's defence; so they offer to surrender both the town and the fort, provided they are granted immunity for their persons, houses and property. When Bolesław learns what has happened, as most of his men are exhausted by the fighting in Bohemia, he presses on with only a small force of volunteers. When he reaches Ujście and sees how difficult, if not imposssible, it will be to storm the fort, he takes a number of captives and burns several villages so as to demonstrate that he has not been defeated in Bohemia, but has returned victorious and will punish the Pomeranians as they deserve, and so withdraws to Poland. Then, having given his troops time to recover, he again advances into Pomerania, now accompanied by his brother Zbigniew, who has joined him with a small body of Mazovian knights. However, instead of trying to retake Ujście, which has a strong garrison, Bolesław attacks Wieleń hoping to catch Gniewomir who has hidden there. During the siege, the Pomeranians, encouraged on the sly by Zbigniew, stage a night attack, but choose a time when Bolesław is making his nightly round of the sentries. Zbigniew is leading the Pomeranians, who attack with considerable dash, but Bolesław manages to get in their rear, routs them and captures a number of them, one of whom is Zbigniew, who is recognized when his helmet is removed. Many clamour for the traitor's death and that they should kill him not just with a sword but that they should tear him apart with their teeth, but in the end Bolesław commutes the death sentence to banishment for life and Zbigniew goes to Bohemia. Not long afterwards, the besieged in Wieleń send messengers to the Pomeranian command to tell them that they are exhausted by the nightly attacks and have suffered heavy casualties and need help. The messengers are told that they can expect no help, so the people of Wieleń come to an arrangement with Bolesław and open the town's gates to him. The Polish flag is then hoisted on the fort, a herald having proclaimed that all who surrender will be pardoned; at this Bolesław's own men complain that, after all their losses and the hardships they have endured campaigning in summer and winter, they should not be deprived of the fruits of victory. Bolesław is unable to calm their anger, which proves stronger than his authority, and the soldiers kill every Pomeranian they find in the town.

A.D. 1109

The Emperor Henry V blames Bolesław for the fiasco in Hungary, in that he helped the Hungarians and defeated the Czechs. Eager for vengeance, he summons men from Saxony, Bavaria, Swabia, Thuringia, Franconia and Meissen for an invasion of Poland. Svatopluk and Bolesław's bastard half-brother, Zbigniew, encourage the Emperor: Zbigniew by assuring him that many Poles will come over to him as the rightful heir, and that forts and strong-points will surrender without a fight. So, at the start of summer, the Emperor invades Poland with a large army reinforced with Svatopluk's cavalry and infantry. He burns and pillages those areas of the country which are now part of either Silesia or Saxony, then he invests Lubusz, in those days a big and powerful city and the first one he reaches on his advance from Germany. But when he realizes that it is going to be difficult to take it, both because of its position and its being defended by knights, he abandons the siege and advances deeper into Poland. His next objective is Bytom, but this, too, he

sees is going to be difficult to capture, more because of its man-made defences than its geographical position, so he attempts to persuade the besieged to surrender. However, the defenders keep sallying out and attacking or ambushing the Emperor's men, thus earning the latter's admiration, and
he turns to Zbigniew and says: "I see how well your promises are being fulfilled; how, at the sight
of you, towns and fortresses and people are coming over to our side. I am sure that I shall encounter
the same enmity from all Poles, for they are loyal to Bolesław". Zbigniew is, indeed, out of favour.

Though Bolesław has a considerable army, which includes a number of Czech exiles, the Emperor's forces seem numerically so superior that Bolesław does not dare risk a pitched battle; instead, he adopts a strategy of harassment, raiding the enemy lines by day and night, using his
cavalry to strike at them here, there and everywhere, picking off those who detach themselves from
the rest in order to forage or loot. Even those who break ranks to answer a call of Nature are liable to
be carried off, and so, at night, are any lone sentries and guards. None now dares go far from the
camp. Every clump of trees, every wood, even every bush seems to harbour danger. Any small
force that ventures out is immediately attacked and forced to withdraw. Because of all this the Emperor's troops now begin to experience hunger, as do the knights' horses, many of which starve to
death. There was, at this time, a popular song about Bolesław's feats of valour, and this now
catches on with the imperial troops to such an extent that the Emperor has to forbid it being sung on
pain of death or confiscation of the singer's property. Finally, after marching up and down the
length of Silesia, devastating as he goes and capturing a few strong points of lesser importance, on
St. Bartholomew's Day the Emperor reaches the town of Głogów, which lies in a bend of the river
Oder. Bolesław has posted guards along this stretch of the river, particularly at the fords, in an attempt to prevent the Emperor crossing. However, a hitherto unknown ford is discovered close to
the town wall and the Emperor gets his army across and captures a considerable number of cattle
and some of Bolesław's troops. The Emperor is now able to tighten his grip on the town, and for
many days his siege weapons bombard its low walls and weak turrets. The inhabitants send to the
Emperor telling him that they will surrender the town unless Bolesław comes to their help within
the next five days.

The Emperor, confident that Bolesław will not dare attack, accepts this and even grants them
a longer respite, though he insists on being sent the sons of the more important citizens as hostages.
Having got his hostages, the Emperor orders the siege to be raised. In the meantime, the people of
Głogów have sent to Bolesław asking him either to agree to their surrender or to to come to their
rescue. Bolesław has now received reinforcements and has a considerably larger army than before,
so that all he needs is the right opportunity, which, he judges, has not yet come. He praises the people of Głogów for having held out so far, but forbids them to keep their agreement with the Emperor. Better, he tells them, to lose their sons than their freedom and their country. He tells them that
he will come and rescue them when the time is ripe, and adds that, if they keep their agreement with
the enemy, when the Emperor withdraws he will put them all and their children to the sword. When
the people of Głogów are told this, they are profoundly depressed and don't know what to do; however, in the end they all agree that the public good transcends private feelings, and decide not to
surrender. They set about repairing the damage done by the Emperor's siege weapons, and, with
every one buckling to, have done all that is necessary by the end of the truce. On the sixth day, the
Emperor demands the town's surrender and is told that this is not going to happen. Furious, he calls
his men to arms and orders a general assault. He decides, too, to play his trump card, the hostages,
and so orders the children to be placed on the mantlets used by the forward troops. This fails to
have any effect, for the besieged still throw stakes and shoot arrows at the mantlets, regardless of
the children, and their aim is so good that many of the Emperor's men, grown careless, are killed.
The Emperor then takes pity on the children and has them removed, but continues the attack with
the utmost fury. Many attackers are killed by the stones, hot tar and boiling water thrown down on

them, but there are always others to take their place. Many succeed in climbing the siege-ladders as far as the top, only to have the ladder hurled off the wall by the defenders, killing those on it before the Emperor's eyes. Such is the courage of the defenders and their loyalty to their Prince, that they are celebrated in Poland to this day. The assault continues for several days. Many Bavarian and Saxon nobles are killed in the fighting, and the Emperor orders their bodies to be sent back home, so that their families can bury them with due respect. In the end the Emperor's losses are so great that he has to raise the siege. The Czechs who have been killed are buried in a field near their camp.

During this long siege of Głogów not a day passed without the Poles attacking the Emperor's camp at some point, both by day and by night, so that the Emperor was never able to employ his entire force in the assault on the town, but had to keep a considerable portion of his men in reserve, in case Bolesław should mount a real attack. Usually, the task of guarding the camp was given to Svatopluk and his Czechs, and Bolesław, who hated him more than he did the Emperor, determines to have him killed. He keeps complaining to those in his entourage of Svatopluk's treachery and promises a huge reward to anyone who will kill him. On September 21, one of his knights, John, a member of the Rawita clan, who has a number of relations and even a brother in the Czech army, rides into the Emperor's camp pretending to be one of Svatopluk's officers. He knows from the Poles' spies the routine of the camp and that he will find Svatopluk in the Emperor's tent. Dis-

An engagement between Polish and imperial troops near Wrocław.
From Joachim Bielski's Chronika Polska. *—British Library.*

mounting, he sees his intended victim standing in the tent and drives a sharp spear into the latter's side with such force that it goes right through him, killing him. He then jumps onto his horse and rides off. He is pursued, of course, but manages to kill his pursuers and returns safely to the Polish camp. For this feat Bolesław rewards him handsomely with castles, towns and estates that are still in the clan's possession. Svatopluk's body is taken to the Czech part of the camp. The assassination of their prince sets the Czech troops murmuring, though few of them really mourned him, and now they have to elect a new leader. By-passing Svatopluk's two sons, they choose Svatopluk's brother, Otto, thus breaking the oath they once swore that they would elect only Vladislav, third son of Vratislav and brother of Bořivoj. The Emperor confirms their choice.

The Czech army is now demanding to go home. The Emperor does his best to prevent this, suggesting that Svatopluk's body should be taken back to Prague by some of his knights, while the rest of the army remains, but the Czechs won't hear of it, and the Emperor has to give way and allow their departure. Zbigniew goes with them, for, knowing that the German nobles and even the Emperor himself are anything but well disposed towards him, he is afraid to remain where he is.

The Emperor holds a council-of-war at which everyone advises him to raise the siege and return to Germany. While the best course of action is being discussed, heralds from Bolesław arrive requesting the Emperor to raise the siege and remove his army from Polish territory, asserting that Bolesław has suffered unjustly from the Emperor's activities, while Bolesław's campaigning against the pagans entitles him to the Emperor's help rather than his enmity. The Emperor's reply is that he will accept this, provided that Bolesław and the Poles submit to his authority, pay him tribute and restore Zbigniew's share of the country to him. He is then told that no Pole will accept the Emperor's suzerainty, nor will any pay tribute; that Zbigniew is his country's worst enemy and they will not have him back. The Emperor then dismisses the heralds.

After the departure of the Czechs, the morale of the imperial troops deteriorates daily. The Emperor's friends all advise him to return to Germany, lest the Poles surround him and finally the Emperor agrees, for the assassination of Svatopluk has made a deeper impression on him than anyone realizes; and so, a few days after dismissing Bolesław's heralds, the siege is raised and the Emperor rides away from Głogów, heading for Wrocław in the hope of being more successful there.

Meanwhile, Bolesław has assembled as large a force as he can, and makes it appear larger than it is by swelling its ranks with peasants. With this he sets off after the Emperor in a forced march that continues day and night. When he has nearly reached the Emperor's camp a mile from Wrocław, he draws up a line of battle, harangues his troops to bolster their courage and make them eager for the fray, and attacks. The two armies close with tremendous shouts. It is morning, and the battle continues until the afternoon. Many fall, and there are times when the Poles are almost thinking of running, but Bolesław is always there where the need is great, encouraging and fighting alongside his men. When the battle is at its height, Bolesław sends in the Saxon unit he has been holding in reserve. This charges one wing of the Emperor's line, crumples it and makes an opening for the others to get in among the enemy, who, realizing what is happening, take fright. Seeing his troops wavering, the Emperor himself turns to escape, first throwing away the imperial insignia lest these betray him. The battle then becomes a slaughter. The Germans run in all directions. Many are caught and brought before Bolesław, who, as always, is considerate and grants them their lives. There are so many corpses on the battlefield that every dog for miles around is attracted and it becomes unsafe to walk anywhere near except in a largish group. The place is still called the Field of Dogs.

A.D. 1110

The Emperor Henry, though smarting from his defeat in Poland, is restrained from invading that country again by domestic problems and preparations for a journey to Rome to be crowned emperor, planned for the following year. He is, however, most eager to negotiate the return of the considerable number of his knights captured by Bolesław. With this end in view, he has mutual friends let Bolesław know that he has changed his mind about Bolesław's earlier offer of peace, which he refused. It is suggested that Bolesław should go in person to the Emperor in Bamberg, where the latter will refuse him neither peace nor friendship, nor whatever is his due. After reflection Bolesław accepts, and sets off with a splendid entourage. In Bamberg, in an eloquent, convincing speech he asks the Emperor for peace, which will bring not shame, but honour and glory upon their two countries. He asserts that he, with the blood of kings in his veins, despite his lesser title of prince, has all the privileges of a king and he knows that Poland and its kings and queens have never paid tribute to anyone and, up to the present, have enjoyed complete freedom. To preserve this, he will, if necessary, take up arms even against the Emperor whose hostility to him is due solely to false insinuations made by Svatopluk and Bolesław's half-brother, Zbigniew. He goes on to beg the Emperor to treat him as a friend, rather than as an enemy, and this the Emperor graciously promises to do and to disregard the evil insinuations of Bolesław's jealous enemies. He is, he says, happy to welcome Bolesław with the respect due to a Christian prince, as his friend and the friend of his country. Bolesław then asks for the Emperor Henry's sister Adelaide as his wife, and Henry's daughter, a pretty girl called Christina, as wife for his son, Władysław. Henry unhesitatingly agrees to both requests; so, after formal betrothals in Bamberg, Bolesław sets off back to Poland with the Emperor's sister and the young Christina, who has not yet come of age, and their two dowries. They are accompanied by an escort of imperial knights. Bolesław now sends back all the German knights he captured in the previous year's fighting, while Henry makes written renunciation of the castles and lands he captured from Poland, specifically of the fortress at Lubusz which he had granted in perpetuity to the Archbishop of Magdeburg.

    When Bořivoj, who for the last couple of years has been in exile in Poland along with a considerable number of Czech nobles, learns that, after the assassination of Svatopluk, his youngest brother, Vladislav, has occupied the capital and driven out the third brother, Otto, he seeks Bolesław's help, because he considers that by rights the principality should be his and he wants Bolesław to help him recover it. He asks for an army commanded by Bolesław in person. Bolesław takes pity on him and conducts him to the frontier together with a large retinue of Czech nobles and a large contingent of soldiers equipped by Bolesław. When they get to the forest of Herczyń, which separates the two countries, they are met by a considerable number of Czech nobles who, having learned of Bořivoj's arrival, have come to greet him. They ask that Bolesław go back to his own country, for they will see that Bořivoj gets his principality back without a fight. Bolesław agrees, and leaving Bořivoj with a large contingent of Polish knights, returns to Poland. Bořivoj is escorted to Prague, which he enters in solemn procession and takes possession of the castle. (His brother, Vladislav, is at this time in Pilzno). Bořivoj imprisons Herman, Bishop of Prague, and would have done the same to the commander of the castle, Fabian, had he not escaped leaving everything behind. Many of the latter's supporters do the same, abandoning wives, families and possessions. Confusion and unrest are rife. Villages are burned, looted and destroyed. Meanwhile, Otto and Baron Vaček assemble an army and try to gain a footing in Prague. Repulsed, they invest the castle at Vyšehrad. Vladislav, wounded by his brother's occupation of Prague and Vyšehrad, marches on Prague, but is refused admittance. He then sends to the Emperor bewailing his exile and asking him to use his authority to have his principality restored. The Emperor responds by sending two princes from his Court to make peace between the brothers. If either cannot agree he is to present himself before the Emperor, who will decide who is to have what. They duly present themselves and are told that the principality must be given back to Vladislav and Bořivoj put in prison. Vladislav then punishes many whom he knows to have supported Bořivoj and he also imprisons his own uncle, Otto, after persuading him to come from Sanczka, and keeps him incarcerated for three years.

A.D. 1111

Bolesław, angered by Vladislav's occupation of Bohemia and the imprisonment of Bořivoj, himself invades Bohemia on St. Michael's Day. He has with him Bořivoj's exiled brother, Soběslav, whom he has been sheltering and whom he hopes may be able to reconcile the two on terms that will allow the release of Bořivoj. His first step is to invite Vladislav to come to him under safe-conduct and allow him, Bolesław, to adjudicate on the quarrel between the three brothers. Vladislav, suspecting treachery, summarily dismisses the envoys and decides to attack Bolesław. Learning of his intention, Bolesław starts looting and burning the countryside as far as the river Elbe. He then bars Vladislav's advance and, on October 6, defeats him in a fierce battle fought beside the River Cidlina. Many Czechs are killed or taken prisoner, and Vladislav has to retreat to Prague, while Bolesław continues to ravage the countryside, before leading his army back to Poland laden with booty. Soběslav goes with him.

Queen Svatává, grieved by the quarrelling of her three sons, one a prisoner, one an exile and the third recently defeated, undertakes to act as referee. She rebukes Vladislav for having opposed his two brothers, who have equal rights to the principality, and reconciles him with Soběslav in Poland. Summoned by his brother and mother, Soběslav goes to Bohemia and takes possession of his inheritance, the town of Žatec and its surrounding lands.

The Ruthenian dukes, encouraged by their recent victories over the Polovtsy, decide to go to war with them yet again; so, on the second Sunday in Lent, placing all their hopes in God and His angels, they lead an army across the River Suda and on to the River Chorol, where they leave their train and draw up line of battle. They advance to the River Olta and there rest for a couple of days, before transferring their camp to another, equally large river, the Vorskla. Crossing this, they continue on to the Tasis, which we know as the Don, a much larger river. There, in battle array and with flags flying, they advance as though the enemy were just ahead of them and thus they reach Sarukan, whose inhabitants greet them with fish and wine. They continue on to another town, Sugrov, which they burn and then set off back to the Don. But, now, the Polovtsy bar their progress and engage them in battle, promising themselves that on this occasion they will rather die than run. However, when the first rank has fallen, the others scatter. Nevertheless, a few days later the Polovtsy return with a fresh army and renew the attack, only to meet with further failure and again be routed. The Ruthenians pursue them for four days and many miles, capturing their camp, horses, cattle, camels, wives, children and all their possessions, and with it all return home to a rapturous reception.

A.D. 1112

The Pomeranians and Prussians, wearied of the peace which has prevailed because Bolesław has been busy waging war on his neighbours, decide to make an incursion into Poland; however, since Bolesław has visited Poznań and Kujawy earlier than usual, and in Pomerania has gained control of a number of forts and installed garrisons in them, the barbarians shift their activities to remoter areas which they have not previously raided. Disguising their intentions, they attack parts of Mazovia, pillaging and burning villages and churches, hoping to be able to return to their fastnesses before Bolesław learns what they are doing. In all this, however, they are disappointed, for Count Magnus, the castellan in charge, summons the local nobility and peasantry to arms and advances on the raiders. He attacks just before dawn, when they are all resting and unaware of any danger, with the result that very few escape death or captivity. Most are slaughtered like cattle, shamefully, with impunity. Some people are convinced that the Poles' victory was largely due to the prayers, fasting and tears of Simon the Bishop of Płock and his clergy, who never stopped beseeching God for victory. The victory is all the more impressive, since those who sought refuge in the woods surrender not only to men, but to women and children gathering strawberries in the woods. Disarmed, their hands tied behind their backs, they are brought before their conquerors. Fate smiles, too, on the inhabitants of Silesia, who in one skirmish defeat some of Zbigniew's soldiers, who are trying to loot and start fires.

Sviatopolk, Prince of Kiev and Bolesław's father-in-law, dies on April 16. The people of Kiev send to his brother, Vladimir, inviting him to take up residence in Kiev, which both his father and grandfather had ruled. When Vladimir delays his arrival, the army mutinies and attacks and plunders the palace of the voivode, a rich man. The soldiers then turn on the Jews in the city. Fresh messages to Vladimir informing him of what is happening bring him hurrying to Kiev, where his very presence quells the mutiny. Iaroslav, Sviatopolk's son and brother of Princess Zbysława, returns to his principality of Vladimir. In an attempt to destroy the Ruthenians' mortal enemies, the Jacwingians, he invades their territory and destroys much of it, before defeating their army and returning home victorious. As far as nationality, language, religion and customs go, the Jacwingians are very like the Lithuanians, Prussians and Samogitians: they practice idolatry. Their main town and fortress is Drohiczyn, on the right bank of the River Bug.

On May 12, Iaroslav marries Mstislav's daughter, Vladimir's grand-daughter.

A.D. 1113

Bolesław is furious with the Pomeranians and Prussians for their treacherous attack on Mazovia and, convinced that Count Magnus let them off too lightly, prepares another expedition against them. He advances on Kruszwica, where, before the eyes of the whole army, an unusually handsome youth appears on the tower of the church of St. Vitus, radiating a miraculous lustre that illuminates not only the town but its surroundings as well. As the Poles stand there, spellbound, the youth jumps from the tower and, putting himself at the head of the army, leads it towards Nakło. Then, throwing a golden apple which he has in his hand in the direction of the town, he vanishes. Bolesław and his men are encouraged by this portent and lay siege to the town and its fort, from which in the past the Pomeranians have inflicted great damage on the Poles. He orders a hail of arrows to cover an assault with battering-rams and other machines, by which the upper parts of the fortress and the town's own fortifications are either destroyed or weakened. The Castellan of Nakło and the townspeople send intermediaries to Bolesław telling him that they will surrender in fifteen days, unless, before then, their princes have sent them help. A truce obtained and the siege suspended, they send urgent messages to the Pomeranian and Prussian princes who are already under arms and preparing to help them, for the Pomeranians are appalled at the prospect of so essential a fort falling into the hands of the enemy. Both veterans and raw recruits, for they have called up a large number of young men of both the nobility and the peasants, take an oath that they will return as victors or not at all. Messages are sent to those in Nakło, giving them hope of receiving assistance before the fifteen days are up; and the leaders then discuss how to fight Bolesław. When they count their army and find that it numbers more than 50,000, they still have doubts about engaging in a pitched battle. They feel that cunning, strategem and treachery may well be their best weapons. Speed and surprise they consider all important: they decide to leave their horses behind so that all are exposed to the same risk and none can seek to escape by riding away, and also because a horse's neighing might betray their presence. So, one night, they leave their camp at midnight and, in silence and close formation, avoiding roads and open country, make their way through the woods and reach Nakło undetected. This being the Feast of St. Laurence, a martyr held in special honour by the Poles, and there being a truce, there is no reason to expect an attack, and the Poles are all hearing Mass. As they make their way back to their tents afterwards, to their considerable confusion they become aware that the Pomeranians are there; indeed, victory might well have been the Pomeranians' had they pressed home their attack, instead of stopping to make a stockade of long stakes hardened at one end in fire, which they stick in the ground together with a number of spears pointing outwards. The construction of this stockade gives Bolesław time to organize his men, whom he divides into two forces, one under Skarbimir, the other commanded by himself, but leaving a force sufficient to guard the camp and the siege engines should the defenders of Nakło sally out. After briefly haranguing his men, he advances on the stockade, then halts out of range of enemy missiles to inspect it. Finding that the rear of the enemy's position has only a rampart to defend it, no stakes or spears, so that this is the place at which to break through, he orders Skarbimir to take his men and attack the rear as soon as he sees Bolesław mount an assault on the front. This Skarbimir does, jumping ditch and rampart, killing and scattering the enemy, for Bolesław's pressure on the front prevents the forward ranks going to the assistance of those in the rear. Then Bolesław, unable to endure not taking part, spurs on his horse and, oblivious to the dangerous stakes and spears, rides straight at the enemy. The stockade takes its toll of the knights' horses; indeed, so many are killed that the cavalry becomes an infantry force. Assaulted from in front and from the rear, the Pomeranians forget their oath and, taking to their heels, head for the woods, but the Poles slaughter many of them before they can get there. Forty thousand Pomeranians and Prussians are killed and 2000 taken prisoner. Others die in the bogs and marshes. The heaped up bodies form a considerable mound, which the Poles cover with earth to prevent the smell causing an epidemic. This mound is there to this day.

Seeing that they are now powerless, the Castellan and citizens of Nakło surrender, as do six other towns in the neighbourhood. All these Duke Bolesław puts under Świętopełk, his baron, a man outstanding not only for his lineage and wealth, but also for his rectitude, kindness and loyalty. Decisive in action and a persuasive speaker, he enjoys the love and friendship of Bolesław, whom he has served well in peace and war. None would have suspected him of treachery, yet he soon becomes arrogant and exhibits a desire to rule greater than his position allows.

Soběslav, warned that his brother, prompted by Baron Vaček, has decided to imprison him, has the baron murdered; then, afraid of what Vladislav may do, he and his supporters make for Sorb territory, from which they hope to get to Poland. Reaching Donin, they accept an invitation from its castellan Ekembert who holds it for the Emperor and treacherously seizes Soběslav and sends him in chains to Saxony. The others manage to get to Poland, which Soběslav, who manages to escape, also reaches later.

A.D. 1114

Bolesław, that restless spirit, still seeks to use his influence, authority and money to restore Soběslav to the princely throne of Bohemia, from which the latter's younger brother has ousted him. He assembles a force of veterans and, taking Soběslav and his fellow Czech exiles with him, crosses the frontier, from where he sends envoys to Vladislav demanding that he restore Soběslav to favour and grant him his rightful part of their inheritance. Vladislav replies that he has treated his brother with great kindness, which has not been appreciated. He has given him what was a considerable share and has in no way wronged him, yet this has been repaid by the murder of Vladislav's adviser, Baron Vaček, after which Soběslav and his associates escaped to Poland, thus making themselves unworthy of further kindness. The envoys try to justify Soběslav's action as that of a man giving way to righteous anger with someone who has habitually sown discord between brothers. Vladislav counters this by saying that he will restore Soběslav to favour, if Bolesław will do the same with his brother, Zbigniew, who is in exile in Bohemia. He says, too, that he has no authority to divide up the country without the approval of the Emperor. Hearing this, Bolesław's immediate impulse is to send his troops deeper into Bohemia and lay the country waste, but Sobĕslav begs him to desist. Meanwhile, Vladislav brings up an army and pitches camp not far from that of the Poles. The two would have been at each others' throats had not the River Cidlina separated them with its muddy bed. The Poles try to cross both upstream and downstream, but the Czechs accompanying them tell them that it is dangerously deep. In the end, Bolesław sends to Vladislav suggesting that one allows the other to cross unopposed, so that they can fight it out. When Vladislav refuses, Bolesław strikes camp and moves towards the Elbe, crossing the Cidlina without loss near the confluence. Hurriedly he marches back to the Czech camp, only to find it deserted, with nothing to be seen but trampled earth and ashes; for, under cover of darkness in a night of mist and thunderstorms, the Czechs have stolen away. Not knowing whether this is a ruse or a real withdrawal, Bolesław holds a council of war: are they to pursue the Czechs and devastate their country or return to Poland? Opinions are divided. The older men feel that they should go back and not fight unnecessary battles, while the younger men wish to finish the job and sack Prague as well. Bolesław is inclined to agree with the younger men, until he learns that the provisions they have brought from Poland are on the point of giving out. He then decides on a return and now allows the troops, whom till then, at Soběslav's request he has restrained from looting, to plunder and burn, indeed, encourages them to do so as widely as possible. Reaching the town of Kłodzko, they find the gates shut, so Bolesław orders the suburbs to be burned. As the wind is blowing towards the town, the latter catches fire too and, although the inhabitants surrender, the whole goes up in flames. The troops are allowed to loot what remains.

After burning Kłodzko and the surrounding villages, the army sets out for Poland by the most direct route, devastating fields and villages as it goes. Reaching the forest that separates the two countries, they learn that the road by which they have come, and many others, are blocked by felled trees. They halt for the night, and in the morning learn from their scouts and spies that the Czechs have occupied the forest, so as to be able to fight in the place most favourable to them and most difficult for the Poles. Bolesław orders a solemn Mass to be sung. Many of his men go to confession and take communion, and then Bolesław harangues his troops. They then move off into the forest, the more experienced troops in front and in the rear, the train and the others in the middle, with the left flank secured by Skarbimir with a picked force, while Bolesław looks after the right flank.

When the forward unit, called the Gnieznian, because its men come from Gniezno, having traversed almost the whole forest, emerges into an open expanse, it halts to await its Prince. Ahead of it, only the fringe of the forest remains. The Czechs feel sure that, when the Poles emerge from the forest, they will abandon their usual caution and break ranks, allowing the Czechs to attack them on all sides. The Czechs do in fact attack, but the Poles have not broken ranks and the fighting is desperate. Skarbimir does not know what is happening to Bolesław, nor does Bolesław know what is happening to Skarbimir; but both are fighting for their lives. At first glimpse of the enemy Bolesław charges and, out in front of the others, kills a Czech with his javelin, while, behind him, one of his knights knocks from his horse and kills a Czech knight who has ridden in from the side. The sight of these two killings so encourages Bolesław's men that they soon gain the upper hand. When Vladislav, who is engaged in the fighting, sees his men perishing so disgracefully, fearful lest the others suffer the same fate, he sounds the signal to withdraw. Hearing this the Czechs run rather than withdraw. The Poles, assuming this to be a deliberate withdrawal, do not at first pursue the enemy; but, when they realize that the enemy are really routed, they go after them and kill or capture a large number, especially those whose horses are exhausted. One who does escape is Poland's arch-enemy, Zbigniew. Vladislav, too, deserts his knights and barons and saves himself. After this victory, Bolesław marches back into Bohemia, taking his wounded with him, and starts plundering and burning all over again; then, with enormous booty, the army returns to Poland, Soběslav with it.

Coloman, King of Hungary, dies on February 3. He had the reputation of being a cruel man; indeed, he tried to kill his close relative, Prince Almus, and when the attempt failed and Almus went into exile in Poland, he ordered Almus' son, Béla, to be blinded. Béla was a child torn from its mother's womb so that he should not prevent Coloman's sons from being next-in-line to the throne, since no cripple can wear the crown. The heir-apparent is Coloman's son, Stephen, son-in-law of Bolesław of Poland, whose daughter by his first marriage, Judith, was his wife. The Archbishop of Esztergom, Laurence, crowns the two, King and Queen, in Székesfehérvár.

A.D. 1115

Bolesław announces another expedition against the Czech prince, Vladislav, for he does not intend to rest until Soběslav, who is still with him in exile, receives his due part of the principality. When Vladislav learns of this, as is inevitable, because of the number of Czech exiles in Poland, he sends envoys to Bolesław proposing terms for peace and promises that, if these are accepted, he will allow his brother, Soběslav, a certain part of the principality, but he requires the release of all the Czechs captured in the fighting. After consulting Soběslav and his Czech supporters, Bolesław replies that he agrees to peace and the return of the prisoners, provided he is given assurances that Soběslav will receive part of his inheritance. He then sends envoys to Vladislav to agree the details. Vladislav welcomes them on arrival. Terms are agreed and Vladislav swears to give Soběslav a just share. It is arranged that the two princes are to meet on St. Procopius' Day beside the River Nysa, where they make peace and confirm it with solemn oaths. Soběslav thus receives Hradec and its four castles, plus its district and province in Bohemia, also the province of Olomouc and the town of that name in Moravia. The reconciliation of the two princes is celebrated with great ceremony. The prisoners are released, and the exiles go home.

Bolesław seldom rests, even during the winter, and then only briefly, for warfare is his greatest pleasure. You might say that Nature made him a warrior and nothing else.

To prevent his knights growing idle once peace has been made with the Czechs, Bolesław takes advantage of the winter to lead a small force into Prussia, where it is difficult to penetrate during the summer because of the many bogs, lakes and marshes. He begins by plundering and burning the frontier areas, then goes deeper in, and there, having heard that the Prussians are arming themselves and so assuming that he will have to do battle with the enemy, he keeps his men in camp.Now, he has gone almost from one end of the country to the other without the Prussians giving battle as he wishes, for, knowing themselves to be much the weaker, they have gone into hiding, so Bolesław alters tactics and orders his men to extend their looting and burning; but when this too fails to entice the barbarians to do battle, he tells them to take booty not only of cattle, but of people as well. This they do and, when almost every town and village in Prussia has been burned, he returns to Poland with enormous booty of cattle and people of both sexes. These captives Bolesław distributes among the settlements to till the land, and with them populates a number of villages which, to this day, are called Prussian.

A.D. 1116

Bolesław's bastard brother, Zbigniew, now realizes that he no longer has any hope of obtaining a share of Poland by force of arms, since the treaty made the previous year between the Czech prince and his brother prevents him arranging an invasion from Bohemia, on which he had pinned his last hopes. He knows, too, that the Pomeranians have been heavily defeated by Bolesław; so, realizing that further plotting will achieve nothing, he can only count on the leniency and kindness of his brother, to whom he sends emissaries asking for forgiveness. When granted audience, these latter stress the misery and penury into which Zbigniew has been plunged by his well justified exile, poverty that shames both Zbigniew and his brother; and say that he humbly asks that an end be

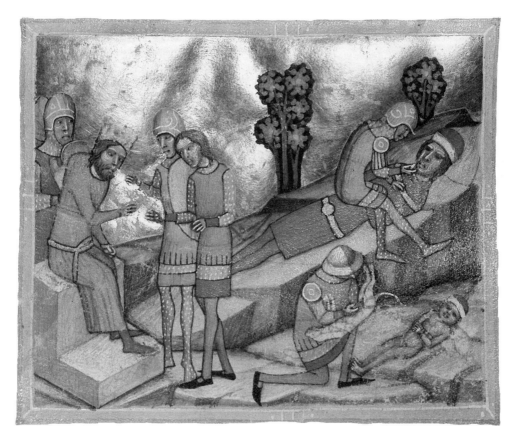

Prince Almus and his young son, Béla, being blinded on the orders of King Coloman, seated on a rock, left. The King had ordered the boy to be castrated as well, but the soldier concerned castrated a dog instead and produced its genitals as proof of duty done.
—*Chronika de Gestis Hungarorum.*—*Országos Széchényi Könyvtár.*

put to his exile and he be allowed back to Poland and given, out of his brother's gracious kindness, a tiny part of the country, so that he should not grow old in poverty, like an exile in a foreign land. They promise that in future Zbigniew will serve Bolesław as his lord with complete submission, loyalty and obedience. Bolesław is won over, though he does remind the emissaries of all Zbigniew's past perfidy and treachery; and, although his advisers vainly advise him not to give his brother any part of the kingdom, Bolesław is prepared to do so if Zbigniew will provide some evidence of contrition and remorse.

The emissaries go back with this message and bring Zbigniew back to Poland, assuring him of his brother's favour and kindness. When Zbigniew comes to meet his brother, whether of his own accord or at the prompting of evil men, he disregards all the promises made on his behalf, and walks in, arrogant, boastful, ostentatious and as proud as ever, his sword carried before him, to the accompaniment of singing, drums, flutes and other musical instruments; thus proclaiming that he is returning not as an exile, but in triumph; not chastened but as one restored to his rights, not humbled, but angered; not to serve, but to rule; not to listen, but to give orders, and that he has returned to Poland of his own accord and will allow himself further treachery and hostile actions such as have already done Poland so much harm. His behaviour betrays his lack of gratitude and his craziness. None could have foreseen, none could imagine a greater insult to his country or to his brother, and what does it augur for the future? Bolesław with laudable forbearance, pretending not to notice his brother's stupid conceit, receives Zbigniew graciously. However, he soon regrets restoring to favour someone so artful, who has designs on his life and possessions, one whose hypocrisy and enmity have been evident for so many years. Bolesław's barons and advisers rebel against Zbigniew and seek to rouse Bolesław's anger against him; indeed, many say that he should be killed, a thing Bolesław has long refused to consider, their argument being that the country will never know peace until so dangerous a beast has been destroyed. The more religious beseech Bolesław to attach more weight to their blood relationship and forgive his brother. Others, shrinking from fratricide, suggest that he be sent to some place on the frontier, there to expiate his crimes. Bolesław entrusts some of his knights to see that this is done. These, at a suitable place and time, confront Zbigniew with all his crimes against Poland. This starts a quarrel in which Zbigniew is killed; though some say that he was not killed, but blinded and died a few years later, deserted by everyone. Bolesław feels that Zbigniew's death is a blot on his life and earlier achievements, and that he would have been happier had he kept his hands clean.

Stephen the King of Hungary and the three princes of Bohemia, Vladislav, Soběslav and Otto, meet on the bank of the river which is the boundary betwen Hungary and Moravia, to settle various disputes and restore peace between them. After a brief discussion, as a result of the whisperings of some Satan, one side, unable to stomach the presumptuous behaviour of the other, suddenly takes up arms as though the intention had been not to make peace, but to wage war. There is a bloody battle in which many on both sides die, and the Czech prince, Vladislav, defeated by the Hungarians, escapes to Bohemia. Soběslav and Otto, who are fighting on the Czech side, renew the fight and after defeating the Hungarians and forcing them to retreat, capture their camp and all their booty. King Stephen is saved thanks to the kindness of Laurence the Archbishop of Esztergom, and returns to his country safe and sound.

A.D. 1117

Having defeated the Pomeranians and the Prussians, the victors start fighting among themselves. Skarbimir, Voivode of Cracow, and Bolesław's chief army commander, who had none superior to him in lineage, intelligence, talent or bravery, becomes overweening in his pride and begins to oppose his Prince, saying damaging things behind his back and claiming earlier victories of Bolesław for himself. When told of this, Bolesław at first refuses to credit it; but, when Skarbimir continues his allegations, this leads to open disagreement, quarrels and hatred. Skarbimir becomes so arrogant that, relying on his influence, his friends, brothers and relations, and those who owe him favours, he openly rebels and takes up arms against his lord. Bolesław, anxious to avoid civil war, orders Skarbimir to be imprisoned and, after three days, has him blinded. In this way, he quells a threatening storm. Skarbimir is divested of his position as voivode.

The Czech prince, Bořivoj, is released after spending eight years in the Emperor's prison. His release frightens his younger brother, Vladislav, who took over the principality and is now afraid lest Bolesław of Poland and his other brother, Soběslav, should together remove him from the throne and imprison him in his turn. Both agree to accept the arbitration of Bolesław, who decides that Vladislav is to have the country north of the River Elbe, while Bořivoj is to rule the rest. Thus is peace established.

Vladimir, who established his capital in Kiev after the death of his brother, Sviatopolk, afraid lest his nephew, Iaroslav, should try to drive him out, decides on a pre-emptive strike. He marches against Iaroslav and besieges him in the castle at Vladimir, where he has taken refuge. Iaroslav, confident of his innocence, goes, unarmed, to his uncle Vladimir and the other dukes, and in a modest speech mollifies and is reconciled with Vladimir, who is embittered because of the false promptings of sycophants. Vladimir lifts the siege and returns to Kiev.

A.D. 1118

Bolesław, seeing that Voivode Świętopełk, to whom he entrusted Nakło and six other towns, is dilatory in his duties, prepares an expedition into Pomerania, but is held up by torrential rain, which starts in the spring and continues throughout the summer, causing enormous damage not only in Poland, but to her neighhbours as well, and such floods as none can remember, which make it impossible to sow the crops, let alone harvest them. This is especially the case in the vicinity of the big rivers, which all overflow their banks. Also at sunset, the whole sky is suffused with red for three hours, which is considered ominous. Further torrential rain follows and people fear they are experiencing a second flood.

Vladimir of Kiev, after hearing all sorts of accusations against his nephew, Iaroslav, especially that the latter is planning to destroy him, angrily summons him by letter and envoy to Kiev. Iaroslav replies that he will come, but only if Vladimir swears not to take any hostile action against him. This Vladimir does, but Iaroslav still refuses to go, having been warned by some of Vladimir's knights—whether truthfully or not one does not know—that he risks being put in prison if he goes. Then, at the treacherous instigation of one of his own knights, to whom he entrusts the castle at Vladimir, Iaroslav takes his wife, children and all his possessions to Poland and Bolesław, who was once married to his sister Zybslawa, and who receives him with sympathy and kindness. There he remains for four years, being provided with all he needs. While he is in Poland, his own knights, fearing that the Poles may occupy Vladimir, surrender it to Prince Vladimir of Kiev, who then sends his son, Roman, to occupy it; but Roman dies on January 14, so Vladimir sends his second son, Andrew, to rule it.

A.D. 1119

Bolesław plans to proceed with the expedition into Pomerania postponed from the previous year, despite the fact that after that year's torrential rain strong gales are blowing, which have destroyed many houses. He orders his troops to muster and marches them into Pomerania, ordering them to destroy and burn whatever remains or has been repaired. The Pomeranians and Prussians assemble a large army, which includes every fit young man and even peasants. Bolesław, never one to decline a fight, at the sight of the enemy orders his men to raise the battle-cry and attack. For a time neither side has the advantage, but when the Poles, who are the fiercer, overcome the enemy's first rank and come up against young, raw troops, the latter begin to waver. Seeing this, Bolesław sends in his reserves and the enemy takes to its heels. Bolesław gives orders that the fugitives, especially the youths and peasants, are not to be killed, but captured, for they are to provide labour for tilling his own fields. After this defeat and the loss of their young men, the Pomeranians and Prussians submit and so, for the rest of his life, Bolesław is to possess both Pomerania and Prussia.

Bolesław now advances on Nakło to deal with Świętopełk. After a long siege in the worst of wintry conditions which prevent Bolesław from taking the town, Świętopełk is captured; he is pardoned after paying a fine and giving his son as a pledge of his acquiescence.

A.D. 1120

Świętopełk has continued to live in Nakło but has now broken their agreement, despite having given his son as hostage, so Bolesław, disgusted, leads his army back into Pomerania to exact retribution. He sees that Świętopełk is relatively weak and that the Pomeranians will not now help him. Having inspected his men, he sends the weak, the ragged and those with little stamina home, and, with his remaining veterans, attacks the forts under Świętopełk's jurisdiction. First to be attacked are the town and fort of Wyszogród, which his siege engines enable him to capture after sixteen days. He then gives his troops a week's rest and, leaving a strong garrison behind, moves on. Capturing other lesser forts, he reaches Nakło, rings it with his men and attacks at dawn, convinced that the inhabitants and the garrison will be frightened into surrender; but nothing of the kind! Instead, they put up a stubborn defence, the women deluging the attackers with hot pitch, boiling water and stones. Bolesław's siege engines destroy buildings and breach the walls in places, but these are immediately repaired. The garrison makes unexpected sorties and once penetrates as far as Bolesław's camp. Finally, having filled in the moats and ditches with earth and timber, Bolesław brings specially constructed towers up to the walls which they overtop and from them his archers are able to do considerable damage. This enables the towers to be pushed even closer, making it impossible for the inhabitants to man the walls. Bolesław now feels sure that he is going to capture Nakło, but those inside pile dry pine wood, straw soaked with butter, tar and other materials against the towers and set fire to them. The Poles try to extinguish the flames, but all the fat and tar makes this impossible and the towers are destroyed. New ones are made, only to be burned in the same way. Bolesław then has a third set of towers made, which are again burned. A fourth set is pushed so close to the walls that the contestants can fight hand to hand. The issue is: can the townspeople burn the towers or the Poles quench the flames? Many are killed or wounded on either side. In the end the Pomeranians sue for peace, asking Bolesław to allow the besieged to walk out unharmed. Bolesław refuses. The Pomeranians then ask for a truce of several days and Bolesław again refuses. The Pomeranians are now running out of missiles and provisions and, more importantly, of the will to fight. Now they ask only for their lives, and this Bolesław grants. Świętopełk is handed over and condemned to life-long imprisonment. With Nakło taken, the other forts governed by Świętopełk also surrender. This whole campaign greatly enhances Bolesław's reputation and the love his men have for him.

The reconciliation of the two Czech princes, Bořivoj and Vladislav, does not last long. Soon there are fresh misunderstandings and quarrels stirred up by both their supporters. In the end, Bořivoj, frightened of what his brother may do, leaves Bohemia and goes to Poland, where he has been before. After some time there, he moves to Hungary to desport himself.

A.D. 1121

The country is afflicted by drought. A heatwave during March, April and May destroys both the winter corn and the spring sowing. This is a difficult year for Poland, because provisions are scarce and food dear. Neighbouring countries are similarly afflicted.

A.D. 1122

After ten years of childlessness, Princess Adelaide gives birth to a son. The delighted father invites a great number of prelates and barons to Cracow for the christening, which is a very pompous and costly affair. The baby is christened Casimir after its grandfather.

Volodar, Duke of Przemyśl, having repeatedly raided and looted Polish territory, Bolesław sends envoys to lodge formal complaints with him and the other Ruthenian dukes. When there is no response, he tells his commanders not to allow such raids to go unpunished. So, on the next occasion, Volodar has Polish knights to contend with. These rout him and deprive him of his loot. Indeed, they pursue and capture him. He is brought, a prisoner, before Bolesław in Cracow. Bolesław requires 80,000 marks in silver for his release. They finally agree on 20,000, 12,000 of which is to be paid immediately and Iaroslav's son given as security for payment of the rest. This amount is later paid in full, fifty silver vessels, drinking goblets, cups and bowls of Greek workmanship being handed over. This debt settled, Volodar and Bolesław are reconciled and conclude an alliance, after which Volodar returns to Przemyśl.

A.D. 1123

The lack of understanding between the Czech princes increases. Soběslav, who holds Moravia, does not wish to be under Vladislav, who has Bohemia. He reproaches his brother for exiling their other brother, Bořivoj, now an elderly man. Their dispute develops into open hostilities, in which Vladislav defeats Soběslav, who seeks safety in flight. Vladislav takes over Moravia. He also exiles Soběslav's wife, making the latter hate him all the more. Soběslav goes to Germany, hoping to persuade the Emperor to help him avenge his defeat, only to find that the latter turns a deaf ear to his requests. He and his supporters then leave Germany and go to Poland. Meanwhile, his wife, Almusza, has gone to her relative, King Stephen, in Hungary, where she spends her exile.

A.D. 1124

Having subdued or defeated all its enemies, Poland has enjoyed three years of peace. Bolesław, whose greatest interest, indeed his hobby, is war, considers this shameful and a waste of good soldiers; so, assembling a picked force, he embarks it in ships specially built for him in Gdańsk and other coastal cities, and sets sail for Denmark, which, the wind being favourable, he reaches safely and without loss. The motive for this expedition is not a desire to invade a foreign kingdom and loot it, but one that is fully justified and honourable. Bolesław's military fame has reached even the remotest nations and knights have come to him from distant countries in order to learn the arts of war and acquire fame for themselves. One of these is a young Dane called Peter, who excels all his contemporaries in handsomeness, wealth, lineage and talent. He is the only son of one of the most eminent of the rich Danish nobles, a man of considerable influence, even a decisive voice in Danish affairs. This Peter came to Bolesław with a letter from the Danish King requesting Bolesław to take him into his service. In a short time, Peter's valour, of which he gave frequent proof, his kindness and friendliness gain him the sympathy of the Court and of all the more important people, a rare achievement for a foreigner. He made great efforts to learn Polish, and in difficult situations showed such attachment to Poland, that one might think he was a Pole by birth and not a Dane. In the hope that he would remain permanently in Poland, Bolesław gave him a number of towns and villages, among others the town of Skrzynno and its adjacent villages. He also provided him with a wife, a Ruthenian princess called Maria, a pretty girl and a close relative of Bolesław's first wife. Then, Henry of Denmark died of wounds inflicted by his brother, Abel, who wished to take over the kingdom. The dead King left a huge treasure, collected over the years by several kings of Denmark, in the charge and control of Peter's father, who, feeling that he himself had not long to live and fearful lest the treasure fall into the hands of the fratricide Abel, sent a trusted messenger to his son in Poland to tell him that he had the treasure and that he would give it only to his son; therefore Peter must come at once to Denmark with a force sufficient to protect himself against the tyrant Abel and take the treasure back to Poland. Peter finds this a daunting assignment, as indeed, it is, and appeals to Bolesław for help. Money is raised to pay the soldiers needed for the enterprise and everything prepared for an expedition by sea, which sets sail as soon as the weather is favourable. When they reach Denmark, the Poles' main concern is to prevent their presence arousing the suspicions of the Danes; so, to gain their sympathy and help, they let it be known that they have come to avenge the murdered King. This brings a number of Danes to their side, so many, indeed, that the tyrant, afraid of falling into Bolesław's hands, leaves the country.

Bolesław takes all the Danish forts and puts them in the hands of various eminent Danish barons, whom he encourages to choose a just and sympathetic king. Then, collecting the whole of the treasure from his father, Peter takes it and the whole clan back to Poland. With this treasure he builds seventy-seven churches, each of dressed stone, a rarity in those days, and, with the King's permission, he also founds and endows two religious houses, one a nunnery. Peter's clan, which bears the arms of a swan on a red ground, becomes one of the great clans of Poland and exists to this day.

When he learns that Bolesław has sailed to Denmark, Volodar of Przemyśl forgets their alliance and sends his son with an army to lay Poland waste. The attack is quite unexpected and there is no defence, so that he lays fields waste and burns houses as far as Biecz and takes a large number of cattle back with him into Ruthenia.

A.D. 1125

Flourishing, peaceful Poland suffers a major disaster. Fire breaks out in Cracow, famed for the number of its beautiful wooden buildings and for its great store of imported goods. Churches, chapels and houses are destroyed and the city made ugly, wretched and poor, and so it remains for a long time. Some hold that the fire was not accidental, but the work of a raiding party of Czechs, who started it in revenge for Bolesław's kindness to his enemy Duke Soběslav, whom the Czechs all despise and hate, and whom the Emperor will not allow into his own lands.

Illness has laid Vladislav of Bohemia low. When his brother, Soběslav, who is still in Poland with Bolesław, learns of his brother's illness, he returns to Bohemia and there, through the intermediary of their mother, who has long grieved over their quarrel, the two are reconciled. Then, on April 20, Vladislav dies and by right of inheritance Soběslav occupies the vacant throne, despite obstacles put in his way by his own son, Otto.

Bolesław is eager to punish Volodar and his son for their destruction of part of his country and for their breach of the alliance. He attacks Przemyśl with all his forces, destroying and burning on as wide a front as possible. Volodar, his own army reinforced with those of the other Ruthenian dukes, bars his further progress at a place called Vilihow, only to be routed by the Poles, who capture the enemy camp. Volodar, unable to prevent defeat, leaves the field of battle and goes to Halicz, where he tries to assemble another force to enable him to continue the fight. Meanwhile, Bolesław continues his devastation of the Ruthenian countryside.

The winter is severe, with fierce frosts which kill both cattle and people. This results in famine.

A.D. 1126

Bolesław, wishing to thank God for all His favours, decides to make Cracow cathedral magnificent. He builds up its walls, which are low and modest, and adds two towers, built on new foundations. He endows it with chalices, chasubles and crosses of gold and silver, and, with the approval of Bishop Radosto, adds twenty to the modest number of prebendary canonnies, for which the Bishop assigns sheaf-tithes and Bolesław several villages and other properties: a monument to his munificence lasting to the present day.

On March 9 Volodar of Przemyśl dies. He leaves two sons, Vladimir and Rostislav, who divide the duchy. They gather a scratch army and, not daring to head it themselves, send it to ravage Poland. It does get across the frontier and burns a few villages, but then takes fright and withdraws. On May 10, Vladimir dies and is replaced by his eldest son, Mstislav. When they hear of Vladimir's death, the Polovtsy raid Ruthenian territory, but are opposed by the Duke of Pereiaslavl, who routs and drowns many of them.

The death of Pope Calixtus is followed by that of the Emperor, who leaves no son to inherit. His lack of progeny is considered God's punishment for having imprisoned his father and starved him to death. Thus does the line of the Henrys come to an end. The Pope sends envoys to Germany to persuade the electors to choose the Saxon duke, Lothar, as the next emperor, which they do.

Once he becomes emperor, Lothar starts persecuting all the relatives and the whole family of the late emperor.

Soběslav and Otto's struggle as to who is to have the capital of Bohemia intensifies. Soběslav arrives with a considerable army in Moravia, deprives Otto of his share of it and transfers this to Vratislav. Otto runs to Lothar for his help, which he is given. Yet, even so, when he joins battle with Soběslav, he is not only defeated, but loses his life. Many of Lothar's men are killed or captured, and Lothar himself has to desert his troops and flee, thus disgracing the start of his reign with a shameful defeat.

A.D. 1127

Bolesław's wife, Adelaide, bears him a second child, who is christened Bolesław after its father and grandfather. He has naturally curly hair, which earns him the nickname "Curly". The covert rivalry and enmity of the two sons of Volodar of Przemyśl turns into open hatred; so much so that each has designs on the other's life and seeks help from abroad: Vladimir from the Pannonians and Rostislav from the Ruthenians. When Rostislav's Ruthenians arrive they advance on Vladimir, whose help from Hungary is late in arriving. Meanwhile, the barons and knights have started talks about reconciliation. When, after several days, the talks fail, military action starts again. Rostislav with his Ruthenian allies lays siege to his brother's town of Zvenigorod, thinking he can easily capture it; however, it is defended by 3000 men, so Rostislav raises the siege and withdraws.

A.D. 1128

After his defeat of Lothar, Soběslav becomes a conceited tyrant and behaves harshly to his nephews, sons of his two brothers: he imprisons Conrad, Lutold's son, in Vyšehrad castle, and then turns his attention to the sons of Conrad the elder, Soběslav and Břetislav, against whom he has nothing but suspicions, yet he imprisons them both.

Bolesław receives envoys from the King of Denmark, together with a number of Danish barons who accompany his son's bride, the King of Denmark's daughter, who comes with a splendid dowry. The wedding is a costly occasion, after which the Danish barons and envoys return to Denmark loaded with generous gifts.

Vladimir, Duke of Zvenigorod, unable to endure the frequent raids of his arch-enemy and brother, Rostislav of Przemyśl, takes his wife and family to Hungary in search of help, for which he is prepared to pay any price.

A.D. 1129

Although Bolesław has done the penance prescribed for the crimes of killing his brother Zbigniew and blinding Skarbimir, and all the clergy in the country have prayed for his absolution, he decides to make a pilgrimage to the monastery of St. Giles, on the assumption that, as he was born of a barren mother made fertile by St. Giles, that saint should be called on to expunge his sins. Before he sets out, he spends the whole of Lent in abstinence, seldom taking food and then only bread and water, mortifying his body with a hair shirt even when resting or sleeping, distributing alms, feeding the poor, washing the feet of unhappy strangers and spending much time in prayer and vigils, to the admiration of many people. Then, after Easter, incognito and accompanied only by his chaplains and a few eminent laymen, he sets out for France. Throughout the whole journey he never departs from his strict regimen. Every day he leaves his hostelry and walks barefoot while he recites the breviary; then he sings the lesser hours in honour of the Blessed Virgin, after them the penitential psalms, often adding vigil for the dead, and only then does he put on his shoes. He never passes a cathedral, abbey or monastery without making it a gift of gold or silver. He is generous to the poor. As he is approaching the monastery at Saint Gilles, the Abbot, informed of his arrival, comes out in solemn procession to meet him, which displeases him mightily. Entering the monastery church, he prostrates himself before St. Giles's tomb, and, with tears pouring down his cheeks, thanks the saint for his intervention which brought him into the world and gave him many victories and a long life. He spends a fortnight in the monastery engaged in devotions and mortifications more severe than those of the monks themselves. He makes splendid gifts to the monastery. On his way back to Poland, he practises the same rigorous regimen as on the way to France. He is greeted with real pleasure and rejoicing that he has returned from so long a pilgrimage in good health, his duty done.

Sviatopolk, Prince of Kiev, dies and is succeeded by his brother, Iaropolk.

A.D. 1130

Bolesław embarks on another pilgrimage, this one to the tomb of St. Stephen in Székesfehérvár. He goes on foot, accompanied by a large retinue of priests and knights and has with him waggons and carriages loaded with provisions and the equipment of a prince. He does not travel incognito, but as himself. King Stephen of Hungary, wishing to honour his father-in-law, a rare guest, sends a number of his knights and courtiers to greet him and to see that he and his courtiers have everything they need. He then comes out from Buda in person, and accompanies them to Székesfehérvár, presenting them all with gifts worthy of himself and his father-in-law. He also provides an escort for their return journey. Bolesław, having paid a visit to the holy tomb, makes generous gifts to the cathedral of Székesfehérvár and other cathedrals, as well as to each monastery church lying on his route. The bishops and barons are all eager to invite him to their palaces and homes, invitations which Bolesław feels it would be discourteous to refuse, though regretting that instead of mortification and penance, as he had planned for himself, he has to accept sumptuous entertainment. When he finally reaches Cracow, although tired, he goes on to Gniezno to honour the tomb of St. Wojciech. Again, he makes this pilgrimage on foot, and the closer he gets to Gniezno, the more pious the exercises and mortifications he performs, often in tears. When he arrives, he spends several day on his knees before the tomb in profound prayer, beseeching forgiveness for his sins. He gives eighty marks in pure gold and a number of unusual stones for the repair of the sarcophagus, and provides the bishops, canons and priests, his knights and each of his companions with splendid garments. Before leaving, he gives gifts to all the cathedral's clerics and its servants.

The Bohemian prince, Soběslav, condemns a number of Czech nobility, especially the members of the Vršovci clan, but also some of his own friends and courtiers, to various punishments, including death, on the grounds that, at the instigation of his nephew, Břetislav, Conrad's son, whom he has imprisoned, they were planning an attempt on his life. Břetislav himself is cruelly blinded.

A.D. 1131

Bolesław's first-born son by his German wife, dies, to his father's profound grief; but this is somewhat mitigated when, in the same year, the Princess gives birth to a fine son, who is christened Mieczysław. In due course, the babe is to evince such sense and enterprise, that he is nicknamed "the Old". Everyone admires his tact, modesty and wisdom, which are evident even when he is a boy.

Stephen, King of Hungary dies. In choosing their next king the Hungarians reject Stephen's sons, because of what their grandfather, Coloman did, and instead elect Almus' son, Blind Béla, whom they take to Székesfehérvár and there, on April 27 they crown him. Over the years, his wife, Helena, daughter of the Emperor of Constantinople, has given him four sons: Géza, Laszló, Stephen and Almus. At her instigation he now executes sixty-eight barons and nobles accused of hav-

Queen Helen of Hungary exacting vengeance on sixty-eight squires and nobles, whom she considers guilty of
abetting or agreeing to the blinding of her son, Béla.
From Chronika de Gestis Hungarorum. —*Országos Széchényi Könyvtár.*

ing abetted or agreed to his blinding. Their children he also has executed and all their possessions
are divided among the cathedral churches.

A.D. 1132

Deprived of their inheritance by the coronation of Béla and afraid lest disaster overtake them,
Stephen's sons go with their mother, Judith, and a few adherents to Poland. Bolesław, wishing to
see one of them on the Hungarian throne, prepares an expedition against that country, all the more
readily as there is no sign of anyone preparing war against him. Here, however, he is wrong, for
Béla, afraid of Bolesław's power has made an alliance with the Czech prince, Soběslav, who is eager to strike a blow at Poland. So, when Bolesław, ignorant of what is being planned, marches his
huge army into Hungary and, devastating it, reaches Spisz, he finds himself confronted by Béla's
Hungarian army reinforced with troops of the Austrian Margrave Albert, whose wife is Béla's sister. In the ensuing battle, Bolesław is victorious, though victory costs him many casualties. He then
advances on Buda. Meanwhile, Soběslav, in accordance with the pact he has made with Béla, has
invaded Poland and is devastating the area round Wrocław. When Bolesław is halfway to Buda he
learns of this, and, after much hesitation and to the sorrow of Stephen's sons who are with him, decides to leave Hungary and take the shortest route home to deal with Soběslav. The Polish army,

which has already marched many miles, moves so slowly that it allows Soběslav to withdraw to Bohemia with his booty.

This year, Bolesław's wife gives birth to yet another son, who, in memory of his grandfather the Roman Emperor Henry is christened Henry; this is the first time that that name has been given to a Polish king or prince.

A.D. 1133

While Bolesław, justifiably angry with the Czechs, is preparing to wage war against them, the sons of the late King of Hungary and some of their compatriots who have deserted Béla and joined them, persuade him to attack Hungary instead. When he sees how strong is the army that is opposed to him, Béla takes refuge in the castle of Vyšehrad and prepares to withstand a siege. Meanwhile, Soběslav is invading Poland with a force of Czechs and Moravians. The knights of Wrocław, convinced that they cannot withstand an assault, withdraw to their camp; but Soběslav, after burning a number of monasteries and churches, as well as more than 300 villages with churches in Silesia and Wrocław, returns to Bohemia with a huge herd of cattle and much booty. When Bolesław learns of the shameful devastation of his lands, he abandons the war in Hungary and marches into Moravia, from which he removes a large number of captives and cattle, after cruelly devastating and burning much of the country. His departure leaves Stephen's sons' enterprise unfinished, indeed, dead; and Blind Béla happily strengthens his position on the throne. Bolesław of Poland never goes to their help again, being too preoccupied with his own wars and afraid of being attacked not only by Soběslav, but also by Lothar King of the Romans. Béla sends valuable presents to the Emperor by envoys who ask for, and obtain, the Emperor's promise to help Béla against Bolesław and Stephen's sons.

A.D. 1134

Deeply grieved by this second devastation of his kingdom by Soběslav, Bolesław assembles a great army from all his territories and, reinforcing it with troops from Ruthenia, invades Bohemia, which he then ravages, plundering and burning as far as the river Elbe. Soběslav prepares to give battle, but when he sees how much stronger than he the enemy is, confines his action to ambushes and skirmishes in inconvenient places, attacking those out foraging or any who may have strayed from their camp. Bolesław, who has plenty of experience of the craftiness of the Czechs, feeling that the enemy is advancing with the intention of doing battle, marches on very cautiously and with closed ranks, securing himself on every side, burning towns and villages in as broad a belt as is possible. Finding that nothing will provoke the Czechs into attacking him, he returns to Poland with his booty and captives. As soon as the Poles are out of the country and have disbanded the army, Soběslav crosses the border with what troops he can scrape together, destroys a few villages and outskirts of towns near the frontier, and marches back again. Winter is at hand.

Prince Vladimir's son, Iaropolk, organizes a series of secret meetings of the Ruthenian dukes with the object of devising ways of throwing off Bolesław's yoke, under which they have been for so long. The idea appeals to the more eminent Ruthenians and it is agreed that they will revolt at a favourable moment, but that until then the plan must be kept secret. This it is not. Bolesław is told of it almost at once, and it disturbs him greatly since he is involved in so many wars this is a real threat. He summons his advisers and although their ideas differ as to how it should be done, all are agreed that unless the conspiracy is squashed at the outset, the country will suffer. One of Bolesław's chief advisers, Peter Włostowic, Castellan of Książa, tells them that it will be useless going to war, unless they first get rid of the main instigator of the conspiracy, and this he offers to see to. Bolesław gives him his full support, cost what it may. Peter Włostowic, selecting a few trusty companions, who are not told what is afoot, presents himself before Prince Vladimir, Iaropolk's father, his demeanour that of a man who has suffered an ugly blow. Vladimir repeatedly asks the reason for his coming and finally is told that Peter is a refugee; that he has been greatly wronged by Bolesław and finally that he has chosen voluntary exile so as to avoid worse happening to him. He has come to the Prince because he has long known him to be noble and kind-hearted. He begs Vladimir to take him in and help him. Peter Włostowic's arrival comes at the right moment for Iaropolk and the Ruthenians, who say that it is as though Heaven had sent him, just at the moment when they wish to start their planned rebellion. Peter's companions keep asking what are the reasons for his flight, for they know of none, but he just tells them to keep quiet and not ask questions, but to be ready to use their arms when the time comes. Thus they wait until one day, when Vladimir's son, Iaropolk, is at breakfast with a few of his fellows, Peter and his companions rush into the room, their swords drawn, and seize Iaropolk. He tries to resist, but is thrown to the ground, tied up, carried away and swiftly taken back to Poland, using boats placed in advance at the rivers they have to cross, and there handed over to Bolesław, a truly splendid gift. For his unusual feat Peter is rewarded with a number of properties and gifts. Iaropolk's imprisonment, which brings the conspiracy into the open and causes his adherents to be punished, ensures the loyalty of the other Ruthenian dukes and nobles, thus is war, that once seemed imminent, avoided.

A.D. 1135

As Bolesław is preparing to avenge himself on the Czechs, an envoy brings him a letter from Lothar, King of the Romans, asking him not to go to war with them, but to come to Lothar, who, he assures him, will be able to make peace between him and Soběslav on equitable terms. The reason for the request is that Lothar is planning to go to Italy to settle disturbances in the Church and be crowned Emperor in Rome, but Soběslav has told him that he must first remove the threat of war between the Czechs and the Poles; otherwise Soběslav, being involved in war with a neighbour, will be unable to send him the requisite help for his expedition into Italy. So, Bolesław, anxious to comply with Lothar's request, one with which many Poles agree, sets out with a magnificent retinue for Bamberg, and arrives there at the same time as Soběslav. For many days the two princes discuss the restoration of peace between them, Lothar acting as intermediary, but in vain, for each exaggerates the wrongs he has suffered. To avoid the two going away with nothing achieved and, perhaps, even more angry with each other than before, and to avoid losing the help of the Czechs, Lothar proposes that Bolesław accept an armistice to last for three years, that is, until Lothar's return from Italy. Bolesław agrees.

Peter Włostowic's astuteness seems to have secured peace and advantage to Poland, so all the greater is the unexpected disaster that it causes, a reminder from Fate that the laws of hospitality and of nations have been broken by his actions. Vasilko, Iaropolk's son, collects all the treasure on which he can lay his hands and manages to pay the amount of his father's ransom. Then, realizing that he is not going to be able to avenge the injury done to him and his father by force, he decides to use cunning and trickery, like that which caused his father's downfall. With large gifts and greater promises he bribes a Hungarian of famous rank and lineage and thus one unlikely to arouse suspicion, as would a Ruthenian, to flee to Bolesław in Poland and pretend to have suffered grievous wrongs at the hands of the King of Hungary for having supported Stephen's sons; to pretend to have been deprived of all his possessions, and that he would have been condemned to death had he not escaped in time. He tells Bolesław that he has come to him as the grandfather and guardian of Stephen's sons. Bolesław, not suspecting treachery or subterfuge, since the man's previous behaviour speaks in his favour, is convinced of the truth of his story. The Hungarian wins Bolesław's trust, at first only in small matters, but goes on to enjoy his favour and generosity and even becomes his intimate and confidant. To help him, Bolesław grants him the town of Wiślica, at that time well populated, with its surrounding villages. The town itself Nature made impregnable, for it stands on an almost circular bluff in the middle of a bend of the River Nida, which there is wide and swollen by waters from other rivers. Then, when Bolesław announces his intention of going to Germany, the Hungarian, sensing that he will never get a better opportunity of carrying out his treacherous plan, lets it be known that he has learned that the Ruthenian dukes are in open revolt and advancing swiftly on Poland, and orders all the knights and barons round about to assemble in Wiślica, as a safe haven, with all their most precious possessions; anyone failing to do this is to have his belongings confiscated. Frightened at the thought of the enemy's advance, the knights and barons do as they are told; thus the entire population from either side of the Nida is concentrated in Wiślica with their belongings. The Hungarian then sends a message to Iaropolk and his son, to come at once with the largest force they can muster. Iaropolk gets there quickly, and, on the night of February 8, when everyone is asleep, the Hungarian treacherously opens the gates and admits Iaropolk and his army. A horrible slaughter follows, one which takes no account of age, sex or status. Very few manage to escape. Then, having sacked and burned the town without resistance or loss, the Ruthenians return to their country taking with them their booty of cattle and people. Iaropolk, wishing to reward the Hungarian for his treachery more lavishly even than he had promised, first has his tongue cut out, then both eyes gouged out, after which he is castrated so that he can breed no more traitors. All too late Bolesław realizes that Hungarians are by nature untrustworthy.

A.D. 1136

Bolesław determines to revenge himself on the Ruthenians. He assembles a huge army, not only of knights and barons, but of peasants and ordinary people as well, and with it invades Ruthenia. Iaropolk, tormented by his conscience and realizing that Bolesław will be inexorable in his anger, abandons towns and forts, even such as are well secured, and moves to the farthest corners of the country, taking refuge in the forests and marshes. Bolesław, out for vengeance, orders every Ruthenian without exception to be killed. The subsequent slaughter claims more lives than a normal war, for no one is allowed to buy his life. Vladimir and its whole area are burned and the people there killed, except for a large number of both sexes, who are driven back into Poland with the cattle.

After spending four years in France, Pope Innocent II returns to Italy. He is met at the borders of Lombardy by Lothar, and by many archbishops and bishops, and is conducted to Rome, where he is restored to the papal throne. Lothar is then crowned Emperor. Bolesław honours him on his return to his own country by going to meet him at Bamberg and presents him with gifts. These Lothar accepts, but he also demands that Bolesław pay him homage and tribute for Pomerania and Rügen, which are subject to the Prince of Poland, asserting that they belong to the Emperor. However, Bolesław is able to show that they are his hereditary territory and have never belonged to the Empire, so the latter withdraws his demand.

A.D. 1137

The Ruthenian dukes and nobles, distraught at the destruction of their country, meet in Vladimir. Many are prepared to declare war on Bolesław, but Iaropolk, speaking from experience, insists that they will achieve nothing by open warfare. If they want to win, he tells them, they must use cunning and stratagem, and he suggests that they leave it all to him. To this they agree. Iaropolk's first move is to expel Iaroslav, Duke of Galicia, who was not prepared to cooperate and was considered likely to inform Bolesław of everything that went on. This Iaroslav takes refuge in Poland, having nowhere else to go, and is there graciously received. Bolesław gives him enough to enable him to live there. After a while the elders of Galicia, duly bribed by Iaropolk, go to Bolesław and ask for the return of their duke. Wishing to make a great occasion of his return, they ask Bolesław himself to escort him back to Galicia. As, on previous occasions, the Ruthenians have gone into hiding at the sight of him, Bolesław sees no reason to suspect any danger, especially as all is peaceful in Galicia. The elders thank Bolesław for sheltering their duke and, in return, promise eternal submission and obedience. Before they receive Bolesław's reply, some of Galicia's neighbours, Hungarian nobles involved in the conspiracy, arrive with the same request, that Bolesław restore Iaroslav to his throne. Bolesław, all unsuspecting, believes them all. Whatever his other virtues, Bolesław has one great fault, credulity, because of which he fails to suspect the fraud. He promises to restore Iaroslav to his throne and to go to Galicia with him. So, he sets off, as if to a banquet, with a retinue of knights and Iaroslav. On arrival at Halicz, he is greeted by some units of Hungarians, who then take up position behind the Polish contingent and mingle with their rear ranks. This at once arouses the suspicions of Bolesław, who already has a premonition of danger.

Next, some units of Galicians appear, pretending to be friendly and submissive. They greet the Polish prince and take up position in the rear of his men. Bolesław now realizes that he has walked into a trap. He summons Wszebór the Voivode of Cracow and commander of the army and they discuss the situation. They agree that their only hope is to attack before more of the enemy appear on the scene, as Bolesław is sure they will. All at once, another Ruthenian unit, led by Iaropolk of Kiev, appears in front of them. The Poles dare wait no longer. They and Bolesław fight as they have never fought before. At one point they almost break through the enemy's line, and, for a while, it looks as though they may well be victorious, but then one of Bolesław's commanders, a voivode whose name and lineage are unknown, giving way to fear leads his men from the line of battle and takes to shameful flight, in which he is followed by a considerable portion of the Polish contingent. Bolesław now fights on, but more as one conquered, than as a conqueror. He is attacked from every side with arrows, spears and swords. His horse, weakened by wounds, collapses under him and almost crushes him. One of his own men, seeing his Prince fighting on foot, gives him his own horse which is relatively fresh and implores him for the sake of Poland to save his life and liberty. Bolesław escapes, but many of his knights are lost, either killed or taken prisoner. Back in Poland, Bolesław sends to the baron who left the battlefield with a large part of the army, the skin of a hare, a spindle and a distaff. The distaff tells him that he is a woman, the hare's skin that he is a coward, and the spindle that he is as erratic as it. This is worse punishment than death, for to have disgraced his honour as a knight is, for a man, worse than death. The unfortunate recipient has no need to have these gifts interpreted. With his own hands he throws a rope over the belfry in his church and hangs himself. The common soldier who gave his horse to Bolesław also managed to escape and return home. Bolesław rewards him by ennobling him and giving him riches and honours. Although the treasury is emptied to pay ransoms, there is not enough to ransom all, and many are sold into slavery and spend miserable existences until they die.

Before the three-year armistice arranged by Lothar expires, the Czech and Polish barons come together to begin discussions for a lasting peace. As each wishes peace, it is thought valuable that the two rulers should meet in person and it is arranged that they do so in Kłodzko. There, Bolesław stresses the injuries he has suffered at the hands of Soběslav in return for the various kindnesses he has done him. Soběslav, in his turn, justifies what he has done and blames Bolesław for injuries inflicted on him; yet, thanks to the mediation of the nobles on either side, peace is agreed. As a sign of sincerity, Bolesław's son, Władysław, stands godfather to Soběslav's son, Václav. It is known that Bolesław agrees to the arrangement readily, because if he is not at war with Bohemia and there is peace in Silesia, he will be able to attack Ruthenia with all his forces, for he is determined to avenge his disastrous defeat there, of which he is so dreadfully ashamed that he avoids meeting and talking with people, and, in solitude, grieves over the knights he has lost.

A.D. 1138

Bolesław's wife gives birth to another son, who is christened Casimir, but not even this can banish Bolesław's grief and shame at his defeat, which is all the more severe, as his lack of knights and empty treasury make it difficult for him to assemble an army large enough to avenge himself on the Ruthenians and Hungarians.

A.D. 1139

Bolesław is still fretting over his defeat at Halicz and will allow himself no pleasures. He is growing weaker and weaker and finally becomes seriously ill. Although his doctors might have cured him with their medicines, Bolesław refuses all treatment and his condition just deteriorates. This goes on for almost a year. When he eventually feels that he is near to death, he summons his prelates and barons and begs them, on his death, to preserve unity and see that squabbles do not destroy the country. He leaves five sons, as a result of which most Poles foresee a disastrous dissolution of their country, and this is what happens, for it soon becomes obvious how impossible it will be for so many princes to agree for long. To avoid them warring against each other, Bolesław divides the kingdom, which, until then, had one prince and ruler, giving Cracow, Sieradz, Łęczyca, Silesia and Pomerania to his first-born, Władysław, who, by the law of primogeniture, is to have the supreme authority and his brothers are to obey him in everything. Bolesław the Curly is to have Mazovia, Dobrzyń, Kujawy and Chełm. "Old" Mieczysław is to have Gniezno, Poznań and Kalisz; Henry gets Sandomierz and Lublin. The infant Casimir is left nothing, which those who were present consider an oversight or the lapse of a sick man's memory. Thus did Bolesław die in the thirty-sixth year of his reign and the fifty-fourth year of his life. It is considered certain that his early death was due to his fretting over his defeat at Halicz. He was of medium height and swarthy complexion; easily moved to kindness or anger; he was well-built and physically strong. He was popularly known as "Wry-mouth", because a painful ulcer, which he had as a youth, left him with a twist to his mouth.

The sons of the Ruthenian duke, Oleg, ask for and obtain help from the Polovtsy, with which they attack Ruthenia and burn towns and villages along the River Sula; but, when they reach Pereiaslavl, they suffer defeat. They go on to burn Ujście and withdraw to Szupon, where Iaropolk and his brothers engage them in battle. Oleg's sons are defeated with heavy losses on both sides, the Polovtsy turning and running. The Ruthenians set off in pursuit and kill or capture most of them. When they return to the battlefield they are attacked by Oleg's sons and routed. Iaropolk and his nephew, Vasilko, are captured, as are many boyars; but Iaropolk manages to escape and makes his way to Kiev. When Oleg's sons besiege him there he does not wish to fight, though he has a fresh army, but makes peace with them on equitable terms.

A.D. 1140

Bolesław Wry-mouth having died so young, the Poles are for a long time reluctant to replace him; indeed, they are so preoccupied with their grief as to dislike the idea of being ruled by anyone other than this man, under whose rule the country became so glorious. They are conscious, too, of the dangers inherent in the coming division of the kingdom into four, which is feared as a kind of pestilence, people rightly foreseeing that it will cause turmoil and domestic discord and bring misfortune upon all. Many say that division of the kingdom will inevitably involve its downfall, since what is divided cannot stand. Now, more and more public affairs are being neglected, since officials are either reluctant to give decisions or overrule those of another; and meanwhile Bolesław's four sons are demanding access to the lands granted them in their father's will. A general assembly is called and after much discussion the country's prelates and lords designate the eldest son,

Władysław, heir to his father's throne; he is to retain his seniority and rights of primogeniture, and be the superior of his brothers, Bolesław, Mieczysław and Henry, who thus owe him obedience. Wars are to be waged jointly by the four who will contribute equal forces, but the right to declare war is to be Władysław's alone. The other three can embark only on defensive, not offensive war. This arranged, the three brothers depart to their inheritances: Bolesław the Curly to Mazovia, Mieszko the Old to Poznań and Henry to Sandomierz. Władysław, as senior prince and monarch remains in Cracow, from where, this being his capital, he will govern his other dukedoms and possessions. The fifth son, Casimir, who is under age, is to remain with Władysław. Thus is Poland torn into parts, so that, when in course of time, disputes arise between the dukes, Poland will take up arms against herself; arms meant to be used against an enemy will be thrust into Polish guts and, in the madness of anger, swords will be drawn to maim Polish limbs and bodies.

Soběslav, Prince of Bohemia, learning that Bolesław is dead and his kingdom disintegrating, in violation of the treaty and alliance he made under oath, invades Poland and Silesia, plundering and devastating. Since Władysław shows no signs of reacting, he goes further and plans to exact tribute from and even annexe Silesia or at least make it his fief. To further this plan, he sets about enlarging a village called Kosczan, which is well protected by surrounding marshes and lakes, intending to make it a town and fort with a garrison. He spends many days laboriously bringing up building material; but Divine Judgment which usually reaches those who break treaties, does so in his case, in that he contracts a fever which forces him to abandon the plan. He is carried back to Prague by his companions, who reproach him for being greedy and breaking the treaty; and there his condition deteriorates and, on February 14, he dies. He leaves three sons: Soběslav, Oldřich and Václav, but is succeeded by Vratislav's son, Vladislav, to which his three sons raise no objection.

On February 10, Iaropolk, Duke of Kiev, dies. By rights, his brother Vyacheslav should have Kiev, but when Oleg's son Vsevolod appears with an army, Vyacheslav, rather than fight, makes an agreement, using the Patriarch as an intermediary, whereby he surrenders Kiev and withdraws to Turov, leaving Vsevolod to occupy Kiev unhindered.

A.D. 1141

Peace cannot long continue after the dismemberment of Poland. Indeed, this causes acrimonious domestic conflict from the very start, in that, although Władysław, as the eldest, has received the larger and more important share, he feels that what his three younger brothers have been given has been at his expense. This thought torments him and he keeps complaining to his friends that he has been robbed. His wife, an ambitious woman, as conceited as she is cruel, keeps urging him to do something about this and tells him that she, daughter of one emperor and sister of another, was betrothed to him at an early age in expectation that he would inherit the whole of Poland, not this cropped and insignificant part of it that he now has. When she married him he was going to become rich and powerful, but now all her own and her father's hopes have been dashed, and her marriage has only brought her misery and humiliation. She can see that, unless he does something about this, she and her children will be plunged into even greater destitution, since he has only a quarter of that to which his late father's will and his seniority entitle him. Because he has let this be shared with his three brothers, who should be his servants and subject to his authority, rather than the equals of princes, he deserves to be called a half-prince. It would have been better for her, she tells him, to have died, than to have contracted such a wretched marriage, which has sullied the lustre of her family. If he considers himself a man and not a woman, she urges, let him demand the dukedoms occupied by his younger brothers, while this is still possible, and so prevent her and their sons being shamed for ever and condemned to a wretched lot. So the Princess goads her weak husband. In the end she has killed all his fraternal feelings for the three young dukes of whom his father's will made him guardian.

A.D. 1142

Władysław is thinking more and more seriously of appropriating his three brothers' shares of their father's inheritance; now he decides to put his wife's whispered promptings into practice. He summons a large number of prelates and nobles from the duchy of Cracow and consults with them. Princess Agnes he allows to take part in the proceedings, hoping this will make it easier to obtain approval of the plan. Cunningly, she advances the argument that Poland ought to have but one prince, one ruler, one monarch, so that, if the country is to remain a whole, the agreed division between the four must be rescinded. The young brothers should be given towns and villages, not provinces, and should not be Władysław's equals, but his subordinates and obedient to him as their monarch, appointed as such by their late father and a general council of the whole country. Otherwise, if things continue as they are, Poland will decline and fall, since it will have been deprived of its necessary strength, and will be plundered by its neighbours. She reminds them, too, of how Bolesław's natural brother, Zbigniew, so often was a threat to his brother and his country. When she finishes speaking, the councillors remain stubbornly silent and it is obvious that they do not support the plan. Later, when asked outright, almost all express dislike of the proposal and tell Władysław and the Princess that it would be wicked, cruel and inhuman to drive the three younger brothers from their possessions. To do this would be contrary to the laws of nations and the just order laid down by God, a precedent that would be most damaging. It could not be done with impunity, they are told, for God takes pity on those who are wronged; and they point out that the case of Zbigniew is not relevant, since he was the child of a concubine, while the three are children of a legal wife. Also the three brothers are not tainted by any of the crimes for which Zbigniew made himself so hated; and they ask Władysław to abandon this disastrous idea which can only harm him and those nearest to him. As the councillors are almost unanimous it is expected that Władysław will take their advice; however, his love for his wife is stronger than anything else, and he lets her pleas and whisperings advocating what is essentially a crime, prevail. First, in order that his tyranny should not be obvious, he orders all the territories which form his brothers' shares to pay him tribute and vassalage as their monarch. Next, he orders that every province in the country is to obey him exclusively. Anyone who rebels or refuses is to be flogged, imprisoned or deprived of their property. He feels that he can safely introduce such a measure, since the nobility and the rich have little sense of loyalty; but even so, he sends for extra troops from Ruthenia (his mother was a Ruthenian) to help him seize his brothers' possessions.

Princess Agnes, puffed up with pride and despising the customs and company of Poles, now refuses to allow any Polish official, master of the pantry or cupbearer to approach her table, pretending to be disgusted by the sight of them and their negligent dress, and also because they stink. In the same way, she despises and looks down on her husband's brothers. She is greedy, too, and pretending that such is her due, gives orders that throughout the country, each in accordance with his means, on the major holy days, is voluntarily to bring for the Prince's table poultry, sucking pigs, geese, honey, wheat and oats. Then, when this has been done on several occasions, she ordains that in future equivalent amounts shall be paid annually to the treasury, thus forcing free people to pay her tribute.

There are disturbances in Bohemia, too, where the Czechs, unable to endure the rule of their prince, Vladislav, who is too energetic in removing people from their offices and clipping the wings of the licentious, have sent for Conrad, Margrave of Moravia, to come and take possession of Prague. So, with the help of his brother, Otto Duke of Olomouc, and Vratislav, Conrad's nephew, and three grandsons of King Vratislav, Conrad leads his army into Bohemia, and there behaves as oppressively as if he were a foreign enemy, killing, burning and plundering. Vladislav takes a small force of knights who support him and tries to halt Conrad's advance. The two armies engage on April 25 and, after a bloody struggle, Vladislav is defeated and takes refuge in Prague; but, not feeling secure there, he goes to the Emperor, whose wife is his sister, to ask for help. Meanwhile, Conrad of Moravia advances towards Prague, defeats Theobald, whom Vladislav left to defend the city, which he then captures and assumes control of. He burns and demolishes the cathedral church, the monastery of St. George and many other holy places and public buildings, brutally murdering clergy and laity alike. After a few days, however, the Emperor arrives to help his son-in-law, and Conrad is driven out.

A.D. 1143

Władysław's behaviour towards his three brothers becomes more and more tyrannical, until they are at a loss what to do. However, acting on advice, they go to Princess Agnes in the hope of being able to gain her sympathy and get her to influence her husband and persuade him to relent towards them. She, of course, insists that her husband has acted correctly and that Poland cannot continue divided. The three go away embittered.

Vladislav, having re-established himself on the Bohemian throne, marches an army of foreign mercenaries into Moravia and devastates first the territories of Margrave Conrad and then those of Otto, neither of whom seem inclined to resist. Having devastated most of Moravia, he returns with his booty to Bohemia.

A.D. 1144

Aware of Władysław's ever-growing hatred of the three young dukes, the influential people of Wielkopolska, Mazovia and Lublin, some of whom have been bribed, decide to give their support to the one who is strongest; so they desert the orphaned dukes and give their support to Władysław. Now, only two openly support the young dukes: Peter of Denmark, the Count of Skrzin, and Wszebór, the Voivode of Sandomierz. On a few minor occasions the latter has had recourse to arms and won, thus incurring the enmity of Władysław. Peter, however, a man famous for his wealth, influence and virtuous life, has achieved a premier position in Poland, though as a newcomer and a foreigner, he has inevitably aroused people's envy. In friendly converse with Władysław, Peter reproaches him for his tyrannical behaviour and points out how dangerous for him this may turn out to be. Władysław first turns a deaf ear, then, becoming suspicious, he conceives a fierce dislike of Peter and decides to deal as harshly with him as he has with his brothers, lest the famous and influential Peter ally himself with the three and so frustrate Władysław's plans and weaken his authority. Princess Agnes is even more fiercely opposed to the Castellan, against whom she bears an old grudge, going back to a time when Władysław and Peter were together out hunting. The chase having taken them far from their camp, in order to placate their rumbling stomachs, they cut themselves meat from their quarry and quenched their thirst with melted snow and ice; then they lay down to sleep on the bare earth, jokingly comparing the delights of their rustic bed with those of their wives'. Władysław is reputed to have said: "I believe, Peter, that your wife will be spending the night more comfortably than we are, perhaps with the Abbot of Strzelno." Peter, reciprocating jest with jest, and taking rather a liberty, replies: "Who knows; perhaps not only my wife with the abbot, but your darling may be enjoying the night with Dobiesz." Dobiesz being Agnes' lover, her intimate relationship with whom has occasioned much opprobious comment. This infuriates Władysław, but he stifles his anger, not only because he values Peter more than any other of his barons, but also because Peter is married to a cousin of Władysław's mother and he does not wish to make an enemy of him. On his return home Agnes suspects that something has happened and pesters him until he tells her what Peter said about her. Ever since, Agnes has not stopped seeking ways of getting her own back. She keeps telling Władysław that he will never achieve complete authority in Poland as long as Peter is left in his present position, and suggests that Peter is planning rebellion, or plotting to remove Władysław from the throne, even of poisoning him. Finally, the two decide to get rid of Peter. To carry out so dastardly a crime calls for an accomplice who can be entrusted with the task without risk of him betraying them. They choose Dobiesz, who agrees to do it, but insists that it is too much for him to do alone. At this time Peter's daughter is about to marry Jaksa, duke of the Sorbs. The wedding is to be held in Wrocław and followed by a tourney. So, Dobiesz goes to Wrocław with a sizeable retinue. He and his men then enter the house, where Peter is lodging, and abduct him, thus spoiling the wedding ceremonies. Peter is conveyed to Władysław, who for a long time hesitates to do anything drastic, being restrained by Peter's innocence and the memory of his services to him and Poland. Agnes is afraid lest Władysław relent and release Peter, so she pesters him until he agrees to have him put to the torture. The executioners are sent for and these cut out Peter's tongue and blind both his eyes; but, by the mercy of God, for whom he performed so many pious acts, Peter miraculously recovers the sight of both eyes as well as the ability to speak, and lives for a further five years, making generous gifts to monasteries, churches and shrines, especially those which he himself built or endowed. To this day there are in Poland many stone-built churches, which, it is said, owe their foundation to this Peter.

A.D. 1145

After this cruel treatment of Peter of Denmark no one dares stand up to Władysław by censuring his actions or saying what is right and in accordance with the law. Władysław now assembles troops from all his principalities and reinforces them with others from Ruthenia, which gives him an army larger than any before, with which he drives two of his brothers out of their castles: Bolesław out of Płock, and Henry out of Sandomierz, and assumes complete control. This leaves only Mieczysław the Old holding Gniezno, Poznań and Wielkopolska and the other two seek refuge with him. The three brothers establish themselves in Poznań castle, see to its defences and prepare to resist Władysław's attack. As soon as he learns of what has happened, Władysław hurries to Poznań, brings up his army and invests the castle, surrounding it with chevaux-de-frises and a close ring of towers, thus making it impossible for any of those inside to escape. He then orders a continual bombardment with siege-weapons and assaults with battering-rams, both by day and by night. The three dukes, seeing themselves thus penned in and in danger of falling into their brother's hands, send emissaries to Władysław asking him to stop hostilities and his attempt to take over their dukedoms, seeing that, after all they all have the same father and thus as good a right to Poland as he has. He is told, too, to remember that Fortune is fickle. Władysław will hear none of it, which reduces the three young dukes to tears. Most of them would have been prepared to give up part of their duchies, if that would have assured them of peaceful enjoyment of the rest, but when this suggestion is refused in its turn, they realize that Władysław will not desist until he has destroyed them and obtained complete authority over all Poland. This decides them to hold out in the hope that Divine Providence, which usually supports a just cause, will come to their help.

All the while, Władysław's troops, especially his Ruthenian reinforcements, are on the rampage, looting, plundering, raping women and children, even those of good family, barbarously murdering, torturing and committing all sorts of crimes, so much so that Jacob the Archbishop of Gniezno puts on his mitre and full canonicals and drives in a four-horse carriage—he is well on in years—to Władysław's camp and right up to his tent. There he gently rebukes Władysław and tells him that the unhappiness he is causing will not go unpunished and that the blood he has already shed, and may yet shed, will cause his own destruction. He reminds Władysław that in his father's will he was made guardian of his three brothers, not their opponent and enemy, and warns him that the dreadful dissension which he has stirred up and which is worse than civil war, can only lead to the complete downfall of his family, and his glorious country. Władysław arrogantly dismisses the

Archbishop's pleas and arguments and makes it clear that he has no intention of altering his crazy plans; then the Archbishop, inspired by the Holy Spirit, rises from his chair and says: "Since you have profaned the laws of God and man, broken trust, the laws of nations and natural laws and decided on this arrogant step, and neither fear of God nor human persuasion nor my encouragement and advice can dissuade you from this unjust and shameful action and incline you to do what is right, I, by the authority of God Almighty, whose deputy I am, because, by unjustly using violence, you have invaded your brothers' duchies and, as an enemy of the faith and of your country, have broken the laws of God and man, despised my paternal persuasion, stubbornly rejected all advice, betrayed a hardness of heart worthy of the Pharoahs, I hereby, before the throng standing here, excommunicate you, and impose a ban on you as a recalcitrant, leaving it to Divine Vengeance to punish you." Then, uttering imprecations against Władysław, his army and his allies, and calling upon Heaven to witness Władysław's violations of honour and faith, and rejection of his advice, the Archbishop leaves the tent, assuring Władysław that any day his brothers will pay him back in his own coin. Władysław suppresses his feelings and says nothing, neither cursing the Archbishop, nor threatening him. As the Archbishop's carriage moves off, the coachman carelessly lets the hub of the rear wheel strike a pole supporting Władysław's tent, causing it to collapse and all but crush those inside. Again, Władysław suppresses the anger to which he usually gives vent.

When the three brothers learn what transpired between the Archbishop and their brother and realize that the latter is as implacable as ever, they all but give way to despair. However, they decide to die rather than to surrender. Their only hope is that, as winter approaches, the bad weather will force their brother's army to disperse in search of provisions; but, of course, they too will grow short of food; however, they decide to go down fighting, a decision on which they shake hands. First, they make frequent sorties against Władysław's camp and fortifications, causing considerable damage. This results in the guards being doubled, but these the besieged proceed to snatch and carry off as prisoners. Often, the snatch turns into a minor battle, and, in this way, Władysław loses a number of men every day, either killed or taken prisoner, the main sufferers being the Ruthenians. Then, all at once, there are no more sorties, and so, there no longer being any danger, Władysław's men take to wandering from the camp and its defences, while others just lie about or indulge in drinking-bouts. The whole camp relaxes, as if the enemy were already defeated; indeed, Władysław expects the besieged to surrender any day and speaks disparagingly and slightingly of them. Often there is a mere handful of men manning the camp's defences, the others having gone off to indulge in licentiousness, feasting or other amusements. Some will be sleeping off their hangovers, stretched out defenceless. No discipline is enforced, as if it were certain that the besieged would not undertake any armed action. When the besieged see that Władysław and his troops have all but written them off and how the rot has set in in the enemy's camp, they determine to chance their hand and order everyone, cavalry as well as infantry, to arms. When all are ready, the dukes order a red standard to be flown from the top of the tower. The sight astonishes Władysław's men, especially the Ruthenians, but when they ask what it signifies, they are told that the besieged are offering to surrender and begging for mercy. While they are thus talking, the besieged attack both with their experienced knights and a horde of men of every age and degree. It is midday, a time when many are still asleep or having a meal, and the shouts of the attackers leave Władysław and his men thunderstruck; their first reaction is that the others have taken leave of their senses. Then as the onrush of the assault assumes the proportions of an avalanche, leaving them no time to consult or get their weapons, panic sets in. Did some deity inspire them with terror? Or was it because they knew they were naked and unarmed; or was it that they doubted the justice of their cause? The confusion and noise is such that fear spreads to men and horses alike. Some without arms, seize the nearest horse and, still half asleep, ride off, only to encounter a well-armed enemy. Some think only of saving their precious possessions. No one seems concerned about

Władysław's cause. When the attackers set fire to the camp, the flames spread from bivouac to bivouac, for these are all covered with straw and brushwood and this is as dry as paper. This causes a
stampede and that a slaughter. In no time at all the huge army of Poles and Ruthenians has been
routed and scatters with the brothers' cavalry in pursuit. Many drown, their bodies all but filling the
rivers Warta and Główna. Deserted by all but a few, Władysław takes to flight with the Ruthenian
dukes and heads for Cracow. By repeatedly changing horses he reaches it safely, but sad and dispirited and without his usual retinue, indeed, almost like an ordinary person. The Ruthenian dukes
also reach Cracow and eventually return home empty-handed and with very few men.

The young dukes exploit their victory with great moderation, granting their freedom to all the
Poles among their prisoners. From now on things take a turn for the better for them, and before long
they have recovered all that Władysław took from them. Not only that, but they capture some of
Władysław's castles and three Ruthenian dukes, enriching themselves with booty. Then, to secure
themselves, they arm some of their people and hire foreign mercenaries.

A.D. 1146

Before Władysław has time to recover from his defeat, his three brothers join forces and
march on Cracow. Their intention is to evict him, for they are convinced that, should he re- establish his authority, he will attack them again sooner or later and get the Ruthenians to help him. As it
is, he has no army and no weapons, is deserted by more or less everyone and is altogether uncertain
what to do. What he does do, is leave his wife and children in Cracow castle and himself go to Racibórz and thence through Silesia to Germany in search of help from Conrad, King of the Romans.

For a few days the people of Cracow deny the city to the three young dukes, but then, seeing
that they can expect no help from Władysław and having got the dukes to agree not to treat them as
enemies, they open the city's gates and the three ride in. A few days later the castle also surrenders.
Princess Agnes is neither punished nor harshly treated, though some, especially the friends of Castellan Peter, urge the dukes to make her pay for her crimes. Though bitter and rightly angry with
her, her brothers-in-law treat her with respect; but, realizing that the country will never be truly at
peace with her in it, and also because they are afraid that Peter's friends and relatives might try to
avenge her maiming of him, and, perhaps, kill her, as well as the fact that she and her three sons
might incite rebellion were they to remain in the country, they decide to banish them all and send
them to join their husband and father.

Peace and quiet now reign throughout Poland. Bolesław the Curly, with the agreement of his
brothers and of the nobility, is given the principality due to the senior prince and the authority of
monarch, while retaining his own share of the realm, Mazovia and Kujawy. The new prince is both
modest and liberal in his dealings with his brothers, relinquishing to them much that is his. As a result, they all trust him, accept his authority and obey his orders without murmuring. He assumes
the guardianship of the youngest duke, Casimir, who was left nothing by his father, and sees to his
education.

A.D. 1147

Conrad King of the Romans gives Władysław a friendly reception, and, when he learns why
he has come, encourages him not to give up hope. When Agnes and her three sons join him, she too
pleads with Conrad. Also she is able to talk to Vladislav of Bohemia in person, and she sends envoys to the Ruthenian prince seeking help to restore Władysław.

In Poland, there are persistent rumours that Conrad, King of the Romans, and Vladislav,
Prince of Bohemia, will attack from one direction and the Ruthenians from the other. Though
slightly scared, the three brothers quietly prepare for war. Though Conrad has promised to help
Władysław and his wife recover their throne, he is restrained from doing anything about it by the

number of domestic and private matters requiring his attention, as well as by the affairs of Empire, the sufferings of the Holy Land and the Christians living in it, especially of the capture by King Alaf, a man of Turkish origin, of the town of Edessa, known in the Bible as Arach, and his subsequent condemnation of all Franks found in the town to death or captivity, involving the forced martyrdom of the Archbishop of the city and all his clergy, who loyally refused to renounce Christianity. Not only that, but the loveliest matrons and girls of noble family were forced to fornicate on the altar of the church of St. John the Baptist. This was the first time that pagans defiled the city which was introduced to the true faith by King Agar to whom Christ sent a letter before his passion. So that it should not be thought that he has given up the plan to help Władysław, or forgotten about it, Conrad provides him with a small force with which he builds two forts at Niemce and Gródek on the frontier, and from these harasses the Poles with frequent raids into their territory. As well as providing this small force, Conrad sends emissaries to Bolesław the Curly and his brothers, demanding that they return Władysław's inheritance to him and relieve Conrad of the duty of helping him and his family in their need. The brothers in replying point out that Władysław cruelly and unjustly appropriated their three inheritances and forced them to take up arms in their own defence, that he then refused to listen to the Archbishop of Gniezno; and that it was only with God's help that they were able to defeat him and remove the threat to their lives that he represented. They tell Conrad's emissaries that they will reconcile themselves with their country's enemies, before they do the same with their brother, adding that it was not they that banished him, but rather the perverseness that blinded him. Their reply partially persuades Conrad, whose ardour for helping Władysław noticeably cools. Władysław secretly lays all the blame for his misfortunes and exile on his wife. He stays on in Germany gradually losing people's respect and finding it more and more difficult to endure his increasing penury.

Conrad, King of the Romans, with many of his barons, receives the cross from St. Bernard in Frankfurt am Main, he decides to journey through Poland and hopes that, while there, he will have an opportunity to reconcile Władysław and his brothers. Conrad has with him a large number of princes and lords and an army of cavalry and foot, which is reinforced with troops from the King of Bohemia. When this horde reaches the Polish frontier, Bolesław, as monarch, comes out with his two brothers to greet the King of the Romans. In every part of the country through which the Crusaders pass they are received with regal pomp and lavishly provided with provisions and whatever they need. Bridges are built for them to cross rivers and other difficult places. This courtesy so charms Conrad and the other princes that they are quite won over to the side of the three Poles, though, as long as he is in the country, Conrad keeps urging the three to make things up with their older brother, as does Vladislav of Bohemia and many of the German princes. In the end, Bolesław and his brothers say that they will yield to Conrad's wishes and do this when he returns successful from the Crusade. The Crusaders then move out of Poland, through Ruthenia and into Volhynia, accompanied and provisioned all the way by Bolesław. When they reach the Black Sea, the Crusaders embark on the ships that await them and sail to Constantinople. Moving on from there, they reach Iconium, where they are joined by King Louis of France and the French and Spanish princes. Conrad has some early military success and captures Ascalon. He does, however, suffer considerable casualties, not due to enemy action, but to the flour they bought in Constantinople which was mixed with lime. Some Polish barons and knights take the Cross and fight in Conrad's army until his return.

With Prince Vladislav absent in the Holy Land, the son of the late Prince Soběslav, who is in exile in Germany, returns to Bohemia in the hope of being able to take over the throne. His efforts to win over a majority of the Czech lords with promises and flattery fail, and he himself is caught and imprisoned by Vladislav' brother, Theobald, who has been left in charge of the country. Thus is civil war avoided.

Vsevolod, Prince of Kiev, dies and his son, Igor, assumes control of the city. The people of Kiev, however, dislike Igor and send for Duke Izjaslav. Igor and his brother, Sviatoslav, oppose Izjaslav, but, lacking the strength to engage him in battle, they both seek safety, leaving Izjaslav to occupy Kiev castle. Four days later, Igor, who has been captured, is brought before Izjaslav and detained in the monastery of St. John in Periaslavl, where, as a means of extricating himself, he seeks permission to become a monk, and Izjaslav allows him to be tonsured. Only a few days after this, Igor's brothers stage a revolt in Kiev. This is suppressed, its suppression involving dragging Igor from his church, where he is at prayer, and murdering him.

Four of the Ruthenian dukes, George, Rostislav, Oleg and Sviastoslav, now start a rebellion hoping to remove Izjaslav, who assembles an army and marches against them, relying on the number of his men and in disregard of the advice of the Patriarch of Kiev that he should agree peace terms. There follows a battle in which Izjaslav is finally defeated. He then withdraws to Kiev, but, fearing that his victorious adversaries will besiege him there, gathers up his wife and sons and heads for Łuck. Duke George, with the support of the other three dukes, now takes Pereiaslavl and then advances on Kiev and occupies the city, claiming it through his father and grandfather. Izjaslav, eager to avenge his recent defeat and recover Kiev, starts making lavish presents to various Poles and Hungarians, and, as a result, that winter, Bolesław of Cracow and Henry of Sandomierz, join forces with him. They are reinforced by a number of Hungarians, and they all spend the winter encamped near Czemyeryn. When the Poles and Hungarians see that Izjaslav is hesitant and timorous, they abandon him. Learning of this, Duke George and his two sons, Duke Sviatoslav and many others attack Izjaslav and besiege him in Łuck. For a long time, Izjaslav is able to hold out, but then the besiegers cut off his access to water and this forces him to negotiate for peace, which he does through the Duke of Vladimir, accepting terms he had originally rejected, and thus the siege is raised.

Conrad's son, young Henry, sends emissaries to the council that Pope Eugenius is holding in Rheims to notify the Pope of his elevation to imperial rank, conveying also a formal complaint against the three Polish dukes, asserting that in their division of the kingdom, they deprived their brother, Władysław, of his share. He lodges a further complaint against the Polish metropolitan and his suffragans, that, contrary to the oath made to his father, Prince Bolesław, they agreed to Władysław being excluded from all authority.

A.D. 1148

After less than six months in the Holy Land, and having rather increased the confusion than restored order, Conrad and Louis of France set out on their return journey. When Conrad arrives in Germany, he is approached by Władysław, who is still there in exile, begging for help for himself and his sons. Remembering that Bolesław assured him, when he was in Poland, that he would carry out his command on his return, Conrad sends to Bolesław requiring him to implement his promise and restore Władysław's share of the kingdom to him. Bolesław receives the imperial messengers with a show of considerable splendour, makes them lavish presents and dismisses them with an equivocal reply.

A.D. 1149

This reply is very badly received. The Prince of Bohemia intrigues with Władysław, who continues to pester Conrad with requests for help. In the end, Conrad announces that he is taking action against the Poles and assembles a considerable army to which the Prince of Bohemia adds his own army of Czechs and Moravians. The larger the army, the higher Władysław's hopes rise. Eventually this great army moves off and reaches the bank of the River Oder, which happens to be in spate, and there it has to halt. While thus halted, rumours reach Conrad of disturbances in Germany and this causes him to hesitate. Meanwhile Bolesław and his brothers have assembled their own army, but do not yet feel equal to a pitched battle; so, Bolesław obtains a safe-conduct and goes to Conrad's camp. There, before a large company which Conrad assembles, he tells the tale of Władysław's crimes and offences. He is so eloquent and convincing that the Emperor's anger is assuaged and he and his princes agree that this is a matter for negotiation, not for war. Conrad also remembers the hospitality he had from Bolesław. The more eminent princes and barons accompanying Conrad, having also been mollified with valuable gifts, mostly agree that the right course is withdrawal and not fighting. This idea is opposed by Władysław and his ally, the Prince of Bohemia, but they cannot alter the decision, so camp is struck and the Emperor and his army return to Germany with a bitterly disappointed Władysław.

A.D. 1150

Władysław never stops pestering Conrad to have another go at the Poles and might well have succeeded in this had not Conrad fallen sick with a long-lasting fever. However, Conrad grants him the income from a number of estates, so that he and his sons can live as befits their station. One of these sons, the under-age Conrad, nicknamed Longlegs because of his thin shanks, is sent to the Abbot of Fulda to be taught reading and good manners, perhaps in the hope that he would later decide on a career in the Church, which his parents consider more suitable for one with such ungainly legs.

A.D. 1151

Bolesław of Poland, nicknamed "the Curly", seeing that the country enjoys peace and that Divine Providence blesses his and his brothers' rule, wishing to ensure that this peace will last, contracts ties of blood with Vsevolod of Ruthenia by marrying his daughter, Anastasia. She and her large dowry are brought to Cracow by her father and other Ruthenian dukes. The wedding ceremonies last several days and are accompanied by tourneys and other knightly games. Bolesław's brother, Mieczysław, follows the other's example and marries Vsevolod's second daughter, Eudoxia, in Poznań, but his bride dies shortly afterwards without male progeny.

A.D. 1152

Conrad slowly recovers, whereupon Władysław starts pestering him again, and, finally, asks only for some soldiers. Conrad, preoccupied with the affairs of the Empire and unable to help him otherwise, gives him a small force, with which Wladyslaw strengthens the defences of the forts he had earlier built at Gródek and Niemce with ramparts, and then proceeds to raid Wrocław, which is not far away, and other places round about. This is an insult Bolesław cannot suffer. He and his brothers assemble an army and lay siege to the two forts; whereupon Władysław goes to Conrad to appeal for help. While he is absent, the two garrisons, seeing no sign of help coming from Germany, surrender on condition that they will not be treated as enemies.

A.D. 1153

The Duke of Wielkopolska, Mieczysław, nicknamed "the Old" because he displayed great prudence and commonsense at a very early age, now marries Gertrude, daughter of Blind Béla, the late King of Hungary. She is King Géza's sister and famous for her goodness and beauty. She arrives in Poland with a magnificent dowry of gold and silver vessels and other valuables, and is married in Poznań with festivities lasting several days. The object of this marriage is to erase the memory of the earlier strife between Béla and Bolesław Wry-mouth, and to ensure lasting peace and agreement between the neighbours, Poland and Hungary.

On February 19, Conrad, King of the Romans, dies; he had been afflicted with illness ever since his return from overseas. He had been ill for a considerable time, because of which he never achieved the dignity of being crowned Emperor, though he had been one in everything but name. To avoid the imperial throne remaining vacant, the Electors choose as King of the Romans, Frederick, son of the Duke of Swabia and nephew of the late Conrad.

A.D. 1154

Wry-mouth's fourth son, Henry, Duke of Sandomierz and Lublin, not wishing to marry, but intent on matters and causes of greater import, takes advantage of the prevailing peace and quiet in his duchy to assemble a force of knights, all volunteers, and with it crosses to the Holy Land, leaving his brother and monarch, Bolesław, in charge of his territories. Before leaving, he endows a parish church in one of his villages, Zagość, on the river Nida, in honour of John the Baptist, and hands it over to the Hospitallers, whose order has earned great respect by its defence of the Holy Land. He reaches the Holy Land safely, pays reverence to the Holy Sepulchre, and joins the army of Baldwin, King of Jerusalem. He distinguishes himself in battle with the Saracens and dreams of a martyr's crown, but Fate does not grant him one. After spending a whole year in the Holy Land, by which time many of his knights have been killed either in battle or by the inclement climate, Henry returns to Poland safe and sound. The many tales he has to tell do much to extend people's awareness of the state of the Holy Land and of the fierce and bloody battles being fought in its defence.

Izjaslav sends his son, Mstislav, to lead a combined force of Poles and Hungarians against Vladimirko of Galicia. The Polish contingent never turns up, but the Hungarians under King Stephen do so. Vladimirko, seeing their numbers, does not dare fight a pitched battle, but makes continual sorties from various hiding-places. When the attackers finally catch up with him, he crosses the river, in doing which many of his men drown, while others are captured or killed, and himself takes refuge in Przemyśl to which Stephen the King of Hungary then lays siege. Shortly after this, Izjaslav comes up with his army. Seeing the situation, he hands over the command to his brother, Sviatopolk, and with only a handful of men sets out to join the King; but when he reaches the River San he finds that Vladimirko has occupied all the fords, preventing him getting across. However, the King moves his army up and Vladimirko withdraws to Przemyśl and from there starts sueing for peace. Izjaslav refuses to negotiate, but the King makes a pact with Vladimirko and returns to Hungary. Izjaslav goes back to Kiev.

In this same year, George with his sons, the men of Rostov and Suzdal and the duke of Riazan, marches into Ruthenia and heads for Kiev. Izjaslav engages them and Vladimir withdraws to Halicz. Then, when George reaches Głuchów, Oleg's son, Sviatoslav, comes to his help with a large force of Polovtsy. Izjaslav sends his brother to help Izjaslav son of David, Duke of Chernigov, but then George also appears on the scene and lays siege to Chernigov. There is a fierce battle between besiegers and besieged; but when it is learned that Izjaslav is approaching, the besiegers panic and run. After this, George also withdraws and marches on Novgorod Siwerski; then, leaving his son, Vasil, in command, he continues to Suzdal. Izjaslav, failing to find George near Smolensk, marches on to Novgorod, makes peace with those who ask for it and so returns to Kiev. Vasilko sends his son, Mstislav, against the Polovtsy, collects a great booty of horses and cattle, and even the Polovtsy's tents, frees a number of Christians and returns home covered in glory.

Vladimir dies.

A.D. 1155

Prince Mieczysław builds the Cistercians a monastery in Lubiąż, traditionally the site of an ancient pagan shrine, and equips it with all the vessels, robes and liturgical ornaments needed for conducting their services. He also builds a church of dressed stone at Kalisz and there installs a prior and body of canons, all suitably endowed.

A.D. 1156

Gertrude, wife of Mieczysław of Wielkopolska, bears him a son. The babe is christened Otto.

Prince Bolesław's wife, Anastasia, gives birth to a son. The delighted father gives the babe his own name, Bolesław. Izjaslav, Prince of Kiev, eager to avenge past injuries, renews hostilities with Vladimir of Galicia. The two armies confront each other along the River Seret. Before the battle begins, it is decided that Vladimir's only son must not take part and he is sent home to Halicz. In the battle that follows, there is considerable slaughter and great confusion, for nobody can recognize anyone. Each side takes numbers of prisoners. For some reason Izjaslav's three brothers desert him, and he, afraid of again being captured, orders all but the most eminent prisoners to be killed, then makes for Kiev taking his captives with him.

A.D. 1157

On his return from Italy and France, Frederick Barbarossa summons the German princes to assemble in Würzburg, otherwise called Herbipolis, and there consults with them about declaring war on Milan, which is in open revolt against him. At this time, too, he marries Beatrice, daughter of the Duke of Burgundy. The exiled Władysław again presses his case for help, this time asking for it not so much for himself, as for his wife, the late emperor's sister, and their sons. During his long sojourn in Germany Władysław has gained the sympathy and friendship of many of the German princes and these now support his plea and call for war against Poland rather than against Milan. Since it is too early in the year for campaigning, emissaries are sent to the Polish dukes to demand in the name of the Emperor that they return his territories to Władysław, otherwise the Emperor will declare war on them. The emissaries find Bolesław in Cracow, convey the Emperor's demand and his opinion that their brother has done sufficient penance for his crimes. The Polish dukes explain that they have never committed any offence against Władysław nor gone to war with him, but only defended themselves when attacked by him. Władysław, they say, is not worthy of forgiveness, pity or intercession, because he has disregarded the ties of blood, the laws of God, man and nations, and never honoured the written, lawful clauses of his father's will. Nor did he heed the pleas of the Archbishop of Gniezno, when he trapped his brothers in Gniezno castle. They can feel pity for their brother in his long exile, but they are also afraid that, should he be allowed to return, with hatred to magnify his ambition, he will be more than ever eager to destroy them. Also, as they see it, their brother's return would inevitably lead to civil war, bloodshed and the ruin of many people. They also make it clear that they will never accept the Emperor's authority, nor pay him tribute. This answer angers, rather than placates the Emperor, and he announces a campaign against Poland for the coming summer, the *casus belli* being the Poles' opposition to his authority, their refusal to take an oath of loyalty and their failure to pay into the imperial treasury an annual tribute of 500 marks in silver required of them.

Princess Gertrude gives birth to a second son, who, at her request, is named Stephen. She dies soon afterwards.

A.D. 1158

Frederick Barbarossa assembles his army from all parts of Germany: there are Franconians, Swabians, Rhinelanders, Bavarians, Saxons, Lotharingians and Meisseners. He invades through Saxony where he is joined by Vladislav of Bohemia with his Czechs and Moravians who, despite being almost of one nation and tongue with the Poles are prepared to fight against them. The enlarged army then moves up to the River Oder, which on August 21 it manages to cross, though not without difficulty, contrary to the expectation of the Poles. The Polish soldiers are better trained, but so outnumbered that Bolesław does not dare risk a pitched battle, but contents himself with harrying and ambushing the enemy in sorties from the marshes and other hide-outs. Here, each of the dukes acts separately with his own force, killing or capturing such of the enemy as have gone off on their own to forage or loot. As well as this, the Poles burn all the places and areas through which the Emperor's army will have to pass, especially fortified towns such as Głogów and Bytom, thereby making it difficult for the Emperor to find provisions and grazing for his horses, with the result that in each camp they leave, they abandon a number of exhausted, starving animals; so that eventually much of the imperial cavalry has to be demoted to infantry. The Germans, being choosy and sensitive and accustomed to wine and beer made from barley, which they cannot get in Poland, have to drink water and this gives them diarrhoea, which spreads through the ranks until the greater part of the army is affected. No herbs or medicines can help, and the troops begin to demand to be allowed to go home, protesting that they should not be asked to continue a war that has started so inauspiciously. Although moved by these demands and the deaths of his men, the Emperor is ashamed to give in to them. He is, however, seriously concerned as to what to do, for he can see no benefit coming from the war, since the Poles will not come out to fight in the open. It is not enough for him to capture castles and towns, of which in those days there are not all that many in Poland, and most of those that there are, have been burned ahead of the Emperor's advance, leaving an army of that size with nothing to do, but devastate the countryside and burn the homes of the innocent. So, after ravaging the greater part of Wrocław and Poznań, in an attempt to find an honourable conclusion to an enterprise he now regrets having embarked on, a conclusion that will allow the withdrawal that hunger and illness now necessitate, the Emperor uses Władysław as an intermediary to persuade the Polish dukes to sue for peace, giving them to understand that any such request will be granted. Provided with safe-conducts, the three go to the Emperor's camp, where, before a number of councillors assembled in the Emperor's tent, Bolesław, speaking on behalf of all three, claims that the Emperor has never properly examined the case against them; saying that, if he had, he would never have had recourse to armed intervention. He points out that, though Władysław is the Emperor's son-in-law, they, too, are his relatives. They are there, he says, solely to present their case against Władysław accurately. The Emperor then says that he will forgive them and take his army back to Germany if Władysław has all his territories restored to him and Poland sends three hundred spearmen to fight for him in his war against Milan. The Poles accept. The agreement is further strengthened by the Duke of Wielkopolska, Mieszko, marrying the Emperor's granddaughter, Adelaide, who is given a considerable dowry.

Bolesław's wife, Anastasia, dies giving birth to a son, who survives and is named Leszek. Bolesław is heart-broken, and for a time refuses to marry again.

A considerable eclipse of the sun is seen at noon. The Sultan of Babylon captures Jerusalem: in the fighting many Christians are killed or taken prisoner. Moreover, following the eclipse there is a terrible famine which afflicts Poland and its realm.

On November 30, Izjaslav son of Mstislav the Prince of Kiev dies. David at once tries to occupy the city, but is frustrated by the dead duke's three sons. Then, Rostislav, the dead duke's brother, arrives from Chernigov and takes over the city. Meanwhile, George's son, Gleb, has brought a force of Polovtsy to Periaslavl, but the townspeople fight him and he has to withdraw. Rostislav then marches on Chernigov; whereupon Izjaslav, son of David, asks Gleb to bring his Polovtsy to help him. Rostislav halts near Białowieża, and Izjaslav and Gleb advance against him. The archers of the two armies contend for possession of the river bank; but, when Rostislav sees how numerous the enemy is, he is intimidated and sends to Izjaslav offering on his own account to surrender Kiev to him and Pereiaslavl on account of his nephew, Mstislav. This angers Mstislav, who withdraws his troops, seeing which the others take to flight pursued by the Polovtsy, who kill many and take as many prisoner. Rostislav escapes to Chernigov and Mstislav to Kiev, from where he goes to Pereiaslavl, collects his wife and takes her with him to Łuck. The people of Kiev then send for Izjaslav, who takes over. He establishes Gleb in Pereiaslavl, where the Polovtsy are on the rampage, burning churches and villages. George now advances on Kiev, which, after some parleying, Izjaslav surrenders to him so George is finally established in the city of his father and grandfather, and he divides its territories among his sons.

A.D. 1159

After thirteen years of living on charity in exile. Władysław now collects arms and horses, waggons and carts to bring his possessions back to Poland. While busied with this, he falls ill and, after a couple of weeks' suffering, dies on June 4 and is buried in Altenburg, where his wife continues to live until her death. Their three sons postpone their return to Poland, lest their uncles avenge their father's misdeeds on them.

There is another account of what happened, namely, that Władysław did return to Poland with his sons and regained his old estates, at the Emperor's expense built three forts at Wlen, Gródek and Niemce, and then declared war on his brothers. A conference was held in Płodek to bring an end to the fighting, and there Władysław was poisoned.

The Emperor Frederick assembles a huge army to which the three Polish dukes each contribute 100 spearmen, and marches into Italy. He proceeds to lay siege to Milan, an enterprise that costs him many of his knights and cavalry. In the end, he comes to an agreement with the citizens of Milan, abandons the siege and disbands the army, telling each to return to his home. The Prince of Bohemia is rewarded for taking part in all the fighting: he is crowned by the Emperor who cancels Bohemia's old emblem of a black eagle and substitutes that of a white lion.

Pope Adrian dies and is succeeded by Alexander III, previously called Roland; but Octavian, who takes the name of Victor, is also elected Pope, thus initiating the dangerous schism that is to trouble the Church for years to come. Octavian is consecrated Pope on the first Sunday in September, and Roland on September 18.

A.D. 1160

Princess Adelaide, recently married to Mieczysław of Wielkopolska, bears him a son, who is given the name Bolesław. At the christening ceremony, which is attended by the other dukes, pressure is put on Bolesław the Curly to renounce widowhood and once more assume the yoke of marriage; so, on his return to Cracow, he marries Helena, the maiden daughter of the Duke of Przemyśl.

A.D. 1161

The Emperor is furious with the Milanese: they who had been on the point of executing his envoys, though these had managed to escape, and who had killed or captured many of his soldiers who had strayed from the camps round the city; so he orders a new campaign and an even stricter siege of the city, swearing not to give up until he has defeated the Milanese. Bolesław the Tall, eldest son of the late, exiled Władysław, disliking the idea of a life of lazy inactivity, leaves his two younger brothers in their mother's care and joins the Emperor's camp before Milan, hoping for an opportunity to prove his valour. Some time after this, a Milanese knight of unusual stature and strength rides out from the city and challenges the Emperor's knights to a duel. He does this several days running without anyone in the Emperor's camp feeling inclined to take so obvious a risk. The huge knight then accuses the Emperor's knights of cowardice and effeminacy. Young Duke Bolesław sees this as an opportunity and, without consulting the Emperor, rides out to take up the challenge. The Emperor's troops stream out from their camp to watch, and the Milanese line their walls and towers. The Emperor's troops are anxious and angry with Bolesław for exposing himself to the danger of so unequal a fight without the permission of his superiors; for, if he loses, it will shame not only him, but the Emperor and his army, and so they watch in silence as the two couch their lances and spur their horses. The Milanese giant misses his thrust, but Bolesław's lance strikes him fair and square and knocks him out of the saddle, mortally wounded. Bolesław, who is unusually agile, leaps from his horse, despatches the recumbent knight, strips the body of its harness and, remounting, rides back to the loud applause of the Emperor's troops, leaving the dead giant on the ground. Later, he takes the armour and presents it to the Emperor in the presence of a crowd of knights, who clamour for him to be fittingly rewarded. The Emperor assures them that this shall be done; but, later he sends for young Bolesław and, in private, reproaches him for his thoughtlessness in embarking on anything so hazardous without permission, and tells him that this must never happen again.

On May 30, Géza, King of Hungary, dies and his son, Stephen is crowned in his place.

A.D. 1162

Jaksa of Miechów, a young Polish noble, owner of extensive estates in the diocese of Cracow, inspired by love of God and Our Saviour Jesus Christ, went with his servants and esquires to help in the Holy Land and for some time was there fighting bravely; now the time has come for him to return to Poland and he obtains permission from the Patriarch of Jerusalem, as head of the monastery of the Austin canons of the Holy Sepulchre, who wear a double red cross, for one of their canons to accompany him home in order to establish a new foundation of the Order in Poland, and this he endows with three villages of his patrimony. Since then the village of Miechów has developed into a populous, wealthy town. Now, with the special permission of Matthew the Bishop of Cracow, Jaksa builds a church there and also the town's first monastery. He also founds a convent in the village of Wierzyniec, near Cracow, for girls wishing to live according to the rule of the Premonstratensians, and this too he endows with several villages. In order to ensure that his descendants should not at any time in the future abrogate or diminish his endowments, he humbly begs Bolesław to confirm the arrangements he has made. Bolesław acquiesces and relieves the new endowments of all duties to the Prince, burdens and dues. He also rules that the inhabitants of these villages need not perform military service, nor be put to building forts, nor pay pradlne (a form of land tax) or strozy (guard tax), should not be subject to the moneyer or obliged to perform powoz (transport) or podwody (cartage). The two foundations are later to expand and grow rich from gifts from dukes, bishops and the nobility.

Duke George breaks his promise and declares war on Mstislav and his brothers. Mstislav seeks refuge in Vladimir castle, to which George then lays siege. Throughout the siege, besiegers and besieged fight many bloody battles. Some Polish knights who have remained in Mstislav's service cover themselves with glory. George declares himself ready to make peace, if the other will sue for it, but Mstislav is stubborn and refuses to do this; so, having achieved nothing, George returns to Kiev with his tail between his legs.

A.D. 1163

After a siege lasting the best part of three years, the city of Milan falls to the Emperor, who orders its walls and towers to be demolished and razed to the ground before his eyes. The conquered city is then looted of its temporal and sacred possessions. Milan having fallen, the other cities of Lombardy and Tuscany, except Pavia, which alone has obeyed the Emperor, also surrender. The Emperor now dismisses the princes and their armies which have fought for him. Among those who now go home is Duke Bolesław taking with him his share of the booty and the Emperor's gifts. The Emperor even writes to Bolesław the Curly and his two brothers recommending Bolesław, prais-

An unknown soldier of the Crusades. This unfinished sculpture of a European Crusader was found in the ruins of Montfort Castle and is now in Israel Museum. Dated to the 14th century.
—Israel Museum.

ing his courage and demanding that, in accordance with the agreement they have made, Boleslaw and his two brothers should have their dukedoms restored to them. This letter is taken by the Emperor's own envoys, who are instructed to repeat the demand verbally, and, if this has no effect, to use threats. Afraid of the Emperor's wrath, the three Polish dukes agree and settle Silesia on the three in perpetuity. Silesia, through which the river Oder flows, extends from its frontier with Saxony to the mountains of Bohemia and contains two dioceses of note: Wrocław and Lubusz. Several knights are sent to escort the three exiles home. They are graciously received and granted the permanent possession of the whole of Silesia from the Alps to the forest of Herczyń. To avoid quarrels, Silesia is divided between the three thus: Bolesław the Tall gets Wrocław; Mieczysław gets Racibórz and Opava; Conrad gets Głogów and Krosno. Prince Bolesław reminds the three that they come under his authority, that they must be careful not to imitate the thoughtless tyranny of their father, lest they suffer the same fate; and that they are to remember that the lands allotted to them are not theirs by right, but charity, the gift of their uncles, and not in any way redress. All three then set about endeavouring to improve their territories which have been so badly torn by domestic

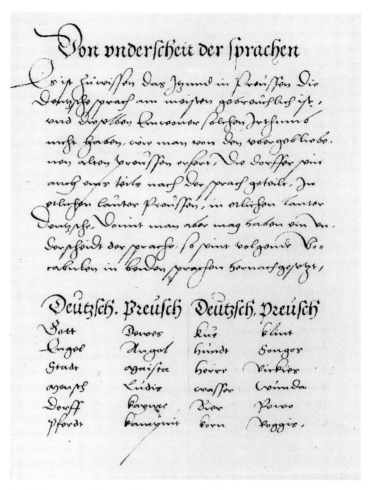

Part of an early 16th century German–Prussian vocabulary now in the Niedersächische Staats- und Universitäts-Bibliothek, Göttingen.

strife and foreign invasion, and before long Silesia is once again flourishing. Only Mieczysław, bewitched by a loose woman, proves crazy enough to give her for her own for ever the important town of Opava, which is part of his share. Later, Conrad dies an early death, when, since he was childless, his share is divided between the other two.

A.D. 1164

With the Emperor and Germany no longer a threat and none of Poland's neighbours showing signs of hostile intent, Bolesław, with the consent of the Polish dukes, announces an expedition against the Prussians, a nation hitherto pagan, in order to convert them to the Christian faith and subject them to his authority. Having assembled an army, he crosses the River Ossa, which divides the two countries, and advances inland with his army arrayed in three lines: the first under the command of Henry the Duke of Sandomierz; the second commanded by Mieszko the Duke of Wielkopolska, and the third by Bolesław himself. However, the Prussians, seeing that they are unable to resist, retreat into their forests and marshes and other impenetrable places, from which, wherever the terrain permits it, they sally out at night and harass the Poles, without ever engaging them in open battle. By the time the Poles have devastated half the country, the Prussians come to Bolesław asking for peace and promising to do whatever he orders. Bolesław tells them that, first, they must renounce the nastiness and errors of their pagan ways and confess the pure Catholic faith, without which they can expect no peace. If they do this, he will guarantee them peace and just conditions. The Prussians find such conditions too severe and arduous, so they go away and report back to their elders. The noise the crowd makes, when the people hear what is required of them, shows that they find such conditions unacceptable, but the elders, having quelled the murmuring, advise the people to accept, for otherwise they will never be rid of the Poles; whereas, if they accept, once the Poles have withdrawn, they can fail to carry the conditions out. So the envoys of this cunning and crafty people go back to Bolesław and tell him that they will renounce their superstitions and pagan error, demolish their shrines, throw down their idols, pronounce their adherence to the Catholic faith and be cleansed with the water of baptism. Bolesław and the dukes then settle with the Prussian elders the extent of their obligations, and, meanwhile, churches are built and clergy, especially those who speak or understand Prussian, are brought in to teach these neophytes. The Prussian district is entrusted to the Bishop of Chełmno. Finally, at Bolesław's suggestion, they issue an edict to the effect that all who now or in the future publicly confess the new faith are to be free men, while those who refuse baptism will be sold at public auction. This frightens even the most obdurate, who prefer baptism to slavery. Bolesław then imposes a small tribute on them, small because of their acceptance of the Catholic faith, the spread of which Bolesław is anxious to aid, and marches his army back to Poland, unaware that he has had the wool pulled over his eyes.

Eudoxia, wife of the Duke of Wielkopolska, gives birth to a second son, who is named after his father, Mieczysław.

The two brothers, Stephen and Lászlo of Hungary cannot agree as to who is to rule the country. Lászlo cannot accept that his brother should have the crown instead of him, and, influenced by certain Hungarians who are always on the look-out for change, invades Hungary and turns for help to the King of Bohemia, who is tempted by his promises. King Stephen, who wants to resist, as he should, obtains help from the Greek Emperor, Kalojan, who is a relative of his wife. Thus does the kingdom of Hungary fall prey to the plundering of its own and foreign soldiery; indeed, the Greek and Czech troops confine their activities to plundering and looting, and never fight officially. In the end, thanks to the intervention of the Greek Emperor and the King of Bohemia, Lászlo makes peace with Stephen, contenting himself with Transylvania. The King of Bohemia now makes the Greek Emperor his relative by marrying his granddaughter to the nephew of the Greek Emperor.

On May 15, George, Prince of Kiev, dies. A number of the Ruthenian dukes make a grab for the capital, but, thanks to the support of the people of Kiev, it is Izjaslav, son of David, who gets it.

A.D. 1165

The Prussians' insincere acceptance of Christianity, forced on them by Bolesław, lasts less than a year. The Prussians have never been accustomed to bowing their proud necks to the yoke of any faith, so now they begin divesting themselves of that of Christianity, so recently assumed, and return to their old pagan rites. The priests and servants of God, whom Bolesław left to educate them, are sent back to Poland and told never to return under pain of death; and at the same time, lest Bolesław declare war on them again, they send envoys to him with gifts and the tribute due. In an attempt to justify their apostasy and avoid another war, they beg Bolesław not to hold it against them, for they do find the Christian faith too arduous and it is difficult for them to abandon the gods of their fathers whom they have honoured for so long or to give up making the sacrifices they have been accustomed to make. They are not refusing submission and loyalty to Bolesław and Poland, and will pay the tribute asked; but in return they ask that they be allowed to retain their old customs and rituals, assuring Bolesław that they will honourably pay the tribute imposed on them, take part in wars on his side, and loyally and sincerely obey all his commands, except the acceptance of Christianity. At the same time they threaten that, should they be forced to live according to Polish, Christian ways and not those of their fathers, they will have to break loose from his authority. Bolesław, whether influenced by their arguments or their gifts, gives in all too easily and accepts this dreadful crime of apostasy. He shows no eagerness to punish it or to end it; but appears indifferent and unconcerned. So the Prussian envoys are dismissed with his tacit acceptance of their revolt and apostasy, and no attempt is made to punish them.

A.D. 1166

The Prussians now go on to break faith in temporal matters, discarding the yoke of subjection and bondage. Not only do they refuse to pay taxes and tribute, but they injure some of the starostas, whose duty it was to collect such dues, even going so far as to kill some and forcibly expel others from the country. Not content with this, they assemble a considerable army of both peasants and nobles, and swiftly invade the lands of Chełmno and Mazovia, neither of which has been anticipating any such move. After devastating many villages and towns, the Prussians collect a great booty of cattle and whatever else has whetted their appetite, slaughter people and carry off many more into captivity. When Bolesław learns of this, he hurriedly gets a scratch force together and sets off to liberate the country. When told that the enemy has retreated with its booty into its fastnesses, he is dreadfully upset and does not know what to do: should he pursue the enemy into the forests and marshes or give up? He can see the sense of waiting until later before dealing with the Prussians, especially as his force is too small to be sure of being safe from an enemy more accustomed to subterfuge than armed conflict. So, leaving garrisons in many sites guarding tributaries of the River Ossa, so as to prevent the Prussians making unexpected raids, he returns home and there proclaims a full-scale expedition against the Prussians.

On October 10, the Bishop of Cracow, Matthew, dies. He had always been a lover of feasting and ostentation, and, it is said that, once, when Bolesław sent officials to ask him for financial help, the Bishop ordered them to be shown the episcopal privy, saying that was where they should seek such treasure as he had, meaning that all his income as a bishop had gone on food, so that it was useless to ask him for money.

A.D. 1167

All arrangements for war on the Prussians having been made, at the onset of summer, Bolesław the Curly's army, all the larger since the country is not under threat from any of its neighbours, advances into Prussia. Bolesław has been joined by two of his brothers, Henry and Mieczysław, whose territories have also suffered from Prussian raids. Such extensive preparations could not be kept hidden from the Prussians, who, seeing themselves faced with defeat and gruesome punishment, decide to have recourse to cunning and deceit. Here they are at an advantage, for there are in the Polish army four Prussian deserters, who over the years have won the sympathy and favour of Bolesław and who, once the army is in enemy territory, act as the army's guides. They choose the camp sites, decide the route the army is to take, what places are accessible and which are to be avoided; in fact, the entire conduct of the advance is left to them. These four the enemy succeeds in bribing with lavish gifts and even more generous promises, also by reminding them that this is their home and their people, and that what is at stake is not just the avoidance of submission, but Prussia's complete destruction. They must remember, they are told, that they were not born in Poland, but in Prussia, where their ancestors lived and their relatives still live. They alone can prevent their country's downfall. The four let themselves be persuaded and agree to betray the Polish army, which has already penetrated deep into the interior, burning as it goes, intending to continue thus into the farthest reaches of the country. The four deserters are with the forward units, which are under the command of Duke Henry of Sandomierz, and these they now lead into trackless forest. Behind them comes the second rank under Duke Mieczysław of Wielkopolska with Bolesław and the cream of the knights well in the rear. They have to cross ravines, forest fastnesses and finally emerge into an area of marsh, bog and quagmire, where everything is slippery because of incessant rain, and the only grass is that which covers the surface of what is a bottomless pit. The four traitors encourage the marchers by saying that once through this difficult stretch they will find a populous area with lots of cattle. Then, when the forward units are jammed in a narrow defile, the Prussians emerge from their hiding places and shoot at them from a distance without themselves coming under attack. Unable to advance or retreat, the Poles flounder in the bog and those who do not drown are picked off by the Prussian archers. Henry, who is in the first line, receives several wounds and dies along with many of his knights, while those behind press forward in a frenzy and are themselves killed by the Prussian spears and javelins, for the Prussians are now in front and behind and on either side; but a worse peril than their spears and javelins is the bog. The number of those who, burdened with armour, sink in and are swallowed by the mud is greater than that of those actually killed. Still the Poles in the rear come on, climbing over the bodies of the dead and fighting, until they, too, fall. Almost the entire flower of Polish chivalry falls here and their banners are gathered up by the enemy. The body of the Duke of Sandomierz, shamefully stripped of its badges of rank, is swallowed by the bog along with those of many others. Bolesław and Mieczysław both survive and with the remnants of the army return to Poland, desperate with grief. Now and for many years the laments and recriminations of the wives and friends of the dead continue to be heard. It is difficult to say how many excellent young men, veteran soldiers and horses; or how much armour, what wealth, was engulfed in this disaster for the Poles and victory for the Prussians, which these of course attribute to their old gods and sacrilegious beliefs.

A.D. 1168

The disaster suffered in Prussia plunges Poland into a depression that is to last for a long time. An ugly glum silence prevails, for people are so ashamed of the wretched conduct of the war. There is hardly a house in the country that does not mourn a brother or a relative. People close their ears to words of comfort. Then Bolesław and Mieczysław summon an assembly of the country's prelates and barons to decide what is to be done with Sandomierz, since Henry, being unmarried, has left no heir. After much discussion, it is decided that Bolesław Wry-mouth's fifth son, Casimir, who was left nothing in his father's will and is now a man of over thirty, should take over the vacant duchy. Hitherto, he has been living off the generosity of Bolesław, who now complains of the heavy demands made on him by the government of the country. So Bolesław is granted for his lifetime the greater part of the duchy of Sandomierz, the town itself, its tolls and the dues of the territories belonging to it; with Casimir having the reversion after his death. Then, giving way to pressure from his brothers and the more influential men in the duchy, Casimir marries Helena, daughter of Vsevolod, Duke of Bełz, a girl of Ruthenian origin. In view of the recent disaster, the wedding is celebrated without great ceremony.

Eudoxia, Duchess of Wielkopolska, gives birth to a son, who is christened Władysław.

A.D. 1169

The wounds of the Prussian disaster have scarcely begun to heal, before Bolesław has a fresh war on his hands. His nephews: Bolesław the Tall, Mieczysław and Conrad the Flat-footed, to whom he had given Silesia when they returned from exile, now take up arms against him in an attempt to avenge the injuries suffered by their father and recover the lands left them in their father's will: claiming the duchy of Cracow and the monarchy by right of inheritance from their father. Having obtained reinforcements from their mother's relations in Germany, they start a civil war more dangerous than the war with Prussia, which destroyed Poland's armed strength and put the three in this favourable position. First, they devastate Poznań. Bolesław, well aware that he has no army left and can scarcely hope to persuade others to do military service, sees that he must negotiate peace, so the prelates and his lay advisers arrange for the two sides to meet. Bolesław starts by questioning the reason for their declaration of war, arguing that the principality of Cracow was never part of anyone's share, but legally can only be inherited by the monarch and thus, on his father's death, the right to it passed to him as the eldest son and elected monarch. The towns in Silesia that Bolesław retained as a symbol of his supreme authority as monarch, he kept legitimately to offset the burden of the cost of government, which fell on him. Part of the duchy of Sandomierz and Lublin he says belongs solely to Casimir, who till then had enjoyed no inheritance from his father. In the opinion of the assembled councillors Bolesław's arguments outweigh the complaints of his nephews and it is agreed that the war on which these have embarked is not justified; nevertheless, to placate his nephews, Bolesław agrees to surrender the towns he holds in Silesia and allow them to be divided among his nephews.

A.D. 1170

Two knights, Jaksa of Miechów and Świętosław as well as nearly all the leaders in the duchy of Cracow now dislike the rule of Bolesław the Curly, whom they consider to be less zealous for the good of the country than he should be, and whom they blame for many of its misfortunes. They now conspire to remove him. In their opinion the duchy and the monarchy should go to Casimir, whose unusual integrity they admire and also because, if this happens, they will not have Mieczysław forced upon them as king when Bolesław dies, which they expect to happen soon, since they consider him exhausted by age. So, they exhort Casimir to accept the government and so avoid the country going from bad to worse, because of Bolesław's sloth and neglect, but Casimir feels that it would be ugly and unjust to expel his ageing brother, who in his youth had been his kind and generous guardian and, still more important, had done his country great service; he will not countenance anything so disgraceful and talk of rebellion dies out.

Mstislav son of Izjaslav, Duke of Vladimir, in a fit of anger, exiles his own son, Vladimir, who has evicted his, Mstislav's, uncle Rostislav from Kiev. When Rostislav then takes refuge with the Polovtsy, Andrew, Duke of Suzdal finds this unacceptable and sends his son Mstislav with knights from Rostov and Vladimir to turn Mstislav of Vladimir out of Kiev. As many people heartily dislike Mstislav, the Ruthenian dukes assemble their forces to help Andrew, and together they besiege Kiev where Mstislav has shut himself up in the castle; he holds out for a time, but then, unable to face starvation, he leaves with his brother and a few companions and goes back to Vladimir. The dukes then capture Kiev castle and take Mstislav's wife prisoner, as well as his son and a number of knights. They then allow the city to be sacked. The soldiers loot not only the private houses, but also the churches and monasteries. Kiev is now given to Gleb, the brother of Andrew, Duke of Suzdal.

For the last fourteen years the see of Płock has been occupied by a man of unusual piety, immaculate life and unusual virtue, Bishop Werner. The Bishop now learns that the governor of Mazovia, Bolesta the Castellan of Wizna, a man of enormous wealth and many friends, has occupied a village which belongs to the see of Płock; first he reminds the Castellan gently and in private that he must not appropriate land that is dedicated to God, and that, if he continues to do so, he cannot avoid God's punishment. The arrogant Castellan replies that if the Bishop tries to reprimand him he will appropriate more of the church's land, and he also threatens to kill the Bishop. The Bishop then summons the Castellan before the land-court in the hope that a severe judgment might put an end to his greedy behaviour. The court pronounces Bishop Werner to be in the right and orders the Castellan to return the village. The Castellan is furious and curses the Bishop and, indeed, does all he can to have him murdered. The Castellan has long had close relations with the pagan Prussians, his neighbours. He is also the highest authority in that corner of Wizna, a post to which Bolesław appointed him, but when people complain of theft, looting, raids and other crimes committed by the Prussians, his judgment always favours the latter: sometimes the Prussian spokesmen, as is the custom of that people, bring him gifts and he reciprocates in kind which makes the Prussians more than ever inclined to do whatever the Castellan wished; so now, when a large number of Prussians happen to arrive in a village under the Castellan's authority and which he happens to be visiting, he first gives them gifts and promises, then takes them to his house and the next night provides them with a splendid banquet. Once they are suitably tipsy, the Castellan, whose spies have told him that Bishop Werner is due to arrive in the Bishop's village of Biskupiec the following day, summons his brother the Prussian commander, Bjebisz, and says: "Why don't you punish Bishop Werner, who is appropriating our possessions under our very eyes? Why not do away with him?" Wishing to do what his brother wishes, Bjebisz collects all the Prussians present and takes them off to the village. This they reach just before dawn, when the Bishop is in a bedroom with Brother Benedict. The Prussians break the lock, rush in and kill the two men. They then cover the corpses with rugs, chaff and twigs and depart. The Bishop's man-servant, terrified, had hidden under the Bishop's bed and so had seen everything, and he now tells what he has seen. After this, the Castellan can never show himself in public. He is never seen and it is popularly believed that the earth swallowed him up three days after the murder. In fact, Prince Bolesław, fearing lest he and the country may be severely punished for the bishop's murder—the Archbishop of Gniezno having already placed an interdict on the whole of Poland—sends soldiers to arrest the Castellan, who is then brought to Gniezno. Bolesław presides over an assembly at which the archbishop of Gniezno, Gideon of Cracow and Bernard of Poznań are present. The Castellan does not dare deny the crime, knowing that there are a great number of witnesses who can testify against him, and he is condemned to be burned at the stake. The method adopted is not the usual one, for the Castellan is wrapped in a freshly woven piece of cloth which has been soaked in wax, and is then burned on a huge pyre in the main square of Gniezno in the presence of Bolesław and his knights.

Since then, Bishop Werner has become famous for performing miracles. The use of his name has enabled the halt to walk, the blind to see, has cured lepers and raised paralytics from their beds, even brought the dead back to life.

On May 6, Mieczysław, or Mieszko, Duke of Wielkopolska and Pomerania, wishing to show his concern for the poor and the unfortunate in Poznań, after seeking the advice of Bishop Radovanus, endows a hospital beside the church of St. Michael, which he entrusts to the Hospitallers of St. John of Jerusalem, granting them in perpetuity nine estates and their revenue. To this the Bishop adds the tithes from these properties and six others in his possession.

A.D. 1171

Bishop Gideon of Cracow builds a church of dressed stone in Kielce, then a remote town in a thick forest far from habitation, and endows it suitably.

A.D. 1172

Prince Bolesław the Curly's eldest son dies, to his father's immense grief.

Duke Gleb dies after ruling for two years in Kiev. Andrew, Duke of Suzdal, replaces him with Roman, Duke of Smolensk, who appoints his son, Iaropolk, to succeed him in Smolensk, but in course of time Iaroslav son of Izjaslav drives Roman out and himself rules Kiev.

A.D. 1173

The passage of time rather than reason heals the pain of the death of Bolesław's son; now a sudden languor makes Bolesław himself take to his bed. When he realizes that his state is deteriorating, he sends for his youngest brother, Casimir, the prelates and barons of the kingdom, and distributes his estates, possessions and valuables. The duchies of Mazovia and Kujawy he grants to Leszek, his only surviving son. He appoints his brother, Duke Casimir, guardian of his son and wife, begging him in his turn to give them the same protection as he had received in his childhood. His valuables and jewels he divides between his wife, Maria, Casimir of Sandomierz and his son, Leszek. Then, having received the sacrament, he dies on October 30, having ruled Poland for twenty-nine years.

After Bolesław's death, Mieczysław of Wielkopolska and Pomerania, Casimir of Sandomierz and Bolesław, Mieczysław and Conrad the dukes of Silesia, all being family members, hold an assembly in Cracow to decide on the new ruler. The Cracovians favour Casimir of Sandomierz, but yield to the insistence of those others who want Mieczysław the Old, Duke of Wielkopolska and Pomerania, who is duly elected prince and ruler, whereupon the castle, city and surrounding country of Cracow are handed over to him.

Stephen, King of Hungary, threatened with rebellion and mutiny, fights it out on the Feast of SS Gervase and Protase. Many are killed and Stephen seeks refuge in Zimony castle, where he dies on April 11, to be succeeded by his brother, Béla.

A.D. 1174

Mieczysław, Duke of Wielkopolska and Pomerania, successor to Bolesław the Curly, fails to live up to people's expectation that under his rule they would be able to lead happy, peaceful lives; indeed, he discredits himself at the very outset of his reign with ugly acts of tyranny. The extraordinary mental maturity that, as a lad, had earned him the soubriquet "the Old", seems to have deserted him on his promotion. He enjoys a certain reputation because of his wealth and his children, especially his five sons: Otto and Stephen by his first wife, a daughter of the King of Hungary, and Bolesław, Mieczysław and Władysław by a cousin of the Emperor Frederick; for Otto marries a daughter of the Duke of Galicia; Bolesław weds a daughter of one of the dukes of Pomerania and Władysław a daughter of the Prince of Rügen; while the other two died without marrying. Of Mieczysław's many daughters, one marries Soběslav of Bohemia, another is the wife of the Duke of Saxony; a third marries the Duke of Lorraine; a fourth is the wife of the Duke of Szczecin, while the fifth marries the latter's son, Boguslav. Because of all this and his other gifts, Mieczysław has been regarded as one of the most fortunate of mortals; nonetheless, he abuses the talents given him and it is now, yielding to the persuasion of perverse councillors, especially that of Henry of Kietlicz, his adviser and mentor in all his undertakings, that he starts extorting tribute from his own subjects. For such a trivial offence as killing a bear, a hind or other forest game, the Prince's officials ruthlessly punish knights as well as peasants, confiscating the culprit's property, partly for the Treasury and partly to fill their own pockets. When their victim's complaints reach Mieczysław, he either turns a deaf ear to them or rejects them out of hand. All that concerns him is money and gifts. He becomes a greedy extortioner, cruel and vindictive; while the duchy's courts of justice and administration are all but ineffective.

At a congress in Nuremberg, the Emperor removes Vladislav from the throne of Bohemia and replaces him with Soběslav, whom Vladislav has held in prison for seventeen years so as to prevent him inciting rebellion, and who has only been released at the Emperor's express command. Vladislav is afraid to remain in the country lest Soběslav, remembering what he has suffered at the latter's hands, should avenge himself, and so he moves to Germany and there dies four months later. His son also leaves Bohemia and goes into voluntary exile at the Emperor's court.

Sobiesław, Duke of Pomerania, dies and is buried in the monastery of Oliwa which he founded. He leaves two sons, Mszczuj and Sambor.

Thomas, Bishop of Canterbury, long a champion of the freedom of the Church, returning after seven years in exile imposed on him by King Henry, suffers a glorious martyrdom, being murdered by the English at the door of his church. After this, his name is added to the role of the saints.

A.D. 1175

Mieczysław's oppression of his subjects becomes more and more onerous. There are endless complaints of how people have been deprived of their possessions as a result of false information laid against them. None of the Prince's councillors has the courage to condemn such acts or to rebuke the Prince, until the Bishop of Cracow, Gideon, a man very zealous and given to plain speaking, moved by the tears of the sufferers, goes to the Prince and, after requesting the removal of all witnesses, courageously puts forward the case of the oppressed and asks the Prince to remove the taxes he has imposed, which are such as no prince before has ever inflicted on his own people, and to relieve the peasants of the illegal, unnecessary burden of having to provide cartage, and to stop the confiscation of people's property for trivial offences, which has reduced so many to penury; in other words, to be a kind father to his people and not a hated tyrant. Mieczysław's only response is a furious outburst in which the Bishop is told that everything that Mieczysław has done has been right and legal, including the new taxes and the imposition of cartage, and that without these he cannot govern the country. What earlier kings and princes have done, the Bishop is told, is no concern of the Prince, who is guided by his own good sense and reason, not by the example of others. The Bishop is further told that, in future, he must confine himself to episcopal matters and leave secular affairs to his Prince. The Bishop then withdraws, a sadder man than when he came.

On May 1, Bolesław the Tall, Duke of Wrocław, removes the black monks from the monastery of Lubiąż on the River Oder, the foundation of King Casimir who was once a monk of Cluny, and replaces them with Cistercians from Porta, a monastery on the River Saale, adding to the latter's privileges and possessions. The first abbot of this new foundation is Florencius, after whom and the brethren who came with him from Porta, is named a kind of apple: Daport, i.e. de Porta; which they had brought with them and which is still very popular.

A.D. 1176

Gideon, Bishop of Cracow, once again rebukes Mieczysław, only this time in public. Again this calls forth a furious outburst, the Prince threatening to avenge himself on the Bishop and those lords who support him by confiscating their possessions and exiling them; the laymen supporting the Bishop are even threatened with death or the loss of limbs. War breaks out between Soběslav of Bohemia and Henry of Austria, with the result that each burns and loots the other's territories, causing considerable damage. During the fighting, Henry breaks a leg while crossing a bridge, and dies. After this, the Emperor takes a dislike to Soběslav, regarding him as responsible for the death of his kinsman Henry.

The Duke of Sandomierz endows a Cistercian monastery in his duchy, choosing for it a beautiful site on the bank of the River Pilica at Sulejów on land that belonged to Count Rasław, who had died childless and made Christ his heir. As its founder and guardian, Casimir endows it with land, tithes, an income from salt and many chattels, as well as exempting its properties from all dues. It is granted thirteen vills and thirteen blocks of salt to be taken in Sandomierz, and a trough of salt from Cracow, plus nine beavers from Casimir's own store. Later, the Archbishop of Gniezno adds sheaf tithes from his own table of six vills and the church in Baldrzyków with tithe of three vills.

A.D. 1177

Bishop Gideon and the chief persons of Cracow secretly discuss what is to be done about Mieczysław, who, they see, cannot be turned from tyranny. The Bishop points to the dangers they and the country will face if they delay taking action, and all agree that they must get rid of Mieczysław and replace him, but with whom? This proves a problem and occasions lengthy discussions, until the Voivode of Cracow reminds them of the dangers of delay and also that not far away is the ideal candidate: Casimir, Duke of Sandomierz, whose manner is charming, and his speech grave; he has great understanding of people and is always eager to help the unfortunate. Though ready to forgive misdemeanours, he hates and severely punishes slanderers, whom he has branded with a red-hot iron on forehead, cheek or nose, their tongue mutilated, or has them blinded or flogged. He devotes all his income to the benefit of his realm. He eats and rests only as much as Nature insists on his doing. Idleness he abhors, and he makes a daily necessity of taking exercise: fencing, hunting, jousting or other knightly exercises, but that only when he has dealt with all important matters of state. This suggestion is adopted unanimously, and the Bishop and the principal laymen go from the meeting straight to Sandomierz, where, granted a private audience, they tell Casimir how, both privately and publicly, they have entreated his brother to give up acts of violence and oppression, yet to no avail, indeed, their pleas have only earned them his enmity and threats of exile or execution. Because of this they have come to ask Casimir to assume the powers of monarch and liberate the country, for they can no longer tolerate the rule of his brother, who acts as if he were an enemy to them and their country. In his reply Casimir reminds them that once before he was asked to do this and refused, because he felt it wrong to displace his brother, Bolesław, who had always been so kind to him. Bishop Gideon then points out that the two cases are quite dissimilar, for Bolesław ruled in accordance with justice and the law, while Mieczysław has taken to tyranny and refuses to give it up; thus Casimir will earn enduring fame and the blessings of them all if he will come to the help of Poland and its downtrodden people.

Having listened to all that they have to say, Casimir finally agrees to take over as monarch, not from any desire for power or out of envious pride, but solely for love of his country. Then, with a modest escort of his knights he sets out for Cracow in the company of Bishop Gideon and the other Cracovians. Mieczysław is not in his capital, but elsewhere in his duchy of Wielkopolska and Pomerania nor does he return but takes up residence with his wife and three sons in Racibórz. When they reach Cracow, they are welcomed by a host of knights and nobles. Villagers come crowding in from outside, calling a welcome to one whom they regard as their country's saviour.

At this juncture, the expulsion of Mieczysław from his duchy enables the starostas and government officials to hand over the city and castle of Cracow without difficulty or resistance. The other castles and fortresses follow Cracow's example and voluntarily submit to Casimir.

The stream of accusations levelled against Soběslav of Bohemia by Frederick, the exiled son of the former King Vladislav, and his Czech supporters, of which Soběslav makes no attempt to clear himself, finally convinces the Emperor, who formally removes him from the Bohemian throne and replaces him with Frederick, whom he invests and presents with the Czech standard. Meanwhile, Soběslav and Conrad, whose territory Soběslav has invaded with evil intent, are fighting each other. There is a pitched battle in which, thanks to the help Conrad receives from the Austrians, Soběslav is defeated and escapes back to Bohemia. This defeat of his enemy encourages Frederick and makes him feel confident that he can expel Soběslav from Bohemia.

There is an eclipse of the sun on September 30.

A.D. 1178

Duke Mieczysław of Wielkopolska and Pomerania has taken his expulsion ill and now seeks both to avenge himself on Casimir and the others who have removed him as monarch, and to get himself reinstated. His advisers are unanimous in demanding military action and insist that on no account must he knuckle under and accept things as they are. However, knowing that, after what he has done to the country, he can expect no help from his former subjects, he seeks the help of neighbouring princes and of his sons-in-law, from whom he asks for armies. Soběslav of Bohemia replies that he has a war of his own on his hands, and the Dukes of Saxony and Lorraine also excuse themselves by saying that they have already sent their armies to the Emperor in Italy, who is now asking for further help for a war to recover the Holy Land.

Sambor the Duke of Pomerania founds a Cistercian monastery in his village of Oliwa and endows it with seven villages and the revenue from tolls, fishing, farms and cattle.

Soběslav, Prince of Bohemia, informed of the approach of his brother, Frederick, with an army of Germans and Czech deserters bent on ejecting him, himself assembles an army and awaits Frederick's arrival. Frederick, however, cunningly delays his advance, whereupon Soběslav, thinking the danger over, disbands his army, thus leaving the way open for Frederick to march into the country. Soběslav tries to bar his way with a scratch force so small—for there is no time to recall the whole army—that it is easily defeated. Soběslav himself manages to escape. Frederick continues his advance and lays siege to Prague, where Soběslav's wife is living, and quickly captures it. He puts in a strong garrison, for he thinks that if he holds Prague, the conquest of the rest of the country will be easier.

A.D. 1179

Mieczysław encounters further misfortunes in his attempts to regain the monarchy. When Otto, his eldest son by his first marriage, discovers that at the honeyed insistence of his second wife, his father is intending to leave the greater part of his duchies to his sons by her, he starts plotting against his father with some of the nobles of Wielkopolska. Choosing a favourable moment, the conspirators occupy Mieczysław's castles and forts in Wielkopolska and eject Mieczysław from his capital. Otto then sends emissaries to Casimir to promise complete obedience and collaboration, and putting all his castles, fortresses and soldiers at his disposal. Casimir takes only Gniezno and its surroundings for himself, and this he does because of its former lustre and fame, all the rest of Mieczysław's holdings he places in Otto's hands; but both parts of Pomerania which were obedient to Mieczysław submit directly to Casimir. In view of their distance from the capital, Casimir appoints Bogusław governor of Western Pomerania, formerly called Słupsk, and places Eastern Pomerania, whose principal city is Gdańsk, under Baron Sambor.

In Silesia the sons of Władysław the Tall are in dispute: young Mieczysław having removed old Bolesław from his duchy; though, initially, they refuse Casimir obedience, thanks to his maturity and perspicacity, the two brothers are reconciled: Mieczysław being forced to give up the duchy of Wrocław which he has been trying to occupy, despite Fate having allocated it to Bolesław, and they accept Casimir's authority. To ensure order now and in the future, Casimir gives Mieczysław two districts taken from the diocese of Cracow and also invites him to the christening of his infant son, who is to be given his father's name, Casimir. Mazovia and Kujawy, which are held by his nephew, Leszek, are governed by Count Żyra, an elderly man of unusual probity, who is also Leszek's tutor and guardian. In this year Casimir regains four districts previously torn from the Kingdom of Poland: Brześć, Vladimir, Drohiczyń and Przemyśl, and installs his starostas in their main castles and settlements, and himself takes over their government. Mieszko the Old, ousted by his son, Otto, has taken refuge in Racibórz, a town which belongs to him, and is living there with his wife and their three sons in dire poverty.

Frederick of Bohemia has been summoned to the Emperor, so Soběslav, who is eager to regain Bohemia, gathers an army and tries to capture Prague. The city, however, has a strong garrison of Germans and he accomplishes nothing. As he withdraws, he encounters Frederick on his way back from Germany with a considerable force. The terrain is unfavourable for Frederick's troops and Soběslav routs them, scattering them so thoroughly that on the battlefield no two soldiers can recognize each other. Frederick obtains a fresh army from Conrad of Moravia and marches on Prague. Soběslav, proud of his recent victory, bars his advance near Prague itself and, defeated in his turn, seeks safety in flight. He dies the following year, leaving Frederick to rule undisturbed. It is said that Frederick was shamefully cruel to the Germans in Bohemia, a thing in which the Czechs encouraged him, having the noses of all those he encountered cut off, sometimes even doing the actual section himself.

A.D. 1180

Having re-established his authority over every part of his kingdom, Casimir sets about restoring justice and liberty to its maltreated people. First, he cancels all the tribute, dues and imposts levied on them by Mieczysław and his officials; then he does away with the illegal courts which have been depriving people of their possessions. Next, he sets about eradicating the more serious abuses which the old law did not treat as crimes or even as offences, and which are commonly practised by dukes, barons, and lords and thus are all the more difficult to suppress. For example, it had long been the custom that, when a knight or lord was on a journey, he could arbitrarily require a villager to supply him with straw, hay, chaff, even oats for his horses, and whatever he needed for himself. Should the villager refuse, he could expect to have his house and stores destroyed, his grazing ruined and even his crops trampled. Also, lords and knights requiring transport to take them to some place where they have to attend to private matters, often quite trivial, can commandeer villagers' horses, which they or their servants can then ride at speed and often over long distances, with the result that the horses are exhausted and often founder; indeed, often such horses are ridden to death or taken so far away that they cannot be recovered, while a really good horse will just be appropriated—all of which involves the villagers concerned in considerable loss and makes it impossible for them to work their fields. Again, when a bishop dies, his possessions have been subject to looting and plundering by the nobles. So, Casimir summons a great assembly of dukes, bishops and knights, who meet in Łęczyca, and to them he details the misfortunes and bloodshed resulting from all these abuses, the losses the country suffers because of them, the perfidy reminiscent of cruel paganism, which, he suggests, is an offence to God, and he proposes that they eradicate these abuses and adopt the sacred laws of Catholic princes. He adds that a man of his upbringing cannot tolerate such shameful, criminal practices in the lands he rules. In the assembly are eight bishops, three princes and a host of lords and knights. The consensus is that these unjust practices must be abolished and that in future anyone who tries to implement any of them is to be punished with excommunication, and this is formally confirmed some days later by the bishops, who don all their robes for the ceremony. To ensure that these salutary laws shall endure for future generations, emissaries are chosen from among the laity and clergy to go to Rome to obtain papal approval and confirmation of them. This delegation is also to request the body and bones of some suitable saint to grace Cracow cathedral. The emissaries find the Pope in Tusculum and are received most graciously. The Pope thanks the Poles for their loyalty to him during the period of schism and praises and approves the laws that have just been passed. As regards the body and bones of a saint, he tells them to be of good heart and to accompany him to Rome. (The original of

Part of Wielkopolska from B. Wapolski's 16th century map of Eastern Europe—Jagiellonian University Library.

the bull recording the Pope's approval is preserved in Cracow cathedral, where I have on several occasions had it in my hands.)

A.D. 1181

All the people of Słupsk were disgusted, when, some years previously, Oward, King of Denmark, maintaining that he was descended from Polish kings and princes through his grandmother,which was true, forcibly occupied the castellany of Słupsk, which belonged to the Duke of Wielkopolska, without the latter bothering to avenge so grievous an injury, but allowing Oward to retain what he had acquired illegally. Now, the barons and people of Słupsk, fearing lest this enforced acquisition of their lands become permanent and leave them in lasting servitude to foreign kings and princes, have refused the Danish king obedience and acknowledged Świętopełk as their rightful lord and duke. Since then, the lands and castellanies of Słupsk have in secular matters come under the kings and princes of Poland and in ecclesiastical matters under the Archbishop of Gniezno.

Mieczysław continues to send letters and messengers to Casimir asking that his wife and children be allowed to end their exile and return not to the throne, but just to the country. He begs Casimir to remember how good Mieczysław was to him as a boy. Being now weak in mind and body, Mieczysław is happy to cede the throne to Casimir.

Deeply moved by his brother's pleas, but not wishing to reach any decision on his own, Casimir summons a full council and lays before it the question of restoring Mieczysław to his duchy. "Gentlemen," he says to them, "I find the exile of Duke Mieczysław, who is my brother, profoundly distasteful. I sympathize whole-heartedly with his misfortune and that of his children, who regard me as a second father. He has repeatedly asked me to return his duchy to him. He cedes to me the right to the authority of monarch, which he renounces. His request I regard as just. In that he has renounced all authority as monarch, I consider it right to restore to him his duchy, for surely it would be wrong that in his lifetime his son Otto, or anyone else, should rule there, while he endures poverty and exile."

The members of the council listen with mounting indignation and, when he stops speaking, there is an obstinate silence. They then ask for time and go aside to discuss the matter, almost in a mood of rebellion. Some even suggest exiling Casimir himself. In the end, they go back and tell Casimir that to allow Mieczysław back would be to endanger their own lives, for they know that his thirst for vengeance would never be satisfied until he had tasted their blood. So, unless Casimir alters his decision, they can only go into voluntary exile or save their lives in some other way. Casimir at once cancels his decision, thanks them all for their sincerity and loyalty, and no more is heard of the suggestion.

When Mieczysław learns from Casimir himself what has happened, he goes in person to the Emperor, presents his case and asks for help in regaining his duchy; but then, having been told that the Emperor is already engaged in a war overseas, has undertaken to help the Holy Land, and has other important matters to deal with, Mieczysław returns to Poland. He marries one of his daughters to Mszczuj, prince of the maritime province, and with the latter's help and that of other volunteers, as well as with the tacit support of Casimir, occupies the castle at Gniezno and from there goes on to occupy the other castles and forts in Wielkopolska, either by persuasion or by force. Otto, through intermediaries, asks forgiveness and is reconciled to his father and returns to submission. Thus, in a short space of time, Mieczysław regains the whole of Wielkopolska with the covert support of Casimir, which could not be given openly.

A.D. 1182

When Casimir is told that the town and district of Brześć on the River Bug have revolted, he assembles a force and advances on the town, invests it and captures it after a siege of twelve days. He has the leaders of the rebellion executed, builds a new fort that towers over the city and installs a strong garrison in it. He then advances into Galicia in order to restore it to its rightful duke, Mstislav, who had been driven from it by his brother Vladimir on the pretext that Mstislav was not legitimate, but a bastard, who had been exposed as a babe. Many of his troops find this extra duty onerous and take part reluctantly. Among themselves they criticize Casimir for going to war to help a foreigner when he has problems enough of his own, and they prophesy little success or advantage from it. They consider it unjust that, far from home, without reward, they should be engaged in dangerous fighting in defence of a bastard and a person of uncertain origins. Though Casimir knows what his knights are grumbling about, he continues his advance. They reach Halicz and, the next day, when they are preparing to invest it, their scouts tell them that Vsevolod of Bełz and Vladimir of Halicz who is Mstislav's brother, are approaching in battle formation together with all the Ruthenian dukes and boyars. At this news, the Poles make no secret of their reproaches and loudly curse the voivode of Cracow, Nicholas, as the real instigator of the war and thus the one who is exposing them to danger, almost handing them over to the Ruthenians, whom they can now see. The Ruthenians are eager to fight, both because of their hatred of the Poles and their own numerical superiority; while their soothsayers have prophesied victory for them and a sad end for the Poles. Casimir, quite undeterred, arrays his army and encourages his men by telling them that, with few exceptions the Ruthenian forces consist of wretched slaves, whom they can defeat without much effort. Entrusting command of the left wing to the Voivode of Cracow, he takes command of the right wing, orders the trumpets to sound "to battle" and engages the enemy. After a period of fierce fighting, the Polish left wing, on whose horses the enemy archers have inflicted considerable losses, begins to retreat. Seeing the danger, Casimir sends in his reserves, which drive off the Ruthenian archers, and the fighting starts up again. The Polish right wing routs the enemy with which it is engaged, and then turns against the rest of the Ruthenian force, which the Voivode is beginning to drive back, and a general rout develops. Vsevolod and Vladimir manage to get away by changing horses, but a great number of Ruthenians are either killed or taken prisoner, and the rich Ruthenian camp is looted. After this defeat the town and castle of Halicz both surrender and are entrusted to Mstislav who swears an oath never to desert Casimir or the Poles either in misfortune or in success. Vsevolod reaches his castle in Bełz with a handful of men, while Vladimir heads for Hungary to seek military and financial help.

The nobles and knights of Bohemia, disliking the rule and habits of their prince, Frederick, accuse him and his brother, Otto, of disgraceful practices, remove Frederick from the throne and elect Conrad, Duke of Moravia, as their prince. The rebels then surround the castle in Prague, in which Frederick has installed a garrison of picked German soldiers, besiege it and force it to surrender. The Emperor, to whom Frederick flies when he sees that all his supporters have deserted him, summons Conrad and the Czech nobles to appear before a tribunal set up to see justice done to Frederick. When Conrad refuses to go, the Emperor summons the Czechs to him and so bullies them that they desert Conrad and once again support Frederick and swear fresh oaths of allegiance to him.

A.D. 1183

Mieczysław is not content with having recovered Wielkopolska and is avid for the monarchy as well, using various cunning ploys to obtain it, bribing one and making promises to another, giving gifts all round in preparation for his return to power. He quarrels with Casimir over which of them is paramount, accusing the latter of arrogance and of having illegally deprived his elder brother of the monarchy. However, he does not dare have recourse to arms, realizing that, if it came to a fight, he could not win; but he fraudulently assures Casimir that he has renounced all claims to the monarchy, holding his own duchy far dearer. However, he tries to persuade Casimir to appoint him successor to Mazovia and Kujawy, when their nephew Leszek dies; he has been ill for some years and is held to be near to death. This Casimir refuses to do. When, later, Casimir goes warring in a distant part of the kingdom, Mieczysław announces that the promises he gave Casimir were made under duress and thus were not binding, and sets about cajoling his nephew, Leszek, Duke of Mazovia and Kujawy, whom Bolesław the Curly had put under the guardianship of Casimir. See-

ing that everything Leszek does is at the prompting of his tutor, Castellan Żyra, Mieczysław wins
the latter over with splendid gifts and by holding out hope that, when Mazovia and Kujawy come to
Mieczysław on Leszek's death, Żyra shall have them. So Leszek deserts Casimir and goes over to
Mieczysław whom he appoints, in writing, as his heir and compels his knights to swear allegiance
to him. This turn in affairs touches Casimir on the raw, but he suppresses his anger against the three
and, in silence, waits for a suitable moment to exact vengeance. Another tragedy afflicts Casimir at
this time, when his young son, Bolesław, is bitten in the neck by a snake lying at the foot of a tree
the lad was amusing himself felling. The skin of one so young is tender and the poison quickly suffocated the boy, who died without a groan or a cry as he was being lifted up. Casimir is distraught.

Conrad of Moravia now drops his claim to Bohemia, so the Czech nobles, eager for a change,
put Václav, son of Soběslav the Old and brother of the younger Soběslav, on the throne. Václav,
trusting in their power, lays siege to Prague, but achieves nothing, since the German garrison defends it stoutly. Meanwhile, Frederick, who has assembled an army in Germany, marches into Bohemia with Adalbert, Archbishop of Salzburg and Duke Leopold of Austria and drives Václav,
who does not dare oppose him, away from Prague which he, Václav, is besieging. Having relieved
Prague and thus regained the friendship or the frightened respect of those who had previously deserted him and gone over to Václav, he manages to pacify Bohemia.

A.D. 1184

Leszek does not long endure the tutelage of his uncle, for Mieczysław seeing how Leszek's
health is so bad that he may die at any time, starts behaving not as his guardian, but as his superior
and, as such, ousts the existing governors and officials and installs his own men in the castles and
forts of Mazovia. Leszek and his tutor, Żyra, soon realize that they are being by-passed and their
authority diminished, so, regretting their desertion of Casimir and fearing lest they incur further
unpleasantness from Mieczysław, the two with the more eminent personages of Mazovia and Kujawy go to Cracow and, falling to their knees before Casimir, beg forgiveness and promise to mend
their ways. Casimir, mild and gentle as always, rebukes them, but forgives them and sends them
back to their duchies. On his return, Leszek removes the officials appointed by Mieczysław and replaces them with his own men. He also cancels the edict appointing Mieczysław as his successor
and confirms that no one but Casimir is to succeed him and has his barons and other eminent persons swear allegiance to Casimir.

On the death of Iaroslav of Kiev the duchy passes to Sviatoslav of Chernigov. At about the
same time, the Duke of Vladimir also dies and is succeeded in all his duchies by his brother, Vsevolod. However, Mstislav son of Rostislav, with the backing of the people of Rostov rebels against
Vsevolod, but is defeated and seeks safety first in Rostov and then in Novgorod. Elated by his victory, Vsevolod advances against the Duke of Riazan with an army reinforced by those of the two
sons of the Duke of Kiev and others. Gleb, the Duke of Riazan secretly appeals to the Polovtsy for
help and swiftly invades the territory of Vladimir and puts it to fire and the sword, looting and robbing churches, monasteries and even the Lord's servants. Learning of this, Vsevolod quickly returns from Riazan and attacks Gleb and his Polovtsy, whom he defeats, though not without much
bloodshed on either side. He captures Gleb and his son, two of Gleb's nephews and much of his
army. The Polovtsy he executes ruthlessly. Later, he has Gleb executed in prison and his two nephews blinded. The others he frees.

The Pope decides to accede to Casimir's repeated requests for the body of St. Florian to be
given to Cracow cathedral, a gift that, according to the old story still being told, was miraculously
confirmed by the Almighty, for when the Pope entered the chapel in which the bodies of numerous
saints were stored and asked aloud—whether seriously or in jest is not known—who of the many
resting there would like to be translated to Poland, an arm appeared out of the tomb containing St.

Florian's body, and beckoned, thus letting it be understood that Florian would like to go to Poland. The Pope at once allocates Florian's body to Cracow cathedral and it is conveyed there by Giles, Bishop of Modena, and installed in the cathedral with great pomp and rejoicing. Bishop Gideon at great expense builds a church in honour of the Saint outside the city walls. From now on Poles of all classes christen their sons Florian.

Frederick, Prince of Bohemia, eager for vengeance on Conrad of Moravia for having tried to deprive him of his throne, sends his brother, Przemyśl, with a large force to burn and loot Moravia and force it into submission. This accomplished, Przemyśl returns to Bohemia although Conrad, who is numerically much the weaker, never dared engage him in battle. Frederick now exiles his brother Theobald, whose presence he considers a threat to himself and his position.

A.D. 1185

In less than three years after being restored to the dukedom of Galicia, Mstislav has earned the dislike and hatred of most Ruthenians by not allowing many of the old criminal abuses to go unpunished, and by granting favours to Polish knights at his court in preference to Ruthenians, whom he appears not to trust. So, the Ruthenian nobles, especially those who support the exiled Vladimir, plan an attentat. Unable to mount one openly, since Mstislav is surrounded by loyal guards who would prevent any outsider approaching him, they secretly administer poison and this kills him. Then they expel the Polish knights, occupy Halicz castle, and send to Hungary to ask Vladimir to come back and recover his duchy. Vladimir consults King Béla, who has taken him in and sheltered him, and asks him for the knights, horses and money he will need to recover his duchy, since he knows that Casimir of Poland is a threat to him, and, indeed, the latter, learning of Mstislav's death, has already sent Duke Roman to replace him. Béla, realizing that this is a good opportunity to get hold of Galicia, puts Vladimir in prison and sends his own son, Andrew, with an army to occupy Halicz castle as quickly as possible. The Ruthenians holding the castle, ignorant of the imprisonment of their Duke and falsely told by Andrew that he has come on ahead of Vladimir, receive Andrew with open arms as their protector and admit him to the castle. Andrew easily overpowers the garrison and ejects the Ruthenians. Some, whom he considers likely to give trouble, he puts in prison. He then proceeds to take over the entire duchy and appoints Hungarians to all the government posts, for he considers the Ruthenians too untrustworthy. He takes particular precautions against being poisoned.

Prince Casimir founds and endows a monastery in Koprzywnica and gives it to the Cistercians.

Frederick of Bohemia, who hates Conrad of Moravia, again sends his brother, Přemysl, with an even larger force to ravage the country as extensively as he can. This time things turn out differently: for Conrad, with his own troops and some Germans to give him confidence, bars Przemyśl's advance at a place called Loděnic. Both sides being eager to fight, the battle is a long one and each side suffers considerable casualties. In the end both armies withdraw, leaving the issue undecided.

A.D. 1186

Leszek, after years of suffering, feeling that he is about to die, sends to Cracow asking Casimir to come to him. When Casimir arrives, Leszek summons the barons of both his duchies and, recommending Casimir to them, surrenders to the latter all his castles and forts. Shortly after this he dies, fortified by the sacraments as befits a Catholic prince. As Leszek has no progeny and Casimir has a document appointing him Leszek's heir, as he also is according to the will of Bolesław the Curly, Casimir takes over the two duchies of Mazovia and Kujawy. Mieczysław complains that he is being wronged in that he is entitled to a half share, as is Casimir, but because of Casimir's strength and the barons' and knights' dislike of him, he stops at armed intervention. Thus, from this time on Casimir and his heirs have held and ruled the two duchies.

Frederick of Bohemia and Conrad of Moravia are brought together in Kunicz and between them agree on peace, thus relieving both countries of civil war.

A.D. 1187

Vladimir, the exiled duke of Galicia, who has spent nearly two years in a Hungarian prison, manages to bribe his gaolers to let him escape and to take him to Ruthenia. He then goes to Halicz and tries to gain entry to the castle, but its strong Hungarian garrison repulses him and he is forced to roam the trackless wastes of the country with nowhere to dwell. He collects round him a band of men, fugitives from justice, who make their living by brigandage, and with them raids Ruthenia's neighbours. Poland, too, suffers from his depredations, when, towards the Feast of the Assumption, when the country is busy with the harvest, he raids the area around Przemyśl, which is under Polish rule. His band loots and burns churches, towns, hamlets and villages, captures the wives and daughters of the barons and some villagers and hurries off with them and the rest of his loot to Kiev, where they are all sold. Casimir cannot tolerate the seizure of his people and sends a force under Voivode Nicholas of Cracow to drive Vladimir from the country. Vladimir does not dare resist or fight, and his prisoners are either freed or ransomed. Vladimir then withdraws with his band into the Carpathian Mountains, where they continue to live off banditry.

The Tatar nation has grown in importance. A few centuries ago, no one had heard of them. They have the same features as the Armenians and speak the same language. They live in the North, near the city of Karakorum, in a vast expanse in which there are no villages or towns, and pay tribute to King Bucham, called Prester John. Having become a huge tribe, they elect a king of their own from among themselves, a very enterprising man called Genghis, and under his leadership start invading neighbouring countries and conquering them; thanks to Tatars from other countries joining them on hearing of this new king, they have grown to such importance that their new king sends emissaries to demand the daughter of King Bucham as his wife. Bucham rejects the demand and insists on Genghis paying him the usual tribute. This results in a war in which Bucham is defeated and shortly afterwards dies. After this the Tatar nation grows into a great power.

A.D. 1188

Having inflicted so much damage on Poland, Vladimir goes into hiding in the marshes and trackless wastes. Casimir, wishing to punish him, searches for him, but Vladimir in an attempt to avoid punishment, keeps sending humble requests for forgiveness. Once assured of his personal safety, he goes and presents himself before Casimir, prostrating himself and promising henceforth to be the latter's loyal and faithful servant. Casimir lets himself be won over and accepts his erstwhile enemy as a friend. He goes even further, for, assembling a considerable army, which he puts under the command of the Voivode of Cracow, he sends it into Ruthenia with the object of restoring the exiled Vladimir to his throne. Poland's neighbours laugh at him for attempting this, for they think it impossible that the Poles shall be able to oust the powerful King of Hungary and his son, who have at their disposal a numerous army and huge resources. The Polish knights, too, are unhappy at being sent on such an expedition, and even the common soldiers are reluctant to make an unjustified attack on a neighbour and a king who is their country's ally. When the Polish army reaches Halicz, it invests the castle there with Andrew and his Hungarians inside; then, having evicted the inhabitants of the surrounding villages, builds a ring of small forts and strong-points round the castle, thus preventing the besieged, who are well supplied, from getting supplies from outside. The Hungarians pin their hopes on King Béla, never doubting that, in answer to their repeated requests, he will come in strength and raise the siege. However, when they find themselves

Four patron saints of Poland: Wacław, Wojciech (Adal-
bertus), Stanisław and Florian.
From Jan Laski: Commune Regni Poloniae Privile-
gium, *Cracow—Jagiellonian University Library.*

starving, they begin to have doubts, and, in the end, send emissaries to the Polish commander who arranges for the surrender of the castle on terms that allow the Hungarians to march out with all their equipment and non-combatants. On the day agreed, the garrison duly marches out and is given a Polish escort as far as the frontier. The castle is then handed over to Vladimir, who has ac-companied the Voivode, and who now swears that he and his successors will be sincere subjects of the Princes of Poland and ever obedient to their authority. This campaign earns Casimir a great reputation among the Ruthenian tribes.

Saladin, learning of the departure of many of the Christian kings and princes who had come to help the Holy Land, and of the dissension among those who remain, brings up a strong army and lays siege to Jerusalem. After fourteen days, unable to hold out any longer, its walls demolished by the enemy's siege machines, Jerusalem surrenders on October 15. The Christian wives and daugh-ters of the knights captured in previous fighting, are now brought before Saladin, who, when they burst into tears, asks the reason for their weeping. They reply that, having lost their husbands, they are now losing their belongings as well, and ask for Saladin's help. Touched, Saladin orders the re-lease of all prisoners who are still alive and gives instructions that all who are unmarried are to be given money from his own purse.

Pope Urban III, grieved by the capture of the Holy City, goes into a decline and dies a few days after sending to the Emperor asking him to organize an expedition to recover the Holy Land.

A.D. 1189

Béla of Hungary, indignant over the eviction of his son from Halicz, lays the whole blame for this at Casimir's door, accusing him of harming a trusted friend by illegally, and in breach of the treaty long in force between their two countries, depriving him of the duchy of Galicia. He feels that this merits not mere protest, but armed reprisal; so, despatching an army into Poland, he plunders and spreads devastation in the frontier areas and puts garrisons of his own men into the frontier forts, from which further raids are to be made into Poland. Casimir is just as eager to prove his superiority, so he heads a Polish force that moves into Hungary and similarly loots and devastates the countryside, and takes considerable booty back to Poland, leaving garrisons in many places to repel unexpected raids. The fighting is desultory, for the Polish knights are reluctant and half-hearted; indeed, they grumble and complain that Casimir has embarked on an unjust war with a friendly neighbour in support of an enemy and a deserter who never keeps faith with anyone.

Pope Clement III, wishing to reform the church in Poland and also to get the Polish clergy to contribute towards the cost of defending the Holy Land, whose reconquest he earnestly desires, sends Cardinal John Malabranca to Poland. The Cardinal goes first to Cracow, where he is received in procession by Prince Casimir and Bishop Fulko. He holds the synod for the Gniezno province in Cracow and promulgates constitutions for the reform of the clergy, telling the bishops that they and all the clergy must hand over the tithes set aside for recovering the Holy Land.

The Emperor Frederick temporarily hands over power to his son Henry, so that he himself can lead a powerful army by land and sea, through Pannonia, Bulgaria and Greece to the Holy Land. Having crossed the Straits and the Sea of Marmora, this great host reaches Armenia. Everyone is optimistic. Then, one Sunday, the Emperor, wishing to wash off his sweat, though many try to restrain him, wades into the River Salef which there runs shallow, and suddenly is swept away, or, as seems more probable, has a stroke and drowns. His knights try to save him, but in vain. His body is recovered by his son and taken to Tyre. The Christian army and the Crusaders elect Frederick the Duke of Swabia, one of the Emperor's sons, a man of unusual endurance, to succeed his father. Under his command, the army advances first on Antioch, where it remains for eight weeks, then to Tripoli, Tyre and Acre, defeating such of the enemy as it meets on the way. Now, however, plague begins to spread through the army's ranks and claims many victims, including Frederick himself, the army's one hope and comfort. His death puts an end to this costly undertaking and all hopes of recovering the Holy Land.

Frederick's son Henry, is unanimously elected Emperor and crowned in Aix-la-Chapelle by the Archbishop of Cologne.

In this year the Prince of Bohemia, Frederick, dies and is succeeded by Conrad of Moravia. Thus at more or less the same time, three Fredericks die early deaths. A fatal year for Fredericks.

A.D. 1190

The barons and councillors of Poland and Hungary meet on the frontier for talks aimed at resolving the dispute that has arisen between their two countries. Each side contends that its cause is the just one, and the discussions continue for several days, then both sides agree to accept an armistice to last for three years on condition that in that period, fresh talks will be held in the same place to work out conditions for a lasting peace.

Meinhard, first Bishop of Livonia, starts proclaiming the word of God on the bank of the River Dvina, at a place where the castles of Üxküll and Doley now stand. The Livonians begin to accept Christian beliefs.

A.D. 1191

No Polish noble much cared for the way in which, two years previously, Casimir restored Vladimir to the throne of Galicia. They complain that this has set a dangerous precedent, in that a man deserving death has not only gone unpunished, but has been granted honour and distinction, thus encouraging others to devastate Polish territory. These complaints gradually turn into active plotting against Casimir, which threatens to turn into open rebellion. The plotters decide to restore

Mieczysław the Old, Duke of Wielkopolska, to the throne in Cracow. This decision is taken at a time when Casimir has just gone to Ruthenia to settle a boundary dispute between Roman and Vsevolod, so the conspirators send messengers with letters summoning Mieczysław to Cracow. To make acceptance easier for Mieczysław, the nobles and citizens of Cracow are told that Casimir has been poisoned in Ruthenia and is dead. Thus an optimistic Mieczysław returns to Cracow with his sons and many of the barons and knights of Wielkopolska. Only the Bishop of Cracow, Fulko, and his brother Nicholas, the Voivode, take no part in the rebellion; indeed, they are opposed to Mieczysław's return. The Bishop does his best to ensure that Cracow castle does not fall into Mieczysław's hands, so Mieczysław builds another fort of baulks of timber and quickly strengthens it with a stout palisade. He also builds a second fort at Bothun. When Casimir learns of what has happened, he at once sets out for Cracow with a small retinue, but accompanied by Roman of Vladimir and Vsevolod of Bełz and the Voivode of Cracow. When told of his arrival, Mieczysław decamps to Poznań, leaving his son, Bolesław, and a knight, Henry of Kietlicz, with strong garrisons to defend the two forts he has just built, as well as the other towns and forts in his hands, until he can return with reinforcements. Casimir, incensed by what Mieczysław has done, assaults the new forts by day and night with knights and others who have rallied to him in great numbers, delighted to see him back. In the end, those of the defenders, who have not been killed, surrender. Bolesław, seeing little hope of his father finding the requisite support, surrenders himself and the castle to his uncle. At this, all the other forts and castles also surrender and are again under Casimir's control. Casimir has the new forts burned and razed to the ground. He is magnanimous in his treatment of his nephew and the knights who supported him, granting them their freedom and sending them home with gifts. The one exception is Henry Kietlicz, whose promptings caused Mieczysław to try and recover the monarchy, thus causing the civil war. He, aware of his crimes, seeks sanctuary in the cathedral crypt. Some raiding Ruthenians try to loot the cathedral and the cathedral officials send urgent pleas for help to Casimir, who succeeds in stopping the Ruthenians. Hearing the commotion, Kietlicz emerges from the crypt and mingles with the throng, hoping to escape, but is caught and hauled before Casimir, who berates him and boxes his ears, before handing him over to Duke Roman of Vladimir to be put in prison; and there he grows old and dies. Casimir's magnanimous treatment of his nephew and the knights who supported him is largely due to the Archbishop of Gniezno, Zdzisław, a man of uncommon intelligence and sense, who persuades him that any other course would only lead to further conflict. The future is to prove the Archbishop right, for as long as he lives, Mieczysław makes no further attempt to recover the monarchy.

Conrad, Prince of Bohemia, dies of the pestilence in Naples, where he was fighting as an ally of the Emperor, and his body is taken back to Prague for burial. The city is now taken over by Václav, son of Soběslav the Elder, but after only three months he is evicted by his uncle, Přemysl. Přemysl is despised by the Czech knights, who proceed to turn him out, but not before he has put a large part of the country to fire and the sword.

More or less at this time, in the pontificate of Celestine III, thanks to the endeavours of Meinhard, Bishop of Livonia, that country is converted to the Christian faith. Meinhard is succeeded by Brother Berthold, but the Livonians murder him, and he is succeeded by Albert who completes the conversion of the country and founds a metropolitan church and a city at Riga under Gothic law, and, with the permission of the Holy See, establishes several bishoprics there and appoints bishops. He introduces an order of regular canons to serve the cathedral, which is to remain in his charge for another thirty years.

A.D. 1192

Casimir, having been reconciled with his brother, Mieczysław, thus ensuring peace in his lands and duchies, decides that he must avenge the death of Henry Duke of Sandomierz and the defeat of the Polish army, when it was betrayed and surrounded by Prussians in difficult country, and announces an expedition against Prussia. Mieczysław the Old sends his son Bolesław with an army, though he himself stays at home. Henry of Wrocław and Mieczysław of Racibórz come in person. When all the different forces are assembled round Chełmno on the Vistula, they move off towards Prussia, taking every precaution to avoid an ambush. They cross the River Ossa and penetrate deep into Prussia, being particularly careful in their choice of camp sites. Precautions are also taken to ensure that the Prussians do not attack those bringing in provisions. The Prussians, not daring to engage the Poles, withdraw into the marshes and the trackless areas of thick forest into which it would be dangerous for the Poles to penetrate, and from them make frequent sorties to harass the invaders. Unable to bring the Prussians to battle, Casimir orders an extension of the devastation of fields and villages, and also of the slaughter of all young people, even children. This last forces the Prussians to beg for peace. Their chieftains come and prostrate themselves at Casimir's feet and beg for mercy, pleading that they have already been punished enough. They promise to pay past and current tribute and to do whatever he thinks right. Casimir is moved by their pleas and stops the slaughter and the burning of villages. He imposes fresh tribute and orders the return of all prisoners, as well as of the standards captured by the Prussians. All this the barbarians do and make unusual gifts to Casimir in the hope of engaging his sympathy. Casimir then returns to Poland, taking with him the hostages he has required, the tribute the Prussians have paid, and the esteem of his troops.

When Saladin, Sultan of Babylon, who captured the Holy Land and inflicted many defeats on the Christians, finds his health failing, he summons his standard-bearer and says to him: "You, who have usually carried my standard in the turmoil of battle, must now carry this banner of my death. Take this tiny rag on a lance and cry all over Damascus: 'Saladin, King of the East, is dying and taking with him of all his fame only this small rag'". And so ends his life.

A.D. 1193

Having dealt with the Prussians, Casimir now turns his attention to resolving the dispute with Hungary and finishing the war, which was interrupted by a truce three years previously. He arranges for a conference similar to that held then. The Polish delegation consists of Casimir himself, Bishop Fulko and Voivode Nicholas of Cracow and other councillors. The Hungarian delegates are the Archbishops of Esztergom and Eger, the count-palatine of Hungary and several barons. After much discussion, tempers are cooled and it is agreed that Béla will content himself with his huge kingdom, and that the Ruthenian territories belong to the Kingdom of Poland. Then the two monarchs meet in Spisz and each forgives the other for past wrongs and renews under oath the alliance made between their two kingdoms long years before. They decide sincerely and without reservation to maintain mutual friendship and accept the duty of each helping the other both in success and in adversity. They then exchange gifts and go their separate ways.

Henry, Bishop of Prague, himself of the princely family, uses persuasion, gifts and promises to get the Emperor to agree that his two relatives, Přemysl and Vladislav, should be granted princely status: Přemysl in Bohemia and Vladislav in Moravia, and assume personal responsibility for payment of the monies promised. When the amounts are not paid on time, the Emperor takes a dislike to Přemysl, both on this account and also because he has made an alliance with the Emperor's enemies, the Saxon princes, and so he transfers the Bohemian title to Henry, Bishop of Prague, who is still at his court, and sends him back to Bohemia to assume princely authority. Although the Bohemian barons have mostly undertaken to support Přemysl, as soon as the Bishop reaches Bohemia with a small force of Germans and Czechs, they all desert Přemysl and go over to the Bishop. Přemysl makes his escape with some difficulty. The Bishop lays siege to the city of Prague, which supports Přemysl, and after five months it surrenders.

Famous in their day. Clockwise from the top-left: John (Ioannes), who fell at Crecy; Conrad II, killed in fighting before Naples; Albert, who died of a surfeit of melons; Wenceslaus V, King of Bohemia and Hungary; Wenceslaus IV, King of Bohemia and Poland; Wenceslaus II, who died in prison.—Alexander Guagninus: Sarmatiae Europeae descriptio.*—Jagiellonian University Library.*

A.D. 1194

Having defeated all the peoples who used to be Poland's enemies and forced them to pay him tribute, Casimir is regarded both at home and abroad, as an excellent and very fortunate ruler. Some even think that he equals his father, Bolesław Wry-mouth. Convinced that he can now rest and spend the rest of his life at peace, he decides to turn his attention to the affairs of his towns and cities, which the recent wars have left dilapidated or seriously neglected, and for the future channel his energies into building and equipping towns and castles. However, fickle destiny does not allow him to fulfill either these hopes or those of his subjects, who are too hasty in rejoicing over their new-found happiness. As is his custom, Casimir spends the Feast of St. Florian, guardian of the city of Cracow and its surroundings, in ceremonial piety: making gifts worthy of a prince and with princely lavishness feeding Christ's poor and those who are wretched. On the following day, the Feast of St. Gothard, there is a reception for the bishops, barons and personages of eminence, followed by a banquet, at which people recall the dangers they have avoided or survived and look forward to the coming era of well-earned peace. When the others, well-dined and wined, are preparing to leave, the King puts to the bishops various questions concerning the nature of the soul and its immortality and the eternal happiness of the saints. Then, having drained a small goblet, he suddenly collapses (some say because of a quick-working poison) and dies a couple of hours later. Some are convinced that it was illness struck him down, others that it was a love-potion administered by a certain woman of Cracow, who wanted to inflame his feelings and passion for her; for, despite the warnings of Bishop Fulko, Casimir had not scrupled to commit adultery and so ran the risk of sudden death by poisoning. When the news reaches the palace, the weeping of Casimir's wife and two small sons, the bishops and knights, can be heard even in the city.

It takes four days to prepare a funeral worthy of so excellent a prince, who is then buried in a tomb built in the choir. The cost is enormous. After the funeral, a general assembly is convened to elect a new prince. Opinions differ, so the discussions are protracted. Addressing the assembly, Bishop Fulko recommends that there should be no delay in electing the new prince, and, bearing in mind the benefits bestowed on his country by Casimir, suggests that they should elevate one of his two sons and do so as soon as possible, and before Mieczysław or another duke with a claim on the capital starts raising objections. Casimir, he tells them, lives on in his sons. They may not have the same character as their father, but they have valuable and unusual traits, reminiscent of their father's. The country, he tells them, cannot long remain without a prince, any more than a swarm of bees can exist without a queen; nor will its rights, or their's, be safe, if, despising a prince brought up in their midst, they should elect a foreign one. He advises them to elect Casimir's elder son, Leszek. Most of the elders and a majority of the knights support him, but one of the barons considers it bad policy to entrust the conduct of a great nation to a boy. An immature boy, he tells them, may turn out to be a madman or may abuse his powers and that would lead to the downfall of the country, and then those nations which now pay it tribute, would be encouraged to rebel. In his opinion, they should think more about the good of the country than of the children, and so, he suggests, they ought to elect Mieczysław the Old, who would seem to have more right to the monarchy than the deceased Casimir had; or, if not him, the other Mieczysław, the Duke of Opole and Racibórz, because one was entitled to expect the country to benefit more from the rule of either of the two, than from that of a boy. He is given some hesitant support; indeed, the majority would probably have sided with him, had not Bishop Fulko quashed the idea by demonstrating that the baron's arguments could only be valid, if the right of election invalidated that of succession. In the present case, he tells them, which is concerned solely with the right of succession, not that of election, the considerations advanced by the baron are irrelevant and have no legal standing. It would be too cruel, and proof of inhuman tyranny, he says, if the inheritance of the sons of a prince, who are not yet of age, should be given to an outsider; for, according to the laws of God, canon law and imperial law, inheritance of a father's share belongs not only to adult sons, but even to posthumous children. Any obstacles in the way of ensuring the security of the country, maintaining its equilibrium and the advantageous resolution of its affairs, can be removed by appointing guardians and trustees and entrusting these with the government and care of the country and of the two boys, especially as kings and princes who have reached adulthood, more often govern through officials, than in person. This point is immediately accepted and all contrary motions voted down. The knights and nobles then rise to their feet and with one voice shout: "Long live, Leszek, our prince and our monarch!"

They then hasten to the prince's apartments, from which the beautifully garbed boy, whose pale hair has earned him the soubriquet "the White", is led into public view. He is then seated on his father's throne and proclaimed prince. Two trustees are appointed for him and his principality: Bishop Fulko and his brother, Voivode Nicholas of Cracow, and the knights and barons present all undertake that, as long as the Prince is under age, they will obey them in everything.

At the suggestion of Voivode Nicholas, Casimir's younger son, Conrad, now takes over Mazovia and Kujawy and their dependencies.

An assembly of the dukes of Ruthenia in Kiev announces an expedition against the Polovtsy, who have been constantly raiding their territories. So, at the approach of summer, the dukes and boyars of Galicia, Vladimir and Łuck under Roman of Vladimir, invade Polovtsian territory and, on June 20, engage the Polovtsy who are barring their advance. In the ensuing battle, with God's help they defeat and rout the Polovtsy despite their vaunted bravery; indeed, only a handful of them escape. The Polovtsian camp and all their tents are captured, and so the Ruthenians return home laden with booty and glory.

Henry, Bishop of Prague and Prince of Bohemia, sends a force into Moravia to evict Vladislav. Then, with as large an army as they can muster, on the orders of the Emperor who has conceived a great dislike of Albert the Margrave of Meissen, they invade the latter's territory and proceed to devastate it, committing many unmentionable acts against both civilians and clergy, monasteries and the servants of God.

Igor, one of the dukes of Ruthenia, eager for fame, together with his two sons, assembles an army of Severian northerners from Novgorod, and, together with Vsevolod, son of Oleg, and the boyars of Smolensk, attacks the Polovtsy. They rout the latter's large army, but then, not content with one victory, decide to advance beyond the River Don, thus penetrating deeper than any other Ruthenian leader, and utterly destroy their enemy; but their advance is halted before they reach the Don by a horde of Polovtsy, which routs them and, indeed, kills most of them, and then, in its turn, advances into Ruthenia near Periaslavl, occupying all the fortresses along the River Sula.

A.D. 1195

Mieczysław is profoundly hurt by the elevation of Leszek to his father's princely throne and that this has been done without his knowledge or consent. He suggests that it is just a ruse on the part of Bishop Fulko and his brother to retain power in their hands. He prophesies that as soon as Leszek and his brother come of age, the knights of Cracow will poison them and so hang on to power. He complains that this is the second time that he has been passed over. On the first occasion, he says, he acquiesced in order to avoid civil war, but he can no longer do so, since by virtue of seniority he has a right to the principality and the guardianship of the two boys; so, this time, the wrong done him can only be expunged by force of arms. When his attitude finds general approval with the knights of Wielkopolska, Mieczysław tells them to arm themselves and prepare for war. Then, by means of promises and other inducements, he gets his nephews, Bolesław the Tall of Wrocław and Mieczysław of Opole, together with his son-in-law, Mszczuj of Pomerania, to lend him assistance.

Next, in order to give his actions the semblance of legality, he sends envoys to Bishop Fulko and the barons of Cracow demanding the invalidation of the election of Leszek on the grounds that it was illegal and only done to shame and humiliate him, and that he, Mieczysław, should be admitted to the monarchy instead. When the Bishop refuses to accept his arguments, Mieczysław advances swiftly on Cracow. The other dukes, who are supposed to be helping him, tend to lag behind, for they are convinced that Fulko and the knights will not actually fight, but compromise. However, the nobles and barons of Cracow are well aware of the preparations Mieczysław has been making and have made their own, calling up troops from Sandomierz, Lublin, Mazovia, Kujawy and Brześć on the Bug and the Ruthenian territories which owed allegiance to Casimir while he was alive, as does Roman of Vladimir. With all these forces organized into three groups, one under Nicholas the Voivode of Cracow, one under Gowórek the Voivode of Sandomierz, and the third under the Duke of Vladimir, they advance on Mieczysław and his army, which has pitched camp beside the River Mozgawa, four miles from the monastery and town of Jędrzejów. The two armies engage at once, the Cracovians wishing to attack before the other dukes arrive with their troops. The battle starts at ten in the morning and continues until evening, the fighting being unusually ferocious, though each side has brothers, uncles and other relatives fighting against them. Neither side will yield, so there are horrible heaps of bodies on either side. The Dukes themselves take part in the fighting and Mieczysław sees his son, Bolesław, spitted on a lance, unseated and killed. Mieczysław himself is wounded by a common soldier, who might well have finished him off had not Mieczysław removed his helm and cried out who he was and demanded to be spared. The soldier, impressed by his rank and grey hair, not only threw down his own sword, but guided Mieczysław from the press, lest anyone else wound him, and allowed him to escape. Roman, Duke of Vladimir, who has received several wounds in the chest, seeing that his Ruthenians have either been killed or have taken to their heels, himself leaves the battlefield. Eventually the fighting comes to a halt without either side winning. No one is found on the battlefield with wounds other than in front. The only one left on the scene is Mieczysław Long Shanks, who arrives too late to take part in the fighting and so can stand there with standards aloft, claiming to be the victor. Mieczysław of Opole and his nephew, Jarosław, withdraw taking with them the Voivode of Sandomierz and a Cracovian knight they captured; then learning that Mieczysław the Old has been wounded and is being taken in a litter to Poznań, they turn back home to Silesia.

Bishop Fulko, who has remained apart in a village a few miles from the battle-field, is told by a deserter that the Cracovians are being slaughtered and Mieczysław the Old is marching on Cracow. Other deserters bring him similar news of disaster; so the Bishop, anxious to learn the truth, sends one of his chaplains in disguise to find out. The chaplain reaches the battle-field as the sun is setting and learns from the wounded lying there and those busy looting the dead and dying, all that has happened and returns to Bishop Fulko with the news. The Bishop, gravely saddened and wishing above all to help the two young princes, goes after Duke Roman, with whom he catches up during the night, and asks him to collect what troops he can and come to Cracow to defend the castle and the young princes, but he is told that Roman has no army, all his men having fled or been killed or wounded. The next day the Bishop and Voivode find each other. The Voivode wants to go after Mieczysław, who has re-formed his forces, and teach him a lesson, but Fulko restrains him and persuades him to return to Cracow and strengthen the garrisons, not only of the castle, but of those in all the other forts and castles subject to young Leszek, so that news of the disaster does not give rise to disturbances or incite anyone to rebel.

A.D. 1196

This shameful battle in which inglorious feat of civil war many were killed and there was no victor, long prevents the two sides from taking any further action. Many of the Cracovian knights are ashamed of having discarded their banners and left the battle-field. The state of the country verges on chaos, and it seems that the best course is to entrust the conduct of affairs to Casimir's widow, Princess Helena. There is one condition, however, namely that in public affairs she takes no decisions, introduces no changes or enactments without the advice and agreement of Bishop Fulko and Voivode Nicholas of Cracow; otherwise, until her sons come of age, she is to make appointments to vacant government posts and offices, allocate the revenue from taxes and what the treasury receives to meet the needs and expenses of the country.

A.D. 1197

Peter Capuanus, the papal legate, cardinal-deacon incumbent of S. Maria na via Lata, arrives to initiate reforms in the church in Poland. He is received with due honour at the gates of Cracow by Bishop Fulko and a procession of clerics. The first synod is held in Cracow, the second in Lubusz, then in the other dioceses in turn. The main reform insisted upon is that the clergy must renounce women and concubines and lead abstemious, pure lives that will be an example to laymen: for at this time many of the priests have wives, as though entitled to them. The Cardinal is eager to eradicate this scandalous custom. He forbids any priest to take or maintain wives on pain of the most serious penalties; and he recommends that even the most eminent laymen contract marriage under church authority. The clergy and the Polish Church as a whole accept this without opposition, but when the Cardinal moves on to Bohemia, the clergy there not only reject the idea, but all but abuse the Cardinal, when, before ordaining some chaplains, he requires them to take an oath of chastity. Indeed, the Czech priests in Prague even plot against the Cardinal's life and it requires all the authority of their bishop, then wielding the ducal authority, to restrain them.

Bishop Henry dies on June 15, but, before this, although ill, he banishes Duke Přemysl, who, anticipating the Bishop's death, was trying to capture the capital, though to accomplish this he has to use the army and there is considerable bloodshed. On the Bishop's death, Vladislav, who as Przemyśl's brother is suspect and has been detained, is released from prison and, with the support of the knights, placed on the throne. He rules for scarcely five months, before his brother re-enters the country at the head of an army of Czechs and Germans to try for the throne. Though he has the larger army, Vladislav, being a man of peace, refuses to fight his brother and, through intermediaries the two make a pact, according to which Vladislav retains Moravia, but relinquishes the rest of the country in favour of his brother.

A.D. 1198

The death without progeny of Vladimir, whom King Casimir restored to the throne of Galicia, leads to stormy disputes between Leszek and Conrad's guardians and the knights of Cracow on the one hand, and the Ruthenian dukes on the other. By rights, and in accordance with the treaty made when Vladimir was restored to the throne, Galicia has to revert to the kingdom of Poland and Casimir's sons, an arrangement by which the knights of Galicia have sworn to abide. However, several of the Ruthenian dukes now insist that Galicia be given to them in fief and this gives rise to disturbances, to quell which Nicholas the Voivode of Cracow is sent to protect the vacant dukedom and arrange matters so that it can be recognized as an appanage and united with Poland. Young Leszek begs his guardians to take him with them on the expedition, and, when both they and his mother suggest that this time he had better stay at home, he asks why dumb, insensitive banners can go with them, while he, their future prince, has to stay behind? He wants to go on the expedition, so that, by associating with brave men, he may himself acquire bravery, and insists that it is disparaging and shaming for him to be all the time with women. If they do not allow him to go, he says, he will follow them, even with only one companion. At this his plea is granted, and when, with a large retinue he enters Galicia, he is met with expressions of submission and the respect due to a rightful lord. First, they beg him to rule them in person, assuring him that they reject with abhorrence the idea of being ruled by a Ruthenian duke and would prefer death to that. Then a rumour spreads that Leszek is intending to appoint Roman, Duke of Vladimir, ruler of Galicia, and this makes them furious. They arm themselves and bar Leszek's path, as if he were an enemy. Their front rank is easily routed and made to run, at which the others, including many foot, panic and take to their heels. Leszek moves forward to invest Halicz, the citizens of which send to beg forgiveness. Granted this, they open the gates and promise to do everything Leszek requires.

Once in possession of the castle and lands of Halicz, the Ruthenian dukes start quarreling among themselves. After much squabbling, they give way to the threats and persuasion of the Duke of Vladimir and abandon their claim to the duchy, leaving Roman to demand that Galicia be surrendered to him, as nephew of the former duke. He uses all sorts of cunning persuasion and daily comes up with fresh arguments that it is unjust that his inheritance from his uncle should go to someone else; that none of the other dukes fully deserve the benefit, as is proved by the services he has rendered to Leszek, the wounds he received at Mozgawa, and the graves of all his knights, who died there.

He fortifies his pleas with threats, saying that, if he does not get the duchy, he will take armed vengeance in the cruellest way. Leszek and his advisers find a decision difficult and discussions continue for several days, during which Roman sends a humble request that the duchy be given to him not as of right, but as an act of grace, not as his property, but as coming under his temporary rule and tutelage. None of Leszek's advisers really wishes to give so rich a duchy to Roman who is already rich and influential in Ruthenia, in case this should go to his head and he rebel and become an enemy, instead of a subject. They would rather see the duchy united with Poland, something they consider advantageous, indeed, essential. They are, too, moved by the objections of the nobles and knights of Galicia, who are afraid that, if they have so devious and perverse a ruler, they will be persecuted in all sorts of ways; indeed, they promise that, if they are not handed over to Roman, they will pay a yearly tribute of various amounts of gold, silver, precious stones, garments, horses, oxen and cattle. Leszek and his councillors find this a convincing argument, yet the threat of war from Roman and of an associated attack by Mieczysław, meaning that they would have to fight on two fronts, inclines them to disregard their own advantage and the pleas of the Ruthenian dukes and the knights of Galicia and give the dukedom to Roman and just hope that he proves a loyal subject. So, Roman is invested as duke and the country handed over to him to the bitter disappointment of the people. These arrangements made, Leszek and his knights return to Cracow.

Sviatoslav of Kiev, one of the most eminent of the Ruthenian dukes, dies and is succeeded by Riurik, son of Rostislav, who, later, will be expelled by the people of Kiev and flee to the Polovtsy.

A.D. 1199

Duke Roman, having obtained the appanage of Galicia, at first tries to humour its people, but he soon conceives a dislike of them and treats them cruelly. Nor does he long keep the undertaking he gave to Leszek, that he would govern in accordance with the law, for on one occasion he summons all the more eminent people of the duchy, who present themselves in all innocence, only to find themselves put in prison. He then proceeds to have some of them publicly beheaded with a sword; others are buried in sand, others again publicly quartered, flayed or disembowelled; many others he has tied to columns, like statues, and used as targets for archery practice or otherwise killed. Then, when the sons and relatives of his victims, aghast at such cruelty, all flee to neighbouring countries, laying all the blame at Leszek's door, since it is he who imposed on them a savage, who, apart from his shape, was all but inhuman, Roman has recourse to cunning and trickery. He flatters and promises, and, for a time treats people with respect and kindliness but soon reverts to killing and torture. He deals thus with almost the entire nobility, justifying his actions by quoting the popular saying: "You cannot eat honey without first destroying the swarm". His cruel behaviour so terrifies not only his own people, but his neighbours as well, that, before long, he has acquired such a reputation that he rules by terror the whole of Ruthenia, a thing that seriously perturbs the Poles. Mieczysław the Old, who has lain quiet after the disaster of Mozgawa, now decides to have another try at settling matters by force of arms. The appanage of Kujawy, part of Leszek and Conrad's inheritance, adjoins Mieczysław's duchies, and this he now occupies and imposes his own authority on it. Leszek does not retaliate immediately, for he is afraid of civil war and this resulting in further disasters; for the two voivodes Nicholas of Cracow, whose clan is the Vulpes, and Gowórek of Sandomierz who belongs to the Rawita clan, are jealous rivals, almost at daggers drawn; indeed, the enmity between them has become so bad that Gowórek has gone into voluntary exile to his brothers and relations in Bohemia, to whom the kindly Prince of Bohemia has restored the lands and possessions they lost because of their treachery, though on condition that they renounce their former coat-of-arms and adopt the emblem of an axe which is to be a reminder of their earlier treachery.

On April 23, Béla, King of Hungary, dies after ruling for twenty-three years, and is buried in Székesfehérvár. His son Emeric is elevated to the throne by general agreement of the country's prelates and nobles, but his rule is to be brief.

A.D. 1200

Having illegally acquired the duchy of Kujawy, Mieczysław the Old employs cunning and treachery, means more powerful than the force of arms, to get hold of Cracow and make himself monarch of Poland. Unable to get the support of the Cracovian nobles, let alone that of Bishop Fulko and his brother, the Voivode, he directs his efforts at Princess Helena. He proposes that, if the principality and the authority of monarch are surrendered to him, he will promise to adopt the two boys, belt them as knights and give them the duchy of Kujawy and ensure that on his death the two will inherit the principality and the monarchy instead of one of his own sons. He persuades Helena that the boys' election by Bishop Fulko and the lords is invalid and that his own proposal is the only way of ensuring that they do succeed to the throne. He emphasizes that he is already an old man, so that they cannot have long to wait. Helena allows herself to be persuaded, despite the opposition of Fulko and the lords, and so, on St. Bartholomew's Day, before a great gathering of prelates and lords, Mieczysław repeats his promise and swears to adopt the two boys, restore Kujawy to them and ensure that they get the monarchy on his death. In addition, it is solemnly proclaimed that should anyone, on either side, dare to neglect, breach, invalidate, circumvent or in any way try to alter the arrangement made, the Metropolitan of Gniezno shall place an interdict on him and he will suffer God's punishment for perjury. After this, Princess Helena, her two sons and many of the lords withdraw to Sandomierz, while Mieczysław becomes monarch of Poland and takes over the city, castle and principality of Cracow. A few days later, he starts building a strong fortress at Bytom, which is to keep the Cracovian nobles loyal, and, in the event of a rebellion, provide him with a safe

Przemyśl Otakar, crowned in A.D. 1200 and reigned for thirty years. Alexander Guagninus: Sarmatiae Europeae descriptio—*Jagiellonian University Library.*

refuge. Letters are sent to Gowórek summoning him home to become principal adviser to the two young princes; for, now that the duchies have been divided up, Gowórek has no reason to fear the enmity of the Voivode of Cracow.

There is an earthquake in the south of the country on May 5. This destroys many houses, towers and fortifications. This unusual occurrence is popularly regarded as a portent and an awful warning.

The Greek city of Constantinople is captured by the Venetians and the Franks, a thing long believed impossible because of a prophesy that only angels can capture the city. However, when the attackers breach a part of the wall on which an angel is painted, this is taken as fulfillment of the prophesy. The Emperor of Constantinople, Askarius, moves to Tersona on the Pontine Sea and from there goes to Galicia, where he is well received and entertained by Duke Roman, and there he remains for some time.

Emeric, King of Hungary, dies and is succeeded by his son, Lászlo.

A.D. 1201

Two years after swearing to fulfill the arrangements made with Princess Helena, Mieczysław has still not implemented any of them, not even restored Kujawy to the young princes; so Helena goes to Cracow and, at first privately, then officially, consults with the Voivode, Nicholas, and asks for pressure to be put on Mieczysław to honour the agreement. At first, Mieczysław assures her that there is plenty of time; then, when he sees that the Princess is still unsatisfied, he tells her that he cannot by-pass his own sons, who are now of age, and that private arrangements cannot invalidate their right to succeed him. Helena returns despondently to Sandomierz, from where she sends to the Cracovian nobles asking for help in recovering the principality for her sons. Mieczysław is now heartily and widely disliked, for he has deprived many of their possessions and official posts, so, while he is away in Wielkopolska, the Voivode of Cracow occupies Cracow castle and installs Leszek the White and his mother there. This action has the support of almost everyone. The government officials installed by Mieczysław and his other supporters are urged to remove themselves to Wielkopolska. Every fort and castle in the principality declares its allegiance to Leszek, with the exception of Bytom, whose garrison, installed by Mieczysław, has done nothing but loot and pillage the countryside.

Přemysl, King of Bohemia, discards his first, legitimate wife Adelaide, sister of the Margrave of Meissen, and marries Constance, sister of Béla III of Hungary.

On December 6, Bolesław the Tall, Duke of Wrocław, dies and is succeeded by the only one of his five sons to survive him, Henry the Bearded, whose marriage is so unusual, in that his wife is saintly Jadwiga, daughter of Berthold, Duke of Merano, who is already famous for her holiness.

Lászlo, King of Hungary, dies on May 7th after a brief rule and is succeeded by Andrew, son of Béla III, whose wife, Gertrude, is another daughter of the Duke of Merano and so sister of Jadwiga.

A.D. 1202

Mieczysław sounds out the lords of Cracow only to discover that their dislike of him is such that there is no question of their assisting him in regaining the monarchy. Armed force being out of the question, he again has recourse to stratagems and trickery. He manages to persuade Helena that his failure to implement any of his promises is due to the prevarication of the nobles and that he is still eager to keep them, if he can. To prove his, he tells her that he is renouncing the appanage of Kujawy and will provide her with whatever legal documents she wants for his surrender of the principality of Cracow to the young princes on his death and appointing them his heirs. He then asks her to banish the Voivode of Cracow, Nicholas, who, he says, will try to prevent him implementing these arrangements. As Helena has long disliked the Voivode, she agrees to do this. Learning of what is afoot, Nicholas goes to the Princess and her two sons begging them to remember his faithful services and not to expel him at the request of his enemies. However, the Princess and her two sons give an unsatisfactory answer; indeed, in a sudden outburst of anger, the Princess refuses to listen to him any further; so Nicholas, seeing that she is indeed implacable, thinking that his own safety will be best assured by joining forces with Mieczysław, goes to him in Poznań, where he is received cordially and treated as a friend, for Mieczysław realizes that, if he has the Voivode on his side, this will almost guarantee that his own son will get Cracow and the monarchy; so, magnanimously he forgives Nicholas all that he has done in the past to thwart him. Now, as he sees it, he has no need to keep any of his promises to Princess Helena. Many of the nobles of Cracow, who all dislike Helena, agree to support Mieczysław, who takes complete possession of the principality, claiming to do so not by virtue of Helena's renunciation, but thanks to Voivode Nicholas. Mieczysław fulfills none of his promises: refusing to give up Kuyawy; occupying Wiślica and three forts in Sandomierz which are under the authority of Leszek and Conrad. He then dies leaving two sons, Władysław and Otto, the others having died before they reached maturity, as does Otto a couple of years later, leaving one son, Władysław, who is still under age and known as "the Spitter".

Ruirik, the exiled son of Rostislav, is given help by the Polovtsy and Oleg's two sons, which enables him to march on Kiev. As no one dares oppose him or even defend Kiev castle, he occupies it on January 2. His savage Polovtsy go on the rampage, killing and looting even churches, monasteries and other places dedicated to God; indeed, they devastate the metropolitan church of St. Sophia. In the end, the old and feeble have all been murdered or blinded, the clergy and monks, boyars and citizens with their wives, children and infants carried off into slavery. Thus is the city Ruirik occupies all but destroyed and empty.

A.D. 1203

Bishop Fulko and Voivode Nicholas summon another general assembly to elect a successor to the now vacant throne in Cracow. Most people favour Leszek, both because of his father's services to the country and because of what they know of his character; but there is one dissenting voice, that of Voivode Nicholas, who feels that it is degrading to be subject to a prince, whose actions are determined by a giddy woman, meaning Princess Helena, against whom the Voivode bears a grudge for agreeing to his exile in the previous year. The others find this objection baseless. There is, however, a more serious obstacle, in that the two voivodes of Cracow and Sandomierz openly dislike each other so much that they seem out for each other's blood and can scarcely be expected to work together. The Voivode of Sandomierz, Gowórek, whom Leszek recalled from voluntary exile, when Mieczysław assumed the throne in Cracow, is held in considerable respect by Leszek and the lords of Sandomierz. In the end, after much discussion, the assembly agrees to elect Leszek the White provided he banishes Gowórek from his presence and dispenses with his services. Leszek does not know what to do. Obviously, someone must take up the reins of government in the principality and so avoid the crop of squabbles and wars that might result if there was no one in authority; yet neither he nor anyone else wishes to see an innocent man exiled. When Leszek and the council are unable to reach a decision, Gowórek, wishing to cut the Gordian knot, tells them that it would be insufferable if the public good were to be neglected solely because of him, who might quit this world any day: or that Leszek should lose his inheritance just because of him. In all that man does, he says, the best thing is to put public interest before private interest. No loyal servant or knight should fear a chivalrous death earned in a just cause defending his prince and lord; how much greater respect will he, Gowórek earn, if he goes voluntarily into unjust exile in order to allow his prince to rule? Leszek is deeply moved by Gowórek's offer, but refuses to accept the principality and monarchy on such terms.

Another assembly now has to be convened in order to decide what is to be done. Most are in favour of exiling Gowórek and electing Leszek, yet Voivode Nicholas and his brother and the other members of the family who make up the old guard and who, like a team of oxen pull in whatever direction Nicholas wishes, dig in their heels, and, in the end, Władysław, Duke of Poznań, is chosen. Emissaries are sent to urge him to come to Cracow as speedily as possible to take over the principality to which he has a dual title: by right of inheritance from his father, and by his recent election. Władysław, however, knowing that the Cracovians originally chose Leszek, hesitates to accept, for he remembers the wars fought by his father and his uncle. When the emissaries insist that Leszek has refused his election, Władysław, wishing to avoid becoming involved in a civil war, sends to Leszek asking whether he is accepting or refusing his election; for, although Władysław has as good a right to the throne as Leszek has, he will not oppose the latter's election if he wishes to accept. Leszek replies, against the advice of his councillors, that he refused his election because of the condition requiring the exile of the Voivode of Sandomierz; and that, if this remains a condition, he will not accept election. Władysław, he says, is to do what is best for him and the country, and neither he nor his brother Conrad, will put obstacles in his way. This reply, given more out of youthful enthusiasm than mature consideration, causes many of the clergy and laity to lament the exclusion of the family of Casimir from its righful succession to the throne and monarchy. Władysław, informed of Leszek's decision, seeks and obtains the support of the Dukes of Opole and Racibórz, as well as of Henry of Wrocław; not that he thinks their support will be of much benefit to him, but he wishes to avoid their envy. These arrangements made, he to goes Cracow, where one and all receive him as their monarch. Once enthroned, he behaves with the most admirable benevolence and mercy to all. One and all have easy access to him: his judgments are objective; he protects the weak from being wronged, and grants requests that are genuine and justified. All his revenue he distributes with unheard-of generosity among the knights. Nature has equipped him with unusual good looks and courage; but his looks are spoiled by long, spindly legs, which have earned him the nickname of Long Shanks.

Henry of Wrocław yields to the requests and encouragement of his wife, Jadwiga, and founds an abbey of the Cistercian Order in a place known as Trzebnica, three miles from Wrocław, and endows it in perpetuity with the town of Trzebnica itself and the revenue from a larger number of villages, enough to support one thousand people; while Jadwiga renounces her right to her dowry in favour of the new nunnery, which, together with its offices, is made of beautiful and expensive bricks. The building of the whole takes fifteen years and costs an estimated 30,000 Polish marks. During these fifteen years, Jadwiga will not allow the sentence of death to be carried out on any evil-doer, whatever his crime; instead, such are put to work helping build the nunnery. The first abbess is a German, Petrusa, the second Gertrude, daughter of the Duke Henry and Jadwiga. The site for the nunnery is a place where Henry once, when out hunting, was thrown by his horse. It was very boggy there and the Prince and his horse began to sink into the quagmire. The Prince, who had become separated from his companions and the hunt servants, was on his own. He called upon the Almighty for help and promised that, if saved, he would found a nunnery. After a long struggle, he managed to extricate himself, but for a long time delayed implementing his promise, made without witnesses and of which he told no one; however, his wife sensed that he had done something of the kind and, after much pestering induced him to keep it.

A.D. 1204

Leszek the White's decision to renounce the duchy of Cracow, as rash as it was unpremeditated, at first appears of little import. In time, however, it proves not only to diminish his reputation and influence, but also encourages his enemies and those who dislike him. Roman the Duke of Vladimir, who acquired the duchy of Halicz thanks to the generosity of Leszek, learning that Leszek has lost the monarchy and the principality of Cracow and is thus left with only Sandomierz, Lublin, Mazovia and Kujawy, begins to despise him both because of his diminished authority and his tendency to act on impulse, thus showing himself still immature, and so refuses the tribute he has till then been paying and announces that he is neither Leszek's subject, nor his vassal, but his enemy. All Poles trading in his territories are stripped of their possessions and his own subjects are forbidden to trade with them. Roman then raids the territories of Lublin and Sandomierz bordering his own and loots them and puts garrisons in a number of their towns. For a while Leszek tolerates these pinpricks, being content to send to Roman requiring him to revert to friendly relations. However, these reminders further incite Roman, rather than incline him to mend his ways; so Leszek puts on the pressure. He places garrisons in a number of strategic places, which rout the Ruthenians who rashly come in search of loot.

Theobald, Duke of Moravia, an enemy of Přemysl of Bohemia, as of all Czechs, invades Bohemia and loots and pillages with impunity, for Přemysl is absent helping Philip against Otto in their struggle for the imperial throne. Theobald even lays siege to Prague. However, when Přemysl, returns from Germany, Theobald decides not to fight and withdraws his forces.

A.D. 1205

Duke Roman, no longer content with minor unofficial raids into frontier areas, declares war on Leszek and Conrad to whom he swore fealty and obedience, and invades their territory. There are several reasons for his action: the huge wealth taken from Ruthenia in the years when almost the whole of the country was conquered; the disbandment and dispersion of his forces, cavalry and infantry, among many of the Polish duchies; the quarrels of the magnates; and, finally, the immaturity of Leszek and Conrad. Also the harsh reply they gave his emissaries when he asked for all the land of Lublin in compensation for the losses and costs he had incurred at the Battle of the River Mozgawa and was told that, having quit the field of battle, he was not entitled to anything. However, before crossing the Polish frontier, Roman sends emissaries to the Bishop of Vladimir, who is of the schismatic confession, taking him gifts and asking for his blessing on his foray into Poland, which Roman intends to be one of devastation and which is to continue for three years. The Bishop, however, declines Roman's gifts and tells his emissaries that he cannot bless Roman or his enterprise, since he has previously started unjust and wicked wars and is again embarking on one that is quite unjustified, considering that the Poles have so often exposed their bodies to danger and death to defend the Ruthenians against the barbarians. Infuriated by this reply, Roman tells the Bishop that he will have his head off when he returns from the war against Poland. The Bishop retorts that threats do not frighten him, nor is it frightening to die for the truth, and, any way, Roman cannot be sure that he will return from his wicked war. So, at the start of spring, Roman advances into the Lublin territory, the part of Poland adjacent to Ruthenia, and lays siege to that city. Lublin has a Polish garrison and is stoutly defended, and for a whole month Roman tries without success to capture it. However, he does capture several of the wives and daughters of the knights of Lublin and these he keeps in an enclosure, like cattle, allowing his Ruthenians to violate them. Meanwhile, Leszek and Conrad have assembled a considerable force of knights and peasants from Sandomierz, Kujawy and Mazovia, which is reinforced with a number of volunteers from Cracow. When this is reported by his scouts, Roman raises the siege of Lublin and penetrates deep into Poland, looting and burning. He threatens not only devastation but eradication of the Latin rite. Bishop Fulko, Vitus the Bishop of Płock and several of the nobles try to parley with him, promising to pay compensation for anything the Poles have done in breach of their alliance. Roman cunningly promises peace and sends the emissaries back, but in the mean time continues his devastation of the country. Some priests he has captured are shot at with arrows to make them divulge where Leszek is hiding. In this way, Leszek reaches the Vistula and gets his army across, partly in boats, partly by fording, for, thanks to a drought, there are a number of places where the river is so shallow as to allow this, and pitches camp outside Zawichost. When his scouts report the approach of the Poles, Roman laughs at them. Then some soldiers confirm what the scouts have said, but Roman still does not believe them, saying that the Poles will never engage him in battle. Then, at dawn on June 19, the Feast of the martyrs SS Gervase and Protase, Leszek and Conrad arrive on the scene. Their army, commanded by the Voivode of Mazovia, is already in battle array and ready to fight. The shooting of the Polish archers and the pressure of the Polish attack is such that, in so narrow an area Roman is scarcely able to array even his first line. The two armies raise a clamour and engage with spears and lances poised. Although Leszek and Conrad are present, they are not allowed to take part in the fighting but have to remain at a distance, where they await the result, torn between fear and hope. The Poles rout the Ruthenian first line, and it seems that Fortune is favouring them; however, having so many knights, Roman is able to replace those who fall or are wounded. The Poles are not angry with the Ruthenians but with their duke, who to them is a traitor, a breaker of faith and a deserter, and they are after his blood. They surround him, where he is fighting in the front rank, identifiable by his ducal emblems. Roman, seeing those with him hewn down before his eyes and realizing that escape is made difficult by the heaps of bodies on either side, digs his spurs into his horse, which tries to throw him, but he manages to get through the press and reach the river and there his horse falls. Now, how is he to get across and escape? A soldier brings him an old jade, which with great difficulty does get him to the far bank, where he mingles with the throng of fleeing soldiery, only to be rounded up by the Poles and, being taken for a common soldier, cut down. A number of Roman's knights and soldiers are standing on the bank of the river they have just managed to cross, watching the flight of their fellows, when the bank, ripped by the hooves of the struggling horses, is no longer able to bear their weight and collapses. The Ruthenians are now all seeking safety in flight, which means flinging themselves into the river. Many are pulled down by the weight of their armour and drown, as do many of those who get across, when the weakened bank again gives way. Some who know how to swim or who have stout-hearted horses, do get across only to be hewn down by the Poles, who pursue the survivors all that night and the following day as far as Vladimir. Some of the fugitives stray into the forest or seek out villages, only to be killed or taken prisoner by the peasants. Only a few of that whole great army survive to tell their compatriots of that dreadful disaster. The Poles capture the Ruthenian camp and enrich themselves with loot, for they find all sorts of things there: gold and silver vessels, clothes, horses, armour. They celebrate their famous victory in various songs that to this day are sung at festivals and pageants. Roman's body is buried in Sandomierz on the orders of Leszek and Conrad. The Ruthenians release all their prisoners, and, on payment of one thousand silver marks are allowed to exhume Roman's body and take it to Vladimir for burial.

Earlier, the Ruthenian dukes, aggrieved that the devastation of their lands by the Polovtsy has never been avenged, vote for war against them; so, when the appropriate time comes, the four dukes invade with their combined armies and penetrate as far as the Polovtsian city of tents, which they call turres, meaning towers, and there kill the old people and round up hordes of the young of both sexes and great numbers of camels, cattle and other domestic animals, which they drive back to Ruthenia without encountering any resistance. When they get back to their own country, Roman Duke of Galicia is sent to arrest Riurik the Duke of Kiev, whom the Polovtsy brought in to help them in their work of destruction. He is put in chains and shaven like a monk. His wife, too, is shaven like a nun, but his daughters are allowed to go free. His sons are arrested too and brought back to Halicz.

Ruthenia is again invaded, this time by the Lithuanians. There is a pitched battle fought in open country, and, though the Ruthenians suffer heavy casualties, the Lithuanians are defeated and all but a handful killed or taken prisoner. This is the first time the name "Lithuanian" has been heard, for, until now, they have lived in hiding, for many years subject to the Ruthenians and paying them tribute in the form of belts and bark.

Sviatoslav son of Mstislav, seeing that the ducal throne in Kiev remains vacant, enters the castle there and with the support of the townspeople tries to occupy the throne, a thing no one else has dared attempt for fear of Duke Roman of Galicia, who set himself up as the ruler of all Ruthenia. Duke Roman considers himself wronged, and brings up an army and ejects Sviatoslav and in his place installs Rostislav son of Riurik, whom he has with him as a hostage. He also releases Rostislav's second brother, Vladimir, so as to make his authority more widely felt and to increase respect for his name and thereby make it easier for him to mount the campaign he is planning against the Poles.

Albert, the third bishop of Livonia or Riga, in order to protect the faithful from the barbarians, founds in Livonia the order of the brethren called the Militia of Christ who carry a sword and wear a surcoat with a cross sewn on it. Pope Gregory IX is to unite this order with the order of the Teutonic Knights and place it under the jurisdiction of the bishops of Livonia.

A.D. 1206

Leszek the White's reputation has been considerably enhanced by his famous victory and he now enjoys far more sympathy among the Cracovians who had deserted him solely at the insistence of Voivode Nicholas. As long as Nicholas is alive, this sympathy is suppressed and covert, for the Cracovians have gone in fear of the Voivode's influence and power, but now that Nicholas is dead, that obstacle is removed. Bishop Fulko hurriedly summons an assembly, at which a majority acknowledges Leszek as their monarch and grants him the principality of Cracow, undertaking to remove the Duke of Racibórz, son of Mieczysław, who has control of the castle, city and environs. Messages are at once sent to Sandomierz to acquaint Leszek of his election and ask him not to delay in coming to occupy his father's throne; and this he does, being received with great respect and cordiality. Having assumed power, he expels Władysław the Duke of Wielkopolska and all his starostas and officials from the principality and assumes control of all the fortified towns and forts. Władysław of Wielkopolska, a quiet, modest man, patiently accepts his dismissal and withdraws with his attendants to Poznań. Leszek then sends the armies of Cracow, Sandomierz and Lublin under Sulisław castellan of Sandomierz to ravage Ruthenia, in doing which they capture Sviatoslav, Duke of Ruthenia and father of Agatha, the betrothed of the Duke of Mazovia, and four of the most eminent Ruthenian knights, whom Leszek has strung up on a gallows.

The Ruthenian dukes, George of Vladimir, Iaroslav of Pereiaslavl and Mstislav, Constantine and Vladimir of Novgorod, long at variance with each other and now unable to conceal their quarrels, come out in open conflict, which culminates in a pitched battle fought on April 12. This ends in victory for Constantine and Mstislav. George escapes to Vladimir in which he is then besieged, but, seeing that he does not have enough men to defend the castle, he makes a peace, under which he cedes the castle to Constantine. The victors then turn on Iaroslav, who has taken refuge in Pereiaslavl. He, too, makes peace on conditions that allow him to retain Pereiaslavl.

A.D. 1207

Once Leszek has taken over the monarchy and the principality of Cracow, young Conrad starts demanding his share of their inheritance. He has long since come of age and naturally wants to be independent. The matter is debated at an assembly attended by the mother of the two princes, Gedko Bishop of Płock and Fulko Bishop of Cracow and, as well as the more eminent lords of all the duchies. After several days of talk it is agreed that the territories involved are to be distributed thus: Leszek, being the monarch and the elder, is to have Cracow, Lublin, as well as the territories of Sieradz, Łęczyca and Pomerania, while Conrad is to have Mazovia, which is extensive, Chełmno, Kujawy and Dobrzyń. Both accept this arrangement, which is then confirmed by the lords who all swear to respect it, while the Bishops pronounce a ban on anyone who breaks it.

The five Ruthenian dukes, among them Vladimir son of Riurik of Kiev, now seek to avenge the earlier devastation of their country by the Lithuanians by attacking them in their turn. There is a great battle in which the Lithuanians are defeated and very many of them killed in the subsequent rout and pursuit.

Bishop Fulko dies on September 11. In his twenty-one years as bishop he obtained from the Pope various rights, privileges and immunities for his cathedral: the right of the Bishop of Cracow to speak first, before all the other bishops of the principality, indeed of all Poland; at the consecration of an archbishop, the Bishop of Cracow being the first to lay hands on him. Fulko is succeeded by another prelate of noble birth, Vincent Kadłubek from Karwów, a man of unusual talents and education, who wrote *The Annals of Poland*, and repeatedly stressed the great importance of literature, pointing out that literary research brings renown, helps to ennoble manners and customs, and indicates norms of proper behaviour. For him study was nobility, fatherland, mother and nurse.

A.D. 1208

When, after the death of Duke Roman, several of the Ruthenian dukes try to follow his example and by force of arms, promises and bribes gain control of all Ruthenia, the country is involved in dreadful civil war. The elders realize that the only way of putting an end to it is to obtain the help of a neighbouring state. Some recommend seeking that of the Poles and submitting to their rule, but the memory of their recent defeat restrains them, so they approach the King of Hungary and ask him to appoint his son, Coloman, as their ruler, promising him fealty and obedience. King Andrew agrees and sends Coloman with a large army to put down domestic strife and take control of Galicia. The Ruthenian elders, dukes and boyars receive Coloman with due honour and he is installed in Halicz castle, after the Ruthenian duke Mstislav has been evicted. Coloman at once orders Vincent of Cracow, Ivo chancellor of Poland, and the other bishops in his entourage to anoint and crown him, and styles himself King of Galicia. This arouses the enmity of the fickle Ruthenians, because it has been done without consulting them and because they are afraid lest his Catholic coronation may lead to the destruction of their religion; so they start conspiring against Coloman, with the result that, when the soldiers he brought with him are sent back to Hungary, as they are as soon as he feels secure, Mstislav, called "the Brave", invades Galicia with the help of the Polovtsy and captures various strongholds and castles, plunders and burns them, and then lays siege to the castle at Halicz. In the course of the siege, the Chief of the Polovtsy is killed, shot from above, and his troops wreak vengeance on the local population, quartering and killing, burning and maiming, and carrying many off into slavery. When the castle is eventually captured, many of the Poles and Hungarians in it are either killed or taken prisoner, those who cannot ransom themselves with ready gold being sold into slavery. The new King is evicted. These events occurred in the year he married Salomea, the maiden sister of Leszek of Cracow, and he lives with her in chastity until his death, thus ensuring the glory of virginity for them both.

A.D. 1209

King Andrew, who feared his son might be expelled has already spent a lot of money assembling a large expeditionary force to send against Ruthenia. He knows that almost all the Ruthenian dukes are preparing for war in the summer in order to prevent him re-installing Coloman and then avenging his eviction and the cruelty of the Polovtsy. He now learns that they are again getting large reinforcements from the Polovtsy, so he sends to Leszek in Poland and persuades him to send him a considerable force of knights, which links up with him in Galicia. The Ruthenians react swiftly: Mstislav, son of Msistlav son of Riurik, Rostislav son of David, Rostislav son of Mstislav and Vladimir son of David combine their forces and to these others contribute contingents, making an army twice as strong as that of the Poles and Hungarians, whose first act is to strengthen Halicz castle which includes fortifying the Church of the Blessed Virgin, which is inside the castle, and installing in it a garrison of knights. In this second stronghold Coloman and his wife now take up residence, along with a number of women and the infirm. The rest of the army then advances on the Ruthenians, the Poles forming the right wing, the Hungarians and Galicians the left, the lightly armoured knights acting as an advance screen and it is they who initiate the assault. The enemy is also arrayed in two parts: one under Mstislav and the other under Duke Vladimir, while the Polovtsy are stationed some distance away, their role being to intervene at the height of the battle, as though from an ambush. The Poles mount a fierce assault on Vladimir's wing and kill so many that the Ruthenians weaken and then turn and run, pursued for miles by the Poles, and it is this pursuit that is to deprive them of victory, for it enables Mstislav to attack them from the rear. The moment the Hungarians are forced to call off the pursuit, the fleeing Ruthenians rally and return to the fray, this time attacking from the flank, and go on to defeat the Hungarians and capture their voivode. At this juncture the Hungarians give way to despair. They are surrounded by the Polovtsy in a ring so tight that they have no room to fight or to flee. The remaining Poles, returning from their pursuit with booty and a number of prisoners, are ignorant of the disaster that has befallen the Hungarians and Galicians, and sing their national anthem in the conviction that they are the victors, but they then find themselves in their turn tightly ringed by Ruthenians and Polovtsy, who show them no mercy. At one point the Ruthenians pick up and raise the Polish standard, to which other Poles then rally, only to be cut down in their turn. The number of the dead is incalculable. The cries of the wounded and dying can be heard in the castle at Halicz. The bodies of the dead are as numerous as grains of sand, too many for anyone to bury. The Polovtsy harvest a huge body of loot: horses, weapons, armour and clothing. Mstislav, overcome with pride at his victory, gives orders that no Pole or Hungarian is to be left alive, which means that those who sought safety in flight are slaughtered like cattle.

Mstislav, with the captured Hungarian voivode, now closes in on the castle at Halicz, from which all the citizens of Halicz have been evacuated as a precaution against treachery and to conserve foodstocks. The Hungarian voivode now calls upon the garrison to open the gates, since God has given victory to the other side. When the garrison refuses to do this, Mstislav sends a personal envoy to advise them to open the gates, and, when he returns unsuccessful, he even goes in person and calls upon them to surrender. When he, too, meets with a refusal, he has the castle completely surrounded. The rear of the castle is not well guarded, and, one night, a sap is made and the Ruthenians get through the wall and into the castle. They manage to capture the gate and let Mstislav and the others in. Mstislav still has to deal with the fortified church in which are Coloman and his wife, as well as some knights and their wives. He makes several attempts to parley with Coloman, which, on the advice of his knights, the latter refuses to do, so Mstislav lays siege to the church. When those inside begin to suffer from thirst, Mstislav sends in a vat of water, which, though rationed, is enough for only half their number. Then hunger, too, makes itself felt and the besieged surrender in return for their lives. The Hungarian men, their wives and other eminent persons, women and well-born maidens, plus some Polish knights, are distributed among the Polovtsy and Mstislav's courtiers for ransom or sale. The last to come out are Coloman and his wife. These Mstislav takes as his share and sends them to Torchesk, where they are strictly guarded. The army is then disbanded and Mstislav installs himself in Halicz.

When the King of Hungary learns of this disaster, he beats his brow in grief and weeps. Then, drying his tears, at his wife's suggestion he sends one of his knights to exhort Mstislav to release his son and daughter-in-law and the other prisoners, and, in the same breath to threaten that, if he does not do so, the King will attack Ruthenia with all the forces at his command. Such a threat carries no weight with Mstislav, who replies that victory is solely in the hands of God, and that, if Andrew attacks him, he will fight him and, with God's help, defeat him. His councillors tell the distraught King that what he did was all wrong and that he must adopt a more conciliatory tone, if he is ever to see his son again; so Andrew sends the knight back with a more modest offer of peace on equitable terms and begging Mstislav to release his son. The Queen sends her own envoy who begs, more humbly than befits a queen, for the release of her son. But Mstislav, fearing that the release of Coloman would just involve him in another war, refuses. He then installs his own starostas in Galicia and goes to Kiev and amuses himself there for several days, before returning to Halicz and taking up the reins of government.

A.D. 1210

Leszek, prince and monarch of Poland, heedful of the weal of the lands that are now his, visits each in turn, restoring the old laws, settling disputes and quarrels, and thereby deadening the pain left in his heart by the disaster at Halicz. He now visits Pomerania, accompanied by a larger than usual retinue of knights and barons, and there spends all the summer and autumn, visiting castles and towns: Gdańsk, Gniew and Słupsk, dispensing justice through the voivode, castellan or other official, for this is the part of the country farthest from his seat in Cracow, where recourse to the ruler and his tribunals is difficult for those who live there. Yielding to the insistent demands of the Pomeranians, he appoints a regent for Pomerania, Świętopełk, eldest son of Mszczuj, a man of excellent family, renowned for his good sense and acumen, and gives him full powers in all matters of justice, defence and the general conduct of affairs. The two voivodes of Gdańsk and Świecie are instructed to obey him, while the new regent himself swears to govern honestly and fairly in the name of Leszek, his sons and successors, always to obey Leszek and never refuse submission to his authority. He further undertakes to remit annually to the treasury in Cracow one thousand marks in silver, and always to use his best endeavour to preserve the monarch's authority and privileges. King Andrew has further talks with Mstislav through intermediaries. At a final meeting held in Hungary a lasting peace is concluded on the following terms: one of the sons of Béla, the late king of Hungary, is to marry Mstislav's daughter, Maria, and at the end of three years Mstislav is to cede the Duchy of Galicia to Coloman and simultaneously release Coloman and his wife.

A.D. 1211

The Ruthenian dukes, puffed up with pride by their unusual successes against the Hungarians, make repeated raids into Poland, helped by the Lithuanians and, indeed, at their suggestion. They collect booty and hurriedly withdraw to their own country. As they never stay long in one place, they do enormous damage and this so encourages them that they come to despise the Poles. Leszek, hurt to the quick, after much consultation, sends Sulisław the Castellan of Sandomierz with a strong force to exact vengeance and put a stop to the raids. The Castellan marches into Ruthenia and proceeds to put it to fire and the sword. He rounds up a large number of captives and sends them back to Poland in chains. The Ruthenian dukes Sviatoslav son of Mstislav and George, Iaroslav, Vladimir and Constantine now bar his further advance and offer to do battle, which, until then, they have cunningly avoided. Early in the battle the Poles break through the Ruthenian first line and scatter it, taking Sviatoslav and four other dukes prisoner, as well as many knights and ordinary soldiers. As many again must have been spitted on Polish swords. The Castellan orders the Ruthenian knights and nobles to be put in chains and sent to Poland, where many of them later regain their freedom, thanks to the generosity of Leszek, while others are ransomed by their families. Sviatoslav and the other four dukes are kept in captivity, both as a punishment and as a safeguard for the future. All in the Polish army are enriched by their share of the booty.

On May 16 Mieszko the Duke of Opole and Racibórz dies. He was a tall man, an unusually expert swordsman and the victor in many a duel and tourney in Germany, where he was brought up. He founded the monastery of the Premonstratensians in Rybnik. His only son Casimir, who succeeds him, moves this monastery to Czarnowąs at the confluence of the Mała Panew and the Oder.

A.D. 1212

Prince Leszek has spent Christmas in Cracow with his mother the duchess Helena, Vincent the Bishop of Cracow and other dignitaries. All is peaceful. The country's enemies are either quiescent or defeated, so there has been time to attend to matters concerning the city and its citizens. New courts are now held in every village, large and small, and justice dispensed. In the month of July, lightning strikes the cathedral's treasury, setting fire to the baulks and oaken beams supporting the roof. The fire is not put out and so spreads into the treasury itself, consuming reliquaries, chests and their contents, vestments, copes and numerous ornaments and jewelry, the gifts of generous kings, princes, bishops and the faithful. Even the clergy accept the fire as God's punishment for their trespasses.

A hitherto unknown Tatar tribe, trying to extend its authority over northern territories by defeating or destroying the Polovtsy, has invaded the areas adjacent to Ruthenia. The Polovtsy, not considering themselves strong enough, ask the Ruthenians for help, pointing out that, if the Tatars defeat them, the Ruthenians will be their likely next victim. As the request is being made, Tatar envoys arrive to ask the Ruthenian dukes not to intervene in the Tatars' war with the Polovtsy, and threatening that, should they ally themselves with the Polovtsy, the Tatars will wage war on them as well. The Tatars suggest that it would be expedient to expel all Polovtsy from Ruthenian territory. The Ruthenian dukes, rashly and without proper consultation, kill the Tatar envoys, thus breaking the law of nations, and send an army, comprising Mstislav son of Roman with the army of Kiev, Mstislav son of Mstislav with the army of Halicz, Vladimir son of Riurik and all the dukes of Ruthenia, all the dukes of Smolensk and Chernigov and all the Polovtsy under their own dukes, against the Tatars in order to help the Polovtsy. Their knights and one of the dukes ride overland, while the rest go by boat as far as the River Protolcza, from where they march in twelve stages to the River Kalka, by which the Tatars have already pitched camp. The Tatars scarcely allow them time to draw breath, but attack them at once, rout them and capture two of their dukes. Those who escape the slaughter run into further danger from the peasants through whose fields they are fleeing, for the peasants kill them indiscriminately, the cavalry for their horses, the infantry for their clothing. A few escape this second hazard and take refuge in the mountains, where most of them starve to death. Others are drowned as they try to cross rivers. Mstislav of Galicia is one who escapes and manages to reach the boats which brought them, and, being afraid of a Tatar pursuit, he has these destroyed. When some fellow fugitives reach the river and find the boats gone, so that they are unable to cross, most of them, now weak with hunger, perish. Vladimir, son of Riurik, escaping back to Kiev, assumes power there.

A.D. 1213

Andrew of Hungary is enjoying success and fame largely thanks to an excellent marriage and his children: three sons and a daughter, St. Elizabeth, who was married at a tender age to Ludwig the Landgrave of Thuringia. Fate now dims the glory, when, on August 28, Baron Bankban, one of the most eminent of the Hungarian barons, runs the Queen through with his sword, killing her. The chroniclers advance two reasons for his action: one, that Queen Gertrude had allowed one of her brothers to dishonour the Baron's wife, while she was in attendance on the Queen, and the Baron, wishing to avenge the slight and unable to reach the actual author, punished his sister instead. Yet, is it not unreasonable to suggest that a woman, until then modest and pure, who had borne a saintly daughter and herself came from a noble, religious family, would aid and abet in dishonouring a marriage and in adultery? The other suggestion is that, when, on the advice of his wife, the King brought in Germans to help him recapture some rebellious castles, he had rewarded them for their services with government posts given over the heads of Hungarians, and for this malcontents conspired to murder him. The Queen was able to warn her husband, who escaped, so, when the conspirators, headed by Baron Bankban, came to carry out their plan and found that the King had escaped, they killed the Queen instead. For this dreadful murder the King orders Bankban's entire family to be wiped out. The Queen bequeathed a golden crown, which she wore on ceremonal occasions, to Wrocław cathedral, and this, in accordance with her wishes, is melted down and a gold chalice made of it.

The youth and maturity of Henry, Duke of Wrocław and Silesia, and of his blessed wife, have been a time of continuing success; now, when they are past their prime, misfortune afflicts them in the guise of increasing enmity between their two sons, Henry and Conrad the Curly, who have now reached maturity, their third son, Bolesław, having already died. These two can be called the Polish Esau and Jacob, for one is backed by his father, the other by his mother. Henry marries young Conrad, of whom he is unusually fond, to a daughter of the Duke of Saxony and grants him the land of Lubusz and its district in Lusatia in perpetuity; while the younger son, Henry, at his mother's suggestion is given Silesia and Wrocław. Conrad, who, by nature, is friendly to the Poles and a fierce enemy of the Germans, takes offence at this and tries to get the arrangement invalidated. When repeated requests prove ineffective, he decides to use force. Furious with both his father and his brother, he decides to expel the latter and all his German supporters from Silesia, and, with this in view assembles his own force of knights and men from Poland and Lubusz and with it attacks his brother. The two parents do their utmost to end the dispute and restore peace, but, when their efforts prove ineffectual, Duke Henry withdraws to Głogów and his wife to Niemcza, their two sons being allowed to do as they please. Henry in his turn collects an army and intercepts Conrad somewhere between Legnica and Złotoryja. Conrad is killed in the subsequent battle, which leaves Henry victorious, and he then goes to his father in Głogów. While there, he goes hunting in the Tarnow forest, where his horse throws him and in the fall he breaks his neck and dies.

A.D. 1214

Duke Władysław, who has become known as "The Spitter", is still not of age when he takes a sudden dislike to his guardian and uncle, Władysław of Wielkopolska, whom some call "the Great", because of his stature, and others "Long Shanks" because of the length of his legs, and demands that his uncle hand over half of Wielkopolska. It is not only that young Władysław is ambitious, but he is being egged on by some of the well-born youths with whom he has grown up. His uncle employs various cunning manoeuvres to prevaricate and this drives the Spitter, who cannot tolerate delay, to take action. Together with a few companions he gains entry into the castle at Kalisz, turns out his uncle's officials, and then takes possession of the town itself.

Learning what has happened, his uncle assembles a force and lays siege to Kalisz where his nephew is shut up in the castle. After a fortnight it is obvious to the besieged that they will shortly run out of food and they send envoys, who arrange a surrender that allows them to leave unharmed and not to fall into disfavour. The Spitter, however, does not trust his uncle, so, one night, he and seven companions steal out and make their way to Cracow and Leszek, only to continue on to Hungary, where King Andrew gives him generous support.

A.D. 1215

Bishop Vincent of Cracow, wishing further to improve his cathedral, grants it in perpetuity eleven sheaf tithes and seven monetary tithes from the villages round Czehów. The revenue this brings in pays for the cathedral's wine, candles and other necessities, and provides the prelates and canons frequenting the cathedral with a daily portion. The neighbouring town of Kazimierz also benefits so that the candles on its altars are never extinguished.

A.D. 1216

This winter the Lithuanians invade Ruthenia and proceed to plunder it. As they withdraw, they are pursued by Duke Iaroslav son of Vsevolod and men of Novgorod, who succeed in making them stand and fight, and then routs them, though not without himself suffering considerable casualties, among them Duke David of Toropek and many of his knights. Later, another Lithuanian army devastates Polotsk and the country round it. Then Duke Mstislav son of David appears with a force of Smolensk knights and kills inumerable Lithuanians. Many of those who flee and seek refuge in farms and forts, are dragged from their hiding-places and killed. Very few escape.

Andrew, Bishop of Prague, being under considerable pressure from King Přemysl and the Czech nobles and knights, who complain that some of the individual assessments on their villages are too high and so are increasingly refusing to pay tithes and various imposts, decides to follow the example of the famous bishop of Prague, St. Wojciech, and excommunicates the King and the Czech barons. When these make light of the ban and do nothing about it, he lays an interdict on the entire Kingdom of Bohemia. Then, fearing the wrath of the King and his knights, he leaves the capital with a few clerics and laymen and goes to Rome, and there he stays until he dies, refusing to return to a people so pig-headed and so difficult to bridle. The pressure on the clergy then increases still further and eventually at every toll, where Jews are made to pay one penny a head, priests and clerics have to pay thirty. This and other barbarous burdens imposed on them make life all but intolerable for the clergy. Indeed, in Bohemia, Christians and priests are more humiliated and disfavoured than Jews.

A.D. 1217

Conrad of Mazovia and Kujawy, brother of Leszek the White, is a cruel man. Mazovia and Kujawy have long been governed by the Voivode of Płock, Baron Christian, under whose rule they have flourished and enjoyed peace; the ducal revenues have increased, criminals have been punished and honest people honoured. Now, seeing the unbridled, licentious behaviour of the young duke, whose tutor he had once been, the Voivode reproaches him, first in private, then in the presence of his councillors, and begs him to give up certain reprehensible activities. The Duke flies into a rage and has the Voivode flung into a filthy prison, at which those who are jealous of the Voivode, invent all sorts of slanderous accusations, which they take to the Duke, who naively believes them and so becomes further incensed with the Voivode, to the extent of having him first blinded, then killed.

After the death of Voivode Christian the fortunes of Mazovia and Kujawy decline. The barbarian Prussians and their neighbours, the Lithuanians and other pagans, who have been forced to pay tribute to Christian and the Polish treasury, seize the opportunity to get their revenge. They make more and more frequent raids into Poland and destroy so much of the country that Conrad has to ask the Duke of Wrocław for help. Together they defeat the invaders and restore the lands of Chełmno to their former state; later, at Duke Henry's suggestion, Conrad invokes the assistance of the Teutonic Knights and hands Chełmno over to them, for them to defend against the Prussians.

A.D. 1218

Vincent, Bishop of Cracow, a man of great piety and unusually well educated, has long wished to renounce his office, but has been prevented from doing so by the pleas of the chapter and of Prince Leszek, who cannot accept the idea of doing without his services; now, however, Vincent gets his way and Ivo, a Pole of noble birth, cantor of Gniezno, canon of Cracow and Leszek's chancellor, is chosen to replace him. Anticipating that the Pope will raise difficulties, Ivo goes to Rome, taking with him one of the Cracow canons, Jacek of Opole. The Pope readily gives his permission for Vincent to relinquish the see and Ivo to take it over, the latter having the recommendation of Cardinal-Bishop Ugolino of Ostia, who has been Ivo's friend ever since they were students together in Paris. Ugolino is in Rome to promote his own business, and is there able to meet Dominic, whose saintliness and piety have been working miracles, and hear him preach. One day, as Cardinal Stephen is on his way to the monastery of St. Sixtus, where Dominic and his brethren live, his horse throws him and he is picked up, apparently dead. One of the bystanders turns to his nephew Dominic and asks what he is going to do, saying that the accident provides him with an opportunity to prove his powers. Dominic, certain of heavenly assistance, says a prayer and restores the dead man to life. Ivo witnesses this miracle. Now, before returning to Poland, he asks Dominic for brethren to accompany him. None being available, he obtains permission for three of his companions to be admitted to the Order, so that they can later return to Poland and there found the first house of the Preaching Order. He himself returns to Rome and is consecrated Bishop of Cracow, while Vincent enters the Cistercian monastery at Jędrzejów, dons the habit and obeys the rules of that Order.

Coloman, son of the King of Hungary, marches into Ruthenia and is received with full honours by the people of Galicia and Duke Mstislav, who, in accordance with the agreement he and King Andrew made in 1210, hands over the duchy and Halicz castle, and himself retires to Torchesk, where he dies twelve months later. Coloman now rules Galicia, but is not left long in peaceful possession of it.

Wishing to implement a vow his father made, King Andrew sails to the Holy Land together with Duke Leopold of Austria and crusaders of various nationalities. In a battle with the Saracens they capture Damietta and recover almost the whole of the Holy Land; yet, after only a short time, Andrew withdraws, despite the opposition of the Patriarch of Jerusalem, who ends by excommunicating him. He takes with him as curiosities a quantity of weapons, helms and animals.

A.D. 1219

On March 22, Henry, Archbishop of Gniezno, dies and the chapter choses as his successor a Polish noble, Vincent of Kietlicz, whose appointment is confirmed by Honorius III. This is the Henry, who, out of the noblest of motives, introduced a number of measures concerning the distribution of benefices and enhanced the liberties of the Church in Poland. Previously, priests could be made to appear before even the humblest of the secular courts, but Henry obtained for them the privilege that priests, monks and converts could only be tried in the ecclesiastical courts of their superiors, and not be compelled to appear before a lay court by their duke or his officials. He obtained a similar privilege for those whose place of birth is one of the Church's possessions. He subsequently went to Rome and obtained papal confirmation of the arrangement. Returning to Poland, he further extended benefit of clergy; but, when the provincial synod met, as the enactment of Cardinal Peter of Capua concerning the dismissal of priests' wives had not yet borne fruit, he insisted that all priests had to give up their wives, and ordered all the clergy to swear on the Bible that they will dismiss their wives and concubines, and thenceforth live in celibacy and abstinence.

A.D. 1220

The nobles of Cracow, afraid that Leszek, who is twenty-eight, might die without progeny and they will find themselves under foreign rule, put pressure on the young duke to take a wife. Opinions are divided as to whom she should be, some advocating a union with Hungary, others suggesting a German, a Bohemian or a Ruthenian bride, the latter suggestion having the greatest support, because, in these stormy times that would provide an opportunity to extend Polish dominion and at the same time restore peace to relations with Ruthenia, which have long been troubled by endless wars and misunderstandings. So, Leszek the White marries Grzymisława, daughter of Iaroslav of Ruthenia. The wedding is held in Cracow with considerable pomp and at great expense. Thanks to this marriage, Poland and Ruthenia enjoy the blessings of lasting peace. It also brings about the release of all prisoners of war, whether of the nobility or the peasantry.

The Ruthenian dukes, jealous of Coloman, who has, undisturbed, governed the lands and castle of Halicz, now incite Duke Daniel son of Roman, who needs no encouragement, since his father once possessed all Galicia, to attack Halicz. Together they occupy the castle and expel Coloman and his Hungarians, who flee back to Pannonia. Galicia they find in a state of utter neglect.

A.D. 1221

A fresh disaster now afflicts Poland, an expression of the wrath of God or, perhaps, a freak of Fate, for incessant rain has deluged the country from Easter until the autumn causing many rivers to overflow their banks, so that people now fear a second flood. Many low-lying villages are destroyed and winter corn cannot be sown. Fields sown in the previous autumn are engulfed, except for a few places where hills or mountains protect them. This causes great unhappiness, not only in Poland, but in all neighbouring countries, where the same thing is happening. One result is a murrain among domestic animals due to lack of pasture; the combined result is three years of starvation, which destroys numbers of people. Indeed, many villages, even towns, are emptied as their inhabitants die. Matters are made worse by the exceptionally severe winter that follows.

In June, Duchess Grzymisława gives birth to a son, who is christened Bolesław.

The King of Hungary, eager to avenge Duke Daniel's expulsion of his son, Coloman, sends the latter and his brother, Béla, with a huge army to teach Galicia a lesson. For three weeks they besiege Halicz castle, hoping that it will surrender quickly, otherwise disaster in the guise of dysentry and hunger may strike both men and horses and force the invaders to withdraw.

A.D. 1222

On his return from Italy with the brethren trained for him by Dominic, Bishop Ivo has to decide where to establish their cloister. After consulting the Duke, the chapter and the town council of Cracow, they are allotted the Church of the Holy Trinity as the new Order's mother and parish church, and are also given a large plot of land on which to build a cloister and offices. These are furnished with vessels, robes, books and other necessities. Accommodation is built and provisions assured for the brethren. Canon Jacek and many others join the Order. Bishop Ivo also builds a new church in the main square in Cracow, and grants to the new church of the Blessed Virgin the parish rights that belonged to the church of the Holy Trinity.

The famine of the previous year still affects Poland, causing much damage.

The Prussians and Pomeranians burn the town of Płock and devastate much of the surrounding territory and that of Mazovia. Andrew King of Hungary again sends his son, Coloman, to attack Halicz. This time he is more successful, for Daniel does not dare resist and Coloman is able to gain control of both town and castle without opposition.

A.D. 1223

Bishop Ivo, concerned by the conditions in which numbers of unfortunates, who have gathered in Cracow, are living, establishes a hospital in the village of Pradnik outside the city gates, which is to provide shelter for those of either sex who may need it.

Such a hospital was originally planned by Bishop Fulko, only his death prevented the plan being carried out. The hospital is endowed with three vills and several sheaf-tithes. Its administration is entrusted to the Brethren of the Order of St. Augustine, known as "de Saxia", who wear a double white cross on a black cloak. Seeing that the site of the hospital has been badly chosen, the Bishop has it moved into the city itself, where he builds a monastery and offices for the hospital and accommodation for the sick and the unfortunate, sending from his own table enough to feed both, for rain has again prevented crops being sown and there is famine once more.

Vincent Kadłubek, former bishop of Cracow, dies on March 8 after five years in the monastery of Jędrzejów and is buried in the middle of the choir there. While still active as bishop of Cracow he wrote a record of the history of his fatherland, the equal in literary worth of those of antiquity.

Otto's son, Władysław, once Duke of Wielkopolska, who has spent almost nine years in itinerant exile in Pannonia, secretly returns to Poland, disguised as a monk, having previously, through intermediaries, made an alliance with Świętopełk, who is governor of Pomerania and also his brother-in-law. His sister, Helinga, who has a large dowry, undertakes to help in demanding that he be given his share of the inheritance.

So, on November 7, with the help of Governor Świętopełk and acting on his advice, Władysław forces his way into the castle at Ujście, which is negligently guarded, though in its position and its man-made defences very strong, being sited at the confluence of the rivers Notéc and Gwda, and captures it. From there he proceeds to ravage the surrounding country.

Cardinal Gregory of Crescencia, legate of Pope Honorius III, arrives in Cracow to be received by Leszek the White, Bishop Ivo and representatives of all the estates. He stays there a considerable time: putting an end to certain abuses among the clergy and issuing instructions concerning their administration.

Bishop Gosław of Płock dies. As the canons of Płock carry out an irregular election, choosing several different people to succeed, the see remains vacant for two years.

A.D. 1224

Two years of famine are followed by a third, and one that is far more severe. This proves fatal not only to domestic animals and people, but causes outbreaks of plague worse than those of the two previous years. Nevertheless, there is no compromise or mercy in the implementation of the law, and justice is administered in exactly the same way as in times of plenty. For example, when the assizes come to Rozegroch, no postponements are allowed. Indeed, Duke Leszek, monarch of Poland, himself presides and dispenses justice in even the most complicated cases to the admiration of all. While there, he is approached by Bishop Klet of Eger, come to tell him of King Andrew's return from the Holy Land with the bones of several saints, and to ask for the suppression of various frontier disturbances that have broken out during the King's absence, as well as compensation for those who have suffered loss because of them. The Bishop also asks that, in the event of King Andrew declaring war on Bohemia, Leszek will personally come to his help or at least send him an army. Leszek declares himself delighted at the safe return of his friend and ally, and promises to punish misdemeanours and make amends for damage done, and for this purpose fixes a day for the two sides to meet on the frontier. He promises, too, to come in person to help King Andrew, or, at least, to send him an army.

The Prussians force their way into the monastery at Oliwa and carry off the abbot, his brethren and all those inside. First, they take them in the direction of Gdańsk, but, in the end, just kill them. After this, the Prussians continue making impudent raids into the territories of Chełmno and Lubawa, to suppress which the Duke of Mazovia calls in the Brethren of the Sword, who are called Knights of Christ and who have a red sword and a cross. The Duke gives them the castle of Dobrzyń from which to fight the Prussians, but this they fail to do; indeed, they put up so meagre a resistance that the lands of Chełmno and Lubawa are soon completely devastated.

Leszek's wife, Grzymisława gives birth to a daughter. Although Leszek is not altogether pleased, they are both delighted that she has been relieved of the shame of barrenness, which means that there is a chance of her having a son in the future. The babe is christened Salomea.

The territory of Lubusz is raided and its castle occupied.

A.D. 1225

Henry the Bearded, having convinced himself that the Polish monarchy and the dukedom of Cracow are his by right of seniority, and that Leszek has usurped them to his detriment and shame, assembles an army of his own men and mercenaries paid for with other people's money, and, urged on by Marek the Voivode of Cracow, now in exile, marches on Cracow with the intention of removing Leszek and so righting the wrong he has suffered. Meanwhile, Leszek has been mobilizing a huge army of his own and that of Conrad of Mazovia, on whom he has called for assistance, so that, when Henry and his army reach the river Dłubnia, not far from Cracow, Leszek is there waiting for them with his army in battle array and ready to fight. Henry is really quite a modest man, and he has been urged by his saintly wife, Jadwiga, to be content with Wrocław and not aspire to the monarchy; now, seeing how much better and stronger Leszek's army is than his own, and that his own troops are intimidated by the strength of their opponents, Henry sends heralds to ask for a parley. To this Leszek and Conrad agree, for both hate the thought of civil war, and a day and a place are fixed. Here the two sides meet, and it is agreed that Henry renounces all pretension to the monarchy and all that goes with it. Each then swears to promote the advantage and renown of the other and to make no attempt to seize any of the other's lands or territory. They then exchange gifts, take part in a banquet and return to their duchies, the best of friends. Leszek invites the other two dukes to Cracow, where he entertains them and their knights most lavishly. Conrad then returns to Mazovia, but Henry stays on for another week; then, laden with gifts, he returns to Silesia, well content.

A.D. 1226

Władysław the Great, alias Long Shanks, wishing to avenge the wrong done him by his nephew and regain Ujście castle, assembles an army and lays siege to the castle with his nephew shut up inside. He mounts an assault with catapults, siege towers and straightforward infantry attacks. The castle is well defended by its position and its garrison, and the besiegers achieve nothing. The siege lasts from early spring until St. Margaret's Day, and the troops lose heart and grow slack in carrying out their duties, whether as guards or as patrols to prevent supplies reaching the besieged. However, the besieged are equally remiss, no longer making sorties, but behaving as if they were exhausted and already half defeated. When, from his vantage point, Władysław observes the relaxation of discipline in the besiegers' camp and how some wander away, others lie asleep, others again neglect to carry their weapons, and some are even drunk, he tells his men that just a little effort will give them victory, so he sallies out in force and, attacking the besiegers' camp, kills or routs all in it. Among the dead are Dobrogost the Voivode of Poznań and a number of eminent knights. After this disaster Władysław abandons the attempt and withdraws. The other Władysław, his nephew, confident that he has the necessary strength, organizes a pursuit of his uncle's forces and occupies Poznań and Kalisz, both part of his inheritance, and thus has recovered it all. He plunders and burns the ducal granaries in Niedźwiedź and several other villages, and makes raids into Wielkopolska.

A.D. 1227

Świętopełk, Governor of Pomerania, proud of being related through his sister to the Duke of Wielkopolska and of the wealth he has accumulated, makes repeated approaches to his sovereign lord, asking to be made duke, quoting as precedent, the Bogusław whom Wry-mouth made Duke of Western Pomerania. Leszek refuses the request which he considers excessive and impertinent. This so angers Świętopełk that he starts thinking of claiming independence and, as a first step, stops paying tribute. Leszek, anxious to stifle the rebellion at birth, arranges a visit to Gąsawa, a village belonging to the monastery at Trzemeszno, and summons the Governor to appear before him in person, pretending that, as monarch, he has to consult him over certain matters and that he wishes to assure him of the permanence of his position, but, in reality, to arrest him. Świętopełk, a cautious and unusually cunning man, who has already forced a number of knights to swear allegiance to him personally, is convinced that the suggested meeting is solely aimed at him and the safety of his person, as, indeed, it is. Together with his relative Duke Władysław, to whom he promises supreme authority over all Poland in the event of their being successful, he plans an attempt on the lives of both Leszek and Henry the Bearded, who, he has learned, is to accompany Leszek. Suspecting neither treachery nor trickery and intending to act in moderation in recovering Pomerania, Leszek comes to the appointed place accompanied by Henry the Bearded and quite a considerable retinue. There they spend a couple of days in discussions with the Duke of Wielkopolska about prolonging the peace arranged between the latter and his uncle, the Duke of Gniezno, all unaware that they have walked into a trap. Next on the agenda is the question of compensation for damage done in the repeated raids by Pomeranians into Polish territory. Świętopełk is now supposed to join them, but delays his arrival, sending instead a stream of messengers, whose real purpose is to spy out the situation and report what is happening in Gąsawa. On the fourth day, many matters having been disposed of, the dukes go to the baths to attend to their bodies. Informed of this, Świętopełk seizes the opportunity and arrives with a considerable force of both Pomeranians and Poles, who force their way into the hostelries and tents of the dukes and knights, killing every one who resists. When the Dukes realize what is happening, Leszek, the youngest and strongest, leaps from the bath and mounting a horse being held by one of his men, rides off with a few companions. Świętopełk or-

A fine bath establishment with most attractive attendants.
From Archiv mesta Brna, *Jakubska Knihovna, Brno.*

ganizes a pursuit, telling his men that victory depends on their bringing him this one corpse. Though Leszek and his companions resist stoutly, they are all killed. Świętopełk is so eager to get rid of the royal progeny and those who came with them, that he has their knights and escort, even those naked in the bath, cruelly murdered. Henry the Bearded is also in the bath and receives several wounds; indeed he would have been killed had not one of his knights, Peregrine of Weissenburg, shielded him with his own body. Peregrine receives several wounds and collapses, but his body still covers that of his Duke, and their assailants depart, considering both to be dead.

Leszek's body is taken to Cracow by the survivors of his retinue and there buried in the cathedral. Świętopełk, having murdered his liege lord, neither regrets it nor attends the funeral. From now on he begins to act as the legitimate duke of Pomerania. Henry is taken home to Wrocław on a litter. Once recovered, he lavishes gifts on Peregrine's children in recognition of their father's loyalty.

A.D. 1228

The murder of Leszek leads to strife between the surviving dukes: Conrad of Mazovia, Leszek's brother, and Henry the Bearded, Duke of Silesia and Wrocław, both of whom strive to assume the authority of monarch and the guardianship of Leszek's children. Disgusted by Conrad's tyrannical behaviour, Leszek's widow, Grzymisława, places herself, her children and their duchies and lands under the protection and rule of Duke Henry, begging him to protect them from Conrad. The result is civil war, with each of the two advancing on Cracow with an army. Grzymisława has possession of the castle and city and denies them to Conrad. Henry builds two new forts, one on a hill near Skala, which is washed by the river Pradnik, the other at Międzyborze, and installs strong garrisons in them, hoping that these will enable him to occupy the whole duchy. Conrad, considering that for him victory depends on the destruction of these two forts, brings up an army to lay siege to that at Skala. Henry bars his advance and there is a fierce battle in which Conrad's young son, Przemyśl, is killed, and which ends in Conrad retreating, leaving Henry the victor. Conrad now marches on the second fort, but fares no better there, and, having lost most of his men, takes refuge in the nearby forest. He then returns to Mazovia in order to get reinforcements and start all over again, but, seeing that his troops are reluctant and not well disciplined, and also that summer is nearly over, he abandons the use of force in favour of deceit and cunning, which, he hopes, will make it easier for him to defeat his enemy.

Henry, thinking that he has defeated his opponent, sends his son back to Silesia with the army, while he, carefree, sets off on a tour of the duchy of Cracow, convinced that the peasants are all his sincere and loyal subjects. Learning of this, Conrad returns to Cracow and with the help of a few discontented knights pounces upon Henry, while he is hearing Mass in a church in Spytkowice and carries him off to a castle in Mazovia. Henry's son, also Henry, assembles a large army of both his own people and mercenaries with which to invade Mazovia should Conrad refuse to release his father. The Duchess Grzymisława, in an attempt to avoid the slaughter, depopulation, devastation and oppression of peasants and the poor, that would otherwise occur, herself goes to Mazovia to prevent civil war. In her presence Conrad is like one defeated and promises to do what she asks. Thus Conrad and Henry are reconciled. The bond is strenghtened by Conrad's two sons marrying two of the Duchess's granddaughters. Henry is released and returns to Silesia. Conrad now considers himself monarch and guardian of Leszek's two sons, despite the opposition of their mother.

The Tatars invade Ruthenia in large numbers and indulge in all sorts of cruelty. They devastate the whole of Riazan, murder its duke, the old and the children, and carry the rest off as slaves. What forts they capture, they burn. During the winter they attack Suzdal and devastate the whole of it, killing Duke Gregory and his sons and many others. They capture Rostov castle from Duke Vladimir, burn it and carry off many captives and much booty.

In January, in his home town of Gdańsk, Świętopełk founds and builds a monastery for the Order of the Dominicans.

Přemysl, King of Bohemia, feeling that death is at hand, has the Archbishop of Mainz in his presence anoint and crown his son, Václav, whose mother Přemysl had married while his first, legitimate wife, Adela, was still alive, she being the sister of Béla, King of Hungary. Václav is thus crowned king and his wife, Cunegund, queen.

Pope Gregory IX canonizes Elizabeth, daughter of Andrew of Hungary and widow of Landgrave Ludwig of Thuringia. The Roman Emperor Frederick exhumes her body, which is in the hospital in Marburg, and, in the presence of many bishops and dukes, produces a golden crown with which to adorn the skull.

A.D. 1229

Fighting again breaks out between Władysław Long Shanks and his nephew. Long Shanks has a force of knights, some his own, others brought in from outside, and hopes to avenge his defeat of the previous year. His nephew, made confident by his earlier success, bars his uncle's advance, but being inferior in number is defeated in the subsequent battle, and, regarding flight from a battlefield as shameful, is himself captured and put in prison. He is released later, thanks to the efforts of his supporters, and he goes to Pomerania to his brother-in-law, Świętopełk, whom he asks to help him in resuming hostilities. Świętopełk not only gives him his army, but himself rides with him against Long Shanks. The latter, knowing that he cannot rely on the loyalty of his subjects, who dislike and despise him because of his nasty, licentious behaviour and other deeds unworthy of a duke, abandons all his strongholds in Wielkopolska and seeks shelter in the castle at Racibórz, where the Duke receives him with great kindness. This allows his nephew to recover his own share, as well as gaining control of his uncle's.

Bishop Ivo, considering this a favourable time to request the restoration of metropolitan status to Cracow cathedral, goes to Italy to Pope Gregory IX, his friend since their student days in Paris, whom he finds in Perugia and who readily grants his request. From Perugia, Bishop Ivo goes to Rome to visit the sacred sites. Here he contracts a fever. He leaves before he has thrown it off, and the ardours of travel and the heat of summer make his condition worse; and, when he reaches Castelvetro on July 21, he dies. His friends bury him in the great church in Modena, and a couple of years later the Brethren of the Order of the Dominicans in Cracow, which he founded, remove his bones to the church of the Holy Trinity in Cracow.

A Tatar horde overruns Smolensk and Chernigov, killing, destroying and capturing castles and forts, which had in fact already been abandoned by their defenders, who, lacking the courage to face the Tatars, had taken refuge in their inaccessible marshes and forests, allowing the Tatars to depart with their spoil and captives.

A.D. 1230

The death of Bishop Ivo leaves the see of Cracow vacant, and so it remains for two years, for the Chapter is unable to agree on a successor. In the end, a Pole of noble birth, Wisław, who is a canon of the cathedral, is elected and his election confirmed by the Pope. The new bishop is of the clan of Zabawa, whose ancestors emigrated from Pomerania to Cracow, and thus he and his family are regarded as newcomers. In his will Bishop Ivo left money to pay for the cathedral tower to be covered with lead. While this work is being carried out, one of the workmen, handling fire incautiously, allows a red hot coal to drop and this falls onto the dry roof of an adjacent building, a church, which that night goes up in flames, despite the efforts of numbers of people to extinguish the blaze.

With the help of the Polish knights Albert and Laurence, the sons of John, the Duke of Wielkopolska plunders the famous abbey at Mogilno, thus demonstrating how far he has departed from the ways of his ancestors, former kings, dukes and heroes of Poland, in that he himself destroys the very monasteries they founded.

The Prussians are behaving with barbarous savagery towards the Poles, making secret and unexpected raids into their territory, burning and carrying people off into slavery. For some time, too, they have been harassing the lands of the Duke of Mazovia, which also border on Prussian territory. Now, on the advice of some wise and pious Cistercians, Duke Conrad sends for seven brethren of the Teutonic Order of the Holy Sepulchre in Jerusalem. These are accommodated in Dobrzyń castle and thus become known as the Dobrzyń Brethren. Later, Conrad grants them the castle and town of Nieszawa with two villages and their appurtenances. With their help Conrad twice defeats the Prussians, after which, with general consent, he ascribes to the Knights and grants them—*de facto*—being unable to do so *de jure*, since to do so would be to the detriment of Poland—those parts of Chełmno and Lubawa lying between the Rivers Ossa, Drwęca and Vistula. At the time the grant was made, it appeared sound and justified, but, later, when the Teutonic Knights try to gain possession of the rest of Poland and the Poles naturally resist, it proves to have been the cause of appalling bloodshed. Indeed, no other Polish king or prince has brought down greater disaster and unhappiness on his country, or involved it in more grievous wars, than this Conrad did. In the document finalizing the agreement, the Master and Brethren of the Order bind

La Vigenére's idea of Poland's bison from La Description du Royaume de Pologne.
—*British Library.*

themselves to divide any territories won from the barbarians equally between the Duke of Mazovia, his sons and successors, and the Order of the Teutonic Knights; also, that, after the conquest of Prussia, the grant of the territories of Chełmno and Lubawa is to become null and void and these territories are to revert with full rights of possession to the Duke and his successors. This document has been seen by reliable officials of the Duchy of Płock, who have held it in their hands. With the Duke's troops to help him, the new Master of the Order, Conrad of Landsberg, builds on the banks of the Vistula a castle, from which he mounts raids into Prussia and which he uses to prevent reciprocal raids from there.

A.D. 1231

This is the fourth year of exile imposed on Władysław Long Shanks by his nephew. Now, with the help of some fellow exiles and a number of other knights who are fugitives from prison for debt or crime, he leaves the town of Racibórz, in which he has spent his exile, and, heading for Wielkopolska, invests the castle at Gniezno, which was part of his inheritance, hoping that, if he can capture it, other castles will come over to him. This proves a vain hope, for the castle is stoutly defended and, after two months during which no one has come over to his side, for everyone is disgusted by his shameful, nasty habits, a rumour begins to circulate that his nephew will arrive any day with Świętopełk of Pomerania and a large army to relieve the besieged. At this, Long Shanks gives up and returns to Racibórz. He dies later this same year, and, as he had no progeny, the rights to the duchy pass to his nephew, Władysław Odonic, who now has both duchies, Poznań and Kalisz, plus the whole of Wielkopolska.

In order to deal more effectively with the Prussians, Conrad of Mazovia and the Teutonic Knights, with some foreigners who have joined them, build a fort of oaken baulks and install a strong garrison. They also found a new town, Toruń. The Prussian reply is to build three forts: one on the Vistula above Toruń, which they call Rogów, another near Toruń, where the old town of Chełmno now stands, and a third by a lake, which to this day is known as Pippin's lake, after the Prussian leader, Pippin, a fierce enemy of Christians. All three forts are quickly captured by the Poles and the Knights and so too is Pippin himself. He is made to pay for his arrogance by having his belly split open and then being driven round and round a tree, until his guts fall out.

Frederick of Austria, desiring vengeance, invades Bohemia with an army reinforced with units sent him by his brother, the Margrave of Moravia, the Duke of Merano, the Margrave of Werd, the Bishop of Bamberg, the Patriarch of Aquileia and yet others. King Václav does not dare oppose so large an army, especially as many Czechs prefer the Margrave to him. However, after capturing the castle at Vetav and doing a certain amount of damage, Duke Frederick falls ill and the army is withdrawn and disbanded.

The King of Hungary, Andrew, dies after thirty years of peaceful, happy rule. He is succeeded by his eldest son, Béla.

A.D. 1232

Władysław Odonic, son of Otto, Duke of Wielkopolska, who is nicknamed "the Spitter", because of his habit of spitting, wishing to repay the many benefits God has bestowed on him: release from dire imprisonment, defeat of his enemies, the increase in the power of his duchies after the death of Władysław Long Shanks, and his two fine sons by his legitimate wife, sister of the Duke of Pomerania, grants considerable liberties and privileges to the two cathedral churches in his duchy: Gniezno and Poznań. He exempts the villages they possess, or may possess in the future, and their inhabitants, from all taxes, services and tribute previously rendered to the Duke and his treasury, as well as from being answerable to his courts, those of the voivodes, castellans, judges, officials and all ordinary or extraordinary courts. He also transfers to the Archbishop of Gniezno and the Bishop of Poznań and their successors all ducal rights over those churches' possessions. He also grants to the two bishops the right to mint coin and to hunt in the churches' lands, hitherto the prerogative of the Duke. In memory of his father Otto, and of Bolesław the Great, the first King of Poland, and of other Polish kings, he grants Poznań cathedral the village of Sulkowa Krob a with its revenues.

Bishop Laurence of Wrocław dies an unusual death, that of excessive smelling of roses, from which he contracts rheumatism, which proves incurable and finally kills him.

A.D. 1233

The lavishness of Władysław's gifts to the Church exasperates the barons and knights of Wielkopolska to such an extent that they secretly plot his death; indeed, when a planned ambush fails, they rebel openly, approaching Henry the Bearded, known to be Władysław Odonic's implacable enemy, promising him the duchy of Wielkopolska. Although hitherto a just and pious man, Henry goes against the advice of his wife, Jadwiga, and accepts the offer, though knowing it to be wrong and conceived of injustice and envy, since it gives him an easy way of punishing Władysław. So, he invades Wielkopolska with a considerable army. Władysław, well aware that his knights have turned against him and afraid that Henry's army is the stronger, as well as that his own knights may well betray or desert him, does not come out into the open. He burns the castles of Bnin and Śrem so as to deny them to Henry, strengthens the garrison in Gniezno and goes to his father-in-law Świętopelk in Pomerania. The barons and knights of Wielkopolska at once transfer their allegiance to Henry. With them on his side, Henry repairs the castles that Władysław burned or dismantled, garrisons them with his knights and hands them over to his nephew, the son of the Margrave of Moravia.

Bořivoj who was the Margrave of Moravia, suitably called "One-Eye", dies in Hungary. His mother, Adelaide, sister of Henry the Bearded, who, on her expulsion from Moravia on the death of her husband, Boleslav, had returned to her parental home with her four sons Bořivoj, Boleslav, Přemysl and Theobald, now dies in the nunnery at Trzebnica, where she was living, and is buried along with her second son, Přemysl, who dies shortly after her. Boleslav's youngest son has become a canon in Magdeburg, while the two others, Boleslav and Borislav, are serving as knights with their uncle, Duke Henry.

Vladimir, Duke of Kiev, fearful lest the Greek rite should suffer from the growing popularity of the Dominican friars in Kiev whose prior was Martin of Sandomierz, expels them from the Church of the Holy Virgin in Kiev.

Leszek's son, Bolesław, rightly nicknamed "the Bashful", being no longer a child—he is almost fourteen—encouraged and prompted by his mother and the Bishop of Cracow, decides that he wants to be free of his guardian, his uncle Conrad, and independent. Conrad, appalled at the prospect of the loss of income this will involve, invites Princess Grzymisława and his nephew to a friendly discussion of the duchy's affairs, and, when they come, promptly imprisons them, accusing them of prematurely attempting to regain ducal authority. He holds them in the castle at Sieciechów on the Vistula, where they are carefully guarded. He confiscates the contents of his nephew's treasury and makes stubborn efforts to gain control of the whole duchy. He even considers killing his nephew, but is dissuaded by the Duke of Gniezno and Marek the Voivode of Cracow. He then sends his two prisoners to the monastery at Sieciechów, where they are kept under strict surveillance, until he can devise ways of resolving his dispute with them.

Meanwhile, Conrad's eldest son, Bolesław, marches into Sandomierz and claims it as "masterless territory". He gains support by making gifts and promises, banishes those who oppose him and confiscates their property. Some of these exiles go to Ruthenia, others elsewhere, but one and all are fleeing for their lives and praying to God to destroy the tyrant.

Herman, Master of the Teutonic Knights, builds a second castle at Kwidzyn in Chełmno and from there gradually gains control of the neighbouring castle at Vilna, recently captured and rebuilt by the Prussians.

A.D. 1234

Wishing to compel the Prussian unbelievers to accept our Faith, Conrad assembles a great army, which, under Duke Świętopełk, crosses the River Ossa and advances into Prussian territory while it is still winter. For two months the army plunders and spreads devastation unhindered, for the Prussians do not dare risk a decisive battle and so never engage them. Over 5000 of the barbarians are killed and the castle at Radzin is captured and in this Świętopełk installs his own garrison. He then returns home with much booty and a large number of captives.

While Conrad is thus engaged, Bolesław the Bashful and his mother escape from Sieciechów, thanks to the Abbot, who bribes the guards, so that, one night when the latter are carousing, they "forget" to set the usual sentries, thus allowing Bolesław and his mother to walk out of the monastery at dead of night to carriages awaiting them and drive off. Two castles, Sandomierz and Zawichost, come over to them, but they do not dare remain in their own lands, lest they end up in prison again, and so go to their relative, Henry the Bearded, by whom they are well received and accommodated. When Bolesław asks for help in recovering his duchy, Henry promises to give it, but he wants to know what recompense he can expect for his trouble and the outlay it will entail. Bolesław assures him that he will have all his expenses refunded and either be paid for his trouble or be given part of the duchies. While this is going on, Conrad's son, Bolesław, with a number of knights from Sandomierz and some of his own, infiltrates Cracow territory and cruelly harasses the population, before returning to Sandomierz with much loot. In revenge, the Cracovians invade Wiślica and devastate as much of it as they can. In return the people of Wiślica mount a series of raids into Cracovian territory and do the same, so that both territories are devastated. When Henry the Bearded learns the full extent of the crimes Bolesław has perpetrated, he advances on Cracow with his whole army, taking young Bolesław with him. They are accepted by almost all the barons of Cracow and Sandomierz and, when Conrad's governors of castles and towns abandon their posts, these, too, submit to his authority. Everyone is so disgusted with Conrad's rule that they rush to receive and acknowledge their rightful duke. Henry, having taken possession of Cracow, Sandomierz and Lublin, proves to be a kindly champion and guardian of Bolesław. He assumes the authority and title of Duke, both of Wielkopolska and Cracow and Sandomierz, principally so as to be able to prevent Bolesław, who is still young, distributing the ducal possessions among the knights.

On January 2 Prussians set fire to the monastery in Oliwa and kill seven of the brethren and thirty-four of the monastery's servants. At the same time, the Teutonic Knights, having overpowered Pomezania with the help of the Margrave of Meissen, force them to accept the Christian faith.

Henry, Margrave of Meissen, occupies the castle at Płock, but Conrad and his two sons swiftly recover it. Some of the Germans they murder, others are burned in the cathedral church, others again are strung up by their feet.

The Duke of Mazovia founds a monastery for the Dominicans in Płock.

A.D. 1235

Conrad of Mazovia gives up his plan to invade Prussia in order to concentrate his efforts on dealing with Bolesław the Bashful and his guardian. First, he invades Cracovian territory, hoping that some of the towns and castles will come over to him. He woos many of the starostas and barons with gifts and promises, but they all dislike him and do not trust his promises, so he then has recourse to more violent measures: he fortifies the church of St. Andrew below Cracow castle, in what has hitherto been regarded as a suburb, since it is not within the city's walls, and he also fortifies the church in Prandocin, the collegiate church in Skarbimierz and the monastery at Jędrzejów, and in each installs a strong garrison, well provided with arms and provisions. He is the first Polish duke who has dared to profane sacred buildings and use them for military purposes, setting a shameful precedent. Henry harasses these forts, but there is no decisive engagement, since he thinks it will be easier to defeat Conrad if he uses delaying tactics. He knows that he himself has enough fortified towns and castles, loyal knights and the means to supply his army with all it needs, while the enemy lack all these. Although Conrad has inflicted enormous damage on Cracow and Sandomierz, he has lost many men and is faced with such difficulties that he regretfully withdraws to Mazovia. After this, Henry and Bolesław surround the church of St. Andrew and put such pressure on the garrison that, after a couple of months, they negotiate a surrender. To deal with Conrad's other fortified churches, Henry builds a small fort of tree-trunks and planks close to each of them. There are frequent minor skirmishes, for the besiegers are scrupulous about stopping fresh supplies getting through to the besieged, and Conrad's men keep sallying out at night to burn villages which have failed to pay their tribute. Thus oppressed, the peasants neglect to till their fields, abandon their homes and go to where they hope they will be more secure. Since both spring-sown and winter-sown grain have been destroyed by enemy action, a severe winter and constant rain, there is famine in Poland for a long time.

Andrew, King of Hungary, dies after reigning for thirty years. He is succeeded by his son, Béla, who is crowned in Székesfehérvár.

When Borzywój, a knight of Wielkopolska, long at odds with Paul the Bishop of Poznań over village boundaries and other matters, goes to the town of Śrem under safe-conduct to attend a meeting arranged by mutual friends in order to try to reach agreement with the Bishop, the latter treacherously throws the knight into prison, and, when he escapes, excommunicates him. The Church regards him as excommunicated and the ban is read out in all the churches. When the knight still avoids giving the Bishop satisfaction, Duke Władysław storms his castle, burns it and has the knight put to death.

A.D. 1236

Henry the Bearded makes another incursion into Wielkopolska and lays siege to the castle at Gniezno, the only one of his castles still loyal to Władysław. Eager to capture the city as well, he brings up a large number of siege engines and bombards the castle with them and with incendiary arrows, hoping to set fire to it, for it is largely built of timber. His infantry make frequent assaults and have stones hurled down on them from above, so that, whenever they withdraw there are many dead and wounded they have to take with them. The castle has a strong garrison, which makes frequent sorties and even attacks Henry's camp and captures a number of his men. The castle appears impregnable, especially when three of the great siege engines, those considered the most powerful, break under the strain of continually launching heavy missiles. The besieged, of course, can see all this and it gives them as much encouragement as it fills their attackers with doubt. Henry, too, begins to wonder if he is ever going to succeed, and in the end he abandons the siege and withdraws to Silesia. Władysław and the knights supporting him thereupon attack the castles and forts which support Henry and burn and destroy the villages which declared for him. One night, having bribed the sentries, they get into Śrem castle, which is under Bořivoj, son of the Margrave of Moravia, who is killed in the fighting. Having looted the castle, they set fire to it, so as to deny it to others, and go to Świętopełk in Pomerania. There, Władysław holes up in the two castles, Nakło and Ujście, which remain loyal to him. He realizes that the barons and knights of Wielkopolska are firmly loyal to Henry the Bearded.

On June 10, at an assembly of Polish dukes held in Danków, Constance and Gertrude, the two daughters of Henry of Silesia, who are present, are formally betrothed to the two sons of Conrad of Mazovia, Bolesław and Casimir. The actual wedding is postponed until later and the two girls sent back to Wrocław. On July 2, Duke Conrad formally divides his duchies between his two sons: Bolesław receives Mazovia and Casimir Łęczyca and Kujawy, and both swear to honour the arrangement.

On May 6, Casimir of Opole dies, leaving two sons, Mieczysław and Władysław. The elder, known as "the Fat", has married Judith, daughter of Conrad of Mazovia, but she is disgracefully barren and has no progeny.

A.D. 1237

The councillors of the two dukes, Henry and Bolesław, start negotiations. After several meetings, the amount of reparations to be paid is agreed as well as terms for the release of prisoners. It is accepted that Bolesław has more than come of age and thus does not need a guardian, but is independent and entitled to all adult rights; that he is to be recognized as duke and may, if he so wishes, appoint a guide and mentor. This arrangement confirmed, Bolesław publicly chooses Henry the Bearded to advise him and again undertakes to obey the latter and accept his advice. Conrad complains that this arrangement does him an injustice, but he sticks to what has been agreed and removes his garrisons from the three churches he has fortified. From now on Henry regards himself as monarch of all Poland and, indeed, is considered the most important of its dukes, but, out of consideration for Bolesław he does not use the title "Duke of Cracow and Sandomierz", but merely calls himself "Duke of Wielkopolska and Silesia". Bolesław, eager to repay the cost of wresting his duchy from Conrad's clutches, assigns to Henry important tolls and other revenues in both Cracow and Sandomierz, as well as some salt revenues and customs dues.

The formal marriage of Bolesław, elder son of Conrad of Mazovia, and Henry's daughter, Gertrude, which had been postponed because of the civil war and the minority of both bride and groom, is now celebrated in Wrocław. Although the blessed Jadwiga arranged the marriage, nothing will persuade her to attend the ceremony. She remains in her nunnery at Trzebnica in contemplation and prayer. She had arranged with her husband, Henry, a pact of lifelong abstinence, and so for thirty years he had not exercised his marital rights.

At the suggestion of his pious mother, Bolesław now sends to Prague for some Franciscans and grants them a large plot of land in Cracow on which to build a church and a friary.

Přemysl the Margrave of Moravia, knowing that his brother, Václav, is his enemy, moves to Hungary, leaving his castles garrisoned by loyal knights. Václav then lays siege to these, but is forced to give up, and the Margrave, welcomed by King Béla, recovers his lands.

Herman the Master of the Teutonic Knights, relying on the help of Conrad of Mazovia and of the Pomeranian dukes Świętopelk and Sambor, invades Prussia both by land and water. At the place where the river Elbing mouths into the Great Bay of Hab, he builds a town and a castle in which he installs a strong garrison. The town is named Elbing after the river.

Duke Bolesław and his mother are so afraid of treachery on the part of Conrad and his son, that they do not dare remain in the part of Sandomierz which Henry assigned to them; they now ask him to accommodate them in some fortified place in Cracow instead, until their enemies forget their inveterate hatred of them and they can make themselves strong by uniting their barons behind them. Henry grants them a fort on the crag in Przegin called Skala and settles a sufficient income on them, and there they live almost in hiding for the best part of five years. Henry retains Cracow and all its revenues for his own use; but he heeds the advice of the prelates and barons and rules sensibly. He abrogates several exactions on the peasants, and he reaffirms the freedoms of the Church. Under his rule of almost ten years the country flourishes.

A.D. 1238

Henry suddenly falls ill, while on a visit to one of the farthest-flung parts of the duchies, near the Bohemian frontier. His wife, the blessed Jadwiga, is informed by express messenger, but, despite repeated requests that she go to her husband, she refuses to do so, lest the sight of him ill should kindle in her a spark of sympathy for him, after the thirty years of their living celibate lives apart and meeting only when a meeting was essential. The Duke's state deteriorates, and, after receiving the last sacraments, he dies on March 19. He acquired the nickname "the Bearded", when, at the request of his wife, he embarked on a life of celibacy and, following the example of a conversus, let his beard grow, discarded his splendid robes of gold and purple and only wore modest woollen garments. His body is brought to Trzebnica for burial, and there all the nuns and a throng of peasants and the gentry of both sexes, gather to pay their respects, indeed, Jadwiga is the only woman there to refuse him the last honours and whose eyes remain dry.

Henry is succeeded by his only surviving son, Henry. This has the approval of the prelates and nobility of Wielkopolska, though Władysław, who has a justifiable claim, keeps pestering them to recognize his rights and return his own and his father's duchies to him.

A monastery of Dominican Friars is founded at Halicz, and the brethren of the Polish province of the Order are given a house there.

A.D. 1239

Władysław Odonic is so embittered by the rejection of his claim that his duchies be returned to him, that his health deteriorates and he dies shortly afterwards, whereupon the fort at Gniezno surrenders to Henry the Pious of Silesia. Władysław leaves two sons, Przemyśl and Bolesław, who get the castles of Nakło and Ujście, all that is left to Władysław at the time of his death.

Conrad of Mazovia once again starts playing an active part in affairs. He hates Bolesław the Bashful for having, as he sees it, slighted him when he chose as his mentor Henry, with whose help Bolesław won several minor engagements with Conrad. So, shortly after Henry's death, Conrad renounces the pact that he and Władysław made, and, at first covertly, then openly, makes forays into parts of Cracow, Sandomierz and Lublin. To stop this, Bolesław sends Clement the Castellan and Janusz the Voivode of Cracow to Béla of Hungary, to ask for the latter's daughter, Kinga, as his wife. Kinga, a girl of fifteen, is considered unusually beautiful and virtuous. At her birth, instead of crying, she is reputed to have said, quite clearly and in Hungarian: "Hail, Queen of Heaven". Also, on Wednesdays and Fridays she would allow herself to be suckled only once, as did St. Nicholas before her. Now, she is conveyed to Cracow with considerable pomp, bringing with her a large dowry of 40,000 marks. The betrothal ceremonies occupy twelve days. Bride and groom are to remain celibate even after their marriage until their dying day, but at the time of their wedding Bolesław accepts celibacy only for a trial period of twelve months, then for another year, another again, and then for ever. Conrad, seeing that his nephew has made such a splendid marriage stops raiding his territories and the two are reconciled.

In this same year, Casimir, the second of Duke Conrad's sons, weds the girl to whom he has long been betrothed, the daughter of Henry of Wrocław. The wedding is celebrated in Wrocław, and Casimir falls in love with his bride and lingers there with his in-laws despite repeated messages from his father requiring his return. Conrad convinces himself that his son is disregarding his orders with the connivance of his tutor, Jan Czapla, an expert in canon law, a scholar, priest and the Chancellor of Mazovia, who is with Casimir in Wrocław; so, Conrad summons the Chancellor home, pretending that he wishes to consult him about his son's behaviour.

When the Chancellor arrives, Conrad has him thrown into a noisome prison and, after a few days, made to ride the wooden horse, after which torture he has him publicly hanged like a common thief. The Chancellor's body is taken down by some Dominican friars, who try to take it back to the city for burial, but are stopped by Duchess Agatha, who has long thirsted for the Chancellor's blood and now, like a second Jezebel, has the body taken from them, put on a cart drawn by two oxen and taken to the river, near the church of St. Benedict, and there hanged on a gallows specially erected. The Dominican prior sends some of his brethren to take the body down from this second gallows and has it buried in the cathedral.

Conrad is reconciled with his nephew and regains the castle at Bydgoszcz, which was occupied by Świętopełk, who now considers that he has been slighted and to avenge the slight, raids neighbouring Kujawy, burns the town of Inowrocław and a number of villages, and then shuts himself up in the fortress there.

The Saxons capture the fort at Santok, which has been negligently guarded by its Polish garrison.

The Archbishop of Magdeburg leads an army into Poland and lays siege to the castle at Lubusz, claiming that, in the time of Bolesław Wrymouth, it was given to his cathedral by the Emperor Henry IV in perpetuity. After several weeks, Henry the Pious of Silesia arrives with a strong force and attacks the besiegers, who are forced to beat a shameful retreat, and so the siege is raised.

Poppo, second Master of the Teutonic Knights, eager to avenge the all but total destruction of his army earlier in the year by the barbarian Prussians, having fresh troops, captures their castle at Balga. In an attempt to recover it, the Prussians erect two forts a short distance away, thus enabling them to cut off the castle's supply of provisions. This quickly reduces the besieged to a state bordering on starvation; indeed, the castle might well have fallen, had not the Duke Otto of Brunswick come to its rescue, driven off the Prussians and captured both their forts.

About this time, the Master of the Order in Livonia, which calls itself the Order of the Knights of Christ, amalgamates his order with that of the Teutonic Knights. He is killed later in the year fighting the Livonians. Poppo founds a monastery for the Franciscans in Toruń and allocates it a site for dwellings.

A.D. 1240

The whole country is appalled by the news of Duke Conrad's treatment of his Chancellor. Peter the Bishop of Płock is afraid to take any action, but the Archbishop of Gniezno places an interdict on all churches in his diocese and sends out an official notice to this effect. The interdict first angers Conrad, then frightens him, and he sends to the Archbishop demanding a meeting. One is arranged, which Conrad attends in person with his councillors. Conrad now exhibits signs of repentance and undertakes to expiate his crime by doing whatever penance is imposed on him. Having thus humbled himself, it is decided that as expiation he must grant the cathedral and its archbishop the right to possess in perpetuity the village of Łowicz and its surrounding woods and forest in which the Duke is accustomed to hunt, the Bishop paying one gold mark annually in recognition of the Duke's overlordship. The archbishop of Gniezno is to have in perpetuity the prebend of a canonry, with all its rights, in Płock cathedral. The cathedrals of Włocawek and Płock are to be granted certain liberties and gifts in perpetuity. Conrad agrees to all this both verbally and in writing, and, with this guarantee, is relieved of the accusation of murder, the interdict is raised and services are resumed. However, the Duke is told that complete absolution can only be obtained from the Pope, but when the application is made, the Pope rescinds the absolution and instructs Thomas, Bishop of Wrocław, and Gerard, scholar of Cracow, to check that Conrad has made the requisite amends, before he can be granted the benefit of absolution. When these confirm that the requisite amends have been made and that Conrad's two sons consent to the transfer to the cathedrals of Gniezno, Włocławek and Płock of the rights, privileges and gifts detailed in the original document, the charge of murder is withdrawn. The document in question is preserved in the cathedral in Włocławek, where I have seen and read it on several occasions.

A.D. 1241

God, the most merciful and most excellent, angered by the manifold sins of the Poles, inflicts upon them not the plague, nor famine, nor the enmity of their Catholic neighbours as in previous years, but the savagery and fury of the heathen. Batu, third of the Tatar khans since the foundation of their state, having conquered many eastern kingdoms and overthrown their kings and rulers, and grown enormously in power and beyond all belief in riches, thanks to the number and wealth of the peoples beneath his yoke, now, as if their abodes in the East were too cramped for the Tatar people, sends his armies into the West and North, hoping to conquer them as he has the East. Having crossed the four great rivers: Don, Volga, Dniepr and Dniestr, and the mountains of Sarmatia, which we also call the Great Forests, he easily defeats those of the Ruthenian princes who dare to fight, and pressing on with unusual speed reaches Poland and plunders and devastates two of its populous cities, Lublin and Zawichost, and the country surrounding them, before returning to Ruthenia by the route of his advance, encumbered with booty and a large number of Polish and Ruthenian captives of both sexes. Having placed his captives in secure places, he swiftly returns and, crossing the frozen rivers Bug and Vistula on the ice, reaches Sandomierz, where he closely invests both the castle and the town. In the end he captures them both and kills the abbot of Koprzywnica and all the brethren in the monastery there, as well as a large number of priests and laymen, who have gathered there in the hope of defending the town and saving their lives. Of these the Tatars slaughter the old and the very young, only a few youths being granted their lives, though they are shackled like slaves. This slaughter is repeated in Wiślica and Skarbimierz. The Tatars then head for Cracow, none dares stand up to them, and while their captives show them the way but after reaching Skarbimierz on Ash Wednesday, they turn and start to withdraw, intending to get their captives, many of whom are of the nobility, across the border.

Because of his youth and feebleness, Bolesław the Bashful, then living with his mother in Cracow castle, cannot deal with so powerful an army, so Włodzimierz the Voivode of Cracow summons the knights and gentry to Kalina to seek ways of putting an end to this series of disasters; but then, learning that the Tatars are withdrawing from Skarbimierz, he orders all there to arm themselves and follow him. The Tatars have reached Połaniec on the River Czarna, where they are encamped, and there the Voivode attacks them with the remaining Cracovian knights, few in number, but determined to conquer or die. Surprise gives the Poles an initial advantage and they kill many of the enemy; but, when the Tatars realize how few are the Poles they are fighting, they regroup and break through the Polish ranks and defeat them. During the fighting, many Polish captives escape and hide in some nearby woods; their initial success sends the Polish knights greedily searching for booty and the battle is lost. Though victorious, the Tatars are horrified by their losses and dare stay no longer in Poland, lest a fresh army should attack them, and they withdraw hurriedly, abandoning their dead by the wayside. They reach Sieciechów without doing further damage, and there they hide in the great forest for a couple of days in order to throw off any pursuers; but when their scouts tell them that there is no pursuit and that all is quiet, they emerge and continue back to Ruthenia, where they replenish their ranks with fresh troops and return to Poland to avenge their defeat. Avoiding areas which they have previously ravaged, they reach Sandomierz, near which they halt for two days, dividing their great host into two.

The smaller force, under Kajdu, makes for Łęczyca and Kujawy, using Ruthenians, who dislike the Poles, as their guides. The larger force, under Batu himself, heads for Cracow, spreading devastation as it goes. Their previous near victory has given the Poles confidence and they now feel that they can defeat any Tatar force however large, so they take to the field, leaving Prince

Bolesław, his wife and mother in Cracow castle. The Poles bar the Tatar advance at Chmielnik near the town of Szydłów. It is March 18. Battle is engaged as the sun rises. The Poles, few in number, are arrayed in a single line and have no reserves. Fighting bravely, they kill many of the Tatar first unit and, after several hours, even force them to retreat towards their reserves, who are fresh and immediately take up the attack. The Poles are physically tired and many of them wounded, and in the end, they, too, break and run. A number reach the cover of the woods and, knowing the terrain, escape; but most find a glorious death defending their country and their faith.

The name of the Tartars came originally from the Tatar river, before that they were called Mongols, but as they grew in number they cam to be called Tatars, for in their tongue Tatar means a multitude. The Tatars are a people vile in temperament and in behaviour cruel. Of low stature, they are short in the leg, have flat, wry noses in broad, hairless faces. They have small, darting eyes, broad, heavy chests, nasty swarthy complexions and powerful bodies. They live on mare's milk, meat and blood, and are content with modest fare that is easy to prepare, eating raw, uncooked food and millet mixed with horse's blood. They are fond of, and ever ready for sensual pleasures and the delights of the flesh. They endure frost as well as heat. To each other they are polite, kind, loyal, truthful and humane, but with strangers they are at first ingratiating, but later become cunning, devious, mendacious and importunate. They are by no means ready to give.

Dispirited by the disastrous defeat at Chmielnik, many of those left in Cracow and Sandomierz make their way to Hungary and Germany, while the peasants hide in the marshes, forests and wastes with their wives and children. Even their prince, Bolesław, leaves Cracow castle with his family and all his possessions and goes to his father-in-law in Hungary; thus, when the Tatars reach Cracow they find it deserted and set fire to it. Convinced that there they will find the country's treasures, they try to capture the Church of St. Andrew, then outside the walls of Cracow, in which many of the poor and sick have taken refuge, but the Poles defend it stoutly and in the end the Tatars abandon the attempt. However, on the Monday after Christmas, the second Tatar army, on its way back from devastating Łęczyca and Kujawy, reaches Cracow.

Leaving Cracow, Batu moves off in the direction of Wrocław. Finding the bridges across the Oder all destroyed or removed, the Tatars, who, if they cannot ford a river, swim across it, do just that, for the Tatars are more expert in the art of swimming than any other nation. Duke Mieczysław of Opole attacks one Tatar unit that lets itself be isolated, and destroys it; but, when the rest of the Tatar army comes up to avenge their fellows, the Duke escapes to Legnica to Henry of Wrocław, whom he knows to be preparing a force to fight the Tatars. The Tatars move swiftly to Wrocław. They find the town deserted, for its inhabitants have all fled with their treasures and provisions, and the knights have removed whatever was left into the castle, before setting fire to the town in order to deprive the Tatars of loot and shelter. The Tatars lay siege to the castle: during the siege Czesław, the Dominican prior of the priory of St. Wojciech, a Pole, saves the castle with his tears and prayers: for a pillar of fire appears above his head and illuminates the whole city with an indescribable brightness. This so frightens the Tatars, that they abandon the siege and withdraw. Meanwhile, the Tatars heading for Kujawy have joined forces with those from Cracow and together advance on Legnica, having learned from their scouts and captured peasants that a large Catholic force is being assembled there.

So, on April 9, Prince Henry, in splendid armour, rides out from Legnica to do battle with the Tatars. As he rides past the Church of the Blessed Virgin, a stone falls from the roof narrowly missing his head. This is regarded as a divine warning or, at least, an ill omen. The Prince arrays his army on level ground near the River Nysa in five ranks: the first consists of crusaders and volunteers speaking several languages, and some gold miners from Złotoryja; the second line is made up of knights from Cracow and Wielkopolska; the third of knights from Opole; the fourth of the Grand Master of the Prussian Knights with his brethren and other chivalry; while the fifth consists of Sile-

sian and Wrocłavian barons, the pick of the knights from Wielkopolska and Silesia and a small
contingent of mercenaries, all under the command of Prince Henry himself. There are many Tatar
units, each more numerous and more experienced in battle; indeed, each consists of more men than
the combined Polish force. Battle is joined. The Poles attack first and their initial charge breaks the
first Tatar rank and moves forward, but, when the fighting becomes hand-to-hand, they are surrounded by Tatar archers, who prevent the others coming to their assistance. These then waver and
finally fall beneath the hail of arrows, like delicate heads of corn broken by hail-stones, for many of
them are wearing no armour, and the survivors retreat. Now two Polish ranks are fighting three Tatar units; indeed, have overcome them, for the Polish crossbowmen protect them from the Tatar
archers, but then someone from the Tatar ranks starts running hither and thither between the two armies shouting "Run, run!" to the Poles and encouragement to the Tatars. The Duke of Opole, thinking the shouts come from a friend, not an enemy, withdraws his men. When Prince Henry sees what
is happening, he laments aloud, but brings up his fourth rank, which contains the best of his troops
and with them is on the point of overcoming the Tatars, when a fourth and even larger Tatar force

*Defeat of Poland's chivalry at Legnica, April 1241. In the centre the Tatar Khan is depicted plunging his
sword into the back of Henry the Pious, who, at the bottom on the left, has just had his head severed by a Tatar.
At the top, right, angels are depicted carrying off the souls of dead Christians, while at the bottom edge of the
picture, on the left, the leviathan is licking up those of the infidel.*
—A. Karlowska-Kamzowa: Zagadnienie aktualizacji w sląskich wyobrazniach bitwy legnickiej,
1972.—British Libray

under Batu comes up and fighting is resumed. The Tatars attack fiercely, but the Poles refuse to re-treat, and for a while honours are even.

Among the Tatar standards is a huge one with a giant X painted on it. It is topped with an ugly black head with a chin covered with hair. As the Tatars withdraw some hundred paces, the bearer of this standard begins violently shaking the great head, from which there suddenly bursts a cloud with a foul smell that envelopes the Poles and makes them all but faint, so that they are incapable of fighting. We know that in their wars the Tatars have always used the arts of divination and witch-craft, and this is what they are doing now. Seeing that the all but victorious Poles are daunted by the cloud and its foul smell, the Tatars raise a great shout and return to the fray, scattering the Polish ranks that hitherto have held firm, and a huge slaughter ensues.

Among those who fall are Boleslav the son of the Margrave of Moravia and the Master of the Prussian Order. Prince Henry does not desert his men. Surrounded by Tatars who are attacking him from all sides, he and a handful of others try to force their way through the enemy. Then, when he has almost won through and there are only four knights left with him, the Prince's horse, already wounded, drops dead. The Tatars, recognizing the Prince by his insignia, press after him. For a while he and his companions fight on; then his fourth knight brings him a fresh horse taken from the Prince's chamberlain. The Prince remounts and the five make another attempt to break through the enemy ranks; but once again are surrounded. Nonetheless they fight on. As the Prince is raising his arm to bring his sword down on an enemy, a Tatar thrusts his lance into the Prince's armpit and the Prince slides from his horse. The Tatars pounce on the Prince and, dragging him two bowshots clear, cut off his head with a sword, tear off all his badges and leave his corpse naked. In this great battle a number of the Polish nobility and gentry find honourable martyrdom in defence of their Faith. The saintly Jadwiga, then in Krosno, is informed by the Holy Spirit of the extent of the disas-ter and of the death of her son in the same hour as it happens, and tells this to a nun, called Adelaide.

Jan Iwanowic, the knight who brought Henry the horse that nearly saved him, joins forces with two of the shield-bearers and another knight, called Lucman, who has two servants with him and himself has twelve wounds. When their pursuers pause for a breather in a village a mile or so from the battlefield, the six turn and attack them, killing two of their number and taking one pris-oner. After this, Iwanowic enters a Dominican monastery and lives there piously, grateful that the Good Lord has saved him from so many dangers.

Having collected their booty, the Tatars, wishing to know the exact number of the dead, cut one ear off each corpse, filling nine huge sacks to the brim. Then, impaling Prince Henry's head on a long lance, they approach the castle at Legnica (for the town has already been burned for fear of the Tatars) and display it for those inside to see, calling upon them through an interpreter to open the gates. The defenders refuse, telling them that they have several other dukes, sons of good duke Henry, besides Henry. The Tatars then move on to Olomouc, where they camp for a fortnight, burn-ing and destroying everything round about. Moving on again, they halt for a week at Bolesisko, and, after slaughtering many of the inhabitants, continue into Moravia.

After the Tatars have gone, the Poles spend several days searching for Henry's body, but, lacking its head, they cannot identify it. Then his widow lets it be known that the Duke had six toes on his left foot, and this enables the body to be identified and taken to Wrocław, where it is en-tombed in the choir of the Church of St. James.

The extent and horror of the disaster are reflected in Pope Gregory IX's bull proclaiming a crusade to help Poland: "Various and painful are the anxieties that beset Our heart, namely the burning question of the Holy Land, the threatening persecution of the Church and the pitiable state of the Roman Empire; but, to tell the truth, We forget these and even Ourself, when We remember how in Our time, because of these Tatars the name of Christianity has almost been obliterated; the very thought pierces Our bone to the marrow, troubles Our mind and weakens Our spirit and causes Us such pain and anxiety, that, as in a fit of madness, We know not where to turn."

The Tatars treatment of Moravia is as cruel and destructive as it has been elsewhere. Since the King of Bohemia has taken refuge in his castles and other safe places, the Tatars are free to range over the whole of the duchy, and for more than a month they burn, kill and torture as they like, since none dares stand up to them or even help the Moravians. While the Tatars are camped near Olomouc, one of their commanders, a man highly esteemed by his own people, accompanied by a mere handful of men, rashly goes too close to the walls and is captured. When news of his capture spreads, there is a great outcry among the Tatars, which is heard even in the town. The Tatars are unable to obtain his release either by threats or in exchange for other prisoners. His companions are handed over to the people of Olomouc. The Tatars move off towards Hungary. King Václav gives to the knight who captured the Tatar commander a star to add to his coat of arms, as well as Castle Sternberg.

When King Béla learns that several hordes of Tatars have entered his kingdom accompanied by a host of civilians: wives, childen and old people, together with their whole train of two- and three-wheeled carts, and have already devastated much of it, he summons a general assembly which meets by the River Tisa. The King arrives with his nephew, Coloman, and the knights of his Court, and is joined by a master of the Templars, the bishops of Pannonia, the archbishops of Esz-

Duke Henry's head is displayed on a lance before Legnica to the horror of the inhabitants.
—Der Hedwigs Chronik.—British Library.

tergom and Kalocz, and the Hungarian bishops, with their men-at-arms and standards flying, as if they were arrayed for battle and not to pray for forgiveness for the sins of their people. King Béla, fearing a night attack, concentrates his entire army in a narrow area, in which they remain encamped for several days. Meanwhile, the Tatar commander, Batu, informed by his scouts of how closely crowded are the enemies' tents, tells his men that, if the Hungarians have crowded into so small an area, they can have no experience, sense or knowledge of the art of war, and orders them to rest and prepare for battle on the following day. At dawn, he arrays his army and attacks. The Hungarian first line resists fiercely; but, in the end, it yields to superior numbers and the others then scatter. Many of the fugitives are chased into bogs and marshes, where they drown. Two archbishops and a bishop are among the casualties, which include many priests and the Master of the Templars. It would have been more sensible had these remained in their chapels and prayed, rather than armed themselves and joined the soldiers. Those who flee into the marshes, find themselves floundering in mud, which prevents them either moving forward, keeping upright or turning to face the enemy and so dying honourably. When the two princes see their men being killed and the Tatars gaining the upper hand, they leave the battle-field. King Béla, too, heads for Austria and finds refuge there for a considerable time. Coloman makes his way to Pest, where he finds a considerable force of Hungarians and refugees, which, he insists, must disband, because he is not strong enough to resist the Tatars. When they do not disband (the uneducated never take good advice), he himself goes to Austria and shelters in a castle there, eventually moving on to Zagreb.

Batu now leads his Tatars towards Pest, where, according to his intelligence, a Christian army is being assembled to fight him. Battle is joined and continues for three days, but in the evening of the third day, by which time more than a hundred thousand Christians have been killed, victory goes to the Tatars, who then go on the rampage. The priests, monks and other servants of the Church come out in procession with their holy relics in an attempt to mitigate the fury of the Tatars, only to be slaughtered and have their churches plundered and their sacred relics flung to the ground. The Tatars then enter Pest, loot it and burn it. Many thousands of captives, men and women are taken back to their camp, where the women deal cruelly with any woman or girl whom they consider pretty or beautiful, cutting off her nose, cheeks or lips, lest their men be attracted and prefer her to themselves. The Tatar boys are encouraged by their mothers to bully the boy prisoners; indeed if any of them can kill one with a single blow, he receives great acclaim.

News of the Hungarians' disastrous defeat so horrifies their German neighbours, that not even the Emperor contemplates resistance, but goes into hiding.

King Béla and his wife take their two-year old son and the body of St. Stephen and the dust of other saints, their jewels, robes and church accessories, to safety in Split. At about this time, Coloman dies and is buried in the Dominican monastery at Czasma.

After the death of Prince Henry, the surviving nobles accept Bolesław the Bald as their liege lord and sovereign. Conrad of Mazovia takes umbrage at having his claim thus disregarded and decides to avenge the slight. He asks the Duke of Pomerania for help, and though, for various reasons the Duke declines to help in person, he promises to send a small force when the time comes.

The Tatars are behaving as if they intended to stay in Hungary for ever. In the great plain between Esztergom and Jawryn they pitch a huge camp of tents, each half-buried in the ground in its own pit, as is their custom. In fact, they do remain for almost two years, turning most of Hungary into a desolate waste.

After their defeat of King Béla, the Tatars hurriedly send a force through Spisz to Cracow, whose inhabitants are unarmed and unprepared; the Tatars slaughter them indiscriminately. They loot the city and return through Oswięcim to their camp in Hungary.

When the disgruntled Conrad learns of the second sack of Cracow, knowing that his nephew Bolesław the Bashful has fled to Hungary and from there to Moravia, and that the flower of the knights of Cracow, Sandomierz, Wrocław and Opole has been killed, so that these lands are all but deserted, he decides to annex them. He assembles as large a force as his means allow and with this and some troops sent him by the Duke of Pomerania, moves in and occupies both territories with all their castles and forts, the inhabitants submitting to his rule and authority, for none believes that Duke Bolesław will ever return. The one exception is the Voivode of Cracow, who prepares to defend the castle at Skala in the name of Duke Bolesław. Conrad does not interfere, but builds a fortress in Cracow itself extending from the cathedral of St. Wacław and the chapel with the altar of St. Thomas to the Church of St. Gereon and thence to the rotunda of the Blessed Virgin. Having seen to all this, he returns to Mazovia. Meanwhile, Bolesław the Bald, wishing to avenge this offence, assembles his own knights and with these and a few German mercenaries marches on Cracow. While he is attempting to take the fort, Duke Conrad arrives with a much stronger force than his, so, not daring to risk a fight, Bolesław withdraws, leaving the Voivode in Skala castle.

A.D. 1242

As soon as he has gained possession of Cracow, Sandomierz and Lublin, Duke Conrad imposes heavy tribute on everyone alike: clergy or knight, inhabitant of town or village, large or small, and this is mercilessly exacted either by his officials or by the Duke himself. People are put to building new forts and repairing the old. It is as if the Duke feels that his dominion will only endure if the people are so repressed that they cannot revolt. As a result, everywhere people complain that, bad as were the ravages of the Tatars, those of their own kind are even worse. So, messengers are sent to Hungary and Moravia to search for Bolesław the Bashful and, when found, bring him back to rescue his tormented country. Meanwhile, Duke Conrad lays siege to Skala Castle and finally captures it, when Clement, the voivode who is defending it, realizing that he can expect no help from Bolesław, seeks and obtains an agreement, whereby he transfers his allegiance to the Duke. Skala is then burned, as is the new castle in Cracow. After allotting the forts and offices to various of his knights, Duke Conrad returns to his own duchy and remains there quietly for a year.

Duke Henry, whom the Tatars killed, left four sons, Bolesław, Henry, Conrad and Władysław, and five daughters. Their grandmother, the blessed Jadwiga, sends the two youngest boys to Paris to study, while the two elder ones take service as knights. Meanwhile, Bolesław called the Bald is guilty of more and more intolerable acts of violence against his knights in Wielkopolska, and promotes any German or newcomer, even a ragamuffin, over the heads of the Poles, thus causing such resentment that at an assembly in Poznań, his barons turn to their lords and natural inheritors, Dukes Przemyśl and Bolesław, who are then in their castle at Ujście, the only one remaining to them, and elect them as their dukes and surrender to them all their forts, castles and towns, thus casting off Bolesław's intolerable yoke. Bolesław accepts this secession of Wielkopolska at the insistence of Jadwiga, best of grandmothers, who knows that her husband, Henry the Bearded, appropriated it illegally. A little later Bolesław marries his sister, Elizabeth, who is in a nunnery in Trzebnica, though she has not yet taken her vows, to Duke Przemyśl.

Świętopełk Duke of Pomerania, a perverse, cunning and clever man, who has fraudulently obtained the duchy of which he had been Leszek's lieutenant, begins to fear the Teutonic Kights, who, called in by Duke Conrad to fight the heathen Prussians, have proved to be stubborn and dangerous enemies of the Poles. For, although Conrad only gave them the territories of Nieszawa and Chełmno on condition that, once the Prussians had been defeated, they should be returned to him and his descendants, this has not been done. Indeed, in this short time the Knights have grown enormously in strength thanks to the support of the Duke and his son, Casimir, who takes part in all their expeditions. They have built numerous towns and castles in Prussia, killed the more eminent Prussians and forced others to accept the water of regeneration and baptism. All in all, the Duke is apprehensive for his continued possession of Pomerania and so decides to try to stop the Knights' progress, while they are still vulnerable. To this end, he joins forces with the Prussian tribes and persuades those who have been baptized to revert to their pagan rites. So, one day, all these rene-gades turn on the Poles and Germans, indeed, on all Christians in Prussia, and massacre them. They then take over all the forts that the Knights have built, except Balga and Elbląg, and elect Świętopełk as their lord and duke, swearing allegiance and obedience to him. The Duke blocks all access to the crossings of the Vistula and kills or captures all who attempt to use them, especially if they owe allegiance to the Knights. Pope Innocent IV sends a nuncio, William Bishop of Modena, to stop this injustice. The nuncio plies the Duke with letters and messages telling him to halt this disgraceful practice, but this the Duke stubbornly refuses to do; instead he sends an army of Pom-eranians and Prussians into Chełmno and puts that to fire and the sword, killing or capturing 4000 people in the process. Meanwhile, the nuncio (the future Pope Alexander IV) divides all Prussia into three bishoprics: Warmińsk, Sambia and Pomezania. It is impossible to calculate the number of Christians murdered by the Duke of Pomerania's men, but in the course of this one year these suffer two disastrous defeats at the hands of the Tatars and Prussians.

While Batu, with one half of the Tatar army, remains in camp, Khan Kajdan moves the other half against the town and castle of Esztergom and captures both. Next, he attacks Székesfehérvár, but this is splendidly defended, so he withdraws and heads for Zagreb. Learning of this, King Béla leaves the area together with three Hungarian bishops and other eminent persons, and moves to Split. However, he does not feel safe even there, and so takes his wife and the entire court to Trogir. Kajdan intends to pursue him wherever he goes. First, he marches into Slavonia, where he has a large number of Hungarian captives marched out into the plain and slaughtered before his eyes; then he moves on into Croatia and so reaches Split. The Hungarians, who have crowded into the town for protection, behave as if this was the end of them; but the Tatars, finding that King Béla has gone elsewhere, quickly move on to Trogir and, when repulsed there, stay in the Bosnian kingdom for several months, roaming through Croatia and Dalmatia, before rejoining Batu and the other Ta-tars, whereupon they move into Serbia and Bulgaria and, to lighten their return journey, slaughter their captives like sheep. When King Béla's intelligence tells him that the Tatars have left Hungary, he and the court return there. After two years of devastation by the Tatars the country is in the grip of famine, made all the worse by a plague of wolves, which roam in packs, attacking and eating all they encounter, even men in armour. Indeed, Hungary has fallen into such a wretched state that, there being no oxen, horses or other draught animals, people harness themselves to their ploughs and so till the soil.

A.D. 1243

Conrad of Mazovia is well aware that the knights and gentry of Cracow and Sandomierz have all turned against him and transferred their allegiance to his nephew, Bolesław the Bashful, as much because of Conrad's oppressive tyranny, as out of sympathy for Bolesław, the true and legal inheritor of these lands. Eager to stifle this smouldering rebellion (he is anticipating the return of Bolesław with some Hungarian knights) he sets out for Cracow. Arriving there early in June, he is received with tokens of honour and obedience and decides to imprison the more eminent of the no-bility and, above all, the Voivode of Cracow. He announces a general assembly to be held on June 29, ostensibly to deal with affairs of state, but in reality to enable him to arrest his opponents and get possession of the city of Cracow. When all are assembled, he gives a signal and his men arrest the knights, who are then shackled and sent to Mazovia and there kept in dreadful conditions under strict guard. The Voivode Clement, his brother and a few others escape to Hungary. However, one dark and stormy night two months later, the prisoners in Mazovia manage to break their chains and escape, one by one, from their ghastly prison. Together they eject the garrison and take over the castle and then the town. That accomplished, they set out joyfully and noisily to meet their prince,

Part of Bernadus Wapowski's Tabula Sarmatiae *showing the eastern part of the Black Sea, with the Bosporus in the middle at the bottom.* —*Jagiellonian University Library.*

who is on his way back from Hungary; Voivode Clement also returns. They swear allegiance and loyalty to him, and accept him as their prince and lord. The gentry and the minor knights follow suit. Perturbed by this news, Duke Conrad marches on Cracow with a considerable force from several countries; but, by remaining within his defences, Bolesław gives him no opportunity to do battle. Conrad then fortifies the Church of St. Andrew outside the city, digging trenches and raising ramparts, and installs a strong garrison commanded by his shield-bearer, and returns to Mazovia to recruit an even stronger army. As soon as he has gone, the shield-bearer surrenders St. Andrew to Prince Bolesław and thus that danger to the city is removed.

Duke Conrad obtains help from Mieczysław of Opole, and is sent re-inforcements by Przemyśl the Duke of Poznań and Lithuanians and Jacwingians, with these he and his son, Casimir, invade Sandomierz. Their advance is barred by Prince Bolesław and his troops near the town of Suchodół, and battle is joined on May 25. Duke Conrad has superiority of numbers and, perhaps, of quality, but Prince Bolesław, whose cause is just and for whom incessant prayers are said, thanks to the mercy of Our Lord, defeats him. Many are killed and many wounded, many forced into shameful flight. After the battle, Prince Bolesław behaves with great moderation, freeing many of those taken prisoner and being generous to others. His men are enriched by their share of the booty. After this triumph, the knights of Cracow, not content to have elected Bolesław as their prince once, proceed to do so a second time, and, in a solemn service conducted by the Bishop of Cracow, he is crowned with a silver crown and conducted to the throne.

Dietrich of Bernheim, Marshal of the Prussian Knights, seeing how Świętopełk's power has grown thanks to the help he has received from the Prussians, and afraid lest the two together bring about the downfall of the Order, summons the senior members of his Order to discuss what should be done. None recommends open warfare, because the Duke's is the more powerful army, but the consensus is that they should harass him with minor skirmishes and raids, and try to capture his castle at Sartawice in a surprise night attack. So, on the eve of St. Barbara's Day, the Marshal moves against Sartawice with only 204 men equipped with scaling ladders, which they put up one night and, the guards being negligent, have no difficulty in climbing in. They occupy the strategic points and the bastions, and tie up the guards. They then fight the remaining fifty of the garrison from midnight until sunrise, killing some and capturing the others. Stored in the castle are the bodies of various saints, among them that of St. Barbara. Some say this was the St. Barbara who was martyred at Antioch, others that it was another saint of the same name from Pomerania; but no one knows the truth, because of the lack of written sources. Having laid siege to Sartawice and failed to recapture it, Świętopełk removes half his force to fight in Chełmno, whereupon the other half is attacked and defeated; thus is Świętopełk deprived of both castles.

The Dukes of Wielkopolska and Mazovia, each with a powerful force, link up with Marshal Dietrich and together they advance on Wyszogrod in Pomerania. That captured, the rest of Pomerania is put to fire and the sword, and a great number of men and women carried off into servitude. They then advance on Nakło, which surrenders at once on condition that those inside are granted their lives and possessions. Świętopełk is now seriously afraid of the combined power of the Poles and the Teutonic Knights, and thinks that together they may drive him out of Pomerania; so, with the mediation of the papal nuncio he makes peace with Marshal Dietrich and the Knights, giving as hostages his own son Mszczuj, the count of We at and the burgrave of Vimar. The Knights then return all their prisoners captured from Świętopełk, but on no account will they return the castle at Sartawice, which is what Świętopełk desires above all else.

On October 9, Princess Jadwiga of Wrocław, widow of Henry the Bearded, dies and is buried in the tomb which she and her husband had built in Trzebnica monastery. Her body, in life sallow and pallid, ravaged by abstention and fasting, after death becomes beautiful. For thirty years she lived a celibate life, protecting her body and soul from temptation, and, what is truly astounding, amidst the thorns of the nuptial bed which she shared with her husband, she flourished as a lily or as gold in fire, and all that time never once became inflamed with the ardour of passion.

A.D. 1244

Duke Conrad of Mazovia, eager for revenge, invades Lublin, which he devastates unhindered and in the most barbarous fashion as far as the river Vistula. He goes on to ravage Sieciechów and Łuków, from which he removes great booty in people with their cattle and belongings, leaving this formerly densely populated and well-cultivated area a waste. This so intimidates its neighbours that they desert their natural lord, Bolesław the Bashful, and voluntarily transfer allegiance to Duke Conrad, whom they know to have loosed the barbarians on Lublin. The only one to remain loyal to Bolesław is Prandota the Bishop of Cracow, and this so infuriates Conrad that he sends an armed force to pillage and burn the Bishop's manors in Sandomierz, the spoils being carried back to Mazovia. The Bishop, a man of real courage, remains loyal to Bolesław despite the destruction of his lands and even uses his ecclesiastical and judicial powers to lay an interdict on the Duke throughout Poland, and this is confirmed by the Archbishop of Gniezno Fulko at the synod in Łęczyca and published in every church.

Learning of the devastation of Lublin, Daniel Prince of Kiev marches in and occupies the castle and town, and illegally makes the entire territory his own. To ensure that his possession of it will last, he builds at astonishing speed in the middle of the castle a round tower of baked brick with a perambulatory and breastwork round the top. He also strengthens the castle and town with ramparts and deep ditches, and forces everyone, knights and citizens, to submit to him.

The heathen Prussian have turned against the Duke of Mazovia for not rewarding them adequately for their help against his nephew, the Prince of Cracow; so now, knowing that the Duke and his knights are busy trying to capture the lands of Cracow, they send their cavalry into Mazovia, which plunders the settlements, burns towns and villages and devastates the entire country as far as Ciechanów. On their way back, burdened with booty of people and cattle, they are attacked by the knights of Mazovia and Łęczyca. Although they put up a stout resistance, they are soundly defeated. Nine hundred fall, 200 are taken prisoner and the rest seek safety in flight. All their booty is recovered and returned to the villages from which it was taken.

Although St. Jadwiga, now in her abode in Heaven, had four grandsons, two serving as knights and two educating themselves, the duchy of Wrocław is divided into two shares only, in the hope that, and on condition that, the two youngest, Conrad and Władysław, will want to continue in the Church—Conrad being already a sub-deacon and bishop-designate of Bamberg; and Władysław archbishop designate of Salzburg—so that what otherwise would have been Conrad's share is added to Bolesław's and Władysław's to that of Henry, for them to enjoy in perpetuity, unless one of them dies or renounces his share. The two now throw lots and Bolesław gets Wrocław and Henry gets Legnica. The division made and confirmed, Princess Anna, mother of the two, together with the Bishop of Wrocław, conducts Bolesław to Wrocław and Henry to Legnica. No sooner is all this accomplished than Bolesław, called the Bald, begins to regret the arrangement, suspecting that Legnica is the better of the two shares; so, feeling certain that his brother Conrad, already a sub-deacon and shortly to be made a bishop, will never claim his share, he does a swop with his brother Henry, who then has Wrocław and Bolesław has Legnica. This is formally set out in a new document, which invalidates the previous one. Meanwhile, Conrad conceives a distaste for the Church and abandons learning and the prospect of a bishopric and returns to his fatherland, demanding that Legnica be divided between him and Bolesław. At first Bolesław is conciliatory, hoping that Conrad will see that the earlier arrangement was more to his advantage, but when Conrad persists, Bolesław dismisses him and refuses to share with him. Conrad then goes to his other brother, Henry, who welcomes him. Meawhile, Władysław, who shared with Henry, is appointed Archbishop of Salzburg and this leaves Henry in possession of the whole of Wrocław.

Świętopełk, Duke of Pomerania, having broken his sworn agreement with the Knights, invades Chełmno and inflicts enormous damage. The Knights, wondering how to recover the booty he has taken and how to defeat him, decide to wait to do battle until half the enemy force has crossed a certain marsh and then attack from the rear, when those who have crossed will be unable to go to the assistance of those in their rear. The sensible commanders agree to the plan, but the new Marshal, Berlewin, does not, and insists that, unless they attack from in front, the enemy will easily remove all the booty and their captives to places of safety. The majority accept this and so, despite the opposition of the others, they pursue the barbarians, who are now across the River Ossa. At their approach, most of the barbarians take their captives and booty into the safety of their forts and castles, and then, seeing how few the Knights are, engage them near the marsh and defeat them. After this victory, Świętopełk sends to certain people in Chełmno promising to reward them well, if they will go into the castle, to which they have access, free his son and the other hostages and return them to him. However, the Order's commander of Chełmno castle is warned of what is afoot and the plotters are refused access to the castle. That night the captain moves Świętopełk's son and the other hostages in chains to another castle, threatening to kill any one who divulges what has been done. Świętopełk, suspecting that his plan has been discovered, secretly sends men to set fire to the towns of Chełm and Sartawice. Then, with a horde of Prussians, Lithuanians and others he marches into Kujawy, of which he is an even greater enemy than of the Poles or the Knights, and ravages it. When the papal legate, William the Bishop of Modena, castigates him for this both in letters and through envoys, Świętopełk tells him that neither for him nor for the Pope will he stop pursuing his enemies, especially the Duke of Kujawy and the Poles. He threatens that, unless his son and the other hostages are returned, he will use every endeavour to harass the Poles and the Knights. He then starts building a castle on the bank of the Vistula at Santir in Chełm territory, and allows no boat to pass until it has paid his dues. The Knights, depressed by all their misfortunes, propose to Świętopełk's brother Sambor, that, if Świętopełk will give assurances that he will keep the agreement he has made with them and stop sending supplies to the barbarians, they will give up the castle at Sartawice which they have captured; but when Świętopełk demands the return of both Sartawice and his son, the Knights send him to Austria under the guard of thirty men-at-arms who are returning there. Świętopełk, desperate to free his son, cannot rest, but starts building another fort at Świecie, in Pomeranian territory, where the Vistula runs in fierce rapids and whirlpools, intending to prohibit all river traffic; but Casimir the Duke of Kujawy and Poppo, Master of the Knights, come in force in boats and stop him. They build a new fort at Putirbork not far away, but accomplish nothing else. Świecie is then demolished and a garrison and provisions put into Santir.

A.D. 1245

The nobility of Wielkopolska are plotting to deprive the Bishops of Gniezno and Poznań of the privileges granted to them with such princely generosity by Władysław Odonic. They do their utmost to persuade the two bishops to relinquish their rights, which, though they harm no one, and are a burden on no one, they find offensive, in that church lands, villages and property are free of taxes, while they themselves are burdened with dues and tribute. They particularly object to the Bishop of Poznań's privilege of minting his own coinage with his effigy on the coins. However, the two dukes refuse to yield to pressure or requests, considering it shameful to revoke privileges granted by their father; instead, they renew and confirm them in new documents, which are read out in all local courts of justice. A general assembly held in Gniezno, at which Duke Przemyśl dubs his younger brother in the cathedral, is accompanied by various games and entertainments at which princely gifts are presented to the wrestlers and boxers.

Casimir of Kujawy and Łęczyca, son of the Duke of Mazovia, assembles as strong a force as he can muster and moves to Chełmno, where he joins up with Brother Poppo of the Order and many knights who come in response to the crusade called to help the Knights, and, having arrayed their ranks, advances into Pomerania to avenge the devastation of Chełmno and Mazovia. Świętopełk decides to wait for the Prussians, whom he has summoned to come to his help, and so does not engage the enemy. In the intervening nine days the Duke and his Knights burn many of the towns in Pomerania and remove quantities of booty; but, when the Prussians arrive, Świętopełk pursues the Duke's force and attacks it from the front and from the rear. The frontal assault easily scatters the Duke's men, while the fighting in the rear is so fierce that some of the Knights break rank and flee. At this juncture, Henry of Liechtenstein arrives with his Austrians and, attacking Świętopełk in the rear, quickly defeats him. One thousand four hundred dead are counted, the rest are either captured or scattered in flight.

A.D. 1246

The Duke of Mazovia harbours a grudge, which the duchess Agatha does her best to keep alive, against his nephew, Bolesław the Bashful, for having ousted him from the duchy of Cracow, and is eager for vengeance. So, with the pagan Lithuanians providing assistance, he advances into his nephew's territory. Bolesław bars his advance at Zarziszow and, though knowing that his is the weaker force, engages him in battle. Many of the knights from Cracow and Sandomierz fall from blows received in the chest; many others are taken prisoner. Bolesław himself leaves the battlefield with a few companions so as to avoid falling into the hands of Duke Conrad, from whom he can expect only the worst. Conrad, having laid the surrounding area waste, returns to Mazovia with his booty. Soon after this, however, knowing that Prince Bolesław's strength has been broken, he marches into Cracow territory and, not wishing to waste time capturing castles and towns, for the citizens of Cracow have disdainfully refused his call to surrender, secures three places with garrisons, and then attacks and captures the fort opposite the castle and town of Cracow, where the Rudawa flows into the Vistula, and another near the Tyniec monastery. These he garrisons with his own men, and then builds a third fort at Lelów and grants it to his son-in-law, Mieczysław of Opole. But, when Duke Conrad returns to Mazovia, Bolesław and his knights besiege and capture this fort, while the other in the fork of the rivers Vistula and Rudawa surrenders without a fight. Shortly after this Conrad's son-in-law dies without progeny. When the news of his death spreads, the castle at Lelów is at once returned to Bolesław the Bashful, so all the Mazovian's plots and plans come to nothing. Mieczysław's share of the inheritance passes to his brother, Władysław, who thus has the entire duchy of Opole.

The knights of Mazovia and Łęczyca bar the advance of the Prussians who have infiltrated into Mazovia and, in their usual cruel way, have been devastating the area round Ciechanów. Battle is engaged and the Prussians are routed. Then, at the instigation of Duke Conrad, the Lithuanians quietly move into Sandomierz and plunder the town of Opatów and its surroundings.

A new legate of Pope Innocent IV, Opizo abbot of Mezzano, vested with full powers, arrives in Cracow, and continues into Prussia and Pomerania. He persuades the Duke of Pomerania to swear that he will not come to any understanding with the Prussian or other heathens against the Christians, nor make secret or covert pacts with them; in return for which he is relieved of the ecclesiastical punishments imposed on him a couple of years earlier by the legate William Bishop of Modena; he then collects from the individual dioceses the St. Peter's Pence that has been accumulating for several years and with it returns to the Pope.

In this same year, Pope Innocent in Lyons canonizes Edmund, Archbishop of Canterbury.

Daniel, Prince of Kiev and Drohiczyń, rich in money, land and soldiers, active and enterprising, is at this time the most powerful of the Ruthenian dukes. He has ambitions to style himself "king"; so, when he learns that a legate of the Holy See, furnished with full powers, has arrived in Poland, he sends eminent envoys with gifts of considerable value, with the request that the Holy See elevate him to royal status and anoint and crown him King of the Ruthenians. He promises that all the lands of Ruthenia under his rule will abandon the Greek rite and transfer obedience to the Catholic church and its Pontiff, and also that he will defend both Ruthenia and other Catholic lands against Tatar raids. The Papal Legate is greatly attracted by the proposal, which he thinks has many advantages, and he agrees to it, though the Polish bishops, especially the Bishop of Cracow, who know the character and ways of Duke Daniel and that his word is not to be trusted, so that in all probability he will disregard his promises and make a fool of the Pope, his legate and his religion, adduce various arguments against him doing this. Still the Legate refuses to change his mind, either because he thinks the arrangement good for the Christian faith or because he just wishes to do something that will make his mission famous, or because he thinks the Polish bishops are not being sincere, but are prompted by envy. So, the Legate goes to Drohiczyń, which is Duke Daniel's principal seat, and in the castle there anoints and crowns him King of Ruthenia. Daniel solemnly promises and swears on the hands of the Legate that in future he, all his dukes and nobles will sincerely and faithfully accept the faith, rites and ceremonial of the Roman Catholic Church and obey its supreme vicar, Pope Innocent IV and his successors.

At about this time the Pope sends some Dominicans and Fransicans to try and convert the Tatars and their Khan and make them less savage. These same Tatars have already cruelly conquered all Persia and Assyria and the whole of Turkey, previously known as Armenia and from there they have occupied Asia Minor, either murdering or expelling their former despotic rulers and their inhabitants, or converting them to their own faith and language.

There is such severe famine in Chełmno, Pomerania and Prussia that many of the Knights are starving. Wydżga a Cracovian knight, who aspires to join the Order, sends three ships down the Vistula laden with wine, honey, wheat, ham, grain, butter and other foodstuffs, while overland he sends a gift even more precious to the hungry—300 head of cattle and horses. When the knight himself arrives in Toruń, he is cordially welcomed and admitted to the Order, in which he remains until he dies. He also brings a considerable quantity of gold which is mined in the hills close to the Hungarian border and gives this to the Order as well.

A.D. 1247

At an assembly held near Poznań, the two dukes of Wielkopolska agree an equitable division of its lands between them: Bolesław, the younger, getting the Kalisz duchy from the River Prosna as far as Przemęt, together with the castle there, and thence to the River Warta, the bogs known as Sepno and on as far as the River Oder, which constitutes the frontier. The elder duke, Przemyśl, gets Gniezno and Poznań with their castles and appurtenances. At the request of these two, the Bishop of Poznań adminsters their vow to respect the arrangement and lays a curse on whomever should break it.

Bolesław of Legnica, wishing to recover Wielkopolska, which he claims as his inheritance from his father, Henry the Pious, starts building a new fort at Kopanica on the Oder, as if those lands already belonged to him. Przemyśl and Bolesław bring up an army to stop this. However, the nobles on both sides intervene to prevent the brothers coming to blows and it is agreed that Bolesław is to have Santok, Międzyrzecz and Zbąszyń castles, and that the fort at Kopanica is to be pulled down. However, the Duke of the Slavs, or Cassubians, Barnim, claims that the castle at Santok belongs to him, and, having assembled an army, proceeds to lay siege to it. It has a mere handful of people to defend it and they are short of provisions, so Duke Barnim might well have captured it, had not Duke Przemyśl quickly come to the rescue, followed almost at once by Bolesław with more troops. Barnim then raises the siege and withdraws, and never attempts to return. Bolesław rewards Przemyśl for his loyalty by returning the castle at Santok to him. Bolesław considers himself shamed and injured by Casimir, Duke of Kujawy, who is turning the monastery at Ląd on the river Warta into a fortress, so he collects an army, captures the monastery, ejects the garrison, demolishes the ramparts, moats and its other defences, and hands it back to the monks.

Worn with age and continual warring with his nephew, Duke Conrad dies. He has scarcely been buried in Płock cathedral, indeed his widow and younger son are still busy with the obsequies, before his elder son, Casimir, still harbouring a grudge against his father for favouring his younger brother, has occupied the castles at Sieradz, Spycimierz and Rozpra, and established himself in them.

Henry de Weida, who became the second Master of the Order, when Poppo died, builds a castle on Pomeranian territory at Christburg and presents it to the brethren and knights to assist them in stopping the pinprick raiding by Duke Świętopełk. However, in a cunning night attack,

Świętopełk captures the castle, killing part of the garrison and carrying the rest off into captivity, and then installs his own garrison. This is a breach of the armistice, which is aggravated when Świętopełk captures a number of Knights near Golub and murders them. He then assembles an army and invades Kujawy, giving his troops orders to spare neither minors nor women, and to put the whole to fire and the sword. He then withdraws, burdened with much loot, into his castle at Świecie. However, while he has been devastating Kujawy, the Master and Brethren have been building a second fort near that at Christburg. That done, they invest Świecie and mount an assault. In the ensuing battle Świętopełk is defeated and forced to retreat, which allows the Knights to capture his train with all his provisions and much booty. Eager to avenge his defeat, Świętopełk assembles a fresh army. He sends several detachments to harass the Knights in the fort at Christburg, but when these are properly engaged, they are forced to retreat. The noise and commotion of their arrival back in Świętopełk's camp causes a panic: men run from their tents and try to escape across the river, with the result that several drown. The Knights then march into Pomerania and devastate it, burning all the barns and granaries of the monastery at Oliwa and removing its horses and cattle, thus reducing it to abject poverty.

A.D. 1248

After the death of Duke Conrad, the lands of Cracow, Sandomierz and Lublin once again enjoy real peace and quiet. Conditions improve and damage done is repaired. Duke Conrad's son, Bolesław, dies.

While all is peaceful in Cracow, a stubborn civil war breaks out in Silesia, where Bolesław the Bald, regrets his voluntary surrender of the better part of Wrocław to his brother, Henry, which he made under the impression that in Legnica he was getting the better share, and is aggrieved that his other brother, Conrad, his co-inheritor, has given up his subdeanery and the promise of the see of Bamberg and embraced the status of knight, and is now demanding his half of the inheritance; while Henry, who shares with Władysław, Archbishop of Salzburg, has both shares for himself. So, Bolesław hires some Saxon mercenaries and declares war on Henry of Wrocław. Henry avoids a pitched battle, for his army is the weaker, thus allowing Bolesław to plunder the whole territory, in doing which he has 500 men and women, who sought refuge in the church at Środa, burned alive. He then advances on Wrocław town and lays siege to it. Wrocław has been recently located under German law by Henry and is under the government of its Germans. It has few inhabitants and is insufficiently equipped with means of defence, nonetheless it bravely endures a siege of three months, during which, by frequent sorties, it inflicts damaging losses on its enemy, this finally forces Bolesław to raise the siege with nothing accomplished.

Jacob Archdeacon of Liège the papal nuncio arrives in Wrocław and holds a synod, at which he explains the difficulties imposed on the Holy See by the long struggle between Pope and Emperor, which have involved the Holy See in debt and financial difficulties, because of which he now begs the assembled bishops to help by surrendering half of their revenues for a period of three years. After much discussion, the Polish bishops decide to contribute one-fifth of the revenues of their clergy for three years (half being considered too onerous), and to make this more acceptable, on the appointed day, they hand over the total amount for three years in coin, which is then converted into gold and sent to the Pope through his penitentiary, Godfrey.

Ever since it accepted Christianity, the Kingdom of Poland has held to the basic principle of a forty-day Lent lasting from Septuagesima Sunday until Easter. This has been the cause of much misunderstanding between clergy and laity, for the latter protest that the custom does not agree with that of the Roman Catholic Church and has been abandoned everywhere else and so is not binding on them. After days of discussion the Papal nuncio uses his powers to abolish the custom and permit the eating of meat by clergy and laity alike, until and including Ash Wednesday.

King Václav of Bohemia, one-eyed and already advanced in years, is so hated by the Czech nobility that he has to yield to their pressure and hand over to his son, Przemyśl, retaining for himself only three castles, to one of which Przemyśl lays siege. However, adherents of his father then attack Przemyśl's own castle and force him and his own people to withdraw. Meanwhile, Václav has obtained help from Austria, which enables him to recover his kingdom. He captures and imprisons his son, who then humbles himself and is reconciled with his father, content henceforth to be Duke of Moravia.

A.D. 1249

Przemyśl, Duke of Gniezno, wishing to prevent the partition of the lands he and his brother Bolesław, the Duke of Kalisz, inherited, with great effort and at great expense builds a castle and town near the cathedral of Poznań, erecting a number of buildings and digging ditches and defensive ramparts. He then summons his brother and forces a new division of their territories, which young Bolesław dares neither dispute nor resist; thus Przemyśl acquires the better land, the castle and lands of Kalisz, while Bolesław has the less fertile area.

Bolesław the Bald of Legnica, still hoping to recover his original share of the territory which he voluntarily surrendered to his brother, Henry, and having Saxon and German support, as well as some foreign mercenaries, organizes a second incursion into Wrocław. When Henry again avoids a fight by confining his activities to defending castles and forts, Bolesław loots and ravages his towns and villages and sends a great deal of booty of cattle and people back to Legnica. He then again lays siege to Wrocław town, but without success, and returns home, where his own people seize him and put him in prison. He is freed, after swearing to behave honourably, but, eager to avenge himself on his own people, he hands his castles over to Germans and, in return for military assistance, gives the castle at Lubusz to the Archbishop of Magdeburg. When his brother-in-law, Przemyśl, learns of this, he takes him into custody and keeps him confined as an honoured prisoner.

Václav the One-eyed, King of Bohemia, imprisons the bishop of Prague, Nicholas, on the pretext that he has conspired against him. The entire diocese is then placed under an interdict, until such time as the bishop is liberated.

As a result of a misunderstanding, Bishop Bruno of Olomouc, despite his cloth, lays siege to, and captures the town of Racibórz and burns it, its churches and monasteries. He brings up siege-weapons to attack the castle, but is repulsed and withdraws abashed. After protracted negotiations Duke Władysław of Racibórz buys Racibórz back from the Bishop for 3000 marks.

Pope Innocent IV sends the Archbishop designate of Ruthenia, formerly the Bishop of Armagh, to Duke Daniel requiring him to swear an oath of obedience to the Pope and the Roman Catholic Church. The crafty, rebellious duke pays no attention to the demand, but rather demonstrates his hostility by dismissing the Papal Legate without due respect.

The Knights garrisoning the castles and towns in Prussia combine forces and march into Natangia, a province of Prussia which they lay waste most cruelly. On their way back, they find themselves surrounded by Prussians in difficult terrain, which allows neither escape nor a battle in close formation, so, despite the opposition of their commander, they surrender and are promptly murdered by the barbarians together with a number of Christian civilians.

A.D. 1250

Prince Bolesław and Prandota the Bishop of Cracow send a delegation to the Pope in Lyons to inform him of a series of remarkable miracles attributed to the former bishop of Cracow, Stanisław. The two delegates are the dean of Cracow, a man of low parentage and mean stature, but of unusually great learning, a doctor of law, wise and energetic, and Master Gerard canon of Cracow, the subprior of the Dominicans there. They report verbally, after which the ever-cautious Pope, sends a bull to the Archbishop of Gniezno, the Bishop of Wrocław and the Abbot of Lubiąz, instructing them to interrogate a certain knight, Gedko, a centenarian, who, though he could not himself have known Bishop Stanisław, must have met and known people who had and so could have told him about the bishop and the miracles he performed in his lifetime and afterwards.

This summer, Bolesław the Bald, for the third time invades his brother's duchy of Wrocław with a mercenary force and, after laying it all waste, invests the castle. Unable to capture this, he returns home burning everything in his path. Pressed by his German mercenaries for their pay, he sells all his horses, weapons, property and jewelry, which brings in about half of what is owing. Because of this many of the new strong points in Legnica and Wrocław are left empty, so these are taken over by brigands and those who have not received their pay. In his financial straits the Duke pledges his castle at Lubusz to the Margrave of Brandenburg for what is a very modest sum, fooling himself that this will induce the Margrave to give him military assistance in his fight with his brothers. Since then, this castle and its lands have been part of the Mark of Brandenburg. Bolesław is now up to his ears in debt, deserted and despised by his own men, as well as by the mercenaries whom he has never paid, and by the brigands who now occupy more and more of the country's strong-points. He is reduced to such penury that, without even a servant, he roams the country not on horseback, but on foot, accompanied only by his page, Surrian, the two of them living off other people. In the end, Bolesław is captured by some of his brother Henry's men and imprisoned in Wrocław castle. Eventually released, he seeks refuge in Legnica, from where he never ceases plotting against his brothers. In an attempt to restore his fortunes, he transfers the towns of Zittau and Görlitz, part of his inheritance, to his barons for a considerable sum, thus further reducing the size of his duchy.

A.D. 1251

Władysław, Duke of Opole, decides to repay his sister-in-law, Judith, widow of Mieczysław of Racibórz, the 500 silver marks she brought as her dowry, thus relieving the villages and properties allotted to her of their obligations; and, with the approval of Casimir of Kujawy, he orders her to be given the territory of Ruda, now called Wieluń, which lies in a fertile valley, well watered with plentiful springs, a territory the Duke acquired when Władysław Odonic's sons were expelled from Wielkopolska and which, he realizes, he is not going to be allowed to keep much longer. On the day that this is done, Przemyśl of Poznań, alerted to what is going on, appears with a force of mercenaries to try to prevent a considerable part of his inheritance being lost to him for ever. As the emissaries of the Duke of Kujawy, who are due to take over the castle, which stands there empty except for its holder and a couple of men, are late in arriving, Przemyśl takes possession of it. All the local gentry submit to his authority and he starts ruling the territory as if it were a legal part of his inheritance. When the soldiers sent by the Duke of Kujawy arrive and discover what has happened, they beat a hasty retreat in case they should be attacked. The Duke himself takes the loss with equanimity and never demands its return. He pays, in ready silver, the amount due to his sister-in-law to Duke Henry, who has married her and by whom she has two children. He then marries Euphemia, sister of Duke Przemyśl of Kalisz, who thus becomes his relation.

A deposit of rock salt is discovered in the village of Bochnia, five miles from Cracow. In many places it is so white that it looks like crystal and it can be quarried in great lumps. To exploit the vein a town is built, which has a parish church, generously endowed by Bolesław. The discovery of the salt is attributed to the good deeds and virtuous life of Bolesław's wife, Kinga.

Bolesław the Bald is convinced that his brother, Conrad, will one day go to war with him, because he feels that he has not been given his due share of their inheritance. Bolesław needs money with which to pay the Germans, who have helped him in his various enterprises, so he orders the arrest of one of those closest to him, Hinko, son of the Castellan of Crosna, intending to use him as a lever with which to extract money from the Castellan, who is reputed to have it in plenty. The arrested Hinko is handed over to the Germans, a thing that further outrages the Polish gentry, who then hand Crosna castle and town over to Bolesław's brother and enemy, Conrad, and transfer their allegiance to him.

Viola, Duchess of Opole, who is of Bulgarian origin, dies.

Some brigands from Lubusz, bent on plunder, raid territory belonging to Zbąszyń castle. There they find a considerable herd of cattle, which they appropriate, siezing the herdsman so as to prevent him running off and raising the alarm. The herdsman, wishing to save himself and his herd, tells the brigands that, if they will leave him and his herd in peace, he will put them in the way of even greater booty. The delighted brigands agree and the herdsman then tells them that the castle at Zbąszyń is now guarded by only three soldiers, because the relief garrison has not yet arrived, and thus can easily be captured. The brigands go to the castle and tell the three guards that they are the relief garrison, and, as such, are at once admitted and tie up the three. When Duke Przemyśl hears what has happened, he assembles a small force from his courtiers and retinue, marches on Zbąszyń castle and pretends to lay siege to it. The brigands, horrified by the paucity of provisions in the castle and surprised that any one should have come to its rescue so swiftly, agree to surrender, if the Duke will grant them their lives. The castle is thus recovered before the real garrison even arrives. The brigands thank the Duke for their lives, a gift they do not deserve.

The disaster inflicted on them at Natangia reduced the Teutonic Knights to poverty and despair. Now they are relieved by the arrival of reinforcements from the Margrave of Brandenburg, the Bishop of Merseburg, and the commander Henry of Schwarzburg. With their help five Prussian tribes are forced to discard their pagan idols and accept Christianity. At this time, the fourth Master of the Prussian Order, Herman of Salza, dies and is replaced by Conrad, Landgrave of Thuringia.

A.D. 1252

Bolesław the Bald, infuriated by the way in which his knights and subjects have gone over to his brother, Conrad, decides to take action, although in reality Conrad has done nothing but demand his rightful share of their inheritance. He plans first to imprison Conrad and then kill him, a task he assigns to assassins recruited with promises. Learning of what is being planned, Conrad goes to the Duke of Poznań, asking for his pity and help, neither of which he can expect from his other brother, Henry of Wrocław. He is well received by Przemyśl and encouraged. Przemyśl then sends to Bolesław and his brother, Henry, asking them to relinquish to their brother that part of the inheritance that is rightfully his, so that he does not have to live in exile on other people's bread. Henry replies that he has nothing that belongs to Conrad and promises to do what he can to get Bolesław to return Conrad's share to him. Bolesław, however, gives a fiercely negative reply, insisting that Conrad is unworthy to inherit, in that he relinquished his post of subdeacon and forfeited the bishopric of Bamberg by abandoning the Church and reverting to lay status. Przemyśl then organizes a small force and, accompanied by Conrad, enters territory in the duchy of Legnica which is in Bolesław's possession. He starts building a fort at Bytom on the river Oder, near Głogów, installs a strong garrison, surrounds the fort with ditches and towers and hands it over to Conrad, who intends to continue harassing his brother until Bolesław gives him back his due share. One day, while this fort is under construction, Bolesław ventures so close in order to see what the others are doing, that he lets himself be captured by a patrol from the fort. He is taken before Duke Przemyśl and put in prison, but escapes shortly afterwards by bribing his guard. The fort at Bytom finished, Duke Przemyśl returns to Poznań, marries his sister, Salomea, to Conrad and gives them a splendid wedding, an occasion he uses to amnesty Thomas the Castellan of Poznań and his son, on their swearing to renounce treachery and be sincerely loyal to him and his brother, the Duke of Gniezno Bolesław.

Despite all their efforts and the wealth of their evidence, the Polish envoys, who have been endeavouring to achieve the canonization of Stanisław, fail to convince more than a minority of the cardinals of the truth of those long-gone miracles, and, as a result, they are asked to present better proof. They return to Poland with fresh instructions for the papal commissioners, who are told to obtain clearer evidence of Stanisław's miracles, both those already investigated and others, and report back to the Pope once again. This set-back would have made anyone else lose heart, but not Prandota the Bishop of Cracow, who remains full of enthusiasm and hails the earlier witnesses and many new ones before the commissioners. Among these is the centenarian knight, whose evidence is carefully recorded. All this takes a good six months, during which time Pope Innocent has left Lyons and gone to Italy. He stops in Perugia where he canonizes a new martyr, murdered by heretics in Lombardy. He then assembles a great army with the intention of invading Apulia.

The Duke of Lower Pomerania, Barnim, seeing that Duke Przemyśl is busy warring in Silesia, attacks the castle at Drezdenko, which is in Przemyśl's territory, and one night, when the guards have fallen asleep, storms it. Przemyśl, with everything settled in Silesia, returns with a strong force and by the grace of God recaptures the castle. He imprisons those left inside and gives their possessions to his men, as their booty.

King Béla of Hungary assembles a big force of Hungarians and Kumans, a people of Tatar origin who settled in Pannonia after the departure of the Tatars, and with this devastates Moravia, Austria and Styria, which, he insists, belong to him, and removes many men and women into servitude. His son, Przemyśl, then marries the daughter of the Duke of Austria. When she proves sterile, he takes as his concubine one of the girls in her retinue, the daughter of the Baron of Kunring, and she gives him a son, who is named Nicholas and granted the duchy of Opava, which Przemyśl took by force when the Duke of Racibórz died. It is, indeed, from Nicholas that the line of the dukes of Opava and Racibórz originate.

Mendog, Duke of Lithuania, having assigned tracts of Lithuanian territory to the Knights, on their advice, pretends to accept Christianity and sends to the Pope informing him of his sincere adherence to Christianity and asking to be crowned king. The Pope sends Brother Heidenrich, previously Provincial of Poland and now Bishop of Chełmno, to Riga, where he anoints Mendog as king.

A.D. 1253

Their second scrutiny of the life, deeds and miracles of Stanisław complete, the Polish envoys return to the Pope, who is now in Italy. They find him in Perugia and present their report. They anticipate a swift and favourable decision, until Cardinal Gaeta informs them out of the blue that their position is all but hopeless, since the Cardinal-Bishop Reginald, a man of considerable authority and intelligence, objects to canonization on the grounds that, if the miracles had been genuine, the fame of Stanisław must have reached the Holy See long before. The Poles then ask Cardinal Gaeta what they are to do, and he replies that Stanisław himself must perform one further miracle to convince the doubters. While the Poles are wondering what to do and discussion of the various proposals drags on, the Cardinal-Bishop of Ostia, the principal opponent of the canonization of Stanisław, falls so gravely ill that his doctors and he himself fear that death is at hand. A little later, during one sleepless night in the privacy of his private apartments, Stanisław appears to the Cardinal. He is wearing bishop's robes and is surrounded by a bright light. He asks the Cardinal-Bishop if he recognizes him. Astounded and somewhat alarmed, indeed, finding it difficult to speak, the sick man replies: "No, I do not recognize you. Tell me who you are that have come to my room in such lustre through doors that are shut". The apparition replies: "I am Stanisław, Bishop of Cracow, whose canonization you so strenuously oppose." Recovering his composure, the Cardinal Reginald replies: "Pardon my ignorance, most holy Bishop, and forgive me, for now I shall be as much in favour of your canonization, as previously I was opposed to it". Stanisław then says: "If you agree that in the eyes of God and the saints I have earned canonization, stand up from your bed of sickness, cured. And take care in future not to oppose my canonization". This the Cardinal promises to do and the apparition vanishes. The Cardinal then calls his servants and orders horses to be saddled, so that he may ride to the Papal palace. At first his servants think that he has taken leave of his senses; but, when he gets out of bed unaided and mounts his horse, they are amazed. When the Pope is told, not, what he has been expecting, that the Cardinal is dead, but that he has arrived and is fully recovered, he asks how it happened. The Cardinal tells him how he received a visit from Bishop Stanisław in a blaze of light he found difficult to endure and was restored to health, and how he, realizing his mistake, now favours canonization as much as previously he opposed it. After further brief consideration, the Pope announces that he will perform the ceremony of canonization of St. Stanisław on the Feast of the Birth of the Blessed Virgin in Assissi. On that day, as the Pope and the College of Cardinals are saying a solemn mass in the city, a certain youth dies and his body is brought to the church by his weeping parents, either to be buried or to be restored to life. Giving way to their entreaties, the Pope falls to his knees and, addressing the Almighty, asks that, if all that he has been told about the holy Stanisław be true, He should give a sign that this is so and that he should be canonized. He has scarcely finished the prayer, when he is told that the dead youth has risen to his feet. Then, in a basilica filled with the blaze of candles, the Pope continues the service of canonization of St. Stanisław, whose day is made May 8. All present at the ceremony are granted a year and forty days remission from any penances imposed.

The Archbishop of Gniezno Fulko keeps telling Przemyśl the Duke of Poznań that he must no longer keep his brother, Bolesław, in prison on the pretext that he has tried to kill him; and so, on Christmas Day, the Duke releases his brother. The two are then reconciled and a fresh division of the duchies made, after which the two live in harmony. King Béla of Hungary organizes another raid into Moravia and, meeting with no resistance, puts most of it, except the stronger castles and towns, to fire and the sword; its churches are robbed of the bones of saints, their bells, vestments and ornaments. Learning of this and of how the Hungarian force includes some Kumans of whose cruelty the Czechs are mortally afraid, King Václav orders the guards to be doubled in all castles and fortified towns throughout the country, while Prague itself is given new walls and fortifications; all the houses in the suburbs are pulled down to deny them to the enemy and their inhabitants moved into the city itself. Both castle and city are hastily supplied with provisions to enable them to withstand a siege.

Bolesław the Bashful, yielding to pressure from his father-in-law Béla of Hungary, also invades Moravia with a large mixed force, including Daniel of Ruthenia and his troops. They plunder and loot the countryside in Opava and Moravia from which many captives of both sexes are removed to Poland and Ruthenia.

Václav, known as the One-eyed, dies in Prague on September 22 and is succeeded by his only son, Otakar, who, for a time, styles himself Prince, not King, of Bohemia. He is an ardent admirer of St. Stanisław and, when he learns of the latter's canonization, he sends to the Bishop of Cracow pleading for relics of the saint; when these are granted and are sent to Prague, he goes out seven miles in solemn procession to greet them, and then has the relics placed in a silver reliquary.

This year is remembered in Poland as that of the canonization of her holiest martyr, Stanisław, of the almost simultaneous deaths of two bishops (Poznań and Płock), and of floods of hitherto unheard-of severity. From Easter to July 25 it rained without pause, day and night, with the result that in low-lying areas the corn was submerged and you could swim in meadows and tilled fields.

What grain is harvested has to be stored on higher ground. Because of these floods and the hostile raids by the Lithuanians, the land called Wiśnieńska became depopulated.

A.D. 1254

The people of Cracow turn out *en masse* to greet the Polish envoys returning with the papal bull of canonization of St. Stanisław. These are honoured like victorious warriors. May 8 is fixed as the day for the saint's bones to be taken from his grave. When the day comes, the city cannot accommodate the crowds that come from all over Poland and even from Hungary. The bones are taken from the grave near the south gate of the cathedral, washed with wine and held up to view to the applause and shouts of those seeking the saint's help. They are then distributed among the cathedral's churches and the more important collegiate foundations, monasteries and parish churches; but the head, hands and other important members remain together with the dust in Cracow cathedral.

Bolesław the Bashful and Władysław of Opole, agreeing that it is intolerable that the Czechs should have been ruling the city and province of Opava, get together a force which includes some Ruthenian contingents and with it invade Opava. They burn all its towns and villages and carry off booty of people, cattle and other things. Meanwhile, the other Polish dukes are all engaged in squabbles or armed strife: Casimir of Kujawy has imprisoned Siemowit and his wife; while their brother dukes, Przemyśl of Poznań, Bolesław of Kalisz and their brother-in-law, Conrad of Silesia, are devastating part of Wrocław, punishing Henry, who inherited one half of it from his father, for never handing the other half on to his brother Conrad, nor seeing to it that Bolesław the Bald gave their second brother his share of their joint inheritance, and also for never paying the fifty marks in silver he undertook to pay as ransom for a certain German he had captured and then released. They wreak havoc on all the villages and towns round Oleśnica and the more hilly country as far as the River Widawa. A mile from Wrocław, they discover a ford in the Oder and, crossing over, capture a huge quantity of cattle and take it all back to Wielkopolska without encountering resistance. Overawed by threats of ecclesiastical sanctions, they have left all towns and villages belonging to the churches and monasteries untouched. The Papal Nuncio complains that these wars reflect on him, since they have taken place while he has been in Wrocław, thus shaming him and the Holy See, so he now places an interdict on Duke Przemyśl's lands of Poznań. This remains in force for only twenty-six days, after which the Duke demands its removal, which is done lest the matter get to the ears of the Pope. The Dukes of Silesia are affected by this plague of war, for Duke Conrad, finding himself unable to extract part of his patrimony either from Bolesław of Legnica or Henry of Wrocław, puts his brother Henry in prison, when he chances to catch him as he is heedlessly travelling through one of Conrad's villages. Although Conrad orders him to be treated more as a brother than as an enemy, he will not free him, until Henry has provided sureties that he will either require Bolesław the Bald to return Conrad his share, or, if he cannot accomplish this, give Conrad part of his own duchy of Wrocław.

On May 29 Bolesław the Bashful founds a nunnery of the Order of Norbertines at Krzyżanowice on the River Nida in the diocese of Cracow and endows it with thirteen villages, which are exempted from all dues and tribute.

A.D. 1255

In order to put an end to the constant raiding of their lands by their brother Conrad, who is claiming a share of their inheritance, as well as by the dukes of Wielkopolska, Bolesław the Bald and Henry of Wrocław summon Conrad to come and negotiate in Głogów. This he does, and it is agreed that Bolesław the Bald is to share the duchy of Legnica with Conrad, while Henry, who is supposed to be sharing with their third brother, now Bishop of Salzburg, is not bound to cede any part of his share to Conrad. Bolesław accepts this judgment, though not without misgivings, and gives Conrad Głogów, retaining Legnica for himself. As soon as Conrad takes over Głogów, Bolesław reduces the taxes on various villages and towns in Legnica and Wrocław and sends his hostages back to Henry.

Mendog, now elevated to the dignity of king by Pope Innocent IV, thanks to the efforts of the Teutonic Knights, burns the timber-built town of Lublin and plunders the surrounding country, before returning to Lithuania with a host of captives. His elevation to king has been a clever and cunning move on the part of the Order, who, within a short time, have reduced him to insignificance by demanding those territories of Lithuania and Samogitia that he had signed over to them.

Scarcely has peace returned to Silesia, than war breaks out again in Pomerania, with Świętopełk, who is unable to endure peace, sending his son, who for some years has been a hostage with the Knights in Prussia, to raid his nephews' territories in Wielkopolska. On the eve of St. Michael's Day, the raiders reach the fort at Nakło, which is held by Przemyśl of Poznań, but which Świętopełk considers to be within the boundaries of Pomerania. The fort is weakly defended and the defenders unsuspecting; so, thanks to the treachery of a bribed crossbowman, it is swiftly captured. When Duke Przemyśl learns of this, he calls upon his brother, Bolesław, to help, and then, with their combined forces, reinforced by 1000 men from Bolesław the Bashful and 800 from the Duke of Mazovia Siemowit, marches on Nakło. When this proves difficult to take, both because of its position and defences, and the stout resistance of its large garrison, they build a new fort to the west of the old one. Within a few days, the new fort is complete with ramparts and moats, well supplied with provisions and given a strong garrison, whose task is to deny the Pomeranians access to or exit from the old fort. After this, there are frequent skirmishes and almost daily sorties by both sides.

The Czech prince, Otakar, having negotiated an armistice with his great enemy Béla the King of Hungary, assembles a force of Bohemians and Moravians and marches it into Prussia. In his retinue are the four bishops of Prague, Chełmno, Warmińsk and Olomouc, the margraves of Brandenburg and Moravia, and the Prince of Austria. Their intention is to fight the barbarians, which they have been induced to do as much by the Pope's pronouncement of a crusade as by the banquets given by the Brethren of the Order at which they are seated in accordance with their rank and fulsomely praised by heralds in defiance of truth and reason. The barbarians withdraw into their hidden fastnesses and refuse a pitched battle, so the country is put to fire and the sword, whereupon the Sambians surrender and Otakar orders the Bishop of Prague to baptize them and give them his own name, Bruno. Then, as a memorial to their having been there, the Knights build two new towns, one on the River Pregola, near the sea, which they call Krolewiec in honour of Otakar, though he is not their king, and another, Brunsberg, where is now Warmińsk cathedral, in memory of the Bishop of Prague. When the invaders have withdrawn, the rest of the Prussians exact cruel vengeance on the Sambians for having surrendered without orders. They also build another fortress opposite that at Krolewiec, which the Knights call Wilhofen.

On July 24, the Prussian Master Conrad dies and is succeeded by Poppo of Osterna.

A papal nuncio, Archdeacon Jacob, who is later to become Pope Urban IV, is sent to Prussia to put an end to the bitter war that has been waged for the last eleven years between Świętopełk Prince of Pomerania and the Order in Prussia. He arranges a lasting peace on equitable terms that both sides eventually keep.

A.D. 1256

Duke Przemyśl, seeing that the capture of Nakło is taking longer than he envisaged, announces yet another campaign against it, in which he is joined by his brother, Bolesław the Duke of Kalisz and by Casimir of Kujawy, one of Świętopełk's great enemies. However, afraid of incurring heavy losses if they should attempt to storm the castle and of disgracing themselves should they achieve nothing and withdraw, instead of halting at Nakło, they march on through the night and reach Raciąz, another fort, just before dawn. Raciąz is one of Świętopełk's fortresses, and it is known that many Pomeranians have taken refuge there with their families and possessions; so they set about investing it, while all inside are still sound asleep. When the defenders awake, there are shouts that the fort has been captured, that the enemy is already inside, that the tower has been taken, and there is such panic that, when Przemyśl's men light fires at various points at the foot of the towers, people come leaping through the flames to surrender. Those who remain inside die miserably in the flames and everything there is destroyed, except what was stored in pits and cellars. The invaders then return home.

Halfway through Easter, Świętopełk reaches Nakło with a considerable force and waggonloads of victuals, which he gives to the garrison, though not without opposition from the garrison of the new fort. He then devotes all his cunning to capturing the new fort. First, he accumulates quantities of dry faggots and resinous wood with which he plans to fill the ditches and moats, using what is left to fire the fort itself. The amount brought in proving wholly inadequate, the soldiers are sent back into the forest to collect more. In the interval, while this is being done and things are otherwise quiet, the garrison of the new fort makes a sudden sortie and sets fire to the piles of wood already stacked and in place. Świętopełk then orders a day of rest for his men, who are told to stand to at ten o'clock the following day, when an attack is to be launched on both sides of the fort. The attackers cross the ditches and, making mantlets of their shields, even reach the lateral bastions, to which, under cover of fire from their crossbows, siege weapons and catapults, they try to set fire. The garrison proves to have as much stomach to resist as the others have to attack, and, after twenty of the attackers have been killed and many others wounded, the latter are forced to withdraw. Denied all hope of capturing the fort, sad and ashamed, Świętopełk returns to Pomerania.

Open, regular warfare having failed, Świętopełk assembles yet another force, but this time decides to rely more on cunning and stratagem. He hides the bulk of his cavalry and foot, which he has brought up secretly and by night, in hilly terrain near the new fort, then sends a trusted messenger, who gains access to the old fort carrying instructions to those inside. Thus, at dawn the next day, they attack the new fort and challenge its garrison to come out and fight. When they do this, the attackers pretend to run and the jubilant Poles pursue them right into the ambush prepared for them. Świętopełk's men then turn and attack, as does the rest of the hidden force. The Poles give as good as they get and kill many of their ambushers; but, in the end, all are either killed or taken prisoner, for Świętopełk has ordered his troops to spare lives, where they can.

This disaster does nothing to diminish the determination of the others in the garrison. Heralds sent by Świętopełk to negotiate a surrender are told that there are still more inside the fort than those whom Swiętopolk has killed or captured, and that these will not allow him the pleasure of his little trick coming off. Świętopełk realizes that he is being dragged into a fierce and cruel war with his nephews and their supporters over a castle, which he himself had occupied illegally; so, through the intermediary of Poppo a noble from Cracow, who had joined the Teutonic Knights and was related through his mother to both Świętopełk and Przemyśl, he seeks to persuade the latter to come to an arrangement with him. Przemyśl is not averse to the idea and the two meet on the eve of the Feast of St. James the Apostle. They agree that Świętopełk is to restore the castle at Nakło to Przemyśl the Duke of Poznań and release all the prisoners he has taken, while the Duke of Poznań will, on certain specified dates, pay Swiętopolk a total of 500 marks to cover his costs and those of the demolition of Raciąz, and will free all his hostages. This is accepted by both dukes, who then go to Nakło and vow that neither will ever again attempt to occupy the castles and lands of the other. Uncle and nephew then kiss and are reconciled. Przemyśl then sends ten noble youths to Świętopełk as hostages until such time as the 500 silver marks have been paid.

No sooner is the war over Nakło concluded, than a new one breaks out in Silesia. This is due to the criminal arrogance of the Duke of Legnica, Bolesław the Bald, who, wishing to recoup the loss incurred when he was forced to hand over half the duchy to his brother, Conrad, now employs various nefarious ways of achieving this, such as extorting money from the clergy. One night, while the Bishop of Wrocław, come to consecrate a new church, in the property of Górka belonging to the abbey of Our Lady on the Sands, is asleep, Bolesław's Germans seize him together with Archdeacon Bogusław and a canon. All three are robbed of their horses, clothes and personal possessions. Then the bishop, still in just his nightshirt, is made to mount a horse, and, when the Germans see that he cannot ride (he is well advanced in years) he is taken off that horse and put on a heavy pacer, which is much more uncomfortable. Then, when the others are laughing at the bishop's nakedness and the chittering of his teeth due to the cold, one of the Germans takes pity on him and gives him an old speckled cloak and his own old boots, so that he should not die of cold. Thus are the three brought to Bolesław's castle at Wlen and put in the dungeon there in chains.

Duke Bolesław now demands changes in the sheaf-tithes. These are normally paid to the bishop and clergy of Wrocław in the field, but he now wants them to be paid in coin, and is also demanding 10,000 marks. There being nobody to stand up to the Duke, the Archbishop of Gniezno summons an emergency synod at which it is decided to send urgent messages to inform the Pope of what has happened and to ask him what is to be done; in the meantime the diocese of Wrocław is placed under an interdict. The Pope, deeply moved, instructs the Archbishop and the bishops of Cracow and Wrocław to use the whole authority of the Holy See to demand the release of the bishop, and, should this be refused, to excommunicate the Duke and his accomplices. And so, in all the churches in Gniezno province, at the end of communion, to the monotonous tolling of bells, the psalm *Deus laudem meam ne tacueris* and the prayer *Exaudi quesumus Domini* are recited in full and Duke Bolesław and his accomplices excommunicated, and an interdict placed on their lands.

Bolesław, Duke of Gniezno and Kalisz, marries Iolenta whom the Poles call Helena, daughter of Béla, King of Hungary, a marriage arranged by Bolesław the Bashful.

A.D. 1257

Bishop Thomas, who is anxious to regain his freedom, without consulting his chapter or his metropolitan, promises to change the sheaf-tithe into a monetary payment throughout his diocese and also to pay the Duke 2000 marks in silver and an amount of scarlet cloth. Half the amount is to be paid in advance and sons of nobles given as hostages for the payment of the rest and the fulfillment of the commutation in sheaf-tithe. This arranged, the Bishop and his companions are freed at Easter. Bolesław then attempts another crime: he invites his brother Conrad to Legnica, ostensibly to a banquet, but in reality to capture him and deprive him of his duchy of Głogów. Though warned about the kind of banquet to which he has been invited, Conrad accepts the invitation and goes to Legnica taking with him a number of his squires and knights. Most of these he leaves in a wood near the city, while he goes in accompanied by a few picked men, whom he tells of the ambush being prepared for them and what he wants them to do. Bolesław receives them with a show of graciousness and conducts them to the castle. Conrad, seeing that Bolesław's Germans are in position on the bastions and at various strategic points on the walls, gets his own blow in first. He seizes Bolesław and, before the Germans have time to come down from their high positions, hustles him through the gate and out. Bolesław's men do not dare pursue them, so Bolesław is handed over to those in the wood and taken back to Głogów under strict guard, and there he is kept until he has handed over all the money Bishop Thomas gave him or was to give him.

When he is informed of Duke Bolesław's disregard of his orders and of his refusal to release Bishop Thomas and his companions, Pope Alexander IV proclaims a crusade against Bolesław and his fellow countrymen, pronouncing them enemies of the Christian Faith. The Archbishops of

Gniezno and Magdeburg are instructed to proclaim the crusade in Poland and Germany, and to call upon all Catholic kings, princes, captains, barons and all the faithful to destroy the Duke and his subjects. A second synod is then called at which all the Polish bishops and abbots are informed of the Pope's enactment and told to inform all the clergy of the province of it. They then all turn on Bishop Thomas and berate him for having agreed to commute the sheaf-tithe, thus violating the freedom of the Church and the estimable practice of Poland, for which it is famed among all other nations. The Bishop excuses himself, pointing out how fear can come over even a brave man, and what suffering he had to endure, and formally promises (though this is a promise he does not keep) never to carry out his promise to convert the sheaf-tithe into money.

Bolesław the Bashful, wishing to develop Cracow which he cannot do under Polish law, appoints a vojt to supervise the change to German law, he alters the arrangement of the buildings and moves some that have been erected here and there without plan or order; but first he delineates the city square and then the corresponding streets.

On June 4, Duke Przemyśl of Poznań dies at the age of thirty-six, after fifteen days of illness.

On January 31, at three o'clock, Cracow and the other towns and cities of Poland suffer a severe earthquake, so severe that those unaccustomed to the phenomenon regard it as an awful warning.

The Prince of Bohemia Přemysl invades Bavaria despite the fact that many of the Czech nobles do not approve of such action, for which there is no justification, and lays it waste as far as the town of Landshut. But then, as he is leading a small detachment across a bridge on the river Inn, the bridge collapses and those following him fall in, all being drowned, except for a handful who know how to swim. The rest of the Prince's men, left on the far bank, are hewn down, except for a few who escape, and the Bavarians capture the whole of the Czech train with all their booty. The Prince and a handful of his followers escape. Some Czechs seek refuge in Muhldorf, which belongs to the Archbishop of Salzburg, and which the Bavarians then invest until peace is arranged.

A.D. 1258

Bolesław, Duke of Gniezno, announces an expedition against Casimir of Kujawy. For some time the two have been raiding and plundering each other's territory in a quarrel over the castellany of Ląd, which unquestionably belongs to Bolesław, but which Casimir unjustifiably appropriated a couple of years earlier, and which Bolesław now intends to recover and so restore the cultivation of its fields and remove the threat of the whole area being turned into a wilderness. So, assembling a considerable force of foot and horse, Bolesław invades Kujawy and invests the town and castle at Inowrocław, just inside the boundary of the duchy. Duke Casimir has not yet called up his men-at-arms and is not sure of being as strong as Bolesław, so he sends spokesmen asking for peace and promising to return the castellany of Ląd and to destroy the castle he has built there, once the garrison has been withdrawn. Bolesław signifies agreement and a day is appointed for the pact to be ratified in a document that both are to sign and on which they will shake hands. So, convinced that Casimir will stick to the spirit of the agreement, Bolesław raises the siege and returns home. Casimir is jubilant at having deceived his enemy and had the siege raised, and keeps none of his promises.

On April 5, Fulko, Archbishop of Gniezno, dies. The Archdeacon, Janusz, is elected to succeed him and sends a delegation to obtain the Pope's confirmation. When this arrives, it is told that new regulations require the new archbishop to present himself in person, so Janusz undertakes the arduous journey to Rome, where he easily obtains Alexander's confirmation of his appointment and is there consecrated. He returns to Poland safe and sound, but two members of the original delegation, the Dean of Poznań and the Canon of Gniezno, die of the pestilence in Lombardy. Bolesław the Bashful announces a general assembly to be held in Korczyn on March 2. This is attended by his cousins, the dukes Casimir and Siemowit. The purpose of the assembly is not to declare war, but to advance the glory of God and the salvation of their fellow men. Bolesław tells them that it has long been his dearest wish and that of his blessed wife, Kinga, to found a nunnery, there being none in his lands, and thus to ensure the safety of the daughters of his nobles and esquires, the weak and the poor or those who scorn marriage, which will thus fulfill the requests of his sister, Salomea, formerly Queen of Galicia. He asks his cousins and the others to help the enterprise, which all applaud. The town of Zawichost is held to be the most suitable place for the nunnery and Bolesław grants it as the nunnery's endowment together with twenty-five of the royal villages round about and in Sandomierz, as well as manors, lakes and tolls, sufficient for sixty women. At his own expense, he builds the nunnery, a church for it and accommodation for the nuns. Its rule is to be that of St. Damian which follows the Order of St. Francis, but which we now call the Order of St. Clare. Bolesław has invited his cousins to take part in order to ensure the continuity of the project, for when Bolesław, being childless, dies, his lands will pass to Casimir and Siemowit and their sons. When all this has been arranged, Bolesław's saintly mother, Grzymisława, dies and is buried in the Franciscan monastery at Zawichost.

A.D. 1259

Warcisław, Duke of the Slavs and Cassubians, wishing to avenge injuries suffered at the hands of Świętopełk the Duke of Pomerania, assembles a force of his own men, mercenaries and some knights sent to him by his ally, Bolesław the Duke of Kalisz, and, accompanied by Wolimir the Bishop of Kamień, who wants to halt the damage being done to villages belonging to his see and to recover his revenues, invades Pomerania and sets about putting it to fire and the sword. When they reach Słupsk, he leaves his train with much of their equipment to be guarded by the Bishop with part of the force, while he moves on with the rest to plunder and burn. When Świętopełk learns of this, he allows Warcisław to continue plundering and burning, and attacks and overcomes the Bishop and his men guarding the train. Only the Bishop and a handful of his men escape. The others are all killed or taken prisoner. Świętopełk then carries off the booty and equipment captured in the train and shuts himself up in his castles and fortresses before Warcisław has time to turn back and attack him. He gains more from the booty he captures than he loses by the damage done by the enemy.

When Duke Casimir of Kujawy learns of Warcisław's defeat, he secretly invades Kalisz and devastates it. When Bolesław the Pious of Wielkopolska is informed of this by special messenger, though half way to Poznań, he turns back and, assembling some thirty local knights, goes after Casimir, whose men are laden with booty and busy driving looted cattle. He catches up with them in a forest of oaks half way between Opatów and Klonów, and attacks them, scattering the rearmost ranks and so starting a general flight, for the others, unable to judge the strength of their attackers because of the trees, think them far more numerous than they are. Many are killed, and many taken prisoner, and all the booty is recovered and returned to those from whom it was taken, except for 300 horses and some loot that Bolesław appropriates. The wounded voivode of Kujawy, Martin, and others, who refused to run, all fall into the Duke's hands. Casimir imprisons the voivodes and others he considers responsible for the disaster, after summoning them to a meeting at Pakość, which belongs to Bolesław of Kalisz, and there builds a new fort, garrisons it and has the garrison devastate the country round about. Bolesław does not take this lying down, but, on November 6, together with his cousin, Bolesław the Bashful, and Siemowit of Mazovia, invades Łęczyca and lays it waste so thoroughly that it provokes the pity of its enemies. He then builds a fortress with ramparts and moats, supplies it with provisions and hands it over to Duke Siemowit. All this so humbles Casimir that he asks for a truce until St. Andrew's Day, when he swears he will accept the judgment of lords from both sides and withdraw from the castles and territories he has occupied.

Jadwiga, wife of the Duke of Legnica and daughter of the Count of Anhalt, dies on December 21.

Duke Casimir illegally appropriates the castle at Raciąż belonging to the see and bishop of Włocławek and assumes control of it. Bishop Wolimir excommunicates him and places his lands under an interdict. That done, he leaves the diocese, so as not to expose himself to attack and resides in Łagów, in the province of Cracow. Casimir, unable to touch the bishop in person, destroys much of his property, burning many of his manors with their granaries and grain.

Although Cracow and Sandomierz have avoided being drawn into the quarrel between the other Polish dukes, they now become involved in a war worse than civil war, when, soon after St. Andrew's Day, a huge Tatar army under Khan Nogay and Khan Telebuga of the Golden Horde, reinforced by contingents from the Ruthenian and Lithuanian dukes, moves against the Polish dukes. The hard winter makes it easy for the invaders, who can cross the Vistula and the other rivers on the ice, so that they appear suddenly near Sandomierz, and, after setting fire to the town and burning its churches, invest the castle in which almost all the nobility of Sandomierz took refuge with their wives, children and possessions when they heard of the Tatars' approach. The castle proves difficult to capture, so Duke Vasilko and the two sons of Duke Daniel, Leo and Roman, send heralds to the starosta of Sandomierz, Peter of Krampa, to persuade him that he can save his life, the castle and those who have taken refuge in it, if he will just humble himself by coming to the Tatar camp and paying the tribute demanded.

The starosta, a simple-minded man to whom the cunning and subterfuge of the Ruthenians is quite foreign, agrees. A cease-fire is arranged and, a few days later, the starosta and most of the more eminent Polish knights go to the Tatar camp, which is not far from the castle. There they pay homage to the Tatar chiefs and confirm their readiness to pay tribute as agreed with the Ruthenian dukes; but the Tatars pay no attention to the Ruthenians' promises or the laws of hospitality, but seize the Poles, rob them, beat them and finally cut off their heads. They then attack the castle, in which few are left but peasants and terrified women and children. There is no one to defend the castle, and the Tatars easily get in and kill all but the better-looking of the young girls, whom they spare to satisfy their lust. The castle is then plundered and set alight. The weak and the sick, who had taken refuge in the Church of the Blessed Virgin Mary, are similarly murdered. Indeed, it is said that so much Christian blood was shed, that it flowed down from the eminence on which the castle stands and into the river Vistula. Bolesław is appalled when news of this reaches him, for he knows that he does not have the strength to stand up to the Tatars. In tears, he entrusts the defence of the royal castle to Clement the Voivode of Cracow and the knights and citizens of the city, and takes his wife to Hungary, where he stays until he learns that the Tatars have returned home, as they do after months of plundering and ravaging the country, during which time many of those they capture are ransomed. In these three months the Tatars inflict more damage than they did eighteen years previously.

A.D. 1260

Within a year of his baptism, Mendog, duke, then king of Lithuania, apostatizes and reverts to his former obscene idolatry along with all those Prussians and Lithuanians who had been baptized with him. The Prussian Knights now have a number of documents in which Mendog asserts, falsely and hypocritically, that on various occasions he has received help and esteem from the Knights, for which he has surrendered to them in perpetuity much of his territory, indeed, almost the whole of Lithuania, and it is his grief at having been tricked and forced to surrender so much of his territory that is the cause of his apostasy. So, Mendog now assembles a vast army, estimated at thirty thousand men, and secretly and unexpectedly invades Mazovia. The Duke of Mazovia, Siemowit, who has not had time even to call up his knights, avoids a fight, so that Mendog and his army find Płock castle deserted and the town abandoned, so they set fire to it. They go on to devastate the remaining towns and villages of Mazovia, sending back great herds of cattle and many captives, male and female. After plundering Mazovia, the army moves on into Prussia, where the Knights can do nothing but defend their forts and castles. Mendog burns and razes all the towns the Knights have built there and murders all the Christians he comes across, so that he returns to Lithuania with only cattle and loot.

Bolesław the Pious of Wielkopolska marries Constance, the eldest of his dead brother's four daughters, to Conrad the Margrave of Brandenburg and, as her dowry, gives her in perpetuity the castle and castellany of Santok, all this without taking advice or considering the unity of Poland. From this dates the secession of Santok, which ever since has provided Poles and Saxons with an excuse for prolonged struggles in which much blood has been shed on either side. Constance's other three sisters, scorning wedlock, take the veil.

The expiry of the armistice arranged by Béla and Otakar gives rise to another war, this time over Styria, to which each lays claim. Béla has the active support of Bolesław the Bashful, the Duke of Sieradz, the King of Ruthenia, as well as of the Bulgarians, Serbs and Bosnians; while Otakar has that of the dukes of Wrocław, Opole and Carinthia and of the Margrave of Brandenburg. On June 10 Otakar bars the advance of Béla's army at the confluence of the Morava and the Danube. The Hungarians are on one bank of the Morava and the Czechs on the other, and there the two armies camp until the Feast of St. John the Baptist, when Otakar moves out heading for the town of Lawa. While on the march, he is attacked by King Béla's son, Stephen, with part of his father's army. Stephen's force is the weaker and is defeated and routed, many escaping back to the rest of the army, but those lost by drowning in the river number more than those killed in battle. A truce is arranged and peace talks held at which sensible conditions are agreed. King Béla renounces his claim to Styria, and to help the agreement to last, Béla's son is married to Cunegund, daughter of Otto III of Brandenburg.

The Prussians and Lithuanians, incensed by the Knights having built a castle at Karsowin on St. George's Hill, attack it with the largest force they can muster. This finds itself faced with two other armies, a Prussian and a Lithuanian, sent to defend the castle, and battle is joined beside the River Durbin in Courland. After much slaughter on both sides, in which the Livonian Master, Henry of Hornhausen, and Henry the Prussian Marshal are killed along with many other knights, the Prussians are put to flight. This victory enables the barbarians to capture Karsowin castle and also that at Heilsberg; but, when they go on to lay siege to the castle at Kinsberg, sited on the bridge across the River Pregor, the Knights force them to raise the siege.

Emboldened by their victory, the recent Prussian converts abandon Christianity and revert to paganism. They elect a leader, arm themselves and in the cruellest fashion rage against every Christian in the country. They kill all the priests and servants of Christ and all who have been baptized, burn the churches, desecrate the holy places and soil the sacred vessels and robes.

A.D. 1261

A punitive Christian army, comprising Poles, Teutonic Knights, Germans and other crusaders, penetrates into the farthest parts of Prussia at the time of the Feast of the Purification, which is the most suitable time of year, for then the marshes and quagmires and rivers are all frozen over. Its aim is to wipe out the pagans and idolators and devastate their land. Burning and destroying everything it comes across, the army reaches a point beyond which the terrain becomes quaggy and extremely difficult, so that a large force risks running out of provisions, for the barbarians sow little corn and hide what they have. Because of the terrain, the waggons and train are left with a small contingent to guard them, while the rest plunge deeper into the interior. The barbarians, not confident of being strong enough, for their scouts have told them of the composition of the Christian

army, attack those guarding the train and easily overcome them, killing most of the men and capturing the entire train. When the few who escape tell the others what has happened, the Christians
hurry back in order to deal with the barbarians. This is just what the barbarians want, and they are
waiting for them where the train had been. A fierce fight ensues. For several hours the issue is undecided, but the Christians are the first to fall back and then they turn and run, a defeat God has inflicted on them as punishment for their sins. The barbarians, satisfied with their victory and afraid
of ambushes, refrain from a pursuit, so that the disaster is not as great as it might have been. However, quite a number of Christians fall alive into the hands of the barbarians, and when, in accordance with their horrible ways, the barbarians wish to make a sacrifice to their gods in thanks for
their victory, they draw lots for which of the prisoners shall be burned. The lot falls on a man from
Magdeburg, Hirtzhals, but some of the barbarians know him and get him reprieved; however, the
lot falls on him a second time and then a third time, after which he volunteers and allows himself to
be burned mounted on his horse, as is the barbarians' impious custom.

When Casimir of Kujawy fails to keep his promise to return the castellany of Ląd, the Duke of
Kalisz, Bolesław, assembles the knights of Wielkopolska and, on St. Bartholomew's Day, invades
Kujawy and proceeds to plunder and loot it. Casimir sends heralds to promise the return of the castellany, but Bolesław replies that, having been taken in twice, he is not going to withdraw his troops
until he has possession of half the castle at Ląd and of the other castles which Casimir has built, and
the other half of Ląd castle has been returned to the Bishop of Włocławek, to whom he, Bolesław,
will return it. Casimir now suffers a further and more serious setback, when two of his sons by his
first marriage, rightly or wrongly accusing their stepmother, Casimir's second wife, of trying to
poison them, turn against their father and take over and, for a long time, occupy, the one, Łęczyca
and the other, Sieradz, with all their castles and forts. This they do with the consent and support of
the local knights and gentry, who dislike the tyranny and unjust rule of their father and are happy to
subject themselves to his sons.

Count Barby, inspired to help the Christians who have suffered a disastrous defeat in Prussia,
arrives there with his own army and starts murdering and plundering the inhabitants of Sambia,
who, in turn, attack him and defeat him, killing many of his men and capturing the Count himself.
They then invest the castle at Heilsberg, which they starve into surrender, rather than capture by
feats of arms. Then, wishing to expunge the concept of Christianity from their territory, they invest
three further forts: Kreuzberg, Königsberg and Bartenstein. The besieged are so starved that they
even lose their teeth and finally surrender. The fort at Bartenstein is abandoned and burned by the
Knights before the Sambians can lay siege to it.

The Flagellants, a sect that apparently started in France and then gained considerably in
strength in Germany, now reaches Poland. Their errors are many and depraved: they go in procession with their heads covered like nuns, but otherwise bare to the navel, and beat each other on the
shoulders with scourges of quadruple thongs knotted at the end. They also perform strange stoops
and genuflexions, sing embarassing songs, each in his own tongue, for the members are of different nationalities. Although they are all laymen, not priests, they hear each others' confession, and
give each other absolution, sometimes for quite serious sins. They recruit those who are doing penance, telling them that their sect is dear to God and brings great comfort and advantage to the souls
of those near them, even of those who have been damned and are in Hell, and those who have
achieved Heaven, as well as their own when they die. When these Flagellants reach Cracow, they
are at once moved on by Prandota the Bishop, who threatens them with prison unless they quickly
remove themselves. When the other Polish bishops expose the falseness of the Flagellant doctrine,
the dukes all order their people not to accept this kind of error under pain of confiscation of property. In other countries the sect is attacked with fire and the sword. It soon disappears.

Casimir of Kujawy, having just finished warring with Bolesław of Kalisz over the castellany that the latter had illegally occupied, suddenly starts another equally irresponsible fight with Bolesław of Cracow, by appropriating the lands of Lelów and its castle, asserting that it all belongs to him. He then builds a castle on a hill near Lelów, but Bolesław captures this.

Otakar of Bohemia dismisses his wife, Margaret, to whom he has been married for many a year, on the grounds of her shameful barrenness and the pretence that, on the death of her first husband, she took an oath to enter a nunnery. He takes as his second wife Cunegund, daughter of Rostislav duke of the Bulgars, their marriage being celebrated in Bratislava. He also arranges for the Archbishop of Mainz to crown him in Prague as King of Bohemia and his bride as its queen; for in those days Prague still did not have the dignity of a metropolitan, but came under the Archbishop of Mainz, who had to be asked to officiate each time the throne became vacant and there was a new king to be crowned and anointed. When the Electors call upon him to take over as Emperor, he refuses to attend, vaunting that it means more to him to be King of Bohemia, than Roman Emperor.

A.D. 1262

An army of Ruthenians and Lithuanians invades Mazovia, making its way stealthily and silently through forest and woods, so as to confound and overcome the unsuspecting inhabitants. On the eve of the Feast of St. John they attack and capture the Duke of Mazovia in his village of Jazowiec, before he has even been told of their incursion, and with him they capture his son, Conrad, and their attendant knights. In those days the Ruthenians so hated the Poles that they maltreated even those who surrendered. The Ruthenian duke has Duke Siemowit bound and then beheads him in his bonds. Siemowit's son escapes his father's fate, for he was captured by Mendog's Lithuanians and ransomed the same year. This disaster brings the Mazovians to their senses. They assemble their knights and men-at-arms and march against the enemy, prepared for a pitched battle, although compared with that of the enemy, their force is neither good nor sufficient. Anyway, on August 5, they attack the combined Ruthenian and Lithuanian force and inflict huge losses on it; but, in the end, the others, being much more numerous, the Mazovians are forced to retreat and victory goes to the others. The proud victors then criss-cross Mazovia killing or capturing people of all classes, burning towns and villages alike and collecting a huge booty in cattle and other things, with which they return home.

Bolesław the Pious takes pity on the Mazovians, whose land has been turned into a virtual waste by these two invasions, and takes an armed force there, together with artisans of different crafts and a large quantity of materials and provisions. Arriving on the Feast of St. Michael, he assembles the remnants of the population, and with generous grants comforts and assists them as far as he can. He then goes to Płock and with much effort and skill rebuilds the castle that the barbarians burned and demolished, providing it with ramparts and ditches. When everything necessary has been done, he hands it over to Siemowit's widow and her two sons Bolesław and Conrad.

The dukes and clergy of Poland, having assembled the necessary material with which to apply for canonization of the blessed Jadwiga, send a delegation to present the evidence to the Pope. The application is heard in public, after which the Pope appoints Salomon archdeacon of Cracow, Master Nicholas the Cracow scholasticus and Herengebert the dean of Vyšehrad who are all canons of Wrocław to investigate the blessed Jadwiga's life and miracles, their investigation having to be completed by 1264.

Bolesław the Bashful is perturbed by the frequent cunning raids into his territory by Ruthenians, Tatars, Lithuanians and other pagans, and wishes to ensure that the servants of Christ, the nuns living in the nunnery at Zawichost, which he himself had founded and endowed, should not be subjected to insult or derision, so, on the advice of the Bishop of Cracow and his lords he moves the nuns to a safer place, St. Mary's Rock, some three miles from Cracow, grants them the town that is being built in a place called Stanków and renews the grants of towns, villages, tithes, lakes and exemptions it had previously enjoyed, even adding to them another village and three tolls, together with one church and its tithes in Żarnowiec.

A.D. 1263

The Ruthenians and Lithuanians again invade Mazovia, but finding the amount of booty not up to their expectations, they head for the castellany of Łowicz, property of the Archbishop of Gniezno, which their scouts have told them is untouched. They move by forced marches, plunder it of cattle and people, set fire to villages and the archbishop's manor and return home without encountering any resistance. The Teutonic Knights in Prussia have the same lack of fortune. Having been attacked in their castle at Wyszembork, it falls to the enemy and they are forced to withdraw to Mazovia, pursued by the Prussians, but when the Prussian prince, Dway, is wounded, his men abandon the pursuit and, instead, advance on the castle at Kreuzberg, which they will eventually capture after a siege of three years.

The other Lithuanian dukes feel the power of Prince Mendog to be onerous and ugly. They feel that unless they remove him, it will lead to their own downfall; so, first, they publicly accuse him of having abandoned their traditional customs and gone over to Christianity, as well as of having surrendered Lithuanian territory to the Knights. Then Mendog's nephew, Strojnat, second in order to Mendog, plots to take over and rule Lithuania. He kills his uncle in his sleep and murders those of his sons who are with him, and assumes supreme power.

The eighth Prussian Master, Hanno of Sangerhausen, on April 4 founds a house of the Dominicans in New Toruń on the River Malera, endowing it with the right to fish for its own use in all its rivers, ponds, lakes and bogs.

An eclipse of the sun which occurred on St. Dominic's Day has grievous consequences in many parts of Bohemia, where hailstorms and drought make the harvest so bad as to cause a famine, in which many people starve to death.

A.D. 1264

Bolesław the Bashful of Cracow and Sandomierz decides to go to war with his immediate neighbours, the pagan Jacwingians, who keep raiding his territory. These Jacwingians live in the North on the borders of Mazovia, Ruthenia and Lithuania; their language is very similar to that of the Prussians and Lithuanians and is understood by them. They are a savage people, martial and so eager for fame that ten of them will take on a hundred of the enemy, merely so as to be celebrated in song by their descendants, a bravado which leads to their destruction, for small numbers are easily overcome by superior numbers with the result that gradually the entire tribe is being wiped out, since none will avoid an unequal contest or seek to escape. Having assembled his army, Bolesław moves into their territory. He appoints a commander for the rearguard, who is to see that none of the men is to be allowed to leave the ranks, which are to be maintained closed. The Jacwingians advance against the invaders, and, on July 24, at sunrise, appear before them ready to do battle. Bolesław arrays his men and battle is engaged. Fighting is fierce and for a long time neither side has the advantage, but with their superiority in numbers the Poles are able to replace, with fresh men, those who have been killed or are exhausted, and, in the end, after the Jacwingians' leader has been killed, the enemy stops fighting and is cut down to a man. This was by no means a bloodless victory, for many of the Poles were killed or severely wounded, while almost the entire Jacwingian tribe was wiped out, so that today the name no longer exists. All their lands and cattle, of which they had great numbers, and their other possessions were appropriated by the Poles, and the few survivors ordered under pain of death to adopt Christianity, the Pope being asked to appoint a bishop to encourage these neophytes to remain in the Catholic Faith.

Henry Bishop of Chełm, a Dominican friar, who, without the knowledge of his metropolitan, the Archbishop of Gniezno, turned his cathedral into a monastic church of the regular canons of St. Augustine, now makes it the church of the Order of Teutonic Knights. He and his chapter, discarding the rule and habit of the regular canons, don the garb of the Teutonic Knights and adopt their rule. This is all due to the influence of the Grand Master, Helmerich, and done with the support and approval of Anselm, Bishop of Warmińsk, at this time papal legate to Prussia.

While the barbarian Prussians are besieging Bergfrid castle, a force of Knights attacks them in their sleep, kills 1300 of them and forces the others to flee. The Knights then burn the castle, so as to deny it to the barbarians, who assemble a fresh force and again invade and plunder Chełmno, destroying and burning whatever they can. In the fighting, the Prussian Master Helmerich and his Marshal Dietrich are killed along with forty of the Brethren. The Prussians' superiority in numbers gives them victory. Ludwig of Baldersheim is elected the new Master.

There is strife in Lithuania and Prussia. After Prince Mendog and his sons were treacherously murdered by Strojnat, Mendog's nephew, Strojnat's cousin Wojsalk plots against Strojnat, who has assumed control, and one day, when he is out hunting, captures him, tortures him to avenge the murder of his father, and then kills him. Wojsalk, although a tonsured Ruthenian monk, has left his monastery and with the help of the Lithuanian dukes, begins to regard himself as Prince of Lithuania.

In order to make the alliance between the kings of Hungary and Bohemia a lasting one, the King's son, Duke Béla, marries Cunegund, daughter of Otto the Margrave of Brandenburg, whose wife, Beatrice, is a daughter of Václav of Bohemia and a sister of King Otakar. However, Béla dies after two years of marriage and Cunegund remarries. Her new husband is the Duke of Limburg. Her sister, Matilda, marries Barnim, Prince of the Slavs.

A.D. 1265

A vast force from nearly all the duchies of Ruthenia under Swarno invades Sandomierz and for a few days plunders, loots and burns. The barons of Sandomierz, without even consulting their duke, assemble a force which they augment with peasants and, taking advantage of a moment when the Ruthenians are out plundering and scattered, attack them. Few put up any opposition, so most are either killed or captured, thus the people of Sandomierz recover almost all that has been looted from them.

Leszek the Black comes of age and receives his share, the duchy of Sieradz. He is also adopted by his relative Bolesław of Cracow as his heir. This special privilege is embodied in a document which makes him the heir to all the latter's lands, duchies and possessions. Leszek marries Gryfina, daughter of the Ruthenian duke, Rostislav, a union supported by Bolesław of Cracow in the hope of bringing peace to his lands. Aware of how negligently the Poles guard Santok castle, the Saxons assault it, capture it and hand it over to the Margrave of Brandenburg as dowry for his wife, Constance, daughter of the late Przemyśl of Poznań. However, Bolesław the Duke of Kalisz claims that their occupation of the castle does him grievous injury and so gets an army together and sets out to recover it; but, before he gets there, the nobles of both sides agree to mediate, and when the Margrave and Bolesław meet, agreement is reached, whereby the Duke of Kalisz demolishes his castle at Santok and the Margrave that at Drzedenko, the two agreeing that if they continue in opposition it will only be to the advantage of robbers and thieves.

On the death of Pope Urban IV, the cardinals are unable to agree on a successor and the papal throne remains unoccupied. Eventually, Guido, a Provençal from Saint-Gilles and Cardinal-bishop of Sabina, is elected as Clement IV. He is a man of great probity and exemplary life. He had once been married and then, after his wife died, became Bishop of Oniksen and then Archbishop of Narbonne. He was sent to pacify England, when it was torn in the struggle between King Henry and Simon, Count of Montfort, and then returned to Perugia, travelling in disguise, because of all the disturbances.

A.D. 1266

Bolesław the Bashful, wishing to avenge the murder of Siemowit of Mazovia by Duke Swarno and to put a stop to the latter's continual raids into Polish territory, mounts an expedition against Ruthenia. He puts it under the command of Peter the Voivode of Cracow, but the latter is so afraid lest he be accused of negligence or irresponsibility, should things go badly, that he never takes a step without consulting all the other commanders, whether it be where to camp, when to march or how to obtain supplies. At the end of the second stage, the Voivode finds his way barred by Swarno and his Ruthenians and Tatars. The Poles refrain from immediately engaging battle, preferring to wait until the following day, which, being the Feast of the holy martyrs Gervase and Protase, should be more favourable for them and inauspicious for the enemy, for it is also the anniversary of their defeat at Zawichost. So, at dawn on June 19, battle is joined. The Ruthenians loose a rain of arrows and the Poles reply with missiles; then, gradually, the fighting becomes hand to hand. Slowly the Poles begin to gain the advantage and, penetrating into the midst of the enemy, start a slaughter. Swarmo renews the fighting in various places and encourages others who may be weakening, but in the end, seeing that his troops are being beaten, he turns and leaves the battlefield so as to avoid falling into the hands of the Poles. More Ruthenians are killed while trying to escape after this, than in the actual fighting. Many are taken prisoner, their lives being spared by Poles grown sick of slaughter. The Ruthenian camp is looted and, a couple of days later, the victorious army returns to Poland. This disaster so curbs and subdues the Ruthenians that for many years they never again dare set foot on Polish soil.

Although Bolesław of Wielkopolska agreed with Conrad the Margrave of Brandenburg, his son-in-law, that the castle at Santok was to be demolished and that the latter would not build another; the Margrave, having refused another more commodious castle, in which the local knights and peasants have been harbouring their cattle, builds a smaller, ducal castle, which he completes in a month by using his considerable army to bring up the building material. In this he installs a garrison, which he supplies with provisions and defensive equipment. The Margrave pursues Bolesław on his way home and then lays siege to Santok and makes every endeavour to capture it. He does such damage with his siege weapons and missiles, that he would have captured it quite quickly had not help arrived, in that Bolesław, shrinking from actual war with his neighbour and son-in-law, and concerned for the freedom and safety of his knights defending the castle, sends to Margrave Conrad promising to renew the agreement and keep its conditions. When Conrad agrees, the garrison marches out and the castle is burned before the eyes of the Margrave and his troops.

Ever since inheriting from their father Henry of Silesia and his brother, Władysław, Archbishop of Salzburg, have lived in amity. However, some knights, suspected of having tried to poison Duke Henry, attempt to sow discord between the two brothers who fall out so seriously that they divide the duchy between them. Now, Duke Henry, feeling that, thanks to his long illness and the poison administered to him, he is likely to die, sends for his brother, the Archbishop, and entrusts to him his two young children by his first wife, Judith, and also his second wife and Henry's part of the Duchy, asking him to look after them all. So, on December 5, Duke Henry dies.

About the same time, the apostate king of Ruthenia, Daniel, dies, leaving two sons.

Pope Clement, he who has so long hesitated to agree to the canonization of the blessed Jadwiga, saying that he required a fresh sign to confirm her saintliness, has a daughter—he was legally married when a layman—who has contracted a disease of the eyes that for many years has blinded her. Now, while celebrating Mass, the Pope asks God that, if the blessed Jadwiga really has performed the miracles claimed for her, she should restore his daughter's sight and health. When, a few days later, he receives news that his daughter has recovered her sight completely, he enters the name of the Polish princess in the roll of the saints and canonizes her in Viterbo on November 14.

A.D. 1267

On June 7 a papal nuncio arrives in Cracow and goes on to Wrocław to address a general synod of Polish bishops, whom he informs at some length of the need for immediate help for the Holy Land. He demands that the Polish clergy should themselves help and encourage the laity to contribute to this pious work, for which they will be granted a year's indulgence. He asks for a crusade against the Saracens now occupying the Holy Land to be proclaimed in every church. All this is granted and collecting boxes are placed in the larger churches, into which all wishing remission of their sins put their money.

Duke Leo of Ruthenia, son-in-law of the late King Daniel, who has succeeded to his father's power and wealth, now quarrels with Wojsalk the Duke of Lithuania, and, when he traps him in a village in which he is staying, kills him.

The Prussians occupy the castle at Ciechanów and burn it.

On December 25 Bolesław, Duke of Legnica, dies.

Thomas the Bishop of Wrocław dies after thirty-five years as bishop. His nephew, Thomas, is chosen to succeed him, but the choice is not confirmed for three years due to the obstacles put in its way by Władysław, Duke of Wrocław, and the Archbishop of Salzburg to whom the Pope finally grants administration of the vacant see and the right to enjoy all its revenues for his lifetime.

Brother Guido, the papal legate sent to deal with the long-standing dispute between the Bishop of Włocławek and Duke Casimir over the castle at Raciąz, which Casimir has occupied, entrusts the case to the Abbot of Our Lady on the Sands. After hearing both sides, the abbot adjudicates: the castle and its area belong to the bishop and cathedral of Włocławek. Then, he gives Duke Casimir absolution and removes the interdict imposed because of his occupation of the castle.

August 18 sees an immense throng of the faithful gathered at the nunnery at Trzebnica, where St. Jadwiga's body is buried, to see Abbot Nicholas of Lubiąż and Abbot Maurice of Kamieniec, together with the canons and priests of Wrocław, raise the bones of the saint from her sarcophagous and wash them in wine. The more important bones are placed in a specially prepared case and others given to Wrocław cathedral and other Polish churches. When the skull is raised, the brain proves to be completely undamaged and healthy. It is to this day preserved in Trzebnica nunnery in the same state. They discover three undamaged fingers of the saint clasping a tiny ivory figure of the Blessed Virgin, which she had treasured and always carried with her. She once dropped it and, to her great grief, was unable to find it; but a pig discovered it and brought it to her in its snout while she was praying in church. After this, she always clasped it in her hand, even during meals and when at work.

After a long siege by the Sultan of Babylon, the city of Antioch, one of the apostolic sees, is starved into surrender. A couple of years previously Jerusalem was occupied because the Catholic kings and princes had not come to its assistance. So, slowly the Saracens are destroying the Holy Land and those of its towns and castles in the possession of the Christians.

A.D. 1268

Queen Salomea of Galicia, sister of Bolesław the Bashful, dies. When her husband, with whom she lived in chastity and complete continence, remote from all pleasures of the flesh, died, she took her vows, joining the Order of St. Clare and entered the nunnery at Zawichost. When the nunnery was moved to Skala, she served the Lord there for twenty-eight years, never taking off her hair habit. She fulfilled the duties of abbess. Though her body lies unburied for seven days, the

The victors, busy with the spoil, are themselves attacked by irate peasants.
—*Konrad Keyser:* Bellefortis.—*VDI Verlag, Düsseldorf.*

nuns who visit it are aware only of a pleasant smell, instead of the stench usual from corpses. Her body is finally buried on November 10 in Skala.

Casimir, Duke of Kujawy, departs this life not from old age, but rather due to illness. He leaves two sons, Leszek the Black and Siemowit, the former having already been given his share of the duchy of Sieradz. Though Sieradz is the least of the three duchies they inherit, Leszek agrees to his brother having the other two (Łęczyca and Kujawy). Casimir married Siemomysł to Salomea, the virgin daughter of Świętopełk of Pomerania, by whom he has had three sons and two daughters by her. One daughter, Fennena, marries Stephen of Hungary, and the other, Constance, becomes abbess of Trzebnica. On Casimir's death, the castle at Bydgoszcz on the River Brda in Kujawy falls to the lot of Siemomysł; but its holder Dietrich, a Prussian who renounced paganism and accepted the true faith, for no reason other than the hope of receiving generous recompense, hands the castle over to Bolesław the Pious of Kalisz. When, too late, he realizes that he has been guilty of perfidy, he falls into such a fit of despair that he decides to commit suicide, so he summons his servant and orders him to kill him, which the servant does, severing the proferred head with a sword.

Świętopełk of Pomerania dies on July 14. On his death-bed he enjoins his four sons, Mszczuj, Sambor, Warcisław and Racibór, to refrain from hostilities with the Teutonic Knights and to maintain genuine friendship with the Polish dukes and, if need be, to elicit their help. So, Pomerania is divided into four, though the eldest of the four sons has supremacy.

A.D. 1269

The new duke of Łęczyca and Kujawy, Siemomysł, is a great admirer of the Teutonic Knights, among whom he spent his youth, and whose customs and disciplines he copies. Now, when the knights and gentry of his duchies complain that he is despising and spurning them, he refuses to sever his ties with the Knights; as a result there are murmurings and finally rebellion. One and all abandon Siemomysł, refuse him obedience and submission, and release themselves from his authority, transferring their allegiance to Bolesław the Pious of Kalisz. Too late Siemomysł realizes how stupidly he has behaved, and sends urgent requests to Bolesław and even offers him the castle at Kruszwica, situated in his part of the duchy, if he will refuse the allegiance of Siemomysł's knights and help to reconcile him with them, and this is achieved on condition that he abandons the councils of the Knights.

The Lithuanians hear of the misunderstandings between Siemomysł and his knights, call up the Jacwingians and other pagan tribes and, on April 2, together they march into Kujawy. None resists them and they are able to collect considerable booty of cattle and people and take it back to Lithuania.

Otto the Margrave of Brandenburg makes an attempt to get hold of the castellany of Santok. He builds a fort at Sulęcin using timbers that have been hewn in advance. Although he considers this almost a declaration of war, Bolesław postpones any attempt to demolish the new fort, instead fortifying his own town of Międzyrzecz with ditches, ramparts and wooden embrasures and breastworks. Margrave Otto takes this to mean that Bolesław is preparing to go to war with him and so mounts an assault on Międzyrzecz. He finds the fort only half completed, captures the town and gives it to his soldiers to sack, and then sets fire to it. Bolesław's powerful army sets off in pursuit of the Margrave's force as it withdraws, but is unable to catch it, so, instead, it lays the whole of Lubusz waste and then marches on the Margrave's new fort, Sulęcin. The Kalisz army makes mantlets of shields and despite a rain of stones from above reaches the castle wall, and after removing the earth covering with axes, piles up pine wood and so sets fire to the castle and captures it. Almost the entire Saxon garrison perishes in the flames, though the Captain and a handful of his men are captured alive, whereupon the Poles start putting out the flames they have so recently kindled.

The booty in the castle: weapons, horses, and provisions is divided among the troops and the army then withdraws.

A.D. 1270

The Margrave of Brandenburg, Otto, takes advantage of the absence of Bolesław the Pious, who is visiting Bolesław in Cracow, to erect a timber fort at Santok, near the Church of St. Andrew. It is built, complete with ditches and ramparts, during February and a strong garrison installed. On his return from Cracow, Bolesław assembles a strong force under cover of which he builds a fort at Drezdenko, which he completes in eight days, thanks to the large number of craftsmen he employs, and installs a garrison with the intention of recapturing Santok. However, the garrison is negligent and hardly keeps any watch at all, with the result that, on the night of December 17, the Saxons get their blow in first, capture the fort and expel the garrison, so that the Margrave has both forts.

Władysław, Archbishop of Salzburg and Duke of Wrocław, dies after a prolonged illness—some suspect certain knights of Wrocław of poisoning his food!—and is succeeded by his nephew, Henry IV, who, being of age, also comes into his father's share.

Mszczuj the new Duke of Pomerania, forgetful of his father's dying injunctions and confident of getting help from the infidel Prussians, embarks on hostilities against the Knights. He ravages the whole of Chełm and part of Prussia, murdering a number of Christians and capturing fifteen boats laden with provisions for the Knights. When he withdraws and disbands his troops, the Prussian Master assembles his own force and, on the Feast of St. Peter and St. Paul, enters Pomerania near Nowe Miasto, which he plunders and burns, freeing some of his prisoners there. He then goes on the rampage round Tczew, which he burns. The Duke of Pomerania starts to negotiate peace through unbiased intermediaries in an attempt to mitigate the extent of the disaster, and peace is finally arranged on mutual payment of damages.

On May 3, Béla, King of Hungary, dies after a reign of thirty-nine years. He is succeeded by his oldest son, Stephen, brother of Cunegund, duchess of Cracow and wife of Bolesław the Bashful.

The Prussian Master, Ludwig of Baldenstein dies and Dietrich is unanimously elected Master, the eighth. Learning of Ludwig's death, the Duke of Pomerania marches into Chełm territory and cruelly devastates it. As he is withdrawing with his loot and prisoners, Dietrich sets off in pursuit, and, taking a leaf out of the latter's own book, devastates a large part of Pomerania.

King Stephen of Hungary decides to make a pilgrimage to the tomb of St. Stanisław and at the same time visit his sister, wife of Bolesław the Bashful. He reaches Cracow on August 26 to be met by the Prince and Princess, who go out seven miles to meet him. Lengthy tourneys are arranged in a number of places and there are lavish banquets and splendid receptions. The opportunity is taken to renew the old alliance between Hungary and Poland: the two monarchs, their prelates and nobles swearing on the Bible and on a piece of the True Cross to share their misfortunes and good fortune, jointly to combat impending and future difficulties, to have the same friends and the same enemies, and to maintain unchanged their pact of friendship.

A.D. 1271

Angered by the way the Margraves of Brandenburg have twice violated his agreement by capturing Santok and fortifying Drezdenko, Bolesław the Pious announces an expedition against him. Having collected a large force from all Wielkopolska and Kujawy which Duke Siemomysł has ceded to his charge, he divides this into four armies and marches into the castellany of Santok, whose towns and villages the Margraves have seen fit to locate under German law, and orders it all to be ravaged and destroyed, so that the smoke of the fires might at least bring the enemy out to fight. When he finds that they are avoiding a decisive battle, he marches on Myślibórz and using siege ladders captures and burns it, distributing the loot among his men, and so returns home with the numerous herds he has captured. He returns the castle of Kruszwica to his nephew, Siemomysł, and orders it to be burned, so as to deprive an enemy of it.

Duchess Gryfina, wife of Leszek the Black, Duke of Sieradz, having summoned an assembly of the nobles, knights and gentry, tells them that for almost six years she has lived with her husband yet is still virgo intacta. She accuses her husband to his face of being impotent and frigid, accusations he accepts in silence. So, removing the hood, with which, as a wife, she covers her head, she thenceforth goes about with her head uncovered, behaving as a maiden and avoiding the company of Leszek. Her aim is to have her marriage dissolved.

One of the first acts of the new King of Hungary, Stephen, is to restart the war between his country and Bohemia, which has been suspended by various pacts and marriages. On April 13 the King of Bohemia, Otakar, captures the castle at Bratislava on the River Danube, along with Trnava and Nitra, sacks them and loots their surroundings. The fighting sees several contests between individual knights from either side fought with varying success, but both kings refuse to agree to a fight between champions that would decide the issue. Now, the King of Bohemia demolishes the bridge across the Raab and, burdened with booty, though having lost a number of men, returns to Austria, which he rules.

Conrad, Duke of Głogów, who has lost his first wife, Salomea, marries again, this time his bride is Brygida, daughter of Dietrich, the Margrave of Meissen, whose first husband, Conrad a great-nephew of the Emperor Frederick, died fighting in Naples. She brings with her a huge dowry in money and jewels, while Conrad makes over to her three castles and towns in Głogów territory. Meanwhile, Bolesław of Legnica, still smarting over his imprisonment by Conrad, occupies the town of Bolesławiec hoping to capture Conrad, who is resting there, and in this he very nearly succeeds, but Conrad is warned a little in advance of his brother's approach and escapes with a few of his men.

Paul, Bishop of Cracow, a man who has always allowed himself forbidden excesses incompatible with the office of bishop, now abandons himself to debauchery and the delights of the flesh, forcibly abducting a nun from the convent at Skala and then living with her as his concubine. He is arrogant and disobedient to his duke, Bolesław of Sandomierz, as well as to the courts of justice. He is so preoccupied hunting in the forests that he is seldom in church or attending to episcopal business, thus calling down upon himself the vengeance of God and of his own people. In an attempt to obtain impunity from his Prince and the law, he starts negotiating with certain disaffected nobles as well as with Lithuanians and barbarians with whom his family has ties of marriage. One day, when he is in the episcopal village of Kunów, two knights called Ota and Żegota attack and capture him. (It is not known whether they acted with the connivance or at the request of Bolesław the Bashful.) The two knights divide the bishop's possessions between them and then, afraid of being attacked by the bishop's servants and friends, they take the bishop through the forest to the castle at Sieradz, where Leszek the Black holds him for a whole month guarded as an honoured prisoner. This strengthens the supposition that Bolesław was the prime mover in the Bishop's capture and incarceration, for Leszek would never have received the Bishop or kept him imprisoned had he not known that this was what Prince Bolesław wished. The Archbishop of Gniezno condemns the bishop's imprisonment, as he must, and places the entire province under an interdict. Bolesław, perturbed by such a turn in affairs and by the accusations made against him, has the bishop released and through intermediaries is reconciled with him, the agreement being that Ota and Zegota are to be punished and removed from the Prince's presence and councils, and that the Bishop is to receive 200 silver marks and the Prince's share of Dzierążnia. So, Ota and Zegota go to prison for a month and, when freed by the efforts of their friends, being afraid of what the Bishop and his minions might do to them, they sell their family possessions in Cracow and Sandomierz and move to Opole, where they settle.

A.D. 1272

Bolesław the Pious wants to punish the Saxons for their treacherous occupation of Gdańsk and his relation, the Margrave of Brandenburg, for his perversity. Having a first-rate army, on January 15 he marches into Pomerania, where he is joined by Duke Mszczuj, and together they advance on Gdańsk and there invest the castle both by land and sea. After nine days of fruitless bombardment with their siege weapons, fruitless because the castle's walls are so stout that the missiles ricochet off them, an assault is mounted. Mantlets of timber are distributed, so that the soldiers can protect themselves from missiles from above and they advance under cover of these. Some reach the walls and hack at them with axes; while others set fire to the wall at various points, so that the smoke and flames drive the defenders back; while others again erect siege ladders and climb the walls under covering fire from their crossbow-men. The Saxons are just as ardent in their defence and hurl down a hail of stones, boiling water and pitch, inflicting many casualties. All day the assault continues, for Bolesław, who is personally in command, keeps sending in fresh troops to replace the wounded and the dead, and so, in the end, lack of missiles forces the Saxons to stop fighting. This allows the attackers to breach the wall at several points, and so, with jubilant shouts they pour into the castle, cutting down any Saxon they encounter. Some Saxons have crowded into the highest tower and they, asking only for their lives, now surrender their arms and all that they have, and are sent in chains into wretched captivity. The castle captured, the city also surrenders. Bolesław disbands his army and returns to Poland accompanied by the Duke of Pomerania, who promises henceforth to be his loyal vassal. The Duke wreaks vengeance on some of the citizens of Gdańsk, especially Arnold and Jacob and their relations, whom he condemns to death and whose property he confiscates, because they are supposed to have plotted against his life and been far too eager to assist the Margrave. The Duke also wishes to render thanks to God, so he gives two of his villages to Włocławek cathedral and its bishop, Albert.

Stephen of Hungary dies after only two years on the throne. He leaves two sons: Lászlo and Andrew. The former succeeds him, while Andrew, being a minor, receives the title of Prince, but remains under the King's authority.

The knights of Kalisz have now had four months in which to rest and prepare for further action; so the Duke announces another expedition against the Saxons and the Margraves of Brandenburg, to punish them for their illegal occupation of Santok castle. Duke Bolesław assembles his forces and, not wishing to go himself, puts his sixteen year-old nephew, Duke Przemysł of Poznań, in command, though the final say is given to Voivode Przedpełk of Poznań and the Castellan Janko of Kalisz, both brave and prudent men, who enjoy the esteem of all. The army advances into territory beyond Drezdenko occupied by the Saxons and lays siege to Strzelce castle, recently built by the Margrave of Brandenburg. This they storm and capture, killing all the Saxons left to garrison it. They loot all the surrounding houses and devastate the whole of Saxony on that side of the Oder. As the army is halted near Wieleń castle, and Duke Przemysł is preparing to return to Poland with his captured cattle and other booty, he is told that the Cassubians in the Polish army have attacked Drezdenko castle from the river and have got as far as the first gate to which they have been able to set fire and burn. So the Duke recalls his men and marches on Drezdenko. The small garrison there fearing lest, were the castle captured, they would be killed, as was the fate of their compatriots in Strzelce, surrender the castle in return for their lives and freedom. They are in fact escorted to the frontier so as to make sure that they come to no harm. The Duke then installs a strong garrison in Drezdenko and returns home in triumph.

On St. Vincent's Day, two counts, de Julich and Engelbert of the Mark, arrive in Prussia each with a body of armed men. They have come to help the Teutonic Knights who, for a good two years, have suffered nothing but disaster at the hands of the barbarian Prussians. Having arrayed their forces the two counts advance into Sambian territory. The Sambians have never been afraid of a fight and they bar the Christians' advance. So, battle is joined. In the end the Sambians yield and retire to a village called Sklunen, where a second battle develops and in this the Knights are completely victorious.

The joys of Conrad of Głogów's second marriage are brief, for his bride soon dies. When he learns of this, Dietrich the Margrave of Meissen sends in his officials who, despite Conrad's protests, take possession of the three properties Conrad granted to Brygida as her dowry, and proceed to pledge them for 10,000 florins to the Archbishop of Magdeburg, drawing up documents to show that the Archbishop and his cathedral are lord, master and heir of these properties, which enjoy the same rights and privileges as previously.

A.D. 1273

King Otakar and Bolesław the Bashful meet in Opava to settle their quarrel over the former's illegal occupation of the Duchy of Opava, which has made them so hate each other in recent years. However, Otakar will not agree to give up Opava, insisting that he inherited it legally under Duke Mieczysław's will, while Bolesław cannot accept that so large a part of Poland should be lost to it and pass into the hands of another king. In the end, the advisors of both sides, eager, if possible, to avoid war, get them to accept an armistice to last for twenty years, during which time the matter is to be left in abeyance.

On his return from Opava Prince Bolesław finds that he has a smouldering rebellion, indeed a civil war, on his hands. Its chief instigator is thought to be Paul, Bishop of Cracow, who has been indulging in licentious living and disregarding the dignity of his office by personally taking part in hunts and openly associating with the Lithuanians, his country's enemy. He seldom concerns himself with his see and associates with knights who live by brigandry, and men who are fugitives either from justice or their creditors. Bolesław decides that he must either exile or imprison the bishop. However, many of the knights dislike Bolesław, because he has punished some of them by confiscating their estates and even condemning some to death, imprisonment or house arrest. The particular complaint of these would-be rebels is that, without consulting them, and so without their agreement, Bolesław appointed as his successor Leszek the Black, Duke of Sieradz, a man they dislike; so, secretly, they send to Władysław of Opole offering him the two duchies of Cracow and Sandomierz. Proud of the offer, the Duke accepts it without stopping to consider its implications, indeed just hoping for an easy acquisition of two duchies, whose duke is childless and so old that his death can be expected any day. He asks the knights of Cracow and Sandomierz to present themselves before him in Opole, so as to confirm their allegiance by taking an oath and signing a document; so, on the advice and with the encouragement of Bishop Paul, a large number of knights sets out, taking almost all their retainers, in case of a possible attack by the Duke, since the whole world knows what they are up to. Indeed, when they reach the monastery village of Boguszyn, they are overtaken by a force of Bolesław's household and nobles and there is a fierce fight. Though many fall where they stand from wounds in the chest, neither side will yield, yet, in the end, victory goes to Bolesław. The handful of knights who escape flee to Władysław in Opole. Bolesław punishes the rebels, the living as well as the dead, by confiscating their property, which he either takes for himself, or distributes among the victors. There were other, more fundamental reasons for this rebellion: the unhealthy phenomenon of false accusation had become so prevalent that many simple, honourable and innocent knights had been fined by the courts or deprived of their patrimonies and made to pay money to the duke, the court and the judges. Again, Duke Bolesław's unbridled love of dogs and the chase, in which he indulged without moderation or regard for the season, is considered excessive and a cause of tangible loss to clergy and laity alike, since everyone is duty-bound to take part in the ducal hunts and in feeding the ducal hounds.

This rebellion quashed, an equally ugly and dreadful war breaks out, when, at the beginning of July, the pagan Lithuanians, together with some Prussians and Samogitians penetrate into Lublin territory. Since Bolesław cannot go to its assistance, both because of the suddenness of the raid and because his forces have been depleted by civil strife, the barbarians are free to rage and devastate the greater part of the territory and carry off considerable booty in people and cattle. It is widely felt that Bishop Paul was responsible for bringing this disaster down on his enemy, Bolesław, by sending letters and messages to the Lithuanians, natural enemies of the Poles and their faith, inciting them to start hostilities and so avenge those who fell at Boguszyn.

While the Lithuanians are putting the lands of Lublin to fire and the sword, the Dukes of Kujawy and Mazovia invade the lands of the Połekszanie and Prussians and there burn, plunder and kill unopposed and carry off a great booty of captives, thus doubly repaying the Lithuanians for the damage the latter inflicted on the Dukes. Bolesław the Bashful, recognizing Władysław of Opole as the prime cause of the affray at Boguszyn, vents all his wrath on him. He assembles troops from all his territories and, with the personal assistance of the dukes of Kalisz, Wielkopolska and Sieradz, marches into Opole on the Feast of St. Simon and St. Jude, and starts burning towns and villages and devastating whatever he can reach. He continues his advance as far as Opole itself and burns and destroys all its suburbs, though refraining from making a direct assault on, or laying siege to the town itself. The clouds of smoke and blazing fires cannot draw the Duke out to do battle, for the raiders have three times as many men as he. However, his men make frequent sorties and attack those bringing supplies for Bolesław's forces or any of his men who are out plundering or just on the roam, thus inflicting considerable casualties. Bolesław now moves from Opole and in a forced march reaches the area of Koźle and Racibórz, and there continues devastating the country until the whole of Opole has been put to fire and the sword.

Przemyśl, the young duke of Poznań, is now sixteen years old. Taking the advice of his uncle, Bolesław the Pious, he decides to look for a wife. First, he goes to Szczecin to make the acquaintance of Duke Barnim's granddaughter, Ludgarda, and, liking her ways as much as her looks, marries her and takes her back to Poznań.

A.D. 1274

War breaks out again between Bolesław the Bashful and Władysław of Opole. Both sides arm their forces and make what use they can of blood ties and gifts to persuade neighbouring dukes to help them. It is a war motivated more by hatred than by military necessity. Bolesław is going to war because Władysław has illegally occupied part of his territory and accepted the allegiance of some Cracovian knights, while Władysław just wants to avenge his burned and plundered duchies and the cinders and fresh ash that keep falling on his nobles' estates. Meanwhile, Bolesław the Pious, though on his namesake's side, tries to persuade the two protagonists to take the path of peace and justice; and, after much effort he does manage to dampen their ardour and arranges peace on equitable terms: an exchange of prisoners and payment of reparations.

The Margrave builds a fort and town in Prussia which he calls Brandenburg.

A man enjoying the greatest fame, a man of unusual excellence in his learning and his life, the famous doctor of the Dominicans, Thomas Aquinas, sets out from Naples in response to a summons from the Pope to attend a synod in Lyons. When he reaches Campania, he falls ill and goes to Fossanuova a monastery of the Cistercians, there being none of his own Order near, and there his condition deteriorates and he dies.

A.D. 1275

Bolesław the Bashful is aggrieved by the fact that for the last four years the Princess Gryfina has lived separately from her husband, Bolesław's brother, Leszek the Black, whom she accuses of frigidity and impotence. Anxious to expunge the shame of this, Bolesław goes in person to Sieradz and after talking to the two, manages to reconcile them and get them to resume marital relations, which they maintain from then on.

Jadwiga, wife of Bolesław the Bald of Legnica, dies and is buried in the Dominican house there. Though he has both sons and daughters, and the omens are altogether unfavourable, Bolesław marries again. His new wife is Adelaide, unmarried daughter of Sambor the Duke of Pomerania. Although he has no real quarrel with her, Bolesław's penchant for adultery, especially with a certain married woman, makes him shun, even hate his new wife. She, unable to endure her husband's affronts and the vileness of his harlot, leaves Bolesław and, taking the only course open to her, returns on foot to her father. Although hard and grim by nature, Bolesław is said to have been so entranced by the charms and songs of his concubine, and impelled by desire for her, that he grants her every wish. She bears him an illegitimate son, Jarosław.

A.D. 1276

The dukes and nobles of Silesia are perturbed by the fact that three of their towns: Crosna, Greifenstein and Przin, have passed into foreign hands. They are afraid, too, lest these be detached altogether from the Kingdom of Poland, and are daunted by the size of the sum required to redeem them. Conrad of Głogów, part of whose lands they are, and Bolesław of Legnica, are already burdened with debt and have little possibility of raising such an amount, so they turn to Henry IV, Duke of Wrocław, whose duchy is large and wealthy, thanks to the amounts saved by his guardian during his minority. Henry is delighted at the prospect of extending his territories and, on the advice of his nobles, repays the 10,000 ducats advanced by the Archbishop of Magdeburg, thereby getting the three castles and towns out of pawn and making Bolesław and Conrad very jealous of his success and increased possessions.

At the end of September a severe frost grips Cracow and its surrounding country. A week later so much snow falls that the Sarmatian alps between Poland and Hungary, and the other mountains, we call the Tatras, are thickly covered and autumn turned into freezing winter.

Anna, wife of Bolesław the Pious of Kalisz, gives birth to a daughter. Though both had been hoping for a son, there is a solemn christening and several days of celebration and junketing. The babe is christened Anna.

Rudolf, King of the Romans, sends envoys to the King of Bohemia calling upon him to relinquish Austria, Styria and Carinthia, Pontus Naonis and Friule, which, he insists, thanks to his marriage, now dissolved, to Margaret, daughter of Duke Leopold of Austria, really belong to the Empire. King Otakar sends a rather arrogant reply, so Rudolf prepares to recover his lands by force. Otakar moves his army up to Těpla to bar Rudolf's advance, but himself stays behind to hunt. Rudolf crosses the Danube into Austria and occupies a number of towns and castles, which either surrender or are stormed. Perturbed by this, Otakar takes to the field in person and, finding Rudolf near Linz, pitches camp on the other bank of the Danube. The two sides then hold talks and peace is arranged and further strenghtened by Rudolf's son marrying Otakar's daughter, Agnes, and Otakar's son, Václav, taking Rudolf's daughter, Gutta, as his wife. The two armies then return to their homes.

A.D. 1277

Bolesław the Bald of Legnica, jealous of the increasing power and wealth of Henry of Wrocław, starts plotting with some of the knights of Wrocław, who are thought to have poisoned Henry's father and are now afraid lest his son seek vengeance. Their idea is to capture and imprison Henry, using the pretext that, when his uncle, Archbishop Władysław of Salzburg, died, contrary to right and justice, Henry appropriated part of the duchy of Wrocław, which was to have been shared between him and his other brother, Conrad of Głogów. The conspirators get their opportunity on the Thursday before Reminiscere Sunday, when Bolesław's minions succeed in dragging the sleeping duke from his bed and carrying him off to the castle at Leben, where he is put in a dungeon in the hope that the hardships of imprisonment will induce him to surrender some of his territory. At this, the knights of Wrocław declare war on Bolesław of Legnica in order to free their duke, and, afraid that they may not be strong enough, they invoke the help of Duke Bolesław of Cracow and Sandomierz, Bolesław of Kalisz and Przemyśl of Poznan and Gniezno, as well as that of Conrad of Głogów and Władysław of Opole. Meanwhile, Bolesław is eagerly preparing his forces in Legnica, to supplement which he recruits mercenaries from Meissen, Bavaria, Swabia and Saxony. His relation John the Margrave of Brandenburg might well have joined these, but the people of Wrocław promise him 4000 marks if he will refrain. When they find themselves unable to raise this amount, they pledge the town and castle of Crosna.

Although the auspices are unfavourable, Bolesław of Legnica and his three sons decide to get their blow in first and thus avoid paying mercenaries for doing nothing, so they invade Wrocław, but on St. George's Day, a Saturday, are themselves attacked by the people of Wrocław. As evening approaches, Bolesław can see that he is not going to win and leaves the battlefield with just one companion. By this time fighting has already come to a stop in many parts of the battlefield, but Bolesław's eldest son, Henry, succeeds in reviving it and his men manage to kill many of the people of Wrocław and their allies, taking prisoner a number of the knights from foreign countries who regard retreat as shameful. So many are killed on either side that, though in the end victorious, the knights of Legnica pay for their victory with so much blood that they cannot scoff at the vanquished. The Duke of Poznań is one of the many taken prisoner. After this disaster the people of Wrocław turn for help to Bolesław's uncle, the King of Bohemia. To ensure his help, they give him Kłodzko town and castle, both due to pass to Henry on Bolesław's death. Thanks to Otakar's intervention, peace between Henry and Bolesław is finally concluded on terms that are, perhaps, not altogether fair, in that, while Bolesław undertakes only to release his nephew, Duke Henry, the Duke of Poznań and the other knights taken prisoner in the recent fighting, Henry agrees to surrender in perpetuity six towns and forts. These conditions accepted, Henry regains his freedom. When it comes to redeeming Kłodzko, Henry finds that it will cost him 6000 marks, for the Margrave unfairly insists on getting 2000 marks more than the sum stipulated to cover his expenses and damage. Since then, Kłodzko town and castle have been subject to the King of Bohemia, and in ecclesiastical affairs under the diocese of Prague, having been detached from the see of Wrocław, for Bishop Thomas preferred to suffer this wrong rather than strive to remove it.

The misfortunes of the Polish dukes caused by their civil strife are capped by another equally shameful, when, on the Feast of St. Luke the Evangelist, a host of Lithuanians unexpectedly invades Łęczyca, then in the possession of Casimir, son of Casimir of Łęczyca and Kujawy. None resists them and they carry off herds of cattle and an estimated 40,000 men and women into servitude.

Following the death of Master Dietrich of Gatirslewe, Conrad of Thierberg becomes the ninth Prussian Master. Two Prussian dukes, Henry of Nactag and Glappo, whom the Knights have captured, are condemned to be hanged and end their lives on a gallows. A third, Dway, wishing to avenge the dreadful death of the other two, invades Chełmno and in the course of two days devastates much of the country, before being himself attacked by the Prussian Master. In the ensuing fight, twelve Knights and 500 Christians fall, and the rest, including the Master, Conrad, take to their heels, leaving the barbarians victorious. Soon after this, the Prussians capture the new fort, which the Master, Conrad, built at great expense between Chełmno and Pomezania, and also that at Radzin in Wartenberg. Every Knight and Christian found in these forts is barbarously murdered. The Prussians cannot hope to keep these prizes, so burn them and return home.

A.D. 1278

Bolesław the Pious of Kalisz, wishing to avenge the illegal erection of Santok Castle, still in the possession of the Margraves of Brandenburg, as well to put a stop to the continual raiding of Polish territory by the Saxons, announces a campaign against the Margraves and proceeds to arm his own men and those of his nephew, Przemyśl of Poznań. He calls on his blood-relation, the Duke of Pomerania, Mszczuj, to come in person to help with his entire army. When these troops are all assembled, Bolesław and the Duke of Pomerania, leaving Przemyśl and his contingent in reserve, invade territory held by the Margraves on the near side of the River Oder and put it to fire and the sword. When they reach Myślibórz, their advance is barred by Otto the Long. In the ensuing battle, Otto, being the weaker, is easily defeated. His force disintegrates and its members seek refuge in castles and forts and take no further part in the fighting. Duke Bolesław, honour satisfied, returns home, where he divides the huge booty with Duke Mszczuj and his Pomeranians.

Bolesław the Bald of Legnica does not long enjoy the castles and properties he has forced his nephew to surrender. Violent in his behaviour to his own people and to others, he remains to the last embroiled in an infamous love-affair with his concubine. His speech, hurried and unclear, was often the cause of laughter and mockery. He was a cheat and a prevaricator, overhasty in pronouncing judgment, so that he earned himself the epithet "Harsh". He left three sons, a fourth having died in childhood: Henry of Legnica, nicknamed "Fatty", Bolesław of Świdnica and Bernard "the Dextrous", all by Jadwiga, daughter of Henry of Anhalt. He also had four daughters by his first wife: one, Agnes, married to the Count of Wartemberg, a second, Anne, who entered a nunnery, while the third, Jadwiga married Conrad of Mazovia and, the fourth, Catherine, died when still a young girl.

In the summer of this year, Bolesław of Mazovia, having been told by the Abbot of Lubin that Henry the Duke of Głogów was secretly preparing an invasion, with the help of Władysław of Sieradz strikes first and routs Duke Henry's army in a battle fought near the castle at Krzywin.

Otakar, King of Bohemia, resenting the loss of Austria, Styria and Carinthia resulting from his pact with Rudolf, King of the Romans, renounces the pact and alliance and renews hostilities in an attempt to recover his lost territories. He invades Austria with all the troops at his disposal and, plundering and burning, advances on the castle at Drossendorf, which he soon captures. When Rudolf hears of this, he assembles his troops from throughout the empire and with this numerous army crosses the Danube and surrounds Otakar's army, which is encamped beside the river Morava. A certain Czech, Milota, to whom the unsuspecting Otakar had entrusted the administration of Moravia, turns traitor together with other Czech discontents, and, as well as informing Rudolf of all that is going on in the Czech camp, promises to desert to him, should he decide on a pitched battle. Rudolf, however, is hesitant to shed Christian blood and sends heralds to Otakar to remind him that he should think twice before engaging in battle with someone stronger than he, especially as he is surrounded by traitors. This only makes Otakar more arrogant and the next day, at dawn, he engages Rudolf in battle. When many have fallen, the advantage swings to Rudolf. Otakar, deserted by Milota and the other malcontents, fights bravely to restore his flagging fortunes, but is killed. His body is taken to Prague and buried there. He is succeeded by his five-year old son, Václav, whose guardian, as arranged before Otakar's death, is Otto, Margrave of Brandenburg, who takes the young boy and his mother from Prague by night and lodges them in his castle at Bezděz, where they are given Saxon instead of Czech servants. Thus is peace finally restored on the terms of the earlier pact and young Václav is married to Rudolf's daughter, Gutta.

With Otakar dead, Henry of Wrocław demands the return of Kłodzko castle, which had been granted to Otakar for his lifetime as a reward for helping Henry against Bolesław of Legnica. In order to remove any doubt as to its ownership, and to prevent the castle remaining in foreign hands, Henry now styles himself not only Duke of Wrocław, but also Lord of Kłodzko. He marries Matilda, the maiden daughter of the Margrave of Brandenburg, now renowned as the guardian of the young king of Bohemia.

Trojden, son of the Duke of Lithuania, divides a combined Lithuanian-Prussian army of 30,000 into three, and sends one part to invade Mazovia, and the other two to invade Chełm. The latter capture the Knights' castle of Bergelow, burn it and then plunder the entire territory, carrying off numbers of Christians into servitude. In this same year, the pagan Sudovici also invade the land of Chełmno and attack Lubawa and the fortress of Chełmno, which they storm after a bombardment, and then go on to devastate the area around Kowalewo. At this time, too, the town of Łęczyca is damaged and plundered in a sudden raid by the Lithuanians.

A.D. 1279

Bolesław the Pious, Duke of Kalisz, contracts a debilitating fever. Feeling worse every day, he sends for his nephew, Przemyśl of Poznań, and entrusts him with his duchy, his wife and their three daughters, Jadwiga, Elizabeth and Anna. He dies on Friday, April 7 and is succeeded by Duke Przemyśl, who now rules all Wielkopolska. He relieves Bolesław's widow, Helena, and her three daughters from guardianship and provides them with an adequate subsistence and dowries. Helena then collects all her possessions and goes to Cracow, to her sister, Kinga, Bolesław the Bashful's wife and a woman of unusual piety. Przemyśl does his duty by his cousins, marrying the eldest, Jadwiga, to the Duke of Brześć, who, because of his small stature, is known as Władysław Łokietek (the Ell); Elizabeth he marries to Henry of Legnica, called the Pot-bellied, while the third, Anna, dies a spinster.

Bolesław the Bashful of Cracow and Sandomierz dies after ruling for thirty-seven years, during which long time, guarding his body against the temptation of marriage, he has remained chaste, earning himself the nickname of "the Bashful", an epithet no other Polish prince has ever earned. His widow, Kinga, had scarcely buried her husband, before she donned the habit of the Order of St. Clare, announcing that she had long yearned for this. She never allowed herself to shed a tear, but, thinking only of Christ, her betrothed. rendered continual thanks for having been relieved of a heavy burden. She sells all her jewelry for the benefit of the poor.

Bolesław is succeeded by Leszek the Black, Duke of Sieradz, a close relative whom Bolesław had adopted and named as his successor. He and his nobles all beg Kinga to remain in Cracow and rule, but no arguments will persuade her to do so.

The Duke of Mazovia marries a Lithuanian, Sophia, daughter of Duke Trojden. The wedding is held in Płock.

Queen Cunegund of Bohemia leaves the castle at Bezděz, where she and her son have been confined, and goes to Prague, ostensibly to celebrate the anniversary of her husband's death, and from there continues to her husband's natural son, Nicholas, Duke of Opava. He persuades her to marry an aristocrat, Zawisza of Ružomberk, by whom she becomes pregnant and bears him a son, who is given his father's name. This marriage, condemned and derided by almost every Czech noble, occasions much distate and jealousy.

The Prussians attack the town and castle of Elbląg, but finding them difficult to take, turn their attention to the mill there, in which the more eminent people of Elbląg have taken refuge. When the Knights fail to send the help they have promised, thus putting the defenders in a difficult position, they surrender, though compelled to provide twenty-five hostages to ensure the lives and liberty of the others. The Prussians, elated at their success, go back on their word and, having cruelly murdered the hostages, proceed to torture and kill all whom they find in the mill. To avenge this breach of the law of nations, the Prussian Master, Conrad, spends several weeks putting Prussian territory to fire and the sword, during which time he also captures the castle at Heilsberg.

A.D. 1280

Many people, jealous of Leszek the Black's success and his inheritance of so many duchies (Cracow, Sandomierz and Lublin), are eager to stir up trouble. One of these is Leo, son of the late King of Ruthenia and now considered the most powerful of its dukes, who decides to try and appropriate Cracow, Sandomierz and Lublin, and so assembles a huge army of Tatars, Lithuanians, Jacwingians and other pagans and with it invades Lublin, despite the unfavourable wintry conditions. Having ravaged it, he crosses the frozen Vistula into Sandomierz and plunders and destroys all in his path as he advances on the town and castle of Sandomierz. When he assaults the castle, he is thwarted by the stout resistance of its defenders and starts plundering the surrounding country from his camp in Goślice, which is some two miles from the town itself. Here, on Friday February 3, he is attacked by a scratch Polish force hastily got together by Warsz the castellan and Peter the voivode of Cracow and Janusz the voivode of Sandomierz. Though they can see that the enemy outnumber them several times over, the Poles put their trust in God and attack, an act I would have called more thoughtless than brave, had it not proved successful.

The Ruthenians' first rank having been hewn down, the others panic, throw down their arms and take to their heels, all but the Tatars, who continue to fight, until they, too, turn and run, pursued for many miles by the Poles. It is said that 8000 died in the battle and 2000 were taken prisoner, while seven standards were captured. Realizing that attack is better than mere defence, Leszek assembles an army of 30,000 horse and 2000 first-class foot in a fortnight, and sets off in pursuit of Leo. He thrusts into Ruthenia and occupies a number of abandoned forts and captures others with weak garrisons and demolishes them. He devastates the country as far as Lwów and carries back to Poland a vast booty of people and cattle, for Leo has fled deep into Ruthenia and does not dare risk another battle.

Hartmann of Helderung is succeeded as Prussian Master by Conrad of Feuchtwangen, and, when he voluntarily resigns, by Mangold of Sternberg, who is to be responsible for building Malbork to replace Santir.

A.D. 1281

Henry IV is still set on avenging his imprisonment by Bolesław the Harsh, but, being afraid he may achieve little by overt action, he has recourse to cunning and treachery. He proposes a conference to discuss peace, good husbandry and administration and such matters, and by letter and envoy invites the dukes of Wielkopolska, Cracow and Silesia to attend. Most make excuses, but Przemyśl of Wielkopolska, Henry of Legnica and Henry of Głogów do arrive, each with a modest retinue and all unsuspecting, for all four men are closely related. Though disappointed that so few have walked into his trap, Henry goes ahead with his plan, and, in violation of the laws of hospitality and nations, as well as of the laws of God, personally and with the assistance of his knights lays hold of the three on their very first day and carries them off in chains to Wrocław castle, where each is guarded separately. There they are kept until Whitsun. After many of the other dukes have demanded their release and been given only the vaguest of replies, Leszek decides to free his brother duke by force. With the help of Mszczuj the Duke of Pomerania and the knights of Wielkopolska he invades Wrocław. No village is spared, nor any town ruled by Duke Henry, and, when the whole duchy has been devastated, the invaders advance on the suburbs of Wrocław itself. Henry remains stoney-hearted and stubborn, and, in the end, Leszek withdraws his army, taking vast booty with him. The three dukes now negotiate their freedom. To get his, Przemyśl has to surrender the territory of Ruda, which Henry insists belongs to him, claiming that it was unjustly taken from his ancestors. Neither Henry of Legnica nor Henry of Głogów will surrender any of their territory, but Henry exacts an undertaking that for the next five years each will contribute thirty spearmen to fight for him in any emergency. The three must give hostages to ensure that they keep their undertakings and have to swear that they will not take any hostile action against Henry because of his imprisonment of them, either personally or through the intermediary of others. They are then freed and return to their duchies.

Lászlo, King of Hungary, is addicted to dalliance and the delights of the flesh. He abandons his wife, who is the daughter of the King of Sicily, and with his knights adopts the dress and manners of the pagan Kumans. He takes three Kuman beauties as his main concubines—there being others as well—and lives with them in unlawful union, as is the barbarous Kuman custom. Seeing this as a danger to the Christian faith, the Pope sends Philip the bishop of Fermo, a very wise and learned man, to Hungary with the full authority of a papal legate, to try to persuade Lászlo to revert to his former ways and take his wife back, but the King just mocks him and treats him with none of the respect due to a papal nuncio, and, indeed, finally refuses even to see him. The legate then suspends the capital's two bishops, who have either tacitly connived at the King's crimes or actually accepted them. He then excommunicates the King and places an interdict on him as being a pagan and abettor of pagans. In response, the King sends his godless minions to seize the nuncio, and then has him placed in a cart and conveyed beyond the frontier, threatening him with death should he ever return. The Hungarian nobles are anxious to restrain their king and end by imprisoning him. Then, having got rid of all his concubines, they establish him and his legitimate wife in Wyszehradz under the guard of certain nobles, hoping thus to curb his lechery and make him abide by the laws of matrimony and so assure the Queen of progeny and the kingdom of heirs and successors.

Margrave Otto of Brandenburg, the appointed guardian of young Václav of Bohemia, knows that Prague cathedral is full of precious objects that the Czech nobility, gentry, clergy and citizens have deposited there as a place of safety; so he sends some of his Saxons, who break all the locks and carry off all the gold, silver, jewels, precious stones and other valuables deposited there. At this time the Czechs are so afraid of the Saxons, that none dares protest, let alone try to stop them.

A large Prussian army invades Chełmno and, as the Master and his Knights do not dare risk a pitched battle or even resist, it ravages and plunders everything. It storms five castles and murders all it finds in them, and then returns home.

A.D. 1282

On September 24 Lublin is unexpectedly invaded by the remaining Jacwingians, who have joined forces with the Lithuanians and want to avenge their defeat at the hands of the Poles. Their army, which has used remote paths, is estimated at 14,000 foot and horse. It is now split into three parts, which ravage and devastate the country as widely as they can for a good ten days, before returning home with immense booty. As soon as Leszek, who was in Cracow, hears of this, he stops dispensing justice, and, with his knights, advances by forced marches on Lublin, calling up more knights as he goes. He expects the enemy still to be in Lublin, but when he gets there, he finds only a few wretches begging for help. He hesitates, uncertain whether to pursue his more numerous enemy, already in their forests, marshes and other secure places, where an invading army would never find food, or to turn back and risk having to face scorn and derision. One night, while he is asleep, an angel, claiming to be the Archangel Michael, appears to him and tells him not to stop the pursuit and promises that he will be victorious. The King then summons his knights and tells them of this, which encourages even the most faint-hearted, for nothing so strengthens a person's spirits as a miracle. So, they collect provisions and arms and, with the train bringing up the rear, set out to follow the still fresh tracks of the barbarians. Learning that these have already crossed the Bug and the Narew, Leszek does so too and, on October 13, catches up with the enemy, whose progress has been slowed by their vast booty. He finds them halted between the Narew and the Niemen. At first sight of the Poles, the Jacwingians overestimate their number and take fright, though Leszek has only 6000 foot and horse, mostly horse. The site of the ensuing battle is an area more of woods than of fields and so does not allow the armies being split into separate units. The Poles initiate the attack and, though the barbarians withstand the first onslaught, they finally begin to withdraw. The withdrawal turns into flight, after which the fight becomes a slaughter. The terror of the Jacwingians is intensified by the growling and barking of the dogs guarding the captives, for these have become very noisy and are threatening to bite, as if they knew who their real enemy was. A remnant of the Jacwingians resists stoutly, and all but a few are killed. Those who do survive, and many of the Lithuanians who escape, are too ashamed to, or dare not return to their homes, and commit suicide instead, either hanging themselves, drowning themselves or killing each other. Strange, indeed almost incredible, is the fact that when the Polish army is mustered, it is found that not one Pole has been killed in the fighting or in the pursuit. This just shows that the prophecy given to Leszek in his dream was not just imagination, but an act of God.

On his return to Cracow, Leszek finds that he has a rebellion on his hands. The knights of Sandomierz, led by Janusz the voivode and Christian the castellan of Sandomierz, in concert with Paul the Bishop of Cracow, all of whom have long been wanting a change, have persuaded Conrad, Duke of Mazovia, Leszek's first cousin, to come to Sandomierz, the pretext being that in law and in age he is more likely to succeed when Bolesław the Bashful dies, and have handed over to him Sandomierz, Zawichost and the other castles and towns of Sandomierz. Leszek, quite undaunted by the news, hastily assembles a force of Cracovian gentry and advances on Sandomierz. Conrad has no faith in his undertaking or in his fickle supporters, and, when he learns of Leszek's imminent arrival, withdraws into Mazovia. Leszek recovers all the castles that went over to Conrad and wins over the voivode and castellan of Cracow and the other rebels without blood being shed, and so stifles the rebellion. (Some writers maintain that Leszek was expelled by the rebels and escaped into Hungary, but, after spending some time there, was reconciled with the knights of Sandomierz and eventually returned to Cracow with a body of his own men and some Hungarians troops.)

These civil and external wars were waged during a famine that affected not only Poland, but Bohemia, Germany and other countries as well. Now, after two years of famine, people are starting to leave their homes and going to Hungary or Ruthenia in search of help. Those who go to Hungary are sold to the barbarian Kumans, and those who go to Ruthenia are given to the Tatars in lieu of tribute, so that, for most of them it would have been better had they stayed and starved to death in Poland.

In Bohemia, the famine is even worse, and to still their hunger, mothers eat their own children. The famine is acompanied by an epidemic, because people's bodies are debilitated and poisoned by the harmful plants, leaves and garbage they are forced to eat.

In an access of pride, the Duke of the Kumans decides to invade Hungary, assuming that the licentiousness of its King will so incapacitate him, that the Duke can conquer the whole country. His advance is halted near Lake Hód and battle is joined. While they are fighting, a violent storm gets up which lashes the faces of the Kumans, blinding them, and so helps the Hungarians to victory. All but a few of the Kumans are killed. Those who escape, flee to the Tatars.

A.D. 1283

The Lithuanians are still eager for vengeance and in October, an unsuitable time of the year for military action, invade Poland, emerging out of the forest near Łuków in Sandomierz. They set about killing and carrying off herds of cattle and humans, while the knights of Sandomierz do no more than guard their castles and the town of Sandomierz itself; though they do send a courier to inform Leszek, who is attending the assembly in Cracow, of what is happening. Leszek, immediately and by forced marches launches a force at the enemy, sending messengers ahead of him to call upon the knights to come from their forts and castles and join him. He also swells his ranks with peasants, so that his army looks far stronger than it is. He presses on, for he knows that once they have collected their booty, the enemy will quickly withdraw; and, indeed, catches up with them near Łuków, for, being overburdened with loot, the Lithuanians have made but slow progress. Knowing that victory depends not on numbers, but on the will of God, they all take holy communion and confess as part of the preparation for battle. The Lithuanians, anxious to avoid another disaster, such as that they suffered the previous year, withdraw with their captives into the nearby woods, which are extensive and, in places, dense and boggy. The Poles hesitate to attack them there; yet the Lithuanians are themselves disquieted by being unable to see what the enemy is doing. Perhaps they will surround the woods! Also, they are seriously hampered by their captives and fear lest these go to the assistance of their compatriots; so, leaving a detachment to guard the train, they emerge from the woods in formation and advance on the Poles' camp, uttering their ferocious war-cries. Their sudden appearance frightens the Poles, if only because of the enemy's superiority in numbers, and the faint-hearted begin to think of flight, but Leszek addresses them and calms their fears. He divides his force into two units, which go on the offensive simultaneously. The right unit under Żegota the Voivode of Cracow gains the upper hand, for it consists of knights from the Prince's household and those with most experience; but then Fortune also favours the other under the Voivode of Sandomierz, and the Lithuanians are routed. The Poles then go to the woods, free the captives and distribute the contents of the train among the soldiers. All the loot taken by the Lithuanians is also recovered. It is difficult to say, whether in this victory Leszek distinguished himself more as a commander or as a courageous knight.

Leszek suspects Paul the Bishop of Cracow of having instigated the Lithuanians' latest invasion of his country and orders some of his knights to arrest him. The bishop is taken in chains to Sieradz castle and kept there for a time, being well treated. The see of Gniezno being temporarily vacant, no interdict is laid on the province because of the imprisonment of its bishop.

Przemyśl II, Duke of Wielkopolska, founds a hospital outside the gates of Kalisz, which is to provide shelter for the sick and unfortunate, and hands it over to the Knights Hospitaller to administer. He also founds a house of the Dominicans in Poznań and endows it with three villages and a lake. When he is later crowned King of Poland he confirms gifts of villages and other properties made in the interim by Vincent the vice-chancellor and his brother, voivode Nicholas.

Depressed by the disasters that have overtaken them at home and abroad, the Czechs are now demanding the return to them of their prince, Václav, who is still under the tutelage and guardianship of the Margrave of Brandenburg, Otto the Long. The Margrave makes sly excuses for not even discussing the matter and dismisses all requests with vague promises, until finally it is agreed that the Czechs will surrender the March of Budyšin with its many towns and villages to the Margrave in perpetuity, and also pay him 35,000 marks in silver. When this has been done, the Margrave sends the Prince to them. He reaches Prague on May 24; but, prompted by his mother, he entrusts the entire administration to his step-father, Zawisza of Ružomberk, whose overbearing attitude makes many of the Czechs hate him as much as they are jealous of him; indeed, they are more hostile to him, than they were to the Margrave.

Warcisław, second of Świętopełk's two sons, considers his share of the inheritance too small. In pique, he joins the Order of the Prussian Knights and then sells them his share of the duchy.

His two brothers, Sambor and Racibór, then follow his example, giving their shares to the Knights on condition that they and their servants are guaranteed a sufficient income and that they can retain secular status and clothing. Duke Mszczuj cannot tolerate this and assumes control of all three parts of the duchy. He also sends to Pope Martin IV complaining of the machinations of the Master and his Order and of their attempt to take over his brothers' shares of the duchy, which should eventually devolve on him. The Pope responds by sending a legate to Prussia, who, after hearing the arguments of both sides, declares the gifts of the two brothers illegal and thus invalid; but he also persuades Mszczuj to gift the town of Gniew and its fifteen surrounding villages to the Order in perpetuity. This arrangement having been accepted, the Master demolishes the fort at Putirbork and builds another of masonry at Gniew.

A.D. 1284

Henry of Wrocław continues his endeavours to take over the remaining duchies of Wielkopolska by making lavish gifts and extravagant promises to some of its magnates, especially those holding the more important positions. One of these is Sędziwój, son of the Voivode of Poznań, John, who is governor of the castle at Kalisz, yet dislikes Przemyśl who appointed him, because he thinks Przemyśl passed him over for certain other posts; thus, at the end of September, oblivious of all decency and honesty, he surrenders Kalisz castle (the town having been burned to the ground some days earlier) to Duke Henry. Rightly incensed by all this, Przemyśl calls up all his knights and advances on and invests Kalisz, into which Henry has put a strong garrison of Silesian knights amply provisioned. He sends heralds to try and persuade the knights of the garrison to surrender the castle, promising that they are safe to leave with all their possessions. The answer he receives is not very positive, so he moves his camp closer to the castle and gives orders for the troops to be ready to storm it in two days time. When the day comes, the assault is launched and continues all day without accomplishing anything, because of the castle's natural position, its man-made defences and the efficiency of the garrison. Towards evening, the Duke gives the signal to withdraw. The eventual outcome is that both sides sign a pact according to which Duke Henry has to surrender the castle at Kalisz and return it to Przemyśl, who, in his turn, is, at his own expense, to build a fort at Olobok and give it with its surrounding villages to Duke Henry. This accepted, the siege is raised.

Duke Henry of Wrocław, called Probus, now makes thoroughly unlawful demands on Bishop Thomas and the clergy of Wrocław claiming considerable sums of money and aid. When this is not forthcoming, he flies into a rage, seizes the Bishop's castle at Ołomuchów and after that the town of Nysa which belongs to the Church. He then goes even further and takes over all the castles, towns and villages belonging to the Bishop or his clergy, ejecting their tenants and ecclesiastical officials. He then orders that, under threat of severe penalties, all tithes in his duchy are to be paid to him. He also lays his greedy claws on the castle at Edelstein, which had been pledged to the Bishop for a certain sum of money. To halt this hurricane that is battering his church, Bishop Thomas sends a delegation to request the return of Church property. He receives a threatening and arrogant response. He sends another delegation and yet another, and, in the end, goes in person to the Duke, but achieves nothing. The Bishop then informs his Metropolitan, the Archbishop of Gniezno, both by letter and by special envoy, of the wrongs he and his church have suffered and asks for protection. Because of the time of year, the matter cannot be dealt with expeditiously, but the Archbishop summons a provincial synod to assemble in Łęczyca and invites all the bishops to attend.

Burchard of Schwander is chosen to be the new Prussian Master in succession to Mangold. He is famous for his rescue of Acre in the Holy Land, long under siege by the Saracens, whom he drove away. Now, after only a few days as Master, despite the prayers of the Brethren, he resigns his post and enters the Order of the Knights Hospitaller. He is replaced by a Saxon, Meinhard of Querinfort.

A.D. 1285

Five bishops and numerous other prelates and abbots attend the Archbishop of Gniezno's, Jacob Świnka, synod in Łęczyca, at which the Church's complaints against the Duke of Wrocław are thoroughly aired. Bishop Thomas tells them how he showed the Duke greater compliance than his dignity as bishop allowed, and the upshot is that, with the support of all the others, the Archbishop imposes heavy ecclesiastical penalties on Duke Henry, his servants and all who helped, advised or supported him, and places an interdict on the town of Wrocław and all other places in the duchy. This is observed by all the churches and monasteries in the diocese, except that of the Minor Friars of the Order of St. Francis in Wrocław itself, which publicly flounts it. The Duke and the city fathers, who support the Duke, expel the bishop and all the Wrocław clergy, as well as the Dominicans, from the city and other towns and villages; so they all go to Polish dioceses and remain there until the storm subsides. Meanwhile, Bishop Thomas goes to Lyons to attend a synod, but fails to get the support for which he was hoping, because Duke Henry's procurators arrived ahead of him and had already obtained remission from the penalties imposed on their Duke and got the interdict lifted, so that the Duke neither repays the Bishop nor provides any compensation for the hurt the latter had suffered. The Bishop returns to Poland a saddened man, and lives in Racibórz as the guest of Casimir the Duke of Opole.

The rebellion against Leszek the Black, which the barbarians' invasion had halted, breaks out afresh and causes even greater confusion. Again, the main conspirator is Paul the Bishop of Cracow, who has the support of Warsz the castellan and Peter the voivode of Cracow, Janusz the voivode and Christian the castellan of Sandomierz, as well as of other magnates who wish to replace Leszek with Conrad of Mazovia. Conrad, confident of his army's strength, moves it up first to Zawichost and then to Sandomierz, where he is met by the Bishop of Cracow and the other magnates. A general assembly is called, at which the knights of Cracow, Sandomierz and Lublin all swear allegiance to Duke Conrad and hand over to him all their castles, forts and towns, with the one exception of the city and castle of Cracow, in which Leszek has taken refuge with his wife and the handful of courtiers who have not deserted him out of fear of being called traitors should the rebellion succeed. The rebels are convinced that success depends on their being able to capture Leszek himself, and the whole army is moved up from Sandomierz to Cracow. Leszek is filled with doubt as to what he should do, though common sense indicates that, if he is to keep Cracow as his capital, he must install a strong garrison with a good number of knights in the castle; but this is far from easy, for most of his knights have deserted him. In the end, he has an inspiration: he turns to the citizens of Cracow who are of German origin, entrusts his wife and the castle to them and promises to reward them generously once the enemy has been defeated. Then, on July 14, he leaves the city with a small retinue and makes as swiftly as he can for Hungary and King László to seek his help. The citizens of Cracow, seeing that there is no likelihood of their being able to defend the city with its low walls and poor defences, leave it and crowd with their wives and children into the castle and prepare to defend it against all attacks. So, when Duke Conrad arrives, he finds the city deserted and quarters himself in it. He sends some courtiers known to the defenders of the castle to tell them that if they will surrender the castle and submit voluntarily to him, whom the other lords and magnates have unanimously elected their duke, he will treat them justly and kindly, granting them immunity for what they have done; but otherwise they will call down upon themselves the full extent of his wrath. After a brief discussion, the city fathers tell the Duke that, having already sworn loyalty to Leszek—as have all the magnates and knights of Cracow and Sandomierz—they cannot stain their honour with such a gross breach of faith and, as long as Leszek is alive, they have no right to, and cannot, renounce the loyalty they have sworn to him. The Duke vents his anger at their reply on the innocent dwelling houses: fires are started in several places and the whole beautiful city burned to the ground. Leszek is now on his way back from Hungary with an army of Hungarians and Kumans provided by King Lászlo. Conrad wants to force an encounter, for he is convinced that with his superior numbers, he can easily deal with Leszek's army; so he moves on from Cracow and battle is joined on August 2, a pitched battle fought on level ground near the river Raba. Both sides suffer heavy casualties; but when Conrad himself is wounded in the head, victory goes to Leszek and Conrad seeks the safety of his castles in Mazovia. Leszek rewards his Hungarian helpers and sends them back to Pannonia. He grants their liberty to any of the gentry he has taken prisoner and restores those who beg forgiveness to their former state of favour. The defenders of Cracow, whose loyalty preserved the city for him, are granted a number of privileges: they are allowed to ring the city with ditches, ramparts, bastions and walls, and also, despite the protests of the knights and nobles, allows the city itself to be administered exclusively by Germans. Leszek now has such sympathy for, and liking of the Germans, that he adopts their manners, dress and way of doing their hair. Przemyśl, Duke of Wielkopolska, is eager for an heir and successor, but his wife Lukerda is barren; so he makes his servants suffocate her and then marries Ryksa, the virgin daughter of the King of Sweden. The murder becomes the subject of popular ballads, but no one is ever punished for it.

At the instigation of the Kumans, who have themselves suffered disaster at the hands of the Hungarians, the Tatars invade Hungary a fortnight after Epiphany and ravage it unopposed as far as Pest and Buda, and there they stay inflicting such damage that there is a shortage of draught animals and people have to harness themselves to their two-wheeled carts and ploughs. The Tatars depart after Easter, but only because of an epidemic that affects many thousands of them and compels them to leave Pannonia. In this same year the Tatars invade the territory of the Emperor of Constantinople and occupy much of his land.

Queen Cunegund dies on September 9 and is buried in the church of St. Francis in Prague.

A.D. 1286

Duke Conrad of Mazovia harbours a grudge against Władysław Łokietek of Brześć, whom he accuses of having deprived him of part of his inheritance: the castle and lands of Gostynin. He now enlists the help of the Lithuanians and Ruthenians to recover these. First, he sends some of his knights to live in Gostynin, so that, when the time comes, they can betray it to him. Thus, when the Lithuanians and the Ruthenians suddenly appear at its gate, the traitors carry out their plan and the castle is easily captured. There follows a ghastly slaughter of the 600 found in the castle, all killed or else carried off into slavery. This shedding of Christian blood restores Gostynin to Conrad, but his satisfaction is not long-lived, for in this same year those who helped him recover it, raid his own Mazovia, occupy the castle at Sochaczew and go on to capture and burn the castle at Płock, which they find negligently guarded.

Duke Przemyśl is eagerly awaiting the birth of his first child. He is hoping for a son, but when the babe is born it is a daughter and he is deprived of his hope and joy. At the christening in Poznań, when the babe is given the name of Ryksa, the prelate and nobles all tell him that he has no need to lose hope of male progeny.

Władysław Lokietek assembles an army and secretly invades Mazovia. One stormy night he makes his way into Płock castle and kills or captures the guards. He then announces that he will not return the castle to Duke Conrad, until he has been given compensation for the damage done to him by the capture of Gostynin and that castle has been returned to him.

The Lithuanian duke, Pelusza, still smarting from the wrongs done to him by his near relative, the Grand-duke, goes in secret to the Captain of Königsberg and persuades him to give him twenty experienced men with whom to harass the Lithuanians. With this band, he then penetrates deep into Lithuania and one night gains entry to the Grand-duke's castle, where many of the nobles are gathered celebrating a betrothal. The celebrants are found in a drunken sleep and some seventy of them and their women are murdered. The raiders loot the bodies of their jewelry and carry the two betrothed and a number of women and children back to Königsberg.

Bernard of Legnica, known as "Speedy" because of his great strength and agility, dies and is buried in his father's tomb in the house of the Dominicans.

On July 5, Wencelas of Bohemia marries Jutta, daughter of Rudolf, King of the Romans, to whom he was betrothed long years before. Rudolf gives the town of Eger in pledge for her dowry.

A.D. 1287

The knights of Wielkopolska rightly consider it shameful that Henry of Wrocław should have been granted the castle and district of Ołobok in exchange for Kalisz, without their duke being asked to give his consent. So, with a small picked force they attack Ołobok on June 14, and storm the castle, which, according to the pact, the Duke had been obliged to build at his own expense. They kill some of the knights stationed there and put others in chains. Thus the castle and district of Ołobok revert to their former status and are reunited with the duchy of Wielkopolska. A force of Lithuanians, Prussians and Samogitians stealthily invades the lands of Dobrzyń, which Duke Siemowit, fifth and last son of Casimir of Kujawy, was left in his father's will. First, they occupy the town itself, which they do on a Sunday, when the unsuspecting inhabitants are hearing mass. Then, having plundered and burned the town, they carry off many captives into servitude. It is estimated that three thousand people were killed.

Leszek the Black, pretending that he wishes to avenge the devastation of Dobrzyń and put an end to the raiding of Lublin and Sandomierz by the Lithuanians, Prussians and other barbarians, proclaims a general call to arms throughout his duchies. As the Holy See has granted permission for a crusade against the pagan barbarians, Leszek and all his knights and companions put on the cross, pretending that both foot and horse are off to fight the pagans. Once he has assembled and reviewed his army, Leszek forgets the pagans and marches against Christians, his mortal enemy and cousin-german, Conrad of Mazovia. He cruelly devastates much of the latter's territory and, as Conrad does not have the courage to resist, Leszek is able to drive herds of cattle and other animals back to his own duchies. However, his hypocrisy and mockery of God do him little, if any good, for on this campaign he loses many of his best troops, who drown while trying to cross rivers, and after this is himself invaded by Tatars and stricken with pestilence, plague, famine and floods, murrain and a plague of wild animals and wolves.

This is the fifth year of Bishop Thomas' and his clergy's exile and of Duke Henry of Wrocław's illegal appropriation of various towns and villages, tithes and other Church revenues. The Duke's greed and appetite for power are still far from satisfied; nor has the interdict placed on his lands and duchies done anything to quell him. Meanwhile, the exiled bishop and his clergy have been living on part of the revenues from lands belonging to Polish dukes, which Duke Henry has not been able to seize. They are living in the town of Racibórz which, though it belongs to the diocese of Wrocław, is held by Casimir the Duke of Opole to whom Duke Henry sends letters and messengers demanding that he should not allow the Duke's mortal enemy, Bishop Thomas and his clergy, to remain in his lands, otherwise he will have another enemy in the Duke. When Duke Casimir treats this threat with contempt, Henry assembles an army of his own men and some mercenaries, whom he hires with money from the confiscated Church revenues, invades Opole and lays siege to Racibórz. The wealthier citizens are prepared to endure a siege, but the populace, to whom it has come as a surprise, soon feels the shortage of goods and begins to experience hunger and so complains loudly and curses the bishop and his clergy. The people's hunger and despair grows with every day, for Duke Casimir is hesitant about coming to Racibórz's assistance; so then Bishop Thomas, with typical benevolence, announces that he would rather that he and his clergy fell into the hands of the tyrant, than that innocent people should be starved to death, dons his liturgical robes and makes his clergy do the same; then, bearing all the bishop's insignia, they go in procession out of the town and head for Duke Henry's camp. The Duke, watching their approach from a distance, is suddenly seized with fear and, leaving his tent, runs to meet the bishop, prostrates himself before him and begs forgiveness of his sins. The Bishop raises him from the ground and, with tears in his eyes, forgives him his perfidy, provided he remains contrite and devout. Then, after embracing and kissing tenderly, bishop and duke enter the nearby church of St. Nicholas and there, after a long discussion without witnesses, they reach agreement and are reconciled with all grudges disposed of, the conditions being that Duke Henry returns all the castles, towns, villages, tithes and property he has taken from the Church, and pays suitable compensation for loss of revenue; also, to atone for his sins, he is to grant the Church in Wrocław considerable freedoms and privileges. The Archbishop now removes the interdict and Duke Henry receives absolution, and divine services are again celebrated throughout the duchy. In recognition of the hospitality and kindness shown him and his clergy by the Duke of Opole during their exile, Bishop Thomas founds a collegiate church in Racibórz and endows it with tithes from the bishop's purse in Wrocław.

The barbarian Tatars, believers in the vile and blasphemous doctrine of the false Mahomet and enemies of all Christians, are suffering from a famine, to relieve which a horde of them under Nogay and Telebuga descends on Poland, devastating as it passes that part of Ruthenia it has to cross to get there, even though its inhabitants are already paying them tribute. Having collected quantities of provisions, the Tatars descend like a cloud of locusts on Lublin and Mazovia, moving on to Sandomierz, Sieradz and Cracow, despite severe frost and deep snow. They burn a number of monasteries, churches and fortresses in which people have taken refuge, but, on the advice of the Ruthenians accompanying them, refrain from attacking the monastery of the Holy Cross on Łysa Góra, only to be shamefully defeated after spending a couple of days vainly attacking the town and castle of Sandomierz. They reach Cracow on Christmas Eve and mount an attack, but lose some of their more eminent warriors and, abandoning the attempt, ravage the surrounding country instead. To do this, they scatter, so that it would have been possible to capture or kill some of them at least, had it not been for the heavy snow and the low morale of the Polish knights. Frightened by the situation, and having no confidence in his knights, Leszek takes his wife and some of his court to Hungary, and when the Tatars learn of this from prisoners, they ravage the country as far as the Pannonian alps.

In these unhappy times, the Dowager princess Kinga with two of her sisters and seventy nuns from Sandek nunnery, together with a number of chaplains and knights, move into the castle of Pieniny, near the town of Krościenko. This castle, on the bank of the Danube, is splendidly defended by its artificial defences and natural position, for the only access to it is by a narrow causeway, and here they all stay as long as the Tatars are active in the area.

The Tatars wage war in a way quite different to that of other nations. They fight from a distance, pour a rain of arrows round and on the enemy, then dart in to attack and swiftly withdraw; and always they are on horseback. Often they pretend to flee and then wound or kill those who thoughtlessly pursue them. They use neither drums nor trumpets. Often they leave the battlefield in the full fervour of the fight, only to return to it shortly afterwards. It is almost as if they regarded war as a sport and are trying to make things more difficult for themselves. By nature they are con-

The Tatars' (Mongols') siege weapons in action. An ancient tracing of a drawing of an old Russian miniature reproduced in S.N. Syrov: Stranicy istorii, *Moscow 1979. The picture shows these being used during the siege of the fort at Kozielsk in A.D. 1238.*
—British Library.

ceited, recalcitrant, sly and arrogant, greedy for plunder or gifts, and taciturn. They are never averse to stirring up civil or foreign disturbances. They are inclined to be dissolute, fond of drink and other delights. They never keep their word or their promises, unless it is to their advantage to do so.

Siemomysł, Duke of Kujawy, dies on November 1 after twelve years in exile. He was exiled because of his inveterate dislike of all Poles and his favouring of Germans, as well as for his attempts to deprive his knights of their rights, appropriate their inherited properties, and remove Poles from his duchies. He leaves no children and his share of the duchy passes to his surviving brothers.

On April 30, Pope Honorius dies in Rome. When the cardinals shut themselves up in conclave to choose his successor, seven of them die of heatstroke and the others then disperse to more salubrious places, postponing the election of a new pope until the following year.

A.D. 1288

Leszek the Black, who has always disliked his cousin, Conrad of Mazovia, makes a second raid into the latter's territory, the first having been unsuccessful. In this the knights of Cracow and Sandomierz, exhausted by the recent fighting, refuse to take part, thus Matthew the Voivode of Sieradz is left to assemble what knights he can from his province, which suffered least at the hands of the Tatars, and lead them against Conrad. Conrad fails to put up any resistance, whether out of weakness or as a strategy, thus allowing the Voivode to ravage almost the whole of Mazovia. On the way back, burdened with cattle and other loot, the raiders march in a rather disorderly fashion. Their every move is watched by Conrad, who has now assembled a considerable force of knights and peasants who have suffered at the enemy's hands. When the raiders reach their own frontier, they halt to rest, and, as the victorious often do, fail to set sentries and are all sound asleep, when Conrad attacks. The suddenness of the onslaught causes immediate panic, though the Voivode and a handful of his knights fight bravely and perish. Thus Conrad captures their camp, the raiders' belongings and arms, as well as their loot, and even takes some prisoners.

The Tatars, having distributed the loot they took from Poland and sold their Polish captives to various peoples, decide to leave Ruthenia and to destroy the Ruthenians before they go; unable to do this overtly, they poison the rivers and waters by placing in all still and running water stakes on which are spitted hearts taken from the bodies of Poles, killed for ritual purposes of divination, saturated with a very strong poison, against which no medicine is of any use, so that all who drink the water die. It is not until the poison has claimed a large number of victims that the Ruthenians stop drinking the water.

A.D. 1289

Leszek the Black's strength has been failing; now his condition deteriorates and, on the last day in September he dies in Cracow castle after receiving the last rites. As he has never appointed a successor, there is immediate squabbling over who is to succeed him. The Duchy of Sieradz having already been detached and joined with Kujawy, the knights and dignitaries of Cracow, Sandomierz and Lublin assemble in Sandomierz to choose their future prince.

Their choice falls on Bolesław, Duke of Mazovia, to whom envoys are sent to invite him to accept, which he does. He is brought to Cracow and takes possession of both city and castle. This the people of Cracow city do not relish, for they are afraid lest Bolesław should punish them for having repulsed his brother, Conrad, so they send for Henry IV of Wrocław, promising to capture both the city and the castle for him. Henry sets out at once with his army. The city fathers, mainly the butchers, at this time the chief guild, order the city's gates to be opened in defiance of Bolesław's order that they be closed. Bolesław then slips out of the castle and retreats to the castles of various knights who are opposed to Henry. Although these knights are prepared to fight and beg him not to desert them, being angry and indignant at having been called upon not to take over a duchy, but to fight a war of uncertain outcome, Bolesław decides to go away. The knights and others who voted for him are appalled at his departure and send envoys to Henry, they lay down certain conditions that he must accept if he is to rule their duchies. When Henry accepts these—they contain nothing unreasonable—he is unanimously elected duke of Cracow, Sandomierz and Lublin. Peace having thus been restored, Henry goes back to Wrocław.

Wisław Bishop of Włocławek grants Mszczuj the Duke of Pomerania permission to found a Dominican house in Tczew to which he grants various privileges; namely, those of gathering wood, splitting and burning stone and lime throughout the duchy, the right to fish in the Vistula, the streams and rivers and all waters round the town of Tczew, as well as the right to sail and ferry across the Vistula free of all dues and tolls.

Casimir, Duke of Opole and Bytom, is induced by promises and gifts from Prince Václav of Bohemia, to forget that he is a descendant of the kings of Poland, never defeated in war nor at present harassed by enemy action, and to agree to submit to the rule and authority of the Prince—who has not yet achieved the dignity of king—recognizing himself as the latter's vassal and liege. This he does not out of necessity, but solely out of greed and thoughtlessness, thus shaming not only himself, but his family and the other Polish dukes, indeed committing a crime against the Kingdom of Poland.

Prince Václav, given certain information by some jealous Czechs, information that is partly true and partly false, turns against his stepfather, Zawisza of Rožemberk and dismisses him from his post of Grand Councillor, just when Zawisza is about to celebrate the christening of his newborn son by his second wife, a daughter of the King of Hungary (some say that she had been a nun), to which he has invited his son-in-law, his father-in-law and the Duke of Wrocław. On the pretext that Zawisza has been planning an attempt on his life during the christening ceremony, Václav has him placed in one of the dungeons in Prague castle and there he is kept for two years, after which he is taken out and is beheaded in front of Freiburg castle for refusing to renounce his right to the castle in favour of Václav.

The Duke of Lithuania invades Sambia with an army of 8000. The Knights decline a pitched battle, so the Lithuanians plunder and burn and return home, having lost only fifty of their men, captured by the Knights.

A.D. 1290

The civil strife, suppressed when Henry IV was summoned to be duke of Cracow and Sandomierz and Duke Bolesław of Mazovia withdrew, breaks out afresh thanks to Władysław Łokietek, who has just made himself master of Sieradz. Angry at Leszek's duchy having been taken over by Henry of Wrocław without him having been given an opportunity to acquire it, he now makes every effort to capture it and remove Henry. In this he is impelled not only by personal ambition, for he is by nature adventurous, quick to act and to judge, but by the persuasion of the dukes of Mazovia, Łęczyca, Wielkopolska and Pomerania, who have promised him troops, with which in early spring he advances on Cracow. When Henry learns of this, illness preventing him accepting the challenge in person, he sends dukes Henry of Legnica and Przemyśl of Szprotawa to secure Cracow. They install a number of knights, so as to keep the townspeople and the populace at arm's length, and set out on their return journey. They halt at the town of Siewierz and there they are attacked by Łokietek and the other dukes. So, on February 26, there is a fierce battle between the armies of the two brothers. Victory finally goes to Łokietek after much mutual slaughter, in which many of the knights of Silesia fall or are captured: the son of Duke Conrad of Głogów is killed, as is Przemyśl, a mere youth, and Bolesław of Opole is wounded and captured. Many of the Silesian knights are killed or captured while trying to escape. The victorious Łokietek, now all the more hopeful of capturing the two duchies of Cracow and Sandomierz, advances on Cracow. The towns-people do not dare resist one who enjoys the support of their bishop and knights and open the gates to him. He is received both in the city and in the castle and proclaimed duke of Cracow. He installs himself in the castle, where he is shown greater submission than in the city. Undeterred by this set-back, Henry of Wrocław sends another force against Cracow. Its approach is kept secret, which al-lows those of the townspeople who still support Henry to admit it one night. Łokietek is all but taken alive, as he is making the round of the sentries in the city, but he manages to escape on foot with a few of his knights, who disguise themselves as Franciscan friars and are let out through the city wall where it runs beside the monastery. Bishop Paul is himself captured and for a time treated as a prisoner of war, thus experiencing imprisonment for the third time. The real rebels and those who either supported Władysław or have been slow in submitting to the Duke's authority are pun-ished by having their crops destroyed, their manors and houses burned to the ground, and after this they submit. Henry then releases the bishop and all the knights he had taken prisoner, installs a strong garrison in Cracow to prevent Łokietek launching another attack, and takes measures to deny the knights the means to defect. The war over, he rewards some of his knights, and even the Franciscans who saved Łokietek, giving their house various privileges.

Conscious of the gradual deterioration of his health, which is due to a poison that the Silesians have been administering to him for the last six months, Duke Henry summons Bishop Thomas of Wrocław and his more eminent nobles so that he can make his last will and testament. Since he has no progeny, he leaves the duchy of Wrocław to his uncle, Conrad of Głogów, and that of Sandom-ierz to Przemyśl of Wielkopolska, while the rest of his possessions are divided up between the vari-ous churches, his wife Matilda and the poor. He dies on July 2 in Wrocław castle, to which Conrad of Głogów, having been told that he is Henry's heir, goes in the hope of being able to take it over peaceably and without dispute. Unfortunately, some of the knights and townspeople dislike the idea of having him as their overlord, because of his quarrelsomeness and his inability to speak the truth, and, though others support him, there is almost a rebellion. Later, when Conrad has been in control for some time, Henry of Legnica, who enjoys the respect and support of most of the Sile-sian dukes, forces his uncle to surrender Wrocław. Conrad is afraid of being imprisoned and leaves the city by one gate as Henry, now successor to the duchy, enters by another at the head of the knights and townspeople who have gone out to meet him. Henry is thus able to exercise his author-ity in peace, but, thanks to Conrad's plotting, not for long. Przemyśl of Wielkopolska took over the duchy after Henry's knights surrendered it to him, but he was not able to do the same with Sandom-ierz, since Łokietek, who enjoyed the support of its knights, had got there first.

Henry IV's widow, Matilda, having had her dowry repaid, leaves Wrocław and goes back to her father, and there she dies and is buried in the convent at Lenin.

Lászlo, King of Hungary, suspects his brother, Andrew, of plotting to deprive him of the throne, a suspicion supported by the fact that the Hungarian magnates, who hate Václav, are known to wish to replace him with Andrew; so he now sends assassins to kill his brother. Learning of this danger and realizing that there is no place in Hungary where he can live in safety, Andrew goes to Poland, first to his aunt, Duchess Kinga, in her nunnery at Stary Sącz. When she recognizes him by certain marks on his body and learns the reason for his leaving Hungary, she entertains him for sev-eral days, during which she intercedes with Duke Przemyśl, who then gives Andrew the ducal resi-dence of Chroberz in which to live and revenues sufficient to maintain him in his rightful status. Andrew now feels safe, yet it is not long before he is deprived of life itself; for Václav sends assas-sins to kill him. These pretend that they have supported Andrew and so have had to escape from Hungary to save their own skins; this is accepted and they are allowed to stay. They wait for a suitable opportunity, drown Prince Andrew in the River Nida, which flows in a loop round the village of Chroberz, and then escape back to Hungary to claim their reward.

Mszczuj, Duke of Pomerania, despite living a dissolute life with a mistress betrothed to Christ (a nun called Sulka from the convent in Słupsk) has no children. He now names Przemyśl II of Wielkopolska his successor and orders the knights of Pomerania to swear allegiance to him.

A.D. 1291

Władyslaw Łokietek, who has both Sandomierz and Sieradz and only lacks Cracow, which is in the hands of Duke Przemyśl, tries various ways of forcing Przemyśl of Wielkopolska to surrender Cracow to him. However, worse still befalls the duchy, in that Leszek the Black's widow, Gryfina, perhaps afraid of being evicted from the properties given her for her dowry, or, because she is depressed by the civil strife that has broken out since her husband's death, sends envoys to her nephew, Václav of Bohemia, with a deed of gift which grants him the duchies of Cracow and Sandomierz in perpetuity and a request that either he come in person to take them over, or send an army to do this, before others, not entitled to them, should try to do so. Anyone but Václav would have taken such a deed of gift as a joke or a leg-pull, for it is inconceivable that a woman from Bulgaria should have been entitled to make presents of Polish duchies. The Duchess, however, falsely insists that her late husband gave her the authority to do this and that she has a document to prove it. This document, if it ever existed, can only have been a forgery; indeed, even Leszek the Black, though himself childless, could not have granted her powers so detrimental to his own brothers, and the other Polish dukes, his relations. But Václav the Prince of Bohemia, who, in the previous year, illegally removed his cousin, Nicholas, from the duchy of Opava, is avid to get his hands on other Polish duchies and so seizes this opportunity, accepts the deed of gift and sends the Bishop of Prague, Tobias, to Cracow with an army. Przemyśl of Wielkopolska, in whose hands Cracow was and who disposed of a larger army and better armaments, could have refused the Bishop entry, but he allows his jealousy of Łokietek to influence him and, encouraged by Duchess Gryfina and some of the Cracovian knights who dislike Łokietek, lets the Bishop occupy the castle, city and duchy of Cracow, assigning them all to the Bishop. The Bishop's Czech troops, having taken over the castle and city, advance into Sandomierz, where the town of Wiślica surrenders to them, despite its being well defended by its natural position. The Czechs go on to storm the fortress of Oblekom, which had a Polish garrison; but when they reach Sandomierz itself, they are shamefully beaten back from the castle and city, losing a considerable number of men killed, wounded or taken prisoner. They then withdraw to Cracow and thence to Bohemia, leaving a small number to garrison Cracow castle and city. They take Duchess Gryfina with them, so as to prevent her ever cancelling her deed of gift. She lives on in Prague for a few years, an object of contempt and ridicule, dies and is buried in the Franciscan church of St. James, beside her sister, Queen Cunegund.

From this time on, Václav Prince of Bohemia considers himself to be duke of Cracow and Sandomierz as well and styles himself as such. With the Czech army out of the way, Łokietek has such superiority in arms that he is able to drive the Czech garrison from Wiślica and occupy that town. He goes on to storm and demolish the fortresses remaining in Czech hands, overruns the country as far as the suburbs of Cracow and exacts tribute from it. The knights and people of Cracow send repeated complaints to Václav in Prague, who, in the end, sends Bishop Tobias back with another army and instructions either to protect the people of the duchy or to arrange an armistice. Łokietek rejects the idea of an armistice or pact and continues his raiding, so the Bishop returns empty-handed and tells his master that the Duke of Kujawy is too powerful for him to deal with.

Conrad of Głogów, incensed that Henry V of Legnica removed him from the duchy of Wrocław, after being named as successor by his father, plans to act to recover it when a suitable

moment arrives, but considering it pointless to do so openly, for Henry has more money and soldiers than he has, he resorts to deceit and cunning instead, harassing the duchies of Wrocław and
Legnica in a succession of nocturnal forays, which pillage, take captives and start fires. He makes a
secret pact with Henry's brother, Bolesław of Świdnica, who is envious of the latter's success and
eager to harm him, the object of which is either to kill or capture Henry. Henry, unaware that his
brother is plotting against his life, sends him an urgent request for help against Conrad. Bolesław
promises to provide this, if Henry will give him a certain part of the duchy of Wrocław to which
both brothers have an equal claim, the towns of Jawor and Strzegom. They make a pact in which
Henry grants him the two towns and Bolesław undertakes to give his brother all the help he can in
defending his duchies against Conrad of Głogów.

On July 9, Lászlo of Hungary, while resting in his tent, is stabbed to death by some Kumans,
the very people whose religion and customs he had adopted. Eighteen days later, Andrew, a Venetian, for such apparently was his origin—he deserves only a passing mention—is elected and
crowned king, the second of this name. When this Andrew was staying with Aldebrandini d'Este
on his way back from the Holy Land, he had made the acquaintance of the Marquis' unusually
pretty daughter, Beatrice, and made her his wife. He now brings her to Hungary and there treats her
as its queen. However, he dies shortly after this, and, when her stepsons put pressure on Beatrice to
go back to her father, she announces that she is pregnant, but nevertheless she goes back to Este and
there has a son, to whom she gives the name of Hungary's kings, Stephen.

About this time, the Sultan captures the castles in the Holy Land still in Christian hands—Jerusalem having been lost already—Tripoli, Acre and Tyre; so that now there is no part of the Kingdom of Jerusalem not in the hands of the Saracens.

The Teutonic Knights under Berthold of Brünhaven invade Lithuania and, after capturing and
burning Kołniany, slaughtering numbers of Lithuanians and capturing several hundred others, return to Prussia. In an effort to prevent further raiding of their territory, the Lithuanians start building a fortress at Mingedin. The Knights assemble a fresh army and advance against them, but,
when they see how many Lithuanians they are facing, they turn aside and attack and capture
Mederabe, where they find a number of captives. They liberate those who are Catholics, but either
kill the barbarians or enslave them. No sooner has this force returned to Prussia, than another under
Meinhard invades another part of Lithuania and puts the provinces of Postów and Gojżewo to fire
and the sword, before returning home with a considerable booty of cattle and human captives. On
their return, Henry the Commander of Balga invades yet again with 1520 knights and devastates
Oukaim and Mingedin. A few days later, the Lithuanian duke, Witenes, invades Kujawy and plunders and ravages the country round Brześć. On their way back with their booty, the Lithuanians are
pursued by Władysław Łokietek and Casimir with their knights, who call upon the Prussian
Knights for assistance, but even with it they achieve nothing.

A.D. 1292

Václav of Bohemia is finally persuaded to send help to his men in Cracow, who are continually being harassed by Łokietek. He calls up his Czech and Moravian troops, but considering this
still too weak a force, gets his former guardian, Otto the Long, Margrave of Brandenburg, to send
him an army, and with this huge force he moves through Opole and into Poland, reaching Cracow
on the Feast of the Assumption. He spends several days discussing ways and means of waging war
against Łokietek. Some advise him to attack Sandomierz, others Sieradz, both of which Łokietek
holds; but since the town of Wiślica bars the way to Sandomierz he moves towards Sieradz, destroying the crops in the fields as he goes. Łokietek, sensibly, does not risk a pitched battle, but confines his actions to nocturnal raids and attacks on those bringing up supplies or out foraging or
searching for plunder in no-man's land away from their bases. These actions are so effective that in

Charles the Master is anxious to obtain any sort of title to Pomerania, if only because of the considerable revenue generated by its port, and is prepared to use any pretext, fictitious or real, to obtain one. To this end he sends envoys to the Margraves of Brandenburg suggesting that he make a pact with them, whereby the Margraves sell to him in perpetuity the lands of Pomerania, all for 10,000 broad grosses. Waldemar is delighted to be offered such a sum for something to which he and his brother have no right or title, and which does not in any way belong to them. So, having received and counted the money, the two Margraves sign a document that states explicitly that they have sold and ceded to the Master and the Order of Teutonic Knights all the lands of Pomerania: that is, the castles and towns of Gdańsk, Tczew and Świecie together with their surrounding lands, which from olden times have belonged to the afore-mentioned castles. "We are selling these", the document states, "with the towns, villages, mints, tolls, taxes, markets, fields tilled and untilled, roads, pastures, groves, woods, lakes and bogs; with the hunting, fishing, beehives and all uses, benefits and fruits that can be gathered from the afore-mentioned lands at this time, with the riches that are now visible to the human eye on the surface of the earth and those which may be discovered in the future below ground such as salt, oil, iron, copper, silver, gold and all metals however named, in perpetuity for free exploitation, with full rights of administration of justice and right of ownership."

This document demonstrates the boundless greed, base desire and ultimate wickedness of both the sellers and the buyer, as well as the studied deceit and fraud employed by the Master in order to obtain Pomerania.

The dislike, even hatred, of their King felt by the nobles of Bohemia grows day by day, as does the spirit of revolt in the populace. King Henry, who knows that he has lost many of his Austrians, killed or captured while fighting in his defence, has shut himself up in the castle in Prague, from where he watches the struggle between his adherents and his enemies. He now receives reinforcements, sent from Austria to secure and defend his person, for even in his own home he is not safe from treachery. The Czech nobles, seeing that open rebellion produces no better results than did their earlier clandestine actions, have to rethink their position. Their next step is to send to Henry, Duke of Luxembourg and King of the Romans asking that he marry his fourteen-year old son, John, to Elizabeth, daughter of the late King of Bohemia, Václav II, and sister of Václav III, a marriage which would entitle John to inherit the kingdom of Bohemia, since this would be his wife's dowry, and so enable him to rule once the hated Henry has been removed. The Duke accepts and agrees to all the Czechs' requirements. Elizabeth, now a girl of twelve, is brought to Speyer, where the Duke is, and, after a wedding of regal ostentation, on the authority of the Emperor and King of the Romans, John is granted the kingdom of Bohemia, and he and his bride are sent with an armed escort and accompanied by the Archbishop of Mainz and certain German counts and nobles to help the Czechs remove King Henry. Reaching Prague, John at once lays siege to the city, which the King seeks to defend; however, thanks to the treachery of some of the townspeople, on December 5 the gates are opened, allowing John and his army to march in. King Henry, seeing that he is surrounded by treachery and trickery, and fearing more serious defeats and disgrace, leaves the castle at dead of night with his wife and his whole entourage and goes to live in the greater safety of the family's home in Carinthia. Other cities now follow the example of Prague and submit to the Count of Luxembourg, who is now anointed and crowned King and his wife Queen of Bohemia by the Archbishop of Cologne in Prague cathedral. Even after this, John styles himself king not only of Bohemia, but of Poland as well, as had other kings of Bohemia though he has no right to the latter title either by election or indirect inheritance.

Witenes, Duke of Lithuania, assembles all the armed men available to him and at Eastertide invades Prussia, turning much of it into a desert of ashes. He returns to Lithuania with 500 captives and much booty, thanking his gods for his success, for which he renders thanks with burned offerings and libations. Meanwhile, two Prussian forces have invaded Lithuania by different routes, burning whatever they come across and killing men, women and children indiscriminately. The Lithuanains do not dare resist and the Prussians return home without loss and with many captives. The Duke, eager to avenge the harm done to his country, assembles another force some 4000 strong and, on the eve of Palm Sunday, marches into Prussia, plundering and laying waste and burning churches after looting their vessels and jewels. Reaching Braniewo, he turns and heads back to Lithuania. Reaching the frontier between the two countries, he halts in a wood on a hill-top in order to distribute the captives among his soldiers. While this is being done, he jeers at the women captives, of whom there are some 1400, asking them what has happened to their god. Then he orders a captured tabernacle containing the body of Christ to be brought to him. He breaks it open, withdraws the Holy Sacrament and flings it at the feet of the girls and other prisoners, spits on it and tramples it with his dirty feet, telling them that his gods are the more powerful. However, God does not long allow this sacrilege to go unpunished; for at dawn the next day, April 6, the Master and eighty Knights of the Order and a number of other troops, arrive on the scene and a fierce struggle ensues. The Lithuanians put up a fierce resistance, but finally are routed. None escapes except the Duke and two of his companions; and all who are captured are hanged or drowned. The Knights recapture the prisoners and regain the loot; and return home victorious and rejoicing. To commemorate this victory, they build and endow a monastery in Toruń.

The Count Palatine of Brandenburg now organizes another raid into Lithuania and devastates the district of Pograude, before withdrawing rather hurriedly, so as to avoid doing battle with the Duke, who comes up with an army of Lithuanians and Samogitians. The Master, Henry Polotzke, himself organizes yet another incursion into Lithuania, which he enters on July 2, putting the district of Soleczniki Wielkie to fire and the sword. He then crosses the Niemen, but when he loses twelve of the Brethren in an ambush, he withdraws.

Pope Clement V, having scrupulously examined the vast number of reports of acts of cruelty perpetrated in Prussia and Samogitia by the Master and the whole Order of the Teutonic Knights, orders the Archbishop of Bremen and his chaplain, Albert of Milan, to investigate the truth of these horrendous accusations, especially that of the slaughter of the inhabitants of Gdańsk by the Teutonic Knights and other utterly abominable crimes. The original of the bull with its twenty-one accusations against the Brethren is to be found in Riga cathedral.

A.D. 1312

Albert the Starosta of Cracow and the City Council feel unable to endure the crushing taxes of Łokietek's rule and the onerous contributions towards financing his war which they are forced to make, to say nothing of his failure to suppress robbery and brigandage, as a result of which the roads are no longer safe; so in secret they send envoys to Bolesław of Opole to conclude a pact for the surrender of Cracow. The Duke duly arrives with a considerable force to take possession of the city. He finds the gates opened wide to receive him and he is granted full honours and submission; yet he is quite unable to extend his authority to the castle, which remains loyal to Łokietek, so the Duke takes up temporary residence in the Starosta's house beside the gate which leads to St. Nicholas. Łokietek realizes that he must put an end to this situation as quickly as possible, so he assembles an army of knights and peasants, but, before laying siege to the city, he sends envoys to the Duke with certain proposals, threatening to lay siege to the city should these not be accepted. Face to face with the Duke, the envoys demand that he withdraw from what is Łokietek's inheritance and admit that it was shameful of him to have come to Cracow at the whim of some of its citizens, especially as Łokietek now has a son. Should he not withdraw, the Duke will be a greater enemy of the Prince, than are the starosta and those who instigated this crime. The Duke, who is well aware of the preparations Łokietek has been making, gives them a mild, humble reply, laying the blame

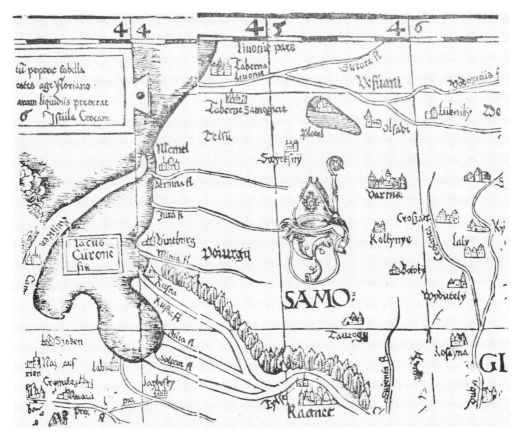

Northern part of Wapowski's map of Samogitia.
—Jagiellonian University Library.

for his actions on the starosta and the city councillors. He points out that he has done nothing hostile or unworthy; and that, now that it has been demonstrated that, contrary to what he had been led to hope, he cannot legally rule Cracow, he will withdraw from the city, leaving it unharmed. So, lest he suffer the indignity of being captured or having to flee, he departs without more ado, taking with him the starosta and certain of the city councillors, who realize that their treachery cannot be forgiven. Łokietek then enters the city with an unusually large contingent of knights and appropriates for his treasury all the revenues of the voivodeship and of the city's mills, shambles, shops and houses. As an example to others and a warning to future generations, he has the chief organizers of the revolt arrested and dragged by horses through the streets of the city, before being hanged or broken on the wheel. He turns the Starosta's house into a fort and builds a tower on the gate of St. Nicholas, in which he places a garrison, thus ensuring the future loyalty of the citizens of Cracow. The Bishop of Cracow is himself unjustly suspected, merely because he comes from Wrocław and is thus a Silesian. This suffices for him to be subjected to persecution and he also suffers imprisonment on the orders of the Prince. He is never able to recover his castle and lands at Biecz. The Starosta, realizing that the Duke, his nobles and the people of Opole all revile him, so that he is not safe where he is, leaves Opole and goes to Prague with his wife and children, and there they lead sad, impoverished lives.

Clement V summons an ecumenical council in Vienne, which orders the Order of Templars, which has existed for about 184 years, to be disbanded because of its unheard-of greed and ill-repute. He distributes its property among the Order of St. John of Jerusalem and other Orders. In the following year, on March 11, the Master of the Templars and some of his captains are publicly burned in Paris in the presence of two cardinals, specially sent to attend.

Charles of Trier, the Prussian Master builds a fort at Christmemel near Ragneta on the bank of the River Niemen and sends ships with 400 men and the necessary provisions to garrison it; but several of these ships are lost in a storm. He also makes two incursions into Lithuania, one by land against the fort at Bisena, and the other under Werner Commander of Ragneta by ship and river against the fort at Mergist, but neither achieves much, beyond taking a few captives and some loot. A third incursion again involves the Master in serious losses, because, without waiting to capture Bisena, he penetrates more deeply and captures a hitherto unknown fort at Sirditin; but, as all its people have taken refuge in the forest fastnesses, there is no food to be found in the abandoned houses and the soldiers are soon starving. Their plight deteriorates every day and finally they are compelled to withdraw. They have to go more than 100 miles, covering twenty miles a day, and many starve to death. Those who do reach home eat too greedily for their weakened stomachs and so kill themselves.

The Duke sends his commander-in-chief, an able, intelligent man, with a fleet of 100 ships to attack Christmemel fort. He finds the Knights' empty boats in the River Niemen, burns them and then attacks the Knights in their fort, only to be forced to withdraw after losing 500 men, where-upon he sails back to Lithuania.

A.D. 1313

Having suitably punished Albert and others, Łokietek pardons a large number of those impli-cated, many of whom are scarcely aware of what they are supposed to have done. Łokietek, how-ever, is afraid lest the spark of anger burst into flame again and reduces the authority of the city by taking away its ancient right to elect its own councillors, which he gives instead to the current Voivode.

On Friday, the Feast of the Assumption of our Lady, Henry VII, recently crowned Emperor, while taking communion, is poisoned, so it is said, by a wafer given him by a Dominican friar; or, what is perhaps nearer the truth, dies a natural death, for he had a carbuncle under his left knee. Af-ter this, various disturbances break out in the Emperor's lands. The Emperor's son, John of Bohe-mia, has started behaving most indiscreetly, in that he treats his knights and nobles with contempt and promotes Swabians and Rhinelanders to all important posts and offices; unable to endure this, the Czechs banish him, yet refuse to allow the Queen to leave Prague.

A.D. 1314

The Prussian Order, still illegally depriving Łokietek of his land of Pomerania, now makes what has been dedicated to God the target of its greed, in that it refuses to send the traditional tithes to the archbishop, bishops and the monasteries, but converts them into cash, thus reducing their value to a twentieth of what it had been, so that farmers contribute as little as two ordinary skojce for each hide cultivated, on which previously they had paid in sheaves. The Order's own farms and those of its commanders and their fellow countrymen are exempt from paying tithes, even mone-tary ones. The Order goes on to appropriate some of the villages belonging to the churches and monasteries in the diocese and puts them under its own authority, thus considerably reducing the revenues of the archbishop and his bishops. The Archbishop of Gniezno and the Bishop of

Włocławek, whose diocese encompasses almost the whole of Pomerania, the Bishop of Poznań and other ecclesiastical authorities, taking advantage of the protection given them by the Church, impose ecclesiastical sanctions on the Master and the Order, both individually and collectively, as well as on the peasants, and also place interdicts on certain places; but the Master and the Order appeal to the Holy See and just laugh at such punishments; indeed, they proceed to appropriate even more of what belongs to the Church, including a number of rich villages, the gifts of generous dukes and princes.

The Electors meet in Frankfurt-am-Main to elect a new emperor, but cannot agree and so elect two: the Archbishop of Cologne, the Count Palatine of the Rhine and the Duke of Saxony voting for Frederick of Austria, while John of Bohemia, the Archbishops of Mainz and Trier and Waldemar the Margrave of Brandenburg, vote for Ludwig of Bavaria, whose supporters then take him to Aachen, where he is crowned by the Archbishop of Mainz. Meanwhile, Frederick receives his crown in Bonn from the hands of the Archbishop of Cologne. This dual election leads to misunderstandings and squabbles. In one battle between the two sides at Muhldorf, Ludwig, who had the support of John of Bohemia and his army, achieved so complete a victory that his rival, Frederick of Austria fell into his hands. After this, Ludwig takes posession of all that belongs to the Emperor and assumes all the authority of the King of the Romans. He even frees his rival, once the latter has renounced all right to the kingdom and the forts under that authority and sworn an oath of loyalty and submission.

A.D. 1315

Poland, all but free of the threat of domestic or external strife, is now visited by something worse than any war: famine. Unusually heavy falls of snow after the seed corn had been sown leave the ground covered, with the result that, when the warm spring comes, all the seed has been destroyed. It is a disaster!

Henry and Władysław, sons of the late Duke of Wrocław, have now come of age. Finding that their brother, Bolesław, continues to squander their revenues, they put pressure on him to divide the duchy between them, so that in future Bolesław's prodigality shall harm only himself. So, the duchy is divided into three parts, Wrocław, Legnica and Brzeg, one part each, though he who is to have Wrocław is to pay 48,000 marks, and he who gets Legnica 32,000 marks, to the one who has Brzeg, so as to equalize the value of the three shares. Bolesław, who needs money, accepts Brzeg as his share. When the other two are asked to pay the agreed amounts, Henry, who has Wrocław, borrows that sum from his knights and the citizens of Wrocław; Władysław, who has Legnica and wants a career in the Church, indeed, is already a sub-deacon, is unable to raise the amount he has to pay and so gives his brother the town of Legnica as security for the amount due; so, Bolesław goes to Legnica and boards there with his brother.

The Samogitians suddenly swoop on Ragneta and lay siege to it. The knights and the castle's other defenders make several sorties in an attempt to repulse them, but are themselves defeated and thereafter confine their endeavours to defending the walls. The Samogitians having lost a lot of time over the siege and realizing that it is not going to be easy to capture the fort, return home after trampling the ripening grain and burning everything they come across. After this, Witenen of Lithuania, wishing to support the Samogitians, marches into Prussia with a combined force of Samogitians, Lithuanians and other tribes and lays siege to Christmemel, which he bombards for seventeen days, during which time 200 men sent by the Prussian Master to try and get through to the besieged, are cut down to a man. When he learns of this, the Master assembles another force, some 6000 strong and marches against the enemy. The Lithuanians, informed by their scouts of the Prussian advance, abandon the siege and withdraw to Lithuania. The Master fails to overtake them, but penetrates into Lithuania, kills a number of the inhabitants and captures others, then returns to Christmemel and repairs the damage done by the barbarians.

A.D. 1316

After his election as King of the Romans, Ludwig of Bavaria sends to Pope John XXII to ask him graciously to come to Rome to attend Ludwig's coronation. When the Pope rightly refuses, Ludwig, in a fit of temper, though with the approval of his own people and of some Romans, appoints an anti-Pope and calls him Nicholas. The true Pope, John, excommunicates the other and places the lands of Bavaria under an interdict, along with Nicholas and his adherents.

Henry Duke of Silesia and Głogów dies, one result of which is that the territories of Poznań and Kalisz, which had broken away from Poland in his lifetime, revert to Wielkopolska thus making it all one kingdom again. So, Łokietek sends Gerward, Bishop of Włocławek, a man of unusual discernment and an ardent patriot, to Avignon to try to persuade the Pope of the need to crown Łokietek king, since, as he is heir to almost all the duchies of the kingdom, his coronation would imbue the whole with fresh vigour in its fight with the heathen and any others who might attack it; while at the same time he wishes to have the authority of the Holy See and its sanctions to compel the Teutonic Knights to return Pomerania, recently forcibly and illegally wrest from the Kingdom, this being the only practicable way of preventing their appropriation of it becoming permanent through desuetude, for Poland is too weakened by previous wars and domestic disputes to recover its territory by itself. As well as verbal instructions, the Bishop is given letters to the Pope and the College of Cardinals, ensuring that the message is twice repeated as proof of its gravity.

Marshal Henry Plotzke now assembles an army of his Knights and invades Lithuania, where he destroys and burns the whole district of Postów, takes 500 captives and so returns to Prussia, where, in Königsberg, he is joined by a number of knights from the Rhineland come to fight the heathen. He at once uses them to organize a further incursion, this time into the district of Miedniki, where he captures and burns the town of Bisena and slaughters the 800 Lithuanians found in it. He organizes yet another incursion, this time with an even larger force, with which he captures and burns the lower part of the castle at Gedemin—the upper part being too well defended—then, seeing that the Lithuanians are not to be enticed into giving battle, he divides his force into four and sends these out to burn and pillage as extensively as they can. When this Christian army reaches home overburdened with loot and captives, the Prussians attack the fort at Ingedin, approaching it on foot in order to keep their presence secret and attacking at daybreak, confident that the sloth and carelessness of the Lithuanians will give them an easy victory. Here, however, they are disappointed, and they have to withdraw after burning only the lower fort. They are pursued and attacked by the Lithuanians. Many fall on either side, but some of the Prussians, screened by thickets, manage to escape. As the grain is now ripening, the Prussians again invade Lithuania, capture two forts, Pistin and Ingedin, and trample or burn all the crops. To avenge this, the Lithuanian starosta of Grodno marches into Prussia with 800 men, devastates the district of Munstorff and carries all its inhabitants off into slavery. On his way back, he is overtaken by Ulrich of Drilebe Commander of Ta ow and battle is engaged. Fifty-five Lithuanians are killed and the rest forced to flee, and their captives are freed.

A.D. 1317

When he learns that Gerward the Bishop of Włocławek has been sent to the Pope in order to try to obtain a crown for Władysław Łokietek and to lodge complaints about the Order's arrogant and impudent behaviour, the Master takes what steps he can to prevent either objective being achieved, steps that are financed by taxes collected from all the appropriated territories. From one part of Pomerania, although devastated in recent fighting, he collects 30,000 marks! Thanks to this and other revenues from the port of Gdańsk and the sale of jetsam or wrecked ships, which he now commandeers, alleging that the so-called Lex Rhodia entitles him to do so, the Order has accumulated an incredible amount. The richer the Knights grow, being by nature arrogant and impudent, the haughtier they become. They now send envoys to Avignon to counter the pleas and accusations of the Poles by whatever means they can, at the same time others are sent to John, King of Bohemia, bearing gifts of considerable value and requesting him not to allow the elevation of Łokietek to the dignity of King, thereby turning King John into an enemy and opponent, for Łokietek probably has the better title, in that the kingdom legally belongs to him by reason of his wife, Elizabeth, being a daughter of Václav, King of both Bohemia and Poland. King John is easily persuaded and sends envoys to Avignon, who both privately and officially do what they can to block the request of the Bishop of Włocławek, contending that in many respects Poland belongs to the King of Bohemia, who still styles himself as such, and promising that at the appropriate time and place they will prove their contention.

The exiled Count John of Luxembourg, avid to avenge his shameful banishment, raises a force, mainly of Swabians, and with the help of Bolesław of Brzeg and Legnica invades Bohemia. He begins by pillaging the country and putting it to fire and sword, but is then confronted by Wilhelm Zając, who first engages the Swabians and defeats them and then drives out Count John. Count John is now regarded as an enemy of the Czechs, to whom he much prefers Germans, and as one who has brought disaster after disaster on their country. The Czech gentry do not have a good word for him, and bitterly regret having chosen as their king a man of German origin, who by nature dislikes them and their language, and who would have done them more harm than good, had they not immediately taken measures to protect themselves.

In this year, starvation in Poland and Bohemia is such that tormented mothers eat their children and wolves attack even people who are armed with crossbows, and devour those they kill.

On December 15, Maria, wife of the King of Hungary and daughter of Prince Casimir of Poland, dies. Charles of Hungary now takes another wife, Beatrice, daughter of Henry, King of the Romans and sister of John of Bohemia. She survives less than a year.

A.D. 1318

Władysław of Legnica, aggrieved by having had to pawn his share of the three brothers' joint inheritance as security for the 32,000 marks he was due to pay his brother, Bolesław, under the agreed division of the inheritance, and needled by the fact that he now lives in poverty, takes the bad advice of his councillors and takes up arms against his brother, hoping that the latter will then cancel the debt and return Legnica to him. He starts ravaging his own duchy of Legnica as well as his brother's duchy of Brzeg. Bolesław resists and, having the better army, routs Władysław's force and, indeed, ends by capturing his brother, whom he imprisons in Legnica Castle, where he spends six months shackled hand and foot. In the end the two brothers are reconciled, thanks to the intervention of mutual friends, and it is agreed that Bolesław is to keep Legnica for the money he is owed, but will pay Władysław 5000 marks a year for his sustenance. Once released from prison, Władysław keeps none of the terms agreed, but stubbornly insists that he had been promised generous gifts. When Bolesław denies this, he is forced to go to arbitration and has to take a triple oath to clear himself; but, finding how differently his affairs have turned out, Władyław goes off his head and joins forces with a certain knight, who has a castle in the mountains from which he and his band of exiles, deserters and fugitive debtors make plundering raids into Legnica and Brzeg. When these attack the villages of Janików and Wierzbno, they are captured by the farmers there, who have engaged a hundred men-at-arms to protect them, and the two are sent with twenty of their companions to Duke Bolesław, who again imprisons his brother in Legnica Castle, where he falls into such a frenzy that he tries to kill himself and all who serve him, so that no one can get near him.

When this frenzy finally subsides, he is released from prison, yet he does not really recover his mental equilibrium, but with one or two companions roams from place to place inflicting himself on the local clergy, knights and baillifs. He continues thus for a considerable time, but in the end he does recover.

There is plague in Poland.

Bishop Gerward of Włocławek has appeared before the curia in Avignon to complain of the injuries inflicted on his church by the Order and demanding official action by the consistory, which he reminds of the Holy See's requirement that the Order return all the property, tithes and villages in Pomerania belonging to Włocławek cathedral, which they had appropriated. The Order's envoys have no answer and have to admit to various acts of cruelty: that in the village of Subkowo they arrested the Bishop's assistant and subjected him to lengthy torture, forcing him to hand over 300 marks for his release. Moved by what he learns from the Bishop and many others, Pope John XXII conceives a profound dislike of the Teutonic Knights and their perverse behaviour and considers dissolving the Order, as he has that of the Templars.

Hitherto, payment to the Church of one St. Peter's penny per lamp originally promised by King Casimir I has been erratic; but now, thanks to the efforts of the Holy See's collectors, it is being made regularly. At first, it amounted to only three pennies in coin and a bolter of oats per house and family, but now every member of a settlement or village has to pay one penny in coin annually, a practice that has continued until this day.

A.D. 1319

The question of Władysław's right to be crowned king of Poland, as petitioned by Bishop Gerward, turns into a protracted squabble with the envoys from the King of Bohemia, who contest his right. Though the evidence provided on behalf of King John is convincingly refuted by Bishop Gerward, who continues to plead with the Pope and the cardinals, even after the King of Bohemia's envoys have left Avignon, Pope John XXII is unwilling to offend one who is related to the King of France through the marriage of his son to the former's daughter, and one who has sent his own son to be brought up at the French Court, and so withholds his agreement, though he does write to the prelates and lords of Poland encouraging them to take the initiative and themselves crown Prince Władysław. He drops hints of his own wishes that encourage the Poles to hasten the coronation, and so Bishop Gerward tells Władysław and the prelates and nobles in Poland that, although he himself will remain with the Roman curia until the question of kingship and church have been satisfactorily resolved, they should perform a coronation without delay. Where Pomerania is concerned, the Pope sends instructions to the Archbishop of Gniezno, the Bishop of Poznań and the Abbot of Mogilno that they are to collect all available evidence, and, if this confirms that the Master and the Order have illegally appropriated the lands of Pomerania, they must compel them to return these under pain of ecclesiastical punishment, and, if necessary, they are to call upon the civil authorities for help.

John of Luxembourg, depressed by the double disaster of his shameful expulsion from his kingdom and his subsequent military defeat, does not know what to do. He realizes that he does not have the power to quell the Czechs' rebellion, so he seeks comfort from the Pope and obtains from him a judgment that his wife, Elizabeth, should be returned to him. The Czechs pay no attention to this, disregarding the possibility of interdict and excommunication; but, at the request of the Czech clergy, it is decided that Queen Elizabeth is to be returned to her husband in Luxembourg, and she is allowed to set out, escorted by some Germans sent for the purpose. However, the Czech nobles regret their decision and go after the Queen and her escort, whom they overtake on the border, near Tachov. There, getting ahead of the Queen's party, they conduct her back to Prague. After this it is not possible to get them to agree to the Queen returning to her husband. They prefer excommunication. After this, King John renounces force and decides to use subterfuge instead, this being more in accord with his devious nature. Through mutual friends he tries to make his peace with the Czechs, vowing that he will mend his ways and suggesting an arrangement whereby, after an interval of some years, he is to be allowed to rule Bohemia again. However, he is still bent on avenging the affronts and disasters that have befallen him in the last few years, which he will have to do clandestinely, since he cannot and dare not do so openly. To achieve this he announces a tourney to be held in a very pleasant meadow, which he proceeds to surround with a wall and several towers; his idea being to have the nobles and magnates taking part in the tourney murdered by German soldiers, whom he will hide in the towers. Queen Elizabeth has a premonition of what is afoot and informs the Czech participants of the fate awaiting them. So, these assemble an armed force near the meadow and dismantle the wall and the costly towers. Shattered by news of what has happened and afraid lest his cunning plot rebound on him, John makes no further plots against the Czechs.

Henry of Wierzbno Bishop of Wrocław dies on September 23. The chapter is divided over whom to elect to replace him, and ends by electing two bishops, Vitus and Lutold, and this gives rise to considerable ill feeling. As neither will give way, the matter is referred to a papal tribunal. The dispute lasts for seven years and involves enormous expense, which is all in vain, for, when the tribunal finally decides in favour of a Canon Vitus, the Canon dies a week later.

Bolesław of Brzeg and Legnica, exasperated by his imprisonment and by being made to pay a ransom for his father, vents his ire on the descendants of those responsible: he declares war on Conrad, son of Henry of Głogów, whose share of the inheritance has been Oleśnica and the towns handed over by his father as ransom. He prosecutes this with such stubbornness that, having devastated the country and defeated his opponent in several engagements, he has reduced him to such misery that he has only one horse and one linen coat with which to cover himself. The nobles of both sides intervene and stop the fighting and compel Duke Conrad to agree to return to Bolesław the seven towns belonging to the Duchy of Legnica which were wrongfully detached from it by Henry V and given to Conrad out of pity, and to renounce for ever any right to them. Thus enriched, Bolesław finds himself more famous than the other Silesian dukes, but, wishing for even more renown, he starts treating his knights, liegemen and vassals with such extravagant liberality that it involves him in damaging expenditure to meet which he incurs further debts bearing interest, these force him to pledge the town and district of Niemce to Duke Bernard, and Chojnów and Złotoryja to the citizens of Wrocław, to whom he already owes several thousand marks.

The famine of the last two years continues into a third year, becoming so severe that parents kill their children, and children their parents, and eat their bodies to appease their hunger. Others tear bodies from the gallows and devour them. Some of these wretches, gorging themselves on a weak stomach die as they are eating or soon afterwards.

A.D. 1320

The prelates, nobles and gentry of all Poland, informed of the Pope's letter and the advice he gave to Bishop Gerward, decide by general acclaim to crown Władysław Łokietek king of Poland, and the Feast Day of St. Fabian and of St. Sebastian is chosen for the ceremony. In order to make the occasion more solemn and to ensure its success, it is decided to deprive Gniezno cathedral of the honour of crowning the kings of Poland and to transfer this to Cracow, which formerly enjoyed the distinction of having an archbishop. The older people and the rich consider this right and proper; so, when the day comes, people of all ranks and conditions make their way to Cracow, where, during a solemn Mass said in the cathedral, the Bishops of Cracow and Poznań and five abbots in their copes and mitres anoint Władysław Łokietek king and his wife, Jadwiga, queen, before a great throng of the rich and powerful. The two are then crowned with regal crowns, which, together with the orbs, sceptres and other royal insignia have been brought from Gniezno. On the following day, King Władysław in his royal robes goes with his prelates and gentlemen to Cracow city, there to seat himself on the throne prepared for him. He then makes a circuit of the city, receiving the homage and oaths of loyalty of its citizens. It is decided by general acclaim to lodge the crowns and royal insignia in Cracow castle, for their safe-keeping cannot be assured in Gniezno.

On February 7 John Muskata, Bishop of Cracow, dies and is buried in the monastery at Mogila. At the subsequent general assembly, the Canon of Cracow, Nanker, the King's choice, is elected to succeed Muskata and is formally consecrated by the Archbishop of Gniezno. The new bishop, seeing how small and modest are the buildings of his cathedral, which had been erected so long before in accordance with the possibilities of the day, and how great the damage done by a recent fire, pulls down the old cathedral and starts building a new one of dressed stone, with its dimensions increased as much as the site allows. Because of this, a number of beautiful old tombs of princes and bishops are buried beneath the new structure. Bishop Nanker meets two-thirds of the cost, the chapter the other third; while the clergy of the whole diocese contribute voluntarily. Every benefice and every parish church, even such as are exempt from contributing to the King and the lay authority, are required to give the fruits of the next year towards the cost of rebuilding. This they do.

After his coronation King Władysław issues various decrees aimed at restoring safety to the public highways and eradicating highwaymen and robbers. Profoundly grieved by the loss of Pomerania, he does what he can to recover it. With the agreement of his councillors, and acting on the Pope's suggestion that proceedings should be started against the Teutonic Knights before the Archbishop of Gniezno, the Bishop of Poznań and the Abbot of Mogilno who have a papal commission appointing them judges-delegate, Władysław summons the Master, Frederick, and the Commanders of Prussia to appear before them. The King nominates the procurators, advocates and attorneys who are to conduct Poland's case against the Knights, and sends them off with the requisite instructions and funds. The King now starts implementing the vows he made while in exile, valuing justice and goodness above all, granting justice to widows, kindness to orphans, allowing easy access to his person, treating rich and poor according to the just decisions of the courts and in all that he does acting in accordance with the laws of God. This shows what a great advantage it is in public affairs for kings and princes once to have been poor and unhappy, humbly to have enjoyed the hospitality of other people's homes and eaten other people's bread, so that, having themselves been under constraint they know how they must be towards God and towards their subjects.

Marshal Henry of Plotzke continuing with his devastation of Lithuania invades once again with a force which includes fifty of the Brethren and puts the entire district of Miedniki to fire and the sword. Meanwhile the Lithuanians and Samogitians, quite undeterred, arm themselves and occupy a narrow defile through which the Knights will have to pass on their return. They fell the larger trees and prepare an ambush into which the unsuspecting Knights fall. The Master himself is an early casualty, being strangled, and all the Knights with him are either killed or taken prisoner. The Lithuanians thank their gods for their victory and the loot, erecting a large pyre on which they burn the body of Gerhard Rude, one of the Knights, together with his horse and armour.

When Łokietek's legal officers restart proceedings against the Prussian Master and his Order the judges appointed by the Holy See, that is: the Archbishop of Gniezno, the Bishop of Poznań and the Benedictine Abbot in Mogilno, decide to issue a summons requiring the head of the Order to appear before them in Brześć. This is delivered in person by the Archdeacon, priest of Laurence. On the appointed day, the King's advocate details the case against the Order, on whose behalf, Siegfried of Papowo, having first presented his authority to represent the Order, questions the tribunal's competence. When his objection is set aside, he announces that he is appealing to the Holy See, and departs. The three judges take no notice of this and the proceedings continue. The tribunal then moves from Brześć to Inowrocław, where for the best part of a year it hears evidence in the absence of the Master and his Order.

King Charles of Hungary has finally triumphed: all domestic disorders have been settled, especially his quarrel with the powerful voivode of Transylvania, Matthew, who has died; the rebellious barons have been either murdered, exiled, killed in battle or imprisoned; so the country can again enjoy peace. The King is firmly seated on his throne, and his only worry is his childlessness. Though twice married, he has no progeny, for his first wife was sterile and the other always miscarried. In order to change this, he now sends envoys to Władysław Łokietek asking for his daughter, Elizabeth, as his wife. The Polish prelates and nobles advise acceptance. A marriage document is drawn up and Elizabeth with the requisite dowry is duly escorted in regal pomp to Buda, where the marriage is performed with the usual ceremonies. The King then has his bride crowned Queen of Hungary in Bialogrod. God grants her such fertility that in the succeeding years she bears the King five sons: Charles, Ladislas, Ludwig, Andrew and Stephen.

Bolesław of Legnica, burdened with debt, directs the sting of his envy against his brother, Henry the Duke of Wrocław, a mild and honest man, whom, through intermediaries, he pesters with requests that, since he has no male progeny, he should exchange Wrocław for Legnica in favour of Bolesław who has numerous sons. When Henry refuses, Bolesław falls into a frenzy of rage and orders clandestine pillaging raids from Marcinkowice and elsewhere into Wrocław territory, all the while pretending to have no knowledge of what is being done. Henry suffers, or disregards, some of these raids, but uses his knights to curb some of the others. This further angers Bolesław and he has his servants drag Nicholas the Canon of Wrocław from the Church of St. Giles and take him to Jelcze, where he keeps him imprisoned for a while; though he is eventually freed thanks to the intervention of his brothers and friends. Another of Henry's councillors, called Molensdorff, he has dragged from the Church of St. Elizabeth on the excuse of his having reviled Bolesław in front of his brother. Molensdorff is put on a horse, from which he calls loudly for help, so his captors, frightened by the gathering crowd, pull him from the horse, kill him and ride off quickly in order to avoid capture. They report what has happened to Bolesław, who is waiting for them outside the city gate, hoping to use Molendorff to force Duke Henry's agreement.

A.D. 1321

The time has come for judgment to be pronounced by the tribunal, which for the last year has been hearing Łokietek's case against the Teutonic Knights for their appropriation of Pomerania. A date and place are fixed: February 12 in Inowroclaw. The Knights keep the judges waiting. Again and again a summons is sent to the Master and the Order, and eventually Siegfried of Papowo appears before them claiming to be the plenipotentiary of the Master and the Order, but all he does is to repeat both verbally and in writing the Order's former objections and refusal to acknowledge the court's jurisdiction. The judges reject his objections as trivial and arrogant and proceed to pronounce judgment, which they do first in Latin, in which language it is written, read by the Archbishop of Gniezno, and then in Polish, read by Abbot Nicholas, thus everyone within earshot can understand it. The judgment requires the Master and the Knights of the Order to return the territory of Pomerania, which they have wrongly seized and to pay 30,000 marks in coin and weight of the kingdom of Poland as compensation for loss of revenue and damage suffered, and to pay 150 marks of broad Bohemian grosses to cover the costs of the tribunal. Judgment having been given in favour of the King of Poland and the Order's appeal having been disallowed, the judges decide to proceed to punitive action, threatening all the sanctions the Church can impose, including placing under interdict these lands and places under the authority of the Master and his commanders. This decision is implemented in all territories and possessions of the Polish Crown. And, in the province of Gniezno, on all holy days the Master and his Knights are to be proclaimed excommunicated and condemned before the various congregations. In the event of either being present, or arriving during divine service, the interdict is to be observed. The Knights employ all sorts of costly ploys to get the judgment set aside, but these are baulked by the King's plenipotentiaries.

On Holy-rood Day, the Lithuanians invade Dobrzyń, now in the possession of Siemowit's widow, and devastate it. They plunder and burn the town itself, capturing men and women and murdering others; then swiftly withdraw.

The Florentine poet, Dante Alighieri, dies in exile in Ravenna, aged fifty-six. His excellent work, written in his native Italian tongue, in which he interestingly describes Heaven, Hell and Purgatory, introducing various heroes and criminals, is, in Italy, considered memorable and famous.

A.D. 1322

John of Bohemia, seeing how simple and unworldly are the dukes of Poland and Silesia, especially those whose lands and his have a common frontier, decides to try and extend his dominion over them and appropriate their duchies, castles, towns and other possessions. By means of gifts and soft talk he persuades some of them to enter into new ties of close friendship with him, then, with all sorts of tricks worthy of his devious character, he wins them over completely. He captivates Bolesław Duke of Ziębice, brother of Bernard Duke of Świdnica, with gifts of money and extravagant promises. Bolesław, who is neither perspicacious nor intelligent, is persuaded to relinquish the castle and town of Kłodzko, situated where the Bohemian and Polish frontiers meet, selling them to the King for a paltry sum. The King then installs a number of professional brigands, whom he instructs to keep raiding and plundering their neighbours, the Silesian dukes. Next he sends his son Charles, the Margrave of Moravia, to lay siege to Frankenstein and force Bolesław to pay him homage. In this, however, he is frustrated; so, instead, he buys the castle from the Duke's son, Nicholas. He sows seeds of discord among the dukes of Poland and Silesia and arms them to fight each other, so that one or another will come to him and ask for armed help, or will choose him to arbitrate in his particular quarrel, with the result that the King can give judgments that suit his purpose, and thus achieve supremacy. Wrocław is another of his objectives, so, after lavishing presents on Bolesław of Legnica and Brzeg, he persuades him to declare war on his own brother Henry, who inherited Wrocław. When Henry, who is a quiet man and unaccustomed to war, and also too poor to engage mercenaries, finds himself unable to repulse the raids and illegal pillaging of his lands, which are financed by King John and are now reducing him to the point of surrender, he turns to his near relative, Władysław of Poland, and makes him an outright gift of the town and duchy of Wrocław, preferring the Poles to have them, rather than the Czechs. So, Władysław takes over the duchy and for a while rules it, thus checking Bolesław's impetus. Later, he takes pity on Duke Henry's straitened circumstances and gives town and duchy back to him, an act that ensures that Henry's four sisters, now of marriageable age, can have dowries and a subsistence. King John is delighted, when he learns that Henry has got his duchy back, and, this time, does not resort to force to gain his ends, but to trickery and flattery. He invites Henry to visit him, plies him with all sorts of honours and gifts and persuades him to renounce both the town and duchy of Wrocław so as to spare them the constant raids and incursions of Bolesław, whom Henry hates enough to let them pass permanently into foreign hands, a thing which many of his knights and many of the citizens advocate, just to spite Bolesław. In return King John gives Henry the town of Kłodzko, but only for his lifetime. Thus is the kingdom of Poland grievously harmed, for the duchy and town of Wrocław are really part of it. Harmed, too, are the Duke's two brothers, Bolesław and Władysław, and three sisters, for Henry, having no male progeny, has no legal right to sign such an act of outright gift. As this arrangement is illegal, when Henry dies, his two brothers, into whose possession the duchy and town should pass, would have been entitled to seize them, but are deterred by the might of the King of Bohemia, who also has the support of the knights and citizens of Wrocław it-self. Since then Wrocław has sought to disassociate itself from Poland, though its payments to the Pope of St. Peter's pence and its subordination to the Archbishop of Gniezno, a metropolitan right instituted by the first king of Poland, are proof that Wrocław used to be part of the Kingdom of Po-land and will return to it, when God takes pity on the Polish people.

Bolesław of Brzeg and Legnica, whom this act of gift chiefly harms, tries to get it invalidated, reminding King John of their close relationship—their wives are sisters—and begs him not to ap-propriate what will otherwise pass to him and his sons, when Henry dies. He also reminds the king of the oath he took on the Blessed Sacrament that he would never try to appropriate lands or prop-erty that in any way belonged to Bolesław, whom he also undertook to help against any person, secular or ecclesiastical. He also asks him to remember how, at one moment of particular danger, Bolesław, at his own expense, came to King John's assistance with a strong force of his own knights, in order to protect him against armed attempts on his life being made by certain Czechs, in doing which he exposed himself to considerable danger and for which he received no reward or re-turn. Let the King remember, too, how he was once shamefully exiled from Bohemia and how Bolesław used his army to restore him; so, after all these good deeds let him at least not attack Bolesław and expose him to loss and disgrace. King John passes most of this over in silence, but he does reply to one point: "I admit", he says, "that I promised to assist you against any person, but not against myself". So, they part company more exasperated with each other than reconciled. King John tells the citizens of Wrocław, who have already put themselves under his authority and prom-ised him obedience, to surrender to him the two towns, Chojnów and Złotoryja, which Bolesław pledged to them, and lets it be understood that, should they not obey, he will take them by force. Meanwhile, Władysław the Duke of Legnica, Bolesław's brother, returning from Mazovia, where he had married the spinster daughter of its Duke Bolesław for her large dowry and stayed there with her, until he had run through all her money and grown disgusted with her person; now goes to King John and proposes to sell him the duchy of Legnica, which he originally pawned to Bolesław for 32,000 marks, claiming that the duchy is his share of the inheritance and that he can produce documentary evidence to support his claim. The King tells him that he will consider the proposi-tion. He then sends for Bolesław and in the presence of judges shows him Władysław's documents and suggests that he follow his brother's example and puts himself under the authority and crown of Bohemia. Bolesław is appalled, because he has so reduced his fortunes by his prodigality and lavishness that he cannot afford to resist, as well as being afraid of a greater danger: that the King might deprive him of his duchy, and so he submits. Thus is the biter bit, and his sons, brother and descendants trapped in servitude.

Knights from Poland, the Rhineland, Bohemia and Meissen, among them Bernard of Świd-nica, the Lord of Swabia and two Rhineland counts, assemble ostensibly for yet another incursion into Prussia; this Christian army, under command of the Knights, advances into Lithuania and Sa-mogitia, pillages and burns three districts and captures the fort at Pestwiany. The heathen now re-sort to cunning: they surrender the three districts and promise to do everything they are ordered, if the Christians will stop murdering and enslaving them and devastating their villages. Meanwhile, the Duke of Lithuania organizes an incursion into Livonia, where he burns and devastates the bish-opric of Dorpat and other districts, and returns to Lithuania with 5000 Christian captives and a huge amount of booty. The Christian army, eager to avenge this loss, despite the onset of winter, or-ganizes an attack on Lithuania and Samogitia. However, the severity of the winter defeats them and they return home having achieved nothing of note. In the meantime, the starosta of the Lithua-nian castle of Grodno, disregrading the severe frosts, raids Prussia with a considerable force and devastates the area round Reval in Livonia, murdering many Christians, burning churches and looting them of their vessels. He kills or takes captive a number of priests and collects considerable loot, burns a town and castle, and then attacking the district of Wilow, defeats the commander of Tapiowa and returns to Lithuania with a large number of captives and much booty. He also harries the duchy of Mazovia, where he plunders and burns several churches and villages, murdering peasants and carrying others off into Lithuania.

The Master of the Order in Prussia, Charles of Trier, dies and Werner of Orseln is elected to succeed him.

A.D. 1323

The Lithuanians, having been able to raid Poland with impunity and gained considerable advantage from plundering Prussia, now assemble an army, which includes some foreign elements, and, using secret paths, penetrate Dobrzyń. They capture the capital, and for several days plunder and loot. Then, in sudden haste, as is their way, they return by the same paths as they came, taking with them a number of captives estimated at 9000 and a huge quantity of loot. Once home, they are attacked by two forces from Prussia, which inflict many casualties on them and mercilessly burn their houses before returning to Prussia with their captives and loot.

Bishop Gerward of Włocławek dies in Avignon, where he has spent the last seven years defending his bishopric against the Teutonic Knights, who are trying to destroy it. To replace him, the Pope, who has the all but exclusive right of appointment, chooses Matthew, the dean of Włocławek.

A.D. 1324

Dobrzyń is threatened with complete devastation from raiding Lithuanians and constant harassment by the Teutonic Knights, carried out sometimes openly, sometimes in secret, but never leaving it in peace. Unable to protect his land against these two powerful enemies and afraid lest he be forced to surrender them, Duke Władysław of Dobrzyń himself goes to the King in Cracow and begs him to help him and his mother Anastasia in their difficult situation. He asks for a place where the two can live decently and which will revert to Poland on his death, since he himself has no children. In exchange, the King is to have the lands, castles and towns of Dobrzyń and so prevent them falling into the hands of the barbarians or of the Knights, for, as the Duke admits, he cannot defend them himself. After consulting his advisers, the King accepts the proposition and grants Duke Władysław for his lifetime the lands and duchy of Łęczyca, which is more than he asked for, since this is fertile land which gives a richer return than that of Dobrzyń, on whose defences and reconstruction the King now spends considerable sums and into which he introduces a number of settlers.

Two envoys of the Holy See arrive in Riga to try to resolve the misunderstandings which, for several years, have made Archbishop Gedymin and the burghers of Riga and the Master of Livonia and his Brethren dislike, even hate, each other. They go first to the Grand-duke of Lithuania and try to persuade him to abandon his idols and accept the Christian faith, but in vain. Meanwhile, on the Grand-duke's orders, David of Garthin, his captain, has marched into Mazovia, attacked Pułtusk belonging to the Bishop of Płock, plundered and burned 130 of the surrounding villages together with thirty of their churches and driven 4000 of the inhabitants back to slavery in Lithuania; while another Lithuanian force has invaded Livonia and ravaged several areas there.

A.D. 1325

The King of Poland is deeply perturbed by the way in which so much of his territory has been devastated and so many of its population carried off into slavery, without the Lithuanians ever giving him an opportunity to do battle with them, but, instead, having collected their loot, like wolves and other beasts, they have returned to their lairs in dense forests, by rivers and lakes and in bogs and marshes. He is afraid, too, that should he lead an army into such country, his men would run out of provisions and go hungry, for, as the Lithuanians rely on hunting and fishing, the land is not cultivated; they would then be forced into a shameful retreat and so expose themselves to greater losses than the enemy could inflict; or else, weakened by enemy attacks, they would starve, or finding themselves surrounded in forests they did not know, be forced to suffer shameful surrender or inglorious death. When no one can devise a way of repelling these savage raids, he decides to try to forge ties of friendship with the Lithuanians by means of marriage, and so, perhaps, incline these savages to gentleness and mutual sympathy. Therefore envoys are sent to the country's ruler, Gedymin asking for his daughter as wife for King Władysław's son, Casimir, asking not for gold and silver, neither of which the Lithuanians possess, for her dowry but only for those Poles whom the Lithuanians had captured during the last few years.

Gedymin is eager to agree. He frees all his Polish captives, men and women, of whatever status, and sends them back to their homes. When his daughter reaches Cracow, she is instructed in the Christian faith by the Bishop of Cracow, abandons her pagan errors and, on the eve of the Feast of St. Peter and St. Paul, is baptised in the cathedral, taking the name of Anna. After this, Władysław's son, Casimir, who has just turned sixteen, marries her in a ceremony of regal splendour held in the cathedral and attended by the parents of both bride and groom and the prelates and nobles of Poland, and accompanied by general merriment and dancing. Now, their security assured, both Lithuanians and Poles start tilling the land they have so long neglected, considering it not worth while cultivating, and before long old settlements are inhabited anew and new ones founded. Since both sides have rejected war and God makes both land and people fertile, the two countries become rich and wealthy again and live in amity.

King Władysław orders some knights from Cracow and Sandomierz to invade Mazovia, which they mercilessly pillage. They capture Płock, and, having looted it, send it up in smoke. Wanko Duke of Mazovia, dismayed by Poland's successes, makes a pact with the Teutonic Knights and helps them in all their hostile acts against Poland.

A.D. 1326

In the summer, King Władysław, conscious of the numerous affronts and injuries inflicted on his country by the Margraves of Brandenburg, and remembering their cunning murder of King Przemyśl, as well as their devastation of much of Pomerania and their illegal sale of it to the Teutonic Knights, organizes an expedition against the Mark of Brandenburg and Waldemar, its Margrave. With a Polish force, reinforced with contingents of Ruthenians, Walachians and Lithuanians. he invades the Mark along either bank of the Oder and puts the whole countryside as far as Frankfurt am Oder to fire and the sword. He does not stop to capture towns or castles, but plunders and burns every village and orchard. He meets with no resistance and so traverses the entire Mark, killing and harrying, the infantry keeping the forts in check and the cavalry thrusting deeper and deeper into territory as yet unharmed. None dares oppose them and they gather an enormous quantity of loot and so return joyfully to Poland. During this campaign the barbarians fighting with the Poles allow themselves all sorts of shameful acts against God's churches and their servants, which the King makes no attempt to stop. Together, Poles and Lithuanians take 6000 captives. It is said that one nun, in order to avoid being ravished by a barbarian, promises him that, if he does not touch her, she will show him how to prevent any sword from wounding him; to prove this, he is to try it out on her own neck. When he does this, and, of course, kills her, he realizes that she has done this in order to preserve her chastity, thus proving how a noble person, devoted to God, is more concerned with purity than with life.

Bernard Duke of Świdnica, father-in-law of Władysław Łokietek, dies on May 6 and is succeeded by his only son, Bolesław.

Bishop Nanker is translated from Cracow to Wrocław.

A.D. 1327

Nine of the Silesian dukes whose duchies border the Czech kingdom, namely the dukes of Opole, Cieszyń, Głogów, Legnica, Żagań, Oleśnica, Ścinawa, Falkenburg and Brzeg, take umbrage when Władysław Łokietek, without seeking their advice, indeed against their will, assumes the crown and styles himself king. The duchies of these nine comprise the most important part of the kingdom, that ruled by Łokietek being smaller and inferior to it; so they now call him not King of Poland, but King of Cracow, and instruct their people to do the same. Their fear is that the King of Poland, or his successors, should grow so strong as to make them, their sons or grandsons, his vassals. So, after many meetings and much discussion, they allow their envy of the Poles and their success in developing better than other peoples to drive them to go to the extreme of transferring allegiance to the King of Bohemia, whose hatred of Łokietek is inveterate. Forgetful of their origins, rank and nobility, the nine dukes assume the yoke of submission to Bohemia and pay homage to its king, swearing oaths of allegiance and loyalty. They commit yet another crime by discarding the white eagle, which is the emblem of the whole kingdom of Poland and which they have borne as their own emblem and princely jewel, and then assuming, some a white eagle on a black ground, others a white eagle on a blue ground, changing the heraldic fields, so as to avoid giving the impression of having anything in common with the kingdom of Poland. Since then, the dukes and nobles of Silesia have so despised the Poles and hated them, that any Polish success or honour has grieved them and they have rejoiced at any failure or loss. No neighbour of Poland has ever been so envious and hostile as have the Silesians.

At the end of July, a force of Teutonic Knights under Otto of Luterberg, Commander of Chełmno, together with the Duke of Mazovia, Wanko, who rides with them, advances into part of Kujawy, which it proceeds to pillage and burn. It surrounds the fort at Kowale, which it then captures and burns. Thus does Wanko, ignoring the ties that link their two territories and the blood and language they share, like a snake, bite his own people and destroy their land in an act of such perfidy as can never be effaced.

On March 9 the Lithuanian dukes assemble a considerable force and, travelling by secret paths and ways, raid Saxony. They make camp on the Oder, near Frankfurt, from where they barbarously pillage the whole of Saxony, which had already been devastated by the King of Poland in the previous year. They meet with no resistance and then hurry back to Lithuania with their loot and captives.

A.D. 1328

King Władysław, seeing that the Teutonic Knights are paying no attention whatever to the sanctions imposed on them by the Holy See, and perturbed by the fact that it is now almost twenty years since they appropriated his inheritance of Pomerania and that they still have it, and are building forts and fortresses with strong walls there, ridiculing and breaking all the laws of God and man by which he had hoped to be able to compel them to return the territory to him, now announces an expedition against them, for which he is promised reinforcements by his son-in-law, the King of Hungary, and other neighbouring princes. Having arrayed his army, he advances into the territory of Chełmno and, without bothering to capture towns, lays waste the whole area as far as the River Ossa, sending all its villages and manors up in flames. He reduces the entire country to ashes without encountering any resistance, for the Knights confine themselves to defending their fortified places and never engage him in battle; he returns without loss and goes to Cracow, where he rewards those who have fought alongside him, especially the foreign troops, each according to his deserts, and sends them back to their homes. Being justifiably incensed by Duke Wanko of Mazovia for overtly and secretly assisting his enemies, the Teutonic Knights, with men and provisions, the King sends a force to burn and pillage the whole duchy. To avenge this, a force of Knights joins Duke Wanko in raiding Kujawy, which it proceeds to plunder and burn. A force of Polish knights attempts to stop them, and, in the ensuing battle, the Knights and Wanko are crushed. Wanko seeks safety for himself and his men in flight, leaving the Commander of Toruń, leader of the Order's army, to be killed with almost all his men.

A.D. 1329

King John of Bohemia, yielding to pressure from the Teutonic Knights, goes to Prussia with a force of Czech and German mercenaries to help the Order in its struggle with King Władysław. Encouraged by its arrival, the Master, Werner of Orseln, decides not to wait for the summer, but at once arrays his army and marches into Dobrzyń at Eastertide. He lays siege to Dobrzyń town, and for several weeks bombards it day and night with his siege weapons. Eventually, the town's walls and defences being battered and broken, the captain, Paul of Spycimierz, voivode of Łęczyca, surrenders along with the rest of the royal forces, it being no longer possible to think of defending the town. The King's starostas and tenants are then expelled from the rest of the territory, together with those of the barons who consider it wrong to break an oath of loyalty given to their king. The Knights now take over the entire territory; however, Łokietek's own knights engage in and win a number of individual contests with the Knights, especially with those out seeking to plunder grain or provisions. The Poles also seize the boats that come down the Vistula with provisions for the Czechs, drowning their crews and then using the boats to harass the Knights. On April 23, the Knight in command of Dobrzyń castle, Brother Kerstan, unexpectedly attacks Włocławek, plunders the cathedral and the houses of the canons and the church itself, which even the barbarians had previously spared. The sacred relics in their beautiful reliquaries go up in flames, and numbers of people are burned. Other churches and villages in the vicinity suffer the same fate. The bishop, clergy and laity are forbidden under pain of death or loss of limbs to rebuild houses or put up any sort of structure. The Knights then occupy Ciechocin, which belongs to the Bishop of Włocławek, and give orders that its taxes, tributes and tithes are to be paid to no one but to the Master and the Order, to whom the inhabitants have to render honour and obedience in everything. King John and the Order then switch their forces to Mazovia, where they attack and for several days besiege the town of Płock, while they burn and plunder the surrounding countryside. The siege is raised when the Duke of Mazovia undertakes to submit to the authority of King John as King of Poland. The invaders show how innate is their cruelty and hatred of the Poles by burning and pillaging not only people's homes, but their shrines as well, even those dedicated to the Blessed Virgin, whose name the Knights hypocritically use in their title. The Master of the Order, fully aware that the Knights have no legal right to Pomerania and may well lose it sometime, now pays King John a huge sum in silver, gold and coin for Pomerania, which he would be entitled to sell, were he king of Poland, as he claims to be. King John, knowing that the previous sale by the Margraves of Brandenburg was invalid and had no standing in law, accepts the deal. Thus do the Knights hope to hide the illegality of their seizure of Pomerania, which they may perhaps do from people, but not from God. The necessary document is drawn up and signed and sealed in Toruń on Invocavit Sunday of the year 1329.

A.D. 1330

King John has been urging the Master, Werner, to seize the remaining provinces of Poland. Now, about the time of the Feast of St. John the Baptist, when excessive heat has ripened the grain abnormally early, the Master moves a considerable army reinforced with mercenaries close to Nakło and on July 9 captures the town, sets fire to it and takes its starosta prisoner. He then withdraws and marches into Kujawy, where he captures and burns the town of Wyszogrod. To avoid him taking Radziejów, from which he could have raided Poland, the royal garrison sets fire to it, before he can reach it. He then advances on Raciąż, the Bishop of Włocławek's castle, and for several days bombards it with his siege and other weapons. At first it is stoutly defended by men and women of the local nobility, many of whom had deposited all their possessions in it, but the constant battering by siege weapons demolishes the ramparts and, when the Knights get possession of the well from which the castle draws its water, Raciąż has to open its gates, which it does on the fourteenth of the month. The Knights find a huge quantity of money, weapons, treasure and other loot in the castle. They also capture many of the nobility and commoners, on whom the Bishop of Włocławek takes pity and ransoms for an agreed 400 Polish marks. In taking these castles, the Knights lose a number of high-ranking members of the Order and ten times as many of the rank and file as do the enemy. The knowledge of this sends the Knights into a sort of frenzy, and they proceed to avenge the deaths by murdering anyone of Polish origin, the old as well as the young, men as well as women, priests and other servants of God, as well as suckling infants. Not content with looting and murdering, they vent their anger on innocent houses and the surrounding villages, though not many of these have survived the previous burning and fewer still have been rebuilt. This accomplished, they return with their loot and a great booty of cattle. On September 15 these same Knights capture and burn the castle at Gniewkowo.

Matthew Bishop of Włocławek is so eager to ransom his brother and others taken prisoner at Raciąż, that, in defiance of the King's orders, he meets Werner the Master of the Order at Toruń on St. Bartholomew's Day and signs a disgraceful document agreeing that all Pomeranian sheaf-tithes, traditionally paid to the Bishop of Włocławek and his clergy in the form of one sheaf of every kind of grain, are to be set at only six grosses, thus considerably reducing the revenue of the See and its clergy, undertaking to have the agreement confirmed by the Archbishop and again by the Holy See.

Meanwhile, King Władysław has been eagerly assembling an army with which to engage the Knights in a decisive battle. He has been sent reinforcements from Hungary, headed by the Duke of Austria, contingents from Lithuania and Samogitia brought by Gedymin, and with these he now advances into the Knights' territory.

He burns and devastates the lands of Chełmno, thus avenging those the Knights had so inhumanely murdered, and then orders the same to be done over a wide area in which all are to be killed irrespective of sex or station. The Knights bar his path on the river Drwęca, defending several miles of both banks with sharpened stakes, logs, pile and faggots, but only on the far bank, where, too, the Prussian and Livonian Masters await the arrival of King Władysław. When the latter reaches the river, he is forced to halt. Wherever he moves his troops, there on the opposite bank are the Knights, who at once bombard them. After several days the King learns of another ford, so he moves his camp back from the river and pretends to be heading for Brodnica, but actually he leaves several thousand of his crack troops in woods and other hiding places with orders to cross by this ford as soon as the enemy withdraws, and to inform him of their withdrawal by smoke signal. All goes according to plan: the Knights hurry towards Brodnica convinced that that is where the King is heading; whereupon the King's troops emerge from their hide-outs and cross the river without difficulty or hindrance. They send the agreed signal and as soon as the King, who is then some three miles away, receives it, he hurries back to the river and crosses it near the mill at Lubicz, which he captures and burns, killing or capturing the entire garrison. He then arrays his army and eagerly awaits battle with the enemy.

When the Knights see that the King's army is stronger than their's and is made up of fresh levies of several nationalities, they decide that it is too risky to engage them in open battle, so they strike camp and withdraw into their castles and fortresses. Thus cheated of his battle, Władysław orders as widespread devastation of the countryside as is possible, so, for the next fortnight the Polish army destroys, plunders and loots the villages and the suburbs of all the towns in Chełm. The King also sends detachments into even the remoter parts of Prussia with orders to pillage and loot. This results in several large herds of cattle being sent back to Poland. The King then moves to Dobrzyń and tries to capture the town, but, several days later, seeing that it is stoutly defended, he withdraws to Chełm and takes up position near the castles of Schönsee and Lipno, intending to operate deep into the country. However, he now receives envoys from the Master bringing proposals for peace and so postpones further action, although with his superior force he could have gone on to devastate all of Prussia beyond the river Ossa, recover Dobrzyń and so get his revenge; as it is, he agrees to strike camp and stop further devastation, and signs an armistice to last until Holy Trinity of the next year, on the sole condition that the question of the occupation of Pomerania and of the damages involved is to be put to arbitration, the arbitrators being the kings of Hungary and Bohemia, whose judgment both sides agree to accept. It is this condition that persuades Władysław to agree to the truce, since he hopes thereby to recover Pomerania without shedding more Christian blood. Peace achieved on the Feast of St. John the Baptist, King Władysław and his army return without loss to Poland and Grand-duke Gedymin to Lithuania.

For many years King Charles of Hungary has led a peaceful, happy life, his kingdom free of all war, domestic or foreign, and is himself considered the happiest of mortals, because of his many children. Now, a sudden upheaval all but destroys it all. Among the Hungarian barons is a certain Felicianus, a man of humble origins who, after being in the service of the voivode of Transylvania, Laszló, transferred to that of the King, thanks to whose kindness and liberality he soon became one of the most influential members of the royal entourage. Indeed, so zealous was he in the King's service that he insinuated himself into the latter's favour to such an extent that even the most private apartments were open to him. In his overweening pride he planned to murder the entire royal family and take over the kingdom; so, on the third day of Easter, a Tuesday, May 18, when the King is dining with his wife and two sons out of doors near Wyszehrad castle, with none of their knights or bodyguard present, but just a few servants waiting on them, Felicianus with his son and some of his servants, walks up with his usual freedom and, drawing a sharp sword from under his cloak, launches a violent attack on them. He strikes both the King and Queen, who raise their hands to ward off the blows, with the result that the King receives a slight, though gory wound in his arm, while the Queen loses four fingers from her right hand, the one which so often nurtured orphans and the poor, helped the unfortunate, repaired chasubles and performed other pious services. Felicianus then turns on the two brothers in an attempt to kill them, but the commotion has brought running the noble youth doing duty as cupbearer and he flings himself on Felicianus and with a single blow between his neck and shoulder-blade sends him swooning to the ground. The other servants and knights then take it in turn to plunge their swords into his body as a token of loyalty. Felicianus' son refuses to abandon his father, but their servants all take to their heels and are pursued and captured, tied, each to a horse's tail, and dragged through the streets and roads until their bones are bare of flesh. Their remains, being considered unworthy of burial, are left lying for the dogs to eat. Felicianus' head is sent to Buda, his hands, feet and other parts distributed among the major towns to be nailed to their gates to inform people of the crime and as a warning to others.

Vengeance is also wreaked on Felicianus' wretched daughter, Clare, one of the girls of noble family who make up the Queen's household, and a very pretty one at that; for, in the confusion, no one believes that she did not know of her father's intentions, so she has her nose, cheeks and the fingers of both hands cut off, and is dragged, half dead, to make public confession of her own and her father's guilt and to admit that her maiming was justified. Her older sister, Zeba, and her husband are beheaded; their sons banished and many of their other relatives either executed or exiled. Some of these latter go to Poland, where they still live under their family name of Amadeus, having as their emblem a white eagle without feet.

Some people maintain that Felicianus' frenzy was induced by Queen Elizabeth giving his daughter, Clare, to her brother, Casimir, when he was in Hungary. Apparently he was captivated by Clare's beauty, and, in order to appease his lust, pretended to be ill and took to his bed, where his sister, the Queen, came to visit him; she loved him more than as a brother, and, knowing that he was not sick in body, but sick of love for Clare, whom she had brought with her, pretended that she had private matters to discuss, and so dismissed their attendants from the room, leaving the three alone. Then, after exchanging a few remarks, she went out, leaving the virgin Clare for Casimir to rape, a sin the Queen considered venial and without significance, confident that it would never come to light or cause trouble. However, Clare confided in her father and asked him to avenge her. Felicianus, finding that the Prince had returned to Poland, decided to kill his sister instead, and his attempt to do so, exposed his entire family to persecution. The Hungarian nobles insist that from that day on, prosperity deserted the country, so that it suffered a succession of disasters at the hands of the barbarians, which has continued until our day.

King Charles, having avoided one mishap, now deliberately exposes himself to another just as serious, in that without cause he starts hostilities against Basarab Voivode of Walachia. In this he is encouraged by the Voivode of Transylvania and others, who have their eyes on that Duchy for themselves. The King's forces do capture the town of Seurinum, which is then handed over to the Voivode of Transylvania; but then envoys from the Voivode of Walachia arrive and, demanding that hostilities cease, undertake to pay 7000 marks in silver and to submit Seurinum to King Charles' rule, the Voivode's own son being given as hostage. King Charles arrogantly replies that he will drag the Voivode from his cottage, as would any driver his oxen or shepherd his sheep, and, although his councillors beg him to accept the Voivode's offer or send a milder reply, he refuses to change his mind and leads his army deeper into the country without proper supplies or adequate reconnaissance. He advances into the Carpathian mountains with their impenetrable forests and great wastes. After several days of difficult marching they are still not out of the mountains and the troops are getting hungry. To avoid what might be even greater danger, the King gets Basarab to agree to an armistice, the one condition being that the latter will provide guides who know the way and will lead the army back to the Hungarian plain by the shortest route. The King and his army then move off, all unsuspecting. The guides, of course, have their orders and lead the army into a ravine, where the Walachians attack them from in front, behind and either side, shooting and pelting them with stones. When the King sees that his best knights are being killed before his very eyes without being able even to fight, he discards his royal robes and insignia, so as to avoid being recognized—actually he gives them to one of his captains, who is then taken for the king and dies under a hail of arrows and stones—and with a few companions makes good his escape, though not without considerable difficulty, and eventually reaches Wyszehrad clad in dirty civilian clothes. The Walachians gather up everything the invaders have had with them; kill the priests accompanying the King and take for ransom all who offer it.

Duke Wanko of Mazovia, a cruel, harsh man, dies on May 17, leaving one son Bolesław whom he had by the daughter of the Grand-duke of Lithuania.

The Teutonic Knights, who have been violating and oppressing their founders, the bishops of Livonia and their subjects, taking advantage of the absence of the Bishop of Riga at the Holy See, attack and capture the town of Riga, which, from its foundation always belonged wholly to the Cathedral of Riga.

On October 19, the Prussian Master, Werner of Orseln, dies at the hand of one of his fellow brethren, John of Ginsdorf, who attacks him in the refectory in the castle of Malbork. He is succeeded by Luther of Brunswick.

King Władysław of Poland sends to Pope John XXII in Avignon to inform him of the invasions, raids and devastation of his lands by the heathen Tatars and Lithuanians, sometimes acting together, sometimes separately, but always destroying, looting, murdering and taking captives, and asks the Pope to help by proclaiming a crusade against these enemies and by granting him several thousand florins to help him resist their attacks. The Pope refuses both requests, but, lest it be thought that he is sending the King's envoys away empty-handed, he grants Władysław the favour of a jubilee to be celebrated in Cracow cathedral during the three days in May of the Feast of St. Stanisław and three days in the autumn during the celebration of the removal of St. Stanisław, when all who wish to have their sins forgiven must give two złoty to the treasury, which money the King may apply to the defence of his country against the heathen Tatars and Lithuanians. Great crowds attend both occasions, coming not only from all over Poland, but also from Hungary, Silesia and neighbouring areas, so that a considerable sum is collected, which the King honestly allots to the defence of his realm.

A.D. 1331

Unlike the Poles, the Teutonic Knights have done nothing to fulfill the conditions laid down in the armistice of the previous year and the dispute has never gone to arbitration. Now hostilities start up again, grievously endangering the kingdom.

The King, who is feeling his age, decides that the burden of conducting a war at the same time as attending to public affairs which demand his presence, is too great for him, and so he calls a general assembly for June 14 in Chęciny Castle. There he consults with his prelates and nobles on how to conduct the war with the Teutonic Knights as well as the management of public affairs. Various measures are decided upon, one of which is to relieve Vincent, Voivode of Poznań, of the post of starosta of Wielkopolska, which is then entrusted to the King's twenty-one-year old son, Casimir, a youth of many talents, whom the King charges to use his best endeavour to recover Pomerania and the other territories belonging to Poland which have been seized by the Knights, Saxons and Czechs, and sends him to Wielkopolska with part of the army, while he himself returns to Cracow there to spend his remaining years in peace and quiet. Vincent is profoundly hurt by his removal from the office of starosta, which involves a considerable loss of income; indeed, he is as angry as if he had lost what was his by right of inheritance, instead of what is usually granted as a royal favour, as it had been in his case. He is, too, afraid of possible retribution for past misdeeds, which might now come to light. He turns renegade and goes to the Master of the Teutonic Knights to stir up trouble for Władysław.

Vincent and the Master Luther meet in Marienburg. Vincent pleads for an immediate invasion of Wielkopolska, insisting that there has never been, nor can be, a better opportunity for extending the Order's possessions, now that he and all his family — than which there is none more eminent on earth! — are eager to assist the Order. He promises that he will take command, gather intelligence and provide everything such an expedition requires, and, finally, promises to surrender the forts and towns of Wielkopolska, which he has hitherto governed and, also, to bring the Master Władysław's son, Casimir. The Master cannot turn down such a proposition or miss so excellent an opportunity of winning the war that is about to break out, so he assembles a considerable force of mercenaries recently recruited in Germany and sends it as secretly as possible into Poland under the Marshal Dietrich of Altenburg with Otto the provincial commander and several other commanders who are to act with Vincent. The Master himself is to remain in Toruń. The force under Vincent crosses the Vistula near Toruń and advances on the castles and towns of Brześć and Inowrocław. The citizens of both towns maintain a lax guard and take the approaching Knights to be friends, rather than enemies. However, the burghers and soldiers in the two towns decisively repulse the attackers, many of whom, being close to the gates and walls, are killed.

The Knights now march rapidly and by secret ways into the heart of Wielkopolska, even before news of their incursion has reached the King or he has been able to call up his knights. Guided by Vincent, the Knights capture the town of Słupca, which belongs to the Bishop of Poznań, and loot it of everything and take off many of the more eminent citizens for ransom. They then set fire to the town, before moving on to Pyzdry, in the hope of capturing Prince Casimir, who Vincent's scouts have reported to be staying there. They launch a violent attack on the town and capture it easily, since its defences have been neglected and no preparations made. However, Casimir has been warned a little in advance and gone with a few loyal knights into the remoter part of the forest. Infuriated by the escape of their prize, the Knights vent their anger on the townspeople, taking many of them captive, killing and torturing others; then they set fire to the town, its churches and monasteries, enriching themselves with what they loot. They then pillage the surrounding country on that side of the river Warta without meeting with any resistance, as Vincent had promised, and return to Toruń with all their plunder. The Knights, wanting still more, plan to gain control of the whole of Poland or, if not that, to destroy it or at least to weaken it so as to make it of no advantage to anyone.

The Master praises Vincent for keeping all his promises. Then, yielding to the latter's insistence, he assembles an army of mercenaries from the Rhineland and Germany to add to his own, and has reinforcements sent from Livonia by the Master there. Command of this huge army is entrusted to Dietrich of Altenburg, who has under him the commanders of all the lands which in previous years the Order had appropriated either by fraud or treachery in Michałów, Prussia and Pomerania. This great army of well-trained infantry and heavy cavalry crosses the Vistula and, not taking anything from Kujawy but provisions—the intention being to occupy the country on the way back—moves into Łęczyca, captures its principal town, despite its being stoutly defended, and pillages and burns the surrounding villages and towns. The army then advances on Kalisz and captures the castle, but is repulsed with heavy losses from the town. It then camps for five days to await the arrival of the King of Bohemia, who has promised to join in with a Czech army; but moves off towards Żnin, before he arrives, and gets as far as Gniezno, where it splits up in order to pillage and burn. One of their objectives is to find the relics of St. Wojciech and remove them, but here they fail, so, like barbarians, they loot the cathedral of all its vessels and jewels and then set fire to it. From Gniezno, the army under Commander Herman of Elbląg and guided by Vincent, moves towards Uniejów and Sieradz, pillaging, raping, carrying off captives, and looting and burning towns and villages, churches and monasteries. When the army reaches Sieradz, Dominican prior Nicholas, who had previously been prior of Elbląg and thus knows the Commander, falls on his knees before him and begs that he stop the slaughter of innocents and the looting and burning of churches and monasteries in which people have taken refuge with their belongings, and to spare the sacred relics. The Commander, pretending not to understand him, forces his way into the monastery, gathers up all the sacred vessels: chalices, crucifixes, ornaments and people's belongings, breaks into the scapularies and even strips the monks of their habits and ordinary men and women of their garments. Having sacked Sieradz, the army returns to Kalisz and attacks the town for several days, but unsuccessfully, for it is well protected by the river Prosna, which all but surrounds it. The disappointed soldiery then scatters and vents its spite on the town of Konin and its surrounding houses and villages. They would never have comittted such wickedness had they not been incited to do so by the traitor, Vincent.

When the Polish knights and barons living on the shores of Lake Niezamyśl hear of the dreadful devastation being wrought by the enemy, they seek to prevent the same thing happening to them by building a rampart seven miles long, extending from the village of Zwola to the town of Głuszyna. Parallel to this they dig a deep ditch into which they admit water from nearby lakes, convinced that the enemy will not try to force such an obstacle. But the enemy, learning that all the cattle from the country they have been devastating have been driven into the area behind the rampart, send 3000 of the Knights' troops to obtain such splendid booty. The Poles, warned by the peasants of the enemy's approach, quickly send news of it to King Władysław, who at once sends them his Marshal and several hundred of his household troops. Encouraged by these reinforcements, the Poles confront the Teutonic Knights, and since they have peasants fighting with them who neither give quarter nor take prisoners, inflict such casualties on the Knights that very few escape. The many bones that still litter the area are evidence of the extent of their disaster.

When King Władysław learns of this fresh incursion by the Knights and of their great strength, although advanced in years, indeed an old man with furrowed brow and a body near to death, by sheer strength of will overcoming his physical weaknesses and making light of the difficulties and burdens of waging war, he assembles knights from all his territories and with them confronts the enemy, who is then threatening Łęczyca. His intention is to make this a decisive battle that will put an end to the ravaging of his kingdom; however, when he discovers that the enemy outnumbers him several times over and has a large contingent of cavalry, he does not dare risk a pitched battle, but, instead, starts harassing the enemy with a succession of attacks on those out foraging or pillaging. The enemy are perturbed by the constant harassment to which they are subjected and do not dare continue burning villages, or even moving; thus the damage they do is not of great significance. Although the King is appalled by the sight of his pillaged kingdom and by the way his mens' eyes are so often filled with smoke and ashes, he dare not risk a decisive battle, while his army is so small; but then, as though inspired, he has recourse to cunning and secretly sends envoys to Vincent, who is directing the enemy's operations. These remind Vincent that his treachery has caused his fatherland to be devastated to an extent that must arouse the sympathy of its worst enemy, and they try to persuade him to switch from destroying his country to saving and strengthening it. They promise him permanent impunity for his treachery, if he will turn traitor again and lead the Knights to disaster. Vincent is moved by what they say, for his anger at his removal from the post of starosta has been sated by the sight of the country that he has reduced to ashes, and he is now begining to regret the awful things he has done which will for ever brand him and his descendants with the stigma of shame. So he agrees to assist whatever steps the King takes to save the country. Having been granted official pardon, he gets down to details and shows how the Knights' army, though numerically superior, is in reality weak, since more of it is train than fighting units, and thus relatively easy to defeat, if anyone but dare attack it. The men are burdened with haversacks stuffed with loot which they are fearful of losing, and so are more ready to run than to fight; indeed, Vincent insists that their great noisy throng will yield to a small experienced force, and reinforces the assertion by declaring himself ready to start the fighting and lead the assault on the enemy; or, if the enemy should attack first, to receive the first onslaught, which is usually the fiercest. These promises embolden the King to agree to do battle and he prepares a plan, while Vincent goes back to the Knights and tells them that, as far as he can see, everything is quiet.

The King sends Prince Casimir to a strongly fortified castle at some distance, so that, should the enemy be victorious, he will still be available to save the country. The Prussian army has now reached Płowce, a wretched royal village near the town of Radziejów, standing in a large, level and completely empty plain without so much as a wood anywhere and thus suitable for drawing up an army, and there the enemy is encamped. Suddenly, at dawn on September 27, King Władysław appears with his army in battle array and banners flying. The Knights cannot believe that he has dared to show himself and accept battle, until the rattle of arms and the neighing of his horses reveal the truth. The realization causes considerable and unusual panic in the Prussian camp; indeed, such confusion and commotion that they have scarcely time to collect themselves and form their ranks. However, they do manage to ring the camp with iron chains set up to prevent the Poles getting through to where others, still frightened and unprepared, are arraying themselves, but more in a huddle than in regular ranks.

A dense, dark mist starts falling and King Władysław orders a halt to his advance and addresses his men to encourage them. He then has the trumpets sound the advance and leads the first of the five units of experienced knights into the midst of the enemy. The enemy has superiority of numbers, the Poles are superior in gallantry. The Knights have more men and can replace those who fall, but the Poles, united by some indissoluble bond move on trampling those they have hewn to the ground. The presence of their King permits none to lag behind. Meanwhile, the autumn clouds have dispersed and the sun has come out, providing perfect conditions for a battle. The King and his knights have their misgivings about Vincent and wonder whether he has not again led the Poles into a disastrous ambush; but the Voivode does not disappoint them and proves more loyal to his King than to the Master and the Order who have done so much for him, and attacks the bewildered Knights in the rear. The Poles press forward and the enemy begins to give ground, then they turn their backs and flight becomes general. Victory appears complete, until suddenly more Knights under Reuss of Plauen, the grand-commander, arrive on the scene on their way back after capturing Brześć. The King has a guard put on Marshal Altenburg, Otto of Bonsdorff and fifty-six other eminent Knights captured in the battle that has scarcely ended; then telling his men that they have a second battle on their hands, assures them that it will be as successful and rewarding for them, engages battle afresh. Reuss of Plauen, acting as if victory were certain, gives orders that no Pole is to be left alive; but it is his men who fall, so many that the others panic and think only of escape, and then the fight becomes a slaughter. The Poles, eager to avenge those of their countrymen the Knights have murdered, prefer to kill than to take prisoners. The King, recognizing that the frightened fugitives must not be allowed a breathing space, loudly calls on his men to go after them and capture and kill, while Fortune smiles on them. Although all but exhausted, the Poles' legs still have the strength to pursue and their arms the ability to kill. They are ready to obey their King, as long as their horses have the strength to gallop and their right hands the force to kill, for they remember how the Knights have raped their women and devastated their country, and they have no pity. The slaughter, that began at dawn, continues until three o'clock in the afternoon. The enemy's camp yields loot of every kind, a wealth of things and provisions that enriches everyone. All the more eminent prisoners and the enemy's standards are taken to Cracow. Among them is Reuss of Plauen, who once threatened to lead his army to the very walls of the city. He now arrives in very different company. The Chronicles tell us that this battle was fought honourably and admirably, as are most, and I would not have described it in such detail, if I had not learned the details from those who took part in it and were still alive in my day.

What courage there was in King Władysław! From sunrise until three in the afternoon he stood in the ranks and was there, wherever danger threatened, attacking the enemy right and left, with sword and buckler, going to the assistance of those who were tiring and replacing the wounded with fresh men. None ever saw fear or anxiety on his face. Always he looked calm and in command, and yet he was a decrepit old man! By sheer strength of will he overcame his physical weaknesses and endured the fatigues of war. No less stubbornly did the Knights fight for victory, especially the commanders, and the mercenaries did too, for they linked themselves in ranks with stout belts, so that the Poles could not break their ranks or the Knights leave their stations.

When the King of Bohemia learns of the disastrous defeat of the Knights both from rumour and from messages from the Master, he is profoundly anxious for the Order; indeed, he is afraid lest Władysław should take even more decisive action and perhaps try to destroy it and so recover the territories seized from him. To prevent this, King John decides to declare war on King Władysław, since that should make him abandon any such plan. This done, with exceptional speed he marches a scratch army into Poland and lays siege to Poznań. When Władysław learns of this, he abandons his advance on Prussia, and turns aside towards Poznań, so as to deal with King John, who, fearing an enemy so recently victorious and so much stronger than he, is content to have saved Prussia from devastation, which was his main objective, and so withdraws to Wrocław in forced marches very reminiscent of flight, in the process losing 500 of his infantry and having to abandon his cannon and siege engines.

Charles King of Hungary and King John of Bohemia, anxious to put an end to further strife between the King of Poland and the Teutonic Knights, meet on St. Martin's Day to try to arrange a peace treaty; but, as it is obvious that the King of Poland will never renounce Pomerania, their efforts are in vain. The Knights, however, having brought in a force of mercenary knights from Germany, among whom are such eminent persons as Count of Bergow and Popo of Kokerzic, penetrate into Kujawy around St. Elizabeth's Day and pillage it for fourteen days, before returning to Prussia with their booty.

Duke Bolesław of Mazovia and Ruthenia marries a pagan girl of barbarian stock, the daughter of Grand-duke Gedymin of Lithuania. When she has been cleansed of the filth of paganism in the water of baptism, the wedding is celebrated in Płock, as is customary.

A.D. 1332

The Teutonic Knights, aggrieved that the disaster they suffered at Płowce has damaged their standing with their neighbours and reduced their influence, repeatedly send to Lower Germany and Bohemia for fresh troops to replace their losses. With these, they march into Kujawy on the Feast of the Circumsion of Our Lord, intending to capture its fortified towns and lay siege to Brześć. They maintain the siege until Good Friday, convinced that they will starve the town into surrender. Disappointed in this, disregarding the sacredness of the day, which even uncouth bullies respect, on Good Friday they mount an assault, and after five days of very heavy bombardment, both town and castle surrender. The Knights put in a garrison and move on to Inowrocław, which surrenders voluntarily. Here, too, they put in a garrison and move on to their next objective, the castle at Gniewkowo, and attack its walls with battering rams and missiles from their bombards. Duke Casimir of Gniewkowo, realizing that he is not going to be able to resist the attack, makes a pact with the Knights, which allows him to walk out with all his people and possessions and burn the castle. The Knights, having now got all Kujawy as well as Dobrzyń, begin building fortresses and towns of brick in places which have the best natural defences, so as more easily to hold their new acquisitions. The knights and barons of these territories, who have been ejected from their hereditary homes and lost all their possessions, take their wives and children to the Duchy of Cracow. Granted audience with the King, they appeal to him to look after them. The King takes pity on them and allots them various royal villages and lands. The only one to escape this disaster is the voivode of Brześć, Albert of Kościelec, and then only thanks to his daring; for he shuts himself up in his castle at Pakość and defends it stoutly, repulsing the enemy again and again and refusing to surrender. The Knights, seeing that the town of Brześć is of little military significance because of its position, raze it to the ground, so as to deny it to Władysław should he ever be in a position to recapture it. They then build a new town and fortress in a more suitable position and protect it with proper walls of brick and deep ditches, which are there to this day.

King Władysław, grieved by the loss of Kujawy and the expulsion of its knights and barons from their homes in the land of which he was especially fond, for it was there that he was born, decides to make an attempt to recover it. Again his spirit triumphs over the obstacle of his years: for, after assembling his own troops and those sent him by Charles of Hungary, who, seeing the difficult situation in which his father-in-law found himself, had sent him several thousand troops, he now marches through Mazovia and into enemy territory. He is accompanied by Prince Casimir, who has almost reached man's estate and has now been given his first command. The enemy, still intimidated, puts up no resistance, as the King's troops plunder and burn the whole of Chełm, its crops and villages. This angers the Master, Luther, and he moves up his army and prepares to fight it out, despite his commander's objection to his readiness to shed Christian blood and his apparent failure to understand that the fortunes of war are fickle, or that Władysław has more men and better weapons.

However, The Master does send envoys to the King asking for peace, for which he promises to accept reasonable terms and to return all that he has acquired by force of arms. The King is more disappointed than pleased, but judges it best to accept and proclaims an armistice to last until Trinity Sunday of the following year. He then marches back into Wielkopolska intending to spend the rest of the summer and the autumn dealing with some of his barons, who had deserted him and gone over to the King of Bohemia, since when they have been making stealthy plundering raids into Poland. With his great army he captures and burns more than fifty of these barons' strongholds and fortresses, plunders and ravages their lands, and ends by laying siege to the town and castle of Kościan, which, too, had gone over to King John. The garrison was composed of Czechs, Silesians and Germans and relied on the strength of the fort's position, it being all but isolated with bogs and marshes on every side, and payed no attention to the siege, until Prince Casimir, against his father's orders led an assault on the fort. Seeing this, the rest of the army joined in. They scaled the walls, cut down the defenders and captured the castle. After this, the town itself hastened to surrender, its citizens being glad to put themselves under the King of Poland once more. In order to avenge those killed or wounded in the storming of the castle, the Prince allowed none of its defenders to be spared, so all are killed. Prince Casimir's name is now on everyone's lips, and he is pronounced an extraordinary young man. Kościan has remained under Polish rule ever since. The King withdraws the entire army into his own territory, disbands its various units and returns to Cracow with Prince Casimir and the Hungarian and Cracovian cavalry. His knights, especially the mercenaries, are rewarded, each according to his services. The King's strength now begins to fade; then he falls ill and decides to take no further part in public affairs.

This has been a year of great heat, so great that crops have ripened before the Feast of St. John the Baptist, and rivers have run dry.

Vincent has been living quietly and without harassment, as the King promised he should, but then, on the Feast of St. John the Baptist, he is clubbed to death by a group of those who were enduring great misery because of the devastation of their lands, for which they hold him responsible.

A.D. 1333

As March, the season of the year most dangerous to the old, approaches, the King grows daily weaker. He sends for Brother Elias of the Dominicans and makes confession. Having received absolution, granted by special dispensation from the Pope, he is given the last rites in the presence of his barons and the prelates, and so he dies in Cracow Castle on March 2, after ruling for twelve years, one month and sixteen days, not counting the earlier part of his rule before his coronation, when he was only a prince, and, later, a private person. He was a man of considerable physical and moral courage, not to be judged by his physical appearance, for Nature was not generous to him as far as looks are concerned; but a courageous spirit enobled his small stature, which earned him the nickname of Łokietek, which means no longer than an ell.

A general assembly is called to elect a new king. It meets in Cracow and is attended by envoys from the King of Hungary who, when invited to speak, plead for the immediate election of the late king's son, Casimir, promising that in case of need, their King will give him all the help he can in the form of soldiers and weapons. Casimir is elected unanimously. The Feast of St. Mark the Evangelist is chosen for his coronation and that of his wife, Anna, though the Queen Mother advances a number of objections to her crowning, mainly on the grounds that, as long as she, the Queen Mother, is alive, it would be a breach of the law to crown another woman. However, in the end her son, whom she loves with more than maternal love, overpersuades her and she announces that she will be happy to see her son on the throne, withdraws to the nunnery in Stary Sącz, puts on the order's habit and spends the rest of her life in prayer and fasting. At dawn on St. Mark's Day, the Prince is robed in the palace by the bishops and conducted to the cathedral, where Janisław the Archbishop of Gniezno, assisted by four bishops, anoints and crowns him King of Poland and his wife, Anna, Queen. The rest of the day and several following days are given over to dancing, tourneys and merriment. As the new king has not yet come of age, the Castellan of Cracow is appointed his councillor. He is Jaszko of Melsztyn an honest, sensible man of proven loyalty, whose advice is to guide the whole kingdom and enrich its treasury.

A.D. 1334

King Casimir has two main aims: to have peace, and so give the country a breathing space, and to stamp out robbery and brigandage and make the roads, public and private, safe once more. To accomplish the former, he suspends military action against the Prussian Knights by extending the duration of the armistice by twelve months. The difficult task of settling the various points in dispute and removing misunderstandings being entrusted to the arbitration of Charles King of Hungary (his choice) and John King of Bohemia (the choice of the Master of the Knights). The sole stipulation is that during the period of the truce the town and castle of Brześć are to remain in the hands of Siemowit Duke of Mazovia, or, if he should refuse, of Matthew Bishop of Włocławek. In the event of the arbitrators being unable to establish peace, Brześć is to be returned to the Knights. It is accepted that the King of Poland, whose country is still smoking from fires kindled by the Knights, will not be able to engage in open warfare with the Knights, who have their own army and can call on the assistance of the King of Bohemia. To achieve his second objective, Casimir has all who are guilty of brigandage and robbery, whether of the nobility, the gentry or commoners, beheaded or executed either on the gallows, by quartering, breaking on the wheel, suffocation, blinding, severance of limbs, or exile. A few of the less implicated he spares at the request of the prelates and barons. As a result, the country soon begins to flourish.

Snow falls in great quantities on St. Wojciech's Day and lies for five days, causing the peasants to fear the complete destruction of their crops; yet, when it comes, the moisture of the thaw assures the crops of unusual fertility, as if they had been dunged.

A.D. 1335

When the time approaches for the royal arbitrators to pronounce judgment, the two kings agree to meet in Wyszehrad Castle on St. Elizabeth's Day and there deliver judgment. King Casimir goes there to present his case in person. King John of Bohemia is there too. The Knights, who have never implemented the condition whereby the town and castle of Brześć were to be transferred to a third party, either the Duke of Mazovia or the Bishop of Włocławek, are represented by Reuss of Plauen, the Governor of Toruń and Świecie. Each side presents its case and the documents to back it. But the King of Bohemia behaves more as an advocate for the Knights, than as an arbitrator, and is especially concerned that his sale of Pomerania to the Knights, which had brought him a very sizeable sum in coin, silver and gold, should not be invalidated. The decision, when pronounced, is that Kujawy and Dobrzyń belong to Poland, and Pomerania to the Teutonic Knights. This is a bitter blow for Casimir, for it deprives him of part of his inheritance, but, knowing how weak he is and afraid lest he become weaker still should hostilities be resumed, for he has enemies enough already and is considering declaring war on Ruthenia, he accepts even the condition that the castle of Nieszawa, though belonging to Kujawy, is to remain with the Order, thus giving the latter control of both banks of the Vistula and enabling it to use the river as a waterway. It is further decided that all liegemen, whether of King Casimir or the Order, who have been expelled from their properties, are to be allowed to return and have their properties and the favour of their liege lord restored to them; or, should they prefer, they may sell their properties and go elsewhere. These decisions are pronounced on November 26.

Anastasia, widow of Duke Siemowit of Łęczyca, who was a brother of the late King Władysław, dies on March 18. Her appanage falls to the King of Poland.

In the summer, when the heads of the grain are full, swarms of locusts appear in such numbers that, while flying, they blot out the sun, and, when on the ground, cover it to such a depth as to hide a horse's hoof. These locusts utterly destroy grain, grass and all other plants. After them comes a hurricane that overturns houses and trees, causing tremendous damage. The Prussian Master, Luther of Brunswick, dies and is succeeded by Dietrich of Altenburg, now released from Polish captivity.

A.D. 1336

After the royal arbitrators have made their award, all concerned depart, except for King Casimir, who, at the invitation of his sister and brother-in-law stays on to spend Christmas with them in Buda. Back in Poland, he sends letters and envoys to remind the Master of the arbitrators' judgment and to require that he hand over Kujawy and Dobrzyń. Master Dietrich with the usual craftiness of the Order, replies that he will implement the award provided King Casimir, his prelates, barons, knights and citizens by means of an official written document and their personal oaths renounce any right to the lands of Pomerania, Chełm and Michałów, and bind themselves to abide by the terms of the award. Without this, nothing will change and the Order will neither return what it has won by the sword nor hand over the brick castles it has built there at its own considerable expense. Knowing that King Casimir is eager for peace, the Master makes things as difficult as he can for the King and takes every advantage for himself, convinced that the King will do all he asks, as, in the end, he does.

In October, the seven Lithuanian dukes and a Ruthenian duke treacherously and secretly invade Mazovia, even though they have family ties with it and a treaty of permanent peace. In Mazovia they behave like enemies, plundering, burning and destroying, before returning home with more than a thousand Christian captives and a considerable booty in cattle.

Bolesław, Duke of Brzeg and Legnica, who has been wantonly and thoughtlessly dissipating his substance on lavish gifts, so that his expenditure is greater than his resources allow, having already pawned the town of Legnica and a considerable part of his inheritance for sums well in advance of several thousand marks, so that his lands no longer yield enough for his subsistence, is now, to his shame, compelled to hand Wrocław over to his creditors as security for the considerable debts of his two sons, Wacław and Ludwig. He is by now so impoverished that he has nowhere to live and nothing to live on. His wife, Margaret, daughter of Václav of Bohemia, dies and this enables him, at the end of the obligatory period of mourning, to marry one Catherine of Cracow, whose dowry he uses to redeem Brzeg and Oława. He transfers the lands of Legnica in permanent gift to his two sons to make what they can of it with its burden of debt. The two ask the knights and peasants for their help and are given it, so that they are able to redeem Legnica from the creditors, some of whom take pity on them and make them a gift of their part of the debt.

The Teutonic Knights, strengthened by knights come from Germany and Austria to help them fight the heathen, again invade Lithuania and for several days lay siege to the castle at Pullen, in which some 4000 Lithuanians from the outlying districts have sought refuge with their wives, children, possessions and cattle, for the castle is protected by both natural and man-made defences. Though their resistance is stout, the castle's defences are damaged in several places by the enemy's bombardment, and the Lithuanians realize that sooner or later it must fall, so they pile all their goods and possessions in the centre of the castle and set fire to them, so as to deny them to their enemies. They then kill their wives and children and offer their own heads for the governor of the castle to sever. When the Knights force their way in, they either kill or capture the handful of survivors. The Christian army then burns the castle to the ground, devastates the area round about and returns to Prussia.

A.D. 1337

King Casimir summons a general assembly to decide whether or not to agree to the Knights' demands for the renunciation of Pomerania, Chełmno and Michałów. The prelates and nobles are unanimous that under no circumstances should they do this, for the Knights' demands go further than the arbitrators' ruling and would for ever deny Poland her rights to Pomerania, Chełm and Michałów. To agree, they say, would be to enter into servitude, not peace, to sow the seeds of future war and hatred, and all agree that the terms are unacceptable. When asked how to deal with the war that would then be forced upon them, they reply that the Poles must not start hostilities, but if hostilities should start, they must defend themselves and in the meantime complain to the Holy See and seek its help. To convey this appeal to the Pope they choose John Grot of Słupcza, Bishop of Cracow, a man of unusual qualities, considerable experience in public affairs and of great commonsense. The Bishop accepts the task without hesitation and agrees to undertake the journey all the more readily as he hopes, by being there in person, more easily to regain for the cathedral the title of archbishopric, of which it was deprived by the negligence and oversight of his predecessors. So, in this same year, the Bishop, well briefed, sets off for Avignon, there to present Pope Benedict XII and the College of Cardinals with details of the injuries inflicted on the Kingdom of Poland, the obduracy of the Teutonic Knights and their utter disregard of the sanctions imposed by the Church.

The King of Bohemia, having by intrigue, flattery or promises subjugated the Polish dukedoms in Silesia and illegally occupied the town and duchy of Wrocław, as well as other castles, towns and forts, which the Silesian dukes had expected to obtain, now plunders the cathedral at Wrocław, which the Silesian dukes endowed. He orders the Bishop and Chapter to surrender its castle at Milicz, and, when Bishop Nanker, a courageous man, disdainfully refuses to obey, the King brings up a powerful force, reinforced by some citizens of Wrocław, and attacks the castle which was held in the name of the Wrocław chapter by Henry of Wierzbno the archdeacon. Seeing that it will not be easy to capture it, for the castle has good defences, and learning that the Archdeacon is an inveterate wine-bibber, he sends him some friendly Silesian knights with bottles of wine in profusion, as a result of which they are eventually able with threats and promises to induce the archdeacon to evacuate the castle with his entourage. The Bishop sends letters and messengers to the King, demanding the return of the castle, and, when this is refused, imposes an interdict on the whole diocese. Further attempts to obtain the return of the castle are made later, when the King comes to Wrocław. When these, too, are unsuccessful, the Bishop, ordering all his clergy to accompany him, goes to the King, so that he can personally excommunicate him should he once more refuse to return the castle. All but four of the canons are too frightened of the tyrant and what he might do, to obey; but with Apeczek the scholasticus and three others the Bishop goes to the Franciscan friary of St. James, where they find the King in a small room adjacent to the refectory. They knock loudly on the door, and, when the King tells them that he is occupied with other matters and cannot give them audience, the Bishop continues to knock until the Silesian nobles and others inside with the King, persuade him to admit the Bishop and his canons. So, in walks the Bishop, his stole round his neck and his crucifix on his chest and says: "I am admonishing you, Your Gracious Majesty, for the first, second, third and last time to return to me and my cathedral in Wrocław the castle at Milicz, which you seized by force". When the King again refuses and insists that he captured the castle legally and possesses it legally, the Bishop takes hold of his crucifix and says: "By the authority of Almighty God I excommunicate you as a plunderer of Church goods and pronounce you excommunicated in the name of the Father and of the Son and of the Holy Ghost." The others in the room are petrified by what they hear and dare not utter. The King, however, is furious and exclaims: "How impertinent and rash is this priest, and how thoughtlessly he seeks death. He wants someone to murder him, so that he can have a martyr's crown, but he must find another tyrant and persecutor". Seeing that he is not going to get satisfaction, the Bishop leaves Wrocław and moves with all the regular and secular clergy to Nysa, ordering all churches in Wrocław to be closed. Nonetheless, the doors of the three parish churches of St. Mary Magdalen, St. Elizabeth and the Holy Ghost are forcibly opened and services are resumed on the orders of the King and the city-fathers. When the common people prove reluctant to go to church, they are driven in and those who resist, have their clothes torn off them. The Bishop, seeing that heavier penalties are called for, orders the King, his advisers and the city-fathers, to be refused all sacraments as excomminicates. This further enrages the King, who responds by confiscating all the property of the Bishop and of the monasteries, telling the Silesian dukes that they can have them; however, they all refuse to take them, all, that is, but the impoverished Duke Bolesław of Brzeg, who seizes the Church's villages in his duchy, their tithes and rents and revenues, thus exposing himself to even more serious sanctions. When the Holy See receives the Bishop's letters and messages detailing what King John has done, Pope Benedict XII, who is in Avignon, praises the Bishop for what he has done and orders him to persist. He also confirms and increases the penalties imposed on the King and the citizens of Wrocław, on whom he pronounces anathema.

On St. Jadwiga's Day the Lithuanians enter Mazovia by secret ways, devastate the towns of Pułutsk and Ciechanow and the country round them; but when they then attempt to carry off a number of men and women, the local knights organize a pursuit and so recapture the prisoners and recover the plunder. Many of the Lithuanians, seeking safety in flight, drown while attempting to cross the River Narew, especially those who had pack-saddles stuffed with plunder to which they clung.

A.D. 1338

Until he sees the evidence produced by Bishop John, Pope Benedict XII is scarcely able to credit King Casimir's accusations against the Teutonic Knights, or that these have shed so much Christian blood and grabbed Catholic territory. Now he decides to remedy the wrongs done to Poland, and for that purpose sends two legates, Galhard de Carceribus and Peter of Montiglio, to that country, giving them extraordinary powers, including that of passing judgment and excommunicating the Master, the Knights and all who in any way have assisted them in committing crimes of which there is proof, and of suspending individuals from their posts, placing an interdict on lands, churches and entire communities, so as to compel the Master and the Knights to return what they have seized and pay full compensation for the hurt they have inflicted. Should, nonetheless, the Master and Knights remain obdurate and recalcitrant, they are to be summoned in writing or by envoys to present themselves in person before the Holy See to be severely chastised and punished for rebellion and disrespect. As soon as they reach Poland, the two papal envoys set up a tribunal in Warsaw, a secure place for both parties and close to the territory of the Knights, and by written edict, which is read out in the cathedrals of Wrocław and Inowrocław and in the Church of the Holy Cross in Opole where Nicholas is the prepositor, summon Dietrich the Master and the Order to appear before it on February 4. On the appointed day, Master Bertold, on behalf of King Casimir, hands the legates, as judges-delegate of the tribunal, a written petition, while Master Jacob, pleban of Arnoldsdorf in the diocese of Chełm, hands them a document challenging their competence and so departs. The two legates, realizing that this challenge has been made solely out of deviousness and has no justification, answer it before the Archbishop of Gniezno, the Bishop of Poznań and others in the name of the Holy See, rebuffing the accusations and asserting that they are fully entitled to pass judgment.

A.D. 1339

Having checked all the evidence presented to them, the two judges feel that they are in a position to pronounce judgment and announce that they will do so in Warsaw on September 15, on which day the written judgment is duly posted in the Church of St. John the Baptist in Warsaw. This awards King Casimir and the Kingdom of Poland the lands of Pomerania, Włocławek, Brześć, Chełm, Michałów, Kujawy and Dobrzyń, these being the rightful inheritance of King Casimir, while the Teutonic Knights must pay some 194,500 marks of Polish coin and weight to compensate the King and his Kingdom for damage done to them, and 1600 marks to refund monies expended.

King Casimir, seeing that he is sterile and will never have sons, is worried for the future of his country and orders a general assembly to be held in Cracow on St. Stanisław's Day. For several days, the assembled prelates and nobles discuss ways and means and who is to succeed their pious king. Various names are put forward: Siemowit Duke of Mazovia, Janusz of Mazovia and Władysław Duke of Opole, all of whom have ancestors in the royal family; but most people feel that they could not endure a foreign king, especially one from Silesia whose dukes have treacherously and unnecessarily submitted to the King of Bohemia; nor would the Kingdom of Poland gain anything from the accession of a Mazovian duke, since these are its feudal subjects, and it is important that they find a successor who will ensure the defence of the kingdom and increase its importance. King Casimir and his supporters put forward the name of Louis, son of Charles of Hungary, a noble youth of many accomplishments and Casimir's nephew. This is the suggestion finally adopted, so King Casimir sets out for Hungary accompanied by Bishop John of Cracow and Bishop Matthew of Włocławek and several nobles. They enter the country on July 7 and there conclude and sign an agreement, whereby, when King Casimir dies, he will be succeeded by his nephew, Louis.

On June 28, after a grievous illness, Queen Anna dies in Cracow Castle leaving her only daughter Elizabeth. She was a noble woman, compliant to her husband, generous, a benefactress of the clergy and of the poor, yet one addicted to games, dancing and other worldly delights, such as she enjoyed as a child with her pagan family and which she never renounced, even after she accepted Christianity. Casimir always looked on this with indulgence, rather than approval. Even when travelling in a coach, the Queen had to have drums, harps, viols and various other musical instruments playing for her. It was said by those, who wished to discredit her, that she died a dreadful and unnatural death.

Bishop Nanker of Wrocław realizes that sterner measures will be required, if the obstinate rebellion of the citizens and city fathers of Wrocław is to be quelled, since those taken by their own bishop and, indeed, by the Holy See, have achieved nothing in more than a year; indeed, the situation is getting steadily worse and doing considerable harm to the Church. So, the Bishop summons the Inquisitor of Heretical Faults in the diocese, Brother John of Schwenkenfeld of the Dominicans, a man of blameless and exemplary life, and explains to him the obduracy of the citizens of Wrocław and requires him to take action against them for disregarding the punishments laid on them by the Church, thus making themselves suspect of heresy. Brother Jan is well acquainted with the misdemeanours of the citizens of Wrocław and promises to try and exert his authority. He goes to Wrocław and, one Sunday, from a pulpit set up before the City Hall, speaks to a huge throng, rebukes them for abusing holy places and for their obstinacy and begs them to return to the bosom of the Church. He concludes by challenging them to appear before him on the next day and answer the accusations laid against them. When the citizens concerned fail to appear, the Inquisitor, inspired by the Holy Spirit, goes in person to the City Hall and calls upon the city fathers he finds gathered there to delay no longer in returning to the bosom of the Church, for otherwise they will call down upon themselves the wrath of God. He tells them, too, that he is determined to use all the means his office allows to quell their intransigence. After a long discussion, the Inquisitor concludes that he is getting nowhere and leaves the City Hall pursued by curses, insults and grinding of teeth; indeed, he is lucky not to have been assaulted.

The Prussian Master Dietrich assembles a force jointly with the Count Palatine of the Rhine and some Germans, and ventures an invasion in winter of Lithuania. He starts by investing the castle at Wielona and attempts to storm it; but he soon realizes that this is a vain endeavour, for the castle is well protected by Nature and well guarded by man, while the severe frost is taking its toll of the attackers, so he is compelled to return to Prussia. Later, in early summer, he makes a further three raids into Lithuania, devastates most of the country and carries off many Ruthenians and Lithuanians into captivity. He also builds a triple rampart and as many ditches and canals to prevent the enemy making sudden stealthy raids into Prussia.

A.D. 1340

On March 24, Duke Bolesław of Mazovia dies when a poisoned drink is administered to him. Various reasons have been adduced for his being so hated: that he was seriously trying to abolish the schismatic form of Church service among his people and replace it with the pure Catholic rite and obedience to Rome; another, that he was exacting too much from his people by way of taxes and tribute; yet another that he debauched people's wives and daughters, while allowing his councillors, officials and courtiers, all of whom were Poles, Czechs or Germans, to abuse and wrong with impunity. In my opinion, the main factor was the difference in faith and rite. When King Casimir learns of the Duke's death, he assembles an army of his courtiers and barons and advances quickly into Ruthenia, actually during Easter Week, and lays siege to Lwów. The city withstands his siege for a time, but, in the end, when hunger is making itself felt, the Ruthenian chief defending the higher and the lower castle and the town agrees to surrender, if King Casimir will promise not to violate or change their rites. The King agrees, for he knows that, should he refuse, the besieged would continue to resist and so would suffer even more. The gates are then opened and the King and his army admitted. The two forts are handed over to the King, homage paid him and oaths of loyalty sworn. Here, King Casimir finds a store of valuables belonging to the ancient dukes of Ruthenia: gold, silver, precious stones and gems, including two golden crucifixes famed for being made of wood from Christ's cross, as well as robes and a splendid throne embellished with gold and jewels, all of which he transfers to his own treasury.

He then advances on Vladimir and captures both the castle and the town and so has control of the whole of Volhynia. In order to prevent a rebellion once his back is turned, he has the castles in Lwów and Vladimir burned down, for, being built of timber, they require a considerable number of men and arms to defend them adequately. He then appoints a starosta for the city and surrounding area and, leaving a garrison, returns without loss to Poland and deposits the treasure in Cracow.

The King does not remain long in Cracow. On the Nativity of St. John the Baptist, he sends an army into Ruthenia, with which he captures the castles of Przemyśl, Halicz, Łuck, Vladimir, Sanok, Lubaczów, Trembowla and Tustań, a number of which surrender voluntarily, together with other forts. Many of the knights and boyars of Ruthenia want him to rule them; so, in the course of one year and a single expedition, he gains control of the whole of Ruthenia and unites it for ever with the Kingdom of Poland. There are a few Ruthenian nobles who are opposed to his rule and these, with the support of Tatar units, make repeated raids to resist the King. Eventually, however, they are broken in battle and killed, or dispersed.

On September 8, a horde of Lithuanians invades Mazovia and, since there is no resistance, devastates it in the most barbarous fashion, carrying off many captives and much loot.

Jadwiga, Łokietek's widow, mother of Casimir II, once Queen of Poland, dies and is given a solemn and costly funeral; she is buried in Stary Sącz.

A.D. 1341

King Casimir wishes to rid himself of the stigma of being a widower and sterile, and also hopes that a fresh marriage will enable him to rid himself of the habit of unrestrained whoring by accepting the restraint of having but a single companion for his bed, so he sends to Henry, Landgrave of Hesse, asking for the hand of his daughter, Adelaide, a girl widely renowned for her virtue and beauty, as his wife. The Landgrave is entranced by the idea of having so splendid a son-in-law and eagerly agrees to the King's request. To honour his future son-in-law the Landgrave personally escorts his daughter to Cracow. They are met by a procession of ecclesiastical and secular officials, and the marriage is celebrated with unusual pomp and ceremony on St. Michael's Day and subsequent days. The Landgrave gives a written undertaking to pay his son-in-law 2000 kops of broad Prague grosses as his daughter's dowry. This modest sum, which, today would scarcely be unusual as the dowry of the daughter of one of the minor barons, shows how modest were the requirements of those days, when Kings were content with dowries that the smallest barons of today would despise; either that, or how poor was the Landgrave of Hesse, whose lands are far from fertile. For the next fifteen years the royal couple maintain the pretence of a happy marriage, but, in reality, Casimir despises his wife and is drawn away from her by his pernicious desire for other women, whose charms he allows to bewitch him. So, he removes Adelaide from his presence and for many years she never sees her husband nor has conjugal love with him. She lives like a widow in the royal castle at Żarnowiec, lavishly supplied with all she might need, enduring her shame with unusual patience and avoiding all prohibited physical temptations.

Bishop Nanker of Wrocław dies on April 10, apparently suddenly, but, it is also said that he was secretly killed on the orders of the King of Bohemia in retaliation for his public excommunication of the king. The city fathers of Wrocław are delighted by the death of their bishop and regard this as a victory over the Church. They now go to King John and register complaints against the Wrocław Inquisitor, alleging that he has insulted and contemned them. The King writes to the Archdeacon of Wrocław, Henry of Baruth, and the Wrocław scholasticus, Apeczek, who are dealing with diocesan affairs while the see is vacant, requesting them to send John the Inquistor to him in Prague, so that, he may, perhaps, reconcile the two sides. He guarantees the Inquisitor complete safety. So, the Inquisitor sets off escorted by Conrad of Falkenheim, Starosta of Wrocław. While spending the night at the Dominican monastery of St. Clement, two thugs come to the Inquistor's cell and knock on the door, demanding to be given confession. The Inquisitor is preparing a sermon and tries to put them off, but they tell him that, if he does not listen to them while they still have a spark of contrition left, it will be too late. At this, the Inquistor emerges, receives three thrusts from their two swords and drops down dead. The King suspects the starosta of having planned the murder with the city council and arrests them, but when they on oath deny their guilt they are released. A year and a half later the two thugs are arrested on another charge and condemned to death. They then confess to the previous crime and tell that they had been bribed by two of the burghers of Wrocław, who gave them thirty marks for the deed.

Following a canonical election Przecław of Pogorzelec, a canon of Wrocław, of the noble Polish house of Grzymala, succeeds to the see of Wrocław. Since Jarosław, Archbishop of Gniezno, hoping to appoint one of his own Poles, delays confirmation of the appointment, the new bishop goes to Pope Benedict XII for confirmation, which he obtains.

On June 15, Dietrich of Altenburg, Master of the Prussian Order, dies while receiving Charles Margrave of Moravia, son of John of Luxembourg, King of Bohemia, who had arrived on a visit. He is succeeded by Luther also called Ludolf, König, a Saxon.

A.D. 1342

Charles King of Hungary keeps falling ill, whether these bouts of ill health are caused by depression resulting from the disastrous defeat he suffered in Moldavia, or are due to natural causes is not clear, but the result is that, if he is to be cured, especially of his painful gout, he has to give up soldiering. However, his condition deteriorates, his strength begins to fail and he departs this world on July 16 after receiving the usual sacraments. The prelates and nobles of Hungary set about choosing a new king, even before the funeral is over, so as to avoid the disorders and possible civil strife that might result from a lengthy interregnum. With Queen Elizabeth present, they unanimously agree to crown the late king's eldest son, the seventeen-year old Louis, and so, on July 21, in the cathedral in Székesfehérvár, Louis is duly anointed and crowned king of Hungary by the Archbishop of Esztergom, assisted by seven bishops and before a throng of nobles and barons. When King Casimir receives letters from his sister and the new king telling him of the death of King Charles he goes himself to Visegrád with a retinue of bishops and nobles, and organizes costly, but splendid obsequies in which Queen Elizabeth and the young King take part.

When the new Bishop of Wrocław, Przecław, returns from Rome, he is received with delight by the clergy and people of his diocese, but, as the city of Wrocław persists in its rebellion, he goes to Nysa and takes up residence there. Charles Margrave of Moravia, son of King John of Bohemia, comes to him in Nysa, and, after much discussion they agree terms for the return of all goods illegally seized. The Bishop, with his clergy and accompanied by the Margrave now returns to his seat of Wrocław. The city fathers come to him at the monastery of St. Wojciech, bare-footed, without cloak or belt, fall humbly on their faces before him, confess their guilt and beg forgiveness, promising never to rebel again. To add solemnity to the occasion, the Bishop has Duke Bolesław of Brzeg and Legnica, Władysław of Bytom, Conrad of Oleśnica, Bolesław of Falkenberg and Bolesław of Opole with many knights take part. Although the Margrave has promised to obtain recompense for the damage and loss inflicted on the clergy of Wrocław by Bolesław of Brzeg and Legnica, he departs without taking steps to implement it, leaving Bolesław disquieted and in a quandary, for Przecław of Wrocław was his friend and ally, and had helped him against Conrad of Oleśnica, but this cannot conceal the fact that he, Bolesław, has despoiled the church of its revenues for several years and so cannot obtain absolution or a relaxation of sanctions.

The people of Wrocław, considering themselves cleared of guilt, take to feasting and rejoicing, which they consider justified, yet God still punishes them, for on St. Stanisław's Day fire breaks out and though everyone hastens to help, the blaze cannot be put out before the whole town has been consumed by the flames.

A.D. 1343

Since the Teutonic Knights, contemn the interdict placed on them and do nothing about returning the lands they have appropriated on the pretext that the matter is under appeal to the Holy See, Casimir, well aware that he is too involved in war with Lithuania and Ruthenia to risk having to fight on another front, decides to accept the conditions demanded by the Knights—although all his bishops are against this—and signs the required document. In this he not only renounces his right to Pomerania and the other two territories, Chełm and Michałów, but also his right to demand their return through the courts. He also undertakes never to use the title, Duke of Pomerania, and to remove these words from the royal seal. The Feast of St. Mary Magdalen is the day set for King and Master to meet in Inowrocław and sign a final peace. King Casimir is only concerned with regaining his ancestral lands of Kujawy and Dobrzyń and the dukes, barons and citizens from the towns agree to the shameful terms in the document, so the only dissenting voices are those of Jarosław Archbishop of Gniezno, bishops John of Cracow, Matthew of Włocławek, John of Poznań and

Clement of Płock who are appalled at this iniquitous treaty, yet it is they who, in the future, are to break the toils the Knights have so cleverly imposed.

I cannot adequately express my dislike of King Casimir, who neglected his military duties so that he might feast and revel, boast of the quantity of gold he had in his treasury, pay homage to the pleasures of his belly and of venery, and live a life free of trouble.

In the same year in which Casimir makes peace with the Teutonic Knights and regains the lands of Dobrzyń and Kujawy, he organizes an expedition against Henry of Żagań and his brothers. With a mixed force of mercenaries and his own knights he advances ready to try his luck with any-one who might wish to do battle. He puts his trust first in God and then in the justness of his cause: he considers his actions justified because, when his father was busy fighting the Knights, who de-feated him, Henry's grandfather, Duke of Głogów and Żagan, seized the town of Wschowa and its surrounding lands, which had long belonged to the Kingdom of Poland, and has held them ever since. Yet, when Casimir now sends letters and envoys requiring their return, he receives imperti-nent, hot-headed replies asserting that Duke Henry would endure anything rather than give them up. First, the King invests the town of Wschowa, then mounts an assault on it lasting several days; having breached and demolished its walls, he captures it. His troops are ordered to refrain from plundering the town, but are granted the belongings of its defenders. So, having captured no small number of prisoners and gained control of Wschowa with its whole territory, he marches into the duchy of Żagań, captures the castle and town of Ścinawa, despite its having adequate walls and good natural defences, and razes its walls to the ground. He then orders the towns and villages in as large a radius as possible to be plundered and burned.

Duke Henry, realizing too late that he is being punished for his hasty words, sends envoys to ask for peace. The King, however, has already moved his army against Henry's capital and castle at Żagań. The envoys plead so humbly for him to spare what little remains, and promise that the Duke will renounce all right to Wschowa, and express their readiness to accept whatever other condi-tions the King may require, that Casimir is won over and sends for the Duke and his three brothers, Conrad of Oleśnica, John of Ścinawa and Przemyśl of Głogów. When they arrive, they are told that their humility and subservience have so disarmed the King that he is going to grant them their in-herited lands, which he has just captured, provided they renounce all right to Wschowa and will take care not to break the present treaty and so call down upon themselves the King's wrath and that of the Almighty. Once the documents have been signed, the King breaks camp and returns to Po-land. Even after it has been returned to Poland, Wschowa has enjoyed, as it still does, certain rights and privileges, particularly that of striking its own coinage.

The Dowager Queen Elizabeth, wishing to visit her son Andrew, King of Naples, and to see Rome, takes ship and sails to Naples, where she is received with due honour by her son and his wife, Queen Joanna. After spending some time with them, she travels on to Rome, pays homage to the holy relics and sends to Pope Clement VI, then in Avignon, asking his permission for her son Andrew to be crowned. This costs her 44,000 in gold and silver ducats. She can see that Joanna is conceited, arrogant, cruel and fickle, and that she both despises and hates her husband, so the Queen returns to Hungary saddened and afraid that her son may be in considerable danger.

Casimir has been irritated by repeated requests from the Duke of Szczecin for the hand of his daughter by his first wife, Elizabeth, a girl who has only just come of age, but, being advised that such a marriage would be advantageous, he agrees to it on condition that Duke Bogusław and his two brothers, Barnim and Warcisław, sign a document solemnly undertaking to be loyal and assist Casimir against all his enemies, especially the Teutonic Knights and their Master, and personally to contribute 400 men-at-arms to any war he may wage and never to desert or abandon him in suc-cess or misfortune.

The King then organizes a sumptuous wedding in Poznań on the Feast of the Apostle Matthew. The dowry of 20,000 Prague grosses is paid over to the bride and her betrothed, and the bride herself is given a rich trousseau of golden and silver vessels, horses, clothes and other valuables, such as one would expect when a great king marries off his daughter. Duke Bogusław makes the bride a written grant of certain castles, towns and villages in his maritime principality, which together have an annual revenue of 2000 in pure silver.

Louis King of Hungary, John of Bohemia, Charles Margrave of Moravia and numerous others assemble in Prussia to implement plans for an expedition against the barbarians. When the Master, Luther König, sees what a powerful force he has assembled, he sends word to the Livonian Master that he need not hesitate to march into Samogitia, where the tribes have reneged their Faith and even murdered their governors and all Christians living among them. When the Livonian Master arrives, the Prussian Master and the King march into Lithuania to destroy it. While their lands are thus being devastated, the Lithuanians themselves have invaded Sambia with their total strength; so, when they learn of this, Master Luther and the kings abandon the destruction of Lithuania in order to try and engage the Lithuanians on their way back. The Lithuanians, however, having devastated Sambia and collected considerable booty, move on into Samogitia, which they find defenceless and so plunder and destroy it too, before returning home, having suffered few, if any losses. This reversal of fortune so depresses the King and the others, that they lay the blame on the Master and accuse him of giving them bad advice and shaming them. Luther takes this very much to heart and becomes deranged. When, some years later, he has still not recovered, he resigns his post and is succeeded by Henry Dusemer.

Siemowit Duke of Mazovia and Sochaczew dies.

A.D. 1344

With the King warring in Żagań and not attending to public affairs, some of the Ruthenian nobility who hate Polish rule and the King himself, start secretly meeting to discuss ways and means of casting off the yoke so recently imposed on them and which, they fear, will eventually lead to the destruction of their schismatic faith. However, they can devise no sure way of achieving what they want. They know that they have been considerably weakened, for many of them have been rebaptized and received into the Roman Catholic Church. Many, too, have fought on the King's side. Many, especially those who have adopted the Catholic faith, have been given official posts and honours, thus it is certain that not all of them can be induced to rebel. Two of the more important, however, do prepare to fight: Daszko, starosta of Przemyśl, and Daniel of Ostrów, and there are some others. Secretly they send to the Tatar khan to tell him that the King of Poland has recently seized Ruthenian territory, which has been paying tribute to the Tatars, and has subjected it to his rule and appropriated all the tribute from it that is normally paid to the Tatars. They suggest that the Khan should not allow this to continue and that he should march into Ruthenia as soon as possible, at which moment those still loyal to the Khan will help him throw off the Polish yoke. The Khan's reply is to send a force with orders to plunder in Poland and restore his authority over Ruthenia. Casimir, is justifiably dismayed by the news of this unexpected war he has on his hands, as well as by what he is told of the size and strength of the Tatar army with its reinforcement of Ruthenian rebels, however, he realizes that he must respond, and so he urgently summons forces from all his territories and leads them against the enemy. Reaching the Vistula, he pitches camp on the near bank with the intention of doing no more than prevent the enemy crossing, thus avoiding a pitched battle. However, when he realizes that he is in a superior position, he decides not to let the opportunity pass, but to take the offensive. What the King foresaw, happens: the Tatar/Ruthenian force is intending to cross the river in the Tatar way, which is for each man to hang on to his horse's tail as it swims across, but when they see that the far bank is full of armed men and cavalry and that the

Poles are prepared to fight, they abandon the attempt. So, for several days, the two armies face each other across the river, firing at one another with bow, crossbow and siege cannon, though to very little effect. Then, realizing that they are not going to be able to cross, the Tatars return the way they came, plundering as they go.

John King of Bohemia, long nettled by Bishop Nanker's reproach that he had to have himself anointed and crowned by foreign bishops, because Bohemia did not have a metropolitan bishopric, with the support of Philip of France, persuades Pope Clement VI to elevate Prague cathedral to the dignity of a metropolitan cathedral, having hitherto been a suffragan of the Archbishop of Mainz; while the church at Litoměřice, which used to be a monastery church dedicated to the use of the monks of St. Benedict, becomes a cathedral church; thus the cathedral in Prague can never again be ridiculed for not having a suffragan.

A.D. 1345

King Casimir now finds himself involved in hostilities against the King of Bohemia. King John has always suffered from weak eyes (a delicate organ) and now has become completely blind, earning himself the nickname of "the Blind". He still feels aggrieved and shamed by the way Casimir reduced to ashes the province of Żagań, which he maintains was a fief of Bohemia, thus depriving the Duke of Żagań of the town and district of Wschowa, while he, King John, has failed to persuade Bolesław of Świdnica to submit and pay homage to the crown of Bohemia; so, on July 12, King John invades Poland with a huge force of Czechs, Germans and Silesians. He is so eager to destroy Poland that he would be quite prepared to die, could he but pitch camp outside Cracow and with his blind man's hand touch that city's wall and ensure its destruction. Three days and nights after invading through Opava, Cieszyn and Oswięcim, the army is encamped outside Cracow, plundering and burning everything on its route from Silesia. The army which Casimir has assembled to resist the Czechs is kept inside the castles and fortresses cunningly awaiting an opportunity to attack. King John, being repulsed from Cracow, divides his great army in two, and, himself heading for Bohemia with a handful of men, sends one part towards Lelów, and the other towards Olkusz, to wreak as much havoc and destruction as each can. Learning of this, the Poles set off in pursuit and catch up with one force at Pogoń and with the other at Biała, two miles away, and then attack them both in the rear. They have no difficulty in crushing the cream of Czech chivalry in a sudden assault, whereupon the front ranks take fright and scatter in flight. There is considerable slaughter and many prisoners are taken. King John, having taken a different direction, avoids the danger, but quickly learns of the disaster and returns to Bohemia, saddened and depressed. The Poles gather up the Czechs' discarded weapons and collect their entire train. Casimir generously rewards those knights who have distinguished themselves by their bravery.

Early in March, the Master of the Teutonic Knights, some Hungarian and Czech knights, the Margrave of Holand and a number of German counts and knights, organize an expedition into Lithuania. But the Lithuanians shut themselves up in their forts and fortresses and the Knights, though well provisioned and supplied, after doing considerable damage, are forced by a thaw and the quagginess of the ground to withdraw, having achieved little of note.

Andrew, brother of King Louis, is summoned to Sicily by Robert, King of Sicily, there to marry one of his son, Charles's, daughters, Joanna, sister of Philip of France, so that the succession to the throne of Sicily should remain in the family of France. For this he needs and has a dispensation from the Pope. For two years the two live together and Joanna produces a son, Jan, yet in a fit of wickedness, Joanna puts a silken cord round her husband's neck while he is asleep, strangles him and throws his body out of their bedroom window. King Louis, wishing to avenge his brother's shameful death, invades Sicily with a large army, pillages much of the country and captures several castles. Meanwhile, Joanna, unable to stand up to the King, has gone to France and there hides in a well-defended castle in Provence. It is said that Joanna perpetrated this monstrous crime because of her taste for harlotry, which she practiced with a certain knight, Louis of Taranto, whom she preferred to her husband and who escaped with her to France. When Louis of Hungary gets to Naples, he decides that the first thing he must do is to raise the siege of Caria Marina, then being besieged by the Venetians, but in this he fails and so really achieves nothing, whereupon he returns to Hungary.

A.D. 1346

John the Blind, considering himself shamed by the fact that the Duke Bolesław of Świdnica is the only one of the Silesian dukes not to have submitted to his rule, starts raiding and harassing the latter's lands. When Bolesław repulses these raiders, the King assembles a large force, marches on Świdnica and lays siege to it. Realizing that he is not going to be able to storm it, he raises the siege and withdraws. He then moves to Kamienna Góra, occupies it and installs a garrison, before returning to Bohemia. Bolesław has a number of waggons filled with soldiers driven towards Kamienna Góra. The soldiers of the garrison assume that the approaching waggons contain some sort of merchandize and so do nothing to stop them entering the town. The soldiers then jump out and take over the town. Half the Czech garrison is held prisoner, the other half is dismissed. Later, when John the Blind dies and Charles ascends the throne, he wins Bolesław over, not by force of arms, but by cunning moves and lavish gifts. On the death of his first wife, who came from France, he marries Bolesław's niece, Anna, only daughter of Henry of Jawor, making it a condition that on the death of Bolesław of Świdnica, who is childless, he is to have both duchies, Jawor and Świdnica, as his wife's dowry. Such an arrangement is detrimental to Bolesław' uncle, Bolesław of Ziębice, his son, Nicholas, the latter's two sons and three grandsons, in that it deprives them of all their rights of inheritance in these duchies. Nicholas, Bolesław's son, coming into his inheritance, sells the town of Frankenstein to the King of Bohemia and goes on a pilgrimage to the Holy Sepulchre, dying in Hungary on his way back. He had two sons, Bolesław and Henry: Henry joins the Teutonic Knights, while his brother dies in June 1412, leaving two sons and five daughters.

Waldemar, Margrave of Brandenburg, who was thought to have died twenty years earlier and to have been buried in Chorin, suddenly turns up claiming to have spent the intervening years as a wanderer and hermit, doing penance for having without dispensation taken as his wife a woman of the second degree of consanguinity. He claims the March of Brandenburg, now held by Ludwig Duke of Bavaria, son of the late Emperor. He finds many supporters, among them the dukes of Saxony and Mecklenburg, the Bishop of Magdeburg and others. I, myself, am convinced that his woes and misfortunes were Heaven's punishment for his having sold the Teutonic Knights the lands of Pomerania to which he had no right or title and which belonged to Poland.

John of Bohemia, wishing to help his relative, King Philip of France, against Edward, King of England, assembles a large force of Czechs and Germans and takes it to France, where he is joined by the King of Navarre and the King of Aragon and Majorca. There is a fierce battle in which the French, though superior in numbers, are defeated. When he sees what is happening, King John has himself led to where the enemy are clustered most thickly and where the fighting is fiercest, and flings himself into the fray. But when the King of France leaves the battle-field with his son and the King of Navarre, King John is found dead. His body is taken to Luxembourg and buried in the cathedral there. As he was killed on St. Rufus' Day, the Czechs have ever since considered this an unlucky day. In this battle, which is said to have lasted from the first hour of the day until four in the evening, 20,000 of the French horse and 40,000 of their foot, some fifty counts and dukes, are killed. The English lose 17,000 archers and ten knights. After the battle, the King of England behaves with great moderation, freeing all the prisoners who are Czechs, Germans, Spaniards and other foreigners. The ransom money he receives for his French prisoners, who are kept under harsh conditions, he uses to build some splendid castles in England.

During this winter, Henry Dusemer Master of the Teutonic Knights invades Lithuania and devastates it. His troops have orders to spare neither women nor children. Duke Olgierd's Lithuanian army has been reinforced by contingents from Smolensk, Polotsk and other parts of Ruthenia, and on the Feast of the Purification of the Blessed Virgin it engages the invaders in a battle, in which the Lithuanians and Ruthenians lose 18,000 of their men before they surrender, leaving the Knights to collect a considerable amount of loot. On their return to Prussia, the Knights celebrate their victory by founding and endowing a convent in Königsberg, as the Master had sworn to do before battle was engaged, should he be victorious. When summer comes, the Master assembles a fresh force and again raids Lithuania and lays siege to the castle at Wielona which surrenders. He burns the castle to the ground, ravages the surrounding area and returns to Prussia with his loot and prisoners. Then, learning that Duke Olgierd has a powerful army with which he intends to raid into Sambia, the Master assembles another force, reinforced with mercenaries, and moves into camp in the frontier area, where it keeps watch to prevent the country being laid waste by the barbarians. Later, bored and their morale low, the Knights strike camp, upon which the Lithuanian army makes an unexpected thrust into Sambia, rounds up several thousand Christians, men and women, and carries them off to servitude in Lithuania.

Pope Clement VI, aware that Ludwig of Bavaria, King of the Romans, is only pretending to submit to the penalties imposed on him and his predecessors, decides to take harsher measures in order to humiliate him. First, he authorizes the Electors to choose Charles, Margrave of Moravia and son of John the Blind of Bohemia, as King of the Romans. Then, in the same year, thanks to pressure from the King of France, whose daughter Blanche has married Margrave Charles, he crowns this Charles King of the Romans in Avignon. His coronation gives rise to a fierce war betwen the two competitors for the imperial throne, a war that is to shake all Germany.

A.D. 1347

King Casimir wishes to end the abuses from which the entire kingdom has suffered under all his predecessors and which have made it difficult to dispense justice and settle disputes, since the provincial courts have been basing their decisions not on a written constitution or laws, but, having heard the evidence, have let personal feelings guide their verdicts and allowed justice to be tempered by personal sympathies or even by bribery. Because of this the King decides to make justice uniform throughout the kingdom by having identical, just laws that will apply to everyone, for he knows that it is not the rich or the nobility who have suffered from the cheating and false witness so prevalent in the courts, but the poor and those of low estate, even when they have had a sound case. He knows, too, how often different judgments have been pronounced on one and the same case according to the prejudices of the members of the tribunals, and that in almost all courts, initial judgments have been overturned and completely contradictory ones substituted. As a result, the princely or royal tribunals have been overburdened with endless appeals; but even these the poor have been unable to make, because they do not have the means and because access to the higher courts is made too difficult. There are other abuses, too, for often those who win and those who lose are both made to pay high fees to the King or Prince for judgment to be given and the sentence to be executed, with further sums having to be paid to the voivode, castellan and judge, while all members of the court down to the usher, also expect to be paid. There is, too, the barbarous custom, one of which even the Scythians have not heard, that has been the cause of so much injustice, namely that whereby the wording of the oath to be taken is presented to the plaintiff and witnesses in writing and this they have to read and repeat in Polish. If, in doing this, the reader makes a mistake or changes a word, even if the one he uses has exactly the same meaning, or if he hesitates, mispronounces or shortens a word, his case, however important, right and just, is endangered or fails altogether. If he speaks badly, incorrectly or in a whisper, he risks being convicted, as though he were guilty. Such courts, in which the innocent are condemned, not for lack of evidence nor because their case is unjust, but because of ignorance or a quavering voice, while the wrong-doer and guilty party obtains all the benefit of the offence he has committed and for which he should be severely punished, these cannot be called Courts of Justice.

The King convenes a general assembly in Wiślica on Laetare Sunday. This is attended by all the bishops of the kingdom, its voivodes, castellans, officials and eminent personages. The King presides and has with him experts in canon and civil law. The assembly then sets about organizing Polish law, writing it all down and publishing it. It confirms the provincial land laws, which are to be permanent and unalterable, so that none can abolish, change or repeal them. All are written down in clear, simple language, so that their meaning cannot be cleverly twisted or distorted.

Various confused enactments of his predecessors are carefully corrected and clauses that have been overlooked, are added, while many that are unnecessary are removed. The King issues a special enactment with orders that, after the old courts which caused such confusion in the affairs of the kingdom and in the administration of justice, have been abolished, all courts of justice, however small or large, and their judges, whatever position they hold and from whatever station they come, are to conduct their cases solely in accordance with the written, published laws and to give their verdicts accordingly; also, that everyone, even the poor and those of humble origin, are to be free to appeal to the written law, if they fear that they have been given an unjust verdict not based on the statutes, and, by thus appealing, can delay execution of the verdict until the statute book has been scrutinized.

Over the years, the towns and settlements of the kingdom of Poland have acquired a large proportion of German and other foreign inhabitants, and, as a result, Polish manners have become gentler, more honest and more moderate. Thus does the King guide his people of the Catholic confession, but of barbarous customs and behaviour, to live honest lives in accordance with their religion. King Casimir is the first giver of just laws in Poland and deserves the honourable soubriquet "Great" of which none of his successors can deprive him or the years efface.

King Louis of Hungary assembles a powerful army in order to avenge the murder of his brother, Andrew. He concludes treaties of friendship with the Italian princes of Verona, Ferrara and the Romagna, which allow him to march through their territory and so into Naples, which he puts to fire and the sword. In Sicily, most of the nobility and all its towns surrender in condemnation of the crime committed by Queen Joanna, who has sought refuge in Narbonne with her second husband, Louis. King Louis executes or confiscates the property of those responsible for killing his brother, and proceeds to rule Sicily. After some months, however, a legate comes from Pope Clement VI with orders to Louis to patch up the quarrel, with the stipulation that Joanna is to regain the kingdom. Louis considers that it would be disgraceful for him to oppose an arrangement made by the Holy See and feels compelled to leave Sicily, all the more so as he learns that a mortal plague has come to Naples, and so he returns to Hungary taking his nephew John, the child of Andrew and Joanna, with him. John dies only a few days after their arrival in Hungary.

Thus is Joanna restored to the throne of Sicily, thanks to the intervention of the Holy See. With the Hungarians gone, she rules successfully and in perfect peace to the end of her days, her feminine judgment ensuring that no king ever made his kingdom flourish more.

A.D. 1348

Henry Dusemer, Master of the Teutonic Knights in Prussia, dies after only five years in office and is replaced by Winrich of Kniprode, who, wishing to start his period of office in a blaze of glory, invades Lithuania and puts the district of Postów to fire and the sword. He had intended to go further, but incessant rain prevents him and he returns to Prussia with his captives and plunder. Hard on his heels comes Duke Olgierd and his two brothers, who, since the Catholic army has been disbanded, are able to plunder and burn more or less with impunity. They return to Lithuania with some 700 Christian captives. The Duke of Smolensk, with a force of Lithuanians and Ruthenians, attacks Labiawa but is defeated by the commander. While fleeing the duke is drowned in the river but his body is recognized and sent to the Lithuanian fort of Wielona where it is cremated.

The Great Plague has now reached Poland and its neighbours: Hungary, Bohemia, Denmark, France, Germany and almost every kingdom, Christian or heathen, causing dreadful mortality. It is said to have been caused by the Jews poisoning the air, so in many places these are beaten, burned, even hanged. Some, to escape the clutches of the Christians, kill themselves, their wives, sons, daughters and near relatives. In some provinces and towns, however, they are able to buy their freedom. The plague begins in January and lasts for seven months. It comes in two waves, the first lasting two months and characterized by constant fever and spitting of blood, those affected dying within three days. The second wave lasts five months and again the symptoms are continual fever, but with tumours and abscesses, particularly on the external parts of the body, usually in the arm-pits and on the genitals, causing death within five days. Both forms are so infectious that infection occurs not only by touch or by inhalation, but by just looking. Frightened parents refuse to tend their children; children avoid caring for their parents. There is no hope. The plague rages from east to west, affecting almost the entire world, which it leaves with a quarter of its previous population.

Louis, King of the Romans, dies a few days after being thrown by his horse, when it stumbled during a hunt, though some think that he was poisoned by a certain duchess. Charles King of Bohemia is elected to replace him, yet some of the electors, including those who elected Louis, elect Gunther, Count of Schwarzburg; thus the conflict between Louis and Charles, which was thought to have been extinguished by the death of Louis, flares up again, and both sides prepare for war. Meanwhile, however, Gunther dies, so Charles quietly occupies the imperial throne after buying the consent of those electors whom he knows to be particularly hostile to him.

A.D. 1349

King Casimir invades the remaining parts of Ruthenia not already under his rule. First, he attacks Łuck, now occupied by Gedymin's son, Lubart, who expelled the ancient Ruthenian princes, and lays siege to it and also to Vladimir, which he captures. He then moves on to Brześć and within a few days has captured its castle and the whole surrounding area. The other fortresses, which are not so strong, surrender voluntarily, and the King advances on Chełm and captures the castle there by keeping up a constant bombardment with heavy catapults. He obtains a considerable amount of goods and valuables. Chełm castle captured, all the others surrender. Casimir, mollified by the pleas of some of the Ruthenian dukes (there were many of them in those days), takes them into favour as his lieges and, after receiving their oaths of allegiance and homage, returns to them all the lands to which, according to witnesses, they were entitled. He installs Polish starostas in the chief castles and, having made all necessary arrangements, returns to Poland in a triumphant cavalcade, headed by a squadron of knights driving their captives ahead of them.

Many people are amazed and delighted that their king has so quickly and easily reunited three such excellent territories with their country, and are full of hope for similar successes in the future. These hopes, however, are soon dashed, for the King, as is natural and almost usual in those who have triumphed, becomes conceited and arrogant. The modesty that previously had been characteristic, deserts him and he indulges in wild debauchery to such an extent that it is not long before people have all but forgotten his former achievements. He despises his wife and, in complete disregard of marital probity, openly lives with concubines, whom he houses in abodes of shame in Opoczno, Czchów, Krzeczów and many other places. Reprimanded by his bishops, and, finally, by

Pope Clement VI himself, who enjoins him to dismiss all his concubines and in future live abstemiously in the bonds of marriage, he refuses to alter his ways. Indeed, he even attacks the privileges of the Church, trying through Otto of Pilcza the voivode and starosta of Sandomierz to compel Złota a village belonging to the Bishop to pay tribute and husbandry service to the King. Bishop Bodzęta of Cracow is unable to stomach this and imposes ecclesiastical sanctions, first on the voivode and, when he proves obdurate, on the King himself. Acting on the Bishop's orders, Martin Baryczka, priest of Cracow and vicar-general courageously confronts the King and, after admonishing him personally, excommunicates him and places a ban on him. The King is furious, dismisses Martin, hurling abuse at him, but does not actually lay hands on him. Later, encouraged, indeed incited by his courtiers, who insist that anyone who dares threaten the King, deserves to die, the King agrees to a dreadful crime: he has the vicar-general arrested on St. Lucy's day and the next night has him drowned in the river Vistula. No one wonders that God, being just, should now abhor the King and his family, oppose him and allow none of his lineage to survive.

On January 24, Henry Master of the Knights in Prussia invades Lithuania with 40,000 men-at-arms who have come from France and England and puts it to fire and the sword, sparing neither sex nor age. As he is withdrawing, burdened with loot, Duke Kiejstut of Lithuania, with a force of Lithuanians and Ruthenians, engages him in battle. There is slaughter on both sides: the Lithuanians lose 18,000 men and the Order's losses include Gerhard of Steegen commander of Gdańsk, the commander of Golub, six brothers of the Order, fifty of its knights and very many of its cavalry and infantry.

The plague returns to Poland, killing many in all stations of life. There being no other remedy, people turn to the practice of their religion, convinced that their misfortunes are due to God's anger at their sinfulness. Some start scourging themselves and others do all sorts of penances, until finally God takes pity on them and removes the plague, ending its dreadful slaughter.

A.D. 1350

God is punishing the Polish people for the murder of Martin Baryczka, vicar-general of Cracow. Poland's oldest enemy, the Lithuanians, putting their trust not in bows and arrows or swords and open fighting, but in secret, cunning incursions and swift withdrawal with their booty, organize a number of sudden raids into Polish territory throughout the summer and the following winter. First it is Łuków, then Radom, then Sandomierz. They slaughter, rape and plunder, and return to their own country with their booty of men, women and cattle. These raids cause grievous loss and damage to the kingdom and leave the common people frightened and apprehensive. On several occasions, the Polish knights and nobles assemble a force of cavalry and foot and engage the Lithuanians in an attempt to recover the captives, who are their peasants, friends and children. God does not grant them victory, for it is the Poles who run, leaving the Lithuanians victorious, though victory costs them much blood. The fact is, that whatever the King does, turns against him or comes to naught.

Louis King of Hungary, unable to forget the murder of his brother, prepares an expedition against the Queen of Sicily. He embarks an army of his own people and some mercenaries on the Dalmatian coast and sails to Naples, captures its castle and destroys the city. Then the Pope intervenes. This angers Louis, but he contains his anger and goes peaceably to Rome, where he is received with due honour, and from there returns to Hungary. However, he is unable to leave matters alone, and sends Charles, son of Robert, with a force back to Naples to demand that Joanna be punished for murdering her husband. Charles crushes Joanna's army, occupies Naples and subdues the kingdom of Sicily, besieging Joanna in Castro Nuovo. But, when Louis of Anjou comes with a large force to free her, and the Pope pleads that no Frankish blood be spilled, he abandons the siege. A little later, Charles, Duke of Durazzo, encouraged and reinforced by Pope Urban (because of whose stupidity, not to say, craziness, the Church is rent by schism) having defeated the Queen's army in battle, suffocates the ageing Joanna by holding a pillow over her face.

Charles, King of the Romans and Margrave of Moravia, son of John the Blind of Bohemia and successor to the throne of Bohemia both by natural law and with the agreement and support of the Bohemian prelates and barons is, in Prague cathedral, anointed and crowned by Arnestus the first Archbishop of Prague, and his wife Blanche, daughter of the King of France, is crowned queen.

A.D. 1351

The Dukes of Lithuania long able to raid and ravage Polish territory with impunity, arrogantly decide to go further, and, with a force of Lithuanians, Tatars, Ruthenians and men recruited from among their captives, advance on Lwów. However, they make no attempt to attack the city or castle, which Casimir has greatly strengthened with high walls and deep ditches, but devastate the surrounding country, its villages and lesser towns, murdering some of the populace, taking others into captivity, and burning everything they can. They then move on to Bełz and, having captured the castle there, continue into Vladimir and Brześć, which they repeatedly assault and, as Casimir goes to neither's help, both are captured and detached from the kingdom of Poland. The Dukes have thus made themselves lords and masters of four very fertile areas: Bełz, Vladimir, Chełm and Brześć, the possession of the latter, which Casimir has been strengthening with walls of fired brick, giving them an open gateway into Poland. Before this, access to Poland had been difficult and dangerous and the Lithuanians had often suffered defeat here or nearby and so been forced to abandon the booty they had collected. Brześć castle is excellently sited, being protected by Nature with extensive bogs and quagmires as well as by the River Bug, in which there are few fords, so that Brześć can be regarded as the port and gateway into Ruthenia. In the end, Casimir, having received reinforcements from Louis of Hungary, organizes a huge operation against the Lithuanians, in which he recovers Vladimir and its fort. In one engagement he massacres the Lithuanians and captures their grand-duke, Kiejstut, from whom he extracts a promise that he with all his brothers, the Lithuanian dukes and all their subjects will embrace Christianity and receive baptism. After this, Kiejstut is treated with every honour, but he fraudulently breaks his promise and one night escapes.

At this time, when God is still punishing the Poles for their crimes, there are plenty of good-for-nothing Poles ready to turn bandit or traitor. Many of these have entered into close, even intimate relations with the heathen Lithuanians, whom, for filthy lucre they will guide through forest, bog, marsh and river, enabling them to make unexpected raids into Poland. Two of the worst of these renegades are Peter Pszonka of Babin and Otto of Szczekarzowice, who, on several occasions, have acted as guides, never worrying about the cruelty with which the Lithuanians have treated their compatriots, but driven by their desire for gold and the gifts they get from the Lithuanians, who also leave the villages and possessions of the two untouched. Now, it seems, God can no longer countenance their shameful behaviour: for, on their next reconnoitre they find the river in full flood; however, with considerable difficulty they find a new ford not far from the town of Zawichost and mark it with the usual tall rods thrust deep into the river's bed. They then go to the Lithuanians and tell them that they can cross safely at the place they have marked. Some local fishermen notice the rods and, guessing their purpose, move them to where the river is much deeper. The next raiding party of Lithuanians led by dukes Jagiello and Skirgiello finds the rods and plunges in with the result that hundreds are drowned. The Lithuanians think that Peter and Otto have double-crossed them, accuse them of treason, and behead them on the river's bank.

Bolesław son of Wanko, Duke of Mazovia and Płock, dies on August 12.

Many Hungarians, afraid of the deadly plague that has again broken out in their country, seek refuge in Poland. They march along in a procession headed by banners; at every church they come across, they halt and go in. Their bodies are bared to the navel. They scourge themselves with twigs and branches until they draw blood; and, as they go, sing a crude, melancholy song. At first, the bishops of the Polish church regard them with indulgence, for they seem to be acting in accordance with some pious principle; but when they discover that this sect has been condemned for various heresies, especially that of granting each other absolution, even for grievous sins and forbidden physical delights (many of their women prove to be pregnant), they expel the sect from Poland.

A.D. 1352

King Casimir is anxious to be given absolution for his murder of Martin Baryczka, priest of Cracow cathedral, and so sends the Chancellor of Dobrzyń to the Pope in Avignon to tell him that King Casimir frankly admits his guilt and is ready to do whatever penance the Holy See sees fit to impose; and further to prevent the severance of Wrocław cathedral from the metropolitan of Gniezno and its subjection to the archbishop of Prague, which the King of Bohemia, who is also King of the Romans, has been trying to engineer through special envoys. The Pope listens to the Poles graciously and grants the King absolution. As to penance: he is to return all the villages belonging to Cracow cathedral; he is to rebuild the church in Wiślica using dressed stone, and he must rebuild five other churches, that of the Blessed Virgin in Sandomierz and those in Stobnica, Szydłów, Zagość and Kargów. The envoys also obtain the Pope's permission for all Polish clergy to remit their tithes for four years in favour of the King, so as to help him deal with the sudden raids by the Lithuanians from which the country has suffered so greatly. The Pope further refuses to allow Wrocław cathedral to be detached from the body of the metropolitan church of Gniezno.

King Casimir now repeals the prohibition of carting sheaf-tithes to the clergy's barns, which he himself had imposed, and rules that all peasants and colonists have an age-old duty to cart sheaf-tithes to the places designated by those who possess the tithes.

For the last sixteen years the Duke of Legnica has had an interdict imposed on him and his duchy for his seizure of Church property; now, enfeebled by gluttony and excessive drinking, and realizing that he is approaching the end of his life (he is over sixty), he has started pleading with his sons to have this interdict lifted. So, while the younger son remains at his bedside, the elder, Wacław, pleads with the bishop and chapter of Wrocław, promising that he and his brother will return everything their father has appropriated. This results in two of the Wrocław canons being sent to Brzeg with powers to grant absolution to the Duke and remove the interdict. The delighted Duke gives thanks to God and, after receiving the sacraments, dies the following day, April 21.

A Tatar horde brought in by Olgierd, Grand-duke of Lithuania, devastates Podole, which belongs to Poland. Olgierd's main grievance is that, on the death of Bolesław son of Troyden of Mazovia, Casimir took possession of the entire territory of Lwów. This same Olgierd is the father of the future King of Poland, Władysław II, who, as long as he remained a pagan, bore the name: Jagiełło.

A.D. 1353

The Lithuanian dukes Olgierd, Kiejstut and Skirgiełło are incensed at the way Casimir and his nephew, King Louis of Hungary, have together devastated Ruthenia and brought the lands of Vladimir back under Casimir's dominion, and are wondering how to avenge themselves. So, on July 7, Duke Lubart with the largest force he can muster steals upon Halicz as quietly as he can, and occupies the town, which belongs to the King of Poland, thus deceitfully breaking the armistice arranged between him and the King. He proceeds to murder most of the burghers and merchants, and then sets about killing the women and children, as is the Lithuanian way. Then, not daring to remain where they are, the Lithuanians set fire to the town and withdraw to their own country with the loot, which they there store in their castles, fortresses and barns.

Again, on August 9, Lubart raids Zawichost with an even larger force and devastates more than sixteen square miles. Before the Poles have time to arm themselves, the raiders have carried their loot back to their forest hide-outs. Now, to stop the Lithuanians raiding the rest of the country, King Casimir fortifies the town and castle of Płock with a wall of fired bricks.

The three dukes of Lithuania now invade Prussia, hoping to avenge the disaster inflicted on them at Labiawa. They meet with no opposition as they spread devastation and return to Lithuania with a number of captives, including 500 of the nobles.

On June 20, having the consent of the Pope, Louis of Hungary marries Elizabeth, the pretty unmarried daughter of Stephen, King of Bosnia. The wedding is celebrated in Buda, as is usual. The bride's mother is Elizabeth, daughter of Casimir duke of Gniewkowo, cousin of the Elder Elizabeth, Queen of Hungary, and thus in the fourth degree of consanguinity with her husband.

On the Saturday before Whitsun, the country witnesses a phenomenon never previously recorded: March, April and the greater part of May have been fine and warm and the grain has put out stems and heads, indicative of a good harvest; suddenly, it turns very cold and the earth is gripped by severe frost. When this relaxes somewhat, there is a sudden tremendous fall of snow which lies two ells deep, covering everything and frightening everyone, especially the farmers. This snow lies for six days and the farmers are afraid that its weight may break the stalks of the grain. Not only does it not do that, but, as it melts, like a beneficial dew, it waters and revives the crops better than could have been done by manuring, and thus produces a bumper harvest.

A.D. 1354

Four of the Lithuanian dukes, Olgierd, Kiejstut, Patrykij and Skiegiełło, assemble as large a force as they can muster and raid the area round Barczewo. As no one dares to stand up to them, they murder and burn and return home with their booty, which includes cattle and captives of both sexes.

A.D. 1355

The old quarrel between King Casimir and Siemowit Duke of Mazovia flares up again. Casimir insists that Siemovit pay him homage for his lands and sign an official document accepting that he has, holds and possesses his lands and title under feudal law, and this the latter has refused to do. Casimir is afraid lest Siemowit follow the example of the Silesian dukes and do homage to another king, especially to the King of Bohemia, so he resorts to harsher measures and takes possession of the castles and towns of Płock and Rawa, both the personal property of the dukes of Mazovia. These he now treats as his property, as having come to him under escheat on the death of Casimir of Mazovia, who died without progeny. The old duke had provided both castles with stout walls and granted the towns a number of freedoms and privileges, so that the nobles and knights all praised him and his impartial justice.

Siemowit follows the dictates of common-sense and abandons his previous resistance—he used to consider it shameful for any member of his family to accept anyone as their feudal superior—and agrees to pay homage to Casimir and to receive his lands in fee. Kalisz is the place chosen for the ceremony and the day the Feast of St. John the Evangelist. The Duke duly arrives accompanied by Nicholas Bishop of Płock and all the eminent persons of Mazovia, and so, on the third day after Christmas, he pays solemn homage to Casimir, who is in his regal robes and wearing his crown, and to the Kingdom of Poland, and in this he is joined by the Mazovian nobles and gentry. In accordance with custom, the Duke lays his standard, coat of arms and shield at the foot of the throne on which the King is seated, and then swears eternal loyalty and due obedience to the King as his sole, natural lord. He then signs an official document in which he asserts on his own behalf and that of his successors, that all the lands, duchies, provinces and parishes of Mazovia (Warsaw,

Sochaczew, Wiskitki, Ciechanów, Nowy Gród and Nowy Dwór, Czersk, Rawa and Liw, and Gostynin) he has and holds from King Casimir and the Kingdom of Poland in fief under feudal law. He promises and undertakes that in any misfortune, need or war he will stand on the side of King Casimir and the Kingdom of Poland with the afore mentioned lands and duchies in his possession or which he may acquire in the future, and that he will never abandon the King and Kingdom of Poland in any adversity. The castle of Płock is returned to the King for his lifetime but thereafter it is to be regranted in fee.

Charles, King of Bohemia and King of the Romans, after he has by skillful and sensible policies reconciled himself with the Italian rulers, with the assistance of the counts of Milan, marches into Italy with a large army of Czechs, Poles and Germans. He is warmly welcomed by all the cities and so reaches Rome, where, on the instructions of Pope Innocent VI, on Easter Day, the Cardinal of Ostia crowns him Emperor and his wife, Anna, Empress. He then progresses through a number of cities, wheedling out of them the taxes due to the Emperor, as well as gifts, so that he accumulates a considerable treasure, of which he gives several thousands of florins to his Austrian dukes, who are his relatives, to be used as dowries for their daughters.

King Casimir now finds it necessary to ask his nephew, Louis of Hungary, to give him an assurance that, when Casimir, who has no sons and is now old and near to death, dies and is succeded on the throne by Louis, in accordance with the pact made long before with King Charles and since renewed by King Louis, the latter will observe and retain in full all the privileges, freedoms and rights enjoyed by the prelates, dukes, barons, knights, nobles and citizens of the Kingdom of Poland, and, especially, that he will not burden Poland with dues, tribute and taxes, nor impose on the Church and laity costs of accommodation and board while he is travelling in the Kingdom through their lands, whether belonging to the Church or to lay persons, but will meet all such expenditure out of the royal revenues. Also, that should he, King Louis, or his nephew, Duke John, die without male progeny, the prelates, nobles and barons of Poland shall be released from all pacts, promises and homage paid to him and his brother, in anticipation of the death of King Casimir. After consulting his advisers, King Louis agrees that these requests are justified and accepts them in a special document.

Duke Casimir of Mazovia dies on November 26.

A.D. 1356

Having removed the injustices to which his knights and the nobility have been subjected, the King is now eager to put an end to the oppression of citizens, bailiffs and others due to the implementation of the Magdeburg Law, according to which all appeals, such as are frequent in country courts, have to be heard by the Supreme Tribunal in Magdeburg itself, whose judgments are final. This not only by-passes the King, but involves appellants in both expense and danger, and these the King wishes to see removed. So, he sets up a supreme court and tribunal of German law under a justice of his own choice, who is to be assisted by seven aldermen chosen by the councils of Cracow and certain adjacent towns, as well as by certain rural justices, all men well versed in the law, who are to be appointed whenever there is a vacancy due to death or absence abroad. This court is to act as the supreme tribunal of German law, dispensing justice and hearing appeals and publishing its verdicts. Should anyone consider a verdict unjust, he may appeal to the royal tribunal whose judgment is to be final. To encourage those serving on the supreme tribunal to accept the duty and be scrupulous and zealous in pronouncing judgment, they are granted various privileges and freedoms. Copies of the books containing the Law of Magdeburg are to be obtained and placed in the treasury in Cracow castle, which, too, is to be the seat of this supreme provincial high court of German law, instead of Magdeburg.

The escutcheons of some of those taking part in the crusade against Lithuania, A.D. 1355–1380. Part of a fresco in Königsberg Cathedral
—Archiwum Państwowe, Olsztyn.

King Casimir is now basking in the glow of his many virtues, justice and moderation, for he is renowned not only at home, but also among other nations, with the result that people, especially Germans to whom he grants special privileges and favours, are moving to Poland with their children and possessions to live there permanently. On the other hand, some of the nobles and gentry, whom he has stopped oppressing and robbing their own peasants, complain that he is too oppressive and hostile.

The King still has a taste for dissipation and debauchery and to satisfy this, as we have already mentioned, he keeps women of easy virtue in many places, having contemptuously discarded his own wife, Adelaide, who lives like an exile and slave in a castle built of rather lovely fired brick at Żarnowiec, seldom even seeing the King, though she is lavishly provided with everything she needs. She has suffered this humiliation for nearly thirteen years, but, now, unable any longer to endure the bodies of slatterns being preferred to her own, pure, honourable one, she sends letters and messengers to her father, Henry Landgrave of Hesse, asking him to rescue her and take her home. It is, of course, common knowledge that the King, despite the admonishments of his bishop and councillors, is becoming more and more dissolute. Though still retaining his concubines, he has entered into a relationship with a certain Czech noble woman of unusual beauty, whom he has brought from Prague, where he had recently been, spending longer time there than usual. He persuades her to share a dwelling and live with him, by marrying her in a ceremony celebrated by the Abbot of Tyniec, who dressed himself in bishop's robes, thus convincing the girl that he was the Bishop of Cracow.

The Landgrave of Hesse, moved by his daughter's appeals, goes to Poland and, without hindrance from the King or his officials, removes her with all her possessions and takes her back to Hesse, where she dies shortly afterwards.

When the King is told by one of the grooms that the Czech girl, whom he dearly loves and whose beauty has bewitched him, is bald and has the itch, he decides to see for himself, and, finding out that it is, indeed, so, summarily dismisses her and replaces her with a woman of Jewish extraction, Hester, another beauty. He has two sons by her, Niemierza and Pełka, and at her request signs a document granting all Jews living in the kingdom of Poland unusual freedoms and privileges, which seriously offend the majesty of God and whose stench endures to this day. (It has been alleged that this document was a forgery.) Pełka dies an early natural death; Niemierza is killed in a riot over his father's death. What is disgraceful and damnable is that the King allowed his daughters by this Jewess to be brought up in the Jewish faith!

On the Eve of the Feast of St. Agnes, the Lithuanians raid Prussia and for several days destroy and pillage at will; indeed, the destruction is so widespread that people consider that they must have ravaged almost the whole of Prussia, while the Knights did no more than guard their castles!

A.D. 1357

Wacław, eldest son of the recently defunct Duke of Brzeg and Legnica, Bolesław, has never got over the fact that, when their father's inheritance was divided among them, the youngest son, Ludwig, was given as his share Legnica and its lands, which, by comparison with what he, the eldest, received, Chojnów, Złotoryja and Lubin, are much more valuable, having become so by a new discovery of gold in the Legnica hills, the mining of which provides the duke with a revenue of 140 gold marks a week which he receives from of his share and from tithes. So, now, spurred on by envy and claiming to have been cheated, Wacław picks a quarrel with this brother in the hope of, perhaps, being able to force him to accept a new division of the inheritance, which would be more to Wacław's advantage. When his brother, after listening patiently to Wacław's argument, refuses to contemplate such a step, Wacław comes to hate him, and goes to Charles Margrave of Moravia and proposes to sell him his entire inheritance, so as to prevent it going to his younger brother when he dies, for at the time Wacław is childless. The Margrave does not reject the proposal, but postpones signing any document to a more appropriate time; so Wacław returns home and proceeds to raid and plunder his brother's lands. The knights and barons of both sides are eager to put an end to the dispute, and, to ensure that Ludwig and his surviving sons, born him by the daughter of the Duke of Głogów and Żagan, should not be disinherited by the sale of Wacław's inheritance; they pretend that Wacław is weak and near to death. and so persuade Ludwig to relinquish his share and exchange it for Wacław's, the argument being that on Wacław's presumed imminent death, both shares will be Ludwig's.

So, it is arranged: Ludwig keeps Legnica and Wacław Chojnów, the condition being that on Wacław's death, even if he then should have children, Ludwig is to have both duchies for the rest of his life; also that during Wacław's lifetime his sons are not to receive any part, but on his death, the whole is to be divided up again, but equally between them. This arrangement having been signed and sworn, Ludwig falls into poverty. He is forced to establish his ducal capital in the village of Bukowiec, for there is no castle in which he can dwell; indeed, he has great difficulty in maintaining a ducal establishment on an annual income of no more than 400 marks, that being his share. Wacław, however, now becomes brave, rather than timid; healthy instead of weakly, and takes to making lavish gifts and throwing his money about, so that in a short time he is again reduced to penury, for even a gold mine cannot sustain such a prodigal life-style. (The vein runs out eight years after its discovery, so that in the end Wacław is unable to afford even the most modest expenditure and often goes hungry.)

King Casimir learns of the death of his second wife, Adelaide, and marries yet again. His bride is Jadwiga, daughter of the Duke of Głogów.

King Casimir's daughter, Kinga, wife of the Duke of Saxony, dies on April 26.

Large numbers of knights from Franconia, England and Swabia, Eanas, the duke of Nuremberg being the most eminent, arrive in Prussia, come in answer to an appeal from the Order issued after the disaster the Knights suffered at the hands of the Lithuanians the previous year. Encouraged by these new arrivals, the Master Winrich announces an expedition against Lithuania, and so, with an army of his own and these foreign knights, whom he puts under the command of Siegfried of Dahenfeld, the Marshal of Prussia, he marches into Lithuania. The Lithuanians grant him no opportunity to fight a pitched battle, so he orders the peasantry to be treated with the utmost cruelty and their homes and villages to be destroyed, for most of them have gone into hiding in the forests, marshes and trackless wastes of their country. After sweeping through most of Lithuania, he returns home with a large number of captives and much booty, without having encountered any resistance whatever.

A.D. 1358

There is in Poland at this time a certain noble of good family and fortune, Matthew Borkowicz, whom the King had honoured by appointing him voivode of Poznań. Matthew has started giving shelter to the thieves and robbers he should have been punishing, and, laterly, has become the chief planner of their thefts and acts of brigandage. When he learns of this, the King first sends mild admonishments, and then threats, in response to which Matthew signs a document in which he officially undertakes to obey the King and desist from his nefarious practices, but, trusting to his family and position, he neglects to change his way of life. The King grows impatient with the number of complaints lodged against his voivode and orders Matthew, who has come to see him in Kalisz, to be arrested and condemns him to death for his crimes. So, Matthew is put in chains and sent to the castle at Olsztyn, where he is flung into a deep and horrible dungeon. The chosen method of execution is that of starvation, so he is given only a goblet of water and a truss of straw. This so infuriates Matthew that, as long as he can, he satisfies hunger by eating the flesh off his hands and elsewhere. The King is then told that Matthew's brother, John, the lord of Czacz, is intending to avenge the other's execution and is plotting rebellion, so he, too, is arrested and condemned to death. The King confiscates the two brothers' castles of Koźmin and Czacz, their lands and all their possessions, which he takes for himself. Some allege that the King punished Matthew so severely because he suspected him of having a romance with the Queen. It takes Matthew forty days to die. Until given the viaticum he cannot die, declaring that he deserved such agony. His son, afraid of reprisals, goes to Saxony and the Mark of Brandenburg. For a time he engages in clandestine plundering raids and arson in various parts of Poland, but when, during one such raid, he and his men are attacked by peasants, he is killed at Rozrażów, as he deserved to be.

On January 12, King Casimir, who was staying in Raciąz, manages to reconcile John Bishop of Poznań and Siemowit Duke of Mazovia and Warsaw, and arrange that the Duke and all his subjects in new lands and settlements are to pay tithes to the Bishop.

The King of Hungary and his wife, Elizabeth, have a daughter, Catherine. She survives only a couple of years.

A.D. 1359

Nobles and knights have been complaining insistently of being overburdened and oppressed by the bishop and clergy of Cracow, who have been enforcing too many laws, collecting too many tithes, hailing them before ecclesiastical courts and making them contribute to the rebuilding of Cracow cathedral, and so the King summons a general assembly to arrange compensation for any damage done and at the same time to put an end to the buying or making presents of tithes, as the same knights and nobles have been doing, a thing of which the Cracow clergy complain. In 1320, Bishop Nanker of Cracow, with the consent of the chapter, ruled that half the revenue from each vacant benefice, based on its value in the first year of its vacancy, was to be surrendered and used for building the cathedral, work on which had just begun. These payments continued until now, when nobles, knights and clergy all demanded their cancellation, as the cathedral has long since been completed. Jarosław Archbishop of Gniezno comes to Cracow to help decide this thorny question, and, together with the King, acts as arbitrator between the clergy and the nobility. The actions of both parties are regulated: half of the building payments are remitted and a thirty year exemption from tithe is granted by Bishop Bodzęta to the lands of Lublin, Sieciechów and Łuków so as to encourage resettlement after the recent devastation by Tatars and Lithuanians. The new arrangements are recorded in a formal document which all parties sign.

Stephen, Voivode of Moldavia, has died while among the Walachians, whose ancestors had been expelled from Italy, it is said they were the Volsci, and who, having cunningly squeezed out the former Ruthenian lords and settlers, as their numbers increased, adopted their faith and customs, thus making it easier for them to assume control. The voivode's death marks the start of a fierce struggle for the ducal throne between Stephen's two sons, Stephen and Peter. The younger of the two, Peter, has the support of the majority of the Walachians, because they consider him the more noble, and he also enjoys the support of the many Hungarians living in the country; so, having chased out his brothers and those boyars he has been unable to win over, he assumes control of Moldavia. His elder brother, afraid lest Peter take even more drastic action, escapes to the King of Poland, who has wealth and soldiers in plenty, and asks him to regain his duchy for him; promising that, if the King does this, he, Stephen, and his successors, his voivodes and boyars will for ever be loyal, obedient subjects of King Casimir and his successors.

The King's advisers recommend acceptance, so he gives Stephen an army of knights from Cracow, Sandomierz, Lublin and Ruthenia, with which to recover his duchy. The army sets out from Poland on the Feast of the Apostles St. Peter and St. Paul and at first enjoys success in a number of engagements and in some individual encounters, but it never comes to a pitched battle, for Peter realizes that that would be too dangerous. So, Peter has recourse to cunning. Between the upper reaches of the rivers Prut and Dniester is a huge expanse of forest, called Połoniny, all uncultivated, indeed uncultivable land, and this the Polish army now proposes to cross. Anticipating such a move, the Walachians cut the trees on either side of the path the Poles must take through the forest, but in such a way that each tree remains upright, though the slightest push will make it fall. The Walachian scouts camouflage themselves with sand and grass and watch the enemy advance and plunge in among the ravines in the forest. Once they are there, the Walachians give a push to the farthest trees, which falling like dominoes, knock down one after the other, breaking arms, legs and other parts of the body of the Poles and their horses, without even having to strike a blow. Those taken prisoner number only slightly more than those who are killed, and none escape, for most have had their horses killed or injured. The victors collect the enemy's weapons, garments and all sorts of supplies. Treachery may have played a part in this disaster. When King Casimir learns of it, he at once sends envoys to ransom the prisoners, and to this the Walachians readily agree, and so all are ransomed without the cost being too great. One of the ransomed was Zbigniew of Oleśnica, grandfather of the later cardinal and bishop of Cracow, who limped for the rest of his life because of a damaged shin.

A.D. 1360

Poland now suffers another and more grievous disaster, though one easier to bear, sent, perhaps, by God to punish mankind's many sins, or the result of some special juxtaposition of the stars, or other unknown cause, a plague-like epidemic which sweeps through almost every kingdom in the West, including Poland, Hungary and Bohemia. It is so severe in towns and villages that, in the course of six months, it kills the greater part of the population, whatever their station or sex. It is said that in the city of Cracow alone 20,000 people died and in the villages and settlements the mortality was such that the countryside became a virtual wilderness, in which there were not people enough to bury the dead. It started about St. Michael's Day and lasted until half way through the following year, by which time in many places only half the population remained. It differed from the earlier plague of twelve years before in that the latter's fatalities were mainly among the populace, but this time its victims are among the gentry and the well-to-do, who suffer the same fevers, abcesses, carbuncles and boils.

The arrival of the Margrave of Brandenburg with other knights from Germany encourages Winrich of Kniprode Master of the Teutonic Knights to organize an expedition against the Lithuanians. He appoints the Marshal, Schindekopf, to command the Order's own army and the pilgrims and he proceeds to put the country to fire and the sword and send back loot and captives. This is followed by a second expedition, despite the onset of winter, and this again by a third, with the result that Lithuania is virtually devastated. On this third expedition Duke Kiejstut himself is captured and exchanged for a large number of Catholics captured in Prussia.

A.D. 1361

At the instigation of Satan, the disastrous quarrel breaks out anew between Bodzęta Bishop of Cracow, the diocesan clergy, and the nobles and knights of Cracow, Sandomierz and Lublin. This concerns the lands ordinarily subject to the diocese, sheaf tithes and their late delivery, sale or theft, as well as the matter of grain grown in orchards so as to avoid tithes. The King, being guardian and defender of the Church, intervenes and calls on Jarosław Archbishop of Gniezno, who is making his visitation of the diocese, to settle the quarrel. Having listened to both sides, the Archbishop pronounces judgment on November 6: the theft of tithes is to be punished by excommunication of the owners of the villages concerned, and of their peasants if the guilty parties endure the Church's punishment for more than six months. Further, if a knight wishes to compound for tithe, he must make the contract and complete the purchase before the Feast of St. James, otherwise the tithes can be sold without hindrance to someone else. Grain of whatever kind is liable to tithes whether grown in an orchard or a field.

A Dominican, Brother Paul, while preaching in Polish in Cracow cathedral, denies that the Virgin Mary was conceived without original sin. He collapses and dies, before he has finished his sermon.

Charles, King of the Romans and of Bohemia, founds and endows a studium generale in Prague which Pope Innocent VI approves. It lasts barely fifty years before the plague of heresy destroys it.

King Casimir is eager to add to his country's glory by giving it an university such as other kingdoms have, so he sends to the Pope in Avignon asking for permission and this is granted. So, near Cracow, between the town of Kazimierz and the vill of Bawoł belonging to the chapter, on a site beside the town wall, measuring a thousand paces and more in either direction, he starts building a beautiful university. This is to have splendid buildings, chambers and lecture rooms, as well as many subsidiary buildings as dwellings for the doctors and magisters. However, building is interrupted by the death of the King and nothing comes of the project. Later, in 1478, Jan Długosz the Elder, canon of Cracow, with the assent of King Casimir III, but against the wishes of the local population, will try to found and build a Carthusian monastery on the vacant site, which the local population had long since cleared of its buildings and gardens and appropriated for its own purposes, claiming desuetude. Although Długosz pledges to maintain all their rights, they prevent the monastery being built.

On July 25 fire breaks out in Wrocław and, because the citizens are too lazy to extinguish it straight away, it spreads and becomes a blaze that no one can put out. Almost all the dwellings in the city are destroyed and the city itself reduced to ashes. The citizens vent their anger on the Jews, then quite numerous, and cruelly slaughter them, irrespective of age, sex or status, as if they had caused the fire, robbing them of their belongings and expelling the survivors from the city.

Winrich the Prussian Master realizes that Lithuania is essentially infertile, a place more of woods and forests than of towns and villages, and has been completely devastated by hostile raids, so he sends a force under Henry of Kranischfeld, the general commander, into the Ruthenian lands subject to the Lithuaninas to punish the Ruthenians for having given armed assistance to the Lithuanians. The part invaded being fertile, there is no lack of cattle and other loot; but the Master's plan is frustrated by continual rain which compels the Knights to withdraw. To avoid the appearance of having suffered a disaster, the army is diverted into Lithuania which it proceeds to ravage. However, three of the Lithuanian dukes, Olgierd, Kiejstut and Patrykig, approach by secret paths and fall upon the Knights, who have never expected to encounter that enemy. The Knights, being better armed and horsed and more numerous, are victorious, victory being made even sweeter by the capture of Kiejstut, who is unhorsed by Henry of Ekkersberg. Duke Petrykig is also unhorsed, but is rescued by his knights. Keijstut is sent to Malbork as a prize capture, put in chains and imprisoned in a strong fortress, where he endures captivity, but only for two years, after which he escapes thanks to a Lithuanian neophyte living in Malbork, who provides him with a white cloak with a black cross on it and also a horse. Thus disguised, Kiejstut fools everyone he meets, whether knights or ordinary people, and when he gets to a large area of forest, he abandons his horse and, in case of any pursuit, spends several days hiding in a bog. He then continues on foot and, travelling by night, reaches Mazovia, where he is recognized by his daughter, Anna, who is married to Duke Janusz. The latter is delighted to see his father-in-law, furnishes him with weapons and horses and sends him back to Lithuania, where he assembles an army with which to avenge his capture, marches into Prussia and lays siege to the castle at Johannesburg, which he captures and burns. He then advances on Jańsbork, which he captures along with its commander, and burns it. He then starts back home laden with immense booty, but two of the commanders of Rastenburg and Bartenstein pursue him, catch up with him and defeat him, thus recovering all the loot and the captives. In the fighting, Kiejstut is again unhorsed, but continues to fight most valiantly on foot, until he is wounded and taken prisoner. While being taken back to Prussia he is slackly guarded and again manages to hoodwink his guards and escape, and gets safely back to Lithuania.

King Casimir, eager to assist the spread of Christianity in the Ruthenian territory under his rule, obtains the permission of Pope Urban V to found an archbishopric in its capital, Lwów, and this he suitably endows. The relevant papal bull is sent to the Archbishop of Gniezno, who then goes in person to Lwów and elevates its parish church to metropolitan status.

A.D. 1362

The plague has receded and all domestic strife has been removed, but Poland suffers yet another disaster: crop failure and famine.

The grain sown before winter and in the spring has produced good heads auguring a good harvest, but, in the month of June, violent winds, torrential rain and thunderstorms flatten every stalk, knocking the swelling grains from the spikes and destroying them completely. The harvesters are left with nothing but empty ears and straw to reap, thus causing a serious famine in Poland and her neighbours. Over the years, the King has always made sure that the peasants and their dependents should till and crop their land, from which, each year, many thousands of stacks of different kinds of grain have been carted to his barns; now, seeing that his country and its neighbours are going hungry, he orders his full granaries to be opened and all who are faced with starvation supplied from them. The King's officials sell the grain at modest prices even to newcomers and peddlers. Those who have no money to pay for grain, are given it in return for work or something else. All over the country the King orders castles, towns and walls to be built, ponds, ditches and canals to be dug, so as to help meet the needs of artisans and villagers. People throng to do the work and so relieve their hunger. Even weak women, children and spent old men are ready to do far harder work than would seem appropriate to their age, just in order to get bread. All are given money for their work or, what is even more precious, grain. The King is lauded at home and abroad for his generosity and for the way in which the royal coffers are being filled with silver and gold from many places, as well as for the construction works he has instituted, the most famous of which, perhaps, is the canal from Cracow to Bochnia, which, filled from the Vistula, provides transport for timber and salt.

In the early spring, the Prussian Master, Winrich of Kniprode, lays siege to the castle at Kaunas. This was defended by walls and battlements as well as by its natural position, for it was washed by two considerable rivers, the Niemen and the Wilia. The Lithuanian dukes, Olgierd, Kiejstut and Patrykig, bring up an army to try and raise the siege, but, on the Wednesday before Reminiscere Sunday they are repulsed and have to withdraw. With them out of the way, the grip of the siege is tightened and the castle is assaulted day and night by relays of troops, and continuously bombarded by bombards and peppered with incendiary missiles, which do considerable damage. Wojdat, son of Kiejstut, commands the defence. Many Knights are killed when they venture close to the walls. Meanwhile, the Lithuanians, now reinforced, are camped on an eminence not far distant, from which they can see all that the Knights are doing, yet they dare not attack, for the besiegers are protected in the rear by a rampart and deep ditches filled with water brought by canal from the rivers. Then on the eve of Easter Sunday, the Lithuanians, watching from their eminence, see part of the castle wall, which has been undermined, fall, killing many of the Knights and opening a way into the castle, which is then captured and set on fire. Some 3000 are captured inside and most of these killed. Duke Kiejstut's son and thirty-six of the most eminent warriors are taken prisoner. On Ascension Day, Bartholomew Bishop of Sambia celebrates a solemn mass, and, the next day, the walls having been dismantled, everything is razed to the ground. The Knights then move off and advance on the fort at Pisten. Finding this abandoned, they set fire to it and advance on Wielona, which they storm after an assault lasting four days. They then demolish the castle and return to Malbork with 500 prisoners and booty.

Charles of Bohemia's second wife. Anna, dies and he marries a third time. This time his bride is Mecellina, a spinster from Bavaria. Charles' son, Václav, also marries. His bride is Joanna, daughter of the Duke of Bavaria. The Margrave of Moravia, Albert Soběslav, is another who marries, his bride being the granddaughter of Count Robert the Red, Palatine of Bavaria. These two marriages into the house of Bavaria were arranged in the hope that they would quench the fierce embers of hatred engendered when Charles was elected King of the Romans during the lifetime of Ludwig of Bavaria.

A.D. 1363

Envoys of Louis, King of Hungary, go to the Emperor Charles demanding satisfaction for his defamation of the King's mother, when in angrily replying to some Hungarian envoys come on quite different matters, he remarked that the King's mother was shameless. This provoked a reply in similar vein and the Hungarian envoys, far from overawed by the person of the Emperor, announced that they were prepared to fight, individually or collectively with the King or anyone else in defence of the honour of their King and his mother. Realizing that the anger of the Hungarians was justified, the officials tell them that the Emperor had spoken in jest, not seriously. The Hungarians reply that such dreadful words have to be atoned for with blood and penance done for them; also that it is not for them, but the King, to grant the Emperor forgiveness. And so they depart, having accentuated the quarrel they had set out to appease. Returning home, they tell the King all that has transpired. The King praises them for their loyalty and the way in which they defended his good name and that of his mother, and also for breaking off relations with the Emperor, and he makes them lavish presents. Not content with the envoys' verbal breaking-off of relations, he sends an official declaration of war to the Emperor. He then begins preparing an army, drawing troops from all his kingdoms and possessions and sending envoys to recruit reinforcements from neighbouring kings and princes. He sends first to his uncle, Casimir of Poland, begging him not to allow the insult to his sister, Queen Elizabeth, to go unavenged, but to bring his whole army and join Louis in waging war against the Emperor. On the advice of his prelates and nobles King Casimir promises not only to help with his own powerful army, which he will lead in person, but also with contingents of Lithuanians, Ruthenians and Tatars. Envoys from Hungary and Poland then go to Denmark, whose King, having heard the reasons for the war, pronounces himself ready to help with all his forces. (He is a relative of Bogusław Duke of Słupsk, son-in-law of King Casimir). When the Emperor learns that several countries are arming against him, he sends repeated letters and messengers to persuade and beg the Electors and the dukes of Germany and Austria to give him armed assistance. Each side uses bribery as well as persuasion to obtain the help of others, whether Catholics or heathens, so that it becomes almost a case of East and West being poised to fight a bitter war. Pope Urban, seeing so many kings angry with and hating each other, is eager to prevent the madness of a war and makes every effort to appease them. He sends a legate, John, a man of unusual common sense and profound learning, a member of the order of the Franciscans, to do whatever he can by honest means to stop these preparations for war. This legate goes first to the Emperor in Prague, then to the King of Hungary in Buda and, finally, to King Casimir in Cracow, telling each of them what the Holy Father recommends and trying to persuade them to stop this unjustified war. He promises that the Pope will give all the help he can to whichever side declines to go to war and does not refuse to make peace with the other. The Emperor, conscious that he has been the cause of it all and fearful lest the action of the Holy See turn the German princes against him, especially as they have repeatedly complained of being dragged into unjustified wars, promises to accept such conditions for peace as the papal legate dictates and to accept the authority of the Holy See in this matter.

Having achieved this, the legate makes repeated visits to King Louis and King Casimir begging them to swallow their anger over such a thoughtless, though insulting remark, for which the Emperor has promised to compensate them. When, finally, the two kings agree not to refuse reasonable, fair conditions, the legate turns marriage-broker and persuades the King of Hungary and the King of Poland to ensure lasting peace by marrying Elizabeth, daughter of the Duke of Słupsk and Casimir's grand-daughter, to Charles, King of the Romans, whose third wife, Mecelina, died shortly after their marriage. After consulting their prelates and nobles, the two kings come to an understanding and, to the glory of the Holy See, the peace of Christendom and the enhancement of the Catholic faith, agree to the proposed match. King Charles, who is father-in-law of the King of Hungary, whose first wife had been the latter's daughter by his first wife, Blanche, daughter of the King of France, cannot refuse to renew an old friendship, though it involves accepting as his son-in-law one who, up till then, had been his mortal enemy. A day during Carnival is chosen for the wedding, which is to be held in Cracow, an early date being favoured so that the war can be called off and an end put to all the suspicions attendant on it. Having arranged all this, the legate returns to Prague and informs King Charles of all that he has done to restore peace. The King cordially thanks God and the Pope to whom he sends envoys with personal letters telling him that he has laid down arms and is ready to obey all the recommendations and requests of the Holy See, and to make friends with the two kings who have been his enemies.

King Casimir, being grandfather of the bride, makes himself responsible for organizing her wedding. He sends special envoys to invite neighbouring kings and princes, especially Louis of Hungary, the King of Denmark, Peter of Cyprus, Otto of Bavaria, Dukes Siemowit of Mazovia, Bolesław of Świdnica and Władysław of Opole, and all the other Polish dukes. The King of Cyprus sails through the Black Sea to Walachia and thence overland through Ruthenia, being everywhere supplied with all his needs by Casimir's starostas. The King of Denmark similarly sails to the duchy of Słupsk and thence travels overland with his relative, Bogusław Duke of Słupsk, and the bride to Cracow, again at the expense of King Casimir. The King of Hungary, who has the shortest distance to cover, travels via Sącz and Bochnia with a considerable retinue. Charles King of the Romans and of Bohemia comes through Silesia and is received in Bytom by officials sent by King Casimir; he and all accompanying him again being provided with all their requirements by the King. The four kings already there (Hungary, Poland, Denmark and Cyprus) come out a mile to meet him. When Charles learns what they are doing, he dismounts and with his retinue walks the remaining distance to meet the four, who are preceded by a large contingent of cavalry. When the four kings are told what Charles is doing, they, too, dismount and walk towards him. Meeting, they shake his right hand to the accompaniment of tears, hugs and kisses in the presence of the papal legate.

The greetings over, they all remount and ride back and into the city, where young Elizabeth and her father, with a numerous retinue of girls, receives them with regal pomp. Then comes a procession of representatives of all the city churches and estates, which lasts until evening. The kings are given bedrooms and special apartments in the castle itself. These have purple hangings, carpets, gold, scarlet and precious stones. The others and their servants are lodged in inns and provided with everything they may need for their comfort. Each of these noble guests has a steward attached to him, one of the barons or nobility, whose duty it is to serve him and help him. Everyone has to obey Wierzynek, a councillor of Cracow, who has charge of the royal palace and is responsible for all the servants of the Court. He, too, is the one who receives and spends the royal revenues, controls expenditure and has charge of all the royal possessions. He also takes part in all councils, manages them and has the deciding vote. To him alone, the King has entrusted the care and organization of everything, as was necessary with such a gathering of kings and eminent personages. During the several days of the celebrations, he, on the King's instructions, shows such ostentatious generosity to the kings, dukes, nobles and other guests, whether invited or come of their own accord, that they not only have food in plenty and their expenses covered, but are without question given whatever they request for their personal use. So that no one may complain of lacking anything, as well as having whatever they need brought to their lodgings, the King has ordered vats and barrels of the best wine to be set up in the market-place and elsewhere and kept topped up, so that all may drink not only what they need, but what they may want. The marriage is celebrated by Jarosław Archbishop of Gniezno in the cathedral on the third day after the kings' arrival. King Casimir gives the bride a dowry of 100,000 florins. After the ceremony, there are tourneys, dancing and caperings which last for several days. There are generous prizes for the winners.

Every day the royal and other guests are regaled with choice dishes and, not only that, but after each course, guests are sent gifts, the value and number of which astound everyone. Then Wierzynek, considering that it is his due to make a personal contribution, invites the five kings and all the dukes and nobles to dine at his house. He has the King's permission to seat them as he sees fit, thus King Casimir is placed in the seat of honour, next to him the King of Bohemia. then the King of Hungary, the King of Cyprus and, last, the King of Denmark, who is not considered to be due more honour than his lord the King of Poland, whose tremendous goodness has made him honoured and enriched, for he is a foreigner and (he was a native of the Rhine) a newcomer. They are all regaled with choice dishes and during the course of the banquet, each is presented with a splendid gift, that which Wierzynek gives to his King exceeding 100,000 florins in value, to the admiration and amazement of many. At the end of all this banqueting, which lasts more than twelve days, the kings and princes, having established friendly relations and sworn to make a pact of eternal peace, exchange gifts, give cordial thanks and praise to King Casimir for the honour done them and the gifts they and their people have received, and so depart for home, again provided on the way with all their needs by the King's starostas.

The Count of Bavaria and many other knights have now come to help Winrich Master of the Teutonic Knights fight the barbarians; so, on St. Agnes' Day, with a large army the Master invades Lithuania and Samogitia and destroys the districts of Parven, Ejragoła and Labima. In this he has the assistance of the Master of Livonia's army, which has been divided into two parts, one under his own command and the other under that of his marshal, and together they devastate almost the whole of Lithuania unopposed, for, though the River Niemen is frozen, the ice on it is thin and it cannot be crossed; thus the Lithuanians on the far side are isolated and suffer considerable losses in loot and captives. The invaders then return, respectively, to Prussia and Livonia without even having been attacked. The Marshal of Prussia makes a further raid on the Lithuanian castle at Gartin but is repulsed by Duke Patrykig, so he just destroys everything round about it and returns home.

Towards the end of the year, the epidemic that has been raging in Poland and neighbouring countries becomes more virulent and causes so many deaths that towns and villages are emptied.

A.D. 1364

Duke Wacław of Legnica and his wife, once relieved of the stigma of sterility they had endured for almost twenty years, now have four sons: Robert, Wacław, Bolesław and Henry, and a daughter, Jadwiga. After he had children, the Duke set about cancelling the agreement he had made with his brother Ludwig concerning the division and inheritance of the duchy, which he now wants his sons to inherit. Some of the barons and knights of Legnica refuse to accept any change, so he drives them from their homes and inheritances; while he forces the burghers of Legnica to recognize none but his sons as his heirs. Now, for the first time, Ludwig of Chojnów, feeling threatened, regrets having exchanged his share of Legnica for part of a duchy that had no fortress or stronghold in which he could dwell in safety, though commonsense requires him to disguise his feelings. He flatters his brother Wacław into giving his assent and then buys back the town of Lubin, which Ludwig had pawned, for this is well protected by its natural position and man-made fortifications. Now that he has this to rule, he will be better able to refuse his brother's blandishments. He invalidates all previous disclaimers, as well as any his brother Wacław might make, and compels a certain Jew, who has been arrested in Legnica and brought to Lubin and to whom Złotoryja was pledged, to return all that he had in his possession.

Wacław is incensed by all this and starts harassing his brother, burning every village he has in Legnica. The Duchess Catherine, their father's widow, now dies and the duchy of Brzeg is divided equally between the two brothers. Now, out of spite, Wacław sells his half-share to Bolesław Duke of Świdnica, who proceeds to harass Ludwig, trying to force him to sell the other half of the duchy. The Emperor and King of Bohemia intervenes and agreement is reached, according to which Ludwig is to receive the whole duchy of Brzeg, and, on the death of the Duke of Świdnica, is to be entitled to buy back the part of the duchy the latter bought; while he permanently surrenders the lands of Legnica and Chojnów to Wacław. Shortly afer this, his ill health aggravated by poverty and debt, Duke Wacław dies. Duke Ludwig takes charge of his children, as his brother has requested, and governs the duchy so carefully, honestly and sensibly that, within a short time, he has paid off his brother's many debts and restored the duchy to the full flower of prosperity. When, in due course, two of Wacław's sons, Robert and Bolesław, decide on secular careers as knights, the third, Wacław, becomes bishop of Lubusz and then of Wrocław; while the fourth, Henry, is equally fortunate, for, after being made dean of Wrocław, he becomes Bishop of Włocławek; while their sister, Jadwiga, marries Duke Henry the Elder of Żagań.

King Casimir founds a new town, Krzepice, on the River Liczwarta in the diocese of Cracow; and, in a marsh not far from it, builds a strong fortress of brick. Casimir asks the Bishop of Cracow to endow a parish church there out of his own revenues, but the Bishop refuses; after which the Bishop of Gniezno steps in and endows the church with two sheaf tithes of his own from the revenue of two royal villages near the Liczwarta and adds to this the monetary tithes from the town of Krzepice, though he has no right to do so, for Krzepice is not in his diocese, but in that of Cracow (the River Liczwarta has always been the boundary between the two dioceses). With the King's consent, the Archbishop claims Krzepice and forcibly incorporates it into his diocese. Bodzęta, Bishop of Cracow, being blind and bowed with age, is unable to stop this act of injustice. Death soon takes him.

Olgierd, Kiejstut and Patrykig, dukes of Lithuania, make a joint effort to rebuild the fortress at Kaunas, which the Teutonic Knights demolished. Using baulks of timber and abatis, they repair most of the damage in just a few days. They then start work on a bridge across the Niemen, a project of considerable importance for the defence of Kaunas, but work involving some danger, because the river there is deep and its current strong. The Knights, wishing to prevent both undertakings, bring up a considerable force under the command of the Captain of Ragneta. He burns the bridge and then, the Lithuanians having fled, razes the rebuilt fort to the ground. In the mean time, the Master Winrich has marched on the fort at Pista with an even larger force, and, finding Pisten empty, burns it, too. He then advances on the fort at Wielona and lays siege to it. He piles up a mass of timber and sets fire to it. There is a very strong wind, which fans the flames, with the result that many Lithuanians are killed and the fort is captured. So, too, is its captain, Gastołd, who is taken to the Marshal's tent and there killed. Before the Knights reach home again, Kiejstut has led an army by secret paths into Prussia and plundered and burned the whole area round Jurgemborg and taken considerable booty back to Lithuania, loosing only a handful of stragglers, whom the commander of the castle managed to capture. Back in Lithuania, Kiejstut advances on the Marshal who is ravishing Samogitia and attacks and routs his rear formation, recovering some of the booty. He inflicts losses on the rest of the army and so forces the Knights to retreat.

The Emperor Charles, having failed to keep his promise that he would personally conduct Pope Urban V back to Rome, the Pope goes there on his own. Later, the Emperor leads an army into Italy in an attempt to restore peace there, but is unable to achieve much, because his troops are going down with plague, which claims among its victims Prince Bolesław of Poland and five hundred Czechs, who are buried in Mantua. When he reaches Rome, the Emperor gets the Pope to crown as Empress his third wife, Elizabeth, grand-daughter of Casimir of Poland.

A severe winter brings harder frosts than usual to Poland and does considerable damage. Continual falls of snow kill many domestic and wild animals, and most birds. The intense cold freezes and desiccates many fruit trees.

Elizabeth, widow of the Duke of Mazovia and daughter of Gedymin of Lithuania, dies and is buried in Płock cathedral.

A.D. 1365

When Władysław Łokietek's brother, Siemomysł Duke of Gniewkowo, died, his duchy was divided between his three surviving sons: Przemyśl, who got Bydgoszcz, Leszek who received Inowrocław, and Casimir who had Gniewkowo. Since neither Przemyśl nor Leszek had heirs, the youngest of the three, Casimir, took over his brothers' shares. Casimir has had a number of sons and daughters, most of whom have died, leaving but one son, Władysław, who, because of his flaxen hair, is nicknamed "the White". There is also one daughter, Elizabeth, whom the Queen of Hungary, her relative, took into her household and eventually married to the King of Bosnia, Stephen, with whom she had a lovely daughter, also Elizabeth, who is well brought up and went on to marry Louis of Hungary on the death of his first wife. They had two daughters, Maria and Jadwiga. Władysław the White has no children by his only wife, the daughter of Albert Duke of Strzelce; he now starts treating Polish knights very high-handedly and puts pressure on Stanisław Kiwała, the judge of Kujawy over his inheritance. King Casimir summons him to appear before a royal tribunal, at which, in a huff, he leaves Bydgoszcz, which he was granted in fief on the death of his uncle, Przemyśl, and renounces possession of both town and castle. Finally, when his wife, whom he loved more than life, dies, he surrenders the whole duchy of Gniewkowo to King Casimir for 1000 florins. He then visits the Holy Sepulchre, spends some time at the Emperor Charles' Court, and in the following year, 1366, goes to Prussia, travelling through Kujawy, but not staying in any of the castles that used to belong to him. In the winter of this year he joins the Teutonic Knights to fight the barbarian Lithuanians, but then leaves them and returns hurriedly to Bohemia by the same route by which he came, and spends Easter in Prague. He then goes to Avignon, stays there a fortnight, and then without consulting or informing any of the Poles with whom he is staying, goes to Citeaux, dons a monk's habit and takes the oaths of the Order. He soon becomes disgusted with Citeaux and the Order and goes to Dijon, where he enters the monastery of St. Benedict, exchanging his grey habit for its black one and taking fresh vows. He remains there for fourteen years, during which time Casimir and Elizabeth of Hungary, his sister, frequently send him sums of money to cover his expenses and those of the monastery.

Duke Kiejstut of Lithuania assembles a force of Lithuanian and Samogitian foot and cavalry and leads it through trackless wastes and forest fastnesses and, unseen by the Knights' guards, captures the castle at Angerborg. The Lithuanians devastate the surrounding country and return home with their loot, pursued by the Vojt of Sambia, but he fails to catch them, so, instead, he devastates the country around Ejragoła and takes loot back to Prussia. Dukes Olgierd, Kiejstut, Patrykig and Alexander, given confidence by the huge army they have assembled and which they now divide into four, invade Prussia and do immense damage to it. They capture the fort at Ragneta and certain other forts and burn several villages, in which, according to their custom, they make sacrifices and feast on the blood of animals; after which they return home without encountering any resistance, taking with them 800 Christian captives and seventy great horses, geldings. Now, Winrich the Prussian Master invades Lithuania in his turn and devastates several parts of it; after which he crosses the Niemen and orders his troops to kill the old people and children, wherever they can, and to burn the houses, for the able-bodied have gone into hiding. He then returns to Prussia with a considerable number of captives.

In the mean time, two brothers of Dukes Olgierd and Kiejstut, some boyars and other eminent Lithuanians have gone to Prussia and accepted baptism and the Christian faith. The Prussian Master again raids into Lithuania, takes several forts, burns them and returns to Prussia with captives and loot. As he is making his way back, the Lithuanians, using secret paths, reach Nidzica, inflict considerable damage, slaughter a large number of people, for the usual precautions have not been taken, and withdraw with booty and captives. This raid is followed by another organized by the Grand-duke, who lays siege to, and captures Jańsbork, which he sacks and burns to the ground. Many of the faithful are killed, the others being put in chains and driven back to Lithuania.

Elizabeth, Queen of Hungary, gives birth to a daughter, Maria.

A.D. 1366

King Casimir, in whom the Lithuanians' illegal appropriation of Brześć, Łuck, Chełm and Bełz still rankles, prepares to try to recover them. He marches into Lithuania on the Feast of St. John the Baptist. The Lithuanians, feeling that they cannot match the strength of his army, decide to use cunning and treachery, rather than armed resistance; thus, when the Poles advance on Bełz, which is occupied by Duke George, he meets the King on the border, is humble and flattering, and begs him not to allow hostile action against him or his lands, for he is no enemy of the King, but his subject and liege. He promises to obey all the King's orders and give him true and sincere service and loyalty, not only in Bełz, but in all the other lands he possesses or will come to possess. He asserts that he considers himself the King's servant and will in future be a loyal and ardent helper against all the King's enemies and opponents. Convinced that there is no deceit or treachery in the Duke, the King weakly forgives him his earlier offences and accepts him as his servant and liege, and so grants him for his lifetime all the lands of Bełz. The King then withdraws his troops from Bełz territory without in any way harming it or the Duke, and advances on Łuck, which is then in the hands of Duke Lubart, a fickle, but very cunning man, whom the King profoundly dislikes, because, when, in a previous war, he was captured and released against his brothers' written and verbal surety, he deceived the King by not returning on the appointed day, and also because he was the originator of the rebellion. Thus, Lubart's word and promises are no longer believed and the King orders widespread devastation of his territory. He then attacks Łuck, Vladimir, Olesko and all the other forts in Vladimir, which in the old days was called Volhynia, with the rest of his army, his bombards and other siege weapons. All these places he captures and expels Lubart, so that he now has all Vladimir under his rule. King Casimir retains Łuck and Vladimir, the two most powerful castles, for himself, giving them as fiefs to Poles; the rest he entrusts to Alexander, son of Duke Michael of Lithuania, a man of proven loyalty and one who will defend it all against raids by Lubart or anyone else.

Casimir starts rebuilding the timber fort at Vladimir, which in many places was crumbling, a task that takes a number of years. No expense is spared, and it is given walls of fired brick. The King moves on to Chełm, which is in the hands of Duke Lubart and his men, and captures the main castle, at which the rest surrenders. These and the capital he grants to George Duke of Bełz, and then, laden with booty, returns home in triumph, having recovered the Ruthenian territories whose loss he had endured for fifteen years. Duke Alexander, to whom he granted the territory of Vladimir, remains loyal, but George of Bełz, repeatedly plots against him and tries to incite rebellion.

His Ruthenian territories recovered, Casimir disbands his army and goes to Łęczyca and Kujawy, then on to Chełm and Prussia, as far as Malbork, for he wants to see the Knights' territory and how it is organized. Master Winrich receives him with all due honour and for three days fetes him, sparing no expense. From Malbork he goes to Pomerania and, after touring round it, returns to Wielkopolska. In whichever place belonging to the Knights he visits, commanders are sent to escort him and to see that he and all his suite are provided with their every need.

Strengthened by the arrival of foreign knights and pilgrims, the Prussian Master organizes an incursion into Lithuania, where he causes enormous damage and returns with many captives. Kiejstut organizes a pursuit and enters Prussia so quietly and secretly that he all but captures the castle at Cherniakhovsk and its commander, who was at breakfast as they attacked. Unsuccessful here, he puts two large areas to fire and the sword and returns to Lithuania with a considerable booty of cattle and many captives. In response, the Master organizes a third incursion, thrusting further into the country than ever before. He also builds a fort and bridge over the Niemen, so as to try and prevent the Lithuanians making their stealthy raids. Twice Duke Kiejstut attacks in an attempt to stop the bridge being built, but without success.

A.D. 1367

The people of Bytom in the diocese of Cracow have been enormously enriched by the silver and lead mines discovered there. Prosperity has gone to their heads and their officials have grown arrogant. Whenever there is a matter of importance on which they require advice, they summon Peter of Koźle their plebanus, who has a good knowledge of canon law, sending a council-messenger not with a request, but with a command. The priest regards this as disparaging, so, one day when he receives such a summons, he sends his subordinate, Nicholas of Pyskowice, with the Holy Sacrament, and himself stays at home. When he arrives, the city-fathers are surprised to see him and not the priest. Nicholas, however, goes into the council chamber and, with his cuff, wipes the table and places the Holy Sacrament on it. Then he removes the Holy Sacrament and returns it to the church. Infuriated by such behaviour, the city fathers, under their leader, Laurence, on September 2 lay sacrilegious hands on the priest and Nicholas in their dwellings and bring them to the city hall, with their hands tied behind their backs, like thieves and evil-doers. Then, acting as plaintiff and judge, they unjustly condemn the two to death without allowing them any means of defence. They are beaten with pickaxes, taken from the court-room pouring with blood and thrown into a pond near the church of St. Margaret, whose waters engulf them. Nicholas' body rises to the surface and floats, whereupon Laurence orders a servant to push it in deeper.

When Florian Bishop of Cracow learns of this dual crime, he summons the chief culprit, the murderer Laurence, and the other councillors, to appear before his tribunal. Here they confess their guilt. They are deprived of all their honours, positions and offices. Their sons and grandsons are deprived of the right to receive the sacrament or any benefices of the Church, while the town of Bytom with its churches and neighbouring parishes is placed under an interdict. It is two years later and after the payment of a large sum in gold into the treasury of the Holy See to pay for the erection of an altar to St. Sigismund, and three annual payments of twelve marks, that the interdict is lifted. No sooner has this been done, than the veins of ore in the Bytom mine are found to be exhausted.

The Prussian Master Winrich sends an army under Marshal Henry Schindekopf to plunder Lithuania, which he does without encountering any resistance. He pushes forward as far as Kaunas and returns to Prussia with 800 captives and numerous herds of cattle and horses.

A.D. 1368

The Lithuanians, who traditionally go to war to obtain booty, are finding the obstacles put up by King Casimir such that they can never raid Poland without suffering serious loss and decide that it would be less risky to raid Mazovia, which is also closer and less on its guard. Now they suddenly appear near Pułtusk, which belongs to the Bishop of Płock. The town has no defences and is swiftly captured, as are those inside and all their belongings.

The castle's defence has been strengthened by those who have sought refuge in it, but the Lithuanians pile pine trunks against the castle wall and set fire to them. Those inside can do nothing to prevent the flames spreading, and the castle and all inside it are burned. The Lithuanians go on destroying the surrounding villages and so amass a considerable booty of people, cattle and other goods, whereupon they return home as suddenly as they arrived, and long before Siemowit Duke of Mazovia has had time to assemble enough troops to deal with them. While this has been going on, the Prussians under Marshal Hennig have invaded Lithuania, destroyed a number of villages and killed many people, and returned to Prussia with captives and loot.

On July 27 Bolesław Duke of Świdnica dies without progeny, thus the duchies of Świdnica and Jawor revert to Charles of Bohemia, who inherits them through his second wife, Anna, only daughter of Henry of Jawor and the brother of Bolesław of Świdnica. There being no more dukes, the duchy is reduced to a province.

Henry I of Opole dies on December 8. He leaves two sons, Władysław and Bolesław, by his wife Elizabeth, daughter of Bernard of Świdnica and grand-daughter of Casimir of Poland.

In many places in Poland a great flood, caused by incessant rain in August, has drowned the crops, herds and draught animals.

A.D. 1369

There now follows a long period of peace in Brzeg during which Duke Ludwig adds lustre to the town of Brzeg by founding a college there, in which he installs a number of canons and obtains from the Holy See the privilege that, on holy days, the deacon may use a bishop's mitre and crozier. He also builds a chapel so that throughout the year the hours may be sung in honour of the Virgin Mary. He also relieves the town of Brzeg of many of its debts and obligations and interest at usurious percentages with which his father had encumbered it. Ludwig has had two sons: Henry and then Wacław, who died prematurely, leaving Henry to inherit both shares. There are three daughters: Margaret, who has married Adalbert, Duke of Bavaria; Jadwiga who is married to the Duke of Oświęcim; and Catherine, who is abbess of the nunnery at Trzebnica.

On February 12, the King presents Cracow cathedral with a large crucifix made of the purest gold ornamented with pearls and precious stones, which is the most splendid of the cathedral's treasures as it still is.

Henry, Duke of Żagan and Głogów, father of King Casimir's third wife, Elizabeth, dies leaving three sons: Henry, Henry Rumpold and Henry, who, between them, share the two duchies.

Master Winrich of the Prussian Order, having received foreign reinforcements from Germany, organizes another incursion into Lithuania. On this occasion the Knights take with them stone, lime and bricks with which to build a fort. However, when they reach the River Niemen, they find there a considerable quantity of building material, which the Lithuanians have assembled for the same purpose. They take this as a gift of Fortune and make an immediate start on the foundations of the fortress, which is to be called Gotteswerder (God's Island). Work is finished in six months. The Knights install a strong garrison and return to Prussia with their loot. The two Lithuanian dukes, Olgierd and Kiejstut, are incensed by the construction of the fort, and, as soon as the Knights have left, mount an attack. The assault lasts five weeks, day and night, and in the end, because the garrison does not maintain the requisite guard, the Lithuanians capture the fort, killing most of the garrison and capturing the rest. Later, an exchange of prisoners is arranged, but on the very day when this is to take place, Duke Kiejstut takes too arrogant a tone with Hennig the Prussian Marshal, and the two sides part having achieved nothing. The Marshal then prepares a large force and attacks the Lithuanian fortress at Beyern and captures it. Envoys from Kiejstut then threaten him with vengeance unless he returns the castle, and this makes him so furious that he burns the town along with 112 people, the others being taken prisoner. Kiejstut now becomes more placatory and, finally, an exchange of prisoners is arranged. Even now, Kiejstut cannot control himself, but threatens to invade Prussia in the coming year. The Master responds by making a winter raid into Lithuania, which causes widespread destruction. The town of Postów is captured, its governor Gerdo expelled, prisoners taken and much booty.

A.D. 1370

The King spends Christmas in Cracow; then, with Lent approaching, he goes to Wielkopolska, taking the Court with him, and there he spends the spring and summer, when he moves on to Sandomierz and Ruthenia, intending to spend the autumn and part of the winter there hunting. He gets as far as Przedbórz, a royal town he himself built of very lovely brick. Then, on the Feast of the Nativity of the Blessed Virgin, as he is about to mount the carriage in which he intends to go hunting, he is taken ill. Pious members of his Court advise him not to go hunting on such a day, there being other days on which he can hunt without impediment.

The King concedes that they are right and decides not to hunt. Then, influenced by the whispering of others, he changes his mind, mounts the carriage and drives off into the forest. During the following day's hunt, the King pursues a hart so vigorously over obstacles in the depth of the forest that he is thrown from his horse, a pacer. The King, being old and stout, falls heavily, so heavily that he has to have a cart before he can be moved, and one is fetched with considerable difficulty from the nearest village. Then, fever sets in. When, thanks to the ministrations of his doctors, the fever leaves him, he continues on to Sandomierz against their advice. There he takes a bath, which he has been told to avoid like the plague, and eats too much, especially of fruit, and has a relapse. Realizing that his condition is deteriorating, he insists on returning to Cracow. Again he disregards the advice of his doctors and drinks cold water, which at once exaggerates the fever, so that, by the time he reaches Chobrzany which is held by his courtier Gowórek, he is in such a state that both the doctors and his knights think that he cannot survive the night. However, the doctors' ministrations reduce the fever somewhat and he leaves Chobrzany the following day and goes to the Cistercian monastery at Koprzywnica, his carriage being carried on the shoulders of his knights, who, like slaves, take it in turns to act as his draught animals, thus showing their great love for their king. He spends eight days in the monastery, and there promises to rebuild the ruined cathedral in Płock, where the head of St. Sigismund is kept. Then, feeling somewhat better, he moves on to Osiek, where, with the permission of one doctor, but against the advice of the others, he drinks mead and this induces another relapse. He is now taken to Korczyn castle, which he built at considerable expense, and there he stays until he feels his strength returning, when, urged by one of his doctors Matthew, he sets out for Cracow. The very next night his fever is higher than ever before, but intermittent, returning every three or four days, though sometimes every day, at times causing him intolerable pain. He reaches Cracow on October 1, so weak that he has to use an interpreter to berate the doctors for having promised to make him better as soon as they reached Cracow and could have the herbs and other medicines available in the apothecaries there and which they could not obtain in the country. The doctors are rather ashamed and promise their help. He insists that they tell him outright what they think are his chances of recovery, or whether he is near to death, so that he may see to his affairs while there is still time. They promise him not only recovery, but a long life; how-

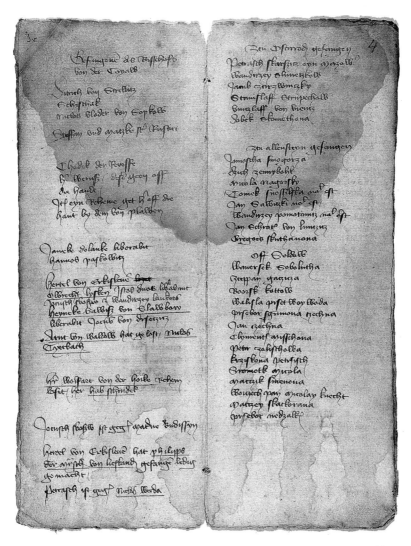

Part of a huge list of Polish prisoners-of-war in the hands of the Teutonic Knights, prepared for a possible exchange. The complete list is now in Historisches Staatsarchiv, Königsberg.

ever, at dawn on November 3, feeling that he is losing strength, he sends for his nephew, Władysław of Opole whom Louis of Hungary has sent to visit him, Florian Bishop of Cracow, the Duke of Opole, the higher prelates and canons, and his knights. First, he recites the creed, then he makes his will: to each of his unmarried daughters by his third wife, Anna and Jadwiga, he leaves a complete dowry of bed, hangings and curtains of batiste glimmering with purple, jewels, pearls and precious stones of rare workmanship, as well as all the spoons of pure silver, one half of all vessels and silver jewelry, the other half going to his wife, Jadwiga. To his grandson, Casimir, son of his daughter, Elizabeth, by his first marriage, he leaves the duchies of Sieradz, Łęczyca and Dobrzyń and four castles. Cracow cathedral is to have a large golden crucifix ornamented with many jewels and precious stones and containing a considerable portion of the wood of Christ's cross, with an estimated value of 10,000 florins. Gniezno cathdral gets a beautiful silver monstrance, gilded, with relics of saints, and a bible. The cathedral at Poznań gets the arm of St. Cosmas in a silver-gilt case. His two natural sons, whom he had by the Jewess, get three estates. The sons of Zbigniew of Brzezie get the royal town of Włodzisław plus a few villages. The town of Międzygórz in Sandomierz goes to Jan Zaklika, and Jásko Zorawsky gets one village. Many of his knights, courtiers and his servants are granted villages, towns, offices, houses, properties and various amounts of money. The Dean of Cracow Cathedral and Chancellor of Poland, John of Strzelce, is to be his executor. Having attended to all this, the King receives the viaticum, is anointed after making several confessions, and so, in the huge, low hall on the south side of Cracow cathedral, he breathes his last on the Wednesday nearest to St. Leonard's Day, November 5. He was sixty. He is buried not in the family sarcophagus, but in a separate place on the right-hand side near the great altar, for everyone agrees that he deserves a special tomb, which is ornamented, little by little, and at the King's expense, with tablets and marble representations of King Casimir as he looked during his life-time.

As soon as Siemowit Duke of Mazovia learns of King Casimir's death, he goes and takes possession of the castles at Płock, Rawa, Wyszogród, Gostynin and Sochaczew. Their starostas and lieutenants submit at once to his authority.

King Casimir was so eager to make his country illustrious and rich, that he went to great expense building churches of brick or masonry, as well as castles, towns, manors etc. so as to make Poland, which he found dirty and with buildings only of clay or wood, a place of bricks and masonry and famous. This he did. He was particularly concerned that prelates, canons and rectors of parish churches should build their private residences near their churches, and that peasants and villagers should not suffer injury from the nobles and the knights. So, too, the peasants and settlers dependent on the knights and nobles, whenever they were oppressed by their masters, obtained some protection from him. The knights and nobles called him "the King of the peasants". He was a tall man, stout, his face one that inspired respect. He had a shock of curly hair and a beard that fell on his chest. He had a slight stammer and a good carrying voice. He took a delight in feasting, making love and other sensual pleasures. Corpulent, of medium height, full-faced, something of a glutton and inclined to drunkeness, throughout his life he paid considerable attention to what he ate and drank. He was sensual and unrestrained in his relations with women.

The two brothers, Kiejstut and Olgierd, dukes of Lithuania, reinforce their army with Tatars, Ruthenians and other barbarians, divide it into two, which jointly invade Sambia and ravage it far and wide. They advance on the castle at Ortelsburg, capture it and burn it; then move on and camp near Königsberg. Here the Prussian Master, Winrich, catches up with them with a small force eked out with armed villagers and townspeople. On the Sunday he attacks and, after much fierce fighting, the Lithuanians withdraw, having lost a thousand men. The Order loses Hennig Schindekopff the Marshal, twenty brethren of the Order and a hundred nobles. The barbarians lose a thousand. Many of the Lithuanians die of their wounds, many others of cold and hunger as they wander in the forests. The Prussians are further reinforced by Leopold of Austria, whereupon they mount a four-pronged assault on Samogitia and destroy almost the whole of it. As they march back into Prussia, they are pursued by Duke Kiejstut, who attacks and captures the castle at Gogelanken and hurriedly withdraws with a large number of prisoners. The Commander of Cherniakhovsk invades Lithuania and ravages the villages not already devastated and returns home with many prisoners and much booty.

Many of Poland's enemies have developed an appetite for that country's territory, fortresses, frontier districts and castles, and now that King Casimir is dead, as if at a given signal, they start grabbing. Thus, when Hass of Huchtenhayn, a captain of Margrave Otto of Brandenburg, is sent

word by two Saxons who are loitering in Santok castle, about the small size of its garrison, the paucity of its provisions and the fact that its captain, Sędziwój of Wiry, is absent, he, in defiance of the
truce arranged with the barons of Wielkopolska, lays siege to the castle and tries to capture it. He is
thwarted for a number of days, thanks to the courage of one young man, Sędziwój of Slesin, but
when Sędziwój becomes exhausted with continually keeping watch and fighting, for these Saxons
never help him in any way, and the help promised by Przecław of Gołuchów, voivode of Kalisz and
starosta of Wielkopolska, fails to materialize, the castle has to surrender. At the same time, the
Lithuanian dukes, Kiejstut and Lubart, have sent a powerful army to lay siege to the castle at Vladimir, which belongs to King Casimir. This lacks for nothing and could easily have repulsed any assault had the starosta and the garrison had the courage. It was a new castle built, with no expense
spared, of fired brick, for the defence of this fertile province. The King had not destroyed the old
castle so as to prevent the Lithuanians interfering with the building of the new which employed
300 men and many teams of oxen day and night for two years, and cost more than 3000 marks in
broad grosses. The King had worried about it even on his death bed, sending the priest Wacław of
Tęczyn, who was in charge of operations, 600 marks to complete the fort. (This amount was retained in the treasury on the King's death.) The besiegers could easily have been repulsed, but for
the carelessness and laziness that is so much a part of Polish nature.

As soon as Queen Elizabeth of Hungary hears of her brother's death, she hurries to Cracow
and, against the wishes of the Poles, who want to raise the siege by force, sends to Duke Kiejstut
asking him to abandon the siege. Kiejstut and the other dukes refuse, for the request has encouraged, rather than intimidated them. So, in the absence of Duke Alexander, the cowardly captain,
forgetful of his honour and his country, makes a shameful agreement with the Lithuanians, which
allows him to leave with all his possessions, while surrendering both castles. The Lithuanians preserve the old timber castle, but raze the King's new one, splendid and all but finished, to the
ground. They then invade Sandomierz through Lublin, aiming to devastate that part of Poland.
When they reach Łysa Góra and learn that Polish knights are advancing against them, they hurriedly withdraw, taking with them the monastery's piece of wood from the True Cross. However,
when they reach the frontier, the waggon carrying this wood suddenly stops and neither horse, nor
oxen nor people can move it forward; indeed, all who try to do so fall down dead. A Lithuanian
priest explains that this is because the waggon has the wood of the Cross in it and that it cannot be
moved until this has been restored to its proper place. One of the Lithuanians' prisoners, a Polish
noble called Chorobat, earns his liberty by taking the wood back to the monastery.

When King Louis of Hungary learned of his uncle's death, he wondered whether or not to go
to Poland with a small army, for he was afraid of fresh disturbances and that Casimir's two daughters, Anna and Jadwiga, might raise difficulties, as might even Casimir Duke of Szczecin, the
rightful successor. Ought he to be there to quell any possible disorders, or should he stay in Hungary until he can discover what the Poles think of him? For a long time he hesitates, insisting that
one shepherd cannot properly protect two flocks so far apart, or that one husband cannot legally
take two wives, or one man act as two bishops. In the end, he yields to pressure and decides to go.
When he reaches Nowy Sącz, a throng of Polish nobles and priests comes out to escort him to the
capital, where he is greeted by processions of the clergy and city guilds headed by the standard of
the city with the city's arms painted on it which is presented to him as a symbol of submission. The
King then rides on into the city, goes to the cathedral and thence to the castle. The next day, Janusz
Suchiwilk, the Dean of Cracow Cathedral and Chancellor of Poland, the executor of King Casimir's will, ask the King whether he confirms unchanged all the depositions his uncle made in his
will and whether he will confirm its grants of dukedoms, land, castles, towns and villages. When
Louis replies that he will, he is told in a whisper that he has given the wrong answer, because the
written will contains a number of forged codicils detrimental to Poland. The King corrects his an-

swer and refers the grants to a committee of prelates and barons, who are to scrutinize the codicils, including those that already have seals attached, and decide which can be allowed and which disallowed. The committee decides that all are allowable but two, these being the grant of the lands of Sieradz, Łęczyca and Dobrzyń and the four castles of Kruszwica, Bydgoszcz, Wielatów and Wałcz to the Duke of Szczecin; the other, the grant of several estates to the late King's natural sons, Niemierza and Jan. King Louis then sends Duke Władysław of Opole to get the committee to pronounce judgment on whether or not the late King was legally entitled in his will to make grants of considerable territories and duchies of his kingdom without consulting his relatives, prelates and the barons. The Committee, wishing to avoid incurring the displeasure of those to whom the King made grants on his death-bed, especially the Duke of Szczecin, gives an evasive reply that fails to answer the question; and then, when pressed, refers the matter to the relevant territorial courts. The Sandomierz court decides that the grants made by the King on his death-bed are detrimental to Poland and thus should not be allowed. This pleases King Louis, who then asks the Polish prelates and barons to set their seals to this judgment and confirm this with their seals; this, however, they refuse to do. The King then initiates talks with the Duke of Szczecin to get him to accept the duchy of Gniewkowo and renounce his rights to the other legacies. The Duke refuses, for he knows that the true heir, Casimir's son, Władysław the White, is as good as a monk in a monastery. The final arrangement is that the Duke gets the duchy of Dobrzyń with the forts of Bydgoszcz, Wielatów and Wałcz, but none of the other legacies. Apart from these, and the legacy to the King's natural sons, all the other legacies are allowed, although many of the codicils were in all probability forged. Neither the knights nor the ordinary people welcome King Louis' arrival. People were too fond of the late King to feel kindly towards Louis or any other successor.

Louis considers that his coronation should take place soon and presses for this. Jarosław Archbishop of Gniezno and the barons of Wielkopolska want the King to come to Gniezno and be anointed and crowned in the cathedral there, while Bishop Florian and the barons of Cracow reject the idea. The King reminds them that his grandfather, Władysław Łokietek, and his uncle, Casimir, were both crowned in Cracow, not in Gniezno, and says that he will not change this custom nor disregard the right to perform the coronation granted to Cracow cathedral. Finally, a compromise is reached: after the coronation in Cracow the King will present himself in Gniezno cathedral in his coronation robes and wearing his crown. So, on Sunday, November 17, in the presence of his mother, Queen Elizabeth of Hungary, Queen Jadwiga of Poland, Casimir's widow and of his two daughters, Anna and Jadwiga, King Louis is crowned in Cracow cathedral by the Archbishop of Gniezno, assisted by the Bishops of Cracow and Lubusz.

Now, at the very outset of his reign, King Louis takes a step that weakens and lessens the kingdom, in that, despite the objections of the Polish prelates and nobles, he grants in perpetuity to Duke Władysław of Opole, son of Elizabeth, daughter of Casimir's sister, and Voivode of Hungary, the lands of Wieluń and all its castles, as well as the towns and castles of Olsztyn, Krzepice and Bobolice in the duchy of Cracow, along with the castle of Brzeznica in Sieradz, whose splendid walls were erected by King Casimir. He goes on to make other grants which weaken and reduce the kingdom as a whole; indeed, it becomes evident that, thanks to the wealth of Hungary, it never occurs to the King to strengthen the kingdom of Poland or to reclaim its lands that the Czechs, Saxons and Teutonic Knights had appropriated. To placate the Polish prelates and nobility, who have been complaining about what he has done and demanding the annulment of the grants, the King accepts the homage of Casimir, Duke of Szczecin and Dobrzyń, for the duchy and land of Dobrzyń, who declares that he has received these lands and duchies from Louis as King of Poland in fief, so that, should he die without progeny, these lands must revert to the Kingdom of Poland.

Now that he has been crowned, King Louis eagerly sets about organizing the postponed funeral of his uncle. This starts at dawn on Tuesday, November 19, with processions from all the churches and monasteries in the city of Cracow; then come four carriages each covered with a pall and driven by a coachman in black, and behind them forty mounted knights in full armour, their horses draped with purple cloths. Then come eleven standards representing the eleven duchies of Poland, each having its emblem embroidered on it. These are followed by a twelfth and larger standard bearing a white eagle, the emblem of the dead King. Behind it rides a knight dressed in the most splendid royal robes, pearls and fine purple interwoven with gold, representing the dead king, and riding a magnificent horse itself with a purple cover. Behind these, two by two, come 600 acolytes, each holding a lighted candle of unusual size (two of them weigh the same as a stone of wax) next come mourners bearing palls of interwoven gold, silver and purple cloth, which is later distributed among the churches and their servants. These mourners are surrounded by more than a thousand knights, in funeral dress. There is weeping, wailing and discordant singing that reduce almost every mortal to tears. Ahead of the mourners rides a knight scattering to either side handfuls of broad Prague grosses, thus making way for the procession behind him, for every road is thronged. Behind all this walks King Louis accompanied by the Archbishop of Gniezno and the Bishops of Cracow and Lubusz, then the Polish and Hungarian nobles and behind them a countless throng. They enter the churches of St. Francis, the Virgin Mary and the Holy Trinity, in each of which they hear mass and give alms (in each church, during the service, two platters are placed beside each mourner filled with broad Prague grosses and from which anyone may take what he pleases and lay it on the altar; when empty each is replenished with more coin); then they go to the cathedral, where mass is said at the High Altar by the Bishop of Cracow and at all the other altars by chaplains; double gifts being laid on each altar. In the cathedral soldiers have to clear a passage to the altars, otherwise none would have reached them. The late King's officials lay gifts in keeping with their rank on the main altar, the treasurer and the Chamberlain giving the King's silver platters, towels and tablecloths; the Master of the Pantry and the Carver give four large silver goblets; the two cup-bearers give cups and bowls, and the Marshal a splendid charger. Finally, after the twelve standards, comes the knight representing the late King, astride a horse. When this horse has been presented by the Second Master of the Horse, the knights break all twelve standards, the signal for one and all, nobles and ordinary people, old and young, to weep and wail.

The King now goes to Wielkopolska, leaving his mother in Cracow to divide the late king's treasure in accordance with the instructions he gave on his death-bed, that is between Queen Jadwiga, whose third share amounts to no more than three hundred and thirty-three and a half silver marks and a thousand marks of broad grosses, with which she returns to her father's house and marries Rupert, son of Wacław Duke of Legnica. Anna and Jadwiga are sent with all their possessions to Hungary; so that, in the event of their making important marriages, there would be less likelihood of their husbands' thinking of conquering Poland. As a further precaution the King has a court declare the two ineligible for the succession, on the grounds that they were conceived on the wrong side of the blanket. Despite this, he marries them off: Anna to William Count of Cilia and Jadwiga to a prince Romer.

While the King is in Wielkopolska, a throne is prepared for him to sit on in Gniezno cathedral, but this he refuses to use, insisting that to do so would make him ridiculous and that it would be unseemly for him and the Poles to repeat the Cracow coronation, as if its legitimacy were in doubt. So, having spent two days in Gniezno, he returns to Cracow via Łęczyca and Sieradz. Not that he stays there long, for, leaving his mother to rule Poland, though there is much unsettled business and the castles of Santok and Vladimir have yet to be recovered, he hurries back to Hungary along the same route by which he came, taking with him the golden crown of Poland, the sceptre, sword and other royal insignia, in order to prevent the Poles crowning anyone else, for he is very much afraid that, in his absence, they might get themselves another king, for some of the Polish dukes and princes do have better claims to the throne. Henceforth, Poland is ruled more by a woman, the

Queen-dowager Elizabeth, than by its King. She now replaces the former councillors, starostas and other officials, mostly with people who have no experience of management, though they do know how to flatter a woman. Under their administration, Poland falters and deteriorates.

Kiejstut of Lithuania organizes an incursion into Prussia, which puts the region of Seesten to fire and the sword, massacring its Christian population. In revenge, the Prussian Master, Winrich of Kniprode, invades Lithuania. He divides his large army into four with which he devastates huge areas and removes many captives and much loot to Prussia. On his way back, the Commander of Bałga marches into Ruthenia and lays siege to Drewik, but, unable to capture it, he devastates the surrounding area and returns to Prussia with a number of captives. The arrival of a number of foreign knights allows him to organize a third incursion into Lithuania, in which he captures the fortified town of Dorsuniszki and burns it, killing or taking prisoner a large number of Lithuanians.

A.D. 1371

The Queen-dowager removes Przecław Voivode of Kalisz from his post and replaces him with Otto of Pilcza, a knight known for his magnaminity. The nobles of Wielkopolska find this difficult to bear and complain that they are being oppressed and their rights and ancient customs violated by being put under the authority of a man with no property in Wielkopolska. At first, they refuse him obedience, but when he appoints some of the more vociferous to the post of starosta and other offices, peace is restored. The numbers of highwaymen, thieves and foreigners making stealthy incursions into Polish territory is growing daily, yet, because of their dislike of Otto, the knights of Wielkopolska refuse to help him stamp them out. This behaviour so annoys Otto that he voluntarily resigns his post. He is replaced by a local knight, Sędziwój of Szubin, under whom Poland's domestic and foreign enemies are allowed to loot and rob with impunity. A more serious disaster is when plague returns to Poland and for the next two years claims so many victims that many houses become uninhabited.

The Bishop of Płock, while on a journey, has an apoplectic fit as he is sitting at table in the village of Górzno and dies without confession or viaticum. He had been bishop for less than three years. Even before he is buried, the Chapter has elected the archdeacon of Płock, Ścibor of Radzimin, to succceed him. Ścibor demolishes the modest, timber church in his native village and builds a splendid new one of fired brick.

A.D. 1372

For almost two years Jarosław Archbishop of Gniezno has been complaining that his property in Łówicz has been looted by a number of Mazovian knights, in particular Pietrasz, son of Christinus Voivode of Płock, yet he has been unable to obtain redress or compensation, while Duke Siemowit has made no attempt to punish the culprits. The Archbishop now unsheaths his episcopal weapon and places the whole of Mazovia under an interdict. He refuses an offer that the perpetrators will be punished if he raises the interdict, insisting on compensation for loss and damage. The matter is then referred to arbitration and this awards the Archbishop two vills in perpetuity, and so the interdict is withdrawn.

However, the Archbishop is failing, and, on December 21, he is struck blind. He decides that he must retire in favour of his relative the Archdeacon, Nicholas of Koszutów and appoints proctors for the election. Although he has not obtained the approval of either his chapter or the King, convinced that his fiat is sufficient, he sets out for Avignon to obtain the approval of Pope Gregory XI. Here he encounters difficulties raised by Janusz Cantor of Gniezno, who is already in Avignon. After a whole year, during which time he has incurred considerable expense and the Cantor has died of venereal disease, the Archbishop returns home having achieved nothing. Nonetheless, he persists in his intention to resign, though Nicholas has died and he has to choose a new candidate,

John Suchilik of Strzelce, who is a doctor of canon law, Dean of Cracow and Canon of Gniezno. He is consecrated in Avignon, which he leaves immediately, because the plague is rife there, and reaches Gniezno on July 1 to be welcomed by a ceremonial procession. The next day, wearing his pontifical robes, he celebrates a solemn Mass and takes over the entire diocese, except for Pomerania and Opatówek and tithes from Kalisz, which the Holy See had set aside for the maintenance of the former archbishop. He, disgusted by living among laymen and associating with them, spends almost two years in the monastery in Ląd, voluntarily doing penance and scourging himself.

King Louis marries his eldest daughter, Maria, to Sigismund Margrave of Brandenburg.

The plague is more virulent than ever in many places; indeed, people are unable to keep pace with the burials.

A.D. 1373

As soon as King Casimir died, some of the barons of Wielkopolska sent messengers with letters to inform Władysław the White, Duke of Gniewkowo, who has spent the last fourteen years in a Benedictine monastery in Dijon, of the King's death. These letters urge the Duke to leave his monastery and return to Poland, since he is next in succession to the throne in the male line and is the choice of the writers and others of their opinion. The Duke is impulsive by nature, and full of hope, he leaves the monastery and goes to Avignon hoping to obtain a papal dispensation that will allow him to accept succession to the throne of Poland. He tells the Poles who have come to escort him back to Poland, that they are to wait for him in Basle, to which he eventually returns without any prospect of being granted his dispensation. Some of the Poles are still in Basle, others in Strasbourg; together they provide Władysław with funds, which, on their advice, he uses to go to Buda, where King Louis receives him rather coolly, and there he stays for two years, deserted by the Poles. However, Queen Elizabeth, who is Władysław's niece, pesters her husband until Louis sends him to the Pope in Avignon asking the latter to grant him a dispensation that will allow him to return to secular life and try to regain the duchy. The application is refused, there being no legal justification for it, and Władysław is left eating other people's bread in Drzeń.

The Commander of Bałga, Dietrich of Elner, declares war on Ruthenia and ravages it as far as Kamieniec. During Lent, Kiejstut manages to avoid all the Knights' guards and, through forest and wilderness, penetrates into Prussia as far as Biberstein, kills or captures a number of Christians and withdraws, as soon as his intelligence tells him that an army of Knights is preparing to attack him.

A.D. 1374

King Louis is not satisfied with the considerable revenue he is receiving from the Kingdom of Poland, a revenue such as no king before him ever received, and orders all the bishops, the rich and more eminent of the nobility of Poland not to reduce the royal revenues, nor to regard him as worse or inferior to his uncle, but to pay the normal tax due on each cultivated field: two grosses plus one measure of wheat and one of oats, the tax normally called the "royal tax" or poradlne. The prelates and nobles refuse to pay, asserting that, thanks to the generosity of King Casimir, they and their possessions were exempt from this tax, which Casimir had abolished. Again and again the Poles' envoys beg that Louis should not violate or remove privileges granted by his uncle, but rather that he deign to confirm these privileges now and for the future. King Louis, aware of the huge amount this tax brings in, replies that his uncle may have promised to abolish the tax known as poradlne, but he had never carried out his promise. He tells them that he is not opposed to reducing much of the tax, so as to aid the growth and prosperity of Poland, its prelates and nobles, but some small part must be paid as a token of his rule, provided that the bishops, nobles and the rich deign to show him submission; so new arrangements are made and embodied in signed documents binding the Poles to recognize Louis' daughters, Maria and Jadwiga, as his heirs and to permit them to possess the kingdom. In order to rid themselves and their successors of the hateful poradlne, the Poles agree to this and undertake that, on King Louis' death, they will accept one of his two daughters as his successor, provided the King agrees in writing to reduce poradlne and restrict it to just two grosses as a symbol of his authority. The Polish bishops, referring to the privilege relieving them from this tax granted them by King Casimir, delay paying even the two grosses; but the royal starostas force the settlers and villagers of monastery villages to pay the full amount, an obvious wrong, yet the bishops do not defend the monasteries, but confine their efforts to defending their own possessions.

The Bishop of Poznań dies of dropsy. He is succeeded by the Archdeacon of Cracow, Trojanus Pałuka.

A.D. 1375

Władysław the White who, for more than a year, has been spongeing on Bodcza of Drzeń hoping that King Louis will show him mercy after his rebellion, now makes determined efforts to recover his duchy. His activities are not so well concealed that they do not become public knowledge. It is said that, by deceit or by force, he intends to occupy several of the castles that once were his. Disturbed by this news, the starosta of Wielkopolska, Sędziwój of Szubin, under whom these castles come, decides to remove Christian, the elderly holder of Złotoria, who is his brother-in-law, and entrust the castle to someone more efficient. Christian takes this as an insult both to himself and to his wife, and insists that he is capable of defending the castle, so nothing is done. Meanwhile, Władysław has bought the assistance of some fishermen, whom he gets to take several casks of fine wine to the castle, as a gift for Christian, who is reputed to be fond of his drink. Christian invites the fishermen to help him sample the wine and before long the casks are empty and Christian is under the table. That night, while Christian is still in a deep sleep, Władysław's men set up ladders and climb in and capture Christian and his servants. These and the castle they hand over to Władysław, who installs a strong garrison. Before long numbers of vagabonds and destitute debtors have rallied to Władysław. Christian is placed in a dungeon, but eventually his friends and the starostas ransom him for 500 marks, enough to have kept him in wine for the rest of his life—if he had exercised restraint!

King Louis, thinking that he is failing, marries his youngest and prettiest daughter, Jadwiga, to William Duke of Austria, who then goes to Hungary and remains at his father-in-law's Court until King Louis dies.

Aware that the Ruthenian territories conquered by Casimir of Poland are largely peopled with Catholics, King Louis sends to the Pope in Avignon and obtains the honour of an archbishopric for Halicz, and of bishoprics for Przemyśl and Vladimir, lands which came to him on the death of King Casimir.

The Knights in Prussia send a further expeditionary force into Ruthenia and Lithuania. At the same time, Dukes Olgierd and Swerdejko make a three-pronged incursion into Prussia and devastate everything around Wielona, Toplanken and Insterburg, massacring the Catholics they find there. They kill 900 Christians, burn the castle at Insterburg and, having met with no resistance, return to Lithuania with 150 captives.

A.D. 1376

Sędziwój of Szubin, starosta of Wielkopolska, realizing that the plethora of small garrisons he has installed all over his province, cannot put an end to the damage being done to Kujawy and Wielkopolska by Władysław and his minions in Złotoria, damage that increases every day, as more and more criminals and brigands join Władysław, thus adding to the harm being done, asks Casimir Duke of Szczecin and Dobrzyń for help: Casimir, with Bartosz of Wezenborg the starosta of Kujawy, lays siege to Złotoria; cannon and other siege weapons are procured and bombard the cas-

tle's beautiful brick walls day and night. The besieged use boats to make night attacks on their besiegers, especially those who may have wandered away from the camp in search of food. In the
castle is a certain Hanko, owner of the mill at Brześć, whom Władysław had captured when he took
his first castle and then released against the usual surety. Now, when Hanko receives a reminder
that he must keep his word, he seeks the advice of his starosta, Bartosz, who leaves the decision to
him; so, when Władysław's men came to fetch Hanko, he voluntarily mounts the waggon and goes
into captivity. Thanks to his skill and that of another miller, the siege machines and catapults in the
castle are trained on the besiegers. Hanko afraid that his having helped the enemy might cost him
his mill at Brześć, and aware that lack of provisions will prevent Władysław surviving a long siege,
through an intermediary makes an agreement with the Starosta for the surrender of Złotoria. He
undertakes to send the starosta his keys to the castle gate. However, his behaviour arouses suspicion and he is arrested and tortured, so that the whole arrangement is discovered. Władysław then
sends Hanko's son-in-law to Sędziwój with the keys and a day and hour are fixed for the surrender
of the castle. The delighted Sędziwój does not tell either Duke Casimir or Bartosz about this, so as
to keep all the glory and rewards for himself; but, selects a force of his best men and with it presents
himself at the castle gate at the time arranged. He opens the postern with the key given him and 260
knights ride in, while he and the rest of the force remain outside. No sooner are the 260 all inside,
than the portcullis, given extra weight with heavy stones to make it fall quicker, is lowered, killing
Frederick of Wedel instantly. The others are then pelted with stones and taken prisoner. The saddened Sędziwój returns to his camp, and, at dawn the following day, attacks the castle with his entire force. The assault continues all day, but without success. Many are wounded, many killed,
before the army returns to its tents. Duke Casimir of Szczecin, who was hit on the head with a
heavy stone, dies shortly afterwards, no doubt because of this injury. Meanwhile, Władysław inflicts suitable punishment on Hanko and his son-in-law by burning them at the stake on a pyre in
front of the castle. Then, afraid of starvation, he makes a deal with Sędziwój and Bartosz, who undertake that he will be restored to King Louis' good graces, whereupon he releases his prisoners
and leaves Złotoria with all his people. As he leaves, he fights a duel with lances with Bartosz of
Wezenborg, who wounds him severely. His wound healed, he is sent at the latter's expense to Hungary, where, after much haggling, he sells his dukedom to King Louis for 10,000 florins and the use
for his lifetime of a rich Cistercian abbey. The Polish nobles and barons who supported and helped
him, are imprisonned and have to endure extreme poverty, for the Duke they served hears neither
their groans nor their accusations and never helps them. Later on, Władysław conceives a dislike
for Hungary, leaves his abbey and goes to Burgundy, and thus dies and is buried in a foreign land.

Przecław, Bishop of Wrocław, dies during Lent after thirty-five years on the episcopal throne.
The Dean of Wrocław, a Czech called Theodoric, is elected to replace him. When he goes to Avignon to seek confirmation of his appointment, the Pope delays granting it until he reaches Rome,
thus enabling him to appropriate the see's revenue, the extent of which rumour has enormously exaggerated. He sends Nicholas Bishop of Majorca, as protector of the see of Wrocław, to collect the
revenue and send it to the Holy See, along with what monies Przecław, "the golden bishop", may
have left. The Wrocław chapter, recognizing the danger of having a foreign bishop, reaches a compromise: namely, that each year while the see remains vacant they will remit to the Papal treasury
from the estate of Bishop Przecław 8000 florins and a further 30,000 as an advance; 2000 as
Wrocław's share of the biennial tribute exacted from the church in Poland, plus 1000 to cover the
cost of sending the money to Rome. Having got 33,000 florins, the Pope still delays confirming
Theodoric's appointment, and eventually decides that the vacant see is not to be filled for two years
from Przecław's death, thus enabling him to get yet more.

Archbishop Jarosław also dies; he had given up his see and ended his days in the monastery at
Ląd. It is told that, when he was rector of Bologna University, the University had condemned an

English student there to death for adultery with a certain woman, whose husband, being in financial straits, condoned the adultery; so the Rector used his powers to remove the university from
Bologna and did not allow its return until the citizens of Bologna atoned for their condemnation of
the Englishman by erecting a special chapel and endowing it adequately.

The number of riots and disturbances in Poland has forced the Queen-dowager to hand the
government of the kingdom back to her son, leaving her to content herself with the revenue from
Dalmatia, which he had granted her; now she is on her way back to Poland with a large and splendid retinue to resume control. The nobles and their wives have orders to await her near Sącz, and
there they are. When the Queen-dowager reaches Bochnia, she is told by her intelligence that there
is a plan for the whole might of Lithuania to invade Sandomierz, and that this could happen any
day, unless she takes countermeasures. She takes the woman's view that there is no need to think
about dangers that are merely threatening and tells them not to worry, for her son is so powerful
that everyone, including the Lithuanians, trembles at the mere sound of his name. Trembling or
not, the Lithuanian dukes Kiejstut, Jagiełło, Witold, Lubart and George, moving at night by the
light of a nearly full moon, set out across the wild parts of Lublin, moving quickly and quietly, hiding by day in the inaccessible depths of the forest. On December 2, they reach the River San, cross
it and spread out, looting and killing over a wide area, indeed as far as the Vistula. They set fire to a
number of churches and return home with much loot, many cattle and captives of both sexes. Their
sudden arrival at the village of Baranów surprises Pietrasz, brother of the Archbishop of Gniezno,
who mounts his horse, seats his wife and as yet unbaptized child behind him, and charges at and
through the enemy. He reaches the Vistula and, despite all the arrows fired at him, escapes.

The widow of Michael of Tarnów, castellan of Wiślica, who is about to set out from her estate
of Wielowies with a splendid cortège in order to greet the Queen-dowager, is also surprised by the
Lithuanians, but her servants manage to get her across the river and to the town of Sandomierz. But
many others, women and children, are made captive. When told of the disaster, the Queen-
dowager puts a brave face on it and tells her subjects that her son will swiftly put things right and
compel the Lithuanians to return the captives and booty. However, the only way to deal with the
Lithuanians is to adopt their tactics and method of fighting, which is to raid for plunder and, having
got the plunder, to hide in forests, marshes and other inaccessible places, avoiding the pursuit and
seldom engaging in any decisive battle. Then, as soon as they learn that the enemy has withdrawn
from the country, at once to invade again. Such teasing tactics have inflicted heavy losses on the
Poles, who cannot take aggressive action because of all the bogs, marshes and rivers, nor go on the
defensive, for the Lithuanians never stand their ground. It is known that the Lithuanians owe as
much to the laziness and lack of unanimity among the Poles, as to their own bravery.

When the Prussian Master Winrich learns that the Lithuanians are busy in Poland, he invades
Samogitia and, being unopposed, devastates Miedniki, Ejragoła, Arwisten, Rosienie, Jezow and
Postów and then lays siege to the fort at Kaunas. This action costs him a number of his best knights
and he abandons the attempt and returns to Prussia.

The Queen-dowager, closing her eyes to the damage done by the Lithuanians, organizes days
of singing and dancing in Cracow castle. On December 7, while she is watching the dancing, her
Hungarian escort plunders several waggons bringing corn and hay to Cracow market. Przedbór of
Brzezie, hoping to prevent his own waggons, which are taking hay to his house near one of the
gates, from suffering the same fate, sends some servants to guard them. When the plundering Hungarians find themselves opposed, both sides call for help. These calls bring a throng of Poles and
Hungarians running, and there is considerable confusion. Queen Elizabeth orders Jásko Kmita starosta of Cracow to deal with the disturbance. He mounts his horse and sets out with a company of
foot soldiers to quell the rumpus. While attempting to do this, he is hit in the neck by an arrow sped
by one of the Hungarians, and falls from his horse, dead. The news of his death brings his servants

and family running and they, in a frenzy, kill every Hungarian they can lay hands on, some 160 of them. The Queen-dowager stops the dancing and orders the castle gates to be closed and guards placed on the walls and towers for the next three days, so as to prevent the other Hungarians being murdered; then, weeping and bewailing her fate, she resigns as regent and handing over to Peter Kmita, the dead starosta's son, for all his tender years, so as to compensate him for the loss of his father, leaves Cracow and Poland and returns to Buda.

Charles of Bohemia, the Roman Emperor, eager that the succession should remain in his family and that one of his sons should be Emperor too, uses gifts and promises to persuade the lay and ecclesiastical electors to make his eldest son, Václav, King of the Romans. So that his election cannot be altered or annulled, he has the Archbishop of Munich crown him in Aachen. Pope Gregory XI and his cardinals do not approve of either the choice or the coronation, since, being sixteen, Václav is still under age and has not yet given proof of his integrity; so the Pope cannot be persuaded to confirm the coronation or to address Václav as King of the Romans.

A.D. 1377

King Louis wishes to avenge the Lithuanians' destruction of Sandomierz, so he announces a punitive expedition, calls up his troops in Cracow, Wielkopolska, Kujawy and Sandomierz, and sends letters to the bishops calling upon them to send armed contingents to help him fight the barbarians. The Bishops, who do not wish to render themselves liable for such dues, refuse to serve, particularly since it is King Louis who has made the request. The King comes to Sandomierz with his Hungarian troops by the most direct route, that is through the Carpathians, and the whole army advances on Bełz.

His army being strong, he divides it and sends the knights of Cracow and Sandomierz, under Sędziwój of Szubin, Starosta of Cracow, to lay siege to Chełm, while he leads the rest against Bełz. It takes the knights of Cracow and Sandomierz eight days to capture Chełm, and they then go on to capture Grabowiec, Horodło and Zawłocie, and so reach Bełz. Bełz proves difficult to take and the King decides to starve it into surrender. But now Kiejstut arrives and peace is arranged on the following terms: the Lithuanians will return all their captives and surrender Bełz. Bełz surrendered, the King, wishing to repay evil with good, entrusts Bełz castle to Duke George, who undertakes in his own name and that of his offspring to govern it as the King's lieutenant and in loyalty to the Kingdom of Poland. King Louis even entrusts another castle to him, that at Lubaczów, and grants him 100 marks a year from the salt revenues for the rest of his life. These matters arranged, the King returns to Hungary.

The late King's nephew, Casimir Duke of Szczecin, dies of a suppurating wound he received during the capture of Złotoria. He had no progeny by his second wife, so Dobrzyń and the castles of Bydgoszcz, Wielatów and Wałcz escheat to King Louis. The late Duke's generosity had bordered on the prodigal. He had so lavished towns, villages and ducal revenues on his knights, as to reduce himself to such poverty that even what he inherited on his father's death did little to relieve it. His sister Elizabeth, wife of the King of Bohemia, took pity on him and frequently sent him money, silver vessels and other valuables, which, much against her wishes, he distributed among his knights and courtiers, thus relapsing into poverty. Courageous and magnanimous, he was impetuous and undignified. He had a poor physique.

Now aware of how fertile and desirable are the lands of Ruthenia of which he had had no previous knowledge, King Louis decides to detach them from Poland and add them to the Kingdom of Hungary. As a first step, he grants to Władysław Duke of Opole in perpetuity the Duchy of Dobrzyń, which had escheated to the Crown on the death of the Duke of Szczecin. After this the Duke of Opole is styled a Ruthenian Duke. To make the duchy's subsequent transfer to Hungary acceptable, the King adds to it the castles of Bydgoszcz, Wielatów and Wałcz, plus the duchy of

Gniewkowo, which the King bought from Władysław the White, and which now, despite the protests of the Poles, are granted to Hungarians. The Poles should have learned from this that disaster is inherent in having a foreigner for a king.

Kiejstut of Lithuania prefers to wage war by subterfuge than by brute force. Now, towards the end of September, he leads an army through Mazovia: Duke Siemowit and Duke John either connive or pretend not to notice, and devastates the regions of Działdowo and Niborg, taking many captives, and returns, again through Mazovia. Around St. James' Day, Kiejstut's young son, Witold, makes his first incursion into Prussia, ravages the districts of Tajnowo and Insterburg and returns home safely with booty and captives.

These two attacks on his country enrage the Prussian Master Winrich, who then moves into Ruthenia and makes camp near Bielica castle. He moves on to Kamieniec and further into Lithuania and Samogitia. The Lithuanians prepare an ambush for him as he is returning with loot and captives. It is laid in the vast forest through which the Knights have to pass, the Lithuanians making various clearings in which the Prussians can be attacked. The first attack kills twenty of the leading Knights. The Lithuanian dukes Olgierd and Kiejstut then organize a three-pronged incursion into Prussia, in which they devastate the country round Insterburg and Wielowo, and continue into Saalan, which belongs to the Canons of Königsberg, and so return to Lithuania via Jurgenburg. Then the Commander of Ragneta and the Commander of Bałga and Kuno of Hattenstein make separate raids into Lithuania, burning, looting and taking captives. To cap it all, Winrich assembles a huge army and marches into Lithuania, where he builds two castles: Bartenburg and Demrin. While these are being built, another force under the Marshal Godfrey of Linda raids elsewhere and returns without loss with his loot and captives. Then some Austrians arrive, coming through Samogitia and in ten days devastate Kaltyniena and Widukle of Rosienie, before moving on into Prussia with their loot and captives.

A.D. 1378

The number of disturbances increases to an extent that might be called rebellion, all because the King's absence allows criminals to act with impunity. The King is pestered with letters and envoys from Poland begging him to remedy the situation, which has driven his mother to resign as governor and leave the country, swearing never to return. The King, who has convinced himself that the Polish climate does not suit him, and has put off returning from year to year, now appoints Władysław Duke of Opole Governor of Poland, gives him wide-reaching powers and sends him there. The townspeople and country people are happy about this and prepared to support him, but assemblies of the barons and nobility of Cracow and Wielkopolska held in Wiślica and Gniezno decide that on no account will they accept the Duke's authority, asserting that it does not befit their dignity or accord with the laws of the kingdom, that they should be ruled by someone they have neither elected nor accepted; while it is an insult to them and the kingdom to be subject to a mere duke. They then chose people to present their views to King Louis and remind him that he swore an oath not to break the laws of the kingdom, and to beg him not to shame them by making them submit to the Duke of Opole. They emphasize that among their number are several to whom the King could entrust these duchies. Afraid of rebellion, Louis removes the Duke from his post.

One difficulty disposed of, another crops up. On the advice of some Poles, who were no friends of the Church, the King has ordered that peasants on Church lands in Poland must pay his bailiffs the tribute known as poradlne, at six grosses in cash, that is half what they have been accustomed to pay, plus two measures of grain, one of rye and one of oats. He insists that the privilege he granted to all Poland reducing this tribute to two grosses, did not apply to Church property. The bishops and clerics regard the reduction of their poradlne by half as a sign of special graciousness and generosity, and are not willing to pay, but when the royal tax-collectors are over-zealous in carrying out their task, the Archbishop of Gniezno sends to Władysław of Opole asking him to restrain the tax-collectors, until the Church has made its representations to the King. The Duke grants his request, and orders collection of the tax to be halted until St. James' Day. The Archbishop, who has been intending to remove it altogether, summons a provincial assembly in Kalisz in order to repeal the King's tax, as the Pope insists. The Bishop of Cracow, Florian, and the Dean of Cracow, then go to the King in Buda and present the Polish Church's case. They convince the King that it was not right for an anointed ruler coming from a royal dynasty who had relieved all the rest of the country of paying poradlne, to leave the Church still paying it. The King accepts the argument and the Church is relieved of paying the tax.

The Knights in Prussia and Livonia make eight armed incursions into Lithuania devastating the country along the rivers Niemen, Wilia, Niewiaża and elsewhere. They create such havoc that the Lithuanians begin to plan going to settle elsewhere, and this they might well have done had not the election of the Lithuanian duke, Jagiello, as King of Poland prevented it.

After Whitsun, pretending to be ill, Kiejstut secretly enters Prussia, captures the castle at Eckersberg and its starosta, whom his men try to burn as a sacrifice to their gods, but are prevented. The castle is burned instead.

The Prussian Marshal again invades Lithuania and gets as far as Troki, which is held by Kiejstut, and devastates the country as far as Wilno. Kiejstut requests talks and the Marshal agrees to suspend hostilities. No sooner has the Marshal withdrawn, than the Commander of Ragneta invades Samogitia and devastates six districts there. The Marshal, Dietrich, then uses new arrivals from Germany to invade again and in five stages reaches Wilno. Kiejstut arranges a truce, but before that half the city has been burned. While the Marshal is vainly trying to capture the castle, Kiejstut with some 500 men gets in ahead of the withdrawing Prussians and captures or destroys all the provisions the Knights have cached for their return journey. As a result both the Prussians and their horses have to fast for six days.

Charles, Roman Emperor and King of Bohemia, dies after reigning for thirty-one years.

A.D. 1379

Sędziwój Castellan of Bnin unable to accept the fact that the death of the Duke of Szczecin means that he is not going to get the money the latter owed him for his help in the war against the Margrave of Brandenburg, goes to the Duke's brother and heir, Świętobor, and demands his money. When Świętobor refuses to pay, Sędziwój and his nephew, the justiciar of Poznań, declare war on the new Duke and repeatedly raid his territory. In retaliation, the Duke invades Poland and invests the family castle of the Poznań justiciar. Finding the castle's moats dry, he mounts an assault the next day. His men reach the castle walls and hack at them with axes, while the defenders shoot at them and throw down stones on them. Having no mantlets, the attackers are faced with disaster and withdraw. A one-day truce is then arranged to enable them to bury the dead. Then, instead of renewing the attack, the Duke splits his force up into a number of units which have orders to devastate the country round Słupsk. That done, he withdraws to his own territory and makes it up with Sędziwój, to whom he pays an agreed sum by way of compensation.

A.D. 1380

On October 20, King Louis using as intermediary the Starosta of Kujawy and the Lord Chamberlain of Poland, whom he sends to Gdańsk, pays Władysław the White the final instalment of the 10,000 florins he owes for the duchy of Gniewkowo. Władysław counts the coin and, without giving a receipt or acknowledgement of payment, secretly sails from Gdańsk with a few servants and goes to Lübeck, which, as is known, was once part of Poland but had broken away.

At about the same time, the Archbishop of Gniezno and his suffragan bishops send a delegation of three to the King in Buda complaining of the grievous harm done to them, their churches and their clergy by the depredations of the Knights. The only reply they are given is that the King will summon a general assembly at which he will right their wrongs.

Bishop Florian of Cracow dies on February 6 after thirteen years as bishop. He is succeeded by Zawisza of Kurozwak, who enjoys the support of Queen Elizabeth.

A.D. 1381

Elizabeth the Queen-dowager dies in Buda on December 29.

Wanting to introduce a new and more just system of government in Poland, which had not been possible while his mother was alive, Louis summons the prelates and nobles to an assembly in Buda in the middle of March, promising to deal there with their complaints, justly and in accordance with the law. The Poles all attend, despite the distance; yet, after several days of discussions no salutary or practical way of righting the situation in Poland has been arrived at. The King has not been attending and it is feared that for that reason any proposal will be rejected. In the end, the King appoints the bishop, starosta and castellan of Cracow, and the voivode of Kalisz joint regents of the entire kingdom. This done, he refuses to hear any more complaints and refers everyone to his regents.

That is the end of the assembly. From now on, Bishop Zawiska of Cracow styles himself regent and surrounds himself with so many knights, servants, horses and conveyances, that his court resembles more that of a king, than of a bishop. There is a document preserved in Cracow cathedral which grants the Bishop complete authority to appoint officials and officers of the Crown as he sees fit, with the exception of the castellanate and voivodeship of Cracow.

Duke Władysław of Opole, having refunded to the widow of the Duke of Szczecin the amount of her dowry, now occupies the duchy of Dobrzyń. He then demands that the peasants in the villages belonging to Płock diocese shall pay him half a mark for each of their fields. As the Duke himself is delaying payment of the sheaf tithe, the Bishop of Płock pronounces an anathema on him, his starostas and other officials, and this is implemented throughout the duchy. He also places an interdict on any places to which they may go. The Duke suffers this for a while, but when he is refused communion at Easter, he goes in person to the Archbishop, admits that he is at fault and promises to pay compensation and make what amends the Archbishop requires. Relieved of the anathema, on May 13, he and the bishops of Płock and Włocławek and their chapters meet in Złotoria castle. The Duke rescinds his tax and returns all the monies already extracted.

Siemowit, Duke of all Mazovia, dies on June 17, leaving three sons: two by his first wife and a third by the daughter of the Duke of Ziębice, as well as two daughters, one married to the Duke of Opole, and the other, first to the Duke of Szczecin, and, on his death, to the Duke of Brześć. When the latter learns from his sister that his wife, whom he adores and of whom he is jealous, is having an affair with a certain noble, he refrains from punishing her, since she is pregnant, but when she gives birth to a boy, he has her suffocated. Her supposed lover is arrested in Prussia and then torn by horses and hanged. His anger assuaged, the Duke regrets and is ashamed of what he has done, especially as the babe is like him. The boy is in due course educated and is his father's special favourite. The Duke eventually arranges for his promotion to be archdeacon first of Płock and then of Łęczyca.

The Duke leaves his duchy to only two of his sons: Janusz who receives Warsaw, and Siemowit who gets Płock.

A Carthusian monastery, the second in Poland, is founded at a place four miles from Gdańsk.

The Castellan, Starosta, Archdeacon and Chancellor of Cracow, whom King Louis has sent to Wielkopolska to see justice done to all, are well received, but the complainants are so numerous and vociferous that they are told that, in the absence of Bishop Zawiska, who is regarded as the chief regent, and who will not join the others until St. James's Day, the others are not authorized to dispense justice or order the return of properties. The angry plaintiffs, loudly cursing the King and his regents, return home disgruntled.

King Louis, disquieted by a number of complaints that Bartosz is using the royal castle at Odolanów as a base from which to plunder the countryside and that he has even captured some French knights and merchants, and is holding them to ransom, orders the starosta of Wielkopolska to attack the castle. After some days fighting a truce is arranged and a conference held in a village belonging to the Archdeacon of Gniezno, the outcome of which is that Bartosz is to surrender Odolanów castle in return for 18,000 florins, its estimated value, less the amounts he extorted from the French. After this no more is heard of civil strife.

A papal legate discovers that the Archdeacon of Gniezno, who collects the Holy See's revenue from Poland, has cheated the Holy See out of 1500 florins, which he is made to refund. Then it is discovered that he has embezzled a further 120,000 florins and for this he is condemned to life-long imprisonment.

The city fathers of Wrocław, wishing to stop beer from Świdnica being sold to the clergy of Wrocław cathedral, impose a strict ban on its import. Nonetheless, a certain carter, bringing several kegs of this beer as a Christmas gift from Robert of Legnica to his brother, the dean of Wrocław, asks the city fathers for permission to deliver them; but they, interpreting the ban more strictly than they should, put the carter in prison and confiscate the beer. Because of this, the Bishop of Lubusz, administrator of the vacant see of Wrocław, places an interdict on Wrocław city and, being afraid of popular protests, moves to Nysa.

Duke Władysław of Opole, anxious to remove the disagreement between the clergy and people of Wrocław, arrives on June 7 and demands that, by virtue of his arrival, services must be resumed. He promises that, if he finds the city fathers at fault, he will compel them to pay compensation. The clergy refuse to commit sacrilege, to which this would amount, and this so angers the Duke that he imprisons the Abbot of the Blessed Virgin in the city hall for a week. The same could have been the fate of Brother Mark of St. Vincent's, had he not lied and promised to say mass for the King on the following day, and then escaped during the night with all his canons and plenty of provisions to the Premonstratensian house in Strzelno, across the border in Poland, where they are safe. The Duke takes his revenge by plundering the Church properties of so many cattle and herds that 200 sheep fetch only three marks, and an ox or a cow goes for a farthing. Even at these low prices not all are sold, so most are sent into Bohemia for sale there. The Duke then allows his troops to sack the bishop's palace, the monasteries and the chapter house, in which they find gold, silver, coins, vessels, valuable robes and a variety of enticing things, not only in locked chests, which they break open, but in hiding places which they seek out with remarkable avidity.

A.D. 1382

The Bishop of Cracow dies on January 20, some say because he fell from a ladder while trying to get into the honey loft.

On March 18 the Bishop of Poznań dies after two years of suffering with cancer of the genitals. His tongue and throat were so covered with abscesses that he was bereft of speech.

On April 5, the Archbishop of Gniezno dies after a grievous illness. Immediately, his nephew and nieces, brother and many other relations plunder his treasury and his episcopal property.

When he learns of the archbishop's death, the Duke of Mazovia collects a force and lays siege to the bishop's castle at Łowicz, now in the hands of the castellan of Gniezno. The Chapter at once sends the cathedral's suffragan bishop to request that he desist, only to be told that the Duke is entitled to have the castle as long as the see is vacant, and that he will only abstain from besieging it if it is put in the hands of one of the canons of Gniezno and not of his mortal enemy, the Castellan. This answer hastens the selection of a new archbishop, a noble called Dobrogost, doctor of law, Dean of Cracow and cantor of Gniezno. The Duke is then asked to raise the siege and agrees to withdraw, if the Castellan is removed and he is given 200 marks to pay the troops taking part in the siege. Thus, the Cantor of Gniezno takes over the castle.

In order to obtain the support and agreement of King Louis to their appointment, the new archbishop and bishops send a three-man delegation to Hungary, and themselves prepare money, horses and equipment, with the intention of going to Rome. The King receives hints that the election of Dobrogost will injure the Crown and his progeny, in that Dobrogost was elected on the understanding that on the death of King Louis, Siemowit of Mazovia would be crowned King of Poland, so he delays receiving the delegates for three days and then tells them that he cannot agree to the election. He also has ambushes laid and traps prepared for the delegates in various places, through which he anticipates they will pass on their way to Rome. Forewarned, when they reach Wrocław they hurry forward as fast as they can, taking every possible precaution. Nonetheless, just before Treviso they fall into one of the traps and are imprisoned on the orders of the Prince of Venice, who wishes to curry favour with King Louis. One of them, Nicholas, is released thanks to Władysław of Opole and continues on to Rome, while Dobrogost, his servants and baggage are turned back. Duke Władysław, having the support of King Louis, puts his own nephew, the son of Bolesław of Opole, into the see of Poznań, despite the fact he was not yet of sufficient age, though he had already been made prior of St. Martin in Spisz. Before Nicholas even reaches Rome, Pope Urban VI, realizing that the see of Wrocław has been vacant for seven years, has appointed the Bishop of Lubusz, son of Duke Władysław of Legnica, to the see, and Jan Kietlic, canon of Lubusz to be Bishop of Lubusz. The Duke dislikes the appointment, mostly because it has been made without his knowledge or approval, and tries to have it annulled, but in the end a compromise is reached: all hurt done by the Duke to Wrocław is forgiven, as is the debt of 5000 marks which the Chapter lent to the Duke's father. The Chapter has the solace that under this agreement the newly elected city councillors may not go from the city hall straight to their own homes, but must first go the cathedral and swear on the hands of the canons that they will defend and preserve the laws and liberties of the Church.

Duke Gedymin of Lithuania had seven sons, among whom, in his lifetime, he distributed the lands taken from the Ruthenians: Monwid receiving Kiernowo and Slonim; Narymunt receiving Pinsk, and Krewo going to Olgierd, who is married to the only daughter of the Duke of Vitebsk and thus is heir to Vitebsk. Jewnuta is given the capital Wilno and designated as Gedymin's successor. Kiejstut gets Troki, Koriat Novogrodek, while the youngest, Lubart, gets no share, because he has married the only daughter of the Duke of Vladimir and as such will inherit the duchies of Lwów and Vladimir. Of the seven, Olgierd and Kiejstut are the most energetic and, also, very close. Together they decide to remove Jewnuta from Wilno and the Grand-duchy. On the appointed day, despite Olgierd's late arrival, Kiejstut occupies Wilno and all but captures Jewnuta, who gets away into the forest and mountains, which he roams until, immobilized by frostbite, he is caught by his pursuers and taken back to Wilno. Kiejstut then informs Olgierd that he has got both Wilno and Jewnuta, and Olgierd hurries to Wilno. When he arrives, there is some dispute as to who is to be grand-duke, but in the end it is decided that Olgierd is to have Wilno and be grand-duke, and to have authority over all his brothers. If he acquires territory this will be divided equally between him and Kiejstut. These two then swear loyalty to each other, and not to make attempts on the other's life or property.

Olgierd is regarded as unusually happy as a father and a duke. He has twelve sons, all handsome youths, whom their mother brought up in accordance with Greek customs and taught the principles of the Greek confession. Jagiello is his father's favourite and loved more dearly than a son, as Kiejstut does his son, Witold, more than the other five. In their youth these two are close friends and love each other like brothers. Each is appointed his father's successor. When Olgierd dies Kiejstut keeps his promise and allows Jagiello to succeed his father as Grand-duke. His uncle is as submissive to him, as he was to his father. He is at his Court, takes part in his councils and gives him advice, yet his sincere loyalty is repaid with appalling ingratitude. One of those close to Olgierd is a man called Wojdylo, a peasant of unknown family, who began as Olgierd's baker, became his chamberlain, then his cup-bearer, and, finally is in such favour with his master, that he is regarded as the first and best of all the King's men. Jagiello is equally attached to him and marries him to his sister, Maria. Wojdylo does not trust Kiejstut and is afraid that the latter may harm his career, so he accuses him to Jagiello and makes the latter so suspicious of him, that he comes to hate him. He alleges that Jagiello has been having secret meetings and has made secret pacts with Winrich of Kniprode Master of Prussia against Kiejstut. Kiejstut suspects this and tells his son Witold, Jagiello's bosom friend. Witold considers it impossible that he, who was so close to Jagiello, should not have known of it. Eventually, Kiejstut quietly raids Wilno, captures Jagiello and takes possession of the castle, where he discovers documents concerning the pacts Jagiello has made with the Knights. He sends a messenger to tell Witold, who hurries to Wilno, covering the distance, some 150 kilometres, in one day. Jagiello is not imprisoned, does not even have his treasury plundered, but he is removed as grand-duke, though allowed to retain Vitebsk and Krewo, which he had inherited from his father. As to the charge of treachery, he clears himself as best he can and promises Kiejstut to be a loyal nephew and help him as much as he can. He renounces his pacts with the Knights. Then, accompanied by Duke Witold and with all his possessions, children and servants, he leaves Wilno and goes to Vitebsk, where he settles.

Kiejstut next attacks Nowogrodek, whose duke, Korybut, has been lax in recognizing his authority. He strings up on a gallows the man he considers his only mortal enemy, Jagiello's brother-in-law, Wojdyta. Meanwhile, Jagiello, who had promised to join him, is, instead, busy suborning the more eminent citizens of Wilno to help him besiege Wilno castle, while Witold remains in Troki. Jagiello returns from Vitebsk with his brothers and an army and the castle is surrendered to him. He then advances on Troki, where the Marshal brings a powerful force to help him.

Witold, seeing what is happening, tells Kiejstut who is still besieging Nowogrodek, and leaves Troki with his mother and seeks shelter in Grodno castle. After some days, Troki castle surrenders to Jagiello. Meanwhile, Kiejstut has abandoned the siege of Nowogrodek and come hurrying back to Lithuania; but, realizing that Jagiello with his Prussian reinforcements is much the stronger and has gained control of the Grand-duchy and the castles of Wilno and Troki, Kiejstut goes to Samogitia to recruit extra forces. Leaving Witold in Grodno, he sends his wife to his son-in-law, the Duke of Mazovia, hoping that he will look after her. The Duke a prudent and enterprising man, who believes that you should never miss an opportunity, seizes Mielnik and Drohiczyn castles, installs strong garrisons and devastates all around, before laying siege to Brześć castle, only to abandon the siege, when he learns that his mother-in-law is there.

Kiejstut with his Samogitian army has reached the River Wilia. His son, Witold, meets him there with his contingent. Joining forces, they cross the river and advance on Troki and invest it. Jagiello, anticipating this move, being assured of the help of both the Prussian and Livonian Masters, whose armies are not far away, advances on Troki to raise the siege. Kiejstut, informed by his intelligence of what is happening, abandons the siege and arrays his troops, ready to do battle. When the two armies are a mere three or four bowshots from each other, Jagiello sends heralds to Witold asking him to adjudicate between Jagiello and his father and so avoid bloodshed. Witold, wishing to discuss things with his father, tells them that he will only go to Jagiello's army, if Duke Skirgiello comes in person and guarantees him safe passage there and back. When Skirgiello comes and gives the guarantee, Witold, with his father's permission, goes to Jagiello under a truce.

Jagiello repeats his pleas for peace and Kiejstut is persuaded to accept the idea. Skirgiello then goes to Kiejstut and guarantees his safety, so Kiejstut goes to Jagiello to discuss terms. Quite unsuspecting, he takes no precautions, does not even leave his son behind. When they arrive, the two are surrounded by Jagiello's men and realize that they have walked into a trap. Jagiello tells them that this is neither the time nor the place for a discussion and insists that they return to Wilno and talk there. They cannot refuse. When they reach Wilno, Witold is placed under guard, while his father is put in chains, taken to Krewo and there cast into a dark and filthy dungeon. After four nights there, he is strangled and his body taken to Wilno and there burned along with his arms, horses, clothes and favourite dogs, as is the ancient custom.

The same fate is intended for Witold, though first he is sent to Krewo with his wife Anna and there kept under strict, though tolerable guard. Witold has his own quarters and his own servants. He is not allowed to leave his room, but his wife, Anna, is permitted to go to him at night, with two of her women, and leave in the morning. Perturbed by rumours that her husband is about to suffer the same fate as his father, she persuades her husband to take a chance, put on the clothes of one of her women and make a run for it. So, one morning, while one of his wife's women remains pretending to be Witold, he leaves his quarters, dressed as a woman, with his wife and that night he lets himself down the castle wall on a rope. First, he goes to his sister's husband, Siemowit Duke of Mazovia, who takes him in and, some say, christens him, he taking the name Conrad. He does not dare stay where he is, lest Jagiello's arm prove sufficiently long to reach him, and so he goes to Prussia. He is followed by a remarkable number of the nobility with their relatives and servants, as well as by his wife, Anna, whom Jagiello had ordered to be released, when he learned of her husband's escape. The Prussian Master Winrich rebukes Witold for not having asked for help earlier, treats him with great kindness and promises him all the help he and the Order can give him. Witold promises that, in return for the help he has already had, and may have in the future, he will always be grateful to the Order and serve it with his men. Then, the Master having provided him with weapons, horses and clothes, he goes secretly to Samogitia and gets the people there to promise to help him against Jagiello.

But to return to Polish affairs! King Louis, realizing that his strength is ebbing and wishing to secure his two kingdoms and his two daughters, choses as husband for the elder, Maria, Sigismund, Margrave of Brandenburg, then fourteen years old; Maria's dowry being the Kingdom of Poland. He then organizes an assembly at which he persuades the prelates and nobles present to accept Sigismund as their king and to pay him homage and swear him fealty. This agreed, he sends Sigismund with a force of Hungarians to take possession of the royal castles and stifle any incipient revolt.

On his arrival, Sigismund is greeted by a host of knights and within a short time has captured Kozmin castle and town and two other forts, part of the property of Starosta Bartosz, which he takes to punish the latter for certain misdemeanours. After this, he makes a fresh agreement with Bartosz, who is promised a certain sum of money secured against some villages belonging to the castle. He then moves his army into Mazovia. In the meantime, King Louis dies on September 13 in the Hungarian town of Trnava.

Sigismund is informed by messenger and hurries to Poznań, where he persuades the people to swear allegiance to him. While he is there, he is all but overwhelmed with requests that he should remove the starosta of Wielkopolska, who, people complain, is too oppressive, promising Sigismund their submission and obedience, if he will only deign to reside in Poland. This the King refuses to do, to the Poles' frustration.

When the Hungarian nobles to whom King Louis granted the more important of the Ruthenian castles captured by King Casimir, with the intention of detaching these Ruthenian lands from Poland and attaching them to Hungary, hear of the King's death, they surrender their castles

(Krzemieniec, Olesko, Horodło, Łopatyn and Sniatyn) to Duke Lubart, then governor of Łuck castle. Heavily bribed, they sell the castles entrusted to them and depart with their shameful gains to Hungary. Queen Elizabeth does not let their infidelity go unpunished. She imprisons many, executes others, and confiscates their goods and family possesions for the benefit of the royal treasury.

When Sigismund, having left Poznań, reaches Gniezno, he organizes splendid obsequies in the cathedral there for the dead King and moves on to Kujawy. While in Brześć, he is again urged to remove the starosta of Wielkopolska, and, when he again refuses, everyone turns away from him. An assembly held in Milosław sends delegates to the prelates and nobles of Wielkopolska asking them to attend an assembly they propose to hold in Radom to consider the state of the realm. Many who attend, consider Duke Siemowit of Mazovia, husband of Louis' second daughter, Jadwiga, as the more suitable ruler, and, after discussion, it is agreed that they will pay homage to one of King Louis' daughters, but she must be married to a sensible prince who will undertake to reside permanently in the kingdom and is one whom they can unhesitatingly accept as king. As this involves a tacit understanding that Sigismund has to be removed, the Archbishop of Gniezno and the starostas of Wielkopolska and Poznań hotly refuse to agree, asserting that they have sworn loyalty to Sigismund. Nonetheless, the proposal is put down in writing, seals attached and sent to an assembly of the knights of Cracow and Sandomierz for them to endorse.

This assembly opens at dawn on the Feast of St. Nicholas. It is attended by the Archbishop of Gniezno, the Starosta of Wielkopolska and Margrave Sigismund, the latter demanding that the knights there swear loyalty to him; but it is also attended by envoys from Queen Elizabeth, the Bishops of Eger and Csanad and two Hungarian nobles. These latter, having demanded a hearing in the name of the Queen, thank the Poles for their unyielding loyalty to her and her daughters, and ask them not to swear loyalty and obedience to anyone, especially not Sigismund, until she has decided the destiny of her daughters. The audience is sympathetic, for Sigismund is out of favour with the Poles for favouring Czechs rather than Poles, whom he has turned out of the room while he was eating. The delegates confirm the decision taken at Radom, and, eventually, the Archbishop of Gniezno and the Starosta of Wielkopolska also agree to it. The Starosta wishes to defend his behaviour, but is told that it is neither right nor suitable to hear him before he has been removed from his post or has resigned it. Sigismund wishes to move on to Cracow, but, on the advice of the Castellan, this is not allowed, as to do so would violate the decision taken at Radom. Instead, he crosses the Vistula at Wawrzyńczyce and goes to Niepołomice, whence, on the pretext of being ill he returns at public expense to Hungary via Bochnia and Nowy Sącz.

Bartosz, the holder of Odolanów, ever with an eye to the main chance, goes to Duke Siemowit of Mazovia, who is avid for the Polish crown, hands Odalanów over to him, promises him his services and makes a secret agreement with him for the use of his army, with which he attacks the castle at Kalisz on the eve of the Feast of St. Thomas the Apostle. The guards being in a heavy sleep, some of his men get as far as the wall, and one of them bores a hole in the gate, which he then enlarges with a saw until it is big enough for men to pass through. The noise of the saw is heard by the castle baker, who gets up early to cut wood for his oven; he goes to the gate, sees the danger and uses his axe to blunt the saw, but so neatly that the sawyer does not feel it. He then rouses the castle's defenders, who hurl down stones and other missiles on to those waiting on the other side of the gate; thus are Bartosz and his men driven off. The next day, Bartosz attacks and captures Koźminek, recently acquired by Sigismund and continues on to Chotecz, King Casimir's brick mansion which has been turned into a fortress. He then hurriedly bridges the river and moves against the neighbouring town and castle of Koźmin, only to be shamefully repulsed. He continues on to Parsko, which it takes him a week to capture.

The Prussian Master, Winrich of Kniprode, dies on June 24 after thirty-one years as Master. He is succeeded by Conrad Zöllner of Rottenstein.

In September, the Duke of Wieluń, with the permission of the Bishop of Cracow, replaces the parish church of St. Mary in Old Częstochowa with a monastery of the hermit brethren of the Order of St. Paul, the first anchorite, who follow the Austin rule, endowing it in perpetuity with the villages of Stara Częstochowa and Kawodrza with their smithies, mills and farmsteads, plus the monetary tithes and dues from Ostrzeszów and Częstochowa, as well as grain tithes from five villages belonging to the castle at Brzoznica, and also tithes in grain and honey from mills recently built and to be built in the future in Częstochowa and Zrach. Also tithes of honey from eight villages, at the same time relieving the possessions of the monastery from all burdens, taxes and tributes.

A.D. 1383

Because of disturbing news from Wielkopolska, the Voivode of Poznań is sent there to sort things out. His troops capture the town of Pyzdry and then lay siege to Kalisz castle, doing considerable damage to Church property. Domarat, the Starosta of Wielkopolska, assembles a force of various nationalities on which the Voivode launches a successful sudden attack. As he then moves on in loose formation, he is attacked in his turn and routed by one of the Starosta's supporters.

Queen Elizabeth receives repeated requests from Poland to send one of her daughters to be married to some prince of whom the Poles approve, who can take over and govern the country, for because of the deteriorating situation the interregnum cannot be permitted to continue. Her response is to send the Bishop of Weszprem and two nobles to a general assembly to be held in Sieradz on February 26. Given special permission to speak, they relieve all the prelates, nobles and magnates of Poland from the oath of loyalty they swore to King Louis' eldest daughter, Maria, and her husband; and tell the assembly that at Easter the Queen will send her younger daughter, Jadwiga, now betrothed, some say married, to Wilhelm, the Duke of Austria, provided they will undertake in advance and in writing and on oath, to crown Jadwiga with the Polish crown and immediately return her to her mother in Hungary, so that she can spend the next three years in her mother's care. The assembly decides that it needs time to consider the proposal and so arranges to meet again in the same place on March 28, while in the meantime the envoys are to remain and wait for an answer. It is then decided to send the Voivodes of Cracow and Kalisz and the Castellan of Zawichost to Wielkopolska to end the strife between its knights and its Starosta, Domarat. Under a commission given them by Queen Elizabeth they order the Castellan of Łęczyca to hand his castle over to them, as they are taking over all the castles under the Starosta's control to end the civil strife. The Voivode of Poznań and the knights of Wielkopolska are reluctant to recognize their authority, but agree that when Kalisz castle surrenders it will be given to the Castellan of Kalisz. The two voivodes then leave to go to Queen Elizabeth in Hungary, and the Castellans of Zawichost and Krzeslaw go to Poznań to quench the smouldering civil war. The two sides agree a truce which ends the bloodshed and damage to property, though the castles remain under the Starosta's control.

At the reconvened Sieradz conference, which starts on March 28, Siemowit, Duke of Mazovia, is all but unanimously chosen to marry Jadwiga and become King of Poland; despite Władysław, Duke of Opole's objection and claim to have a better right to the succession. (A plan to imprison him is foiled.) The Archbishop of Gniezno now gets up and asks the assembly whether it wishes to see Siemowit crowned, as the shouts of approval die down, Andrew, son of the Voivode of Cracow, tells them that they are being shamefully and dangerously over-hasty, since, as they all know, they owe a duty to the Princess Jadwiga, and he suggests that they require her to present herself no later than the coming Easter and wait until then, before taking any further steps. They must ask her to come before them with a husband dear to her and to them. Should she not arrive by that date or refuse their request, they can begin to choose and appoint a king. One and all approve the idea and it is decided to postpone the election of Siemowit and to send their reply to Queen Elizabeth, which is that the long interregnum has so damaged Poland that they can wait no longer: they will keep the oaths of loyalty they swore to King Louis and his daughters, so that if his daughter, Jadwiga, will come at Whitsun and promise to remain in Poland with her future husband and to recover all the territory torn from Poland, especially Ruthenia, Wieluń and Dobrzyń, they will accept her as their lady and queen; otherwise, they cannot allow Poland to suffer any longer and must search for a suitable king.

So, at Whitsun, the great men of Poland foregather at Nowy Swiąt to await the arrival of Queen Elizabeth and her daughter; but, instead, come the Voivode of Kalisz and the Starosta of Cracow with greetings from the Queen, who wishes them to know that she and her daughter have reached Košice, but can go no further because of floods. She asks them not to be angry with her and promises that she will try to get to them, even if that means incurring danger. In the meantime, she begs that the most important of them should deign to come to her and allow decisions to be made. Some of those of lesser rank now go home, but the more important go to Košice, where they agree a different arrangement, setting aside that agreed at Sieradz, namely that Princess Jadwiga will come to Cracow by next St. Martin's Day and take possession of the kingdom, and she and the Polish prelates and nobles are jointly to decide her choice of husband. Should the Princess not have progeny, on her death the succession will pass to her full sister Maria and vice versa. It is further decided that the bonds linking Hungary and Poland are to remain indissoluble; while the progeny of one or of both sisters are to have the right to succeed to either kingdom. Though many feel that further postponement of the Princess's arrival augurs disaster, it is accepted.

Duke Siemowit, eager for his election and looking forward to gaining the hand of a daughter of King Louis, goes in secret to Cracow together with the Archbishop of Gniezno and Bartosz of Koźmin. When it becomes known that they have arrived and are accompanied by a number of Mazovian knights and 1500 spearmen, they are not allowed into the city. The Duke has to remain outside the city wall, in a manor belonging to the Prior of St. Florian in Płock. That night the city fathers post guards in case of an attack. The next day, Siemowit moves on to Korczyń, where he awaits the outcome of the Poles' discussions with Queen Elizabeth. The large number of armed men he has with him suggests that, after the Princess's arrival, should she not give herself voluntarily, he intends to take her by force. It is said that, knowing this, and to prevent ambushes being prepared, the Poles who went to Košice, deliberately postponed Jadwiga's arrival, so as to compel Siemowit to withdraw, also that they advised the removal of several starostas busy preparing a hotbed of treachery. Such an unexpected turn to his plans decides Siemowit to leave Cracow and return to Mazovia. He is furious with the Voivode of Cracow, a youth not yet eighteen, for having opposed him, so, on the way back he burns the young voivode's town of Książ, as a warning to him and to others. Now, learning that Queen Elizabeth and the Poles with her have sent Ścibor to govern Łęczyca, Kujawy and the castles there, removing Peter Maloch, who is suspected of supporting Siemowit, Siemowit gets in first by sending a force under the Voivode of Płock to seize the castles of Kujawy. He is admitted into Brześć on May 23, just ahead of Ścibor, to whom the townspeople of Brześć, who dislike Siemowit, give a great welcome. Siemowit's troops at once invest Brześć town. Realizing his difficult situation, Ścibor arranges for his unmolested withdrawal, whereupon Maloch imprisons many in Brześć who had welcomed Ścibor, confiscates their possessions and hands that castle and others in Kujawy, to Siemowit. Siemowit then moves on to Kruszwica, which surrenders.

Having imposed his authority on Kujawy, Siemowit summons the prelates and lords of the rest of the kingdom to an assembly in Sieradz on June 15, saying that he will reward those who obey his instructions and agree to his coronation, and that he will take armed action against any who oppose him. Almost all the great and powerful disregard the summons, so that only the Archbishop of Gniezno turns up on the appointed day together with a few knights from Wielkopolska.

There, in the friary of the Dominicans, the Archbishop proclaims Siemowit King of Poland, and, had it not been for the protests of a small group, he would even have crowned him with the royal insignia, assisted by the Bishops of Cracow and Płock, whom he summoned specially to conduct the ceremony. After this, Maloch hands Łęczyca castle over to him. Siemowit moves his army into Wielkopolska, hoping to gain control of that too.

Wielkopolska is now aflame with war and rebellion, demonstrating what happens when there is no king. The Archbishop of Gniezno bows to the superior power of the Castellan of Poznań and surrenders to him the castle of Żnin. The Duke of Głogów, Henry the Sparrow, unable to recover the lands of Wschowa that King Casimir had taken from him, puts them to fire and the sword. The Starosta of Wielkopolska makes an attempt to raise the siege of Kalisz, but succeeds only in recovering the castle of Poniec.

In Cracow and Sandomierz peace reigns. Appalled by the civil and external strife taking place in Wielkopolska, an assembly is called for the Feast of St. James the Apostle. This is attended by Duke Siemowit. Its purpose is to see to the security and peace of the Kingdom. Much discussion leads to no conclusion, but a grudging truce is arranged to last until St. Michael's Day.

An army of 12,000 Hungarians under the Margrave of Brandenburg, Sigismund, in whose suite is the Archbishop of Esztergom, moves into Poland to stop the hostile activities of the Duke of Mazovia. Crossing the Carpathians that separate Hungary from Poland, its first halt is at Nowy Sącz. After some days Margrave Sigismund breaks camp and, reinforced with knights from Cracow and Sandomierz, moves through Radom to Mazovia, as he goes burning whatever belongs to Duke Siemowit. The part of Mazovia belonging to Duke Janusz of Warsaw he allows no one to harm, since the Duke has remained faithful to the oath of loyalty he swore to King Louis' daughters.

Domarat the Starosta of Wielkopolska, having failed to defeat his country's enemies, avenges himself on the Archbishop of Gniezno. He attacks the town of Żnin, but, being repulsed, brutally ravages the surrounding villages and their innocent inhabitants, burning farmsteads and plundering. Having collected a considerable booty of cattle, he advances on Gniezno, where he loots the Archbishop's palace and the houses of the canons.

Margrave Sigismund, having, with his Hungarians, Cracovians and men from Sandomierz, cruelly burned and looted all Mazovia belonging to Siemowit, on September 25 invests the town of Brześć, which also belongs to Siemowit. Throughout the eleven days of the siege Sigismund's troops treat the surroundings as if they were enemy territory. In the end Duke Władysław of Opole, Wieluń and Dobrzyń arrange a truce between Sigismund and Siemowit, as a result of which Sigismund and his cruel Hungarians return to Hungary. The Castellan of Poznań, who, hoping to curry favour with Sigismund and Queen Elizabeth, has come with troops from Pomerania and Saxony to help Sigismund, collects a considerable booty only to be deprived of it by the Duke of Opole, when he tries to cross the latter's territory with it.

The Archbishop of Gniezno, having learned that Margrave Sigismund and Queen Elizabeth are trying to get the Pope to ban him from Żnin on the grounds that he was using it as a base from which to raid and plunder, demands that the governors of Żnin clear him of such unjustified accusations. When they refuse to do so, unless first repaid the considerable sum they have already spent on his behalf, the Archbishop secretly arranges with the governor of Żnin to have the gates opened, and, on October 9, marches in with a large force, ejects the Saxons and Pomeranians and thus recovers Żnin, which he hands over to the Dean of Gniezno.

The Lithuanian leaders, hearing that Poland is torn by civil strife, as is the duchy of Mazovia, pluck up courage and decide to recapture Drohiczyń, still in the Duke's hands, whose holder, the Marshal of Mazovia, is not in residence.

The Marshal, knowing how small is the garrison he had left in Drohiczyń, goes to its rescue with 300 spearmen and sixty crossbowmen. He marches straight through the enemy's camp and, recognized by those inside, the gates are opened to admit him.

However, some Ruthenians in the town, who have been bribed by the besiegers, light fires in a number of places and then let themselves down the outer walls on ropes and escape to the enemy's camp. The Lithuanians then attack, thus preventing the fires from being put out, and in the end the Marshal has to surrender to the Lithuanian duke.

The Knights' army in Lithuania suffers a similar fate, for, when, after a long siege and bombardment, the fortified town of Troki surrenders to the Prussian Master, he puts in a strong garrison with plentiful supplies, and then leaves. No sooner have the Prussians gone, than Jagiello lays siege to it in his turn, before any repairs can be carried out, and forces it to surrender.

This year is memorable for the plague that rages almost throughout the world. Every part of Poland suffers and very many victims are claimed.

A.D. 1384

The Voivode Sędziwój of Kalisz and the Starosta of Cracow, accompanied by sons of some of the more eminent Polish nobles, are sent to Queen Elizabeth in Hungary to protest at her failure to bring her daughter Jadwiga to Cracow by St. Martin's Day. They are granted an audience in Zadar, the capital of Dalmatia, at which, after making their complaint, they again ask her to end the harmful delay and send her daughter to Cracow, where she will be crowned and, with order restored to Poland, returned to Hungary to stay there until she comes of age. Should the Queen not trust them to do this, they will give her the noble youths they have brought with them as hostages. The Queen's reply is ambiguous. Voivode Sędziwój, angry at this further disappointment, decides to return to Cracow. The Queen forbids his departure, afraid lest she lose Cracow castle, and sends the Castellan of Sandomierz, Jan of Tarnowski, to occupy it and hand it over to the Hungarians she is shortly going to send. Sędziwój guesses what is afoot and sends a messenger to Cracow, who uses the horses stationed ready for Sędziwój's return. The message is that under no circumstances, even if they were to see their voivode burning at the stake, are they to surrender the castle to anyone. Sędziwój then leaves Zadar with a handful of companions, and, by changing horses, reaches Cracow in one day, exhausted, and before his messenger, having covered a distance of 600 Hungarian miles. The lords, perturbed, move the venue of the March 2 assembly from Lelów to Radom to make it more accessible to the barons of Wielkopolska.

Those attending the assembly duly meet in Radom on March 2. There is fierce discussion of whom to choose as successor to the throne, about public order and how to put an end to civil strife. One great problem is whether or not reneging on the oath sworn to King Louis would, or would not occasion worse civil strife and warring with neighbours; so they decide to send to the Queen one envoy she does not know, a sober person who can convince her of their profound exasperation. Orders are issued forbidding all official or private visits to Hungary. The chosen envoy is despatched and finds the Queen in Buda and delivers his message, begging her at least to keep her word and send her daughter to Cracow by May 2, stressing that they can wait no longer and will not ask again, but have sworn an oath that, if the Princess does not reach Cracow by St. Stanisław's Day, they will elect their own king.

This worries the Queen. She sends for her councillors and despatches her son-in-law Sigismund with a large, well-equipped force to govern Poland until Jadwiga grows up. When the news reaches Cracow, the Poles are indignant at being subordinated to a man imposed on them by a woman and a Hungarian, a man who has already earned their dislike. They quickly assemble an army and move up to Sącz, from where they send to the Margrave, who is already in Lubowla, warning him not to cross into Poland, for under no circumstances can they accept him as king or as regent, and telling him that they will resist if he attempts to move in. Somewhat intimidated, Sigismund sends envoys to ask them to send delegates to him to discuss Poland's problems and how to resolve them. The four chosen are the voivodes of Kalisz and Cracow, the starosta of Cracow and Jan Tarnowski castellan of Sandomierz. They succeed in persuading Sigismund to do his utmost to see that Jadwiga arrives by St. Stanisław's Day. He also promises on the quiet—a promise he immediately forgets—to see that the Chamberlain and the young hostages are released from prison. Meanwhile, in Wielkopolska, the barons are squabbling among themselves: Dobiesław of Golancz captures the son of Janusz of Głuchów after burning his manor and pillaging his property. Martin of Zwanowa imprisons and mortally wounds Jaracz of Siedlec and the son of Dobrogost of Szamotuły; while the wojt of Obarnik dies at the hand of Swidwa of Galowoi, and other quarrelling knights are killed.

On St. Stanisław's Day, the nobles and barons of Poland reassemble in Sącz to await the Princess's arrival. When she does not appear and there is no indication that she will, they hold further discussions. A proposal to send further delegates to Hungary is defeated, when Przecław Wawelski points out that it would disparage him and the others who have just come back from there after telling the Queen that no further envoys would be sent, and brand them as liars. Orders are then issued that no one may go to Hungary either officially or privately; but the Starosta of Cracow defies the ban and goes there to try and get the release of the hostages and persuade the Queen to send the Princess quickly, else the whole project will fall through.

Queen Elizabeth now realizes that she can no longer safely prevaricate and sends her daughter with a regal dowry of gold, silver, vessels, cloths. jewels, pearls and rugs and a huge cavalcade of nobles and knights headed by Cardinal Demeter Bishop of Csanad. A delighted throng of prelates, nobles, gentry and the guilds go out to greet her with a display of affection, indeed, behaving as if she could govern Poland alone, without a husband. So, on October 15, St. Jadwiga's Day, in Cracow cathedral she is anointed and crowned Queen of Poland in a ceremony performed by the Archbishop of Gniezno and the Bishops of Cracow, Poznań and Włocławek in the presence of the Cardinal-archbishop of Esztergom and a vast throng of the great of both countries, thus granting her complete authority to rule the kingdom until they find her a suitable husband, knowing that since childhood she has been brought up to put nobility before beauty, modesty before a fine figure, virtue before prettiness, modesty and restraint before fame and wealth, gentleness before authority.

A.D. 1385

When Jagiello, Grand-duke of Lithuania, hears that King Louis' daughter, Jadwiga, has been brought from Hungary to Poland, crowned Queen of Poland and entrusted with full authority over all Poland, and knowing of her reputed exceptional beauty, he sends two of his brothers and the captain of Wilno to Cracow and the Queen to ask for her hand in marriage. At the council, which is convened, the Grand-duke's brother, Skirgiello, tells them that his brother, Jagiello, his brothers, fellow dukes, the nobles and, if possible, the entire population of Lithuania and Samogitia, will convert to the Roman Catholic faith. He promises to free all Christian captives, especially those captured while raiding Poland. He proposes that they should form an indissoluble union of the Kingdom of Poland and all territories subject to Lithuania and Samogitia, together with some Ruthenian land conquered by force of arms. He further promises to recover and reincorporate into Poland the territories of Pomerania, Chełm, Silesia, Dobrzyń and Wieluń and all other territories surrendered, appropriated or wrest from the Kingdom. He further promises that his brother will bring to Poland all his treasure and that inherited from his father and grandfather and employ it for the benefit of Poland. He further promises to repay to Duke Wilhelm of Austria his surety of 20,000 florins. (So much for a pagan!) Though the proposal is scarcely to the liking of Queen Jad-

Iagiclo ſiuc Vladiſlaus
Lituanus.

Hic gentilis erat Lituanus de ſtirpe *IAGELLO*
Vir bonus, & tanti est inter benefica apex.
Mox est cœleſtis Princeps Baptiſmate tinctus,
Quem ſubact est Dominum gens ioncatſa ſonus.   *Hinc do-*

wiga, it is very much to the liking of the Poles, and it is referred to Queen Elizabeth in Buda for her to decide. In its favour are the spread of Christianity and the material advantages offered, against it is the fact of the agreement made between King Louis and Duke Wilhelm and his solemn betrothal to Jadwiga.

Queen Elizabeth's reply is that she will allow whatever is advantageous to Poland and insists that her daughter and the prelates and nobles of the Kingdom must do what they consider will benefit Christianity and their kingdom. The council rejects the claim of Duke Siemowit of Mazovia, as that of Władysław Duke of Opole, since the choice of either would be of little benefit, while that of Duke Wilhelm is dismissed out of hand, because they would have to wait a very long time for any help from him. That leaves only Jagiello, who, with Kiejstut destroyed and Witold gone over to the Knights, is the best of the Lithuanian dukes, even though uneducated and simple and better suited to the chase than to government. Some, however, find it distasteful to promote to royal degree a foreign, pagan duke over the heads of their own Catholic dukes, but the majority of the more sensible, having regard to the good of Christianity and the peace this would bring to Poland, consider they should choose Jagiello, Jadwiga's dislike of the idea being outweighed by the glory this extension of Christianity would bring to Poland. This decision removes the Queen's dislike of the proposal, for she is a pious woman already ardent in her faith, and it is easily accepted by the others. Envoys are at once sent to Lithuania to obtain confirmation of these promises and bring Jagiello to Cracow to marry the Queen and rule over Poland.

The loose morals and dissolute behaviour of Margrave Sigismund, whose marriage to Princess Maria is set to bring him the throne of Hungary, incenses his mother-in-law, who, with her councillors, has him expelled from Hungary in June, whereupon he goes to his brother, King Václav of Bohemia. Queen Elizabeth, who now hates her son-in-law, tries to annul his marriage to her daughter Maria, so that she can marry the Duke of Orleans, brother of the King of France. To arrange this she sends envoys to propose it, but nothing comes of the idea, because the Duke has already promised to marry the daughter of the Duke of Milan. Some Hungarian nobles, supporters of Margrave Sigismund, dislike what the Queen is trying to do and plan to put her in prison or exile her. The Queen and the Princess Maria take refuge in a strongly fortified castle. The King of Sicily,

Charles of Durazzo, learning of this strange dissension in Hungary, in defiance of an oath he once took that he would never try to get Hungary or Poland, or do anything to the detriment of King Louis' two daughters, and forgetful of the late King's goodness to him, brings a large armed force from Sicily to Hungary—whether of his own accord or at the instigation of Queen Elizabeth is not known—and there, with the help of some Hungarian nobles has himself crowned King of Hungary. This is too much for Queen Elizabeth, who, yielding to repeated pleas from Václav of Bohemia, who seeks to justify his brother's behaviour and promises that the latter will make amends, relents and recalls Sigismund from Bohemia. She realizes that as Maria and he are legally married, Maria cannot properly marry another man. This leaves Charles of Durazzo to be got rid of, and she entrusts the task to a Hungarian called Forgacz. When he tells her that the only way of accomplishing this is to cut off his head; he is told that she does not mind how it is done, as long as she is rid of him. So, one morning a few days later, Forgacz enters Charles' bedroom in Buda, jestingly pulls out a sword and starts jokingly brandishing it—he and the King often joked together—and then kills him in his bed. For this shameful act he and his descendants are given the notable castle of Gimel. Sigismund now renews his marriage vows and consummates his marriage to Maria. Other sources tell us that Charles' wound was not mortal and that he was taken from the bedroom to a castle and there poisoned. Forgacz did not escape general condemnation for the part he played. It is said that from that time on, whenever he or one of his descendants went to the royal palace, the King's sword would be unsheathed and brandished before him, until Forgacz or the member of his family had left the palace.

Duke Wilhelm of Austria, to whom King Louis had promised Jadwiga as his wife, disturbed by rumours of what is happening, sets out for Poland with a considerable retinue of knights, all his jewels, treasure and possessions. His unexpected arrival puts the Castellan of Cracow in a difficult position, lest the arrangement with Jagiello should now come to nothing, for the Queen favours the Duke and, some say, had summoned him, promising him personal immunity. The Duke stays on and on in Cracow, for none dares go against the wishes of the Queen, who would have preferred to marry this young man she knew, rather than a barbarian she had never even seen, and of whose manners, looks and savage behaviour she has been given exaggerated accounts. The Governor of the Castle refuses the Duke access, so, again and again, the Queen rides out with her retinue of knights and ladies and goes to the monastery of St. Francis in Cracow, and, in the refectory there, amuses herself dancing with the young Duke. Rumour has it that she so disliked the idea of marrying Jagiello that as soon as she learned that he was on his way, she told her ladies that she had decided to marry Duke William, because her betrothal to him had been made publicly and in church long before. But, when Wilhelm is brought to the royal apartments, to the Queen's bedchamber, certain Poles, who were his enemies, have him removed in a shameful and offensive manner and driven from the castle. The Queen then sets out to go to him in the city, but finding the gate closed, she calls for an axe and tries to break it open. In the end, one of her knights, Dymitr, persuades her to desist. Duke Wilhelm is now afraid of being wounded or killed, so, having deposited his treasure and jewelry with the Chamberlain of Cracow, he secretly leaves the city. The Duke is never able to ask for his treasure back and the Chamberlain uses it for his own purposes, buying up large properties, villages and woods, a fortune which his sons will later squander.

A.D. 1386

Grand-duke Jagiello, his brother and a huge retinue arrive to marry the Queen and take over the kingdom. He comes with waggons loaded with his vast treasure. Guides are sent to conduct him and they take him first to Lublin, where he remains for a week, so as to allow the news of his arrival to spread. While there a few nobles, including the Voivode of Cracow, come out to greet him. Meanwhile, in Cracow, the other prelates and nobles are begging the Queen to think of the enormous benefit her marriage to Jagiello will bring to her faith; but for a long time she puts her duty to Wilhelm first. Finally, she secretly sends a confidant, Zawisza of Oleśnica, to go to Jagiello and report to her on his figure and looks, and manners, ordering him not to accept any presents from the Grand-duke. Jagiello, well aware why Zawisza has been sent to him, receives him graciously and then has him accompany him to the bath, with the result that her envoy is able to tell the Queen that Jagiello is well-built, of medium height, graceful and well-shaped, has a merry expression, a long face without trace of disfigurement; that his manner is serious and worthy of a prince. This reassures the Queen and, her prejudices removed, more nobles go out to greet the Grand-duke, now in Sandomierz, from where he sends Dymitr, the royal treasurer, to Prussia to invite the Prussian Master to come to Cracow to act as his godfather and attend his marriage and coronation. So, on February 20, the huge splendid cavalcade enters Cracow. Jagiello is conducted to the castle and goes first to Queen Jadwiga, who is in her chamber with a large retinue of her ladies and girls.

The Grand-duke is so impressed by her unusual looks—she was, indeed, a beauty—that the next day he sends three of his brothers to her with gifts of gold, silver, jewels and garments. It is said that, in the mean time, Duke Wilhelm had returned to Cracow in disguise, perhaps not without the Queen's connivance, and was hiding in the castle at Łobzów or in the house of the Morsztyns, where, during a search, he climbed onto beams in the chimney in order to avoid detection. He then comes to the conclusion that he is not going to get Poland and its Queen, and marries Joanna, daughter of the King of Sicily and sister of the present one. He dies shortly afterwards.

The contention that she was not really bound by a betrothal made when she was under-age mollifies the Queen and eventually she agrees to marry the Grand-duke, not to satisfy passion or to savour the delights of the flesh, but to ensure the spread of Christianity and peace. So, having got her word, on February 14 the Grand-duke, his brothers, their boyars and nobles, now properly instructed in the Catholic faith, confess and accept the true Faith and reject paganism, and so are christened in Cracow cathedral by the Archbishop of Gniezno and the Bishop of Cracow, the Grand-duke rejecting his pagan name of Jagiello and assuming that of Poland's princes: Władysław. The other Lithuanian dukes, except the Grand-duke's brothers, had long before adopted the Greek Orthodox rite and could not be induced to abandon it. So, Duke Władysław Jagiello takes his first sacrament and, later the same day, returns to the cathedral and is there married by the Archbishop to the enchanting, lovely Queen Jadwiga. He then ascribes Lithuania, Samogitia and Ruthenia, territories over which he has complete sway, to the Kingdom of Poland, to be united with it and incorporated in it, and undertakes under oath to baptize their peoples in the true faith.

Pressure had been put on the new King to let himself be baptized two days before his coronation, but he had refused to accept the gift of baptism before his coronation, out of fear of the Poles not keeping their word, and Queen Jadwiga, it is said, hesitated a long time before agreeing to marry him. She knew, of course, that to enter into a second marriage could not be legal and, recoiling from committing adultery, felt the shame of a second marriage worse than death. She knew, too, that many people knew that, having officially agreed to the marriage, she had for a fortnight shared her bed with Duke Wilhelm and that there had been physical consummation. Thus she was troubled by her conscience. It was generally thought that this criminal act of compelling an unwilling woman to marry a pagan after removing her from her legal husband, would call down the vengeance of Our Lord on the Poles. On Sunday, four days after receiving the two sacraments, the Grand-duke Władysław Jagiello leaves the bedchamber and proceeds with great pomp to the cathedral to receive the insignia of royalty and be anointed, as is usually only done to kings. There, watched by his wife, he is crowned with a new crown of gold and jewels, the crown previously used having been removed to Hungary by King Louis to prevent any but his progeny ascending the throne. The day after his coronation, Władysław II of Poland, as is the tradition, rides round the city of Cracow and there in the market-place seats himself on a throne set up in the open near the city hall, and there receives the homage of the mayor, the city fathers and the whole city. There follow several days of celebration, including jousting with lances and swords, and dancing.

The Prussian Master, Conrad Zöllner, full of foreboding that the union of Poland and Lithuania will prove disastrous for him and his Order, disregards his invitation to act King Władysław's godfather and, instead, invades Lithuania, well knowing that all the dukes and nobles will be in Cracow. In his retinue is Jagiello's brother, Andrew, who belongs to the Ruthenian rite, and who had defected to the Knights in the hope that they would help him to gain control of Lithuania and Ruthenia. Zöllner finds the country deserted, so splits up his force and orders pillaging and destruction on the largest possible scale. He storms Łukomka castle and hands it over to Duke Andrew, to whom the people of Polotsk also surrender their castle and lands after renouncing obedience to King Władysław. Learning of this Władysław sends his brother, Skirgiello, and his cousin, Witold, to Lithuania with a strong force of Polish knights to deal with the invaders. When they discover that the Knights have done their worst and returned to Prussia, they move straight against Łukomka and capture it in a couple of days, killing or capturing Andrew's garrison. They then move to Polotsk and when neither Andrew nor the Knights go to the people's assistance, they forgive them, though beheading the ringleaders of the revolt with axes.

King Władysław rewards the more eminent Poles with lavish gifts, being particularly generous to the Voivode of Cracow, to whom he gives his sandals, which are embroidered with precious stones, valuable pearls and jewels of price.

Swiecislaw, Duke of Smolensk, and his two sons, die.

Half-way through Lent, at the urgent request of the prelates and nobles of Wielkopolska, King Władysław leaves Cracow with his bride and goes to Wielkopolska to end the domestic strife from which the duchy has long suffered. He has with him a number of armed knights from Cracow and Sandomierz. When they halt in Gniezno, at the suggestion of the laity, the King demands that they be quartered and provisioned by the Chapter, and, when this is refused, he demands this be provided by the Chapter's villages. The protesting villagers take their wives and children to Gniezno to complain, at which the Archdeacon places an interdict on them and then leaves Gniezno. Moved by the peasants' distress, the Queen corrects her husband's mistake and repays the amounts extracted, and also tries to have the interdict lifted. She is reputed, in her bitterness, to have said: "We have, indeed, returned the peasants' cattle, but who can repair their tears?".

The King spends Easter in Poznań, where he puts an end to the squabbles between the Castellan and Voivode of Poznań and the Castellan of Nakło. Church goods that have been appropriated he has returned to their rightful owners, he annuls the sentences passed by the Justiciar of Poznań, locally called the "Red Devil", whom he puts in prison (where he stays for many years). He summons Bartosz of Odolanów, instigator of much of the strife, to appear before him, and, when he fails to turn up, exiles him and confiscates his fortune and his castle. In a very short time the clash of civil strife is silenced and peace restored to Wielkopolska, where the King spends all summer and the autumn.

A.D. 1387

The King goes to Lithuania with the Archbishop of Gniezno and many pious priests, who, he hopes, will sow the seeds of Christianity among its pagan people. He takes Queen Jadwiga with him, so that she can see her new country and her husband's people. He calls an assembly in Wilno, at which he and the clergy spend many days trying to persuade the King's brothers and the nobles and people of Lithuania to abandon their false gods and accept the faith and rites of the one, true Faith. The ordinary people protest and insist that it is unworthy, irrational and against the tradition of their ancestors to expose themselves and their idols to destruction. The King then orders the eternal fire maintained in Wilno with daily supplies of fresh firewood to be extinguished, and the shrine from which a priest gives petitioners answers allegedly from the god of fire, to be demolished. The sacred groves are to be cut down, and the snakes kept in people's houses as tutelary idols are to be killed.

When this has been done, thus proving the falseness of their gods, the people agree to accept the Christian faith. Instructed by Polish priests, or, rather, by the King, who knows their languages and to whom they will listen, they are, in the course of a few days, cleansed with the water of Holy Baptism. The pious King gives those of the populace who receive baptism a new set of clothes, a shirt or cloth brought from Poland. Such generosity brings people accustomed to linen clothes running to obtain the woollen garments that are to be had with baptism. It being difficult to christen so many individually, the King has groups of either sex sprinkled with holy water, each group receiving a common Christian name: Peter, Paul, John, Jacob, Stanisław etc. for the men, and Catherine, Margaret, Dorothy etc. for the women.

Knights and the gentry are christened individually. Pope Urban VI sends a special bull praising and thanking King Władysław for what he has done.

The King now builds a cathedral in Wilno, siting its great altar on the spot where the fire, falsely thought to be everlasting, used to burn. Its bishop is Andrew Vasilko, a Franciscan of Polish origin, who formerly had been confessor to Queen Elizabeth of Hungary. To enable bishop and clergy to live fittingly among primitive people, they are given a parish church in Kłodawa, in the diocese of Gniezno, which has a considerable revenue. A further seven parish churches are founded and suitably endowed, and these are all given Polish priests to conduct services and instruct the people in Christian beliefs and rites. The Queen herself provides Wilno cathedral and the parish churches with chalices, books, monstrances, crucifixes, chasubles and other beautiful jewels and robes.

This done, the King sends the Queen back to Poland and himself remains in Lithuania for the rest of the year, travelling the country and encouraging those not yet baptized to be christened, building and endowing churches and chapels, so that he can rightly be considered the apostle who converted the Lithuanians. He also issues rules that Lithuanian catholics should avoid marriage with schismatic Ruthenians and those who do not acknowledge the Roman Church. If they should make such a marriage, the Ruthenian wife should accept the faith of her husband, or a Ruthenian husband accept that of his believing wife. (The Greek rite is not mentioned.) He also orders that Church property, including that which may be acquired in the future, is to be relieved of all taxes, dues, tribute and services.

Joanna, wife of the King of the Romans and Bohemia, dies on the last day of December.

On Palm Sunday, the Margrave of Brandenburg, Sigismund, with the approval of Queen Elizabeth, is anointed and crowned King of Hungary by the Archbishop of Esztergom in Székesfehérvár. Some days later, Queen Elizabeth and her daughter, Maria, are seized by some Hungarian nobles and taken to Slavonia and kept in a well-guarded castle. In the end, King Sigismund brings up a powerful force and lays siege to the castle. During the siege, her captors suffocate Queen Elizabeth and hang her body from one of the windows. Maria, however, is returned to her husband, Sigismund. To avenge the death of his mother-in-law, Sigismund has thirty-two Hungarian nobles responsible for her death, publicly beheaded, all on one day. Others are exiled and their properties confiscated.

A.D. 1388

After celebrating Christmas in the new cathedral in Wilno, King Władysław, accompanied by Lithuanian nobles and gentry, goes to Vitebsk and thence to Polotsk, where he spends some time suppressing an incipient rebellion, imprisoning the leaders and confiscating their possessions. He then returns to Lithuania, and, everything settled, he appoints his brother, Skirgiello, regent of Lithuania, marries his sister, Alexandra, to Duke Siemowit of Mazovia, and Witold's sister, Danuta, to Janusz, Duke of Warsaw. That accomplished, he heads for Poland. He turns aside to Łuck and puts Tarnow Castellan of Sandomierz to govern it in his name. In order to placate his sister, Alexandra's husband, Siemowit, and compensate him for the loss of a kingdom—for he did have a right to the succession—he plans to grant him Radom in perpetuity, but, realizing that the Poles would never allow a grant of this kind, he grants him his sister's dowry, the lands of Wielz, which are very fertile, well-watered and with plenty of pasture; indeed, better in every way than those of Radom, but even this does serious damage to the Kingdom of Poland, which shed a lot of blood in conquering the territory. The King returns to hear from the Chamberlain of Cracow that Duke Wilhelm of Austria is said to have paid a secret visit to Cracow and had several meetings with Queen Jadwiga. Though angered by these insinuations, people intervene to show them to be false and there is no quarrel between King and Queen.

A.D. 1389

Once Władysław has gone back to Poland, his brother, Skirgiello, and his cousin, Witold, fall out. Skirgiello is naturally courageous and as good with his hands as with his tongue. He would have been formidable had not his inveterate drunkenness earned him general contempt, for, when drunk, he could wound friends and associates, and then, when sober, he would bandage their wounds, for he was an able surgeon. Witold, a modest and sensible man, always sober, is afraid of Skirgiello. Being of the same confession as the Ruthenians, he has their support. He receives many a warning that Skirgiello would be glad to see him killed with poison or by any other means, and so, to ensure his own safety and that of his family, he installs strong garrisons in Grodno and Brześć, which he governs, and takes his wife, Anna, his boyars, knights and servants first to his sister's husband, Janusz of Warsaw, and when he proves reluctant to provide the support expected, he goes to Siemowit, and, when he, too, is unwilling to give him the help he wants, indeed, even deprives him of a gold cup—an act for which he never forgives him—he again goes to the Prussian Master, Conrad Zöllner, who is King Władysław's enemy. The Knights welcome him and, for several years, treat him well. He learns their language and adopts their ways. When he fled from Lithuania, that country and Samogitia became divided into two camps: one supporting Witold and the other Władysław, so that there was danger of civil war.

In order to secure Wilno and prevent it being surrendered to Witold and the Teutonic Knights, the King sends his Vice-Chancellor with cannon, crossbows and other military equipment, to take over the castle from Skirgiello and to get rid of certain Lithuanians and Ruthenians, whose loyalty is suspect. The deserter, Witold, makes a permanent alliance with the Order, sworn and documented, accepts baptism and the Christian faith. He sends secret envoys to King Władysław and the two are reconciled; indeed, at one stage the King hints that he might entrust Witold with the Grand-duchy, whereupon, without consulting the Knights, Witold secretly takes a force into Lithuania and occupies the castles at Jurgenburg, Mergenburg and Nawandz, where he is received as a friend and ally and provided with everything he needs. He then kills most of the Knights, throwing them into the moat and sets fire to the castles, rounding up the rest of the garrisons as his prisoners. Later, when he sees that the hopes raised by Władysław are not going to be fulfilled, he makes an attempt to seize Wilno castle by sending a number of waggons, in which soldiers are concealed under the carcasses of game, said to be for his sister's wedding feast, with orders to try and get into the castle. However, the subterfuge is discovered in time and Witold flees with his wife and friends back to Prussia, where he renews his alliance and for two years occupies three forts built for him by the Knights on Lithuanian soil, Ritterswerder, Neugarten and Metemberg, from which he raids Lithuania.

Misunderstandings between the King and the Queen have become frequent, as have scenes of jealousy, the result of the insinuations of flatterers, so the two agree to reveal the source of the accusations laid against the other. These prove to be one and the same, namely the Chamberlain of Cracow, Gniewosz. The two are now reconciled and united. They agree to summon the Chamberlain to come before them. When the day comes, the Castellan of Wojn, convinced by the Queen that she had known no bed but her husband's, takes up her defence. Before a large audience, he complains that the dirty, false accusations of Gniewosz have brought the Queen's purity and innocence under suspicion and defamed her to her husband. He demands that the Queen's unjust accuser should be compelled to retract his slanderous denunciations. When Gniewosz does not have the courage to deny the accusation—he knows that there are twelve knights ready to duel with him in defence of the Queen's honour—the tribunal declares the Queen innocent of the accusations. After this, the relations of the King and Queen could not have been better.

King Václav takes as his second wife the unmarried daughter of the Duke of Bavaria, Sophia. They are married in Prague. Shortly afterwards there is an ugly incident, when the Chaplain of St. Valentine, taking the holy sacrament to a sick person, is pelted with stones by a throng of Jews. The news causes an immediate riot, which leads to a massacre and burning of Jews in Prague.

The announcement in Rome of a Jubilee year brings countless hordes of pilgrims from Germany, Poland, Hungary, Bohemia, England and other countries. Their contributions permit many churches in Rome to be restored and enrich the Pope. This is not all, for the Pope sends almoners to various kingdoms, who sell indulgences for the equivalent of the cost of a journey to Rome.

On December 26, the Archbishop of Gniezno dies. Jan Kropidlo, Bishop of Włocławek, without bothering to get the King's approval or that of the Chapter, and in contravention of electoral law, tries to get Boniface IX to approve his transfer from Włocławek, where he has been for six years, to Gniezno cathedral, thinking that in those days of schism it would be as easy for him to get Gniezno, as it had been for him to get Poznań and Włocławek, thanks to the influence of his family and that of the Dukes of Opole. His hopes being dashed, he incurs the wrath of King Władysław, who removes him from Gniezno. He also loses Włocławek. Although he henceforth styles himself Archbishop of Gniezno, he is imprisoned by the Marshal of Poland and deprived of all his possessions. Later, the King frees him. As the dispute continues for seven years, Jan Kropidlo incurs enormous debts, which impoverish him, though he receives some help from the Knights, with whom he finds a safe refuge.

A.D. 1390

King Władysław, grieved by the domestic strife in his fatherland, assembles an army and, at the beginning of February, when it would have been better to remain in winter quarters, advances on Brześć, Mały Kamieniec and Grodno, which are in Witold's hands. He invests Brześć and captures it after ten days. Then, his troops being short of provisions and finding themselves in barren, uncultivated land, most of them return home against the King's wishes. This leaves the King with only his courtiers and household knights, altogether scarcely thirty spearmen. Leaving Brześć, the King moves on with the troops left to him and a number of volunteers, not quite 900 cavalry, but all experienced and tough. Kamieniec falls to him easily, so, at the start of Lent, he crosses the Niemen and invests Grodno. The siege lasts throughout Lent, during which time his brothers send him Lithuanian and Ruthenian reinforcements. Indeed, Korybut, the Duke of Novgorod, who is of the Greek persuasion, comes in person with probably more than anyone, at least where armour and horses are concerned. Witold now arrives with Knights from Prussia, and, knowing that Grodno is not in a position to withstand a long siege, makes camp nearby, but on the other side of the river. He starts throwing up a mound, so as to build a new castle on it, but this is of no help to the besieged, most of whom are now wounded, or were killed when the lower fort was stormed, as well as by the constant bombardment by siege catapults; so they tell Witold that they cannot hold out much longer. Witold now fixes an iron chain across the river with the intention of fastening boats to it in which the sick and wounded can be ferried from the castle and replaced with fresh troops, and the castle supplied with provisions. The King's troops then fell a number of trees upstream and throw them with all their roots and branches into the river. The current is considerable and the trees, sweeping down, break the chain and destroy several of the boats, drowning those in them. One of those in the water starts swimming towards the bank, where the King's camp is. The Knights call out in German, telling him to seek death in the river, rather than fall into the hands of the enemy, but when one of the Poles reaches out a spear, the man grasps it and is pulled ashore. From him the King learns details of Witold's position, as well as how this deserter and his fellows had been planning to desert the following day, which, indeed, they do. On April 8, the besieged, having lost hope, surrender the castle. They were so short of provisions that for some time they had been living on coarse black bread and their horses on leaves, branches and old thatch from the roofs of houses, for which they foraged for fourteen miles round about.

While her husband is thus occupied in Lithuania, Queen Jadwiga, intending to enlarge her kingdom, assembles another army of knights and gentry, who are so attached to her that they obey all her commands, and with this invades Ruthenia. Within a short time, she has captured Przemyśl, Jarosław, Grodek, Halicz, Trembowla and Lwów, thanks, in part, to the generalship of a Hungarian knight, called Bebek. She removes all the Hungarians and Silesians installed there by her father and the Duke of Opole and replaces them with Poles, thus reuniting lands unjustly torn from the kingdom of Poland.

The King and his wife now wish to obtain for their country the grace, accorded to no other language but Latin, Greek and Hebrew, that all rites and offices, both diurnal and nocturnal, even the Holy Mass, may be conducted in the Polish language.

Witold and the Knights, anxious to avenge their recent failure, assemble an army, which includes many new arrivals, among whom is the elder son of Henry, Duke of Lancaster, the Margrave Frederick and a number of Germans. With these they mount a three-pronged invasion about the Feast of St. John the Baptist. One force is commanded by the Prussian Master, Conrad Wallenrod, and is made up of English, French and German knights; the second is commanded by the Livonian Master, and the third by Duke Witold.

First, all attend a banquet in Old Kaunas, and then they move against Troki and burn both the castle and town. Next, they put further pressure on Wilno castle, Witold taking up position near Krzywy Zamek and the Prussian Master on the Polish bank of the Wilia, near Ponary, and the Livonian Master, also on the Wilia, but near Mejszagola. The Lithuanians and Ruthenians who claim to be loyal to the King then set fire to Krzywy Zamek. Enemy action prevents the fire being put out, and, when Korygiello tries to escape through the flames, he falls into the enemy's hands and is immediately beheaded, his head being placed on a long spear and shown to the Poles defending the castle, which is then bombarded day and night with missiles from siege engines, which demolish the castle's walls for the extent of a bowshot. In order to give the impression that the walls have been rebuilt, the starosta has the gaps filled with a drapery of skins, the loose folds of which cause many of the missiles to fall harmlessly. The upper castle would have suffered the same fate as Krzywy Zamek had not the Lithuanians and Ruthenians in it been relieved of their duties and replaced with Poles. The Poles earn considerable renown with their courage and endurance, for they fill the gaps in the walls with their own bodies and do not allow the enemy to approach. The gaps in the inner wall are filled in with earth, dung and hides. Those killed are immediately replaced. Repeated sallies are made against the enemy. But their most effective defence is the use of hides and skins to repair breaches and destroy the effectiveness of the enemy's missiles. The siege lasts from the Feast of St. John the Baptist until the Friday after the Feast of St. Michael. The casualties are enormous.

The upper fort at Wilno is commanded by the Vice-chancellor of Poland, the inner fort by the King's brother, Skirgiello, who uses his Lithuanians and Ruthenians to attack the enemy more by night than by day, inflicting heavy casualties and never suffering defeat. This so infuriates Witold, that when Duke Narymund is captured, he has him strung up by the legs from a tree in a meadow, where the Prussians have their guns, and has him used as a target. The besieged squabble among themselves, the French accusing the Poles of helping pagans in preference to the faithful, while the Poles contend that they are protecting neophytes against subversive monks. To decide who is right, they finally agree on a foursome duel to be fought on a suitable day in Prague. When the day comes, the Poles are represented by the Castellan of Dobrzyń and three others, and there are four Frenchmen. The contestants are brought before King Václav, when he is at table, and he entertains them and manages to reconcile them.

One day, when the Poles and Lithuanians are having a meal, the enemy get into the lower fort in Wilno, where the cathedral of St. Stanisław is and where the bishop's palace now stands, climb onto the wall and claim victory. One of the Prussians on the wall calls out: "Kater er Kater", but is at once flung off the wall by a Polish knight. The others there are either scared off or flung off. So, on October 7, seeing that they are getting nowhere, Witold and the Knights abandon the siege, having first set fire to Władysław's newly built church, impaled children and infants and performed other acts of cruel vengeance. Back in Prussia, Witold asks for fresh troops and is joined by the Captain of Ragneta and the governor of Insterburg with a large group of German and other foreign knights, with which he organizes frequent raids into Lithuania and Samogitia. In November, the King arrives in Lithuania with a train of waggons laden with cannon, crossbows, arrows, clothes and provisions, which do much to restore morale. Even so, when the Vice-chancellor resigns as starosta of Wilno and governor of Lithuania, the King cannot find another Pole to replace him, for all are afraid of the enemy, of treachery and of the King's brother, Skirgiello. Eventually, however, he manages to persuade Jasko of Oleśnica to take over. To make things easier for him, the King sends Skirgiello to Kiev to oversee the administration there, and, when he gets back to Poland, he sends the new starosta some knights and some of his best troops as reinforcements, as well as provisions and siege machines to strengthen the castle's defences.

A.D. 1391

At the beginning of the summer, Witold and the Prussian Master return to Lithuania and advance on Wilno hoping that treachery will enable them to capture its castle. The new starosta has prudently burned the city, so as to deprive the enemy of help and shelter, and has had abatis of tree trunks set up in various places to prevent access to the castle. The advancing enemy finds its way barred by a force of dismounted knights at the Church of the Blessed Virgin Mary. This attacks them fiercely and, having killed or wounded many, withdraws into the castle without any casualties. As they accomplish nothing in the next few days, Witold and the Master abandon the siege, but in order to avoid people seeing that they have achieved nothing, they advance on the two forts that Skirgiello built on the Wilia and after a few days capture them, taking a number of Polish knights prisoner. These they take back to Prussia and imprison them in Elbląg castle, where they spend seven years in shameful captivity. Witold and the Knights further burn Miednim and Welże.

During the winter, Witold and the Prussian Master again move into Lithuania. Reaching Kaunas castle with its Polish garrison, they start building three wooden forts on the Niemen there: Neugarten, Rittersswerder and Metemburg. The Master installs strong, well-provisioned garrisons in the first two, while Witold occupies Metemburg. Now, with the help of the Knights, he devastates the surrounding country, convinced that by doing this he will recapture, or, at least, recover that part of his inheritance that Władysław took from him. The starosta assembles an army, which he puts under the command of the King's brother, Alexander Wigunt, and sends it to lay siege to Neugarten. When it reaches Neugarten, though not yet in battle array, it mounts an immediate assault and all but captures it.

Throughout his lengthy conflict with Witold, the King has had to send, month by month, military equipment and troops, as well as huge quantities of grain, lard, millet and other victuals to replace what Witold and the Prussians have destroyed, for which he uses his own means of transport. All this is fairly distributed. Had this not been done, many of the gentry and ordinary people would have abandoned the country, leaving it an easy prey for the Knights.

The Margraves of Meissen raid Bohemia, and, after causing a great deal of damage, assume control, while King Václav does nothing to try and stop them.

A.D. 1392

Early in this year Alexander Wigunt dies, poisoned by his servants. He is buried in the same grave as his brother Korygiello, who had his head chopped off by Witold. After his baptism, he so completely rejected his family's pagan customs, their dress, ways of speaking and cutting their hair, that he was regarded as a life-long Christian, rather than a neophyte. Many suspected Witold of engineering his death. Although married, he had no progeny.

In order to ensure peace in his beloved fatherland and prevent his remaining brother being poisoned, the King decides to be reconciled with Witold and make him ruler of Lithuania and Ruthenia; for most of his brothers, ever ready to drink or hunt, seemed little suited to rule nations. So, in secret, he sends Henry, Duke of Opole and also Bishop-elect of Płock, who, for the last two years, has been enjoying that cathedral's revenues, to negotiate a reconciliation. As go-between, he succeeds in reconciling Władysław and Witold. He had gone first to the Captain of Bałga, who welcomed him and sent him on to Ritterswerder, where he stayed for three weeks, and, having finally abandoned the priesthood, wedded Władysław's sister Rynalla. Witold, having assured himself of the King's favour, seizes and ties up all the Knights and merchants in his castle at Ritterswerder and, having set fire to the castle, returns to Lithuania with all his knights, boyars and servants, all his armour, guns and crossbows.

He is received, on the King's orders, by the starosta of Lithuania and well treated. When the Knights in the castles of Neugarten and Metemburg learn of Witold's defection, they chase after him and bring him to bay. There is a fight and the Knights are defeated, leaving Witold with more booty. He then turns back and easily captures the Knights' two castles, plunders them and then burns them.

Informed of Witold's return to the fold. Władysław goes to Lithuania at the end of July. He reaches Ostrów on August 7 and there Witold and the more eminent of his supporters come out to meet him. A tearful Witold makes repeated humble requests for forgiveness for himself and others. The King forgives him everything and they go to Wilno. The King removes the starosta there and entrusts Witold, whom he knows from childhood to be skilful and enterprising, with complete authority over Lithuania; he returns to him his share of the inheritance and the castles taken from him, granting him as well, all the Lithuanian and Ruthenian castles. Witold swears oaths of loyalty and signs documents undertaking to administer the lands in the name of the King and Kingdom of Poland and never to abandon the two whether in prosperity or adversity, for there was no one better able to rule Lithuania and rebuild it out of the ruin and destruction of recent wars.

The Knights are disgusted by Witold's defection and his burning of their two castles. When a force under Marshal Engelhard Rabe goes to the Castle of St. John and there holds a banquet in honour of some recent arrivals, they advance against the Lithuanian castle of Surzaz. The Lithuanians sally out and there is a battle at the end of which the castle surrenders and is occupied. Wi-

Part of the coast of the Mare Svetti (Baltic) showing a city with a long jetty and, on the beach, a small military camp.
—Codex Picturatus Balthasuris Behem. Jagiellonian University Library.

told's son-in-law just manages to escape. A further incursion is organized in the winter and two castles in Lithuania captured, Barten and Stramel. Part of the population is murdered and the rest, some 3000 men and women, are marched back to Prussia.

A.D. 1393

The deserter and now enemy of Witold, Boleslaw Świdrygiello, joins forces with an ally inside Lithuania, and thus all the more dangerous, Władysław's own brother, Skirgiello, who has taken offence at having been passed over. He now starts stirring up his supporters so successfully that it appears as if the duchy is threatened with open revolt. Hearing of this, the King and Queen hurry to Lithuania, and to them the two dukes present their cases. It then transpires that Skirgiello's charge against Witold is not justified, and the two are reconciled and become friends again. As a sop, Skirgiello, who already has Kiev, is given Krzemeniec, Starodub and Stare Troki, on condition that he obeys Witold in all things. It is further agreed, and put in writing, than any further misunderstandings or squabbles are to be referred to Queen Jadwiga.

The Queen Elizabeth, widow of the Emperor Charles, dies on February 12.

Václav of Bohemia, at the insistence of the Czech gentry, expels the Teutonic Knights from the whole kingdom on the grounds of their being useless, confiscates their castle at Kadan, their towns, villages and all their revenues, and either distributes these among the Czech nobles or transfers them to the royal treasury.

King Władysław sends craftsmen under a strong guard to rebuild the castle at Grodno, which the Knights from Prussia had destroyed in the previous year. When the Prussian Master learns of this he sends some knights and foreign mercenaries to cross the Niemen, which they do with difficulty and considerable loss of good men, capture the fort and burn it down again. Later, the Marshal makes a further incursion into Lithuania, this time with troops from Wurtemberg, France and Germany. They cross the Niemen by boat and for several days devastate Samogitia, removing 400 captives.

The Prussian Master, Conrad Wallenrod, dies and is succeeded by Conrad of Jungingen.

King Władysław uses fired bricks to increase the modest height of the walls of Cracow castle. He also increases the fifty marks endowment given to the burgraves by Casimir II by ten marks a year, which is given on condition that throughout the year each of them maintains in Cracow one horse and one archer, to be assigned in the event of an emergency, to the starosta or his deputy to help him repulse an enemy.

A.D. 1394

Towards the end of June, the Prussian Master, Conrad of Jungingen, wishing to avenge the capture and maltreatment by Witold of some of his Knights, invades Lithuania with a well-equipped force made up of Lithuanian and Ruthenian deserters, many Frenchmen and Germans, as well as 150 archers from Genewel. With him is Świdrygiello. He reaches Wilno without meeting resistance and for the next two months lays siege to the castle there, but achieves nothing. Witold does not have sufficient troops to confront the Prussians head on, so he occupies all the forest roads with the intention of attacking from inaccessible places. When he learns of this from prisoners, the Master sends a force through marshes and trackless areas, building itself bridges where necessary. Even so, it loses many of its draught animals and horses by drowning or being sucked down in the bogs, as well as many of them shot by Lithuanian sharpshooters; but it does capture one of the Lithuanian boyars, who is killed by being hung up by the feet from a tree. Władysław sends a number of experienced knights to help Witold, and with them a number of volunteers. Many of the barons send their own armed contingents at their own expense. On Witold's orders these refrain from any pitched battle, but by frequent attacks on the enemy's camps and positions they achieve as much. Świdrygiello's best hope lies in treachery. By giving lavish presents and promises he persuades some Ruthenians to set fire to the castle, but the plan is discovered in time and Witold punishes the plotters as they deserve. The Prussian Master then abandons the siege and returns to Prussia with Świdrygiello, losing many men on the way from attacks, especially at night and when they are in boggy or awkward places. King Władysław continues to send fresh knights to help Witold. The cost of this is a burden on the treasury.

The Prussian Master again sends a force which includes a number of French and German knights, into Lithuania. It finds Neugarten burned and moves on to Lida, whose inhabitants burn it and abandon it before the Prussians get there. The Marshal devastates the country far and wide, and drives a horde of captives back to Prussia. Then the Wojt of Sambia tries his own invasion, hoping for loot and fame, but when he gets to Rosienie he suddenly loses heart and hurries back to Prussia. Meanwhile Witold has marched into Prussia and devastated much of Insterburg. When he has withdrawn, the Captain of Bałga raids Drohiczyn and removes a great deal of loot and 300 captives.

Henry of Opole falls ill on his way back from the university at Bologna and dies.

Sigismund of Hungary arrives in Poland on a visit to Queen Jadwiga, his wife's sister. He spends several days there, during which a number of pacts confirming peace between the two kingdoms are concluded.

The Duke of Mazovia starts building a new fort in the Narwa basin, which he calls Złotnia. Then, to hasten its completion, he goes there in person, only to be captured along with his knights by the Captain of Bałga. The Prussians burn the timbers of the fort; then seat the Duke on a mare, tie his feet under her belly, despite his loud calls that he be given a time and place to which to report. He and the others are then taken before the Prussian Master and insulted. When he learns of this, Władysław sends to the Prussian Master complaining that this is a breach of their alliance and so has the Duke freed; yet many considered the breach so serious that it should have been answered with war.

Duke Skirgiello, who has always been harsh to his subjects, especially when drunk, dies. He was poisoned by a Ruthenian friar in Wyszogrod castle. The poison was given him in a cup into which, once it had been tasted, the friar dipped a finger on which was a ring containing the poison. He had no progeny.

In order to restrain the thoughtless extravagances and cruel behaviour of their king, Václav, the Bohemian nobles shut him up in the royal palace of Velevary, three miles from Prague. They dismiss his scatter-brained advisors and give him mature, serious men to attend to affairs of state. Unfortunately, Duke Jan and the Margrave of Moravia free him, but he is apprehended a second time by King Sigismund of Hungary, who is said to have been the main instigator of all this, and sent for safe-keeping to the Duke of Austria in Vienna. However, he is not carefully guarded there and escapes and recovers his throne. He does not change his way of life.

A.D. 1395

King Władysław sends to Duke Władysław of Opole demanding the return of Wieluń, Dobrzyń and Ostrzeszów, which had been shamefully wrest from the kingdom by King Louis. The Duke dismisses the claim and war seems imminent. The King, however, does not want war and so sends the Duke a very fair proposal: the Duke has neither sons nor daughters, so that, if he will just pay homage to the King of Poland and affirm that he is a subject of the King and Kingdom of Poland, when he dies these territories would revert to Poland without them going to war. This suggestion, too, is rejected contemptuously, the King being told that the Duke has no authority to accept, and that he is not so faint-hearted that he will agree to be the subject and vassal of the King of Poland because of lands which belong to him and his successors by virtue of a right conferred on him by Louis, King of Poland and Hungary. Władysław then considers going to war at a council attended by only five of his advisors. In the meantime, the Duke has had a large number of mounds thrown up to act as a frontier. Some are still to be seen near Zytniów.

Sigismund of Hungary, urged on by a number of Catholic princes, who have promised him support, assembles a huge army and advances into Turkish territory. He has troops sent by the King of France, and some from Burgundy headed by the Duke in person; indeed, so many nations are represented in his army that a special coin is struck for its use. This huge army, however, lacks a leader and also discipline. There is no joint command and Sigismund, to whom they all look, does nothing except to tell them that the Turks can never stand up to such an army. Yet, when they reach Nikopol in Romania, they learn that the Turkish Sultan, Bayazid or Kalapin, is scarcely two miles away with a powerful army ready to do battle. Sigismund remains in his tent, tending his body, resting and amusing himself; thus, when the Sultan attacks, he finds the Christian army scattered and in complete disarray, many, indeed, wandering about like sheep, unarmed. The Hungarian lords and the King abandon the army and head for the Danube estuary—it mouths near Nikopol —intending to get across by boat and so out of danger. The French, Poles, Czechs, Burgundians, Spaniards and some of the Hungarians do put up a fight, but are easily routed. A few take to their heels, but most are either killed or taken prisoner. Among the latter is the Duke of Burgundy, who considered flight shameful, and many of his knights. The Duke is ransomed two years later for 100,000 florins. The Turks loot the Catholic camp.

Among the Poles who escaped was Ścibor of Ściborzyc, who, when trying to get into a boat with King Sigismund, was pushed back by those in the boat, who were afraid of it becoming over-loaded and sinking. Ścibor, although in armour, dived into the river which there was rapid and wide, and swam across. Others, trying to get into boats had their hands cut off. King Sigismund was so afraid of falling into the hands of the Turks that he put to sea and sailed on as far as Constantinople, where he stayed for a whole year, at the end of which, the Venetians ferried him back to Dalmatia and from there he returned to Hungary.

So great a victory encourages the Turks and gives them fresh strength, with the result that in the following winter the Sultan invades Hungary, plunders it and carries off several thousand Christian captives, both men and women.

King Sigismund's wife, Queen Maria, dies in Buda on May 17. The Hungarian lords now begin considering electing a new king, as if Sigismund has ceased to be king on his wife's death.

A.D. 1396

King Władysław makes public his intention to send an expedition against Władysław of Opole in order to recover the lands granted to the latter by King Louis. First, he sends the Castellan of Sandomierz with part of the army to recover Dobrzyń, letting it be known, falsely, that he intends to follow with the rest of the army. The Castellan closely invests Bobrowniki, thus distracting the Duke, so that he fails to secure the castles at Wieluń, Ostrzeszów and elsewhere, which the King intends to attack first. After a while, the Prussian Master arrives to help the besieged in Bobrowniki. The Castellan, realizing that he is not strong enough, withdraws. Meanwhile, the King, whose aim is to conquer the territory of Dobrzyń, heads for Olsztyn and sends the Voivode of Cracow with part of the army to invest Wieluń, Ostrzeszów and Bolesławiec. On the third day of his siege of Olsztyn, the King orders an assault on the castle, which stands on a tall cliff, and captures it. He takes pity on those in the castle, and, although it would have been enough to grant them their lives, he gives them good properties near Tłumacz in Ruthenia.

After capturing Olsztyn, the army advances swiftly on Krzepice, Wieluń, Bolesławiec, Brzeznica, Bobolice and Grabów. Those in these castles are at a loss what to do, and few put up any resistance, for, seeing that Olsztyn has fallen, they see no shame in surrender. As a result, all but Bolesławiec are in the King's hands within a week. The starosta of Wieluń does resist for a time, hitting various people with stones thrown from the castle, and for this he is condemned to be beheaded with a sword, but is graciously reprieved at the last moment, indeed, just as the executioner has raised his sword. Having lost all his castles in little more than a day, the Duke sends all his weapons, troops and provisions to Bolesławiec, which is surrounded on all sides by the River Prosna and has good man-made defences. For seven years the King's men besiege it, building a chain of forts round it. After the Duke's death, it is defended in the name of his widow, who, when the two sides are later reconciled, gives it to the King. Before this, however, in order to spite the King, the Duke pawns Dobrzyń, Bobrowniki, Rypin, Lipno and Złotoria to the Prussian Order for 40,000 florins. The pledge bears interest and is thus a considerable loss to Poland. The Order should never have accepted the pledge, had it had any respect for God or the pact it had made with Poland.

Unable to act openly, Władysław the Duke of Opole, in the middle of March, arrests some Polish merchants who are attending Wrocław market, and puts them in prison. He deprives them of their money and goods, and boasts that now he has got some of his own back. King Władysław then sends envoys to Władysław of Opole. These are told that there can be no return of goods. Meanwhile the Duke is employing brigands, deserters and debtors fleeing from the courts, to make further raids.

King Władysław is incensed with the Duke of Opole for pledging Dobrzyń to the Prussian Master, for he foresees that this will result in the Master breaking their pact of everlasting peace, and so he starts preparing for war. When advised not to do this, for his object was more to regain Samogitia than to avenge the pledging of Dobrzyń, he decides that he and the Master must meet, lest the latter think that the King acquiesces in what has been done. It is decided that the Queen should deal with the Master, lest the damage done to his old country by the Order should cause the King to employ language that would lead to war. So the Queen goes to Inowrocław with a splendid retinue and spends several days trying to persuade the Master and the Prussian Commander to return Dobrzyń territory, but, as the only conditions they will accept are that they are be repaid the 40,000 florins, the Poles depart thoroughly disgruntled.

A.D. 1397

Duke Alexander Witold, now reconciled with Bolesław Swidrygiello who has settled in Poland, organizes the first campaign against the Tatars in the hope of gaining recognition as a Catholic prince. He crosses into Tartar territory and devastates it as far as the River Don, which in Latin is called the Tanais.

Meeting with no opposition, when near the greatest of those rivers, the Volga, he infiltrates one of the Tatar permanent camps called ordas, captures several thousand Tatars with their wives and children and cattle and conducts them back to Lithuania. Half of these he sends to the King as proof of his victory, and the rest he retains in Lithuania. The King settles his Tatars in Poland, where they abandon their pagan errors, accept Christianity, and, by intermarrying, become one nation with the Poles; while those kept in Lithuania persist in their Mohammedan faith and continue to live in accordance with their old ways and religion.

At the end of February, Henry of Głogów dies from a wound received during a tourney in Legnica.

Queen Jadwiga founds a special college for students from Lithuania in the expanding university of Prague. For the college she buys, in the old part of the city, not far from the royal palace and near that of the Queen, a stone-built house with many comfortable bedrooms, halls and workplaces. The house backs onto the moat that divides the old from the new town, which is near the College of St. Václav. She obtains special permission from the King to endow it with a permanent income of 600 score of broad Prague grosses, to provide which she spends a considerable sum buying villages near Prague. The college still exists and is known as the Queen's House.

A.D. 1398

Henry, Bishop of Włocławek and Duke of Legnica, dies on December 12 and, since he disliked Włocławek cathedral, is buried in that at Wrocław.

Sigismund of Hungary pays a surprise visit to Cracow and spends several days with the King and Queen. A tourney is held in his honour. King Sigismund's armour is so splendid that everyone challenges him to a joust.

Disregarding the rights and wishes of the Archbishop and Chapter of the metropolitan church, the Pope sells the city of Riga with all its castles and properties to the Teutonic Knights, a sale that flatters the vanity of the Master of the Prussian Order in Livonia. The price is 15,000 florins, less a certain sum paid to agents and promoters of the transaction. Thus is the Chapter, which ever since its foundation had an archbishop, prelates, canons and monks of the Order of St. Augustine, transferred against its wishes to another order by employing falsification and trickery equal to that employed when the Margraves of Brandenburg sold Pomerania to which they had no right or title whatever. For fifty years the Archbishops and Chapter dispute the legality of the sale with the Curia and are finally proved right.

A.D. 1399

The Grand-duke Witold, encouraged by his first campaign against the Tatars and wishing to acquire fame among both Christian and barbarian princes, against the advice of King Władysław and Queen Jadwiga, announces a second expedition against Tartary. He establishes a base in Kiev and there, all June, awaits the arrival of the foreign knights who are to join him. When these arrive, he breaks camp and moves into Tatar territory with an army of Poles, Germans, Lithuanians, Ruthenians, plus the Tatar khan, Toktamish, with several thousand Tatars. They cross the Dniepr, the Cold Water, the Psioł and the Sula and by St. Laurence's Day have reached the wide plain along the River Worskla, where they sight a Tatar army, commanded not by Timur, but by Edyga, the size of which strikes fear into their hearts. Witold is advised to sue for peace, and Edyga is prepared to negotiate, but when his conditions prove unacceptable and people start accusing Witold of cowardice, a battle becomes inevitable. The Tatars are by far the more numerous, and before long the Christians have begun to give way. To avoid the disaster of being captured by the Tatars, Witold leaves the field of battle asking the Voivode of Cracow to accompany him. The Voivode, however, considers flight shameful and continues fighting, until he falls pierced with several arrows. Many of Witold's courtiers are also killed. Among those who flee is his treasurer, who, when he gets back to Poland, buys so many properties that he is suspected of having purloined the treasure. King Władysław, seeing to his delight that the Queen is pregnant, informs the Pope and other kings and princes of the fact and invites them to the christening of the babe to be. Everyone in Poland is delighted with the news. In a special bull the Pope instructs Wojciech Jastrzębiec, a scholar of Cracow, to represent him, and asks that the babe be given the Pope's name, adapted to its sex, as one of its names. OnJune 12 the Queen gives birth to a daughter, who is christened in Cracow cathedral and given two names: Elizabeth Bonifacia. The Queen now falls gravely ill, and, three weeks later, her infant daughter dies, the news reaching her almost at the moment of her own death.

A.D. 1400

After his wife's funeral the sorrowing King withdraws to Ruthenia and stays there for some time, afraid lest he be removed from the throne. Indeed, he makes preparations to leave the kingdom, saying that it scarcely befits him to remain in someone else's kingdom, when she who inherited it was dead. His councillors come to talk him out of this faint-hearted attitude and tell him that they want him on the throne. They explain that there is another heiress, close to Queen Jadwiga, namely Anna, daughter of the Count of Cilia and great-granddaughter of King Casimir II, and say that he should marry her. They persuade him to send envoys to Cilia, where the girl's paternal uncle, her father being no longer alive, receives them delightedly and without hesitation hands his niece over to them. They travel back through Hungary and reach Cracow on July 16 to be received with considerable pomp. Anna speaks nothing but German and so the King keeps her in Cracow for the best part of eight months, while she learns Polish. When she has learned to understand, rather than speak the language, she is betrothed to the King, who, for some time avoids her, thinking her not attractive enough, because of which the envoys are also out of favour.

On the Feast of St. James the Apostle, in the royal city of Cracow, King Władysław founds the university for which Queen Jadwiga has so earnestly striven. Doctors and Masters in every faculty are brought from Prague and the new university provided with an income from salt dues and other royal revenues. A College of the Arts and Theology is established in St. Anne's Street and a College of Law and Medicine in Grodzka Street, both built by Queen Jadwiga's executors with money left by her for the purpose.

On January 1, while travelling by coach between Gliwice and Cieszyn, the young Duke of Oświęcim is killed by a Czech at the instigation of the Duke of Racibórz. His father is so eager for revenge that he buys the Czech concerned for 1600 kops of broad Prague grosses and brings him to Cieszyn with an escort of 600 horse and there executes him in a strange, ingenious fashion, placing him on a brazen horse, with glowing coals inside it, on which he is conveyed through the streets, alleys and all round the town, while three executioners with red-hot tongs pull off his flesh and eventually his innards.

During the summer there is a great struggle between the Tatar khan, Timur, and the Turkish sultan, Bajazet, which ends in the latter being captured.

A.D. 1401

After spending most of the winter in Lithuania, King Władysław returns to Cracow in time for Carnival with quantities of wild game of different kinds. He then officially marries Anna, the daughter of the Count of Cilia, after which the two attend a tourney lasting several days.

The Electors, enraged by King Václav's behaviour and manners, especially by his procrastination in seeking the imperial crown, assemble in Frankfurt-am-Main and deprive him of the throne of Rome, replacing him with Rupert, Duke of Bavaria and Palatine of the Rhine. When the latter, having received the first crown in Aachen, hurries to Italy to get the other, he is refused entry to Milan by its Duke and returns empty-handed to Germany. After this, both regard themselves as King of the Romans, and, as long as Rupert lives, the Roman Empire is thus split.

The nobility of Hungary, hating the manner and behaviour of their king, Sigismund, call an assembly in Buda at the end of April and imprison him in the castle there, before handing him over to Miklós Garai, whom they expect to kill him in order to avenge the murder of his father. King Władysław repeatedly tries to obtain Sigismund's release. The one most loyal to King Sigismund is Ścibor of Ściborzyc, a man of Polish origin, with whom the King has shared his worries, thoughts and hopes, and who now organizes Poles and Hungarians to raid Hungary, capturing forts and taking prisoners in order to try and force the King's release. However, Miklós Garai treats Sigismund well the whole time and in the end releases him.

The Pope, wishing to elevate Ladislas, King of Sicily, exempts him from all tribute to the Church and grants him the tithes from Sicily for three years, and, to the detriment of Sigismund, has him crowned King of Hungary by the Cardinal-Bishop of Ostia in the Dalmatian town of Zadar, where the body of St. Simeon is said to rest. Hearing of this, King Sigismund sends a strong force to Dalmatia and shamefully ejects Ladislas and his supporters.

A new dispute breaks out between the Grand-duke Witold and the Knights in Prussia and Livonia. The Master of Livonia invades Lithuania and devastates it. The Grand-duke does not dare resist, so keeps his knights and troops in Wilno. As the Livonians withdraw, not expecting to be attacked, Witold, who has been sent help by Władysław, organizes a pursuit. This moves so quietly as to deceive the Livonian sentries, entering each camp they leave while the fires are still burning and bits of oats and straw bestrew the ground. As soon as the Livonians reach their own country and disperse to their homes, Witold marches in and devastates a number of villages and towns and captures the fortified town of Dzwina, which the troops are allowed to sack. He then tries to capture the fort there in which a number of people have taken refuge. This proves difficult, but in the end the Teutonic Knights surrender in return for preferential treatment. The sack enrichs Witold's troops. A Polish knight, called Peter Ryterski, is hit during the fighting by an arrow, and this the surgeons are unable to extract. For three years he endures considerable suffering from it, but finally it passes down his leg and comes out through his foot.

Duke Władysław of Opole dies on May 8, leaving no progeny.

A.D. 1402

On the Sunday before Easter, in Cracow cathedral, the Archbishop of Gniezno crowns and anoints the King's wife, Anna, Queen of Poland. This is followed by several days of tourneys with prizes for the victors.

While King Sigismund is under arrest in prison, delegates from the prelates and nobles of Hungary arrive in Cracow to explain why they imprisoned their king and to ask King Władysław to accept the throne of Hungary, to which he is entitled as husband of the late Queen Jadwiga. The King does not reply immediately, but, perturbed, goes to Nowy Sącz, where the Hungarians repeat their request. On this occasion they are told that it does not befit Władysław to deprive a rightful king of his throne, while he is still alive. Ashamed, the Hungarians return home and Sigismund is released. Władysław offers him military assistance, should he need it, and this delights Sigismund.

A.D. 1403

For the last ten years the Grand-duke Witold has been harassing the rich and fertile lands of Smolensk, each year being sent reinforcements by King Władysław, without which he could have achieved nothing. This year he marches in again and, after laying much of it waste, invests its capital and principal town, Smolensk, in which the nobles have placed their wives, children and treasured possessions. First, he bombards the buildings, then orders his men to advance up to the very walls.

They encounter no lasting resistance and so capture it, though at considerable cost, mainly in wounded. The Duke of Smolensk flees to Hungary when he learns that he has lost his capital and there he remains for many years in the service of King Sigismund. The nobles of Smolensk are not brave enough to resist and surrender their forts to the Grand-duke, and ever since Smolensk has been part and a province of the Grand-duchy. A great quantity of treasure (gold and silver vessels, jewels and precious stones) falls into the hands of the Grand-duke, who sends part of it to King Władysław and distributes the rest among his own knights.

The Grot of Słupca, who turned against Poland on account of the murderous attack made on the Castellan of Wiślica, while he was rightly defending the collegiate foundation's village of Dwiekosy, and the Castellan of Włocławek are both arrested and exiled from Poland because of their plotting. They establish themselves in the Moravian castle of Szowsten, from where they harass Polish territory, capturing merchants and nobles and carrying them off. Finding this intolerable, King Władysław sends a force, largely made up of his household troops, which storms Szowsten castle and sets fire to it. The Castellan of Włocławek is captured and taken back to Poland, where he spends many years in prison, until released at the request of Zawisza the Black of Garbów, who, at the same time, negotiates the release of several Poles imprisoned in Hungary. The Grot escapes prison, but all his possessions are confiscated and he is sent into permanent exile. The Grot's castle at Konary in Sandomierz, whose walls were built of stone, is demolished on the orders of the King, who decrees that it must never be rebuilt or repaired without his permission or that of his successors. At the beginning of February, the Prussian Master together with Swidrygiello, who has a weak and fickle nature, again invades Lithuania. Watched by Witold from the castle in Wilno, he first advances on Merecz which he captures and burns, but then, unexpectedly, he heads for Troki. He halts for a day beside Lake Dawgen and then moves on to Zamiennik, where he halts for a further two days and so moves on to Oława, a mile from Troki; then, though Witold feared he was going to invest Troki castle, he moves to the village of Steigwick on the River Strawa. From there he proceeds via Semeliskes, Stokliszki and Nerowena, making camp seven times and devastating the surrounding country as he goes, and so reaches the frozen River Niemen, which he crosses on the ice without difficulty and marches back into his own country near Ragnetha. He has with him a thousand captives, who are released when Witold promises to ransom them and to release an even larger number of Prussian prisoners held in Lithuania. No sooner have the Prussians gone than the Master of Livonia invades in his turn, wreaks havoc and returns to Livonia with a number of captives.

In order to stop Świdrygiello's raids into Lithuania, Władysław recalls him and, having paid off his huge debts, grants him the part of Podole he bought from Spytek of Melsztyn's widow and her sons for 5000 broad Prague grosses, as well as part of Zydaczów and four other parishes and grants him an annual income of 1400 marks from the salt revenues. Even this is not enough to bind the thoughtless Świdrygiello who, having installed Poles and Ruthenians in his new lands, goes back to the Knights in the hope of getting Lithuania, which, apparently they promised him. When the King demands the return of the Podolian castles, the Poles and Ruthenians installed by Świdrygiello rebel.

Poles and Prussians at very close quarters. The Polish army has been reinforced with Czech mercenaries. Maciej: Chronika Polonorum—*British Library.*

A.D. 1404

With Whitsun in the offing a general assembly is held in Raciąz in an attempt to bring about peace between Poland and the Grand-duchy and the Teutonic Knights and to remove misunderstandings caused by the occupation of Dobrzyń and Samogitia. The King and the Prussian Master both attend in person, and at once appoint referees to settle the dispute. After several days of discussions, this is achieved on the following terms: Samogitia is to be handed over to the Order, its people giving their sons as hostages, paying homage and signing a document agreeing to this. King Władysław is to buy Dobrzyń back for 40,000 florins and confirm the endowment made to it by the Knights. Both sides agree not to accept deserters or give them shelter, and also to free their prisoners.

The Prussian Master invites the King, his captains and most of his councillors to Toruń, where a three-day tourney is to be held. At first, the Poles are not very successful, so the King orders one of his knights, Dobieslaw, to take part. He jousts so successfully that by three in afternoon he finds himself alone in the lists. One day, when the King and the Master are riding round the town, a cook pours slops all over the King. She is seized and condemned to be drowned, but is reprieved at the King's insistence. No one knows whether this was an accident, or whether the Knights put the cook up to it in order to shame the King, but as the King was the only one hit, it looks as if it was not an accident.

Without any excuse or justification the Prussian Knights treacherously invade the duchy of Mazovia, and the Duke of Mazovia's other duchies of Czersk and Warsaw, capturing the Duke, his family and all his household. Forgetful of honesty and humanity, as well as of the fact that the Duke, an excellent man, was the benefactor of the Order, which ought to honour him, they are all shamefully tied up with cord and carted off to distant towns and castles. When informed of this by special messenger, the King complains to the Prussian Master and they are all swiftly freed, the Prussian Master falsely pretending to have known nothing about it.

Leaving Toruń, the King spends all summer in Wielkopolska and organizes local assemblies, so that all the nobility can contribute from their private means towards the cost of Dobrzyń. Another assembly is held in Korczyń in the Autumn at which it is agreed that the owner of each cultivated field is to pay the King twelve grosses in addition to the two he normally pays, to help pay for Dobrzyń. Such payment, it is stressed, does not constitute a precedent. When counted the amount brought in totals 100,000 marks.

At the insistence of Václav of Bohemia, he and King Władysław meet in Wrocław on the Feast of St. James the Apostle. Władysław is accompanied by such a throng of prelates, knights and barons that he appears to have more than 5000 with him. When the advance party of the Marshal of Poland and his assistants, numbering 600, arrive to arrange quartering, Václav thinks they are the King arriving and rides out to meet them. Władysław spends eight days there, being provided with all his needs by Václav, who insists, as do the Czechs and Silesians, that the two kings make an everlasting alliance, whereby the King of Poland sends the other help whenever he needs it, especially against Sigismund of Hungary, in return for which Poland is to be given back the Silesian territory taken from it, including the towns of Wrocław, Namysłów, Świdnica, Środa and others. Though Władysław himself would have agreed to this, the Polish prelates and lords are afraid that acceptance might cause enmity between the two, and so it is not accepted.

Once back from Wrocław, the King has to recover Podole from some Poles and Ruthenians who have occupied it in the name of Bolesław Swidrygiello. Krzemieniec receives him with open gates as its rightful lord, and, entering the town he starts an immediate assault on the castle, bombarding it with his cannon. The starosta, having received written assurance that the lands and castles of Podole will not be granted to any one duke, but to Polish knights, surrenders to the King, after which all the other castles do the same. The King makes Peter Szafraniec governor of Podole.

As Witold has failed to honour the agreement made at Raciąż to return Samogitia to the Order, the Master invades Lithuania with a force so strong that Witold does not dare risk a pitched battle and confines his action to harassment. When Władysław learns of this, he sends a medium-sized force to help Witold. The Knights, overestimating its size, withdraw to Prussia.

A.D. 1405

When Władysław, the Prussian Master and their advisers meet in Gniewkowo over Whitsun in order to ratify the Raciąż agreement, a fresh obstacle is encountered, when the Knights produce a document signed by Casimir II in which he renounces his right and title to Pomerania and undertakes not to use the title "heir to Pomerania" and to have those words erased from the royal seal. As this has not been done, so that the seal on the document now presented contains the old wording, the Knights refuse to accept it. They further insist that both nominally and de facto Pomerania is accepted as belonging to the Order and that no one else can lay claim to it. The King will not agree to this and the two part company having settled nothing.

The outcome of another meeting between the Grand-duke Alexander Witold and the Prussian Master held at Salin on the Niemem on the Feast of St. Peter and St. Paul, to which the King sends the Castellan of Wiślica and the Marshal of Poland to see that the Knights do not cheat, is equally disastrous. After much discussion of peace and the surrender of Samogitia to the Order, the delegates take their departure, though not without loss of temper, for some Knights accuse the Grand-duke of breaking his word and make other insulting allegations which Witold swallows rather than start a war. There is a further meeting at which the Grand-duke concludes a necessary, rather than a suitable peace, in which he agrees to surrender Samogitia and to compel its people, if necessary by force, to submit to the Master and his Order, a thing which King Władysław strenuously opposes though in vain. A document is drawn up in both Latin and German confirming the permanent transfer of Samogitia to the Order, and this, at the insistence of the Grand-duke the King also signs.

The people of Samogitia put up a stout resistance mainly in night attacks on the Prussians, so effective that the latter have to double their guards; and from the forests come unhappy pleas that the Grand-duke should not allow the people to be separated from their fellow Lithuanians, for they are one tribe and one nation and have the same language and customs, nor should he make them subject to the Knights. Though sympathetic, the Grand-duke has to keep to the agreement and must compel them to give some of their sons as hostages to the Knights. To ensure that the Order has secure and lasting possession of their new lands the Grand-duke builds two forts on the River Niemen and a third at the confluence of the Dubissa and the Niemen, as governor of which latter the Knights appoint Michael Küchmeister, who knows both Samogitian and Lithuanian.

A.D. 1406

King Władysław decides to end the Hospitallers' occupation of Drahim, lest it become permanent and the place be considered their property, as happened with Santok; so he sends emissaries to the Master of the Order requiring him either to return Drahim or to discharge feudal duties to Poland and its king. The Master disdainfully rejects both suggestions, so the King sends the Castellan of Sandomierz and the Starosta of Wielkopolska to retake Drahim, which they do in just four days, for the Knights scarcely bother to defend it, and ever since Drahim has remained part of Poland.

The Grand-duke, relieved by the recent pact of the recurrent raids into his territory by the Knights, assembles an army and embarks on his first incursion into Muscovite territory. Foregoing the capture of towns, he concentrates on pillaging and plundering, ordering his troops to make the devastation as widespread as possible. When this fails to induce the Muscovites to come out and fight, he continues laying the land waste and then returns to Lithuania laden with spoils.

In Cracow, a Jew, called Feter, is arrested for importing coins from two Silesian principalities and mixing their metal with the Polish coinage to his considerable profit and an equally considerable loss to Poland. He is paraded round the streets and the city square, garlanded with counterfeit coins, while the driver of his cart loudly proclaims his crime. He is then burned.

On the eve of the Feast of the Holy Rood, the members of the commune of Wrocław allow the anger they have long felt with its councillors to find expression in rioting. With arms in their hands, they force their way into the City Hall in which the frightened councillors have shut themselves, compel the latter to resign and elect new ones in their place.

A.D. 1407

The Jews in Cracow have increased greatly in numbers and, by the unlawful practice of usury, also in wealth; so much so that they have become proud and objects of envy. They indulge in various wickednesses, but with impunity, for those in authority hesitate to stop them. Nonetheless, they incur divine vengeance, which can be even more severe and this compensates for the negligence of the authorities. Thus, on the Tuesday after Easter, as the canon who has been preaching to the congregation in St. Barbara's church, is leaving the pulpit he has in his hand a piece of paper which, he says, has been left in the pulpit with a request that he inform the congregation of a certain event, a dreadful crime, about which he has deliberately kept silent, since the announcement of a similar occurrence in Prague led to riots there. The congregation demands to be told the news that is being withheld from it, so the canon climbs back into the pulpit with more levity than befits a magistrate and a preacher, and tells them that the paper contains the news that the previous night, Jews living in Cracow killed a Christian child and used its blood for nefarious purposes, and also that they stoned a priest who came to administer the last rites to the child. Hearing this, as if at a signal, the congregation starts exacting a cruel revenge on the Jews. They destroy the whole of one of the Jewish streets, killing many of its inhabitants. Eventually, the Castellan and Starosta arrive with armed men and suppress the riot and stop the looting. Once the crowds who came rushing in to loot or just to watch have dispersed and gone to their homes, a bell rings from the City Hall summoning the councillors and officials in order to punish those who perpetrated the riot and the looting. Then a voice is heard saying that the councillors ordered the looting and killing of Jews in the first place by ringing the bell; at which, as though in accord, people come thronging back and start killing and looting all over again. None dares oppose them; indeed, it would have been impossible to restrain so crazy a crowd. The rioting only stops, when someone—whether a Jew or a Christian no one knows—sets fire to some of the houses. As the fire spreads, the Church of St. Anna and several more streets go up in flames, for no one fights the fire. The College of Arts is with difficulty saved by a tremendous effort on the part of its noble students. Several Jews who took refuge in the belfry of St. Anna, hold out until almost dusk, when fire is put to the belfry and they come out of their own accord. The riot lasts from six in the morning until dusk. Many of the Jewish survivors have themselves baptized. Many of the Jewish children, whom Christians spared or rescued from the flames, are regenerated in the sacred water of baptism. A wealth of precious objects is looted from the Jewish homes and many a Christian enriches himself thereby; yet, when the riot is over, many valuables are still to be found in Jewish houses, hidden in sand or in the privies. This is the year of slaughter of the Jews, which, by God's righteous judgment, also takes place on the same day in two Silesian towns, Nysa and Frankfurt, and, indeed, in the English city of Canterbury as well.

On October 12, King Władysław, his jealousy aroused by foul sycophants, charges one of his knights, Jacob of Kobylan, with fornicating with Queen Anna. Jacob is put in chains and flung into prison in Lwów, where he is kept for close on three years. Another knight, Nicholas Chrzalowski, suspected of the same disgraceful crime, goes into voluntary exile. Thus is Queen Anna put into general disrepute—in the opinion of most people, unjustly—though foreshadowed by what had happened a few days earlier, when her apartments in the castle suddenly collapsed without there being any violent shock. Another knight, Andrew Tęczynski, is similarly suspected, having been discovered with the Queen in a secluded apartment at a compromising hour. However, he is less suspect than the other two. At the next assembly held in Niepołomice, the King is accused of irresponsibility in thus defaming his wife. The Archbishop of Gniezno, speaking on behalf of the King, pronounces her innocent. The main authors of these accusations, the Castellan of Wiślica and the Starosta of Cracow are proved guilty of defamation at the hearing of the case brought against them and have to withdraw their false accusations.

A.D. 1408

The misunderstandings between Lithuania and Prussia grow more and more serious, so Władysław arranges to meet the Master of the Order in Kaunas in an effort to secure peace. The King has with him his prelates and various eminent Poles and they spend several days in discussions with the Master and his officials, who are lodged on an island near the city. The Master, haughty and proud, refuses to accept any proposals for peace and the two sides part, disliking each other more heartily than ever, though they do not yet regard each other as declared enemies, since Władysław has sent the Master gifts worthy of a king, which have been accepted and reciprocated.

The Grand-duke now prepares a second expedition against Vasily, Prince of Muscovy, who is married to the Grand-duke's only daughter, Anastasia, and yet has been nibbling away at the frontier, much to the Grand-duke's detriment. King Władysław sends the Grand-duke five companies, amounting to 1000 veteran spearmen, under the command of his Marshal. A number of Polish lords and knights go with them as volunteers or send armed units of their own, and the Prussian Master one company of picked men. So, on the day after the Feast of John the Baptist, the Grand-duke moves this army of Poles, Lithuanians, Teutonic Knights and Ruthenians out of Wilno and into Muscovite territory, where it proceeds to put the country to fire and the sword. He now finds that he has a new enemy to contend with, Prince Świdrygiello, the brother of Władysław of Poland, a perverse, unstable character, who now, having burned down two castles which he holds in gift from the Grand-duke, whom he hates, has shamefully deserted with a few adherents to the Prince of Muscovy and begun to organize ambushes and attacks by night on the Grand-duke's forces. Thus, when the Grand-duke's army tries to cross the wide River Oka, which flows through the middle of Muscovy, although the Muscovite forces have withdrawn into their castles and fortresses, it is prevented from crossing by Świdrygiello. Envoys now arrive from Vasily asking for peace, and, after much deliberation, equitable terms are agreed, namely that Vasily will return all that he has been trying to appropriate and is reconciled with his father-in-law. No sooner is peace signed, than the uxorious Grand-duke leaves his army in the field and hurries to his wife, using a relay of horses to get to her quickly.

As it returns to Lithuania without its commander the army suffers considerably, especially from hunger, for this is an area mostly of forest, in which are very few villages, all of which have already been plundered either by the enemy or by the army itself. It is the horses that suffer most, for the Tatars whom Wasyl had summoned to help him, will not allow any but their own horses to graze. As a result many waggons with provisions have to be left behind in the forest for lack of draught animals, thus adding to the men's hunger. Some try to stifle their pangs by eating acorns, but these kill them. There had been continual rain and, the land being very low-lying, the track is slippery, with the result that almost all the horses, being weakened by hunger, founder. In one part of this immense forest, the mud is so deep that the track has to be built up with the bodies of the dead horses or bridges built, without which they could have gone no further. The Polish knights, too, lose their armour, their horses and many of their servants, and it is St. Martin's Day before they get back to Poland. They petition the King to recompense them for their losses and this he does most generously.

Continual rain which destroyed the autumn- and spring-sown corn has caused a serious famine in Lithuania. When envoys arrive requesting King Władysław's help, he orders the grain that has accumulated in the royal barns over the last few years, thanks to the efforts of the starosta of Kujawy, to be threshed and put into twenty large barges, which are to be sent down the Vistula and on up the Niemen to help relieve the famine. However, when the barges reach Ragnetha, they are confiscated on the orders of Ulrich of Jungingen, who justifies his action by pretending that the barges contain arms which are being sent to the pagan barbarians for use against Christians, when, in fact, they are full of grain. The real reason is that this year Lithuania has refused to buy grain from the Knights at inflated prices, as it had had to do in previous years, and is getting it from Poland instead. This illegal seizure of grain is the beginning and decisive cause of the war between the Teutonic Knights and Poland and Lithuania, a war that is to go on for several years.

Władysław is persuaded by his advisers that it will be better to stomach this wrong, than to embark on a war, so he first sends the Archbishop of Gniezno and the Castellans of Sandomierz, Kalisz and Nakło to request, indeed, demand the return of all the corn. The Master, a very arrogant man and one quick to anger and to quarrel, is quite unimpressed by the mild tone of the Polish envoys and tells them that he did not confiscate grain, but arms sent for use against him, his Order and other Christians, and that in no circumstances will he return them. He then makes matters even worse by arresting some Lithuanian merchants, who were in Ragnetha on business, and confiscating their goods and possessions.

The Grand-duke will not suffer such an injustice and says that the return of stolen goods is not a matter for diplomacy; so, having secretly obtained the approval of the King of Poland, he decides to retake Samogitia, which had previously been given and assigned to the Order. He entrusts the task to the Justiciar of Samogitia and a Lithuanian marshal, who are provided with the requisite force. They set to work and soon have expelled the garrisons from the forts they have just finished building and captured all the knights in them. The Samogitians are very ready to submit once more to the Grand-duke's authority, so Samogitia returns to Lithuania.

On Palm Sunday, Queen Anna gives birth to a daughter, who is christened Jadwiga.

A Council is held in Pisa in September. It is attended by the bishops of Cracow, Poznań, Płock, Wrocław, Chełm and by other clergy. In an attempt to restore unity to the Church, the cardinals remove from office Benedict XIII and Gregory XII and in their stead appoint Peter of Crete, a Greek by birth, who is given the name of Alexander V. After the Council, the Bishop of Cracow continues on to the Holy Land to visit the birth-place and tomb of Our Saviour. Returning to Venice, on the advice of his physician, he takes a strong purgative, which so weakens him that he falls prey to sleepiness and lethargy, of which no one can cure him and of which he dies shortly after returning to Cracow.

Benedict and Gregory, though deprived of their titles, both behave as if they were still Pope. Władysław of Poland is moved by the letters he receives from Gregory's cardinals and announces his obedience to him and that of Lithuania as well.

Peter de Luna falls into a rage and appoints new cardinals, thus widening the schism in the kingdoms of Spain and Aragon. Meanwhile, Gregory leaves the town in Austria where the Council was held, with only two companions, on foot and in disguise, which enables him to avoid an ambush laid for him by the Patriarch of Aquileia, whose enmity he had aroused by depriving him of the patriarchate in Lukka. He manages to reach two ships sent to rescue him by the King of Sicily, which take him first to Abruzzi and thence to Gaeta, where he lives for a long time under the protection of the King.

Sigismund of Hungary, having announced an expedition against the King of Bosnia, who had renounced his loyalty and obedience, now invades that country with a strong force, which includes a number of well-known Polish knights. The force captures several fortresses, decapitates many of the garrisons or throws them from the walls; thus does the whole of Bosnia again become a dependency of Hungary and pays tribute to its king.

A.D. 1409

When King Władysław, on a progress through Wielkopolska, reaches the Warta, he is met by envoys from Ulrich of Jungingen, sent more to publicize the Order's complaints, than with any hope of obtaining what they are demanding. They complain that the Grand-duke has annexed Samogitia, despite having previously signed a document surrendering it to the Order and renouncing all right to it; and, also, that he has shamefully murdered the starosta governing it; and further that, though the Order has repeatedly and urgently demanded the return of the territory and those taken prisoner, its demands have been ridiculed. Thus, the Order now feels compelled to have recourse to force in order to recover its lost territory and avenge the hurt done to it. The envoys have come, they say, to ask the King to tell them frankly, whether or not he intends to give his brother, the Grand-duke, armed assistance, so that the Master may know where he stands. Władysław, suspecting that the envoys are up to some crafty trick and not having an answer ready, tells them that, because of the importance of the matter and his having few advisers with him, he cannot give them an immediate answer, but will call a general assembly for St. Alexander's Day and will then send his reply by his own envoys.

The Order's envoys are not satisfied with this answer and publicly protest, proclaiming that the Master and the Order are ready to observe the pact for permanent peace made with them by Casimir II; but since the present King of Poland will not disassociate himself from the Grand-duke of Lithuania, but intends to assist him in an unjust cause, the knights and nobles of Poland have no cause to wax indignant with the Order, if it declares war on their country. Having made their protest, they ride off without waiting for a response, angry and indignant, their gestures and expressions demonstrating a greater lack of tact than befits envoys; indeed, making it obvious that, as soon as the right opportunity occurs, they will declare war on Poland. Władysław is left hesitant and uncertain what to do. On the one hand, he does not want to leave Alexander Witold in the lurch; yet neither does he want to be involved in an arduous war against which his advisers have spoken unanimously.

On St. Alexander's Day the prelates and nobles of Poland arrive in their numbers for the assembly in Łęczyca at which they are to decide on the answer to be sent to the Master of the Teutonic Knights. This decided upon, the Archbishop of Gniezno, the Voivode of Sandomierz and the Castellan of Kalisz are sent to deliver the King's reply, which is as follows:

"King Władysław is convinced that you and your Order well know that Grand-duke Alexander Witold, of whose occupation of Samogitia and other injuries you complain, though an excellent duke and linked to the King with ties of fraternal blood, is still a subject of the King and holds the lands of Lithuania during his life-time solely as the gift of, and with the permission of the King. For this reason the King is not at liberty to desert him even in this war, which you intend to undertake against the Grand-duke, or in any other adversity, but rather it behoves the King to help the Grand-duke with all his power and might. Nonetheless, the King is resolved to abstain from war and so intends at a suitable place and time to arrange a meeting at which he promises to make amends for any wrongs and injustices done and so end them. He will induce Grand-duke Alexander, his brother and his subject, to accept what will ensure peace and justice."

The Master is quite unmoved by this conciliatory answer and in inflated language and with much exaggeration renews his complaint against the Grand-duke and asserts that he will no longer suffer the wrongs done to him and his Order, but will at once invade Lithuania with his whole army. At this, the Archbishop of Gniezno, unable to stomach such threats and forgetting his brief, addresses the Master somewhat rashly, thus: "Master, stop trying to frighten us by declaring war on Lithuania, because if you decide on that, be sure that while you are invading Lithuania, our King will invade Prussia. The enemies of Lithuania are our enemies, and, if you attack them, we will take up arms against you." No one knows whether the Archbishop gave this rash answer on his own initiative, or whether, as some suggest, he was just saying what he had been told to say. The Master is delighted by such frankness: "I am grateful, Worshipful Father, for your not disguising your King's intentions. Now, knowing how he will act, I shall attack the head rather than the limb, settled land rather than deserted land, towns and villages rather than woods and forest." And that is what he does. As soon as the King's envoys have left, he prepares an army and on the eve of the Assumption sends a letter to Władysław repudiating their pact, and immediately lays siege to Dobrzyń castle and captures it by continually bombarding it with cannon and incendiary arrows. He kills the Polish knights of the garrison, burns the castle and goes on to devastate three towns, murdering many of the girls and women in them. He then advances on the fortress of Bobrowniki, attacks it in the same way and captures it, though this time by surrender, for the eminent knights the King had sent to defend it give it up without there being any need to do so, for it had a sufficient store of provisions and the walls and ramparts were intact except for one section.

The Master next lays siege to the castle at Złotoria. Before mounting an attack, he assembles all the women and girls from nearby Toruń to witness the action. He does, indeed, capture it, but only after an eight-day siege in which most of the knights defending the castle are killed by cannon balls and the others can no longer endure the bombardment and are taken prisoner. The Grand-duke arranges an exchange for them, as he has some Teutonic Knights captured earlier, but though he releases his prisoners, the Knights fail to keep their side of the bargain and release none of theirs.

The Master then sets his sights on Bydgoszcz, but, seeing that it is too secure to be captured by similar means, he bribes the Burgrave of the castle to surrender it. The news of this kills the starosta in charge.

Dismayed by the loss of so many castles, Władysław orders general mobilization and orders all under arms to assemble in Wolborz during the week before the Nativity of the Blessed Virgin. From there they are to advance into Prussia. The King sends letters and messengers to the Grand-duke fixing a rendez-vous near the Prussian frontier.

By the time appointed a large army has assembled in Wolborz and with this the King moves to Łęczyca, where a halt for four days is ordered to enable the others to catch up. Moving on after this, the army reaches the lake near Radiejów in three days, and, then, on St. Michael's Day surrounds Bydgoszcz with a wall of bucklers and wicker shields. Władysław then bombards the castle there with his cannon, which kill its castellan and governor. Seeing that the castle must fall, the Master sends to Władysław demanding that he abandon the siege, in which event the Master will surrender the castle to the King of Bohemia, who will adjudicate between them. Władysław replies that if the Master promises to hand over to Václav not only the castle, but the lands and city of Dobrzyń as well, he will raise the siege. This is not accepted, and Władysław spends the next week in the forest, while the castle is besieged. He then launches a fierce attack and captures and destroys the castle. Meanwhile, the Master has been assembling a force near Świecie. As soon as Władysław learns of this, he sends several companies to deal with it, but before these arrive, the Knights withdraw, leaving all their tents and a large quantity of booty, which the Poles acquire. Exasperated, Władysław sends to all the Catholic kings and princes a lengthy letter complaining of the Teutonic Knights' behaviour.

The Grand-duke sends his clerk on a confidential mission to tell Władysław that, for the time being, he cannot help him and, begging him not to take this amiss, suggests that he conclude a year's truce with the Order, which will give the Grand-duke time to make his preparations and be ready to assist the King with an army, which would be larger, better equipped and well-trained.

The King and his advisers must consider their next step. Many say, that since the King has assembled so powerful an army, he should advance deeper into Pomerania and put it to fire and the sword. Others, remembering that so large an army cannot be kept in the field during the winter, which there is severe, consider that the King should negotiate a truce and return home, renewing the campaign in the coming year. Before anything has been decided, envoys arrive from Václav, King of the Romans and of Bohemia, asking Władysław to agree to a truce and to accept Václav as adjudicator on any outstanding misunderstandings between him and the Order. If the King accepts, he is to send plenipotentiaries to Prague on the First Sunday in Lent, and there they will be told Václav's decisions. Władysław is persuaded to agree and signs and ratifies a truce with the Teutonic Knights, which is to last until sunset on the Feast of St. John the Baptist. He accepts the First Sunday in Lent for discussions and the conclusion of a permanent peace through the intermediary of King Václav. The Poles consider this rather a shameful arrangement, considering the powerful army the King has under his command, but still the right one, considering the time of year.

Before the Grand-duke can be informed of the truce and suspension of hostilities, he has secretly sent his brother, Duke Sigismund, into Prussian territory, where he loots and burns a large number of villages, sacks three towns and carries off a number of men and women captives. Although this expedition was undertaken in ignorance of the truce, there is no way of persuading the Knights that it was not just a heinous crime and dishonest behaviour on the part of the Grand-duke; and they are just waiting for an appropriate moment to exact their usual vengeance. Secretly, they assemble an army, which invades through the waste country between Grodno and Bielski Podlaski. Near Jaskra, its captures and murders some of the Grand-duke's men who are keeping watch there, and whose presence was betrayed by the smoke from their fire. On Palm Sunday, they attack Wolkowysk, and capture a crowd of Lithuanians assembled in the church there, men and women, Lithuanians and Ruthenians alike. Then, having sacked and burned the town, they return with their captives by the way they came. The Grand-duke, who was then only seven miles away, is appalled by the news, and withdraws with his wife Anna into the thick forest, full of lakes and marshy hiding-places round Zdzilow, and there he stays until he is assured that the Knights have withdrawn. The passage of the Knights through this waste and back again leaves a broad track which is still visible. From this time on, guards in the area have made their fires only of oak bark, which does not give off smoke.

The common people, ignorant of the reasons for the truce, dislike it and even accuse those responsible of having been bribed to make it. Once made, Władysław disbands his army and, leaving Bydgoszcz, goes to Poznań, where he announces a general assembly to be held in Niepołomice, so that the prelates and lords can try Warcisław of Gotarłowic for having broken faith and needlessly surrendered the castle at Bobrowniki. Justifying his actions, Warcisław maintains that he surrendered the castle with the knowledge and on the orders of the Archbishop of Gniezno, and produces a letter to support the assertion. A careful reading of the letter leads to the conclusion that Warcisław acted wrongly and is rightly accused, so he is handed over to the King as worthy of punishment, and is, indeed, condemned to life imprisonment in the castle at Chęcin. A year later, after the victory over the Teutonic Knights, he and all other prisoners are released in an amnesty, but he does not long survive.

The assembly also appoints those who are to represent Poland in Prague, when the court of arbitration pronounces its judgment on the dispute between King Władysław and the Teutonic Knights.

Jan Hus preaching in Kostnic.
—Litomerice gradual—Atelier Paul, Prague.

The heresy of John Wycliffe, which during the last several years has taken firm root in England, is now introduced into Bohemia and its flourishing university in Prague by Jan Hus. Václav himself pretends to be unaware of the new heresy, while his Queen and some of her advisers actively support it; thus it spreads quickly. Jan Hus began advocating the heresy out of spite and envy, when he was, rightly, removed from his Prague living. He was a man of great learning and an excellent preacher. He had lead an exemplary life and was worshipped by the populace because of his impressive sermons, thus the plague of his heresy found easy root in the hearts of the Czechs, who are naturally inclined to seek out novelties and to take pride in not being as others are. As Hus increases his advocacy of the heresy, the Holy See recommends that the University of Prague be closed. After this all foreign students and any of the clergy or monks who have expressed dislike of the heresy are expelled from the city, indeed, many of them are murdered. Civil strife and highway robberies become widespread. The unity and order that used to grace Bohemia are now things of the past. As the heresy spreads and its strength increases, lay people everywhere rob the churches and their servants of their temporal goods. All priests who refuse to adopt the heresy are murdered, wounded or expelled. Churches are set on fire, defiled and destroyed. The bones and larger reliquaries of the great patron of the country, St. Václav, and the other saints, are scattered and trampled. The famous Carthusian monastery is razed to the ground, as are many other shrines. Since all good people have now been either killed, expelled or have fled, only the worthless are left. As the number of criminals increases, so does wickedness. Some of the servants of Satan even practice the rites of the Pikard sect, which permits people physical enjoyment of each other in public.

Hus's perverse doctrine is further encouraged by the arrival in Prague of an Englishman, Peter Payne, who remains in the country until he dies. He instills in the Czech nation the poison of the English doctrine which he has got from reading Wycliffe's books. Such are the misfortunes that involve the Kingdom of Bohemia—Oh, horror!—in differences of opinion, ill-considered interpretations of Holy Writ based on the arrogant ideas of puffed-up masters and lascivious doctors who seek to know more than is needful. Now, this famous country and honoured Slav nation has become an object of loathing and lost all its renown.

While the assembly is being held in Niepołomice, an envoy of the Roman Church arrives with letters from the Cardinals asking the King to support their action in deposing the two competing popes and electing Alexander of Crete in their place, and to renounce his declared obedience to Gregory and to acknowledge Alexander instead. The matter is put to the assembly. The King's advisers recommend that he abandon Gregory, even though he has been a good friend to the King, for it was he who gave Władysław the right during his lifetime to appoint the dean of Cracow and the Archdeacon of Gniezno, and to announce obedience to Alexander V, who, having once visited Ruthenia, when he was of humbler rank and Władysław was still a heathen, is an old acquaintance.

Leaving Niepołomice, Władysław goes to Lithuania to confer with the Grand-duke. He reaches Brześć in Ruthenia on St. Andrew's Day and goes out a mile to greet and thus honour the Grand-duke. The two work out a plan for the coming war against the Teutonic Knights, a plan that is kept secret from all but the Vice-chancellor. The Grand-duke has brought with him a Tatar khan, whom he and Władysław court so as to enlist his help in the fighting. They agree a date and place of assembly for the Polish and Lithuanian armies, and decide on how they are going to cross the Vistula, for which they order the construction of a bridge to be supported by boats, a thing never yet seen. The construction of this bridge is entrusted to the Starosta of Radom, who has it built in Kozienice by that excellent Master Jarosław. The bridge takes all winter to build. The cost is defrayed by the King.

The King now leaves Brześć in the company of the Grand-duke and makes for the forest of Białowiez. Before he reaches it, he receives a special messenger from Pope Alexander V bringing the latter's bull informing the King of his election as Pope and asking him not to refuse him obedience. The King replies that he and the Grand-duke acknowledge him as Pope, in accordance with the decision taken at the assembly in Niepołomice. The Grand-duke now proceeds to Lithuania together with the Tatar khan, who remains there with all his soldiers and their wives throughout the winter, indeed, until the Feast of St. John the Baptist. Władysław continues on to the Forest, where he hunts for a week, killing a great quantity of game, which he orders to be salted in barrels and stored in Płock for the coming war. He then goes to Chełm and so to Lubom, where he spends Christmas and in one day builds a wooden church for the local Catholics, which he endows and orders the Bishops of Vladimir and Łuck to consecrate.

This winter the King does not go to Lithuania as usual, since it would have been too onerous for the Grand-duke to have to entertain him at the same time as making preparations for the coming war. Also, there were too many domestic matters awaiting his attention at home for him to have been able to go.

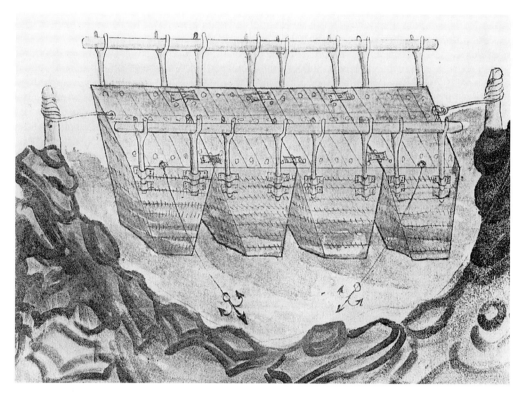

Conrad Kyeser's book of designs for military weapons, Bellefortis, *which he published in 1405, contains a design for a bridge of boats, a thing, to the Poles "never yet seen". While lashing together available boats had been done before, by Caligula and by the Mongols, a specially constructed pontoon bridge, as built during the winter of 1409–10 by the Poles to cross the Vistula and then dismantled and stored for re-use, was probably innovative.—VDI Verlag, Düsseldorf.*

A.D. 1410

The King spends Christmas in Lubomla and then moves on to Ratno to hunt, this being his passion. Again he orders the kill to be salted down for use in the coming war with Prussia. From Ratno he progresses in five stages to Kozienice and is there joined by Queen Anna, who has come from Cracow. They move on to Jedlna, where they are joined by the Queen's brother, Count Herman of Cilia. The King orders races, dancing and merrymaking. To honour his guest he treats the Count as a member of his Court which then moves by three stages to Sandomierz, where the Count leaves them, departing laden with gifts worthy of a king and well-satisfied. At the Count's insistence, Władysław and his brother, the Grand-duke, agree to meet Sigismund, King of Hungary.

On May 23, Przemyśl of Cieszyń, who, disabled by gout, for the last thirty years has been carried everywhere in a chair, having returned from Prussia, where he made great efforts to persuade the Teutonic Knights to make peace with Władysław, dies in Cieszyn and is buried in the monastery there. He was a sensible, helpful man and divided his dukedom between his two sons, Bolesław and Przemyśl.

When the time comes for Václav of Bohemia to adjudicate in the dispute between Władysław and the Master of the Teutonic Order, Bishop Wojciech of Poznań is sent with a splendid retinue to represent the King of Poland in Prague. He is accompanied by the Marshal of Poland Zbigniew of Brzezie, also by Vincent of Granow, castellan of Nakło and starosta of Wielkopolska, and by the King's notary. With them come the representatives of the Grand-duke of Lithuania: a knight, Butrym, and the Grand-duke's notary; there are also two marshals representing Janusz and Siemowit, the dukes of Mazovia. Reaching Prague, the delegates present King Václav with documents detailing their argument and claim, as the Knights have already done. Václav, an inveterate optimist and quite scatter-brained, attaches no importance to the briefs and does not even bother to look at them. To avoid being accused of frivolity and to prevent the envoys departing with the matter unresolved, also due to pressure put on him by his advisers and the envoys of both sides, Václav co-opts certain Czechs and Germans into the decision-making. Chief of these is Jodok, Margrave of Moravia, who thoroughly dislikes King Władysław, because on several occasions Władysław has given assis-

Khubilai Khan crossing a river on a bridge of boats during his conquest of southern China.
—Jami al-Tawarikh of Rashid al-Din. British Library.

tance to Jodok's brother and rival, Procopius. Jodok proposes several new clauses, which are childish and obviously unjust, yet he persuades Václav to adopt them.

Warned of what is afoot, the envoys of Poland, Lithuania and Mazovia, put forward their own solution, but as a draft, rather than a finished text, so that the King and the dukes pronouncing judgment cannot take offence. When the day for the pronouncement arrives, the envoys of the two sides assemble in the royal palace. Silence is called for, and, while Václav amuses himself whittling a stick, from behind a dais his secretary starts reading the judgment, but in German. He has scarcely begun before the Polish, Lithuanian and Mazovian envoys, without asking permission, file out, even though several of them have a good knowledge of German and can understand and speak it. When Václav asks why they are leaving, he is told that it is because the language used in the judgment is German, which, as Poles, they do not understand, so they are off to find a Polish version. When told to be patient and stay where they are, for in a short while they will hear the judgment in Czech, they tell him that they do not know Czech either. Václav then points out that Polish and Czech sound so alike that whoever speaks one of the two can understand the other. The fact is that the Polish, Lithuanian and Mazovian envoys, knowing how unjust and iniquitous will be what they are to hear, have no wish to hear it in any language. However, Václav sends them a complete copy of the judgment with his seal attached. This includes two of Jodok's absurd clauses, namely that the province of Dobrzyń, now occupied by the Knights, should be handed over to Jodok along with all its castles and everything appertaining to them, after which he will, within a year, decide to whom it is to belong. The other ridiculous clause is that, in future, Poland must never choose a king

La Vigenére's idea of the aurochs, biggest of the big game hunted by the Kings of Poland to provision the royal kitchen, or to salt down for the army's use in a forthcoming war.
La Description du Royaume de Pologne. —*British Library.*

LE POVRTRAICT DE L'VRVS.

La Vigenére's idea of Poland's elk from La Description du Royaume de Pologne.
—*British Library.*

from Lithuania or any of the eastern countries, but only someone from among western rulers. This is itself sufficient to demonstrate the absurdity of the judgment, since it introduces a new element that has never been in dispute. The only civility accorded to the Polish, Lithuanian and Mazovian envoys is when Václav invites them to dine at his table and, after the banquet, orders dancing, during which the Queen, splendidly gowned and wearing a diadem, frolics with her ladies and maidens.

While they are there in Prague, a Czech baron, Boček of Poděbrady, quite without provocation insults the Poles and Lithuanians, and when they ask Václav for assurances for their personal safety while in his kingdom, they are told that the King knows nothing of any affront being offered them and that they have no need of his protection. Convinced of Václav's frivolity, the envoys decide to put their trust in God and their escort of 600 armed men; so they ride away and reach Poland, safe and sound, despite having been dogged all the way to the frontier by Boček and his men, who keep level with them, seeking an opportunity to harass or pick off a straggler. The two parties are, indeed, so close that time and again the outriders are within sight of each other; in fact, one day, the Polish company, seeing that it was the stronger, attacked Boček's men and gave them such a drubbing, that they had to jump into the River Elbe and swim or ford it. It was this same Baron Boček, a man who lived by brigandry, was arrogant with his king and inclined to stir up rebellion and disorder, who fathered the godless George of Poděbrady, who, later, was treacherously to poison Vladislav, King of Bohemia and Hungary; or, as others say, kill him by crushing his testicles; and thus make himself heir to the throne of Bohemia, which, by bribing the great ones of the realm, he eventually obtained, though he did not long keep it.

King Władysław leaves Sandomierz on the Wednesday after Dry Sunday and goes to Przyszów for more hunting. He kills enough bison and elk to fill fifty barrels and these are sent by water to Płock to be added to the other stores for the coming campaign. From Przyszów he moves in five stages to Lwów, which he reaches on White Sunday. From there he makes a quick tour through Podole and reaches Halicz on Palm Sunday, but returns to Lwów for Easter. While there, he learns that Sigismund King of Hungary wishes to meet him in Kežmarok. He sends to Grand-duke Alexander to give him warning, so that he too can be there. Then, he goes in three stages to Łańcut, where the Grand-duke joins him on the first Sunday after Easter, and together they move on to Nowy Sącz, to which the king has summoned a large number of prelates and barons to meet him. Having discussed the rather difficult situation, it is decided that the King and Grand-duke should not both go to Kežmarok, but that Władysław is to remain in Nowy Sącz, while the Grand-duke with a retinue of prelates, knights and barons, is sent to meet Sigismund. The main reason for their meeting is to try to ensure that Sigismund honours the terms of the armistice which has another four years to run; for, if he does so, Władysław and the Grand-duke will be free to embark on their campaign against the Teutonic Knights, for they will not then have an enemy in their rear. However, when the Grand-duke and the King of Hungary meet and the Grand-duke insists that Sigismund should continue to honour the armistice, he is told that he will be unable to do so, if the Grand-duke and Władysław go to war with the Teutonic Knights. However, Sigismund does promise, that, should war break out, he will intervene personally and send envoys to the Master of the Order to try and end hostilities. At this time Sigismund is hoping to attain the dignity of Roman Emperor and is doing everything he can to get the German princes to look favourably on his claim. He has also had a secret meeting with Ulrich of Jungingen, the Master, at which he promised to send considerable reinforcements to help him fight the Poles, if the Order would pay him a certain sum in gold, being confident that such an offer would unloose the Order's purse-strings.

During this meeting in Kežmarok, a fire breaks out, which spreads and inflicts considerable loss in horses and personal belongings on the Poles. It is at this meeting that Sigismund takes the first step towards implementing a pernicious plan to woo the Grand-duke away from his loyalty and obedience to the Polish crown. At one juncture he takes the Grand-duke aside and, dismissing all witnesses, tries to persuade him to desert his royal brother and ally himself with Sigismund, promising him that the authority he has as King of the Romans is sufficient to allow him to make Alexander king of Lithuania and relieve him of his oath of allegiance to the King of Poland. He promises, indeed swears, to be his friend and give him genuine and disinterested help against Władysław or anyone else. Although aware of the treachery inherent in Sigismund's proposal, in view of the place and time of its making, the Grand-duke gives a favourable reply; but, as soon as he returns to his hostelry, he mounts his horse and rides off without taking leave of the King, who has already sent him valuable presents. Learning of the Grand-duke's sudden and unexpected departure, Sigismund hurries after him and catches up with him in a village scarcely a mile away and there bids him farewell, but without concluding any agreement, for he can now see that his proposal has been rejected. On his return to Nowy Sącz Alexander informs Władysław of all that passed between him and the King of Hungary. Then, in the greatest secrecy, the two men discuss ways and means of waging war on the Knights. After which the King hurries home by coach and in four days reaches Brześć where his wife, Anna, awaits him.

Seeing that there is no hope of maintaining peace with the Teutonic knights, Władysław issues a general call to arms and declares war on Prussia. To secure his frontier with Hungary, he appoints John of Szckekociny, the Castellan of Lublin, to be starosta for the town and district of Sącz and to take command of the soldiers of Sącz plus the knights of Biecz which, at this time, was granted to the Bishop of Eger and his brother, two refugees from Sigismund's Hungary. These are all absolved from the Prussian campaign but, under John of Szczekociny's command, are to defend the Hungarian border in case King Sigismund invades. The King also arranges for sufficient supplies for the area being made available, then leaves Sącz and goes to Cracow. He now sends his remaining knights and courtiers home to prepare for the war with Prussia, and sends for certain mercenary Czechs and Moravians, experts in the art of war, who are reputed to know how to lead an army, order lines of battle and how to choose places for quartering troops. He recruits these foreign mercenaries, not because he doubts being able to raise an adequate staff from among his own troops, but because, as his advisers point out, if he is victorious those he conquers will have to pay him whatever he asks, at any rate enough to pay for any mercenary force he employs, while, if he is defeated, most of the mercenaries will have been killed or captured; so, in neither event, will they be able to demand their pay. A further argument is that mercenaries already engaged or about to be hired, being bribed by the gifts they have already received, will never go over to the enemy. John of Tarnow, Voivode of Cracow, and others protest, saying that it would be better to use the money to pay Polish knights owing no military service but still inclined to be loyal to their fatherland. However, Zbigniew of Brzezie's plan to hire foreign mercenaries is adopted.

Before leaving Nowy Sącz, Władysław sent Zbigniew of Oleśnica, who speaks Hungarian, and the notary Stanisław Ciołek to King Sigismund urging him yet again to honour the terms of the truce arranged between them. Sigismund, disquieted by this succession of Polish envoys, tells them that he intends to go to Prussia in person in order to re-establish peace between the Teutonic Knights and King Władysław, provided the latter will allow him free passage through his kingdom. He promises that, if peace is re-established, not only will he honour the truce during its remaining term, but he will make a treaty of permanent peace with Poland. Władysław, who wishes to avoid a war with the Knights if this is at all possible, sends Stanisław Ciołek back with a letter to Sigismund guaranteeing his personal safety while travelling through Poland. However, Sigismund changes his mind and postpones his journey, pleading unexpected obstacles; so, instead of going himself, he sends Nicholas Gara, voivode of Hungary, and Ścibor of Ściborzyce, voivode of Transylvania, a man of Polish origin, and also a Silesian called George Kercz, ostensibly to prevent war breaking out, but in reality to collect the 40,000 florins which the Master has undertaken to pay, if Sigismund prevaricates with King Władysław.

These three, with a mounted escort of 200 men, arrive in Cracow while Władysław is still there. Władysław receives them most graciously, plies them with gifts and allows them free passage to Prussia; indeed he gives them guides, who see not only to their personal safety, but also lavishly meet all their needs. Władysław urges the Hungarians to go to Prussia and make peace, or conclude a truce, insisting that the whole blame for war, if it comes, will attach to the Knights.

All his preparations for war complete, Władysław appoints the Archbishop of Gniezno, Nicholas Kurowski, his Vice-regent with power to attend to all matters that may require attention during the King's absence and leaves Cracow on the Wednesday before Whitsun. He reaches Korczyn in four stages and there spends Whitsun, Trinity Sunday and Corpus Christi together with Queen Anna and the young knights whom he is leaving as her bodyguard. They are joined here by Queen Anna's mother, Princess of Teck by her second marriage, daughter of the Polish king, Casimir II. She spends several days with them and returns home laden with gifts. Władysław spends a further week there before moving in three stages to Słupia, where he spends two days, on one of which, at dawn, he climbs on foot to the monastery of the Holy Cross on Łysa Góra. Here he spends all day on his knees, praying. Then, having distributed alms, he commends his person and his cause to God and the Holy Cross and, at dusk, descends to Słupia for his first meal of the day.

When a number of Polish knights in the service of the King of Hungary learn that their mother country is preparing to go to war with the Knights and that the Kings of Hungary and Poland hate each other, they relinquish the valuable properties they have been granted in Hungary and, with that King's permission, though he does try to persuade them to stay, go to Poland to fight for Władysław. Władysław receives them most graciously and rewards them fittingly for their unusual loyalty.

As the truce with the Knights is about to expire, Władysław sends 400 mounted knights to protect the frontier at Inowrocław. Borowiec, Starosta of Inowrocław, provides them with every-thing they and their horses require. Other knights are sent to Brześć on a similar mission. On the day when the truce expires, the Feast of St. John the Baptist, the two forces combine and lie up in the woods near Toruń; then, at sunset, they sally out and set fire to some cottages on the banks of the Vistula and several lovely villages belonging to the Order, whose Master Ulrich is at the time dining in Toruń with the King of Hungary's envoys.

These see the blaze, a beautiful, if displeasing spectacle, but to the Master it is more a humilia-tion than a loss, and he turns on the Hungarians, saying: "The pact, you, as intermediaries, are pro-posing to me is a fraud, for before my very eyes fires are being kindled, people slaughtered and villages plundered". The Hungarians reply: "This small insignificant fire is no hindrance to peace-making or to talks towards that end. War has its necessities and its rights. You draw our attention to the slight damage the Poles are inflicting on you, but you overlook the damage, slaughter and fires you have already inflicted on Poland, devastating its territories and occupying the province of Do-brzyń, which belongs to Poland. It would seem sensible, if we are to discuss peace, that we should agree to a cessation of hostilities for several days." The Master agrees to the suggestion and a ten-day truce is arranged and documented. This is essential for Władysław and Poland, since such a pause will allow individual knights and starostas to prepare for war without having to keep a look-out for the enemy, while the frontier areas will be spared enemy incursions, before the King gets there with his powerful army and assures their safety by invading enemy territory.

On June 19 Władysław moves to Bodzentyn, where two days are taken up with discussions with envoys from the dukes of Słupsk, Szczecin and Magnopole, who have come to offer him troops for use against the Knights. They speak of these reinforcements as if they were numerous and powerful, but in fact they consist of units hastily scratched together and ridiculously modest. Having disposed of the envoys, Władysław moves on to Sulejów, which he reaches on the Tuesday.

He hears Mass in the monastery there the next morning and, after breakfast moves on to Wol-borz, where some of his prelates and advisers await him, as does the bulk of the army. Here, too, are the Czech and other foreign envoys, and also the waggons of the commissariat, four-horse teams for the cannon, and the rest of the army's equipment. The one big contingent missing is that from Wielkopolska, which only joins him, when he reaches the Vistula. Here Władysław spends three days consulting with his advisers and the Hungarian envoys, Nicholas Gara and Ścibor, who have come to inform him of the ten-day truce from the Feast of John the Baptist they have arranged and request that he observe this and not allow raids into enemy territory. Władysław agrees to this; in-deed, it is to his advantage, since it allows him to assemble his and the Lithuanian forces and move them up close to the Order's territory. So, after breakfast on June 26, the army moves off and reaches the Archbishop's iron ore mine and huge fishpond on the following Saturday. Here, light-ning kills several horses and one man, leaving another half dead. It also destroys a large dish of boiled fish in the tent of one of the knights, yet without harming any of those who have sat down to eat it. The next day, the army moves on to Kozłów on the Bzura, where the King receives a message from the Grand-duke telling him that the Lithuanians and the Grand-duke's Tatars have reached the Narew and are asking for some squadrons of cavalry to be sent to cover them as they cross the river, which the Grand-duke hesitates to attempt without protection. The King at once sends him twelve squadrons. On the Monday, the army moves on again and reaches the Vistula near the mon-astery of Czerwińsk, at the spot where the pontoon bridge made in Kozienice has been assembled. Then, in one day, the entire army, its four-horse waggons, a number of cannon, a quantity of provi-sions and other baggage are all moved safely across the river and camp pitched. Here are assem-bled the might of Poland, the armies of Janusz and Siemowit of Mazovia, the mercenary knights, as well as the Grand-duke's army and its contingent of 300 Tatars; and here they remain for three days to allow contingents from the more distant areas to arrive and cross to their side of the river. One of the King's best units remains on duty at the bridge-head, ensuring that there is no jostling or confusion on the bridge itself; while at its either end the bank itself is protected by strong baulks of timber that prevent people standing on it. Those moving onto the bridge have to keep to a strict, pre-arranged order for men, waggons and horses. Once everyone and everything are across, the bridge is dismantled and sent back to Płock to be stored there against the King's return.

During the three days spent on the bank of the Vistula, the King and the Grand-duke attend a service in the monastery at Czerwińsk, at which Jacob Bishop of Płock delivers a sermon to the whole army, explaining how wars can be just and unjust, and demonstrating the justness of the one they are waging on the Teutonic Knights. A Polish knight, Dobiesław Skoraczewski, in the service of the King of Hungary now arrives to make arrangements for Sigismund's two envoys, Nicholas Gara and Ścibor, to wait on Władysław and be informed of his intentions regarding peace in the future, having already been acquainted with those of the Master. Władysław tells him that he will receive the two Hungarians on the following Saturday or Sunday, but that he cannot say where, since an army never has a permanent site and he cannot say in advance what route he will follow. When Dobiesław returns to Toruń, the Master questions him as to where in the Polish camp he had been

A bridge of conventional design being used by the Poles to cross a river of modest size and no great depth.
—*Andreas Krzycki:* Ad Sigismundum Ploniae regem post partam de Moschis victoriam carmen. *A.D. 1515.*—*Jagiellonian University Library*

and where it was when he left it; and also whether he had seen the Grand-duke. He is told that the Grand-duke had just arrived with a powerful, excellently equipped and numerous army. The Master retorts: "In Alexander's army you will find more men fit to wield a spoon than a sword." Dobiesław insists that Alexander's army is powerful and excellently equipped, only to be told that the Master knows better than he. The Master then asks to be told about the bridge Władysław is said to have built "in the air". Dobiesław explains that what he saw was a bridge built most ingeniously of boats, and not in the air, which only serves the birds, and how with his own eyes he saw the whole army, even its heavy cannon, cross over dry foot without the bridge even trembling under the weight. The Master laughs contemptuously and, turning to the two Hungarians, says: "What nonsense this fellow talks! It's all lies, for our most reliable scouts have reported that Władysław is roaming the bank of the Vistula trying to cross, and cannot. Already, many of his men have been drowned searching for fords. As to the Grand-duke, he is on the Narew and does not dare cross." The Pole replies that if the Master will send someone he can trust with him, he will take him to the Polish camp and show him that everything he has said is true; but the Master just says that, being a Pole, he naturally exaggerates the power of his liege-lord, whereas the reality is quite different.

On the Thursday after the Feast of the Visitation of the Virgin Mary, Władysław and the Grand-duke move the army towards enemy territory. While on the march, they are given news of a disaster inflicted on the Knights by Janusz Brzozgłowy, the starosta of Bydgoszcz. What happened was this: as soon as the ten-day truce expired, the starosta, ever ready to strike a blow at the enemy, assembled a strong force and marched by night on the town and fortress of Świecie. Having set an ambush in a suitable place, he sent a small force forward to start fires and collect booty, which it did without losing a man. When the Knights in Świecie saw what was happening and how small was the Polish force, they mounted their horses and set off in pursuit of the withdrawing Poles. Their withdrawal, however, was a strategic one that led the Knights into the ambush prepared for them. The Knights fought desperately, indeed, more fiercely than their numbers would have led you to expect; yet, in the end they were all either killed or taken prisoner.

This start to the war is a good augury for the future, and Brzozgłowy's boldness makes the Master and the Knights strengthen their precautions: so they leave in Świecie Henry Plotzke the commander with the knights of his district and they also send him no small number of mercenaries to deter Brzozgłowy from any further action. On July 4 the King moves the army onto level ground near a village, whose name is not known. That night, seeing distant fires, some of the Poles, in disregard of their orders, slip away into enemy territory, a thing they would never have dared do by day, and return with splendid loot.

The next day, Władysław pitches camp near the village of Jeżów, and there receives the Hungarian envoys in audience. These try to persuade him and the Grand-duke to make peace on terms which they set forth. George Gersdorf has accompanied them, seeking only to discover the strength of the combined Polish and Lithuanian forces. After discussing the proposed terms with the Grand-duke, Władysław tells the envoys that the idea of peace has never been foreign to him, so that he will certainly never refuse equitable terms, if that will avoid shedding Christian blood; but a just peace would necessitate the Grand-duke recovering the whole of Samogitia, which since time immemorial has been his by natural right; while the province of Dobrzyń, unjustly seized by the Knights, must be returned to Poland. The question of damages, the King would be willing to leave to arbitration by the Roman King Sigismund. The Hungarians are delighted and breakfast with the King, sure in their own minds that the Master of the Order will agree to such terms.

After breakfast, Władysław breaks camp and moves the army to a village near the River Wkra, where the Grand-duke arrays his forces in the traditional manner, that is with those on smaller horses and those less well armed in the middle of each line, shielded by those on larger horses and those better equipped, thus avoiding any looseness in formation, though each line marches separately and at quite a distance from the others. The whole force is given forty banners.

King Władysław and the two Hungarians go to the top of an eminence from which the two armies can be seen on the level ground below. Later in the day, in order to ensure that his men remain alert and ready to fight, the King tells them that the enemy is advancing. The next day he breaks camp and moves to the village and the whole valley of the Wkra that rightly belonged to Mazovia, but had been occupied by the Knights, who were demanding 5000 broad grosses for its return. Because of this, the Lithuanians and their Tatars start devastating the area as though it were enemy territory. They kill adults and young people, babes in their cradles, drag some with their mothers to their tents and into captivity, despite the fact that all the people in the area are Polish by origin and speak Polish. The mothers of the murdered children, with hair dishevelled, come wailing before Władysław's tent. Their protests are supported by the Polish prelates and nobles, who beg the king to put an end to this barbarous cruelty and threaten to leave the camp unless all those taken prisoner are released. Władysław and the Grand-duke agree that they are right and order the release of all prisoners, who then assemble round the tent of Wojciech Jastrzębiec, Bishop of Poznań, to be given their freedom. Henceforth, any soldier behaving in such a barbarous fashion is to forfeit his life. The Bishop of Poznań, who has accompanied the King from Poland, obtains the latter's permission to return home.

On Wednesday July 9, the Polish–Lithuanian army advances a further two miles through wooded terrain into an extensive plain, where the combined forces, consisting of eighty-two squadrons of knights, are drawn up in line of battle. Władysław, with tears in his eyes, then unfurls a great standard embroidered with a white eagle with spread wings, open beak and a crown on its head, the arms of the Kingdom of Poland. He then prays aloud, a prayer heard by many and so moving that it reduces most who hear it to tears. The Grand-duke and the Mazovian princes similarly pray for victory as they unfurl their standards. The whole army then sings the Polish anthem: *Bogu Rodzica.*

Since none of the experts Władysław has hired feels competent to assume supreme command of so huge an army, command is entrusted to Zyndram of Maszkowicze, Sword-bearer of Cracow, a man of small stature, but great experience and courage. The combined armies then move forward and pitch a new camp between two lakes near the town of Lidzbark Welski, which has already been plundered and burned. Later in the day some Lithuanians and Tatars are seen barbarously destroying churches, raping women and girls, and, in one church even jestingly throwing the Holy Sacrament from the tabernacle. The sight elicits a protest from the Polish knights, who demand that the King put an end to such barbarous behaviour and punish those responsible, otherwise they will not rally to the standard. This worries the King, who orders a search for those responsible. This results in two Lithuanians, the main culprits, being brought before the Grand-duke, who orders them to hang themselves. The two first make a gallows and erect it with their own hands; then without physical compulsion, they mount the gallows and each puts a noose round his neck; one, who hesitates, being told by the other to hurry up, lest the Grand-duke become even more angry. Thus, they hang themselves watched by the whole army, which is so impressed that thereafter none dares reach out greedy hands for any Church treasure.

Early on Thursday July 10, before the dew has fallen, the King again moves camp and once more pitches it beside a great lake, Rubkowo, near the town and castle of Kurzetrik. Meanwhile, the Knights' army has halted not far away, by the River Drwęca, both banks of which it secures with tall, closely-spaced stakes so as to prevent anyone crossing. Learning that the enemy is so close, some Polish knights set out to harass them. They capture fifty of the Knights' horses, which are being watered in the river, and, making their grooms dismount, themselves ride them back to the Polish camp. Their sudden appearance there on horseback causes great confusion, for they are assumed to be the enemy, and many abandon the meal to which they have just sat down and rush to arm themselves. Dust rises and the sun blazes down, but eventually calm is restored. That evening, when the heat has somewhat subsided, the King calls his council and appoints commanders. They work out a strategy and decide on the route the army is to take and where it is to pitch camp. The Grand-duke is particularly concerned that they find the driest route and camp where there is sufficient drinking water, grazing and firewood.

Guides, who know the area and are familiar with its paths and roads, are sent for. The troops are strictly forbidden to break ranks before Marshal Zbigniew of Brzezie has moved ahead with the King's standard, when all are to follow him. All blowing of trumpets is forbidden, except by one of the King's trumpeters, at the first sound of whose trumpet, whether before dawn or at any time, all are to stand to and arm themselves; at the second call, they are to saddle their horses and, at the third call, to move off behind the Marshal and his standard.

In a last bid for peace, Władysław sends one of his knights, Peter Korcbog, to the Hungarian envoys, who are with the Order's army, demanding a guarantee that the Order will agree to peace and that this will be on the terms already agreed. The Hungarians go to the Master and do their best to persuade him to accept peace, emphasizing that the conditions proposed by King Władysław are equitable and urging him not to procrastinate, lest that lead to war, and, also, pointing out that Mars may prove to be with either side, so the outcome is far from certain. The Master consults his commanders and advisers in private. These all harbour a vain superstition that, because they are in possession of certain holy relics, no enemy can defeat them, and so they are inclined more to war than to peace; in consequence, the Hungarians are told that had Władysław asked for peace before invading the Order's territory, the Master might have agreed to it, but since he is making the request from territory that he has already pillaged and burned, the Order would consider it shameful to conclude peace with such an enemy. The Hungarians try to get him to change his mind, but this only angers the Master and he refuses to reconsider his answer. Seeing that they can do no more, the Hungarians inform Władysław that they have achieved nothing and that a special envoy will bring him the Master's official reply the following day. Władysław is persuaded that there is really no hope of arranging peace, but nonetheless he and the Grand-duke move their armies closer to the River Drwęca and the Knights' camp, just in case negotiations should start, when it would be an advantage to have the two parties one on either side of the same river. Peter Korcbog, whom Władysław sent to the Master, tells the King on his return that the Master will never accept a reasonable arrangement and that the Poles cannot cross the Drwęca without a fight, because of barricades of stakes set up on both its banks. The King then decides that his best tactic will be to withdraw, move upstream and cross dry-foot at the river's source. Though this will involve a short delay, he considers that better than having to fight a regular battle just to get across. Such a manoeuvre also saves the army the labour of rebuilding the pontoon bridge.

So, on Friday July 11, the trumpet sounds at dawn in the Polish camp, and the army withdraws by the way it had come. Reaching Lidzbark Welski, it turns left and moves through hillocky country to near Działdowo, where it pitches camp and, the men being tired, rests for two days. While there, a messenger arrives from the Hungarian envoys and, in private audience, tells the King how the Master would not listen to reason, so the Hungarians have achieved nothing, and he continues: "Since the King of Hungary, on whose behalf the envoys are acting, is Regent of the Roman Empire and, as such, is not at liberty to abandon the Order and its Master in their need, for they are part of his Empire, the Hungarian envoys have ordered me to hand to Your Majesty this letter, a declaration of war by the King of Hungary, who now breaks with Your Majesty and sides with the Master and the Order". Before he leaves, the Hungarians' messenger whispers to the King that he must not take this breaking-off of relations too seriously, for that letter is to cost the Order 40,000 florins and will have little other effect. The King, he says, is not to worry, but to continue with his plans and not delay starting hostilities, for the Knights are in all respects inferior, so that, with God's grace, the King will be victorious. He further gives the King to understand that Sigismund did not send the two envoys to Prussia to make peace; indeed, he would have preferred war to break out and hostilities to continue, but only to extract gold from the Order, which was falsely reputed to have a tower full of it. The Hungarians have frankly told the Knights that they have a letter from Sigismund to King Władysław breaking off relations between the two countries, but that their instructions are not to deliver the letter until the Order has paid them 40,000 florins. The Master considers such a letter worth the money and has agreed to pay half the amount there in the camp and the other half when the Hungarians reach Gdańsk. For this huge sum the Order receives nothing, now or later, but a written declaration of war, which was handed over in private, so that none but the King and his eight advisers knew of it. The King orders the letter and conversation to be kept secret, lest the news reach his knights and dampen their ardour.

On the day of the Poles' withdrawal from the Drwęca, a Prussian scout, covered in dust and pouring with sweat reaches the Knights' camp with the news that the king of Poland and his armies are retreating, even fleeing. The delighted Master goes to the Hungarians and says: "A scout we have sent out, a Pole by origin, tells us that for several days he has been looking for the Polish camp and has been unable to find it. He found places where the army had halted with some empty food containers and a few abandoned, exhausted horses and some cannon balls; but, after that the tracks brought him to a crossroads, where he was unable to determine the direction which the army had taken. I believe it certain," he said, "that the King of Poland, afraid of my greater strength, is on the run; for retreat is always clear evidence of fear. Now that my enemy has escaped, I hesitate as to my next step. Tell me, please, am I to pursue the escaping enemy or stay where I am?" The Hungarians reply: "Abandoning a few empty utensils and some exhausted horses is scarcely sufficient evidence of retreat or flight. Indeed, one might think it stupid of anyone to take empty containers and lame horses with him. However, leaving cannon balls behind does suggest a sudden withdrawal or retreat. But it calls for proper investigation, for one cannot accept as true one report that so large an army is in flight." The Master decides not to order a pursuit, but, instead, to strengthen the defences of his towns. He orders twelve bridges to be built across the Drwęca, so that he can move his army across, and then, moving quietly, he advances in the direction where he thinks the enemy may be, persuaded by his flatterers that the outcome of battle will be the one he wishes.

On Sunday, July 13, the King and almost the entire army take the last sacrament in the conviction that they may shortly encounter the enemy, as, indeed, they will. The King then breaks camp—the waggons and train having been sent on ahead two hours previously—and advances on Dąbrówno, whose walls and bastions are washed by the waters of the lake that all but surrounds it. He pitches camp on level ground some half a mile from the town. The heat is unusually intense, but, that evening, when it is not so fierce, many soldiers leave the camp to take a look at the town. The town's garrison, thinking that these sightseers are attacking them, makes a sortie and suddenly every one is fighting. The Poles have the upper hand and force the garrison to retreat within the walls, with the Poles, who see a chance of capturing the town, at their heels. The town is defended by high walls with towers and bastions, as well as by its position, which is that of being almost surrounded by the lake with only a narrow strip of land providing access. There is such confusion in the Polish camp that the King has to order a general assault, lest the troops already attacking the town should be defeated and rendered useless for further action. The inhabitants of the town are not slow to defend themselves, firing cannon and throwing stones to drive off the attackers. Many of the Polish knights now wade into the lake and start undermining the walls; while others set up siege ladders and these succeed in climbing the walls and quickly capture the town, which is crowded with men and women and stuffed with supplies of every kind, collected during the years of peace. In addition, the knights and gentry from the surrounding area have sought refuge in it with all their possessions. All this the victors capture and the booty is so huge, that everyone in the army is enriched and the supply waggons are filled with an incredible amount of provisions. Fire is set to the town before all the booty has been removed, with the result that many who had sought refuge in the churches are killed in the blaze. Thousands of men and women are captured and brought to the King's camp. All knights who have been captured are handed over to the King and many of them are executed; indeed, none escapes death or captivity, except the few who flee across the lake in boats. No mercy is given to the aged, behaviour that is not only in accord with the laws of war, but motivated by hatred for the way the enemy had devastated the province of Dobrzyń. When the Master, Ulrich, hears that Władysław has captured and burned Dąbrówno and is advancing on Malbork, he is greatly perturbed and realizes that he can no longer avoid a fight.

On this same day, Matthew of Wąszosze Voivode of Kalisz and Starosta of Nakło had marched the force he had been given to guard the frontier into Pomerania and started looting and pillaging. Michael Küchmeister, wishing to put a stop to Matthew's activities, brought up an army and, in the ensuing battle, Matthew left the field and his discouraged troops scattered. Many, who considered flight shameful, were taken prisoner. News of this disaster is suppressed and the King only hears of it, when, after his own victory, he is besieging Malbork and there discovers one of Matthew's men, Jarosław of Iwno, who had been taken prisoner.

Instead of moving camp on July 14 as he had planned, the King stays where he is for one further day, Monday, so as to collect the remaining provisions and valuables hidden in the cellars and basements of the houses in Dąbrówno. He has, too, to decide what to do with the prisoners. He releases every one but those who are the members of the Order or of the local gentry, that is to say all citizens of Dąbrówno, whether commoners or peasants, as well as all women and girls and maidens of whatever class, who are guaranteed immunity from assault or abuse by the troops. Then, as the sun is setting, the King orders details of the next day's march to be issued, while the troops are ordered to their tents to rest.

The King had decided to hear Mass at dawn, but, at daybreak on Tuesday July 15, the violence of the wind is such that it is impossible to erect the tent in which to celebrate Mass, so, on the advice of the Grand-duke the army moves on a couple of miles through a countryside of burning villages and pitches camp among woods and thickets on the level plain surrounding Tannenberg and Grunwald. He orders the chapel tent to be pitched on an eminence above Lake Lubań, so that he can hear Mass while the troops are pitching their tents. Meanwhile, the Master of the Order has arrived in Grunwald village, though the Polish intelligence is unaware of the fact. Then, just as the King is about to hear Mass, one of his knights comes to tell him that he has seen a squadron of the enemy quite close. As he is speaking, a string of other knights comes hurrying with the news that they, too, have seen the enemy quite close and ready to do battle. The King is quite unconcerned and, considering it more important to praise the Lord than to start fighting, he hears two Masses, during which he prays for divine assistance. Meanwhile, the Grand-duke Alexander, who cannot bear procrastination, has been sending messages urging the King to stop praying and start fighting. He now comes in person to do this, though he and Zyndram have already ordered the troops to stand to arms, the Poles on the left wing and the Lithuanians on the right. The Poles have fifty standards and the Lithuanians forty.

The Knights, seeing the enemy in woods and thickets, think that they are being enticed into an ambush and so miss an opportunity; for, instead of attacking, they wait for both sides to be drawn up in ordered ranks under their banners. It has been said that before and during the battle, the wind favoured the Poles by blowing dust into the eyes and mouths of the Knights. At this juncture, 300 Czech mercenaries decide to withdraw from the field, either because they are afraid or because they have been bribed by the enemy. As they are leaving the camp without the knowledge or permission of the King, they are met by the Polish Vice-chancellor Nicholas, who asks them where

The battle of Grunwald (Tannenberg), one of the illustrations in B. Paprocki: Ogród Królewski
(1599).—Jagiellonian University Library.

they are going and why. They tell him that the King has not paid them the money they have earned.
The Vice-chancellor then tells them that he knows that they have been rewarded generously for all
that they have done, even being paid in advance. The Czechs are so impressed that they abandon
their intention of deserting and return to the Polish camp and get themselves ready for battle.

Having finished his prayers, the King dons his armour, a magnificent suit that covers him
from top to toe. Meanwhile, everyone is begging him to give the word for battle to be joined; for
though the two armies are lined up and ready for battle, scarcely a bowshot apart, and individual
duels are already being fought, it is felt that the King's command is required before general hostilities can start. The Poles are determined to conquer or die; while the Teutonic Knights, who are
made up of a number of nationalities speaking different languages, are not so single-minded, and
they have with them, too, a host of artisans, servants and camp-followers, who are useless in battle.
However, the King just mounts his horse and, leaving all the banners but the royal standard with its
embroidered white eagle in the camp, moves to an eminence from which he can survey the enemy
forces between the two woods. He then dubs several young knights, makes an encouraging speech
and, changing his mount for a very powerful, carefully chosen chestnut gelding with a small blaze,
asks for his helm; but, before putting it on, he orders Vice-chancellor Nicholas to take all the
priests, secretaries and other non- combatants to the train and wait there for him to come, which he
will do after he has ordered the line of battle, it having been decided that the King should not take
part in the actual fighting, but remain with the train in the camp.

Suddenly, the King is informed of the arrival of two heralds from the enemy's camp. These have brought two swords, without scabbards, which they say the Master has sent to encourage the King to start fighting and to take his place in the ranks. Władysław recalls the Vice-chancellor and, in his presence and that of those who constitute the King's bodyguard, tells the heralds to deliver their message: this they do, but in German, which Jan Mężyk interprets: "Your Majesty! The Grand Master of the Prussian Knights, Ulrich, sends you and your brother (not naming Alexander or giving him his title) these two swords, so that you may fight him and his army without further procrastination or hiding in woods and thickets to deceive him, but to fight him now. If you think the field of battle here too cramped to deploy your ranks, the Master will, to help you, withdraw as far as you wish, or you may choose any other battle-field, as long as there is no further procrastination." As the heralds are speaking, they can all see how the Knights' army is withdrawing some distance, as though to confirm the instructions given to the heralds. The King then tells the heralds that he has no need of other people's swords, for he has plenty of his own; but, in the name of God, he accepts these two sent to him by an enemy that desires his blood and the destruction of his army, so that they may further strengthen the help being given him by God, into whose hands he entrusts everything." (These swords are preserved to this day in the royal treasury in Cracow.)

The King dismisses the heralds, who are conducted back by one of his knights, and orders the Vice-chancellor back to the camp. He then puts on his helm and orders the bugles to be sounded throughout the army; whereupon the entire army sings the country's anthem, *Bogu rodzica*, then brandishing their lances the knights prepare to engage the enemy.

It was considered obvious, as had been decided, that the King, whose person was considered the equivalent of ten thousand knights, must remain in a safe place and at a distance, out of sight of both the enemy and his own troops, and with a body-guard of sixty knightly lances, while saddled horses had been placed in advance in various places, so that, should the enemy gain the upper hand, the King could escape by changing horses. The Grand-duke, however, entrusts care of his person to God alone. With just a few men and no bodyguard he is everywhere among the Poles as well as the Lithuanians, changing horses, restoring order where ranks have been broken. On his orders, the Lithuanians are the first to engage the enemy, which they do in the middle of the level ground between the two armies, both sides uttering the cries that soldiers shout before battle. The Knights vainly try to repel them with two salvoes from their cannon. Here, in the middle of the battle-field are six tall oak trees, their branches now occupied by people—whether from the Polish army or that of the Knights is not known—who have climbed up to watch the first encounter and its outcome. As the two armies engage, the noise of lances breaking and swords striking armour is as loud as a rock-fall and can be heard several miles away. Armour crumples and swords thrust at faces. The ranks become confused and so close together that you cannot distinguish the cowards from the brave, the valiant from the heedless. Positions change and men advance or retreat as one repels or kills an enemy and moves into his place. Their lances broken, knights fight hand to hand; pressed close by their mounts, they can fight only with swords or battle-axes. The sound of battle is that of clanging hammers in a blacksmith's forge.

For the first hour it is impossible to tell who is getting the better of the fighting. This is fiercest on the Polish left wing, where the Knights seem to be having a difficult time; so the Knights increase their pressure on the right wing, where are the Lithuanians, whose ranks are thinner, their horses smaller and their equipment inferior, so that they might be considered easier to defeat. If that can be achieved, it will allow the Knights to attack the Poles on the other wing more effectively. The plan is a good one, but it does not wholly succeed. Under the increased pressure the Lithuanians, Ruthenians and Tatars begin to weaken and withdraw nearly half a mile. The Knights keep up the pressure, forcing them back again and again, until finally they turn and run. The Grand-duke uses his loud voice and whip to try to stop them, but in vain. The fleeing Lithuanians take a number of Poles with them, and they are all pursued for several miles, the Knights cutting them down and taking prisoners, for they think that they have won the day.

The only unit of the Grand-duke's army not to run is its three squadrons of Ruthenian knights from Smolensk, who fight fiercely under three banners. At one point, one of these banners is thrown down and trampled, but the other two squadrons fight as befits men and knights and emerge victorious and join up with the Polish right wing.

Another to give up is Jan Sarnowski, the Czech standard-bearer of the Czech and Moravian mercenaries, fighting under the banner of St. George. He withdraws his men to the grove, where the King girded the new knights and there they stay, apparently not intending to return to the fray, until the Vice-chancellor notices them and, mistaking their white cross for the emblem of a Polish knight, Dobiesław of Oleśnica, whose device is very similar, storms out of his tent and bitterly berates them. Sarnowski pretends that their withdrawal was solely due to pressure from some of the knights fighting with them; but his men protest that the blame rests with him and that they will no longer obey him, but return to the battle, which they do. After this, Sarnowski is regarded as a man without honour and one not to believed. When, after the war, he returns from Poland, his own wife refuses to admit him to the castle or her bed, telling him that he is a coward. His shame is such that he does not long survive. It is not known whether he deserted out of cowardice or because he had been bribed.

The Grand-duke, perturbed by the flight of his troops and afraid lest this dishearten the Poles, having vainly sent several messengers to the King begging him to attack without delay, now goes to him in person and urges him to encourage his troops with his presence and to take part in the fighting.

After the rout of the Lithuanians, a gentle rain begins to fall, which lays the appalling dust that hangs over the battle-field, and fierce fighting breaks out again in several places. At one point the enemy presses forward so fiercely that the royal standard with its white eagle, borne by the standard-bearer of Cracow, falls to the ground in the press, but the knights quickly raise it again. Ashamed that this should have happened, the Poles attack more fiercely and completely rout their opponents.

The Knights who have been pursuing the Lithuanians thinking that the battle has already been won, gleefully return to their camp with a crowd of prisoners. There, seeing that fierce fighting is still going on, they abandon their prisoners and booty and fling themselves into the fray. Many fall on either side, but the Knights suffer the greater casualties, and gradually confusion creeps into their ranks and the Poles sense that the Czechs and Germans are beginning to think of flight; yet the Knights of the Order stiffen their resolve.

Meanwhile, the King is still on his eminence watching the fighting and putting his trust in God, while he placidly awaits the final defeat of his enemy, who suddenly bring up sixteen fresh squadrons which have not yet fought. When these turn in the direction of the King's eminence with their lances couched, it looks as though they are about to attack the King. Thinking he is in danger, Władysław sends his secretary, Zbigniew of Oleśnica, to the nearest Polish unit ordering it to come to his assistance immediately. The unit concerned is on the point of engaging an enemy force and its commander brandishes his sword at the King's secretary and angrily tells him to be gone and asks if he cannot see that they are about to be attacked, so that, if they now turn away and go to the King, to the enemy it will look like flight and this will endanger the King and all of them. The King's secretary goes back to Władysław and tells him that all the knights are engaged and that those fighting or about to fight are not to be persuaded to do otherwise or obey contrary orders. He explains that he did not go to other units, because the noise and confusion was such that it was impossible to hear what anyone said. The small banner with a white eagle, which marks where the King is, is now taken down, lest it betray the King's presence to the enemy.

Władysław is now eager to enter the fray and his bodyguard is obliged to restrain him from putting spurs to his horse. Suddenly, out of the Prussian ranks rides a German Knight from Lusatia in full armour, mounted on a chestnut horse, and charges straight towards where the King is. The King prepares to defend himself, but his secretary, who is unarmed and without armour, parries the German's lance-thrust by knocking it up with the shaft of a broken lance with which he then pushes the Knight out of his saddle. The King points his lance at the recumbent knight's forehead, which is exposed as his visor is raised, but does not strike home. However, the King's bodyguard swiftly dispatches the fallen Knight and some foot-soldiers strip off his armour as their spoil. No deed could have been braver than this unarmed youth's defence of his King, in which he unseated a knight in full armour, a mature man and a veteran. When the King, wishing to reward the youth, proposes to gird him with a knight's belt, the young secretary will not accept it, and, when the King persists in wishing to honour him, he tells the King that he would rather join the spiritual army and fight for Christ. The King assures him, that, if he lives, he will see that his secretary is made a bishop. (He does later become bishop of Cracow, Pope Martin V granting him dispensation for the stain his brave act left on him.)

When they see how the German knight has been unseated and killed, the fresh enemy squadrons start withdrawing, a withdrawal prompted by one of the Knights who gives the signal for retreat to those in the front rank, using his lance and calling out, in German, "Herum! Herum!" They turn aside and move in the direction of one of the largest of the Polish banners. Some Poles, seeing the throng of men under sixteen different banners rightly take them to be the enemy, but others, the confirmed optimists, hope they may be Lithuanians, because of the light javelins they carry, and so they are not immediately attacked. Then one of the Polish knights, Dobiesław of Oleśnica, brandishing his lance, spurs his horse at the advancing throng, from out of whose ranks another knight rides to challenge him. With a deft movement of his javelin the Prussian knight parries the thrust of the Pole's lance, knocking it up above his head, and, when the Pole tries a second thrust, bends his head aside, so that the thrust misses him again. The Pole, seeing that his thrust has failed and being disinclined to take on an entire enemy squadron, turns and rides back. The Prussian spurs after him and with a thrust of his lance wounds the Pole's horse in the loins, but not mortally, and quickly rejoins his squadron so as to avoid capture. The Poles, having now got over their hesitation, attack the enemy, who have been joined by yet other units, and a mortal fight begins. In the end, surrounded by the Poles who outnumber them, the Knights are cut down and almost all killed or taken prisoner. Among those killed is the Master of the Order, Ulrich, his marshals and many of their famous knights and commanders. The rest of the Prussian army then begins to retreat, and the retreat turns into a flight. Thus King Władysław obtains a late and hardly won, but decisive victory.

George Gersdorf, the knight who carried the banner of St. George for the Knights, held it more honourable to be taken prisoner than shamefully to run, so, along with forty of his companions-in-arms he dropped to his knees and, as he wished, was taken prisoner and surrendered his banner. Two princes, Casimir of Szczecin and Conrad of Oleśnica, who were fighting with the Prussians under their own banners and with their own men, were also taken prisoner, as were many knights of different nationalities and from different armies, who, in escaping, sought refuge in the Prussian camp with the train.

The Knights' camp is full of valuables and in it, too, are waggons loaded with the Master's possessions and those of his knights. All this is plundered by the victorious Poles. In the camp, too, they find waggons filled with wooden handcuffs and chains, which the Knights, telling themselves that God would give them victory, had brought to put on the many prisoners they intended to take. The Poles use these chains and handcuffs on their prisoners, a just form of divine punishment! Seeing the Prussians in their own chains is, indeed, a thrill and a sight worth seeing. The enemy waggons, numbering several thousand, are plundered in a short quarter of an hour. In the camp, too, are waggons laden with barrels of wine, to which the weary Poles turn to quench their thirst, the knights using their helmets, gloves, even their boots to drink from; then the King, afraid lest his men drink themselves stupid and incapable of defending themselves, orders the barrels to be broached. This sends wine spurting over heaps of dead bodies and, flowing on, mixes with the blood of men and horses, and in a red stream cuts itself a channel through the meadow that leads to the village of Tannenburg. Seven of the enemy's standards are then found in a thicket of birch trees and at once taken to the King.

The King moves up on to the eminence on which the Knights' tents were pitched. From there the Prussian infantry and cavalry can be seen scattered in flight, the sun's rays reflected back from the armour that almost all are wearing. Seeing this, the King orders a pursuit, but forbids a general slaughter. The fleeing soldiery are pursued for several miles. Many are captured and brought back to the camp, but, because of the confusion and crowding, a number are drowned in a fishpond two miles from the battle-field. A few escape as night falls and the pursuit is called off. In all fifty-one enemy standards are taken, and so much booty that every one of the victors finds himself considerably enriched.

Throughout the fighting, the Grand-duke went from unit to unit, replacing those exhausted with fresh men and always alert as to how his troops were faring. Now, after the victory, he meets King Władysław for the first time since the battle began and tells him how two of the Order's Knights, who have been captured, are those who at a meeting between the Grand-duke and the Master on the bank of the Niemen, had made slanderous and indecent insinuations concerning the Grand-duke and his mother, whom they accused of being anything but modest; he adds that he intends to punish them as they deserve and behead them. Władysław forbids vengeance for past deeds being wreaked on those taken in battle or who have surrendered, and the Grand-duke would have accepted this, had the two arrogant and impudent Knights not again incensed him by refusing to ask for mercy or even to address him humbly; so he orders them to be beheaded on the following Sunday. The King does not oppose this. I do not presume to say whether or not the Grand-duke was right in thus treating prisoners of war.

As the sun is about to set, the King leaves his eminence and has the vast number of the enemy's waggons moved a quarter of a mile towards Malbork. Camp is then pitched beside a lake, where the army is already assembled. When he reaches the camp, the King dismounts and stretches out on a couch of maple leaves with only his secretary, Zbigniew, beside him, and there he rests until his tent is ready. He is so hoarse from shouting encouragement and orders to his knights that for the next couple of days, it is difficult to understand what he says. Once in his tent, he removes his armour and orders a meal to be prepared as speedily as possible, for neither he nor his men have tasted food all day. After nightfall it begins to rain and continues to do so all night, throughout which odd groups keep coming in with more prisoners and booty, the prisoners being handed over to the King for him to deal with in the morning. When Mszczuj of Skrzynica informs him that Ulrich of Jungingen the Prussian Master has fallen and, as proof, shows him a golden pectoral full of sacred relics, which his servant had torn from the dead man, the King sighs deeply and bursts into tears. "My knights", he says, "see what an ugly thing is pride; for he who yesterday claimed to be the master of many a country and kingdom, who was convinced that he would not find another as powerful as he, now lies beyond help, killed in the most wretched manner, proof that pride is worse than modesty." He then thanks his Creator for having defeated his opponents and made him and his people famous. The cold rain kills many of the wounded from either side who have been left on the field of battle. During the night, too, orders are given for all to assemble round the King's tent in the morning to hear a solemn Mass of thanksgiving; after which the army is to remain in camp for the rest of the day. Some of the King's advisers think it should spend three days at the scene of its victory; but others insist that it should march on Malbork as soon as possible, or, at least, that a considerable force be sent to invest the castle there, saying that, if they can now capture the enemy's main fortress, while they are still fearful and apprehensive, the others will all surrender without force having to be employed. This was good advice and, if acted upon, would have been most advantageous. Indeed, those expert in the profession of arms consider that King Władysław's greatest blunder was that he neglected to send troops to capture Malbork, which could easily have been done; for, until Henry of Plauen, Commander of Świecie, reached it with reinforcements the castle was as good as deserted and defenceless.

Wednesday, July 16. The rain stops and the sun comes out. The King orders a search for the bodies of the Master and other eminent officers of the Order, so that they can be handed over for honourable burial in a church. When the King is shown the body of the Master, in which are two wounds, one in the forehead and the other in the chest, and those of Frederick Wallenrod, Conrad Lichtenstein and others, he says not one word expressive of insult or scorn, allows himself neither laughter nor delight, but, instead, tears course down his cheeks in sympathy with their fate, and he orders them to be wrapped in clean cloths, placed in a waggon with a purple cover and sent to Malbork for burial. Other bodies he orders to be buried in the wooden church at Stębark. He sees to it that any surviving wounded have their wounds dressed. He takes the view that his victory will earn him greater fame and occasion less hatred, if he practices moderation. The Polish dead who can be identified are also buried in Stębark church, their funeral being no more splendid than that of the defeated. The wounded are brought into the Polish camp and their wounds dressed. Once their numbers have been counted, it transpires that only twelve eminent Polish knights have been killed. It is indeed, remarkable that the Polish knights suffered so few casualties in defeating so powerful and numerous an enemy, almost all of whose own knights were either killed or captured.

The royal chapel tent has a nave and choir, like a church, and here three Masses are said, while the whole army gathers round to hear: one of the Blessed Virgin Mary, one of the Holy Ghost and one of the Holy Trinity. At other altars Masses are said for the souls of the dead. All round the camp are the captured enemy standards and banners, their fluttering quite loud in the light breeze. Later in the day, the King gives a banquet to which are invited his chief commanders, the Grand-duke, the two Mazovian princes and also two of his prisoners: Conrad the White of Oleśnica and Casimir of Szczecin, to whom he has granted their freedom, though their unworthy behaviour had really earned them punishment.

Meanwhile, in Malbork, the two Hungarian envoys, Nicholas of Gara and Ścibor of Ściborzyce, and the Knights left to guard the castle, have anxiously awaited the outcome of the battle, which they know will be fought any day. An exhausted soldier reaches the castle and tells them that he has galloped all the way from the Prussian camp, and that there has been a dreadful slaughter in which the Master has been killed and his army routed. The Knights in Malbork insist that until now there can have been only odd encounters, but no pitched battle; but then the two Hungarians venture outside the gates to see what they can discover, and come across a group of soldiers who have fled from the battle and these tell the same story. In this group is a knight, Peter Świnka, formerly standard-bearer of Dobrzyń, who deserted the King before the battle and went over to the Master, and he gives them a full account of how the Poles have been victorious and the Knights defeated. Hearing this, the Hungarian envoys' attendants, most of whom are Polish, cheer loudly, but are ordered to confine expression of their delight to within their own circle, since they are quartered in Prussian homes. At first, a victory for the King of Poland seems so incredible that the news is treated not only as empty, but insane talk; but, when others arrive and tell the same story, it is finally believed and those in the castle give way to despair. No one now thinks of anything, but how to escape, no matter where; so, had the King advanced swiftly on Malbork after his victory, as he had been advised to do, he would have captured the fortress without loss of life.

After the banquet, the King has his knights hand over their prisoners. These are paraded on a stretch of level ground, on which six secretaries have set up desks at which they record the name, family and rank of each prisoner, these having already been segregated according to whether they are knights of the Order, of Prussia, Chełmno or Livonia, citizens of the Prussian towns, Czechs, Moravians, Silesians, Bavarians, knights of Meissen or Austria or the Rhineland, Swabians, Frisians, Lusatians, Thuringians, Pomeranians, inhabitants of Szczecin, Cassubians, Franconians or Westphalians. When that has been done, each knight is required to swear an oath and give his word of honour that he will present himself in Cracow castle on the next St. Martin's Day. After this, he is allowed to go, generously provided with provisions for the journey, clothes and a guide to take him to Osterode, the nearest town. The only ones to whom this does not apply are the Dukes of Szczecin and Oleśnica and all who are Knights of the Order, the latter being sent to various Polish castles as prisoners-of-war.

While this is going on, the King has mounted his horse and sets out with the Grand-duke to inspect the battle-field. He returns to camp as dusk falls, when he sends a special messenger, Nicholas Morawiec, with one of the captured banners, that of the Bishop of Pomezania, and letters to Queen Anna and the others telling them of the defeat he has inflicted on the Order, and ordering services of thanksgiving to be held in all churches. This news is received in Cracow with great jubilation: people light up their houses and Mass is sung in the churches.

Thursday, July 17. The army moves to Olsztyn and makes camp there; whereupon both town and castle surrender. The King's mild and generous treatment of those who surrender or are captured is regarded as a more successful exploitation of his victory, than the victory itself. An emissary arrives from John Bishop of Warmińsk to tell the King that the Bishop will surrender and submit to him, if he will not allow the Bishop's lands and properties to be plundered or burned. The King declines to accept the proposal, because the envoy is regarded as untrustworthy, but he is told that the King will not reject the proposal, if the Bishop comes in person to make submission.

When he learns of the death of Ulrich of Jungingen and of so many of the Order's Knights, realizing the dire situation in which the Order now finds itself, Henry of Plauen, Commander of Świecie, collects all the infantry and horse at his disposal and marches to Malbork with a further 500 mercenaries he has persuaded to be hired. Their arrival injects new hope into those who have sought refuge in the castle and brings in others from outlying forts and castles, which are thus left deserted.

In the end, there are 5000 knights defending Malbork. But for this swift and clever action, it would have been the end not only of Malbork, but of the whole Order of Teutonic Knights, which Władysław would undoubtedly have utterly destroyed, had he at this time captured Malbork castle.

Friday, July 18. The King advances as far as a lake between Morąg and Olsztyn and there halts. Refugees arrive here from other camps and are distributed among the Polish units. On this day, too, the Hungarian envoys leave Malbork and go to Gdańsk to collect the 20,000 florins the Master arranged for them to be paid there.

Saturday, July 19. The army advances to Morąg. Though the castle there is splendidly defended by the lakes and marshes that surround it, it immediately surrenders. After this, almost all the Prussian castles and towns surrender, for, after the Poles' victory at Grunwald, all are afraid of them and feel that, now that the Master is dead and his army defeated, none can stand up to the victors.

Sunday, July 20. The army moves from Morąg and camps near the castle of Preussmarkt. The King is quartered in a village on Lake Czołpie, to which many of the Knights left to garrison Preussmarkt come to surrender themselves and the castle, the tenure of which the king grants to a knight from Wielkopolska, Mroczka of Łopuchow. However, since the castle is reputed to contain many hidden valuables and treasure, he sends his secretary, Jan Socha, with the knight when he takes possession in order to make an inventory of all that is in the castle. The inventory made, Socha sets out to return to the King, but he and his retinue are set upon and murdered, thus the King never learns what his secretary found in the castle. Mroczka, strongly suspected of having arranged the murder, is formally accused by the murdered man's brother and relatives, but clears himself in court by giving his knightly word that he was innocent.

The army now advances to Lake Dolstath and so to the town and castle of Dzierzgoń, which is occupied without let or hindrance, the knights left to guard it having fled. The Poles find fires burning in kitchens, tables laid for a meal, cellars and larders full of wine, oats, honey, fish, meat and all kinds of grain. There is a room, called trapparia in German, filled with clothes made of purple and precious cloth and also those clothes which are specially worn by the Knights. The King generously gives these to his knights and finally allows the whole army to help itself to what each wishes of the clothes and provisions that are there in profusion.

The King hears Mass in the chapel in the castle, which has a number of beautifully carved wooden figures, which he orders to be sent back to Poland, where they are given, together with a silver-gilt crucifix later taken from Brodnica, to the church of the Blessed Virgin in Sandomierz, where they are to this day.

Thursday, July 24. Leaving Marshal Zbigniew in command of Dzierzgoń the army moves on and pitches camp half way between Dzierzgoń and Malbork. Emissaries from Henry of Plauen come from Malbork requesting safe-conduct for a number of knights whom he wishes to send to parley with the King. Władysław tells them, that, God willing, he will get to Malbork on the following day and will then grant safe-conduct. Meanwhile, Henry of Plauen has the town of Malbork burned, so as to prevent it providing cover and defences for the Poles should they capture it.

Friday, July 25. The King sends several squadrons ahead of the main force to occupy strategic positions and deal with possible ambushes and other dangers, and camps at Lake Grinhau, from which he invests the castle at Malbork. Throughout the day there are minor skirmishes between the Lithuanians, posted below the castle, and the garrison for possession of the burned town, still in enemy hands, though it has no proper defences and, the citizens having fled, is as good as deserted.

Saturday, July 26. In the evening, fighting breaks out between some Poles, who are trying to enter the town, and men from the castle, many of whom are killed, for the Poles vastly outnumber them. In the end, their enemy has to withdraw into the castle, surrendering the town. Their blood up, the Poles with couched lances and loud shouts advance as far as the church near the wall, hoping to capture the castle. If the King had sent troops to back them up, they would have been able to do so, for there was access to it through a breach in the wall. However, again a good opportunity is wasted. In the evening, the enemy sets fire to the bridge across the river leading to Tczew, denying it as a means of access to the Poles. This is greatly to the Poles' advantage, for it provides them with secure grazing for their horses on the far side. The enemy spends all night repairing the breach in the castle wall with huge baulks of oak; while the King brings his cannon up under cover of darkness and positions them, some near the ramparts in the Lithuanians' sector, and others at the head of the burned bridge, from where they maintain a continual bombardment of the castle.

King Władysław's own tent with its chapel and outdoor dining-space has been pitched on an eminence above the river, from which the King can survey his whole army and the castle it is besieging. The siege is maintained for a good two months, during which the Bishop of Poznań arrives, but he contracts a fever and is ordered home by the King.

With Malbork castle under siege, the nobles and knights of Prussia and the councils of Gdańsk, Elbląg, Toruń, Chełmno, Kinsberg, Świecie, Gniew, Tczew, Brodnica and Brandenburg as well as Bishop John of Warmińsk, Bishop Arnold of Chełmno, Bishop Henry of Pomezania and Bishop John of Sambia all come and submit to King Władysław, each taking an oath of fidelity and homage. Those taken prisoner during the fighting, plead to be released from captivity before taking an oath of allegiance, their excuse being that they are not at liberty to give an oath of homage as long as theoretically they are prisoners. The King grants them their former rights and liberties and even some new ones. The town of Elbląg, whose citizens threw out their commander, Werner Tettingen, when he fled the battlefield and returned there, surrender both town and castle and these remain unplundered. The King grants tenure to the Voivode of Cracow, John of Tarnow, who, when he takes possession of the castle, finds many valuables there and sends a hundred golden and silver vessels to his King.

One day, the Knights inside Malbork make a sortie aimed at the Polish cannon, but those guarding the guns anticipate their attack and halt it at the river. Fierce fighting ensues and in this most of the enemy are killed, the rest retreat towards the castle, pursued by the Poles as far as the round tower. Here, a wall, weakened by the Polish bombardment, collapses on the Poles, wounding many of them, while others are hit by arrows shot at them from above. The helm of one knight, which had been struck by a heavy stone, required the use of blacksmith's hammers before it could be removed.

The King grants tenure of twenty-three of the castles and towns that have surrendered to him to his own knights. In one of these, Brodnica, a quantity of golden and silver objects is found, as well as a number of wonderful books, including five parts of Vincent of Beauvais' *Speculum*, some lovely paintings in golden and silver frames, crucifixes and ornaments, all of which are duly handed over to the King, who gives some of them, including the *Speculum* to Cracow cathedral; others to Wilno cathedral and various churches in Lithuania. He also distributes the castles of Prussia between his nobles.

The only castles and towns that do not surrender to the King are Malbork, Radzyń, the castle of Gdańsk, Świecie, Płochow, Brandenburg, Balga, Ragneta and Memel. Radzyń is besieged, but Gdańsk escapes being besieged by undertaking to surrender the moment Malbork is taken.

Early in August, Henry of Plauen sends to the King asking for a meeting. This is agreed and takes place near the castle's walls. The gist of Henry of Plauen's proposal is that the Poles, having achieved their great victory, should not try utterly to destroy the Order, but be content with the territories, castles and towns of Pomerania, Chełm and Michałów, which they consider to be theirs by right and usage and to regain which they have so often gone to war and which they have now recovered, and to leave the Order, which was created to defend Christendom against the pagans, with their other lands which cost them so much blood. The King's councillors are divided in their advice: some, thinking that Malbork cannot withstand a lengthy siege and that, if the Order is left with any territory in Prussia, it will eventually try to regain what it was now willing to surrender; and so, forgetting that success is seldom long-lasting and that fortunes can change, they recommend rejecting the proposal. Indeed, the Poles are puffed up with pride and, as usual, want more than they are offered; so, it is decided to tell Henry of Plauen that the Poles have no need to be grateful for the return of lands that are theirs and that the Order must also surrender Malbork and all other towns and castles that have not yet surrendered. Henry of Plauen replies that, as his proposal has been rejected, he will henceforth rely on God and the Blessed Virgin, who will not allow the Order to be destroyed. He then withdraws with his retinue into the castle and Władysław returns to his tent.

There is a general feeling that the Poles' rejection of Henry of Plauen's reasonable proposal did much to help the Order's cause. Certainly, from that day the tide turned in favour of the Order. For example, a few days after this meeting, the Knights make another sortie and attack the Poles' guns, which are guarded not very efficiently by the Wieluń company, for the Knights capture the Commander of the siege train, wound a number of his men and damage a few of the cannon. Some time later, when the cannon are being used by Duke Janusz of Mazovia, their fire demolishes a wall in one of the burned-out houses in the town, which falls and crushes twenty Polish knights.

So many flies breed in the bodies of the dead horses, the heaps of guts of slaughtered cattle and sheep, and the huge amount of human excrement, that they are more than a nuisance, a real torment. On the other hand, there are foodstuffs in profusion and no one lacks for anything. Almost all the army's horses have been put out to graze on the island in the river, where they feed on the corn in fields abandoned by the farmers, in whose houses those guarding the horses live and where they find plenty of everything and are able, not only to recuperate physically, but to take grain to neighbouring markets and come back with plenty of money or clothes which they have bought. Quantities of grain are found in underground stores in many of the villages of Prussia and Pomerania.

The Livonian Master, Herman of Wintkinschenk, wishing to help Malbork, comes with a force of 5000 and quietly camps near the town of Königsberg. The Polish intelligence informs the King of their arrival and the Grand-duke is sent with twelve standards of Polish knights to deal with them. Contact is made near the River Pasłęka and an assault planned for the following day. However, the Livonian Master, who has always intended to employ cunning rather than force to get the Order out of its predicament, requests and obtains a meeting with the Grand-duke at which the two talk in private, without witnesses. The Master tries to win the Grand-duke over with promises, one of which is that the Order will relinquish its claims to Samogitia and Sudawia. The Grand-duke prefers the idea of recovering Lithuanian rather than Polish territory and supports the idea. The Livonian Master sends the bulk of his force to the castles at Balga and Brandenburg and with only fifty mounted men accompanies the Grand-duke to Władysław's camp outside Malbork. There, Władysław is persuaded to allow the Livonian Master to enter Malbork, ostensibly to try to persuade Henry of Plauen to surrender and make a pact with the Poles. There the Master stays for several days conferring with Henry of Plauen how best to recover the castles and territories the Order has lost, after which he departs, leaving von Plauen much encouraged and no longer prepared to talk peace or accept the terms he had proposed to the King, who is now prepared to accept them, having, belatedly, come to see how good a proposition it was, and also because he sees that the Grand-duke is against prolonging the siege and sees no benefit to Lithuania in the lands proposed being returned to Poland. The Poles now meet with further discomfiture, in that, when the Livonian Master leaves the castle, the plebanus of Gdańsk, a member of the Order who happens to be in the castle, is allowed to leave with him, ostensibly to spare an elderly man the hardships of a siege; when, in actual fact, the priest has with him 30,000 złoty to be distributed among the commanders of Gdańsk, Człuchów and Świecie, who then use the money to hire mercenaries from Bohemia, Silesia and Germany.

At the beginning of September, the Grand-duke thinks up various specious excuses for withdrawing his army and returning to Lithuania. One excuse is that, due to the unusually rich fare his men have been enjoying, they are all suffering from diarrhoea and he is afraid lest this develop into something more serious unless he takes them home, despite the fact that with a little good-will it would have been easy to cure them. The King does his best to get him to give up the idea, but then, realizing how the Grand-duke's sympathies have changed and that he is no longer sincere, he agrees to him leaving with his whole army. So, the Grand-duke breaks camp and abandons the siege; however, he dare not leave without a Polish escort, lest he be attacked by the Livonians or other Knights and their mercenaries, so Władysław provides him with six standards of his own men, who escort them to the Lithuanian frontier and return safely to the King's camp at Malbork. Soon after this, the Dukes of Mazovia, Siemowit, Janusz and Siemowit the younger, also leave and take their troops with them. King Władysław continues the siege.

From the time the Livonian Master promised the Grand-duke to return Samogitia to him, the Grand-duke has been prepared to stick at nothing to achieve this: indeed, it was this promise that induced him to change his plans and abandon the siege of Malbork. From now on, the Grand-duke is a different person and afraid lest the King gain control of all Prussia, and then deprive him of his dukedom.

The Czech mercenaries defending Malbork are worried by the way the siege is dragging on and are beginning to fear for themselves, so they enter into secret negotiations with the Poles through Jaśko Sokół for surrendering Malbork. The two sides agree that one night, when the Czechs are on guard duty, they will open the gates and allow the Poles in; for this they will receive 40,000 florins and be guaranteed complete immunity. When the deal is put to the King's council, however, it is rejected as a shameful and unworthy way of capturing an enemy castle, while they still have arms with which to do it, and thus nothing comes of the project.

A false rumour now spreads through the camp, that Sigismund King of Hungary has invaded Polish soil with a powerful army and is creating havoc there. From now on the Poles begin to lose some of their dash and there is even talk of abandoning the siege; indeed, many of them actually advocate doing so. Shaken by this change in attitude, the Polish knights and the Prussian ones fighting with them go the King and impress on him that under no circumstances should he give up the siege, since the capture of Malbork, which they have every reason to expect to happen any day, will itself give him the full fruits of his great victory; while, if he abandons the siege, he will lose all the benefit of it, since all the towns and castles which have submitted to his authority will revert to the Teutonic Knights.

When the King complains that he is running short of money and that this is causing difficulties with the mercenaries, for which reason he wishes to go back to Poland to replenish his coffers, it is suggested that were he to impose tribute on all the Prussian towns now under him, that would bring in enough to pay the mercenaries and finance the further conduct of the war. The King is reluctant to take any such step at the start of his rule, lest it upset those whose loyalty and submission are still in the balance, since it would infringe their rights and give them an excuse for secession. It is then suggested that the towns and castles in Prussian territory should give the mercenaries promissory notes for the amounts due to them, if the mercenaries will agree to accept them and undertake to continue the siege. The King does not consider even this excellent suggestion acceptable, as it might cause the mercenaries to become a burden on the townspeople and villagers, whom they might even plunder, or else make the mercenaries open to bribery by the enemy. So, refusing to burden others, the King decides that he and his people alone shall meet this extra expenditure. The most stubborn supporter of continuing the siege is the Vice-chancellor, Nicholas, its most ardent opponent the Castellan of Wojnicz, Andrew of Tęczyn, who is head over heels in love with Anna of Kraśnik the daughter of Demetrius the vice-treasurer and whose only wish is to get home to her.

The mercenaries keep sending repeated, aggressive reminders that they are owed money, and this, plus the persuasion of those who wish the siege to be abandoned, decides the King to do just that. Though he orders the plan to be kept secret, news of it spreads throughout the camp and, to their delight, reaches the besieged. So, on Friday, September 19, the King orders fire to be set to the Polish camp and marches away, still only half way to fame, and returns home more as one defeated, than as a conqueror. As the chestnut horse from whose saddle the King had watched the great battle is brought to him, it neighs loudly and paws the ground with its hooves; then, as the King puts his foot in the stirrup, the horse drops down dead, thus foretelling the end of the run of successes the King has enjoyed.

It is all but certain that Malbork would have been in the King's hand within the month, because the Order failed to send it the supplies prepared years before for just such an eventuality, so the besieged were reduced to eating boiled wheat and this had given them diarrhoea and caused a serious epidemic of which many were dying every day, with the result that the civilians were complaining that they could endure the siege no longer and wished to leave the castle so as to avoid the death that threatened them all. This frightened the Commander Henry of Plauen, who distributed several thousand gold coins, begging the besieged to hold out for just another fortnight, for he had certain information that the King of Poland was about to abandon the siege. The civilians agreed to this on condition that if, at the end of the fortnight, the siege still continued, they would be allowed to surrender. As it was, Władysław abandoned the siege before the fortnight was up, thus casting a shadow on his title to fame. Thus, once again, the public good was harmed by private interests prevailing, in this case when the King, due to his innate weakness, failed to act as he himself thought right, but, instead, obeyed the promptings of others.

So, the King leaves Malbork, the waggons of his train laden with loot of every kind. He reaches Kwidzyn the same day. There Bishop Henry of Pomezania comes out in procession to greet him and conducts him to the cathedral, where he is shown the cell and dwelling of a very pious woman called Dorothy, who leads a solitary and very arduous existence and is famed for a number of miracles, though she has yet to be canonized. The King grants the town and Bishop the freedom they request and returns to his camp, which is half a mile from the town, and there he spends two days. When he moves on, he sends several waggons laden with provisions to the garrison at Sztum, which is later to inflict considerable damage on the Knights, even attacking one of their convoys and capturing 10,000 florins being sent to pay the Knights' mercenaries in Malbork.

Henry of Plauen is now elected the new Master of the Order. Wishing to avenge its defeat and regain its lost Prussian territories, he sends emissaries to Václav of Bohemia to arrange the sale to the King of one of the Order's properties in Bohemia, Chomutov, which has an annual revenue of 4000 florins. The price is 115,000 florins in gold, the seller retaining the right of re-purchase, a right not yet exercised.

September 21. The King reaches Radzyń, where the castle is already under siege, though the town itself has sworn allegiance to him. He pitches camp beside Lake Melno, a quarter of a mile from the castle. He now has to decide whether to continue or abandon the siege of the castle, which has a strong position and excellent defenders. First, he announces an assault on the castle for the following day, and then summons the townspeople for talks, hoping to persuade them to get the castle to surrender without bloodshed, telling them that he is postponing the pretended assault on the castle. This clever move proves successful, for, when the news spreads that the King is intending to storm the castle on the following day, the army, which has just finished breakfast, takes matters into its own hands and, without waiting for the order, mounts its own attack and furiously engages the enemy on all sides. The Knights resist stoutly for a good five hours, but being shot at with so many darts and arrows that none dares raise even a finger above the parapet, they finally lose heart and surrender. In the fighting, Dobiesław of Oleśnica, while using his shield to cover a knight battering at one of the gates, is wounded by a bullet from a handgun, which passed through his shield. The King enters the castle in the evening and grants the survivors their lives. Inside are fifteen elderly Knights and these are taken prisoner. The castle is found to be full of treasure and provisions. The treasure is distributed among the King's knights, but the provisions are left in the castle, tenure of which the King grants to a Czech, Jaśko Sokół, a man of proven loyalty and daring, with whom he leaves a large garrison of Poles and Czechs among them Žižka. The King now moves on to Rogoźno and, on the Wednesday, to Golub, where, after breakfasting in the castle, he crosses the River Drwęca into Dobrzyń territory. On the Thursday he reaches Przypust, where the pontoon bridge, sent from Płock, has been assembled so that the army can cross the Vistula there. For some unknown reason there has been difficulty in positioning and securing the bridge, which previously had taken only half a day to assemble. This is further evidence of how Fortune has turned away from the King. Once across, the army is disbanded and each returns to his home laden with silver and other precious objects.

September 28. The King reaches Raciąż, where he and a small retinue embark and sail to Toruń. As Władysław is disembarking there, he is met by the local clergy and people and conducted
to the parish church, where he hears a sung Mass although the plebanus is a priest of the Order. He
then goes to the castle for a meal. While he is there, Jásko Sokół arrives from Radzyń. He is entertained by one of the townspeople with a dish of pike and falls dangerously ill. The King orders him
to be moved to Brześć, where he dies and is buried. None of the Czechs fighting with the King was
dearer to him than was Jásko Sokół and he rewards his services by taking paternal charge of his two
sons, Nicholas and Jaroslav, whom he has educated in Cracow, where they are taught Latin and
German literature and other sciences from which they can acquire polish and refinement. In the
evening, as he is leaving to board a boat to take him to the castle at Nieszawa, the women and girls
of Toruń crowd round him and, half jokingly, half in earnest, beg the King to have pity on them and
grant them husbands and protectors, since the battle at Grunwald has deprived so many of them of
their husbands, fathers and brothers. He promises to do what he can.

The King spends three days in Nieszawa. Here news reaches him that the castle at Tuchola,
which was left under Janusz Brzogłowy, has been invested by the Knights and that the town was
surrendered by the townsfolk. This means that, unless they are opposed, the Knights will soon be
burning and pillaging in Poland itself. Although perturbed by this news, the King allows many of
his officials, who have been asking to be released from their duties, to go home, and, because of
this, he can now count on scarcely more than a hundred lances. Reinforcing these with men from
several districts of Wielkopolska, he sends them all to Koronowo, which is weakly defended, having but a poor situation and no fortified walls. This force is not well supplied with arms, provisions
or clothing; indeed, the men's armour is rusty, their horses jaded, their clothing worn thin by heat
and rain and long service far from home.

The King leaves Nieszawa on Saturday, St. Francis' Day, and moves to Inowrocław, where he
sets up permanent residence. He sends knights with detachments of Kujawy and Dobrzyń yeo-
manry to Brodnica, Brześć, Nakło and Rypin, to help secure the defences of the realm. Now news
comes that the castles of Osterode, Nidzica and Działdowo, which he had entrusted to the Mazovians, have been recaptured by the Knights. Then two knights from the garrison at Koronowo, which
has received some reinforcements from Poznań, reach Inowrocław through enemy-occupied territory to tell the King that, unless he withdraws its garrison, Koronowo will be in great danger of being captured. Though disquieted by the news and reduced to tears by his anxiety, the King does not
consider it safe to withdraw from Koronowo, lest this allow the Knights to penetrate even deeper
into his country, which, having disbanded his army, he can no longer adequately defend.

The castle at Tuchola is still being besieged by the Teutonic Knights, but when they learn that
the Polish force sent to Koronowo is weak and poorly equipped, while their own is strong and composed entirely of mercenaries, one of whom is its commander, Michael Küchmeister, vogt of
Nowa Marchia, with knights from the court of Sigismund of Hungary, sent at the latter's expense,
they advance on the Poles, confident of being superior in numbers and that this will give them victory and loot. When the Poles learn that an enemy force is advancing against them, two knights are
sent out to estimate the enemy's strength. They venture out farther than is wise or necessary and
halt in an area of slippery mud, and here some of the enemy come up from behind and capture
them. They are at once subjected to close interrogation as to the size and composition of the Polish
force, and cunningly give false answers, saying that their force is composed of untrained, inexperienced troops, almost in disarrray, which, if attacked, could easily be defeated. The Knights, convinced that they have been told the truth, press on towards Koronowo, and, when close to the town,
dismount with the intention of entering the town on foot. The Poles, when they see the enemy advancing, abandon the meal which they have just started and hurry to the monastery at the foot of the

hill on the bank of River Brda. Here, they swiftly put on their armour and, using a crossing unknown to the enemy, move on in close formation to do battle.

Dismayed by the sight of them, the Order's troops hasten back to their horses and start to withdraw. Their idea is that, if the Poles, who are on foot, get far enough from the town, the rest of the
garrison will be unable to come to their assistance should fighting start. However, the Polish archers fire flight after flight of arrows at the withdrawing Knights which wound many of them and allow the Poles to get in among them and kill many more. Every time the enemy turns to attack the
archers, these withdraw in among their own knights, where they are safe, and from where they
emerge later and start shooting again. This skirmish continues for over a mile, until the enemy
reaches a village, Łączko, belonging to the monastery at Koronowo. Here they reform and await
the Poles' attack, confident that the terrain will give them an advantage. However, instead of advancing straight at them, the Poles make a detour to the steeper side of the hill. The men of both armies are well experienced in the art of war, men who will fight with the greatest courage. However,
before the two sides actually engage, Conrad of Niemcza a Silesian in King Sigismund's army, on
his own initiative rides out and challenges the Poles to a duel. The challenge is taken up by Jan
Szczycki, who unseats the challenger and tramples him. The two ranks then close with great
shouts. Each stands firm and the outcome is long uncertain, for the two sides are equal in armament, skill and experience; but eventually they become exhausted and fighting stops, as if a truce
had been agreed. One is then arranged, and for a short period the ranks separate, wipe away their
sweat, and rest. After a while, the truce is declared at an end and fighting resumes. Many are killed
or taken prisoner. When exhaustion again overcomes them without Fortune having given any indication of where the advantage lies, a fresh truce is arranged, during which the knights rub down
their horses and themselves, bandage wounds, rest, talk, exchange prisoners and captured horses,
send each other wine and clear the ground of the wounded and those thrown from their horses and
unable to get up, lest these be trampled when fighting resumes; indeed, the scene is such that all of
them might have been thought the greatest friends, instead of enemies. Fighting then starts up for a
third time. None can remember so bitter a struggle betwen two armies of veterans experienced in
the profession of arms, who fight on until wounded or taken prisoner. Still the fight is equal, each
side fighting under a single standard, that of the Poles a dark-red dual cross stitched to a white
background, that of the Teutonic Knights a white and a red field joined diagonally, which is borne
by Henry a knight of French origin. Suddenly, a Polish knight, Jan Naszan, knocks the enemy's
standard-bearer from his horse, seizes the standard, rolls it up and fastens it to his saddle. At once
the Poles begin to have the advantage and, the enemy, appalled at the loss of their standard, begin to
weaken. The Poles press ever more fiercely and the enemy begins to think of retreat. Then, as fear
begins to outweigh shame, the enemy starts to withdraw and so their defeat becomes a certainty.
Many are killed or taken prisoner; the others forced to flee, pursued by their victors as long as these
have the strength to run and kill. Then nightfall hides the fugitives.

Later, the family of the knight who lost the Knights' standard reproaches him for its loss; and
he would, indeed, have been accounted dishonoured, had not King Władysław, at the man's own
request, given him a letter absolving him of the shame. Experts in the art of war consider this battle
more important than that fought at Grunwald; and, if you consider the dangers, ardour and endurance of the combatants, it certainly should rank higher.

Sunday, October 12. The Poles leave Koronowo with their prisoners, Michael Küchmeister,
Conrad of Niemcza and many of Sigismund's courtiers, and booty and move to Bydgoszcz, where
they spend three days distributing the booty equally among themselves. They then go on with their
many horses and waggons to Inowrocław, where the King is. Behind them come the prisoners,
some in the sixty waggons sent by the King for that purpose, some on horseback, others on foot.
The King orders a banquet to be prepared for them and for their wounds to be carefully dressed. He

even details several knights to wait on the prisoners at the banquet, and, later in the night, goes in person and by candle-light visits the Polish wounded in their quarters. There is none who has not received the medicine he needs, and the King speaks to each, so that one might have thought him a private individual and not a King. Each Polish knight receives a truly regal gift in reward for his services. The next day, after recording the name, station and rank of each prisoner, the King appoints the day and place at which they have to report, and dismisses them all, with the one exception of the Vogt of Nowa Marchia, Michael Küchmeister, who is sent in chains to the castle at Tęczyn.

Their defeat at Koronowo finally reduces the pride of the Teutonic Knights, for even their own members and the people of their towns begin murmuring that the Order is waging an unworthy war, one that contravenes the pacts they have made, and that the Order will never be successful if it does not return the lands and possessions it has taken from Poland. For many years to come the Teutonic Knights and their leaders dare not do serious battle with the Poles, but confine their activities to minor skirmishes and affrays.

The Poles' victory at Koronowo is swiftly followed by misfortune, when, on October 11, the Knights besieging Tuchola produce a number of Polish-speaking soldiers, among whom is a knight of Dobrzyń called Nawir, who had deserted to the Order. These are shown to the besieged, who are told that they had all been taken prisoner when the Knights were victorious at Koronowo. To make this credible, Nawir is wearing a woven headband, stitched with pearls, which a German knight had torn from the head of Nicholas Powała, when he was thrown from his horse and almost taken prisoner. The commander of the Tuchola garrison, recognizes the headband as belonging to Powała and asks Nawir, who he is. Nawir lies and tells him that he is Powała and that the King's army has been defeated. The garrison commander believes him and starts negotiating the surrender of Tuchola. This arranged, the garrison marches out and goes to Inowrocław to the King. When the garrison commander learns the truth, he bursts into tears and tears his hair, horrified that he, a man experienced in war and well versed in the profession of arms, should have let himself be so grievously tricked into losing his King's strongest fortress.

The Prussian Master Henry of Plauen now assembles another and larger force of mercenary knights of several nationalities, speaking various languages, provides it with a large number of cannon, waggons and other military equipment and sends it to Tuchola with the intention of mounting an attack on Poland, which he hopes to find more or less defenceless. Learning of this, Władysław orders mobilization in Wielkopolska, Wieluń, Poznań, Łęczyca, Kujawy, Sieradz and Dobrzyń. He himself leaves Inowrocław on October 26 and on the following Monday reaches Bydgoszcz, where most of the troops mobilized are assembled. The King decides that he himself will remain in Bydgoszcz, and puts the assembled force, amounting to twelve standards, under the command of the Chamberlain of Cracow, Peter Szafraniec. The next day, this mixed force of cavalry and infantry, the mixture making it appear larger than it really is, leaves Bydgoszcz accompanied for the first half mile by the King, who then has the entire train sent back, so that the force can have maximum flexibility, and it advances swiftly, plundering and burning whatever belongs to the enemy, and reaches Tuchola that same day. An ambush is set up and 600 of their mercenary crossbowmen sent to harass the Knights. The crossbowmen start by plundering and driving off cattle, and, when the Knights sally out to attack them, pretend to take fright and fake a retreat. The Knights, thinking that the crossbowmen are the enemy's entire force, pursue them right into the ambush prepared for them. Suddenly they find Poles in their rear with banners waving, Although far superior in numbers, the Knights scatter in disorderly flight. Szafraniec forbids pursuit, fearing an ambush such as he had prepared, but when he sees that the fugitives are really widely scattered, he does order a pursuit, which is continued up to the very gates of the town, thus capturing the enemy's camp and their waggon train.

As night falls, the weary Poles, now burdened with the captured waggons, roam the environs of Tuchola in search of food for themselves and their horses. They have no guides. There is no moon and no stars are visible, thus they have little idea where they are going and at dawn find themselves scarcely more than half a mile from Tuchola and still in view of the castle. Afraid lest the enemy find the courage to attack them while they are famished and exhausted, they decide to withdraw to Bydgoszcz, which they reach safely, being screened by the mist that hangs all day so thick that the sun never breaks through.

Meanwhile, Władysław, informed of their success and intended withdrawal, has horses saddled and rides off to stop them and have them lay siege to Tuchola instead. Though he rides quickly, he arrives too late, the little army being scattered and straggling and impossible to re-assemble; so, after spending the night at Łabiszyn, he returns to Inowrocław. On the following Monday, the crowd of prisoners taken before Tuchola is brought before the King. After their names and rank have been recorded, they are released on their word of honour to report later at a place and on a day appointed. One of the prisoners is a Czech, Jan Zając, who had been at the Polish court and then gone over to the Knights. Władysław asks him how it is that he, who had served him at his Court, deserted to the enemy and how he can justify such behaviour. The Czech replies: "I do not deny that I was your courtier and servant. What made me leave you and go over to your enemies was my daring spirit, because of which I am considered to be brave and intrepid. Knowing of your famous triumphs over the Teutonic Knights, I considered it more noble to fight for them, the under-dogs. If I had fought for you, my comforter, (meaning Sophia, wife of King Václav of Bohemia) might have reproached me for cowardice in joining one who previously had always been victori-ous; so I joined those who had not enjoyed success in order to demonstrate my courage; and this, indeed, I did, for when the Germans ran, I, considering flight shameful, let myself be captured by your knights. Do with me as you like." Asked by the King what, in his opinion, a victor should do with him, his prisoner and former courtier answers: "What the leniency with which you treat the conquered and which turns victory to your advantage, prompts you to do." The King, won over by this answer, releases the Czech against his word of honour.

The King's household knights, who so crushingly defeated the mercenary knights at Tuchola, now send a herald with a stern letter to Duke John of Ziębice and all those in the Order's pay who are in Tuchola reminding them that, in accordance with the usages of war they must hand over all the armour, horses and military emblems with which they went into battle, especially their surcoats called Wappenrokken, all of which are forfeit to the victors, since, having gone out to fight, they had not done so, but turned and fled, and so must be considered worse than defeated. The merce-nary knights reply that they have always cherished their honour and cannot see that they have stained it in any way, and are prepared to defend it in the customary manner at the court of any prince or king, where, arms in hand, they may refute any accusation of fault or shame. In order to demonstrate their innocence, they suggest tourneys and duels in some neutral place. The Poles then offer to entertain them at the court of the Grand-duke Alexander or at that of the Mazovian princes, promising them complete security, but the mercenary knights, hoping to evade a trial by arms and to hide their shame, suggest the court of the King of France, England, Spain or Naples instead.

Henry of Plauen, having come to the conclusion that the Polish resistance is too strong for his planned invasion of Poland to succeed, turns aside into Prussia and lays siege to the castle at Sztum, from which Andrew Brochocki has been inflicting considerable damage on the Knights in Malbork. After an assault lasting six weeks, there is still no sign of Sztum surrendering, but then, either by accident or treachery, the tall tower over the gate catches fire and all the gunpowder, darts, screens and provisions stored in it, go up in flames. The besieged now become doubtful of being able to hold out and start negotiating terms of surrender with the Master, though not intending to conclude any arrangement until they have consulted the King and received his orders. For this purpose two knights are, with the Master's permission, sent under an escort provided by the Master, to the King at Inowrocław. When told of Sztum's predicament, the King orders its garrison and that at Morąg to surrender provided that they are allowed to march out with all their horses, arms and equipment.

The surrender of these two fortresses encourages Henry of Plauen to lay siege to a third castle, Radzyń. Though he bombards it with his cannon for six weeks, the garrison defends it stoutly and the Master has to abandon the siege, leaving a considerable number of wounded in the town. The withdrawal cannot be concealed, so the next night the garrison sends messages to the Polish garrison in Brodnica asking for help in capturing Radzyń town, in which the Knights have left many of their possessions as well as their wounded. The force from Brodnica arrives at the time agreed, the garrison sallies out and the two join forces and together break down the town's gates. The few men the Knights left to guard the wounded surrender and the Poles occupy the town and return safely to their camp with all they find there and their prisoners.

Henry of Plauen has already been negotiating in secret with the townspeople of Toruń and Gdańsk, who have renounced their allegiance to King Władysław, for the surrender of their two towns. So, having abandoned the siege of Radzyń, he moves his army towards Toruń. In the mean time, the people of the two towns, wishing to conceal their underhand, perverse behaviour, send two officials to the King to tell him that they expect the arrival of Henry of Plauen any day and to ask for the King's protection. Władysław replies graciously, telling them not to despair, but to be of good cheer, for he will come to their assistance with five, eight or as many thousands of cavalry as he thinks necessary, and that, in the mean time they must assemble enough boats to ferry his army across the Vistula. The two then return to Toruń. The King keeps his word and sets out the very next day. He gets as far as Gniewkowo, where the two officials again come before him. He questions them about the number of boats they have assembled. The two remain silent, and then admit that they have come with very different news.

"We have come to tell Your Majesty that we are in such a difficult situation that unless you come to our assistance by sunset tomorrow, we must surrender the towns". The King replies: "I promise that I shall be there by sunset tomorrow as long as you can provide the boats to ferry my men across". Now the truth comes out: the two have to tell the King that they have already made a pact with the Knights to whom they are to hand over the towns on the following day. Instead of this eliciting a furious outburst, the King quietly and gently rebukes them: "So this is what your loyalty, oaths and promises are worth! Were you not ashamed to make a pact with my enemies?" The two, not daring to reply, can only stare at the ground. Those with the King want him to have them beheaded as an example to others, but are reminded that you must not inflict violence on emissaries who have come in good faith and that it is more important to uphold this principle than that the emissaries have broken faith. Thus, though circumstances in no way made it necessary, the towns of Gdańsk and Toruń are handed over to the Teutonic Knights, who straightway lay siege to Toruń castle, which is in Polish hands, but without being able to capture it; indeed, by making frequent sorties, the garrison is able to inflict considerable damage on the enemy.

King Władysław now returns to Inowrocław. Then, wishing to fulfill a vow he made before the great battle, namely that he would go the monastery at Poznań to venerate the Blessed Sacrament, he goes to Trzemeszno and from there on foot to Gniezno. From Gniezno he goes to Pobiedziska and from there, again on foot, to Poznań and the monastery of Corpus Christi. There he spends three days in religious exercises and returns to Inowrocław by the same route, thus by his presence protecting Poland from her enemies. He also orders mobilization in the lands of Wielkopolska and in Sieradz, Łęczyca, Kujawy and Dobrzyń. When the troops reach Inowrocław, he places them under the command of the Voivode of Poznań, Sędziwój of Ostroróg, and sends them into Pomerania, where they capture the town of Nowe, burn it and go on to sack the whole of Pomerania, for the enemy never comes out to fight. They then return home laden with booty. Both sides are now weary of waging war in winter-time and in need of rest; so, it is decided to arrange a truce and the Vice-Chancellor of Cracow is sent to Toruń to agree terms. This proves impossible, so it is agreed that King Władysław and the Master of the Order should meet in Raciąz.

At about this time, the Voivode of Transylvania, Ścibor of Ściborzyce, with twelve squadrons recruited from Czechs, Moravians and Austrians, but not Hungarians, for they, remembering their alliance with Poland, which they considered sacred and permanent, could not be persuaded to take part, are sent by the King of Hungary to make an incursion into Poland with the object of demonstrating that, in return for the 40,000 florins the Teutonic Knights had paid him, he has kept his promise and broken off relations with Poland. He finds that most of the troops King Władysław left to guard the frontier, bored by long inactivity, have gone home, so the Voivode is able to sack and burn the town of Stary Sącz and the suburbs of Nowy Sącz, together with a few villages, and return to Hungary by a difficult mountain route which involves crossing the Poprad.

The Poles do not take this lying down, but, having hastily re-grouped, go after the Voivode and, indeed, catch up with him, but not until he is already across the Carpathians. In the ensuing battle, the Voivode is defeated and many of his men killed or taken prisoner.

King Władysław leaves Inowrocław at the end of November and goes to Brześć. While he is there, Polish arms achieve another victory over the Teutonic Knights. Herman Master of Livonia brings up a considerable force to help Henry of Plauen in Prussia. The larger part is sent to Golub, as being a good point of entry into Dobrzyń, while with the remaining mere handful of Knights he heads for Malbork. Learning of this, the Polish garrisons under Dobiesław Puchała at Borowniki and Rypin put together a scratch force, which makes for Golub. When it reaches the area, an ambush is prepared and several small detachments sent towards the town's gates with orders to destroy what they find and seize what they can. These light several fires and do considerable damage and drive off the cattle that have been put to graze outside the town. At this, a large detachment of superbly armoured Livonian knights sallies out and pursues the Poles, who pretend to panic and run to where the ambush has been prepared. The waiting Poles get in the rear of the pursuing Livonians, who caught unawares, turn and hurry back to the town. Those on the walls, dismayed by what they see and afraid lest the Poles should be able to force an entry, close the gates. There is then such crowding, jostling and trampling underfoot in the gateway by those unable to get in, that more than half the Livonians surrender and thus many Brethren of the Order and some noble knights are captured. These are then divested of their armour and marched off towards Rypin. The prisoners naively believe that there is another, larger Polish force concealed in the surrounding woods. They keep asking their escort, where the rest of the Polish army is, and the Poles, afraid of what might happen if their prisoners learned the truth, tell them that the others are keeping level with them, but screened from them and out of sight. So, thanks to having this ghost army to subdue their prisoners, the Poles reach Rypin. Once safely in chains, the prisoners are told that there never was another force but that which captured them. The Livonians attributed their defeat and capture to the fact that the war they were fighting was an unjust one. Next day, the prisoners are brought before the King, who has all the Teutonic Knights and members of the Order sent to various fortresses together with those laymen considered unreliable. All other knights are released on their word of honour to present themselves at the place appointed at the time required.

King Władysław and Henry of Plauen meet in Raciąz as arranged, but it again proves impossible to agree terms for a truce and the King returns to Brześć. Later, Peter Szafraniec, the Vice-Chancellor of Cracow, is able to agree terms, but for one month only. The King then moves to Wiskitki, where the Duke of Mazovia and his wife, Władysław's sister, Alexandra, and their five sons receive him with due pomp. Here Władysław spends four days hunting and then moves on to Jedlna, where he spends Christmas.

A.D. 1411

December 27. The King arrives in Opatów, where Queen Anna already is. This is their first meeting since the great victory. Here the King finds a number of prisoners sent on from Cracow, where they had reported as arranged. They are given a new date and place for reporting, while the King moves on to Radoszyce, where he spends Twelfth Night. After this, he sends the Queen back to Cracow, while he returns to Brześć, where the troops he has called up are already assembled. Here he is joined by Grand-duke Alexander with his army. Their forces combine at Old Włocławek and cross the Vistula, which presents no difficulty, since the river is frozen; indeed it has already borne the weight of hundreds of Polish waggons. Then, instead of devastating the country round the town of Toruń, in which the Master and his troops are shut up, which would have been an advantageous move, influenced by the Grand-duke, a man who prefers subterfuge to direct action, the army moves in the direction of Przypust to a forest a mile from Raciąz. Here the troops are put to cutting firewood, while camp is pitched by the river and there the army stays until February 2, during which time the advisers of both sides meet on an island in the river near Toruń trying to negotiate terms for a lasting peace.

While all this is going on, Janusz Brzogłowy, realizing that the old truce has expired and that a new one has not yet been proclaimed, knowing that the Order's best horses and those of the mercenary knights are corralled outside the defences of Papowo castle, crosses the Vistula from Bydgoszcz at Solec where the ice has already thawed, and, with only forty troopers, makes for the castle whose outer defences are negligently guarded, since a truce is in course of negotiation. The Poles then set fire to the outer defences, gather up the herd of superb horses and drive it towards the Vistula. When the mercenary knights in the castle come out in vigorous pursuit, Janusz orders most of his men to keep going and get the horses across the river, while he himself, with only a dozen knights, by continually attacking and then pretending flight, keeps the enemy in fear of an ambush and hesitant, and thus reaches the waiting boats ahead of them. Boarding a boat, he turns and shouts "Good-bye" to the enemy, who only then realize how they have been tricked. The Poles return to Bydgoszcz with all the Master's horses and those of the mercenary knights.

Thanks to the intervention of the Grand-duke, who is eager to recover Samogitia, which the Knights had taken from him, the negotiators on their island in the river finally arrange and sign a pact, the terms of which are unjust and injurious to Poland. The main points are that Poland is to return to the Order the castles it has won in Prussian territory; that the King will free all members of the Order taken prisoner in whatever battle, in return for which the Master and the Order will, in three instalments, pay the King and Poland six million broad Prague grosses, though the King could well have demanded sixty million for these same prisoners. Further, the territory of Samogitia is to remain in the Grand-duchy of Lithuania, but on the death of both King Władysław and the Grand-duke Alexander, is to return to the Order. The opportunity to restore to Poland the lands of Pomerania, Chełmno and Michalów, unjustly removed, is again neglected, as at Malbork the King had the chance to recover them. However, he and Alexander are content if Lithuania is preserved and Poland mutilated, so the treaty is signed and ratified at a meeting of King Władysław and the Grand-duke with the Master, to which the latter comes with a splendid retinue. The meeting is held on a stretch of level ground opposite the town of Złotoria, where the King's tent is pitched. When all necessary documents have been signed, the Master presents the King with twelve beautifully chased silver- gilt dishes, which Władysław reciprocates with several sable cloaks.

At this meeting Nicholas Powała complains that a certain German, a mercenary fighting with the Knights, whom he claims to have defeated and taken prisoner during the battle of Koronowo, had failed to present himself as he had promised, as a matter of honour, to do. The case is referred to a military tribunal, whose members are drawn from both sides, where the German insists that he defeated and took Powała prisoner, and demands that the judges hand the Pole over to him and that they compel Powała to admit that he had been made prisoner. When Powała asks if the German has any proof or token he can show to prove his assertion, the German replies that he has and triumphantly produces the headband stitched with pearls that Powała was wearing when he went into battle. Powała is delighted, for the German has destroyed his own case. He turns to the judges and says: "It has long been accepted and is so to this day that, in war, tourneys or battles, whenever headbands, ornaments or badges of any kind fall from those fighting, if they are picked up, it is not by those engaged in the fighting, as the appellant seeks to make out, but by rogues or scoundrels, the most worthless of men. Thus the headband produced by my opponent does not prove that he defeated me, but only that he, motivated by greed, busied himself picking up badges and tokens fallen from others, instead of fighting. If he pretends to have defeated me, he must present the Court with very different proof that befits a knight and not a rascal." The Court, having carefully considered the evidence, decides that Nicholas Powała was not taken prisoner and so is not bound to surrender himself to the German. The meeting ended, the King and the Grand-duke return to where their armies are camped, and the Prussian Master to Toruń. The next day the King grants Podole which had been held in fee by Peter Włodkowicz, who is now bankrupt, to the Grand-duke, little realizing the harm to the Polish Kingdom that shall later come of it.

The Polish and Lithuanian armies are now disbanded, and the King, after spending a night in Inowrocław, goes to Sandomierz, where he spends Shrove-tide with the Queen, whom he had summoned to meet him there.

In order to secure the frontier with Hungary, the King sends knights to guard it; but, instead of doing only that, these raid towns, villages and forts in Hungary itself. Their activities are soon stopped and a truce arranged by Zawisza the Black of Garbów, a courtier who enjoyed the respect of both kings.

Queen Anna having returned to Cracow, Władysław goes to Chełm and remains there, hunting, throughout Lent. Now he has a truce with the King of Hungary, whom he has always considered hostile, Władysław is able with an easy mind to go to Lithuania, which he has long wished to see again. So, half way through March, he goes there and spends the whole spring and summer travelling the lands of Lithuania and Ruthenia with Grand-duke Alexander. Then, in Wilno, he boards a ship and sails to Kaunas, whence he goes to Jurborg and there again devotes himself to the delights of the chase.

While he is at Jurborg, Władysław sends Zbigniew of Olésnica his secretary and two others to present Pope John XXIII with four golden goblets, two gold vases of unusual size, three sable cloaks, a large bedcover one side of which is of ermine, the other of various other skins, as tokens of his obedience. When the three are received in audience, they ask four things of the Pope: that he pronounces Władysław's war against the Master and the Order justified; that he agrees that Władysław is entitled to retain goods taken from churches in Prussia and give these to other churches in Poland; that Władysław be allowed to mount a general crusade against the Tatars, and, lastly, that the Pope issues a bull confirming the indulgences traditionally offered on June 2 by the Church of the Virgin Mary in Sandomierz. The Pope recognizes the justice of the first, second and fourth requests, but cannot accept the King's wish to start a crusade against the Tatars, since he has already arranged for a campaign against the King of Naples, so that, to authorize another military expedition would put obstacles in the way of the first and might even cause it to come to nothing. After spending ten weeks in Rome, the three are dismissed on Christmas Day.

When he leaves Jurborg, the King spends time in Polotsk, Vitebsk and Smolensk then goes to Zasław, from where he sails down the Dniepr to Kiev. He is everywhere accompanied by the

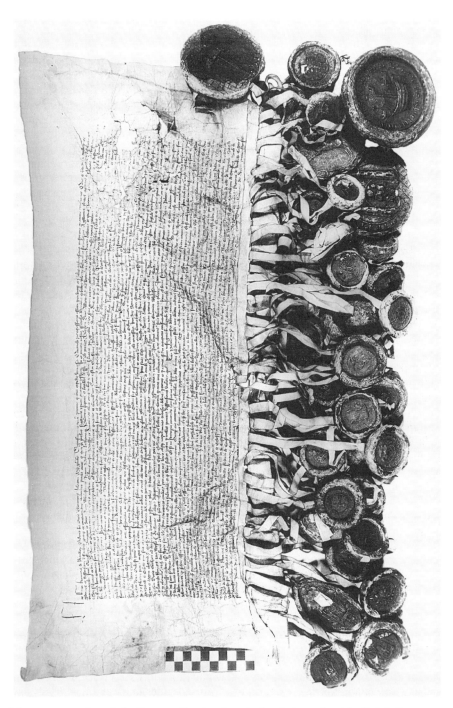

One of the treaties made with the Teutonic Knights furnished with the seals of the Polish "signatories".
—Now in Archivum Główne Akt Dawnych, Warsaw.

Grand-duke and his wife, Anna, who provide him with everything he needs and shower him with gifts. In Kiev, he takes leave of the Grand-duke, crosses the Dniepr and continues on to Czerkasy, Bracław and, finally, Kamieniec, from where he proceeds to Lwów and so to Gliniany, where he meets the Grand-duke, a secret arrangement made some time before, for here they are to try the Archbishop of Gniezno, Nicholas Kurowski, whom Queen Anna has accused of enticing her to commit adultery, a serious lese-majesty. However, the Archbishop, who has been hurt falling from his horse, dies the night after reaching Ropczyce, refreshed only by confession. His body is sent to Gniezno and buried there.

Over the years, the Archbishop had acquired considerable wealth in gold, silver, pearls and landed property by sending shiploads of meat and grain for sale in Flanders. His brother and other relatives now try to lay their hands on this treasure, but the King makes considerable efforts to prevent them, even sending troops to surround the castle at Uniejów, where the treasure was reputedly kept. The Archbishop was said to have taken a considerable amount of gold with him, when he set out for Gliniany, hoping to be able to bribe his way out of his predicament.

Władysław, wishing to pay his respects to the remains of the three saints: Stanisław, Wacław and Florian, goes first to Niepołomice, where he remains for a fortnight, and then, on November 26, sets out on foot for Skałka, though first making a detour to Kazimierz with a huge retinue of prelates and lords carrying the unfurled standards of the Teutonic Knights captured in the great battle. Having honoured the holy relics, he continues on to Cracow, where he deposits the Knights' standards in the cathedral of St. Stanisław, where they hang to this day. All Poles should cherish them and, if necessary, new ones should be woven to replace the old.

A.D. 1412

Advent the King spends in hunting round Goniądz, then goes to Grodno for Christmas. Meanwhile, the Archduke of Austria, Ernest, has arrived in Cracow, incognito and with only his marshal and a small retinue, hoping to be able to conclude an alliance with Władysław to help him in his quarrel with Sigismund of Hungary over Dalmatia. When news of his arrival reaches the King in Lithuania, Władysław returns home as quickly as he can. It is dawn when he reaches Cracow, and he goes straight to the house where the Archduke is staying, and, finding him still in bed and drowsy, jokingly asks how he has dared enter his kingdom and city without a safe-conduct, and thereafter entertains him with great friendliness. After some days of talks, it is agreed that the Archduke is to marry Władysław's niece, Cymbarka, daughter of the Duke of Mazovia, a maiden whom her uncle provides with a splendid dowry in gold, as well as concluding an alliance of friendship with the Archduke. The wedding is celebrated before Shrove-tide in Cracow with all the splendour worthy of the high rank of the bride and groom, who then return to Austria, escorted by 600 Polish knights sent in case the King of Hungary should contemplate staging an ambush. Back in Austria, the Archduke organizes a magnificent tourney at Neustadt, after which the Polish knights of his escort return home via Vienna and Moravia. In due course, Cymbarka bears the Archduke a son, Frederick, who is to become King of the Romans and Emperor.

The Doge of Venice, Michael Steno, writes to King Władysław begging him not to give up his war with Hungary or make an alliance with King Sigismund, and promising, in return, to cover in gold the cost of maintaining 600 of the King's knights for as long as the war between Venice and Hungary continues. Though this is an advantageous proposal Władysław feels that he cannot accept it.

Sigismund of Hungary, afraid lest Władysław ally himself with Venice, thus putting Sigismund in danger of having to wage a war on two fronts, decides to try and win Władysław over. With this object he sends Cardinal Branda and the Voivode of Transylvania, Ścibor of Ściborzyce, to him. The two try to excuse the hostilities against Władysław of which Sigismund has been guilty and ask Władysław to make a new, permanent alliance with Hungary, suggesting that the two kings should meet in person, which they can do in Spisz, to which Sigismund has gone in order to attend the conference arranged in the previous year for November 19. Władysław, who considers Sigismund unstable, complains of the harm the latter has done to his country; so the two envoys go from one king to the other, trying to reconcile them. When negotiations drag on, Queen Anna, who has received a number of invitations from King Sigismund, with Władysław's permission goes to Kežmarok with a splendid retinue of eminent knights to visit her aunt's sister, Barbara, King Sigismund's wife. Then Władysław lets himself be persuaded to meet Sigismund in Lubowla and sets out for there on March 12, accompanied by Bolesław of Mazovia and Zygmunt of Lithuania, as well as by a number of Polish prelates and nobles. He is met by King Zygmunt Korybut in the Carpathians. After greeting each other and exchanging kisses, the two kings return to Lubowla, where their two queens receive them. For the next week the kings and their advisers discuss peace without being able to agree terms. Then, on March 19, as Władysław and those with him are preparing to leave, Sigismund persuades Władysław to meet him in a separate room for a tête-à-tête without advisers. As soon as the two are seated, Sigismund says: "Dearest Brother, since we are linked by blood and a dual relationship, and each of us rules a country traditionally linked to the other by a number of necessities, I feel it shameful and wrong for us to part without concluding a peace treaty, especially since our estrangement can easily be remedied with a little good will. I ardently desire to remain at peace with Your Majesty and your territories. However, since I started a war in defence of the Teutonic Knights, a war I now regret and of which I am ashamed, I promise and swear that, if you will agree to return to permanent peace with me, from that day on and for ever I shall abandon the Teutonic Knights and with all my forces give you my personal support in destroying them, on this sole condition that, when, with God's help, the Knights have been defeated and destroyed, the territories of Chełmno, Michałów and Pomerania, which—I admit—are part of your kingdom by natural law, shall be yours and your kingdom's solely, but the territories of Prussia shall be divided between us, the larger share going to whichever of us has provided the larger army."

Upright, naive Władysław believes Sigismund's specious, cunning promise, assuming that with him, as with himself, promises are sacred; so, on his own initiative and without telling his advisers, he agrees to the proposal as it stands, without even mentioning the damage and losses inflicted on his country by Hungary, when he was struggling hard with his enemies. The two kings then shake hands and swear on the Cross to keep and fulfill the agreement they have made. Thus was King Władysław induced to accept what was to be to the detriment of his country then and in the future; for example, although Poland traditionally, and legally enjoyed possession of the lands of Ruthenia and Podole, by making this pact Władysław allowed this right to be put in question, thus giving rise to a problem that had not previously existed and one that was to continue for five years after both kings were dead. Again the territory of Walachia, which was a fief of Poland and paid it tribute, would now have to be divided equally between Poland and Hungary, as would any extension of his frontiers Władysław might achieve. Sigismund had, indeed, obtained everything he had envisaged and wanted; though he would never have achieved any of this had Władysław's advisers been present at the talks, as Sigismund well knew.

Their secret talks concluded, the two kings go to where their queens are. In their presence, Sigismund doffs his head gear and urgently persuades Władysław to come to the populous and important town of Košice, Lubowla not being a suitable place in which to entertain a king. Władysław again agrees without consulting his advisers, who, when they hear of it, rebuke him for agreeing to go off with the enemy without taking measures to ensure his own safety. Władysław tells them that they do not know the situation and are to shut up, for, when they are acquainted with the secrets of the matter, they will praise his decision. This same day, Władysław entertains King Sigismund and Queen Barbara, and the more eminent Hungarians, to a splendid banquet. After this, Władysław, his prelates, knights and nobles accompany King Sigismund to Košice, where they spend a whole week.

While in Košice, the two kings, each with four advisers, hold a secret meeting at which the advisers are told the terms of the agreement Sigismund and Władysław made at their tête-à-tête in Lubowla. The four Poles, Nicholas, Archbishop of Gniezno, Albert Bishop of Poznań, John of Tarnow voivode of Cracow and Zbigniew of Brzezie Marshal of Poland, are unable to praise the agreement, for they consider it dangerous and harmful, but, of course, they cannot repudiate what their King has agreed and so reluctantly accept it.

The draft agreement has as its first and main clause the destruction of the Order of Teutonic Knights and the division of their Prussian territories; but, when envoys from that Order arrive, Sigismund feels that he must get Władysław to agree to its removal, lest the envoys hear of it; so, first he suggests that Władysław send Queen Anna back to Cracow and then himself accompany Sigismund to a number of places where the hunting, Władysław's favourite sport, is particularly good. He then says to Władysław: "You must know, dearest Brother, that I have just been elected King of the Romans, but have not yet fully taken over the imperial capital; thus I must ask you to agree to our not including in the formal document the clause relating to the destruction of the Teutonic Knights and the division of Prussia, which we have mutually agreed and sworn to implement, as this would expose me to a considerable amount of ill-will, the result of which could be that the Electors, who favour the Knights, would remove me from the imperial throne. So, dearest Brother, please have a care for my good name and allow this clause to be removed from the treaty, for otherwise it will undoubtedly expose me to considerable odium and the reproaches of the Electors and other princes of the Empire. I, of course, will sincerely adhere to it and all other points in our agreement, just as if they were formally included in the document, as I have promised and personally sworn to do." Again Władysław agrees to Sigismund's cunning move and allows the clause to be removed. He does not even consider it a blot on his fame, that, by falling into such a trap, he has made a laughing-stock of himself. Thus the formal treaty is written and sealed without the all-important clause being in it.

Władysław, having agreed to mediate between Sigismund and the people of Venice, sends Thomas Canon of Cracow to Venice to try and induce the Doge to abandon the war and agree to peaceful plans. To make this easier, the Canon tries to persuade the Doge to send envoys with full powers to Buda to negotiate through him as intermediary and, perhaps, achieve the restoration of peace on equitable terms.

On Friday, March 25, Queen Anna sets out to return to Poland with an escort of prelates and nobles. King Sigismund, who is seeing them off, falls from his horse and, when picked up, appears half dead. The Hungarian nobles at once start telling each other that, if Sigismund dies, they want no other king than Władysław of Poland; however, Sigismund quickly recovers and the two kings are able to ride away. They spend a night in Tokay and from there go to Varaždin, where lies the body of St. Lászlo, whom the King wishes to honour. King Władysław goes there on foot, with King Sigismund riding ahead of him. The two kings spend a fortnight in Varaždin, that is until after Easter. While there, a Venetian envoy, a master of theology and a brother of the Order of St. Augustine, arrives to collect a letter ensuring the inviolability of Venice's envoys, who are to come and discuss peace and a text for a treaty. Władysław and Sigismund move on to Buda before April 22, having occupied themselves with hunting, when, in the course of three days they killed a considerable quantity of game. They stay in Buda until June 22.

A tourney is held on July 3 with a hundred knights fighting in the lists. The jousting lasts for two whole days and from morning until evening. Those taking part are of many nationalities: Greeks, Italians, French, Poles, Czechs, Hungarians, Austrians and Franconians, knights from Meissen and the Rhine, Lithuania, Bosnia, Bulgaria, Italy, Albania and Raško. On the first day,

Archduke Ernest, whom Sigismund hates and has not invited to the tourney, dubs several knights and, after taking his official leave, departs, but secretly returns and is present throughout the tourney. Extra splendour is given to the occasion by the presence of the King of Bosnia, Charwen, and his wife, especially as his knights, tall men of slender build, acquit themselves well, showing great endurance and courage. Before the King leaves Buda he is waited upon by envoys from the Tatar khan, Zeledin, who presents him with three camels with woven coverings and other gifts. The envoys suggest sending all the Khan's forces to reinforce Władysław against any of his enemies. The presence of the Khan's envoys causes consternation among the representatives of the other nations. Władysław, wishing to reciprocate Sigismund's kindness, wants the Khan to make the same offer to Sigismund, who uses their presence to threaten the Venetians.

Sigismund is afraid lest Władysław invoke the treaty they have just concluded and confirmed by oath, and demand his help in dealing with the Teutonic Knights, who have already broken their pact with King Władysław, in that, having paid the first instalment on the due date, they have at the instigation of Sigismund, refused to pay the other two instalments, and so, even if they now pay the outstanding amounts, Władysław would be entitled to declare war on them, because of their failure to pay on time. However, Sigismund induces Władysław not to declare war on the Knights by the following stratagem: when the Order's plenipotentiaries arrive in Buda and put all the disputes in Sigismund's hands, leaving it to him to decide them, he persuades Władysław that it will not harm him to do the same and leave Sigismund to decide the dispute, since he is bound to Władysław by ties of the sincerest friendship, as he assures him again and again, and so will pronounce a judgment that is favourable to his friend. Władysław naively believes him and accepts Sigismund as arbitrator and judge. There follows a solemn hearing of the case, under the direction of King Sigismund, before a court consisting of the prelates and nobles of Hungary, each side presenting its own case, answering the other side and producing what evidence it has. Sigismund could easily have settled the matter then and there, but he keeps procrastinating, so that Władysław is kept from declaring war on the Knights or emptying their money-bags, and finally pretends that he has been urgently summoned to Italy to conduct the war with Venice over Dalmatia, so he entrusts the rest of the hearing to the Archbishop of Esztergom, Nicholas Gara, and other Hungarian nobles.

Meanwhile, two Venetian envoys, one of whom is the future Doge, Tomas Mocenigo, reach Buda. They have come to use Władysław as intermediary in talks with Sigismund on Dalmatia. Although adamant that Venice will never relinquish possession of Dalmatia, they have a solution: namely, that Venice will allow Hungary to be titular owner of it, for which Venice will pay Hungary a tribute of a white horse with a purple covering. When Sigismund learns of this, he feels that Venice is making fun of him, falls into a rage and has five Venetian flags, which had been captured the previous year, when the Hungarians defeated the Venetians at Forum Julia, dragged along the ground through the streets where the Venetian envoys are staying, and then along the most frequented streets of Buda to the castle. By chance Sigismund and Władysław are together, when they see this being done. Władysław is disgusted at the sight and he and his retinue refuse to tread on the flags, but Sigismund does so and is rebuked by Władysław, who tells him that it is not fitting thus to mock an enemy's flag; but that Sigismund should be expressing his gratitude to God by exhibiting a little humility; in other words, he should model himself on Władysław who, having defeated an unworthy foe in Prussia, treated the defeated with the utmost kindness, took their flags to his capital and had them placed in the cathedral there in honour of God, by whose help, he admits, they were captured.

Władysław leaves Buda on June 22 and goes to Székesfehérvár, where he spends the Feast of John the Baptist. He then moves on to a village on the Danube, where, after eating too greedily of cheese made with curdled cow's milk and certain heavy foods and refreshing himself with a two-hour-long bathe in the river, he contracts a severe fever, which lasts for three days. Nonetheless, he moves on to Moroch, where the Archbishop of Esztergom has hunting, and here he is visited by two doctors sent by Sigismund. He then moves back to Esztergom, where he spends five days generously supplied with everything he needs by the Archbishop. He then goes by boat to Visegrád, where his illness forces him to stay a week. Here he is joined by Sigismund, who has the castle cleared to accommodate him and his retinue. The two kings then go together to Warprim, where they hunt and Władysław recuperates for several days. Then, Sigismund, seeing that Władysław, who has now recovered, wants to return home, presents him with a golden crown, actually that of the Kingdom of Poland which the Emperor Otto III placed on the brow of Poland's first king, Bolesław the Great, the sword "Szczerbiec", nicknamed the Crane, as well as the golden orb and sceptre, together with other Polish treasures that King Casimir's sister, Elizabeth the Elder, carried off when she was afraid that the Poles were intending to dishonour her son, King Louis, by replacing him with another king, because of his neglect of the domestic affairs of the kingdom. Sigismund also presents Władysław with various sacred bones and relics in a silver-gilt monstrance, embellished with the ring of the late King Louis, and also three lengths of velvet, three woven Florentine hangings and three geldings. King Władysław rewards the bearer of these gifts with two villages in Poland and a hundred marks of broad grosses, and reciprocates by presenting Sigismund with a fur cloak lined with sable, marten, ermine and squirrel, some saddle- and running-horses and various birds trained to hunt.

On July 22, the two kings ride into the wasteland to the monastery run by the Brethren of the First Hermit. They discuss a number of matters in a spirit of sincerity and friendship, then take their leave of each other and go their separate ways, Władysław to Moravia, where Baron Laczko receives him with every expression of humility and kindness, and, for two days, provides him with all the provisions he needs. The King moves on to Cieszyn and so enters his kingdom. For his entrance into Cracow, he orders the true crown of Poland, the orb and the sceptre to be carried before him for all to see. Queen Anna comes out to meet him at the head of a great procession and there is general rejoicing.

On August 16, the King leaves Cracow on a tour of inspection of his towns and fortresses. This takes him to Hrubieszów on the river Bug, where he meets the Grand-duke of Lithuania, whom he informs of all his conversations with Sigismund and the pacts they have made, and also gives him several of the gifts he has had from Sigismund. Here, too, he receives the Bishop of Cracow, Peter Wysz, who has come to persuade the King to right the wrong the King has done him, namely that, having been told that the bishop was mentally ill and like one in a state of lethargy, Władysław got the Pope to transfer him to the see of Poznań and appoint another, Albert Jastrzębiec, to the see of Cracow, as if Poznań was so inferior that it could be administered by a man who was crazed. Many people speak up for Peter Wysz, but the King is implacable. This affair does considerable damage to the King's reputation and causes much ill-feeling between laity and clergy. One knight of Wielkopolska, a relative of Peter Wysz, even planned to kill Bishop Jastrzębiec, but nothing came of that.

After meeting the Grand-duke, the King moves on to Medyka and there spends a fortnight. Here he receives emissaries from King Sigismund, John Archbishop of Esztergom and Michael Küchmeister come to ask him to lend the latter the 40,000 broad Prague grosses the Teutonic Knights are due to pay him. As security, Sigismund will hand over the territory of Spisz, which belongs to Hungary. After consulting his advisers, Władysław agrees, hoping that this will strengthen the ties of sympathy and friendship between them and, especially, confirm Sigismund's undertaking to help him destroy the Teutonic Knights. From Medyka the King and Michael Küchmeister go to Przemyśl, where the King orders the re-consecration of its cathedral, which was built of stone and sited in the middle of the castle, and which hitherto had come under a Ruthenian bishop and practiced the Greek rite, he does this to show the Germans how untrue is the slander that he protects schismatics. Now it is to be a Catholic cathedral and use the Latin rite. The bones and dust of all the Ruthenians buried there are to be removed, a thing the Ruthenian clergy and people consider shameful and complain about loudly.

Having dismissed the Hungarian envoys, King Władysław inspects a number of other towns and castles and, on November 11, reaches Niepołomice, where he spends a fortnight with various prelates and nobles who have come to see him. He then moves on inspecting still more towns and reaches Lithuania, where he spends most of the winter. He distributes most of the remaining gifts given him by King Sigismund, some to the Grand-duke and his daughter, Anastasia, wife of Basil, Duke of Moscow, who is visiting her father. Another visitor there is Benedict of Makra, a Hungarian knight sent by King Sigismund to inspect Poland's boundaries with Lithuania and Prussia, and see how the various rivers divide the territory and the places in it. This he does scrupulously, investigating and noting details of topography of the lands mentioned in their depositions by King Władysław and the Teutonic Knights, and then departs laden with presents from the King and the Grand-duke, having seen with his own eyes the subject of the dispute between Poland and the Order.

Pope John XXIII agrees to a council being held in Constance with the object of mending the many schisms in the Church. Ladislas, King of Sicily, assembles an army and tries to shut the Pope up in Bologna, but dies of St. Anthony's fire of his male organ before he can carry out his plan.

A.D. 1413

King Władysław spends Christmas in Lithuania. As agreed, he lends the King of Hungary the 40,000 marks of broad Prague grosses he receives from the Teutonic Knights and gets Lubowla and fourteen towns in Spisz as security for its repayment, granting them to Paul Gładysz, who speaks Hungarian, for him to hold until such time as Sigismund has repaid the whole amount. The King reaches Poznań during the week after Corpus Christi and realizes, unfortuately too late, the mistake it had been to remove Peter Bishop of Cracow from his see and forcibly transfer him to Poznań. He summons the bishop to his chapel and there falls to his knees before him and begs forgiveness. The Bishop raises him to his feet and forgives him.

The King spends Ascension in Wiślica and as he continues, turns off the highway into the forest, so as to evade the plague which is rampant throughout Poland, and slowly makes his way to Chełm, avoiding every town and village on the way. Even so, many of his Court fall victim to the plague.

On October 2, the King reaches Horodło on the River Bug for a meeting, arranged long before, with the Grand-duke, which is also attended by a large number of prelates, knights and barons, as well as the councillors of the two rulers. The purpose of the meeting is to conclude a permanent union of Poland and the territories of Lithuania and Samogitia. The Lithuanians are to be allowed to sport the arms and badges of nobility, which the ancestors of the Polish nobles had won long before by their deeds of valour and services to their King. Those who, previously, had not enjoyed the status of nobility are to receive Polish titles and arms, as well as the rights and freedoms for which the Kingdom of Poland was famed, being exempt from tribute, services, and taxes. The daughters, sisters and female relatives of those thus enobled are to marry only Catholics, as was the custom in Poland. They will have to pay taxes for building fortresses and castles.

All important officials will have to be Catholics. On the death of the Grand-duke Witold the Lithuanians are not to elect anyone unacceptable to the King of Poland. Similarly, if the King of Poland dies without an heir, his successor must be approved by the Lithuanians.

This advantageous pact having been concluded, King Władysław goes to Lithuania accompanied by the Grand-duke, Queen Anna and their daughter, Jadwiga. Feeling ashamed of the fact of the Samogitians still being in the blind toils of paganism, the King directs all his efforts to enlightening them, and, for this purpose, leaving the Queen and the baggage in Kowno, he embarks and sails to the River Dubissa and so to Samogitia. Here, the King summons an assembly of the entire population, tells them that it is wicked and illegal for them to persist in the old, false beliefs, when all the dukes and knights of Lithuania believe in the one true God. He then has the altars of their pagan gods destroyed and the woods they consider sacred felled. The Samogitians regard fire with special reverence, considering it sacred and eternal. They keep one burning on the top of a tall tower on a hill by the River Niewieża, and this tower is now burned to the ground and the sacred flame extinguished. There are certain groves considered to be the home of the Samogitians' gods and thus sacred, as are the birds and animals in them, and, indeed, whoever enters one, so that no Samogitian dares fell trees or hunt in these groves, for evil spirits will twist off the hands and feet of whomever does this, thus the wild animals and birds living in these groves, like domestic creatures, have no fear of man and do not avoid him. The Samogitians are amazed, when the soldiers cut down the sacred groves belonging to individual families, in which they are accustomed to burn the bodies of their dead along with each dead person's horses, saddles and finest garments. Here are altars beside which stand tables made from cork-trees on which they set soft foods, such as cheese, while they pour mead over the altars, naively thinking that the spirits of the dead they have buried there will come by night, eat the food and drink the mead long since absorbed by the ashes. It is obvious that the food is eaten not by spirits, but by crows, ravens and other birds and creatures of the forest.

October 1 is always the occasion for a special ceremony to which everyone of either sex comes bringing food and drink, each according to his station, and on this they all feast for several days, sacrificing to their false gods, especially to the one called Perkun (or Piorun). This land of Samogitia lies mostly on the cold northern frontiers of Prussia, Lithuania and Latvia, and, being surrounded by forest, hills and rivers, is fertile. The Samogitians are barbarians, uncouth, savage, ready to commit any crime. Tall, of slender build, they are content with modest fare of bread or meat. Their thirst they usually quench with water, seldom with mead or beer. Gold, silver, iron, brass, wine, fish and fat for bread are unknown to them. A man is allowed many wives. When a father dies, a son will marry his stepmother, as a brother will his brother's widow. They are pot-bellied, yet otherwise their bodies are slim. Their houses are made of wood and straw, broad at the base and tapering towards the top, rather like a boat, with a window at the top to let light in. Beneath this opening lies the hearth, over which they cook, when they do cook. Their houses shelter themselves, their wives, children, slaves, servants, cattle, horses, pigs and their grain and utensils. They have no other buildings: no refectories, palaces, stores, barns or stables. A harsh, savage, uncouth people, given to soothsaying and fortune-telling.

As none of the priests accompanying the King can speak Samogitian, the King preaches to them himself. First, he teaches them the Lord's Prayer, then the Creed. Then, in a lengthy speech, he tells them that they must honour only one god, the only God, in the person of the triple, most bountiful Creator and Redeemer of the world. He explains that their false gods: fire, lightning, woods and groves, cannot of themselves bring them salvation, as they have seen, when their main god, Fire, whom they considered eternal, was destroyed, as were all his altars. Influenced by the destruction of their idols and by the King's gravity and by the incentives offered them, the Samogitians abandon their idols and agree to accept the Christian faith and be baptized. The more eminent of them are instructed in the new faith and its articles and are then baptized in the presence of the King, who gives them Christian names. All who thus accept Christianity and baptism are given lavish presents of beautiful clothes, horses, cloth, money and other things, so as to encourage others to accept the true faith. Then, in the most important of their places, Miedniki, the King endows and builds a cathedral, as well as parish churches elsewhere, each being provided with sufficient revenues. When the King's chaplain, Nicholas Wężyk, is preaching through an interpreter, telling them about the creation and the fall of Adam, one of the Samogitians, thinking that Wężyk is describing something he has himself witnessed, calls out: "He's lying. Man does not live long, so how can anyone pretend to remember the creation of the world? We have many who are older than he, over a hundred years old, and they cannot remember the creation; everyone knows that the sun, moon and other planets shine thanks to the same changes and in the same time." The King tells him to be silent, and explains that the preacher did not mean that the creation took place in his time, but that it happened six thousand six hundred years ago.

As King Władysław is preparing to leave their country, he learns that the fickle Samogitians, deeply hurt by the destruction of their idols and the extinguishing of their sacred fire, are secretly planning to rekindle the fire once the King is out of the way, for its ashes are still warm. If they succeed in this, they will feel sure that their god cannot be destroyed. So the King stays on for a few days longer and has his soldiers bring quantities of water from the River Niewieża, which they pour on to the sacred pagan hearths. He appoints one of the Lithuanian barons, Kinzgalo, a devout and pious man, a starosta, and orders him to take special care of the neophytes and see that they do not revert to their old superstitions, and to ensure that those who refuse the new faith are not able to worship or make sacrifices to their false gods. The King then returns to Lithuania and spends Christmas in Wilno with Grand-duke Alexander and Queen Anna.

The plague, which has raged throughout Poland and Silesia, killing many people, checks around St. Jadwiga's Day, but breaks out again around St. John the Baptist's Day.

While Władysław is in Lithuania, some of the Prussians' castellans and knights deprive the Prussian Master, Henry of Plauen, of his office and imprison him. This they do, it is said, either out of envy, for he has revived the all but defunct Order by his courageous defence of Malbork and his recovery of castles captured by King Władysław, or because of his extravagance. The real reason is that some of these commanders under Michael Küchmeister suspected Henry of Plauen of conspiring with King Władysław against the Order and so, one night, they went to his bedroom pretending to wish to consult him, seized him and took him quietly and secretly by water to Gdańsk, where they imprisoned him in the castle tower. Ulrich commander of Gdańsk was Plauen's own brother, and he, sensing that he would probably suffer the same fate, escaped that same night with a few of his men and went to King Władysław, with whom he was to stay for seven years, respected and lavishly entertained, giving loyal help in all that is done against the Knights. (When Plauen's replacement, Michael Küchmeister, dies, Plauen is released and moved to Lochstaedt by the sea, where he dies six months later from the effects of the torture he had undergone during his seven years in prison.)

A.D. 1414

Learning that at home the plague has abated, the King leaves Lithuania and returns to Poland. He travels through Mazovia, while Queen Anna takes a different route through Pinsk, Vladimir and Chełm. The King reaches Cracow on the fourth Sunday after Lent, then moves to Wielkopolska and spends Easter in Kalisz. From there he goes to Słońsk in Kujawy, where he meets the new Master of the Order, Michael Küchmeister, from whom he tries to obtain compensation for the damage inflicted on Poland by the Teutonic Order despite their pact of permanent peace; but his efforts are in vain and the two men part in anger.

Still wishing to settle his quarrel with the Knights by legal means rather than by force of arms, King Władysław sends four envoys to Buda to continue the arbitration undertaken by the King of the Romans and press for judgment on the basis of the evidence presented, which the King is convinced can only be to his advantage. The four reach Buda on the first Sunday after Easter and present John Archbishop of Esztergom with the evidence supporting the Polish case. The Knights are also there presenting their own case, using gold and bribery as arguments rather than justice. The

Archbishop judges the case not according to common sense and conviction, nor in accordance with the obvious evidence of the documents laid before him, but as instructed by King Sigismund. His judgment, given in writing, disappoints King Władysław's dearest hopes. It is not detailed, as the Poles had hoped, but terse and incomplete, for it fails to mention the fact that King Władysław has kept all the conditions of the treaty for a lasting peace made with the Master and the Order, or that the Order has paid the King only 40,000 of the 100,000 marks of broad grosses awarded to him.

Grievous and unpleasant as the judgment is, the King and his councillors decide to honour it and so ensure peace with the Order; but the Knights, their hopes revived by the appointment of the new Master, become bumptious and start inflicting further damage and this the King cannot endure. Some Polish merchants, citizens of Poznań, who, trusting to the treaty, had gone to Gdańsk with quantities of goods, had all been killed on the way home and robbed of everything they had. To add insult to injury, the local people had placed dead dogs on their graves. Also, the Knights have used the least excuse to remove Polish knights living in the vicinity from their homes and strung them up on the gates of their manors. They had also invaded Dobrzyń and started burning it, but frightened lest King Władysław arrive, suddenly withdrew. As overt hostilities have not succeeded, they revert to underhand measures, sending highly paid agents of either sex into Poland to start fires in towns and villages. Many of these are caught and confess that the Knights had paid them to do their nefarious work. Although the King again and again claims compensation for the damage all this has done and demands that the terms of their pact be adhered to, the Knights just reply with mockery, forcing the King to conclude that he must, with God's help, humble the Knights; so, after consulting his prelates and nobles, he organizes a punitive expedition. His troops are ordered to assemble in Wolborz on the Sunday after the Feast of the Visitation of the Blessed Virgin, and he calls upon the Grand-duke to send him certain contingents, while some Silesian dukes and foreign knights make cash contributions.

The King spends Corpus Christi in Buk and from there moves to Kościan, where, in answer to pleas from two Silesian dukes, Conrad of Oleśnica and Wacław of Żagań that he stops the raids being made into their territory, he appoints officials to see justice done and repair the damage. Moving on, he reaches Wolborz on the Sunday after Visitation Day to find troops from all over Poland assembled there.

The army moves off following the same route as that taken at the outset of the Great War. On July 17 it reaches the Vistula near Zakroczym, where the Grand-duke Alexander and his Lithuanians, Ruthenians and Tatars are already encamped. Although the pontoon bridge is there and ready, they are unable to use it until the waters swollen by the summer rain subside, which they do a week later. In the mean time, the entire army has to remain in Mazovia. When it finally gets across, it moves in four stages into enemy territory and is drawn up in battle formation. It is larger and stronger than any the King has previously assembled for such an expedition; indeed, there is no level ground extensive enough to accommodate it and its camp. The King gives his permission for its arraying to be watched by envoys from the Knights, who eagerly note all that happens. They had come to inform the King that, if he would abandon hostilities, the Master would undertake to settle all grievances with William Margrave of Meissen. However, as it is obvious that this is a ploy to stop the invasion, the envoys are dismissed and given no hope of peace. If they had genuinely wished peace, they would have put forward very different proposals.

The King moves on, captures the town of Nidzica and invests the castle which stands above it, and storms it a week later. The capture of this castle is a considerable gain, as it opens up a supply route and so prevents the huge army from being weakened by hunger. Next, the King advances on Olsztynek and both town and castle at once surrender. He moves on to Olsztyn itself, whose town and castle belong to the chapter of Warmińsk. The castle does not resist and the town is given to the army to loot. Waggon after waggon is filled with provisions of all kinds. As was to be expected, the Knights, hoping to win by starving the King's army, which they cannot defeat in battle, have burned almost every bakery and mill, especially in those areas through which they expected the enemy to pass. The King now orders a halt for five days, during which the army provisions itself with flour from the best mills along the River Łyna. He then moves on Dobre Miasto, which was built of brick at great expense by the secular canons of its collegiate foundation and which had already been captured, plundered and burned by the advance force, so that all that remains is the college and the house of one of the canons, which had been saved from the flames. Moving on, the army halts near Lidzbark Warmiński, a town belonging to the Bishop of Warmińsk. Some of the servants and camp-followers set out on their own accord to plunder the town. The town's defenders, seeing how few they are, attack them, driving off some and killing others and mutilating their bodies, cutting off their male organs and stuffing these into their mouths. The King is told by his scouts that 500 Czech cavalry, hired by the Knights, are hidden near Lidzbark and preparing to attack the camp by night. The King sends three squadrons to deal with them, but the Czechs, scenting danger, have already withdrawn into their fort. A number of other knights from various countries, come to join the Czechs, are roaming the countryside, plundering and burning what they are there to protect.

At the urgent request of John Bishop of Warmińsk, whose loyalty had made him abandon his see and retreat to Poland, the King calls off the siege of the Bishop's castle of Heilsberg and moves his camp to Kluczbork, which, some days previously, was captured, plundered and burned by his own troops, now roaming all over Prussia. While the King is at Kluczbork, the Archbishop of Riga arrives with three commanders of the Order, come to ask for talks. They are received by the King's household officials, who tell them that the King does not reject the idea of peace, but as the Knights are not proposing equitable terms, but just hoping that the King will give up, when he finds himself unable to feed his troops, there is nothing to discuss. After this, the commanders depart, having settled nothing.

The Grand-duke is anxious to return to Lithuania, which is near, but the Polish captains condemn the suggestion, insisting that should their horses founder, they will follow their King on foot, and the Grand-duke grudgingly gives up the idea. Władysław's plan is to move the army deeper into Prussia and there use it to devastate all that part adjoining Lithuania, as the Grand-duke requested; but incessant rain makes it impossible to move the army into such boggy terrain, and, instead, he advances to the River Pasłęka, which he bridges and moving on, lays siege to the town and castle of Pasłęk. Some Lithuanian knights stupidly go searching for loot in the orchards and gardens outside the town. Seeing them, the mercenaries employed by the enemy sally out and capture some of them, including the Grand-duke's Marshal, Butrym of Żernina. Other of the King's cavalry units go searching for loot towards the sea as far as Frombork where the cathedral church of Sambia is and, meeting with no resistance, make a considerable haul and return with herds of cattle and waggons laden with wine and equipment.

The King next advances towards Elbląg and lays the country waste for miles around it. Then, on the Eve of the Nativity of the Blessed Virgin, he moves on to Dzierzgoń, which he finds empty, its garrison and knights having fled, so he spends the holy day there. The next day, he burns the fort to the ground and advances on Riesenburg and, although this has been captured and plundered the previous week by the Lithuanian duke, Zygmunt Korybut, they still find quantities of wine, mead, beer, meat and other delicacies with which to fill their waggons. Then it is the turn of Biskupiec and this the King captures two days later. Unexpectedly, there they find a quantity of gold, silver, cloth and a number of horses, which enrich them all. The King's plan is to move on against Chełm and Toruń, assuming that both will surrender immediately; but, thanks to the treachery of one of the King's coucillors, I do not know which, the Knights learn of his intention and with guile and duplicity distract him from an undertaking that would have benefited him enormously, and, instead, get him to attack Brodnica, which, being well sited, strongly garrisoned and well provisioned, is capable of enduring a siege of many days. This is done by the Commander of Brodnica sending a runner with a letter addressed to the Prussian Master telling him that Brodnica has no reserves of food, no guns and very few men and asking the Master to send him these by night, otherwise the town will undoubtedly fall into the King's hands. The runner, who was ordered to use roads known to be patrolled by the King's scouts, is duly caught and, as the letter is held to be genuine and not a trick, the King alters his plans and sends sixteen detachments to invest Brodnica and prevent anything being brought in to it. When, after a week, it is obvious that he is getting nowhere, the Grand-duke departs for Lithuania, as he has long wanted to do, but via Mazovia, for he is afraid of the enemy. His departure sours relations between him and King Władysław.

When Brodnica has withstood his siege for a whole month, the King realizes that he has been tricked. The length of the siege has adversely affected the troops, in that, though well provided with meat, there has been a serious shortage of bread, as a result of which many of the men are suffering from dysentry, which in some cases has proved fatal. The enemy, who know all that is going on in the Polish camp, are delighted and feel certain that the Poles will give up without their having to strike a blow. At this juncture, a Papal Legate, John Bishop of Lausanne, arrives. He has been sent at the instigation of the Knights, who are paying his expenses, to try to end the war. He persuades King Władysław to conclude a truce to last for two years and leave the dispute to be settled by the General Council due to be held in Constance on November 1. The King agrees, for winter is approaching and dysentry rife among his troops, and appoints Nicholas, Archbishop of Gniezno, John Bishop of Włocławek, Jacob Bishop of Płock, Tuliszkowo Bishop-elect of Poznań, Janusz of Tuliskowo castellan of Kalisz and Zawisza the Black of Garbow to represent him at the Council. So, on October 6, the siege is raised and, on the following day, the army is disbanded, the men crossing the Vistula on the pontoon bridge and then dispersing to their homes.

The King now progresses in eleven stages to Opatów, where Queen Anna awaits him, and so gradually reaches Biecz, where the Archbishop of Gniezno comes to receive his instructions for the Council in Constance and the gold, silver, jewelry, fur cloaks and horses he is to use as gifts. Having attended to all this, the King moves on to Niepołomice and then by the usual stages to Lithuania. He spends Christmas in Grodno, but avoids meeting the Grand-duke with whom he is still angry, though his councillors make every effort to bring about a reconciliation. In the end, the Grand-duke admits that he is in the wrong and, in order to placate the King, invites him to come to Lithuania again in the summer.

While their King is away attending the Council in Constance, the nobles of Hungary, on their own initiative, assemble an army and, without outside help, mount an expedition against the Turks. There is a battle in which the Hungarians are decisively defeated and a number of the more eminent taken prisoner, a huge sum being required to ransom them. After this victory, the Turks move in and devastate most of the country as far as Cilia, capturing many thousands of Christians. King Władysław, who is genuinely sorry for the Hungarians and wants to remove the threat hanging over them, sends two of his knights, Skarbek of Góra and Gregory the Armenian, to the Sultan, demanding that he stop his invasion of Hungary, release all his prisoners and conclude a truce for six years, otherwise the King will attack the Sultan with all his forces. The Sultan receives the two envoys graciously and generously provides them with everything they need. He invites them to several banquets and finally promises to end hostilities and conclude a six-year truce with Hungary. To add weight to his promise, he agrees to send his own envoys to Hungary. Skarbek travels through Walachia and returns safely to Poland to report to Władysław; however, the Turks hesitate to set out without a written safe-conduct, so Gregory goes ahead to arrange for one, but when he applies for it to the Ban of Temessna, he is thought to be a spy and put in prison, where his goods, clothes, parcels and even his bootlaces are rigorously searched in case he is carrying letters from the Turks. When the Turks learn what has happened, they resume ravaging Hungarian territory and even King Władysław cannot stop them, though repeatedly asked to try. The Polish envoy is finally released and returns to King Władysław.

Jan Hus, who had long since become infected with the false doctrine of the disciples of John Wycliffe, which was brought to Bohemia from the English city of Oxford by a Czech, has now started openly preaching it. He is a man of outstanding intelligence, a gifted speaker and a master of debate, a lover of foreign ideas and an enemy of the Germans, whose masters he now baits in the hope of frightening them into leaving the University. When this does not succeed, King Václav arranges for the University to be administered by Czechs. The disgusted German masters and scholars found their own university in Leipzig, near Meissen. Jan Hus, being a good speaker and renowned for his honesty, easily gains eminence among the scholars who are left and the ordinary people. When he sees that they like listening to him, he propounds many of Wycliffe's dogmas and imbues the Czechs with the false English doctrine. He maintains that Wycliffe was a worthy and excellent man, and that he wrote and confessed only what is true. He himself, he says, yearns that he may be able, after death, to reach where Wycliffe's soul has gone. Hus finds many adherents among the clergy. Any who are in debt or known for crime or rebellion hope that the new arrangements will help them avoid the punishment they deserve. They are joined, too, by a number of eminent scholars who, with jaundiced eye, have watched the well-salaried posts in the Church go to those of superior family though of inferior learning, instead of to them. Those who have joined these mad Waldensians begin to inveigh against the clergy, for they hold that Rome is the equal of any other bishopric and that there is no difference between priests. A priest can rise no higher than the services he renders in his lifetime. Souls, on leaving the body, are at once subjected to everlasting torture or achieve eternal bliss. There are no fires of purgatory. There is no advantage in praying for the dead; that is an invention of greedy priests. Images of God and the saints should be destroyed. Holy water and palms are ridiculous. Evil demons invented the mendicant orders. Priests should be poor and content with alms. Any one is free to preach the word of God. No serious sin can be condoned even to avert a greater misfortune. Whoever is guilty of mortal sin cannot achieve lay or spiritual office and cannot claim obedience. Confirmation and the use of holy oil, chrism and the extreme unction are not church sacraments. Aural confession is nonsensical. It is enough to confess one's sins to God in one's own house. In baptism only river water should be used and without the addition of holy oil. Cemeteries should not be a source of revenue, for there is no difference in the earth that covers a human body. The world is an open temple of God. To build churches, monasteries or houses of prayer and pretend that God's goodness is greater in them, is to diminish His majesty. What priests wear is without significance, as is what decorates altars, corporals, chalices, patens and all such vessels. A priest can consecrate the body of Christ and administer it to those who ask for it anywhere and at any time; it suffices if he pronounces the words of consecration. It is no use petitioning the saints: they are in Heaven with Christ and cannot help. It is a waste of time to sing and recite the canonical hours. There is no need to stop work on any other day than the one we call Sunday. Saints' days should be abolished. There is no benefit to be had from the feast days appointed by the Church.

At this time the Chapter of Prague is administered by a man renowned for his common sense, courage and good family, Zbinko. The Archbishop wishes to nip this false doctrine in the bud and so has more than 200 books beautifully written by John Wycliffe burned and forbids Jan Hus to preach. Hus then leaves Prague and goes to his native village, from where he reviles the Pope and other bishops and tells people that tithes should be given to priests only as alms. This false doctrine is now being further spread by Peter Drazenski, who, exiled from his native Meissen, has returned to Prague as an asylum from which he had earlier been evicted. He, too, instigates Jakubek, also from Meissen, to preach to the masses and incite people, telling them on no account to neglect communion in the kind of wine, without which no-one can be saved. All heretics agree and rejoice that now they have an article based on evangelical truth, which shows up the stupidity and unworthiness of the Holy See.

Archbishop Zbinko gets no help from the King in combating this growing evil, for the King allows the heretics to attack him with impunity, so he goes to the King of the Romans and begs him to come in person to Prague and extinguish the flames of misfortune that are being fanned by his brother's negligence. King Sigismund does, indeed, promise to do this, but procrastinates. Then the Archbishop dies and is succeeded by Albicus, a Czech by origin and one dear to the King because of his skill in medicine. Albicus is also extraordinarily mean. He carries the key to his cellar on his person, and dislikes having many servants, whom he has to feed and clothe. This makes him a laughing-stock to the heretics, whose numbers both he and the King allow to increase.

A.D. 1415

The King leaves Lithuania after Christmas and goes on the usual progress to Jedlna. Queen Anna joins him in Parczew, from where he goes to Lwów on the Thursday before Easter. Whitsun finds him in Śniatyń, where he receives a visit from Alexander the Voivode of Moldavia with his wife and a great retinue of his boyars. The King receives them graciously and with all due honour. The Voivode and his boyars all pay solemn homage to the King, as he sits in all his splendour on his throne. The Voivode personally swears loyalty to the King and throws their standards down at his feet. A document is also drawn up and this is lodged in the treasury. The Voivode then invites the King to a banquet at which they are all presented with gifts, which the King later reciprocates. During all this, envoys from the Patriarch and Greek Emperor arrive with letters and sealed documents asking for help in the form of corn. The King grants them the amount they ask for, which they are to collect in Odessa. The King sends the Queen to Cracow and himself goes to Kamieniec in Podole and so by stages to Lithuania to take up the Grand-duke's invitation. On a Saturday afternoon, while he is between Kobryń and Myło there is an eclipse of the sun so complete that frightened birds sit on the ground and the stars shine as though it were night. It is so dark that the King has to halt and cannot continue until the eclipse is over. As the King approaches Troki, the Grand-duke and the Master of Livonia come out a mile to greet him. He and his knights are then entertained in a tall castle in the middle of the lake. The next day the King is conducted to the grand-ducal treasury and presented with 20,000 marks in broad grosses, forty cloaks of sable fur, 100 horses and 100 purple cloaks, while his knights all receive individual gifts. The King's gifts are sent to Cracow and eventually distributed among his knights and retinue.

The King and the Grand-duke go together to Kaunas and there they part. The King sails on to Wielona and thence up river to Wilkomierz and on to Dubinki, where the Grand-duke has built a new fortress. From there he goes to Niemenezyńiany, Bezdan and Kostyka, where he hunts. He reaches Wilno on the Feast of the Visitation of the Blessed Virgin and spends a week there, before moving on again and so returns to Poland in fourteen stages. The Queen joins him in Wiślica and they continue together to Przyszów and Dobrestanow, and thence by the usual stages to Ruthenia, While they are there, Janusz Castellan of Kalisz arrives to render his report on the Council in Constance and to get the King and the Grand-duke to swear on the Bible that they will continue the age-old alliance between them and Sigismund, King of the Romans and of Hungary, as Sigismund will also do, when the Castellan returns to Constance. Władysław then returns to Lithuania, where he spends November and December hunting.

The proceedings having started in Constance, the Council summons the Czech, Jan Hus, to appear before it. Hus, a man of low origin and station, is accused of the heresy now spreading in Bohemia. He stubbornly denies the allegation, though shown a book written in his own hand, one

The initial letter depicts scenes from the Creation. To the left of it, Hus is shown being burned at the stake.
From the fifteenth century Orationale regis Ladislai Posthumi. *Narodni knihovna, Prague.*

we have seen in Cracow, with all the heretical doctrines he preached to the people of Prague in it. He cannot deny that the book was written and published by him, and refuses to renounce the pernicious doctrine and errors he has sown in the hearts of the Czechs, who are always attracted by new ideas; so the just judgment of the Council is that he be deprived of his office and, in accordance with the words of St. Paul: "Let sinful body suffer destruction" is condemned as a heathen to be burned at the stake by the civil authorities. To prevent his ashes becoming an object of reverence to his adherents, they are to be thrown into the nearby lake. Despite this, his adherents solemnly celebrate his birthday, July 6, as that of a saint and martyr. Another Czech, Hieronymus, also appears before the Council accused of the same heresy as Hus, whom he excelled in learning and eloquence. Hieronymus has already spent almost a year in prison, and, though there was no concrete evidence of instigation, he too was ordered to be burned at the stake. Both men suffer the stake calmly and without uttering. Hieronymus's ashes are also thrown into the lake and the Czechs likewise honour him as a martyr. When news of all this starts to circulate in Prague, the adherents of the two men call a meeting at which it is decided to honour their memory every year. Since King

Václav has given them possession of the churches, they are able to preach to the people and distribute the sacraments. They demolish the famous Dominican monastery outside Kłodzko and then go round all the other churches and monasteries destroying their sacred shrines. Some 30,000 of them assemble near Bechyne and set up 300 or more tables in the open, from which communion in the kind of wine is administered. Václav scents rebellion and fears that he may lose his life and his kingdom; but his chaplain, Conrad, persuades the people that, though their King is lazy and a drunkard, he is well-inclined towards them and will allow them to live according to their convictions and not harm them or their rites. This appeases the rebels, but the madness of a people once noble and sensible has not been cured; indeed, to this day the Czechs persist in their opposition and lunacy.

A.D. 1416

King Władysław is a little later than usual in leaving Lithuania. When he reaches Lublin, he is told that the Queen is ill, but he continues as usual to Jedlna and remains there during Lent before moving on to the monastery on Łysa Góra, where he learns that the Queen's condition has deteriorated and he hurries to Cracow, which he reaches just in time to see her before she dies. After the funeral, the King goes to Wielkopolska and spends Easter in Kalisz. He then moves on to Kujawy and Dobrzyń. He gets to Wschowa on Annunciation Day and there receives a visit from William Margrave of Meissen, who, after talks, returns home laden with gifts. Moving on to Śrem, the King reaches Wiślica on Assumption Day and then, avoiding Ruthenia, goes to Lithuania, where he has arranged to meet the Master of the Prussian Order in Wielona, to which he goes by boat accompanied by the Grand-duke, and there they are joined by the more eminent of their councillors headed by Bishop Albert Jastrzębiec of Cracow. On the other side of the river are Michael the Prussian Master and Lander the Livonian Master, Dietrich Bishop of Dorpat and a number of commanders. After a number of meetings, they all disperse without having reached any conclusions. The Prussian Master has stated that the Order will never attack the King or the Grand-duke in defence of Samogitia, and promised to renounce the rights given to him in the act of gift enacted by King Władysław and the Grand-duke, provided that Władysław agrees to renounce all claim to the Polish territories occupied by the Knights. Władysław, who is eager to obtain the return of Samogitia and sees this as an opportunity to do so, is prepared to accept such a condition and suggests concluding a treaty of everlasting peace, which would leave all disputed matters and the question of compensation to be settled by the courts; however, the Master arrogantly rejects the proposal and departs in anger without taking leave of either the King or the Grand-duke, apparently considering it beneath his dignity to go to the King, although he is scarcely a bowshot away, and also forbids his councillors to make personal visits; while those quartered in the ships anchored in the middle of the river are not even allowed to go ashore, where the tents of the King and Grand-duke are pitched. The Prussian Master allows himself this display of arrogance because he is certain that, in accordance with the agreement his envoys have made with the Tatars, the Khan is about to invade Lithuania, Ruthenia and Poland in considerable force, whereupon the Knights intend to invade Poland from the other direction. It has been agreed between them that neither would withdraw until both Poland and Lithuania have been put to fire and the sword.

This meeting over, the King and the Grand-duke go to Kaunas, where they win over to our faith more than 3000 Samogitians, men and women, who are baptized and given presents. They then return to Troki, where the prelates and nobles disperse to their homes and the King hunts, spending Christmas in Grodno. Both King and Grand-duke are worried that Samogitia may be wrested from Lithuania and send special envoys to the Council in Constance to ask that the Knights should not be allowed to put pressure on the Samogitians, who, thanks to the King and the Grand-duke, have just been led from the darkest paganism to the light of our faith: maintaining that the Knights should be made to observe the strictest amity with the neophyte Samogitians and not bully them into reverting to paganism. The Council is also asked to have set up the cathedral church which Władysław has already planned, built and endowed there. The Council agrees to all this and categorically forbids the Knights to invade Samogitia and authorizes the Archbishop of Lwów and the Bishop of Wilno to establish a diocese in Samogitia.

King Władysław, who has two marriages behind him, is now contemplating a third. He sends John of Rzeszów and Peter Niedźwiedzki to Brabant to have a look at Anna, daughter of Charles of Bohemia and now widow of the Duke of Brabant, and propose marriage. Anna tells him that she has no desire to remarry; however, shortly after this she changes her mind and marries the Elector of Utrecht with whom she has fallen in love. He is a subdeacon, but gives up his office and the prospect of a bishopric in order to marry her.

The Tatar Khan, Ediga, who exercises absolute sway over the entire Tatar empire and at whose behest commanders are made or dismissed, sends a powerful force into Ruthenia, which makes a sudden attack on Kiev, loots it and burns it and the surrounding churches and country, taking a great number of captives. Kiev castle is itself invested and subjected to a number of assaults, but its Polish and Ruthenian garrison defends it stoutly and the Tatars have to withdraw. After this Kiev loses much of its lustre and its population is now shrinking.

Sigismund of Hungary, who went to Aragon to try to persuade Peter de Luna to renounce his claim to be pope, returns to Paris in an attempt to arrange peace between the kings of France and England. He is accompanied by Nicholas Archbishop of Gniezno, Janusz Castellan of Kalisz and others sent by King Władysław. The Archbishop, who has written instructions from his King, repeatedly raises the question of war breaking out between the Prussian Knights and the King of Poland on the expiry of the truce and whether or not the truce can be renewed. King Sigismund persuades the Poles to extend the truce for a further two years and this Władysław ratifies.

When they reach Paris, Nicholas of Gniezno, wishing to enhance Poland's image, lays on a splendid, most ostentatious reception to which he invites all the masters, scholars, doctors and others connected with the University, and here he is handed a book, a libellous lampoon on King Władysław written by a Dominican friar, Jan Falkenberg, whom the Prussian Knights hired to write it. The Archbishop takes the book to the Council, where he runs into its author. When the book is laid before the Council to be judged, it is pronounced full of errors and falsehoods and its author is condemned as a heretic to lifelong imprisonment, every cardinal present putting his signature to the verdict. Eventually, at the instigation of Pope Martin V, Falkenberg is released and goes to Malbork, convinced that he will be generously rewarded; but the Master, Paul of Russdorf, gives him only four Prussian marks, telling him that the book has been of no benefit to the Order. Falkenberg then flings the coins at the Master's feet and tells him what he thinks of him, and only the kindness of the people of Toruń saves him from the death by drowning to which the Master condemns him. He escapes to Kamień, where he writes another, even more scurrilous lampoon, this time on the Master and the Order, which he proposes to publish at the Council in Basle; but, while he is on the way there, friends of the Master rob him of it. He then goes to Legnica and there dies.

A.D. 1417

The King leaves Lithuania earlier than usual and goes to Chełm, where by arrangement he is met by his sister Alexandra, Duchess of Mazovia, and by Elizabeth, widow of Vincent of Granow, Castellan of Nakło, with whom he is violently in love, some say bewitched by her, for she suffers from a chronic disease of the lungs, is well on in years and has already had three husbands and numerous children; yet the King is not ashamed to offer to marry her, though to do so must weaken the royal authority. The intended marriage is kept secret from the prelates and nobles, who would not have allowed it. When she leaves Chełm, Elizabeth takes with her furs and other gifts, the lavishness of which arouses the suspicions of many people. The next few days the King spends hunting, then he goes to Jedlna, where many of his councillors have foregathered. Then he moves to Sandomierz, which he reaches on the Second Sunday in Lent. Heavy snowfalls have covered the ground and destroyed the sown corn in many parts of the kingdom. Moving on, the King reaches Łancut in eight stages and there Elizabeth entertains him ostentatiously for two days. The King continues his progress and reaches Lwów in time for Easter. From here he sends Jan Mezyk to the Grand-duke to inform him that he intends to marry Elizabeth. The news annnoys Grand-duke Alexander, especially as it has been arranged without his consent, and because the King could have made another marriage that would have greatly benefited both countries. After Easter, the King crosses the Carpathians to Sanok, where the Archbishop John Rzeszowski of Lwów, Albert Jastrzębiec Bishop of Cracow, John Bishop of Chełm, Christian of Ostrów the castellan and John of Tarnow the voivode of Cracow, Zbigniew of Brzezie the Marshal of Poland and Peter Szafraniec the chamberlain await him, ignorant of why they have been summoned. Here, too, is the Duchess of Mazovia, who is in favour of the marriage. The next day sees the arrival of the woman, who is to make a marriage so much above her station. On the following Sunday, the King summons the prelates and others and informs them of his intention to marry Elizabeth Granowska. None likes the idea, but as they can see that the King is not going to change his mind, some agree, while others just accept it. The marriage is finally celebrated in the parish church in Sanok by the Archbishop of Lwów. Now, since the bride's mother Jadwiga, wife of Otto of Pilcza the Voivode of Sandomierz, is god-mother to King Wladyslaw, it can be said that Elizabeth is the King's spiritual sister. When people realize this, it brings tears to the eyes of many patriots, who consider that this impairs the sanctity of the kingdom and of the King. When the Knights in Prussia hear of it, they spread the news in Constance, tell the King of the Romans and the other Catholic kings and princes, from whom the Polish envoys first hear the news, news that reduces them to tears. They and the entire kingdom deplore the King's shame.

When this Elizabeth's father, the Voivode of Sandomierz, died, she found herself the sole heir to a fortune. A man of little note, called Wiseł, abducted her from the castle at Pilcza and took her to Moravia, where a Moravian nobleman, Hiczynsky, a baron of the Odrowąż clan, tempted by such a huge dowry, seized her from her abductor and married her. Wiseł then accused him of having taken her by force and claimed that she was his lawful wife by reason of their physical and spiritual ties and so denounced the other as an adulterer. At this, Hiczynsky secretly took a dozen crossbowmen with him to Cracow and killed Wiseł as he came out of the bath in a house belonging to Spytek of Melsztyn, Voivode of Cracow. After this, with the King's permission, he enjoyed possession of his wife and her dowry. When, shortly after this, Hiczynsky died, Spytek, a close relative of Elizabeth, constituted himself her protector and married her to Vincent of Granow, a man of modest means, later made Castellan of Nakło.

The King and his bride go to Lwów, where the new Queen remains, while the King goes by five stages to Halicz, where he has arranged to meet the Grand-duke, whom he has to pacify about his marriage. After this, he goes on to Sambor, where he is joined by Queen Elizabeth and together they go to Nowy Sącz, where they are joined by the King's daughter, Jadwiga. Moving on again, they reach Niepołomice by Assumption Day and there spend a week. Next they move to Lublin. While at Żuków, on the way, the King sent an envoy to the Council in Constance to obtain the dispensation he requires to remain married to Elizabeth, given their spiritual relationship, and this he is eventually granted, though with the proviso (not fulfilled) that on her death he is not to take another woman.

The King spends the autumn in Ruthenia and then returns to Cracow, where, despite the objections of all the prelates and nobles, especially of Sędziwój of Ostroróg Voivode of Poznań, he has his bride crowned Queen of Poland by the Archbishop of Lwów, which so perturbs Nicholas

Archbishop of Gniezno, lest this should eventually lead to Gniezno losing its primacy, that he asks the Council to pronounce him Primate of Poland, since when he and his successors have called themselves Archbishops of the cathedral of Gniezno and Primates of Poland. On the Friday after the coronation, the King leaves the Queen in Cracow and goes by the usual stages to Lithuania to hunt. He spends Christmas in Grodno and returns to Jedlna for Easter and there the Queen joins him.

A.D. 1418

Grand-duke Alexander Witold, tormented by suspicions that his and King Władysław's brother, Prince Bolesław Świdrygiello, and some Ruthenian nobles, who have a great affection for the Prince as chief of their rite, are plotting to kill him, has the Prince arrested. Strictly guarded, he is moved from place to place, until, afraid of treachery, the Grand-duke takes the fortress of Krzemieniec from the Ruthenians and incarcerates him there. Here, he is in charge of a Polish knight, Conrad of Frankenberg, who, being a good and just man, provides his prisoner with humane conditions and gives him decent treatment; indeed, he even allows some Ruthenian nobles to visit him, and with these Bolesław plans his escape. Thus, on Good Friday night, these nobles set up siege ladders against the wall and climb into the castle. They make a dash for where Bolesław is kept, causing a commotion that brings Frankenberg running, armed with sword and buckler, but he is killed and the castle captured without further fuss. However, Bolesław dares not stay where he is, so, at dawn, he and his rescuers set out for Hungary.

On July 19, a crowd in Wrocław, incensed by the imposition of more and more taxes for which the city councillors never account, breaks down the doors of the city hall and summarily seizes six of the councillors and one ordinary citizen thought to be in league with them, strips them naked and, without even allowing them to speak to their wives or family beheads the six councillors and throws the citizen from the tower of the Town Hall.

King Władysław sends Matthew of Łabiszyn, voivode of Brześć, and Peter Szafraniec, the Chamberlain of Cracow, and his secretary to the Grand-duke to try and reconcile him and Świdrygiello, so that the latter might be able to return from Hungary. The Grand-duke consents and grants Świdrygiello Bransk and Novgorod Seversk in fee where he lives until the death of Grand-duke Alexander.

Grand-duchess Anna dies on August 1. The Grand-duke's grief is profound, but short-lived.

On the day after St. Michael's Day, the King and Queen Elizabeth set out for Lithuania, where they are to attend a general assembly aimed at concluding a lasting peace with the Prussian Order. They embark at Dubno and sail to Grodno, where the King's councillors join them. They then continue by water to Derszunik, where they are joined by the Grand-duke, and from there sail to Kaunas, where they leave the Queen, and continue to Wielona, where the Prussian Master, Michael Küchmeister, and his councillors already are. After several days of talks, they disperse with nothing agreed. The King's councillors are sent back to Poland from Troki, while the King, Queen and Grand-duke return to Grodno, to which the Grand-duke summons his nobles in order to tell them of his intention to marry Juliana, widow of Ivan Kareczawski and aunt of the Grand-duke's first wife, Anna. The Bishop of Wilno is asked to perform the ceremony, but refuses to do so without a papal dispensation. The marriage is finally celebrated by the Bishop of Włocławek, Jan Kropidło, though canon law forbade it. The next few days are devoted to celebration.

Queen Elizabeth now returns to Cracow, while the King stays on to hunt at Troki and in the forest of Wigry on the River Niemen. While there, he receives a visit from the commander of Rastenberg and three of his knights, who really have only come to see how many men the King has with him. Having made their reconnaissance, the Captain, who has a force of 500 cavalry, makes an attempt to capture the King, but the King's suspicions have been aroused and he has left Wigry and is already on his way back to Grodno, from where he continues to Poland.

The Tatar Khan, Kerim Birdj, who ascended the throne on the death of his uncle Zeledin, is no friend of the Grand-duke. The latter, eager to give tit for tat, appoints a different Tatar, Betsub Ulan, in Wilno and sends him with an army against Kerim Birdj. In the ensuing battle Betsub Ulan is defeated and forfeits his head. A few days later, Kerim Birdj is killed by his own brother, Dżabak Berdi, who then ascends the throne. He, like his father, respects the Grand-duke and, sensibly, makes friends with him.

A.D. 1419

Back in Cracow, Queen Elizabeth falls ill with her old complaint, while the King receives an urgent request from Sigismund King of Hungary to meet him and legates from the Pope sent at the request of the Knights to try and arrange a permanent peace or a truce.

The King goes to Spisz, where he meets the legates, Jacob of Camplo Bishop of Spoleto and Ferdinand of Spain Bishop of Lucca. They travel through Poland with the King who explains his case and makes clear his readiness to conclude peace. The legates move to Toruń to see the Master of the Prussian Order. He insists that the Order's rights and privileges be properly scrutinized, and to this the legates agree; but, as it is obviously too dangerous to send the original documents to Rome, the Master insists that the legates go to Prussia to see and copy them. In the end, the documents are sent for from Krołowiec. When they arrive and the coachman gets off his box, the horses bolt and the coach ends in the waters of Lake Melno. Everything inside the coach is soaked, except the documents, which have been wrapped in waxed linen and are unharmed. The legates then read them and copy them and end up more on the side of the Knights, than of the Poles. King Wladyslaw is so incensed that he writes to the Pope to complain that his legates have not listened to him or properly examined the documentary evidence, and goes on to justify all his actions, now in dispute, and asks the Pope to tell his legates to discard their bias against the Poles.

The legates are now dismissed and Władysław, while awaiting the arrival of the King of Hungary, makes the round of the thirteen towns in Spisz, which provide him and his huge retinue with all that they need. When King Sigismund fails to appear, Władysław sends his Marshal, Zbigniew of Brzezie, to complain. King Sigismund tells him that illness has prevented him from coming. Władysław then moves to Sanok, where another of Sigismund's envoys arrives to invite him to return to Hungary for another meeting. Władysław at first refuses, but is persuaded to go and reaches Košice on May 11. Again Sigismund fails to appear, and, just as the King is preparing to leave at the end of a week's wait, he does arrive, again pretending that he has been ill. Władysław urges the Order's envoys to accept Sigismund as an arbiter but they are reluctant to do so: Sigismund is enraged by their impugning his good faith and seeks to revive the agreement made at Lubowla whereby, once the Order was defeated and Pomerania, Chełm and Michałów returned to Poland, Prussia would be divided between him and Władysław. Back in Poland, the King orders quantities of wine and provisions to be got ready in all towns through which his Hungarian reinforcements are to pass, but none ever arrive. Władysław then goes to Sanok, where he announces an expedition against the Prussians, sends to the Grand-duke for his army and orders all Poland's knights to assemble in Wolborz. He spends Corpus Christi in Lwów, then goes to Łysa Góra to pray, and here envoys from King Sigismund catch up with him and beseech him to put off the expedition. Unable to believe King Sigismund's promises, Władysław refuses. He then joins Queen Elizabeth, who is still ill, but nonetheless accompanies him to Wolborz, from where he goes on to join the Grand-duke at Czerwińsk. The whole army then crosses the Vistula on a pontoon bridge and marches into enemy territory. Here the Archbishop of Milan, acting on behalf of King Sigismund, arrives, come to try to persuade King Władysław to accept arbitration. The King wishes to refuse, but the Grand-duke persuades him to agree to a truce to last for two years, which he does grudgingly. The army then crosses back into Poland and is disbanded. Almost all the provisions, mostly farinaceous, which the army took into Mazovia, are handed over to the villages there, as their crops have largely been destroyed.

News that Václav King of Bohemia has died is followed by an envoy from King Sigismund requesting a meeting in Nowy Sącz, to which Władysław hurries and there has several days of talks about the vacant throne. Władysław advises Sigismund to get to Bohemia as quickly as he can and settle matters there, and above all, to quash the Wycliffean heresy, which, otherwise, will spread. Sigismund, however, considers this unnecessary and prefers to arrange his plan for a campaign against the Turks; however, he is badgered into agreeing to arbitrate between Poland and the Order.

In the absence of Queen Sophia, who does not dare enter the city, and for fear of disturbances on the part of the followers of Wycliffe, King Václav's body is buried in the cathedral of St. Vitus.

Władysław returns to Lwów with the Queen, who is still ill and who continues on to Łancut, where the King again visits her before going to Lithuania to hunt during Christmas.

The strength of the Czech heretics is now such that they are able to attack the true faith and force the faithful to take the Eucharist in both kinds. As the heretics maintain that it is a crime for the Church to possess temporal goods, a mob under Jan Žižka first robs the Carthusian monastery in Prague, murdering some of the brethren and ejecting the others, and then razes the building to the ground. It then moves on to the Cistercian monastery a mile away, loots it and takes the body of the late king and throws it into the river, from which a fisherman later rescues it. Conrad who was made bishop of Prague, when Albicies abdicated the see, now joins the heretics, though whether he does so out of fear or because of a mental aberration is not clear, but that is what he does and is then deserted by almost all his flock. The Czechs are now afflicted by an even more shameful madness known as Picardism. It is almost criminal to describe the practice, which is that people of both sexes foregather naked in one place and at the same time, and perform sexual acts without consideration of whether the partner is married or their own relative. Many follow this path. A Czech, Jan Opoczenski, robs the Cistercian monastery at Opatowice of its many relics in gold and silver cases, which during the worst of the disorders had been put in a silver car, taken from the sacristy and placed on the main altar. Almost every other monastery or place of worship in Bohemia is plundered and destroyed. Every monk or person connected with the Church, who will not accept the heresy, is burned, murdered or expelled. The sacred relics of SS. Václav, Vitus and Ludmila are tipped out of the reliquaries and trampled. All church vessels and jewels used in church services are broken up and made into rings, bits, saddles and other things. The books belonging to the churches, monasteries and Prague university are taken and sold. The pious who are not affected by the heresy are driven from their homes and their possessions taken from them. Some are killed. The scholars of the university are dispersed. Jan Žižka, a veteran of the Prussian wars in which he lost an eye, becomes poisoned with the heresy and, greedy for plunder, recruits 50,000 heretics, occupies Pilsen, puts a strong garrison in it, and advances on the castle at Vyšehrad. Meanwhile, Queen Sophia, still waiting for the help promised her by Sigismund of Hungary, raises an army to defend the castle and the old city of Prague. This, however, put up little resistance and, after five days and nights of fighting, in which many are killed and many houses near the city destroyed, the castle surrenders.

King Sigismund moves his army to Belgrade in Serbia, where it is confronted by a Turkish army, but, as there is the Danube between them, there is no fighting. After wasting several weeks doing nothing the King withdraws to Buda, leaving the Turks free to plunder the Christians and devastate the best of their lands: Serbia, Albania and Transylvania, carrying men and women off into slavery.

The Queen and her doctor. A.D. 1420.
—Statni vedecká knihovna, Olomouc.

Ediga, the powerful leader of the entire Tatar Empire, wishing for an alliance with the Grand-duke Alexander, with whom he has been warring successfully, sends special envoys with gifts of three camels draped with purple cloth and twenty-seven horses, also a letter in which he writes: "You and I, most honourable Prince, have reached an age when death is near, and it behoves us to spend the rest of our time in peace. Let the earth swallow the blood shed in battles between us. Let the wind sweep away the maledictions and insults we have exchanged. Let fire purge our anger and madness, and let water wash away the traces of the fires we have started in each other's country." The Duke agrees to the proposal and sends the envoys back with splendid gifts.

A.D. 1420

King Sigismund announces that he will give his judgment in the dispute between the Teutonic Knights and the King of Poland in Wrocław at Epiphany and that he intends to arrive a fortnight earlier in order to scrutinize the documentary evidence of both sides. However, although all the others are there on time—the papal envoys, the Archbishop of Mainz, the Duke of Saxony, Frederick Margrave of Brandenburg, Bartholomew Capra Archbishop of Milan, as too nearly all the princes and barons of Silesia and the leading barons of Bohemia and Moravia—Sigismund is not, nor has he sent judges to act for him, as he could have done. At midnight on the Feast of Epiphany Sigismund and his Queen, Barbara, arrive in a simple coach. The King's judgment is heavily biased in favour of the Knights; it is to the effect that both sides must be able to use and carry their goods along the old routes in complete safety; that Pomerania, Chełm, Michałów and the fort at Nieszawa are to remain with the Knights in accordance with the earlier Toruń agreement; that the Order is to pay the King of Poland 20,000 florins in two annual instalments for the castle at Złotoria; that the Order will within six months demolish the castle at Lubicz along with a small mill on the river Drwęca; that the boundary betwen Mazovia and the territories of the Prussian Order is to be that laid down in the document drawn up by the former Master, Rudolf König; that all prisoners on either side are to be set free within three months; as to Samogitia, the Order is to have the territory betwen the River Niemen and the waste-land below the River Rodaw as far as Klaipeda Castle and thence to the sea. As long as both the Grand-duke and the King of Poland are alive, the Grand-duke is to have all Samogitia and the territory between its forests and the River Niemen, from the waste-land as far as the confluence of the Rodaw and the Niemen and straight on across the river for five miles through Sudawia and Geicwen as far as Lithuania, together with both banks of the Niemen. During the life-time of the Grand-duke and the King of Poland neither is to put up buildings in these territories. Each side is to forgive the other all wrongs, hurts and any damage inflicted. Any breach is to be punished with a fine of 10,000 marks in pure silver. The King of Poland is to return the fortress at Jasienic within two months. As soon as the Polish envoys are presented with these terms, the document is copied and sent by courier to the King in Lithuania. Leaving on a Saturday, the messenger covers more than 200 miles in seven days and reaches the King in Dawgi.

Meanwhile, the Polish delegates have all left Wrocław without taking leave of King Sigismund, that is, except for Janusz of Tuliszkowo castellan of Kalisz and Zawisza Czarna, who have to wait for the Polish copy of the judgment with King Sigismund's seal. King Sigismund tells them how sorry he is that the papal envoys and others have compelled him to pronounce so harsh a judgment and asks that he be allowed to mitigate it. The Poles tell him that they have no instructions about this and will send a message to King Władysław informing him of what King Sigismund has said. Sigismund asks them to remain in Wrocław until the reply comes, but they feel that the King is just mocking them and decline.

King Władysław and the Grand-duke are dismayed by this turn of events and weep convulsively. The next morning the Grand-duke goes to the King in his bedroom and tells him that they must think of the future rather than dwell painfully on what might have been. Wounds, he tells him, cannot be healed with sadness, but with wise advice and a trusty arm. Then, having consulted their councillors, they decide to send delegates back to Wrocław to tell King Sigismund that the King and the Grand-duke cannot accept his unjust award and, with God's help, will take up arms to get what rightly belongs to them. The requisite documents are drawn up and, on the Monday before the Feast of the Purification, the King's delegates, splendidly dressed, set out for Wrocław. When they get there, they demand an audience with King Sigismund.

On Tuesday, January 30, Sigismund reassembles the dignitaries: his councillors, the papal legates, the Duke of Bavaria, the Margraves of Brandenburg and Meissen, the Duke of Silesia and many of the nobles of Hungary and Bohemia, to hear the delegates from Poland and Lithuania, Zbigniew of Oleśnica and Nicholas Cebulka. These begin by reminding King Sigismund of the old alliance between him and King Władysław, which the latter has never broken, though this is what Sigismund has done in his unfair award. They further accuse the King of wrongly including Samogitia and Sudavia, as these are not mentioned in his terms of reference. At this point the King interrupts them to say that this is something he did not, and could not, have known. Next they remind the King of the help given him in his dealings with the Turks and of the money lent him so that he could ransom his knights. After this, the Grand-duke's delegate, Nicholas, expresses the hope that he will not give offence, when he stresses that the Grand-duke never considered friendship with him nor of concluding an alliance with him, whom he always suspected of being an enemy, and that he had strongly advised Władysław of Poland to stick to those friends he already had; thus the alliance was not of the Grand-duke's choosing but made to please the King of Poland, even so it had always been observed. The envoy then goes on to explain that what his lord must do is what King Władysław has already done, renounce the pact with Hungary and from now on treat King Sigismund as his enemy. It is with difficulty that the furious Sigismund is restrained from having the two envoys drowned. Then, on the last day of January, the two envoys are told that King Sigismund will send special envoys to King Władysław to answer his main objections. The two Poles then return to Jedlna, where Władysław is staying and render a full report. The King's councillors are unanimous in recommending that the King neither accept nor obey the award; yet, in the end, it is decided that, since the King earlier agreed to abide by the King of Hungary's award, he must let it be seen that he is doing so and must just hope that in due course something may turn up that will amount to a breach on the part of the Order, after which the King will be entitled to have recourse to force.

While King Sigismund is still in Wrocław, Czenko of Wartenberg, Ulrich of Rožembork and other nobles of Bohemia come and, after initial talks in private, publicly invite him to come to their country and rule it as the rightful heir. King Sigismund wants to humiliate the Czechs who, so far, have just rebelled against him, so he tells them that he will only come to Prague if the city walls are breached, so that he and his army can enter, not through a gate, but triumphantly through a breach in the wall; also that all weapons in the city of whatever kind are first to be deposited with his captain in the castle. He, then, beheads twenty-three of the more eminent citizens of Wrocław, who, some years previously, out of spite executed the city councillors, even though these had managed the city's affairs competently. Appalled by these cruelties, the Czech delegates return home and themselves raise the standard of revolt and inform King Sigismund that they will not have him as their king, even if he withdraws his previous stipulations. As a token of rebellion they return the symbol of their alliance, a dragon on a large cross, while many of them sign a threatening open letter. King Sigismund then proclaims an expedition against the Czechs, with the object of crushing the rebellion by force of arms, and orders the dukes of Germany, Silesia and others to take part in it. The captain of Prague Castle, Czenko of Wartenberg, well rewarded for his actions, now orders that Sigismund is not to be granted admittance, since he is an inveterate enemy of the Slavonic race and has no other aim than to destroy their kingdom and their language, and also because it was he who pawned Stara Marchia to the Teutonic Knights, tore the Mark of Brandenburg from the Bohemian crown and, at the Council in Constance, to the nation's shame, had Jan Hus and Hieronymus burned at the stake, and has sought by every means to destroy the teachings in which the Czechs believe.

On the first Sunday in Lent, two envoys from King Sigismund arrive in Iłża to give his reply to the Polish envoys' speech in Wrocław; this is that Sigismund was ignorant of the facts adduced and could not have known them. The Hungarians are then reminded that their King had not come to Wrocław a fortnight in advance, as he had promised, but had only arrived at midnight on the actual day and neither made any attempt to acquaint himself with the facts nor given himself time to do so. The Hungarians then again assert that their King is prepared to correct his unfair verdict and prove himself a just arbitrator. King Władysław accepts this at its face value and sends to Albert Jastrzębiec, Bishop of Cracow, and the other Polish delegates, who are still in Wrocław and tells them to demand correction of the king's verdict in the place, where it was originally pronounced. King Sigismund, however, denies that his envoys were entitled to promise that he would alter his verdict and insists that, without the agreement of both sides, it would not be fitting for him to alter his award, a written copy of which, with his seal attached, was already in the hands of the Knights. He insists that it would shame him as King and Emperor to do this.

King Władysław has moved by the usual stages to Wielkopolska to which Albert the Bishop of Cracow and the other delegates now go to make their report. When the King realizes that there is really no hope of Sigismund changing his award, he vents all his ire on the Bishop, accusing him of signing the text of the award against his orders. The Bishop is able to refute the accusation. Now, Queen Elizabeth persuades the King to make Jan, her son by her previous marriage to Vincent of Granow, a castellan. When the requisite document is drawn up, the Bishop of Cracow objects to the appointment most vigorously and the voivode of Cracow, John of Pilcza, refuses to set the royal seal on it. The appointment is withdrawn. The Queen is furious and in the privacy of their bedchamber incites her husband against the Bishop. Some evil men encourage the King to deprive the

Bishop of the royal seal. Other honest and pious councillors consider this stupid and tell the King that, if the Bishop is at fault, the matter must be dealt with legally and that he should be arraigned before the general assembly to be held in Łęczyca on St. James's Day.

The King continues his progress through Wieluń, Sieradz and Brodnica and reaches Kalisz, where he spends Easter and then continues to Kujawy. When he reaches Brześć on the eve of Ascension Day, he is told that the Queen has died in Cracow and been buried in the cathedral there. The news delights the Court and the whole country. People attend the funeral ceremonies in their Sunday best, cheering and laughing.

The King now sends Zbigniew Oleśnicki prior of St. Florian and the Voivode of Włocławek, Janusz of Kościeliec, to Toruń to collect the 12,500 Hungarian florins awarded to him by the Wrocław arbitration. The Knights produce a few thousand florins in gold and propose to pay the rest in pure silver; this the Poles, refuse to accept, seeing the Knights' failure to adhere to the terms of the award as the breach the King wants, and leave Toruń on the day after the due date, being accompanied to their ships by the Knights begging them to accept silver. The King receives the good news in Brześć. This failure on the part of the Knights provides a minor, but not insignificant pretext for war, and justifies the King in bringing troops to Brześć in the summer.

The King moves from Brześć to Kowale, where Czenko of Wartenberg, Ulrich of Rożembork and Werner of Rankor, envoys of the Bohemian barons, come to him. After presenting their letters of authority, they tell him that King Sigismund has scorned their offer of the crown of Bohemia and in such terms that they could never submit to his rule, and that they have now chosen King Władysław as their king and ruler and beg him not to delay in taking over the government of their country. The King receives the offer graciously and promises a reply after he has consulted his councillors. He then goes to Łęczyca to attend the assembly called for St. James's Day, at which he publicly accuses the Bishop of Cracow, the Marshal of Poland, Zbigniew of Brzezia, and Janusz of Tuliszkowo, Castellan of Kalisz, of agreeing to King Sigismund's award against his orders. The three have many supporters among those present and there is quite a commotion; indeed, the situation becomes so threatening that the members of the tribunal leave their seats. Fighting breaks out in the castle and spreads to the knights in the town itself. A big crowd arms itself and advances on the castle. There is a great scramble and much shouting. The King takes refuge in the royal apartments above the gate. There would have been fatalities had not the castle gate been shut and the drawbridge hauled up. The commotion subsides and in the end the King is reconciled with Bishop Albert and the others. The assembly proceeds to discuss the offer of the crown of Bohemia. The decision is that the King cannot accept, because of the heresy that blemishes so many of the Czechs and also because there is a legitimate heir to the throne in Sigismund of Hungary. However, it is agreed that the King should not give the Czechs a straight answer, but prevaricate, so that Sigismund, who appears to be Poland's mortal enemy, may be worried by this indecision and stop harming Poland.

From the Belgian part of France there comes a certain man of Picardy, who quickly wins over to his practices many of the country's men and women; who then go about naked and call themselves Adamites. The man from Picardy calls himself a son of God and tells his followers to call him Adam. They are allowed to swap partners, but not without first consulting him. These Adamites settle on an island in the River Luznica, from which they proceed to rob and even murder the neighbouring peasants. Jan Žižka, though himself a transgressor, is disgusted by the Adamites and sends a small force to occupy their island and kill all of them but two, from whom he hopes to extract details of their practices. Those to be killed sing and smile as they are taken to the stake and burned.

King Sigismund assembles a large army at Wrocław and, about the Feast of St. John the Baptist, invades Bohemia through Świdnica and Kłodzko. He lays siege to Prague on the assumption that, if he captures that city, the other towns will capitulate. The siege is prosecuted for six weeks, but so ineffectually that the citizens never close the gates and make frequent sorties by day and night to harass the besiegers. They also send for Žižka and give him supreme command. He lays siege to Vyšehrad castle, which supports King Sigismund. The latter, realizing that he is not going to capture Prague, forces his way into the castle of St. Václav and has the Archbishop of Prague, Conrad of Westphalia, anoint and crown him King of Bohemia. After his coronation, disgusted by his troops' demands for their pay, the King abandons the siege of Prague, removes from Karlstein castle the Holy Lance and Nail of the True Cross and all the other sacred relics, jewels, treasure and books that are stored there and takes them back to Hungary. (In the course of time his extravagance will force him to sell all these treasures, as he does the royal crown of Bohemia.) From now on he styles himself King of Bohemia. With Sigismund gone, the citizens of Prague attack Vyšehrad castle, while Žižka starts demolishing churches, which, he says, should not be dedicated to anyone but God. When he captures a shrine or any place occupied by the Faithful, he kills them all, or burns them at the stake, priests, men, women and children. Finally, the Vyšehrad garrison, suffering more and more from hunger and shortages of everything, indeed, reduced to eating horse-flesh, agrees to surrender on a certain date, unless by then Sigismund has rescued them.

Back in Wolborz, King Władysław receives a new Czech delegation under Hinek of Waldstein, which, after explaining how Sigismund refused their offer of the crown and then invaded and ravaged their country, and, then when he withdrew, took with him the Czech crown, the bones and relics of their saints, their treasures, books and jewels, so that they cannot consider such a person worthy of being their king, thus they are again offering the crown to Władysław, on condition that he promises to protect them from raids by their neighbours and to practice the articles of their faith: communion in both kinds, public confession of sins, freedom for all to preach the word of God, and forbidding churches and clergy to have temporal possessions. They warn the King that, should he be unable to accept the throne of Bohemia, he will not be able to rule Poland in peace, for King Sigismund, having destroyed Bohemia, will seek to do the same to Poland. Žižka and his adherents do not support this offer, for they maintain that free people should not have a king, but live together in freedom, obeying laws rather than kings.

Replying, the King tells the Czechs, that he intends to do all that he can to end the quarrel between them and King Sigismund, and that he cannot answer their proposal until he has consulted the Grand-duke Alexander, to whom he has sent express messengers requesting a meeting. He suggests that Hinek and Simon the Prague councillor should go to Lithuania and put the matter to the Grand-duke, and that the others, who are under the interdict the Pope imposed on all Czech heretics, should go to Niepołomice, where they will be well looked after, but not allowed to mingle with the Faithful, thus maintaining the interdict.

King Sigismund, having assembled a huge army to relieve Vyšehrad, himself leads it there and pitches camp near the castle. The citizens of Prague, convinced that Sigismund will try to end the siege, seeking to defeat him by cunning rather than by force of arms have dug pits and trenches in all the approaches to the castle and then covered these with branches and sand to make them invisible to any who might tread on them. Thus, when Sigismund's troops prepare to attack and press forward eagerly, they fall into a trap in which many are killed, including the flower of Czech chivalry. King Sigismund, appalled, withdraws to Hungary, whereupon Vyšehrad surrenders.

Žižka burns five rich monasteries in Moravia and installs a garrison in the monastery at Kladrov, which has good fortifications and on which Sigismund now advances; yet, when Žižka moves against him, the King retreats shamefully and withdraws from Bohemia altogether. Žižka now returns to Pilsen, and, in later fighting, loses his second eye, yet he does not give up his command because of that. Thus does a blind people follow a blind leader.

King Władysław reaches Niepołomice on St. Martin's Day, and here a messenger informs him of the disastrous defeat of King Sigismund at Prague. The Czech offer is further discussed, but no one is favour of the King taking on Bohemia with its heretics, rebellions and domestic strife, especially as there is a legal heir in the person of King Sigismund. So, the King tells the Czech delegates that the kingdom of Poland is enough for him, and that he cannot accept Bohemia whose articles of faith are condemned by the Catholic church. The delegates depart and the King moves on to Lithuania, where he spends the entire winter.

A.D. 1421

The King engages in hunting after Christmas.

There now arises the question of a husband for the King's daughter, Jadwiga. When Sędziwój of Ostroróg, the Voivode of Poznań, was in Brandenburg arranging for the release of certain Polish knights taken prisoner during the fighting between Frederick Margrave of Brandenburg and the Dukes of Szczecin, the Margrave raised the subject of such a marriage, promising to give Władysław every assistance against Poland's enemies, particularly the Knights in Prussia, and to incorporate certain of his lands into the Kingdom of Poland in perpetuity, if Władysław would allow his daughter to marry the Margrave's eldest son, Frederick. Having examined the proposal, the Voivode sends a special messenger to the King in Lithuania suggesting a quick meeting between the King and the Margrave. The King replies that he is not declining the proposal, but must first discuss it with the Grand-duke, and suggests meeting the Margrave in Cracow shortly after Easter. During Carnival the King and the Grand-duke receive yet another Czech delegation, which includes Peter, the Englishman who infected the Czechs with the false English confession, and several others. These renew the Czechs' request that Władysław assume the crown of Bohemia, or, should he still decline it, that the Grand-duke should do so instead. The Czechs are given no definite answer; in fact they are kept guessing for a whole year. The King makes his usual progress back to Poland, now accompanied by the Czech delegation, which is then quartered in Niepołomice to await the Grand-duke's decision.

The King gets to Cracow on Palm Sunday, where the Margrave of Brandenburg arrives a day or two later, the King going out as far as Prądnik to meet him. The discussions last a fortnight, at the end of which it is agreed that the Margrave's eldest son, Frederick, and the King's daughter, Jadwiga, should marry, the conditions being detailed in a special document. These are that, should Władysław leave no male heir, Frederick and Jadwiga are to have the Kingdom of Poland and that Saxony will be incorporated into Poland, as will Lubusz, previously so unjustly detached from it. Should the King have a son, he will give the Princess 100,000 florins as her dowry. Some Poles would have preferred to see Jadwiga marry Bogusław, the Duke of Słupsk, but that idea was rejected as the naval support that the Duke of Słupsk and his ally the King of Denmark could offer would be of less benefit to Poland than the help the Margrave could provide. The King, having decided on a summer campaign against the Knights, now asks the Margrave for assistance, only to be told that the Margrave cannot afford to give any this year and, instead, suggests concluding a twelve-month truce, which will give them time to seek ways of overcoming the Knights without recourse to force, perhaps reducing them so that they will do whatever the King orders, even carting their own excrement. The King accepts the suggestion as though it were offered in good faith and, through Sigismund of Hungary, arranges a truce for one year. So, King and Margrave exchange lavish gifts and the Margrave departs, delighted with what he has achieved.

On the Feast of St. John the Baptist the King gives audience to a Burgundian knight, William de Lannoy, who is on his way to the Holy Land and has a letter of recommendation from King Henry of England. He presents the King with a piece of satin interwoven with gold, an iron helm with a magnificent golden crest, two English bows, and various other gifts and requests safe passage through the King's territory. The King not only grants this, but gives him a letter of recommendation to the Turkish Sultan, thanks to which the Sultan's servants escort de Lannoy all the way from Constantinople to Jerusalem.

The Bohemian question is debated again during the assembly held in Lublin, with the result that the Czechs are told that neither the King nor the Grand-duke can consider accepting the crown of Bohemia as long as there is a legitimate heir; but that, should Sigismund renounce his claim and the Czechs give up their false doctrines, they might reconsider the matter. Władysław now sends two envoys to King Sigismund, whom they find in Trnava, to tell him that he and the Grand-duke consider it their most important task to restore peace to Bohemia and cleanse it of heresy; and to ask whether, in the event of Sigismund refusing the throne, he would allow them to try to restore peace there and banish heresy, if need be, by force of arms; but, since Sigismund has failed to keep his promise to help Poland against the Knights, Władysław cannot in future rely on what the other swears to do, but only on what he does, so he proposes that they now intervene to restore peace and the true faith to Bohemia, after which they will recognize Sigismund's authority there. Should they not succeed, Władysław promises to assist Sigismund militarily against the Czechs in return for armed assistance against the Knights, which he is already bound by treaty to provide; but only on condition that, if together they are successful, Sigismund will assign to him the whole of Silesia, and that, if Sigismund helps Władysław destroy the Knights, the two kings will share Prussia in proportion to the size of the forces each contributes, once Pomerania, Chełm and Michałów have been restored to Polish sovereignty. If these conditions are fulfilled and Sigismund keeps his promises, Władysław will return Silesia to King Sigismund, otherwise it will remain for ever under Polish rule. Sigismund must realize that Władysław is not so naive as to take the other's words and promises at their face value. Sigismund gives his reply the next day. This is that he does not consider it right to use Silesia as surety for fulfilling his obligations; instead, he proposes that Władysław marry Sigismund's only daughter, Elizabeth, who will have two kingdoms as her dowry, for, on her father's death, she will inherit not only Silesia, which Władysław wants, but the kingdoms of Hungary and Bohemia as well, for Sigismund has no other children, nor will he have any—the envoys, he says, can ask his wife about that!—Should Władysław consider the eleven-year old Elizabeth too young to be his wife, Sigismund proposes that, instead, he should marry Sigismund's sister-in-law, Offka, widow of his brother Václav, who is as dear to him as a daughter and whose dowry will be Silesia and 100,000 florins. The King's envoys then go to Bratislava to see Queen Offka and check her age and looks. They have several days of friendly talks with her, before they return to Poland, laden with gifts, and report to the King. The King postpones his decision until after the general assembly on St. Martin's Day, at which he will discuss the offer with his councillors and the Grand-duke, who is being informed of it by a special messenger, who is also to have a look at Sonka the daughter of the Duke of Kiev, niece of the Grand-duke, who has suggested her as an alternative bride.

At the assembly in Niepołomice it is decided that the King should accept Queen Ofka and her dowry, and Zawisza of Garbów is sent to Hungary to make the necessary arrangements. When he gets there, King Sigismund is just setting out with an army to invade Bohemia and asks that the matter be held over until his return. Zawisza, considering it shameful to do nothing, accompanies the King's great army of Hungarians, Czechs, Poles, Germans and others, which first advances on the town of Gora and captures it at the first assault. After this, many of the Czechs and Germans, who oppose the heresy, join the King's army. Meanwhile, the heretics' army, composed largely of debtors and people accustomed to live by robbery, under its blind commander, Žižka, having assembled a great number of waggons, advances on Sigismund's much larger army, which effectively surrounds it in a closed ring. The heretics expect an assault at any moment, but when this does not happen, they decide to attack themselves. They find the King's army in loose formation with men wandering about the fields and these scatter as they are attacked, those who dare fight being either killed or taken prisoner. The King withdraws with the bulk of his troops into Niemecki Brod, leaving the heretics to capture his camp, waggons and much plunder. The heretics then lay siege to Niemecki Brod, thinking the King to be there still, but he has already left. Zawisza could have left with him, but he considered it his duty to stay with the other knights and so, when, thanks to the treachery of some of its citizens, the town is taken, he is captured and carried off to Prague with the others, and there endures a long and grievous captivity. Because of all this, the idea of King Władysław marrying Queen Offka is not taken any further.

Žižka's repute is now greater than ever. He rages against the Catholics and the Church. He will no longer tolerate idols or pictures of saints, nor will he allow anyone in canonicals to conduct a service. He sets fire to Niemecki Brod, which then remains deserted, without a single inhabitant, for fourteen years.

King Władysław sends two envoys, Master Paul, canon of Cracow, and Jacob of Paravesino, to Pope Martin V to renew his claim that the Teutonic Knights must return Pomerania, Chełm and Michałów to him. The two are provided with the necessary money from the royal treasury. As a result of their insistence, the Pope sends a nuncio, Anthony Zeno, a Doctor of canon and civil law, to Poland to interrogate witnesses.

The King goes to Lithuania to hunt and stays there until Christmas.

The councillors of the city of Prague decide that they can no longer tolerate the arrogance of an apostate Premonstratensian monk called Jan, who, ready for any villainy, has by his gift of oratory been inciting people to crazy deeds; so, now, they summon him to the Town Hall, ostensibly to discuss public affairs, but, as soon as he and some companions, enter the hall, they are run through with swords. The City Fathers then return to their homes, as if nothing had happened, confident that peace and quiet will now reign. However, when the news of what has happened spreads, there is an outcry; the Town Hall is stormed and eleven of the city councillors are killed. The Charles University is plundered and its entire library scattered. Some women, who considered Jan a saint, gather up his head and for many days go round the churches and public places, weeping and crying out that this is the head of a holy man who has died for the truth and the traditions of his fathers. The head is finally anointed with fragrant unguents and placed with the sacred relics, where it is revered as the head of a famous saint.

A.D. 1422

King Władysław goes to Wigry after Christmas for more hunting. When, to his delight, the Grand-duke hears that Sigismund's army has been defeated and Władysław's envoy taken prisoner, he increases his pressure on Władysław and finally gains his agreement to his marrying the Grand-duke's niece, Sonka. She has no dowry, and all the King's advisors are against the idea, preferring the advantages of marriage to Queen Offka, though at the same time considering it quite unnecessary for their decrepit King to remarry at all. Nevertheless, on February 24, King Władysław weds the young Sonka, formerly of the Greek Church, but having now accepted the Roman rites and been baptized Sophia. Her looks are better than her manners.

The King and his bride go to Lida, where they find the papal nuncio, Anthony Zeno, who has come to hear witnesses and scrutinize the documentary evidence in Poland's dispute with the Knights. The King and the Grand-duke ply the nuncio with splendid gifts, which he is forbidden to accept, whatever their value. They then set out for Cracow. On the way there, the King receives an envoy from the Duke of Berg, a place of which he has never even heard, so remote it is. (In fact it lies between Burgundy and Germany.) The envoy has come to ask the King to accept the Duke as his vassal. The King courteously declines the offer on the grounds that he could not protect his liege as he should, nor could the Duke perform his feudal duties to his king; so the envoy is dismissed and departs, laden with gifts.

Having spent some weeks in Cracow, the King moves on to Wielkopolska, leaving his wife and daughter in Cracow, to which the papal nuncio now summons the witnesses he wishes to interrogate. This done and the relevant documents scrutinized, the nuncio himself goes to Wielkopolska to visit its cathedral churches, colleges and monasteries and to question witnesses too advanced in years to go to him. Meanwhile, the King has sent Nicholas Archbishop of Gniezno and Andrew Łaskarz, Bishop of Poznań, a demand for the 5000 florins the Pope has assigned to him from the Polish clergy. After consulting the other bishops, the two tell the King that they cannot accept the Pope's award, because it is so grievous an imposition that they are afraid of its consequences, and also because the award was made conditional on the King sending an expedition against the Czech heretics, which he has not done. The matter is then allowed to drop.

On April 19, the King reaches Radziejów, to which John the Bishop of Lubusz and some eminent knights of Brandenburg have brought their eight-year old margrave, Frederick, Princess Jadwiga's future husband, to present him to his father-in-law. The King receives him graciously and entrusts him and his upbringing jointly to the Deaon of Sandomierz and the knight Peter of Chełm. The boy is to reside at Court and be seated on the King's right at table, so that the Polish nobles may get to know their future king.

The Grand-duke equips an army and, with the King's approval, sends it under Zygmunt Korybut into Bohemia in order to take possession of the country in the name of the Grand-duke. King Sigismund is, at the time, trying to capture the town and fort of Ostrov in Moravia. Now, afraid lest the Lithuanians attack him, he destroys all his siege engines, raises the siege and withdraws to Hungary, furious with both Władysław and the Grand-duke. Zygmunt Korybut then marches into Moravia and attacks Unczów, which is well defended both by its position and its walls, yet he captures it without difficulty and allows his troops to plunder it. He then moves on to Prague, where he is received with sincere delight by most of the Czech nobility and by the people of Prague, who present him with the keys of the city and its two castles. Within a short time, he has improved conditions quite considerably. He is gracious to the nobility and to all who wish to live in peace and quiet, but harsh to rebels and criminals. He decides to lay siege to Karlstein castle because of the documents and charters relative to Bohemia that have been deposited there.

The castle is well defended by a garrison of 400 put there by King Sigismund. The siege lasts six months, during which the castle is assaulted day and night and bombarded with great stones. When these appear to have had no effect, close on two thousand containers of human excrement and corpses are hurled over the walls and the stench of these causes the teeth of the defenders to fall out. This continues all winter, but then the besieged secretly obtain medicine from Prague, thanks to which their teeth are saved. Then the Margrave of Brandenburg, Frederick, invades the country and forces the besiegers to abandon the siege.

King Władysław spends Whitsun in Wrocław, to which a number of his prelates and nobles come to urge him to renew or extend the truce with the Knights, which is due to expire on St. Margaret's Day. Such, too, is the advice of the papal nuncio, who has accompanied the King from Cracow and who now writes to the Knights advising them to agree to a renewal and to arrange for the two sides to meet to discuss it. Thanks to the efforts of Anthony Zeno the nuncio a truce is agreed in principle, but when the details are discussed, at the instigation of King Sigismund, the Knights demand the insertion of a new clause to the effect that the truce shall become null and void should this be ordered by either the Emperor or the Holy See. The Poles know of this in advance, for a man disguised as a beggar, who was travelling through Poland on his way to Prussia, had fallen ill in Konin and, as he lay dying, had asked that his beggar's rags be sent to the Commander at Toruń. The local tax-collector, Gnero of Konin, reported this to the King's secretary, Oleśnicki, who ordered a search for the rags, which had already been distributed among other beggars. They were, however, traced and in them was found a letter from King Sigismund, in which he told the Teutonic Knights that almost the whole of the Polish army was in Bohemia with Zygmunt Korybut, so that this would be an excellent opportunity for the Knights, once the document had been signed, to break off the truce on his orders and attack Poland. When the Knights now refuse to sign the truce without this new clause to which the Poles will not agree, the two sides part with mutual recrimination. King Sigismund's letter is then shown to the papal nuncio.

Now that it is obvious that there is no possibility of peace with the Knights, all the King's councillors agree to an expedition against Prussia, so letters are sent to the Grand-duke and the other dukes and the knights of Poland telling them to be ready by St. James's Day. The nuncio, having now examined all the documents and heard the witnesses, summons the King and the Master and the Order to come to Głogów on the Feast of St. John the Baptist to hear his award. When the Silesian dukes close Głogów to him, so as to demonstrate their support for the Knights, he places an interdict on the town and so compels them to give him access. However, when the time comes for him to announce his award, which is that Pomerania, Chełm and Michałów have been unjustly torn from the kingdom of Poland, he is prevented from doing so by special order of Pope Martin, who intervenes on behalf of the Knights at the instigation of King Sigismund. The nuncio now returns to Rome to make a detailed report on the justness of King Władysław's case. The Knights, afraid lest the Pope's final award go against them, bribe King Sigismund to ensure that King Władysław's claims are never allowed.

King Władysław arrives in Wolborz on the Feast of the Visitation and there graciously receives the Duke of Mecklenburg, who promises him help against the Knights, a promise which he puts in writing, and is then dismissed with gifts. The King moves the army from Wolborz to Czerwińsk, where he is intending to cross the Vistula, and here he is joined by the army from Wielkopolska. The next day the entire force crosses the river on a pontoon bridge and a day later is joined by the Grand-duke with his army. On the last day but one of July the great army advances into enemy territory and camps beside Lake Lidzbarkskie Wielkie. On August 1, arrayed as if the enemy were already in sight, the army advances on Lubawa, prepared to be engaged by the enemy at any moment. The Knights' army, commanded by Ulrich Czanger, Marshal of Prussia, consists of their own forces and mercenaries. Ulrich is determined to try his luck and takes up position on a stretch of grassland surrounded by ditches near the castle of Lubawa, which is itself surrounded by woods, which hide the Knights' army so effectively that for a long time the King's scouts are unable to discover where the enemy is. Both sides are eager to do battle, but Ulrich who thinks that the Poles are the weaker, is restrained from launching an immediate attack by an experienced Silesian knight, Conrad Niemcza, who insists that he first establish the strength of the enemy. So, the knight and Ulrich mount their coursers and ride out to survey the scene. They see Poles everywhere, like locusts, so many of them that they cannot assess their number. Dismayed, they ride back and order the Knights to withdraw into castles, to do which they have to cross the river Drwęca, which they do, destroying the bridge behind them.

The King spends the night in a wood two miles from Lubawa and, the next day moves on a mile and a half and then halts for two days, while he tries to establish where the Knights' army has got to. Learning that it is has dispersed in various directions, the King moves his army closer to the town and fort of Lubawa and spends four days trying to capture them, but when he learns that both belong to the bishopric of Chełmno, he desists and moves to the Drwęca, where the enemy tries with bullets, arrows and other means to stop him crossing, but fails to do so. The first squadron across the river drives the enemy back, kills and captures many of them. The rest of the army then crosses between the fort at Bratian and the bridge that had been destroyed, and pitches camp a mile further on. Many of the King's men roam about in search of booty, some even going as far as Rie-

senburg, nine miles away, which they assault and capture, despite its stout walls and favourable position. They collect everything worth having and then set fire to the town, in which is Chełm
cathedral, the walls of which collapse.

On St. Laurence's Day, the King pitches camp beside a lake near a burned-out village. The
next day he moves on to the River Osa and camps there. Here a messenger from Peter of Zeech
Bishop of Corbavia, who has been sent to him by King Sigismund, arrives to tell him that the
Bishop is afraid to continue his journey, because of the soldiers who are everywhere laying the
country waste, as, indeed, they have been ordered to do. The messenger has been brought from
Malbork by some Polish prisoners from there, and he is now sent back together with a Pole and a
Lithuanian, who finally bring the Bishop safely to the King.

The army reaches the great lake on the eve of the Assumption and rests there for two days, because it is a holy day. The next day it advances on Golub, which it attacks and easily captures. The
troops are allowed to sack it. During the assault, a knight from Meissen fighting with the King is hit
by a stone as he leans against the wall of a tower and is killed. The King now lays siege to Golub
castle on its eminence outside the town and subjects it to a severe bombardment by his big guns. On
August 12 the King's knights launch an attack, which is stoutly resisted by the garrison of Silesians
and troops from Meissen; but, even so, they have to set fire to the lower fort, even though that kills
their best horses which are stabled there, so as to deny it to the enemy. In the end they have to surrender the upper fort, too, this having been considerably weakened by the King's siege engines.
Fifteen of the Order's knights are killed in the fighting, as are forty mercenaries. With great reverence the Holy Sacrament is removed at night from the castle and taken by candlelight to the tent of
Zbigniew Oleśnicki, Prior of St. Florian, for use the following day. The town's tower, the tallest
and stoutest of its buildings, having been undermined, topples into the river with a great roar, its
bulk filling the river bed and for a time hindering the river's flow.

While the King is besieging Golub, King Sigismund's envoy, Bishop Zeech, arrives and asks
for an audience with the King, the Grand-duke and their councillors, to whom he presents a letter in
which his king expresses surprise at Władysław's breach of their pact by ravaging part of his territory and calls upon Władysław to withdraw Zygmunt Korybut and his entire army from Bohemia
and forbid him to lend assistance to the heretics. If, he writes, Władysław considers that he has suffered hurt, he suggests that they should submit the matter to the arbitration of mutual friends. He
begs the King, as earnestly as he can, to withdraw from the territory of the Order and cease devastating it; while if the Order has been guilty of harming the King, King Sigismund, under whose
authority the Order comes, will see justice done. The King and the Grand-duke give their answer
the next day. This expresses surprise at Sigismund being surprised after giving so unjust an award
without deigning to consider Władysław's claims, a thing even the Scythians would consider unfair. Władysław complains that Sigismund has deprived him of his rightful inheritance, that the
Order has still not paid the money awarded against it, nor destroyed the castles it was ordered to demolish, nor yet returned occupied territory, because of which Władysław has had at great expense
to refer the matter to the Holy See, whose award Sigismund has blocked. Since then, Władysław
has tried to renew the truce, but again his efforts have been nullified by King Sigismund's letter, the
original of which Władysław now returns to him, a King on whose word and promises Władysław
can no longer rely. Władysław points out that it was not he who sent Zygmunt Korybut to Bohemia, a statement the Grand-duke confirms. With this answer the Bishop returns to Malbork and
thence to Hungary. He realizes that Władysław and his councillors have reason to be angry and are
not going to give up the war, especially as they are getting the better of the enemy.

The Voivode of Moldavia's Walachians, some 400 strong, sent to help King Władysław, get
as far as Malbork in their search for loot and provisions and there are attacked by knights from the
garrison. Seeing that the enemy are stronger than they, the Walachians withdraw into a nearby

wood and dismount, for they consider it easier to fight on foot. They then camouflage themselves with leaves and branches as is their habit. The Knights, thinking that the Walachians have really run away, hasten after them into the wood, where they are showered with arrows, which wound and kill both men and horses. This disposes of the first file and the rest are forced to retreat. The Walachians then return to the Polish camp laden with booty and with a number of prisoners, some Knights of the Order and some mercenary knights, whom they hand over to King Władysław.

In order to protect Kujawy from being raided from Nieszawa, which is in the hands of the Order, the King installs the starosta of Brześć, Andrew Brochocki, there with a force of Kujawian knights and those of Matthew of Łabiszyn voivode of Brześć and Janusz of Kościeliec voivode of Włoclawek, who have orders to obey the starosta. The two voivodes consider this subordination a slur on their abilities and leave the camp with their men, ostensibly to fetch provisions from home. The starosta, thus weakened, doubles his sentries as a precaution. The Knights, learning from their scouts what has happened and how few are left in the camp, assemble a force of 800 horse and prepare to make a night attack on the camp, the rear of which they expect to find unguarded. So, on September 7, they move up in silence and manage to kill the first sentry, but a second escapes them and shouts out that the enemy are there and this alerts a third sentry, who raises the alarm. The starosta jumps from his bed, puts his armour on over his bare flesh and runs at the enemy, who have just reached the tents. Thus, with God's help—for the starosta is a virtuous and pious man—the attackers are cut down or forced to run. Not knowing the lie of the land, the Knights straggle all over the place in the dark and many of them are captured or killed by the peasants. The vice commander of Toruń, twelve of the Brethren and some other knights are among those captured, and they are incarcerated in Brześć.

In one attempt to storm Kowale, the Polish knights, having broken through the first line of defence, find themselves falling into a ditch which has been planted with sharpened stakes and then covered over with straw, to which the garrison sets fire as soon as it sees the enemy floundering there, so that few of the attackers escape death or capture. One who does escape is the Castellan of Kamieniec, he who, earlier, had lost the fort at Drahim, though this was retaken shortly afterwards by Paul Wasznik, who, having a bedroom in a corner of the castle, in which he hid from the enemy, was later able to let down hunting nets and pull up a number of Poles, with whose help he recaptured the fort.

Abandoning the attempt on Kowale, Władysław moves towards Toruń, but on the Saturday after the Feast of St. Giles he drops his plan to attack it, because plague is rife there, and, instead, has his troops destroy the vineyards round the city and burn whatever they can. He then withdraws and moves into Chełmno territory intending to ravage it. He has provisions brought overland from Poland by waggon. The Knights, seeing that they are too weak to resist, send a delegation headed by Bishop Gerhard of Pomezania to treat for peace. The King agrees and moves from Chełmno town to Lake Melno to conclude arrangements. He appoints his own delegates who, like those of the Knights, have full powers to conclude peace, and this they finally do. On St. Stanislaw's Day, the King moves camp to near Brodnica and, after building seven bridges, crosses the Drwęca and again makes camp. Mass is heard, after which the standard-bearers in their harness all come and kneel before the King and hand back their standards. The King then allows the departure of the Grand-duke, with whom he exchanges the kiss of peace, and of the Dukes of Mazovia, and, finally, disbands his own army. Some Tatars attack the few remaining Poles, but are swiftly defeated; indeed, fifty of them are killed.

Now, the King goes to Poznań to render honour to the Holy Sacrament, as he has always done on his return from an expedition against the enemy, and from there to Mazovia and Wiskitki to hunt bison. After hunting, he goes to the monastery on Łysa Góra and from there to Opatów, where Queen Sophia joins him and together they progress in six stages to Niepołomice, where a conference is being held. The Hungarians attending the conference are afraid to go further than Lubicz, lest hostilities break out again, for the Prussian Knights have not yet honoured the terms of the peace concluded at Lake Melno, nor made the stipulated payment. The King sends an escort to fetch them, and himself goes to Lithuania. Since neither of the Kings is present, the two delegations reach no conclusions other than arranging for their kings to meet during Easter near Spisz to which the Order is to send plenipotentiaries to confirm the peace agreed at Lake Melno.

A.D. 1423

Nicholas Archbishop of Gniezno dies in Lubicz, he was the first to use the title of primate, which he obtained at Constance. Albert Jastrzębiec, Bishop of Cracow, is elected to succeed him in the see of Gniezno and Zbigniew Oleśnicki succeeds to the see of Cracow. King Władysław arrives in Nowy Sącz at the head of the Polish delegation on the Fourth Sunday in Lent. The two kings then ride out to meet each other. Meeting, they dismount, shake hands and embrace. They then return to Sromowiec, where the two delegations thresh things out and prepare fresh documents confirming a treaty of perpetual peace, which is finally signed in Kežmarok.

The new alliance having been signed and sealed, the King recalls Zygmunt Korybut from Bohemia, so as to protect King Sigismund's interests there; while the Master and the Order at last demolishes the fort at Nieszawa and fulfills the other conditions of the pact made at Lake Melno. Władysław then accepts an invitation for him and the Court to go to Lewocza, where they spend Easter being supplied by King Sigismund with all their needs.

The Polish delegation to the conference held in Wielona just before Ascension Day leaves its carriages and baggage at Grodno and is ferried across the Niemen and taken to where, hidden among trees, it finds quarters all prepared and stocked with all sorts of provisions. The conference is attended by the Grand-duke and the Prussian Master, Paul of Russdorff. After a week of discussions, conditions for peace are settled and the boundaries between Lithuania, Samogitia, Sudovia and Prussia agreed and marked by the erection of cairns and by accepted landmarks. The delegates then go to Troki, where the Grand-duke distributes gifts and they all return to Poland safe and sound.

King Władysław spends the Feast of the Assumption in Cracow with Bolesław Duke of Cieszyn, in whose honour there are ceremonial tourneys and knightly combats with lances.

In the absence of the King, a general assembly held in Warta agrees that the laws of property promulgated by Casimir II no longer meet the needs of the kingdom and new laws are derived from many and various sources, written down and added to the old laws of King Casimir: for example, that the widows of nobles and knights are to be content with their dowries and jointure, instead of, as before, being allowed to, or, by twisting the law, able to enjoy all their husband's property throughout their widowhood and use it according to their whim or desire to find a new husband.

Zygmunt Korybut, back from Bohemia, demands that the King grant him Dobrzyń in fee. The King's reply is that he cannot grant the kingdom's lands without the approval of his councillors and refers the request to the assembly, which rejects it. Zygmunt Korybut, incensed by the refusal, starts inciting certain knights to plot against the kingdom, and from then on, he is regarded as a dangerous pest. King Sigismund thinks that, with Korybut out of the way, the heretics in Bohemia will do what he tells them, but he is badly mistaken. Indeed, the heretics' army moves from Bohemia into neighbouring countries, especially Austria, looting and destroying. In order not to be left unsupported, Sigismund gives Moravia to his son-in-law, Albert Duke of Austria, although many of the Moravian nobles have already gone over to the false Hussite doctrine.

The coronation of Queen Sophia is fixed for the last Sunday before Lent. Invitations go to the kings of Hungary and Denmark, as well as to all neighbouring dukes and the Polish nobility. In the mean time the King goes to Lithuania, where he spends the winter hunting game with which to feed the coronation guests.

Ludwig Duke of Brzeg and Legnica founds the first Carthusian monastery in Poland.

A.D. 1424

The Grand-duke has been sent many invitations to the coronation, but he so hates the new Queen that he prefers not to attend. The first arrival is Eric, King of Denmark, who reaches Poznań immediately after Christmas and from there, escorted by the more eminent of the Polish nobles and without a safe conduct, travels to Poland and on to Hungary to visit King Sigismund before returning to Cracow in time for the coronation. King Sigismund delays his arrival, demanding a written safe-conduct, instead of which Władysław sends King Eric, Zbigniew Oleśnicki the Bishop of Cracow and the Marshal of Poland, Zbigniew of Brzezia, to escort him from the frontier. The two kings and Queen Barbara dine and spend the first night at Nowy Targ and, on the next day, continue to Myślenice, where they are received by King Władysław and conducted to Wieliczka. Here they dine together at a single table in the upper chamber and leave the same day for Cracow, where they are met outside the city by the prelates, dukes and nobles of near and distant countries with their retinues of varying sizes, as well as by the noble women and girls riding in carriages that glitter with gold. They are also greeted by Cardinal Branda, representing the Pope, and by Duke Korybut at the head of 500 mounted men. Queen Sophia receives Sigismund and his Queen on an eminence covered with rugs. The two queens then drive together in a superbly decorated coach to Cracow, where Queen Sophia conducts Queen Barbara to the apartments prepared for the royal couple, which include a painted bedroom. King Eric has the apartments on the floor above.

After the coronation, the three kings dine at one table, Sigismund sitting between Władysław on the right and Eric on his left. Cardinal Branda is seated on Władysław's right and then come the bishops in order of precedence; the eminent laymen are seated on King Eric's left. A protracted banquet is followed by dancing that continues late into the night. The following three days are devoted to tourneys and the nights to dancing. On the Friday, the three kings and the cardinal are the guests of Zawisza the Black, a knight yielding to none in Christendom in excellence.

While they are in Cracow the kings have confidential discussions about preserving peace and how to deal with the Hussite heretics. The kings of Hungary and Denmark try to persuade Władysław to cancel the betrothal of his daughter, Jadwiga, to Frederick the young son of the Margrave of Brandenburg and, instead, marry her to Bogusław, Duke of Słupsk, a near relative of Eric of Denmark. This is an attractive proposition, because it would add to Poland a number of peripheral territories to which the Duke is heir; but Władysław tells them that he cannot decide so important a matter without consulting the Grand-duke, so envoys are sent to the latter. Most of the King's councillors are against the betrothal being broken off and the King tells the Grand-duke that he leaves the decision to him. It is decided that the betrothal remains valid.

After a fortnight in Cracow, the two kings leave with many assurances of friendship and lavish presents of gold and silver vessels, jewels, horses and furs, and travel together to Hungary, whence King Eric continues to Jerusalem. Władysław remains in Cracow to assemble the 5000 men he has promised to send to help Sigismund.

On the Feast of the Blessed Virgin, King Władysław leaves for Wiślica, where the Czechs come to ask him to send them Zygmunt Korybut with a strong army, so that they can make him king. The King replies that he will neither send them Korybut nor assist them, until they have abandoned their false beliefs and reverted to the Catholic faith. If they refuse to do this, he can only treat them as enemies of Christianity and, as such, will send King Sigismund a strong force to help him wipe them out. At this time there was a Czech priest in Wiślica, and he now starts loudly praising the heretics; at the urgent request of Bishop Zbigniew the King has him turned out of the town and imprisoned.

His army now reinforced by contingents sent by King Eric and Peter, brother of the King of Portugal, King Sigismund is able to lay siege to Lutemberg in Moravia, but, since Žižka's second-in-command, the priest Procopius, entrusted with the defence of Moravia manages to send provisions in to the town, the siege is ineffective. Meanwhile, Žižka himself, confident of receiving help from the citizens of Prague, lays siege to the town of Usti, which is loyal to the Margrave of Meissen, who then assembles a force and goes to the help of the besieged. The two forces engage and for a long time the outcome is uncertain, but in the end blind Fortune favours the blind leader and gives victory to the heretics, and the town is captured and demolished.

This victory makes Žižka even more arrogant and hostile to the nobility. He imposes heavy tribute on the towns, and this makes the citizens of Prague seek the help of the nobles. The citizens and nobles combine to attack Žižka, who, seing himself outnumbered, withdraws into the mountains. Here he induces his enemies to accept battle in a narrow ravine, where thousands of them are killed and the rest routed. Žižka immediately recaptures Kutná Hora, which has just been rebuilt, burns it and then lays siege to Prague itself. In the end, the citizens of Prague and Žižka are reconciled thanks to the efforts of a most eloquent priest, John of Rokičan, a one-time follower of Jacobellus and a man of very humble origins.

King Sigismund, seeing how successful Žižka has been and how the fate of Bohemia seems to lie in his hands, secretly tries to win him over. He promises him complete authority over the whole country and the army, as well as a large annual income, if he will recognize Sigismund as his King and make the towns swear allegiance to him. Žižka, that blind old man, rogue, heretic and church-robber, accepts these conditions and sets out to meet the King and conclude arrangements, but dies of the plague before this can be done. When asked on his death bed, where he wishes to be buried, he orders his corpse to be skinned and then put out for the birds and animals, while his skin is to be used to make a drum, the sound of which will send the enemy fleeing. After Žižka's death, the army divides, each part continuing to fight the enemy on its own.

Zygmunt Korybut lets himself be tempted by the empty promises of the Czechs and, without the consent or orders of King Władysław, assembles a force of Poles, mostly men who have squandered their inheritance or burdened themselves with debt, or are avoiding a sentence imposed by a court, and with it invades Bohemia at Whitsun, hoping for an easy conquest. He and his men now start taking communion in both kinds, a thing formerly considered heretical. This encourages the rebellion of the heretical Czechs and casts suspicion on King Władysław, who again and again has to send to the Catholic kings and dukes disclaiming responsibility and justifying himself, and especially to King Sigismund to whom he sends the promised force of 5000 men-at-arms at the time and to the place agreed. When this force reaches Olomouc, Sigismund's son-in-law, Duke Albert of Austria, who is in command there, refuses to admit it on the grounds that he does not wish the two armies to mingle, but in reality because he considers the Poles' intentions suspect, because of the presence of Korybut in Austria. The Poles spend a fortnight encamped outside Olomouc, apprehensive lest the enemy attack them there and the Duke not come to their assistance, before they return to Poland. King Władysław punishes many of those who joined Korybut against his orders by confiscating their property, if they had any, if not, with permanent banishment and exile.

Returning to Cracow the King continues on to Ruthenia. While he is there, Queen Sophia gives birth to a son, their first. When he learns of this, the King sends his notary to Pope Martin V to inform him and to ask him to christen his son. The Pope is delighted with the news and loads the notary with gifts and sends others to Queen Sophia, velvets interwoven with gold thread. He also sends a special bull authorizing Zbigniew Bishop of Cracow to christen the babe in his name. Sigismund of Hungary, the Duke of Milan and many other heads of state send their representatives.

The King returns to Lithuania and spends the winter there, hunting, as the guest of the Grand-duke.

A.D. 1425

Władysław's first-born son is christened by Albert Jastrzębiec Archbishop of Gniezno and the bishops of Cracow and Poznań and given his father's name: Władysław. The Pope and King Sigismund send representatives, several neighbouring princes attend and the Master of the Teutonic Knights, Paul of Russdorff, sends Martin Kempnater the Grand Commander and Henry Hold the commander of Elbląg. The Grand-duke sends the babe a silver cradle which weighs 100 marks. After the christening the King goes to Wielkopolska and spends Easter in Kalisz, to which King Eric of Denmark comes on his way back from Jerusalem and spends several days there. Władysław then moves on to Poznań and other towns in Wielkopolska and so by the usual stages to Ruthenia to escape the plague, which has been raging throughout the kingdom all year, claiming many victims.

Cardinal Orsini, Bishop of Ostia, sends King Władysław and his Queen one of the nails used to nail Jesus to the cross. It is received in solemn procession and presented to Cracow cathedral.

A provincial synod in Łęczyca attended by all the bishops of the province of Gniezno, except Jacob bishop of Płock who is ill, unanimously votes to refuse to pay the 12,000 florins the Pope has allowed the King to collect from the Church in Poland for his campaign against the Czech heretics. The King, realizing that the Pope has contributed nothing from his own treasury and that to impose this impost on the Polish clergy will only vex them, stops demanding it and does nothing about the campaign he is supposed to lead in person against the Hussites. At this synod, the Archdeacon of Płock, Stanisław Pawłowski, speaking for his bishop, announces that the Pope's award to the King does not apply to the diocese of Płock, since that duchy and all the lands of Mazovia within the diocese of Płock, have their own independent dukes not subject to the kingdom of Poland or regarded as belonging to it and thus are not due to pay. When told of this, King Władysław is furious with his brother-in-law, Duke Siemowit, at whose suggestion the Archdeacon raised the objection, and at once announces a general assembly to be held in Brześć in Ruthenia on the Feast of St. Martin, which is to discuss how best to block the Duke of Mazovia's move.

This assembly is attended by the King, Queen Sophia, the Grand-duke of Lithuania and all the prelates, boyars and nobles of both countries, but not by the Duke of Mazovia, Siemowit, who sends delegates to explain that sickness prevents him attending. His absence means that the matter has to be postponed until later. At this assembly the Grand-duke tries to insist that the mill at Lubicz, demolished under the terms of the pact of perpetual peace entered into by Poland and the Knights, be returned to the Order, for he has promised to help the Prussian Master obtain the return of this potentially profitable mill. The Polish delegates explain that this is a matter they are not competent to decide, but which must await a general assembly.

The King and Queen leave Brześć and go to Lithuania, which the plague has not yet reached, intending to spend the winter there, hunting. However, the plague breaks out there in the middle of the winter and the royal couple and the Grand-duke seek refuge in the great forests, while the infant Władysław is sent to Chęciny castle, where he stays as long as the epidemic lasts. While the King and the Grand-duke are in Grodno, the Prussian Master, Paul of Russdorff, arrives and so pesters the Grand-duke for the surrender of Lubicz that the latter undertakes either to persuade Władysław to surrender the mill there or himself give the Master the territory of Połaga on the Gulf of Samogitia. Władysław yields to the entreaties of the Grand-duke and is prepared to hand the mill over provided his councillors do not disapprove, for in such matters he cannot decide without them.

Pope Martin V, considering that Władysław has been extravagant, rather than sensible, in the way he has been giving away castles, towns and villages instructs the Archbishop of Lwów to annul all these documents and deeds of gift and save Poland by pronouncing all such grants of land as null and void.

A.D. 1426

The King and Queen spend Christmas in Wilno; then, since the plague has died out, they decide to return to Poland; but, before they can do so, the King breaks a leg while hunting bear in the chase known as Białowieża and is taken to Chełmno. He spends Carnival and Lent in Krasnystaw to allow his leg to heal. It is, however, so painful that he is prevented from attending the assembly called to decide on the reply to be given to the Grand-duke's request that the mill at Lubicz be returned to the Knights. The reply agreed is that to do as requested would be a breach of the treaty with the Order, and that the Grand-duke is under no obligation to give Połaga, which is worth a hundred mills at Lubicz, to the Order instead. So, Władysław Oporowski doctor of canon law and the standard-bearer of Kujawy are sent to the Master of the Prussian Order to inform him of the decision and to point out that, were the mill to be returned, that would lead to a degree of discord between the Grand-duke and the King, and also that the Grand-duke cannot give away bits of Lithuania without the consent of the King of Poland. The Master insists that he never asked for the Grand-duke's help in getting the mill back, but he continues to badger him for this, not because he really needs the mill, but because its surrender would damage relations between the King and the Grand-duke.

His leg healed, the King goes by boat to Kujawy, and, at Whitsun, attends an assembly at Łęczyca, at which he is asked to confirm the rights and privileges of the nobles and to grant certain new ones, a move against which King Sigismund advises in a special message. The King refuses both requests, at which there is an outcry, and Zbigniew Bishop of Cracow produces an ordinance of the realm with the seals of its prelates and nobles affixed, in which the signatories undertake, on the death of the King, to accept his son as king, and announces that he is returning this ordinance to the King, since 'our King is refusing to keep his promises'. The nobles present seize the document and, drawing their swords, cut it into tiny pieces before the King's eyes. The King leaves the assembly saddened and disquieted. For the next few days he allows them to hope that he may yet grant the confirmation and rights for which they are asking, and, in the meantime, requires individual undertakings from many of them, there being few who do not yield to their King's gifts and promises, disregarding others' rights and binding themselves to accept the King's son, thus putting private gain before public good.

The assembly also decides that, in order to avoid friction with the Grand-duke, the Knights should be given the demolished mill at Lubicz and allowed to rebuild it; so, a delegation is sent to the Grand-duke to inform him of this, though also pointing out that it is a breach of the pact made with the Knights and a shame on Poland, so it is to be hoped that the concession will make the Grand-duke more than ever loyal to the King and that in future he will refrain from asking for what would harm the Kingdom. The four delegates are graciously received when they reach Troki; indeed, the Grand-duke even sends Matthew Bishop of Wilno out two miles to greet them, and himself descends from his apartments on the first floor to receive them in the gateway of the lower fort. It takes the Bishop of Cracow three days to deliver all the messages with which the delegates have been entrusted, and this he does in such mild. modest and eloquent language as to evoke the admiration of his audience; but, at the same time, his castigation of the Grand-duke angers the latter almost beyond endurance, yet he replies calmly and promises to repair any hurt he has done to his King or his country. The four delegates are finally dismissed with splendid gifts and given 4000 broad grosses for the King. The mill at Lubicz is then returned to the Order in Prussia.

From Łęczyca the King goes to Cracow to see Queen Sophia and their second son, born a short time before. The infant is baptized and named Casimir. The occasion is marked by games and tourneys.

Yielding to a number of requests, Władysław agrees to send King Sigismund 5000 men to help him fight the Turks. To provide this force, he calls up only Ruthenian knights, who muster a splendidly equipped force of more than 5000 under the command of Janusz Kobylański Starosta of Sanok and Huntsman of Cracow. This reaches the appointed place on the Danube on the very day required, only to discover that Sigismund is postponing the campaign. The Ruthenians spend almost two months encamped there, before they are told that the King is abandoning the project altogether and will they all go home.

Some Ruthenians knights, who had refused to join the force unless they were to be paid five Polish marks for every spearmen and thus incurred the wrath of the King, are now punished with imprisonment; though the King later relents and frees them and returns their confiscated property; that is, of all but the Vogt of Krosno, whom he keeps in prison.

The King now returns to Lithuania by the usual stages and spends the entire winter hunting big game, gifts of which, salted if mild weather threatens, he sends, as is customary, to the Queen, the archbishops, bishops, voivodes and nobles, the dukes of Silesia and the chapters, masters and doctors of Cracow University, as well as to that city's councillors. This generosity greatly enhances the love and devotion of his subjects.

Bolesław, Duke of Cieszyn, dies leaving four sons.

Siemowit the Elder, Duke of Mazovia and Płock, who also held Bełz as dowry for Alexandra his wife, King Władysław's cousin, blinded by age, dies in Gostynin. His widow, Alexandra, dresses his corpse in costly garments, girds it with a silver belt and knight's sword; has it booted, fitted with thigh-pieces and gilt spurs and placed comfortably on a bed in the grave, more in accordance with barbarian custom than with that of the Church. Stanisław Pawłoskinow, Bishop of Płock, is unable to countenance this pagan horror and has the gold, silver, garments and bed coverings removed from the tomb after the funeral and applied to the service of God and His people.

A.D. 1427

The King spends Christmas in Grodno and the next few weeks hunting in the forest there. Early in March he moves to Chełm, about which time his infant son, Casimir, dies in Cracow, to the grief of both King and Queen; indeed, the Queen is thought to grieve excessively, which, plus the fact that she is again pregnant, is taken as confirmation of the Grand-duke's suspicions that she is being unfaithful to her rather decrepit husband, suspicions that are echoed in popular gossip. When this gossip even reaches the King's ears, he and the Grand-duke agree to meet in Horodło on the River Bug to try and quash it and preserve the good name of both King and Queen. They meet one Sunday in September, the Queen having been sent to a manor at Medyka. Those of the King's councillors who usually agree with him (the others are not summoned, so as not to complicate matters) are sent for privately, as is the Grand-duke. The Grand-duke asserts that he is certain from what he has been told that the Queen has relaxed the restraints of modesty and bound herself with unlawful sentiments to certain Polish knights, whom he names. He maintains that unless this evil is swiftly removed, the Queen will give way to the weakness of her sex and indulge in worse crimes and so bring shame upon the King and his kingdom, abetted in this by her youth, beauty, breeding, success and wealth. He tells them that the knights involved must be imprisoned and the Queen herself placed under strict guard and kept on a very frugal diet.

There is no knowing whether or not the Grand-duke, whom the Queen had earlier angered, was just out to slander and ridicule her; whichever it was, the King and his councillors agree with him and it is decided that the knights who have been named are to be arrested in the utmost secrecy and certain ladies with whom the Queen associates, removed from the Court. The Queen herself is to be placed under strict guard. So, Hińcza of Rogów, Peter Kurowski, Laurence Zaremba and Jan Kraska are arrested and imprisoned. Three others, Jan of Koniecpol and the two brothers, Peter and Dobiesław of Szczekociny, escape. There are at the Grand-duke's court two sisters, Catherine and Elizabeth, who used to attend on the Queen and whom she took with her to Lithuania, where they married and have lived there ever since. These are now interrogated about the Queen's infidelities, even put to the torture, and tell the whole truth. After this, the Grand-duke demands the death penalty for all concerned, but some of the King's councillors advise against this. The Grand-duke appears to have been the moving force behind the proceedings. People are more afraid of him than they are of the King, because the Grand-duke is prone to exact immediate retribution and is twice as effective in getting what he wants. The most suspect, Hińcza of Rogów, manages to escape, but is recaptured and put in a deep and filthy dungeon, the stench in which all but kills him.

After this meeting, the King returns to Ruthenia and spends the autumn there, before going back to Lithuania for a winter's hunting. Meanwhile, the Queen, grieved and disquieted by the shame cast on her name by the imprisonment of the knights and the removal of her ladies-in-waiting, has laid a plaint of defamation and, on the King's orders, now goes to Cracow, where, on the eve of St. Andrew's Day, she gives birth to a third son, whom the Bishop of Cracow baptizes on December 21, naming him Casimir. Whereas the birth of the Queen's first son had been an occasion of rejoicing, that of her third boy causes the people to curse her and tell naughty stories about her, much to the amusement of foreigners. To remove the shame attaching to her, the Queen is ordered to purge herself in the company of six other women, and this she does in the presence of Bishop Zbigniew, Christian of Ostrów, the Starosta, and Jan of Tarnow, the Voivode of Cracow, and Nicholas of Michałów, Voivode of Sandomierz, attended by seven of the most eminent matrons: Catherine, Nicholas of Michałów's wife; Anna, widow of Marshal Zbigniew; Kachna, wife of the Voivode of Sieradz, Jacob of Koniecpol; Jadwiga, wife of Jan Głowacz, Voivode of Mazovia; widow Klichna; Helen, wife of Paul Bogumiłowice, the Justiciar of Cracow; and one spinster, Helena Kotka, who, later, is to marry Florian Pacanowski.

At this time there was at the University in Cracow a Master Henry, a man of Czech origin, who was unusually expert in astrology. He had been admitted to the Queen for each of her previous births, and, on the basis of the stars in the heavens at those times had predicted that her first child would rule many kingdoms and dukedoms, if Fate allowed him a longish life; while the second, Casimir, would ardently love his mother, but live only a short time. He now predicts that her third son, Casimir, will live longer, yet never enjoy success. Under him, the kingdom of Poland is to suffer a variety of misfortunes and be threatened with disaster, should God in His mercy not rescue it.

A.D. 1428

The Silesian dukes, frightened by rumours that the Wycliffean heretics of Bohemia are about to declare war on them for having helped King Sigismund, have been sending appeals for help to the Pope and to the Roman Emperor. Pope Martin orders Zbigniew Bishop of Cracow to intervene; but any suggestion of his acting as arbitrator is rejected by Bishop Conrad of Wrocław and the Silesian princes, who suspect that the Bishop will favour the Czechs. At a conference of the Electors and German princes held in Nuremberg, a campaign against the Czech heretics is announced, and, although the idea is rejected by King Sigismund, almost the whole of the Rhineland takes up arms to ensure its success, and is later joined by the dukes of Silesia prompted by the Electors. The Bishop of Cracow does put forward peace proposals, but these are rejected, because people are convinced that the Czechs will soon be forced to plead for peace. The Poles are unjustly accused of being ready to help the Czechs, should they be threatened with complete destruction, but, after their peace proposal is rejected, the Poles put their army on a war footing and go to the assistance of the Electors, who have assembled a large, motley force, which is joined by a thousand English bowmen under an English cardinal, Henry, Bishop of Winchester. Together they now advance against the Czechs. It is a huge army, one almost impossible to defeat, certainly powerful enough to defeat the Czechs. It now invades in a three-pronged attack: one prong being directed at Tachov, which surrenders. Meanwhile, the heretics have been assembling as large an army as they can, one consisting largely of peasants and with this advance on Tachov. Due to some decision of Our Lord that we cannot fathom, the sight of the Czechs causes such panic among the Catholics, that this strong army of German and English troops takes fright and retreats in disorder. Cardinal Henry meets them in full flight, as he is coming up to join his archers, and vainly tries to rally them and get them to continue the fight. Thus, the Czechs not only recapture Tachov with its enormous wealth, but all the German troops' siege weapons as well. They go on to ravage Meissen and then, having been bribed to leave Brandenburg and Nuremberg alone, they return home, enriched. Delighted, the Czechs now declare war on the Silesian dukes, who were so quick to help the Emperor. They meet with no resistance and devastate the country, occupying several fortresses and burning villages and manors.

King Sigismund, who is repeatedly being reminded that he ought to be defending the Church from the Czech heretics, assembles an army of Hungarians and Poles and moves it up to the Turkish frontier, so as to make it look as though he were fully engaged and thus could not be accused of not doing anything about the Czech heretics. He advances on the castle at Golubak on the Danube, which the Turks had recently acquired: its holder offered his allegiance and services to King Sigismund for 12,000 złoty, an offer which the King was advised to accept, but, he pretended that the deeds were suspect and procrastinated so long that the holder took his offer to the Turks, who immediately accepted it. Now, the holder is defending the castle for the Turks, and does so successfully until Sultan Murad sends a relief force, at which Sigismund takes fright and withdraws his army across the Danube, or at least the bulk of it, for there were not boats enough to get them all across. He then moves into Transylvania. He sends envoys to the Polish assembly in Niepołomice asking when Władysław will bring the help he has promised; Władysław replies that he did send a force as far as the Danube but that they became tired of waiting and returned home, a reply that does not please Sigismund.

Frederick Margrave of Meissen assembles a large force with which to attack the Czech heretics, who are besieging the town of Most. When the Czechs learn of its approach, they send a small force to bar its advance. There is a fierce battle, the outcome of which hangs in the balance for several hours. The great heat favours the Czechs in their light armour, rather than the Germans, whose armour is heavier; but the latter are fighting for their lives and start gaining the upper hand, and, indeed, are convinced that they are going to win, until suddenly Zygmunt Korybut appears with his Poles and helps the Czechs rout the Germans, many thousands of whom are killed.

The Grand-duke, well aware of the wealth and riches of the Ruthenians of Novgorod, peaceable people accustomed to indulge in drunkenness and the pleasures of the flesh and thus disinclined to fight, declares war on them on some spurious pretext, but really just to subject them to his rule and so enhance his own reputation. He assembles a huge army and advances on Novgorod, which lies in a marshy lowland surrounded and protected by lakes, ponds and bogs, which the people consider impossible for an army to penetrate in summer, when it is accessible only to birds and wild animals; indeed, merchants can only reach Novgorod in winter, when frost has covered the water with ice. So, the people of Novgorod laugh at the Duke and announce that they will prepare mead for his reception. When the Duke's army reaches the Czarnilas, the width of which is a whole day's travel, he does not let himself be put off by the slipperiness of the ground, which makes progress difficult, but sets tens of thousands of his men to felling trees and cutting brushwood with their axes, and with this he builds a succession of causeways, several miles in length, over which the en-

tire army crosses on to dry land and there pitches camp. Advancing, the Lithuanians reach Opoczno, fourteen miles from Novgorod, and lay siege to it. However, the castle has a garrison of 3000
and as many horses, and is prepared to defend itself. The Grand-duke orders a bombardment of its
walls with cannon, siege-weapons and crossbows. The sudden appearance of the Lithuanians and
their subsequent bombardment give the defenders of Novgorod a double fright and promises them
even worse to come, so they decide to sue for peace or a truce, and send their bishop and fourteen
citizens to Opoczno to negotiate. The Grand-duke, forewarned of their arrival, sets up a throne
with a purple canopy to shelter him from the sun and there he sits at the end of two intimidating
lines of men in armour. When the ambassadors see the Grand-duke thus enthroned, they fall on
their faces, foreheads touching the ground, recognize him as the victor and their lord and, in the
name of all the people of Novgorod beg him to lay down his arms and stop waging war and destroying their fields. They promise to stay within the boundaries he may draw for them and to bring
splendid gifts. The Ruthenians in the Grand-duke's army, anxious for those with whom they share
a religion, language and customs, also beg the Grand-duke to stop hostilities; so, after some discussion with the Bishop and his fourteen citizens, the Grand-duke promises to do so in return for
10,000 roubles in pure silver, all the people and horses in Opoczno castle, fifty cloaks lined with sable and a similar number lined with other skins, and thirty purple cloaks. This is agreed without demur and three days later it is all piled at the Grand-duke's feet, and with it he returns to Lithuania.

Many blame the Duke for making terms that were too lenient and for not capturing the rich
city of Novgorod itself, to whose walls his scouts had penetrated more than once. The Grand-duke
thinks otherwise. He knows that if the city had been stormed, the treasures in it would not have
gone to him, but to whomsoever first grabbed them, and so he preferred to take what he was offered
and leave the city untouched.

Tradition has it that, on this expedition, the Grand-duke did what was unusual for him and directed the entire operation himself, giving orders that were binding throughout the army, such as
that no one was to take grain or foodstuffs without his permission, thus securing the safety of the
property of his allies, friends and subjects. Anyone found disobeying the order was at once hanged
on a huge gallows, round which the army was marched before breaking camp on the following day.
The Grand-duke provided his troops and horses with plenty of what they needed to live. Alexander
Witold was then over eighty, yet throughout the campaign he never made use of a carriage or a litter, and always made his inspection on horseback. He did, however, have one trait worthy of condemnation: impatience. The call of the delights of domesticity he found so strong that the moment
a war ended or a truce was declared, he would mount the horse that always awaited him and ride
back to his wife as swiftly as he could, leaving someone else to command the army, and this, too, he
did on this occasion.

A.D. 1429

King Władysław spends Christmas in Grodno and then goes to Łuck for a meeting with King
Sigismund, the Grand-duke of Lithuania and the prelates, dukes and nobles of Poland, Ruthenia
and Lithuania. King Sigismund is at a diet, but he does, for once, send notice that he has been delayed and this allows Władysław to spend some days hunting in the chase between Łuck and Ży-
tomierz. This year Carnival lasts six weeks and thus it is January 23 before King Sigismund, his
wife and the prelates and nobles of Hungary reassemble. The Grand-duke and his retinue go out a
full mile to meet their King. The greetings over, King Władysław mounts the carriage in which is
Queen Barbara and rides with her back to Łuck, followed by the Grand-duke and King Sigismund,
flanked by Zbigniew Bishop of Cracow. Trumpets sound. The open space is filled with a huge
crowd, standing shoulder to shoulder and horse to horse. Each, even the kings and dukes, tries to
outdo the others in magnificence of dress, mount and arms. As they cross the River Styr, they are

met by a procession of the city's dignitaries: Bishop Andrew of Łuck with his chapter, then the Ruthenian, Armenian and Jewish clergy, who greet the King of the Romans, and he, saluting the
Catholic Bishop, dismounts and pays honour to the holy relics, but disregards those of the other
confessions. Then the Grand-duke entertains them at a magnificent banquet.

For the conference, each delegation is given a room of its own and is presided over by its own
King or Duke. Sigismund sends Władysław a demand that, in accordance with the terms of their
treaty, the original of which is presented to him, they shall in the coming summer mount an attack
on Moldavia and, after expelling its dukes, divide the territory between them in the proportion laid
down in the treaty. One of the reasons for doing this is that the Walachian nation does not owe allegiance to anyone, is accustomed to live by theft and brigandage and so is everyone's enemy. They
had come and settled on fertile land, from which they then removed the native peasants and their
rightful lords, and ever since have refused to help King Sigismund, whenever he has tried to arrange an expedition against the Turks. Władysław replies that it would not be right to wage war on
the Walachians, who confess the Christian faith and have given him and his kingdom obedience
and submission; indeed, to do this would be an act of savagery. Though some may live by brigandage, they cannot all be tarred with the same brush, nor can they be blamed for not helping King Sigismund against the Turks, because they had gone with the Poles to the given rendez-vous on the
Danube and got there on time, yet had to waste two months waiting there, and then return home.
Rather does the blame for this attach to King Sigismund, who failed to turn up at the appointed
time. The squabbling continues for several days, at the end of which Władysław's stubbornness
compels Sigismund to abandon the plan and seek other ventures. Later, when the two kings and the
grand-duke meet, Sigismund tells them that he is asking the Pope for a council with the object of
winning back the Czechs and introducing reforms of the Church. Should the Pope not grant one,
Sigismund will use his own authority to convene one. There is no need, he tells them, to force the
conversion of those of the Greek rite, for, he says, they and we hold the same beliefs and all that divides us is beards and wives. Not that the fault was theirs alone, for the priests of the Greek rite restrict themselves to one wife, while some of those of the Latin rite have ten or more. This makes the
Ruthenians praise him for recognizing that the Greek rite is more distinguished than the Latin. He
ends his speech by pretending that France, England, the Germans, Italians, Czechs and Hungarians, almost all countries of the West, are engaged in rebellion and bloody war, while only the Poles
are successful and at peace. When the latter pay no attention to his jibes, he starts making treacherous plans to involve them in civil strife, which was his real objective in convening the conference.

Sigismund now reverts to the suggestion he made twenty years before, namely that the
Grand-duke should allow himself to be elected king of Lithuania. He tries to win over the Grand-
duke, the other dukes and boyars, even those of quite humble origin, to the idea with gifts of gold,
silver, chased vessels, horses, gorgeous materials which they put on and so parade for several
hours in public. The Grand-duke is easy to persuade, but he tells Sigismund that he cannot go
ahead without the approval of his brother, King Władysław. Sigismund promises to remove this
obstacle, and so, one morning, he and Queen Barbara enter Władysław's room, while he is still in
bed, dismiss the secretaries and then tell the King that it is unfair that Alexander Witold should be a
grand-duke and not a king, and ask him to agree to his brother being made king of Lithuania, a
thing which Sigismund, as Roman Emperor, has the power to do. Władysław agrees that his
brother is worthy of a crown, even of being emperor, and he would be prepared to let him have his
own crown, but he cannot take such a step without first consulting his prelates and nobles. Sigismund replies that it would be a slight to Alexander Witold to give him his brother's crown. They
should both be kings. Nor does Władysław need to consult others, for the Emperor's consent
suffices.

Apparently, Władysław neither assents or disagrees, just says nothing, so Sigismund tells Witold that his brother does agree, at which Witold sends his secretary, Nicholas Sępiński, a Pole, to the Polish prelates and nobles. Entering their council chamber, the secretary tells them that he is speaking for the Grand-duke and has come to tell them that King Sigismund wishes to elevate Lithuania to a kingdom and make Witold its king; that Władysław has agreed to this and has sent him to obtain their consent. Before he stops speaking the Grand-duke himself enters the chamber with his prelates and boyars, thinking that in their surprise the Poles will let themselves be rushed into agreeing. He repeats what his secretary has just told them and asks them individually for their opinion. The first speaker, Albert Jastrzębiec Archbishop of Gniezno, makes a long speech that indicates neither agreement nor disagreement: but the next speaker, Zbigniew Oleśnicki Bishop of Cracow, tells the Grand-duke that he has heard what he has said with surprise, pain and sympathy, and reminds him that, when his brother, King Władysław, married Jadwiga, who had refused other Catholic princes who wished to subject their realms to Polish rule and unite their lands with it, he was accepted as king of Poland on condition that Lithuania accepted the Catholic faith and that Lithuania and Ruthenia were to be united with, and become part of Poland. There are, he reminds him, documents signed and sealed which make this binding on Władysław, himself and the other Lithuanian dukes. He also reminds him that this pact was renewed only a few years previously, when, to further strengthen the bond, and at King Zymunt's suggestion, arms of nobility were made interchangeable. Now, this same King is trying to destroy the union and set the two countries fighting each other. Yet, if the Poles and Lithuanians continue to stick to the terms of the treaty, Władysław will still be regarded as king, even now after Queen Jadwiga's death. He has sons by a Lithuanian, Queen Sophia, who will succeed him on his death. You and your brother, he says, seem to be trying to tear from Poland lands permanently united with it and to carve it up into little pieces. He, the Bishop, he says, will never attend Witold's coronation, but will oppose it tooth and nail. The next speaker, Jan of Tarnow Voivode of Cracow, agrees with the Bishop in such strong terms that, despite the presence of the Grand-duke, there are murmurs of assent, and the Grand-duke leaves the council chamber, a saddened and disappointed man.

As soon as the Grand-duke has left the chamber, Władysław's councillors go to their King and berate him for seeking to tear the country apart, but they are told that the King never agreed to his brother being made a king, and eventually they are reconciled and leave Łuck. Shortly before they leave, however, news arrives that a powerful force of Czechs have invaded Silesia and are wreaking havoc there. It had been challenged near Brno by Duke John of Ziembic, whose wife Elizabeth is the widow of Spytko of Melsztyn Voivode of Cracow, but unsuccessfully, the Duke himself having been killed.

Alexander Witold has now agreed to accept the dignity of kingship from the hands of the Roman Emperor, doing so without the agreement of King Władysław and despite his sworn oath of loyalty to the latter and the documents he had signed in which he pledged himself and all the lands of Lithuania and Ruthenia to serve the Kingdom of Poland.

Early in March, King Władysław goes to Korczyn, where the prelates and more eminent nobles are already assembled. All agree that they must act in moderation, so they send Zbigniew Bishop of Cracow and Nicholas of Michałów Voivode of Sandomierz and Captain of Cracow to Lithuania to try to reconcile the Grand-duke and obtain his cooperation. They find the Grand-duke in Grodno and acquaint him with their mission and point out that his coronation could only diminish his good name and would inevitably lead to bloodshed. They suggest, too, that a prince of his age should not need to deck himself with little twirls of gold or pearls, or bring war to the two nations which had united at his express wish. Replying, the Grand-duke tells them that he has never wished nor intended to be king, nor sought such advancement, but that, years before, King Sigismund himself had begged and advised him to do just that. Since the suggestion has now been made public, they cannot now withdraw, but must finish what has been begun. With this reply the Polish delegates return home, while the Grand-duke, more avid than ever for a crown, sends his secretary to King Sigismund, then in Vienna, to get him to send the Grand-duke a crown and the other insignia of royalty.

King Władysław spends the summer in Wielkopolska, from where he twice sends councillors to meet their Hungarian counterparts in an attempt to revive the old friendship between their two kings. However, on neither occasion do the Hungarians turn up and the Poles, justifiably annoyed, come to consider King Sigismund as an enemy. After this, it is decided to impede the Grand-duke's coronation by all legal, and other means.

Back from Wielkopolska, the King meets his councillors, who are perturbed by a spate of rumours that Sigismund has sent, or is about to send, a crown to Alexander Witold. After some discussion, it is decided to send the two envoys to Lithuania with a new proposal: namely, that if the Grand-duke must have a crown and the glory of kingship, his brother will abdicate in his favour, on the ground that Alexander Witold being the younger, is as capable of ruling a kingdom as a duchy, indeed, perhaps better than the ageing Władysław or his under-age children.

Władysław returns to Wielkopolska on St. Martin's Day. He decides against spending the winter in Lithuania and, instead, goes to Ruthenia. First, in order to prevent Sigismund's threatened action, he lodges an official complaint against it with the Holy See. This results in Pope Martin sending a special bull to King Sigismund forbidding him to send a crown to Alexander Witold, and a similar bull to the Grand-duke forbidding him to accept a crown.

During the summer, the Czech heretics devastate almost the whole of Silesia, most of its principal towns being either captured or abandoned to the enemy, who are to occupy them for a long time.

A.D. 1430

At the end of February, King Władysław meets his assembled prelates and nobles in Jedlna. Here he tells them that, after much thought he has decided to reward their loyalty to him and his sons with new benefits and privileges, namely, that henceforth all cathedral churches and all monasteries of whatever Order, all villages which are the property of an Order and all places used in connection with the Church, are no longer to be used as stages in his progresses, and that all churches in the kingdom and all individuals attached to them, are to be relieved of the duty of providing staging. He further promises to remove all oppressive abuses and burdens. He elucidates many of the legal points which have so often aroused doubt. This is all detailed in a long letter addressed to "To whom it may concern" in which it is laid down that, on King Władysław's death, whichever of his two sons the prelates and nobles of the kingdom consider best fitted to govern, is to be prince, lord and heir to the kingdom of Poland and all the lands of Ruthenia and Lithuania. The territories in the possession of his dear brother, the Grand-duke, are to remain with him until his life ends, when they will pass to his legal successor; the King of Poland, his sons and the crown. When King Władysław's own son comes of age, he is to be crowned and given the sceptre. All consecrated places and churches are to retain their rights, freedoms and privileges previously granted to them in their entirety. The dignitaries of Church and State are to continue to enjoy the rights and liberties they have previously enjoyed; if any one of these offices shall become vacant, they shall not be given to a foreigner, but only to a noble of the territory concerned: in Cracow to a Cracovian, in Sandomierz to a noble of Sandomierz, and so on. The nobility are to be obliged to defend the country's frontiers at their own expense and risk; but, if anyone has to go beyond the frontier in order to repulse an enemy or a threatened attack and is captured, he is to be compensated for imprisonment and loss. All enemy prisoners taken within the frontiers of the kingdom are to be handed over to the King and used to ransom the kingdom's own prisoners held abroad. If, and when, the inhabitants of Poland are required to serve beyond the country's frontiers, they are to receive five marks for every spear, and, if, by two years after receiving his money, service has not been required of him, the recipient is not required to repay the money, nor further to supply the service in question. Whichever of the King's two sons is made king, he shall not mint coin of any metal without the consent of the prelates and nobles.

All peasants, without exception, on the lands of the country's nobles, are to be relieved of all taxes, tributes and levies, of cartage, labour or provision of horses, tribute of grain, other than the obligatory two grosses of ordinary coin in common circulation in their country. These two grosses each peasant must pay every year between Michaelmas and the Feast of St. Nicholas for every hide in his possession; even if possessed by more than one person, except for bailiffs and servants, who are to be exempt altogether, as also are millers, the owners of inns, orchards and cottages, and those who cultivate the orchards and cottages, and those who cultivate the fields, that is whole hides or halves of a hide. if an innkeeper, miller or cottager cultivates a whole hide, he must pay two grosses; if half a hide one gross. Should a village neglect to pay this amount at the stated time, the King's tax-collector shall be entitled to seize one ox without hope of restitution. If, after fourteen days, the amount is still unpaid, the tax-collector is to seize two oxen, again without hope of restitution.

Any citizen or inhabitant of a town under the King's rule living there with his wife, children and servants, who cultivates his land himself or by the hands of a cottager or peasant, is not due to pay furrow tax, but, if he dwells in the suburbs or outside the town, he must pay furrow tax, as if he dwelled in a village, although it is recognized that he does not come under the jurisdiction of the town and is not bound to provide cartage.

The King further promises not to quarter soldiers or set up supply depots or staging posts in any of the towns, villages, inherited properties, manors and possessions of the Church, nobility and those born in the country. Should any of these be necessary, nothing shall be taken by force or high-handedly. The King wishes to pay in cash for whatever is essential.

If, while a trial is in progress, the dispute is settled out of court, the defendant is not to have a punishment imposed on him by the court.

For the next ten years all inhabitants of Kujawy and Dobrzyń are to be responsible for supplying the oats they are accustomed to supply to the King, but thereafter they are to be free of this tribute.

Those elevated to the dignity of notary are to take part personally in all hearings, unless justifiably prevented, and are not to send substitutes or those who just sign on their behalf.

The Grand-duke writes to King Władysław, his prelates and nobles, whom he knows to be in Jedlna, renewing his accusation that the King is trying to damage his good name with the Pope and the Catholic kings and urging them to agree to his coronation. So, Zbigniew of Cracow and Nicholas of Sandomierz are sent back to Lithuania to answer these accusations and to complain about Witold's requiring the prelates and boyars of Lithuania to swear fresh oaths that are incompatible with their duty to the King and the Kingdom of Poland, and of his strengthening of castles along the frontier with Poland. The two wait on the Grand-duke in Grodno during Easter and point out that the King is not so thoughtless as to try and denigrate one whose opinions he has always shared and whose growth in importance he has watched with satisfaction. If he complained to the Pope, it was because the other's coronation would diminish his own rights. The Grand-duke replies that he is only strengthening the frontier castles against the Czech heretics, who keep trying to get Władysław's permission to pass through his territory on their way into Prussia and Lithuania, requests that Władysław has kept to himself.

The King leaves Jedlna and returns to Cracow, where he spends some days before moving to Wielkopolska. He spends Easter in Kalisz. Certain Polish nobles, who have squandered their for-

tunes and inheritances and are overburdened with debt, thinking that the monastery at Częstochowa has money and treasure galore, recruit a number of brigands from Bohemia, Moravia and
Silesia and attack the monastery at Easter time. Disappointed at finding no treasure, they seize the
liturgical vessels and even strip the picture of the Virgin of the gold and pearls with which the faithful have adorned it. They thrust a sword through the face on the picture and break its frame, so that
people should think the perpetrators were Czechs, not Poles, as, indeed, for a time they do, though
in the end the culprits are discovered and severely punished.

     After Easter, the King moves on to Jędrzejów, where he meets the chamberlain of Poznań, Jan
Czarnkowski, who has property adjacent to Saxony and Nowe Miasto. He suggests that Czarnkowski should station well-paid, armed guards on all the roads and have them keep an eye out for
King Sigismund's messengers, who are known to have left Vienna with letters and the crowns,
while others should keep a watch on the crossing-places out of Saxony. The Grand-duke's coronation has been announced for the Assumption, but when the envoys with the crowns are delayed, a
fresh date has to be fixed, that of the Feast of the Birth of the Blessed Virgin, so fresh invitations are
sent to many of the Ruthenian dukes, the Master, the eminent Prussian commanders and the Tatar
emperor. The crowns are expected to arrive any day, for Sigismund has assured the Grand-duke by
messenger and letter that they will, and has even sent a doctor of law to reassure him as to Sigismund's right, as King of the Romans, to create a king, a matter about which doubts are being whispered. As Sigismund's envoys, having negotiated Saxony, are about to cross into Prussia, they are
caught by Czarnkowski's guards, who take all the documents they are carrying, their armour and
horses, and then release them against their undertaking to present themselves in Czarnków on a
certain day—a stupid thing to have done—whereupon the envoys cross into Prussia and on to
Lithuania, where they report to the Grand-duke and tell him not to worry, for the crowns are still on
their way and will arrive at any time.

     When Władysław breaks the seals and reads the documents Czarnkowski brings him, he finds
that they all concern the elevation of the Grand-duke to king, arrangements for the coronation of
the Grand-duke and his wife, Julianna, and plans for an alliance between Lithuania, Hungary and
Bohemia, perhaps extended to the Order in Prussia and Livonia. Władysław and Poland are mentioned again and again, but either disparagingly or derisively. There is much that borders on treachery. Władysław is delighted and rewards Czarnkowski richly. He now knows that the envoys with
the crowns are to travel via Saxony and Prussia, so Czarnkowski is sent back to keep watch on all
the roads along which they might travel. However, the envoys are so perturbed by the way in which
all the messengers they have sent ahead by various routes have been captured and afraid lest the
same thing happen to them and they lose the treasure they are carrying, that they dare not continue,
but return to King Sigismund with the crowns and the gifts they are carrying.

     Czarnkowski has mounted his guards along the frontier and even some way out to sea. There
may even have been some the other side of the frontier. News that Sigismund's envoys have turned
back comes while the Grand-duke's guests are assembling in Wilno. Now, for the first time, the
Grand-duke realizes that, perhaps, he is not going to get his crown; but, to lessen his shame, he retains his guests until Michaelmas—just in case! The guests are then finally sent home. Because of
the pain and shame of all this, the Grand-duke contracts what is known as cancer.

     King Władysław now moves to Lublin, where he receives an envoy from the Grand-duke
asking if he will deign to come to Lithuania in the winter and begging him not to bear malice, for
the Grand-duke has abandoned all his plans and has no intention of being crowned king. Although
Władysław is eager to go hunting in Lithuania, he first consults his councillors, many of whom are
suspicious of the invitation, for Sigismund's special envoys are still in Wilno. Nonetheless, on the
Thursday after the Feast of St. Francis, Władysław, his prelates and nobles, but not the Bishop of
Cracow, whom the Grand-duke regards as his prime enemy and who is already in the city, arrive in

Wilno. They are received with great pomp outside the city by the Grand-duke and his wife, the Master of the Prussian Order, the dukes of Moscow, Tver and Odejów, and a number of Lithuanian and Ruthenian dukes. Next day a general council is held at which the Prussian Master tells them that much as he dislikes any misunderstandings between the Grand-duke and the King, he has, after all, been invited to a coronation. Bishop Zbigniew tells him that his words are noble, but not his deeds, which show that he is trying to sow discord. At this, the Grand-duke gets to his feet and walks out of the Council Chamber, thus nipping a potential quarrel in the bud. Now, a letter arrives from the Holy See in which the Pope expresses his delight that the two are meeting and his hope that they will become reconciled and renew the ties of brotherly love.

The Bishop and Chapter of Wilno, afraid lest the gift of certain lands to them by the Grand-duke should not be valid unless confirmed by the King of Poland, insistently ask Władysław, while he is in Troki, for a document to this effect and this they obtain.

A number of the Silesian dukes send specially to the King promising him and his realm their every support against any of his enemies, now or in the future, and telling him how Sigismund is boasting of having instigated the quarrel between the King and the Grand-duke, likening this to throwing down a bone before two dogs, who thereafter fight over it to the end of their lives, and telling in colourful language how he has ensnared King Władysław like a wild animal, surrounding him with hostile countries, so that it is not humanly possible for him to escape.

Duke Witold is increasingly debilitated by an ailment called a carbuncle or prurient ulcer, which has formed betwen his shoulder-blades; but whether this is something hereditary or has been caused by the disappointment of not getting a crown, is not known. As he grows daily weaker, he pesters the King to agree to his coronation and to set aside the objections of Poland's prelates and nobles. Władysław tells him that he does consider him worthy of a crown, but that he cannot override the objections of his prelates and nobles, especially those of the Bishop of Cracow. The Grand-duke at once sends two Poles to the Bishop, who beg him not to oppose the Grand-duke's coronation to which all but a few now assent; if he will do this, the Bishop is promised access to the Grand-duke's treasury and the freedom to take from it whatever he likes. The Bishop replies that the courage, deeds and manners of the Grand-duke are, indeed, worthy of a crown, yet he wonders why he should want one, when he knows that his coronation can only result in loss of repute for himself and Lithuania, in more fighting than peace, more bloodshed than pleasure, more weakness than power; for King Sigismund has only kindled the Grand-duke's hope of a crown in order to destroy the union of Poland and Lithuania and so weaken them both and give the Knights an excuse to invade Lithuania as a pagan country. He points out, too, that he was given the task of preventing the coronation by the whole of Poland and cannot by himself agree to it. At this the Grand-duke threatens the Bishop with loss of his see and exile, but the Bishop remains unmoved. The Grand-duke now realizes that there is no hope of his being crowned, and is full of praise for the Bishop's courage.

The Grand-duke's pain grows worse and worse. He abandons all hope of his coronation, a thing he confides to Władysław, Bishop Zbigniew and others. His thoughts now are not of further life, but of life's ending. Władysław displays genuine brotherly love, sitting by the other's bedside and comforting him. He sends Bishop Zbigniew, Duke Siemowit, the Vice-Chancellor Władysław Oporowski and other nobles back to Poland, although, in view of the imminent death of the Grand-duke, they would have done well to have stayed; but the King does not want them there when the Grand-duke dies, as they might prevent him making Świdrygiello the new duke, as is his wish. The Grand-duchess Julianna tries to persuade Bishop Zbigniew to take her jewels, gold and silver, precious stones and pearls back to Poland with him and keep them there for her, or, should anything happen to her, to use them for good works; but this the Bishop refuses to do, as it would be open to misinterpretation. On St. Jadwiga's Day, Władysław leaves Wilno for Troki. At the start, the

Grand-duke rides with him, but pain soon forces him to dismount and he takes to his wife's carriage. He reaches Troki prone and, indeed, does not leave his bed again. Duke Świdrygiello starts behaving as if he were Grand-duke already, then, suddenly and unexpectedly, he rides away.

After a fortnight in Troki, the Grand-duke realizes that death is near and summons the nobles of Lithuania and Ruthenia, and, in their presence and that of his wife, says to King Władysław: "I see, Your Majesty and dearest brother, that my last hour is imminent and that at any moment I must leave this world and you; so, I am handing back to you the Grand-duchy of Lithuania that I received from your hands. Rule it as your own or through some honest man. To Your Majesty I entrust my wife, the prelates, dukes and nobles here present and others elsewhere, and beg that you care for them and respect the rights and gifts I have given them. I beseech you to forgive any harm I may have done you in my endeavour to get a crown". The Grand-duke then confesses, receives the Holy Sacrament and extreme unction. Then, having entrusted the keys of the castles to King Władysław, he dies at dawn of the Eve of St. Simon and St. Jude, October 27.

The Grand-duke's only relaxations were hunting and dicing, but he indulged in them infrequently, for he considered it stupid and bad to go hunting, if that meant neglecting affairs of state. With the help of certain merchants, with whom he was on friendly terms, he accumulated a fortune in gold, silver, pearls, cloth, furs and other valuables, with which latterly he demonstrated his generosity. Throughout his life he never took wine or must, but drank only water; yet he was more ready to make love than was decent. Harsh to his subjects, whom he never allowed to go unpunished, he was kind and polite to his guests. Those who enriched themselves by theft or by exacting excessive tribute, he deprived of their possessions; yet, on the principle of setting a thief to catch a thief, he often appointed such a person to an important post. He was remarkable for his small height and slight stature; but he was distinguished by his unusual munifence and magnaminity. Services he repaid with equal readiness. His right arm was notably longer than his left. He was a womanizer, sensual and avid for love-making; he would sometimes anticipate victory and leave the field of battle, while fighting was still in progress, and, with frequent changes of horse swiftly return to his wife, or concubine, to quench his ardour.

The death of the Grand-duke without progeny sets everyone wondering who is to succeed him. There is his brother, Duke Zygmunt, a man of good character about whom people had forgotten; and there is Duke Świdrygiello, Władysław's brother, a man all too fond of drink and revelry, and, though kind, fickle and rash, without much common sense and not quick-witted; yet his generosity and fondness for drunken revelry have endeared him to many people, especially to the Ruthenians, to whose rite he inclined, though officially a Catholic. However, all depends on King Władysław, who could himself take over or replace Witold with some one else. The King loves his brother, Świdrygiello, and feels that the time has come to give him preferment and the chance to acquire fame and glory; so, without consulting or informing his councillors of either part of the realm, he sends his secretary, Jan Mężyk, to Świdrygiello with a special ring appointing him to govern the Grand-duchy. At this, the nobles and knights of Lithuania and Ruthenia desert Władysław and attach themselves to Świdrygiello (typical of people who change faith as fortune changes!) and there is even talk of imprisoning Władysław and killing the Poles. This is the first of a series of misfortunes awaiting the King.

The Pope sends Władysław a letter commiserating with him on the death of his brother and expressing the hope that, having arranged matters in Lithuania, he will devote his efforts to destroying the heresy in neighbouring Bohemia.

It is hoped that Świdrygiello will soon calm down; but in actual fact his behaviour becomes more and more violent, especially when he learns that, when they heard of the Grand-duke's death, the Bishop of Kamieniec Podolski, a man of low birth, and the Polish nobles of Podole assembled in Kamienica and invited the starosta of the castle, the Voivode of Wilno, who had not heard the news, to come to them, and, when he did so, promptly imprisoned him, occupied the castle and placed it under the authority of the Polish crown. They go on to do the same with all the other fortresses in Lithuanian hands in Podole. From this point, Podole, which the King granted to his brother only for his life-time, has been re-incorporated into Poland. The news of this sends Świdrygiello into a fury. Again and again he storms into the King's bedroom, scolds and curses him and his nobles, and, when drunk, even threatens to put them in prison or kill them all, if they do not return Kamieniec castle and the other fortresses. Władysław keeps his temper, but many of his nobles are attracted by the idea of killing Świdrygiello. They feel, too, that they should fortify Wilno castle in which the King is living and evict all Lithuanians in it, for the castle is well provisioned and could be defended until a Polish army comes to the rescue. At the same time, Świdrygiello is considering either killing the King's courtiers or putting them in a dungeon. He even has chains and shackles prepared in case he should decide to do this.

When he learns that his nobles are planning to kill Świdrygiello, the King is profoundly disturbed and so fearful of the consequences that he decides that he had best return Kamieniec Podolski and the other forts, to pacify Świdrygiello. So, despite the opposition of the Poles, he writes to the holder, Michael Buczacki, ordering him to hand over Kamieniec and the other forts, and sends Tarlo Zaklika to see that the order is carried out. The delighted Świdrygiello now tries to make it up with his brother: he sends him gifts of a thousand silver roubles, furs and fur cloaks, jewels and various fabrics. Meanwhile, the nobles with the King are wondering how to prevent the surrender of Podole. One suggestion is that they should destroy the royal seal on the letters and so make their authenticity doubtful and thus delay the surrender; but the fact that Tarlo is to take the letter makes this impracticable. Instead, they write a letter to Michael Buczacki telling him of the danger threatening him and how this is not the King's own decision but one forced on him by fear of imprisonment for himself and the others; and they call on Buczacki not to surrender the castle, but to arrest Tarlo and the bearer of the King's letter. As it would be impossible openly to hand a letter to Buczacki, since the King's messenger would query it, the letter is folded and covered with a ball of wax. To make this less suspect, two partially burned candles are stuck in the wax and this given to Tarlo's page, who is easily persuaded for one mark of broad grosses to give it to Buczacki as soon as they arrive and to tell him and the city councillors, that they must seek enlightnment in the candle, unless they wish to make a grievous mistake. This the page does and Buczacki, convinced that the candle contains some secret, breaks open the ball of wax, finds the letter and then arrests Tarlo and the carrier of the King's letter and imprisons them both. Thus is fertile Podole, whose lands abound in honey, grain and cattle, saved for the Kingdom of Poland.

While all this is going on, news that the King has been imprisoned by his own brother spreads throughout Poland and neighbouring countries, and even reaches the ears of Pope Martin V, who is profoundly troubled and writes to King Władysław and the Polish councillors, the King of the Romans and Duke Świdrygiello himself urging them all to free the King. Then, John of Oleśnica Marshal of Poland arrives back in Poland with the thousand roubles and other gifts Świdrygiello made to the King and this is all placed in the royal treasury. The Marshal secretly urges that immediate steps be taken to free the King. Though they all know that the King has brought this on himself, this is not the time for recriminations and they all assemble in Warta on the Feast of St. Nicholas, though plague is everywhere. Some recommend sending an army immediately, others that they send the Queen and her Court; but it is decided to proceed cautiously and first send to Świdrygiello demanding that the King and those with him be given their freedom, and advising Świdrygiello to refrain from re-occupying Podole, which has always belonged to Poland. It is decided, too, to assemble the entire armed forces of the kingdom and for these to muster a week after Epiphany on the river Wieprz, from where it will be easier to cross into the marshes of Lithuania, once winter has covered them with ice. This agreed, the chosen envoys spend Christmas in Warsaw awaiting the arrival of the letter of safe-conduct, to obtain which a special messenger has been sent to Lithuania. While he is away, those at home receive a letter from the King telling them that, when Świdrygiello learned that a general call to arms had gone out, he freed the King and all with him and sent them out of Lithuania. The King assures them that he needs neither envoys nor an army, for he is already at liberty and in no danger.

Meanwhile, two tutors, Master Vincent Kot of Dębno and Peter Ryterski, have been appointed to educate the King's two sons, Władysław and Casimir, to teach them to read and how to behave correctly. This displeases some of the councillors, who think that education will enhance the boys' acumen excessively and that it would be better to have a simple, uneducated king, who would be more impressed by the deeds of others, than would one who had been educated.

A.D. 1431

Safely back from Lithuania, the King goes to Sopoth in Chełm, to which Queen Sophia and a number of barons come to congratulate him on his safe return. The King then goes to Sandomierz to attend the general assembly, at which the whole question of Lithuania is discussed, as well as that of the harm done by Świdrygiello, his occupation of several forts in Podole, the raids of his people into the Polish districts of Trebowla and Lwów and his continued siege of Smotrycz. Repeated written requests that these matters be put right having had no effect, a delegation is sent to Lithuania to require the surrender of the forts and territory of Łuck and the return of the forts occupied in Podole; but this, too, has no effect.

At this assembly, Queen Sophia lays a plaint before the King that Jan Strasch has defamed her by publicly accusing her of fornication and asks for justice. Trial by combat having been refused, his peers condemn Strasch to imprisonment in a dungeon in Sandomierz castle. Here, fumes from some live coals all but suffocate him and he is dragged out, half dead; thus he neither pays a proper penalty for his crime, nor gets off scot free. In the middle of Lent, the King reaches Nowe Miasto Korczyn, where he receives envoys from Bohemia asking that he permit public celebration of their rites. The King decides to refer the matter to the University of Cracow, but before it can be disputed, Zygmunt Korybut moves out of Gliwice, which he has occupied with the help of a throng of Poles and Bohemians infected with the heresy and starts ravaging the adjacent part of Silesia. The Carthusian monastery at Lechnica on the River Dunajec on the border of Hungary and Poland, is savagely attacked by him in the belief that it houses a large treasure. He strips it of its vessels, robes and ornaments and books, and, in his disappointment, kills some of the monks, wounds and scourges others, and also abducts the prior, an old man, whom he hopes can be compelled to tell them where the treasure is hidden. When he hears of this, Zbigniew Bishop of Cracow assembles a force and, the next day, after dining, marches out of the city heading for Lipowiec and hoping to encounter the Duke's troops and recapture both the Prior and the spoil. Failing in this, they return to Cracow regretting being too late by the space of a meal. Ever since, Duke Korybut has hated the Bishop.

The King returns to Cracow, where Zygmunt Korybut and the principal heretics already are. The King arranges for a disputation with the doctors of Cracow university in the great hall, whose windows look out onto the houses of the canons. The King reads the heretics a lengthy sermon and beseeches them to mend their ways and return to the true faith. The heretics remain unmoved, and, though defeated in the disputation, they refuse to accept defeat and stay on in Cracow, at which an interdict is put on them. Then, one day, having gone outside the city, when they wish to return, they find the gates shut against them; and this makes them more than ever angry with Bishop Zbigniew Oleśnicki. In the meantime Duke Conrad the White of Oleśnica and Koźle recaptures Gliwice, which Świdrygiello and the heretics had made their seat.

The King moves to Biecz and announces an assault on Łuck. Here he receives Ludwig of Landsee, an envoy from Duke Świdrygiello, who hopes to persuade the King to hand over the castles in Podole. He also receives the Commander of Toruń and the Prussian Master, Paul of Russdorff, offering their good offices in making peace with Świdrygiello. For these talks the King requires an interpreter, as he knows no German. From Biecz the King sends his secretary to Świdrygiello to point out that he is behaving neither sincerely nor in a brotherly fashion, and to ask him to revert to brotherly relations. The Duke takes offence and in his anger strikes the envoy on the chin and puts him in prison, which inclines the King more than ever to renew hostilities. The King now moves into Ruthenian territory and, on the Feast of St. John the Baptist reaches Przemyśl, from where he sends to Cracow for bombards, arrows and other military equipment for use against Łuck. Moving on to Horodło, the King camps beside the Bug and here he stays for a twelve days, awaiting the arrival of the rest of his army from Wielkopolska. He learns here how Łuck has been turned into a wilderness; how the forts are deserted, the people gone into hiding with their serfs, flocks and treasured belongings, the whole area empty. The King now sends Świdrygiello a formal declaration of war, detailing his reasons for this step: the latter's occupation of Podole and his treatment of the King's envoys. On the Eve of the Feast of the Blessed Virgin, the King and his army cross the Bug on bridges specially built, make camp and stay there for a further two days, during which some sixty of the King's knights engage some Ruthenians and Tatars, some of whom they capture and bring before the King. Again the King sends to Świdrygiello offering fair terms for peace, but this has no effect on a man, who is by nature irascible and demented. Now, the King moves on again and makes camp on the other side of Vladimir, where he stays for three days, during which he captures three wretched islands and a wood in a lake, in which a crowd of Ruthenians had taken refuge with their families, flocks and treasures. The King captures Vladimir and grants it to Theodore Fieduszko, Korybut's son, who is a schismatic. The huge amount of loot is distributed among the troops. Vladimir and several other towns are burned.

After the Feast of St. James the Greater, the King moves camp again, but lack of water and the filthiness of what there is force him to move on again to a pleasant site among hills covered with oaks. After some days he again moves camp, this time to Sadowa, where his envoys to the Duke return with two of the Duke's own envoys asking for peace and to arrange a meeting between the two in person. Moving camp again, the army advances on Łuck, but finds that the enemy has destroyed the bridge across the River Stir, so not knowing the fords, it is unable to cross and attack the town, which meanwhile has been sent more people and provided with ramparts, provisions and arrows. What is more, the Duke has assembled some 6000 Lithuanians, Ruthenians and Tatars on his side of the river, denying access to it. To this the King replies by bombarding the enemy with his two bombards. One evening, the King, having discovered fords, gets most of the army across the river, and arrays his troops. Now, for the first time, the Duke sees how strong the Poles are, and retreats. A couple of days later emissaries are sent into Łuck to demand its surrender. On the same day Andrew Bishop of Łuck sets out to go to the King to proclaim his loyalty, but on the way he is stripped of everything including his clothes, and has his horses taken from him by some Poles. Half naked, he is conducted to the tent of John of Oleśnica, Marshal of Poland, who provides him with clothes. The bridge across the Stir has now been rebuilt, making foraging easier for the King's troops. Casimir Duke of Mazovia rejoins the army with six knights after a successful foray into Bełz. The rest of the King's troops and their equipment is now brought over and the fort ringed with a pallisade, thus preventing foraging and denying the besieged access to water. The King transfers his tents to a part of the bank opposite the fort. He then brings up his great bombards, whose missiles demolish a large part of the wall and several of the towers. One night several Poles make their way into the fort and secretly treat with the enemy, encouraging them to resist and offering food of which there is a great shortage. Though some are caught by the King's guards, others escape. One

Chess players.
—Jacobus: de Moribus et de officis nobillium
super ludo scaccorum—National Museum Li-
brary, Prague.

night there is a great commotion in the camp, that sends everyone rushing to arm themselves, and, at dawn, the army marches out ready to do battle, but as there is no enemy in sight, it returns to its tents.

Though an expert in arms, the Duke is now using wiles and stratagem. He sends a messenger to the King with forged letters purporting to be from the Emperor of the Tatars and addressed to the King and his nobles, requesting them to stop their invasion and ravaging of Lithuania and Podole and to restore these to the Duke. It is realized that the letters are forgeries.

On the Feast of St. Hippolytus the King orders an assault on Łuck fort whose walls are breached in several places, but this is made with more enthusiasm than skill, and with no great effect, for the troops are fighting with nothing but spears, swords and arrows. This gives the enemy confidence and, using bombards, slings, arrows and stones, they fling the Poles from the walls and ladders, killing and wounding many, and forcing them to abandon the assault. This setback is attributed to the fact that the Poles, no different to the barbarians, have laid waste and burned, put things dedicated to God to their own uses, despoiled priests and given other causes of offence. The same day, after sunset, the commander of the fort sends a message asking for a three-day truce, after which, if the help asked for from the Duke has not been forthcoming, the fort will be surrendered to the King. No one doubts but that this is a cunning trick, but the King does not see how he can refuse. The very next day the fort has been repaired with timber, stone, brick and stakes, and the King is told that there is no need for a truce. However, this same day, two Lithuanian envoys arrive asking in the Duke's name, that the truce be confirmed, allowing either side to send twelve nobles to conclude peace. The King agrees to a truce that is to last until a week after the Assumption. All this while, the Duke, more arrogant than ever, deaf to all sensible warnings, has made a secret pact with their common enemy, the Teutonic Knights.

As soon as the truce expires, guards are mounted on the camp, yet the King's men are carefree and playing chess and other games, so that when, at midday, the enemy sallies out from the fort and attacks, many are killed and wounded. On the Sunday, two Ruthenian dukes, Olelko and Basil, and some Lithuanians arrive, sent by Świdrygiello to treat for peace; but they go away some days later having achieved nothing, except that they have arranged for the truce to be extended for another week, much to the disadvantage of the King's army, for summer is almost over and autumn's rains are in the offing.

The King's fort at Ratno is betrayed to the enemy, who burn it to the ground. The enemy then goes on the rampage in Chełm, where people are carefree and unsuspecting; however, the burgrave with difficulty assembles 130 men with whom he attacks, killing 300 of the invaders and so stops the devastation of Chełm and avenges the betrayal of Ratno. Elsewhere, Peter Szafraniec and three other nobles have sallied out from their castles in search of the enemy. Dukes Basil and Balaban have left Krzemieniec with a host of Ruthenians and Walachians and been defeated by some Poles grazing their horses who were more numerous than the Duke realised. The Poles return to their camp and are able to revive their fellows with all the cattle they had captured. In the camp there is a horrible stench from rotting bodies of horses and a plague of the flies feeding on them. Many of the remaining horses are dying on their feet, because they are being fed mouldy wheat instead of being grazed, as they are accustomed. The loss of horses is so great that most of the cavalry has been demoted to infantry.

As the siege continues, so does the cruel struggle between Poles, Ruthenians and Lithuanians. If the enemy capture some Poles they chop these into little pieces, or else they fill them up with water till they suffocate, or inflict other tortures. Five Polish Dominicans, who took refuge in Łuck fort are put to death, and the Poles reciprocate by torturing the Lithuanians and Ruthenians they capture.

On the Sunday after St. Bartholomew's Day, the King concludes peace with Świdrygiello and the Poles look forward to returning home; but, before that can happen, it is reported that Świdrygiello has cunningly used the peace to invade Poland with an army of Tatars and Walachians. This, plus the fact that autumn and winter are at hand, mean that the King will have to leave Łuck. The envoys are dismissed and take with them Sędziwój of Ostroróg voivode of Poznań and Laurence Zaremba starosta of Sieradz who are to discuss outstanding details. But now the Duke makes more difficulties, insisting that he cannot agree to such terms unless the Knights and the Walachians are included. This gives rise to a suspicion that he has already made a permanent peace with the Knights.

Duke Theodore Fieduszko, a Ruthenian and the King's nephew, dies, leaving his treasure, jewels, horses, clothes and everything he has to King Władysław, who generously has it all distributed among his men.

The truce having expired at three o'clock on St. Augustine's Day, the bombardment of the castle begins again. The defenders make a stout reply, much to the admiration of the Poles. Some eminent Poles are suspected of selling gun-barrels and gun-powder to the castle. This arouses great indignation and Laurence Zaremba is challenged to a duel.

The King's inability to give proper attention to the war has gravely hampered the army, so he now entrusts the conduct of the war to a committee under Siemowit Duke of Mazovia and includ-

For quite a long time after the introduction of firearms stones remained the besieged's most effective weapon. No time was lost in reloading, and at the short distances involved a stone could be thrown with greater accuracy than a bullet fired from a handgun. The cross-bow was accurate, but re-loading it was quite a lengthy process. From Diebold Schilling's: Spiczer Chronik.

ing Nicholas of Michałów starosta of Cracow, the five voivodes of Sandomierz, Poznań, Sieradz, Łeczyca and Breść, John the Marshal and three others.

On the Feast of St. Giles, from a tower cleverly made of fire-wood and sited on the far bank, the castle is bombarded with huge stones and the rotting carcases of horses, much to the horror and terror of the defenders. Indeed, the castle could have been captured in a few days and the war thus ended, had not the King's clemency towards Świdrygiello and the Lithuanians made him defer an assault. Now, after many talks, a temporary peace is agreed and signed between the King and the Duke, a lasting peace being deferred to a conference to be held in Parczów, till when all hostilities are to cease. Much of the Polish army's meat, lard, butter, flour and other victuals are offered for sale to those in the castle, but then the sale is forbidden by the King.

The King now gives permission for the army to be disbanded and the siege raised. The camp is moved back across the river, and the next day the King begins a progress towards Vladimir. He spends the night in the home of the Bishop of Łuck and from there moves on into Chełm. Some greedy Poles, who stayed behind to try and sell the army's victuals once the King was out of the way, are given short shrift, being either killed or captured and stripped of all they have.

While the King has been busy with the siege of Łuck, the Prussian Master, Paul of Russdorff, has invaded Poland and put Kujawy and Dobrzyń to fire and the sword; while Nieszawa has been betrayed to the Knights. Toruń is ravaged by fire and the costly houses of the nobility, built of brick and timber at great expense, are all destroyed, as is the Church of St. Mary after it has been despoiled of its chalices, books and treasure. The whole kingdom is thus ravaged by fire. The Prussian Master announces rewards, which his treasury will pay to incendiaries: one mark for each house and for each manor three marks. The effect of this is to send the Master's men rushing to Dobrzyń and Kujawy, so that within a few days every manor and house there has been demolished. The crowd of the displaced, whose houses have been burned, their flocks driven away, their wives and daughters debauched, are prepared naked to fling themselves at armed men, but are dissuaded.

The truce with Świdrygiello signed, the King sends to the Knights announcing the signing of the pact and requiring them to stop devastating Poland, but too late for Dobrzyń and Kujawy, where twenty-four towns and more than a thousand farms have been burned. All this furthers the suspicions of his councillors that the King may have been responsible for the devastation.

A Livonian army under Dietrich the Marshal broke away from the Prussian army and marched into Poland and started putting it to fire and the sword. A number of Kujavian and Dobrzyń knights seeing the familiar sight of burned houses, pursue the Livonian force and, catching up with it near Nakło, attack it. The sound of voices singing *Bogu rodzica* resounds everywhere and so the few fight the many, the naked the clothed, peasants the soldiers. The slaughter is huge. Finally, the Livonians run, abandoning their camp. Few are captured, but four of the enemy's standards are taken and sent to Cracow. Most of those who escape, not knowing either the terrain or the language, tormented by hunger and cold, are captured by the peasants.

Poland receives a similar wound from the Walachians. The Voivode of Moldavia, Alexander, although a vassal of the King who has granted him castles in Poland and elsewhere in fee, has been bribed by Duke Świdrigiello, who follows the same rites, to make a foray through Podole and Ruthenia and carries off numbers of people and many flocks and herds. Shortly after this the Voivode dies.

The proposal for a campaign against heretical Bohemia to be led by Sigismund of Hungary is turned down by the Council in Basle and the task of dealing with the heretics entrusted to Frederick of Brandenburg, who assembles an immense army of units from most of the German principalities, which assemble in Nuremburg. From there the army moves to Eger and from there makes its way, with considerable difficulty, through the forest between Meissen, Bavaria and Bohemia, and makes camp in open country. When the small Bohemian army under Zygmunt Korybut which is advancing against them, is reported to be some two miles away, unaccountably, panic strikes the entire German army and they all take to their heels, abandoning their camp, their baggage and waggons, full of every kind of riches and food, to the enemy for their enrichment. When the Bohemians arrive on the scene there follows a massacre, rather than a battle. After which the peasants spend several days collecting the packs, weapons and clothing discarded by the fugitives.

A.D. 1432

Having spent Christmas in Cracow, the King reaches Lublin by Purification and arrives with the Queen in Jedlna for Carnival.

Moving on, he reaches Korczyn, where he spends some days discussing affairs of state, then moves on to Kalisz for Easter and so with the Queen and their two sons, Władysław and Casimir, to Sieradz, to attend a general assembly. Here, the King draws the delegates' attention to his advancing years and the fact that his death cannot be all that far away, and asks them which of his sons they would wish to succeed him. They choose Władysław.

While the King is in Wiślica an embassy arrives from John, King of Jerusalem, Cyprus and Armenia. This is headed by the Marshal of Cyprus, Baldwin, who has in his company 200 knights, among them his two handsome sons; with them is Peter of Bnin, a Polish knight who arrived in Cyprus seeking his fortune and rose high in the king's service. They have crossed, in their own galley, to the port of Walachia, Belgrade, where they bought horses and so travelled to Ruthenia and Poland. Władysław receives them with every honour and provides them with all their needs. Baldwin presents the King, Queen and their eminent officials with gifts of aloe wood, valuable spices and joss sticks. They then recount the grave wrong inflicted on the King of Cyprus, when, in 1426, the Sultan of Babylon invaded Cyprus and captured King John and his son. These have had to buy their freedom by paying to the Sultan an annual tribute of 1050 florins. The purpose of the embassy is to ask Władysław to lend King John 1000 gold ducats with which to hire soldiers and right the shameful harm done to Christianity; in return for which he offers Wladyslaw a share in the crown of Cyprus, Wladylsaw to have two voices and two shares, while John retains the third share. Secondly, Władysław is to give his daughter, Jadwiga, whom they believed to be still alive, to King John's only son in marriage. Władysław's reply is that he would have been glad to help with money and men had not his resources been tied up in his continuing war with the Tatars. Indeed. he might well have asked a similar favour from King John to enable him to maintain that war. So, the embassy departs laden with gifts, Baldwin and his sons receiving horses as well the valuable vessels and furs, that the others all get. They plan to cross from Venice, shrinking from the shorter route by which they had come, because of the way they had been harassed in Walachia.

From Korczyn the King sends Laurence Zaremba, Castellan of Sieradz, to his brother, Duke Świdrygiello, to exhort him to stop being stubborn and allow the two to make it up. He has another mission: to sound out the boyars and, in particular, Duke Sigismund Starodubsky, about the alternative plan of expelling Świdrygiello, both because of his bad rule and his favouring of the Greek rite. This is what is finally decided upon. Władysław intends to capture Oszmany in which Świdrygiello is living with his consort. She is captured, but Świdrygiello makes good his escape to Ruthenia. Thus Sigismund regains possession of the castles in Lithuania: Wilno, Troki, Grodno, though Smolensk and Vitebsk remain loyal to Świdrygiello. A proposal that the King should go to Lithuania himself is abandoned and, more wisely, a body of the King's councillors is sent instead. (The King does send a force of his household troops to invest Olesko, which is quickly captured and thereafter remains part of the kingdom of Poland.) The King's envoys leave Lublin and reach Grodno, where Sigismund and all his officials come out half a mile to greet them. They are sincerely and blithely welcomed and then conducted to the lodgings prepared for them, where they are provided with everything they might need. A few days are spend in agreeing terms and drawing up and signing the necessary documents, after which Sigismund is sworn in as Duke of Lithuania, a Lithuania that does not include Podole, Łuck, Olesko, Hrodło or Łopatyn.

Having attended to domestic affairs in Lublin, the King moves on to Lwów in Ruthenia, to which his army has returned after capturing Olesko. Reinforced, the army moves into Podole to deal with Duke Fethko of Ostrog, one of Lithuania's most successful military commanders, who has been raiding Poland from the castles he holds in Podole, using a mixed force of Tatars, Wala-chians, Ruthenians and Bessarabians. When the King's army reaches Podole, Fethko decides not to risk a pitched battle, but to adopt a policy of frequent skirmishes and attacks on individual tar-gets, and this enables the King to capture all the castles held by the Duke in Podole, except for Brasław. The Duke then recruits a further force of Tatars, Walachians and Bessarabians, with which he attacks the Poles, who narrowly escape defeat.

Świdrygiello has recruited an army of 20,000 Ruthenians and Tatars with which he now marches into Lithuania, where he is joined by an army from the Knights in Livonia. Grand-duke Sigismund assembles a force of Lithuanians, Samogitians and Poles living in Drohiczyn and with it hastens to Oszmiana and succeeds in defeating the invaders. Among those captured is one of the King's nephews, who had joined Świdrygiello. The latter escapes. Sigismund then builds a church on the site of his victory and endows it.

At the beginning of July, a Hussite army of Taborites and Orphans invades Silesia. It burns the monastery at Lubiąż after looting its treasures and removing its bells and lead roof, and lays waste to several towns. The inhabitants of Olesko are so terrified of the Hussites that they set fire to their town and take refuge with their families and valuables in Wratisław. The Hussites are able to put out the fires and collect enormous spoil.

A.D. 1433

The King celebrates Christmas in Cracow, and there spends several days discussing with his barons and prelates ways and means of waging war with the Knights now that the truce is at an end, a war in which the King, worn by age, his eyesight dimmed, cannot personally take part. The Lithuanians are preoccupied with their own war, while for a number of reasons, neither the Tatars nor the Walachians can be involved. The King then moves to Korczyn and Jedlna, where he stays over Carnival, and then continues to Sandomierz and from there to Wielkopolska.

About Easter, an army of Bohemian Taborites, on its way from Silesia to Hungary, from which Sigismund is absent, being in Italy trying to obtain the imperial crown, approaches the fron-tier. The Poles try to stop their advance by blocking the roads with felled trees, but the Hussites burn or otherwise remove these and move on. Some Hungarian barons, aware of their approach, collect an army and advance against them, at which they break camp and make for Kežmarok, which the frightened inhabitants abandon on their approach, leaving them free to loot it, which they do along with several other towns, before continuing on home through the mountains with all their spoil.

After spending Easter in Kalisz, Władysław goes to Poznań, where Duke Bogusław is to marry Amelia, daughter of Siemovit of Mazovia. Here, the King receives envoys from the Hussite army, which calls itself Orphans, and which has been ravaging Meissen, Saxony and Nuremburg, who offer him whatever military aid he might wish against the Knights. The offer is welcomed and the envoys sent with the whole army against Nowa Marchia, now under control of the Knights. The King's councillors consider that the quickest and most effective action would be for the Bohemian army, which all its neighbours fear, together with the force from Wielkopolska, to ravage Nowa Marchia, and then join up with another force from Cracow and march into Pomerania.

During Rogation, legates from the Council in Basle come to tell the King that they have per-suaded the Knights to embrace peace and ask him to send his officials to Słupsk to agree terms. When these arrive there, they find neither officials from the Knights nor the legates. The latter ar-rive the next day, making all sorts of excuses for the absence of the Knights and asking for a fort-night's postponement and this they obtain. Returning then, again they find none of the other parties and go away once more.

War against Prussia is now decided upon. The combined armies march into Nowa Marchia which thus once more comes under the authority of the King of Poland.

An army of Samogitians makes a secret foray into Livonia, which is called Courland, and, meeting with no resistance, for twelve days ravages the country and carries off captives of both sexes and much booty.

By using wiles and bribery, Duke Nos, a Ruthenian of the Greek rite, has obtained possession of Łuck fort, from which he has been making frequent raids into Chełm, whose Governor puts up a stout resistance and finally defeats him.

On the King's orders, the combined armies assemble in Koło. There, the prelates and barons, meeting in secret, decide that the King is too nearly senile to be entrusted with the conduct of the war, so they entrust it to the Castellan of Cracow, Nicholas of Michałów, who marches the army into Pomerania and puts this to fire and the sword. Another army from Wielkopolska and the Bohemian army having devastated Nowa Marchia, are directed to Pomerania; while the King moves to Konin and makes it his temporary residence. In Pomerania, the Polish forces attack the town and castle at Tucholya. They destroy the suburbs and surroundings, but bombardment from the castle prevents them taking up position there and they have to camp in woods a mile away. Another force of Bohemians from Nowa Marchia now joins them and invests Chojnica. Neither town is captured, but Tszchow is stormed and all those in it, numbering 10,000 or more, sent to the Polish camp and placed in the custody of the principal Polish nobles, all, that is, but those who are Bohemians, identified by language, who are handed over to the Bohemian commander. In the middle of the camp is a huge pyre on which all are thrown. Imitating this, a certain Pole builds a wooden cage of his own in which he places the Pomeranian commander and some others, then surrounds the cage with dry combustible materials and sets fire to them. Seeing flames all round them, the Pomeranians break down the door of the cage and try to get out. A number of Poles, who have come along to see the sight, intercept them and would have killed them, had not the Polish commander, who had learned of what is happening, come running, forbidden the sacrifice and had the flames put out. One of those who escaped had his feet badly burned, he managed to get to a nearby lake to quench the pangs, but then, unable to bear the pain, he drowned himself. No further cruelty is inflicted on the captives. The women and children captured in Tszchow are not only respected, but granted their liberty and treated with humanity. Polish soldiers are sent to guard them and see that none is molested, maltreated or robbed of her possessions. This adds lustre to Poland's fame, and when the women see that not only their persons, but everything they have are safe, they are loud in their praises of the Poles. How different these are to the Knights, who, when in the previous year, they raided this same area, satisfied their lusts to the full, prostituting their women captives. As the fires in Tszchow have made it impossible for the women to return there and they would not be safe in the houses outside, they are all brought to the Vistula and taken by ship to where they can be safely housed. The army's camps are searched and any women found in them released.

The Poles now move against Gdańsk, burning farms, towns and manors as they go. Reaching the city, they halt for four days, before heavily bombarding it with their siege engines and bombards, and reducing the port to ruins. Here many Poles and Bohemians discover a taste for the sea. Then, after the Feast of St. Laurence, the Polish army leaves Gdańsk to the applause and delight of its inhabitants, and, in six stages, reaches Tucholya. Here a bombardment from the castle prevents them making camp opposite the castle, and they have to move half a mile away. The King then moves on Jasieniec, and, in his camp there, civilian and military envoys from Prussia arrive to discuss peace. When Jasieniec falls, the Knights try to hasten the talks, and it is agreed that they will conclude a truce to last until the Epiphany; that a conference is to be held in Brześć on St. Andrew's day to discuss terms; and that the Knights' captives, debilitated by hunger, who, like locusts, destroy the places where they are kept, are to be released.

Pomerania has been so ravaged that only fourteen manors are left intact. There is really no more to be done and Nicholas of Michałów disbands his troops and sends them home. The Bohemian troops are similarly disbanded and they go to Sieradz to which the King went on St. Bartholomew's Day after spending almost the entire summer in Konin, and here he rewards them for their services with money, gold and silver vessels, clothing and fine horses. The King moves on to Przyszów, where he receives Master Christian, an envoy from Prague and the most famous astronomer of his day. He is also what one might call an elder of the heretical Bohemian sect, and, when Zbigniew Oleśnicki Bishop of Cracow learns of his being received in private audience, he demands, and obtains, his instant dismissal, though the King insists that they had discussed nothing but eclipses, the unusual conjunctions of planets and other such things that the Master maintains presage the deaths of Kings and Princes.

When St. Andrew's Day comes and the delegates assemble for the conference in Brześć, they are quite unable to agree on anything, and, after a while, the Poles decide to prepare for war. Their plan is to mount a campaign in the winter and spring, when the army cannot run short of food and most damage can be done to the enemy, while the Vistula, being frozen, will make it easy to transport troops and their equipment across. Epiphany is made the date for the troops to assemble. There is, however, one difficulty: where to get the money to pay the troops adequately? The commanders are afraid to engage in war without money, for they remember how, during the siege of Chojnica, the troops mutinied and announced that never again would they fight without being paid in advance. Then, just as the King is about to leave Łęczyca, envoys arrive from the Prussian Master and his Order offering to accept the peace they had refused in Brześć. As this cannot be arranged quickly, a truce is agreed that is to last twelve years.

Świdrigiello makes a foray into Lithuania with a mixed force of Livonians, Ruthenians and Tatars, taking advantage of the fact that the Grand-duke is unable to help the Poles, who are fully occupied fighting the Prussians. Although Zygmunt has assembled a force of Lithuanians and Samogitians, he never risks a pitched battle, but moving his force through trackless country worries Świdrygiello's foragers; nonetheless, Świdrygiello puts most of Lithuania including Wilno, Troki and Lida to fire and the sword, at the same time as his Tatars cross the Dniepr and cruelly devastate the area of Kiev.

A.D. 1434

The King goes to Jedlna for Epiphany. There, he receives envoys from the Grand-duke inviting him to Lithuania, an invitation which he accepts, and so, after spending several days hunting, he goes to Krynki, where the Grand-duke, his prelates and barons come out to greet him and welcome their benefactor with humility and devotion, loading him, and his, with gifts of gold and silver, clothing and horses. The King confirms Zygmunt as Grand-duke, but refuses an invitation to visit the remoter parts of the country and returns to Poland by the usual stages.

The King appoints the bishops of Cracow and Poznań and the Chancellor of Poland and Deacon of Cracow, as his delegates to the Council in Basle. They are provided with the necessary funds from the royal treasury. Then, in the presence of all the King's councillors, the Bishop of Cracow berates the King and lists his deficiences: spending his nights in debauchery, so that he has to sleep during the day and is fit for little else; neglect of law and order, failure to protect the Church, orphans and the oppressed, etc. etc. and suggests that he mend his ways before Death, which is imminent, overtakes him.

After Easter, the King leaves Cracow and progresses to Ruthenia. He intends to go to Halicz, where Stephen, Voivode of Moldavia, is due to come and pay him homage and swear allegiance. But by the time he gets to Medyka, a sudden return of winter has replaced the gentleness of spring, killing the corn and the young flowers and leaves on the trees. After the Feast of St. Wojciech, in accordance with the old pagan custom that he has observed all his life, the King goes into the forest to listen to its magic sounds and hear the song of the nightingale, and there he spends the greater part of one night and in doing so becomes chilled to the marrow, for he was one whom cold never worried and was wearing only sheepskin, having all his life refused to put on expensive furs. As a result he is stricken with a high fever while dining in the house where he is staying and he has to take to his bed.

For a fortnight the King's doctors are unable to do anything, and finally the King makes confession, receives the last rites, makes his will and commends himself to God. Thus, he dies in the third hour of the night of the last day in May. His body is placed in a wooden coffin, smeared with pitch and resin and taken to Cracow for burial. It is met outside the city by Queen Sophia and her two sons, Władysław and Casimir, and conducted to the Church of St. Michael.

Meanwhile, the delegates to the Council in Basle have been recalled from Poznań, which was as far as they had got. To avoid civil strife, the coronation of one or the other of the two boys is hurried forward and the Feast of St. Peter and St. Paul fixed for the ceremony. Special messengers are sent to the Grand-duke inviting him to attend in person. The funeral of the dead King is held on June 18. The ceremony is conducted by Albert Archbishop of Gniezno, in the presence of the two boys, Queen Sophia and a throng of nobles and other dignitaries. Paul of Zathor makes a speech in the vernacular detailing all the good things the late King did for his country. The corpse is then placed in a marble sepulchure, specially built, and buried.

Because of indecision as to which of the two boys to crown, the coronation of the new king is postponed until the Feast of St. James the Apostle, which involves sending out fresh invitations. As the day approaches, those invited: prelates, nobles and dignitaries from all over the kingdom, converge on Cracow. The Grand-duke has felt unable to leave his country, in case Świdrygiello should invade it, but sends representives fully empowered. The Voivode of Mazovia and Duke Siemowit do the same. Voices are now heard saying that the new king will be too young to rule by himself and must be given tutors and mentors. Some say they would prefer the second son, Casimir, but these are overruled, and on the Feast of St. James the prelates, dukes, nobles and dignitaries assemble in the White Hall in Cracow castle; then, after some more wrangling, the procession sets out for the church, where, despite the late hour, Albert Archbishop of Gniezno and his assistants in all their robes with great merriment and eagerness robe Władysław in the sacred garments: sandals, humeral, alb, maniple, stole and dalmatic, and, on top of all this, a rain-cape; he is then led to the great altar, anointed and crowned. In view of his tender years, he is made to swear to observe the laws, statutes and liberties and preserve the muniments of the Kingdom. Thus, is the coronation, begun about midday and retarded by the opposition of three barons, duly concluded in the late evening. The following day is equally propitious for the King, who in full regalia, diamond cap on his head, and surrounded by his bishops, descends to the city to allow the populace to see him. After this he returns to the palace, but does not go to the apartment prepared for him, where he is to receive the city councillors who are to swear allegiance, because the bishops and dukes of Mazovia cannot agree on which side of the King they are to be, when he dismounts. During the next few days, there is much discussion as to the extent to which a King of Poland, who is a minor, should govern on his own. Many want his near relative, Siemovit, Duke of Mazovia, who is there in Cracow, to assume the task of tutor and guide. This idea is finally turned down and instead, administrators are appointed for each part of the kingdom, except for Cracow, which is to have two: one to attend to the coinage, the other to the affairs of the capital and seat of the monarch. The administrators are to have restricted powers.

In the summer of this year, hostilities break out between Poland and Silesia. Each destroys what it can of the other's lands; but, in the end, a conference is held in Bandzin at which peace is refashioned and reparations agreed. However, no sooner are the documents signed, than the peace is broken by raiding parties from Moravia and Silesia again ravaging Poland.

A.D. 1435

As before, Władysław is living with his brother, Prince Casimir, in Cracow. He and the Court spend Christmas there. Lent he spends in Sandomierz, returning to Cracow for Easter. On Laetare Sunday an assembly is held to fill the post of voivode of Sandomierz vacant after the death of Spithko of Tarnów. The post goes by majority vote to the Castellan of Sandomierz, John of Cziszow. It is also decided that, in order to avoid dispute in the future, such posts are to be filled by appointment. Thus, the Castellan of Lublin, Dobiesław of Oleśnica, becomes the new castellan of Sandomierz, the Castellan of Wojnicz, Domarath of Kobilany, goes to Lublin, John of Thanczin of Biecz to Wojnicz, while Clemens Wątrobka is chosen as Castellan of Biecz. Thus are the vacant posts in the kingdom filled while the King is still a minor.

On St. Florian's Day delegates of the Poles and Teutonic Knights assemble in Brześć in Kujawy to discuss, *inter alia*, the question of a permanent peace; but the Knights put so many difficulties in the way of achieving this that the assembly moves to Słuszow, as if Brześć were not the right place in which to conclude peace. However, the new venue proves no better, for the Knights do not want peace. At this time the Grand-duke of Lithuania is at war with the Livonian Master, to help whom the Prussian Knights have sent a considerable force. Now, just as the Poles are on the point of going home, two messengers arrive, one sent to the Poles, the other to the Knights, each bringing the news that Barthor de Lo the Master of Livoniia's army has been routed. The horrified Knights, who hitherto have turned down all offers of peace, hurriedly send a delegation to Brześć to say that they are ready to make peace. So, a truce is arranged and another meeting fixed for the Feast of St. Nicholas. That done, they all set out for Sieradz to attend another meeting to be held on St. Stanisław's Day. This is attended by the King, his brother and the Queen Dowager. They have to decide whether or not to free the Voivode of Moldavia, Elias, who is imprisoned in Sieradz. His supporters among the Walachians press for him to be freed, while the representatives of Voivode Stephen want him to stay where he is. It is decided not to free him as long as the King is a minor, and thus ensure Stephen's loyalty and obedience. However, shortly after this Elias escapes and makes his way unhindered to Walachia, which at once becomes the stage for civil strife. The Sieradz meeting also discusses the serious quarrel that has arisen between the dignitaries of the Church and the laity over tithes and their collection and certain other burdens. In Cracow it is about the payment of tithe on the harvest and the voluntary payment of tithes on fields from which a peasant has been removed. In Wielkopolska, the main dispute is about tithes not having to be paid on new cultivation, a privilige formerly granted by the Archbishop and Chapter of Gniezno, but one which is now disputed. At a meeting of the provincial synod in Łęczyca on Ascension Day the Church is represented by Albert Archbishop of Gniezno and almost all the other bishops of the kingdom, the abbots, doctors and masters; the laity by a smaller number of the barons headed by the castellan and starosta of Cracow, Nicholas of Michałów. The chief matter of discussion is perhaps, whether a noble who has removed a peasant from his land should continue to pay tithe in the same way. While the barons of Cracow duchy demand the extension to them of the privilige granted to those in Wielkopolska by Archbishop Jarosław of Gniezno, because he was the primate of Poland, the Church contends that Jarosław's priviliges cannot extend to Cracow as they were obtained contrary to the custom and practice of the Church; and they were granted in Poznań not in Gniezno. The Church in Cracow has its own priviliges granted at about the same time by Bishop Bodzęta at the request of Prince Casimir and the barons. The lay delegates, seeing that they are losing the argument, decide to withhold tithes until the Church grants them what they want, but when Archbishop Albert threatens to place an interdict on all who do this, nothing more is heard of the matter.

The Roman Emperor Sigismund sends envoys to the Czechs calling upon them to wipe out the bands of criminals in their country, and, with peace restored, accept him as king. Crowds come to meet him in Ratisbon and acclaim him king. Then, at the request of the Hungarians, he goes by boat to Buda to attend to Hungarian affairs.

Bolesław Świdrygiello, who has been banished from Lithuania, is being encouraged by Emperor Sigismund to demand the return of the duchy, a large part of which, i.e. the Ruthenian territories, is still loyal to him. Now, he receives the support of Sigismund Korybut, who in previous years had considerable experience of fighting in Bohemia. Świdrygiello, who knows how honest the latter is and how skilled in the arts of war, is delighted to have him on his side, as are the Knights, with whom he was once allied against the Poles, and these have promised to help him with money and troops. So, about Assumption, having assembled an army of Ruthenians, Czechs, Tatars and Silesians, he moves secretly into Lithuanian territory, where he is further reinforced by troops from the Prussian and Livonian Masters. All this is known to the Grand-duke, who assembles as large an army as he can, but, realizing that the enemy is much the stronger, and also that many Lithuanians, whose fathers, brothers or relations he had murdered, are hostile to him and favour Świdrygiello, he sends to King Władysław begging him not leave him in the lurch, but to send him help. This Władysław is advised to do, even though he realizes that he is sending men to fight his own uncle. The delighted Grand-duke takes his courage in both hands and advances against Świdrygiello.

The two armies then zigzag about the country, destroying it as they go, and finally reach the vicinity of Wilkomierz, where they pitch camp with only a small river between them. For three days and nights they just eye one another. Each expects an attack and none goes about without his arms. The cavalry are always on the alert. And, all the while, rain deluges down, to the great discomfort of those on guard and of the horses. The swollen river fills them all with fear, lest they be ordered to cross it or be forced to do battle in so unfavourable a place. Sigismund Korybut makes every endeavour to resolve the conflict peacefully and spends three days in negotiations; when he realizes the enemy is not going to agree to arbitration, he moves his army to where he can more easily link up with the reinforcements coming from Livonia. Duke Sigismund is said to have told some who were speaking disparagingly of the Poles and Lithuanians, most of whom fight half naked or wearing only their black armour, that there was more strength in them than in the splendidly equipped Germans of his own army, and that, were he free to choose, he would choose the former. Thinking that the enemy is afraid and retreating, Jacob Kobilensky commander of Świdrygiello's army orders a pursuit. There is a great clamour and the Poles, as is their custom, start singing *Bogu Rodzica* and, after a few verses, engage the enemy. There is a loud clashing of lances, swords and armour. Many jump from their horses. Many are killed or horribly wounded. The battle lasts for an hour, at the end of which the Knights, Livonians, Tatars and Ruthenians are put to flight, sweeping along with them those who are coming to help them, so that these never even fight. The Poles and Lithuanians harry the fleeing enemy, killing many and capturing many. Many drown in the River Święta. Świdrygiello himself escapes with a handful of Ruthenians who know the forest tracks, but most do not know them and almost the whole of the army of Knights and Livonians is killed or captured. Indeed, for the next fortnight, stray Knights and Livonians are still being rounded up. The rest of the Livonian army which has not yet arrived, learning of the disaster and not knowing what to do, builds wooden bridges and lurks by a lake where it hopes to find safety, only to be met by Lithuanians, so that all are captured with their equipment. In this engagement Barthor the Livonian Master and Marshal Dietrich Croe are killed and the Livonian forces so weakened, that, for a long time, there are no men to garrison their forts, which could easily have been taken by their enemies had the Prussian Master not provided the requisite troops. Among those taken prisoner was Sigismund Korybut, who was wounded, and Sigismund Roth, a fierce enemy of the Poles and one whom Czarnkowski had earlier taken prisoner, and who then, though having given his word of honour, had failed to surrender. Both of these the Grand-duke orders to be drowned. It is said that Sigismund Korybut was not drowned, but died while his wounds were being treated, either from the wounds themselves or from poison added to the ointment with which they were dressed by a doctor specially sent by the Grand-duke. After this, all the Ruthenian towns and castles desert Świdrygiello and submit to Grand-duke Zygmunt.

Emperor Sigismund the King of Hungary sends to King Władysław asking him to intervene and stop the fighting between the Grand-duke and Świdrygiello, or, at least, to arrange a truce. The King replies that matters have gone too far and must be decided by fighting, but Sigismund's envoys have not yet left the palace before news arrives that the Grand-duke has defeated his enemy and the war is over. The next night bells are rung and bonfires lit all over Cracow.

A peace conference arranged for the Feast of St. Nicholas in Brześć is attended by the representatives of the Grand-duke, the Dukes of Mazovia and of Poland's ally the Duke of Słupsk. The Poles do not reject peace, in their favourable position they are eager to arrange it. They are represented by Albert, Archbishop of Gniezno, Bishops Zbigniew of Cracow, Stanisław of Poznań, just returned from the Council of Basle, Władysław of Włocławek and Stanisław of Płock; by Nicholas of Michałów castellan of Cracow and John of Cziszow the voivode. Dobiesław of Oleśnica castellan of Sandomierz, Dobrogost castellan of Poznań and several others. The Prussian Master is represented by Bishops Francis of Warmińsk and John of Pomezania, the judge of Chełm, several knights and commanders and the leading councillors of the Prussian towns. So many difficulties are adduced that the suspicion grows that there is no way in which peace can be arranged and many leave the gathering. One of the main difficulties is the large amount of money demanded by the Poles as reparations, and also their refusal to recognize as Grand-duke anyone not nominated by King Władysław. More than once the delegates send their servants home ahead of them, only themselves to be prevented from following. In the end, peace is proclaimed in the parish church in Brześć by the Bishops of Cracow and Warmińsk, and a *Te Deum* is sung. When a list of the different conditions is drawn up and carefully checked, it is found that there are so many that there is not room for them all on a single parchment; indeed, a whole scroll is hardly long enough.

A.D. 1436

A general assembly is held in Sieradz on Reminiscere Sunday. The King does not attend, but a large number of prelates and nobles confirm the conditions for peace agreed with the Knights and each attaches his seal. Two captains, specially sent by the Prussian Master, see to it that each signatory swears a personal oath that the peace will be observed. This done, the two go to Cracow and Sandomierz to require the same of the prelates and nobles there. At the same time, two Polish envoys are sent to Prussia to require in the name of the King that the Prussian Master, his commanders and the other nobles swear similar oaths.

A Hungarian–Polish conference is held in Kežmarok to consider the Hungarian demand that Poland return the territory of Spis without recompense. This the Poles reject on the grounds that, in his hour of need, the King of Hungary borrowed 50,000 score of broad grosses from the King of Poland and gave a part of Spis as security. The Poles contend that it is inequitable to require the return of the territory without the loan being repaid, since, for that amount they could have bought outright twice as much land as was pledged. After much friendly discussion, the Hungarians, seeing that their claim is not going to be accepted, abandon it and they all go home.

Seeing how the unfortunate Walachia is being torn by civil strife as the two brothers, Stephen and Elias, vie with each other for supremacy, King Władysław makes repeated efforts to restore peace and, in the end, succeeds. The territory is divided: one part, which includes Biały Zamek and the sea-port, going to Stephen, and the other part with Soczawa and the surrounding area to Elias.

To ensure that both parts remain under his authority, the King requires the two voivodes to pay him the requisite homage. Stephen devises excuses, but Elias gives a solemn undertaking to do this. The ceremony is to take place in Lwów on St. Michael's Day, and shortly before then the King, his brother, the prelates and eminent personages of the realm arrive in Lwów, where Elias and his councillors already are. On the day appointed, after hearing Mass in the cathedral, the King wearing his crown, his brother and the Polish prelates and lords, seat themselves in a decorated chamber specially built for the occasion in the market square. Voivode Elias, holding his military standards and insignia and the arms of Walachia, then approaches the throne on which the King in his royal robes is seated. Humbly the Voivode bends his knee and, as a further sign of submission, breaks the wooden shafts of his standards and places them at the King's feet and swears to remain loyal, obedient and submissive to the King. The King then embraces him and gives him the kiss of peace. Next, he gives his hand to the Walachian boyars and promises to treat them as loyal subjects and to defend them from enemy raids. He grants Elias a place on his left and the boyars places appropriate to their rank and services. To make the act of homage more lasting, the proceedings are published in an official document to which the participants attach their seals. A separate agreement is made whereby Elias and his successors undertake to provide an annual tribute of twenty waggons of fish and forty oxen for the royal kitchen, forty purple garments and one hundred horses; also that Siepien is to revert to Poland. The King grants Elias the castle at Halicz as a repository for his treasure and a refuge in case of need. Elias and his retinue are then entertained at a splendid banquet and given lavish gifts. Next day, it is Elias' turn to entertain the King and his officials, who each receive silver spoons and utensils and purple garments. After the banquet, Elias urges the King to appoint Jan Odrowaz archbishop of Lwów, and, although the King has already chosen another candidate, he agrees, being reluctant to refuse the Voivode's very first request, though what he is doing is not strictly legal. Bishop Zbigniew of Cracow is the only one to object.

Realizing the advantage of being related to the Roman Emperor and aware that neither King Sigismund, already old, nor his daughter can have male heirs, Władysław proposes that Sigismund adopt him and his brother Casimir as his sons and marry them to his nieces, the daughters of Duke Albert of Austria. Such marriages would guarantee lasting peace to several kingdoms. Sigismund is delighted with the idea. He and Queen Barbara go to Ilawa, where he has talks with the Czechs and confirms acceptance of the arrangement they made with the legates and promises the Czechs that Church property can be retained until it has been bought back from those to whom it was pledged. Although exiled priests still have no hope of returning, Jan Rokiczan is promised a post in Prague, once the ban has been lifted which Philibert, chief of the legates, does shortly afterwards. All this arranged, the Emperor moves on and, on August 24, reaches Prague, where he, who so recently was considered an enemy of the Czechs, the son of Antichrist, a bastard, sacriliegeous and damned, is received with special honour, and, as if his original coronation were invalid, Bishop Philibert crowns him anew King of Bohemia and his wife, Barbara, Queen. The Emperor takes over the monastery of the Minor Friars, hears Mass there and hands the monastery back to the Order. He also allows the Taborites to live according to their rules. And all the while, the poison of heresy is spreading.

Now, the King tries to repair and rebuild what has been destroyed and here he is far too generous, for his generosity extends even to the peasants, monks and priests, who have used force to make themselves knights and nobles. He grants castles, towns and villages to those who had arbitrarily seized them and even grants them considerable sums of money. Although this wins him immediate popularity, he reaps only harm. The people's defence of the heresies of Wycliffe is as strong as ever, if only because thereby they hope to retain what temporal goods they have seized and which, otherwise, they would have to relinquish.

When the Polish envoys arrive, the Emperor loads them with gifts of imperial generosity and tells them that, much as he likes Władysław's suggestion, he is too preoccupied with Bohemian affairs that should have been attended to years before, to be able to embark on discussions of such a pact; but he urges Władysław to bring the matter up again, once the Emperor is back in Austria or Hungary, promising that then he will not refuse his consent.

A.D. 1437

During Lent an unusually large number of the King's councillors foregather in Cracow to discuss a number of matters concerning the capital, Gniezno, especially that of the coinage.

The more sensible ones advocate stopping minting the small coins that are everywhere, since, as their number grows, their assay is less, so each increase in their number reduces their value. They are told that many counterfeit coins are being brought in from Cracow, Moravia, Silesia and Bohemia, to everyone's detriment. Although Bishop Zbigniew of Cracow warns them that even gold and silver can become valueless if there is too much of it, he finds it difficult to convince those in favour of the present situation out of which they are profiting, thus the import of counterfeit coins is allowed to go unpunished, and so not only the nobility, but commoners as well continue to enrich themselves to the detriment of the Kingdom.

The King remains in Cracow all spring and summer. Again and again messengers from his uncle, Bolesław Świdrygiełło, arrive bringing him rich gifts and beseeching him to take the latter under his protection, a request that he repeats in person on August 13. An assembly is called to meet in Sieradz on St. Jadwiga's Day to discuss the matter. To strengthen his case, Świdrygiełło makes a present of the castle in Łuck to the castellan and starosta of Olesko. The main difficulty is that the King and his councillors have already assured the Grand-duke in writing and on oath that they condemn Świdrygiełło, regard him as a mutual enemy and will give him no support. The Grand-duke has repeatedly complained that, although Świdrygiełło was utterly defeated in April, some Polish nobles still receive him and seem to wish him well. The Grand-duke is also pressing for the return of Łuck. In the end the assembly decides to send a delegation to the Grand-duke to try to reconcile him with Świdrygiełło and get him to agree to Świdrygiełło being supported in Poland. The Grand-duke rejects both proposals and, with tears in his eyes, begs them to preserve the alliance and not give comfort to his enemy. The delegates then give the Grand-duke written assurances confirming the original agreements and adding certain clauses that consolidate the alliance and ensure peace. These documents make it perfectly clear that the Grand-duchy of Lithuania, being subject to the Kingdom of Poland and united with it, will, on the death of the Grand-duke, be put at the disposal of the King of Poland, despite the fact that the Grand-duke has a son, Michael, who, on his father's death, will have to be content with only part of his inheritance.

A.D. 1438

Christmas sees an outbreak of lawlessness. No one is any longer restrained by fear of the King, and everyone is enjoying unusual affluence. It all began when Spytko of Melsztyn, thinking that Bishop Zbigniew of Cracow falsely suspected him of adhering to the Czech heresy, of taking communion in both kinds and of sheltering heretical priests and so was trying to have him excommunicated, assembled a small armed force from his household and those of some friends, and tried to capture some of the Bishop's properties. The King is aware of what is going on and repeatedly sends to Spytko telling him to desist, yet Spytko stubbornly persists. He refuses mediation and then invades the estate of Uszwicki, occupies the manor and, with the help of a Ruthenian duke, Frederick Ostroski, plunders and destroys the farmstead and barns and all that is in them. The King summons Spytko, as a rebel, and forces him to pay compensation and withdraw from the manor.

The Emperor Sigismund falls ill in Prague. Being advanced in years and so liable to die at any time, the Empress Barbara, who is anxious to preserve the monarchy, secretly sends for certain Czech nobles and demands that, in the event of Sigismund's death, they will arrange for her to marry the King of Poland. When Sigismund realizes that he is soon to die, being uncertain of the loyalty of the Czechs, he leaves Bohemia and goes to Znojma. He has a guard put on the Empress, summons the Czech and Hungarian nobles to his chamber, tells them that he is dying and names his son-in-law, Albert of Austria, king of the two countries. He keeps enquiring whether envoys from Poland are on their way and, if not, asks for them to be sent for, saying that he would die more peacefully, if he could marry his granddaughters to King Władysław and his brother; but he dies on December 7, before this can be arranged. The Hungarian nobles duly elect Albert as their king and, on January 1, he and his wife, Elizabeth, are crowned in Székesfehérvár. The Empress Barbara is then released and granted an annual pension of 20,000 in gold. The Electors agree on Albert of Austria as the new emperor and that he is to receive the sceptre in Frankfurt; but Albert considers it unwise to accept the office without the consent of the Hungarian nobles, as he had promised, but in the end the Hungarians do give their assent and Albert becomes Emperor.

The people of Bohemia are divided over their choice of new king: some prefer Albert, King of the Romans; others would like Casimir, the thirteen-year old brother of the King of Poland; so both parties send envoys to their chosen one to ask him to accept election. One goes to Casimir in Cracow and urges Władysław to allow his brother to accept the Bohemian crown. The King summons an assembly to discuss the offer, and, meanwhile, sends to the Grand-duke, as chief duke and councillor of the kingdom, to ask his opinion. The assembly spends several days discussing the matter: the Mazovians advise against acceptance, since their country has been so weakened by internal division and is infected with a condemned heresy, and, especially, because the Hungarians have chosen a different king. The Lithuanians all insist that the offer should be accepted, as, if this should lead to war, they would not be required to produce accounts of the royal revenues for which they are responsible. Others vote for acceptance, merely to prevent the King of the Romans and Hungary having it, because, should he by peaceful means acquire a second of Poland's neighbouring kingdoms, he, being a German, could harm Poland. So, Casimir accepts the Bohemian crown and King Władysław sends the Voivode of Poznań Sędziwój Ostrorog and Jan of Tęczyn Voivode of Sandomierz with a considerable armed force to see that his brother's election goes through. Not everyone likes the decision, especially not Bishop Oleśnicki of Cracow, who thinks that it will mean that the Czech heresy will be bound to spread to Poland.

King Albert, knowing that Casimir has accepted the crown with the knowledge and approval of his brother, sends envoys to King Władysław to explain the basis of his claim to the kingdom: first because his wife, Elizabeth, is the only daughter and heir of Sigismund, the late king; secondly, by virtue of old treaties made between Hungary and the House of Austria, and, thirdly, by reason of his recent election; and to ask that he restrain his brother from accepting the offer made by a handful of people who had no right to make it. Władysław replies that he is aware of what has happened and that his brother accepted the offer all unaware that he might in any way be wronging the King of the Romans, as it is common knowledge that women do not succeed to a throne; further, that, even if there had been a document or agreement that entitled Albert to claim the throne of Bohemia that claim must have been invalidated by the difference in customs and established practice of the two countries, for which reason the King has sent the voivodes of Poznań, Sędziwój of Ostrorog and of Sandomierz, Jan of Tęczyn, with a small force to implement the election, but with orders first to cleanse Bohemia of its heresy and restore the true Catholic faith and to bring back peace; for it was not the intention, nor the desire of his brother to rule Bohemia on any other conditions. But, at the same time, his brother cannot be deprived of the right that eminent men have bestowed on him. The Czechs and the Poles have one language and one origin, while neither has anything in common with the Germans. The people of Bohemia are loyal to its choice. He has no fear of external force. With this reply, and many gifts, the envoys return to King Albert, who, warned of the approach of the Polish force, is afraid lest Casimir take possession of all Bohemia, for now every Czech, even those who sent for Albert, seems eager to give his allegiance to Casimir. Dropping everything, Albert hurries to Prague, which, hitherto, has supported him, and on the Sunday before the Feast of St. James has himself formally crowned by Bishop Philibert, the papal legate to Bohemia. Meanwhile, the Polish force, having avoided a number of traps and ambushes laid for it, advances on Prague, its ranks swelled by nobles and barons. King Albert takes fright and informs the prelates and barons of Hungary and the German Electors and princes of the danger in which he finds himself and asks for help to be sent to him quickly. As a result, all Germany takes to arms and many of its princes, Meissen, Saxony and Brandenburg, personally head their armies, which assemble, intent on destroying the King of Poland's army. Albert moves out from Prague and sends to the Poles demanding that they stand and fight. The Poles reply that, in the first place, they have come on an errand of peace: to restore peace and the Catholic faith to Bohemia, and that, whatever right Albert has to the throne of Bohemia, that of Casimir is greater. As servants of a Catholic king, they shrink from shedding Christian blood, but it is not for them, but for God, to choose the place and time of battle.

Having thus avoided having to fight in an unfavourable position—for the site of a battlefield is of prime importance—the Polish command moves its entire force to Tabor, which is loyal to Casimir, and there pitches camp, which is surrounded with several deep ditches and a ring of waggons. Albert, informed of all this by his scouts, hurries there full of confidence until he sees the strength of the Poles. He then pitches camp on an eminence within a balista's range from the town and surrounds it with ditches and waggons. The two armies being so close to each other, there are daily skirmishes, a spectacle watched by either side, like a second Trojan war, yet in which numbers are killed and prisoners taken.

Not a day passes without cannon and mortars being fired, swords, lances and other weapons used. 30,000 men are under Austrian command and 14,000 under Polish orders. Both camps have numbers of brass arbalests, though the Austrians have the most. Both armies tire. All places within reach have run out of provisions and it is dangerous to go farther afield because of the hostility of those whose crops they have already consumed. The Poles withdraw into the town of Tabor and King Albert disbands his army and goes to Prague while the Margrave of Meissen with his army makes for home, but, when nearly there, he is pursued by a force from the towns of Luna and Zator which support Casimir and seize the opportunity to try to defeat the Margrave. He sends an urgent message to King Albert asking for Jacob Berlin and some other Czechs to help him. When they arrive the Margrave manages to defeat his attackers and returns safely home. Informed by messenger and letter of the great army King Albert has assembled, Władysław is quick to send Casimir the help for which he asks, issuing a call to arms and summoning all to muster in Częstochowa by the Feast of the Nativity of the Blessed Virgin. So, the knights and barons of Cracow, Sandomierz, Lublin and Chełm assemble there and the King, without waiting for the knights of other duchies, officially breaks off relations with the Silesian dukes on the pretext that they have refused to swear allegiance to Casimir as King of Bohemia, that they have secretly plundered his lands, coined counterfeit Polish money and let it be introduced it into his kingdom. He then invades their territory and devastates it as far as Opava, then marches back to Poland via Racibórz ravaging the country as he goes. He then orders the troops from Wielkopolska, who are also ravaging Silesia, to return home.

About Whitsun, the Tatar Khan, Szadchmath, leads a great army into Podole and, as is the Tatar way, plunders the land and carries many off into permanent slavery. His troops have with them instruments of intimidation: images of people astride a horse; but these have no effect. The knights and nobles of Ruthenia, considering it better to die in war, than to watch the destruction of their own people, assemble a sufficient force and organize a pursuit of the Tatars, whom they outnumber. The Tatars withdraw into a boggy area, part of which they cleverly harden, as if it had been asphalt, and there await the others' attack. The Poles, unaware of the unsuitablity of the terrain, rashly do attack, only to sink into the bog, which costs many their lives. Yet good might have come of it, had the others circumvented the area and attacked the Tatars from the rear. As it was someone in the van raises a cry which those in the rear, ignorant of what is going on, misinterpret as a general call to retreat and take to their heels. Seeing this, the Tatars attack, causing general confusion. The Tatars press home their attack, and, suddenly, the entire Polish army takes fright and runs. So savage are the Tatars, that they take not one prisoner, but spear them all.

This disaster, the tale of which is to be told down the ages, encourages the Tatars to increase their raids into Ruthenia. In one of these a certain Jan Włodkowicz, weakened by several wounds, collapses between two piles of the dead stacked to await burial. Some Tatars start stripping him, where he lies pretending to be dead. Unable to remove a ring, they cut off the finger with the ring on it. To get his thigh-pieces and boots they slit these open with a sword, leaving a long cut down each leg from thigh to foot, the scars of which I myself have seen, for he survived both death and slavery.

The increasing import of counterfeit coin causes a popular revolt in Cracow aimed in particular at the Inspector of the Salt Mines, Michałów Serafin, the city councillors and others. Everyone stops work and crowds round the castle demanding that these men be handed over to them. They, feeling guilty, have taken refuge in the castle itself. When the commotion has subsided and most people have returned to their homes, Serafin and the others still do not dare leave the castle. Perhaps they would never have been safe had not Bishop Oleśnicki of Cracow, after much persuasion from the King, spoken to the proletariat in their own tongue, and pacifed them. Serafin and the others are made to do a fortnight's penance in the castle prison.

In the middle of summer, the Sultan of Turkey invades Hungary, ravages Transylvania and carries numbers of people off into captivity.

King Albert yields to pressure from various Hungarian nobles whom the Empress Barbara, while her husband was still alive, had vilified and insulted, and turns her out of all the castles, towns and properties in Hungary given her as her dowry and strips her of all the treasure and jewels she has collected over the years. The Empress then goes to Poland and asks King Władysław to take her in as a poor orphan. The King is sympathetic and agrees; indeed, with regal generosity he provides her with her every need and grants her the revenue from the castle, town and lands of Sandomierz, so that she can live in accordance with her station.

A shortage of corn affecting Poland and her neighbours has raised the price of a measure of wheat to a whole florin. This is due to the sown corn being destroyed by violent rains, and to the damage done by the army as it passed through on its way to invade Silesia and again on its way back. The shortage is aggravated by the circulation of counterfeit money secretly imported in such quantities that it is to be met with everywhere; indeed, many people are unable to distinguish the counterfeit from the genuine and sometimes reject the latter.

Helped by the Poles, Grand-duke Zygmunt has now taken possession of all the duchies and castles that used to belong to Bolesław Świdrygiello except Łuck, which the latter had handed over to two Poles to hold for the Kingdom of Poland, which they have loyally done. The Grand-duke has complained about this at every general assembly, insisting that it was unjust to him, since it had been agreed that the castle and lands of Łuck were to be returned to Lithuania, no matter how they had come into Polish hands, and then, on the death of Grand-duke Sigismund revert entirely to the King and Kingdom of Poland. This year, the Grand-duke is more insistent than ever that this arrangement be adhered to, and, although many of the King's councillors feel that to surrender these rich and fertile lands would be a considerable loss, they come to the conclusion that to keep the promise made to Sigismund is worth more than the advantage of breaking it. So, on the King's or-ders, two officials are sent to Lithuania to hand Łuck over to the Grand-duke and his son, Michael, who are personally to swear an oath and sign a document binding them to return the castle and its lands to Poland on the Grand-duke's death and that they will not appoint any governor or starosta of Łuck, who has not undertaken to see that this is done. On the Feast of the Immaculate Concep-tion, the prelates, dukes and barons in general assembly renew the oaths they swore to King Władysław, who, robed in the royal vestments and seated on the throne, is, with the full agreement of all present, given the right to govern without guardians, for, having just begun his fifteenth year, he has reached maturity. Among the measures passed by the assembly is one to deal with counter-feit money, one of these being that assayers are appointed in every town so that good money should be everywhere accepted and counterfeit refused. Though these measures would have greatly bene-fited the entire kingdom, it is only in Cracow and Ruthenia that they are applied, for the officials in Wielkopolska and Mazovia, though repeatedly promising to observe them, never do so.

Pope Eugenius IV, who has been writing and sending envoys to King Władysław urging him to make peace with King Albert, now suggests a conference to be held in Wrocław to which he would send his own delegates. To this the King agrees.

A.D. 1439

Pope Eugenius is represented at the Wrocław conference by Bishop John of Siena, Bishop Al-phonse of Burgos, a man of great learning and judgment, the son of a converted Jew, and also by Michael Amici a master of theology. Hungary is represented by King Albert and a number of his prelates and nobles; and Poland by King Casimir, the Archbishop of Gniezno, and others. The con-ference begins with both sides giving a lengthy exposé of their claim to the kingdom of Bohemia. Casimir tells them that he is not greedy for another crown, but acting out of sympathy for the diffi-cult situation of the people of Bohemia, whose language is so closely related to his; nonetheless, for the sake of Christendom he is prepared to renounce his right, if King Albert will do the same and allow the nobles and barons of the two kingdoms freely to choose whom they want as their king: Casimir, Albert or some other prince. This idea is generally thought a possible way of achiev-ing peace, and a fortnight is spent in discussing it. Then Albert sends for the Archbishop of Gniezno, dismisses the arbitrators, and tells the Archbishop how dearly he loves Władysław and Casimir and suggests that if the former marry Albert's elder daughter and Casimir marry his younger daughter, Albert could renounce the crown of Bohemia; all he wants is that it should be done in such a way that he should not appear to have been yielding to pressure. The Poles find this a good and speedy way of achieving peace, but then King Albert wishes to make various alterations and this so angers the Poles that, without even breaking off the discussions, they make a rather dis-orderly departure. Albert is hurt by this behaviour and tries to restrain them. The Poles, though thinking it shameful to return to their inn once they are in the saddle, yield to the tears, rather than the pleading of the papal legate, and agree to go to Namysłów to renew discussions, and Albert sends his councillors to them there. Even now they cannot agree on peace, but they do arrange a truce to last for some years, on condition that, on St. George's Day, the two kings or their delegates should meet on the Polish/Hungarian frontier and arrange for further talks. While he is in Wrocław King Albert falls down some steps and, at first, appears to have been badly hurt, but later he is able to return to Austria via Moravia, though he still has a bad limp.

Neither King is able to attend the meeting arranged for St. George's day, but their representa-tives and the papal legate Philibert foregather in Lubowla at Whitsun. Without the kings, however, they cannot reach agreement and it is decided that the two Kings shall have a further meeting on the Feast of the Nativity of the Blessed Virgin, when Władysław will go to Biecz and the King of Hun-gary to Bardejov and then the two will meet somewhere in the middle. When the time comes,

Władysław duly goes to Biecz, but Albert is unable to go to Bardejov, because the Sultan of Turkey has come with a large army and occupied and annexed all Raško and is laying siege to Smederevo on the Danube, with its ring of twenty-five towers, which the governor of Raško had recently built at great expense. Albert assembles a scratch force of Hungarians and Austrians and, without waiting for reinforcements marches against the Turks. After several days in the field he realizes that his craven Hungarians have no stomach for a fight and also that his army is the weaker, so he postpones doing battle. Meanwhile the Turks have captured Smederevo by bribing its commander. As a good Catholic, Albert is crushed by all these misfortunes. Then, one day, after he has eaten a lot of melon, he is afflicted with severe and persistent diarrhoea. As he makes his way home, he makes his last will and testament in a village on the Danube, where he dies. He is buried in Székesfehérvár. He was a gentle, modest prince and an ardent Christian. He was strong and healthy, had black hair, large eyes and a merry, ruddy complexion with fat cheeks. His teeth were uneven and, when he smiled or spoke, these slightly distorted his face.

Murad, the Turkish Sultan, sends an envoy bearing splendid gifts to King Władysław seeking his friendship and an alliance; then, learning that the King is waging war against Albert of Hungary, the Sultan also promises him financial help and 100,000 men. Władysław decides to retain the envoy until he sees what is going to happen to Hungary now that Albert is dead, for Albert had only two daughters and, though his widow is pregnant, there is no knowing what will be the sex of her babe. Meanwhile, the Hungarians, afraid lest the Turks are aiming to annex the whole of their country, after much discussion decide that Władysław of Poland is the best prince they can choose as their new king. Queen Elizabeth agrees to this, provided Władysław marries her, even though, should she have a son, when the boy comes of age he will have to be content with just his inheritance from his father: Austria and Bohemia. This agreed, envoys are sent to King Władysław, who arrives in Cracow about Septuagesima.

A.D. 1440

King Władysław sends his brother, Casimir, to go out to greet the Hungarian envoys, whom he orders to be lodged in the best inns and to be provided lavishly with all that they may need. There follow several days of private discussions, which reveal considerable differences of opinion. The King himself does not relish the prospect of leaving his father's kingdom to take over Hungary, nor of making a not altogether attractive marriage for the sake of a crown. Some actually think that it would harm Poland, should her king also be king of another country, in that it is difficult enough for a king to rule one country, let alone two. The wiser majority, however, think that he should accept, because it will be easier to defend the Catholic faith and the kingdom of Hungary against the Turks, than to defend Poland with Hungary already occupied by the Turks. So, the public good takes precedence over private interests and, as usually happens, the opinion of the majority prevails. An official is sent to Hungary to discover what ordinary people there feel about it, and, when he reports that the majority favour it, the Hungarian envoy is told that the Poles are ready to make an agreement. At this juncture an express messenger arrives bringing a letter to inform them that Queen Elizabeth has given birth to a son, who has been named László. This news robs King Władysław and his councillors of any desire for the crown of Hungary, and the Hungarians are told that, now that there is an heir to the throne, there is no chance of them reaching agreement. However, the Hungarians are insistent and eventually Władysław is persuaded to agree, out of love for his faith and the true religion. The conditions are that the King will protect the country against the Turks; that he will marry Queen Elizabeth and find suitable husbands for her two daughters and provide them with adequate dowries; that he will do everything he can to obtain the Kingdom of Bohemia for the Queen's son, the posthumous László, when he reaches man's estate; that any sons the King may have by Queen Elizabeth will be heirs to the kingdom of Hungary; and that, if there are no such sons, on the King's death Lászlo will succeed him. All this agreed, a solemn Mass is sung in Cracow cathedral, at which Bishop Zbigniew, speaking in Latin, proclaims King Władysław the unanimous choice of the Queen, prelates and nobles of Hungary for their king. Then, in the presence of the envoy of the Turkish Sultan, the Bishop falls on his knees and begs the King to accept election. In a short, but beautiful speech, the King emphasises that for him the kingdom of Poland suffices, so that he has never aspired to another, yet it seems to be God's wish that he accept the crown of Hungary in order to ensure peace there, defend the faithful and destroy the barbarians, and so he does accept. There is a delighted response; a Te Deum is sung in all churches and on the following night the bells are rung and bonfires lit all over the city.

Three of the Hungarian delegates are now laden with gifts and sent home to report to Queen Elizabeth, all unaware that in the meantime, influenced by the Austrians and Germans, she has changed her mind—though without telling anyone—so that, when she hears what they have to tell her, she sends them and their servants to prison, where they are put in chains and robbed of their possessions. The Queen then sends to inform the nobles and cities of Hungary that she does not accept the delegates' decision, but will oppose it with all her strength. This decision causes considerable disagreement: some favour Władysław, others Elizabeth, and yet others, her infant son. Hungary appears threatened with rebellion and civil strife.

Meanwhile, Władysław has sent Sędziwój of Ostrorog the voivode of Poznań and Chancellor Jan of Koniecpol to Queen Elizabeth with truly regal gifts and various suggestions. When the two are approaching Komárno, they hear that their fellow ambassadors have been put in gaol; so, despite having a safe-conduct from the Queen, they slacken their pace, not daring to complete their mission. Simon Bishop of Eger advises them not to proceed, so they turn back. Many people remain convinced that had they gone to the Queen and delivered their King's messages, these would have restrained her and persuaded her to abide by the decision of her delegates, and thus avoided the disasters of the years ahead.

Władysław is unperturbed when he learns of this, but he does hurry on his preparations for his departure for Hungary. However, other news now reaches him that puts any such journey out of the question: namely that Duke Ivan Czartoryski, by origin and religion a Ruthenian, is plotting with certain Lithuanians and Ruthenians against Grand-duke Zygmunt, whom they accuse of holding the country down by terror. Afraid lest news of the conspiracy leak out, they hasten their preparations, and, on Palm Sunday, after the Grand-duke has heard Mass in Troki castle and most of his courtiers are in the parish churches, they enter the Grand-duke's apartments with swords concealed under their cloaks, kill their victim and mutilate his body more horribly than any barbarian would and then throw it outside the castle. It appears that the Grand-duke had been dabbling in soothsaying and divination and, acting on what was told him, killed numbers of innocent people; thus many people maintained that his death was God's just punishment for this. He was a man of boundless coarseness and greed, ready to punish the least offence, to steal and to murder; a man of medium height, taciturn, avid for luxury, quick to anger and violence, greedy of possessions; he would have been happier to have fallen in battle, but it was his subjects killed him, including those who owed their high posts to him.

The country is divided by this murder of the Grand-duke. Some wish to honour the written agreements and have King Władysław as their overlord, and these occupy some important castles on his behalf; others, those of lesser importance, who owed their positions to the Grand-duke, favour his son and only child, Michael, and in this they have the support of Samogitia. King Władysław's uncle, Bolesław Świdrygiello, steps in and occupies the castle at Łuck, which Władysław Jagiello renounced in favour of the Grand-duke and which was due to revert to the Kingdom of Poland on his death. At the same time, Bolesław Duke of Mazovia takes possession of Drohiczyń and its three castles, reasserting a claim under rights granted to his grandfather by the then King of Poland, and of which he had been maliciously deprived by the Grand-duke Alexander Witold, an act to which Władysław Jagiello had turned a blind eye.

Władysław is worried by this threatened dismemberment of the Grand-duchy. Many advise him to renounce the Hungarian crown and devote his attention to his own possessions, peace in Lithuania and the treasure left by Sigismund; indeed, he finds it distasteful not to do this, yet even more distasteful to fail the Hungarians, who keep asking him to come and deal with Queen Elizabeth. A compromise is reached: Władysław is to go to Hungary and accept the crown, while his brother, Prince Casimir, is to go to Lithuania and govern it, not as Grand-duke, but as his brother's deputy and regent, until such time as his brother may decide otherwise.

This winter is hard and grievous in Poland and her neighbours. The severe frosts kill many fruit trees and animals. The harvest having failed, prices soar and many people starve to death. People make bread of fat and bits of wood, or of herbs, bones and roots, all of which can prove fatal. The gentry and farmers get out their old bedding and straw and with this satisfy their hunger and that of their cattle and sheep, as best they can. Heavy snow falls and lies from St. Martin's Day throughout the winter and spring, accompanied by severe frosts. There is no thaw until St. George's Day, so that rivers are crossed on foot, as if they were land. When the storks arrive from their warm countries, they find it still winter and have to go into people's houses like domestic creatures and stay there until the thaw and milder weather comes. Many other birds die because of the cold.

The Archbishop of Kiev, Isidore, a Greek by origin, recently appointed cardinal, comes from Italy as papal legate to Ruthenia. He brings with him a papal bull bearing the Pope's leaden seal and the silver seal of Emperor John Palaeologus in Constantinople, the subject of which is the unification of the Greek and Latin churches. Written in Latin, it is signed in both Greek and Ruthenian. The Cardinal is entertained by Bishop Oleśnicki of Cracow, who supplies him with whatever he needs and allows him to say Mass in the parish church. Later, as if the two churches were already united, he says Mass according to the Greek rite. However, both Greeks and Ruthenians ridicule and reject the idea of unification. Indeed, when the legate speaks to his suffragans in Ruthenia and Moscow, trying to convince them of the need for union, he is seized, imprisoned and robbed of all his valuables, of which he had acquired quite a number. Later, he manages to escape.

Władysław leaves Cracow in the company of Prince Casimir on the first stage of his journey to Hungary, and reaches Sącz three days later. Here his mother, Queen Sophia, and Bishop Oleśnicki of Cracow await him, and here, too, he is joined by Bolesław of Mazovia and a large number of nobles from all over the kingdom. With these he carries out an extensive reorganization of castellans, starostas and voivodes, aimed at ensuring peace and quiet throughout the realm. This includes sending his brother, Casimir, as regent to Lithuania. The King has to wait in Kežmarok for ten days to allow the bishops, royal treasurer, vice-chancellor and other eminent persons who are to accompany him, to catch up, each with his own retinue and his own silver table utensils and other equipment, in the splendour of which each vies with the other. News of Władysław's arrival in Kežmarok causes turmoil in Hungary. Many are delighted by the news, others fearful and sad. Queen Elizabeth writes to the main towns in Hungary ordering them not to admit King Władysław, and herself goes to Visegrád, then in the hands of the Ban of Slavonia, and there, having secretly broken the seals and padlocks on the chest containing the royal insignia, takes the actual crown used to crown the kings of Hungary, intending later to crown her infant son with it. The Bishop of Eger, who favours King Władysław, has sent him message after message begging him to hasten his arrival. When he learns that the King is in Kežmarok, he occupies the town of Apperiasch and installs a garrison of his own servants, and with a number of Hungarian nobles goes to Władysław in Kežmarok, to which there also come messengers from Lithuania begging the King not to delay in sending Prince Casimir, as otherwise Duke Michael might well take over. The King assures them that Casimir will soon be there, but himself begins to hesitate about continuing to Hungary. Indeed, the Voivode of Cracow and others are advising him to return to Poland, telling him that it is both dangerous and harmful to attempt to acquire the throne of Hungary by force of arms. However, Bishop Oleśnicki of Cracow and Sędziwój of Ostrorog Voivode of Poznań take the opposite view, which is the one that eventually prevails and, on May 4, the King moves off towards Buda. He halts for the night in Nowa Wies. In the morning having heard a sung Mass and dined, he moves on to Podegrod. On the Friday, the day after Ascension, he reaches Sobinow, where he gives audience to a nuncio sent by the Council in Basle to inform him of the election as pope of Felix V, so that now there are two popes: Eugene IV in Rome and Felix V in Basle, a schism that is to last for many years.

The King moves on to Apperiasch, where he is greeted by numbers of Hungarians. While he is there, there is an extraordinarily fierce hail storm, and this is considered a bad omen.

On the Tuesday, the King moves to Rozgon, where the Bishop of Eger supplies him with all his needs. The next day he moves to Wislów, and spends the evening there hunting duck with hawks, during which hunt his secretary drowns in the river Arnath while trying to rescue a hawk from the water. This, too, is considered a bad omen.

Władysław hastens his advance to Buda, but just in case Queen Elizabeth should get there first, sends the Bishop of Eger, the Castellan of Międzyrzecz and a number of Polish and Hungarian knights on ahead. In Buda these are given a rapturous reception; thus, when the Count of Cilia, whom Queen Elizabeth had sent with fifty horse to occupy Buda for her, learns that the Poles have got there first, he returns hurriedly to the Queen in Komárno. One day, before Władysław gets to Buda, where Simon Bishop of Eger is in command, the Bishop has one Hungarian and his horse killed and quartered, because the rider had in the coarsest language mocked the election of Władysław.

Władysław reaches Ciksów on the Friday before Whitsun. He dines in Smeth on the Saturday and so reaches Eger, where he is lodged over Whitsun in the castle. Meanwhile, Queen Elizabeth has Archbishop Dionizy of Esztergom crown her three-month old son in Székesfehérvár using the crown she had purloined from Visegrád. News of this, which is quick to reach King Władysław, though unpleasant, does not deter him from the enterprise.

The King leaves Eger on the Wednesday after Whitsun, sups and spends the night in Kompolth and the following night in Hothwan. On the Friday, he continues towards Buda, ordering the waggons and companies as he approaches. The Voivode of Hungary, the Starosta of Buda and a throng of the eminent come out as far as the seventh stone to greet him. The King continues, but only as far as Pieczek, not entering Buda until the Saturday before Holy Trinity, when he crosses the Danube by boat, to be met by those he had sent on ahead, fully armed and in three companies: one of knights and barons, one of their servants armed with crossbows, and the third of youths armed with spears and shields, who finally conduct him to the castle, built of stone with great skill and labour by the late King Sigismund.

Learning of the King's arrival, the dukes, nobles and gentry throng into Buda to declare their loyalty and swear allegiance. The ruler of Raško excuses his absence by the fact that Raško has just been invaded by the Turks, and so does the King of Bosnia.

Queen Elizabeth is now fearful of losing her support, especially as all the prelates of Hungary and most of the nobility sympathize with Władysław. She has no strong castle left in which to seek safety should the need arise. So, with flattery and promises she persuades the Bishop of Jawrinum to give her the use of his fortified town, into which she then puts a garrison of Czech mercenaries. Władysław replies to this by sending a force to lay siege to Jawrinum, where the Count of Cilia has taken refuge. (Later, when the Count escapes, the siege is raised.)

After several days of debate in the Franciscan friary, King Władysław, seated on an eminence, speaks to the assembled Hungarians. He tells them that he came expecting to find a united

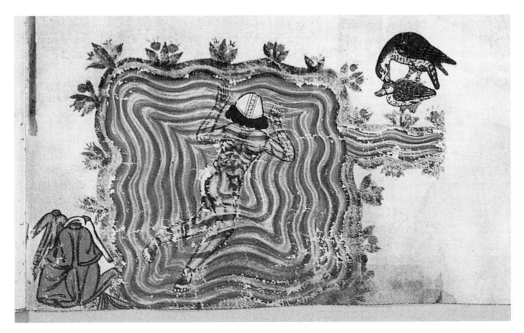

Rescuing a bird in such circumstances was the job of the falconer, who, in the Middle Ages, was expected to be able to swim.
—Frederick II: De Arte Venandi cum Avibus.

country, which he had undertaken to defend against the Turks; but instead he finds a country divided and on the verge of civil war. Of this he does not wish to be the cause; indeed, he would rather return to Poland than cause civil strife. They must make up their minds: do they want him or Queen Elizabeth and her infant son. He is told that they see in him their only defence against the Turks and that they reject the coronation of the infant László and will get it invalidated.

They then fetch the wood of the True Cross and on it the Archbishop of Esztergom, the bishops and the nobles swear loyalty to King Władysław. The King is then brought in among them, raised aloft and with great shouts proclaimed king of Hungary. The following day, they start discussing details of the coronation, which it is decided to hold on St. Alexis' Day. But then they remember that there is no crown, the old one having been appropriated by Queen Elizabeth. In the end, so as not to have to postpone the coronation, it is decided to take the crown off the head of St. Stephen, and use that instead. (Two officials are sent to Visegrád to examine the chest from which the crown was said to have been taken. These find the seals and padlocks broken as reported, but that the other insignia are still there. Only the crown has been taken.)

On the Saturday before St. Alexis' Day, the King and a cavalcade of prelates, nobles and gentry leave Buda for Székesfehérvár, where Władysław is to be crowned king of Hungary. Having spent the night in Pest, they reach Székesfehérvár in time for dinner. The next morning the King goes to the shrine in Székesfehérvár, which is already so crowded that he has difficulty in making his way in. To make the ceremony easier the throng is turned out of the church, leaving only the prelates, nobles and barons of the two kingdoms, as well as some citizens of Buda who have a traditional right to take part in the coronation of their king, which they do wearing their armour and holding the old standard of the Kingdom of Hungary. As the Cardinal-Archbishop starts the Mass, Władysław takes off the splendid royal robes in which he entered the church, and these the canons at once remove. The King is then blessed and anointed. He is provided with sandals, stockings, humeral, alb, belt, stole, two tunicles, two necklaces, a pectoral, mantle, apostle's cross, sceptre, banner and round orb with the requisite symbols and prayers. All these, made for the first king St. Stephen and now damaged by age, are considered more precious than if they had been new. Apparently every king of Hungary is given an apostle's cross at his coronation, because the Pope had sent a cross of this kind to Hungary's first king, St. Stephen, for him to give to the bishops of his churches on their investiture. The crown taken from St. Stephen's tomb is then placed on the King's head. The King takes the oath and the sacrament of the Eucharist. Thus crowned, in accordance with sacred custom the new king of Hungary goes to the church of St. Peter and St. Paul in the square and there seats himself on a specially prepared throne. Here he hears two cases, which he does to emphasize that the King's first duty is to administer justice and to protect the weak from the more powerful. The King then mounts his horse and rides round the city. When he reaches the church of St. Martin outside the walls, he enters it and before everyone's eyes points his bare sword at the four quarters of the compass, thus signifying that he should and will defend Hungary from unjust invasion from whatever quarter. He then returns to the royal palace, where he gives a banquet to the prelates and nobles of his kingdoms. The rest of the day is devoted to merriment, games and dancing.

When Queen Elizabeth, who is in Bratislava, learns of the successful coronation of King Władysław, she leaves Bratislava and goes to Austria, where she entrusts Prince Frederick with her infant son, asking that he act as a father to him. Frederick agrees and takes charge both of the boy and of the crown, which the Queen brought with her.

The King spends four days in Székesfehérvár, during which time he appoints Simon Bishop of Eger Chancellor of the Kingdom of Hungary, confirms and renews all the privileges granted by his predecessors. The royal insignia and the new crown are put in a chest and sent to Visegrád to be used to crown future kings of Hungary should the original crown not be recovered. The country's prelates, nobles and commoners sign a document binding themselves to be loyal and obedient to their duly elected king, the document being translated into Polish and lodged in the Royal Treasury.

King Władysław leaves Székesfehérvár on The Feast of St. Mary Magdalen and reaches Buda a week later. There he stays all summer occupying himself with domestic affairs, though now and again finding recreation in hunting on the island of Czepel.

For three months now, the Sultan of Turkey has been besieging the fort of Alba Nandor, on the border between Hungary and Raško, the first point of access to Hungary, hoping to capture it, as he has Smederevo, by force of arms, bribery or starvation. Władysław sends an envoy to inform the Sultan that he now rules Hungary and to demand that the Sultan raise the siege of Alba Nandor and cease all armed attacks on his new country, thus giving practical expression to the friendship they have already put into words. This the King does to test the attitude towards him of the Sultan. When the King's envoy finally arrives after avoiding the dangers of the road, he tells the Sultan everything. The Sultan says that he requires three months in which to give his reply and sends the Polish envoy to Smederevo to await it in the castle there; while he makes every endeavour to capture the castle he is besieging, convinced that he will never have a better opportunity to do so. Having failed to buy its surrender by shooting into the castle arrows carrying messages in Bulgarian offering bribes, he bombards it with his cannon, which demolish a large section of the wall. All the ditches round the castle are filled with timber and a number of boats full of soldiers stationed in the Danube, which flows round one side of the castle, in preparation for an assault planned for the following day. During that night, however, the commander of the castle spreads gunpowder all over the timber with which the Turks have filled the moats and ditches. Thus, when the Turks launch their attack and are swarming all over the ditches and setting up siege-ladders, the defenders throw down burning logs and red-hot coals, which ignite the gunpowder in many places. The Turks suffocate in the fumes and sudden flame. Those who attack from the water are no more fortunate, for many of their boats are destroyed by gunfire from the castle, while a strong wind drives many others onto the castle walls, where they are captured. The fighting is fierce and lasts from the first hour of the afternoon until evening. His hopes of victory dashed, the Sultan raises the siege and withdraws into his own territory, after which he sends to King Władysław telling him that, if he wants peace, he must give up the castle at Alba Nandor and withdraw from Raško.

The coronation and most affairs of state having been dealt with, Bishop Zbigniew of Cracow is granted permission to return home. He leaves Buda on Saturday, July 29, and reaches Kijewies the following day. The inhabitants of Kijewies, who have suffered by having grain forcibly taken from them by the King's men on their way to and from Buda, now use threats in an endeavour to recover from the Bishop what they are owed. The two sides start arguing, and then fighting breaks out between the townspeople and Bishop Zbigniew's men. The Bishop's bodyguard close round him and get him safely out of the town, leaving his escort and the townspeople hard at it. Fires are started, and half the town, including the church, goes up in flames. The townspeople take to their heels and many are shot at with arrows and killed as they run. None of the Bishop's men is killed, though many are wounded.

Bishop Zbigniew Oleśnicki enters Poland between Jaslisk and Lymanow, turning aside to Santok to visit Queen Sophia, whom he tells of all that has happened. He reaches Cracow on August 13 and a few days later the Voivode of Cracow follows, after which a council is held in Korczyn. This is attended by Queen Sophia, but illness, brought on by drinking wine mixed with water in Hungary—perhaps by the air of Hungary—prevents Bishop Oleśnicki from being there. The Council decides to help the King by raising a levy of one farthing on every field in Cracow duchy, while any noble who does not have a peasant or bailiff is to pay one mark. Any barons or nobles with their peasants, who elect to go in person to help the King are to be exempt.

While King Władysław is still in Hungary, his brother, Casimir, sets out to take over the Grand-duchy of Lithuania. Lavishly supplied with treasure and all that he might need: horses, carriages, cloth and jewels, he travels with a numerous retinue that includes two dukes, four castellans, two voivodes. He spends Whitsun with his mother at Korczyn and reaches Sandomierz on Holy Trinity. He continues to Lublin, where a force of more than 2000 first-rate lances awaits him. Continuing, he halts on the River Swislo, where he is joined by Duke Michael of Grodno with 500 horse. The Duke presents him and his officials with gifts, swears obedience and loyalty and asks for his father's murder to be avenged. Continuing, Casimir fords the River Niemen and heads straight for Wilno, where he is received by the bishop, castellan and voivode of Wilno and is conducted to the castle to the sound of trumpets, but first he must enter the cathedral to give thanks to God for his safe arrival. Many castles such as Grodno, Brześć and Lida are still in the hands of Duke Michael. After a few days, prelates and nobles from all over the duchy come to request that Casimir be confirmed as Grand-duke. The Poles cannot agree to this, as it would be contrary to their instructions, which are that Casimir is to be regent until such time as the King decides otherwise. The Lithuanians, however, feel that there is a real danger of Duke Michael taking over, unless Casimir is made Grand-duke, especially as earlier they had all been forced to swear obedience and fealty to the Duke, who could now accuse them of breaking their oaths. So, afraid of civil war, early one morning, when the Poles are still in bed, to the ringing of bells and the singing of a *Te Deum*, the Lithuanians publicly proclaim Casimir grand-duke and not just regent. Michael Gotygin, who holds the upper fort at Troki for Duke Michael, cannot be persuaded to hand it over without the latter's consent, even though cannon are moved up, as a threat. Jan Szczekocki is sent to Ivan Czartoryski, the killer of the Grand-duke Sigismund, to require in the name of Prince Casimir that he surrender the lower fort at Troki and its treasures. Czartoryski replies that he will agree to this, but only if the Poles promise him complete immunity. The older Poles refuse to promise this, but are overruled by the younger ones, and the castle and its treasures are handed over.

The local Poles and the Polish lords and prelates cannot restrain the arrogant behaviour of Prince Casimir and the lords of Lithuania and Ruthenia, and neither do they condone it. So, neither the Poles nor King Władysław, of whom they are equally critical, ever call Casimir grand-duke. The King is not to be persuaded and keeps everything in suspense by delaying his return to Poland. Eventually, having settled things in Hungary, he does return and then goes to Lithuania, where he grants Duke Michael his share, thus honouring his promise, but retains certain castles including Brześć and Kamieniec for himself and the kingdom of Poland. He gives the territory of Drohiczyn to Bolesław Duke of Mazovia and grants the rest of the Lithuanian and Ruthenian duchies to Casimir, hoping that the grand-duchy thus divided would never dare rebel against Poland, and that lands hitherto not cultivated would now be tilled.

Enjoying the protection of the Poles, yet afraid of being besieged in his own castle, Ivan Czartoryski demands Casimir's forgiveness. With a safe-conduct, he goes in person to Casimir. Despite all the voices raised against him, the Lithuanians and Ruthenians make light of his guilt and even suggest that he deserves not punishment, but a reward for disposing of a cruel tyrant. So, Czartoryski is pardoned and he surrenders Troki castle. The next day he is violently attacked and robbed of all his possessions. He would also have lost his life, had not the Poles protected him. The Poles now return home with modest gifts from Casimir, whose permission to leave they have obtained. The few who remain are gradually ousted by the cunning machinations of the Lithuanians, and then attach themselves to Lithuanian dignitaries and learn their language and customs.

The departure of Bishop Oleśnicki has so encouraged Queen Elizabeth and her supporters that they embark on outright war with the King. The Queen wins over to her side four major towns, which swear to be loyal to her. These the Queen puts under Jan Giskra, a Czech, whom Władysław had recently released from captivity. He brings in mercenaries from Bohemia, Moravia, Austria and Silesia, who use violence to compel people to abandon their loyalty to the King. They succeed with the town of Aperiasz and are often the victors in a number of violent clashes with the forces of the starosta of Kežmarok. The country round Spis is in flames. Giskra bribes the garrison of the castle at Skaracz to come over to him. He lays siege to the castle at Kyszik, undermines its walls with a number of saps and demolishes them. He goes on to capture a number of other towns either by cunning or by force and styles himself Chief Lieutenant of Lászlo, King of Hungary. The captured towns all pay him the monies due to the king. In Krempnica they strike gold and silver coin in the name of Lászlo. The Queen persuades the Ban to break his oath of loyalty to King Władysław and declare war on him, and he persuades others, who are rich and influential, to do the same, among them most of the nobles of Slavonia. Others join them just because they hate the Bishop of Eger. One and all desire to expel Władysław and deprive his supporters of their lives and estates. The Ban recruits an army of the nobility, a well-armed force that is not to be despised. Certain of victory, Queen Elizabeth goes to Esztergom, where Archbishop Dionizy has already broken his oath of loyalty and is ready to support her, if the result of the war the Ban is about to wage is the one they want.

Władysław is well informed of what is happening and, convinced that the situation calls for action, not deliberation, sends a force under Nicholas Frystacki and János Hunyadi against the Ban and his accomplices. Battle is engaged near the town of Balta, and, after many hours, victory goes to the King's men. Much of the glory attaches to Hunyadi, till then scarcely known, a man of unknown origin, but of excellent spirit and avid for greatness. The Ban escapes and goes to the Queen, who, distraught, begs him to try again and to lend her 100,000 florins to finance the war.

The Ban refuses to do either and departs. After roaming the country, he is arrested by King Frederick and spends a long time in prison, having, in the end, to pay 70,000 florins for his release.

King Władysław magnanimously releases most of the prisoners taken in the battle, thus winning them over to his side. He suitably rewards the two victorious commanders: Frystacki and Hunyadi, making them joint voivodes of Transylvania. He also appoints Hunyadi, whose abilities have greatly impressed him, commander of the army fighting the Turks and puts him in charge of all the castles adjacent to Turkish territory.

Meanwhile, the prelates and nobles of Cracow have held two assemblies in Korczyn, at which they eventually agree to send the King both military and monetary help. The money is rapidly collected and a new army assembled and sent to the King in Hungary, much to the surprise of the Hungarians.

Learning of King Albert's death and of Prince Casimir's rejection of Bohemia in favour of Lithuania, the Czechs call an assembly at which they fix a day on which to elect a king. Rokiczano, originally an exile from Greece, returns to Prague and, as is his custom, rages against the Pope and the Church, insisting that the sacred truth is only to be found among the Czechs. He admininsters the sacrament in both kinds to tiny children and those whose minds are disordered, and expels any priest who opposes his crazy behaviour. He refuses church burial to those who refuse to take communion in both kinds. Queen Elizabeth sends emissaries to attend the election of a new king, demanding that the electors remember King Sigismund and King Albert and should not discard their progeny, but have pity on her fatherless boy. Some greet the emissaries delightedly, yet no one proposes that they should elect a helpless child as their king. So, rejecting the child László, posthumous son of King Albert, they elect Albert, Duke of Bavaria, as the new king of Bohemia. A delegation of eminent persons is sent to him, an unusually modest man, whom the Emperor Frederick instructs not to accept the throne of Bohemia, which the Duke rightly refuses. The Czechs summon a new assembly which sends to the King of the Romans asking him to accept the crown on behalf of the infant László. Frederick, realizing that the Czechs will refuse loyalty unless they are richly rewarded, and knowing that the country's revenues and silver mines are exhausted, rejects the proposal and suggests that the Czechs rule themselves until the child, László, grows up. Fearing similar rejection by any other prince, the Czechs appoint two adminstrators for the country: Plachek and Meinart.

A.D. 1441

With the help sent him from home King Władysław assembles a further force of Hungarians loyal to him and, about the Feast of the Purification of the Blessed Virgin, takes to the field with it. His objective is to recapture the castles and towns on the frontier, which have been occupied by the Austrians, who have used them to raid into Hungary. He appoints two men to act as starostas and councillors in his absence. Neither the severity of winter, the quantities of snow nor shortages of provisions inhibit the King or his army, though it takes them all winter, up to Lent, to retake all the castles. Władysław does not encroach onto Austrian territory, eager as he is to regain the actual crown of Hungary, which Queen Elizabeth gave to King Frederick for safekeeping, not realizing that Frederick had already decided to surrender the crown rather than have his lands devastated. Władysław wants to attack the remaining rebellious towns and force their submission and obedience and then mount an expedition against the Turks; yet in no way can he persuade the prelates and nobles of Hungary to go with him. Perhaps, they were put off by the ugliness of war, or had already had more than enough of warring; or, as is more likely, because they were afraid Władysław might leave them and go to nearby Poland, never to return. So, the King disbands his two armies and returns to Buda.

(It is said that during the earlier hostilities, some of the Polish troops rashly ate hare during Lent and died sudden deaths.)

The King spends the summer in Buda, though with frequent expeditions to Czepel island to hunt or rest, or just to avoid the plague which was rife both in Hungary and Poland, though the King pays so little attention to its dangers, that he neither avoids meeting with, or talking to people. Nor does he live in seclusion, but openly, especially in Buda, where the pestilence is rampant. Any morning bodies might be found in the King's bedroom of those who have died there overnight. People fall dead before his eyes during divine services, giving up the ghost and lying on the ground, jerking. So the plague rages all summer, autumn and winter; indeed, until the spring.

Florins bearing the arms and name of King Albert's son, László, have been minted in Krempnica and the salt mines there as a token of rebellion; but coins minted elsewhere bear the arms of the true king, Władysław; those of gold and silver carry his mark as well. Thus a Władysław florin is quartered with his own arms, with the arms of Hungary, four lines, with the arms of Poland, an eagle with a crown and outspread wings, with the arms of the Grand-duchy of Lithuania, an armed horseman holding a glinting sword, and with a cross of Lorraine. On the obverse is the likeness of St. Lászlo.

Władysław sends Jan Czepek to replace the governor of Kežmarok, who has been altogether too lax, and be more vigorous in resisting the Czechs; however, before he reaches Kežmarok, thanks to the treachery of one of its burghers, the Czechs are able to take possession of the town. Many of the Poles and Hungarians there crowd into the tower, while the governor and a number of Hungarians escape. At this juncture, the barons of Wielkopolska, realizing that, to their shame, they have never sent their King the military help for which he has repeatedly asked, collect tribute from the people and send the King in Hungary a considerable force under the Castellan of Sieradz. By chance, this reaches Kežmarok while the Poles and Hungarians are still defending the tower against the Czechs and could easily have turned the tables on the Czechs, had not its command insisted that it had not been sent to capture or recapture towns, but to help King Władysław. Learning of this, the defenders in the tower come to an agreement with the Czechs and surrender the tower. The army from Wielkopolska marches on from Kežmarok to Buda. The whole burden of the war devolves on Kežmarok, which was then governed by Nicholas Komorowski on behalf of the Cardinal-bishop of Cracow. For many years it will bear the whole brunt and burden of war.

Queen Elizabeth, proud of having captured Kežmarok, lays siege to the castle at Bratislava, convinced that she can easily take it, since the town itself is loyal to her and well provisioned, while the castle, as she knows, is not well supplied. The Governor, perturbed by the situation, goes to Buda to ask for help. The King at once sends a force under Andrew of Tęczyn to Trnava with orders to do its utmost to prevent the Queen's men from ravaging the country, while they themselves are to destroy everything round Bratislava and get supplies into the castle there as speedily as possible. After reaching Trnava, the force captures and loots Bratislava, seizing all the cattle, sheep and goats, burning the suburbs and supplying the castle with a wealth of provisions to forestall any danger threatening it.

The prelates and nobles of Poland and Lithuania meet on the Feast of St. Nicholas in Parczów to consider the dispute between Grand-duke Casimir and the Duke of Mazovia over Drohiczyń territory, which the latter ruled. Unexpectedly Duke Michael of Lithuania turns up complaining that Grand-duke Casimir has deprived him of his inheritance from his father, so that he has had to live on funds supplied by his wife's brothers, the dukes of Mazovia. The Mazovians produce documents that prove that they are entitled to Drohiczyń, but the Lithuanians will not acknowledge them, nor accept that they can discuss returning his inheritance to Duke Michael, this being outside their terms of reference. Thus, everyone departs with nothing arranged or decided. This is a matter that disquiets King Władysław and his advisers, who are with him in Buda, and after some discussion it is decided that Lithuania ought to be divided into a number of duchies, to reduce its power.

A number of eminent knights from Cracow and Ruthenia have at their own expense and without official help, gone to King Władysław in Hungary. They are so numerous as to amount to a regular army. With them is Peter Odzowąż Voivode and Starosta of Lwów with a considerable retinue. They reach Buda and, on the King's orders, set out to capture the castle at Roznawa, which they accomplish in a couple of days. All the Czechs taken in it are killed.

A.D. 1442

When Queen Elizabeth launches an all-out attack on the castle of Bratislava, Władysław, despite the severe frost and snows of winter and that this is a time when people's granaries are more or less empty, sets out to rescue it. When he gets there, he finally ends the long siege and sets about rebuilding and strengthening the castle; meanwhile laying siege to the town itself, from which the Queen fled when she learned of Władysław's approach. Cannon from the castle demolish many of the houses and there is no doubt that it would have been forced to surrender had not the King abandoned his siege, because there was no pasture for his knights' horses within a reasonable distance; nor was there any chaff to be had and for many days there had only been branches to give the starving horses, which were collapsing. The army then returns to Trnava and thence to Buda, where the King celebrates Easter.

After Easter the knights from Poland are rewarded, not just suitably, but magnificently, for the King divides among them not only his Polish revenues but also money raised illegally by mortgages on Crown lands. With this and the King's permission the knights set out for Poland. The Bishop of Eger accompanies them as far as Eger, where he supplies them with whatever they need, and there they rest, secure, as they think. Then, one day, at sunset a Czech with a small force of the Queen's supporters attacks the town. The sound of the enemy's trumpets and the clang of armour and swords startles the Poles and Hungarians, who are all resting or asleep. The Czechs plunder the town and the Poles' waggons, remove numbers of their horses and, seizing the Voivode of Lwów as he steps out of his inn to see what is going on, withdraw with their loot. Angered rather than frightened by what has happened, the Poles and Hungarians sieze up their weapons, mount what horses are left and set off in pursuit. They soon overtake the Czechs, whose horses have been ridden all night, while the Poles' mounts are fresh. To make sure of his prize captive, Peter Odzowąż Voivode of Lwów, a servant of the Czech commander is ordered to take him to a nearby camp, but the servant, afraid of being captured himself and becoming booty in his turn, takes him to a nearby fort which supports Queen Elizabeth. The commander of the fort seeing an opportunity of currying favour with Władysław, takes Odzowąż to Buda and hands him over to the King. The Czechs turn on their pursuers and in the fighting most of them are killed.

The papal legate, Cardinal Julian Cesarini, having spent much of July at King Frederick's court, leaves Vienna and goes to Buda, where he is received with all honour. He tries to persuade the King to make peace, which Władysław is willing to do, though hitherto his efforts have been baulked by Queen Elizabeth. The Cardinal, convinced of Władysław's sincerity, goes to the Queen in Győr and tries to persuade her to make peace. This the Queen is eager to do, for she has sold almost all her jewels and spent her cash on the war and also contracted huge debts. Both sides impose conditions: the Queen wants Władysław to renounce his right and title of King of Hungary, but, at the same time, she wants him to proceed with the marriage to her eldest daughter and to continue to rule Hungary until her son, Lászlo, is fifteen. Also, so as to compensate Władysław for his outlay in Hungary, the lands of Spis, their towns, villages and castles, are to be returned to the Kingdom of Poland: Silesia is to be transferred to Władysław in lieu of a dowry of 20,000 florins. Again, the Kingdom of Hungary will withdraw from Ruthenia and Walachia, renouncing them for ever, so that there may in future be no doubt as to the King's right and title to them, which the Kingdom of Poland rightly possesses. What is more, in the event of László dying before he comes of age or of having no progeny, Władysław is to be his successor. The Queen further proposes that Władysław's brother, Duke Casimir of Lithuania, should marry her second daughter, who is to have a dowry of 120,000 florins in cash. Władysław considers these conditions advantageous both for him and for Poland, but the Hungarians do not like the idea of having to revoke the coronation and all Władysław's enactments. So Cardinal Cesarini goes from Győr to Buda and back again many times, and even gets Władysław to go himself to meet the Queen; thus, in the end, agreement is reached and the conditions published in Hungarian, Polish and German in Győr cathedral. Władysław presents the Queen with some lovely sable cloaks and she gives him a number of geldings and accepts an invitation to spend Carnival in Buda. The Queen is now full of admiration for Władysław's virtues and moderation, and discreetly lets him know that she wishes to support him on the Hungarian throne and, now that she has given him her eldest daughter, she wishes him well and loves him as if he were her own son. She also earnestly asks him to help free her son, László, and the actual crown of Hungary from the clutches of the Emperor Frederick, whether by honest means or by war; for Frederick, having taken possession of what her son inherited from his father, has appropriated for himself its entire revenue. The King does not turn down the request; so he leaves with her the Deacon of Cracow, Nicholas Lasocki, to act as secret adviser and discreet intermediary. However, when the Deacon has been only three days in Győr, the Queen's diarrhoea and pains in the womb, which were usual with her, but of which she was ashamed to tell her doctors, so weaken her that she is beyond helping and dies. Her death does much to restore equilibrium to Hungary, although some of the starostas and governors of castles who were her supporters, transfer their support to Frederick, King of the Romans.

In July, at the instigation of Macek, the Ban of Dalmatia and Croatia, the Sultan sends an envoy to Buda with the proposal that the Sultan and Hungary should conclude either a treaty of permanent peace, or a truce. The Sultan's envoy is received in audience in the presence of the papal legate, Cardinal Julian Cesarini, and officials of Władysław's two kingdoms. The King receives him seated and with such majesty that the Turk is speechless with admiration and exclaims that never has he seen such dignity. He explains his mission in a few words, as is the custom of barbarians: the Sultan, he says, is prepared to make peace or conclude a truce, whichever the King prefers, if the King will surrender the castle at Alba Nandor or pay an annual tribute for it, conditions which Macek has assured the Sultan that Hungary, ruined by external and civil war, would be prepared to accept. This proposal the King regards as insulting, in that it suggests that Hungary has sunk so low that it must buy peace from barbarians. While the Sultan's envoy is still in Buda awaiting an answer, a messenger arrives with news that János Hunyadi has just won two major victories over the Turks; so the envoy does not receive a favourable answer.

Silesian brigands have been repeatedly raiding and plundering parts of Wielkopolska, the nobles of which assemble an army and send it into Silesia, where it captures and burns the two forts, which have done the most harm, and returns unharmed to Wielkopolska. At Whitsun the Tatars invade Ruthenia and, meeting no resistance, penetrate as far as Lwów, roaming all over the country and carrying off into slavery men and women of every class. As the Tatars are making their way back, the governor of Gliniany attacks them with a force of his own people. Though he kills many of them, he is himself killed with all his men; yet he liberates many of the Tatar's captives, providing an opportunity for them to escape. If others had shown the same courage, the Tatars would never have captured so many thousands, nor would Ruthenia and Podole been so continually devastated. As it is, most were more concerned with personal advantage and would sooner go to Hungary and beg gifts or one of the royal possessions, than defend what they already had; thus there was scarcely a town or village that did not have such refugees living in it at the King's expense.

A.D. 1443

Queen Elizabeth dead, the prelates and nobles of Hungary declare for King Władysław except for those rebel towns and castles occupied by Jan Giskra. The King, considering that the country has largely recovered from the civil strife, decides to implement the policy, that originally induced him to accept the throne, that of freeing the country from the oppression of the barbarous Turks. In this he is encouraged by Cardinal Julian, who, on behalf of Pope Eugenius IV, provides him with a considerable sum of money, and promises the assistance of Catholic kings and princes in the form of armed men. The idea is supported by the exiled ruler of Raško and Albania, Stephen, who, thanks to the generosity of King Władysław has been living in Hungary with his wife and a large part of his army, since the Sultan has annexed his country with its exceptionally fertile soil and rich gold and silver mines, and deprived Stephen's two sons of their eyes and instruments of propagation. Cardinal Cesarini also approaches the King of the Romans, but Frederick refuses to help, being afraid lest at a later stage Władysław attack Austria; but he does agree to an armistice to last for two years. Another who refuses to help is the Master of the Teutonic Knights in Prussia. All this Cesarini reports to the Pope. Meanwhile, Władysław spends the summer preparing for war: buying weapons and horses, and recruiting in Poland and Walachia.

With everything prepared and ready, on the Feast of St. Mary Magdalen, King Władysław and Cardinal Julian, who has with him men of many nationalities who have taken the Cross, march out from Buda. They spend the first night at Pieczki and then head straight for the castle at Alba Nandor. They cross the Danube near Stare Kamienie, capture the town of Sofia, which the troops are allowed to loot; that done, it is burned to the ground. The same is done with a number of castles and towns, which the Turks have occupied in Bulgaria and Raško. When they reach the river locally known as the Morawa, their intelligence reports the presence of a Turkish army concealed and ready to attack at a propitious moment. The King decides to send a force of several thousand under János Hunyadi to stage a night attack. This takes the enemy completely by surprise. Few are not killed or captured. Their camp is captured and looted. After this victory several Bulgarian towns surrender. So, for a considerable time the King's army marches on. Again and again it is attacked, but on each occasion it routs its attackers. Thus, having traversed all Romania it reaches the frontier with Macedonia. The army is now running short of provisions and has already lost so many horses that much of the cavalry has had to be incorporated into the infantry.

Meanwhile, the Sultan has been assembling his forces, which he places under the command of the governor of Natolia, who is ordered to defend the Rhodope Mountains between Romania and Macedonia, which are difficult to cross, and not to allow Władysław's army to penetrate into them, but at the same time forbidding him to engage with the enemy. This command the proud Turks cannot obey. Again and again they attack Władysław's army, which they know they outnumber, and are suitably punished by losing their commander, the governor of Natolia and much of his staff. The Turks withdraw to their camps in the mountains, but Władysław does not leave them in peace. He launches a fierce attack on Christmas Eve. The Turks shower the Poles with arrows to which the King replies with bullets, crossbow bolts and other missiles. The King himself is hit in the chest by several arrows, but his armour prevents them wounding him. It is long since his men have eaten and the King, afraid to let them fight on, withdraws. The Turks think the withdrawal is flight and attack, but the King turns back and routs them. The only voice raised against withdrawal is that of Stephen of Raško and Albania, who even offers the King 100,000 ducats to replenish their provisions. But it would have been wrong to keep the army in the field in the middle of winter, thus ruining its transport, killing the horses and exposing the debilitated troops to defeat at the hands of an enemy they have just defeated. As it is, many of the King's men die of starvation on the march. They can be seen staggering from side to side as though about to fall; with their pallid faces and sunken eyes, they are more like ghosts than humans. In order to make things easier for his men, the King orders the weaker horses to be killed, armour and weapons to be buried, and everything that is heavier than its usefulness: tents, waggons, saddles, clothes and whatever they cannot carry to be burned and so prevent the Turks getting them and using them against them. They then continue back along the normal route. Bare of foot, the King enters Buda in triumph, the clergy and city-fathers going out in procession to greet him. The captured Turkish standards are placed in the Church of the Blessed Virgin in Buda, and the King orders the arms of twenty of the foremost Polish nobles and the same number of Hungarian devices to be painted and hung in the same church in honour of their heroism.

A.D. 1444

Learning of Władysław's triumphant return, the Catholic kings and princes send envoys and letters to congratulate and thank him. The Pope sends not only Cardinal Cesarini, but gifts as well. The kings of France, England, Spain and Aragon; the dukes of Burgundy and Milan and the cities of Venice, Florence and Genoa send envoys to thank him and beg him to organize another expedition, offering their help on land or sea. The Pope, the Venetians, the Genoese and Philip of Burgundy offer to provide a fully equipped fleet to guard the coastal waters and prevent Turks crossing over from Anatolia. But, from the kingdom of Poland, come messages that their King should not embark on another such dangerous exercise, but rather think of returning to Poland and stopping the destruction being inflicted on it in his absence by the Tatars, who, this year, have again invaded and wreaked havoc as far as the suburbs of Lwów. Again the Silesians have been secretly raiding the country.

Bishop Zbigniew of Cracow, eager to increase his Church's possessions and widen his country's frontier, buys the duchy of Siewierz from Bolesław Duke of Cieszyn for 6000 marks in broad grosses, but is prevented from enjoying his purchase by the machinations of the Duke of Racibórz. War affects other Silesian dukes, some of whom now demand compensation from the King. Thus the presence of the King in Poland is generally considered essential, and so, in the hope of his coming, a conference held on April 1 suspends hostilities for a year.

It is thought certain that Prince Casimir and the Lithuanians are preparing to fight Bolesław Duke of Mazovia in order to recover Drohiczyn for Duke Michael of Lithuania, though it has been in Bolesław of Mazovia's possession for some three years or more. The Poles deplore that Bolesław should be deprived of his inheritance from his father and grandfather by a Lithuanian army. All these questions, envoys, happenings leave the King not knowing what to do or whose advice to take; but he finally decides not to abandon his defence of Christendom and the kingdom of Hungary as requested by Pope Eugenius and so many kings and princes. For, having already been victorious, the Hungarians are eager for another fight. Even so, love of his country and the advice he receives from his councillors cause him to hesitate. However, his own fervid faith, the persuasion of Cardinal Oleśnicki and the prognosis that a second expedition against the Turks will succeed, win the day. He summons a general assembly that meets in Buda on St. James' Day and promises that on a suitable occasion he will go to Poland and repair the damage that has been done.

The purpose of the assembly, which is also attended by all the prelates, dukes and nobles of Hungary, is to organize the new expedition against the Turks and to restore peace in the country without which any such campaign would be too risky. It is also attended by Stephen of Raško, as well as by Jan Giskra and representatives of all the rebel towns to whom the King has promised immunity. Frederick King of the Romans has no liking for the assembly, which he sees as yet another triumph for Władysław. The King's main concern is to restore peace to Hungary. Various suggestions are made and in the end, Jan Giskra, who alone has espoused the cause of young Lászlo, for all the others have gone over to Władysław, agrees to a truce. Next comes the question of financing

Polish and other Christian troops fighting the Turks in Hungary in 1443. —Joachim Bielski's Kronika Polska, *1597—Jagiellonian University Librray.*
This illustrates how hand-to-hand fighting was in those days, and for long to come. A battle was, in effect, a series of duels, each victor having to fight again and again until the battle was over.

the coming war. The royal treasury is empty, for the King has been generous in his rewards and indeed extravagant, for he has given away more than he has received. In the end, it is decided that every town and village is to contribute a certain amount and their every inhabitant will pay a certain sum to be assessed. The country is divided into a number of areas to which collectors are sent. János Hunyadi is made responsible for the supply of waggons with iron tyres, cannon, firearms, gunpowder, horses and other necessary materials. As the time approaches when King Władysław promised to return to Poland, the Hungarians become afraid lest he be retained there so long as to be unable to lead the army against the Turks, and so do their best to prevent him leaving, greatly to the disadvantage of Poland. When he learns of this, Bolesław, Duke of Opole, who has covered himself with shame by embracing the Hussite heresy and by discarding his legal wife, Elizabeth of Pilcza, and taking a concubine, plucks up courage and, while a number of Cracovian merchants are in Kreuzberg resting, he attacks and imprisons them, together with a number of other people, mounted and on foot, who have waggons of merchandize which they are taking to a fair to be held in Wrocław on the Feast of St. John the Baptist. Duke Bolesław's men, whom many think to be real soldiers, seize all the merchandize and everyone's gold and silver, the whole amounting to some 200,000 złoty. The Poles decide to avenge Duke Bolesław's rash act and declare war on him officially: yet for this to succeed, they agree that they must ensure their action cannot be misunderstood as they are waging their war in the King's absence; anyway the King, whatever his other preoccupations, cannot fail to react to such a crime. However, the King tells them to leave matters in abeyance until his return, promising that the robbers will not long enjoy their loot. At the same time the King sends letters and envoys to the Master of the Teutonic Knights in Prussia asking him to send military help, at least for this second war against the Turks, for the Master had failed to help him in the first. Again the King's request falls on deaf ears.

The fervour for war against the Turks receives a sudden check, when it is learned that Stephen of Raško and the Voivode of Transylvania, János Hunyadi, have secretly made peace with the Sultan, Murad, largely because Stephen is eager for the return of his castles and possessions, which the Turks have taken from him and thinks that this will be easier to achieve by peaceful means than by force of arms. The Sultan fully informed of the preparations for war against him being made in Hungary and with his defeat at Władysław's hands in the previous year fresh in his memory, becomes convinced that Fate is against him, especially when he learns that the Tatar khan, Karaman, is attacking Natolia with a huge army, and decides that at all cost he must make peace with Hungary. The governor of Natolia urges both sides on, for he is eager to obtain his freedom; indeed, he is released even before peace is concluded, being ransomed by the Turks for 70,000 florins. King Władysław informed of all this, is asked to go to Szeged in early August to hear the Sultan's envoys, who are coming to sue for peace.

This is good news for King Władysław and for all Hungarians, for hitherto it is the Hungarians who have had to ask the Turks for peace; but it is not good news for Cardinal Cesarini who sees all his efforts to free Europe from the Turks being frustrated, as well as having to face the prospect of being accused of deceiving the Duke of Burgundy, the Venetians and the Genoese whom he has persuaded to send fleets to guard the Straits. All Władysław's land forces have been given orders to assemble in Szeged, from which they can swiftly attack the enemy, should peace not be agreed. When the Turkish delegates arrive, Władysław and Cardinal Julian Cesarini are already there. The Turkish delegation is headed by the Sultan's chancellor, a Greek who had renounced the Catholic faith and become a Muslim. The others are all Turks and they are all mounted. They have brought the King gifts of golden and silver vessels. They propose the following terms: that the Sultan surrender all the castles in Raško that he and his predecessors have captured and garrisoned with Turks (fifteen are named); that the Sultan renounce for ever that part of Albania held by Stephen of Raško; while the whole of Bulgaria is to remain under Turkish rule. Stephen's two sons are to be freed. That is all. The Hungarians are all agreed that such an advantageous offer must not to be refused. They remember how much blood was shed when Golub was besieged and now it can be recovered without a further drop being spilled. The final decision—one to which Cardinal Cesarini does not agree—is that they should conclude peace with the Sultan for ten years, during which time Władysław will be able to remove all civil strife from Hungary and when the ten years are up, will be free to start another war with the Turks.

When the Turks have left with the peace treaty agreed, letters arrive from the commander of the fleet of the Apostolic See, the Duke of Burgundy, the cities of Venice and Genoa, as well as the captains of the galleys and other ships, informing the King that they have a powerful army ready to sail with the fleet and that they have been watchful and prevented the Turks crossing from Anatolia to Romania. They now ask the King to keep his promises and send his army overland to Romania, anticipating that it will be possible without great effort to recover the whole of Europe, especially as all the Sultan's forces are busy fighting the Tatars. The King also receives letters sent by special messenger by the Emperor of Constantinople, John Palaeologus, assuring him that there was every hope of victory and of liberating Europe. He warns Władysław against false, deceitful peace treaties, for which the Turks may ask, and pleads that he should not allow the desire to heal old wounds to damage the whole of Christendom. Władysław, perturbed by these letters, yields to the arguments of the Cardinal, who depicts all the misfortunes that will befall them, should Hunyadi's peace treaty be upheld, and what advantages will accrue to them, if it is rejected. Indeed, the King and his advisers are beginning to regret having made the treaty, especially as it now looks as if they will be able to recover not only all that the Turks are proposing to hand back, but the whole of occupied Europe, and to drive the Turks back across the Straits. Hunyadi is won round to this view, when the King gives him a written promise that, if they win the war, Hunyadi shall be made king of Bulgaria. There follow days of intense discussion, and the issue is decided when, three weeks after the Turks made their offer, they find that Smederevo, Golub and the other castles the envoys had promised to surrender, have still not been handed over and so conclude that the Turks have been deceitful and their promises empty. That being so, they decide to abrogate the treaty they have just made and wage war on Turkey.

Cardinal Cesarini salves their consciences by telling them that what they are doing has the authority of the Holy See and that the treaty they made was invalid, since it was made with an enemy of Christendom and without instructions from the Holy See. The Cardinal even persuades the King and his councillors to swear an oath to wage the war to the best of their ability. People in Poland, however, are perturbed by this turn in events, and an assembly held in Piotrków on St. Bartholomew's Day votes to send the Bishop of Włocławek to the King in Hungary to try to persuade him not to go to war with the Turks, but to return to Poland. The King, informed of what is going on, sends Peter the Warden of Cracow and his own notary to Piotrków to tell the assembly that he is not going to give up warring with the Turks, indeed, is already planning to move the entire army from Szeged towards Orszawa. He enjoins the Poles to help Bolesław of Mazovia against the King's brother, Casimir, Duke of Lithuania, who is seeking to conquer Mazovia. He promises that he will try to bring the war with the Turks to a swift conclusion, and that he will put matters right should Casimir try to attack Mazovia. At this point, Casimir has already invaded Drohiczyń territory, built fortifications and is attempting to capture Drohiczyń castle. Duke Bolesław moves up his army, which has been strongly reinforced by Polish nobles and barons, to prevent his territory being laid waste. The other duke of Mazovia, Władyslaw, though moving his army into the field, delays linking up with his brother, thus making it look as if he were deserting, rather than helping him. Had the two dukes joined forces, the Mazovians would have considerably outnumbered the Lithuanians, many of whom were really peasants and non-combatants; while the Mazovians had numbers of tyred waggons laden with firearms and cannon, with which they ringed the army, protecting it like a wall against attack, which both gave them courage and so perturbed the Lithuanians that they sent the best of their gold and silver vessels to nearby castles for safe-keeping. In the meantime, the assemby at Piotrków has sent Vincent Archbishop of Gniezno and Jan of Tęczyn Voivode of Sandomierz to Mazovia to arrange a truce, promising to refer their dispute to the King, as soon as he gets back from fighting the Turks. This proves unnecessary, the two sides having made peace on their own. This involved the Lithuanians paying the Duke of Mazovia 6000 threescore of broad Prussian grosses for which he renounces his claim and right to Drohiczyń and surrenders the document he has confirming his right to it. He is, however, to retain the district of Wingrów. The Lithuanians soon regret making this pact, especially when the Bishop of Wilno reproaches them for betraying the ways of their ancestors by using money, instead of arms, to fight their battles.

Władysław's new army is not so strong or numerous as before, when, about September 20, he moves out from Szeged. His heart is heavy, for he is breaking the treaty he made with the Turks and he is without many of his Poles, who had asked far too high a reward and been told that they were not needed. Following the Danube, the great army enters Bulgaria on November 3. The King himself crosses the Danube at Orszawa and reaches Florentinum four days later, and Bidinum two days after that, heading for Adrianopole and then Gallipoli, where he intends to link up with the Venetian and Genoese fleet, which is already in position preventing the transfer of Turkish troops from Asia, where the Sultan, Murad, and Karaman, the Tatar khan, are already warring. The shortest route from Bidinum is through the mountains, a distance an army could safely cover in a fortnight at the most, but the King and his councillors consider the King's army too small to be able to transport its waggons through the mountains, so it is decided to follow the Danube, which will allow them to retain their waggons and provide better access to provisions. So, they cross the mountains to the Danube and after traversing the rich province of Macedonia reach Nikopol in 26 days. Nikopol is half surrounded by the Danube, the other, eastern half, being protected by a high hill, while the rest of the city is girdled by a line of low hills. Outside the city itself are people's huts, which are at once looted and burned. Although the city's walls appear to have been built of small stones, the King does not try to capture it, both because he is eager to get to Greece and also because, in order not to overburden the army, he has brought with him only a few small cannon. Nikopol is a modest-looking place, its appearance less than its fame as capital of Bulgaria; yet once it enjoyed many privileges. Its soil is fertile and it is a port and provides the Turks with easy access to Volhynia and Transylvania, and so to Hungary.

While the King and his army are resting outside Nikopol, the Voivode of Transylvania, Dracula, crosses into Bulgaria and comes to beg Władysław's forgiveness for having made friends with the Turks. Having inspected the King's army and seen how small it is, he earnestly advises the King to abandon the expedition and return to Hungary, insisting that Władysław's army is far too weak, smaller indeed than the number of men with which the Sultan normally goes hunting. If the King should insist on going ahead with the campaign, the Voivode promises to send him his son with his whole army, and also a pair of very powerful horses and two men who know the country and so can get him out of any tight corner. The King accepts the horses and guides, but not the Voivode's advice. He has no intention of abandoning the expedition, especially when his men are reinforced with 4000 troops from Transylvania. To tell the truth, the King now has scarcely 5000 horse and more than 2000 waggons laden not only with provisions, but with gold, jewels and so much domestic equipment, that it looks as if every knight had brought his own household with him.

Leaving the Danube, the King advances through fertile Thrace, where they find numbers of costly buildings and marble plaques with Greek or Latin inscriptions, memorials of the old Roman emperors and commanders, as well as arches and tall columns, most overthrown by age or Turkish neglect. During the march, the King comes across a river, in which the Sultan has hidden twenty-eight barges, which were to be moved to the Danube at the appropriate time and used to transport troops to the gates of Buda. These craft the King orders to be burned.

The King, seeing how his troops are looting and destroying towns, shrines and villages, indeed behaving worse than the Turks, and finding that he cannot stop their cruelty, fears God's vengeance.

Cardinal Julian receives a letter from the Cardinal of Venice, commander of the fleet of the Apostolic See, telling him that 40,000 Turks have crossed secretly and by night from the lower part of Pharos into Europe unhindered by the fleet and its guards, whom some think may have been bribed, though the pious cannot accept that Venetians and Genoese would go so far as to sell the blood of Christians to the Muslims. Others say that the Apostolic fleet has been withdrawn, because of lack of provisions. Whichever it was, the waters are now open to the Turks. The King remains unperturbed by the news and determined to continue the planned advance to the shores of the Moorish Sea.

Having stormed and burned Petrziec, the army advances through open country. On its right, to the south, are the mountains between Romania and Bulgaria, which run from Bidinium and Nikopol to Galata and the Moorish Sea leading to Mesambria and Constantinople. At the foot of these mountains is a lake, one end of which is near Petrzec and the other in a small bay near Galata.

King Władysław fighting the Turks at Adrianopole.
—Joachim Bielski's Kronika Polska, *1597—Jagiellonian University Library.*

To their north are other hills, beyond which is another empty plain that stretches northwards to the Danube, Moldavia and Transyslvania, a distance of some eight days, for in this part of the world no one measures distance in miles.

The army continues its advance until it reaches Varna, some five hundred paces from Galata both of which have already been abandoned by the Turks. At the sight of the Polish standards, Hawerina and several other towns surrender, despite the protection of triple walls and access to the sea. At night the King can see the fires in the camps of those Turks who had crossed from Natolia and gone first to Gallipoli and then to Adrianopole, and who now together amount to a considerable army, following the King's army and finally pitching camp some five thousand paces from it.

At dawn on the Wednesday, scarcely an hour after sunrise, there is a great cry that the Turks are advancing; indeed, all but upon them. The men seize up their arms, dismantle their tents and load up their waggons, and take up position in front of them, instead of deploying the waggons in the customary three rings, from inside which they could have fought as in a fort. It was the King who decided on this, so that those who normally would have been behind the waggons, would be in the front rank with him, making the army look larger than it was. It is not known why he had not provided the army with cannon or arbalests. Perhaps his state of health had prevented him, for he had an ulcer on his left foot. János Hunyadi deploys the various units in a wide arc across a depression between the lake and the mountains, each a thousand paces from the other. On the left, near the lake, he places five standards of his own and Hungarian troops; then the King and his standards, with the Walachians on the right; then the black Hungarian standard and beyond this the Bishop of Eger's troops, then the Ban of Slavonia's troops under the command of the Ban's brother; beyond them the standard of the Holy Church under command of Cardinal Cesarini, and lastly, at the end of the right wing, some two thousand paces distant, the standard of St. Ladislas under the command of Duke Waradyn. In this array, with the waggons all behind them, they await the Turks for the best part of three hours. The weather is fine; the sea calm; but suddenly a wind gets up from the West, a wind so strong that it breaks the poles of all the standards but that of St. James, of which the King had charge.

Meanwhile the Turks have been advancing not through the open country, but through the woods and hills, sending scouts ahead of them and moving slowly. In the van are their foot archers, whom they call janissaries. First, they mount a weak attack on the right wing under Duke Waradyn. Why it was, I do not know, but the Hungarians in the first ranks with four standards, i.e. those of Duke Waradyn, the Legate, the Ban of Slavonia's brother and Bishop Simon of Eger, are unable to withstand the Turks' first assault, and retreat towards Galata, which lies between the bay and the lake and the mountains towards Romania. The Turks pursue them for a couple of miles, i.e. ten thousand paces. When he sees this, the King mounts his own attack, and so does Hunyadi. The two then link up and rout the Turks, whom they pursue for four thousand paces. However many the King and his men kill, it never looks as if they have achieved much, so great is the number of the enemy, some of whom, many people say, were women, recruited to swell their numbers. The Turks had, too, a number of camels laden partly with silks, partly with arrows and other necessary equipment. Others carry gold and silver coin, which, when they see themselves defeated, they spill on the ground to slacken the pursuit of the enemy, a cunning old trick of the Cossacks. These camels so frighten some of the knights' horses as to make them unmanageable; though the Walachians and others greedy for money showed themselves brave enough to attack the camels.

The janissaries have now grouped in one place and from behind their tall shields pour such a rain of arrows on the King's men, that the air is filled, as if with hail. Many are killed and the air resounds with the cries of dying horses. The King's infantry suffers the most, though he also loses many of his eminent Polish knights. Those who are expert in the art of war maintain that the King brought about his own defeat in that, at the beginning, he pursued the enemy far too far. If he had shown restraint here, there is no doubt that victory would have been his. The King is always in the centre of the fray; Hunyadi repeatedly sends to the King suggesting that he withdraw and save himself; as Hunyadi does later.

For a third time the King renews the attack. When he advances, the Walachians show themselves more eager to strip the bodies of the fallen than pursue the enemy; and when the King has to withdraw, they take to their heels. So the fight continues until dusk. The King's men have by then driven the Turks thirty thousand paces back from their base at Varna. The King is now in the middle of the fray, surrounded on all sides, and there he dies together with all his knights, a grievous loss to Christendom and Poland.

When night falls, both sides consider themselves defeated. The Hungarians under Hunyadi have left the battlefield, and what is left of the King's army remains halted some distance from the waggons, which they no longer dare approach, in case the Turks are there already, and there they wait for their King to come to them. Nor do the Turks, who, likewise, consider themselves defeated, dare approach the waggons for two whole days. Meanwhile, fear has lent wings to the heels of the retreating Hungarians, Walachians and others, so that they reach the Danube in two days and two nights. Many of them not having eaten for two, three, even five days, nor had anything to drink.

The King was never seen again after night stopped the fighting. No-one has ever been found who saw him being captured or killed. Of the many others who never returned, definite news came of their having died or been captured, but none of the King's fate. Cardinal Julian left the battlefield together with Hunyadi, but then the two separated, no one knows why. The Cardinal reached the Danube with a small company, and there was killed by a Walachian who was ferrying him, his sole passenger, in a tiny boat. The Walachian probably noticed that the Cardinal was carrying gold, and this must have weighed down the boat. The Cardinal's naked body was later recovered from the river.

A.D. 1445

Neither the Hungarians nor the Poles can credit the rumours of disaster having befallen their armies. When, at the end of the month, these rumours are confirmed by the few survivors who reach home, people still insist that the King himself must be alive and either in Constantinople, Venice, Transylvania or even Albania. Finally, it is decided to send people to Romania, Greece and Bulgaria, at public expense, to try and discover the truth. Meanwhile, an assembly meets in Sieradz to discuss the future government of the kingdom. This is attended by more people than usual. Some want to wait for more certain news, others just to do nothing, but, in the end, they accept the advice of Bishop Zbigniew Oleśnicki of Cracow and elect the King's brother, Grand-duke Casimir of Lithuania, as their new king. Casimir is informed of his election, but told that, in case definite news of his brother's fate should be received, it is not to be put into effect until St. Bartholomew's Day, when he is requested to present himself before an assembly to be held on that date in Piotrków.

The Hungarians, too, for a long time refuse to believe in the death of their king; but, in the end, an assembly in Pest unanimously elects King Albert's posthumous son, László, to be their king and a delegation is sent to King Frederick to ask for the boy and the crown itself to be sent to Hungary. Meanwhile, other people are sent to Poland to seek news there. They have talks with Queen Sophia, but learn nothing new. King Frederick tells the delegation sent to him that there is no need to crown young László, since he is already legally king and Hungary his by virtue of inheritance from his father, mother and grandfather. This by no means pleases everybody and in the end, for the sake of peace and the unity of the kingdom, Frederick agrees to allow a fresh coronation, but without anointment, and insists that the coronation document emphasizes that the first coronation is not thereby invalidated, and that both boy and crown be returned to Bratislava, since it would not be right to remove the lad from the care of the person to whom his mother and the other executors entrusted him. However, he promises to confirm the coronation document, so that in the event of the boy dying, Hungary should not lose either its right to coronation or to Bratislava.

When St. Bartholomew's Day arrives, Queen Sophia and the others assemble in Piotrków. They are told by those sent to Lithuania that Grand-duke Casimir is sending his own envoys with his reply, which, when it arrives, is that the Grand-duke is so upset by the misfortunes of his brother, that he does not have the heart to undertake further duties, and, also, that he considers it too early to declare the throne vacant, and that they must wait for some considerable time yet to be sure of the King's fate, and, meanwhile, should continue to search for him. In the meantime, the country can continue to be governed by the regents, whom the King appointed. This answer disappoints the Council and leads to further discussion, the conclusion of which is that there is no more suitable candidate, so again they send to the Grand-duke begging him to accept the crown without further delay.

Although Casimir is himself inclined to accept, he is held back both by a feeling that his brother may still be alive and by his Lithuanian councillors, who are afraid that, should he move to

Poland, the bad old days of Witold and his brother, Sigismund, will return. They are afraid, too, lest Casimir incorporate Łuck in Poland. In the end, Casimir promises to give his answer at the close of an assembly of all Lithuania, Samogitia and Ruthenia. Should he accept the crown, he promises to come to Cracow at Epiphany, unless in the meantime definite news that King Władysław is alive has been received.

A.D. 1446

As Epiphany approaches, the delegates begin to assemble in Piotrków to hear the Grand-duke's reply. He tells them that he did not go to Lithuania as a temporary ruler acting on behalf of the King of Poland, but as its legal inheritor. He has no desire to leave it or to rule a larger area. He has never sought to rule Poland nor to occupy its throne. He is content to rule a duchy, especially as it is still by no means certain that his brother is dead; indeed, many things point to his still being alive. He finds it unworthy that the prelates and others in Poland should be in such a hurry to choose a new king, instead of waiting, for years if need be, for certain information. Poland is enjoy-ing such ideal peace, that it can perfectly well continue to be governed by those who have been do-ing so for a number of years already. The Poles must be careful lest in their haste they create war and strife, for Casimir cannot accept that anyone else should occupy the throne of Poland without his consent.

This reply angers the Poles and they decide to look for another king; however, Queen Sophia, who is attending the assembly, is against the proposal, for she realizes that, if someone else should occupy the throne, her son would be in danger of assassination. Indeed, if people are to be believed, seven plots have already been laid against his life. In the end, it is decided to delay taking a decision and to send one further delegation to Lithuania. Again the reply comes back that the death of King Władysław is not yet certain and that in the mean time Casimir is content with Lithuania, though, should anyone else occupy the throne of Poland without his approval, he will be regarded as an en-emy and the Grand-duke will devote all his skill and energy to having him removed.

When the Grand-duke's answer is made public, people are convinced that in reality Casimir desires the Polish crown, but the Lithuanians will not allow him to accept it, because they are afraid that, should he do so, they could only play a subordinate role and would lose all hope of recovering the lands and castles of Łuck and Podole. So, now, people from all over the kingdom converge on Piotrków, where an assembly is to decide whether or not to elect a new king. Before taking the de-cision, in accordance with ancient custom, the prelates and councillors take Holy Communion, at a Mass celebrated by Vincent Metropolitan of Gniezno, where an act of expiation is performed by the bishops and nobles. After this, humbly and in silence they walk to the council chamber. First, they discuss whether or not to proceed immediately to the election of their future king, thus annul-ling the earlier election of Grand-duke Casimir, or, despite everything, to continue to urge Casimir to accept the crown. After some discussion it is decided to elect a new king, but, that they should also give Casimir a chance to change his mind, for they are convinced that the election of anyone else could lead to civil war.

The first speaker is Archbishop Vincent, who discusses the merits of a number of princes from far and near and finally advocates chosing Frederick of Brandenburg, both because of his common sense, his knowledge of the Polish language and the proximity of his lands. This proposal is seconded by Bishop Oleśnicki of Cracow, who points out that as long as Bohemia was ruled by its own native princes, it remained small and insignificant, but, as soon as German princes from Luxembourg were called in to rule it, it became renowned. Presumably, the same thing would hap-pen, should Poland chose Margrave Frederick. Further approval comes from the bishops of Włocławek and Poznań, but that choice is opposed by the Bishop of Płock, who dislikes the idea of having a foreign prince, however virtuous, when there are the two dukes of Mazovia, available, both eminent and virtuous and descendants of the old family of Polish kings. His objection is seconded by the Castellan of Cracow, who, of the two dukes prefers Bolesław, as do the voivodes of Cracow and Poznań. Opinion among the others is almost equally divided, with the majority of the nobles voting for Bolesław. The bishops who voted for Frederick then change their minds and vote for Bolesław, after which the Archbishop of Gniezno proclaims Duke Bolesław of Mazovia Poland's future king, unanimously elected in accordance with ecclesiastical law. The clergy then sing *Te deum laudamus*, and the populace sing *Bogu Rodzica*. The next day a delegation of five is chosen, which, unless in the mean time Grand-duke Casimir has changed his mind, is to go to Duke Bolesław after Whitsun and ask him to accept the throne and come to Cracow to be crowned. All these proceedings have been attended by an unofficial Lithuanian observer, who now departs sorrowfully to report to his master.

The Lithuanians consider that with Bolesław of Mazovia on the Polish throne, there would be danger of civil strife, in that Duke Michael, son of the late Grand-duke Zygmunt and son-in-law of Bolesław, in whose house he was brought up, and under whose influence he must be, so that Bolesław might use him to involve the country in civil war, and, if he did, he would have the support of the many who are angry with Grand-duke Casimir for governing not in person, but through others, which they consider unworthy. For the sake of preserving peace, some would like to see Casimir humbled and forced to do what they wished, or even expelled from Lithuania and replaced with Duke Michael. Casimir, aware that he has escaped assassination several times already, is disquieted, because he has been told that he will lose his life if there is anyone else on the throne of Poland, and he realizes that, if they start fighting, he will be lucky to survive. Now, he begins to regret having acted as he has done and, in the greatest secrecy reveals his change of heart to his mother and a small number of trusted friends, telling them that only now does he realize the danger to which his refusal of the Polish crown exposes him.

The time is at hand, when the delegates are to go to inform Duke Bolesław of his election, but now some of the Cracovian nobles have turned against the idea, being afraid that, if Bolesław became king, he would not allow them to continue to enjoy the royal demenses they have appropriated, the loss of which would reduce their standard of living, the number of horses and servants they could keep, and the amount they could spend on their womenfolk. These nobles now get together and, with the encouragement of Queen Sophia, privately send the Castellan of Sanok to Grand-duke Casimir, who gives the Castellan a more favourable hearing than any of the others have had. The Castellan reports back that Casimir has changed his mind. Though uncorroborated, this news causes a split between those who wish to believe it and those who want to send to Duke Bolesław, and so Bishop Oleśnicki of Cracow summons an assembly of the prelates and nobles of Wielkopolska in Koło to decide what is to be done. These agree that they should invite Casimir to attend a general assembly on the Feast of the Assumption in Korczyń, so that the decision taken at Koło can be confirmed in the presence of Queen Sophia, with whom everyone sympathizes, when she begs that, having already lost one son, she should not be deprived of the other. There is one proviso, however, namely that, should Grand-duke Casimir prevaricate or refuse to accept the throne, the election of Duke Bolesław of Mazovia will be proceeded with.

Shortly before St. Michael's Day people start foregathering for a new assembly, only to hear that a horde of Lithuanians and Tatars is heading for Parczów intending to seize and carry off the delegates.

Grand-duke Casimir gets as far as Brześć, from where he lets it be known, that he is there at his mother's request, and, though happy to discuss the state of Poland, has neither promised to accept its crown nor to attend the assembly in Parczów. If they wish to see him, let them come to him in Brześć. The assembly decides that it is not going to leave Parczów, and, instead, sends an eight-man delegation to Brześć. This is given a friendly reception and has several days of discussion with the Grand-duke; however, as Casimir makes it a condition that Podole, Łuck and Olesko must be surrendered to Lithuania—and who in his senses would consider that anything but a dangerous and humiliating dismemberment of Poland, which must impoverish it?—he is told that this is unacceptable. Some delegates are even ready to up sticks and go straight to Mazovia; however, those who are afraid of losing the crown properties they have appropriated should Bolesław become king, tell Casimir that, as King of Poland, he will have the right to detach the three territories and give them to Lithuania, as his father did, when he granted them in turn to Spytek, Świdrygiello and Witold, and they promise that they will do everything they can to help bring this about. At this, the Grand-duke, while justifying his procrastination by his hope that his brother might still be alive, finally agrees to accept the Polish crown. Before leaving Brześć, he orders several villages, which his brother had added to Parczów to be taken from it and given to Brześć, thus showing that already he was thinking more of Lithuania than of Poland.

A.D. 1447

Casimir, Grand-duke of Lithuania, has moved to Lublin, where he is generously provided with all that he and his retinue require. He continues to Sandomierz, where he is received by Queen Sophia on the Saturday after Corpus Christi. Leaving on the Monday, he reaches Polaniec on the following day and Korczyn on the Wednesday. Here he is received by Bishop Oleśnicki and Jan Tęczyn voivode of Cracow. He leaves on the following day, and, after dining at the manor of Podolana, continues on to Proszowice. He reaches Cracow on the Friday and is met by dignitaries of the city and university in procession, as well as by the Archbishop of Gniezno and three bishops. Entering the city, he first goes to the cathedral of St. Stanisław and, having done honour to the sacred relics and donated fifty florins, proceeds to the palace. On the next day, the two dukes of Mazovia, Bolesław and Władysław, appear with a retinue of a thousand mounted knights, a beautiful sight that arouses general admiration and surprise that two dukes should have a retinue worthy of kings.

On the Sunday, after being robed in the castle, Casimir is crowned before the altar in the cathedral in the presence of Queen Sophia, the dukes of Mazovia, Szczecin, Racibórz and Oświęcim, a number of Ruthenian dukes and many of the barons of Lithuania, Bohemia, Moravia and Silesia. The new king places on the altar a gift of 100 florins, all of which, as is the law and custom, must go to the vicars of Cracow.

The dukes and gentry of Lithuania now take their leave, departing enriched with costly gifts from the King, who conducts them to the city gate, and then goes to Niepołomice to divert himself with hunting.

On the Tuesday before St. Margaret's Day, the King leaves for Wielkopolska and eventually reaches Poznań. While he is in Kalisz, Duke Michael of Lithuania comes and flings himself at his feet and humbly begs for forgiveness, grace and the return of his father's property. The King, whom such a change of heart should have inclined to clemency, scorns the suppliant and, having exchanged scarcely one word, dismisses him with nothing settled. The Duke departs without taking leave, feeling that the King is not to be propitiated and that he has humbled himself in vain.

On the night that the King reaches Poznań fire breaks out and burns until sunrise, destroying almost the entire city, except for those houses built of stone. When the King's escort of Poles, Lithuanians and Tatars starts looting, many of them are killed on the King's orders, some being beheaded. It was said that the fire was God's punishment for the shameful homosexual practices in which the Court has indulged with impunity.

The King now goes to Piotrków for a general assembly, at which the following laws are approved: firstly, that the first-born or eldest brother may not by reason of seniority be allowed to take or dispose of his father's possessions other than that part which belongs to him, unless the extent of the father's debts makes this essential, in which case no more shall be sold than will cover the father's debts, and, should there be a surplus, this must be honestly divided equally between the brothers; secondly, that the rivers Vistula, Warta, Dunajec, Bug, Dniestr, Dniepr, Wislok, Wisloka, Pilcza and others within the kingdom of Poland are to be accessible to all without hindrance. No obstacles or impediments to their flow are to be built, and all and sundry are to be allowed to cross them and to float on them goods of every kind with free access upstream and downstream; thirdly, that in peace time the people's courts are to be held and justice given to the poor without interruption; that all voivodes, castellans, judges and officials are to attend in person, except in the event of serious illness or absence on the King's business, in which event they must provide a substitute; fourthly, that anyone accused of theft or robbery must prove his innocence before twelve honest witnesses chosen from among eighty; and the same applies to a second or third incident; but, if one be accused a fourth time, he must be punished in accordance with local law.

At this assembly King Casimir is asked to swear to confirm the privileges his predecessors had granted to the inhabitants of the kingdom and also not to detach from the kingdom any of its lands, especially not Ruthenia, Łuck or Podole; also that, when he goes to Lithuania, he should take with him mature, sensible people and take their advice on matters affecting Poland. The King replies that he can grant none of these requests because of promises made earlier to the Lithuanians; and so, on St. Felix's Day, he departs.

With its new king out of the way, all Poland's enemies, especially the Silesians, start raiding and plundering its territories, taking captives and killing nobles and barons. With the help of certain Silesians, two nobles from Włocławek treacherously make their way into the town of Będzin with two waggons carrying armed men disguised as merchandize. These secure access for the rest of the raiding party, which then sacks the town, sets fire to it and withdraws, all without opposition.

On the Wednesday after St. Michael's Day, Lublin and Żmin are destroyed by fire so completely that not one house survives. Bochnia, Ksiąz and Sieradz suffer the same fate. Thefts are common this winter, mostly committed by Silesians and Hungarians, who plunder merchants' waggons and rob the merchants themselves of their money and jewelry. Even a knight and his son were attacked and killed while out hunting. In Vladimir, the cupbearer of Sieradz and some others are seized and put in prison. But none are more daring than those members of the Polish nobility who, with their minions, now live by theft and brigandage and, in the King's absence, do so with impunity.

The Regent of Hungary, János Hunyadi, assembles a sizeable army and, pretending to be going to attack the Turks, enters Bessarabia with the man whom he intends to make voivode of it, after he has expelled Vlad, the present incumbent. Finding the unsuspecting Vlad unattended, he has him and his son killed, all this just to pay Vlad out for having helped and looked after him, when he escaped from the Turks at Varna. He then blinds the very man he promised to make voivode of Bessarabia and seeks to appropriate the province for himself.

While the King spends his time hunting, many of the Lithuanian boyars are holding secret meetings at which they discuss way and means of obtaining supreme power for Duke Michael, and in this are encouraged by the Duke himself. When the King learns of this, he removes all the suspect boyars from their posts and replaces them with others loyal to him, at the same time making preparations to capture Duke Michael, who is then with relations in Mazovia. He even sends envoys to the Prussian Master asking him to arrest the Duke should he attempt to escape through the Order's territory, and hand him over. The Master is happy to help and places guards on all the wastes and woods betwen Mazovia, Lithuania and Prussia through which the Duke might try to pass; and, indeed, this is what he and six pages attempt, hoping to get to friendly Samogitia. As it is they run into the Prussians, eight men under a commander. The Commander draws his sword, bends low over his saddle and spurs at Duke Michael, who seizes the Commander's sword with his bare hands and wrests it from him, cutting both his hands in the process. Nine being superior to seven, the Duke makes a dash for it into the surrounding bog, but his pages are captured. The Commander, with local help, captures the Duke the following day, holds him and his pages until the Duke's hands have healed, and then dismisses him with gifts. Duke Michael gets back to Mazovia and from there to Silesia.

A.D. 1448

King Casimir spends Christmas in Wilno, to which envoys from the dukes of Moscow and Tver, the Tatar Khan, the city of Novgorod and the Master of the Order in Prussia and Samogitia, come to congratulate him. They are all entertained and dismissed with gifts. The King then goes to Brześć and remains there over Easter, before returning to Wilno, where he is joined by Queen Sophia, but her court being so numerous, she cannot stay long because of the famine from which Lithuania is suffering. However, they are together again after Corpus Christi, in Lublin, where an assembly is being held. The delegates are all accomodated in tents along the bank of the River Bystrzyca. Now, the Lithuanians again raise the question of the pact made by King Władysław and the Grand-duke Alexander when they united Poland and Lithuania for all time, disputing the meaning of some of the documents, especially those texts which can be interpreted as reducing the prelates, dukes and nobles of Lithuania to inferior status. They also demand the return of Podole, the fort at Olesko and the departments of Wielzy, Łopatyn and Horodło, contending that these were illegally detached from the Grand-duchy on the death of the Grand-duke Witold. The Poles' reaction is conciliatory, and, in the end, it is agreed that the intention of King Władysław and Grand-duke Witold was that Poland and Lithuania together were to be under one king and that henceforth both countries were to be called the Kingdom of Poland, the term of grand-duchy no longer being used, and that Lithuania, Samogitia and Ruthenia, which then came under the grand-duchy, were to enjoy exactly the same rights and conditions, privilegies and liberties as did Cracow, Sandomierz, Lublin, Lwów and all the others. The Lithuanians are then asked whether they wish to continue with Poland under one king and one grand-duke, because, if so, there is no question of detaching Podole and the rest because you cannot detach a whole from a part. After consideration, the Lithuanians reply that they do wish to continue under one king, but not for ever, only as long as King Casimir and the descendants of his generation and family are alive. However, they cannot agree to Lithuania being part of the Kingdom of Poland and on a par with Cracow, Sieradz and the rest: it would be shameful were the name of the Grand-duchy of Lithuania, with all its glory and renown, to be subsumed under the joint name of Poland. They, therefore, request, indeed, demand, that the relative documents be amended and that Podole and the other territories mentioned be given to them. The Poles then remind the Lithuanians of the various stages of the union and finally propose referring the matter of Podole and the other lands to arbitration. The Lithuanians, realizing that they have no legal basis for their demands, refuse to discuss the matter further.

The assembly concluded, the King leaves Lublin and reaches Cracow shortly before the Feast of St. John the Baptist. Here he receives the dukes of Racibórz and Oświęcim come to promise him assistance and loyalty. They are duly rewarded and dismissed.

At this time, Duke Bolesław of Cieszyn marries Queen Sophia's sister, Anna, Duchess of Ruthenia. The King generously gives her a dowry of 2000 florins taken from the treasury, thus emphasizing his wish for close friendship with Cieszyn. He expresses his wish that in time all the Silesian duchies may be reunited with Poland.

Leaving Cracow, the King goes to Wojnicz, where he receives news of the death of his half-brother, Roman, voivode of Moldavia, and son of the voivode Elias who was poisoned by his own knights. He hurries to Ruthenia intending to restore peace and order in Moldavia. Reaching Lwów, he stays there for eleven days wondering whether or not to take an army into Moldavia, for he has been told that voivode Peter is preparing to resist, relying on help from János Hunyadi. Finally, he orders mobilization throughout Ruthenia and shortly after St. Peter's Day goes to Halicz, where he receives a visit from Maria, the widow of Voivode Elias, who arrives with an escort of 200 mounted Walachians, who used to support her brother and are now inclined to put themselves under King Casimir. The King sympathizes with his aunt's predicament and grants her the town of Kolomyja as her residence. Her Walachians receive generous gifts of money and are asked to accompany the King to Podole.

The King now goes to Halicz, the point of assembly for the troops from Ruthenia, and there goes hawking. While thus engaged, a Polish noble, who had long served him in Lithuania, dies while testing a ford in the River Lipia. Although the water is shallow, it is several hours before his body is recovered. Moving on, the King spends twelve days at Wawrzyniec to the delight of its nobles and landowners, who voluntarily pay double the amount due for his subsistence. The King has sent to Voivode Peter in an attempt to win him over and persuade him to pay homage and also to surrender Duke Michael, whom he has hitherto supported. Peter agrees to pay homage and be loyal, as were his ancestors, but, as he is afraid to present himself in person, for he has been warned that, should he do so, he is likely to be imprisoned; he sends his own emissaries to ask the King to forgive him for being afraid to come, and to explain that it would be too shameful to hand over Duke Michael, who came to him as a friend, though he will undertake not to allow the Duke to continue to stay in his territory. The King now disbands his troops and sends Peter a long letter assuring him of his personal safety. With this Peter sets off to go to the King, but the latter, being impatient to get back to Lithuania, leaves Kamieniec before Peter arrives. Before he left, the King received an envoy from the Tatar Khan, Kalin, offering to provide military help against Peter, should the latter refuse to submit. The Khan's envoy is received in secret and departs laden with gifts and with various messages for the Khan, of the content of which we have no knowledge.

King Casimir reaches Novgorod on the Feast of the Nativity of the Blessed Virgin, and has secret discussions with the local prelates and nobles, before continuing on to Grodno and thence to other places famed for their hunting, where he remains for a long time; though not until he has sent a joint Lithuanian–Samogitian force against the Grand-duke of Tver, who had sent troops to recover a castle the King had captured.

A fortnight after the King left Podole, the Tatar Khan suddenly invades Kamieniec and ravages it savagely, carrying off numbers of people and cattle. However, he is pursued by the starosta, who catches up with him in a boggy place and so frees many of his captives. This Tatar raid must have been made with the compliance of those trying to appropriate the territory, for it is known from letters received by certain Polish nobles, that the Tatar envoy, who had been sent to the King in Kamieniec, was seen with the Tatar force, when it returned to Bratislava.

János Hunyadi, a man of very modest origins, promising lavish pay and rich equipment, assembles a mixed force with which he plans to raid the Turks As he is preparing to cross the Danube, the Sultan, Murad, through the rulers of Serbia, sends proposals for peace, offering to liberate the whole of Bulgaria, which he and his predecessors have ruled for many years, and to pay a considerable sum. Hunyadi discusses the proposals with the Dean of Cracow, Nicholas Lasocki, and some of the Hungarian nobles and then asks for considerably more; namely that the Turks vacate Romania and withdraw within their own bounds to Anatolia. This the Turks refuse and talks are broken off. Hunyadi then crosses the Danube and heads for Turkish territory, but making a detour through land subject to the rulers of Serbia and Albania, who have sullied themselves with murder, pillage and arson, and who have horrified Hunyadi and his Hungarians by refusing to take up arms against the Turks, though the war was started to right their wrongs and recover their possessions now in Turkish hands. Confident that his army can defeat an enemy more powerful than the Turks, Hunyadi pushes on for several days, destroying everything in his path, and so reaches Kosovo, where, on the Thursday before the Feast of St. Luke the Evangelist, his advance is barred by the Sultan with 300,000 horse and 60,000 foot. Battle is joined. During the first day, the Thursday, fortunes are equal. On the Friday, the Turks are almost everywhere superior, their huge numbers engulfing the Hungarians. The following night, that between Friday and Saturday, the Hungarians weaken and then take to flight, leaving most of the Poles and Czechs with the waggons: but these fight on from dawn to dusk of that Saturday, protected by their guns and crossbows; at last the Turks close in and they are utterly defeated, the Turks capturing their prisoners, weapons and booty. It is said that 15,000 Catholics were killed and 20,000 taken prisoner, including almost all the remaining Hungarian nobles.

János Hunyadi, seeing that he is losing, leaves the battlefield before noon on the Saturday, having first removed all insignia of rank, so as not to be identified by any pursuing Turks, and dismissed his servants and aides. Although alone, he is captured by three Turks, who divide his clothes, horses and money among themselves. One of them then goes off to hunt other fugitives, leaving the others to guard Hunyadi. These now quarrel over a golden crucifix he wore under his shirt, which they had not previously noticed. As they are squabbling, Hunyadi picks up a sword and kills one of them and wounds the other, and so recovers his possessions. He wanders for several days and eventually reaches Serbian territory and, trustingly, goes to a castle, where he is seized and kept prisoner for three months, being freed only after giving his son as hostage, until all the Hungarian prelates and nobles have sworn to give Serbia's rulers certain castles in Hungary.

The army Hunyadi abandoned is severely punished for the damage it did to Serbia, for as they are marched back to Turkey, almost all have their horses and possessions taken, several lose limbs and many their lives. Most of those who do escape, suffer hunger, before being killed by the peasants, who remember how they had been plundered by them, as they marched through their country against the Turks.

A.D. 1449

The King remains in Lithuania, hunting, until the summer. Then, about Ascension Day he leads an army of Lithuanians, Ruthenians and some Poles, against his enemy, Duke Michael, who has occupied a number of castles, and, with the help of the Tatars, invaded Lithuania, where he has already routed one army sent against him. Learning of the King's advance, Duke Michael decides to withdraw and advises those holding the castles he has occupied, to surrender them. Thus the King gets what he wants and returns to Wilno without loss.

On August 1, Pope Nicholas, considering that Zbigniew, Bishop of Cracow, has been appointed cardinal by both Pope Eugenius IV and Felix V, sends him his red hat by the hand of Jan Długosz, canon of Cracow. When the latter reaches Cracow, he is met at the door of the cathedral by Cardinal Zbigniew and a number of notables, members of the University, nobles, barons and city fathers. He is then conducted to the choir and the chanting is interrupted, while he presents the Cardinal with the cardinal's insignia: red hat, cape and silver staff, as well as the document of his appointment. The choir then resumes singing. At the end of the Mass, the Rector of the University makes a speech thanking Jan Długosz for successfully carrying out a mission that has brought honour to his country and to his church.

Around Assumption Day, János Hunyadi moves his army against Koszów so as to deal with the rebellious Czechs. It pitches camp in a village near Koszów and remains there waiting for Jan Giskra to bring up his army of Poles and Czechs and attack. This he eventually does and in the ensuing battle many of the Hungarians are killed and many taken prisoner, while their camp is plundered. This is the second serious defeat the Hungarians have suffered in a year. Giskra's army goes on to ravage the surrounding country and captures the fort at Moldawa. Meanwhile Hunyadi assembles another army and marches on the Poles, who seek the safety of their forts. Hunyadi retakes

Moldawa, and every Pole or Czech he discovers here has both hands and the tip of his nose cut off and one eye gouged out, making him useless for fighting. Hunyadi then marches against Krempnica, which his intelligence has assured him he can capture, but Jan Giskra has anticipated the move and put in a detachment of his Poles; so, instead, Hunyadi burns all the surrounding villages as well as the delicate wooden structures erected at great expense and over many years and used to purify water. He then goes on to devastate the lands of Spis.

In an effort to stop this dreadful war, Queen Sophia and Cardinal Zbigniew send Jan Długosz to Hungary to negotiate in the name of King Casimir, who is in Lithuania. After six days of talks, Długosz persuades Hunyadi and Giskra to accept a truce. This is as welcome to the Hungarians, as it is to the Holy See, which has already sent a special letter to the Cardinal instructing him to go to Hungary in person and conclude a peace.

Having arranged matters in Lithuania, King Casimir returns to Poland and summons a general assembly to meet in Piotrków. He invites Cardinal Zbigniew to attend, but he at first refuses, but, learning that some of the nobles of Wielkopolska are threatening action against him, he changes his mind and arrives with a huge retinue in the middle of the procedings. At this, Władysław Archbishop of Gniezno, afraid that now he will have to play second fiddle, takes his leave and with him go the Bishop of Poznań, two voivodes and a number of other personages, who are jealous of Zbigniew's promotion. However, the King continues the assembly and a number of matters are settled. The King also receives envoys from Frederick, King of the Romans, and from Duke Conrad both demanding that he does not harass Władysław Duke of Mazovia, who is King Frederick's uncle. King Casimir agrees to defer his demand for the return of the territory involved, so as to allow the matter to be settled judicially. The Archbishop and his supporters, chagrined that the King has settled the matter without them, demand a private discussion. The King agrees to see them without any Cracovians being present, other than the Castellan and Voivode of Cracow, Jan of Tęczyn, and the Voivode of Lwów, Peter Odrowąż. The Cracovian prelates and nobles feel that this humiliates them and blame Cardinal Oleśnicki for their humiliation. They even ask the King not to allow them to be treated in this way, but the King merely reiterates that time and again he has asked the Pope not to promote Bishop Zbigniew until all grounds for disagreement have been removed, but his wishes have been ignored.

Two matters discussed at the assembly are the defence of Ruthenia and Podole against the Tatars, and the widespread increase in brigandage and robbery in Poland resulting from the King's absence. A resolution is adopted that all thieves and robbers are to be interrogated and subjected to judicial enquiry; but this and many other useful decisions are immediately invalidated by the King's refusal to confirm any law that disadvantages the Grand-duchy. People are outraged by this and turn from the King, telling him that they cannot accept his injunctions or fulfill them or give him their customary obedience, until he confirms the rights of the Kingdom in writing and under oath.

A.D. 1450

The King leaves Sandomierz after Christmas and, after spending some days hunting in Niepołomice, goes to Cracow,where he remains until after Lent, attending to public affairs and receiving visits from neighbouring dukes, to entertain whom several days of tourneys and other spectacles are arranged. During Carnival the King summons an assembly to consider renewing rugi throughout Cracow in order to compel the disclosure of the identity of thieves and robbers, especially such notorious ones as those who robbed some Cracovian merchants, including Nicholas Wierzynek, who lost 5000 florins in cash and various merchandize. The assembly is attended by Cardinal Oleśnicki and the more eminent persons of Cracow and they favour the proposal, but a minority, headed by the voivode of Cracow cannot agree, arguing that such a court would invalidate the resolution so recently passed at the assembly in Piotrków and, as a result, enhance the power of the King. This outcome only encourages the thieves and robbers, who become more active.

In response to pleas from the voivode of Moldavia, King Casimir sends an army from Ruthenia and Podole against Bogdan, who has appropriated the territory on the grounds that he is a natural son of the late voivode Alexander, whose legitimate sons have all died, so that Moldavia now belongs to him. The army advances swiftly into Moldavia, expels Bogdan and entrusts the more important castles to Ilichnon, another natural son of the former voivode. No sooner do the King's troops leave Moldavia, than Bogdan emerges from his mountain fastness with a band of robbers and brigands and again enters Moldavia and compels the supporters of Ilichnon to swear allegiance to him, and forcing Ilichnon to flee with his mother to Podole. Before leaving Cracow the King spends several days discussing whether or not to send another army to Moldavia or to let matters rest. The King is advised not to lose this opportunity of obtaining for himself the lands of Moldavia that flow with milk and honey and with them the port of Bialy Zamek, expelling or capturing Bogdan and compensating Ilichnon with part of Ruthenia and incorporating the rest of the territory into the Kingdom of Poland. There are difficulties in such a course and the King decides to leave the territory in Ruthenia and just help Ilichnon to expel Bogdan. This matter settled, the King leaves Cracow heading for Kalisz, Poznań and Gniezno.

The army being sent to Moldavia reaches Lwów on St. John's Day and continues to Kamieniec, where it is joined by forces from Podole and Walachia. It then advances on the castle at Chocim, which is held by Voivode Ilichnon and stays there for several days. Reaching the River Prut, it continues to Lipowiec expecting to find Bogdan there; but he, relying on cunning rather than strength, has withdrawn into the forest, and from there he sends to the King asking for peace. This is generally considered desirable, so, after arranging a truce, a week is spent discussing terms. It is agreed that Bogdan is to govern Walachia until Ilichnon reaches the age of fifteen, paying an annual sum of seventy Turkish gold coins to the King. The relative document having been signed and ratified, they shake hands and embrace, and the same day the King's army is withdrawn from Lipowiec. Bogdan orders his men to assemble in some woods near a place through which the one narrow road from Lipowiec runs and orders them to attack first the waggons and train of the King's men, and then the soldiers themselves. However, the plan is betrayed and the King's men are prepared for an attack, but decide to rush the waggons through the forest so as to be unhampered when attacked. So, at sunrise on Sunday, September 6, Bogdan and several thousand Walachians emerge and the King's men immediately arm themselves.

After battling almost the entire day the King's men can claim victory, though a costly one. Too tired to pursue the fleeing enemy, they are content to shoot out of the trees those who are hiding in them, as many as seventeen out of a single tree.

The Tatar Khan, learning of the absence from their country of the nobles of Ruthenia and Podole, seizes the opportunity to raid these territories with a considerable force. This he splits into units, which then ravage the two countries and carry off numbers of people of both sexes, as well as cattle, sheep and goats. One detachment, while at Grodek on the border with Bełz, all but captures Duke Władysław of Mazovia, who is hunting there.

A.D. 1451

At a general asembly held in Wilno after Christmas, the insistence of a noisy few succeeds in having the old question of detaching Podole and Łuck from the body of Poland, brought up yet again. Whatever method is suggested proves to be either illegal or too difficult to accomplish, and the majority decides that it wants to let the matter rest, but, in order to avoid it looking as if the idea has been abandoned, the Poles are invited to attend an assembly to be held at Brześć on St.

Stanisław's Day. The Poles refuse the invitation, because the date is inconvenient and the venue more remote than is customary. After this, the King goes to the Ruthenian districts of Vitebsk, Smolensk and Polotsk, which belong to Lithuania, and spends most of the winter inspecting them.

The Whitsun assembly in Piotrków is attended by all the more eminent with the exception of Cardinal Zbigniew and the Voivode of Cracow, who is ill. The barons and gentry of Wielkopolska lodge a complaint that the Cardinal has deprived the Metropolitan of Gniezno of his primacy. Castellan Jan Cisów speaks up for the Cardinal, telling the assembly that it should be proud of its cardinal and reminding it that previous kings had unsuccessfully sought to persuade the Pope to grant this honour to one of their bishops, and that Zbigniew Oleśnicki has been appointed by three Popes, a thing unprecedented, and solely on merit. He reminds Archbishop Vincent that he is not the only one inferior to a cardinal, for so are the primates of Munich, Cologne, Leon and all other primates in the Catholic Church. Finally, it is agreed to treat Zbigniew Bishop of Cracow as a cardinal and to honour him as such. If the Archbishop should really feel that the promotion of Bishop Zbigniew has in any way diminished him, though they cannot see how that can be, he is to remain in his lodgings when the Cardinal is present and give his opinion from there. There is, however, no question but that he is inferior to the Cardinal. It is also agreed that, in future, no Polish bishop or archbishop shall endeavour to obtain the dignity of a red hat or of papal legate without first consulting the king and his council. The assembly also decides that throughout the kingdom small coins are to be accepted without demur and foreign ones refused. Any who do not comply are to be severely punished. The regulations governing the salt works are renewed.

The King arrives in Cracow on St. John the Baptist's Day and has discussions with his council. Many decisions are taken, but few are implemented. One matter discussed is the siege of the fort at Welczyn, from which a notorious Silesian brigand, who bought it, has been carrying on his nefarious activities. The King is urged to declare war on Bolesław Duke of Cieszyn who has been ravaging Siewierz territory, and also to lay siege to the castle at Berwald, from which the holder and his wife have been living by brigandage, in defiance of the law and the orders of their King.

But the King, having other things on his mind, remains unmoved by the wrongs of his subjects. Pressure, too, is put on him to confirm the rights, privileges and freedoms granted to his subjects by his predecessors; but the King insists on such matters being deferred until after a Lithuanian assembly and all outstanding boundary questions have been settled.

The Kingdom's merchants are now told not to go to Wrocław for the annual markets there, at which they have been burdened with ever-increasing dues, and to use the money thus saved to promote three new annual markets: one in Poznań on St. John the Baptists's Day, one in Wieluń on St. Elizabeth's Day and the third in Kalisz, half way through Lent. The merchants of Cracow dislike the proposal and demand its abrogation, but they are told that they must give it a trial, so that it can be seen how much good or harm it will do. Further orders are issued expelling merchants from Nuremberg from Cracow and other cities, because they were depriving the Poles of their profit and are exporting more than they imported.

The King attends an assembly at Korczyń, at which it is agreed that, in the event of general mobilization, landholders will pay six grosses for each of their fields for the defence of their country, but these sums will be raised only in extreme necessity. Cardinal Zbigniew, who attends the assembly, tells the King that the reason why all his undertakings are ending so disastrously, is that God is punishing him for exiling his brother ruler, Michael, embezzling the latter's inheritance and then refusing to forgive him, when he humbled himself and sought to appease the King by renouncing his inheritance. He begs the King to return to his brother ruler what was his by right and to recall him from where he is living among Tatars and other barbarians, who have repeatedly raided the King's lands. The King replies that he never thought to hear such ugly words from his Bishop and that no argument can persuade him to do what the Cardinal is asking. The Cardinal then calls upon God Almighty to witness that he has encouraged the King to save his soul, and prays that he should not be blamed for whatever innocent blood may be shed by the King's subjects in the misfortunes that will result from the King's obduracy.

The King then goes to Sandomierz where he spends a fortnight. The weather is such as none has ever experienced: for fifteen days and nights rain pours down, at first incessantly and then intermittently; thus, not only is the harvest interrupted, but the grain is swept from any fields in low ground near a river. It is the same with the hay.

While in Sambor, the King has secret discussions with his more eminent councillors. Świdrygiello being ill and near to death, the King is urged to set aside his other worries and order the occupation of Łuck castle, to which the Kingdom has the most obvious right and which Grand-duke Sigismund expressly disclaimed—there are documents to prove this!—and agreed that its lands were not to be detached from the Kingdom of Poland, for has he not been elected to protect the boundaries of the kingdom, as well as to extend them? Should he fail to do this, let him be certain that they will combine to see that Poland is not deprived of so valuable a part. Similarly, should Łuck be occupied by the Lithuanians as a result of the King's remissness or his tacit consent, his councillors could never attend the assembly at Parczów. Let the King consider how unbefitting it would be, were he and his nobles to be at loggerheads and they fail to render him the usual obedience. The King replies that he will answer all this later, and that in the meantime they are not to do anything further about Łuck castle. He has been brought up, he tells them, to favour Poland rather than the Grand-duchy, but he has to be careful lest Lithuania refuse him obedience.

This summer, the famous John of Capistrano, a man of noble family and a member of the Franciscans, who has spent many years in Italy, arrives in Moravia and enters the monastery of his Order in Olomouc. There he remains for several months. As not even the largest church can hold all who wish to hear him, he sets up his pulpit in the middle of the square and from there, using two interpreters, a Czech and a German, he preaches all day. He tells the people that it is not essential for their salvation to receive the Eucharist in both kinds. His message is confirmed by the miracles he performs: his mere use of the words "In the name of Our Lord Jesus Christ" being enough to restore the dead to life, their sight to the blind, their speech to the dumb, the ability to walk to the halt and to the paralyzed the use of their limbs. Throughout Moravia and Bohemia, thousands of those imbued with heresy, into which many have been born and in it brought up, are renouncing their heresy and turning to the Catholic faith. Those of the gentry who belong to the heretical sect are urging its chief spokesman, Jan Rokiczan, to challenge Capistrano to a public debate, defeat him and so stop him preaching, or, should he himself be defeated, they will themselves be converted. Full of misgivings, Rokiczan issues the challenge, which Capistrano eagerly accepts, and, his safety guaranteed by the Catholics, goes to Bohemia, where he is welcomed enthusiastically. Cardinal Zbigniew writes to him there, telling him that should the Czechs reject him, he must come to Poland, an invitation that is repeated by the King.

When he reaches Parczów for the assembly, the King finds all the Polish delegates, but none of the Lithuanians, for these have refused to come unless their safety is guaranteed. The Poles all agree that such a request must be refused, lest it is made to appear that the union no longer existed. The King goes as far as Łomza to meet the Lithuanians and returns with them to Parczów. Here the Bishop of Wilno insists that the old treaties and agreements are both burdensome and insulting to his people, since they employ such phrases as "subject to the yoke of servitude", "make our property", "unite the territories of Lithuania and Ruthenia in the Kingdom of Poland", and demands that the documents in question be invalidated and new ones drawn up, asserting that the Lithuanians originally agreed to the old because ordered to do so by the Grand-duke, but without knowing what was in them. He further demands that Podole, Łuck, the castles at Olesko, Wietly and Ratno and the country surrounding them be handed back, claiming that Grand-duke Witold used to have them. Cardinal Oleśnicki urges the King not to give way, telling him that it would be ridiculous to annul pacts made by two such sensible rulers and reaffirmed and renewed by them and their successors, as well as being tacitly accepted by the Lithuanian dukes and nobles, when they swear their oaths of allegiance. He points out that there is no doubt but that Łuck and the other territories demanded have always belonged to Poland, having been settled by Poles after the Tatars were removed from Podole in days when the name Lithuania was unknown. The Cardinal offers to produce documents that will prove him right, but the Lithuanians will not look at them and stubbornly continue with their demands. The Cardinal then suggests putting the dispute to arbitration by kings or princes of the Catholic faith, but this too the Lithuanians refuse. Further discussion is then deferred until the next assembly in a year's time. After this, instead of going to Walachia, the King goes to Lithuania, sending Jan of Koniecpol the Chancellor, Przedbor of Koniecpol castellan of Sandomierz and Peter Szamotuł castellan of Poznań to Walachia in his stead.

The King spends the winter and spring hunting in Lithuania. St. Martin's Day finds him in Kaunas, to which comes an envoy from Duke Philip of Burgundy asking for help for himself and the King of Aragon in their proposed attempt to recover the Holy Land. The King tells him that, as he is engaged in more or less continual war with the Tatars, he cannot undertake other wars without exposing the Catholic countries to Tatar raids. The envoys, laden with gifts, then go to Prussia and the Order with the same request, only to meet with another refusal.

This year, the plague has been especially severe in Wielkopolska, only a few villages in the diocese of Cracow being free of it.

Now, thanks to the efforts of Cardinal Zbigniew, the Pope grants a Jubilee year for all Poland and Lithuania. This is to last from October to the end of the following September, during which period anyone wishing to obtain remission of his sins must lodge with his cathedral half of what it would cost him to go to Rome, stay there a fortnight and return home; also he must visit the church in question on three consecutive or separate days. Half the money thus obtained is to go to the King for the defence of Catholics against the Tatars, a quarter is to go to help finance Queen Sophia's maintenance of a number of poor girls, while the final quarter is to go to the Pope for the upkeep of the churches in Rome. Thanks to the Cardinal, what the individual has to pay is reduced from a half to a quarter of the cost of a pilgrimage to Rome, and the period extended to January 1. After this, the money starts flowing in, especially into Cracow cathedral, whose great chests end up full of golden grosses, half grosses, broad grosses and small coin.

János Hunyadi and Jan Giskra are again at loggerheads. Hunyadi is suspected of having tried to kill Giskra while he was attending the wedding of the latter's widowed sister. After this, Giskra occupies the monastery at Luzeniec and pronounces Hunyadi his enemy. Hunyadi then invests Luzeniec town which is protected neither by Nature nor by artificial defences; but the fort there is defended by 500 brave and resolute men, who repulse all assaults. Hunyadi surrounds the fort with a double ditch, fenced and reinforced with baskets of earth, and expects it to surrender. The defenders, many of whom are Poles and Czechs, though short of water and provisions, are afraid that if they surrender they will lose eye, nose, face or hands, and so they fight on. In the meantime, Giskra has assembled a scratch force of some 4000 foot and horse obtained from outside, and advances against Hunyadi's army, reputed to number some 17,000. Hunyadi is ready to do battle and issues from behind his ramparts, leaving only a handful to guard the camp and the waggons, and a small force to see that the besieged do not make a sortie. But this is just what the desperate besieged do and attack their besiegers. Hunyadi sends the latter reinforcements, but when the besiegers see them, they think they are fleeing, not coming to their assistance, and so themselves take to their heels; whereupon the rest of Hunyadi's troops follow their example. Giskra's men become exhausted with killing and taking prisoners, one of whom is the Bishop of Eger. Hunyadi's camp is given to the troops to loot. Hunyadi himself escapes.

A.D. 1452

On February 10, Świdrygiello dies in Łuck castle. Forgetting how the Lithuanians had deprived him of Łuck and the Poles restored it to him, forgetting his sworn oaths and written undertakings to hold Łuck for the Poles, and that on his death it should revert to the Kingdom of Poland, for which undertakings he had received an annual subsidy of 2000 marks; his mind on his death bed being even more sick than his body, Świdrygiello orders Łuck to be surrendered to the Lithuanians. In anticipation of his death, Duke Radziwił and another have been sent to take over the castle, and Świdrygiello makes the starosta, nobles and boyars swear to hand Łuck over to them on his death, and this they do, the Poles being in no position to prevent them. Shortly before this, Duke Michael who had sought refuge in Moscow, dies there after being poisoned with a poison so powerful that it split his skull as with a sharp sword.

The prospect of loosing so fertile and important a part of the country as Łuck arouses great indignation in Poland. After holding various meetings, the protesters take up arms, lay siege to Łuck castle and capture it. A message then comes from the King, telling them not to take any action against Łuck and promising that the King will quickly return to Poland and seek ways of resolving the dispute, for otherwise, he fears hostile raids into the kingdom. The messenger, when asked why the King did not restrain the Lithuanians from annexing Łuck, replies that the King had told him that, whenever he tried to do this, the Lithuanians said that they would refuse to obey him. It is decided to send three eminent Poles to Lithuania to ask the King whether he agreed to the Łuck castle being detached from the body of Poland in such an ugly and shameful manner, seeing that the Kingdom had by far the better title to it, and to request that he confirm the rights of the Kingdom in writing and by sworn oath. The three set out, but are recalled when only half way, a letter having been received from the Castellan of Cracow telling them that on the King's orders Łuck castle had been handed over to the Lithuanians. It is then decided to call an assembly on St. Urban's Day, which will seek ways of extracting the Kingdom from its many difficulties. In the mean time, troops are called-up in Sandomierz, Lublin and Ruthenia and sent towards Łuck. At the same time, a start is made rebuilding the castle at Vladimir, a third of which had been destroyed by the Lithuanians to prevent it being occupied by the Poles. This done, a garrison is to be installed and an attempt made to recapture Łuck which has no proper defences and no store of provisions. Not every one likes this idea, especially not those who are hoping for high office from the King, and in the end the plan is abandoned and nothing decided.

King Casimir, seeing how the Poles are turning against him, conceives an even greater dislike of Cardinal Zbigniew and the Voivodes of Cracow and Sandomierz. He arrives in Cracow at Corpus Christi, which is celebrated with special solemnity and ceremonial because of his presence. He attends a council at which the Cardinal and two Voivodes strenuously reject accusations made against them and the things that are said about them. The whole matter is then referred to the next general assembly, which is to be held in Piotrków, though the barons of Wielkopolska object to that venue and want Sieradz instead. The Cardinal and the Voivodes go to the King in council and, the Cardinal speaking first, accuses him of neglecting the weal of the Kingdom, of failing to confirm the rights of the Kingdom, although repeatedly urged to do so; and of having in many ways violated them and oppressed churches and monasteries by the imposition of quartering and stabling, to which they are not accustomed, making the whole Kingdom liable to quartering and conveyance; also of appointing a foreigner to a Polish see, and of severing Łuck and Podole from the Kingdom; of having none but Lithuanians in his household, of never doing anything to defend Poland, and that all the revenue from the Kingdom goes to the benefit and enrichment of Lithuanians; that he seldom listens to the complaints of widows, orphans and the oppressed. The Cardinal again calls upon the King to improve his ways and not call down God's vengeance upon himself and his subjects; for, although the Cardinal has often rebuked him in fatherly fashion, both in private and in public, he has never mended his ways nor taken the advice of his Council. In future, he tells him, he will take no part in the King's councils, lest he be suspected of complicity in the King's evil deeds; though he will continue to defend his churches, monasteries, widows and orphans unto bloodshed or death. The Cardinal is supported by almost every other speaker. There follow days of endless discussion and prophesies of the end of the Polish state. Eventually, all decisions are deferred until the next assembly, now to be held in Sieradz.

While the King is in Cracow the Tatars raid Podole and create havoc there, even carrying off into servitude the governor of the fort at Row, with his wife and children.

The King leaves Cracow and goes to Nieszawa, where, on the Friday before St. Jacob's Day, he entertains the Prussian Master and others to a splendid banquet, at which each guest is presented with a sable cloak and other gifts. The next day, against the advice of his councillors, the King goes to Toruń, where he is entertained by the Master and presented with magnificent gifts. The pact of perpetual peace is confirmed and renewed and disputes settled. The King continues to Gniezno, where a messenger brings him the news that Duke Bolesław of Opole has abused the King's trust, broken off relations and is ravaging Siewierz territory, where he has seized treasure and used it to hire mercenaries from Bohemia and Moravia, thus, he hopes, making himself the stronger. The King despatches all his household troops to Wieluń, even though plague is rampant there, and issues a general call to arms. He himself goes to Sieradz to attend the assembly, for the prelates and nobles have refused to take part in the fighting unless he first confirms the Kingdom's rights and liberties. All are present in Sieradz, except Cardinal Zbigniew and those who are ill. The assembly is attended by two Lithuanian delegates, who demand that Lithuania retain its present boundaries., which include Podole and Łuck. They insist that they do wish to be in union with Poland, but as equals, not as subjects; at the same time they do not want to be incorporated into Poland nor made subject to it; indeed, they would prefer death to incorporation or subjection. Should their demands be refused, they intend to seek other partners. They are told that the Poles have always treated the Lithuanians as brothers and allies, not as subjects, and that incorporation is no shame, but an honour; also that Podole and Łuck have belonged, and still belong to Poland, the Grand-duke having held them only for his life-time and always paying tribute for them. The discussions get nowhere. The King insists that he cannot confirm Poland's rights, since to do so would be contrary to other oaths made to the Lithuanians, and he asks for a further year in which to settle matters. This being refused, he summons eight of his Polish councillors and, swearing them to secrecy, he tells them that for him to do what they want, would endanger his life and, perhaps, lose them Lithuania. Thus he needs another year in which to gain possession of the stronger Lithuanian castles, Łuck in particular, and to transfer the Duchy's treasure to Poland. It takes the eight two days to reach a decision, which is that they will agree to the extra year provided the King will provide a written undertaking to confirm the Poles' rights within the year, which document is to be placed in a casket sealed with the seals of the eight and entrusted to the Archbishop of Gniezno. This done, those in Wielkopolska who are eligible to serve march into Silesia, destroying many of their own villages as they go. Plague forces the King's troops to leave Wieluń, but not before it has claimed many of them as its victims. Plague is also rampant in Silesia and much of Cracow, because of which the troops, afraid of the entire army becoming infected, think more of a truce than of continuing to fight. A letter from Duke Bolesław of Opole requesting justice and peace, provides an opportunity, and a truce for one year is agreed, one condition being that the two sides meet on the Feast of the Circumcision to settle claims for compensation.

On September 3, the King leaves Sieradz for Lithuania, not knowing that the plague is there everywhere rampant and so severe that people fall suddenly while they are walking, eating, even sleeping: the King cannot enter Wilno or Troki, so he goes hunting in the forests round Grodno.

The Tatar Khan, Sadachmela, takes advantage of the absence of the nobles of Ruthenia to devastate their country as far as Lwów. When the peasants come out of hiding to harvest their crops, he rounds them up like cattle, then he feigns a withdrawal and returns suddenly to capture any who had earlier escaped him. The Lithuanians send the Tatars various expressions of gratitude for their raids, hoping to encourage them to keep up this form of pressure on Poland; but before their envoys reach Sadachmela's camp, another Khan, Eczigeri, has attacked and defeated Sadachmela, who, with his wife, seeks refuge in Lithuania. Later, he does something to arouse King Casimir's suspicions and is put in prison together with his servants and family. He is eventually released and sent to Kaunas, where he dies miserably much later.

Frederick, King of the Romans, sets out for Rome where he is to be crowned Emperor. Avoiding Milan, where his predecessors used to receive their second crown, he reaches Siena, where he is joined by his betrothed, the pretty daughter of the King of Aragon, who has only just arrived from Pisa, her ship having been delayed by a storm. Together, and accompanied by László, King of Hungary, they reach Rome on March 8 to be greeted by all the cardinals and envoys of kings, princes as well as the other dignitaries of Rome. They are conducted to a small house by the gate in the wall of St. Peter's and there they rest. On the following day, the Emperor enters Rome preceded by King László, and goes to the Pope who awaits them both with his cardinals and prelates on the first flight of steps of St. Peter's. The Pope kisses the Emperor's feet, hands and lips, but only the feet and hands of the Empress, on whose head and shoulders he also lays his hand. Then, having placed their offerings on the altar of St. Peter, they are taken to their quarters in rooms specially prepared for them in the apostolic palace.

On the Wednesday before Laetare Sunday, during a sung Mass celebrated by the Pope, the Emperor, clad in the dalmatic of a deacon, is, in the presence of his betrothed, crowned by the Pope with a second crown, the one with which he should have been crowned in Milan. Voices of protest are raised, claiming that the Milanese are being wronged, but the Pope has the protesters removed, saying that one who had transferred the empire from Greece to Germany, may also transfer the coronation from Milan to Rome. This same day, the Pope personally marries Frederick and his betrothed, who exchange kisses and rings. They then hear mass. The stole joining them is then untied and they are conducted back to their apartments. The Sunday sees the coronation of King Frederick as emperor and his wife as empress. It is performed in this manner: in the chapel of the basilica, Frederick is dressed as a deacon and then two cardinals conduct him to the altar. Here he drops to his knees and one of the cardinals and the Cardinal bishop of Albano recite prayers, keeping one foot on the Emperor's nape. He is then raised and as he stands with bent knees beside the altar, his clothes folded back, he is anointed and conducted to his apartments, where he is again dressed as a deacon, The Empress is then conducted to the altar by King László and Duke Albert; here she bares only her right arm and a little chrism is poured on it and she is conducted back to her room. The Mass is still being celebrated by the Pope, on whose right the Emperor now stands, as his server. The moment comes for the solemn reading of the gospel, the Pope stands up and walks to the main altar. The Empress is led forward. The Pope recites certain prayers, then places an imperial crown on the Emperor's head and another on the Empress's head. The Emperor is given the sceptre and orb. The Pope girds him with the sword; whereupon the Emperor lays down the orb and thrice draws the sword from its scabbard and brandishes it in time with the prayers the Pope is reciting. The gospel is sung, while the Emperor remains standing wearing his crown, holding the sceptre in his left hand and the sword in his right. The gospel sung, the Emperor and Empress take the sacrament. The Mass concluded, the Empress retires to her house. The Emperor puts a cope specially consecrated by the Pope over his dalmatic. The Pope then mounts his horse and rides off, the Emperor walking on his right, but he has taken only three or four strides before the Pope invites him to mount as well, and so he rides on the Pope's left and somewhat behind him. As they approach the tomb of Remus, the Pope gives the Emperor a rose he has been holding and dismisses him. The Emperor goes to St. John Lateran, where he dines and at five o'clock returns to St. Peter's.

On the way back from Rome, at the instigation of his tutor, King László makes several attempts to escape, but each time is captured and then kept under guard; but when the Emperor reaches Florence, he is met by a delegation of Hungarians, Czechs and Austrians demanding that their lord and king, László, be returned to them or else the Emperor can expect war. The Emperor's reply is silence, so the delegation continues to Rome, where the delegates complain to the Pope, that the Emperor is holding their King, despite repeated requests for his release to them. Finding no comfort in Rome, they return home and pin their hopes on force. The Austrians lay siege to Neustadt, where the Emperor is. They bring up a siege gun so powerful that after three salvoes the entire surround of the double gate is demolished and then battle is joined. Eventually, the Emperor's troops are overcome by sheer numbers and compelled to withdraw into the town, which is all but captured with the Emperor inside. Frightened by this defeat, the Emperor agrees to allow the return of László.

While Casimir is in Lithuania, the envoys he sent to ask for the hand of Elizabeth, daughter of the late Albert, King of the Romans, return with the news that they have the full agreement to the marriage of the girl's brother, King László, and of the Regent of Hungary, János Hunyadi, and other high officials. With them are envoys from Hungary come to hear from the King himself that he is assuming the bonds of matrimony of his own free will and has not been compelled to take this step by his advisors; they are also there to assess his habits, character and physical appearance. This done and with the King's assurance that he is anxious to agree to everything they want, they return to Austria, an envoy being sent at the same time to inform László and the Emperor of Casimir's decision, and to agree a place and date for the wedding.

In the autumn, the dukes of Ciezsyn and Oswięcim, having taken offence at being required to pay 2000 florins towards the cost of the war against Stodek of Berwald, have raided Cracow, despite the fact that one has a treaty of perpetual peace with it and the other a truce. The two dukes have hired 9000 mercenaries, who are busy plundering the province, which is all but empty, as the gentry have all fled the plague, thus the raiders can do almost whatever they please. Although informed of what is happening, King Casimir does nothing. But the Chamberlain of Cracow captures the castle at Malec and another at Będzin and installs garrisons of a hundred horse and as many foot, with which he forces the two dukes to pay him tribute. The dukes have already collected a considerable booty, including thirteen waggons loaded with merchandize, yet they realize that the Kingdom is bound to exact revenge and that what they will have to pay is increasing from day to day; thus, wounded by their own sword, they sue for peace. To obtain this, they have to sign a document to the effect that they started an unjustified war with the Kingdom, that they will return all the prisoners they have taken and pay the 2000 florins already due, as well as 800 florins as damages. This done, the fort at Malec is liberated and its people given an exemption from paying tribute.

A.D. 1453

About the time of the Feast of the Circumcision, a modest force of Tatars makes a foray into Łuck territory and roams almost everywhere unopposed, especially around Olesko, and then returns home with a vast booty of cattle and, it is said, some 9000 men and women captives.

The assembly being held in Lublin decides to send a force of mercenaries to lay siege to Oświęcim and avenge the misdeeds of the Dukes of Oświęcim and Cieszyn. They would have captured Oświęcim had not its duke already gone to Cracow, now free of the plague, and humbly begged for forgiveness. A truce is arranged according to whose terms the castle at Oświęcim is to be governed for the King by the Castellan of Cracow, who is to hold it until the Duke of Oświęcim has paid an amount equivalent to what has been spent on mercenaries and to compensate for damages already incurred; either that, or he is to hand over his lands and pay homage to the King, who is to choose the course to be followed.

Duke Michael of Lithuania arrives to conclude the arrangement and further hostilities against Oświęcim are stopped; indeed, further action has already been made impossible by snow and cold, as well as by the fact that the treasury is empty, for the whole of the royal revenue is being sent to Lithuania and spent on the King's personal needs.

Early in April, the Tatars raid Podole and carry off captives and cattle. A certain Jan Laszcz and two others raise a small force and set off in pursuit. They use surprise to make up for their lack of numbers and attack the Tatar camp by night. This they do successfully and so recover the loot.

The King arrives in Parczów for the assembly on June 3. None of the Lithuanians are there, for they have stopped in Brześć, having been told that the Poles are preparing to waylay and kill them. The Poles, afraid of wasting their time and incurring the expense of attending for nothing, blame the King, for they feel that he must have known what the Lithuanians were up to. However, a delegation of five Lithuanians does arrive. They demand that Podole, Ratno, Olesko and Wietlo be returned to Lithuania, which is once again to have the boundaries it had under the Grand-duke Witold; that the old treaties are to be annulled and new ones drawn up. Cardinal Zbigniew points out that there is no call to annul documents drawn up with such care, for, if this were once allowed and new documents substituted, the procedure could be repeated quite legitimately in a generation or

Clients of the crossbow-maker in his workshop. From Baltharius Behem: Codex Picturatus. *—Jagiellonian University Library.*

two. The Poles, having no wish for unilateral action, suggest that, if the Lithuanians consider that they have been deceived over the documents and boundaries, they should refer the matter to the Pope or some Catholic King and the Poles will accept his decision. The Lithuanians ask if the Poles will accept the Tatar khan as arbitrator, but, when told that this would be an insult to Christendom, they are unable to suggest anyone else. Another assembly is called for the Feast of St. John the Baptist and, at this, the Mazovian delegates demand the return of Goniadz and Tykozin which the Lithuanians have occupied. The King, without taking advice, gives a harsh, even threatening reply that prompts Cardinl Zbigniew to tell him that the Crown should never threaten, for among bees the queen has no sting. The Mazovian dukes are of royal blood and the King's nearest relatives; they possess a large army and, he tells him, the King should be proud to have such vassals; yet, instead of giving them the justice for which they ask, he threatens war. It is impermissible for Polish dukes to be so humbled or harassed.

To this same assembly come representatives of the Order in Prussia and the nobles, cities and people of Prussia, the two being in dispute about certain interpretations of the pact, which the Master now wishes to annul, because of doubts as to its validity. The Master asks that the others be given no help, while the Prussian subjects ask the King to recognize their rights and support their just claims. The King insists that he must remain neutral. The assembly convened in Piotrków on the Feast of St. John the Baptist is attended by Queen Sophia, the prelates and numbers of the nobility. The casket containing the King's written undertaking to confirm the Poles' rights is produced and the document read out, after which the King is asked to fulfill his undertaking. He is granted twenty-four hours in which to consider his reply. This, when it comes, is that, much as he would like to fulfill his undertaking, he can do so only as King of Poland, not as Grand-duke of Lithuania, and thus cannot use the latter title in a document confirming Poland's rights, lest it appear that he is breaking his vow to the Lithuanians. If the Poles do not like "Grand-duke of Lithuania" being deleted from their King's title, he suggests substituting "Supreme Duke of Lithuania", the title used by his father and brother. Although manifestly reasonable, the Poles realize that this is a cunning and dangerous suggestion, since it questions the validity of an accepted document and annuls rather than confirms their rights. For the next few days, the Queen and the Cardinal both put pressure on the King, though for different reasons, yet nothing will make him change his mind and the situation becomes desperate. Some say that they should challenge the King's authority and refuse him obedience; others that they should elect another king. This latter course is considered previous and distasteful, and finally they decide that, if the King refuses to confirm their rights, they will do this themselves: all the prelates, nobles and city fathers will swear an oath and give a written undertaking never to abandon the rights and privileges of the Church and laity, and to defend and maintain the boundaries of the Kingdom, if necessary with their blood. Any who violates these rights or liberties is to be punished. The King is to be given four advisers without whose assent he shall take no action in matters of moment; and, if he should, such action is to be invalid. All the Lithuanian advisors are to be sent back to Lithuania. The old customs are to be observed in all stages of the royal progress, as, too, is conveyance, once the new burdens and compulsory labour have been abolished. All this is read out to the King, who is also asked to grant the Grandy-duchy in fee to someone both loyal and sympathetic, so that he can devote himself to ruling Poland, since, as things now are, both countries are endangered. The King is distraught, though he seems to consider the requests justified. Then, hoping to be able to act in secret, he summons the Cardinal and eleven others to whom he hands a signed document to this effect: "I, Casimir, King of Poland, Grand-duke of Lithuania and Heritor of Ruthenia, hereby undertake, promise and swear on the Holy Bible that I shall keep, maintain and observe" all the rights and privileges in question; he also promises that he will defend the frontiers of the Kingdom and, if possible, recover lost territories. The Poles consider this sufficient and just hope that in time, as he realizes how uncertain is the loyalty of the Lithuanians, the King's spirit will grow stronger.

The Dukes of Opole and Cieszyn are granted a truce to last for two years. The assembly lasts nine days in all, involving the participants in great expense, for their presence there has quadrupled the price of everything in Piotrków.

Early in July, while he is in Cracow, the King receives a letter from the Voivode of Moldavia with the grievous news that Constantinople has fallen to the Turks.

The time is approaching when the kings of Poland and Hungary are to meet. Casimir sends ahead of him a group of eminent Poles and Lithuanians who, with their retinues, all mounted, number some 1200, and they reach Wrocław on St. Laurence' Day. The following day, a Saturday, they start discussing arrangements for the wedding of King Casimir and the Princess Elizabeth, daughter of the late King of Hungary. The talks last ten days, at the end of which, with all the necessary documents signed, a proclamation is issued from the town hall to the effect that the King is to marry the Princess on the Sunday after Purification, that she is to be crowned, and that the King of Hungary is to give her a dowry of 100,000 florins, not repayable even if she dies early and without offspring. Similarly, King Casimir is to transfer to her, as her dowry, three towns in Sandomierz and Łęczyca. This is the first time that details of dowries have been officially published.

The King has been spending the autumn and winter hunting in Lithuania. In his absence there, the Duke of Oświęcim lays siege to Oświęcim castle, now governed for the King by the Chamberlain of Lublin, and occupies the Dominican monastery there and turns it into a fortress. Unable to capture the castle, the Duke has the old ruined castle at Wolek rebuilt and installs a garrison, which proceeds to raid the surrounding country and even into Poland. The Poles retaliate by laying siege to Wolek castle, which could have been taken in a matter of days, had not the Polish commander been unwilling to risk the lives of his young soldiers by storming a fortress so well defended by Nature. Talks are held and peace arranged, the conditions being that the Duke is to be paid 20,000 broad grosses for the whole of Oświęcim, his inheritance, to which he will renounce all right and which will then revert to the Kingdom of Poland, of which it was once part. The documents of sale and purchase have been deposited in the royal treasury in Cracow.

On the Feast of St. Simon and St. Jude, Lászlo, King of Hungary and Duke of Austria, is crowned King of Bohemia by the Archbishop of Esztergom. He confirms the Czechs' rights and customs, especially the right of the individual to choose how to take Holy Communion, whether in one or two kinds, a privilege that offends many good Catholics. The Czechs all contribute one third of their income to help meet the cost of the coronation, of maintaining the Court and of redeeming certain objects belonging to the crown. The new King remains in Prague for some time, yet he neither enters a church of the heretics, though strongly urged to do so, nor takes part in any of their ceremonies, so that his presence is unwelcome to the heretics, who find themselves condemned and despised by all who have influence with the King, with the result that a great number of them go over to the True Faith.

Hostilities have broken out between the Master of the Teutonic Knights, Ludwig, his captains and Order, and the knights, nobles and townspeople of Prussia, as fierce as they are unexpected, and conducted with such ferocity that the Knights are driven out of their castles, towns and fortresses, bereft of their goods, and find themselves shut up in one castle, Malbork.

A.D. 1454

After many days of successful hunting, most of the quarry being sent back to Poland, the King returns to Wilno and spends Christmas there, before returning to Sandomierz, where he is to meet certain Prussian prelates and nobles to discuss their proposal that fifty-six of the more important towns in Prussia should become subject to him.

The King is making every effort to ensure that his coming marriage shall be celebrated with regal magnificence. He sends a cavalcade of eminent persons and noble youths from his Court, some 2000 in all, to meet his bride in Cieszyn and escort her to Cracow. The Princess arrives in Cieszyn one hour ahead of them. Here, the two parties halt for two days. The Princess is then delivered to the Poles and the Austrians return home. The Poles could have got to Cracow with the Princess by the Thursday, but the King orders them to halt for three days in Skawina, to the horror of those accompanying the Princess, who wonder whether the King is having second thoughts and, perhaps, is going to refuse to marry the girl. The reason for the halt, however, is that preparations for receiving the princess have been delayed by a severe frost and a return of winter, which has covered the roads with deep snow, killed numbers of horses and domestic animals and destroyed many villages in Podole. Then, on the Saturday, the King and his Mother with a retinue of important people ride out to greet the bride. The King looks splendid: his saddle, bridle, stirrups and the horse's harness are all covered with velvet interwoven with gold thread and together valued at 40,000 florins. Some of the others have followed his example and arrayed themselves, their horses and servants in magnificent garments of gold and purple. However, the weather is atrocious: rain pours down from morning until evening ruining most of this precious cloth. A procession of clerics and eminent laymen also goes out to greet the bride, but in the downpour no one can keep his place and they all beat a hasty retreat. Queen Sophia invites the Princess into her own carriage and so, to the sound of trumpets, she is conducted to the castle, where she is welcomed by Bishop Zbigniew of Cracow and his prelates. After offering a prayer and making gifts to the cathedral, the Princess is conducted to the royal palace.

The clergy now start quarrelling among themselves as to who is to conduct the marriage service: most of the Chapter accept that Cardinal Zbigniew has the greater right, but no agreement is reached, and, in the end it is decided that, for the future, the matter should be referred to the Pope, and that on this occasion the papal legate, John Capistrano of the Order of the Minor Friars, should perform the ceremony. When he is asked to do this, he insists that the Cardinal alone is entitled to perform the ceremony, and that he, a legate, can only do this, if he has the Cardinal's permission. Meanwhile, the Cardinal, fully robed, has started saying Mass at the altar. The legate drops to his knees and humbly requests, and is granted permission to perform the ceremony; but then it transpires that he can speak neither Polish nor German and so cannot officiate, so, after all, it is the Cardinal, who speaks both languages, who has to do it. This part of the ceremony performed, Mass is sung in great haste for evening is approaching and the Queen has yet to be anointed and crowned.

The following week is devoted to dancing and entertainment; and all this time the guests, Hungarians, Czechs and Austrians, are supplied with whatever they need; and, on the following Monday the bridesmaids attending the Princess, now Queen, set out, laden with gifts, to return to their own countries.

A delegation of Prussian subjects arrives in Cracow and, after giving the King a long recital of the wrongs and injuries the Prussians have suffered at the hands of the Order, and told him how they, the Prussians, have captured twenty-five of the Knights' fortresses, they ask him to accept them as his loyal subjects and to allow their lands to return to the Kingdom of Poland, from which they were detached in the past. With their help, they insist, the King can recover the rest of Poland's former territories, giving him an empire that would stretch from the Baltic to the Black Sea.

Opinions are divided: Cardinal Zbigniew earnestly advises against accepting the Prussians' offer, as to do so would be a breach of the King's pact with the Knights and of oaths sworn; however, the Castellan of Cracow and others think this too good an opportunity to be missed. Discussions continue for a whole fortnight, and even younger men are consulted. Some want to defer a decision until the Lithuanians have been consulted, but, when they learn of this, the Prussians, who are already on their way home, return and beg that there be no delay; otherwise they may have to seek another prince to accept their allegiance. Indeed, it almost looked as if they were about to set out for Bohemia, for it had already been hinted that King László might be prepared to accept them. This very suggestion induces immediate acceptance of the Prussians' offer. Further news comes, showing that Fortune is still favouring the Prussians, for all the towns and castles remaining in the Knights' hands have either been captured or have surrendered voluntarily; so that the Master and his Knights have only Frombork and Sztum. Nevertheless, some of the King's councillors still consider the whole thing suspect.

The Order's treasurer, who was sent to represent the Order at the King's wedding, had been given 50,000 florins to use at his discretion and had authority to bind the Order to pay homage to King Casimir, if that, plus the money, would prevent acceptance of the Prussians' offer; now see-ing that the King is inclined to accept the offer in any case, he leaves Cracow and goes to Silesia, Meissen and Saxony, where he uses his florins to hire an army to defend the Order. Before he leaves, he sows seeds of discord by bribing the Chamberlain of Cracow, a man hated for his asso-ciation with thieves and brigands, as well as for his fraudulence, to incite civil war. Although the two meet only by night, it is all reported to the King, and so they achieve nothing. To bring home to the gentry and townspeople of Prussia how their fortunes have changed, they are relieved of the general tribute known as funtczol, to them the most onerous, as well as of the annual impost known as wieprz, a relic of the old days; while the King, for himself and his successors, relinquishes his right to levy dues on land and sea, as well as his right to goods from shipwrecks, which must now be returned to those to whom they belonged before the ship was wrecked or to their heirs. The Prus-sians are to enjoy the same rights and privileges as people in Poland, especially in having an equal say in electing a king. Four voivodeships are set up: Toruń, Elbląg, Königsberg and Gdańsk. Thus do the territories of Prussia, Chełm and Pomerania return to Poland, where they belong, only now as provinces. Sensible people see that this is an arrangement that cannot last.

On their return the Prussian envoys are greeted with delight: before they even reach home four of the Knights' castles: the new one at Toruń, the ones at Gdańsk, Elbląg and Königsberg are demolished by the local townspeople, much to the displeasure of the King and the Prussian nobles. An army is immediately sent to Malbork to lay siege to the castle there. Meanwhile, Chojnice, which has not submitted, is reinforced with a thousand cavalry sent to help the Master. The Voivode of Inowrocław then arrives with 1200 horse and 700 foot and occupies Tuchola and Slu-chovia. In a series of duels, his champions repeatedly defeat those of the Chojnice garrison and this prevents the crops there being destroyed. At Easter, all the nobles of Prussia pay homage in Toruń to the Bishop of Poznań and the Chancellor, representing the King, after which the bulk of the army and its guns are sent to continue the siege of Malbork.

Frederick Margrave of Brandenburg takes the chance of appropriating Nowa Marchia. The King pretends not to know what is happening; so, once again, towns, villages and forts are wrest from the hated clutches of the Order.

The King sends a canon of Gniezno to the Pope, the Roman Emperor and to King László in Prague, so that he can counteract any complaints the Knights may lay against the Poles. Then, leav-ing his wife and his mother in Cracow, he goes to Brześć in Ruthenia for a conference and there or-ders the Lithuanians to deny passage to a Livonian force that is wishing to go to the help of the Order. They are to use force to do so, should that be necessary. Next the King goes to Sandomierz, where his wife and mother await him, and spends Easter there. Then all three go to Łęczyca for an assembly that lasts a week.

The main matter under consideration is Prussia. It is unanimously agreed that the King should go there and stay in Toruń, sending his household troops and those from Kujawy and Dobrzyn to continue the sieges of Malbork, Sztum and Chojnice. While in Toruń he is to receive the homage of the nobles and people of Prussia. In Łęczyca, he receives envoys from Margrave Frederick of

Brandenburg asking him not to make difficulties about the Margrave's appropriation of Nowa Marchia. Then envoys arrive from the Duke of Słupsk to ask for help in recovering Nowa Marchia, which, the Duke says, is his by right of inheritance, in return for help the Duke promises to provide 2000 horse to help the King in any of his wars, including the present one. Both sets of envoys are told that the King cannot make a decision about territory claimed by two friends, as well as by the King of Bohemia. The King's own envoys now return from Prague bringing the news that the brother of the Margrave had come there to inform King László of the defection of the Prussian territories, and to complain of the way in which the Poles are seeking to bring these under their dominion. There is a Czech suggestion that in return for 500,000 florins, the amount offered to the King of Bohemia, King Casimir should renounce his right to Prussia, which would then become a perpetual fief paying him 10,000 florins a year. The Dukes of Mazovia also arrive, come to demand the return of Goniadz and Tykozin occupied by the Lithuanians, but they do not get a proper answer and leave with feelings of considerable bitterness, though both are ready to support Casimir with all their forces, if he will see justice done them.

After this, the King, with a vast throng of knights and young people, goes to Prussia, where his voivodes, bishops and castellans are already assembled. He has so many troops with him that they form twelve good companies, six preceding him and six bringing up the rear. Thus he comes to Toruń, and, on the Tuesday before Ascension Day, wearing his cloak and royal diadem, girded with the coronation sword and holding the orb and sceptre, he seats himself on a throne set up in the market place and there receives the homage of the lands of Chełm. The voivodes and nobles of Chełm cast their standards and emblems at his feet in symbolic submission and swear oaths of enduring loyalty, obedience and submission. He then goes to the parish church, which is so crowded that he has difficulty in making his way in. After Mass sung at the high altar and the singing of a *Te Deum laudamus*, the rest of the day is devoted to merry-making.

While the King is in Toruń, envoys from the King of Hungary and Bohemia come to tell him that their King looks with disfavour on the way King Casimir has, without consulting him, accepted the submission of the Prussians, and to demand that he sends envoys to Prague with full powers to negotiate new agreements concerning Prussia and, in the mean time, to stop harassing Malbork, Sztum and Chojnice, because King László is the patron and benefactor of the Order. Casimir expresses surprise at hearing such harsh words from envoys of his neighbour and relative who, by reason of his tender years, cannot judge such matters, but, remembering how the Knights wooed George Poděbrady and the Czech heretics, he considers himself entitled to decide whether it be war or peace. He stresses that he has never agreed to consult László, but he will send envoys with his answers to the other questions. The envoys now take a milder tone and, indeed, individually hint that Casimir should continue to deal with Prussia as he is doing. They do ask, however, that their clerks be allowed to go to Malbork to collect money that has been promised them. This is refused categorically and the envoys then return to Prague laden with gifts. King László realizes that he sent the wrong envoys and quickly sends another, Jan Rabstein, who asks Casimir to forget what the previous envoys said without their King's approval and explains that in many respects he supports the King's actions in Prussia and promises to do nothing to disrupt it. Casimir now realizes that he had better come to an agreement with László and sends the Voivode of Cracow and Peter Szamtoł, Castellan of Poznań, to Prague. Back in Prague, Rabstein tells his King that only a madman would go to war with the King of Poland with his huge army of superbly trained troops, just to recover Prussian territory all of which, except for three castles, is already in that King's hands. Hearing this, many of the Czechs who had been thinking of going to help the Knights, now have second thoughts.

At Whitsun, King Casimir goes to Elbląg, where, in full regalia, he seats himself on a throne set up in front of the town hall and there receives the homage of three of the bishops and their chap-

ters, but of only the chapter of Warmińsk since the bishop is shut up in Malbork. After the ceremony, the three bishops and their chapters, who hitherto had worn the garb of the Knights, discard
this and put on regular dress, requesting the King to allow them to revert to the rules of the Order of
the regular canons of St. Augustine, which each had abandoned at the insistence of the Knights: for
none except a member of the Order could become canon or bishop. Unable to go to Königsberg in
person, the King sends the Chancellor, Jan of Koniecpol, to receive their oaths of allegiance in his
stead, and himself returns to Toruń, where he grants the citizens of Gdańsk, Elbląg, Toruń and
Königsberg generous grants of villages, mills and other revenue. The people of Gdańsk have 700
marks of interest remitted and are given the island's mills and villages, leaving the King with only
thirteen villages and two manors, on condition that the city pays him 2000 florins a year and supplies him and his court with all their needs for four days, and at his own expense he replaces the ruined castle with a royal mansion of fired brick. In return the King is granted all he needs for the
continued siege of Malbork, Sztum and Chojnice. During all this, the Queen and her Mother pay
them frequent visits from Nieszawa for dancing and other entertainment, just as if there were
peace.

On St. Margaret's Day the King attends an assembly at Grudziądz, the main purpose of which
is to pay off the Czech mercenaries besieging Malbork, who are now considered unreliable and
who, having been granted pay as high as 26 florins a quarter for every horse, are making a great
deal of money and doing very little for it. They are now to be replaced with the household troops.
Back in Toruń, the King receives envoys from the Emperor asking him, in the name of justice, to
return the lands of Prussia to their previous owners, the Master and Order of Teutonic Knights, and,
instead, to devote himself to recovering Constantinople. They are told that the King will send envoys to give his reply at the council being held to discuss the whole question of the Knights; while
their request to be escorted to Malbork and for the sieges of Malbork, Sztum and Chojnice to be
suspended, cannot be met. So, the envoys depart, laden with gifts.

Lack of bread and beer after six months of siege has caused an outbreak of dropsy and dysentry among the garrison in Sztum, fifty of whom have already died. Now, seeing no hope of receiving help, they surrender, being allowed to march out with their personal belongings, but leaving
their guns, powder, cannon balls and other equipment in the castle. Only fifty of them go to Malbork, all the others. including some Knights, join King Casimir. On Assumption Day there is a
regular battle between the King's troops and the garrison of Malbork. So much blood is shed that
the Master's mercenaries, most of whom are Mazovian and Czech peasants, lose heart and send to
the King asking for forgiveness for their breach of faith. At the same time, a fire-ship, prepared in
Gdańsk where it was filled with tar, sulphur and other incendiary substances, is floated downstream without a helmsman and would have burned the bridge at Malbork had not the garrison sallied out and poured enough water on it to quench the fire.

Learning that the Order is using the last of its resources to recruit an army in Germany, the
King orders the barons of Wielkopolska to send their troops to Chojnice. These cause more damage by their looting and plundering on the march, than would any enemy; and, when they link up
with the besiegers a couple of miles from Chojnice, they find that the latter have everything in profusion and are amusing themselves, rather than besieging a castle.

News now comes from Frederick Margrave of Brandenburg that the Order's new army of
German, Silesian and Czech mercenaries, to which he has granted passage through his territory, is
approaching Nowa Marchia, which supports the Knights. The King, having wasted a lot of time
settling up with his Czech mercenaries, who have been demanding their pay, finally moves out
from Toruń. Cardinal Zbigniew repeatedly warns him against going into battle without his veteran
household troops, which he should now recall from Malbork, for, if he does not win his battle, he
will lose Malbork as well; however, Jan of Koniecpol the Chancellor gives his King contrary ad-

vice and the result is that the veterans from Malbork are never sent for. On the Wednesday before
Holy Cross, the King's army reaches Cerekwica, where he finds the troops from Wielkopolska in
complete disarray and so forgetful of their duty of obedience, that they are refusing even to muster
until their old rights have been confirmed and some new ones granted. This conceded, on the Saturday, the King arrays his forces in seven units, and, on the Monday, advances on Chojnice anticipating that he will be attacked by the Knights trying to raise the siege. The Knights' approach is
cautious, as if they were reluctant to fight. However, the King is so appalled by the lack of discipline among his troops and by the almost total lack of experienced soldiers, for most of his are mere
youths ill-armed and unaccustomed to war, that he decides to send for his household troops from
Malbork and for another 500 that the Castellan of Gniezno has available, and not to engage the enemy before these arrive. Then, however, his scouts report the approach of what is only a small enemy force and he yields to the importuning of his commanders and decides to engage it; although
his Czechs advise him to allow it into Chojnice, where, shut in with the garrison, the two could be
defeated without a fight. So, battle is joined and there is a fierce and rather bloody fight, in which
the Poles come off best. The next day the King's army stands to from morning until dusk awaiting
attack. Finally, the enemy does come into sight, but only three squadrons, which, when they see the
King's huge army, think only of escape. The King's inexperienced commanders now move their
men in unusual formation into a marshy and thoroughly unsuitable position, without attacking or
doing anything to discomfort the lightly armed enemy, a tactic on which victory largely depends.
The commanders of both forces now urge their troops on and battle is engaged. Fortune favours the
Poles, who break and then rout the first enemy formation, several of whose commanders are killed.
Then, however, the enemy presses harder, yet without success, until, for no good reason. the Poles'
rear-guard takes fright and runs, turning certain victory into shameful defeat. The King very nearly
falls into the hands of the enemy, while trying to rally his troops. The whole of the King's train of
4000 waggons is captured and the siege of Chojnice raised. With a mere handful of men, the King,
angry and regretting not having listened to Cardinal Zbigniew, goes to Bydgoszcz, to which emissaries from all over Prussia come begging him not to lose heart, but to organize a fresh army, and
promising to give him all they possess to help repair his losses. The King tells them that the disaster
has angered, rather than broken him, and that, with God's help, he will within a short time have
turned the tables on his enemies. He now raises the siege of Malbork and withdraws his household
troops from there, giving them the new task of garrisoning and holding all the castles in Prussia.
Although winter is at hand, he orders all Poland, except Lwów and Podole to mobilize quickly.

    The Knights now move on Tczew, which surrenders, as does Gniew. Meanwhile, the Master
has sent to all the towns and nobles of Prussia urging them to abandon the King and return to his
authority, promising to forget all their misdemeanours; but only one, the Bishop of Sambia, breaks
his oath to the King and surrenders his castles and towns to the Order, only to have all his properties
and those of his churches confiscated by the Master. The Order's mercenary army having crossed
the Vistula, reaches Malbork, where it at once demands its pay. The Order's treasury is empty, so
the Master gives them what he has confiscated from the Bishop of Sambia and what he can borrow,
as well as what he gets from melting down sacred vessels and crucifixes, but this amounts only to
six grosses apiece. Pretending that the Order has transferred its treasury to Rome, the Master persuades the mercenaries to allow him to postpone payment of the rest. In the end, it is agreed that
they are to receive 40,000 florins during Lent, in default of which the castles they are garrisoning
will be handed over to them.

    The troops for which the King sent have now reached the assembly point at Opoka, having
plundered the country through which they passed on the way there. The King is expecting mercenaries from Bohemia, Moravia and Silesia, and only when these arrive, does he break camp. He
crosses the Vistula and halts for some days near Toruń before moving on and so reaches the Ossa

between Radzyń and Łasin, which latter is in enemy hands. The Knights have put troops into a mill there to try and prevent the King crossing, but these decamp as soon as the Poles appear, allowing them to cross and make camp in a wood a mile from Chełmża, whose garrison has firewood and provisions enough for itself and its horses. The Polish train is so huge that it is still crossing the river the following day, delayed because rain has made the ground slippery and a hindrance to quick progress. This is obviously a winter campaign. In order to prevent Łasin obtaining provisions from outside, the King remains camped in the forest. Meanwhile, two of the Bishop of Sambia's towns have been captured, given to the troops to loot and then burned. Any eminent prisoners taken in them are handed over to the King.

A.D. 1455

The King had decided to starve out Łasin, but this is taking so long that already snow has fallen, and thus there are no more provisions to be had from the surrounding country, so the King strikes camp and disbands the army. He appoints governors for Chełm, Pomerania and Prussia, and gives each a strong force of mercenaries with which to protect their castles. The castle and town of Działdowo on the border with Mazovia are considered too remote to be endangered and are entrusted to the standard-bearer, a man in whom the King has complete confidence; but no sooner has the King left, than the standard-bearer without any necessity breaks his oath and surrenders the castle and town to the Master.

The Poles claim that they have crushed the enemy in Prussia, while the Knights say that the Poles have spent a lot of time under the walls of one wretched little town and then marched away with nothing achieved.

The disbanded army crosses the Vistula near Toruń and reaches home ahead of the news of its disbandment. The King attends to various matters in Nieszawa and Toruń, before going to Łęczyca to attend an assembly. From there he sends their pay to the governors of the castles in Prussia. Next, he send tax-collectors to collect the levy laid on every field throughout the kingdom, which is intended to finance the army in Prussia; but as this cannot be collected immediately, it is decided to mint a new coin in Cracow, a half-gross, which is to go into general circulation and so enable the treasury to finance the continuance of the war. The Queen who, throughout the war, has been in Sieradz castle, now joins the King in Łęczyca.

The King dismisses most of his Polish courtiers and goes to Lithuania, where he has to suppress a number of minor disturbances, and here he spends the whole spring and receives a number of dukes come with gifts. The Tatar Khan, Eczigari, sends messages of condolence over his defeat and promises either to bring his own powerful army to help him in his next battle, or to send his son with it. The Lithuanians promise military help against the Master and his Knights.

Cardinal-bishop Zbigniew Oleśnicki dies in Sandomierz on the Monday after Palm Sunday. Three red hats are hung beside his grave to show that he had been appointed by three Popes, something unprecedented. The Cardinal left his money not to his relatives, but to students, the poor and the unfortunate, as well as to churches and monasteries.

Although it is still winter, the Master has moved an army of 3000 on Toruń, hoping to capture the old town, two of whose city fathers have conspired to surrender it. The plot would have succeeded had not a Pole, who is held prisoner there, sent a page to hurry up three women who were making wax moulds of the keys of one of the gates, bribing the boy with fifty florins to tell no one of his errand. However, the women are caught in flagrante delicto and killed. People now realize that something untoward is afoot, but no one knows what, until the Master turns up at the place agreed, but, finding none of the plotters there to greet him, sends two heralds and a number of Knights to the gates. This arouses suspicion. One of the traitors is arrested and he betrays the other. The two are then marched to the castle, holding aloft letters from the Master as proof of their crime, and there they are beheaded, their corpses quartered and displayed on the city's gates. Several other guilty citizens are either beheaded or drowned; thus the town is cleansed of treachery. The disappointed Master lets his troops loot the new town and heads back to Malbork, setting fire to a number of villages on the way. The King's army, now far the stronger, could have done battle, but unpaid wages keep the troops in their quarters.

Even the remoter parts of Prussia are not free from the clash of arms. Two towns near Königsberg open their gates to the Master; while a third, Knipow, gets reinforcements from Gdańsk and remains loyal to the King. Two other towns are bombarded by the Knights' cannon, which demolish so many houses and so terrorize the inhabitants, that they, too, go over to the Master. Elsewhere, one, Jan Kolda, pretending to be the Commander of Elbląg, gains admission to Działdowo, where he kills several of the Knights' mercenaries, seizes seventy of the more eminent townspeople and sets fire to the town itself. In the course of one fortnight four battles are fought in each of which the Poles defeat the Knights, many of whom are killed along with their mercenaries and 200 others taken prisoner. The booty is divided among the troops.

The King, his wife and her mother, arrive in Piotrków on the Saturday before Ascension Day. Here the King has discussions concerning the future conduct of the war in Prussia and how to pay the mercenaries he has hired, who, being unpaid, will now do no more than defend their towns and castles. It is generally felt that to order general mobilization in order to prosecute the war in Prussia would be too costly, especially as mercenaries can easily deal with the Knights, if only there is money to pay them. So, it is decided to raise a further levy on every field. The barons of Wielkopolska accept the need for this and start collecting it, but the barons of Cracow will not pay up, unless the King's lands produce at least half the total, a condition the latter will not accept.

Two disasters now strike the city of Cracow. On the day the new bishop, Thomas Strzepinski, is elected, a fine bell with a very pleasant ring, a gift of the late Cardinal-bishop Oleśnicki, is dislodged and falls and breaks the upper part of one ear, thus making it useless, until it can be recast. Then, on the following day, fire breaks out in the house of Thomas the Armourer, which is close to the church. The attempts to put it out are only half-hearted, for almost all the apprentices are outside the city shooting at a popinjay or watching others do it; then the wind goes round to the north and the flames break out again, and the fire spreads rapidly. Some of the houses affected have gunpowder stored in them and this only increases the blaze. People are more concerned to rescue the contents of their houses than to put out the fire, which, in the end, consumes over a hundred houses and four churches, as well as the college of the students of canon law, only two of the canons' houses being saved, one that of the cantor and the other that of Canon Jan Długosz. The fire spreads as far as the castle, killing many, especially those who take refuge in their cellars. Many attribute the outbreak to the hurt done to God's name, when the Jews, who used to deposit most of their possessions with Thomas the Armourer, were granted their liberty.

Their own mercenaries have turned the Knights out of Malbork and other castles for failing to pay them their due, now amounting to millions. Having neither money nor provisions, they now turn to King Casimir in the hope that he will pay them and take over the castles. The King sends the Bishop of Włocławek and the Starosta of Sandomierz to negotiate.

The besieged in Knipow are now feeling the pangs of starvation. Its two neighbours, which have already gone over to the Master, are so eager to prevent supplies getting through to Knipow, that they have diverted the river that flows through the town by damming it with baulks of timber. The King orders help to be sent to Knipow, but this involves first finding several thousand florins to pay some mercenaries; but the people in Knipow cannot be told of this and, despairing of receiving help, they surrender. Their example is followed by other towns in the lower part of the country, news that depresses the King and makes Margrave Frederick of Brandenburg believe that Fortune has deserted his ally, so he cancels a meeting with Casimir and, instead of going to Poland, goes to

Gniew and makes a treaty with the Master, doing so, he says, at the request of the Emperor. Afraid of further misfortune, although the summer is already over, the King sends out a general call to arms and obtains reassurances of their loyalty from his towns in Prussia. The Knights, meanwhile, have been advancing on Friedland, held by one of the King's mercenary knights, a Czech called Skubela, who, pretending to be afraid of them, allows some of the enemy to reach the walls and even to climb the outer wall; then, with the enemy crowded into the narrow space between the two walls, he fires on them with handguns, cannon, bows and arrows, and hurls stones on them from above. In a short time, there are 500 dead between the walls and a hundred others have been taken prisoner. Those outside panic and run to their camp, but the defences of this are poor, so that, when the King's men sally out and attack it from the rear, it is captured.

Despite the fact that summer is over and the winter in Poland usually cold and wet, the King decides on one further campaign in Prussia. He orders troops from all over the kingdom to assemble, which they do, though most complain that they ought to be going into winter quarters instead. Those, who assemble on the appointed day, have to wait a further six weeks before all the others arrive. As the army moves towards Prussia, it devastates the country through which it passes. The first to reach a staging-post bring in grain from the surrounding fields, as if intending to winter where they are, and build huge stacks of it; yet, when they move on, they burn what they have not consumed, thus depriving the others of it. This just shows how great was their love of their country and how good their discipline!

Meanwhile, the King has been in Brześć conferring with emissaries from the gentry and towns people of Prussia and his own prelates and nobles on how to continue the war, and, above all, how to pay the mercenaries what they are due, for their representatives are threatening to go back to the Order unless they are paid. The collection of the field levy of the previous year having proved a failure, the only other source of money is the property and jewels of the Church. The Archbishop of Gniezno and the bishops of Włocławek and Poznań agree to surrender their's against a guarantee of it all being replaced eventually, so their churches are stripped of their plate and jewels. There is something of an outcry, when it is learned that all this silver has brought in only 6000 florins. (Cracow, being too far away to have sent representatives, is not affected.)

The new army crosses the Vistula near Toruń on the King's pontoon bridge, and continues to Bydgoszcz, where Frederick Margrave of Brandenburg, who has just spent several days with the Master in Malbork, now making much of his loyalty to King Casimir, begs to be allowed to mediate, promising that he will be able to obtain better terms than the King is entitled to expect. Naively the King accepts in principle and, taking no further military action, sends a five-man delegation to meet the Margrave and hear what he proposes. When these come face to face with the Master, they discover that the latter is demanding that Casimir remove all his troops from the Order's territory and surrender all the towns and castles in Prussia that have gone over to him. Any matters in doubt are to be decided by the Pope, the Emperor or the Electors. The Poles give the necessary reply and castigate the Margrave for having made fools of them. The Margrave then suggests that, if they will agree to surrender Chełm and Michałów and to pay the cost of the war, they can wait until peace has been signed and the Germans have mostly withdrawn, and then renew the attack and so conquer all Prussia. This suggestion is dismissed with contempt and the Margrave's emissaries return home.

The Poles now advance towards the River Ossa with the object of laying siege to Gniew and Tczew, and, having captured these, of gaining control of both banks of the Vistula, thus making life difficult for the enemy and easier for the people of Gdańsk who, as things are, are prevented from moving their goods and possessions by water. There is a good prospect of achieving this, for Gdańsk has promised to provide enough cannon and powder to demolish the walls of both towns. It takes the King three weeks to capture the wretched town of Łapczyce. Now, the army is finding

The young men of Cracow shooting at the popinjay, as they were on the day of the Great Fire. From Baltharius Behem: Codex Picturatus. —*Jagiellonian University Library.*

difficulty in feeding its horses, for after such lengthy hostilities there is no pasture left anywhere, and the grain, having been harvested in the summer, is all in the forts; and the villagers themselves have all sought refuge in Ruthenia, Prussia, Germany and elsewhere. So, the horses have to be fed on chaff, thatch from roofs and what sods are left in the empty fields. There is grain to be bought in the castles, but only by the wealthy; other people's horses have to starve. A quarter of the army's horses die.

King Casimir, now regretting having embarked on this dangerous enterprise, raises the siege, leaving the townspeople boasting of having twice endured a siege by the great King of Poland. The townspeople of Prussia are furious about the way in which the King's troops have plundered the countryside and are beginning to wish that the Master and his Order were again lords of Prussia.

In the King's absence, a Moravian and a Pole, both of whom have a private quarrel with the King, raid Poland between Olkucz and Slawkiew with a force of volunteers avid for plunder and loot. They seize eighty of the horses used to work the pumps at the lead mines in the mountains, and burn the town of Slawkiew. After this success. they try to repeat the process in Wieluń district, where a few of them, pretending to be peasants coming to pay their taxes in kind, gain admittance to the fort at Kepno. With these inside, the others emerge from their hiding-place and together they occupy the fort and capture its governor. The Burgrave of Wieluń hurriedly assembles a force and lays siege to the fort. He sends for reinforcements, but, as winter is at hand, he allows the bandits to march out with all that they have purloined.

On the Wednesday before St. Lucia's Day, Władysław, Duke of Mazovia and Płock, dies of tuberculosis, which runs in his family. He leaves two sons.

A.D. 1456

After Christmas, an assembly in Piotrków votes to make all clergy and officers of the Crown pay two farthings for each of their fields and to contribute half the revenue from the Church's holdings. The bishops complain that they are being imposed on. Next the assembly discusses the troublesome Prussian question and eventually decides to mount another expedition immediately after Whitsun and continue hostilities throughout the summmer; but also that they must examine ways of achieving peace. The Knights are now proposing terms which will involve the release of some of their Polish prisoners, who, of course, are begging for their liberty. It is accepted that, if terms are agreed. Poland will have to pay the considerable sum which the Knights' mercenaries are demanding in back pay and compensation; should it come to this, half of the total revenue of Church, King and the nobles will be required to meet this new demand.

On the first Monday in March the Queen gives birth to a pretty infant. The astronomers prophesy him great success. He is christened Władysław.

On the Sunday before St. Wojciech's Day, the King and Queen leave Cracow for Wielkopolska, where they spend the whole summer. Because of persistent rumours that many of the German dukes, Margrave Frederick of Brandenburg in particular, are planning to help the Knights, the King orders another invasion of Prussia. Meanwhile, people are wearied of war and desire peace, so there is much discussion of possible terms. This takes the King to Toruń, where he spends a fortnight, at the end of which conditions are agreed that are quite impracticable: namely, that the King is to pay the Order's former mercenaries thirty-seven florins each in back pay and compensation for losses. This paid, Malbork and all the other castles in the enemy's hands are to be surrendered to the King and all Polish prisoners-of-war freed. The real worry is how is such a sum to be raised? Although the Prussian estates are proposing to find half the amount by means of a poll tax, how is the King to raise the other half, when he already owes his own mercenaries as much again? The matter is referred to the next assembly.

A.D. 1457

Bishop Osmund of York in England, who for 350 years has been lying in dust and performing miracles, is canonized by Pope Calixtus III on January 1.

King Casimir spends the whole winter in Lithuania, where he succeeds in silencing those who have been openly voicing the need for a new grand-duke. At the start of Lent, he goes to Piotrków to attend an assembly, for which he arrives late, the Vistula's flooding being worse than anyone can remember. He then goes to Koło to attend another assembly, at which it is decided that, the royal treasury being empty, Słuchow, Świecie and Tuchola castles are to be garrisoned not by mercenaries, but by the King's own troops. Chojnice, still under siege, is starving and in urgent need of supplies.

In Hungary, Lászlo Hunyadi, elder son of János, has murdered Ulrich Cillei; King Lászlo, with the backing of his principal advisors, imprisons Hunyadi and his brother Matthias and has Lászlo Hunyadi beheaded in Buda. He then hands the Bishop of Varaždin over to the Archbishop of Esztergom for him to deal with. Shattered by the news of the fate of her two sons Hunyadi's widow, instead of having recourse to womanly tears, takes up arms. Having the huge fortune collected over the years by her husband, she hires several thousand mercenaries, some of whom she installs as garrisons in her late husband's castles, and with the others, still a considerable army, she declares war on the King, who has to bring in troops from Bohemia and Austria to stop her from besieging him in Buda. Eventually, peace is restored.

While Casimir is in Bydgoszcz, the Archbishop of Gniezno, two bishops and a number of lords and knights, all in splendid battle armour, arrive, come to accompany the King to Prussia, there to take possession of Malbork; however, in the meantime the King's officials in Toruń have started paying the mercenaries in Malbork, instead of in Gdańsk, as had been promised. The mercenaries refuse to accept payment in Malbork, so the officials have to take ship to Gdańsk. With them is Ulrich the Red, who has been having secret talks with the King about the frauds of the Poznań justiciar, Jan Siepenski, who had been entrusted with the money from Wielkopolska. Easter, the last day for paying the mercenaries having passed and more remaining to be paid than had already been paid, it looks as if all the Germans and some of the Czechs will refuse to accept payment because of the king's default. Ulrich negotiates an extension of the term, during which period 160,000 is paid, leaving 30,000 florins still outstanding, for neither Poland nor Prussia have come up with the amounts they promised.

The amount due is now greater than was originally estimated, for the Malbork mercenaries have claimed for an exaggerated number of horses and losses. The realization that such a sum cannot be raised in so short a time causes considerable anxiety, lest by defaulting Poland should lose all that has already been paid. Not only that, but Prussia might be lost as well and Poland itself collapse. However, the King's commissioners do not lose their heads, but demand further money from the citizens of Gdańsk, stressing the unpleasant consequences of the money not being paid and promising that, when the King takes over Malbork, he will deposit with the city the silver image of the Virgin and the reliquary with the bones of St. Barbara, as security for the loan. This is accepted, but the people of Gdańsk require the King to come in person. The King, who has spent the last three weeks in Bydgoszcz arranging a supply of provisions for starving Słuchow, sets out for Gdańsk. He spends the Saturday night in a village a mile from Stargard, intending to go to Gdańsk the next morning; but then the King of Sweden, recently expelled by his people, suddenly arrives on foot, and he is followed by processions of all the churches and states, all in their best clothes, come to see their king, who is clad in armour as if going into battle. As the King of Sweden approaches, Casimir dismounts and receives him not as an exile, but as an equal, whom he then mounts on a regally caparisoned horse, prepared in readiness, and the two ride together through the crowded streets to the Church of the Blessed Virgin. The next few days are given over to displays of swordsmanship and jousting, which everyone watches, forgetful of their work. It was estimated that the King had with him 6000 foot and horse.

The arrival of King Casimir in Gdańsk considerably strengthens the position of Poland and weakens that of the Order. The citizens of Gdańsk set about collecting the money with renewed enthusiasm. Some of the German and Czech mercenaries seize control of Malbork, pretending that they are entitled to do this, since the King has defaulted. This is done in the absence of their officers who now hurry back, manage to get into the castle by boat and calm the unrest; after which Ulrich the Red arrives with 18,000 florins for the mercenaries. The money is handed over and the mercenaries made to surrender the upper castle. The King then sends the Castellan of Gniezno to Malbork with the rest of the money; but these become involved in an argument as to the true number of horses involved and the extent of the losses incurred and end up having to hand over a further 12,000. Even then the Germans cause further trouble by secretly removing the castle's greatest treasures, the silver crucifix with part of the Cross, the silver-gilt image of the Virgin, and the head and image of St. Barbara. When this is discovered, the Poles, who now outnumber the mercenaries, take up arms and swiftly recover them. The Master of the Order, who has continued to occupy his usual quarters in Malbork, although his furniture and belongings have been sent to Prussmork, now leaves Malbork with his Czechs and Hungarians, shaking his fist at the Poles and the men of Gdańsk as he goes and telling them that he will soon be back and have his revenge.

Trouble breaks out in Cracow duchy, where some mercenaries, Czechs, Poles and Silesians, who have not been paid for their service in Prussia, incited by two brothers who bear a grudge against the King of Hungary for not paying them what they think he owes them, fortify a hill near Oświęcim and from there plunder the countryside. They could easily have been dealt with, but for the negligence, even compliance of the local governor, for neither he nor anyone stands up to them and before long they have taken over the town of Mysłowice, in which they are eventually besieged. To end the siege, they agree to accept half what is due to them, but when the siege is raised, they start demanding the whole again and hostilities are resumed. To prevent the trouble spreading, any mounted soldier with the necessary equipment, who is willing to serve, is offered twelve Polish grosses a week. To meet the cost of this, the salt works are relieved of having to pay rent, so that all their revenue, except what is due to burgraves and salt-makers, can be used to pay for the war, the treasury having no other revenue.

On September 21, in Cracow, the young Queen gives birth to a full-term daughter, who is christened Jadwiga.

The King's household troops are laying siege to Gniew, the one remaining town on the Vistula still in enemy hands. The besieged are so short of provisions that people are dying of starvation every day, and the town's surrender is expected within the week; yet the King's troops, forgetful of their oaths and discipline, at the instigation of the starosta of Lublin, abandon the siege and depart, wasting all their previous effort and expense. The enemy are so encouraged by this, that they set about recovering Malbork town and castle. In the town are some traitors, men forgiven when the King assumed control, and these secretly admit others during the vigil of the Feast of St. Michael and together they seize control of all the towers and fortifications of the town itself and kill or capture the King's knights as they lie, unsuspecting, in their beds. A few do manage to escape and alert Ulrich the Red in the castle, so that when the enemy reach the ditches between the town and the castle they are pelted with stones and repulsed. For the next several days the streets of Malbork are so exposed to gun-fire that none dares show himself on them and people knock holes in the walls of the houses so as to gain access from one to the other. In an attempt to capitalize on his good fortune, the Master brings 800 cavalry by ship down the Vistula towards the confluence with the Nogat, hoping thus to collect taxes and homage from the area; however, he is prevented in this by the King's troops still besieging Gniew. He attempts to build a wooden bridge across the river at Malbork, but men from Gdańsk guarding the river prevent this. The town of Malbork once more in his hands, the Master returns there in triumph, confident that the castle will soon surrender; but King Casimir sends 6000 well-equipped troops provided by the nobles of Wielkopolska, who have agreed among themselves that whoever has yearly rents of 100 marks shall provide one lance, and the towns will provide infantry. Thanks to this, a considerable force is assembled in a short time and it is this that the King sends to relieve Malbork, making its way through Pomerania, crossing the Vistula near Tczew.

The next assembly at Piotrków is much concerned with the problem of the unpaid former mercenaries from Prussia, who are raiding the kingdom from their fortified strongholds at Mysłowice, Żebracz and Wapienna Gora, but again the matter is deferred to the next assembly at Koło. Now comes the sad news that Lászlo of Hungary, betrothed to Magdalena, daughter of the King of France—the invitations to the wedding having already been sent out—has suddenly died of an unexplained illness. The rumour is that he has been poisoned at the instigation of Joanna, wife of George Poděbrady.

A.D. 1458

After attending a memorial service for King Lászlo, the King and Queen go to Lithuania and remain there all winter. Although this is somewhat superfluous, reminders are sent to both Hungary and Bohemia that only King Casimir and his sons have any right to these two thrones. These reminders are unwelcome, for both countries have someone else in view; indeed, in Buda, on St. Vincent's Day the Hungarian assembly unanimously elects as the new king of Hungary, Matthias, the thirteen-year old son of János Hunyadi, who is still a captive of George Poděbrady. The young King's uncle, Michael Szilágyi, arrives with 5000 mercenaries, mostly Poles, intent on quashing any attempt to elect anyone else. 50,000 złoty are collected to ransom the new king, and the castles at Buda and Visegrád are handed over to his uncle. A huge gallows is erected on the bank of the Danube. From it dangle a rope and an axe as a warning to anyone inclined to resist the election of Matthias. The Roman Emperor sends messengers with letters drawing the Hungarians' attention to the fact that King Casimir, through his wife, is next in succession to the throne, but to these the Hungarians pay no attention. The fact that they have chosen a young man of unknown family, a prisoner of war, whose release has not yet been accomplished, is an indication that the Hungarians themselves had plotted against the late King's life.

The Czechs are no more sensible, for an assembly held in Prague during Lent elects as their ruler George Poděbrady, a man well fitted for the task, but tainted with the heresy of Wycliffe. The King of France is contemptuous and, through his envoys still in Prague, lets it be known how grieved he is by the premature death of Lászlo and exhorts the Czechs to elect one of his own sons in Lászlo's place, promising that, if they do so, he will return the County of Luxembourg, currently held by the Duke of Burgundy, to Bohemia and will restore all the ecclesiastical and royal goods that had been pledged to him. However, he admits that he knows that by right the Bohemian throne belongs to King Casimir, and is ready, should Casimir decide to give the crown of Bohemia to his own son, who is not yet of age, to give the young king his own daughter, or, should Casimir prefer to see his daughter on the throne, she can marry one of the sons of the King of France. These suggestions are refused, as is the claim put forward by the Margrave of Meissen, whose wife is the elder sister of the late King.

The dukes of Silesia are offended, when they learn of Matthias' election, both because they were not invited to have a say and because now they will have to obey a man of low origin, younger than they and a heretic. They let their dissatisfaction be known, but prefer to accept a heretic rather than involve Silesia in war. Even so, in order to be ready for any eventuality, each duke and town agrees to raise a certain number of cavalry and infantry, and anyone who possesses 1000 florins has to pay the wages of three infantrymen. In Moravia, the nobles accept George Poděbrady, but the towns follow the example of Silesia and refuse to do so. Nonetheless, on the Sunday before St. John's Day, Poděbrady is crowned king and his wife, Joanna, crowned queen.

At an assembly held in Piotrków on St. Philip's Day, it is decided to mount a further expedition against Prussia, the troops having to assemble in Gniewkowo on St. Vitus' Day. It is also decided that the rebellious mercenaries in Mysłowice and elsewhere are to be given the pay owed them from Prussia, the money to come from the field tax being collected throughout the kingdom. This assembly is attended by Jan Giskra from Hungary, who, having obtained permission to address it, urges the King and his councillors not to accept Hunyadi's son Matthias as king of what belongs to King Casimir, but for the latter to march his huge army into Hungary as quickly as possible and take possession of it. He announces that he is transferring the support he gave King Lászlo to King Casimir and his progeny, and that many of Hungary's nobles will do the same; also that, as he controls many of the castles in his own country, these, too, will accept the King, if he will come to Hungary. Giskra is told that the King is too modest to accept the offer, one kingdom being enough for him, and also that the war with Prussia, which he cannot neglect, makes it impossible for him to do this. However, if, on conclusion of this war, the prelates and nobles of Hungary still want him, he will gladly come. Giskra then offers to send his troops to help the King in Prussia and this is accepted; but before anything further is done, Giskra himself goes to Prussia and discusses peace with the Master, though without achieving anything.

The army, having assembled at Gniewkowo, crosses the Vistula near Toruń on the King's pontoon bridge and advances on the castle at Papów, recently captured by the enemy. The castle is equipped with stout walls and moats on all sides, and there seems little hope of storming it; yet the squires, grooms and drivers take the initiative and rush to the walls and set about undermining them. The entire army then takes to arms, positions its guns and starts an assault, which is so effective that the defenders are unable even to man the walls and, finally, beg for mercy. With the King's permission, the commander enters the castle by a secondary gate, breaks down the main gate and leads the garrison out, thus preventing his angry troops from killing them, much to the latter's indignation. The troops are further angered, when the nobles send in their servants to occupy closets and storerooms, thus denying these to the ordinary troops when they come to loot the captured castle. Indeed, some are so indignant that they hurl lighted torches into the castle, setting it on fire and burning not only the provisions there, but also those trying to keep them for themselves. The walls are then razed to the ground.

The army now advances on Chełm, which is rambling and defended neither by its position nor by man-made defences and so considered easy to capture, but the King leaves it alone and continues to the River Ossa, which he crosses and so reaches Łasin, which he could have taken at the first assault, but, afraid of casualties, he forbids it to be attacked, to the considerable anger of his troops. The army now advances on Malbork; but suddenly news comes that the enemy has left Chełm and is heading for Sztum. The King fails to give any orders and the impatient troops take matters into their own hands and set off in pursuit. The enemy has plenty of time to get away, but gets lost during the night and in the morning all but bumps into the King's army. To mitigate the danger, the Knights' Commander orders his men to disperse and seek their own safety. As a result many are killed and many taken prisoner.

Casimir now lays siege to Malbork, the capture of which many expect to be quick and easy. Reinforcements arrive from Gdańsk and Elbląg bringing cannon, cannon-balls and other equipment necessary for capturing towns. Guns are brought from the castle and the walls and towers of the town bombarded. Meanwhile, Giskra is having talks with the Master and this induces the King to hold his hand, so that no positive action is taken for several weeks. When nothing comes of the talks, the King has the town ringed with towers, shelters and fences; then, leaving the troops from Gdańsk and Elbląg to continue the siege, he moves his huge army inland, ravaging and accepting the surrender of other towns. News now comes of how, when the mercenaries got to Nowe, which the Order had occupied and which they were sent to capture, they were told that the garrison was holding the castle for the King and thus that their presence was unnecessary. The mercenaries have now exhausted what provisions the countryside can supply and there is no pasture left. In the King's own camp, more and more horses are dying. The men throng round the King's tent begging him not to allow procrastination to destroy so excellent an army. The troops are ready to attack Malbork town and beg the King not to allow the summer and fine weather to be wasted. Even the King's commanders are divided: some wish to attack, others to avoid bloodshed. All this encourages the besieged, who can see how sentries are not being set and how even the guards on the guns sometimes wander away. On one occasion the impatient troops mount their own attack, but the King orders an immediate withdrawal. The Governor of Prussia, an energetic and clever man, keeps reminding the King that it costs 100,000 florins to maintain an army of the present size in the field and that he should not allow so much to be wasted. However, all such good advice is received with contempt.

The length of the siege and the ban on any assault are making the troops suspicious, and when people are found visiting the besieged and these tell who sent them and why, these suspicions are strengthened. In the King's camp they hear people shouting from the walls that they have bought off an assault. Again the troops draw the King's attention to their plight and that of their horses, not always mincing their words and insisting that they prefer to die fighting than to starve or die of disease. This results in a decision to attack, which is cancelled the very next day, destroying the men's spirits. In this way nine weeks are wasted, during which almost the whole of Chełm is being ravaged by the four hundred Tatars fighting with the King. Eventually, Jan Giskra negotiates a truce to last until St. Margaret's Day, the conditions being that until that date Malbork is to be handed over to Jan Giskra and, in the meantime, seventeen arbitrators chosen by both sides are to meet in Chełm to put an end to the war. Should their decision not be unanimous, Albert, Duke of Austria, is to have the casting vote, or should he refuse to act, Jan Giskra will do so. The King decides to stay where he is until he receives written confirmation of the agreement; but the army, angered by being deprived of the opportunity to loot Malbork and unable any longer to endure the hunger to which they and their horses are being subjected, strike camp and, after burning all that they cannot take with them, march away. Now, as well as hunger, they have to endure the winter's rain. The King is advised to take up residence in Malbork castle, but the people of Gdańsk, having had considerable success at sea during the summmer against pirates and other enemies, promise to provide enough to pay for 4000 mercenaries, so the King, who longs for Poland, his wife and children, is enabled to go home.

The departure of the army without waiting for orders makes King Casimir swear that never again will he go to war with such undisciplined troops; while the men in their turn swear that never again will they go to war under the King's command without being paid. No previous war has involved such losses: 700 dead of starvation and disease; 7000 horses dead of starvation. Those whom they were besieging claim that even pigs could have forced their defences, which the Poles never even tested. Many of Poland's neighbours mockingly say that the Poles prefer to endure a war rather than to wage it.

The returning army makes but slow progress, for its draught animals are so starved that they can scarcely walk. It crosses the river at Toruń by the pontoon bridge and is there disbanded, each man returning to his home. The King reaches Cracow on the Sunday before All Saints, just in time to see the Bishop of Cracow baptize his second son, born in the red dawn of October 3. He is christened Casimir. The King then attends to various matters, in particular seeing to the payment of what he had promised to the 11,000 mercenaries who all the previous year had caused such trouble throughout the country.

During the King's absence a small assembly has been discussing ways of ensuring that Poland's knights are not exhausted by frequent spells of military service and by the support they have to provide out of their own resources. At the same time envoys come from George Poděbrady King of Bohemia to explain that their King is aware that on László's death the crown of Bohemia should, by right, have passed to King Casimir and his descendants, and that he intends to see that on his death it shall pass to them and accordingly he has ordered that none of his sons should occupy the throne of Bohemia after him, and that these latter have indeed renounced their right to it. King George is well aware that he is not of royal blood and does not pretend that he is. If he allowed himself to be crowned, he did so in good faith and in reponse to the wishes of the Czechs. He asks that King Casimir live in friendship with him and they be allies rather than enemies. He is prepared to go in person to Prussia with an army and endeavour to ensure that King Casimir enjoys peaceful possession of the whole territory once the Order has relinquished it. Also he will punish lawless Silesia, so that the King suffers no hurt from that quarter.

Hungary is torn by civil strife instigated by the many Poles and Czechs who have settled there in recent years. In this, victory is mainly with the Hungarians. Some 6000 fine young Poles die of their wounds, a splendid death, one would say, had they fallen for their country. King George Poděbrady harasses Austria, from which Duke Albert shamefully flees after suffering two defeats, after which King George, with Polish reinforcements, goes on to put the country to fire and the sword. But then, on St. Martin's Day, the Czech Marshal, Henry, and his 1600 men are routed by the Austrians, who, then pluck up courage and turn the tables on the Czechs and Moravians, burning Olomouc, Brno and other towns. The Czechs were never as strong as they were reputed to be; indeed, it is known—shameful to write it!—that, when he fought the Austrians King George had no more than 2000 cavalry and 7000 foot, some of them mercenaries.

A.D. 1459

King Casimir spends Christmas with his family in Sandomierz and then goes to Piotrków for an assembly, which spends a fortnight discussing ways and means of ending the war with Prussia either by agreement or by military action. One great difficulty is that the nobles are refusing to support their King either financially or in person because of the wretched way in which the previous year's campaign was conducted. Five emissaries from Prussia arrive with the news that the Master has been writing to all the German countries telling them that the decision of the arbitrators is certain to give him back all the territory he had before the war began; also, that he will be left with not only the original territory of Prussia, but also with everything round it, and lands and kingdoms as far afield as Syria and the Holy Land. Such rumours embolden the German dukes and princes, who have come to regard the Order's cause as lost. However, at an assembly in Elbląg, the people confirm their allegiance to King Casimir and agree that they would risk anything rather than again be subject to the Order, and they beg the King not to allow the arbitrators in the dispute to remove them from his authority.

Some of the King's councillors consider that the Master's offer of 100,000 florins and an annual tribute of 20,000 florins, plus the services of two squadrons in any war the King might wage in return for the lands he, the Master, held before the war and for which he is to pay homage, are more to the advantage of Poland, than if the King had to adminster these territories himself. Nonetheless, in view of the Knights' cruel treatment of the people of Chocen and Kinsberg, it is felt that to accept these terms would be disastrous for the inhabitants of Prussia. Also, it looks as if the King would never have another opportunity of recovering these lost territories, were he to neglect this one. There is as yet no crisis: the country is not without men, weapons, horses or money for provisions. Should it ever come to that, the Prussians will have to be told that they must fend for themselves; but they cannot now be abandoned like cattle. So, it is agreed that they will appoint people to represent the King at the forthcoming arbitration and instruct them how best to present Poland's case. Business concluded, the King goes to Lithuania, where the Queen already is, and there spends the winter and spring.

The Polish contingent arrives early for the adjudication of the dispute with the Knights, whose representatives are delayed in reaching Chełm by a sudden thaw that floods all the rivers, making them impossible to cross except by boat. Earlier the King had suggested to the Master that for greater security and because of the amount to be discussed, the Order's delegates should go to Nieszawa, but the Master refuses to change the venue; so for three weeks nothing happens, except that the Poles keep sending to Chełm asking the others to come to Nieszawa or Bydgoszcz. When the Order's representatives continue to refuse, the Poles agree to go to Chełm, if they can be guaranteed complete immunity. The document sent to them guaranteeing immunity contains so many

George Poděbrady, self-elected King of Bohemia.
From Alexander Guaginus: Sarmatiae Europeae descriptio—*Jagiellonian University Library.*

mistakes and omissions, that the Poles send it back asking for a better guarantee. Confident of obtaining this, they all, except for Canon Długosz, set out for Chełm by boat. They spend the night in
Solec, where, in the morning, a messenger brings them the news that the Master is refusing to provide another document or give further assurances, so they return to Nieszawa and Toruń.

On the Friday after Easter, in the city hall in Toruń, Bishop Thomas of Cracow in a portentous
speech pronounces his judgment: the King was justified in what he did. After detailing the arguments put forward by the Knights, the agreements made, the laws of God, Nature and Man, the
Bishop dismisses the Knights' case and clearly demonstrates that the King was justified in starting
and continuing the war with the Knights, and states that he, a bishop and Master of Law, already
advanced in years, will die in that conviction. His speech heartens the people of Prussia and helps
those undecided to make up their minds; but, this being an unilateral decision, final judgment is referred to the chief arbitrator, Albert of Austria, who accepts the task at the insistence of the Polish
envoys, the Master and the German princes.

In Hungary, a few nobles, rejecting Matthias, elect Frederick, Duke of Austria, as their king,
and his acceptance of the crown involves the whole of Hungary in a fresh and bitter civil war,
largely because Frederick is dilatory in taking steps to implement his acceptance. Each side assembles an army and when these finally engage, the fighting is cruel and stubborn. In the end, Frederick's troops prevail and the Hungarians are wiped out. Matthias discards his royal garments so as to
avoid recognition, and escapes to Buda. There, he decides to relinquish his right to the throne and
asks the Emperor to allow him to remain in his fatherland as a private person, enjoying his father's

property and castles. However, his uncle, Michael Szilágyi, and other friends persuade him to change his mind, so envoys are sent to Vienna who negotiate a treaty of everlasting peace according to which the Emperor is to retain the title of King of Hungary for himself and his successors, though returning the actual crown; while Matthias is granted administration of the Kingdom of Hungary for his lifetime, though the Emperor is to succeed him, even should Matthias have a child. The Emperor then accepts Matthias as his son and Matthias is crowned in Székesfehérvár. Thus, contrary to expectations, Matthias acquires Hungary, despite the sons of Casimir of Poland being its rightful heirs.

Casimir reaches Radom, where his mother already is, on the eve of Corpus Christi and, together, they go to Wielkopolska for an assembly to discuss the war with the Knights. This assembly decides to renew the campaign, using troops which Wielkopolska will provide and equip to the best of its ability. The people of Cracow, however, refuse to take part until the country is in better shape and ask for a further assembly to be held in Piotrków. This the King refuses, and after further meetings it is agreed that whoever has an income of 100 marks is to send three-score men and all towns and royal manors whatever infantry they can. Thus is an army assembled, which, when the truce expires on St. Margaret's Day, is sent to Prussia, where it achieves nothing of note, though it does prevent the enemy harassing the King's subjects. The King's men in the castles and towns deeper in Prussia obtain considerable victories over the Prussian Master, who almost lets himself be captured. Two hundred Knights are taken prisoner and as many, or more, killed. The amount of loot is such that every soldier receives twenty złoty.

Lubowla, which belongs to the King, goes over to the Order so as to avoid destruction of its crops. Meanwhile the King is having frequent discussions with the Order about peace or a truce, and even sends two officials to Malbork, but these return with the arrogant reply that the matter is now one for the mercenaries. The King also demands the return of a number of merchant ships carrying corn and timber to Gdańsk, which had been seized during the truce by the Commander of Gniew, but is told that Fritz, the Commander, would never obey the order, should he be told to surrender the ships. Thus was more damage inflicted by the enemy during the truce than during hostilities.

While the King is in Łęczyca, officials from Wrocław, who are also acting for Namysłów, come with the request that, since the death of the King of Hungary and Bohemia they belong to neither kingdom and cannot accept the heretic George Poděbrady, who is illegally occupying the throne, Casimir, as their sovereign, should come in person, or send a deputy, and take possession of the two towns and rule them. They are told that the King is so involved in war with Prussia that he cannot accept their offer, and that they must go back and look after their towns as best they can.

When the time comes for the next assembly in Piotrków, the delegates from Cracow halt some distance away and refuse to enter the town without the King's assurance of their immunity, for the King has ordered the members of his Court, more numerous now than usual, to arm themselves, for there are rumours of an attempt being made to remove him. The Cracovians are themselves armed, so both sides feel that they are meeting not as brothers and friends, but rather as strangers or enemies. At the assembly, the Starosta of Sandomierz, speaking for the entire kingdom, demands reforms and a stabilized economy. He complains that two nobles of Chełm have been beaten, imprisoned and robbed by their starosta, that the King seems to regard Poles as his enemies; that he has detached the territories of Łuck and many villages near Brześć and attached them to Lithuania; and that he is now trying to detach Podole from the Kingdom and give it to Lithuania, as he has parts of Mazovia; that he has brought the Lithuanians to the point of not wanting to take up arms against their common enemy, the Knights, nor to obey the King's orders; that the minting of light-weight coin is ruining the economy; that he allows brigands and robbers to flourish as well as counterfeiters; that he is consuming the royal revenues to no purpose; that taxes and quartering are exhausting the kingdom and emptying villages and even towns; that the complaints of widows and orphans go unheeded; that he is denuding Poland of its horses, its gold and its silver. The starosta reminds the King that it was thanks to the kindness of the Poles that his father, duke of a small part of Lithuania, became king of Poland and Lithuania and a Christian, and that it was thanks to the assistance of the Poles that his father was able to give Lithuania lands appropriated by the Knights, and that, when his father died, the Poles exalted his brother, Władysław, to the throne of both Poland and Hungary; and, when Władysław died, honoured Casimir with a splendid marriage. Because of all this, they are profoundly grieved that he puts the Lithuanians, who have done nothing for him, not even been faithful, before the Poles, whom he is now oppressing and whose country he is weakening to the point of destruction. Now, he says, they are demanding the return of Łuck, the villages of Parczów and that part of Podole that had been illegally detached; demanding that the minting of light-weight coin cease and that they be relieved of quartering and other impositions; that he remember that he is King of Poland and thus their father, not their step-father. If he does all this, they will obey his orders and give him their all, should that be necessary; but, if not, he can be sure that they will give him nothing of their private possessions and will not fight for him unless they are paid. The King tries to exonerate himself, telling them that Łuck and the other places were not taken by him, but by the Lithuanians, an excuse the Poles counter by pointing out that he is also Grand-duke of Lithuania and thus responsible for these having been taken, for had he not been the King of Poland, the Lithuanians would never have dared seize them. The King then tells them that the minting of light-weight coin was done with the consent of his councillors, and has now been stopped; that he makes no greater use of quartering nor extracts more taxes than his father did, that he loves the Poles as much as he does the Lithuanians, and gives justice to everyone who asks for it; he does care for the defence of the kingdom, he tells them, but as the treasury is empty and in debt, he cannot do so properly; let them see that he receives his possessions and he will see to the needs of the kingdom. The main business after this is the question of Prussia, for the Prussian estates are pressing for help. Some of the mercenaries have now been paid part of what they were promised, but to complete payment an impost of six grosses on every field will have to be levied. The Cracovians will not agree to this, but demand further discussion in Korczyn. The bishops now tell them that they all ought to make a small contribution towards the Pope's endeavours to recover Constantinople.

The Master has been trying to induce the Prussian town of Passenheim to expel the King's starosta and his garrison and surrender the town to the Knights. About St. Michael's Day, with the connivance of the starosta, the townspeople let the Master know that they are ready to surrender; but when, on the day agreed, the Master's men arrive to take possession of the town, only some of them are admitted, the others being told to wait outside. The gates are then shut and the Master's men killed if they try to resist, taken prisoner, stripped of their armour and deprived of their horses.

When George Poděbrady and his army arrive in Silesia, which is a breach of the agreement, he is welcomed by all the dukes, except the Duke of Żagan. The only town to refuse to admit him is Wrocław, which dislikes the idea of being ruled by a man tainted with the Wycliffean heresy. Poděbrady plunders and burns many of the towns, manors and villages belonging to Wrocław, installs garrisons in a number of places and returns to Bohemia. These garrisons have the support of the Czech army and the Silesian dukes, and these make various attempts to capture Wrocław, which repulses every attack. The Czechs then assault the monastery of St. Vincent, which is near Wrocław and is a good base for attacking it. The people of Wrocław prepare a number of ambushes and then sally out to attack the Czechs. As battle is engaged, the people of Wrocław emerge from their hiding-places, attack the Czechs in the rear and the flanks and have no difficulty in routing them. The Czechs then return to Bohemia. The people of Wrocław refuse to conclude a truce with their neighbours, the Silesian dukes, on the grounds that they are not to be trusted; but, in the end, the persistence of the dukes compels them to do so. Now, two papal legates arrive, sent to persuade the people of Wrocław that George Poděbrady is obedient to the Pope and is intending to unite Bohemia and discard the false doctrine, so they should show him obedience as a king at one with the Catholic Church. The townspeople of Wrocław, eager for peace, agree on condition that their rebellion is not held against them, that they should not have a governor of whom they may not have approved imposed on them, and that, after a truce of three years, they will give Poděbrady their obedience, should he have shown himself a loyal Catholic.

The assembly in Piotrków agrees to help the Prussian campaign, in which the King's forces have had more than usual success, and for this a levy is to be imposed on all merchants and all who trade for profit, but for one year only, and a farthing paid for every field under cultivation, while the laity and clergy promise an eighth part of their income to pay the troops. This so encourages those fighting in Prussia, that they volunteer to extend the time for repayment of back pay and promise to fight more doughtily in the future.

Jacob of Sienna, archdeacon of Gniezno and canon of Cracow, has been sent to Mantua to attend the Pope's council about declaring war on the Turks and recovering Constantinople. Once there, he asks the Pope to absolve the knights and gentry of Prussia from obedience to the Master and the Order as he, the Pope, had previously commanded. He strongly advocates that the Order should be removed from Prussia, so as not to involve the neighbouring Catholic kings in strife, and transferred to the island of Tenedos, where they can engage in battle with the barbarians as their Rule dictates. Most of the kings and dukes support the proposal, but the Pope will not agree. A representative of the Order is there in full uniform, and he, in a speech prompted, as many think, by the Pope, castigates King Casimir for laying claim to Prussia to the detriment of the Pope and the Catholic Church.

A.D. 1460

For the last couple of years the King has been urged to conclude an alliance with George Poděbrady, but has procrastinated. Now, the Czech Duke Przemyśl arranges for the two to meet in Bytom; but, of course, terms have first to be agreed. For this the King appoints a commission of three, who are to confer with Jan Zajíc chief burgrave of Prague and Poděbrady's brother-in-law. The chief difficulty to be disposed of is that of Queen Elizabeth's right to the crown of Bohemia, which she has inherited from her grandfather, father and brothers. A proposal to annul this is rejected, the Czechs contesting that no woman, nor man, can inherit their kingdom. The Czechs now propose another, short conference at which the two kings may meet in person and conclude an alliance. The Polish trio insists that it is too early for a personal meeting, since they must first establish the exact terms of alliance, especially the question of compensation for the damage done to Poland by the Silesian dukes. Eventually, it is agreed that representatives of both sides should meet in Bytom on St. John the Baptist's Day to agree terms and a venue for the meeting.

On the Saturday in Transfiguration Week a delegation from Archduke Albert arrives in Cracow and is received in audience. After reminding the King of all the good turns the Archduke has done the Poles, the delegates suggest that the Archduke is the one best fitted to undertake the trouble, cost and effort required to establish peace between Casimir and the Knights. The King can rest assured that he is entrusting his cause to a true friend, whose decision will bring him benefit rather than harm. In replying, Casimir reminds the Austrians that a similar arrangement made by his father and the King of Hungary led to dreadful wars and much bloodshed, and caused such hatred of each other that the two kings never ceased attacking and denigrating each other. Because of this, the King fears lest his best friend be turned into his mortal enemy in the event of an unfair judgment depriving the King of territory which he has inherited. He goes on to say that he has resolved to make the Archduke arbitrator with restricted authority in the dispute, and that, in the middle of

Lent or at some more suitable time, he should come to Wrocław and, after hearing both sides, try to reconcile them. The envoys then return to Austria, each with a sable and marten cloak. No sooner have they departed, than an envoy arrives from Duke Ludwig of Bavaria, a close relation of Queen Elizabeth, with a proposal that Duke Ludwig mediate between the King and the Knights and asking for an alliance with the King. The latter request is granted and the Duke told that his offer of mediation would have been accepted had the King not already entrusted the task to Archduke Albert. At this time, too, a request for safe-conducts comes from three papal legates, who have been given the task of persuading the King to end the war in Prussia. The King refuses the request, for one of the three is a Venetian merchant recently turned priest and a man of ill repute, another a Spaniard and a long-time supporter of the Knights. However, out of consideration for the Pope, the legates are told that the Archduke has already undertaken the task, while King Casimir is intending to go to the remoter parts of Ruthenia to investigate the state of the country and the Catholic Church there. Before leaving, the King learns that the castle and town of Wałcz have been captured by the Knights. He at once orders the knights of Wielkopolska to recover it; but they, unable to storm it, fail even to lay siege to it.

Criss-crossing Ruthenia the King eventually reaches Brześć and there stays for a week conferring with eminent Lithuanians and trying to counter a dangerous tendency among them to think that the time has come to declare war on Poland and so, perhaps, recover Podole. The King then continues on to Sandomierz, where he receives news that George Poděbrady has declared war on Poland, because after certain Czech towns had been burned and the culprits caught, the latter pretended that they had been acting on the orders of the King and Queen Elizabeth. Undeterred, the King prepares to declare war on the Prussians and also to resist the Czechs. The Poles are becoming increasingly indignant at such blatant, slanderous attacks on their King and Queen, and feel that, with God's Grace, they can easily defeat the Czechs. Messages are sent to the Tatar Khan and to the ruler of the Walachi, asking for their help should Poland have to go to war with the Czechs. It is thought that the burning of the Czech towns was the work of the Knights so desperate are they to ease the Poles' pressure on them. The King spends the next three weeks in Łęczyca discussing the possibility of sending an army into Prussia and of laying siege to Wałcz on the border with Saxony. From here, too, he sends two knights to Bohemia to clear him and the Queen of the false accusation of responsibility for burning the Czech towns, although some people think it wrong to react to such a trumped-up charge. The two tell George Poděbrady that King Casimir has enough swords, armour and military equipment to deal with his enemies openly without having recourse to subterfuge. If anyone dares to doubt them, the two are ready to duel and demonstrate the innocence of their King and Queen. Poděbrady tells them that he never believed the story. The Czech nobles all say the same and the two Poles are sent home laden with gifts, but not before they have arranged for the councillors of both sides to meet on St. Martin's Day, apologizing for the misunderstanding that prevented the Poles attending the previous conference.

Malbork has now been under siege for almost four months. The besieged could easily continue as they are, but they are so afraid of the enemy gaining access through subterranean saps, which are being rapidly extended, that they surrender the castle to the Voivode of Włocławek and the Starosta of Malbork, not knowing that the Master is on his way from Moravia with a force of Czechs and Germans estimated at 3000. When this reaches Frankfurt on the Oder, the assembly point of Poland's enemies, for the Margarve is jealous of the Poles' successes, and they learn of Malbork's surrender, the troops all turn back, except for 500, whom the Master with difficulty retains. Meanwhile, the King's troops are besieging the town and castle of Wałcz; but, when it is rumoured that the Master is coming with an army, the Polish commander raises the siege and withdraws to a place where he can best engage the enemy. Cunningly keeping to side roads and covering twelve miles in a day and a night, the Master outwits the Poles and reaches Chojnice, having lost only 100 horses. Those inside Wałcz now abandon the castle and, having set fire to it, try to link up with the Master. As they move by night, the Poles fail to catch up with them and there is no battle. The Master now moves his enlarged army towards Gdańsk. He ambushes the garrison of a fort a mile from Gdańsk, killing sixty of them and taking 200 prisoner. This raises the enemy's spirits and gives the people of Gdańsk reason for criticising the King. Not only this, but the strong town of Golub is treacherously surrendered and a number of nobles from Dobrzyń captured in it with all their belongings. However, the castle above the town, held for the King, is reinforced and provisions sent in. The situation in Prussia is now very uncertain. Dobrzyń is paying tribute to the enemy; and for no reason whatever the Duke of Szczecin, a near relative of the King, breaks faith and surrenders two of the towns entrusted to his stewardship, Lemberg and Bytów, to the enemy. A third town, Puczkow, which the King of Sweden holds against money lent to King Casimir, is also taken over. Bielawa and Bartelstein go the same way. Kwidzyn is looted and burned. The city of Warmińsk is plundered and burned by mercenaries from both sides, the loot being enough to give each man 200 florins. Some of the King's men in Paradyż monastery defeat the enemy in two major engagements. On St. Martin's Day, the upper fort at Świecie is captured by a hundred of the enemy, who are hauled up the wall in fishing nets by a Prussian inside; but, alerted to the situation, knights from Kujawy and Bydgoszcz, and some men from Gdańsk, come down from Toruń by boat, surround the upper fort and recapture it.

On St. Catherine's Day, a Polish delegation, including Jan Długosz, canon of Cracow, meets emissaries of King George in Bytom. After six days of talks an alliance is arranged, the terms are that the two kings are to maintain a pure and lasting friendship, neither harming the other personally or by the use of arms, nor going to the help of any cleric or lay person, other than the Pope, and that at the end of one year, at the latest on the first of May, the two kings will meet in Głogów and personally confirm the alliance.

King Matthias, who has captured many of the castles and fortresses in the hands of Jan Giskra, or held in his name, yields to pressure from King George and withdraws from two castles he is besieging, and makes a pact with the latter in which he undertakes to go to Trenczyn on the Feast of the Circumcision and pronounce his final verdict in the dispute between him and Giskra. The fact that in the mean time the Turks have invaded Hungary, makes Matthias more ready to agree.

Boleslaw, Duke of Opole, dies on May 29. An evil-doer who robbed God's churches of their temporal goods, and a tyrant, he died without confession, which he had neglected for many years, and without any viaticum. He left no progeny, for he had discarded his legal wife, Elizabeth. with whom he had one son, who died prematurely, and thereafter lived with his concubine, Jadwiga. He was buried in the collegiate church in Głogów, from which he had ejected the canons and appropriated their possessions. He is succeeded by his brother, Nicholas, a simple, honest man, who is at once attacked by the former Duke of Oświęcim, who pretends that the succession is his through his grandmother. It takes 1000 florins, which Nicholas has to pay, to pacify him. Another claimant is the King of Bohemia, who invokes feudal law, but abandons his claim in return for half Opava and its villages, which Bolesław had bought for 40,000 florins, the town of Ziegenholz and the gift of several golden goblets.

A.D. 1461

After Christmas, a severe frost having made it possible to cross the Vistula on foot, the King moves his court and army to Brześć Kujawy in order to defend it against hostile raids. Angered by the Pope's appointment of Jacob of Siena as Bishop of Cracow in preference to his own candidate, the Bishop of Włocławek, the King banishes Jacob, his friends, relatives and supporters and confiscates all their property. He, then, goes to Radom, where his wife and mother are, and thence to

Lithuania and Ruthenia. Everywhere, he is begged to reside permanently in Lithuania, or else to make the Duke of Kiev the Grand-duke. He refuses to commit himself,and returns to Poland, where the struggle over the appointment of a new bishop for Cracow continues, the King sending emissaries to ask the Pope to cancel the appointment of Jacob and appoint the Bishop of Włocławek instead. The emissaries have instructions to continue on to the Emperor in Vienna and request his support.

At the end of June the King goes to Włocławek to await the troops for his campaign in Prussia; but these do not arrive until the Feast of the Assumption, by which time three castles are being besieged by the Knights and begging for help. They are told to be of good cheer, for the King is coming to help them any day, but for the besieged that is not good enough, and one garrison, in despair, sallies out prepared to conquer or die, and actually defeats its besiegers and captures their entire camp. However, a larger enemy force arrives and the siege is quickly renewed.

While the King is in Włocławek, there is an unfortunate episode in Cracow, one that is to poison relations between the city and its knights for years to come. On July 16, Andrew of Tęczyn angrily rebukes the armourer Clement for failing to deliver a suit of armour on time and for not making it fit; and, when the armourer makes a vigorous reply, strikes him, but only lightly. The armourer goes to the town hall and complains that he has been grievously assaulted, and, on the way back from lodging his complaint, he is accosted by Tęczyn, whom he berates for hitting him and, brandishing his fist, threatens to repay the blow with interest; he was, of course, angry, and he may have been hoping for compensation; but, as a result, Tęczyn and his servants fall upon him and beat him. When they learn of this, the City Fathers are indignant and more angry than is justified; indeed, they seem to have been more inclined to inflame the quarrel between the artisans and the nobility than to compose it; for they close the city's gates and report the incident to the young Queen. She demands sureties of 8000 marks and enjoins both parties to keep the peace and await her judgment, which she will give in the morning, for it is already late in the day, indeed, ten o'clock. The City Fathers return to the town hall and order all householders to arm themselves and assemble there. Meanwhile, the Queen and his friends are advising Tęczyn to leave the city and go to the castle. To Tęczyn this smacks of cowardice and, with his brothers and friends, he shuts himself up in a house in Bracka Street intending to resist any attack. Then a bell in the Mariacki Church starts pealing—on whose order no one knows—and this proves the signal for a riot, which the City Fathers could have quelled with a little common sense and exercise of their authority. Everyone stops work and a crowd, not only angry, but tipsy, presses round the house, intending to kill Tęczyn, who, seeing that the house cannot withstand such an attack, escapes with three companions and some of his servants to the monastery of St. Frederick and takes refuge in its tower. Then, convinced that he is not safe even there, though his companions try to restrain him, he leaves the tower and hides in the sacristy. The rioters break down the monastery door and, after a long search, find Tęczyn and split his head open. His corpse is dragged through the streets' open sewer to the town hall and kept there for two days, riddled with stab wounds and with the hair singed off its face. It is then moved to the Church of St. Wojciech and finally handed over to the victim's friends and relatives. Tęczyn's friends in the tower are besieged there all the following day and night, after which they are released. Because of this, the knights of Cracow and Sandomierz at first refuse to take part in the Prussian campaign, but, when the King promises that Tęczyn's death shall be avenged, they agree to take part.

On August 5, the young Queen gives birth to a fourth son. In view of the recent disturbances and the absence of the King, the christening is a simple, modest affair.

Several of the enemy's forts and towns have been captured, while the King's forces are slowly assembling in Włocławek; but the enemy would have lost considerably more had the King's troops destroyed the pasture and corn, only there were not enough of them to do this, for many were ill and others remained at home. The King cannot decide where to fight: some advise him to advance into the remoter parts of Prussia and, after devastating Sambia, relieve the three towns under siege. This is good advice, but he does not take it. Instead, he heads for Pomerania, but does not go through Toruń whose citizens have prepared a bridge of boats to enable his army to cross. On the advice of some, who are alleged to have been bribed by the Knights, he makes for Friedland and Chojnice, where the towns have no garrisons and so are more likely to surrender, after which he can continue to Szczecin to avenge the infidelity and defection of Duke Eric. All the King's Prussian supporters consider such a move disastrous. It certainly encourages the enemy besieging the three towns, who now jeer at the besieged, telling them that they have made sure with money, not arms, that their King will not come to save them. The wretched besieged feel that under their ill-starred King nothing will go right.

So, with a force of Poles, Lithuanians and Tatars, the King heads through western Pomerania. He avoids Nakło which, though it belongs to him, is paying the enemy an annual tribute estimated at 50,000 marks, and so reaches Friedland on August 5. After a siege of a week, he concludes a pact, whereby the besieged are granted immunity and allowed to march out with all their possessions, and the town is surrendered. The King installs a garrison and grants tenure to the Starosta of Nakło. He then sets out for Chojnice, but quite unnecessarily halts for a fortnight a quarter of a mile from the town and thereby incurs considerable losses, for many foragers, who go out without an escort, are killed or captured by the enemy. While there, some volunteers and a party of Tatars, having nothing to do, set about devastating the countryside; they even capture the fortress at Szczecin and other forts, and acquire considerable loot. As they are taking this back, they are attacked by some of Duke Eric's Saxons, many of whom they capture and hand over to the King, while the loot is sold. Frightened by this reverse, Duke Eric's wife, Sophia, goes to the King in his camp, admits that her husband has been guilty of a serious breach of faith, to which she was no party, and begs the King to have mercy on the Duke, herself and their children, and promises that in future she and her husband will be loyal and energetically help the King against the Knights. The Duchess is as pretty as she is eloquent, and shows humility. After much discussion, it is agreed that Duke Eric is to be forgiven. It is said that the King, seeing the cleverness and beauty of the Duchess, regretted not having chosen her when she was suggested as his bride; for, apart from her beauty, she would have brought him the large amount of gold which came to her on the death of her grandfather, King Eric of Romania, as well as the lands of Szczecin, themselves no mean dowry; yet he sets aside his regrets, remembering the love and modesty of his wife Elizabeth, mother of his five children.

The King's troops are justifiably angry at being kept so long before Chojnice in useless inactivity and complain that this is costing them more than it does the enemy. The King is a prey to anxiety and cannot make up his mind what to do, for autumn is approaching; indeed, in the last few days snow has fallen, as has rain, and there have been deaths from cold. In his heart of hearts he is ashamed of not having helped the three towns under siege. Now, he demands financial help from his knights, each of whom with an income of 100 marks or more is to contribute five marks and this most of them do, thus making it possible to send 2000 mercenaries under Peter Danin Chamberlain of Sandomierz to the other Pomerania. At this juncture, the knights of Wielkopolska mutiny against the Castellan of Poznań, whose appointment they consider illegal and whose harsh actions, they say, are motivated by greed. To stop the mutiny spreading, the King breaks camp and moves to Bydgoszcz and there disbands the army. He remains there for a few days, paying off the Tatars who have been six weeks in the field at considerable cost and have had nothing whatever to do. They are sent back to Lithuania.

Sophia, the Queen-mother, contracts a high fever after eating melons, but refuses medication on the grounds that Nature will effect its own cure, but then becomes paralyzed and on September 21 she dies.

A.D. 1462

After Christmas, which the King spends in Cracow, he yields to pressure from Tęczyn's son Jan and reopens the case against the City Fathers and citizens of Cracow. These claim that they are entitled to have the trial held in the city, not in the castle, and not before the King or under Polish law, but under Magdeburg law, but this is refused and they are tried and condemned to be fined and beheaded. Sentence is to be carried out on the following Saturday, but when the Castellan of Kalisz arrives to implement it, the assembled City Fathers and townspeople demand that sentence be carried out only on four of the Fathers and five of the artisans. Feelings are so high that this is accepted and the nine retained in the town hall and the next day taken to the castle and put in the dungeons. After five days there, they are given confession and taken to the Tęczyn mansion, where Jan Tęczyn swears to their guilt; then, to avoid a disturbance, they are taken back to the castle and executed. They are buried in one grave.

Perturbed by repeated reports of danger threatening Brodnica castle, and troubled by the mercenaries' demands for overdue pay, the King leaves Cracow earlier than planned. Matters have now come to a head in Prussia and this has brought the Voivodes of Chełmno territory and two officials from Gdańsk, representing the gentry and townspeople of Prussia, begging the King to deal with the situation and, in particular, to end the siege of Brodnica, the loss of which would be highly damaging. They ask that he bring a considerable force to Malbork and stay there. If he will do this, they are prepared to hand over half their income from tonnage and other revenue, even from their own property, in order to pay for mercenaries. The King feels that he must discuss this question of Prussia with the King of Bohemia, so sends two envoys, who arrange for the two to meet in Głogów on May 15. Casimir is prepared to do whatever the other might want, as long as he will promise to acknowledge Casimir's title by right of inheritance to Chełm, Pomerania and Michałów. So, on February 10, he leaves Cracow with the Queen, to whom he has handed over, as her endowment, all the castles, towns, properties and villages which had constituted Queen Sophia's dowry, but, after deducting her previous endowment, which amounted to a considerable sum. He has arranged, too, for his first-born son, Władysław, to be taught to ride, and has paid several thousand florins to his knights and mercenaries. Now, he moves in four stages to Łęczyca, where he reinforces Peter Danin's army with many from his own household, some recently arrived mercenaries and the troops under the Voivode of Brześć; yet, still considering the army not strong enough to deal with the enemy, he pulls his forces back. The news of this so discourages the garrison in Brodnica that, though not yet in an extremity, they make a pact with the enemy that saves their lives and possessions, but betrays, rather than surrenders, Brodnica. Had the King not been so lax and hesitant, but had acted in good time and relieved the castle, he would have defeated the enemy almost without a fight. As it is, the advantage has now passed to the Order, who rejoice, as if this were the end of the war.

The early death, on February 6, of the young Mazovian duke of Płock, due, some say, to poison, like that of his father, gives rise to considerable squabbling over who is to inherit Płock and Bełz, for there are five claimants to the two: first King Casimir, who claims them under feudal law; second, the five sons of the late Mazovian duke of Warsaw, who are of the dead duke's family, though of the fourth generation; third, Katerina, stepmother of the late duke and widow of Duke Michael of Lithuania; fourth, the two Bohemian princes, sons of the second stepmother, Ofka, and, last, Margaret, wife of Duke Conrad of Oleśnica and only daughter of Siemowit of Mazovia and cousin of the dead duke, who claims them by right of succession. At the request of the King's envoys, the knights of Bełz take an oath that the lands of Bełz came to the Mazovian dukes not by right of succession, but as the grant of Władysław II, King of Poland, by reason of which they surrender them to King Casimir, who grants tenure to Jan Lissinowski, who had till then been the starosta.

The wishes of the people of Płock are quite different. They are considerably under the influence of their bishop, who is no friend of King Casimir and eager for the duchy to continue under the same family; and so accept first, the widow of Duke Michael, but, as she seems unable to guarantee that she will have progeny, they pay her off and, instead, summon Conrad, Duke of Warsaw, the oldest of the five brothers, and give him the castle and lands of Płock, except for Rawa and Gostynin, which insist on remaining neutral until it has been legally established, who is the rightful successor to the duchy. Then the Duchess Katerina comes to Rawa with some nobles and men-at-arms and tries to capture the castle, but fails, and, having suffered a few casualties, returns to Płock. Then, on May 1, King Casimir arrives in Łowicz, from where he gets in touch with the people of Płock and demands the surrender of the duchy's castles and forts, to which they agree, since no one appears to have a better title. A meeting is arranged for May 2 in Łęczyca, which is attended by the King and the widow of the Duke of Warsaw, but not by the Bishop of Płock or the Mazovian nobles. The King is asked to produce the documents that prove his right of succession, but in the absence of so many who ought to have been there, he refuses and postpones the meeting until St. Martin's Day, in Piotrków.

On April 27, fire breaks out in Cracow in the monastery of the Dominicans, some of whom are dabbling in alchemy. The flames quickly reach the roof of the church and so spread to the neighbouring streets. There is no containing the fire and by two in the morning the monastery and the Church of St. Francis, the court of the Bishop and seven streets have all gone up in flames; thus is almost half of the city destroyed. The repairs cost 200,000 florins.

The King's emissaries return with the King of Bohemia's full agreement to compromise over Prussia. The King leaves Łęczyca with a large retinue and goes to Wschowa, where he finds a number of Czech dignitaries who have come to conduct him to Głogów. He leaves Wschowa on May 18, his men drawn up in six companies, in the last of which is the King, his prelates and nobles, all in wonderful armour and with splendid accoutrements. King George, his bishops and nobles come out a mile to meet the King of Poland. The two kings greet each other without dismounting; then they return to Głogów, where Casimir is lodged in the palace. The next two days are spent in talks; on the third day, King Casimir entertains his hosts to a magnificent banquet. and this is followed by a further week of talks resulting in a pact, which is to last until the death of either of the two kings. The conditions are the same as those laid down in Bytom, but with two additional clauses; namely, that if the Turks invade Poland the King of Bohemia will go to its assistance with all his forces; similarly, if the Turks invade Bohemia, the King of Poland will help the King of Bohemia with all his forces; secondly, that the King of Bohemia is not to harass King Casimir over Oświęcim, Walek, Zator, Żywiec, Szewior or Berwald, while, for the rest of his days King Casimir will not invoke the agreement made with Lászlo of Hungary and Bohemia, that, if the two kings meet, they will do so in a place within the Kingdom of Poland. No decision is taken about Prussia and the two kings part after presenting each other with gifts. During these discussions, an envoy arrives from the Duke of Bavaria requesting King Casimir to declare war on the Margrave of Brandenburg and promising to send his whole army to help the King against the Knights, should he do so.

The King now goes to Poznań and remains there for three weeks, during which time the Knights are laying the country waste as far as Paluki. When he leaves Poznań to go to Włocławek, he has his courtiers take a host of peasants armed with scythes into Chełm, where they cut all the corn, so as to deny it to the enemy.

At about this time, a thousand men accustomed to live by rapine arrive in Poland with their two leaders and pitch camp in Oświęcim country. They proceed to take over the town of Zar, which lies in a bend of the River Sola, fortify it and from there proceed to devastate the countryside, even though the Starosta of Cracow hires mercenaries to stop their activities spreading. In the end, the brigands are shut up in their fortress and starved into surrender. They have to abandon all their armour and equipment, and are granted only their lives and their clothing.

After spending some weeks in Kujawy, the King moves on to Toruń, where he spends the summer and autumn with the Queen who is staying in the castle at Nieszawa. He sends a force under Peter Danin Chamberlain of Sandomierz to relieve the castle of Warmińsk, which the Master is besieging, and to wreak havoc in Pomerania. About this time, the Master in nearby Chełm embarks some troops in boats and sends them towards Nieszawa to attack the King's forces there. The King, though warned of what is afoot, does not think it necessary to take precautions; thus, when the enemy craft reach Nieszawa at dusk as they had planned, they are able to disembark and spend the night in the only square open to the river. At dawn, they set fire to the houses and return to their boats. Once recovered from their initial fright, the King's troops in the fortress and a squadron of Tatars mount and set off in pursuit of the boats. The enemy is hoping that the width of the river will allow them to escape, but the current forces them over to the near bank, from which the King's men can kill most of them with their arrows. Only six escape in two boats with the wounded.

As the King's army approaches Warmińsk, the Prussian Master, fearing defeat, raises the siege and withdraws, abandoning a camp full of provisions and this the King's troops plunder. Meanwhile, an army from Gdańsk, acting without orders, invades Sambia, which, so far, has not been touched this year, the peasants all being away with the Master's troops, and carry off their herds of cattle. When news of this reaches the Master's troops, most of whom are peasants, they desert en masse to go to help their wives and children.

Having relieved Warmińsk, Peter Danin moves his army into Pomerania. Burning villages as he advances, he reaches the sea. The devastation he causes provokes an attack by the Knights, who have received reinforcements from Austria. Learning of this, Peter sends to the King for reinforcements, which he sends and which the Knights try to attack before the two can link up. However, they manage to avoid the Knights and get across the Vistula. The Knights then attack Peter's army. They engage on September 17, near the town of Pack. After more than three hours, the two sides are so exhausted that, as if by agreement, they stop fighting and withdraw to their waggons. After resting a while, they return to the fray or, rather, to pursue the enemy, for each thinks that the other has been defeated and is fleeing. The Poles capture 200 waggons, fifty cannon and all the Knights' armament. They then rest for three days, attending to the wounded and burying the dead, and there they are joined by the reinforcements the King has sent.

The assembly in Piotrków, held to determine to whom the vacant duchy of Płock should go, considers King Casimir's feudal right paramount, but, as the legality of this is in doubt, the matter is referred to the Holy See.

The King, who has sent Queen Elizabeth ahead of him to Radom, is preparing to leave Piotrków, when the papal legate, whose arrival has been expected for over a year, at last makes an appearance. His mission is to settle ecclesiastical disputes in Cracow and to put an end to the Prussian war. He has spent over a year in Pannonia trying to bring about peace between the Emperor Frederick, the King of Hungary and Jan Giskra, and it is this which has prevented him reaching Poland. King Casimir receives him somewhat impatiently. The legate reminds the King that his mission is threefold: to restore peace to the Church in Cracow, to stop the war in Prussia, and to persuade the King to declare war on the Turks. After some discussion it is decided to postpone all decisions until January 17, and the King leaves Piotrków together with the Archbishop of Gniezno and the Bishop of Włocławek and goes to the camps in Rowa.

When the Emperor asks the Viennese for six thousand florins with which to pay for mercenaries to defend the city and the country, four of the city councillors are sent to protest and are put in prison. Vienna revolts and besieges the Emperor in the castle, but welcomes Duke Albert, the Emperor's brother, when he sails down the Danube with twenty ships, and entrusts him with full authority. Meanwhile, King George of Bohemia has called his people to arms, crosses the Danube by boat at Klosterburg and is secretly advancing to free the Emperor; but one of his scouts is captured, so that they are expected and lose 1000 men; while King George's son loses a further 500 in an attempt to capture Eczinsdorf. After this, peace is made, the conditions being that the Viennese elect the Emperor's son, Maximilian, and Duke Albert is made his guardian. The Emperor is allowed to return home.

A.D. 1463

On Sunday, January 16, an assembly begins in Piotrków. Among those attending it are emissaries from the Mazovian dukes and others demanding that the King should relinquish the duchy of Płock and return it to Duke Conrad of Warsaw and his brothers. As regards his feudal right, they demand that this be tested by impartial judges. The King replies that his own lawyers are fully competent and he does not wish to throw doubt on a matter that has already been decided. Should feudal law be held not to apply, he will demand the duchy not for himself, but for Margaret, daughter of Duke Siemowit and wife of the Duke of Oleśnica. There are also envoys from Lithuania demanding the return of Podole, Bełz, Oleśnica and Ratno. This, too, the King rejects on the grounds that it is without legal foundation and unjust. Having settled this and other matters, and given the officers and men fighting in Prussia their pay, Casimir leaves Piotrków on January 29 and returns to Radom, where the Queen awaits him. Together, they go to Lithuania and there spend Lent. The papal legate, having been repeatedly invited to visit the Master of the Prussian Order, obtains an armed escort from the King and goes to Prussia via Mazovia, hoping to be able to end the war either through a peace treaty or a truce, and so allow the King to direct his endeavours, and those of other Catholic kings, against the Turks, who this year have captured Macellina and carried off a great number of Greeks into captivity. He hopes to achieve this, as the Knights have recently suffered several defeats at the hands of the King, and, presumably, are eager for peace.

Although he has sworn allegiance to the King, the Bishop of Warmińsk goes over to the Knights, with whose help he tries to capture the King's town of Warmińsk in the darkness of one night. However, when the traitors admit the Master's men, most are either captured or killed; those who do escape flee onto the thin ice of the lake near the town and are drowned. Again, on January 12, 300 cavalry, sent from Brodnica to plunder Dobrzyń, are defeated near Skampa and few escape. Eighty are captured and the rest killed by a force from Golub, which arrives before the King's men from Brześć.

The Bishop of Płock, who has long suffered from the itch, dies on January 27 after a pontificate of twenty-three years. On March 6 the Chapter meets to elect a new bishop, though it has been told not to do this until the King has informed it of his choice, which is Jacob of Siena, Bishop of Cracow. Disregarding this, the Chapter elects the Canon of Płock, one of three candidates.

The King sends the Voivode of Sandomierz and the royal Treasurer to Cracow to settle the outstanding quarrel between Jan Tęczyn and the City Fathers, who have been fined 40,000 florins, in addition to which Tęczyn is demanding 8000 florins for himself, this being the sum he has been given to understand he may expect, yet is being offered only 6000. In the end, thanks to the intervention of the Bishop of Cracow, he accepts 6200 to be paid in instalments. This agreed, the city's three hostages are released after a year and eight weeks in prison.

In Königsberg the papal legate has long discussions with the Master, whom he assures of his support, for in his eyes King Casimir is in the wrong. The Legate's bias, at first rumoured, becomes evident when two letters he has sent to the Master are intercepted. Having thus encouraged the Knights, the Legate returns to Poland accompanied by emissaries of the Knights, hoping for a lasting peace or a twelve year truce. For this objective, a meeting is arranged for May 1 in Brześć in Kujawy. There, quarrelling starts before they have even started to discuss terms, because the Legate has seen fit to place an interdict on delegates from Gdańsk, Elbląg and Toruń. Now comes news that the King's forces have captured a castle in Prussia and taken much booty and many prisoners. At this, jubilant soldiers flood into the churches, where they ring the bells and sing *Te Deums*. The clergy are unable to restrain them, and the irate Legate complains that this is an insult both to him and to the Pope, and becomes even more angry when services are held for the absent delegates from Gdańsk, Elbląg and Toruń. The King's councillors in their turn complain that the Legate has done more to stir up strife, than to bring about peace, as was his mission. The Legate then demands that he be taken back to Cracow to await the King's return from Lithuania, but this is refused, so he leaves Brześć and goes to Włocławek, where he stays for several months. While there he writes to the King complaining of being treated with discourtesy and insulted, for which he blames the Bishop of Włocławek. Though promising to work for peace, the Legate has men and women, who have come from Pomerania and Prussia to obtain the indulgence available in this Jubilee year, brought to his quarters, where he cajoles and threatens them, telling them that they should desert the King and give their allegiance to the Master of the Prussian Order. Wives, who cannot persuade their husbands to do this, are enjoined to leave their husbands.

The King and Queen spend all the spring in Lithuania. To them come emissaries from Kaifa, who stress how dangerous it would be for their city, should the Turks attack it, and asking the King's permission for half of their tribute to be used for the defence of the town, as well as for Polish troops to be sent to Kaifa. The King agrees to this and 500 men from Ruthenia, all of Polish origin and paid by the citizens and nobles of Kaifa, are sent there. When they get as far as Bracław, then under Lithuania and governed by Duke Michael Czartoryski, they become embroiled in a brawl with the townspeople, one of whom is killed, and even set the town on fire. When they move on, the Duke, eager to avenge the hurt, attacks them four times, but is repulsed on each occasion and forced to retreat. He then assembles a number of peasants and gets them to fell trees, which are used to fill the channel of the River Bug, which the Poles have to cross, so that, when they attempt to do this, they are caught as in a trap and all but five mercilessly killed. Czartoryski's men collect booty to the value of 30,000 florins.

King Casimir returns from Poland in order to arrange a foray into Prussia, a thing he has been advised not to attempt. On June 7, he goes to Łęczyca, where he orders general mobilization, but the knights protest and, eventually, he agrees to postpone military action, but imposes an impost of six grosses on every corn-field, mill and tavern, which is to be paid by St. Bartholomew's Day. He also agrees to make one more attempt to reach peace with the Master, using the papal legate as an intermediary, who is thought to have lost his bias in favour of the Knights, and who is now recalled from Włocławek, and also asked to revoke his excommunication of the gentry and people of Prussia, since the Pope had done so as long ago as the synod of Mantua. This the Legate says he cannot do. He then returns to Rome.

In response to complaints from Prussia, especially from the people of Gdańsk and Toruń, that those who hold Gniew are hampering their ships from sailing the Vistula, the King sends a force of mercenaries to lay siege to the town and castle of Gniew, which has a garrison of 500 excellent soldiers. Though this force is helped both by land and water by units from Gdańsk, the besieged repeatedly sally out to do battle or fight individual duels, and the King's men see no hope of capturing Gniew, nor of starving it out.

This turn in events exposes Gdańsk to grave danger; in that twelve of its citizens plot to surrender the city to the Master. However, as they recruit more and more conspirators, the plan becomes known, as well as the date of the intended coup, July 13. When the day comes, the Master is not far away with 1500 horse, while the conspirators are all in the city together with a number of veteran foreign soldiers they have brought in disguised as merchants come by sea with their goods. However, one of their number betrays them and all are summoned to the town hall, ostensibly to discuss some public matter, and there they are forced to confess. Most are then killed with swords, though some are drowned and a few given long terms of imprisonment. Among them is their chief, Matthew Schumann, who is so terrified that he can neither speak nor hear, and is more unconscious than confused. (When freed later, at the request of the Bishop of Włocławek, he enters the service of the Master.) Covert treachery having failed him, the Master has recourse to open hostilities. He fits out twenty ships in Königsberg, embarks some Knights and sends them to destroy the Polish fleet at Gniew. Twelve ships from Gdańsk intercept them, while they are still a mile from Elbląg, with the result that several of them are lost, 1000 men killed and 600 captured along with their craft and equipment. Eight weeks later a Livonian fleet tries a similar attack, but again it is intercepted and most of those aboard killed; though two of the larger ships are captured together with 200 soldiers, 100 horses and much equipment. When news of this defeat reaches the Commander of Elbląg, who is leading a force overland to relieve Gniew, he turns back.

Earlier in the year, the Sultan of Turkey assembled a huge army, but so cleverly that no one knew what his intentions were, and invaded first the island of Lesbos and then Bosnia, a country where they speak a Slavonic language and, though professing to be Christians, practice the rites of the Monophysites, which the Catholic Church condemns. The Sultan's victories are so swift. that news of them is received before that of the outbreak of hostilties. Every town and castle in Bosnia was well-secured both by Nature and by artifice, yet they were all swiftly captured and all, except for the six the Sultan considered the strongest, demolished. The King of Bosnia was himself captured in Jajca castle, where the Turks found a huge quantity of gold and silver, in which metals the country is rich. The King and all his subjects, an estimated 100,000 men and women, are carried off into captivity, where 30,000 of those with the vigour of youth become janissaries. The King, mocked for failing to provide himself with adequate protection, when he had all that money, is stripped naked, planted in the earth and used as a target by the archers. Vexed by this occupation of Bosnia, Matthias King of Hungary captures five of its castles with their Turkish garrisons, and appoints a very rich and enterprising man, Emeric Diak, to be king of Bosnia.

At this same time, the Sultan has sent 4000 picked troops to ravage Hungary, which they do and carry off 17,000. King Matthias who is then in Futa and Zaslonia, fearing similar raids into Hungary in the future, sends 500 of his Polish cavalry and 700 Hungarian horse to recover what the Turks have looted. The Turks withdraw into a fortified town called St. Gregory. Anxious about the Catholic captives, the Poles decide to launch a night attack on the town; but, when the Hungarian cavalry see that they are being involved in what is obviously a dangerous enterprise, they withdraw to their King's camp, all, that is, but Duke Peter Sokół, who, considering it shameful to abandon the Poles, joins them with seventeen of his own people. Meanwhile, the Turks have moved on with their captives to the River Sava, where they demand boats to be sent to ferry them across. There the Poles find them and attack. Knowing how few they are, the Poles cleverly attack in a series of waves, each withdrawing when exhausted and being replaced by the next wave. When day returns after a night of fighting and the Turks see how small a force has inflicted all this damage on them, they are ashamed. They then split their force, one part attacking the Poles from in front, the other from the rear. The Turks' captives are grouped in several places under guard, so as to prevent them going to help the Poles, or the Poles from recapturing them. Fighting starts up again. This time the Poles, having broken their spears, use sword and arrows. The boats to ferry the Turks across the river having now arrived, the Turks throng to the bank, the Poles at their heels, abandon their horses and crowd onto the boats, almost every one of which is overloaded and sinks as soon as it gets into midstream. When King Matthias sees how his Polish contingent has returned victorious and almost without loss, yet with much booty and with many of those the Turks had captured earlier, he praises them publicly and gives them special awards. At the same time he castigates the Hungarians for having left their companions in the lurch and orders them to have their heads covered with their breeches and thus to be driven from the camp and not allowed back for three days.

A general assembly begins on the Sunday before St. Jadwiga's Day in Piotrków, to which the King and Queen come from Brześć. It is assumed that the matter of the duchies of Mazovia and Płock will not cause much trouble, but it is one that requires to be settled by agreement, rather by imposed judgment. When this proves more difficult than expected, some demand arbitrators, even that the matter should be referred to an Italian university, whose decision would be binding, so the whole question is referred to the next general assembly. The office is offered to the second duke, Conrad the Black, Duke of Koźle and Oleśnica, acting for his wife Margaret, daughter of Siemovit, the late duke of Mazovia. He is offered full powers and the right to appoint judges from among the members of the Kingdom. Duke Conrad of Warsaw does not like this and departs.

The maritime city of Lübeck, which the Poles know as Bukowiec (it once belonged to Poland) is demanding that war with Prussia be stopped and peace concluded on equitable terms. The Master agrees to talks to be held at Whitsun between the King in Bydgoszcz and the Master in Chełm.

When, during the assembly in Piotrków, troops from the King's garrison in the town of Holand sally forth to loot, the townspeople close the gates behind them and send to the Master for some of his men, whom they then admit. The rest of the Polish garrison still holds the castle and one gate and the two towers near it. When he learns what has happened, Peter Danin, who is besieging Gniew, hastens to Holand and invests it. As he arrives during the night, this gives the impression that his force is larger than it actually is and the commander of the Knights in the town takes fright, sets fire to the town in several places and escapes with all his men. The Poles then move in, put out the fires and punish those guilty of treachery.

A.D. 1464

The siege of Gniew is now in its second year. The besieged are trying to get rid of their servants and the common people, who, they know, will never endure starvation; yet, at the same time, people keep streaming in, for they regard the castle as their safest refuge. Now, with no more provisions than will last for a fortnight at the most, and no hope of help from outside, the Commander of Gniew surrenders both the castle and the town, on condition that the garrison be allowed to march out taking with them fourteen waggons loaded with their possessions. Four hundred of the Knights and their commander are escorted to Königsberg, while all the townspeople are spared, thanks to the kindness of the Poles. The soldiers are paid what they are due.

The Bishop of Kamień sends 500 of his own men-at-arms with 700 of the Knights' horse by secret paths to stage a night attack on Kołobrzeg. In this he would have succeeded had not the citizens of Gdańsk send warning to their fellows in Kołobrzeg and obtained some mercenaries, who lie in wait for the Bishop's force. They allow it to reach the walls, even get on to the bulwarks, and then destroy it. All are either killed or captured.

The garrison the Knights put into Friedland complains that they are being reduced to extreme misery, because they have not been paid, so they march out, after looting and setting fire to the place.

The King and Queen go to Lithuania and spend Christmas in Grodno. Realizing that trouble is brewing between Poland and Lithuania over Podole and Łuck, which both claim, the King proposes that the assembly, due to be held in Parczów, should be postponed until the Feast of the Nativity of the Blessed Virgin. The Lithuanians are now behaving more as spectators of the war, that has already lasted ten years, than as participants, for nothing will induce them to help the Poles, who reasonably insist that the part of Prussia bordering on Samogitia belongs to the King and

Kingdom of Poland. The Lithuanians are convinced that the situation of both the Poles and the Knights is so unfavourable that the only winner will be themselves. Indeed, they are on the point of declaring war on the Poles, who are occupied with the Prussian war, and would have done so, had not the King intervened. The King spends Easter in Brześć in Ruthenia and returns to Cracow on April 20.

Wishing to relieve the pressure being put on Christendom by the Sultan's shaming capture of Constantinople, the Pope proclaims a general crusade against Sultan Mehmet, in which he will personally take part. He has the support of a fleet commanded by the all but senile Duke of Burgundy and the Doge of Venice. All who take part are to be granted remission of their sins and, when this is everywhere announced, many thousands of Poles take the cross. In the evening of the Tuesday after Easter, the Cracow crusaders attack the Jews and loot and destroy their homes and synagogues. More than 300 Jewish men and women are killed. A number seek refuge in the house of the Castellan of Cracow, and, the next morning, they, too, are threatened by the crusaders, who wish to kill them, and are only protected by some armed men sent by the Bishop and starosta. They are then taken to the castle. The same thing would have happened to the Jews all over Poland, had they not sought refuge in castles and other places of safety. The City Fathers of Cracow are fined 3000 florins for not preventing the slaughter of the Jews.

The King now goes to Korczyń, where an assembly is held. Here, it is decided to postpone the King's long-planned campaign against Prussia, it being considered too difficult and dispiriting an undertaking for the summer. The people of Wielkopolska and Prussia find this postponement very onerous and insist that it will only prolong the war, which they had hoped to see concluded. By the time the King returns to Cracow 20,000 well-equipped men have taken the cross and are ready to go and annihilate the Turks.

On May 6, Queen Elizabeth gives birth to a daughter, who is called Sophia. The christening is an occasion for games, at which the winners are given prizes.

Towards the end of June the King pays a quick visit to Koło to arrange for an expedition against Prussia using mostly men from Wielkopolska, but, when the latter refuse to take up arms without the knights from Cracow, the idea is abandoned and it is decided that, later in the year, the King should attack the Knights with a force composed of his household troops and mercenaries. Meanwhile, the Prussians themselves complain that the cowardice and inexperience of the Poles have caused Prussian affairs to be dealt with laxly and laughably, and the war thus prolonged.

The King moves to Brześć, where he finds a number of his councillors, the Bishop and delegates from Lübeck, come, belatedly, to arbitrate between the Prussians and the Poles. The men from Lübeck have with them representatives of five other Hanseatic towns: Rostock, Wismar, Lüneburg, Riga and Dorpat. The Knights are censured for not sending anyone; but then the Master sends the Bishop and Marshal of Livonia and several others, including the city council of Reval. When all are assembled in the town hall in Toruń, Poland's case is presented: this is formulated in fifteen separate points: 1. Pomerania, Chełm and Michałów are inhabited by people speaking the Polish language, who gave the towns, hills, rivers and places their names long before the Order of the Teutonic Knights existed; 2. the first king of Poland, Lech, and his descendants obtained these lands many centuries previously and they have always belonged to the Polish monarchy; 3. the lands in question and Prussia have frontiers with Poland; 4. the kings and princes of Poland had complete legal right to these lands and have given them their laws and appointed their officials, until they were wrest from the Kingdom; 5. it was the kings and princes of Poland who founded the cathedrals, churches and collegiates of these lands; 6. all these lands pay Peter's pence like other parts of Poland; 7. and 8. the Master of the Teutonic Knights forcibly appropriated these lands from the King of Poland; 9. and 10. Popes John XXII and Benedict XII both awarded these territories to the king and Kingdom of Poland; 11. Prussia and Pomerania are within the boundaries of the Kingdom of Poland and pay it tribute and taxes; when the Master of the Knights appropriated Prussia, he not only refused to pay the usual tribute, but ravaged the territory of Poland with his own troops and mercenaries at a time when its King was busy warring against the barbarians; 13. the nobles and people of these territories cannot endure the arrogant tyranny of the Master and have legally approached the King to receive them back; 14, the Master of the Order has engaged in hostilities against these territories and prevented their natural ruler from taking possession of them; 15. the King of Poland, wishing to endorse his right to all of Prussia, bought it from the Master's mercenaries, who were fully entitled to sell it, for 4000 marks of broad grosses paid in gold and silver, and for this he now demands his rights. The Knights give their reply three days later, one that is weak and unsatisfactory. The Master also puts forward specific points, which the King's lawyers refute three days later. The arbitrators then announce that they will start formulating a peace treaty; but, a month and a half later, though some are still hopeful, others consider it time to have recourse to arms.

The King and his advisers are prepared to accept that the Order of the Teutonic Knights should be preserved, not destroyed, and that the more distant areas of Prussia, other than Elbląg and the castle at Malbork, should remain with the Order. The Knights on their part are prepared to relinquish Pomerania, Chełm, Michałów and Elbląg for ever and to let Malbork castle and its lands remain in the King's hand and under his rule for thirty years; but the Germans, especially the Margrave of Brandenburg and his brothers, as well as the Margrave of Meissen, are piqued that they should have been by-passed in the peace process, and keep sending knights to the conference with orders not to agree to such terms. So, two further conditions are put forward, one by either side: one, that King Casimir will not conclude a lasting peace unless the Master and the Order thenceforward and for ever pay homage to the King and Kingdom of Poland, of which they are subjects, because, otherwise, no peace can be lasting; the other, put forward by the Knights, is that King Casimir pay the wages, amounting to several millions, of all who for the last eleven years have been fighting on behalf of the Order, especially the mercenaries, who have provided the garrisons for the castles now going to the King, because the Order itself cannot afford to do so. In the end, when they are all about to leave Toruń, having accomplished nothing, the Dukes of Pomerania produce four documents from the years 1255, 1293, 1294 and 1298 drawn up by their predecessors and confirmed by Władysław Łokietek granting to the town of Lubicz a church in Gdańsk city and various privileges, as well as freedom from all dues and duties throughout Pomerania, and demand confirmation of these grants. In themselves these documents prove that the war was completely justified. When the arbitrators reach Lübeck, they find that city in the grip of the plague and almost all their friends and relations dead. The King, having lost hope of concluding peace, starts preparing for war and a siege of Nowe. He puts in command of this a brave, but rather stupid person, who begins the siege without waiting for some cavalry, as he had been ordered to do; thus, when the besieged see how small is the force besieging them, they sally out and attack it from in front and the rear and easily force it to make a shameful retreat, in which more than a hundred are killed. The casualties would have been higher had there not been some of the King's ships on the river, which rescued many of them.

On July 28, the captain of Działdowo, recently returned from Mazovia with much booty, is defeated by the governor of Nidburg with some of the King's men. The King, wishing to make good the disastrous defeat of his infantry at Nowe, when he tried to recover the town, which treachery had given to the enemy and so ensure that the King's ships should again be able to sail on the Vistula, which flows close to that town's walls, and its waters be denied to the enemy and, so perhaps, induce them to make peace, sends two forces, one of Prussians and mercenaries under Peter Danin, and the other of his household troops under Paul Jasienski, to lay siege to it. The first starts out on August 6 and the latter on August 13 and soon the fort is surrounded by bastions and pallisades. Though the besieged have asked for assistance, they receive none. Coming to the conclusion that they dare not risk a pitched battle, but can only pursue a policy of harassment and ambushes, the Knights again bring up the subject of peace. Because of this, and to arrange certain other matters, Jan Długosz, Canon of Cracow, is sent to Gdańsk, where he spends several days in discussions with representatives from Prussia, Gdańsk, Toruń and Elbląg; but, as the plague is rampant there, he has to leave without achieving his objective.

The plague keeps spreading and the King moves to Kłodawa, where he spends several weeks with the Queen, before moving to Piotrków for an assembly at which the claims of the two dukes to the Mazovian duchy of Warsaw are discussed. It proves impossible to reach a friendly solution and so the question of Duke Conrad the Black of Oleśnica's claim to the duchy of Warsaw is deferred to the next assembly at Whitsun. Nowe is still under siege, but Łuck and Działdowo have both surrendered, the former after a siege of twenty-six weeks.

The pestilential air has now reached Wilno, brought there by troops of the Order from Livonia. One night, during the assembly in Piotrków, Commander Henry with a small force secretly approaches Toruń, hoping to capture it. They get in through the southern and most unlikely part of the ramparts on the river side, where the dwellings of the fishermen are, and start erecting ladders against the main wall. Fortunately, dawn reveals the danger and the guards call the entire town to arms. The shouts of the defenders so frighten the enemy that they withdraw hurriedly, leaving their ladders. Some days later these capture the fort at Czarnoszyn, which was negligently guarded by Duke Conrad of Warsaw's men; the Duke at once invests it in order to prevent supplies getting in, and the besieged, fearing death should the castle be taken, surrender it and their possessions, content to keep just their lives.

A.D. 1465

King Casimir and Queen Elizabeth spend Christmas in Grodno; then, unable to go to Wilno or any lovelier place, because of the plague rampant in Lithuania, they move to Kaunas and there spend a good part of the winter. The siege of Nowe has already lasted seven months. Now, Kasper Nostwicz brings 600 cavalry and 400 foot from Germany, recruited for many promises but little pay, to raise the siege of Chojnice. It being winter, and one that is unusually severe, and they are marching in their armour, by the time they reach Chojnice many have died and others are ill. The rest, realizing that they have been duped, return to their homes. The besieged in Nowe, exhausted by the cold and on the point of revolt, realizing how little effort is necessary to breach the walls, voluntarily surrender on February 1, being granted their lives and possessions. The Knights then cross the frozen Vistula and burn Zulawa so as to deny Malbork a source of provisions, and finally withdraw to Königsberg. In order to give his mercenaries something to do during the winter, the Master sends them across the still frozen Vistula into Lower Zulawa, most of which they burn, collecting and removing to Stargard all the corn, cattle and whatever else they can find.

Bishop Jacob of Siena returns to Włocławek on March 21. A week later, the son of the former starosta of Golub with a company of armed men, most of them mercenaries, complaining of not having been paid, fortifies Dobrzyń Hill, which rises beside the Vistula and on which once a royal castle was built to control Mazovia and Kujawy and to force all ships sailing up and down the river to pay dues on their goods. Bishop Jacob institutes discussions and after three days persuades the starosta's son to accept 150 florins to relinquish the hill. The danger to Włocławek thus averted, a similar danger is found to be facing Gniezno, where 1000 mercenaries are threatening to occupy the cathdral and monastery of Trzemeszno in lieu of payment of the monies due to them. At this, the cathedral's treasures are removed to Uniejów castle, and the clergy all leave. The Archbishop then meets the chief of the mercenaries and agrees to give them 1000 florins, 200 of which he provides from his own pocket, thus this danger is averted until the King returns from Lithuania.

Crossbowmen shooting firebombs against a besieged town. The defenders are using both crossbows and handguns. Illustration from a German manuscript firework book, about 1440.—The Board of Trustees of the Royal Armouries.

A similar situation has arisen in Hungary, where a band of mercenaries calling themselves the Brethren, almost all of whom are Poles, claiming that they have not been paid, have fortified a few places and are extracting tribute from the local people. They have defeated the starosta of Spis in several engagements and have plundered thirteen towns in Spis, which belongs to the King of Poland, and extracted 7000 florins from them. There is talk of war being declared on Hungary, but the starosta of Cracow forbids this, while their neighbour is engaged in war with the barbarian Turk. Then King Matthias promises compensation and the fuss subsides.

King Matthias imprisons the Duke of Upper Moldavia, whom he suspects of plotting against him with the Turks. At this, the Duke's second brother goes to the Sultan, submits to him and undertakes to pay him tribute, and so takes over Upper Moldavia and the castle at Kilia on the bank of the Danube, which the Greeks used to call Lykostomos. The Voivode of Walachia, a vassal of the King of Poland, afraid lest the proximity of the Turks should lead to the devastation of Walachia, agrees to pay them tribute, a thing King Casimir forbids both in writing and by emissary. When the Voivode sees how the people of Kilia favour King Casimir, he gets a letter to them from King Casimir outlining terms for surrender and advances on Kilia with a large force. The City Fathers close one of the gates, so that they cannot be accused of treachery, and that same night the Poles occupy the castle, in which they find its two captains, rather tipsy, for they have been to a wedding. The Sultan is furious at the news and orders the Duke's brother to retake Kilia. The Voivode has to order everyone to arms, leaving only women and children in the houses, and marches out to do battle; but the Sultan considers it dangerous to fight any one so determined and accepts the situation.

After spending the winter and Lent in Lithuania and Easter in Grodno, the King goes to Brześć, from where he sends the Queen and their baggage to Korczyn and himself goes to Lwów and from there, travelling in light coaches, he reaches Korczyn to attend the assembly called for May 6 to discuss the Prussian question. It is decided to impose yet another levy on fields and towns, to be paid by St. Margaret's Day and used to pay mercenaries to prosecute the war in Prussia. Also, the barons of Wielkopolska are to call up their forces, who are to fortify and surround Chojnice with a palisade and then go home, after which the mercenaries can be left to continue the siege. While he is still in Korczyn, delegates from Chełm, Toruń, Gdańsk and Elbląg wait on the King to report on the recent talks with the Master's supporters, at which all but the Prussian delegates agree to press for a new lasting peace with the Order on the terms agreed the previous year in Toruń: that the Master is to be permanent duke, councillor and vassal of the King of Poland. The Prussian delegates' objection being that in the present situation it was not fitting to make peace on these terms, since the King had latterly incurred considerable expense, due to the Order having refused the terms. The Order's emissaries beg that they should not be sent home without hope of peace, for the lengthy hostilities have left them with nothing but their bodies. When asked if they have the Master's authority to make peace, they reply that they have not, but will endeavour to get it; and they ask the King's approval to enter into discussions, which he gives them.

On May 9 Queen Elizabeth gives birth to a seventh child, a daughter, who is named Elizabeth. (She is to die in Sandomierz exactly a year later.)

Having paid the mercenaries several thousand marks, the King leaves Cracow and goes to Łęczyca, where he equips the mercenaries who are to go to Prussia. Then he has a meeting in Kalisz with Duke Conrad of Oleśnica, who is demanding the return of various territories which he is continuing to claim in the name of his wife, Margaret, daughter of the late Duke of Mazovia. The King and Duke cannot come to an agreement and decide to meet again in the same place on the next St. Michael's Day, together with two of the King of Bohemia's councillors, who will act as mediators.

On August 8 the King arrives in Brześć to receive unwelcome confirmation of rumours that the Castellan and Starosta of Nakło has suborned 500 of the King's knights with many promises and the meagre pay of half a florin—against the three florins in gold suggested by the King—and that these have defected. The King is appalled at this possibility of civil war, which would force him to abandon the campaign in Prussia; but, of course, his enemies there are delighted. Having repeatedly, but vainly, sent to the rebels promising to forgive them all, if they will return to his service, the King decides on armed action. He installs strong garrisons in various strategic places and prepares to lay siege to Nakło and Damoborz, at which the rebels take fright and sue for peace. They come before the King and are given such a dressing-down that they fall on their faces before the throne and beg for forgiveness. The King forgives them and restores them to favour and a share in his councils. Then, he gives the mercenaries some of their pay and sends them to Prussia to lay siege to Stargard.

In Prussia, things are changing for the worse. On June 13 some Mazovian knights, relying on their superiority in numbers, let themselves be ambushed, and are heavily defeated, many being killed, and even more taken prisoner. The helmsmen of some ships laden with goods belonging to merchants in Gdańsk and Toruń abandon their craft, which are then captured near Kwidzyn. Finally, on the last day in June, the Prussians garrisoning Toruń, hithterto successful in their sorties, attack some of the enemy's cavalry far too rashly with the result that ten are killed and eighty taken prisoner. Three weeks later, taking advantage of the absence of their starosta, fifty-five of the garrison of Gniewkowo go out pillaging, but encounter a large enemy force and all are either killed or captured. Then the Starosta of Stargard intercepts a letter from the commander in Gniew asking Gdańsk to send him reinforcements, as town and castle are almost without defenders. The Starosta at once marches on Gniew with all the men he can muster and lauches an assault. For many hours a mere handful of men under one of the Prussian knights defends the place stoutly, killing so many of the assailants with the stones he throws down, that these have to be taken away by the waggon-load. News of this brings sixty cavalry from Malbork and seventy foot from Gdańsk. Fortune again favours the King when, on August 10 Duke Henry of Słupsk rounds up 300 enemy raiders and announces that he will only release them if the fortified towns of Bytom and Lemberg are surrendered to him.

On August 1 a force of the King's men reaches Pomerania and lays siege to Stargard and puts an end to the enemy's activities there. On September 21 the Poles start investing the suburbs of Gdańsk and the castles of Gniew, Tczew and Nowe. However, at Tczew there are as many besieged as besiegers, and the former are able to come and go as they please. On October 18, sixty troopers secretly leave Stargard and that evening, by arrangement, join up with those who have remained in the town and start a mock fight. When the Polish commander, all unwittingly, rides up and sends a squire to ask what is going on, he is told that the combatants are inhabitants of Tczew, who have captured some of the enemy. The Polish commander walks in among them to congratulate them, and is at once captured together with two of his men and taken off to Stargard. The delighted enemy ring church bells and beat their drums, as if the capture of the enemy's commander was tantamount to victory. (The commander is immediately replaced.)

While the King is in Inowrocław, envoys arrive from Duke Henry of Słupsk to ask for a renewal of the treaty made long ago between Poland and the Duchy; and also that one of the Duke's sons should be taken into the King's household and live with the King's sons. They are told that they can expect a favourable reply, once the King has consulted his councillors.

The King returns to Kalisz for another meeting with Duke Conrad of Oleśnica; at which, a number of difficulties having been resolved, it is decided that Margaret, daughter of the late Duke of Mazovia, and her husband, the Duke of Oleśnica, are to surrender and renounce all rights to Mazovia and Bełz and that they undertake on the death of the Dowager Duchess Anna not to claim their inheritance. In exchange for this, King Casimir will pay the Duchess and her husband 20,000 złoty spread over five years: 5000 on St. James's Day of the first year and 15,000 during the next three years. The King then moves to Poznań, where the Duke and his wife officially confirm the agreement both verbally and in writing, and depart with splendid gifts.

In the middle of December, the enemy around Stargard are harassing those on the roads leading to it to such an extent that the Poles are unable to bring up supplies, with the result that the situation of the besiegers of Stargard is worse than that of the besieged, and the former are almost faced with hunger. To avoid that situation coming about, the Starosta and a number of knights ride to Tczew to obtain provisions. This ride convinces the Starosta that the besieged are more numerous than the besiegers and thus capable of defeating them in the field. This, indeed, is what the besieged decide to attempt, especially when a deserter from Gdańsk tells them that the commander there is sending a large force to Tczew to get provisions for the besiegers. So, 300 horse and a horde of infantry assault the Poles in their two bastions. For several hours, the Poles put up a stout defence. Again and again their assailants reach the galleries, only to have their supports cut from under them. At the fourth attempt they withdraw leaving piles of dead and wounded, whom the Poles allow them to cart away for burial. After this, whenever the Poles go out any distance from their camp in search of firewood or pasture, the besieged are quickly aware of it and sally out to attack them. Now, the Poles' only proper source of supplies is what is brought in at night by young women; so that in reality the besiegers are themselves besieged. Nonetheless, they decide to hold out in the hope that endurance will give them what they lack the strength to get for themselves.

Pope Paul II has sent Ludwig of Bavaria, Patriarch of Antioch, to Khan Hadzigerej. With a mounted retinue of twelve the Patriarch passes through Hungary to the River Stryj, then, with the consent of the King of Poland, who provides him with guides, continues through Ruthenia to the Khan's camp on the River Elza, which he reaches on August 10. A few days previously, in a very bloody battle, the Khan had defeated another Tatar khan, Chiczinachmeth, whose territory was on the Volga, thus acquiring all the latter's territory, towns, forts, army, wives and a wealth of possessions. The Khan is more gracious than befits a barbarian monarch and accepts the Pope's bulls and gifts. The Patriarch tells the Khan of the ghastly bloodshed the defeated khan had, for no reason whatever, inflicted on the Christians and the countries he had captured, from which he had expelled or exterminated the Catholics, and asks Hadzigerej to persuade Sultan Mehmet to stop the bloodshed and his occupation of Christian lands, or, if he will not, to declare war on Mehmet, when he shall have all the help Pope Paul and Emperor Frederick can give him. The delighted Khan says that he must have time to think this over. Some weeks later, the Khan moves to a stronghold called Kercher. He tells the Patriarch that he sincerely sympathizes with him, especially over the disasters the Christians have suffered at the hands of the Turks; so he is sending to the Turks to tell them in future not to wage war on Christians, especially not on Walachia and Hungary, nor to conquer them; but, as to declaring war on the Turks, that does not depend solely on him, but on King Casimir as well, whom he honours as a brother and a lord, and that he must first consult him; indeed, all will depend on what Casimir wishes to do. To prove that there is no deceit, he will give his reply in writing, so that it can be shown to King Casimir, who will give a quick decision, and by this the Khan will abide. The Patriarch then takes the letter to Casimir, who is in Wilno. Casimir tells him that he has long wished for the destruction of the Turks, but he must first lay the matter before the prelates and councillors of his realm, these being due to meet in Piotrków on March 17. The Patriarch then departs with this reply and many gifts, and goes back to report to the Pope and the Emperor.

A.D. 1466

The King and Queen spend the winter in Lithuania attending to local affairs, going hunting, and receiving envoys. Then a crime is committed, such as, I believe, had not been known in Poland since the country became Christian: on Monday, January 6, Jacob Boglewski, an excellent knight, whose crest was goat's horns, while resting in bed in his village, was killed by Jan Pieniązek, arch-dean of Gniezno and deacon of Łęczyca, a man of the same clan and the same arms—three jave-lins—all because of Jacob's wife, Dorothy, in whose vulgar crimes the dead man had earlier re-fused to believe, though repeatedly told of them by reliable people. Nor would he take measures to prevent attempts on his life, though warned of them. The murderer was assisted by Boglewski's secretary and member of his household, along with two of the servants. He was murdered before the very eyes of his wife, who, allegedly, was Pieniazek's mistress, and this at a time when he had been sleeping badly and having dreams of attempts being made on his life. He was hacked with swords and axes, carved into so many pieces that it was difficult to identify which was which. At dawn the next day Jacob's brother, the voivode of Warsaw, arrived and arrested the wretched woman's servant, who knew all about her mistress's shameful doings, as well as the murdered man's secretary who had been the first to strike his master. (Jan Pieniązek and two of his men had, during the night, fled twenty miles in the direction of Łęczyca so as to make it easier to deny their guilt.) The discovery of a letter written by Pieniązek to Dorothy, proved that the murder was planned. The Voivode then released Dorothy and her servant, a spinster, saving them from a prob-able sentence of being buried alive; while Pieniązek was condemned to be disembowelled alive and then quartered.

Early in February, the Livonian Master sends a force of 700 of his infantry and horse to assist the besieged in Stargard. It travels overland, a sea route being out of the question because of the winter's gales. When it reaches Samogitia, the Samogitians march out and pen them all within a ring of felled trees. After several days, hunger forces the Livonians to make for the sea, but many fall into pits dug long before and covered with brushwood, and in these all but two are killed. These two later tell their captors that, shortly before this happened, forty ships carrying Knights from the Rhine had been wrecked in a great storm. The few who avoided the pits try to flee across a frozen lake, but the ice breaks under them and all are drowned.

The new bishop of Warmińsk, convinced that the Master and his Order are enemies of peace, breaks off relations with them and summons Polish forces from Passenheim, Nidburg and Ornoc, installs them in five of his castles and authorizes them to use these as bases from which to attack the enemy. When he learns of this, the Master writes to King Casimir in Lithuania asking for the peace he had previously scorned.

Despite pouring rain, the King arrives on horseback for the March 14 assembly. The main item on the agenda is the question of Płock, Wizna and Sochaczew, and whether the King's right to them is feudal or by succession. The dukes of the six Mazovian duchies concur that the rights to these territories do not belong to them, but to the King of Poland; yet Duke Conrad of Warsaw him-self, having given up any right by succession, which earlier he had been eager to claim, now de-mands his right be recognised as hereditary. When this is rejected, he demands that all Mazovia be granted him as a favour, the King retaining only Bełz for himself. The King considers this unjust, pointing out that he has already paid 20,000 złoty for Bełz, so that it would be wrong to give it to anyone else. However, he is prepared to grant the Mazovian dukes Wizna, if they will surrender Płock. No agreement is reached and the matter is referred to the next assembly. The Voivode of Warsaw brings up the matter of Jan Pieniążek's murder of his brother Jacob Boglewski. The major-ity verdict is that Pieniążek, now in custody, should be handed over to the Archbishop of Gniezno, and the murdered man's widow and her maid, who have already been granted their liberty, are to be re-arrested and sentenced. Before the sentence can be carried out, Dorothy escapes and makes her way to Prussia, while Pieniążek also escapes by hiding among his relatives, but is deprived of his posts of dean and archdeacon. Next there is the Prussian question: it is decided that the King, his councillors and an army of several thousand should go to Prussia and take up residence in Malbork. To help finance the move, the King is granted twelve grosses for every cornfield and mill, plus two grosses from such of the landless nobility; and there is a church levy as well. These funds are to last the King a year.

On April 10, the King's chief starosta in Prussia, having assembled a force drawn from a number of garrisons, makes a surprise night attack on the Knights' town of Melzak, takes sixty of the garrison prisoner and carries off most of the provisions the peasants have stored there. This at a time when most of the Order's commanders have been summoned to Königsberg to keep an eye on Sambia, which the Gdańsk fleet is intending to raid. Five days after receiving news of the loss of Melzak, the Master, assuming that by now the King's troops will have withdrawn and only a small garrison be left in Melzak, sends a force of 3000, which launches a four-fold assault on the town. One gate is destroyed and the attackers are convinced that they are about to regain the town, when such a hail of arrows is shot at them from above that two hundred are killed and many more wounded, some even taken prisoner. The Knights remove their wounded and lay siege to the castle at Holand, which they think they can easily capture and so compensate for the defeat at Melzak. But as many of the Knights' troops are killed in a battle with the King's troops there as fell at Melzak.

Osiek is now under close siege by the captain of Nowe. The Knights in Chojnice and Stargard go to its assistance, but are defeated so thoroughly that the King's men capture their arms, horses and guns. Seeing this, the men of the Osiek garrison set fire to the fortress and jump into the water, only to be taken prisoner. The King's men have no difficulty in getting into the fortress and extinguishing the fire.

King Casimir, being unable to go to Malbork as planned and wishing to have the enemy's grain crops trampled—and the enemy prevented from trampling his—sends the starosta of Nidburg with 500 mercenary horse to join the King's household troops in Passenheim and do this.

King Casimir is being accused of not giving a clear answer to the papal legate sent to negotiate peace between the King and the Knights, so he sends Jan Długosz the Elder to the legate in Wrocław to try and obtain an assurance that the legate is not biased in favour of the Knights, as was the previous legate. In this Długosz appears to have been successful.

The Prussian Master lays the whole blame for the loss of Melzak on the Bishop of Warmińsk, asserting that the Bishop has done him more harm than has King Casimir; so, early in July he marches in with 600 horse and as many foot and tramples all the grain round six of the Bishop's towns. The townspeople blame the Bishop's attachment to the King for this, saying that it could have been avoided had they followed the example of other towns and submitted to the Master; or if the King's men had got there first. The King's captains are afraid of not being strong enough, but when they are finally ordered to act, the enemy have withdrawn into Bartenstein Castle and they are able to trample the crops and burn the houses in enemy territory.

Two envoys from Duke Henry of Słupsk arrive to tell the King that the Duke is prepared to give him the assistance of his whole army on certain conditions, but these are such as to make the King and his councillors suspect that the Duke's real aim is to take over the whole of Pomerania.

The King spends nearly two months in Brześć and, while there, receives delegations from the gentry and townspeople of Prussia, Chełm, Elbląg and Gdańsk complaining of the severity of the burdens imposed on them and asking that he come soon with his army and put an end to this lengthy war, which, they maintain, has all but destroyed them and their properties. They also ask that the administration of Malbork and the other castles in Prussia and Pomerania be entrusted to them, for it would be an affront were Prussians to be passed over and outsiders made governors of the royal castles, outsiders who might never exert themselves to see that the crops were sown and the enemy driven off, but just steal from the royal treasury, demanding cash and giving nothing. The King's reply is a mild one: that, when the time is ripe and he has assembled an army, he will come to Malbork and see to everything; and that delays here cannot be attributed to him or his officials, but rather to the times and the unprecedented shortage of bread and provisions due to the last autumn's incessant rain, which turned the soil into a quagmire and prevented sowing. At the end of July, the King, accompanied by the envoys of the Duke of Słupsk, goes to Bydgoszcz, where he receives the unwelcome news of the loss of Slochów castle, captured by Martin Syczowic and his two brothers. This Martin had earlier been captured by the Captain of Słochów and imprisoned in that castle. As he was supposed to be rich, a large ransom was asked for him and he was treated with greater leniency than his status of prisoner allowed, even being permitted to go home on several occasions. Now, perhaps with the tacit agreement of Duke Henry of Słupsk, Martin decides to capture the castle, which is not well guarded. On the day on which he was due to pay his ransom, which, the castle being short of grain, had been set at four waggon-loads of flour, Martin arrives at the castle with four waggons each drawn by four horses and accompanied by four stalwart infantrymen. These are allowed in and then, with the treacherous connivance of the Saxons in the Starosta's employ, they have no difficulty in taking over the castle and consign the captain and the other officials to the dungeons. The news of this convinces the King of the duplicity of the Duke of Słupsk, who has been asking to be allowed to buy back Stargard, Chojnice and other forts in Pomerania, so he summons the Duke's envoys and tells them that their duke has not been honest with him. The envoys express their horror at what has happened and promise to do what they can to see that Słochów is returned to he King. The King also sends one of his starostas to Duke Henry to complain and demand the return of the castle.

The King is waited on by the Captain of Chojnice offering to buy that castle for cash. Another arrival is an envoy from the Margrave of Brandenburg, who comes with forty mounted men, hoping to obtain a share in Słuchów and then eject Martin. Martin has as much Saxon cunning as any of them, and tells the King's envoy that, as the Duke and the King are allies, he is in fact holding the castle for the King. The King now summons his councillors to discuss what is a dangerous situation and whether he should go to Malbork or turn his attention elsewhere. He tells them of a plan he has long been considering, namely that he should give up Malbork and concentrate on Chojnice, since there can be no end to hostilities until this has been captured. The siege of it must be tightened and no more provisions from Poland be allowed in; while its corn, of the abundance of which the people of Chojnice are so proud, must be trampled. To do this would also frighten those who have occupied Słuchów, who will be equally affected. All acclaim the plan, but the Prussian gentry, who keep reminding the King of his promise about Malbork, but in the end they, too, are persuaded to agree. To hasten things, the King sends a company of mounted mercenaries to start the siege, but when these see how greatly they are outnumbered by those they are supposed to be besieging, they take shelter in Tuchola to await the King's household troops. These arrive on July 25, with reinforcements from Gniezno, Włocławek, Poznań, Sieradz and elsewhere; and three days later the siege is started, but only on the side facing Bydgoszcz. Those in Chojnice can scarcely believe their eyes and laugh at the enemy, but eventually they find themselves encircled with obstacles and ditches. They then start firing their guns and other siege weapons so rapidly as not to allow their besiegers rest by day or by night, and so, each day, a number of the King's men are killed or wounded. The King now sends them a force of Lithuanians and Tatars strong enough to prevent sudden sallies being made by the besieged, who, angry and feeling their situation hopeless, start using poisoned arrows.

On July 23, the besieged in Stargard, impelled by a sense of hopelessness and beginning to feel the pangs of hunger and anxious to avoid falling into the hands of the Poles, abandon their guns, siege engines and prisoners, and in the darkness of midnight march out so quietly as to deceive the besiegers. Their cavalry divide into several squadrons and ride for Chojnice; while the infantry makes for the church of Zantyz on the Vistula, which the Knights had fortified to hinder river traffic and force the peasants on the larger island to pay them taxes. One and all might have been destroyed, had the Poles gone after them, but it being dark and their horses half starved, pursuit was impossible. The next day the town itself is surrendered to the King's captains, who transfer their main force to Chojnice, now besieged by six thousand men.

The Knights contend that the capture of Słuchow quite outweighs the loss of Stargard, but now they are to lose the former, too. This happens on July 29, when the Voivode of Włocławek sends forty infantrymen to see if they can get into Słuchów or at least lay their hands on some plunder. When the commander of the garrison sees them in the distance, he sallies out with his Saxons beyond the outer gate, leaving the castle empty. Inside, are two priests of Pomeranian origin, a scholar and other clergy, all aggrieved at the King being deprived of his castle; these now close the gate of the upper castle, break down the door of the prison tower and extract the former governor and seventeen of his company, hauling them up on ropes, as if they had been wild animals. Having captured the upper castle, they hurl stones down on the Saxons below, who are nonplussed and do not know whether to attack the advancing enemy or try to get back into the upper castle. When the King hears of the feat he rewards Dąbrowski and his companions with sets of new clothes.

With Słuchow captured, Friedland and Hammerstein surrender and accept the King's garrisons. All this news makes the Knights feel hopeless and so threatened that they can see no good coming to them in the future.

With the siege of Chojnice daily becoming more effective, the Prussian Master summons his knights and commanders to Krolewicz to discuss the situation. The first to speak, the Prussian Master, tells them that he is familiar with the Poles' character and how magnaminous they can be, but they have long been angered by the loss of Pomerania and will not rest until they have recovered it. Everything, he says, inclines him to accept peace, if that is possible on reasonable conditions. he is worried, too, as the enemy is squeezing them by land and sea, lest the other Prussian towns should side with the Poles, for many, he feels, are eager for a change. Also, the German dukes, being engaged in their own wars, have all deserted him and are refusing to help him other than verbally. So, he sends the Bishop of Chełm to King Casimir to propose talks. The King considers it unwise to reply until he has consulted his advisors, or to leave Bydgoszcz until Chojnice has been taken or has surrendered, and dismisses the Bishop with the promise that he will give his reply in a fortnight. At the end of the fortnight, he sends Jan Długosz the Elder and a companion to fix a day and a place for talks. These catch up with the Master on August 4, and agree the Nativity of the Blessed Virgin as the date and Toruń as the place for the King to go to and Chełm for the Master, with Chełmża, halfway between the two, as the venue for those who are to work out the details. A special messenger is sent to summon the papal legate.

At about this time, George Poděbrady assembles a scant 2000 foot and horse, a wretched lot, composed mainly of brigands and those accustomed to live by looting, but among them is a Pole, who maintains that the King of Poland owes him certain monies. This little force, without any declaration of war, enters Poland and seizes the town and monastery of Częstochowa and several surrounding villages. The starosta of Cracow could easily have dealt with the raiders, but delegates the task to the starosta of Spis, who procrastinates and so allows the raiders to move to Dorniowica, and thence to Namysłów, which they besiege for a fortnight. Then, feeling that pressure on them is mounting, they plunder the immediate country and cross the Oder into Moravia at Welczyn. When the King learns what has happened, he immediately complains to George Poděbrady, who tells his two envoys that the raiders had no orders to do what they did, but acted on the prompting of the Pole who claimed that King Casimir owed him money; so that the King must either pay up, or, if he denies the debt, as he does, allow the matter to go to arbitration. A date is fixed for the hearing: the Feast of St. Andrew the Apostle, and the place, Bytom. (This is later postponed until the following Trinity Sunday, because plague is rampant in Bytom, and then postponed again because of civil war in Silesia.)

On August 17, Duke Henry of Słupsk arrives in Bydgoszcz. Having been granted an audience, he humbly requests the renewal of ancient pacts, which is granted; he then proposes to send his whole army to assist the King should the latter's troops besieging Chojnice be attacked, and also to defer payment to the enemy of what is due for Bytów and Lwów as long as the King likes; he promises, too, that he can easily make the captains of Chojnice surrender to the King. In return, he asks that his eldest son be taken into the King's household to live and serve with the King's own sons. This, too, is granted, which just shows that this was nothing unusual, but, rather, the custom. Then, having spent four days in Bydgoszcz, provided with all that he and his men needed, and having asked for and been given six very lovely cloaks, money and horses, he goes to Chojnice, where, through an intermediary he has talks with the captains, but these hinder, rather than hasten capitulation, and he then returns to his duchy. Shortly after this, he sends his chaplain to Chojnice to negotiate its surrender not to the King, but to the Duke himself, who is ready to pay the amount due in cash; however, the chaplain is not even allowed into Chojnice, and returns covered with shame. All the commanders and most of the men in the garrisons of Bytów, Lwów and Chojnice are Silesians and averse to surrendering to the King of Poland, for the Silesians are more hostile to the Poles than are the Knights or the Germans; indeed, no people is more inclined to hate the Poles than are the Silesians. They are grieved if the Poles enjoy any success. Like traitors and worse than foreigners, they hate to see any development of our nation and tongue. This is the cause of considerable anxiety to the King and his advisers, whose only concern is that the siege of Chojnice should not prove vain, for its capture would bolt the door through which reinforcments from Germany have been reaching the Knights. So, the King orders artisans and peasants from every town, village and fort in Wielkopolska and Kujawy to come with their tools and waggons and encircle the town with ditches and ramparts, adding their endeavours to the slow digging of the soldiers, and thus the work is soon completed to the dismay of the besieged. The presence of so many new mouths causes a dearth of almost everything, but particularly of corn and drink, the worst affected being the horses. Those in Gniew and Nowe are better able to support a siege, not because there is no timber there with which to build towers and ramparts, but because alongside each castle flows the Vistula, which allows those inside to obtain provisions and whatever else they need.

As the time approaches for the Toruń conference, the King leaves Bydgoszcz, where he has spent almost two months because the plague is rampant in Cracow and elsewhere in the kingdom, and reaches Toruń on August 7. The Papal Legate arrives the next day and in a speech to the dignitaries assembled in the town hall explains his mission as peace-maker. Replying, the King assures him that, although he has victory in his grasp, he does not reject peace, and, so as to prove that the war on which he has embarked can be ended peacefully and equitably, he is not going to ask for more than the territories illegally wrest from his kingdom and those parts of Prussia to which he is entitled. So impoverished has the Prussian Master become, that he has not been able to attend, though his subjects have offered to defray the cost of the journey. Chełmża having suffered such damage as to make it unsuitable for talks, these are transferred to Nieszawa.

Fierce struggles between besiegers and besieged have been a daily occurrence at Chojnice; but now, on August 14, the besieged make a last desperate attempt to defeat their besiegers. For several hours the fighting is furious and casualties heavy; but, in the end, the besieged are forced back inside; however, in order to prevent the Poles getting in with them, they have to close the gates before all their number are inside and those excluded are either killed, taken prisoner or thrown into the water-filled ditches. The Poles then start building two long, wide ramparts and trenches to deprive the besieged of any hope of outside help; also, during the night of August 15 they shoot flights of incendiary arrows into the town, causing fires which the besieged vainly try to extinguish, for the roofs in Chojnice are made of thatch, and thus a quarter of the town goes up in flames; indeed, the whole would have burned, had not a strong wind got up and blown the flames in the opposite direction. The Poles, now in possession of half the town, keep up the pressure by setting fire to the remaining roofs and eventually terms for surrender are agreed, which allow the besieged to leave unharmed and with all their possessions, but leaving their guns and other weapons. Both sides then release their prisoners and, on August 28, the town, the besieged's guns, projectiles and all their weapons are handed over, the besieged mount their horses and, weeping copiously, ride out, heading for the seats of the German dukes, who never gave them the help they had promised them. They are escorted by the Poles as far as Lwów and Bytów, which, a fortnight later, are handed over to the Duke of Słupsk in exchange for 8000 florins. The King, thanking God for the surrender of Chojnice, moves the besieging force to Toruń, where each is rewarded in accordance with his service.

For several days the Knights in Nieszawa refuse to credit rumours of the surrender of Chojnice; but then a letter from the Prussian Master arrives, which confirms the news.

The papal legate now goes to Chełm and over the next several days the more important points of the treaty are agreed with the King's secretary and the two then return to Toruń, where they are joined by the Prussian Master and his officials. It is nearly two months before all the minor points are settled; but, although plague has broken out in the town and members of his Court and councillors are dying every day, and he himself is advised to leave, the King is so eager to conclude the treaty that he remains there until peace is assured. So, on October 19, when all the articles have been drawn up in Latin and confirmed by the signature of the papal legate, the three official notaries and the seals of King Casimir and the Master of the Prussian Order, as well as of the prelates and councillors of either side, the King and Master head a great procession to the Guildhall in Toruń, where, after greeting and embracing each other, they hear the terms of the treaty read first in German by the papal legate, who does not know Polish, and then in Polish by the King's secretary; the King and the Master then kneel and swear on the wood of the True Cross proferred by the legate, to observe all its conditions. The archbishops and bishops present and all the King's and the Master's officials do the same. All then go to the cathedral, where a *Te Deum* is sung and a solemn Mass said. Then all are invited to dine with the King.

Now, Poland is to have the territories that naturally belong to it: Chełm, Michałów and Pomerania, and the Master and the Order for all time renounce any right to them, except for three villages in Neryndza, which the King has graciously granted to the Order, as their possession makes fishing in the River Haba easier, though the King retains for himself hunting rights throughout Neryndza. Similarly, Malbork, Sztum and Christburg, the old and new towns of Elbląg and the town of Tolkmit and its forest, six villages of the castle at Holand and all its dependencies are to belong for ever to the King and Kingdom of Poland, and the Master and the Order forever renounce any claim to them. Next, all Prussia, its towns, castles, fortresses, manors and villages, except for those of Malbork and Elbląg, with the right to defend them, appoint the bishops of Pomezania and Sambia are forever to belong to the Order and be ruled by it. Again, half the fishing rights is to belong to Poland and half to the Order. Next, that the Prussian Master and his successors are to be dukes and permanent advisers of the Kingdom of Poland, and the Order's principal commanders, such as the Master appoints, are to act as advisers, but under the King and subject to him, to be treated with favour and their rights maintained. Within six months of his election, each new Master is to present himself in person before the King and swear, for himself, his commanders and the lands of Prussia, to respect the peace and never to seek relief from his oath, and, even if granted this, never to make use of it; also that the Master is to have the right to sit on the King's left. Similarly, that the Master, the Order and the lands of Prussia and such other territories as the Order may conquer from the barbarians are for ever linked to the Kingdom of Poland, united with it and incorporated in it, so as to form one indivisible body, one people, one nation, united in friendship. Apart from the Pope, none but the Kings of Poland shall be regarded as their head or ruler, and the Kings

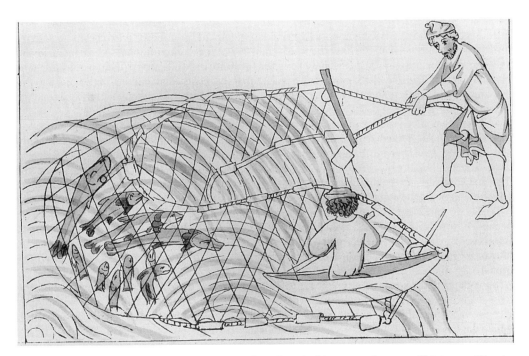

The right to fish in rivers or lakes was eagerly sought and a valuable source of revenue. This is one of the pictures in the Hedwig Chronik. —*British Library.*

of Poland will give them assistance against all enemies, will never abandon them whether in success or adversity, nor will they wage war or make alliances with Catholics without their cognizance and agreement; that the church in Chełm is to return to its maternal church in Gniezno and remain united with it; that its chapter shall be changed from a regular to a secular observance and remain for ever administered by the King. Also, that the Church in Warmińsk with its chapter, its castles and towns are to be subject to the authority of the King, the Master and the Order renouncing all right to it. Also, that the King's secretary will now be transferred to the Church in Chełm and have, for his lifetime, authority over it, but that, on his death, the church shall revert to the authority of the Master. Similarly, all castles, towns, fortresses, villages and other places rightly belonging to the Church are to be surrendered by either side to the churches involved. Both sides are to free all their prisoners of war. The highways are to be used as before, exempt from new taxes or regulations. The Order of the Teutonic Knights is to admit suitable subjects of the King of Poland as members, though their number is not to exceed half of the whole, and such are to be eligible for consideration when new captains or other officials of the Order are being appointed. The King has to approve new Masters of the Order, and these are not to be removed without proper cause or the King's consent. Neither the King nor the Order will apply to any ecclesiastical or lay authority to be relieved of this agreement; nor, if granted such relief, will either make use of it. All castles, fortresses and towns occupied by the Order in the King's territories, or transferred to the Order in Pomerania, Chełm or Michałów, on the Feast of St. John the Baptist, are to be returned to the Kingdom of Poland and vice versa. All hostile or rebellious acts performed by private citizens are to be forgotten and the perpetrators assured of their lands and possessions. All gifts or sales of goods made by either side during the hostilities are to be completed to the advantage of the second party or else be made invalid. All deserters and exiles, especially of the nobility, are to be allowed to return to their properties and to enjoy them. All transfers of their properties are to be cancelled and their properties, houses or lands that may have been sold are to be returned to them or they are to be given the amount paid by the purchaser. To ensure that this peace shall endure, both sides will endeavour through their delegates to have it confirmed by the Pope. Sanctions will be imposed for any breach of it.

It is common knowledge that neither the King of Bohemia nor the Lithuanians like the treaty: the Czechs because it means that Poland no longer has to worry about Prussia; the Lithuanians because, having previously failed to contest the loss of Podole or the grant of independence to Łuck, once called Volhynia, now that Poland's might has been increased by that of Prussia, they have lost the opportunity to hurt Poland. Even some Poles, are worried by this sudden, advantageous peace, which they consider shameful, because the country was not consulted, and also because now they will have no opportunity to enrich themselves with plunder and, too, will lose the royal domains, because now the King will have plenty of money. Thus they denigrate the achievement and pretend that those, who made the peace, could have obtained better terms had they not been in such a hurry. Nor do the mercenaries like the peace, because, without war, the demand for their services will diminish, as will their value.

As the papal legate is preparing to leave Toruń, the King, wishing to reward him for his services, sends him four silver platters worthy of his achievement, two goblets, forty gold florins, four gilt boxes, a number of sable and marten furs lined with purple, and various other objects, gifts which the Cardinal's office forbids him to accept. Instead, the King appoints the Cardinal his permanent adviser with an annual fee of 200 florins to be paid by the salt works in Cracow. The King's generosity extends to others: the Master is given three lovely sables, 300 florins, two goblets, two silver dishes and two very good horses as a parting present. Others of the Knights are given equally lavish, though smaller gifts. Learning how impoverished the Master is, the King gives him 15,000 florins with which to pay his mercenaries, hoping thus to ensure his loyalty.

The Cardinal, having obtained an audience with the King, tries to persuade him to turn his attention to the Bohemian question and urges him not to allow that vile, cunning heretic, George Poděbrady, to continue trampling the faith in the country which he rules illegally. The King, he says, must remember that the two countries have almost the same people and language, and that the King of Poland is the only one with a title to Bohemia, which he has through his wife, Queen Elizabeth, heiress to the kingdom through her father, her grandfather and her great-grandfather. He tells the King that, in Bohemia, are many eminent persons loyal to the orthodox faith, as are many towns; but, even were there none, Wrocław on its own would provide a secure centre for his rule. There are, too, Silesian dukes eager to get rid of George Poděbrady. So, King Casimir should liberate Bohemia and earn a reward from God even greater than the renown he would have in the world. Should his concern for Poland prevent him himself accepting the throne, let him give it to his eldest son, Władysław, or, indeed, his second, third or fourth son. The Pope is prepared to help generously with finance and will promise him all Silesia and Lusatia. The King tells the Cardinal that these are difficult questions and, as there is so little time for discussion, since they are having to leave Toruń because of the plague and they are all exhausted by dealing with Prussia, they cannot give him a proper answer: but, if he will attend the May assembly in Piotrków he will, God willing, be given an answer.

The date for paying the mercenaries is postponed until the Feast of St. John the Baptist.

The papal legate now leaves Toruń and goes to Wrocław, the Master and his officials to Prussia; and so, on October 28, the King leaves for Nieszawa, making his way through the remoter villages in order to avoid the plague. On November 8 he moves on to Kozienice, where he deals with a number of local matters and goes hunting. There he stays until January 29.

Meanwhile, the mercenaries of both sides, being made to wait for their money and having nothing to do, unite to form a force of some 2000, which moves into Słupsk, where it occupies a town and remains there all winter, despite being repeatedly ordered to move out. The holder of the town responds to this by occupying the royal town of Draheim. Eventually, both relinquish possession.

In the middle of August, the Tatar khan, Hadzigerej, dies, some say, poisoned by his own people. As long as he ruled, he maintained peace between Poland and Ruthenia. Benevolent, gracious and eager to do good, he even offered his huge army to help the Christians against the Turks, should Casimir just ask for his help. He turned his Tatars from looting and plundering and set them to cultivating the land and the exercise of crafts, so that they now lived by work and trade. He was humane, generous and gracious to the Poles, many of whom served under him, and to all Christians in his empire. His death was a greater loss to the Christians than to the Mahomedans.

This year and those of the recent past have been bad ones for the Poles, perhaps because of the long war and the severity of the times. Crime has gone unpunished, and men have formed the habit of curling their hair and of dressing in order to evoke the admiration of women; they go bareheaded indoors and out, compete with women in the softness of their bodies and vie with them with dangling locks and ribbons with which they swathe their breasts, a thing previously scarcely allowed to women, but now a speciality of men. The perversity of the dissolute has increased enormously and crime multiplied beyond measure. Many, unable to take care of their inheritance, squander their possessions and take to robbery and plundering. In others you can see greed, pride and depravity in their refusal to accept the rules of the Christian religion. They despise the Church. They vaunt the deeds and virtues of their ancestors; talk big and puff themselves up, as though they were the authors of these deeds. When high-ranking posts are vacant, business and bribery see that they are granted not to the most respected or most able, but to him who pays most.

This year is memorable for the removal by Pope Paul II of George Poděbrady from the throne of Bohemia. When it became obvious how fraudulent had been many of the oaths the latter took at his coronation, the Pope, on December 23, stripped him, as a heretic, of all royal or princely status, and freed all subjects of Bohemia from subjection to him or his jurisdiction, and deprived him, his son and their progeny of the right to acquire any high office or honours.

The winter is exceptionally warm, much to the benefit of the plague from which all Poland is suffering, though not Prussia, Pomerania, Ruthenia and Mazovia.

A.D. 1467

To avoid the plague, the King and Queen spend Christmas at their country residence in Kozienice, which is on the Vistula, near Radom; and here, on January 1, the Queen gives birth to her eighth child, a fine son, who is christened Sigismund. A few days before he is due to leave Kozienice, the King receives an envoy from George Poděbrady, who asks him, both verbally and in writing, whether the rumour that the King is intending to take over Wrocław is true, and also whether or not he intends to honour the pact that he and Poděbrady made in Głogów. Poděbrady already knows that the Pope has stripped him of his titles and he has a presentiment that Cardinal Rudolf, speaking for the Pope, has prevailed upon the King to accept the throne of Bohemia and so Poděbrady has sent this envoy to flatter Casimir and find out the truth.

The King sends the Queen, their children and their baggage to Korczyn and himself leaves to attend the assembly in Piotrków on May 3. There, he receives delegates of the Teutonic Knights bringing the legal document confirming the pact of lasting peace concluded in Toruń. Attached to this are the seals of the Master, the various Knights and captains of the Order and of the citizens of Prussia, and a corresponding document with an equal number of seals is requested from Poland. There are also delegates from Pomerania, Chełm and Elbląg requesting that, in view of the changed situation the King create three new sets of offices: voivodes and castellans for Malbork, Gdańsk and Chełm. Another arrival is an envoy from the Tatar khan, Nurdula, successor to his father, Hadzigerej, who proposes ties of friendship and an alliance, asserting that the Khan continues to regard the King's friends and enemies as his own, and that he is ready to help King Casimir against his enemies, an offer that is graciously accepted. The next problem is that of the payment of the soldiers, who have served in Prussia for thirteen years, many of whom have come to Piotrków with their wives and children; but the Treasury is empty. The question of how the money is to be raised is the main one facing the assembly. In recent years the outlay incurred by private individuals has so impoverished them, that it takes them seventeen days to find a solution. The local diets, held previously, had reached no conclusions, since most of the knights were against providing any help. Now, two new diets are announced for Wielkopolska and Cracow. In the meantime, each soldier to whom pay is due is to receive two gold coins and a promise of a further four in a few months time.

By promising to pay them out of a large sum allegedly owing to him for military help against the Knights given in previous years, the castellan and starosta of Nakło induces some mercenaries to try to capture Słuchów. Failing in this, he exacts a large tribute of cattle from the surrounding country and imposes a monetary tribute on the district of Nakło. Refusing to surrender his arms when called upon to do so, he is captured on May 13 and handed over to the castellan and starosta of Poznań, who takes him to Kalisz, where he is beheaded in public, thus squashing an incipient rebellion.

Yet another envoy from George Poděbrady now arrives, again requesting that King Casimir honour the Głogów agreement and not support those rebelling against him or interfere in the struggle. Should Poland have suffered any hurt or injury, the envoy promises that anything taken will be returned or replaced and all cause for further raids removed. The King's reply is that hitherto he has honourably kept the agreement, though the King of Bohemia and the Czechs and their ruler have broken it repeatedly, and that he will continue to honour it, provided that the Czechs and their ruler will do the same, and, if they break it, pay the necessary compensation. The delighted envoy returns home promising that all shall be done as King Casimir wishes.

The King, still in Piotrków trying to arrange payment of the money due to his Prussian veterans, receives letters from the Catholic nobles in Bohemia begging him not to allow a heretic to rule a Slav kingdom, which by rights belongs solely to King Casimir and his sons, nor to allow a heretic to rage against the faithful, but to help them in their predicament of having six towns under siege by Poděbrady. Replying, the King tells them that his councillors, without whom he cannot decide so complex a matter, have already left. Being cautious and anxious not to get involved in another war, the King prefers to procrastinate and wait upon events. Already the barons of Wrocław are under arms and in the field with some mercenaries devastating parts of Silesia that are loyal to George Poděbrady, their purpose being to draw him away from the six castles in Bohemia. The Wrocławians capture Frankenstein and George Poděbrady brings up a force which the barons of Wrocław could easily have defeated had they attacked at once, but, instead, they shut themselves up in the castle, allowing the Czechs to receive reinforcements: 1000 cavalry from Meissen and 500 from Brandenburg, whose two dukes, despite the papal ban, have allied themselves with George Poděbrady by marrying their daughters to his sons. As the city of Wrocław is preparing a force to relieve Frankenstein, now under siege, a violent quarrel breaks out among the knights there, and this allows the enemy to scale the walls and get into the town. The cavalry from Wrocław escape, but all 4000 of the infantry are either taken prisoner or murdered, thus the Czechs get possession of the town, the castle and a considerable booty, including 600 siege engines and cannon.

The King's envoys return from Rome, their mission unaccomplished, for the Pope has decided to leave it to Cardinal Rudolf to confirm the peace and lift the punishment imposed on the gentry and townspeople of Prussia.

At the end of June, the King and Queen go to Cracow where, on July 2, other papal legates arrive and, in audience, beg the King to accept the crown of Bohemia for himself or one of his sons, for the Catholic nobles have declared George Poděbrady deposed and have elected Casimir as king. Their arrival is followed on July 28 by that of Cardinal Rudolf, preceded by a few days by the Grand Inquisitor of Heretical Iniquity and the Dean of Akwin, who have escaped the hazards of having a price of 4000 florins put on their heads by Poděbrady. The King is given a document, confirming his election by the Czechs, and is asked in the name of the Pope to accept the crown of Bohemia for himself or one of his sons; if he does so, he will have the help of the Pope, the Emperor and of all the German and Silesian dukes and princes, the Catholic Czechs and Moravians, as well as those of Lusatia, who, having rejected Poděbrady on the orders of the Pope, are now anxious for King Casimir to rule them. The Cardinal produces two bulls, one an instruction to confirm the Prussian peace treaty, and the other an order to raise the interdict placed on the knights and citizens of Prussia, but only if the King accepts the crown of Bohemia for himself or one of his sons and gives practical help to whomever accepts it. It grieves the King to see peace being made dependent on his becoming involved in a civil war in Bohemia, when he has only just finished fighting one in Prussia. He and his councillors cannot devise an answer that will not deprive the King and his sons of their right to Bohemia and yet not involve them in a dangerous civil war. The reply finally given is that the King thanks the Pope and the Czech nobility for the offer of the crown that legally belongs to him, but that it is not fitting that he should decide such an important matter without consulting the prelates and nobility of his own kingdom, who will have to help him rule the country, should he accept the crown, so he is transferring the assembly due to be held in Korczyn, where plague is rampant, to Cracow and will give his answer after that. Meanwhile, he proposes to send a delegation to try and stop the domestic strife in Bohemia and to persuade George Poděbrady to return to the true faith and humble himself before the Supreme Pontiff, and asks that in the meantime there should be no pronouncement of punishment on Poděbrady, nor any announcement of a crusade.

The King sends officials to Prussia to discuss the question of financial help in paying what the King owes the troops who have been fighting in Prussia for thirteen years and who have agreed to accept eight florins for each year of service for the cavalry and half that amount for the infantry, this to be both pay and compensation for any injuries suffered. This means that the King owes 270,000 złoty which has to be paid in two instalments over the next two and a half years. The King himself remains in Cracow for another three months, during which he distributes gold and goods to the value of 70,000 złoty among the troops. He appoints Jan Długosz tutor to his sons. Then he and the Queen travel by country roads to Lithuania, where they spend the autumn, winter and spring. To avoid the plague, the King's sons are moved from Cracow to the monastery at Tyniec.

The Polish envoys reach Prague on October 1, their mission to get George Poděbrady and his people to obey the Pope and use the service and ritual of the Catholic kings and princes, for unless this is achieved peace cannot prevail. The idea appeals more to George Poděbrady than to his court, and, his heart softened, George Poděbrady leaves everything concerning peace to King Casimir. As far as religion goes, George Poděbrady insists, wrongly, that he has kept his agreement and never refused obedience to the Pope; he asserts, too, that he will repair whatever damage he has done, provided that the town and castle at Konopisk are surrendered to him. The Polish delegates suggest that there should be a truce to last a whole year after which King Casimir will give his final decision. George Poděbrady makes the delegates gifts of gold and horses, but these they refuse and so set out for home. When they reach Wrocław, the papal legate, the dukes of Opole,

Głogów and Żagań, and others from Moravia, Silesia and Bohemia demand to be shown the text of the delegates' instructions, and to be told whether they are prepared in the King's name to accept the throne of Bohemia or give an assurance that the King will help them in defeating those who in previous years have twice helped the heretics, asserting that with Bohemia conquered, Austria, Hungary and Romania would all pass into the hands of the King of Poland and his sons; for, as the King has five sons, he will presumably wish to conquer not one, but several kingdoms, it being be a bad thing having so many princes inside one kingdom, and civil war being worse than war with foreigners. When the envoys repeat King Casimir's refusal to accept the crown, they are pressed to send the King's eldest son with a thousand horse, so that he, after being crowned in Wrocław by the papal legate, can rule from there. They reply that they should not be asked for this either, and return to Prague to await events. No one expects George Poděbrady to honour the terms of the agreement, but rather to resort to lies and cunning; but, once certain difficulties have been overcome, a truce is arranged to last until Ascension Day. As soon as this has been confirmed, Poděbrady sends an army under his son, Victor, to start hostilities against Austria and the Emperor.

In Prussia, the King's delegates have a series of meetings with the Prussian Estates in Gdańsk, Elbląg and Malbork, which are also attended by delegates of the Order. The mercenaries hired by the Order are stubbornly demanding their pay, while the Order is calling upon Toruń to hand over the 15,000 florins promised as soon as peace was concluded. When, Gdańsk and Elbląg are also asked to contribute, they refuse, saying that they are already in debt and poverty-stricken; so that it now looks as if there must be fighting, for the mercenaries are furious. In the end, thanks to the efforts of the Poles, Gdańsk, Elbląg and Toruń agree to pay 12,000 florins, 6000 on the Feast of the Purification of the Virgin and the rest two weeks after Easter.

Some years previously, the King had appointed as voivode of Moldavia a certain Stephen, a member of the Duke of Moldavia's family. This Stephen's rule has been so strict and just that no crime has gone unpunished and people now obey his every order. He has insisted that not only the knights and nobility should bear arms, but that farmers and villagers do so as well, for everyone has a duty to defend his fatherland. If the Voivode learns that a farmer does not have a bow, arrows and a sword, or has mustered without a spear, the culprit is condemned to death. The King now appoints this Stephen governor of Walachia, promoting him over the heads of other candidates, one of whom, Berendeja, has gone to the King of Hungary, promising to restore Walachia to him. As a result, King Matthias has assembled a considerable army, which, in the middle of October, marches through the forests and mountains into Walachia, burns a town, which the troops are allowed to plunder, and continues along the foot of the mountains, burning towns and villages as it goes. When Voivode Stephen now bars its progress near Tortrusz, King Matthias, not being sure of the loyalty of his troops, avoids a pitched battle and limits his efforts to surprise attacks and ambushes, yet is himself prevented from foraging or doing further damage. When he reaches Barni, he fortifies the town with ramparts, ditches and a ring of waggons for he is still afraid of Stephen's army which is encamped between the rivers Moldau and Szamos. Stephen sees this as an opportunity to do battle; so, leaving the horses and baggage in his camp, he advances on Barni, sending small detachments on ahead to set fire to the town in a number of places. When, in the early evening, flames burst out, Stephen launches his attack. Fighting continues with varying success until dawn. Many of the Hungarians fall or are consumed in the flames, and King Matthias, thrice wounded, has to be carried from the battlefield on a stretcher, to avoid him falling into the hands of the enemy. When, moving on, the Hungarians again reach the hills, they find the roads barricaded with tree-trunks and, after burning their three-horse waggons and burying all 500 of their guns, so as to deny them to the enemy, they manage to escape. Some of the Hungarian standards are captured and these are sent to King Casimir in Wilno as proof of Stephen's victory, which has provided a huge booty of tents, waggons and guns. Back in Hungary, the King imposes a fine of 400,000 florins, to be paid in gold, on the knights and citizens of Transylvania for having deserted him. This money he uses to organize another and larger army, mainly of foreign mercenaries. This year plague has affected almost all Poland, emptying villages and even towns: as a result foodstuffs have become expensive, though not as expensive as they would have been had the plague not killed off so many. There is, too, a plague of mice that destroys the crops in the barns and then takes to the fields and there destroys the winter-sown crops.

A.D. 1468

The King and Queen leave Lithuania and reach Cracow on April 13. At Easter, the King bathes the feet of twelve of the poor and gives them new clothes; and, on the following day, takes Holy Communion.

The Bishop of Olomouc arrives on April 8 and, three days later, is received in audience, when he tells the King that he is there in his private capacity, having left the King of Hungary in Bratislava. He is able to tell the King that, at the request of the Holy See, King Matthias has undertaken the defence of the Faith and of Czech Catholics against George Poděbrady and his heretics, and has given a written undertaking—the Bishop shows the King the original document—to wage war against Casimir and that he already has a force under arms. The Turkish sultan has sent Matthias lavish presents which the King has reciprocated, hoping to arrange a three-year truce. The Roman Emperor has also prepared an army to help fight George Poděbrady, and many people have joined the crusade against the heretics. The Czech catholics have already joined the Hungarians, whose troops are well-trained and well-equipped and eager to fight; the Bishop asks the King to trust the Pope and join him and the other kings and princes in freeing from the tyranny of George Poděbrady the Bohemia that belongs to him and his sons. The King can be confident that King Matthias has taken up arms solely to support him and his sons, so that Bohemia shall the more quickly pass into their hands. Then, in a private audience attended by only five of the King's councillors, the Bishop proposes that King Casimir give his eldest daughter, Jadwiga, to Matthias as his wife, and his youngest daughter, Sophia, to Maximilian, son of the Roman Emperor, thus creating a useful alliance between the three and relieving the other two of any fear that, should Poland take over Bohemia, the one might be turned out of Hungary and the other out of Austria. After much discussion, the Bishop is told that King Casimir does not refuse the crown of Bohemia offered him by the Pope, but that he reserves his decision until after the general assembly that has been called. Should anyone in the meantime try to take over what belongs to him and his sons, he will look to Almighty God to protect him and will make every endeavour to see that any such occupation is of short duration. He also reminds the Bishop that King Matthias has broken their agreement and inflicted considerable damage on Poland by twice ravaging the territory of Spis and, more recently, Moldavia, and it would not be fitting for King Casimir to forget such hurts and choose a son-in-law from among his enemies. If the King of Hungary wants to be related to the King, he must know that nothing can be done until after the general assembly and until he has repaired the harm he has done and put an end to such violence. The Bishop then departs, disappointed, but laden with gifts.

The following day an envoy from George Poděbrady arrives. He is received in audience on May 17, when he thanks the King for having sent a delegation to Bohemia to try to stop the war and reminds him that George Poděbrady has placed the whole matter in his hands, as he still does, though the truce that was to last until Ascension Day has not been honestly observed by either side. He begs the King to renew his efforts to stop the dreadful war King Matthias is waging against Bohemia and to reconcile George Poděbrady with the Holy See. Because, if he can arrange a place for an audience which George Poděbrady can attend in person, he will be able to clear himself and will gladly repair any damage he has done; on the question of religion he will yield to kindness but not to force. He goes on to say that George Poděbrady is excluding his own sons from the succession and ordering that his successor is to be none but a son of King Casimir, not by right of inheritance, but solely from the goodwill of the Czechs. So, the King is invited to send delegates to a future general assembly of Bohemia to receive official confirmation of Poděbrady's promise as to his successor. Replying, the King assures the envoy that he will gladly help in stopping the civil war and will send people now, but only if their security is assured. Also he will try to reconcile Poděbrady and the Pope, provided Poděbrady gives proof of his purity and renounces his errors. The envoy sets out for home laden with the gifts that have been sent to his hostelry, but still apprehensive lest King Casimir march into some part of Bohemia and so involve the Czechs in war not only with the Hungarians, but with the Poles as well, an even a greater enemy.

George Poděbrady's son, Victor, after several weeks fighting in Austria, expels the nuns from Polger nunnery and fortifies the building like a castle, from which he plunders the country as far as the Danube, stopping all trade and work on the farms, and forcing the frightened Duke of Austria to send a force of mercenaries to eject him. Anticipating this, Victor and his brother, Henry, join forces and withdraw out of danger to Spilburg castle in Moravia. The Emperor's force, which is commanded by a Swede, Groffenekker, attacks the nunnery. Using cannon to breach the ramparts they capture it and the town, and kill all but a few of the Czech garrison; before moving on into Moravia against Victor. Learning how small is the enemy force, Victor advances to do battle and would have, had the enemy not sought safety in the town of Znaim.

King Matthias has long hated George Poděbrady because of the ransom of 70,000 florins the latter exacted from him, a thing Poděbrady now considers past history seeing that the two are now related, Matthias having married one of George Poděbrady's daughters. So, having assembled an army of Polish, Czech and Hungarian mercenaries and equipped it suitably with waggons, cannon and other armaments, he marches into Austria and takes up position near the town of Lawa in a watery, boggy area by the River Taja, intending from there to wage war on the Moravians and Czechs. Undeterred, George Poděbrady assembles another force, mainly of peasants, which he himself heads despite the impediment of his gross belly. Reaching Lawa, he pitches camp not far from the Hungarians, so as to deny the latter pasture for their horses, and surrounds his camp with ramparts. Though so close to each other, for more than four weeks neither side attacks the other, the Hungarians being afraid of the Czech infantry, and the Czechs of the Hungarian cavalry; but the Czechs do take the fort of Martnic with its large Hungarian garrison, which surrenders to avoid the bloodshed inevitable if it was stormed. Its capture, in full view of the Hungarians, is followed by days of discussion, which result in a three-year truce being agreed, but this is not implemented as Poděbrady refuses to surrender to their rightful owners the forts, towns and lands captured during the previous year, while the Hungarians, who lost them, refuse to make peace without them. The Czechs are now suffering from hunger and have lost many of their horses, so Poděbrady strikes camp and—no one dares attack him—marches back to Bohemia and establishes himself in the town of Poděbrady. His son, Victor and most of the cavalry have been left in the Moravian town of Trzebiczow, which has strong fortifications and is well sited. King Matthias also breaks camp and advances on Trzebiczow. He starts his assault by setting fire to the suburbs; a very strong wind fans the blaze and the whole town goes up in flames. Victor and two knights manage to escape with 500 horse and seek safety in the monastery which, long before, they had fortified after ejecting the monks. The fire kills many men and horses and destroys much equipment; indeed, is a disaster. The King then besieges Victor in his monastery, which he rings with a triple rampart, confident that hunger will soon deliver them into his hands. But Victor prolongs his resistance, he and his men subsisting on horse-flesh without salt, and water. Each day sees a number of skirmishes, which cause considerable casualties. Then, Poděbrady's other son, Henry, arrives with a fresh army, flanked by four-horse waggons and pitches camp so close to the Hungarians that bullets easily pass from one to the other. This proximity causes difficulties, in that there are skirmishes every day, which prevent the ramparts being finished and interrupt the cartage of provisions and foraging. Since both sides have been ravaging the countryside, especially the Hungarians who have many more horses, they now have to go six miles or more to find pasture, a dangerous expedition. Both sides lose horses from hunger, and the troops, themselves short of provisions, eat their flesh; while the rich find that a florin will buy only four loaves. Now, the Duke of Bavaria arrives with a force of Swabians and Swiss. The Catholic Czech nobility and the people of Pilsen capture a number of towns. Victor requests a personal meeting with King Matthias, but this is refused; then, seeing that he is in real danger of having to surrender, he decides on one last effort. One night, just before Whitsun, he marches out with 1300 infantry, leaving a garrison of only 500 in the castle, makes his way through the enemy's outposts and reaches Henry's camp and then goes on to his father's camp four miles away. Trzebiczow castle now surrenders on condition that the garrison may walk out leaving half their arms and horses. Poděbrady has now lost so many men, arms and horses that he never recovers; yet for a long time both armies remain in the field probing the possibilities of battle, but doing nothing. Poděbrady now secretly arranges a meeting with King Matthias and this might have led to an agreement, had not the King's councillors called him back to Olomouc before he could do any harm.

Three Polish officials arrive and have talks with Poděbrady in Prague at which they urge him to reconcile himself with the Pope and then to step down from the throne in favour of one of Casimir's sons. This Poděbrady refuses to do, but promises to leave the throne not to his sons, but to those of King Casimir, which promise he will confirm in writing, if the Poles will arrange a truce and a meeting with the Pope. The Poles move on to Olomouc where King Matthias and the two papal legates are. Meanwhile, hunger forces three castles to surrender to the Hungarians. The men of Wrocław capture Frankenstein castle and demolish the town there, and the Czechs are driven from Samba. It is not a happy year for George Poděbrady.

King Casimir sends two officials to Walachia to pacify the voivode of Moldavia and assure him of help against the Hungarians or any other enemy, and also to fix a day and place for the voivode to pay homage to the King. The King and Queen go to Wiślica to attend an assembly at which the King demands assistance in paying the mercenaries. Although this is agreed in principle, the matter is referred to the general assembly to be held in Piotrków in order to allow Wielkopolska to have its say. The King then goes to Koło, where the matter is again referred to Piotrków.

The King now moves to Bydgoszcz where he spends several days and sends the Archbishop of Gniezno home, as he is ill and paralysed down his left side. Then, sending the Queen to Nieszawa, he and the court move to Gdańsk, which is being asked to provide a considerable sum to help pay the mercenaries. This, however, is refused on the ground that the city is already in debt to the extent of 700,000, but it agrees to pay tonnage for the next eight years, which will pay its own and the King's debts. Of this the King is to receive three-quarters of the revenue for the first three years, the remaining quarter going to Gdańsk, Toruń and Elbląg, which towns will receive the whole of the revenue for the next four years. Gdańsk will then return to the King three parishes, relieving the King of having to pay what is due on them and also sparing Gdańsk 2000 a year for fifteen years. The city agrees to lend the King 5000 florins to be repaid out of the tonnage which is expected to produce 15,000 florins.

A stubborn war is being waged by the Kings of Sweden and Denmark. The Danish king, not having the means to pay an army, has been robbing English ships bound for Gdańsk, taking goods to an estimated value of 20,000 florins, and has been using this to pay his troops. The English, unable to avenge themselves, have been retaliating upon the Gdańsk merchants, confiscating all their goods on which they can lay their hands. King Casimir tries, not without difficulty, to compensate the merchants. Fighting has broken out between the Margrave of Brandenburg and the Duke of Słupsk, who appeals to King Casimir to remember their agreement and help him against the Margrave, who has received reinforcements from Meissen and elsewhere, and suggesting that if the agreement is not enough, the duke is ready to pay the King homage and swear obedience. The King tries to arrange a truce. On the Feast of the Nativity of the Blessed Virgin the King goes to Malbork, where he spends almost a month conferring with the deputy Master and his captains. Matters arranged, the latter are dismissed with splendid gifts, and Nidburg is returned to the Order and the Order encouraged to elect a new Master soon; but the election has to be postponed because of the absence of the German and Livonian Masters, who according to the constitution have to take part.

The search for the means to pay the mercenaries is the only matter to be dealt with by the next assembly at Piotrków, but since the delegates of the knights and gentry say that they have no brief to agree to provide help, it is decided to hold two further assemblies: one for Wielkopolska in Koło, the other in Korczyń. The King now moves on to Radom and Jedlna, where he spends more than a month hunting. After this he attends the assembly at Korczyń, visiting the monastery on Łysa Góra and presenting it with wood from the True Cross. There is much discussion over helping the King pay the mercenaries. None of the knights wishes to give out of his own purse, so, finally, they agree, though with difficulty, on an impost of twelve grosses on each peasant and to this even the delegates of Wielkopolska agree, though with the proviso that half the amount is to be paid by whoever owns a farm or village and the other half by the peasant who has the field. In practice few of the knights respect the proviso, but shift the entire burden onto the peasants who are already in dire straits because of a poor grain harvest caused by heavy rain the previous year, and because rain has also hampered the autumn sowing. The King postpones his return to Cracow until Christmas, so as to avoid being pestered by the mercenaries, who have been promised payment by then and many of whom have come early to collect it.

A.D. 1469

After Christmas the King goes to Niepołomice, where he hunts. He distributes most of the game among the dignitaries of Cracow and Włocławek.

On Twelfth Night he and the Queen return to Cracow, where they are welcomed by their four sons, the eldest of whom makes a beautiful speech of welcome. Casimir spends three weeks in Cracow, during which he persuades the mercenaries to agree to a postponement of payment until Passover, by which time the revenue from the new impost should have come in. Each receives twelve grosses on account.

The King goes to Lwów to receive the homage of the voivode of Moldavia, who has been specially summoned, yet delays his arrival on the pretext that he is afraid that if he leaves the country, the Turks, Hungarians or Bessarabians might occupy it; but, in reality, because he is afraid the King may put him in prison. However, to avoid angering the King, he pays homage and swears fealty to the King's envoy and undertakes to come in person as long as he is given two months notice. The King receives envoys from the new Tatar Khan, Mengligerej.

On Christmas Eve the Emperor arrives in Rome with 500 teams of horses. After secret discussions with the Pope he and his son, Maximilian, are confirmed successors to the thrones of Hungary and Bohemia. The Pope, playing for time, defers confirming the Prussian peace.

When the Emperor Frederick returns to Vienna, at the instigation of King Matthias, one of the Emperor's courtiers, Bankkirchner, to whom he has entrusted Austria, cunningly occupies a number of castles and fortified towns, his excuse being that he has not been paid money due to him. He then attacks the Jews, whom the Emperor has treated with exceptional favour, murdering and robbing them, and even sends an army against the Emperor. When the Emperor prepares a large army to deal with him, as he must, Matthias, no longer able to hide his hostility to the Emperor, sends his own army to help Bankkirchner with the object of extending his power over Austria, and thus involves Austria, Styria and Carinthia in bloody war.

In the first days of spring, having already taken over the whole of Moravia, King Matthias invades Bohemia with an army of 10,000 horse and 6000 infantry and heads for Kutná Hora, burning and devastating the country for seventeen miles in either direction, to the terror of the heretics. George Poděbrady has his force of 5000 horse and 18,000 infantry camped in the meadows of the monastery at Siedlec, but, being afraid of treachery, does not dare risk a pitched battle and so sends to the King asking for a meeting. This is granted and the two meet. George berates his father-in-law for attacking him and is told that this has been done on the orders of the Pope, because Poděbrady is a heretic and persecutes the Catholics. Poděbrady insists that he will not leave this world outside the true faith and tells the King to summon the legates, promising to obey their orders. This leads to an armistice and the two legates are summoned to Olomouc for peace talks, as are most of the bishops and nobles of Hungary. The two rulers then meet in private and have further long talks. Neither dares try his luck in battle, for though the Hungarians have more cavalry, the Czechs have three times as many infantry, and both feel that defeat would be disastrous. These talks arouse the suspicions of the Hungarian councillors and, especially, of the papal legates, lest the King is betraying the true faith and the Holy See. King Casimir's envoys sent to Rome are also present, their aim being to prevent the two from coming to any decision which Casimir would consider prejudicial. The prelates are glad of their presence and ask them to stay until everything is settled; but when the matter drags on, they continue on to Rome.

Fire breaks out in Olomouc during a riotous dicing session at which the King is present. The fire is contained, but the King's troops start looting the houses, whether burned or not, which adds considerably to people's losses.

Despite all the discussions, the only document to be signed is that for a truce to last until the Feast of the Circumcision.

On May 3, King Matthias is finally elected King of Bohemia by the bishops of Olomouc and Wrocław and a few eminent Czechs. The new King then goes to Wrocław to receive the homage of the people and dukes of Silesia, which most of the latter are willing to give. The King is accompanied by one of the papal legates and a bishop sent by the Emperor. The Archbishop of Esztergom and the Bishop of Eger and some prominent Hungarians are also present, and it is their presence that induces the Silesian dukes to pay homage. The Margrave of Brandenburg, who has been invited, is there too. The King demands that he support him, and this the Margrave does, but he refuses his other demand that he make an alliance with him against all and sundry, on the grounds that he cannot take up arms against the King of Poland, because the two countries have a common frontier and the King of Poland could devastate Brandenburg before King Matthias could come to the Margrave's assistance. The King then goes to Legnica and Świdnica to receive homage, after which he returns to Wrocław, where he spends several days watching jousting with lances; then, at the Emperor's request he goes to Austria to help the latter there; however, the Emperor's army of mercenaries is defeated in a fierce engagement with Bankkirchner and Groffow before Matthias gets there.

King Casimir leaves Lwów after Easter and reaches Cracow on April 27 to be received with great ceremony and a speech made by his second son, Casimir, in Polish. Here he remains for eight weeks, during which time he pays the troops who served in Prussia a first instalment amounting to 140,000 florins, half of it in cloth bought with the impost on peasants and townspeople. He obtains further postponement of the second instalment for a whole year.

On June 17, delegates from the bishops and catholic lords of Bohemia and Moravia arrive in Cracow. They are received in audience and begin by justifying their action in rejecting Casimir and his sons and choosing Matthias blaming Casimir's procrastination and attributing to this much of the harm inflicted by George Poděbrady. They ask that the King stop supporting the heretics and support them instead, for, should he do so, the heresy might easily die out. They further ask that he be generous to King Matthias since friendship between the two will benefit the Faith and the two kingdoms. Though hurt by the rejection of himself and his sons, King Casimir realizes that the people of Wrocław, Lusatia and the Silesian dukes have been afraid of him and afraid that, as their king, he might involve them in war with Hungary, which was itself involved in war with the Turks, and whom they would be expected to help. Nonetheless, he is gracious to them, presents them with furs and tells them that he will reply to their requests after he has discussed them with his councillors, of whom at the moment there are too few present. The Czechs now begin to regret having chosen Matthias, and one of them, having seen and talked with the King's sons, announces with tears in his eyes that he is sorry that they transferred their choice from these boys, the true heirs to Bohemia, to the King of Hungary and that he himself had not agreed to it, but had been overpersuaded. While the Czechs are still in Cracow, news comes that George Poděbrady, who still considers himself King of Bohemia, and all his supporters have, in the presence of the Polish envoys sent to examine the conditions of the truce with Hungary, repudiated the earlier election and chosen King Casimir's eldest son as their king. Though more pleased than displeased by the news, the Czech delegates' advice is that, if Poděbrady, who is a trickster, really has left Prague, the election should not be refused, for Matthias' marriage to King Casimir's daughter would surely stop him from persisting in his claim to the throne of Bohemia. As George Poděbrady has done this in the presence of his three sons, he cannot be insisting on their succeeding him, and he must have done this because King Matthias has told him that he cannot stick to their secret agreement, especially that of getting the Pope to allow George Poděbrady and his subjects to receive the Eucharist in both forms, despite the papal legates having banned such an arrangement. The truce having come to nothing, fighting breaks out again with even greater bitterness.

An unofficial assembly is held in Radom to ensure the defence of the realm in the event of an attack by the King of Hungary. The long-expected envoys from Poděbrady now arrive and confirm that considering the state of the country and the infirmity of George Poděbrady, the result of affluence and overeating, they have elected King Casimir's son, Władysław as their future king, on condition that George Poděbrady is to retain the sceptre as long as he lives; that the King of Poland will defend him against any enemy, will seek to obtain an audience with the Pope for him, and, should this prove impossible, not to desert him in any need; that the King's son is to succeed only on George Poděbrady's death; that Poděbrady's wife, Joanna, retains the right to her dowry and his sons their rights to their dukedoms, and all the nobles retain their rank and office, and, once those to whom the King of Hungary has given Bohemian positions have been expelled, the posts are to be returned to those from whom they were taken. In addition to these rather onerous conditions is one much more difficult, namely that the King's son, Władysław, is to marry George Poděbrady's eleven year-old daughter, Ludmila, which marriage is to act as confirmation of his election as king, but, if he refuses the marriage, this will negate his election. Almost no one likes the idea of marriage to a heretic and one who has inherited gluttony from both parents. Most of the King's councillors are against exposing Władysław to the double danger of heresy and war; so envoys are sent to Bohemia to object to the worst conditions, especially the marriage. Another two officials are sent to Prussia to deal with complaints and to quash possible disturbances. It is suspected that the Order has been persuaded by the King of Hungary to break the alliance and is now contemplating war.

Fighting breaks out again when King Matthias arrives in Wrocław and lays siege to a number of forts. In the fighting, Poděbrady's son, Victor, and his troops are encircled by the Hungarians and in trying to escape Victor is captured and sent to Buda for safe-keeping. When he learns of his son's capture, Poděbrady lays siege to three towns belonging to Jan Zając, in one of which is the latter with his infant son, Poděbrady's intention being to capture Zając and exchange him for his own son. Zając escapes, but the towns are besieged nonetheless. At this time the Voivode of Moldavia makes an incursion into Hungary and plunders much of Transylvania. He defeats the Hungarians in two engagements and triumphantly returns with his booty to Walachia. Meanwhile a force of Silesians assembled at the urgent request of Jan Zając to raise the siege of his towns sets out for Bohemia. Then, having a presentiment that the Czech heretics are having talks with the besieged over surrender unless relieved within a certain time, the difficulty of getting so large a number of four-horse waggons through the mountains between Silesia and Bohemia causes them to lose heart and they disperse to their homes. Learning of this, the Czechs, numbering a scant 2000, lay siege to Zylawa and at the third assault capture the mill and 100 of the people, killing twelve of the defenders. Then they move into Silesia and devastate the countryside near the mountains. No one comes to its defence, despite King Matthias' call for help, and although some villages and buildings can pay to save themselves from being burned, none can be saved from looting. This immunity costs 12,000 florins, which does not cover any of the Church's possessions. The people lay the whole blame for this on the bishop and city fathers of Wrocław, because they chose Matthias. King Matthias then sends the dukes of Cieszyn and Rybnic a thousand florins in gold to hire troops and force the other Silesian dukes to take up arms. These two lay siege to Opava, while the other half of Silesia is attacked by Poděbrady's starosta. Meanwhile, the Czech army, having sent home its booty of cattle and other goods, enters Moravia to raise the siege of Hradiště and starts ravaging the area round Trenczyn. King Matthias, then attending an assembly in Bratislava, asks it for a large amount of gold to help him fight the Czechs, but the Hungarians, feeling insulted by his continual demands for money and hating his cruelty, for most of them have had castles and properties taken from them, and disliking his impulsiveness, start talking of driving him out. Matthias collects an army and marches against the Czechs besieging Hradiště, only to be defeated by Poděbrady's son, Henry, though himself escaping with but three companions. The Czechs collect splendid booty, but are unable to raise the siege of Hradiště; but from now on they are in the ascendant and many of the Czech Catholics desert Matthias and join George Poděbrady.

The Tatars plunder Lithuania, not daring to enter Poland because of the army there already under arms. The Voivode of Wołów boldly condemns one of the Khan's sons to death.

While the King and Queen are in Lithuania, a large Tatar force, made up of deserters and exiles, whom the Tatars call Cossacks, under Khan Maniak, crosses the Volga and penetrates into Poland. Part of this Cossack force captures some 10,000 captives in Vladimir, Krzemieniec and Zytomir, for the Lithuanians sent against them did not defend the area because of the great difference in their numbers. Also, because of the long period of peace, the peasants and villagers, forgetting what they have so often been told about the Tatars, fail to take refuge in their marshes, forests and other hiding places. King Casimir sends to his friend and ally, Khan Medigerej, informing him of this incursion, and, assembling an army from all over Poland and Lithuania, makes camp near Treboula. When the second part of the Cossack force learns of its presence, it turns aside and moves off quickly. The third part of the Cossack force which has entered Walachia is twice defeated, but in a third engagement captures a number of prisoners, but loses the son of its own Khan, Maniak, who, convinced that threats will bring about his son's release, sends a delegation a hundred strong to the Voivode of Moldavia, threatening vengeance if he does not release his son. The Voivode, a man of spirit, is not intimidated, but reminds Maniak of his treachery in starting hostilities without a declaration of war and then has the Khan's son quartered before the eyes of the delegates, who are then impaled, except for one who is sent back to Maniak without his nose, to report what has happened.

While attending the November assembly in Piotrków the King receives delegates from the Margrave of Brandenburg and a very clever envoy from the Duke of Słupsk, who ask him to adjudicate on the long drawn out squabble between the Duke and the Margrave over certain feudal rights. The Margrave's delegates produce numerous documents signed by the Roman Emperor and other kings as proof of his entitlement, but these are rejected by the Duke's envoy on the ground that feudal possession of Słupsk belongs to neither of them, but solely to the King and Kingdom of Poland, of which Słupsk was originally a dependency. This complicated matter has been examined by the doctors of Cracow university, who have left it to the King to decide. The Brandenburg delegates are also asking for the King's youngest daughter as bride for Albert, the ten-year old son of the Margrave by his second marriage. The King does not reject the idea, but a decision is deferred until a later date. The King supplies all these delegates with whatever they need and dismisses them with splendid gifts of clothes. With them goes the Justiciar of Poznań entrusted with the task of reconciling the two or at least of stopping the fighting.

The new Grand Master of the Prussian Order, Henry of Plauen, arrives with two of the Brethren and are graciously received. The Grand Master in person takes the oath of loyalty and obedience to the King of Poland laid down in the peace treaty. He and the King discuss their problems. The Grand Master then departs laden with gifts and the King and Queen having spent six weeks in Piotrków go to Lithuania.

On the last Sunday in December, the Grand Master, then in Morag, suffers a brain haemorrhage during breakfast and falls from his chair. He loses his speech and dies two days later. The post is temporarily filled by Bernard of Schumborg who, five days later, dies poisoned, it is said, by a woman. He dies in such poverty that he is given no honours, not even a pyre.

The severity of the winter has covered bogs, ponds and rivers with thick ice, which allows a huge Turkish army to invade Hungary and Slavonia and devastate them as far as Cilia, for neither the Croats nor the Hungarians hinder them.

A.D. 1470

After Christmas in Grodno, the King moves to Wilno and, having spent some time there, sets out with the Queen and some eminent Lithuanians to inspect the duchies of Polotsk, Vitebsk and Smolensk, which he has not visited for close on seventeen years. This done, he returns via Lublin to Sandomierz, stays there over Easter, and then moves to Korczyn, where he receives a papal legate, who has come to insist that the King take action against the heretic and rebel, George Poděbrady and remove him and his supporters from Bohemia, and also to persuade him to make an alliance with the King of Hungary by marrying his daughter to the latter's son; for, though the Pope would prefer to see Bohemia go to one of Casimir's sons, he cannot agree to let Matthias, who has done him considerable service, go unrewarded. Meanwhile, an envoy from Emperor Frederick, a Pole who has been in his service for many years, arrives with a colourful retinue, having had to avoid a number of traps laid for him by King Matthias, the danger of which had prevented any of the Austrian lords accepting the mission. The envoy tells King Casimir how latterly the Emperor has wished King Matthias well and has considered his assumption of the throne a matter of little importance, yet, when the two met in Vienna to consolidate their friendship by giving Frederick's daughter, Cunegund, to Matthias as his wife, Matthias demanded that the Emperor relinquish his titular right to Hungary in favour of Matthias, reimburse the 70,000 florins, which the latter had paid for the actual crown of Hungary, and also return certain Hungarian castles given to the Emperor as surety for that sum, together with those illegally seized by Bankkirchner, to whom the Emperor is to pay 40,000 złoty in compensation. At this meeting, the two became so angry with each other, that King Matthias departed in a hurry without taking formal leave, the Emperor riding after his boat in an effort to preserve appearances. The envoy goes on to say, that, though many seek an alliance with the Emperor, Frederick considers friendship with King Casimir more important than friendship with other kings or princes, and he urges Casimir to send envoys to the Emperor, fully empowered to conclude an alliance and so strengthen their friendship. He also warns the King to be circumspect in dealing with Matthias and never to conclude an alliance with him or stand surety for him. The King listens graciously and dismisses the envoy with lavish gifts and sends with him two of his voivodes, who have instructions to conclude a treaty of friendship with the Emperor; and also to arrange ties of blood by giving the King's daughter, if asked for, to the Emperor or his son, Maximilian, and getting the Emperor's own daughter, Cunegund, for Casimir's first-born, Władysław. The Emperor is also expected to help Casimir conquer Hungary and Bohemia and himself renounce all claim to either kingdom.

King Casimir now sends yet another envoy to George Poděbrady to urge him to abdicate in favour of Casimir's first-born, Władysław, and allow him to be crowned during Poděbrady's lifetime. The envoy is also instructed to go to the Catholic lords supporting King Matthias and reconcile them with George Poděbrady, since force-of-arms has not advanced their cause. However, it now looks as if George Poděbrady is gaining the upper hand. He has equipped his troops with battle-waggons and sent them against Matthias in Moravia; but, when the latter does not dare risk a pitched battle, for he has lost many men by desertion, Poděbrady withdraws his army and tries to put an end to the protracted siege. Having captured three of the bastions and supplied the hungry townspeople with provisions, he is planning to go to Trnava, but then Matthias' army of mercenaries arrives on the scene and it looks as though they are going to have to fight it out; but the two armies avoid each other: the Hungarians as they cannot attack Poděbrady because of his waggons fitted with scythes, the Czechs because they cannot pursue the Hungarians in such precipitous, awkward places. In the end, Poděbrady sends to Matthias suggesting that the two of them fight a duel in front of the two armies or else fix a place and a day for a pitched battle. While Matthias is hesitating, Poděbrady ravages Silesia. Matthias, in an attempt to stop him, makes a forced march into Bohemia and starts burning the villages round Kutná Hora. However, Poděbrady's wife, Joanna, raises a force to stop him and Poděbrady himself comes up with another force by a different route. Afraid for himself and his army, Matthias withdraws in some disorder, abandoning many exhausted horses. Back in Hungary, the King furls his standards and disbands his troops. Lack of money prevents him assembling another army for the rest of the year.

Wrocław and the other Silesian towns, having no money with which to pay their mercenaries, dismiss them, leaving themselves incapable of opposing Poděbrady, when he sends a force of 4000, which fortifies Oleśnica in Opole, and Labacszów, near which he builds another fort and also bridges the Oder. He imposes heavy tribute on the whole country, and sets fire to some of the villages and unfortified towns. The despairing Silesians send to Matthias to ask him either to defend them or to allow them to make a treaty or truce with Poděbrady.

After eleven weeks in Korczyn, King Casimir sets out for Lwów with 3000 men and reaches it in easy stages on July 13, having arranged to receive the homage of the Voivode of Moravia there. For nine weeks he waits, for the Voivode is tied up in war with the Voivode of Bessarabia and insists that he and his country would be in real danger were he to leave it. In the end he sends the King a written undertaking, bearing his own seal and those of his councillors, that on May 1 of the following year he will pay homage to the King, and that, meanwhile, will the King help in putting an end to the war between him and Bessarabia. The King, being in a hurry to attend to other matters and his troops being short of provisions, agrees, only advancing the date by six months, when he does send envoys to arrange peace, fearing lest otherwise Bessarabia obtain help from the Turks, and so strengthen its position.

On October 14, the King attends an assembly of the knights and barons of Cracow in Korczyn. In his address he asks for financial assistance in paying the outstanding wages of his troops. Continuing to Piotrków for the general assembly there, his first act is to ask for the financial help already voted, but not yet paid. Here, he encounters several difficulties, one being that although he has ruled for more than twenty-three years, he has not yet confirmed the rights of the kingdom with the royal seal. Also, the knights of Wielkopolska have deliberately stayed away, so as to avoid being asked for help; while the Ruthenian knights are refusing to contribute unless their country is given effective protection against the Tatars. Matters are so complicated that the assembly has to be prolonged and, in all, lasts for thirty days, the King finally yielding to necessity and promising to use the royal seal, which will be the first time it has been seen. It is also agreed that the levy on fields under crop in Cracow is to be paid by the Feast of the Purification. The King also asks the Church for help but this is promised rather than voted upon. A levy is imposed on all towns in the kingdom. The soldiers owed money are asked to accept a delay in payment, and do so. The Papal Legate, summoned to the assembly, is plied with gifts and told that, on his return to the Holy See, he is to ask for confirmation that none but the sons of King Casimir has a right to the throne of Bohemia, a thing the Pope has already accepted, and not allow this to be altered before the arrival of the King's envoys, who are to leave in a matter of days, and who will have fresh instructions about this and other matters.

On November 17, the new Master of the Prussian Order, Henry of Richtenberg, is escorted in by seventy mounted knights and, three days later, before the assembly and in the presence of the papal legate, personally swears loyalty and submission, as he is bound by the treaty to do, and departs, well pleased with gifts from the King.

The King's three envoys to the Pope have been instructed to go first to Prague and urge George Poděbrady to show submission to the Holy See and to provide an assurance that the Czechs will not change their minds about accepting Casimir's eldest son, which rumour has it they are thinking of doing and then putting themselves under the King of Hungary. After this, when they reach Rome, they are to demand confirmation that the Kingdom of Hungary will pass to King Casimir's son, and also confirmation of the peace with Prussia.

The envoys sent to the Emperor return and report to the King in Poznań. The terms they arranged being manifestly unfair, the King will not confirm them, lest they invalidate his son's right to the kingdoms of Hungary and Bohemia.

On July 30, the Turkish Sultan invades the Greek island of Euboea, which is under Venetian rule, and lays siege to the town of Negropont, which, after an assault lasting three days and nights, is captured with the loss of 30,000 men. The immature children are taken away to Constantinople to be subjected to the Turks' obscene practices, and the wealthy town itself is razed to the ground. This creates a new danger to Catholic shipping and augurs badly for many, especially the cities and kingdoms of Italy. The Pope urges the Catholic kings and princes to fight the Turks.

On October 11, a small Turkish force makes its way by secret paths through the mountains and forests into Transylvania and, meeting with no resistance, penetrates as far as Zagreb in Croatia. Encouraged by this success, the Turks make a similar foray around Christmas and again find themselves unopposed.

Envoys from the Pope and Venice arrive in Buda to remind King Matthias of his undertaking to fight the Turks, for which he was granted a suitably large sum of money. The King's reply is that he will assume this burden, if Venice will return to him the Kingdom of Dalmatia, which it took from him by force. This answer shocks the envoys, who then return to Venice. The Venetians would rather entrust the task of fighting the Turks to the King of Poland, for they feel that, if he has any more of their money, the King of Hungary might become so powerful as to constitute a threat.

As the King and Queen are leaving to go to Wilno, news reaches them of the death of the Duke of Kiev, who, when he felt that he was dying, sent to King Casimir entrusting him with his dukedom and his wife and two children, and giving him the horse and sword with which the Duke had so often overcome the Tatars. The Lithuanians, being eager to have Kiev, as one of their Ruthenian dukedoms, persuade the King to appoint a starosta for Kiev. The people of Kiev are horrified, when they discover that the man chosen follows a different rite and is not even of noble birth, and protest that they would rather die or seek another duke, than obey and entrust themselves to a Lithuanian, and they ask the King to appoint someone belonging to the Greek Church, rather than the Latin or perhaps one of his own sons. The dispute keeps the King in Lithuania, for he is afraid of fresh disturbances should he leave before the matter has been resolved. In the end Kiev accepts the new starosta.

At assemblies in Malbork, Gdańsk and Elbląg the King's officials again ask for help in paying his soldiers' outstanding wages, even though previous requests have been refused on the grounds of poverty. Now, they agree to a turnover tax on trade. The officials then go the Prussian Master in Krolewiec and settle a dispute involving those of his troops that have not yet been paid.

War is now the only way of deciding disputes in Silesia. Each plunders, burns and kills the other; but, what is even worse, King Matthias has started minting counterfeit coins in Wrocław, using a little silver from broad grosses to mix with base metal, and these coins are circulating in Silesia at twice their value, so that poor peasants are giving two heavy Meissen coins for one bad Wrocław coin. This is considered most harmful and there are numerous protests. People begin to regret having put themselves under Hungarian rule.

A.D. 1471

Matthias had come to fear that his own people would seek to replace him with one of the King of Poland's sons, and so decided to make peace with George Poděbrady and his Czech supporters, some of whom he bribed. His proposal was that Poděbrady should have the entire kingdom as long as he lives; that Poděbrady's son, Victor, whom Matthias has already freed, should be made Margrave of Silesia and Moravia and succeed Matthias if he dies without progeny. The Czechs are now more inclined to favour Hungary than Poland, especially as they feel that, with Hungary and Bohemia one, they will enjoy peace. An envoy is sent to King Casimir in Lithuania to explain and excuse what they are doing; and, indeed, the matter might well have been resolved in Hungary's favour, had not the Chancellor of Poland, on his way to Rome, gone to Prague and there emphasized that they could not with impunity fail to keep their promises, and persuaded them to keep the matter in abeyance until his return from Rome.

On March 22, George Poděbrady, weakened by disease and the spread of the great swelling in his legs, dies. When his body is eviscerated the following day to avoid any stench, its liver is found to be half destroyed and the gall bladder to contain a stone the size of a pigeon's egg, while the stomach is no larger than the palm of one's hand. His people mourn him as one reluctant to shed human blood.

King Matthias is informed of Poděbrady's death by special messenger. Convinced that the crown of Bohemia is to be had without fighting, if he acts at once, he leaves Bratislava earlier than intended and goes to Beroun with his main army, sending 2000 cavalry ahead to show the Czechs and anyone else that they had better accept Matthias. Czech opinion is divided: some support the King of Poland, others the Emperor, others Hungary, yet others Poděbrady's son, Henry, especially those who are heretics and thus afraid of what would happen to them under a Catholic king. The Margrave of Meissen is a staunch supporter of King Casimir, whose daughter he has married; others favour Louis of France, who has promised to redeem all church and crown possessions that have been pawned; some favour the Margrave of Meissen because he is a neighbour and has married George's daughter, while others would like the Duke of Bavaria, because of his reputed wealth. All this time Matthias remains in Beroun, having spent a fortune bribing the Czech nobility. The Margrave of Meissen arrives for talks in Prague with 5000 men-at-arms, pretending to have come to help the Czechs should Hungary put pressure on them, but in reality hoping to get it for himself. King Casimir returns to Cracow on May 12 and sends three envoys to remind the Czechs of their earlier promises to accept his eldest son Władysław as their king. The final choice is to be made by a newly-convened assembly to be held in Kutná Hora. The Margrave of Meissen remains in Prague.

Matthias sends special envoys to the new assembly. These seek to justify the King's previous cruelty and promise that henceforth he will be benevolent. A Polish envoy is also present and is heard with great approval. The assembly rejects the King of Hungary out of hand, and, at twelve o'clock on May 27, elects King Casimir's eldest son, Władysław, their new king. When he hears that his hopes have been dashed, Matthias falls into a rage and indulges in a fury of burning and killing.

A nine-man delegation now goes to Poland and is received in audience on Wednesday, June 13, when it informs King Casimir that Władysław has been unanimously elected King of Bohemia, and that they are there to ask him to accept the crown and to come to Prague as soon as possible to be crowned and to see to the defence of the realm. A document is drawn up and, on June 15, in a private painted room in the royal apartments, Władysław agrees to accept election. This he repeats in the Great Hall and again on the Sunday during Corpus Christi ceremonies, when the Czechs recite the text of their mission, and Władysław, in a beautiful speech in Polish, accepts the throne of Bohemia for the greater glory of God, for the furtherance of Christianity and the honour of the Slav people. Rashly he gives a written promise to return to anyone whatever Bohemia may owe them, thinking such debts to be small or, at least, not large.

After spending three days in Oświęcim to allow his retinue to assemble, the new king orders his men and waggons, takes leave of his father and sets out. He is accompanied by three bishops, six Silesian dukes, two Polish voivodes, the canon of Cracow, Jan Długosz the Elder, and many others, the whole numbering 7000 men on horseback and 2000 on foot. While at Kłodzko he receives a document announcing the breaking-off of friendly relations by the Voivode of Transylvania and a number of Poles, Czechs, Hungarians and Silesians serving in the King of Hungary's army, then encamped near the Moravian town of Lipnik. Undeterred, but making sure to send scouts ahead, he continues; however, before he even reaches the hills beyond Kłodzko popularly considered the boundary between Poland (Silesia) and Bohemia (the true frontier being the Forest of Herczyń) he is welcomed by Henry Duke of Frankenstein, one of George Poděbrady's sons, and various knights and lords, as well as by representatives of the clergy and people. He reaches Prague on Monday, August 19 and, on the 21st, is crowned king of Bohemia and anointed in the metropolitan church of Prague by the Bishop of Podole in the presence of representatives of the Duke of Meissen and the Margrave of Brandenburg. The next few days are spent paying off the debt of 30,000 złoty accumulated during the war, the whole burden of which falls on the new King's shoulders.

After spending six weeks in Prague, King Władysław goes to Kutná Hora and forcibly takes possession of it. He then sends back to Poland the two voivodes in his retinue, and Canon Jan Długosz of Cracow and all the courtiers, who have kept reminding him that he must be wary of being poisoned, a thing, it is said, many would like to see happen. What is remarkable is that on their way to and from Prague, not one Pole was captured, wounded, killed or assaulted.

While all this is going on, the Hungarians, burning with hatred of their King because of his failure to defend the country against the Turks and for all the shameful things he has done, have been pestering King Casimir to send his second son to be their king, promising to defray the entire cost, and also threatening that, if he hesitates in accepting, they will ask the Turks instead, for they would rather obey a barbarian than a shameful king and cruel tyrant, who acquired his kingdom by force. Dangerous as such an undertaking would be, but believing the Hungarians capable of carrying out their threat, the King sends them his second son, Casimir, with a mixed force of 12,000, including 100 Tatars, though some of his councillors would have preferred to see this particular young man stay at home and eventually become their king.

Learning of all this, Matthias goes to Buda, summons his troops from Bohemia and Moravia, and arranges a series of assemblies at which, with bribes and promises, he wins back many of the older men previously opposed to him. This makes others change their minds, among them János Vitéz Archbishop of Esztergom and the Bishop of Transylvania, largely because Casimir has not yet arrived. The latter reaches Hatvan on November 8 and there pitches camp, but, after a short time, lack of firewood forces him to move to a monastery and town on a river, where he can get provisions and firewood. He then moves on to Nitra, where the Bishop of Transylvania joins him; but, for the rest of the war, none of the Hungarian nobles follow suit, not even those who, earlier, had sworn to die for him. Now, they all side with Matthias, who, lest it look as if he were hiding in Buda, moves his army, estimated at 17,000, most of them mercenaries, into the field, as though he were ready to do battle, and pitches camp three miles from Casimir's camp. From here he devastates the villages and properties of Archbishop Vitéz of Esztergom and of the Bishop of Transylvania, but he does not engage the enemy. Then, feeling uncertain of the loyalty of his Hungarians, he disbands them, and returns to Buda with his mercenaries.

The new Pope, Sixtus IV, sends his chamberlain to King Casimir to persuade him to abandon his action against Hungary. The King is prepared to listen and sends the chamberlain on to his son in Hungary with the message that he does not wish to refuse peace, if its conditions can be just and fair.

The period of service for which young Casimir's German mercenaries have been engaged having come to an end and there being no money to continue to pay them, they are dismissed. Along with them go many of the Prince's Polish courtiers. Casimir withdraws the rest of his troops to Nitra, but when Matthias advances against him, in order to avoid being besieged, he moves to the fortified town of Ilawa, leaving 4000 men to defend Nitra. While this move was being made, no sentries were ever set and this allowed sixty of the Poles' four-horse waggons to be stolen.

The Turkish viceroy in Bosnia makes a surprise raid into Kraina and for three months puts it to fire and the sword, devastating the country as far as Ljubljana, and carrying off some 30,000 Catholics. Then, learning that the Roman Emperor was attending an assembly in Ratisbon, 15,000 of his cavalry make a lightning dash through Croatia. By sunset on the day after Whitsun the Turks are almost at the walls of Ljubljana and might well have captured it, had they not set fire to some villages, the smoke from which was seen, thus betraying their presence. The Viceroy now divides his army and sends one part through the mountains between Karniok and Styria into the famous Sava valley, as far as Cilia, where it rounds up 30,000 and carries them off into captivity; the other part is sent to wreak havoc throughout Slavonia along the Danube, and continues into Istria, as far as the town of Gorz.

A.D. 1472

King Casimir and the Queen spend Christmas in Cracow beset with worries: Casimir, their second son, having accomplished nothing in Hungary has returned to Poland and, on his father's orders, is living in Dobrzyń castle. The commander of the Polish troops remaining in Nitra having been successful in a number of duels with Hungarians besieging Nitra, has made a truce which allows Nitra to remain under Prince Casimir and, leaving 300 to guard it, has withdrawn the rest of his men, much to the discomfort of the Hungarian gentry. However, Matthias breaks the truce and organizes a pursuit of the Poles, thinking that his superior numbers will give him an easy victory, but then he changes his mind and calls off the pursuit. Many of the Poles fighting with the Hungarians not for glory, but for money, complain of Matthias' breach of the truce.

One reason for the Poles' lack of success in Hungary is that, while on the march, they respected neither sacred objects nor people's rights. They plundered churches, robbed and beat people, raped girls and young mothers, all because their commanders either acquiesced in such behaviour or failed to curb it by punishing the offenders. Another of the King's worries is that he has depleted his treasury to ensure the success of his Czech and Hungarian ventures, and is now deeply in debt and, having pledged almost the whole of his revenue, has scarcely enough for the daily sustenance of himself and his family. The King's men in the four places in Hungary which they have fortified and which are now under siege, give up all hope of receiving help from their King and surrender, losing their freedom, belongings, horses and armour. A fifth fort, at Stropkow, is not threatened, for Matthias rightly thinks that should he lay siege to it, King Casimir, being so close, would come and relieve it.

Matthias captures the Archbishop of Esztergom and, despite having guaranteed him immunity, has him put in a pillory and threatens to let barbarian archers use him as their target unless he surrenders his castle at Esztergom. When the officials there refuse to obey the order to surrender, he lays siege to it and five others. Some surrender on condition that they are in future to be under the jurisdiction of the Bishop of Eger, now paralyzed by fear and the torture to which the King has subjected him, and that, on the latter's death, he should not be replaced by a Pole.

The knights, who have returned to Poland after fighting in Hungary, find their pay withheld, because the treasury lacks the necessary funds, and they start plundering churches, especially those in the diocese of Cracow, and destroy some 500 villages belonging to the clergy. The delegates to the assembly in Piotrków spend five days discussing ways of providing the money to pay these knights, but nothing is decided. The King then goes to Korczyn, where he begs the assembled lords to give him financial assistance and these do consent to pay an agreed sum for every field of theirs under cultivation. The barons of Wielkopolska do the same, and the clergy of its four deaneries also provide considerable help, all, that is, but the Cracovians who give half what the others contribute. Many of the unpaid knights become highwaymen.

On May 13, Queen Elizabeth gives birth to her fifth daughter and tenth child. She is christened Elizabeth.

After five weeks of talks, the Castellan of Sącz, sent to Hungary to end the war, arranges a truce and returns to Poland to find out if the King and his councillors will abide by its terms. They do not find the terms entirely acceptable, but they do agree to a truce, which is to last until the Feast of St. John the Baptist, when officials from the three kingdoms will meet in Olomouc and conclude a temporary peace. All agree that for Poland and Hungary to be at war with each other is both wrong and dangerous, because of the Turkish Sultan Mehmet, who has already occupied a large part of Hungary and is threatening Austria, Styria and Carinthia, and is said to be preparing a huge army with which to attack Belgrade and Raško in the summer.

Now, out of Persia and Lower Armenia comes another sultan, Hussenkassen, a man of unknown—even to himself—family, who has made himself famous by his conquests and is opposed to Mehmet and his sons, though he does not dare risk a pitched battle. Mehmet's son assembles a huge army and with the help of his relations and the Tatar khan, routs Hussenkassen decisively, and, advancing on Trebizond, which Hussenkassen had captured some years previously, kills the Greek Emperor of Trebizond and most of his supporters. Then, with surprising speed he captures Sunopta in Anatolia, and, summoning the Venetians to help him, advances on Gallipoli. He sends an embassy to King Casimir, which reaches Cracow in the middle of July, its purpose to request the King's help against Sultan Mehmet, a request that is refused. Meanwhile, Mehmet who feels that his downfall is imminent, having vainly asked the Sultan of Babylon for help, has started fortifying all his towns, especially those on the coast.

Plague breaks out, so on August 12 the King leaves Cracow with the Queen and their children, and moves to Niepołomice and, after a few days there, to Korczyn, where he receives another visit from the papal legate. During the eight weeks he spends here, the King calls a special assembly to discuss payment of the money still due to the soldiers from Prussia, who are making their presence felt through robbery, brigandry and the theft of church goods and tithes. Then, leaving the Queen in the monastery at Sulejów, the King goes to Piotrków for the assembly. There he finds himself compelled to fill many vacant posts, though his choice of officials is not popular. Messengers arrive from Władysław in Prague asking for money and troops, and the King at once sends 500 men-at-arms. who set up their base near Kutná Hora, which the King of Hungary is said to be intending to attack. Władysław is also granted 10,000 złoty, which is to be raised by a levy of six pennies on every field of knights' holdings and a farthing from all fines imposed in the dioceses of Gniezno, Włocławek and Poznań.

From Piotrków the King goes to Toruń to put an end to the civil strife that started when the Pope transferred Michael Tungen from Warmińsk to Kamień and various posts in Prussia were given to Poles. The wrathful Tungen has hired 500 mercenaries and with these and some impressed peasants captured Brunsberg and Galstadt. He has also fortified Frauenberg and Ressel. Four weeks of talks produce no result, largely because of the Prussians' insistence that all Prussian castles be entrusted to Prussians of whom the King approves. Though the King does not refuse this, he insists that it must be accompanied by a monetary contribution with which to pay the present incumbents what they are owed. Tungen, who is afraid to present himself in person, sends messengers who promise complete submission and loyalty, and beg the King to restore him to the see of Warmińsk. In the end the whole matter is deferred until after Whitsun.

While in Toruń, King Casimir receives envoys from King Christian of Denmark, who suggest that the King's eldest son, Władysław of Bohemia, should marry Margaret, daughter of the Marquis of Mantua and niece of the Margrave of Brandenburg, whose virtues, noble blood and large dowry they emphasize, pointing out how such a marriage would ensure the King the friendship of the Dukes of Meissen, the Margraves of Brandenburg, the Cardinal of Mantua and many other Italians. The suggestion is well received, but, of course, has to be referred to Władysław and his councillors.

In the summer of this year, a Turkish army from Bosnia raids Illyria and devastates the country along the River Sava and the Slavonian march. In September, it reaches the territory of the Patriarch of Aquileia, which is under the Venetians, and raids as far as Pryul and the castle of St. Daniel, carrying more than 12,000 off into slavery. In November it devastates the town of Gorica and the whole of Istria, and no king or prince opposes it.

Through the intermediary of the papal legate, the Emperor Frederick concludes an alliance with the King of Hungary. The conditions are that the Emperor is to confirm Matthias' rights and privileges as King of Bohemia, is to appoint him an elector and imperial cupbearer; while Matthias is to renew his undertaking not to marry, so that the succession will pass to the Emperor, and to undertake to free Austria from the tyranny of that rabble of soldiery, the so-called Brethren. The King agrees with less hesitation than does the Emperor, who does not relish the idea of war with Poland and Władysław of Bohemia. The aim of the alliance is to drive Władysław from Bohemia and to deprive the balding king of Poland of the rest of his hair. Once he has removed the rabble of soldiery from Austria and exacted heavy tribute from the Hungarians, Matthias is to assemble a force of mercenaries, which is to inflict all the damage it can on Poland.

A.D. 1473

The King and Queen spend Christmas and the following few days in Toruń. They then progress through Gostynin, Sochaczew and Warsaw to Grodno, where they remain for a fortnight, before continuing on through Berszta and other princely manors to Troki, from where they go to Wilno for Lent. Everywhere in the Grand Duchy they collect the agreed levy of six broad Prague grosses for every plough. The papal legate has repeatedly asked the King to attend a peace conference to be held in Nysa on St. Matthew's Day. Instead of going in person, the King decides to send a delegation of nine, but he is so late in appointing its members that only six arrive and then rather late, the other three having declined to go either because of illness or for some other reason. The late arrival of the six angers the papal legate and the Hungarian delegates, who have been in Nysa for three weeks already. King Władysław was to have sent nine delegates, but in fact sends only one. The papal legate is most active and has high hopes of reaching an agreement; but one of his conditions for peace is that Casimir's daughter, Jadwiga, should marry Matthias of Hungary, being given Spis and Moravia as her dowry; but this the Poles will not accept on account of the constitutional difficulties involved; however, discussions continue until the first Sunday after Easter. In a bid for support, Matthias frees Victor on condition that, as soon as the Duke recognizes Matthias as King of Bohemia, Victor will be made governor of Kolin. Matthias then sends 1000 cavalry and 800 foot to seize Kutná Hora from Władysław, hoping eventually to drive the latter from the kingdom. Matthias himself remains near Beroun to await the outcome of the conference.

King Casimir pays little attention to these preparations for war; for he has no troops with whom to oppose an enemy but his unpaid mercenaries, who, for the last year and a half, have been devouring the Church's goods while he does nothing to restrain them. Even worse is the situation in Bohemia, where a number of eminent Czechs have undertaken to pay Victor 30,000 as king, while the Emperor has again renewed surety for the 32,000 owed as the dowry of Elizabeth of Poland. Casimir sends his son 10,000 złoty, which he uses to buy Hradec back from Poděbrady's son, Henry.

After six weeks of vain discussion, with neither side willing to surrender its right to Bohemia, the papal legate finally gets the delegates to agree to the following: another conference will be held in Opava on Assumption Day at which peace will be concluded; to this conference Poland and Hungary will each send eight delegates and the two disputants for Bohemia six. The Kings are to hold themselves in readiness nearby: Casimir in Oświęcim, Matthias in Olomouc and Ladislas in Kłodzko. Should the delegates be unable to agree, the Duke of Burgundy is to be brought in as arbitrator; in the event of the latter dying or refusing to act, the King of France is to be co-opted. To help the process, both Władysław and Matthias are to absolve their subjects from their oaths of obedience, thus enabling them to obey whomever is awarded the kingdom. The arbitrator is to assess the damage suffered by each country and, once lasting peace has been restored, both countries will release their prisoners. The three kings comply, but reluctantly and late, cursing the prospect of having to send envoys to Burgundy to plead their cause.

After Easter, the King goes to Lublin, where he is told the decisions taken at Nysa. Though some protest and complain that the delegates have accepted unfair conditions, the King is delighted and summons an assembly to meet in Piotrków. In the event this is attended only by delegates from Wielkopolska, for those from Cracow and Ruthenia stay away, because they are angry with the King for having overlooked them when making appointments. To placate the absentees, yet another assembly is summoned to meet in Radom at Whitsun, and here the King manages to placate the representatives of Cracow and Ruthenia, so that, after discussion, it is agreed to accept the Nysa proposals, as the other parties have already done in Bienaszow, where the two kings had relieved their subjects of their oaths of allegiance and appointed those who are to attend the Opava conference.

Various things incline the Emperor to contemplate war with Hungary, and to him Casimir sends the Dean of Poznań to tell him that Casimir will attack Hungary with three armies, if the Emperor will give expression to their alliance in deeds and not, as hitherto, just in empty words, and if he and his Electors will acknowledge Władysław as King of Bohemia and style him as such, his legal title. This will enable Władysław, with help from his father, to avenge himself on his most stubborn enemy, Matthias, whom the Hungarians hate, and who is trying by every means to rob the Emperor of the duchy of Austria, which is his by right of inheritance. The Emperor will then be able to pay the 30,000 he has owed Casimir for the last twenty years, for his failure to do this has jeopardized Władysław's position as King of Bohemia and required him to use resources, which his brother Casimir might have had, against Matthias of Hungary.

As Assumption Day approaches, a host descends on Opava: prelates, knights and nobles from Poland and Lithuania, eight of the King's councillors and an estimated 6000 troops, 1000 of whom are the Tatars the King pays to accompany him wherever he goes. The Papal Legate is there, but only two delegates from the King of Hungary, though the full complement of those from Władysław.

Matthias is highly suspicious of the Czechs now that they have been released from their oaths of loyalty and is demanding that they swear a new, more specific oath. When this is refused, he threatens to kill the more eminent should he lay hands on them, and informs Casimir that he cannot let himself be bound by people who have betrayed him. Matthias' failure to honour the agreement delights Casimir and Władysław, since it means that they are no longer bound to accept the decisions of an arbitrator.

Those at Opava have now waited twenty days for the Hungarian delegates, who have not come, because, a short while before, 4000 Poles calling themselves 'the Brethren', who were in fact mercenaries who had been paid a small sum to leave Poland, had entered Hungary and captured and fortified two hills near Košice. A local noble is intimidated into handing his castle over to them and in no time at all the Brethren are exacting tribute from a large part of Hungary. This so frightens Matthias that he feels he must forget Opava and try to deal with the Brethren; but when he discovers that he can only recruit a few foreign mercenaries and is more or less helpless, he decides to send delegates to Opava after all. When these arrive, several days are wasted in sulks and squabbles, the Poles and Czechs accusing the Hungarians of coming late, the Hungarians countering this by claiming to have been delayed by having to deal with the Brethren, whom the Poles had wished on them. They then decide to reduce the total of delegates to twenty, plus the Papal Legate. When this produces no result, the number is further reduced to eight and then again to two. When even the two cannot reach a decision, the whole costly enterprise proves to have been in vain.

The Archbishop of Gniezno has told King Matthias that he can expect to marry Casimir's eldest daughter and that she will have Moravia, Silesia and Lusatia, Spis and Walachia as her dowry, but Matthias insists on most awkward terms: namely that Władysław is to recognize Matthias as his father, and vice versa; Bohemia is to be governed by a competent Hungarian, who will undertake to pay off its debts and, when this has been done, will resign in favour of Władysław, who will then rule, and, should Matthias die without issue, take over Hungary as well. Further, Władysław is to reimburse Matthias half the cost of his fighting in Bohemia, estimated at three million, plus a further million and a half, or, should he not have the money, pledge Moravia, Silesia and Lusatia, one third on each, so that he should have the possibility of redeeming each individually. Further, King Casimir is to marry his daughter, Jadwiga, to King Matthias, her dowry being the value of the three provinces in question. If Matthias dies without progeny, half the debt is to be written off and half paid to the King of Hungary. If Jadwiga dies without progeny, 500,000 is to be written off, and King Władysław is to be entitled to the million.

The Polish and Bohemian delegates recognize the artful cunning of the proposals and decide to leave without agreeing to anything. The Hungarians then put pressure on the Papal Legate to pronounce that the whole question has passed into the hands of the Duke of Burgundy. The Poles and Czechs strongly oppose this and, though the Cardinal is inclined to support the Hungarians, he accepts the others' view and leaves for Bratislava and Rome.

Peace restored and the clash of arms hushed, a rumour spreads that poison has been prepared for King Władysław. This is investigated and a Czech-speaker, George Lucky, is arrested in Kutná Hora, where he is living modestly, even poorly, with his wife and children. A tin box of poison is found in his house, which poison he had bought for 250 florins, part of the 2000 promised him through an intermediary by King Matthias. He bought the poison in the presence of the man who betrayed him. This poison is so powerful that you do not even have to swallow it or have it rubbed on your body, for the very smell and vapour of it are lethal. Lucky is taken to Karstein Castle and there put in a noisome cell, where he takes his own poison so as to avoid a trial.

On August 10, encouraged by his wife, daughter of the Emperor of Trebizond, the Sultan of Persia and Lower Armenia does battle with the Turkish Sultan, Mehmet, in defence of the Christians near the town of Harsuthszan on the Euphrates. Although Mehmet has called up so many men that none but women, children and the aged are left in the houses of Anatolia, victory goes to the Sultan of Persia, a victory that costs the Turks 56,000 men.

In Austria, the Brethren, debilitated by eating flour mixed with chalk, are defeated by Baron Ettinger.

The Turks occupying Bosnia invade Carinthia and Styria and, as no one puts up any resistance, devastate the whole of it.

In Ruthenia, the district of Mniszczeniec, near Kiev, is plundered by Tatars and 700 of its inhabitants taken off into captivity.

The splendid delegations prepared by the kings of Poland and Bohemia now set out for Augsburg, where a conference is to be held on September 1, at which the delegates are to have full powers to conclude a new alliance and at which the Emperor Frederick is to pronounce his final judgment in the matter of Władysław and Bohemia. However, convinced that neither the Emperor nor the Electors are going to go to Augsburg, they turn aside to Taldesberg in Brandenburg, where they are to stay for more than twenty weeks, while the Emperor, more concerned with his personal affairs than with public matters, has gone to Trier to meet the Duke of Burgundy and discuss the marriage of the latter's daughter and the Emperor's son. The result is that the Emperor promises to propose, elect and crown the Duke of Burgundy King of the Romans in Aachen. In return, the Duke, as King of the Romans, will pay solemn homage to the Emperor in Trier, marry his daughter to the Emperor's son, Maximilian, giving her a dowry of 100,000 gold crowns and all the lands he has acquired in Swabia and Alsace from the Duke of Austria, some pledged, others bought, on condition that all these and the whole dowry are to remain for ever with the House of Austria, even if the two have no progeny. Shortly after this agreement, however, the Emperor learns that the Duke is refusing to give up his alliance with King Matthias, so he tears up the agreement and leaves Trier, to the fury of the Duke. Having spent all this time and money for nothing, the Emperor finally reaches Rotenburg on February 13. Here he is joined by the King of Romania and the Polish and Czech delegates, who have been so long and so generously supplied with all their needs by the Margrave of Brandenburg. These delegates he receives most kindly. They are then conducted to Nuremberg, where are Cardinal Mark, the Patriarch of Aquileia, the papal legate and a number of German princes. The Emperor is most gracious to the Kings of Poland and Bohemia, and, when he finally pronounces judgment, it is that Władysław the first-born son of the King of Poland is the natural and righful King of Bohemia, whom he now promotes to Elector in place of the King of Hungary. The three rulers then make a new pact that they will unite all their forces against the King of Hungary and destroy that plague so harmful to all Christianity and that they will not withdraw from Hungary until they have achieved this. The Polish delegates then return to Łęczyca at Easter, happy and deserving of praise.

The Brethren still have their two fortified hills and live by robbing the country people. Unable to countenance this any longer, despite its being winter, Matthias assembles a force of mercenaries, which he equips with an unusually large number of cannon. The force easily captures the first hill, in which a Hungarian garrison is then installed; but the fort on the second hill is well defended by a steep rocky approach and man-made defences, and has provisions enough for a whole year;

however Matthias has already bribed its commander and his two brothers, it is said with 2000 florins, and these sabotage the fort's armament before the King makes his assault. A surrender is then agreed: the fort's defenders being allowed to walk out with all their clothing, but leaving their horses and armour behind. Their shame is made all the greater, when the King insists that they come to his camp and there lay down their swords, in the place of which they are given sticks and told to walk home.

This year the whole of Europe has suffered from a disastrous drought. Ponds have dried out and even big rivers have been crossed on foot. Heath- and forest-fires have broken out everywhere, killing the wild animals and burning towns.

A.D. 1474

The King and Queen spend Christmas in Wiślica, where they ask an assembly of nobles to provide money to enable the King to retain his mercenaries and so be ready to repel the threatened attack from Hungary. The assembly passes a number of useful measures, such as: if a knight deliberately kills another knight, he shall suffer a year's imprisonment in a dungeon; but, if the killing is accidental, he shall pay 100 marks; or that, in accordance with the amount of heritable property he has, each knight shall fight in every war, instead of restricting his services to light military duties; and, again, such knights are to pay the King six grosses for every field they possess. Actually, none of these measures is ever acted upon.

The King of Hungary is now an inveterate enemy of Poland. Secretly, he sends a force a thousand strong through the forest between the two countries, and, one day, at midnight this force puts up ladders and climbs into the sleeping town of Śmigród and captures it without difficulty; for, despite repeated warnings, the Poles there have never maintained a proper watch. The Hungarians then capture the castle, or, rather, it surrenders after being bombarded and having its walls undermined. The new occupants fortify both the castle and the town with new ditches and ramparts and other defences. They drive the peasants into such woods as would have provided excellent cover for infantry, and then devastate the surrounding country, burning six towns and some twenty villages. They then go on to Pilzno, to which, the King having refused to pay 4000 florins for its immunity, they set fire and then raze to the ground. After this, the Hungarians lay siege to Krisno which is well defended, until traitors open its gates to the enemy. Perturbed by these disasters, King Casimir calls for general mobilization; but, as the country has grown weak after so many years of peace and prosperity, and also because it is wintertime, the response is tardy, and little is accomplished except that peasants are moved into the towns.

The Hungarians keep asking for talks and, when these are arranged, King Matthias, who still pretends that he did not start the war, sends a six-man delegation, while the Poles send only four. Before they even meet, while the Hungarians are still in Lubocza and the Poles in Sącz, and both are squabbling about immunity for their persons, the talks themselves are endangered by a spate of killings, suspicious fires and ambushes. The King of Hungary even imprisons some of his delegates: the Bishop of Zagreb and some of his junior captains whom he suspects of being friendly to the enemy. Eventually, the Hungarians assemble in Stara Wies and the Poles in Szramowice, and, on February 1, a new pact for permanent peace is signed. The Polish army is then sent home, having achieved nothing except that it has filled its waggons with loot.

Leaving Wiślica, the King goes to Opatów to await the arrival of his forces. While he is there, two Venetians arrive bearing wonderful gifts of damask interwoven with gold thread. They ask for escorts to take the one to Kaffa, where he has to discuss Catholic matters with the King of Persia, and the other to Moscow, where he wishes to discuss certain matters of the Holy See with the Grand-prince there. The two are given the requisite escorts.

Another Venetian now arrives, this time an envoy from the King of Persia. He brings letters written in Chaldean requesting King Casimir to join other Catholic kings and princes in a spring offensive against the Turkish sultan, Mehmet, the enemy of Christendom. The King of Persia will join them with an army of tens of thousands. This envoy has already been to the kings of Naples, France and Hungary, and to Venice. He offers all his resources, monetary and military, to defeat the King of Hungary and so ensure peace there and in Bohemia. At the same time, the papal envoy proposes that one of Casimir's sons should marry the elder of the two beautiful daughters of the King of Persia, whose wife is the daughter of the Emperor of Trebizond, though the girl has first to be baptized. Her dowry would be the whole of the Greek Empire less Constantinople, which the King wants for himself, and Georgia, once these have been freed from the Turks. However, Casimir sees no virtue in either proposal and replies that he will send his answer by his own envoys.

He then spends several weeks in Opatowiec awaiting the arrival of his army and his Tatars from Lithuania. The army's progress is slow, for the troops are busily looting the Church's and other people's property, and do this with impunity, for the perpetrators are never punished. When peace is eventually concluded, the King disbands his army and dismisses his mercenaries, on whom he has spent so much for nothing. He then goes to Korczyn and those places which the Hungarians have evacuated in accordance with the pact. Many of the Hungarians, as they left, were set upon in the woods and elsewhere and killed, for the peasants suspected them of intending further plundering.

The pact is not well received by the nobles of Transylvania, who go to the King and offer themselves and all their possessions to assist him, if he will but continue the war against their inveterate enemy, Hungary. Meanwhile, King Matthias, seeking an excuse to provoke the King of Poland, has equipped the Duke of Żagan to fight Wielkopolska. The Duke assembles 4000 Silesian troops, many of whom are just tanners, tailors, cobblers and other artisans, and with them and some of Wrocław's guns, made available on Matthias' orders, fords the Oder below Ścinawa. Then, since King Casimir, as is his habit, is prevaricating and doing nothing, for he considers the matter unimportant, the Duke is able to use the bridge as well as the ford, and so penetrates into Wschowa where he attacks the town. Some of those inside, whom he has suborned, set fire to the town in several places, but the watchful townspeople put out the fires and drive their assailants from the walls. The Silesians then withdraw to an inn, called the Devil's Inn, a mile from Głogów, where they camp and from there they make raids into Poland. The knights of Wielkopolska are too afraid to do anything, except for one, Peter Gunicki, who, with thirty of his followers, attacks 300 of the plunderers and, having routed them, foolhardily attacks the rest of the army round the waggons. Here he finds a glorious and memorable death, though one or two of his men do escape.

At about this time, Michael Tungen, with the support of the knights and towns of Prussia, takes over the castles of Elsberg and Scheburg and, eventually, the entire bishopric of Warmińsk and all its towns and does this with impunity, thanks to the Bishop of Warmińsk. This stains the Poles' hitherto unblemished opinion of the people of Prussia. To put matters right, the King leaves Wielkopolska and goes to Prussia, where he summons an assembly to meet in Toruń. Although he has written assurance of immunity, Tungen is afraid to attend. There has been a recent outbreak of plague and this is spreading round Toruń and its neighbourhood, so the King, afraid of it, as he should be, settles a few minor matters, leaves to attend the assembly at Piotrków. Here he receives messages from his son, the King of Bohemia, asking for money and military assistance. He sends him 24,000 złoty to help pay his debts, and intends to send armed help as well, both to him and to help the Emperor fight Matthias, who has been putting Austria to fire and the sword, even setting the suburbs of Augsburg ablaze, while the Emperor Frederick is there attending a conference. The King now creates a new post, that of voivode for Lublin, which has expanded considerably. He orders all regions to send their troops to Mstawa by Ascension Day, hoping thereby to avoid having to hire mercenaries, and also to prevent his own people growing soft. The summons is also sent to the Lithuanians and Tatars.

The King now goes to Korczyn to make arrangements for the coming campaign. While there, he receives several messages from the starosta of Kiev telling him that a horde of Tatars has, without the knowledge of their Khan, encroached onto Polish territory with hostile intent, and asking him for money and men with which to repulse them. The King, never one to respond to such appeals, sends help neither to Kiev nor to Podole and Ruthenia, which are also threatened. The result is that, when all are peacefully engaged getting in the harvest, some 7000 ill-armed Tatars invade Podole and Ruthenia, devastate an area some hundred miles by thirty and carry off a number of captives to be sold into slavery. The Archbishop of Lwów is so enraged with the King for never helping, that he begins saying outright that Casimir should be replaced. This disaster is followed by yet another, when Sultan Mehmet, more arrogant than ever now that he has every fort and castle in Bessarabia, sends to the Voivode of Walachia demanding that he hand over Belgorod and Cilia, and, in future, pay him tribute, otherwise he will be regarded as an enemy.

Half way through August, the King moves to Mstów and there camps. After six weeks, he moves to the River Istwarta to await the arrival of the rest of the army, whose progress is reluctant and slow, the troops doing a great deal of damage to the country through which they pass. Most of them are men from Cracow, who have refused to serve outside their country unless they are paid. Their reluctance is eventually overcome and, on September 20, the King, after sending a written declaration of war, moves his army, now swollen with Lithuanians and Tatars to 60,000, into Opole. He captures two towns, in which he installs his own garrisons, then moves on, destroying everything as he goes. Near Chapkowiec he crosses the Oder, intending to do battle with King Matthias, who is in Wrocław with 6000 men-at-arms, but the latter never comes out to fight.

The Poles start quarrelling among themselves. Those from Wielkopolska consider that they should not go so close to Wrocław as to leave that part of the kingdom next to Silesia unprotected and thus give the enemy a chance to attack it. The men from Cracow do not like the idea. The dispute goes on for several days, after which the army moves to Opole and could easily have captured it, had not the King, afraid of more squabbling, forbidden an assault and moved on to Brzeg in Oława, where he receives envoys from the Margrave of Meissen sent to try and stop the fighting.

One night, Matthias secretly sends his entire force out of Wrocław with orders to attack the Poles. To do this, it has to cross the Nysa, but is unable to do this, and so, instead, attacks the Polish foragers stationed near Oława, whom it easily routs. A scratch force is sent to help the foragers, who then rally and battle is engaged again. When the King then sends in his largest squadron of household troops and his Lithuanians, the Hungarians turn and run; indeed, the entire force could have been wiped out had the Polish knights kept up the pursuit. The envoys from Meissen cannot believe that Casimir has had such an unexpected victory over the powerful King of Hungary; but, when they see eminent prisoners being brought before King Casimir, they confess their surprise and, a few days later, realizing that an armistice is out of the question, return home, taking as a gift for the Margrave an undertaking that the Poles will not harm the Duchy of Żagań, which the Margrave has bought from Duke Jan.

On October 24, while the Poles are still near Oława, King Władysław arrives with a splendid army of some 20,000, mostly infantry. After a little discussion the two armies are merged and together they invest Wrocław. When Matthias sees the combined army, he tears his hair and bewails his lot. There are frequent skirmishes; then, realizing that he is no longer safe in Wrocław, Matthias moves to the vicinity of the monastery of St. Vincent and fortifies the whole area, using ramparts, ditches and stakes, hoping that this will make his foraging easier and also that it will act as a base from which to raid into Poland.

Their captains advise Casimir and Władysław to station several thousand troops in Oleśnica and so hinder the enemy receiving supplies, and also to demolish the dam built to divert the Oder to Wrocław and allow the river to return to its old bed, thus depriving Wrocław of part of its defences. To do this they use carters, not soldiers, and the whole thing is completed in a matter of days. The army is then moved to the other side of Wrocław and the blockade maintained day and night.

The combined armies now set about devastating Silesia, which they do without plan or order, with the result that Poles out foraging are killed by their countrymen. As they roam the countryside many of the soldiers become infected with the plague and bring it back to their camps, where now there is a shortage of bread and honey, the former due to so many mills, which could have supplied them with the flour they need, having been burned down. There are several thousand waggons laden with provisions uselessly parked near Wieluń and unable to move, because no one bothers to give the necessary orders; nor, if they had been given, would there have been any one to carry them out! A sudden thunderstorm sets fire to the Polish camp at Wrocław, which burns furiously, killing people and horses, and destroying 4500 waggons with supplies.

Seeing how inactive the enemy is, Matthias sends troops to the boundary between Wieluń and Wielkopolska, an area that is undefended, and sends much of it up in flames, for though Casimir is not far away, he never sends it help. Near Bolesławiec the peasants actually take on the Hungarians, but are easily defeated. The enemy get into Kłobuck, but the townspeople throw them out. At Międzyrzecz, the castle is captured one dark night by a force of Hungarians which also sets fire to the town. But now plague and hunger force Casimir and Władysław to take pity on their men, who are suffering from dysentry and calling for peace, as, too, is the King of Hungary; so, it is decided that the three kings should meet in person. When the meeting takes place, Władysław and Matthias won't even look at each other as they shake hands, and they find it impossible to discuss all that should be discussed, so, they arrange that each is to send officials to meet in Wrocław and agree terms for a truce, which is to last for eighteen months. Terms are eventually agreed, namely that all castles in Poland and Silesia that have been occupied are to be returned to their previous owners, and that all prisoners are to be released. Thus do the kings go home having accomplished nothing of note.

Envoys from the two dukes of Bavaria, who all this time have been waiting in Wieluń at the King's expense, catch up with him as he reaches Łęczyca. They have come to propose Duke Ludwig's son, George, as a husband for Casimir's daughter, Jadwiga. The King agrees in principle, but, as Christmas is at hand, he takes the envoys with him to Radom, where terms are agreed, and, on the second last day of December, Jadwiga is betrothed to the twenty-three-year old son of the Duke of Bavaria. The bride is to go to her husband on St. Michael's Day and is to have a dowry of 32,000 złoty to be paid over five years. Matthias feels aggrieved by the marriage and at once sends envoys to arrange for him to marry the daughter of the King of Naples.

A.D. 1475

On January 17, the Voivode of Moldavia routs Sultan Mehmet's army of 120,000, which was ravaging Walachia, and thus recovers all the castles in Bessarabia that had gone over to the Turks. Many of his men are promoted from infantry to cavalry, and a few dubbed knights. Many of the fleeing Turks are killed by the Walachians, who have the swifter horses; others are drowned in the Danube. The Turks' horses, like their owners, are excessively skinny. All but the most eminent of the Turkish prisoners are impaled. The bodies of those killed in battle are burned. The many piles of their bones have long borne witness to this victory.

The Voivode sends four of the captured Turkish commanders, together with thirty-six of their standards and much splendid booty, to King Casimir in Lithuania, begging him not to abandon the Voivode, but to help him with troops, money and military equipment, for the Sultan is eager to avenge his defeat. He also begs the King to come to Ruthenia to receive the Voivode's long-delayed homage. The Voivode also sends a few prisoners and Turkish standards to the Pope, requesting his help in defeating the Turk. Similar trophies are sent to the King of Hungary seeking his help, but, when he gets these, the arrogant Matthias writes to the Pope, the Emperor and other kings and princes, telling them that he has defeated a large Turkish army with his own forces under the Voivode of Walachia. That done, he sends a delegation with splendid gifts to the Sultan Mehmet to complain that some brigands and Turkish exiles have attacked the King, which they must have done without the Sultan's knowledge, for Matthias cannot believe the Sultan guilty of perfidy and hostility, and asking the latter to break up this band of brigands and to send to the King any that may have fled to the Sultan's territory. This angers, more than it mollifies the Sultan, who, and, contrary to the laws of nations, first claps the envoys in prison, then, having stripped them all but naked, sends them back to their King on foot.

A conference of Czechs and Hungarians held on February 12 and attended by their respective kings agrees that Władysław is to have all Bohemia, the two duchies of Lusatia and two other duchies in Silesia, while Matthias is to have all Moravia and the rest of Silesia; also that, should Matthias die first without progeny, everything is to pass to Władysław; but, if Matthias has progeny, when he dies his sons are to receive 2000 florins and renounce everything else; the same is to apply to King Władysław. It is also agreed that the appointment of the bishop of Olomouc and of the marshal of Bohemia are to be the sole prerogative of the King of Bohemia. A further conference at Beroun confirms these terms, but then Matthias has second thoughts and pretends that he is not at liberty to accept the agreement without the consent of the Pope and of the various princes that have been helping him, after which everything is left in abeyance and a new conference arranged for the Feast of St. James the Greater in Bratislava, but even there nothing is decided.

While Casimir is in Lithuania he receives an envoy from the King of Persia. This envoy is a Greek, called Isaac, a convert to Islam. He has come to request King Casimir to join the other Catholic kings and take part in the King's intended offensive against the Turks. The King is friendly, plies the Greek with splendid gifts and sends him, full of hope, to Cracow, a place which the Greek is longing to see and where he spends the best part of a month before moving on to Hungary, Venice, Rome and the other Christian kings with the same request.

At eight in the evening of the last Friday in March fire breaks out in the brewery of Jan Gehan in Cracow. It destroys all the houses from New Gate to the Gate of St. Michael, a hundred in number, among them the Tarnowski mansion, two lovely towers; and also some cannon.

The Voivode of Walachia, who keeps an eye on all that the Turkish sultan is doing and so knows that he is concentrating his forces in Adrianopole, sends message after message to the King in Lithuania alerting him to the threat and asking for speedy assistance. He sends a similar appeal to the Ruthenians. He is asking for 2000 foot to keep watch on Belgorod and Cilia, and for the King to order mobilization in Ruthenia and set up a camp near Kamieniec. The Voivode's plan is that he should not risk a pitched battle with so numerous an enemy, but would withdraw on Kamieniec, where the King can deal with them. He also asks that, should the need arise, the Voivode and his troops are to be allowed into Kamieniec. The Lithuanians are happy to mobilize and fight the Turks, but the King is convinced that the Voivode is imagining the danger, and so he does nothing. He remains in Lithuania until Whitsun and finally gets to Lublin on June 5. Here everyone begs him not to leave the successful voivode in the lurch, but to use his whole army to help him and in one campaign put an end to the fighting with both Turks and Tatars. The King pleads poverty both in money and in men, and does nothing, hoping that war will never happen. He is then accused not only of sloth, but of deliberately causing dissension between his two countries by having detached all Łuck and part of Podole from Poland and handing them over to Lithuania. He is told that, if he does not alter his behaviour or hand over to someone else, his sloth and shameful rule will in the end destroy him, even if his external enemies do not do so first. He remains unmoved; indeed, all that he does is to send a Turkish-speaking envoy to the Sultan to ask him not to harass Walachia, which is a constituent part of Poland, and so not compel King Casimir to take up arms against him. He is to tell the Sultan that the Voivode has acted on his own and, if he has in any way hurt the Sultan, he must suffer the penalty. He is to ask for a day and place to be fixed, so that their councillors can meet and put an end to any misunderstandings by friendly discussion, rather than by bloody, unjustified and uncertain conflict.

On June 30, the King arrives in Zawichost, where he is given a letter from his secretary, whom he had sent to Khan Megligeren with certain instructions. This letter tells him that Sultan Mehmet, having routed the army at Adrianopole, has moved his large army both by land and by sea, and, together with a Tatar force, attacked the Genoese town of Kaffa, which has withstood the Turks ever since the fall of Constantinople, twenty-three years before, and captured it on June 5. Part of the Sultan's success was due to his having bribed certain citizens of Kaffa to betray their city; these were then taken on board the Sultan's ships together with their families and households. The ordinary people of Kaffa were spared and allowed to remain in their homes, though they had half their possessions taken from them. (Later, many of them are carried off into servitude.) Khan Megligeren, who happened to be in Kaffa at the time, and two of his brothers, have been taken prisoner and removed to Constantinople, along with other eminent prisoners. All forts and castles in the vicinity of Kaffa have fallen into Turkish hands, and all envoys and spies in them, totalling some 160, have been put to the sword.

Now, at last, the King credits what the Voivode has been telling him and calls a conference for July 2 in Korczyn to arrange support for the Voivode and Walachia, Podole and Ruthenia. Meanwhile, the Voivode, having received none of the help for which he has asked, and realizing that he is too weak to take on the Turks by himself, has dispersed his troops into the mountains and forests to await a more suitable occasion for launching an attack. Meanwhile, the Turks have sent a fleet of seventy large ships to Constantinople carrying a huge amount of treasure and a large number of captives, including 250 young boys from Kaffa, who are handsome and suitable either for castration or as partners in unlawful union. These boys are in the charge of a Greek, who, when the Turks are not watching, detaches his vessel from the rest and, after killing the few Turks on board, sails her into Cilia harbour, where he hands the boys over to Voivode Stephen, for them to be castrated or sent to brothels, a rich gift that delights the Voivode.

Rivers are everywhere low, except in Cracow, where days and nights of rain have caused unprecedented flooding of the Vistula on July 24 and the following three days, when the water rises to the level of the altars in the churches of St. Bernard and St. Agnes. The great bridge joining Kazimierz and Cracow is swept away, and the orchards are all destroyed, yet food remains cheap all the rest of the year.

Matthias continues his cunning, evil ploys. He uses a papal legate, sent to try to end the fighting between the Emperor and Charles of Burgundy, to ask the Emperor to agree to assign to him the royal insignia of Bohemia, promising that, although he has an alliance with the Duke of Burgundy, he will help the Emperor against him and obtain a grant of some 10,000 gold coins for the Emperor. Knowing how wily Matthias is, the Emperor rejects the idea, for he knows that, should Hungary become powerful, he himself would be threatened. He tells King Władysław's envoys, who are claiming the long promised insignia that, on his return from Austria, he will hand them over in either Leipzig or Berlin, if the kings of Poland and Bohemia will meet him there; or, if not there, in Freistadt, some eighteen miles from Prague.

King Matthias sends envoys to Voivode Stephen to try to wean him away from Poland by promising to protect him from the Turks. The Voivode accepts the offer of help, but can not be induced or frightened into detaching his country from Poland.

A swarm of locusts, each as long as a man's finger and with the head of a bat, flies into Sieradz from Hungary by way of Moravia and Silesia. The swarm is three miles long and a mile and a half wide. It moves with military precision, devouring the fruit on the trees and bushes, leaving nothing but bare earth and the insects' droppings. If the swarm settles on a wood, even stout trees bend to the ground beneath its weight. The sun can scarcely pierce its cloud.

The King and Queen progress to Poznań, where they receive messages from Ludwig of Bavaria asking for a speedy completion of the marriage of his son George to Casimir's daughter Jadwiga; so, on October 10, the bride, on whose trousseau and dowry her father has spent 100,000 florins, accompanied by her parents, her brother and a vast company, proceed to Wittenberg, where they are received by the knights and barons of Bavaria. They then proceed to Łańcut along more than a mile of road laid with carpet and lined by soldiers. First to greet them is the bridegroom at the head of a splendid company; next, comes the Emperor Frederick heading a cavalcade of 7000 horse, who come out as far as what is called the seventh stone, whence they are conducted to Lancut. The wedding is celebrated the same day and is followed by several days of entertainment. One absentee, is the King of Bohemia, who, though invited and supplied by his father with the necessary funds, would not go, because the omens were inauspicious.

The King has incurred huge debts to provide his daughter with her trousseau and dowry, so he calls an assembly in Sieradz in the hope of obtaining help in paying them. He is asking for twelve grosses for every field, but only the delegates from Wielkopolska have turned up and they will only agree if Cracow and Ruthenia do so too; but the latter, knowing what would be expected of them, have refused to send delegates. The King, disappointed, spends Christmas in Koło, to which the knights and matrons and others who escorted his daughter to Łańcut now return, all with splendid gifts from the Bavarian dukes and infected with the plague, which was rampant in Bavaria and Germany.

Towards the end of the year, the King of Hungary, having paid his troops lavishly in gold, advances against the Turks with an army of 20,000 well equipped with cannon, waggons and siege weapons. He tells the Pope and many of the Catholic kings, that he intends to pursue the Sultan, who is withdrawing. This huge army reaches the River Sava, where it encounters a Turkish forward position, manned by 500. Not daring to continue his advance, lest he be surrounded, Matthias calls a halt. The Turkish position is eventually captured at considerable cost to either side, and Matthias returns to Buda having really accomplished nothing. From Buda, Matthias sends to the Emperor, whose provinces of Carinthia and Styria have been ravaged by Turks from Bosnia, demanding that he be given the royal insignia. Meanwhile, a large Turkish force has entered Hungary unopposed and devastated it as far as Varaždin, the castle there having difficulty in defending itself.

A swarm of locusts inflicts considerable damage on Hungary.

A.D. 1476

The King sets out for Sochaczew to take over its lands and castle as agreed with the late Duke of Mazovia's widow, Anna. Duke Conrad of Warsaw and Duke Conrad of Oleśnica try to forestall him, only to find the castle already in the hands of the Archbishop of Gniezno. Informed of this, the King rides day and night and reaches the town, while it is still dark. Having heard Mass in the church, he is conducted to the castle by Duchess Anna. The two dukes now arrive protesting that they are the rightful heirs to Sochaczew. The King points out that all Mazovian lands, including Sochaczew, fell to him on the death of the late duke Siemowit, both as his fief and by right of purchase from the true heir, Anna daughter of Siemowit and wife of the Duke of Oleśnica, and that the Duke of Warsaw never had any legal right to it. Having heard this answer, the two dukes return home and no more is heard of their claim.

King Casimir arrives in Brześć Kujawy with 2000 mercenaries intending to advance into Prussia and settle certain matters which his absence has complicated, and especially to remove Michael Tungen from Warmińsk. Here he has to stay longer than he anticipated, since his councillors are so late in arriving from Cracow that, by the time they do arrive, the King has run out of money with which to pay his mercenaries. Leaving Brześć, the King sets out for Toruń, accompanied by two of his sons, Casimir and Albert.On April 25, he enters Malbork, and here all the voivodes, castellans, officials and nobles of Prussia wait upon him. A week later the Prussian Master arrives with some of the commanders and, on the Sunday after the Feast of St. Sophia, is formally received. He is ushered in by two bishops, several voivodes and all the King's courtiers, and presented with splendid gifts. Two days later, having been granted permission to speak, the Master repeats all that his envoys have repeatedly said, namely that he, as Master, is a true and loyal ally and subject of the King and Kingdom and that he never has and never will breach their agreement. He promises that he and the Order will adhere to the terms of the peace pact. When accused by the King of having given audience to envoys from King Matthias and making secret agreements with them to the detriment of the King and Kingdom, he denies the charge, insisting that he refused their demands that he break off the alliance.

The quarrel between the city fathers and the townspeople of Gdańsk has intensified, due to German law having been wrongly invoked to deprive certain clerics of their estates. These, with the consent of the King, referred their case to the Holy See, which imposed an interdict, to foil the city fathers, and the King now gets this annulled.

Queen Elizabeth, made pregnant by the King, feeling that her time is near, goes to Nieszawa and there, on March 12, gives birth to a fifth daughter, her eleventh child, who is christened Anna.

King Matthias, having arranged a truce with Poland, Bohemia and the Turkish sultan, now turns his attention to domestic matters. He sends a delegation to Naples to fetch his bride, Beatrice, daughter of the King of Naples, unmarried, but highly educated. She is to bring a dowry of 100,000 florins. This is a marriage arranged by the Pope. An invitation to the wedding is sent to King Casimir in Prussia, but he cannot accept, for he expects to be attacked by both the Tatar khan and the Turkish sultan, and cannot leave his lands even for a day. Meanwhile, Sultan Mehmet, who hates the Voivode of Moldavia, has assembled an army near the town of Sophia with the intention of invading and capturing Walachia. As he advances on the Bulgarian town of Varna, he is met by an envoy from King Casimir, who, long before, had been instructed to go to him, but had been prevented from doing so. Having obtained an audience on May 2, the envoy reminds the Sultan of the old friendship between him and the King of Poland and begs him not to make an armed incursion into Walachia, a fief of the King of Poland, and so compel the latter to take up arms against him. The Sultan graciously accepts the sable cloak presented to him, and, after he and his councillors, who are called pashas, have listened to what the envoy has to say, tells the envoy that he could never have refused King Casimir had his envoy come to him in Adrianopole, even though to have abandoned war with Walachia would have involved him in considerable expense, but, now that he is almost at the enemy's frontier, he cannot break his promise to the Voivode of Bessarabia and the Tatar Khan, who instigated the war. However, he will do this even now, if Voivode Stephen will agree to pay outstanding and future tribute, return Cilia to Bessarabia and release all his captives. The envoy quite rightly regards such terms as inequitable, and departs, having noted that the Sultan is ferrying his troops across the Danube in ships and also bridging the river in four places. He tells Voivode Stephen of this and continues on to Malbork to report to the King.

Meanwhile, a Tatar army has crossed into Walachia to help the Turks and has already started creating havoc. Undeterred by the strength of his opponents, Voivode Stephen daringly attacks the Tatars and, in fact routs them, killing more of them in the subsequent pursuit than in the actual battle. The fleeing Tatars discard their weapons, their saddles and clothes, while some, as though crazed, jump into the River Dniepr. Voivode Stephen now attacks the Turks and kills many of those who have already crossed the Danube in the Sultan's ships and rounds up all their foragers. Those he captures he has flayed alive irrespective of age or status, or else he has them impaled. Eventually, the Turks, who have plenty of men, manage to surround the Voivode and so force him to withdraw. The Turkish losses are estimated at 30,000.

The Voivode has sent repeated pleas for help to King Casimir, asking him for 20,000 men, sufficient, he assures the King, to drive out the Turks, who are suffering from plague and also starvation, even though the Voivode of Bessarabia, on whose account the war was started, is doing his best to send them provisions and other necessities. The Bessarabian soldiers, who share a language and customs with the Walachians and know their secrets and domestic affairs, are able to inflict more damage on them than can the Turks. The Sultan, uncertain what to do, continues his policy of destruction, thus making things even worse for his hungry troops. Then he moves into Podole and continues the destruction there; but he is forced to withdraw from Soczawa and Chocz, when he tries to capture them. Had Casimir sent the troops he had in Prussia to deal with the Turks, they could have done so, but all that he does is to repeal an old law so that a woman can now inherit her parents' property, where there is no male heir, as is the Polish practice.

The King goes to Nieszawa, where the Queen has been living while he is Prussia, and so to Piotrków to discuss the Walachian question at the assembly. On his orders almost the whole of Ruthenia is called to arms, and the army then goes into camp near Kamieniec, intending to assist Voivode Stephen; yet there it remains for several weeks to the discomfort of its fellow-countrymen, but not of the Turks, who assume that it cannot move without orders from the King. Meanwhile, a Turkish fleet with reinforcments and siege-weapons is lost at sea. The Sultan, depressed by the news and afraid that Casimir may be about to attack, withdraws to Constantinople. King Matthias claims the credit for this and so pockets 20,000 złoty for his war chest from the Pope, the King of Naples and several Italian dukes. Suddenly, a large Turkish force arrives from Bosnia and starts ravaging Carniola, Carinthia and part of Styria, and then tries to capture the five, strong wooden bastions King Matthias has built on the bank of the Danube in the rear of Smiderow castle and garrisoned with 5000 men. Four of these the Turks storm and the fifth then surrenders, a thing that could have been avoided had Matthias, who was not far away, himself attacked the Turks.

Pope Sixtus IV and the Italians now realize how Matthias and the King of Naples have fooled them. The latter's daughter, Beatrice, is sent to Hungary, to Székesfehérvár and there married and crowned.

After a fortnight's parleying, a special assembly held in Korczyn grants the King four grosses for each field held, this to be used in the defence of Ruthenia. Wielkopolska promises to pay a similar amount if Cracow will do the same; which it does and pays promptly, but Wielkopolska fails to keep its promise, because of the objections of some of its knights. From Korczyn the King progresses to Lublin, where the Queen awaits him. After spending five days there, he moves to Chełm and so to Bełz, where he stays for a fortnight. He declares himself ready to resist the Turks, should they move out of Walachia and deeper into Poland, but when, instead, the Turks withdraw to Constantinople, he heads for Lithuania, where he spends the rest of the autumn, all the winter and part of the spring, hunting. The weather is fine, and there is plenty of hard snow.

The Emperor Frederick, suspecting that the havoc wreaked by the Turks was done at the instigation of the King of Hungary, abandons his long wait for peace and by siege or surrender captures a number of Matthias' castles. Władysław King of Bohemia also breaks the truce, sending 4000 Czechs to help the Emperor. Thanks to this, the Emperor enjoys considerable success, though postponing a final, decisive encounter with the enemy until later. Matthias, seeing how the Emperor and his allies are harassing him and afraid lest this harassment increase, cunningly uses the occasion of his wedding in Buda to plan with the Prussian Master's representatives to ally himself with the Master and go to war with Poland. He gives some of his Walachian councillors 14,000 florins with which to hire mercenaries to help the Master. He then demands that the Duke Przemyśl either re-imburses him in cash for what he, Matthias, has spent on his behalf, or else permanently surrenders the lands and castle of Cieszyn. The Duke, realizing, rather belatedly, how deceitful Matthias is, goes to Władysław of Bohemia and puts himself under his protection. At this, Matthias releases Dracula, the former voivode of Bessarabia, whom he has kept imprisoned for twelve years, and tells him to join Voivode Stephen in recovering Bessarabia. In their first encounter they defeat the Bessarabians and capture some castles, but in a second engagement the Bessarabians, reinforced by the Turks, drive the two from the country. Dracula is then treacherously murdered by one of his slaves.

A.D. 1477

The King, Queen and two of their sons have spent Christmas in Wilno, and Carnival and Lent in Troki. Acting on messages from the Emperor and rumours that Matthias is intending to invade Poland, King Casimir arranges for a force of mercenaries to assemble in Silesia, and then goes to Piotrków for the assembly called for April 13. Here, it is arranged that, in accordance with their pact, Poland is to send 4000 troops to help King Władysław; but then an excuse is found to avoid having to do this, namely that the men are refusing to take part in so distant an expedition and reject the idea of contributing to pay for mercenaries to replace them, the treasury being empty. As no definite answer can be given to Władysław's envoy or that of the Emperor, they are told that King Casimir is too preoccupied with his own wars with the Tatars and Turks and with the threat from the Teutonic Knights to be able to help others. For the Order has not given up their idea of renewing hostilities with Poland, and in this are encouraged by King Matthias who promises to cover all their costs. On several occasions, one of the Knights' commanders has gone from Prussia to Hungary to make arrangements for this, travelling in disguise through Poland under the aegis of Michael Komorowski, a Pole ready to betray his king and an associate of Matthias. In this they are abetted by some Prussian knights, especially the voivodes of Malbork and Chełm and a councillor of Gdańsk, who are eager for freedom greater even than that they presently enjoy. A document detailing all this falls into Casimir's hands, and he then sends the Starosta of Łęczyca with 600 cavalry and 400 infantry to Malbork to prevent a rebellion. Meanwhile, Matthias and the Knights are trying to persuade the dukes of Mazovia to keep their part of the bargain and join them against Casimir. The Mazovians are attracted by the idea, but inhibited by their fear of the Poles and by the loyalty of some of their number. The knights and gentry of Prussia discover the Order's intentions and, while in assembly in Malbork, take a solemn oath never to deny the authority of King Casimir. They promise that, if war threatens, they will take up arms, and the towns of Prussia undertake to provide a fixed number of men-at-arms, while the villages are to send four men each and pay for a fifth.

On August 5, the Knights elect a new Grand-master, the commander of Osterode, one of their number recently returned from Rome, who is considered modest and sensible.

The office of Castellan of Cracow, the highest in Poland, has fallen vacant. The King appoints the Voivode of Cracow, who is already Castellan of Sandomierz and Marshal of Poland, to fill it. This is considered an outrage and illegal. It is, indeed, the first time that three such important posts have been held by one and the same person. When the King refuses to cancel the appointment, it is decided to boycott the assembly. King Matthias and the Knights bribe Komorowski, who holds three castles near the frontier with Hungary, to rebel. From these three castles it would be easy to deny anyone access to the salt works. The King repeatedly sends to Komorowski to persuade him to abandon his treachery, even offering to repay any money Komorowski may have raised on his castles, a generous offer that is also refused. Faced with the prospect of having to fight Komorowski in the south and the Knights in the north, the King sends a mixed force of Poles and mercenaries to lay siege to one of Komorowski's castles, which is in a favourable position, has good moats and walls. It takes seven months of bombardment by the King's heavy guns, before it is captured. The King then orders it to be demolished. This, too, is the fate of another of the castles, and the third is handed over to the man from whom the King borrowed money against its security. Komorowski is hailed before the King, who refuses mercy, even though Komorowski is willing to submit, but he soon manages to escape to Hungary; but, getting no encouragement there, returns to Poland and is now permitted to eat humble pie and be reconciled with the King.

King Władysław goes to Austria, where Emperor Frederick comes out to meet him and conducts him into Vienna. Although Pope Sixtus IV has repeatedly asked the Emperor to give the Bohemian royal insignia to Matthias rather than to Władysław, or, at least, not to give them to either, the Emperor keeps his promise to Władysław, and, in the cathedral of St. Stephen, arrayed in his imperial robes, he presents Władysław with the insignia and the Czech standards: appoints him imperial cup-bearer, and, after banqueting him, sends him home laden with gifts. This grant of the insignia frightens all the rebels in Moravia, Silesia and Lusatia, who now think only of submission. Even the Teutonic Knights in Prussia feel that their position is hopeless. King Matthias is so furious that he writes to Casimir and all the other kings and princes telling them that he would willingly suffer even death, if thereby he could avenge this slight. The Pope writes to the Emperor condemning his action. Władysław returns to Bohemia, his troops exhausted by the long campaign and lack of provisions; while the Emperor, perhaps because of an empty treasury, or in the vain hope that Hungary will not start a war, dismisses his mercenaries, who are at once recruited by Matthias, who sends them and his big guns across the Danube at Bratislava, despite the fact that a Turkish army some 5000 strong has entered Hungary not far from the King's own camp, and is creating havoc almost before the latter's very eyes.

Matthias is accompanied by his bride, who suddenly expresses a desire to witness the storming of a town; so the King advances on Heinburg, a town without natural or even man-made defences. Three times the assault is repulsed and enormous losses inflicted on the attackers. The King then withdraws and vents his frustration on the countryside almost as far as Vienna. The Emperor has entrusted the defence of Vienna to Count Haug, who has 5000 men-at-arms, with whom he makes frequent sorties and inflicts defeat after defeat on the Hungarians, taking so many prisoners that, although he beheads or drowns a large number of them, the huge prisons in Vienna are unable to house all the others.

In the meantime, the Emperor has sent to Poland and Bohemia for help. Winter weather being in the offing and the Poles reluctant to fight so far from home, Casimir sends the Emperor ten thousand złoty. In the end, under pressure from the Pope and the Venetians, the Emperor agrees to peace on shameful conditions; namely, that he renounces any right to the Kingdom of Hungary, that he provides Matthias with a duplicate set of Bohemian regalia and pays him 180,000 florins; that Matthias is to retain the towns and castles he has captured in Austria until this amount is paid, and that each will assist the other against anyone except the Pope and the King of Sicily. Although the Emperor could have fulfilled the first two conditions, he cannot afford to pay the 180,000, so the Austrians, afraid of such a burden of debt, weakly accept Hungarian rule.

Voivode Stephen of Walachia, having recruited a fresh army, makes another foray into Bessarabia, where he captures Dracula's son, Radulon, whom the people of Brašov voluntarily surrender to him. He captures almost all Bessarabia and drives out the Turks, at least those whom he does not kill. He then proclaims Bessarabia independent and places it under a governor.

The Turks, who receive the monthly intelligence reports sent to the Sultan by the Jews and thus know all that is going on, take advantage of the outbreak of hostilities between Hungary and the Emperor to invade Friuli and devastate the country as far as Cunianum.

Bolesław, Duke of Mazovia, having fallen violently in love with the daughter of the former voivode of Bełz, marries her on July 20. After the wedding, when his brother and friends are teasing him about his bride, he discards her as casually as he took her, and proceeds to choose another wife. This is a woman of low station, whom he takes from her husband and with whom he remains for several years; indeed, until she dies, when he gives her a princely funeral and marries another girl of low station, thus writing his infamy in triplicate.

A.D. 1478

Because of illness, many are absent from the assembly at Piotrków. The King does not know how to deal with the situation the country is in, his main difficulty being his lack of funds to meet the cost of what ought to be done. One proposal is that all peasants should pay a tax, but as many of the knights are against the idea, the proposal is shelved until the next assembly. At this, all but Poznań accept the tax. Another absentee from Piotrków is the new Master of the Prussian Order, Truchses, who has been summoned to take the obligatory oath of loyalty, a summons to which his only reply is to go into hiding. Having achieved nothing at Piotrków, the King goes to Łęczyca, where he receives a secret envoy from some Hungarian nobles. With the Queen acting as interpreter, the envoy asks the King to invade Hungary. If he does this, the envoy asserts, everyone will desert Matthias. Casimir gives an evasive reply.

The King now goes to Lithuania to attend to its domestic affairs. The Lithuanians are eager for him to appoint one of his sons as his successor. Although Albert, one of his sons with him, supports the idea, the King tells them that, as long as he lives, he will never surrender rule of the Grandduchy to anyone. While here in Lithuania, he receives an envoy from the Sultan of Turkey, who is accompanied by a Tatar envoy. The two present the King with numerous gifts and tell him that the Sultan is most favourably inclined towards him and ready to sign a treaty of friendship with him, and he requests the King to send his own envoys to agree terms and sign the necessary documents. Each will then regard as his enemy whomever attacks the other. The Tatar envoy supports the idea and asks for a similar document for his Khan, Nasrdub. The two envoys are lavishly rewarded and told that, grateful as the King is for their offers, he can only reply through his own envoys.

In the middle of March, a special Council is held in Beroun to conclude peace between the kings of Bohemia and Hungary. After much discussion, the following is agreed: Władysław, eldest son of the King of Poland and his natural heir, is to have Bohemia, and all the inhabitants, castles and towns of Bohemia are henceforth subject to him. The King of Hungary is to style himself King of Bohemia and to consider Władysław as his son and himself as the latter's father. Matthias is to rule Moravia, Silesia and Łuczyce until Bohemia has paid him 400,000 florins; but the Czechs are to be relieved of making this payment if, in the event of Władysław dying, they elect Matthias as their king. These are very different conditions to those agreed at Wrocław, but, as neither side seems anxious to adhere to the latter, the new conditions are finally accepted, thus leaving both Władysław and Matthias styling themselves "King of Bohemia", while Władysław rules Bohemia and retains the dignity of Elector, and Matthias has Moravia, Silesia and Lusatia. If Matthias should die first, Władysław is to pay Hungary 400,000 florins and so regain Moravia, Silesia and Lusatia and become perpetual heir to the kingdom of Bohemia. Should Władysław die without progeny, Matthias is to succeed him on the throne and Bohemia will be relieved of having to pay 400,000 florins. The King has difficulty in getting the assembly in Piotrków to agree to the whole kingdom paying a farthing tax. However, it does agree that, in order to stop the import of salt from

Saxony, salt works are to be established in Wielkopolska, which are to be managed by the salt works at Cracow. Władysław sends thanks for the 80,000 florins he has been sent.

An envoy is sent to the Pope to complain of the behaviour of the Papal Legate, Balthazar, who has stupidly called Władysław King of Bohemia a heretic and King Casimir a supporter of heresy, and placed an interdict on all the adherents of the heresy.

On July 15, in Sandomierz, the Queen gives birth to a sixth daughter, her twelfth child, who is christened Barbara.

The new Prussian Master, having refused the King's summons to swear allegiance, is just waiting for an opportunity to renew hostlities against Poland. Meanwhile, a certain Szumborski has illegally seized two of the King's towns in Chełmno and then, at a time agreed with the King of Hungary, moved his force, consisting mainly of peasants, to Osterode, where it remains for several days in quarters, until Szumborski realizes that Matthias has deceived him and is not coming with assistance, but is still in Buda occupied with dancing, jollity and carousing; whereupon Szumborski shamefacedly breaks camp and takes his troops home. The garrisons he put in the two towns he captured are dispersed.

Sultan Mehmet, seeking to take advantage of the civil strife in Italy, sends a large army from Bosnia into Carinthia, which it ravages almost to Salzburg, without encountering any opposition. It reaches the River Drawa and if the bridge had not been destroyed and the river itself in flood, the Turks would have advanced into Podole with the intention of overrunning Ruthenia; but, learning that a large Polish army is there ready and waiting, it withdraws and, feigning retreat, hides in the Black Forest. When it learns that the Polish army has been disbanded, it emerges and advances by night on Bracław, then in the possesion of Prince Czartoryski. When the inhabitants flee, the town is burned and the surrounding country ravaged. The castle itself is very nearly captured.

When he learns of the Prussian Master's rebellion, the King sends a force of mercenaries to deal with him. The Master takes to the field with a force composed largely of peasants, but, when the Poles advance swiftly and are in position to do battle, and the Master realizes that the help promised by King Matthias is not forthcoming, he disbands his own force and retires into his castles.

King Casimir now sends Matthias a reminder of the treaty between their two countries made long before and recently renewed, according to which Matthias is not to interfere in Poland or Prussia. Matthias replies loftily that it would be ignoble were he to leave his allies in the lurch and he suggests that, if Casimir really wants peace, he should halt his war against Prussia, put in writing the reasons for the Master not being bound by the terms of their alliance, and compel the Master and the Order to renew their allegiance to the King. The King, too, wishes to test this. He sends two more envoys: Jan Długosz and Stanisław Marszalkowiec, to tell Matthias that their King will agree to cease hostilities if it can be shown that the suggestions are genuine, for Casimir knows that Matthias has sent troops into Silesia on the pretext of assisting the Duke of Żagan against the Margrave of Brandenburg, but in reality to be where they can easily be transferred to Prussia. The two envoys find Matthias in Visegrád and soon realize that they are being hoodwinked. They scarcely know what to do; but, at least, they can see that Matthias is preparing four different armies, which are to invade Poland at four different points, and that these are already equipped and ready. A fifth army of 7000 has orders to get to Pomerania by whatever route it can and from there go into Prussia to help the Master. Realizing the danger of the situation, the two envoys make a pact with King Matthias according to which neither side will start hostilities before the Feast of the Purification, when the two kings are to confer in Olomouc. Meanwhile, King Casimir is to retain the castles he has taken in Warmińsk and repatriate all his troops not needed to guard them.

A.D. 1479

In the middle of January, King Casimir receives an envoy from the King of Hungary asking for their meeting to be postponed until May 2, and that Casimir be sure to attend in person and thus facilitate the return of peace to Prussia. Should the proposed date and place be unsuitable, let the King propose others; the main thing is to halt the war in Prussia. Some of the King's advisers are suspicious of the proposal, but, in view of the excellent terms Matthias had suggested to the earlier delegation, Casimir agrees. He sends his daughter, Sophia, with a splendid retinue and escort to Frankfurt, where she is to marry the young son of the Margrave of Brandenburg, Frederick; while he and the Queen go to Łęczyca and from there to Koło, where the assembly, like the rest of the country, votes a grant of tonnage in all the King's towns.

Sophia's wedding in Frankfurt is a very modest affair. It is celebrated on a Sunday, February 14. The Polish courtiers accompanying the Princess are not even fed by their hosts, but have to provide for themselves, and they and the bride's escort of knights receive either only very modest gifts or none at all.

As the Italian dukes are fighting among themselves, Venice feels compelled to make peace with the Turks, even though the conditions are unfavourable, involving surrendering Scutari and its neighbouring towns.

A Polish delegation waits on King Matthias in Buda and tries to make him see that it is unworthy of him to start wars with friendly kings and neighbours in support of the Master, who is a subject of their King and pays him homage as a vassal, and they demand that he adhere to the terms of the pact he made long before. In return, Matthias complains that the terms of the truce have not been kept. In the end it is agreed to hold a council in Sieradz at Whitsun and to cease hostilities in the meantime. In the event, Matthias pleads illness and does not turn up for the council, but neither does he send delegates.

The Knights in Prussia have been led to hope that, since Matthias has surrenderd Moravia, Silesia and Lusatia to King Władysław, the latter's father, King Casimir, will voluntarily withdraw from Prussian territory and allow the Order to have back the lands that have been incorporated in Poland and allow it complete independence. The Master persists in this hope, in which he is encouraged by Matthias, as it allows the latter to attend to his own affairs and the decisions he and King Władysław took at Olomouc.

King Casimir goes to Korczyn to receive the Master, and there for several weeks the two await Matthias' envoys, who eventually arrive on October 2, excusing their tardiness by their King's preoccupation with his war with the Turks. For the next ten days, however, they work eagerly to reconcile the Order and King Casimir. The Master makes difficulties about swearing the necessary oath of allegiance and submission, saying that God and man (i.e. King Matthias) had promised something very different. However, his own people are soon advocating that he take the oath and so avoid disaster, for, as the Poles keep pointing out, because of Hungary's involvement with the Turks and others, the Order can never rely on getting help from its king. The Master then agrees to take the oath and renew the pact of lasting peace, which he had broken. So, on October 9, in the great hall of the castle in Korczyn, the Master, protesting that he would rather have let himself be skinned alive and chopped into little pieces, takes the oath of loyalty and submission and undertakes that the Brethren of the Order, the knights and citizens of Prussia, will take the same oath, and that, on the approaching St. Margaret's Day, he will hand over the castles and towns of Chełm, Bodice and Stargard, which King Casimir is buying back for 18,000 florins. A panel of nine judges is to assess the damage inflicted by either side. Four of the nine are to be Poles, four members of the Order, and the ninth, chosen by both sides, is to have the casting vote. This settled, the King forgives the Master and the Order, and they all shake hands. The Master and those with him, as well as the Hungarian envoys, all receive splendid gifts of sable and marten cloaks lined with purple, or horses. The Master is made to send the original document of their alliance back to King Matthias and to require the return of his copy, which had been lodged with the Bishop of Wrocław. When it comes, it is cut into little pieces before anyone can see it.

The war is over, but civil strife breaks out when the King's great army of Czechs, Moravians and Silesians is told that the men cannot be given the pay they have earned, and that to cover this a farthing is being levied on the peasants and tonnage on the towns. Hearing this, the troops go on the rampage, burning towns and villages, especially those belonging to the Church, with the result that cries and groans are everywhere to be heard.

On October 13, a Turkish army, reinforced with Bessarabians and estimated at some 100,000 strong, invades Transylvania, near the town of Sobinow, which people of German origin call Ekthorn. It has five commanders, called pashas, each in command of part of the army and marching not far apart. The Hungarians are in three divisions, one of which takes on the far more numerous enemy and, after three hours, is forced to withdraw; but then it regroups and returns to the attack, now together with the other two divisions, which attack the enemy's either flank and force them to retreat. Fifty eminent Turks are captured, the smallness of that figure being due to the Hungarians' preference for killing rather than capturing. The country is jubilant.

The King hands over responsibility for paying his unpaid troops to three men: the Bishop of Cracow, the Castellan and Starosta of Cracow and the Castellan of Sandomierz, and goes with the entire Court to Lithuania, where he spends the winter, spring and summer mostly in hunting, though he does have friendly discussions with the two princes of Moscow about the Lithuanian territories they are alleged to have occupied illegally during the King's absence. The elder of the princes, Ivan, is a daring, versatile person, who cast off the Tatar yoke and freed himself and all his lands from the servitude that so long, indeed, since the days of Alexander Witold, had oppressed all Moscow. Shaming and oppressive this servitude had been, for in those days, the Prince of Moscow was expected to run barefoot to greet envoys from the Khan, who never even deigned to dismount. Even when some junior official of the Khan, filthy and wretched as he might be, came to demand tribute or give orders, the Prince had to do the same, and then humbly present him with a cup of mare's milk and lick from the Tatar's horse's mane any drops of the milk that might be spilled on it. A sable cloak had to be placed under the feet of the one reading the translation of the Khan's letter, which was written in Tatar, and, while it was being read, the Prince and the others had to kneel and pretend to be listening avidly. They had had to help the Tatars against Catholics. But now this Prince had become a powerful man and a rich one: he saw how the King of Poland and the Grand-duke seemed to have abandoned Novgorod even though its people paid them an annual tribute of 100,000 shekels and how the people of Novgorod had grown effeminate from being overburned with riches, greater perhaps than those of Venice; so he moved in, seized the Bishop's priceless treasure of gold and silver and fine furniture and made the people surrender two-thirds of their gold, silver and precious stones, all of which he loaded into 300 waggons and drove off with others laden with furs and purple cloth. Thus enriched, the Prince is now feared by his neighbours and, now he has seized some territory from the Grand-duchy is considered a threat to the rest. The Lithuanians plan to stand up to him, but Casimir advises them to do nothing until veteran troops can be brought from Poland. Help might be had, too, from the Ruthenians, who are known to be hostile to the Prince, because of religious differences.

A.D. 1480

King Casimir spends Christmas and the following days in Grodno with his wife and three of his sons, and then returns to Lithuania for Lent. He is in Wilno over Easter, despite receiving a stream of messages urging him to return to Poland, for the Lithuanians keep begging him not to go, or to leave them one of his sons in his place.

Rumour has it that the King of Hungary has been poisoned by oil made from olives brought from Venice to be sold in Buda, and, as everyone, even the Hungarians, long to see him dead, the rumour is believed. However, it is only severe gout from which he is suffering and this is easily cured by his doctors—to everyone's disappointment. Before he is properly recovered he sends a force to invade Austria, and this captures Radkerburg despite its strong position and good defences, after his guns have demolished its walls. The Hungarians then advance on Graz and start bombarding both town and castle.

Epilogue

Though lying in bed, gravely ill, yet am I no little pleased that, after protracted, uninterrupted labour, much thought and deliberation, extensive travel and journeying in search of the chronicles of our own and other lands and in so doing subjecting myself to censure, abuse and rebuff, I have come to the end of this work, which all others have neglected. Gladly would I continue it for the honour of God and the benefit of my Fatherland, but Fate is preventing me, for I strongly suspect that the Cruel Sisters are even now drawing their threads. I have, by the Grace of God, reached an age that not all attain, having lived for sixty-five years. My afternoon being over and I having reached the actual evening and term of life, when I am to enter the Kingdom of Eternal Light and enjoy everlasting life with all the saints, I confess, what I admitted long ago, that not absolutely everything I have written has accorded with the truth. Some of things I have described have been trivial and ephemeral, though amusing, things that I have taken from the writings of others either on my own initiative or at the suggestion of others, thing that I have found in minor works or in other people's maps, or matters of hearsay, taking as worthy of belief what I have merely been told to be true. I beg those who are better endowed by Minerva and have ready tongues to correct my errors and misconceptions. Should they find what they read, even the whole, confused or amateurish, may they undertake the editing of it, and may they forgive my language and incompetence. With such a wealth and variety of topics, only an angel could explain and verify it all. It is not a gospel or a canonical letter I have been writing, as the holy apostles did, but, as an intellectual exercise, I have described things that are variable and ephemeral. I accept responsibility for verifying them or for failing to do so, should that be what what I have done.

Though for more than a year now I have been ill and in pain, I have sought to record all that has happened, whether good or bad. All my life, in humble prayer I have besought Our Gracious Lord not to remove me hence too early and that in His Mercy He should see that I am free of offence and dereliction and that illness that I could endure has expunged all my hidden sins. I feel that the hour has come when, due not to me, but to His Grace and Mercy, I have been cleansed. May I add that for close on twenty-five years I have occupied, should carry on *The Annals* and not allow them to stop. Indeed, I beseech them to see that each myself day and night writing *The Annals* not only with my own hand, but also with those of my copyists. Discovering a mistake, has led to the recognition of other truths. After the sixth reading there are few residual mistakes and further readings have not changed any essentials. Finally, may I beseech all connected with the Church, whether cleric or laity, in particular our esteemed doctors, professors, magisters, students and copyists in each faculty of our university in Cracow that, on my death, each , according to his seniority college assigns one of its members to this task and that he be given another, specially trained and experienced in research , who is to be relieved of all other tasks, so that he may occupy himself solely with *The Annals*, loving them and rejoicing in them, talking of them day and night. May he also care for the good repute and advantage of our Fatherland, yet still more for the honour and glory of God, and the truth. I beg all who read or will read this Chronicle to kneel and say for me, first and last of sinners, one Paternoster and one Hail Mary, so that Our Lord Jesus Christ, son of the Immaculate Virgin, through all his torments borne with strange love for me, for him and every mortal, may deign to free me of eternal and temporal torment and lead me to see His Blessed Trinity, whose is the honour and the glory, now and for ever. Amen.

A Commentary to *The Annals of Jan Długosz*

The father of Poland's greatest historian, also called Jan Długosz, had distinguished himself at the battle of Grunwald (1410), where the power of the Order of the Teutonic Knights was broken: he rose subsequently to high office in the service of King Władysław Jagiello: his career path matching that of another Grunwald veteran, Zbigniew Oleśnicki, who was in course of time to be his son's patron and the most significant influence in his life. Successive appointments took the Długosz family (which came originally from the Wieluń district on the border between Silesia and Wielkpolska) first to Breźnica, where Jan was born, probably in 1415; and then, from 1421 to Nowe Miasto Korczyń. Breźnica is rarely mentioned in the Chronicles, but Korczyń very frequently, as befits its importance in the public life of the Jagiellonian kingdom. As a royal town, Korczyń was a more congenial place for conducting the often uproarious business of government within Cracow duchy than the city of Cracow itself, where a number of powerful semi-independent authorities uneasily coexisted: chief among them, and in that order, the Bishop, the Voivode and the town council, any and all of whom were quite capable of generating riot and mayhem on their own account even when no public issue existed to excite them.

Zbigniew Oleśnicki as Bishop of Cracow was not content simply to play the strongman on his local stage: such parochial tasks as quelling the city mob, expelling the Hussites, and reprimanding Spytek the Voivode for heretical associations although performed with gusto and panache were, so to speak, small change to Bishop Zbigniew. He also sought and found a national stage. Young Jan Długosz must have heard from his father, who can not have approved, of the sort of scenes Bishop Oleśnicki regularly generated at national assemblies in order to get his own way, long before he entered his service: doubtless Jan also heard of them direct from his patron on many subsequent occasions; nor can there be any doubt from his recording of events in the Chronicles that he entirely approved of the great man's outlook and behaviour.

Beyond doubt, Zbigniew Oleśnicki was a splendid figure, the greatest Polish churchman of his age. Three popes sent him three cardinal's hats: and the King himself ordered the Archbishop of Gniezno, when he showed himself disgruntled at the elevation of his suffragan, to defer, as he ought, to the wearer. The third of these celebrated hats was brought from Rome by Canon Jan Długosz, who later declared his ceremonious entry into Cracow cathedral bearing the hat to be the proudest moment in his life.

All this and greater glory still lay in the future when the young Jan Długosz entered the university of Cracow in 1428; which he left after three years without a degree to enter Oleśnicki's service. However, this conclusion to Długosz's formal studies was a mark of distinction rather than the reverse, a sign that he had outgrown what the university could offer one who had no desire for an academic career. Even so, Długosz retained a life-long interest both in academic life and in the formal study of history; which was well established in Poland as a series of rhetorical procedures, and which continued in spite of some academic recognition of Długosz's individual achievements, along its own highly arcane path.

Some two hundred years previously Master Vincent Kadłubek, himself to become Bishop of Cracow, had written his Chronicle of Poland, which was to remain the epitome of historical writing: a judgement to which Długosz himself could not help but defer even though his own Chronicles are unquestionably superior if both works are judged by present-day historiographical criteria. By the accepted standards of Długosz's day, however, to suggest that the comparison could produce a verdict in his favour would have been ridiculous: for Kadłubek's history had the advantage of an elegant impenetrability which made it highly suitable, not to say, convenient as a text for academic study; thus there could be no question of rivalling or superseding it, and the literary production of the most eminent academic historians might be safely confined to the writing of commentaries on the work of Master Vincent.

The view still persists to some extent that Długosz was highly dependent on Kadłubek for the early part of the Chronicles, but this idea can not be seriously entertained. It is very clear that Kadłubek's chronicle was one of a number of sources, albeit an extensive, helpful and well-organised one, which Długosz approached in a spirit of investigation. Kadłubek's influence is most apparent in certain passages of the Chronicles where the display of due literary deference is intentional: one example being the treatment of King Casimir I's return from exile, a solemn and ceremonious moment, where the elegant formulations of Kadłubek are reproduced in their entirety.

By far the greatest formative experience of Długosz's life and the greatest influence on his intellectual development was the time he spent in Oleśnicki's service. Długosz embarked on a lifetime of involvement in public affairs, acquiring proficiency in foreign languages, and travelling as far afield as Rome and Kiev. Promotion came rapidly: by 1436 Długosz was already a canon of Cracow cathedral, although he did not enter Holy Orders until 1440. This dignity, although one within the reach of a well-born imbecile or infant (as the author on occasion notes), was for Długosz a source of justified pride. In 1438 he was appointed Oleśnicki's chancellor, and throughout the Cardinal's lifetime continued to acquire distinguished appointments of the Cracovian cathedral chapter: custos in Wiślica (1444), and canon in Sandomierz (1456). Taken together these marks of distinction are enough on their own to identify Długosz as the right-hand man of the most powerful churchman in the Kingdom of Poland: and as such he could expect himself to be advanced to the highest rank in due course, perhaps even to the see of Cracow, the obvious summit of his ambition. Indeed, his ultimate prospects of obtaining this goal were good, since he was well-placed within the dominant faction, and the chapter of Cracow was sufficiently strong to resist the depradations visited by the King, and, in one uniquely shocking case, by the Pope on other Polish dioceses when vacancies arose. Długosz may well have come to think of himself as the next bishop but one or two.

However, when Oleśnicki's successor died and the see fell vacant in 1461, events took a disastrous turn. Jacob of Siena, Oleśnicki's nephew, secured the appointment from the Pope by the simple, if unsportsmanlike, expedient of being on hand to solicit it in person. Unfortunately, King Casimir Jagiellończyk, who had already appointed the Bishop of Włocławek to the see proved to be not only angry, but resolute in his opposition. Długosz could not, in principle, approve of Jacob's manoeuvre (the cautionary tale of the two rival Gniezno churchmen who died respectively of the pox and disappointment in Avignon, while their aged and decrepit archbishop struggled backwards and forwards between Poland and Rome in a futile effort to resign his see may be a barb aimed at Jacob), but he threw himself whole-heartedly into the fray in his support. It is hard to imagine any other cause that would have excited to such effect the public passions of this staid, cautious, vituperative man, save this one only. Like many men of pacific, or pacifist, temperament Długosz was highly argumentative and quite evidently gloried in this bruising conflict, for he remained unrepentant in defeat. In a departure from his usual conventions, Długosz's entry for Jacob of Siena in his catalogue of Cracow bishops celebrates the uniquely stirring occasion of the chapter's mutinous election of Jacob with a tableau vivant of the specific ways in which the individual (all named!) dissident canons were intercepted, detained or otherwise suppressed when they sallied forth in defiant procession.

The reaction of King Casimir is of interest. He evidently saw in this conflict, which he had not directly provoked, a chance to move against the so-called Małopolskan faction, the political heirs of Bishop Zbigniew, who had long been a thorn in his and his father's side. The self-elective culprits, electors and elected, would be allowed, after an interval in exile, to continue to serve: they could not be permitted to maintain their control of Cracow. Jacob was within a few years installed as Archbishop of Gniezno, and Canon Jan Długosz was appointed tutor to the King's children; but neither was to be Bishop of Cracow.

From the time he took up his appointment in 1467, Długosz became a feature in the royal household. The canon, from 1471 also canon of Gniezno, was nursing his grievance, was sharp-tongued and valued fearless frank talk to monarchs as a virtue. The atmosphere at times must have been sticky. Długosz's references to King Casimir in the Chronicles are not so much disobliging as grossly abusive. He starts by insulting the King's mother (his recollection that Louis of Hungary started a war with Charles of Bohemia under similar provocation may be an extra taunt) and questioning his legitimacy, before going on to suggest that he only accepted the Polish throne out of cowardice and a fear for his personal safety.

One wonders whether Długosz believed this sort of thing was in the spirit of Zbigniew Oleśnicki's fearless and forthright tirades directed against King Władysław Jagiello and the Grand-duke Alexander Witold: but cannot help noticing that the most extreme examples of out-spokenness Długosz records date from before his service, and so his main source must have been the Cardinal's own account of his actions. Possibly, just possibly, Cardinal Zbigniew was a trifle more fearless in retrospect than he was at the time: or perhaps he really did respond with great steadfastness to the Grand-duke's threats when baulked of his crown (the main threat was alleg-edly to treat Bishop Zbigniew as Bolesław the Bold had served Bishop Stanisław, and this if Zbig-niew's own report is the source is suspiciously self-regarding); with the result that the Grand-duke gave way and praised the rectitude of his positions; and perhaps the Grand-duchess really did beg the Cardinal to take her jewels away with him "for safe-keeping". However this may be, King Ca-simir and his family probably had to endure a considerable quantity of unwonted candour; but the evidence is that they took it well. Perhaps like Władysław Jagiello, who had the scurrilous lam-poon on himself of the Dominican friar Jan Falkenberg read aloud to his court at Christmas even while his archbishop was busy soliciting the cardinals and the Pope to condemn it, King Casimir derived some amusement from vehement, futile attacks. Certainly he valued Długosz highly for his personal qualities, telling his children, "You have two fathers, myself and Father John".

Following his appointment as tutor to the young princes in 1467, Długosz concentrated his at-tention on the completion of the Chronicles, an intended masterpiece in which all of his earlier la-bours and very considerable historiographical achievements could be incorporated.

In 1471, Władysław Jagiellończyk accepted the Czech throne and Długosz was of the party that accompanied the young prince to Prague on the somewhat perilous venture of taking posses-sion of his kingdom. Władysław intended making Długosz archbishop of Prague, or at any rate he made the offer, which was declined. Perhaps Władysław felt some relief since it is quite clear that Długosz was fussing over the new King his former pupil like a mother hen. Not wishing to be arch-bishop in Prague for personal reasons which are more than once rehearsed in these pages Długosz was packed off home, begging the King as he left to take care the Czechs did not poison him.

Was there a touch of devilment in Władysław's offer, and an element of paying the canon back in his own coin? Czechs were very much not to Długosz's taste, and he always took pains in his writings to stress that anyone assuming pastoral responsibility for them was taking on a more than Sisyphean labour. It was absolutely clear to Długosz, and should have been clear to his pupil if he had attended to his lessons, that the canon could not be archbishop of Prague. Consider the evi-dence: St. Wojciech had been forced to relinquish the see, Christinus a man of normal human (Długosz was fair!) but not saintly piety, who reluctantly, after much hesitation, shouldered the charge St. Wojciech placed upon him was invaded by demons at the moment of his consecration. Bishop Henry of Prague, who was a doughtily efficient prince of the country, still could not curb or bridle the Czech clergy. When papal legates urged them to set aside their concubines they all but attacked them. Ever and anon the prophesy of St. Wojciech was proved correct: worse was to come! The emergence of the Hussite heresy simply confirmed the single salient fact touching Bohemia's historical development, that this nation must progress along a predictable path to ever greater horrors that no saint, and certainly no ordinary human agency, could hope to divert it from.

Perhaps more importantly, to accept an archbishopric precluded translation to Cracow at any future date, if Długosz still realistically could hope for that. In the meantime, in what proved to be the last year of his life, there came another offer of an archbishopric, this time the see of Lwów. Ruthenians, having a different but no less reprehensible propensity to unorthodox belief, were little better than Czechs in Długosz's estimation. However, there were strong patriotic motives which could impel a Cracovian to accept a Ruthenian archbishopric. Of the achievements listed in Długosz's Catalogue of the Bishops of Cracow for Oleśnicki's pontificate four were singled out for particular praise, among them the foiling of a Ruthenian plot to detach Lublin from the diocese of Cracow and attach it to the Ruthenian diocese of Chełm. Just such an ambition in the political sphere expressed by Roman of Galicia three centuries earlier was probably sufficient in itself to prompt Długosz's denunciation of the Ruthenian prince as "a fiend in human shape". We may also note the rare appearance at this stage of the Chronicles of a Ruthenian (Orthodox) bishop who is conveniently on hand to raise pious objections to Roman's undertaking and to warn him that he deserves what is coming to him. Długosz could usefully imagine himself into the role of such a bishop. It is worth remembering that, while the Chronicles were originally projected as an account of Oleśnicki's life, Długosz himself no less than his hero is present in their pages.

From the earliest stages of his career Długosz had been encouraged to write history, and at his death he left behind a quite unparalleled mass of historical writing. His first work, as so often is the case with medievalists, was an inventory of ecclesiastical possessions, lost, in this version, in the 19th century, although he later reworked it as the *Liber Beneficiorum Cracoviensium*, the book of benefices of the Cracow diocese. A vast background of knowledge of church estates forms part of the fabric of the Chronicles; so much is evident, but it is also desirable, as part of any assessment of Długosz's general capacity, to stress the unique and astonishing competence he displayed as an ecclesiastical historian: his descriptions of the original endowments of the great abbeys of Poland and Pomerania, (only a few of which appear here, and in a truncated form, for obvious reasons) are models that could not be improved upon. They address questions which are among the most challenging in medieval historiography. Długosz's magnificently sensitive reduction of the earliest Polish administrative documents to a common standard of expression, and adaptation of their language to restate their contents with minimal distortion, can not help but appear the most prosaically uninteresting of tasks to those who have not themselves laboured in this driest of historical dust-bowls: but those who have can hail the canon as a master in the field.

More common, and more sensible in practical terms was it to argue for any practical interpretation that happened to suit, and such was the inevitable practice in law-suits. The disappearance of the Teutonic Knights' treasured "documents" (and their subsequent rescue) in the waters of Lake Melno was certainly made more piquant and ludicrous a comic situation for Długosz by the certain knowledge that the documents in question could bear no relation to the specific questions they purported to address: that is, unless they were rewritten, or to put it more plainly forged.

Accordingly, Długosz allows himself a certain slyness in the Chronicles when reporting the question that arose over the feudal service that might or might not be owed by the duchy of Słupsk to the Polish crown. The matter, he says, was referred to the doctors and masters of Cracow University, and their answer was that the King must decide. Enjoyment of the discomfiture of the scholars is a quintessentially Długossian situation, for they reveal themselves to be ineffective on every level. The scholars do not know the genuine answer; they can not guess the answer they are supposed to give; they do not know what answer they dare give. Długosz would have known all three; but in addition he knew how to keep his counsel, and he knew how to laugh up his sleeve.

Nonetheless much sober labour preceded the piquant laughter. The remainder of the early works, all of which found their way with some adaptation into the Chronicles were utterly sober and serious. Długosz's first venture into contemporary history was the *Banderia Prutenorum* (1448), which is no more and no less than a description to accompany illustrations of the standards captured at Grunwald. It is a work of the greatest simplicity, which has nonetheless defied the efforts of several publishers from the earliest days of printing to reproduce it accurately. It is reproduced in the Chronicles, but provides another example of one of the many elements of that work that are utterly unsuited to any form of abridgement, and have necessarily to be omitted. Obviously this exercise was a satisfactory means for one of Długosz's temperament of response to that great battle, scene of his own father's glory as well as Oleśnicki's: but the imaginative, even poetic, power of the narrative of the Chronicles could find no place in such a work. However, when he came to write the account of the Grunwald campaign, he approached the similar problem of "reporting" the Grunwald campaign from a different angle, collating the material from oral sources to such effect that the end result can be accepted as equivalent to a campaign diary. We can surely recognise this startlingly human and humane account, drawing on our own experience of the new achievements of this century's communications media, as bearing the hallmark of great authenticity and veracity. Indeed the events of Grunwald, in Długosz's version, have acquired an undying resonance, so that the words of Władysław Jagiello, since immortalised in Sienkiewicz's great novel *The Knights of the Cross* and in the film made from it, are recognisable as Długosz reported them, and seem inviolate from alteration.

Some brief mention should be made of the remaining works, whose essential and relevant parts contributed also to the supreme achievement of the Chronicles: a separate geographical work, regarded as outstanding in its own right, the *Chorographia*: the "Jewels of the Polish Kingdom" (*Insignia seu Clenodia Regni Poloniae*), the oldest Polish work of heraldry (which has a published edition of 1851); finally, the two hagiographies, the *Life of St. Stanisław*, completed in the years of exile, and the *Life of St. Kinga* (1471–4), saint of the fearsome Hungarian stable and willingly-suffering wife of the equally insufferable Boleslaw the Chaste. As a result of his court service Długosz produced for a time, and had continued access to the written royal itineraries. Little-edited portions appear in the later parts of the Chronicles and have been omitted of necessity in the present edition, but they should be mentioned as an unrivalled primary source, and of course, as with our Tudors, the framework of exact chronologies. Długosz also produced catalogues of bishops for all the Polish bishoprics, paying particular attention to the dioceses of Gniezno and Cracow. It is the reproduction of these driest of details in the Chronicles that give signs of that incipient psychological rebellion that was to work a transformation in the historical writing of Długosz's maturity, and help to make the Chronicles a masterpiece.

The Chronicles were begun after Oleśnicki's death in 1455, and here one may suspect a further psychological impulse. They were written backwards, which we should remember is a method that has a logic quite as compelling as the reverse. The *Life of Oleśnicki* did not progress. A moment's glance at the fragment which survives is sufficient to reveal the problem, for it begins "To write the life of Cardinal Oleśnicki we have to go back two hundred years". The Chronicles were the posited response to this conundrum.

It is unlikely that there is any humour to be found in the literary productions of Długosz's youth. The Chronicles are full of it, and it is of a very particular kind, which might be termed purposed, since pointed is barely sufficient. The jibe at Jacob of Siena and the taunting of King Casimir have already been alluded to, but these are barely the start. On an initial reading the most startling, since unexpected, are the curious insertions (and they are mostly manuscript insertions) in the brief lives of the Polish bishops, most usually detailing their bizarrely discreditable deaths. This can not be dismissed as a freak of Długosz's humanism, for one comes to appreciate that the whole of the Chronicles are coloured in this way.

The stories about the early life of Elizabeth Granowska furnish a good example of Długosz laying it on thick. One can tell easily enough that the canon disliked the Queen, since he informs his readers that laughing and cheering crowds attended her funeral: but one might have suspected something of the kind long before. The story of her abduction (of considerable length before abridgement, and clearly every moment relished) is contrived in such a way as to reflect the maximum discredit on all involved. The initial comic premise is that the Queen was in her early life abducted by one Moravian, and once abducted became a source of dispute between the first abductor Wiesel, (or Weasel), and a Moravian of slightly more elevated rank, one Hiczynsky who became her second abductor. This, in effect, was how the future Queen, who later rose above her station in marrying the King, had made her first social advances. An additional jibe is contained in the inference that neither would have bothered to marry her had she not become a bone of contention between them: and further that neither gallant was prepared go to the trouble of fighting for Elizabeth, one having recourse to the law, and the other to assassination. The more cowardly "noble" Hiczynski chose to have his "unarmed" rival (Długosz was a roaring snob) bumped off with ludicrous excess by twelve crossbowmen as he emerged from a bath-house, which might or might not have been owned by Spytek of Melsztyn. Długosz also had it in for the Melsztyns.

Some of what Długosz finds funny is frankly distasteful. The second string of his humourous bow drawn on Elizabeth Granowska is aimed at the lung disease which killed her. Decrepit archbishops of Gniezno and blind Bohemian rulers are stock characters. The transformation of events into farce occasionally becomes routine. It is comic, since shocking, that the Bishop of Olomouc, despite his cloth, should lay siege to Racibórz; but ludicrous that he should react to being rebuffed by calling up siege-engines and heavy artillery. Thus, some of the comic transformations may appear routine, but we should note that they are more pronounced in situations that excited Długosz's strong disapproval: and Bohemians, whether of clerical or secular estate assailing Silesian towns was certainly such a situation.

The fact that humour was directed against those of whom the author disapproved offers some slight mitigation of the conventionally harsh tone with which Długosz writes of the Jews. What he writes is distasteful but receives no additional twist. Nor is it special pleading to say that some expressions of his disapproval are conventional rather than heartfelt. King Casimir the Great did much to excite Długosz's conventional disapproval including the taking of a Jewish mistress, and this disapproval is duly recorded: but although Długosz breaks into his narrative to declare that he finds it impossible to express adequately his dislike of the King, it is hard to believe that he actually disliked the King more than he disliked Elizabeth Granowska and a number of others.

Very much of Długosz's life and personality is recorded in the Chronicles, and the bulk of the material for his biography must be sought there. Some of his own activities are recorded: he bought land for the development of Cracow University, inheriting the work from Oleśnicki, but neither were to have a college there, nor was the Carthusian monastery, the second project on the site (to which he refers in the Chronicles) brought to fruition. Most of his actual achieved benefaction was made in Sandomierz, a town whose glory was already in the past as it waned before the rise to prominence of Lublin, and was a place for which Długosz always had a great fondness: also in Cracow's Pauline monastery: and finally, perhaps remembering the glory of that great legendary founder of parishes the magnate Peter Włostowic, in small stone churches, called the Długosz churches after his association with their builder. In one of these was placed an image, likely to be life-like, to endure within his one chosen form of monument, if any additional were required.

Although the Chronicles are divided into twelve Books, the logic of the division is not continued throughout. Books 1 and 2 which deal with the pre-historical and the earliest Christian period respectively have certain distinct characteristics. Book 1, which has been omitted entirely in the present abridgement, merits its place in the work as a whole, but demands adjustment to an unfamiliar logic for appreciation of its merits.

It is, of course, quite justifiable for an historian to offer a prehistory of the land and the people who lived on it which predates any written record. Indeed, ultra-modern historians have earned praise for their "imaginative" use of archaeological, in extreme cases also geological records. However, since a precondition of ultra-modernism would appear to be sniffiness about medievalism, it is not to be expected that authentically medieval solutions will be judged equally impressive. Długosz nonetheless was in tune with modern thinking to the extent of realising that Book 1 was the correct resting-place for his geography. Henryk Łowmiański, the greatest historian of Poland's prehistory accords considerable respect to Długosz's treatment of Slav mythology. Although the Slav pagan gods are arranged by Długosz in Book 1 according to a classical pantheon, Łowmiański is prepared to accept the veracity of the two original names for which Długosz is the only source, those of Dziewanna and Marzanna (also the names of plants) who reappear in Book 2.

For present purposes it is sufficient to note the continuing resonances of the early, omitted legends. It was obviously important to Długosz that there should be an integral unity of Polish history, which necessarily comprehended recurrence of events or incidents between the documented and mythological period. This accounts for the fate (also omitted here) of a prince of Kujawy in that most obscure of periods for Długosz, the late thirteenth century, who came to be devoured by mice, just as Piast of legend had been consumed in the dungeons of the Wawel castle.

It is hard to know how seriously to allow one's sense of historical propriety to be affronted by this sort of thing. On one level it is clearly nonsense. Yet the resonances between all parts of the Chronicles are very striking and should not be ignored. Długosz's examination of Władysław Herman's presumed motives in declining the monarchy quite clearly derives some of its force from the analagous dilemma of Casimir Jagiellończyk after his brother King Władysław went missing at Varna. The earliest history of Polish–Pomeranian relations, a subject about which Długosz is deeply ignorant, is covered by recourse to the extended family of Piast. This seems ludicrous, but is it? The family of Piast, however fancifully conceived, is a political fact, indeed the central political fact of Polish political history for four hundred years. The question of what political structures existed in Piast Poland is inextricably linked to this single ruling family. Likewise, the genealogies of the Chronicles, only abandoned when they become unmanageable in the fourteenth century remain the narrative backbone of political history. There would be susbtantively less Polish history without Długosz. Indeed, Polish culture owes its sense of history in large part to the work of the canon. It is no coincidence that the tradition of Polish medievalism, which has its roots in the middle of the nineteenth-century, although barely known outside Poland, is one of the strongest in Europe.

Book Two of the Chronicles presents a different set of problems, being based almost entirely on the Lives of the Saints. A modern readership, unprepared to swallow the mice that swallowed Piast, is little more inclined to stomach demons, possessions and a range of religious phenomena, unless these can be reinterpreted in terms of some form of psychological disturbance. There has, in fact, been some sanitising of demons, but one should by no means ignore the fact that such matters interested him. For example, Długosz adduces as evidence of Wojciech's holiness the fact that the very demons in the possessed shrieked out the worthiness of his election. The ejculations of demons proved a thorny problem for theologians. It took St. Thomas Aquinas to formulate the proposition that demons must not be believed even when they told the truth. Prior to this pronouncement and conditioning its necessity, was the belief that demons under certain conditions might prove more than naturally truthful, the authority being that Christ had constrained demons to tell the truth. It followed, that although the Devil was a liar and the father of lies, the presence of a person of extreme holiness would constrain a demon to absolute truth. Much of the interest of this argument is necessarily lost if one does not happen to believe in demons. It is natural for the reader of the present text who comes across a demon, to say nothing of St. Wojciech and St. Vitus, contributing to the Polish war effort to react with disbelief, but that should not extend to characterising the whole of the information given as unreliable, for Długosz is essentially truthful, truth being the historian's distinguishing virtue.

On one level, Długosz's truthfulness takes the form of attempting to reconcile conflicting accounts; where no reconciliation is possible, two separate versions (in the case of the loss of the Lubusz territory, some half-dozen) are retained. Strict hagiographic conventions were adapted to make the Lives of the Saints accessible as a historical source. The result is a new synthesis which is entirely Długosz's own. The Five Martyrs appear both in Wojciech's story and in their own, to our confusion. Elsewhere the retention of inconsistency may be productive. The alternative to the story that King Casimir became a monk at Cluny, which only appears in Długosz, is that he was driven into exile in Hungary. Długosz conscientiously gives both versions, to our relief. For this, in fact, is the most likely fate not only of Casimir but of Mieczysław his father and Bolesław the Bold his son, the Polish nobility and the family of Sieciech in particular being at the fore of opposition to the Piasts. The historical truth arising from this, an important one, is that while the Piast dynasty was not secure in the monarchy through the eleventh century, only they were able to fill the position of supreme authority. The tutors of the early period, whom Długosz clearly conceives of in somewhat whimsical terms, perhaps remembering his own role, can be more plausibly identified as something akin to kidnappers. Długosz's sense of the historically appropriate, if distinct from that which at present applies, nonetheless marries well with it, and it his fundamental honesty that allows the marriage to occur.

Długosz's achievement in extracting a sufficient chronology from the raw material of his sources should not be underestimated. The material on which he had to work was in some ways barely improved as the first recognisable synthetic or narrative accounts became available to him. The Anonymous Gaul, biographer of Bolesław Wry-mouth, as befits one who wrote his history in hexameters and without including a single date, declared that Bolesław the Bold had "set the bounds of his realm in iron". Master Vincent Kadłubek, that sublime paragon, in an act pardonable in one whose history took the form of dialogue between immanent spirits expanded this information into the erection of pillars: while Długosz, who in the majority of his historical moods, tended to be sober, diligent and prosaic, offered best guesses on where these pillars might be found and how many might be appropriate to each site. It was left to a modern German scholar to write an article about them.

There is something of a characteristic pattern of treatment in the handling of early Lithuanian information, which is of course of the highest interest since the subject matter is Lithuania's prehistory. The established written record begins with a passage from Janko of Czarnków which Długosz reproduces without significant alteration, including its characteristic desciption of the Lithuanians slinking away like wolves. The new material which is worked in clearly derives from oral sources and legends: one wonders indeed how much of the Polish material, traditionally dismissed as "simply" imagined by Długosz has a similar historically valid foundation. Under close examination all of the information can be shown to have some justification. Even his errors can tell in Długosz's favour. The date of the murder of Becket is incorrectly given, but that is the date given in the Cracow chapter annals which were his source. The formulation of the brief notice on the events of 1066 is sufficiently cautious to take account of the fact that two King Harolds died in England in that year. Amusingly, the Polish editors of the Academy of Sciences text of the Chronicles unquestioningly identify Harold Hardrada as the victim. There are some errors of enthusiasm. Two of the earliest references to Prussians are misreadings, one of a Czech, the other of a Ruthenian source.

The fact of Długosz's veracity has long been appreciated by Polish scholars. The details he gave of the Łęczyca bull were confirmed by its rediscovery. Professor Labuda has argued convincingly for the existence of an unknown set of Silesian annals on the basis of careful internal examination of the notices in the Chronicles.

For the most part the Chronicles can and should speak for themselves. There are at first sight some few unusual features. Długosz refers to the princes of Kiev Russia as Ruthenians, and certainly the focus of his interest is provided by a desire to integrate the earlier history of those Ruthenian lands that became part of the Polish Kingdom into its national story; although it must be said that the dubious eye with which he regarded that process finds reflection in the certain awkwardness with which the textual integration is accomplished. The state of the Teutonic Order in Prussia, regarded as aberrant even at the time, and its historical development is a persistent theme in the Chronicles, and Długosz's Polish perspective, although less than comprehensive, and certainly one unredeemed by empathy, since it remains absent from modern accounts deserves to be presented, as it is here, on its own terms. While Germans are present in this story, Germany is for the most part remote: this, too, a simple fact of geography, should be remembered before facile speculation on the nature of "frontier societies" is indulged in. Poland was no frontier society. These pages, detailing five hundred years of its history and national story establish a historical fact that only the operation of ignorance and prejudice has obscured: participation in the life and culture of the Latin West was as complete in Cracow, Wrocław and Poznań as in those other obscure centres Winchester, York and Canterbury, which were equally distant from its heart.

A bibliographical note

Most points of curiosity that will have been stimulated by a reading of the preceding pages can be satisfied by consulting Norman Davies *God's Playground: A History of Poland* (Vol. 1) Oxford University Press, Oxford (1989); which contains, for example, a Turkish account of what happened to King Władysław after Varna, or at least what happened to his head (the Polish equivalent of King Charles'): indeed, this is a work tailored to suit all intelligently interested readers, with the possible exception of those determined to don the regulation hair-shirt of medievalism. A number of academic works in English exist on topics related to Długosz's Annals and could be termed required reading, were East European medieval history a taught subject, among them: Eric Christiansen, *The Northern Crusades, The Baltic and the Catholic Frontier 1100–1525,* Macmillan, London (1980), which is light on Polish content; Paul Knoll, *Casimir the Great and the Rise of the Polish Monarchy: Piast Poland in East Central Europe 1320–70,* Chicago (1972); and the same author in Robert Bartlett and Angus Mackay (Eds), *Medieval Frontier Societies,* Oxford (1989), where his contribution "Economic and Political Institutions on the Polish–German Frontier in the Middle Ages: Action, Reaction, Interaction" doubles as an up-to-date bibliographical essay; A.P. Vlasto, *The Entry of the Slavs into Christendom,* Cambridge (1970); Oscar Halecki, *The Crusade of Varna,* New York (1943); Simon Franklin and Jonathan Shepherd, The Emergence of Rus 750-1200, Longman, London (1996); Otakar Odložilík, *The Hussite King Bohemia in European Affairs 1440–1471,* Rutgers, New Brunswick, NJ (1965), an account of George of Poděbrady more sympathetic than Długosz's, as one might expect; and finally a rare excursion into ecclesiastical history, Piotr Górecki, *Parishes, Tithes and Society in Earlier Medieval Poland ca. 1100–1250*, in Transactions of the American Philosophical Society Philadelphia (1993).

There are two available editions of the Latin text: the earlier of which appears in the Cracow edition of the Collected Works (Opera Omnia) of Długosz, where a complete Polish translation is also provided. The modern Polish Academy of Sciences edition of the Latin text, with its useful notes, has now reached (in the British Library holding at any rate) the end of Book 10 of the Annals, which is roughly where the extant manuscript source also ends. Dr. Mrukówna's published Polish translation of Book 11 continues to provide footnotes, which are naturally more directed towards a Polish readership than those accompanying the Latin text. There is a substantial weighting towards passages from the final book of the Chronicles, Book 12, in Henryk Samsonowicz's selection. Otherwise, for a complete text of Book 12 it is necessary to fall back on the Cracow edition.

The most recent short biographical notice of Długosz appears in Andrzej Brożek and Stanisław Chankowski (Eds), *Słownik historyków polskich,* Warsaw (1994) which provides a short bibliography. A short listing of essential Dlugossian titles may be permissible here: Marian Biskup and Karol Górski, *Kazimierz Jagiellończyk. Zbiór studiów o Polsce drugiej połowy XV wieku,* Warsaw (1987) includes one article (pp. 316–337) specifically devoted to Długosz, but all in this volume are relevant and important; Gerard Labuda, *Zaginiona kronika w Rocznikach Jana Długosza. Próba rekonstrukcji,* Poznań (1983), demonstrates the high evidential value of the early part of the Annals; "Dlugossiana. Studia historyczne w pięćsetlecie śmierci Jana Długosza", in Stanisław Gawęda (Ed.), *Zeszyty Naukowe Uniwersytetu Jagiellońskiego*, Warsaw–Cracow (1985); Feliks Kiryk (Ed.), *Jan Długosz w pięćsetną rocznicę śmierci,* Olsztyn (1983), the last two being commemorations of the 500th anniversary of Długosz's death, Feliks Kiryk's own essay on Długosz's association with Sandomierz being particularly fine; Tadeusz Chrzanowski and Marian Kornecki, *Sztuka ziemi krakowskiej,* Cracow (1982) contains some information on the Długosz churches; finally, one might mention as of interest a recent Polish translation of the Chronicle of Master Vincent, *Mistrz Wincenty Kronika Polska*, translated by Brygida Kürbis, Warsaw, Ossolineum "Biblioteka Narodowa" series (1996), and a splendid scholarly study of Polish Christian names, Maria Malec, *Imiona chrześcijańskie w średniowiecznej Polsce*, Polish Academy of Sciences, Cracow (1994). Paul Vincent Smith, *Crusade and Society in Eastern Europe: The Hospital and the Temple in Poland and Pomerania 1145–1370*, unpublished Ph.D. thesis School of Slavonic and East European Studies, London (1994) contains more on the Hospitallers and Templars and smaller military orders encountered in these pages for anybody who is pleasantly surprised to find them there.

Index

Guide to the index

A few abbreviations have been used in the preparation of this index; s. for son, d. for daughter, m. for married. Additional symbols are Dl for Długosz, ? to indicate a query or some dubiousness in the information offered, ! to identify some few cases where the fact that the information is definitely incorrect should be signalled, either because this is of interest in itself, or because it would lead to confusion or misunderstanding if accepted as correct. Some few geographical terms that make a frequent appearance have been abbreviated, namely Wp for Wielkopolska, Mp for Małopolska. Pol. for Polish, Ger. for German indicate equivalents in those two languages for place-names or personal names where two versions exist. Selection has been made on a number of grounds, principally that of convenience and internal consistency, rather than with reference to any broader consideration or sensibility.

J

N

S

W

Wacław (Polonisation of Václav) patron of Cracow cathedral 2; 183, 408, 416

Wacław Duke of Legnica 314

Wacław of Tęczyn builder of castle in Vladimir 323

Wacław s. Bolesław Duke of Brzeg and Legnica 286, 302, 307

Wacław s. Ludwig of Brzeg 319, 323, 325

Wacław s. Waclaw of Legnica 314; becomes Bishop of Lubusz 315

Wacha of Belus Hungarian devil–worshipper 38

Waggons, fitted with scythes, a military weapon 575

Walachia 273, 278, 308–9, 313, 410, 419, 439, 449, 460–4, 468, 471, 488–9, 496–7, 503, 506, 509, 552, 555–6, 569, 573–4, 583, 587, 589–90, 593–4, 596; Italian ancestry 308; Voivode Basarab 278; Voivode 552

Wałcz Wp/Mark/Pomerania fort 324, 332, 537–8

Waldemar Margrave of Brandenburg 252, 259, 263, 273; reappears 296

Waldensians Hussites called 419

Waldstein, see Hinek

Walek 543

Wallenrod, see Conrad, Frederick

Wapienna Góra 528

Warasz (as text) Ruthenia 3

Warcisław brother of Bogusław Duke of Szczecin 293

Warcisław Duke of Slavs and Casubians, attacks Świętopełk 202

Warcisław of Gotarłowice, tried for surrendering fortress 371

Warcisław s. Świętopełk 212; joins Teutonic Knights in fit of pique 226

Warmińsk (Ermland) diocese and Christianised territory of Prussia 184, 198, 208, 393, 395, 417, 470, 520, 538, 543–4, 555–6, 561, 581, 587, 592, 598; Bishop Anselm 208; Bishop John 393; Bishop Francis 470; Bishop 198; diocese founded in Brunsberg 198

Warprim Hungary 412

Warsaw Mazovia town and duchy of 289, 304, 308, 335, 342, 350–1, 364, 457, 542, 544, 547, 550, 555–6, 582, 592; Duke Siemowit 308; Duke Conrad 542; judgement of papal tribunal posted in as a neutral locality 289; Church of St. John Baptist 289

Warsz, see Peter

Warta River 112, 190,–1, 241, 280, 369, 441, 457, 501

Wartenberg (Barczewo) Pomerania (Count of) 220; see also Hincza

Wasznik, see Paul

Wąszosze, see Matthew

Water, polluted 70, 118, 232, 248, 276, 280, 283, 307, 311, 320, 349, 352, 360, 366, 377, 383, 414–5, 419, 425, 428, 447, 455, 458, 460, 480, 483, 503, 505, 509, 520, 525, 546, 556, 560, 569, 590

Wątrobka, see Clement

Wawelski, see Przecław

Wawrzyńczyce Mp 339

Wężyk, see Nicholas

Weddings 19, 33, 45–6, 62, 75, 78, 99, 110, 115, 126, 163, 174–5, 195, 222, 245, 259, 283, 294, 303, 313, 351, 408, 509, 513, 516, 518, 529, 552, 591–2, 594, 596, 598

Wedel, see Frederick

Welczyn fort 507, 559

Werd Margrave 170

Werner (St.) Bishop of Płock 126ff

Werner of Orseln Teutonic Knights Prussian Master 272, 275–6, 279

Werner of Rankor envoy of Bohemian nobility 431

Werner Tettingen Teutonic Knight Commander of Elbląg 395

Werner Teutonic Knight Commander of Ragneta 262

Westphalia 393; see also Conrad

Weszprem Hungary 340

Wezenborg, see Bartosz

Whoring 291

Wiar River Ruthenia 67

Widawa River Silesia 197

Widukle Lithuania 332

Wiedukki Lithuania 252

Wielatów castle 324, 332

Wieleń Wp/ Mark/Pomerania fort 83, 216

Wieliczka 441

Wielkopolska 13, 71, 79, 109–10, 115, 117–9, 123, 125–8, 130–1, 134–5, 141, 146, 150, 155, 160, 164, 166, 168–75, 179, 183, 186, 188, 190, 193, 197–8, 202, 204–5, 209, 214, 217, 221, 223, 225–6, 228–9, 233–5, 239, 241–5, 249–51, 256–7, 264, 279–80, 284, 318, 320, 323–9, 331, 333, 335, 339–44, 349, 365–6, 369, 376, 381, 394, 399, 401, 404, 413, 416, 422, 431, 436–7,

SCANIA

MARE GER[MANICVM]

NVBR

IDNAGAN

ILADIA

LALANT

BERNHOLM

PRVSSIA

PRVS

SANBI

HEYLA

DAZAG

LEBEPORG

MOLT·EL·

BIRSAV

MARI·E·PVRG

ELBINGEN

VARNE·ECCLESIA

EMERN

LVDIS·GRIPSEVALD

OVAL PE·

EGELBORG

POME RANIA

POLONIE

BARZO

NSVBORG

GRIMDENES

POMEZANESIS ECCLESIA

TOCH MAGNA

BOLSTAT

SCHIVELBEM

MENA

STRASPORG

DEMYN

EVALD

PARS·

KVIAVIA

OTORVN

SI·ROCZVZS·

PARCHE

STETTIN

PIS

GOEDODO

MESTAZ

STARGART

CARNKOV

BYDGOSTIA

NAGAT

GV

RAPIN

MZVRA·FL·

RCHA ANTIQVA·

GOMEBORG

GISMA GEN

STRZYELNO

FLATESLAV

PLAZKO

BRADEBORG

HENEZBATH

POLONIA MA

VARKA

ELBIA·FL·

BOONNVLI

SNENA

TREMEZNA

RABOM

KICZYVO

DVCA

IOR

WILSNACK

QNIESNA

LOVYCZ

PILZNI

BYELAN

VAKSOVIA

BORVE

SLVPCZA

ISZLSA

STEZICE

BISCHEGRA

EMYCK

FRIVALT

POSNANIA

SZOHOVA

SKODA

KONYN

VYSKO

VIBERS

ZEPVS

COSTAN

LENCICIA

SYDLOF

OPATONIA

FRANCK

MESARIZA

PIS·DRI

TVREK

ADERK

SANDOMIRIA

RETELIS

FODIA

CROBYA

VARN

KALYS

SCVDLA·SC

PETERKOVIA

PACZANOF

LVBLYN

MADEBVRG

MORSPERG

XANSCH

OSZMYN

CIVITAS NOVA·

VKZEDOF

SLESIA

PRZEDBORS

VISLICIA

PREVORS

HAREZPERG

GOVLVZ

FOVESTA

GEMSTO

BILIZA

LELOVO

COSYCZE

RZESOFO

SANOKO

PREMI

TARGA

GLAGONIA

CAVIA

MSTGF

PILZNE

GVRZELOF

VAPOVICA

Y BEZIG

HAGE

LIGTRVZ

PIOS

MYECHOF

PRESOVLA

ROPEZVZO

PELSNG

FAVDISEM

SCALA

TARNOF

VRATIS·ZA VIA

ILKVS

POLONIA MI

LITATRA

ORE·IS

LEMEO

KOSVECZYM

GOGASIMIRA

CRACOVIA

NOR

BVCHNA

ISNA

NIZA

VELYZKA

BORG

GOLT·FERG

GLOOZ

OYESZYN

LIPNIZA

SANOK

THOTEPERG

ATHOT

HVIZFELT

GVMIZA

SILVA HIRTIMA

ZVNDEIZNOVA

HEMVZ

SESLAVIA

GRA IZ

OLMVZ

MORAVIA

FRIDERK

RESGEMA

ZVMBIZ

TROP

TRENS·FL·

IERG

ANTIQVA·

NIA